NOT FOR CIRCULATION

D1202225

NOT FOR CIRCULATION

# ENCYCLOPEDIA OF
# RELIGION IN AMERICA

CQ Press would like to thank the First Church Unitarian (www.fculittle.org) of Littleton, Massachusetts, for use of its Sanctuary Quilt, "Many Paths, One Congregation," as this encyclopedia's cover. The quilt was made by members and friends of the congregation, the turtle design was created by Bruce Curliss, and the quilt was photographed by Barbara Peacock.

First Row

*Left:*  A stylized human figure in the form of a capital H represents the American Humanist Association.

*Center:*  A flaming chalice within overlapping circles, which represent Unitarianism and Universalism, is the symbol of the Unitarian Universalist Association.

*Right:*  An empty space acknowledges the quilt's incompleteness and our own, and affirms humility in the face of mystery, celebrating our continuing journey toward understanding.

Second Row

*Left:*  The yin and the yang show opposites intertwined and represent Taoism.

*Center:*  The Hindu symbol is the word "Om" in Sanskrit, evoking the infinite Brahman and the entire Universe.

*Right:*  The Buddhist symbol is the wheel of dharma. "Dharma" means law or teaching.

Third Row

*Left to right:*  The familiar symbols of the three Abrahamic faiths: the Jewish Star of David, the Christian cross, and the Muslim crescent and star.

Fourth Row

*Left:*  The turtle represents the Nipmuc people, who lived in Massachusetts before the Europeans.

*Center:*  The Tree of Life links the three worlds: upper, middle, and lower.

*Right:*  The triple moon symbolizes the Goddess, the feminine face of the divine. The three lunar phases—waxing, full, and waning—represent the three stages of women's power: Maiden, Mother, and Crone.

# ENCYCLOPEDIA OF RELIGION IN AMERICA

## VOLUME I

Charles H. Lippy

Peter W. Williams

*Editors*

CQ PRESS

A Division of SAGE
Washington, D.C.

CQ Press
2300 N Street, NW, Suite 800
Washington, DC 20037

Phone: 202-729-1900; toll-free, 1-866-4CQ-PRESS (1-866-427-7737)

Web: www.cqpress.com

Copyright © 2010 by CQ Press, a division of SAGE. CQ Press is a registered trademark of Congressional Quarterly Inc.

All rights reserved. No part of this publication may be reproduced or transmitted in any form or by any means, electronic or mechanical, including photocopy, recording, or any information storage and retrieval system, without permission in writing from the publisher.

Composition: C&M Digitals (P) Ltd.
Copy editors: Matthew H. Adams, H. Glenn Court (Formandsubstance.com), Ann Davies, Robin Gold (Forbes Mill Press), Carolyn Goldinger, Tina M. Hardy, Sabra Bissette Ledent, Jon Preimesberger, Janine Stanley-Dunham (Eagle Eye Editorial Services), Pam Suwinsky (Thalia Publishing Services), and Tracy Villano
Indexing: Indexing Partners LLC
Proofreading: Catherine A. Farley, Ingeborg K. Lockwood, and Kate Macomber Stern

⊖ The paper used in this publication exceeds the requirements of the American National Standard for Information Sciences—Permanence of Paper for Printed Library Materials, ANSI Z39.48-1992.

Printed and bound in the United States of America

14   13   12   11   10        1   2   3   4   5

LIBRARY OF CONGRESS CATALOGING-IN-PUBLICATION DATA

Encyclopedia of religion in America / edited by Charles H. Lippy, Peter W. Williams.
     p. cm.
Includes bibliographical references and index.
ISBN 978-0-87289-580-5 (alk. paper)
1. North America—Religion—Encyclopedias.  I. Lippy, Charles H. II. Williams, Peter W. III. Title.

BL2520.E52 2010
200.97'03—dc22

2010018656

# Contents

# Alphabetical Table of Contents

## Volume 3  L–P

## Volume 4  Q–Z

# Thematic Table of Contents

## Judaism, Jewish People, and Jewish Culture

## Latino/a Religion

## Liberal Religious Movements

## Literature

## Lutherans and the Lutheran Tradition

## Mainline Protestantism

## Mass Media and Popular Culture

## Methodists/Wesleyan Tradition

## Methodological Approaches to the Study of American Religion

## Mexico

## Mormons/Latter-day Saints

## Native American/Indigenous/Aboriginal Religions

## New and Non-Traditional Religious Movements

## Organization, Forms of Religion

## Philosophical and Theological Movements

## Spirituality and Devotionalism

## Visual Arts and Material Culture

## War and Peace

## Women

## Worship, Music, and Architecture

### Architecture

### Liturgical Arts

### Music

# Preface

This collection of essays provides an opportunity for students at any level to acquaint themselves with all facets of religion in North America. Two major factors have conspired to necessitate a new encyclopedia on this subject since we last collaborated on a reference work more than two decades ago. The religious landscape of the United States and its North American neighbors has changed significantly: since the mid-1980s, the religious right has coalesced as a significant force in both religion and politics; the Episcopal Church has split over the implications of its having elected an openly gay man as bishop; the Roman Catholic Church is reeling from the reverberations of child abuse scandals among its clergy; and unprecedented numbers of Buddhists, Hindus, and Muslims have entered the country legally, as a consequence of the 1965 Hart-Celler immigration reform act. The widespread public alarm over the menace of exotic "cults" in the 1960s and 1970s rapidly subsided as the novelty and numbers of such organizations as Krishna Consciousness and the Unification Church began to wane.

American religion has changed, and its study has been transformed in both quantity and quality. The impact of the expansion of American higher education institutions in the 1950s and 1960s and the upgrading of professional expectations for faculties of these institutions in subsequent decades resulted in a veritable explosion of scholarship in this and other fields. Beyond a simple, if exponential, increase in the number of scholarly books and journal articles that continue to be published, the viewpoints from which the phenomenon of religion in America has been examined have also undergone significant changes. Although historical and sociological investigations have continued unabated, the "ethnological turn" in methodological approach that began in the 1980s has produced any number of significant participant-observer accounts of contemporary American religious phenomena. Topics such as economics and environmentalism are now included here. Similarly, the realm of visual studies in religion has attained a remarkable sophistication in recent decades and is well represented in this work. So, too, the increased awareness of what an examination of material culture tells us about religious life and a deepening appreciation of popular culture and mass culture have left their mark on how we explore religion in American life. Gender and sexuality studies continue to push us in new directions as well, and the number of entries reflecting those arenas of inquiry has likewise expanded. In addition, although our earlier work attempted to include the remainder of North America as well as the United States in its purview, the coverage of Canada, Mexico, and the Caribbean appears here in greatly enhanced form.

The contents of these volumes are arranged in alphabetical order. We would like, however, to call the attention of our readers to the alternative, thematic table of contents included at the beginning of each volume. This feature clusters articles that are related in content into coherent units, so that readers interested, in say, a broader area than that covered by any individual article can easily access the whole gamut of essays dealing with that topic. Similarly, each article concludes with a list of cognate articles included in these pages, as well as a bibliography.

In pulling these volumes together, the editors—who mutually acknowledge the ease and pleasure of having worked with one another for many decades—are pleased to recognize the extraordinary contribution of the many others who have made this new set possible.

First, our editorial advisory board, an outstanding group of scholars whose individual and collective expertise straddles a broad range of fields, has been most helpful both in formulating the shape of the content of these volumes and in tracking down potential authors. Calls for help to our far-flung colleagues for assistance in the latter enterprise have resulted in gratifying and indispensable responses from, among others, Mary Ellen Bowden, John Corrigan, Marie Griffith, Amanda Porterfield, Jon Roberts, and Grant Wacker. The editorial staff at CQ Press, especially David Arthur and John Martino, have been uniformly pleasant, efficient, and cooperative in bringing the entire operation together. And, without the unrelenting determination of our literary agent, Victoria Pryor, this work would not have seen print at all, at least not in its present form.

In addition to those who have provided direct aid to our enterprise, we would also like to acknowledge others who have provided deeper levels of support. The two of us, and many of our colleagues, were nurtured academically by an extraordinary generation of scholars who combined erudition with magnanimity and shared their wisdom with their own students as well as with their entire professional community. These include Daniel Walker Howe, Martin E. Marty, and John F. Wilson, as well as the late Sydney E. Ahlstrom, Robert T. Handy, and William R. Hutchison. On behalf of the company of American religious historians, we salute them.

We also salute Ruth Ann and the multigenerational cohort that provided the context for our summertime stays at Buffalo Bay in Madison, Connecticut, where we happily sorted out the complexities of this enterprise while contemplating Long Island Sound, fortified by refreshing beverages and savory meals.

Finally, we acknowledge our many canine companions, past, present, and future, who have so amply enriched our lives over the years.

Charles H. Lippy
University of Tennessee at Chattanooga, Emeritus

Peter W. Williams
Miami University, Oxford, Ohio

# About the Editors

**Charles H. Lippy** is LeRoy A. Martin Distinguished Professor of Religious Studies Emeritus, University of Tennessee at Chattanooga. He holds degrees from Dickinson College, Princeton University, and Union Theological Seminary (New York). Lippy was a Fulbright scholar in India and has served as president of the American Society of Church History. He has written or edited more than twenty books on various aspects of American religious life, including the three-volume *Faith in America* and his most recent book, *Introducing American Religion*. Lippy also developed a teaching website with Peter Williams on Reinhold Niebuhr in conjunction with the public radio *Speaking of Faith* series.

**Peter W. Williams** is Distinguished Professor of Comparative Religion and American Studies at Miami University in Oxford, Ohio. He holds degrees from Harvard and Yale universities and is a past president of the American Society of Church History. Williams is the editor of a number of reference sets and the author of several books, including *Houses of God: Region, Religion, and Architecture in the United States*. His research interests include American popular religion, religious architecture and sacred space, and the Episcopal Church and American culture.

# About the Associate Editors

**Randall L. Balmer** is professor of American religious history at Barnard College, Columbia University. He holds a PhD from Princeton University and is the author of more than a dozen books, including *God in the White House: How Faith Shaped the Presidency from John F. Kennedy to George W. Bush* and *The Making of Evangelicalism: From Revivalism to Politics and Beyond*. His second book, *Mine Eyes Have Seen the Glory: A Journey into the Evangelical Subculture in America*, now in its fourth edition, was made into an award-winning, three-part documentary for PBS.

**Kathleen Flake** is associate professor of American religious history in the graduate department of the Religion and Divinity School at Vanderbilt University, where she also teaches on the interaction of American religion and law. She holds degrees from the University of Chicago and the Catholic University of America. Her primary research interests are the adaptive strategies of American religions and First Amendment questions. Flake is the author of *The*

*Politics of Religious Identity: The Seating of Senator Reed Smoot, Mormon Apostle* and several scholarly articles. She serves on the editorial board of *Religion and American Culture: A Journal of Interpretation*.

**Philip Goff** is director of the Center for the Study of Religion and American Culture and professor of religious studies and American studies at Indiana University–Purdue University Indianapolis. He is senior editor of *Religion and American Culture: A Journal of Interpretation*, and his books include *The Companion to Religion in America*, *Themes in Religion and American Culture*, and *The Blackwell Companion to Religion in America*. Goff has coauthored amicus briefs for church-state cases before the U.S. Supreme Court and is a scriptwriter and interviewee on documentaries related to religion in American life for the BBC, HBO, and PBS.

**Paula M. Kane** is John and Lucine O'Brien Marous Chair of Contemporary Catholic Studies at the University of Pittsburgh, where she is a faculty member in Religious

Studies and a core faculty member of the Program in Cultural Studies. She is the author of *Separatism and Subculture: Boston Catholicism, 1900–1920,* and a coeditor of *Gender Identities in American Catholicism.* Her areas of interest include American Catholicism, religion and film, lived religion, religion and the arts, and U.S. history.

**Timothy Matovina** is professor of theology and the William and Anna Jean Cushwa Director of the Cushwa Center for the Study of American Catholicism at the University of Notre Dame. He studies religion and culture, with a specialization in U.S. Catholicism and particularly in Latino/a religion. His most recent book is *Guadalupe and Her Faithful: Latino Catholics in San Antonio, from Colonial Origins to the Present.* Other publications include *Tejano Religion and Ethnicity, The Alamo Remembered,* and, with Virgilio Elizondo, *San Fernando Cathedral: Soul of the City* and *Mestizo Worship.* He has also edited nine volumes, including *Beyond Borders.*

**Anthony B. Pinn** is Agnes Cullen Arnold Professor of Humanities and professor of religious studies at Rice University. He is the founding director of the Houston Enriches Rice Education Project. Pinn has served on the American Academy of Religion board of directors and executive committee and was the first executive director of the Society for the Study of Black Religion. He is also the author or editor of twenty-two books, including *Why, Lord?: Suffering and Evil in Black Theology; By These Hands: A Documentary History of African American Humanism;* and *African American Humanist Principles: Living and Thinking Like the Children of Nimrod.*

**Jonathan D. Sarna** is Joseph H. and Belle R. Braun Professor of American Jewish History at Brandeis University. He also chairs the Academic Advisory and Editorial Board of the Jacob Rader Marcus Center of the American Jewish Archives in Cincinnati and is chief historian of the National Museum of American Jewish History in Philadelphia. Sarna is the author or editor of more than twenty books on American Jewish history and life, and his *American Judaism: A History* won six awards, including the 2004 Jewish Book of the Year Award from the Jewish Book Council.

# Contributors

Abolitionism and Antislavery
**JONATHAN OLSON**
*Florida State University*

Abortion
**DEBORAH VESS**
*Georgia College and State University*

Adventism and Millennialism
**GARY LAND**
*Andrews University*

Adventist and Millennialist
  Denominational Families
**GEORGE R. KNIGHT**
*Andrews University*

African American Religion: Colonial
  Era through the Civil War
**JOHN M. GIGGIE**
*University of Alabama*

African American Religion: From the
  Civil War to Civil Rights
**LAWRENCE H. MAMIYA**
*Vassar College*

African American Religion: Post–Civil
  Rights Era
**ANTHONY B. PINN**
*Rice University*

African Traditional Religions
**MONICA REED**
*Florida State University*

Amana Communities
**LANNY HALDY**
*Amana Heritage Society*

America, Religious Interpretations of
**CHARLES H. LONG**
*University of California, Santa
  Barbara*

American Revolution
**PHILIP N. MULDER**
*High Point University*

Anabaptist Denominational Family
**STEPHEN LONGENECKER**
*Bridgewater College*

Anabaptists
**DAVID L. WEAVER-ZERCHER**
*Messiah College*

Angels
**PETER GARDELLA**
*Manhattanville College*

Anglican Tradition and Heritage
**ROBERT BRUCE MULLIN**
*The General Theological Seminary*

Anglicans in Colonial and
  Revolutionary America
**EDWARD L. BOND**
*Alabama A&M University*

Anti-Catholicism
**ELIZABETH FENTON**
*University of Vermont*

Antinomian Controversy
**WILLIAM K. B. STOEVER**
*Western Washington University*

Anti-Semitism
**GREGORY KAPLAN**
*Rice University*

Apocalypticism
**ROBERT BRITT-MILLS**
*Florida State University*

Appalachian Mountain Religion
**W. PAUL WILLIAMSON**
*Henderson State University*

Architecture
**PETER W. WILLIAMS**
*Miami University (Ohio)*

Architecture: Asian Religions
**ARIJIT H. SEN**
*University of Wisconsin–Milwaukee*

Architecture: Early America
**PAULA A. MOHR**
*Des Moines, Iowa*

Architecture: The European Protestant
  Background
**PETER W. WILLIAMS**
*Miami University (Ohio)*

Architecture: Jewish
**DAVID E. KAUFMAN**
*Hebrew Union College–Jewish
  Institute of Religion*

Architecture: Muslim
**AKEL ISMAIL KAHERA**
*Prairie View A & M University*

Architecture: New Religious
  Movements
**PAUL ELI IVEY**
*University of Arizona*

Architecture: Protestant, from the
  Nineteenth Century to the
  Present
**DAVID R. BAINS**
*Samford University*

Architecture: Roman Catholic
**RYAN K. SMITH**
*Virginia Commonwealth University*

Atheism, Agnosticism, and Disbelief
**ROBERT C. FULLER**
*Bradley University*

Atlantic World
**CARLA GARDINA PESTANA**
*Miami University (Ohio)*

Bahá'í
**CHRISTOPHER WHITE**
*Vassar College*

Baptists: African American
**SANDY DWAYNE MARTIN**
*University of Georgia*

Baptists: Denominations
**BILL J. LEONARD**
*Wake Forest University*

Baptists: Sectarian
**KEITH HARPER**
*Southeastern Baptist Theological
Seminary*

Baptists: Southern
**BILL J. LEONARD**
*Wake Forest University*

Baptists: Tradition and Heritage
**JAMES P. BYRD**
*Vanderbilt University*

Benevolent Empire
**MARY KUPIEC CAYTON**
*Miami University (Ohio)*

Bible: As Sacred Text, Translations,
Cultural Role
**PETER J. THUESEN**
*Indiana University–Purdue University
Indianapolis*

Bible: Interpretation of
**DONALD K. MCKIM**
*Westminster John Knox Press*

Bioethics
**DENNIS PLAISTED**
*University of Tennessee at
Chattanooga*

Book of Mormon
**TERRYL L. GIVENS**
*University of Richmond*

Buddhism in North America
**JEFF WILSON**
*Renison University College
University of Waterloo*

Buddhist Tradition and Heritage
**ELIZABETH WILSON**
*Miami University (Ohio)*

California and the Pacific Rim
Region
**RANDI JONES WALKER**
*Pacific School of Religion*

Calvinist/Reformed Tradition and
Heritage
**KATHRYN GIN**
*Yale University*

Camp Meetings
**DICKSON D. BRUCE JR.**
*University of California at Irvine*

Canada: Aboriginal Traditions
**JENNIFER REID**
*University of Maine Farmington*

Canada: Anglicans
**ALAN L. HAYES**
*Wycliffe College, University of Toronto*

Canada: Catholics
**TERENCE J. FAY S.J.**
*St. Augustine's Seminary*

Canada: Church and State
**MARGUERITE VAN DIE**
*Queen's University*

Canada: Pluralism
**EARLE H. WAUGH**
*University of Alberta*

Canada: Protestants and the United
Church of Canada
**REBEKKA KING**
*Centre for the Study of Religion
University of Toronto*

Caribbean Religious Culture and
Influence
**ADÁN STEVENS-DIAZ**
*Executive Council of the International
Society for the Comparative Study
of Civilizations*

Celebrity Culture
**DON LATTIN**
*University of California, Berkeley*

Chabad-Lubavitch
**JONATHAN D. SARNA**
*Brandeis University*

Charismatics/Charismatic Movements
**M. ANNETTE NEWBERRY**
*Assemblies of God Theological
Seminary*

Children and Adolescents
**SAMIRA MEHTA**
*Candler School of Theology
Emory University*

Christian Science
**PAUL ELI IVEY**
*University of Arizona*

Church and State: Revolutionary
Period and Early Republic
**DONALD L. DRAKEMAN**
*Princeton University*

Churches of Christ
**KEITH HUEY**
*Rochester College (Michigan)*

City Missions
**LYLE W. DORSETT**
*Samford University*

Civil Religion in the United States
**CHARLES H. LIPPY**
*University of Tennessee at
Chattanooga*

Civil War
**LUKE E. HARLOW**
*Oakland University*

Common Sense Realism
**DANIEL WALKER HOWE**
*University of California, Los Angeles*

Congregationalists
**MARGARET LAMBERTS
BENDROTH**
*Congregational Library*

Congregations
**R. STEPHEN WARNER**
*University of Illinois at Chicago*

Constitution
**BETTE EVANS**
*Creighton University*

Cult of Domesticity
**MOLLY ROBEY**
*Bridgewater State College*

Death and Burial Practices
**KATHLEEN GARCES-FOLEY**
*Marymount University*

Death of God Theology
**CHRISTY FLANAGAN**
*Florida State University*

Deism
**KERRY WALTERS**
*Gettysburg College*

Demographics
**PHILIP L. BARLOW**
*Utah State University*

Denominationalism
RUSSELL E. RICHEY
*Candler School of Theology*
*Emory University*

Devotionalism
CHESTER GILLIS
*Georgetown University*

Disciples of Christ
SAMUEL C. PEARSON
*Southern Illinois University at*
*Edwardsville*

Dispensationalism
PAUL S. BOYER
*University of Wisconsin–Madison*

Dutch Reformed
JOHN M. MULDER
*Louisville, Kentucky*

Eastern Orthodox Tradition and
Heritage
SCOTT KENWORTHY
*Miami University (Ohio)*

Eastern Orthodoxy
SCOTT KENWORTHY
*Miami University (Ohio)*

Economics
SEAN MCCLOUD
*University of North Carolina at*
*Charlotte*

Ecumenism
SONJA SPEAR
*Indiana University–Purdue University*
*Indianapolis*

Education
EUGENE BARTOO
*University of Tennessee at*
*Chattanooga*

Education: Bible Schools and Colleges
B. DWAIN WALDREP
*Southeastern Bible College*

Education: Boarding Schools
PETER W. COOKSON JR.
*Yale Divinity School*

Education: Christian School
Movement
SUSAN D. ROSE
*Dickinson College*

Education: Colleges and Universities
BARTON E. PRICE AND KASEY
PRICE
*Florida State University*

Education: Court Cases
ISAAC WEINER
*University of North Carolina at*
*Chapel Hill*

Education: Home Schooling
Movement
MILTON GAITHER
*Messiah College*

Education: Parochial and Private
Religious Day Schools
ROBERT F. LAY
*Taylor University*

Education: Religious Issues
ANN DUNCAN
*University of Virginia*

Education: Seminaries and Theological
Education
GLENN T. MILLER
*Bangor Theological Seminary*

Education: Sunday Schools
BARTON E. PRICE
*Florida State University*

The Electronic Church
JAMES Y. TRAMMELL
*High Point University*

Emerging Church Movement
WARREN BIRD
*Leadership Network*

Emotion
JOHN CORRIGAN
*Florida State University*

Enlightenment
KERRY WALTERS
*Gettysburg College*

Environment and Ecology
SARAH E. FREDERICKS
*University of North Texas*

Environment and Ecology: Colonial
Era through the Early Nineteenth
Century
SUSAN POWER BRATTON
*Baylor University*

Environment and Ecology: Current
Ethical Issues
LISA SIDERIS
*Indiana University*

Environment and Ecology: Native
American Cultures
KENNETH LOKENSGARD
*Gettysburg College*

Environment and Ecology: Since the
Mid-Nineteenth Century
BERNARD ZALEHA
*University of California, Santa Cruz*

Episcopalians: Early Republic
ROBERT W. PRICHARD
*Virginia Theological Seminary*

Episcopalians: The Gilded Age and the
Progressive Era
PETER W. WILLIAMS
*Miami University (Ohio)*

Episcopalians: Twentieth and Twenty-
First Centuries
WILLIAM L. SACHS
*Saint Stevens Episcopal Church*
*Richmond, Virginia*

Esoteric Movements
ROBERT C. FULLER
*Bradley University*

Establishment, Religious
ANN W. DUNCAN
*University of Virginia*

Ethnicity
MARK GRANQUIST
*Luther Seminary*

Ethnographic and Anthropological
Approaches
BETH ANN CONKLIN
*Vanderbilt University*

Evangelicals: Colonial Era
FRANKLIN T. LAMBERT
*Purdue University*

Evangelicals: Current Trends and
Movements
RANDALL BALMER
*Barnard College*

Evangelicals: Nineteenth Century
JOSEPH S. MOORE AND ROBERT
M. CALHOON
*University of North Carolina at*
*Greensboro*

Evangelicals: Twentieth Century
**RANDALL BALMER**
*Barnard College*

Evolution, Creation Science, and
  Intelligent Design
**CHARLES A. ISRAEL**
*Auburn University*

Faith-Based Community
  Organizations
**HEIDI SWARTS**
*Rutgers–Newark*
*The State University of New Jersey*

Faith-Based Initiatives
**MICHAEL LEO OWENS**
*Emory University*

Feminism
**LAUREN DAVIS GRAY**
*Florida State University*

Feminist Studies
**S. SUE HORNER**
*American College of Greece*

Film
**S. BRENT PLATE**
*Hamilton College*

Folklore
**LEONARD NORMAN PRIMIANO**
*Cabrini College*

Food and Diet
**CORRIE E. NORMAN**
*Converse College*

Freedom, Religious
**ERIC MICHAEL MAZUR**
*Virginia Wesleyan College*

Frontier and Borderlands
**QUINCY D. NEWELL**
*University of Wyoming*

Fundamentalism
**DARRYL G. HART**
*Westminster Seminary California*

Fundamentalism: Contemporary
**CHRIS R. ARMSTRONG**
*Bethel Seminary*

Gender
**MARY BEDNAROWSKI**
*United Theological Seminary of the*
  *Twin Cities*

Geographical Approaches
**PHILIP L. BARLOW**
*Utah State University*

Glossolalia
**VINSON SYNAN**
*Regent University*

Great Awakening(s)
**BARTON PRICE**
*Florida State University*

Great Lakes Region
**BRIAN C. WILSON**
*Western Michigan University*

Great Plains Region
**ROBERT STODDARD**
*University of Nebraska–Lincoln*

Harmonialism and Metaphysical
  Religion
**PAUL ELI IVEY**
*University of Arizona*

Hasidism
**SARAH IMHOFF**
*University of Chicago Divinity School*

Healing
**HEATHER CURTIS**
*Tufts University*

Health, Disease, and Medicine
**JONATHAN R. BAER**
*Wabash College*

Hindu Tradition and Heritage
**BRIAN PENNINGTON**
*Maryville College*

Hinduism in North America
**STEVEN RAMEY**
*University of Alabama*

Hispanic Influence
**ROBERTO LINT SAGARENA**
*Middlebury College*

Historical Approaches
**HENRY WARNER BOWDEN**
*Rutgers, The State University of New*
  *Jersey*

History of Religions, Approaches
**ANTHONY PETRO**
*Princeton University*

Holidays
**HOLLY FOLK**
*Western Washington University*

Holiness Denominational Family
**ROBERT F. LAY**
*Taylor University*

Holiness Movement
**SUSIE C. STANLEY**
*Messiah College*

Holocaust
**ZEV GARBER**
*Los Angeles Valley College*

House Church Movement
**WARREN BIRD**
*Leadership Network*

Idealist Philosophy
**MATHEW A. FOUST**
*University of Oregon*

Immigration: From the Colonial Era
  to the Mid-Nineteenth Century
**ROBERT BRITT-MILLS**
*Florida State University*

Immigration: From the Mid-
  Nineteenth Century to World War I
**MARK GRANQUIST**
*Luther Seminary*

Immigration: From World War I to the
  1965 Immigration Act
**JENNIFER SNOW**
*Independent scholar*

Immigration: Since the 1965
  Immigration Act
**DAVID ENGSTROM**
*San Diego State University*

Independent Bible and Community
  Churches
**B. DWAIN WALDREP**
*Southeastern Bible College*

Internet
**DOUGLAS E. COWAN**
*Renison University College*
*University of Waterloo*

Invisible Institution
**TORIN ALEXANDER**
*Rice University*

Islam in North America
**KATHLEEN HLADKY**
*Florida State University*

Islam Tradition and Heritage
**AMIR HUSSAIN**
*Loyola Marymount University*

Jainism
**KAY KOPPEDRAYER**
*Wilfrid Laurier University*

Jehovah's Witnesses
**ANDREW HOLDEN**
*Lancaster University (United Kingdom)*

Journalism
**MARK SILK**
*Trinity College*

Judaism: Conservative
**SHULY SCHWARTZ**
*Jewish Theological Seminary*

Judaism: Jewish Culture
**LAUREN B. STRAUSS**
*The George Washington University*

Judaism: Jewish Identity
**EDWARD S. SHAPIRO**
*Seton Hall University*

Judaism: Jewish Science
**ELLEN M. UMANSKY**
*Fairfield University*

Judaism: Orthodox
**JEFFREY S. GUROCK**
*Yeshiva University*

Judaism: Reconstructionist
**ERIC CAPLAN**
*McGill University (Canada)*

Judaism: Reform
**DANA EVAN KAPLAN**
*Congregation B'nai Israel
Albany, Georgia*

Judaism: Sectarian Movements
**DANA EVAN KAPLAN**
*Congregation B'nai Israel
Albany, Georgia*

Judaism: Secular
**ELI LEDERHENDLER**
*Hebrew University of Jerusalem*

Judaism: Tradition and Heritage
**JACOB NEUSNER**
*Bard College*

Krishna Consciousness
**ROBERT D. BAIRD**
*University of Iowa*

Latino American Religion: Catholics, Colonial Origins
**ROBERT E. WRIGHT, O.M.I.**
*University of Iowa*

Latino American Religion: Catholics, Nineteenth Century
**TIMOTHY MATOVINA**
*University of Notre Dame*

Latino American Religion: Catholics, Twentieth Century
**GERALD E. POYO**
*St. Mary's University (Texas)*

Latino American Religion: Mainline Protestants
**PAUL BARTON**
*Seminary of the Southwest*

Latino American Religion: Pentecostals
**ARLENE M. SÁNCHEZ WALSH**
*Azusa Pacific University*

Latino American Religion: Struggles for Justice
**ANTHONY M. STEVENS-ARROYO**
*Brooklyn College*

Latino/a Religious Practice
**LUIS D. LEÓN**
*University of Denver*

Latter-day Saints
**KATHLEEN FLAKE**
*Vanderbilt University*

Liberation Theology
**MICHELLE A. GONZALEZ**
*University of Miami*

Literature
**JANA RIESS**
*Westminster John Knox Press*

Literature: African American
**KIMBERLY RAE CONNOR**
*University of San Francisco*

Literature: Colonial
**BRYAN ADAMS HAMPTON**
*University of Tennessee at Chattanooga*

Literature: Contemporary
**AARON SHAHEEN**
*University of Tennessee at Chattanooga*

Literature: Early Republic and the "American Renaissance"
**CAROLINE LEVANDER**
*Rice University*

Literature: From the Civil War to World War I
**CAROLINE LEVANDER**
*Rice University*

Liturgical Arts
**VIRGINIA C. RAGUIN**
*College of the Holy Cross*

Lived Religion
**DAVID D. HALL**
*Harvard Divinity School*

Lutheran Churches
**L. DEANE LAGERQUIST**
*St. Olaf College*

Lutheran Tradition and Heritage
**L. DEANE LAGERQUIST**
*St. Olaf College*

Mainline Protestants
**JAMES W. LEWIS**
*Louisville Institute*

Marriage and Family
**ANNE C. ROSE**
*Penn State University*

Masculinity
**STEPHEN C. FINLEY**
*Louisiana State University*

Material Culture, Approaches
**KELLY J. BAKER**
*University of New Mexico*

Megachurches
**MYEV REES**
*Miami University (Ohio)*

Methodists: African American
**STEPHEN W. ANGELL**
*Earlham School of Religion*

Methodists: Since the Nineteenth
Century
ANDREW TOOLEY
*Wheaton College*

Methodists: Through the Nineteenth
Century
D. E. "GENE" MILLS JR.
*University of Tennessee at
Chattanooga*

Methodists: Tradition and Heritage
CHARLES WALLACE JR.
*Willamette University*

Mexico: Colonial Era
JAVIER VILLA-FLORES
*University of Illinois at Chicago*

Mexico: Independence to the Mexican
Revolution
MARGARET CHOWNING
*University of California, Berkeley*

Mexico: Indigenous Religions
LEAH SARAT
*University of Florida*

Mexico: Protestants
CARLOS GARMA NAVARRO
AND VIRGINIA GARRARD-
BURNETT
*Universidad Autónoma Metropolitana
Iztapalapa, México and University
of Texas, Austin*

Mexico: Twentieth Century
ADRIAN A. BANTJES
*University of Wyoming*

Ministry, Professional
WILLIAM B. LAWRENCE
*Perkins School of Theology
Southern Methodist University*

Missions: Domestic
ANNE BLUE WILLS
*Davidson College*

Missions: Foreign
AKINTUNDE E. AKINADE
*School of Foreign Service in Qatar
Georgetown University*

Missions: Native American
HENRY WARNER BOWDEN
*Rutgers, The State University of New
Jersey*

Moravians
CRAIG D. ATWOOD
*Wake Forest University School of
Divinity*

Mountain West and Prairie Region
DONNA RAY
*University of New Mexico*

Music: African American
CHERYL A. KIRK-DUGGAN
*Shaw University Divinity School*

Music: African American Gospel
CHERYL A. KIRK-DUGGAN
*Shaw University Divinity School*

Music: African American Spirituals
CHERYL A. KIRK-DUGGAN
*Shaw University Divinity School*

Music: Appalachian Religious
BEVERLY PATTERSON
*North Carolina Folklife Institute*

Music: Christian
DAVID W. STOWE
*Michigan State University*

Music: Contemporary Christian
JAY R. HOWARD
*Butler University*

Music: Coritos/Spanish-Language
EDWIN DAVID APONTE
*Lancaster Theological Seminary*

Music: Hymnody
STEPHEN A. MARINI
*Wellesley College*

Music: Jewish
MARK L. KLIGMAN
*Hebrew Union College*

Music: Roman Catholic
JAMES L. EMPEREUR
*San Antonio, Texas*

Music: White Gospel
RYAN HARPER
*Princeton University*

Nation(s) of Islam
LAWRENCE H. MAMIYA
*Vassar College*

Native American Religions
LISA J. M. POIRIER
*Miami University (Ohio)*

Native American Religions:
Contemporary
CHRIS JOCKS
*Durango, Colorado*

Native American Religions:
Post-Contact
JOSHUA FLEER
*Florida State University*

Native American Religions:
Pre-Contact
LISA J. M. POIRIER
*Miami University (Ohio)*

Nature and Nature Religion
BERNARD DALEY ZALEHA
*University of California, Santa
Cruz*

Neo-Orthodoxy
K. HEALAN GASTON
*Harvard University*

Neo-Paganism
HELEN A. BERGER
*West Chester University*

Neo-Thomism
SANDRA YOCUM
*University of Dayton*

New Age Religion(s)
PHILLIP CHARLES LUCAS
*Stetson University*

New England Region
ELIZABETH C. NORDBECK
*Andover Newton Theological School*

New Religious Movements
CHRISTOPHER G. WHITE
*Vassar College*

New Religious Movements: Black
Nationalist Movements
LAWRENCE H. MAMIYA
*Vassar College*

New Religious Movements:
Nineteenth Century
JEREMY RAPPORT
*Indiana University*

New Religious Movements: Twentieth
Century
PHILLIP CHARLES LUCAS
*Stetson University*

Occult and Metaphysical Religion
**ROBERT C. FULLER**
*Bradley University*

Oneida Community
**ROBERT S. FOGARTY**
*Antioch College*

Pacific Northwest Region
**PATRICIA O'CONNELL KILLEN**
*Pacific Lutheran University*

Pacifism and Conscientious
    Objection
**JEFFREY WILLIAMS**
*Brite Divinity School*

Pentecostal Denominational Family
**DAVID G. ROEBUCK**
*Dixon Pentecostal Research Center*
*Lee University*

Pentecostals
**KIMBERLY ERVIN ALEXANDER**
*Pentecostal Theological Seminary*

Pentecostals: African American
**DAVID D. DANIELS III**
*McCormick Theological Seminary*

Philanthropy
**THOMAS J. DAVIS**
*Indiana University–Purdue University*
    *Indianapolis*

Philosophical Theology
**DAVID S. PACINI**
*Candler School of Theology*
*Emory University*

Philosophy
**DAVID R. PERLEY**
*University of Toronto*

Pietism
**JEFFREY BACH**
*Elizabethtown College*

Pilgrims
**MICHELLE MORRIS**
*University of Missouri*

Pledge of Allegiance
**R. JONATHAN MOORE**
*Denison University*

Pluralism
**CHARLES H. LIPPY**
*University of Tennessee at Chattanooga*

Politics: Colonial Era
**JONATHAN DEN HARTOG**
*Northwestern College*

Politics: Nineteenth Century
**JASON C. BIVINS**
*North Carolina State University*

Politics: Twentieth Century
**MATTHEW AVERY SUTTON**
*Washington State University*

Polity
**THOMAS FRANK**
*Candler School of Theology*
*Emory University*

Popular Religion and Popular Culture
**PETER W. WILLIAMS**
*Miami University (Ohio)*

Popular Religion and Popular Culture:
    From the Colonial Era to the Civil
    War
**KYLE T. BULTHUIS**
*Colby College*

Popular Religion and Popular Culture:
    From the Civil War to the Mid-
    Twentieth Century
**KATHRYN J. OBERDECK**
*University of Illinois at Urbana–*
    *Champaign*

Popular Religion and Popular Culture:
    Since the Mid-Twentieth Century
**JUAN FLOYD-THOMAS**
*Vanderbilt University Divinity School*

Populism
**JOE CREECH**
*Valparaiso University*

Positive Thinking
**CATHERINE BOWLER**
*Duke University*

Postmodernism
**JAMES K. A. SMITH**
*Calvin College*

Practical Theology
**BONNIE J. MILLER-MCLEMORE**
*Vanderbilt University*

Pragmatism
**ADAM NEAL** AND **JOHN**
    **SNAREY**
*Young Harris College and Emory*
    *University*

Preaching
**WILLIAM B. LAWRENCE**
*Perkins School of Theology*
*Southern Methodist University*

Presbyterians: Colonial
**K. S. SAWYER**
*McCormick Theological Seminary*

Presbyterians: Nineteenth Century
**MATTHEW PETERSON**
*University of Pittsburgh*

Presbyterians: Since the Nineteenth
    Century
**RICK NUTT**
*Muskingum College*

Progressivism
**SCOTT BILLINGSLEY**
*University of North Carolina at*
    *Pembroke*

Prohibition
**ANDREW S. MOORE**
*Saint Anselm College*

Protestant Liberalism
**CARA BURNIDGE**
*Florida State University*

Psychology of Religion
**CHRISTOPHER F. SILVER**
*University of Tennessee at*
    *Chattanooga*

Puritans
**DAVID D. HALL**
*Harvard Divinity School*

Quakers: Through the Nineteenth
    Century
**THOMAS HAMM**
*Earlham College*

Quakers: Since the Nineteenth
    Century
**MAX L. CARTER**
*Guilford College*

Qur'an
**FREDERICK S. COLBY**
*University of Oregon*

Race and Racism
JAMES B. BENNETT
*Santa Clara University*

Radio
TONA HANGEN
*Worcester State College*

Reformed Denominational Family
DARRYL G. HART
*Westminster Seminary California*

Religion, Regulation of
DEREK H. DAVIS
*University of Mary Hardin-Baylor*

Religious Prejudice
JOHN CORRIGAN
*Florida State University*

Religious Prejudice: Anti-Cult
KERRY MITCHELL
*Global College, Long Island
    University*

Religious Press
BRUCE J. EVENSEN
*DePaul University*

Religious Right
SUSAN FRIEND HARDING
*University of California, Santa
    Cruz*

Religious Studies
MARK HULSETHER
*University of Tennessee at Knoxville*

Religious Thought
DAVID R. BAINS
*Samford University*

Religious Thought: African American
JAMES A. NOEL
*San Francisco Theological Seminary*

Religious Thought: Feminist
DARRIS C. SAYLORS AND KELLY
    JO FULKERSON
*Harvard Divinity School*

Religious Thought: Gay Theology
J. MICHAEL CLARK
*Warren Wilson College*

Religious Thought: Jewish
NOAM PIANKO
*University of Washington*

Religious Thought: Latino/a
MICHELLE A. GONZALEZ
*University of Miami*

Religious Thought: Lesbian Theology
MARY E. HUNT
*Women's Alliance for Theology, Ethics
    and Ritual*

Religious Thought: Mujerista
ADA MARÍA ISASI-DÍAZ
*Drew University*

Religious Thought: Reformed
Protestant
DONALD K. MCKIM
*Westminster John Knox Press*

Religious Thought: Roman Catholic
JUSTIN D. POCHÉ
*College of the Holy Cross*

Religious Thought: Womanist
STACEY M. FLOYD-THOMAS
*Vanderbilt University*

Revivalism: Nineteenth Century
CHARLES H. LIPPY
*University of Tennessee at
    Chattanooga*

Revivalism: Twentieth Century to the
Present
ROBERT F. MARTIN
*University of Northern Iowa*

Roman Catholicism: African American
Catholics
CECILIA MOORE
*University of Dayton*

Roman Catholicism: Catholics in the
Atlantic Colonies
ANDREW STERN
*Southern Catholic College*

Roman Catholicism: Catholics in
the New Nation and the Early
Republic
JASON KENNEDY DUNCAN
*Aquinas College*

Roman Catholicism: The Impact of
Immigration in the Nineteenth
Century
KATHLEEN S. CUMMINGS
*University of Notre Dame*

Roman Catholicism: The Age of the
Catholic Ghetto
MARGARET M. MCGUINNESS
*La Salle University*

Roman Catholicism: The Cold War
and Vatican II
CHESTER GILLIS
*Georgetown University*

Roman Catholicism: The Later
Twentieth Century
PAULA M. KANE
*University of Pittsburgh*

Roman Catholicism: Early Twenty-
First-Century Issues
PATRICIA O'CONNELL KILLEN
*Pacific Lutheran University*

Roman Catholicism: Cultural Impact
UNA M. CADEGAN
*University of Dayton*

Roman Catholicism: French
Influence
MICHAEL PASQUIER
*Louisiana State University*

Roman Catholicism: Tradition and
Heritage
CHESTER GILLIS
*Georgetown University*

Romanticism
TODD M. BRENNEMAN
*Florida State University*

Same-Gender Marriage
MARVIN M. ELLISON
*Bangor Theological Seminary*

Santería
MIGUEL A. DE LA TORRE
*Iliff School of Theology*

Science
ADAM SHAPIRO
*University of British Columbia*

Scientology
EUGENE V. GALLAGHER
*Connecticut College*

Scriptures: American Texts
PETER J. THUESEN
*Indiana University–Purdue University
    Indianapolis*

Seeker Churches
**WARREN BIRD**
*Leadership Network*

Serpent Handlers
**RALPH WILBUR HOOD JR.**
*University of Tennessee at Chattanooga*

Settlement Houses
**RIMA LUNIN SCHULTZ**
*Oak Park, Illinois*

Seventh-day Adventists
**GEORGE R. KNIGHT**
*Andrews University*

Sexuality and Sexual Identity
**MARVIN M. ELLISON**
*Bangor Theological Seminary*

Shakers
**JANE F. CROSTHWAITE**
*Mount Holyoke College*

Sikhs
**KAY KOPPEDRAYER**
*Wilfrid Laurier University*

Social Ethics
**DENNIS PLAISTED**
*University of Tennessee at Chattanooga*

Social Gospel
**EUGENE Y. LOWE JR.**
*Northwestern University*

Social Reform
**JENNIFER GRABER**
*College of Wooster*

Sociological Approaches
**JOHN SCHMALZBAUER**
*Missouri State University*

The South as Region
**SAMUEL S. HILL**
*University of Florida*

The Southwest as Region
**DONNA RAY**
*University of New Mexico*

Spiritualism
**BRET E. CARROLL**
*California State University, Stanislaus*

Spirituality
**MARGARET LAMBERTS BENDROTH**
*Congregational Library*

Spirituality: Contemporary Trends
**DOUGLAS BURTON-CHRISTIE**
*Loyola Marymount University*

Sport(s)
**ARTHUR REMILLARD**
*Saint Francis University*

Stone-Campbell Movement
**KEITH HUEY**
*Rochester College (Michigan)*

Suburbanization
**EILEEN LUHR**
*California State University, Long Beach*

Sunday and the Sabbath
**ALEXIS MCCROSSEN**
*Southern Methodist University*

Supreme Court
**KATHLEEN FLAKE**
*Vanderbilt University*

Systematic Theology
**GEORGE STROUP**
*Columbia Theological Seminary*

Television
**MICHELE ROSENTHAL**
*University of Haifa, Israel*

Theocracy
**PETER J. THUESEN**
*Indiana University–Purdue University Indianapolis*

Torah
**JONATHAN D. SARNA**
*Brandeis University*

Tourism and Pilgrimage
**THOMAS S. BREMER**
*Rhodes College*

Transcendentalism
**DANIEL VACA**
*Columbia University*

Transcendental Meditation
**BILL BAKER**
*Miami University (Ohio)*

Unaffiliated
**ARTHUR FARNSLEY II**
*Indiana University–Purdue University Indianapolis*

Unification Church
**M. DARROL BRYANT**
*Renison University College University of Waterloo*

Unitarians
**LAUREN DAVIS GRAY**
*Florida State University*

Unitarian Universalist Association
**MARK W. HARRIS**
*First Parish of Watertown (Massachusetts)*

Universalists
**CHARLES H. LIPPY**
*University of Tennessee at Chattanooga*
**PETER W. WILLIAMS**
*Miami University (Ohio)*

Utopian and Communitarian Experiments
**SUSAN LOVE BROWN**
*Florida Atlantic University*

Violence and Terror
**JOHN CORRIGAN**
*Florida State University*

Visual Culture
**KATHRYN LOFTON**
*Yale University*

Visual Culture: Painting, Sculpture, and Graphic Arts in Early America
**GRETCHEN BUGGELN**
*Valparaiso University*

Visual Culture: Painting, Sculpture, and Graphic Arts from the Revolution to the Civil War
**DAVID BJELAJAC**
*George Washington University*

Visual Culture: Painting, Sculpture, and Graphic Arts from the Civil War to World War II
**KRISTIN SCHWAIN**
*University of Missouri–Columbia*

Visual Culture: Painting, Sculpture, and Graphic Arts since World War II
**SHEILA F. WINBORNE**
*Independent scholar*

Voodoo
**CHARLES REAGAN WILSON**
*University of Mississippi*

Wicca and Witchcraft
**HELEN A. BERGER**
*West Chester University*

Women
**JEANNE HALGREN KILDE**
*University of Minnesota*

Women Religious
**DARRIS C. SAYLORS**
*Harvard Divinity School*

Women: Evangelical
**PAMELA D. H. COCHRAN**
*University of Virginia*

Women: Jewish
**PAMELA S. NADELL**
*American University*

Women: Muslim
**SHANNON DUNN**
*Florida State University*

Women: Ordination of
**BARBARA BROWN ZIKMUND**
*Hartford Seminary*

Women: Protestant
**KELLY JO FULKERSON**
*Harvard Divinity School*

Women: Roman Catholic
**MARY HENOLD**
*Roanoke College*

World War I
**JONATHAN EBEL**
*University of Illinois at Urbana–Champaign*

World War II
**JILL K. GILL**
*Boise State University*

Worship: Anglican
**RICHARD D. MCCALL**
*Episcopal Divinity School*

Worship: Contemporary Currents
**DAVID R. BAINS**
*Samford University*

Worship: Eastern Orthodox
**SCOTT KENWORTHY**
*Miami University (Ohio)*

Worship: Jewish
**LAWRENCE A. HOFFMAN**
*Hebrew Union College*

Worship: Muslim
**DANIEL C. DILLARD**
*Florida State University*

Worship: Protestant
**DAVID R. BAINS**
*Samford University*

Worship: Roman Catholic
**DAVID R. BAINS**
*Samford University*

Zen Buddhism
**JEFF WILSON**
*Renison University College*
*University of Waterloo*

Zionism
**YAAKOV ARIEL**
*University of North Carolina at Chapel Hill*

# A

# Abolitionism and Antislavery

American abolitionism was an antislavery movement that began in the early 1830s. It gradually faded after issuance of the Emancipation Proclamation in 1863 and ratification of the Thirteenth Amendment in 1865 and the Fifteenth Amendment in 1870. American abolitionism was characterized by violent conflict, heated debate, political action, and religious fervor.

Questions over the legitimacy of buying and selling slaves often surfaced within the early Republic. Amid the animated debates between state governments and political parties, the Slave Trade Act of 1807 was eventually ratified, banning the importation of slaves to the Americas and British colonies. By 1827 the termination of the African slave trade had led to the complete abolishment of slavery in all northern states.

Apart from political legislation, opposition to slavery before the 1830s came primarily from religious groups that considered the practice of slaveholding unethical and immoral. The Society of Friends, more commonly known as the Quakers, argued that the buying and owning of slaves was inappropriate for a true follower of Christ. In a similar fashion, the Methodists in 1789 forbade congregants from buying and owning slaves, citing that the practice was antithetical to the sovereign laws of God. A significant number of Unitarians, Mennonites, and Transcendentalists, along with some Presbyterians and Congregationalists, also condemned slavery in the late eighteenth and early nineteenth centuries and would later play a prominent role in antislavery initiatives.

Although opposition to slavery was evident in the eighteenth and early nineteenth centuries, not until the mid-nineteenth century did antislavery sentiments begin to emerge in American public discourse. During this time the Enlightenment ideas of inalienable rights and democratic equality—remnants of Jeffersonian democracy and the founding of the new Republic—combined with the nation's budding economy to produce a strong sense of progressivism. Young men and women began leaving the small towns of their childhood and moving to urban centers to capitalize on the tremendous job growth produced by the post–Revolutionary War industrial boom. Heeding the call of "Manifest Destiny," others began migrating westward, seeking to claim a niche on the frontier. Also during this time persecution and a protracted famine in Europe spawned a mass migration of Jewish and Catholic immigrants to America's shores. Moreover, in the late 1840s the first wave of feminism began sweeping portions of the nation. In the wake of such extraordinary cultural change, the boundaries that once differentiated genders, religions, and ethnicities were forcibly redefined, making room for more equitable convictions.

The early nineteenth century in America was also a time of profound religious transformation. In what has since become known as the Great Revival or the Second Great Awakening, post–Revolutionary War America was inundated with an overwhelming sense of religious fervor, manifested in Protestant revivalism. Evangelists such as Charles Finney (1792–1875), Lyman Beecher (1775–1863), and James McGready (1760–1817) avidly preached to large and diverse gatherings at lengthy camp meetings in upstate New York and on the American frontier. Their message emphasized conversion that hinged on an individual, dramatic, and often emotionally turbulent experience. Congregates were encouraged to display physically feelings of anguish toward previous sin, as well as feelings of jubilation for redemption and salvation. This salvific experience was open to all who were willing to participate, regardless of social class, gender, or even race.

This evangelical style of conversion tended to provoke both moral and social reforms. Many nineteenth-century revivalists assumed that if an individual could be

William Lloyd Garrison founded the American Anti-Slavery Society in 1833 and produced antislavery literature, including a weekly newspaper titled *The Liberator*. Garrison chided religious denominations for their lack of commitment to the antislavery agenda and their quick willingness to compromise on the issue.

materialize in the mid-nineteenth century as a visible social force. In 1833 the American Anti-Slavery Society was established in Philadelphia by journalist and social reformer William Lloyd Garrison (1805–1879). Like many of his contemporaries, Garrison emphasized peaceful social activism with the ultimate goal of purging the nation of its moral failures. Although he shared with Finney, Beecher, and other revivalist leaders a sense of perfectionism, as a native New Englander he was most heavily affected by the pacifistic and social concerns of American and English Quakerism.

With the adoption of the Missouri Compromise of 1820 and the various pro-slavery concessions that characterized Andrew Jackson's presidential administration, Garrison became disenchanted with the ability of the U.S. political system to eradicate slavery. Garrison also chided religious denominations for their lack of commitment to the antislavery agenda and their quick willingness to compromise on the issue. Instead of lobbying for legislation or appealing to the rhetorical power of clergy, Garrison and his followers—known commonly as Garrisonian abolitionists—protested the institution of slavery primary through the written word.

As a young man in the early 1820s, Garrison coedited with fellow abolitionist Benjamin Lundy (1789–1839) the Quaker antislavery newsletter *Genius of Universal Emancipation*. Having experienced first-hand the efficacy of the written word, Garrison's American Anti-Slavery Society also produced a weekly newspaper, *The Liberator*. Throughout the 1830s, Garrison, along with other abolitionist publishers such as Theodore Dwight Weld (1803–1895), inundated the southern states with antislavery literature. This flood of abolitionist rhetoric prompted southern clergy to respond.

### Disputes and Violence

More often than not, the debates between northern abolitionists and southern clergy centered on interpretations of the biblical text. For abolitionists such as Angelina Grimké (1805–1879), the Bible had to be interpreted contextually. In her treatise *Appeal to Christian Women of the South*, Grimké pointed out that slavery in the Bible and slavery as it existed in the American South bore "no likeness." Although the Law of Moses protected slaves from the cruelty of their masters, the southern American slave system facilitated injustice and brutality. By contrast, members of the southern clergy such as Thornton Stringfellow

dramatically transformed through a vivid conversion experience, so, too, could American society be rescued from its perpetual state of moral and spiritual decline. Social movements such as temperance and suffrage, the outgrowths of this perfectionist mentality, became popular modes for enacting social change, especially among the women who experienced a degree of authority as lay leaders during revival meetings. In the eyes of many, however, the institution of slavery was at the core of America's moral iniquity. Heeding the call, many revivalists, including Finney and Beecher, began advocating the immediate disbandment of slavery throughout the nation.

### William Lloyd Garrison and the Early Years

Strongly influenced by nineteenth-century cultural change and revivalist perfectionism, American abolitionism began to

(1788–1869) argued that a literal reading of various biblical passages justified the institution of slavery. In his tract "The Bible Argument, or, Slavery in the Light of Divine Revelation," Stringfellow observed that slavery was not abolished anywhere in the Bible, and therefore it should not be abolished in nineteenth-century America. He wrote: "If pure religion, therefore, did not require it abolition under the Law of Moses, nor in the church of Christ—we may safely infer, that our political, moral, and social relations do not require it in a State."

Many northern Democrats also disapproved of emancipation, at times even violently. On November 7, 1837, Presbyterian minister and abolitionist publisher Elijah Lovejoy (1802–1837) became the first victim of pro-slavery mob violence while defending his printing press from destruction. Like their pro-slavery rivals, abolitionists also were prone to certain acts of indiscretion. In response to the ransacking of Lawrence, Kansas, by pro-slavery ruffians, radical abolitionist John Brown (1800–1859), along with a few of his supporters, murdered several sympathizers near Pottawattamie Creek, Kansas, in 1856. Brown's most famous, and ultimately unsuccessful, insurrection occurred in the fall of 1859 when he and twenty-two followers led a raid against the federal armory in Harpers Ferry, West Virginia, in the hope of seizing its munitions and arming the local slave population.

Disputes, though relatively nonviolent, also arose among abolitionists in the late 1830s and early 1840s over the role that political and religious institutions should play in the antislavery movement. Even though Garrisonians severed all ties with politicians and denominations, other abolitionists, believing Garrison's actions to be rash, sought to maintain an alliance. For these non-Garrisonian abolitionists, political and religious institutions provided the necessary resources for enacting genuine change.

## Political and Denominational Abolitionism

Non-Garrisonian abolitionists established the Liberty Party in 1840, which advocated full emancipation and opposed extending the practice of slavery to the western territories and newly formed states. In 1848 the Liberty Party was joined by other "non-extentionist" Whigs and Democrats to create the Free Soil Party, whose platform, like that of the Liberty Party, opposed the extension of slavery to the West. However, with the ratification of pro-slavery legislation such as the Compromise of 1850, the Fugitive Slave Act of 1850,

and the Kansas Nebraska Act of 1854, the Free Soil Party became obsolete and eventually was absorbed into the new Republican Party.

In addition to engaging in partisan politics, many non-Garrisonian abolitionists worked closely with various religious denominations, including Methodists, Baptists, Presbyterians, and Congregationalists, as well as non-Protestant religious groups such as Unitarians, Mennonites, and Shakers. Non-Garrisonians also aligned themselves with some religious institutions. Schools of higher education, such as Congregationalist-run Oberlin College—the second president was Charles Finney—became centers of abolitionist activity, admitting African American students as early as 1835. Also unlike Garrisonians, non-Garrisonian abolitionists used the influence and charisma of the clergy to further disseminate the antislavery message. Famous abolitionist ministers such as Charles Finney and Lyman Beecher preached openly against the immorality of slavery to large congregations and gatherings. Yet in spite of their strong opposition to the buying and selling of slaves, Finney and especially Beecher were hesitant to suggest that all races be treated as equal.

Non-Garrisonian abolitionists may have cooperated with a variety of religious denominations and institutions, but most remained steadfast in their anti-Catholic sentiments. And yet, even though many American Catholics in the mid-nineteenth century were pro-slavery, liberal Catholics pursued an abolitionist agenda. Catholics such as James McMaster (1820–1886), editor of the antislavery *New York Freeman's Journal,* and Archbishop John Purcell (1800–1883) of Cincinnati were highly vocal in their criticism of slavery as a blatant violation of basic human rights. Although skeptical of President Abraham Lincoln's proposal of immediate emancipation, the Vatican itself, during the early years of the Civil War, also characterized slavery as a tragic and regrettable institution.

## The Final Years

By the beginning of the Civil War in 1861, antislavery sentiments in the United States had reached a fever pitch. The Republican abolitionist contingency in the North pressed the Lincoln administration for decisive action. In response, the executive branch issued the Emancipation Proclamation of 1863, which was followed shortly by ratification of the Thirteenth (1865) and Fifteenth (1870) Amendments. With slavery officially abolished and freed male slaves given the right to vote, the American abolitionist movement quickly faded, but not before leaving an indelible mark on nineteenth-century American culture.

**See also** *African American Religion: Colonial Era through the Civil War; Bible entries; Benevolent Empire; Civil War; Episcopalians: Early Republic; Evangelicals: Nineteenth Century; Politics: Nineteenth Century; Quakers: Through the Nineteenth Century; Transcendentalism; Unitarians.*

Jonathan Olson

## BIBLIOGRAPHY

Andrews, Dee E. *The Methodists and Revolutionary America, 1760–1800: The Shaping of an Evangelical Culture.* Princeton, N.J.: Princeton University Press, 2000.

Essig, James D. *The Bonds of Wickedness: American Evangelicals against Slavery, 1770–1808.* Philadelphia: Temple University Press, 1982.

Fehrenbacher, Don E. *The Slaveholding Republic: An Account of the United States Government's Relations to Slavery.* New York: Oxford University Press, 2001.

Friedman, Lawrence J. *Gregarious Saints: Self and Community in American Abolitionism, 1830–1870.* New York: Cambridge University Press, 1982.

Grimké, Angelina. *Appeal to Christian Women of the South.* 1840. Reprint. New York: Arno, 1969.

Kraditor, Aileen S. *Means and Ends in American Abolitionism: Garrison and His Critics on Strategy and Tactics, 1834–1850.* New York: Pantheon Books, 1969.

McKivigan, John R. "Abolitionism and American Religion." In *History of the American Abolitionist Movement: A Bibliography of the Scholarly Articles,* edited by John R. McKivigan. New York: Garland, 1999.

———. *The War against Proslavery Religion: Abolitionism and the Northern Churches, 1830–1865.* Ithaca, N.Y.: Cornell University Press, 1984.

McKivigan, John R., and Mitchell Snay, eds. *Religion and the Antebellum Debate over Slavery.* Athens: University of Georgia Press, 1998.

Nash, Gary B. *The Forgotten Fifth: African Americans and Age of Revolution.* Cambridge, Mass.: Harvard University Press, 2006.

Stringfellow, Thornton. "The Bible Argument, or, Slavery in the Light of Divine Revelation." In *The Cotton Is King and Pro-Slavery Arguments,* edited by E. N. Elliott. Augusta, Ga.: Pritchard, Abbott, and Loomis, 1860.

Strong, Douglas M. *Perfectionist Politics: Abolitionism and the Religious Tensions of American Democracy.* Syracuse, N.Y.: Syracuse University Press, 1999.

# Aboriginal Traditions

See *Canada: Aboriginal Traditions*

# Abortion

Abortion is a medical procedure used to terminate a pregnancy by removing the embryo or fetus from a woman's uterus. Nonsurgical means for abortion include longtime herbal options and modern drugs such as RU-486. Surgical abortions became legal in America in 1973 with the U.S. Supreme Court decision in *Roe v. Wade.*

Prior to *Roe,* most religious groups, with the exception of Roman Catholics, did not view abortion as a significant moral issue. Rather, it was a medical issue, and physicians drove the debate. After *Roe,* religious views colored the issue, and it became a focal point of domestic politics and foreign policy, eventually affecting world population policies. Though pro-life positions are often motivated by belief in the dignity of human life, antiabortion politics have at times perpetuated racial inequities in the United States, and American antiabortion transnational activism has arguably contributed to greater social and economic burdens for women in underdeveloped areas of the world.

## Abortion as a Medical Issue: Antiabortion Legislation

Prior to the enactment of antiabortion legislation in the nineteenth century, abortion was common in America. The most common indicator of pregnancy was quickening, the point at which a woman first felt fetal movements. Early antiabortion legislation, such as in Connecticut in 1821, outlawed abortion using poison after quickening and imposed life sentences on abortionists. Nevertheless, women effected their own abortions with pennyroyal or other herbs, and physicians commonly treated women for "menstrual blockage," even after quickening. Untrained abortionists such as Ann Trow Lohman, more widely known as Madame Restell, made fortunes catering to wealthy socialites. Abortions were even more dangerous than childbirth, and without antibiotics they often resulted in infection or death.

During this period there was surprisingly little religious opposition to abortion. Instead, changes in English law and medical concerns first inspired antiabortion legislation in the United States. Quickening disappeared as a dividing point after the British declared abortion via poison (Lord Ellenborough's Act, 1803) or surgical means (Lord Lansdowne's Act, 1828) illegal. New York embraced its own Lansdowne Act of 1828 and brought charges only upon the death of the woman or the successful termination of her pregnancy. It did, however, make exceptions for the mother's life when two physicians deemed the procedure necessary. By 1840 eight states had enacted antiabortion legislation, including Connecticut, where abortion before quickening became a crime in 1860.

Lobbying by physicians in response to the health risks posed by untrained providers escalated the legislative movement. Physician Horatio Storer led the effort to organize the medical profession, and in 1859 the American Medical Association (AMA) called for an end to abortions both before and after quickening. The AMA rejected the common belief that a fetus was not alive until after quickening and declared it a living being before birth. It also claimed that women seeking abortions had abandoned providential roles, a sensitive issue at a time when more and more women were entering the workforce and experiencing its effects on their role in family life.

The debate soon addressed birth control. Protestant women were more likely to use birth control than Roman Catholic women, and Protestants feared that their declining birthrates might promote "race suicide" if Catholic and other "inferior" immigrants increased in numbers. Although Protestants had little to say against abortion, Antony Comstock and other Protestant politicians became the chief opponents of legalized birth control measures. The Comstock Act of 1873 made it illegal to send any contraceptive or abortion-related item through the mail. Connecticut promptly banned the use of contraceptives, forbidding physicians to dispense them or to provide information even to married couples. Authorities eventually prosecuted both Madame Restell and birth-control advocate Margaret Sanger under the act.

The Comstock Act was very unpopular, but by the end of the 1870s over forty states had passed antiabortion statutes without reference to quickening, often allowing exceptions for a woman's health. Nevertheless, abortions continued to be common, especially for privileged women, but physicians had gained control of the process. Often states required the opinion of two concurring physicians for abortions. The debate over contraceptives followed a similar pattern. Margaret Sanger supported physician control of contraceptives and won a victory over another birth control activist, Mary Ware Dennett, who advocated women's control over their own bodies. For both abortion and contraception the debates focused solely on medical concerns; moral issues never became a focal point.

## Physicians Drive Abortion Reform

By the 1940s physicians were making their decisions to grant therapeutic abortions via hospital boards, but medical advances had made pregnancy safer, and doctors routinely denied abortions, even in cases of maternal cancer. Boards subjected women to humiliating interviews and examinations, and women approved for abortions were often perceived as psychologically unstable. Over 40 percent of U.S. hospitals performing abortions insisted that women consent to simultaneous sterilization.

This was particularly true for impoverished African American women, many of whom were unwed mothers. A 1970 study conducted by Princeton University researchers reported that 20 percent of African American women had been sterilized. Politicians blamed unwed African American mothers for juvenile delinquency, poverty, and inflated welfare rolls. African American women sometimes sought abortions so their children would not suffer from miserable social conditions, and by 1950 the rate of population growth for African Americans had been cut in half. According to an article in the magazine *Ebony,* eight thousand of the abortions undergone by African American women every year resulted in death.

As medical care advanced, physicians once again led the battle to reform antiabortion laws, and in 1959 the AMA stopped classifying abortion as a homicide. An epidemic of German measles from 1962 to 1965 that resulted in 15,000 babies with birth defects, as well as the well-known case of Sherry Finkbine, who took the sedative thalidomide while pregnant with her fifth child but could not get an abortion in America, inspired further reform (thalidomide causes severe birth defects).

The abortion issue was, however, not yet a moral controversy, nor were race and political persuasion decisive factors. The few pro-life movements before *Roe* were largely Roman Catholic. Pope Paul VI defended the sanctity of life and defined it as beginning at the moment of conception (*Humanae Vitae*). Consequently, abortion reform bills failed in states with larger percentages of Catholics, such as Maine and New Jersey, whereas they passed easily in states such as Georgia with small percentages of Catholics. Indeed, southern states passed most of the reform legislation. Generally, no large, well-organized antiabortion groups were active in the South during this period, and many Protestant groups openly supported abortion reform bills.

By 1972 Alaska, Florida, Hawaii, New York, and Washington had repealed antiabortion laws. Meanwhile, feminist organizations such as the National Organization for Women (NOW) and the National Abortion Rights Action League (NARAL) continued to agitate for reform. Other organizations such as Jane, founded in 1969 and officially known as the "Abortion Counseling Service of Women's Liberation," provided underground though safe abortions for poor women. Some doctors even performed illegal abortions, such as Jane Hodgson, the only licensed physician ever convicted for performing an abortion in a hospital. Other doctors referred women to providers such as Ruth Barnett, "the abortionist," who performed tens of thousands of abortions. Nevertheless, no further legislation was passed, because physicians drove the movement and it never touched the masses.

### The Supreme Court's Impact on Abortion Law

When the courts stepped into the picture, abortion became a polarizing moral issue. In 1965 in *Griswold v. Connecticut,* the U.S. Supreme Court overturned the Comstock laws, which criminalized the delivery or transportation of "obscene, lewd, or lascivious" material as well as methods of or information about birth control. Justice William O. Douglas's majority opinion referenced "penumbras and emanations" from the "specific guarantees in the Bill of Rights," including the right to privacy, which became a factor in the 1973 *Roe v. Wade* decision.

The case of Norma McCorvey, better known as Jane Roe, was controversial from the beginning. Texas denied an abortion to McCorvey, who had pleaded economic hardship. She already had children and claimed to have been gang-raped, but news leaked out that she was a lesbian and that her pregnancy was the result of a brief liaison rather than a rape. By the time the case came before the Court, McCorvey had given birth to her child. Her attorneys, Sarah Weddington and Linda Coffee, were recent law school graduates, and Weddington did not provide a constitutional foundation for her arguments. Although the Court found in Roe's favor, Weddington reargued her case when Justice Harry Blackmun's majority opinion did not convince the Court.

Justice Blackmun based the majority opinion on the due process clause of the Fourteenth Amendment and also on the penumbra of privacy from *Griswold*. However, he argued that the right to privacy was not unqualified, because the state's legitimate interest to protect the welfare of its subjects and "the potentiality of human life" increased over the course of a pregnancy. *Roe* did not guarantee the right to abortion on demand, nor did it forbid physicians or the state from regulating the process. In the first trimester, it gave a woman the unqualified right to an abortion in consultation with a doctor. The state had the right to regulate but not prohibit abortion in the second trimester, and in the third

trimester and after fetal viability the state could proscribe abortion unless the mother's life was in danger. *Roe* subjected the state's right to regulate abortion to a standard of "strict scrutiny," but this standard did not negate state requirements that licensed physicians perform abortions. In an especially controversial statement, the Court declared in *Roe* that a fetus was not legally a person before birth and before viability had no rights of its own that superseded those of the mother.

The Court further confirmed physicians' control over abortion in *Doe v. Bolton,* issued the same day as *Roe*. It upheld a Georgia law requiring medical review of abortions by a board of physicians, but expanded grounds for therapeutic abortions to include economic hardship. In 1977 the Court upheld the conviction of an untrained abortionist (*Menillo v. Connecticut*).

The Court issued inconsistent decisions, however, on the principle of "strict scrutiny," refusing to require spousal or parental consent for abortions involving underage, unwed girls, but upholding mandatory prior written consent in *Planned Parenthood v. Danforth* (1976). Later, in *Belotti v. Baird* (1979) and *Planned Parenthood of Kansas City v. Ashcroft* (1983) it reversed itself on parental consent laws for minors as long as judicial approval or other alternatives were available. Simultaneously, in *Akron v. Akron Center* (1983) the Court overturned Akron's hospitalization requirement, a twenty-four-hour waiting period, and its informed consent requirement for the second and third trimesters. In *Planned Parenthood of Kansas City v. Ashcroft,* Justice Sandra Day O'Connor dissented and advocated an "undue burden" standard for determining whether state attempts to regulate abortion violated the spirit of *Roe*. The Supreme Court then gradually retreated from *Roe,* ignoring its own precedents.

After *Roe,* pro-choice groups such as Planned Parenthood and NARAL fought for abortion to be available in clinics. As a result, the number of safe abortions increased. Deaths from legal abortions were ten times lower than from illegal ones and five times lower than the death rate of women who gave birth. Inequities were apparent, however, as abortion often remained inaccessible to young and poor women who lived far away from urban centers. When Congress passed a "conscience clause bill" in 1973 allowing hospitals to refuse to perform abortions, they became even more inaccessible. Only 17 percent of public hospitals in 1975 performed abortions; 28 percent of non-Catholic private hospitals offered them. Consequently, more than 500,000 women in America had to seek abortions outside of their state of residence.

## *Religious Responses to* Roe v. Wade

*Roe* sparked a great deal of outrage among Catholics. The National Right to Life Committee was formed in 1973, spending $4 million lobbying Congress for a constitutional amendment banning abortion. The 1976 election proved pivotal to the pro-life movement, and for the first time Protestant involvement became more of a factor. Ronald Reagan, who as governor of California had refused to veto the state's abortion reform bill in 1967, became a favorite of pro-life groups. Although Gerald R. Ford eventually won the Republican nomination, Reagan's supporters pushed through a plank in the party platform supporting a constitutional amendment banning abortion. Democrats refused to support an amendment. By 1978, however, thirteen state legislatures had called for a constitutional convention.

Medicaid was funding over 33 percent of all abortions. In response, pro-life agitation led to the drafting of the 1976 Hyde Amendment, which called for a ban on the use of Medicaid funds for abortions. The amendment eventually passed the Senate, with an exception clause for the life of the mother. When the Supreme Court upheld this ban in *Harris v. McRae* (1980), the rights provided by *Roe* were now largely inaccessible to minorities.

In the 1970s pro-life advocates were a very diverse group that reflected an odd marriage of Catholics, Protestants, and Jews. They were not yet clearly divided along party lines, even in Congress and in the White House. The Republican pro-life plank was criticized for being contradictory—that is, Republicans who supported the right to life for the unborn and interpreted abortion as murder were often in favor of the death penalty. Nor did a pro-life stance on abortion translate into advocacy for a minimum quality of life for all people, because pro-life Republicans were generally opposed to welfare. By contrast, Catholic pro-life advocates tended to be liberal on government programs for the poor and to condemn the death penalty and euthanasia. Protestants tended to see abortion as a by-product of premarital sex and focused on this issue more than on the right to life of a fetus, whereas Catholics focused on right to life issues. More broadly, pro-lifers tended to be generally more conservative in their worldviews, single-issue voters, and supportive of traditional roles for women.

Unlike the view put forth by the Court in *Roe v. Wade,* pro-life advocates maintained that a fetus is a human being from the moment of conception. Pope John Paul II's theology of the body underscored this view, because he emphasized the centrality of the Incarnation in Christian theology and the importance of human embodiment as the only medium through which God is revealed. But there was lack of agreement even here, because Catholics protected fetal life over the life of the mother, whereas the Seventh-day Adventists and the Union of Orthodox Jewish Congregations of America allowed exceptions for rape, incest, or the mother's health.

The official positions of many religious groups on abortion and the status of the fetus evolved over time, especially as a result of the political activism during the 1980s. For example, the Southern Baptist Convention initially endorsed *Roe v. Wade,* but by the thirtieth anniversary of the decision it had firmly retracted its endorsement.

Pro-choice advocates tended to maintain that a fetus is not a fully individuated person; it is not a human being. Scientific studies supported these views, demonstrating that a fetus could not feel pain prior to the third trimester. However, the demarcation between antiabortion and pro-choice positions was not, and is not, always clear. Even within the pro-choice group opinions often differed and positions evolved over time.

In 1973 a group of pro-choice clergy formed the Religious Coalition for Abortion Rights in response to *Roe v. Wade.* Later renamed the Religious Coalition for Reproductive Rights, this group includes, among others, Methodists and the Presbyterian Church (USA). In 1970 the General Assembly of the Presbyterian Church in the United States declared that abortion should not be regulated by law; in 1992 the General Assembly declared that abortion should not be used as a form of birth control; and in 2006 it affirmed that the life of a child ought to be respected both before and after birth. Simultaneously, however, the General Assembly insisted that humans could not claim to know when life begins. Although the Presbyterian Church (USA) can be classified as pro-choice, its position is complex and it cannot be said to favor abortion on demand. Similarly, although the United Methodist Church favored abortion as a choice in the 1970s and its 1996 *Book of Discipline* still included pro-abortion statements, it also included texts that affirmed the sanctity of unborn life.

Demarcation of the pro-life movement by political party lines did not occur until the 1980s, when the Christian Right allied with the Republican Party. After 1980 there was also more Protestant pro-life involvement. The Moral Majority, founded by Jerry Falwell, a Baptist minister, had a significant impact on politics in the 1980s and drew supporters from a broad spectrum of society. Together with Pat Robertson's 700 Club, the Moral Majority added some eight million voters to the rolls. Falwell had an enormous influence on the Ronald Reagan administration, and pro-life representatives met with Reagan every year on the anniversary of *Roe v. Wade*. Reagan failed, however, to deliver the constitutional amendment banning abortion desired by the pro-life movement.

Pro-life activism took a decidedly violent turn in the late 1970s and early 1980s. Joseph Scheidler, a former Benedictine monk, founded the Pro-Life Action League (PAL) in 1980, which harassed women as they entered clinics, followed them home after appointments, jammed clinic phone lines, and harassed workers. Bombings and arson began in 1977 and reached a high point in 1984, with the release of the emotionally stirring film *Silent Scream,* depicting an actual fetus during an abortion. Randall Terry, a protégé of Scheidler, formed Operation Rescue in 1986, and thousands of evangelical Protestants joined him in picketing abortion clinics in Atlanta in 1988 and in Wichita, Kansas, in 1991. In Wichita a federal judge issued an order to stop the picketing, which resulted in over two thousand arrests. Another controversy erupted when the administration of President George H. W. Bush filed a brief of amicus curiae in *Bray v. Alexandria Women's Health Clinic* supporting the activities of Operation Rescue and similar groups. The Bush administration argued that authorities could not use federal civil rights law to protect clients of clinics from blockades. John G. Roberts Jr., who worked in the Bush Justice Department and Office of White House Counsel, helped to develop some of these briefs, a controversial factor in his later confirmation hearings as chief justice of the United States. Despite the support of the Bush administration, two court cases, *National Abortion Federation v. Operation Rescue* and *National Organization of Women (NOW) v. Scheidler,* resulted in restrictions on clinic picketing, and Terry himself was later incarcerated. In the 1990s, during the Clinton administration, the Justice Department also prosecuted Operation Rescue under the Racketeer Influenced Corrupt Organizations (RICO) laws, imposing fines in the hundreds of thousands of dollars by the 1990s.

Although the activities of Operation Rescue and similar organizations dwindled as a result of legal difficulties, violent activism succeeded in reducing the number of abortions performed. By 1985 only about one-quarter of medical schools were offering training in abortion. By 1991 only 12 percent were offering training in performing first-trimester abortions, while only 7 percent trained physicians in second-trimester procedures.

## Planned Parenthood v. Casey

In 1989 pro-life forces believed they had won another victory when a Supreme Court decision in *Webster v. Reproductive Health Services* upheld state regulations prohibiting abortions in public hospitals and requiring that physicians check for fetal viability before performing an abortion. The Court left untouched a portion of the Missouri statute that defined human life as beginning at conception. The fetal viability requirement potentially undercut *Roe's* provision of privacy during the first two trimesters, prompting Justice Blackmun to remark that "a chill wind blows." *Webster* was the beginning of the Court's reconsideration of various planks of *Roe*.

In 1992 the Court continued its assault in *Planned Parenthood of Southeast Pennsylvania v. Casey*. The *Casey* decision upheld a twenty-four-hour waiting period before an abortion. Previously, in *Thornburgh v. American College of Obstetricians and Gynecologists* (1985), the Court had ruled against such a period. The Court also refused to force a woman to obtain spousal consent, basing its argument on the principle of *stare decisis* (prior decisions), but this refusal implied that other state restrictions, once upheld, would be permanent. Although the Court had not completely overturned *Roe,* it had negated its trimester system and abandoned *Roe's* standard of "strict scrutiny" for restrictions in favor of Justice O'Connor's "undue burden" standard. State court decisions also retreated from *Roe's* statement that a fetus is not legally a person, convicting African American crack addicts on charges of endangering their unborn children and determining that frozen embryos were "persons" who should be considered "children" of a divorced couple (*Davis v. Davis* [1989]).

Ironically, *Webster* and later decisions energized the pro-choice faction and women's rights groups became a significant factor in the debate over abortion, although antiabortion groups softened their stance throughout the 1980s and 1990s to accommodate exceptions for rape and incest. They favored freedom from governmental intrusion into areas in which the family should be sovereign and parental consent laws for minors. Even NARAL softened its support for abortion to accommodate what journalist William Saletan calls the "mutant version" of abortion rights, based on data gleaned by professional pollster Harrison Hickman. NARAL orchestrated a massive campaign based on the motto "Who

Decides—You or Them?" In 1989 Douglas Wilder used this strategy and won the Virginia governor's race, becoming the first African American governor in U.S. history. In 1992 even Democrats Bill Clinton and Al Gore ran on a plank that included parental consent laws and opposed government funding of abortion. By the early 1990s Republican Newt Gingrich could refer to America as "pro-choice, anti-abortion."

## Partial-Birth Abortion and RU-486

The introduction of partial-birth abortions, technically known as "intact dilation and extraction," further ignited the debate. The procedure involved dilating the cervix over several days, partially delivering the fetal body, piercing the skull in order to suction out the contents of the cranium, and then delivering the rest of the fetus intact. Less than one-third of fetuses aborted in this way were dead when the procedure was performed, making it especially controversial. The American College of Obstetricians and Gynecologists pointed out that it was never the only option available, and the AMA called for a ban based on the "inhumane" nature of the procedure. In addition to expected opposition from the Catholic Church, the Presbyterian Church (USA), which historically had advocated for a woman's choice in the matter of abortion, issued a statement of concern about the procedure, departing from the position of its fellow members of the Religious Coalition for Reproductive Rights. Some pro-choice senators, such as Daniel Moynihan of Massachusetts and Tom Daschle of South Dakota, did not support the procedure, and in 1995 a ban on partial-birth abortions passed both houses of Congress. President Clinton vetoed the bill and did so again in 1997. Many religious groups protested Clinton's veto, including the Orthodox Church in America.

The states then took matters into their own hands, and by 1998 twenty-two states had passed bans on the procedure. However, in *Stenberg v. Carhart* (2000) the Supreme Court refused to uphold Nebraska's ban on partial-birth or late-term abortions. Because the ban did not include an exception for "health" and removed an option for women, the Court held that it constituted an "undue burden" on women's rights. The decision, however, contradicted public opinion, and in 2003 President George W. Bush signed the Partial-Birth Abortion Ban Act into law.

New nonsurgical options are equally controversial. In 1982 French physician Etienne-Emile Baulieu invented RU-486, an antiprogestin that breaks the bond of the fertilized egg with the uterine wall. A dose of RU-486 is followed thirty-six to forty-eight hours later by a dose of synthetic prostaglandin. A miscarriage then occurs in 96 percent of cases. Although RU-486 has a wide safety margin, physicians restrict its use to women under age thirty-five who are nonsmokers. In 1996 the U.S. Food and Drug Administration (FDA) approved the use of RU-486 in the United States at the request of President Clinton; it is marketed as Mifeprestone. As expected, pro-life forces reacted vociferously to RU-486. The Catholic Church condemned its use, and in view of the multimillion-dollar pro-life campaign against RU-486, drug companies are wary of marketing the drug. Germany, Spain, and France have banned RU-486.

Other new technologies have brought the issue out of a woman's womb and into the test tube. Surrogate mothers have already given life to frozen embryos. Eighty-four families have adopted children born from frozen "snowflake" embryos, obtained from *in vitro* fertilization programs by Nightlife Christian Adoptions.

## Abortion and U.S. Foreign Policy

The parameters of the abortion debate extend beyond the unborn. What is less recognized is that the antiabortion stance of the New Christian Right has molded U.S. foreign policy and had a dramatic impact on women in developing regions of the world. In 1973, the same year as *Roe v. Wade* and well before the Hyde Amendment passed the Senate, Congress prohibited the use of U.S. population funds to either pay for or encourage abortion. In January 1974 the U.S. Agency for International Development (USAID) stopped funding abortion-related services. Prior to 1974, presidents Lyndon B. Johnson and Richard Nixon had argued that it was inappropriate for the United States to export its abortion policies to other countries. Thus USAID policy before 1974 gave priority to funding for research on early abortion technologies and considered abortion an essential component of effective family planning programs. After 1974 Congress prohibited the use of foreign aid to pay for biomedical research on abortion as a method of family planning (1981) or lobbying for abortion (1982), but left open the ways in which organizations could use funds from other sources.

In 1982, it was argued that USAID had an impact on the Alan Guttmacher Institute's freedom of speech when it cut funding for its *International Family Planning Perspective*. Two articles in the journal discussed abortion in developing countries, thereby allegedly violating USAID's policy on promoting abortion. One article contained only one sentence about the legalization of abortion in Tunisia in 1973. The Guttmacher Institute took the case to court. In 1986 a circuit court upheld the district court and ruled that because USAID regulations did not prohibit the publication of neutral information on abortion at the time that funding was denied, the agency could not impose funding restrictions that applied retroactively. The court did not explicitly address the freedom of speech issue raised by the case.

In 1984 the United States released the Mexico City Policy, a radical departure from previous policies, in preparation for the UN Population Conference in Mexico City that same year. In this election year, the New Right of the Republican Party figured prominently. The leader of the U.S. delegation to the conference was former senator James L. Buckley of New York, who had lobbied for the failed constitutional amendment banning abortion. The Republican leadership hoped that transnational antiabortion efforts might ensure success for their domestic planks.

The Mexico City Policy contained the controversial assertion that population growth was a neutral phenomenon not necessarily connected to underdevelopment. For the first time, the policy restricted foreign funding for nongovernmental organizations (NGOs) that engaged in abortion-related activities, even if with non-USAID funds. This restriction included counseling women to obtain abortions in countries where abortion was legal or performing abortions for victims of rape or incest. Effectively, this policy meant that funding NGOs in Asia, Latin America, and Africa risked violating the policy. Many of these NGOs were important providers of contraceptive services and had only limited connection with abortion-related activities. Government agencies that provided abortion services without coercion could receive funds so long as USAID funds were not used for such purposes.

These restrictions on NGOs came at a particularly inopportune time. Since 1980 twenty developing countries had softened harsh abortion laws. Whereas only three African countries had population policies before 1974, African economic ministers endorsed the Kilimanjaro Programme of Action on Population shortly before the 1984 Mexico City conference. The Kilimanjaro Programme was intended to respond to population issues in order to promote socioeconomic development. Family planning services were considered integral to the program's success. Algeria and Brazil were much less confrontational on the subject of family planning than they had been in 1974 at the UN population conference in Bucharest, whereas China had implemented its one-child policy in 1979 and was prepared to defend population programs. Even the location of the conference was conducive to population reform, because Mexico was then the leader of the Group of 77, the caucus of developing countries in the United Nations, and since 1974 Mexico had worked to solve its population issues. The World Bank encouraged these efforts when it released data suggesting that countries would have to quadruple population assistance to meet current needs.

Although the United States articulated a policy prohibiting funds for abortion-related activities, it allowed the Vatican to demand that the conference exclude abortion as a method of family planning. Attendees ultimately agreed not to promote abortion (the word "promote" meant anything from providing services to referring a client to a provider).

One of the first casualties of the Mexico City Policy was the United Nations Population Fund (UNFPA), which provided funds to China. U.S. support for the UNFPA had already declined from about 50 percent of its total revenue to 25 percent by 1984. Since 1980 China had been the second largest recipient of UNFPA funds. James Buckley, under secretary of state and a leading antiabortion advocate, linked the use of funds for abortion or forced family planning in China to UNFPA funding, and pro-life advocates demanded that President Reagan cut UNFPA's funding at their annual meeting on the anniversary of *Roe v. Wade*. Although several senators challenged the Mexico City Policy and the majority of Americans did not want to see funding for population programs tied to abortion, eventually the New Right won, and the United States cut off aid in 1985, despite having previously provided China multilateral development loans without reference to human rights issues. The percentage of funds lost by China for its family planning programs was negligible, but China relied on Western technologies acquired through UNFPA for its population program.

## The Mexico City Policy and the Status of Women

The United States did not include any reference to the status of women in its statement released before the 1984 Mexico City U.N. Population Conference. In an election year in which the traditional views of the New Right were pivotal, a public statement was too risky, but the United States did endorse a section of the conference document strengthening the stand on women's issues. Not coincidentally, many American women were at the conference lobbying for NGOs.

Ironically, the official conference statement on women emphasized persistent links between high rates of fertility and women's inferior social status. In fact, since the 1950s demographers had argued that rates of population growth in underdeveloped areas of the world outpaced those of industrial areas, and they insisted that economic growth was dependent on a reduction in fertility rates. Because the Mexico City Policy often affected NGOs that provided contraceptive and abortion services, its biggest impact was on developing countries with high fertility rates. The population of Kenya, for example, increased threefold after it gained independence. The largest NGO that offered family planning services in Kenya was the Family Planning Association of Kenya, whose parent donor was the International Planned Parenthood Federation (IPPF), an agency that lost funding as a result of the Mexico City Policy. Meanwhile, the Roman Catholic Church and transnational right-to-life groups from the United States have successfully blocked attempts to reform antiabortion laws in Kenya.

The Roman Catholic Church also agitated against abortion and family planning with great success in Mexico, and again transnational groups with support in the United States aided the Church. In 1989 Catholic transnational organizations such Pro-Vida opposed a Mexican government plan to legalize abortion, with the result that the political leadership ceased to make any public statements on the issue. Members of U.S. antiabortion movements attended two international conferences organized by Pro-Vida in the 1980s. Mexican bishops regularly attend meetings of the Knights of Columbus in America, and Pro-Vida receives materials from Human Life International. Traditional views about women's roles continued to dominate the debate in Mexico, as evidenced by results from a 1991 Gallup poll which showed that 43 percent of Mexicans believed that the decision to get an abortion should be a woman's and another 48 percent believed that a woman need not consult the Church, only 38 percent believed that health care organizations should provide abortion services. Some shift in thinking occurred in 2007, when Mexico City's legislative assembly voted to legalize abortions obtained during the first twelve weeks of pregnancy; one year later the Supreme Court of Mexico upheld the law. In other parts of Mexico, abortion is legal only in cases of rape or when the mother's life is endangered.

## The Cairo Conference and Beyond

By the 1990s the alliance between the United States and the Vatican had crumbled after U.S. policy took a decisive turn away from the Mexico City Policy. Within two days of taking office Bill Clinton repealed the Mexico City Policy. In 1994 the U.S. supported a very liberal policy toward women at the International Conference on Population and Development in Cairo. The U.S. contribution to population aid reached its peak early in Clinton's administration. The Vatican, by contrast, assumed a rigid stance at Cairo, and was alarmed by the growing influence of women's rights movements in America. It feared Clinton might promote abortion on demand, and it held up the debate over language on abortion for three days, offending many of the delegates. Clearly, 1994 signaled a new era for women, and the chair of the main committee at Cairo believed the conference had achieved unimagined success.

However, the impact of the Clinton administration was short-lived. Agitation among antiabortion activists, among other factors, resulted in the restoration in 1995 of a Republican-controlled Congress. In 1998 Congress essentially withheld payment of the back dues owed by the United States to the UN and called on Clinton to restore the Mexico City Policy. By 1999 the back dues amounted to almost $1 billion, and Clinton feared loss of the U.S. vote in the General Assembly in 2000. In 1999 Congress passed legislation once again implementing the Mexico City Policy, also known as the Global Gag Rule, and Clinton signed it into law.

Once again, NGOs had to certify that they did not use USAID or any other funds to provide abortion services or to engage in efforts to change foreign abortion policies. USAID interpreted the last restriction to encompass communicating with political leaders on abortion, trying through the mass media to alter policies, or organizing demonstrations. Clinton had the discretion to waive the restrictions on $15 million of the funds, and he immediately did so. Many organizations that certified compliance with the policy later also protested U.S. attempts to curb their autonomy within their native lands. Enyantu Ifenne of Nigeria described the Global Gag Rule as retrogressive, repressive, and undemocratic. Ironically, this reversal of U.S. policy came at a time when global policy was focused on the links between reproductive rights and women's economic and political status, but in 2001 President George W. Bush reaffirmed the prohibitions of the Mexico City Policy. Nonetheless, despite the events chronicled here, at the end of the twentieth century the United States remained the largest single donor to population assistance programs, amounting to fully one-third of the total contributed from all sources.

On January 21, 2009, newly inaugurated President Barack Obama rescinded the Mexico City Policy. On the thirty-sixth anniversary of *Roe v. Wade*, Obama issued a statement criticizing the policy as unnecessarily broad and affirming a woman's right to choose. USAID announced quick action to implement the change, while antiabortion groups protested the decision.

In November 2009, as the House of Representatives debated a sweeping health care bill, Democrat Bart Stupak of Michigan proposed an amendment to the bill that barred the use of any federal funds to pay for an abortion or to purchase a health care plan that covered abortion, except in cases in which the mother's life was in danger or in cases of rape or incest. The Stupak Amendment did not prohibit women who wanted abortion coverage from purchasing supplemental policies, but they could not do so with federal funds.

## Conclusion

Though the policy articulated by President George W. Bush in 2001 did not forbid postabortion care, legal and cultural restrictions continue to pose challenges to programs offering such care. Worldwide, contraceptives are still not readily available to 120–165 million women, and safe abortions are out of the reach of one in four women who live in countries where they are illegal. In developing countries as many as 68 percent of patients treated for complications from abortions are under twenty years of age. Family planning issues are among the most pressing global issues.

Even though the abortion issue played a very important role in the 2004 U.S. presidential election, it did not play a similar role in the 2008 presidential election, perhaps signaling a decline in the political influence of the New Right. Nevertheless, there can be no doubt that the rise of the New Right's antiabortion politics in late twentieth-century America combined with Vatican activism have had an impact on America and the world in ways still being measured.

**See also** *Bioethics; Feminism; Gender; Health, Disease, and Medicine; Politics: Twentieth Century; Religious Right; Roman Catholicism: Early Twenty-First-Century Issues; Supreme Court.*

Deborah Vess

### BIBLIOGRAPHY

Blanchard, Dallas, and Terry Prewitt. *Religious Violence and Abortion: The Gideon Project.* Gainesville: University Press of Florida, 1993.

Brodie, Janet Farrell. *Contraception and Abortion in Nineteenth Century America.* Ithaca, N.Y.: Cornell University Press, 1994.

Burns, Gene. *The Moral Veto: Framing Contraception, Abortion, and Cultural Pluralism in the United States.* Cambridge: Cambridge University Press, 2005.

Crane, Barbara. "The Transnational Politics of Abortion." In *Population and Development Review.* Vol. 20, Supplement: "The New Politics of Populations: Conflict and Consensus in Family Planning" (1994): 241–262.

Davis, Angela. "Racism, Birth Control, and Reproductive Rights." In *Women, Race and Class,* edited by Angela Davis, 202–222. New York: Random House, 1981.

Dienes, Thomas C. *Law, Politics, and Birth Control.* Urbana: University of Illinois Press, 1972.

Finkle, Jason L., and Barbara B. Crane. "Ideology and Politics at Mexico City: The United States at the 1984 International Conference on Population." In *Population and Development Review* 11 (March 1985): 1–28.

Hall, Robert E., ed. *Abortion in a Changing World.* Vol. 1. New York: Columbia University Press, 1970.

Herring, Mark Y. *The Pro-Life/Pro-Choice Debate.* Westport, Conn.: Greenwood Press, 1993.

Luker, Kristen. *Abortion and the Politics of Motherhood.* Berkeley: University of California Press, 1984.

Mohr, James C. *Abortion in America: The Origins and Evolution of National Policy, 1800–1900.* Oxford: Oxford University Press, 1978.

Pope Paul VI. "*Humane Vitae.*" *The Pope Speaks* 13 (Fall 1969): 329–346.

Reagan, Lesley J. *When Abortion Was a Crime: Women, Medicine, and Law in the United States, 1867–1973.* Berkeley: University of California Press, 1997.

Saletan, William. *Bearing Right: How Conservatives Won the Abortion War.* Berkeley: University of California Press, 2003.

Savel, Lewis E. "Adjudication of Therapeutic Abortion and Sterilization." In *Therapeutic Abortion and Sterilization,* edited by Edmund W. Overstreet. New York: Harper and Row, 1964.

Solinger, Rickie, ed. *Abortion Wars: A Half Century of Struggle, 1950–2000.* Berkeley: University of California Press, 1998.

Thomson, Judith Jarvis. "A Defense of Abortion." *Philosophy and Public Affairs* 1, no. 1 (1971): 47.

# Adventism and Millennialism

The adventism formulated by William Miller in the 1820s—the expectation of Jesus' imminent Second Coming or, as the adventists say, Jesus' "soon" Second Coming—developed within a tradition of Anglo-American millennial thinking that began in the seventeenth century. Millennialism looked forward to the Second Coming of Jesus, but its thinking took two major forms. Postmillennialists believed that the biblical prophecies of the millennium referred to a future time when God's spirit would reign in human hearts, after which Jesus would return to earth. Premillennialists understood the prophecies to foretell a period of increasing doom that would end with Christ's return in judgment, after which the millennium would begin. Until the mid-nineteenth century most premillennialists took a historicist position—that is, they believed that the prophecies described historical periods—but in the 1830s an alternative futurist view emerged, which asserted that the prophecies told of events that would occur just before the end of time. The futurist interpretation, however, did not become prominent in the United States until after the Civil War.

## Eighteenth-Century American Millennialism

Although millennialist thought was widespread in seventeenth-century Anglo-American religious movements, it gained greater prominence in the eighteenth century, particularly in the thought of Jonathan Edwards (1703–1758), a minister and theologian in Massachusetts. As early as the 1720s Edwards had expressed his expectation that the future would bring the church both civil and religious liberty, a postmillennial outlook he developed more fully in a series of sermons preached in the 1730s and published after his death as *History of the Work of Redemption* (1774). The Great Awakening of the 1730s and 1740s, in which Edwards played an important role, spread similar millennial hope throughout the New England and middle colonies.

In the aftermath of a series of earthquakes in 1755, most importantly in Lisbon, Portugal, liberal preachers Charles Chauncy and Jonathan Mayhew drew on biblical prophecy to support their conviction that the world would undergo a fundamental transformation. By the 1770s, these millennial expectations had become a significant element in American political thought as the revolutionaries interpreted Great Britain as the antichrist, believed that America would bring the kingdom of God, and thought that the latter days were at hand. Although millennialist enthusiasm subsided during the Revolutionary War, the French Revolution of 1789 and subsequent reign of terror sparked a revival of interest in the biblical prophecies. Works of prophetic interpretation began attracting attention, among them a new edition of Edwards's *History* as well as Samuel Hopkins's postmillennialist *Treatise on the Millennium* (1793) and Elhanan Winchester's premillennialist *Lectures on the Prophecies that Remain to be Fulfilled* (1795). During the 1790s the two versions of millennialism became more distinct.

## British Premillennialism

The French Revolution also awakened interest in the biblical prophecies among British observers. Believing that Daniel 7 and 13 were being fulfilled before their eyes, such writers as George Stanley Faber in *Dissertation on the Prophecies* (1804) and James Hatley Frere in *Combined View of the Prophecies* (1815) developed a literal, premillennialist interpretation that took a pessimistic view of the future. Another premillennialist, Lewis Way, introduced the idea

that before Christ's Second Advent, the Jews would return to Palestine.

British premillennialism was organized through the Albury Conferences of Henry Drummond (1786–1860), a former banker and member of the House of Commons. The conferences, which were held annually from 1826 to 1828, brought together leading premillennialist clergymen, mostly Anglican, and lay persons, thereby consolidating the premillennialism theology. In 1829 Drummond established six points of belief on which the conference participants largely agreed: (1) the current dispensation would end cataclysmically; (2) the Jews would return to Palestine; (3) Christendom awaited judgment; (4) the millennium would take place after this judgment; (5) Jesus would physically return before the millennium began; and (6) the 1,260-day prophecies of Daniel 7 and 13 were to be understood as historical years, extending from Justinian to the French Revolution, while Revelation 16's vials of wrath should be interpreted as referring to the present time. Christ's Second Advent, therefore, would occur very soon.

Beginning in the 1820s several societies formed to study the prophecies, and premillennialist periodicals began to appear. William Cuninghame and Edward Irving, who had translated Manuel Lacunza's *The Coming of the Messiah* in 1826, emerged as leading preachers, although the exhaustion arising from a controversy over speaking in tongues led to Irving's demise in 1834. Meanwhile, John Nelson Darby (1800–1882), founder of the Plymouth Brethren, adopted a futurist/dispensationalist interpretation of the book of Revelation, which asserted that nothing in Revelation's prophecies had yet taken place and would not occur until very near the end of the present age. The differences between these two versions of premillennialism became clearer at the Powerscourt Conferences in Ireland, held between 1831 and 1833, which were ultimately dominated by Darby's views. Despite these differences in interpretation of prophetic chronology, the premillennialists were agreed that the present age would end in destruction as Jesus physically returned to earth and the millennium began. Their outlook toward the future contrasted sharply with that of the postmillennialists.

## Second Great Awakening

Despite the interest in millennialism in late eighteenth-century America, the new nation was rather secular in outlook and active involvement in religion seemed to be in decline. This situation changed dramatically during the first half of the nineteenth century with the series of revivals known as the "Second Great Awakening." The spiritual renaissance had both eastern and western origins. Its beginnings were marked by Kentucky's Cane Ridge camp meeting (1801) and a major revival at Yale College (1802). From there it spread across the country, becoming most intense in upstate New York in the "Burned-Over District," where the fires of revival spread back and forth across the region from the 1820s to the 1840s. Charles G. Finney (1792–1875), who was converted in 1821, became the most famous of the Second Great Awakening preachers and developed several evangelistic techniques, known as "New Measures," that were to shape the tradition of American revivalism.

Although many of the Awakening preachers, such as Finney, regarded themselves as Calvinists, they moved in an Arminian direction that emphasized the role of the personal decision in conversion. Influenced by Methodism, Awakening theology also stressed that Christians should not only accept Christ's forgiveness of sin but also strive to overcome it through an infusion of the Holy Spirit. As Thomas Hastings wrote in the popular hymn "Rock of Ages," "Be of sin the double cure/Save from wrath and make me pure." Most of the revival preachers also believed in postmillennialism and looked forward to the reign of God's spirit on earth prior to Christ's return. The combination of perfectionism and postmillennialism contributed to the establishment of many voluntary associations that sought to advance God's kingdom by engaging in activities ranging from foreign missions to temperance to antislavery. By the time the Second Great Awakening reached its end in the 1850s, it had transformed the American religious landscape. Whereas in the eighteenth century American religion was dominated by the Congregational and Presbyterian churches, by the mid-nineteenth century these denominations had been replaced by the Methodists and Baptists.

With religious revival flourishing, millennial language achieved widespread expression, even in the old-line churches. In a hymn written in 1840, Arthur Cleveland Coxe, an Episcopalian, asked, "Hark! What Soundeth? Is Creation/Groaning for its latter day?" A few years later, Samuel H. Cox, moderator of the Presbyterian General Assembly, observed that "God has got America within anchorage. . . . He intends to display His prodigies for the millennium." More directly connected with the Second Great Awakening, Alexander Campbell, founder of the Disciples of Christ, entitled his journal the *Millennial Harbinger* and explored the meaning of the 1,260-day and 2,300-day prophecies of Daniel using the day-year principle of interpretation.

Although postmillennialism dominated most millennial thinking, a few Americans turned toward British premillennialism. Between 1840 and 1842 Joel Jones and Orrin Rogers reprinted various British premillennialist works in *The Literalist,* which ran to five issues. Their effort was continued by Isaac P. Labagh, the rector of Calvary Episcopal Church in New York, who published the *American Millenarian and Prophetic Review* from 1842 to 1844. In the pages of this journal, Labagh recommended British premillennialist authors and offered copies of *The Literalist.* American works that reflected British premillennialism included those by Episcopalian Edward Winthrop, *Lectures on the Second Advent* (1843), and Presbyterians William Ramsey, *Second Coming . . . Before the Millennium* (1841), and George Duffield, *Millenarianism Defended* (1843).

On the fringes of Christian orthodoxy, other movements that developed during the Second Great Awakening also held millennial expectations. The Shakers, who were established in the Revolutionary period but grew significantly during the revival, adopted as their official name the Millennial Church of the United Society of Believers in Christ's Second Appearing. In their view, the Second Coming of Christ had already occurred in the person of Ann Lee, their founder, who had inaugurated the millennium. In the early 1830s, John Humphrey Noyes, who later established the Oneida community, fully expected that the millennium was near. Later, he reinterpreted the scriptural passages, concluding that Jesus had returned in spirit in 70 CE. Meanwhile, Joseph Smith, founder of the Church of Jesus Christ of Latter-day Saints, or the Mormons, called his periodical the *Millennial Star* and through the early 1840s advocated premillennialism. As the Mormons were forced to move west to Utah, however, they increasingly connected the millennium with a geographical location rather than time.

## William Miller

Before this transatlantic interest in the millennium had fully developed, William Miller (1782–1849), a New York farmer, had concluded that Jesus would return about the year 1843. Born in Massachusetts and reared in Low Hampton, New York, Miller was largely self-educated. He had been raised a Baptist, but became a Deist as a young adult while living in Poultney, Vermont. There, he read works by Voltaire, David Hume, and Ethan Allen. After moving back to Low Hampton, he held some minor public offices and was elected a lieutenant of the local militia raised for the War of 1812, later becoming a captain in the regular army. After participating in the Battle of Plattsburgh on September 11, 1814, in which an outnumbered American force defeated the British, Miller began to question his Deistic beliefs, for it seemed that a divine power must have been involved in that victory. Upon returning home after the war, Miller began attending a Baptist church. He was sometimes asked to read the sermon, but he did not yet profess belief in Christianity. While presenting the sermon in 1816, however, he underwent a profound conversion experience in which he was drawn both emotionally and intellectually to Jesus as his savior.

Challenged by his Deist friends who alleged inconsistencies in the Bible, Miller began a systematic study of the scripture. In line with his faith in reason and common sense that he had held as a Deist, he established fourteen rules of interpretation, which he wrote down in a two-column chart with the rule on one side and a supporting proof-text on the other. By 1818 he had proven to his own satisfaction not only that the Bible contained "a system of revealed truths" that were both simple and clear but also that Jesus would return in about the year 1843. Focusing on Daniel 8:14, "Unto two thousand and three hundred days, then shall the sanctuary be cleansed," Miller combined the common interpretive principle that a prophetic day represented an actual year with his belief that the seventy-week prophecy of Daniel 9:24–27, which referred to the rebuilding of Jerusalem, was part of the 2,300 days. As for Artaxerxes's decree in 457 BCE to rebuild Jerusalem as a fulfillment of Daniel 9, through simple arithmetic Miller determined that the 2,300 days ended in 1843. Because he understood "sanctuary" to mean the earth and "cleansing" to refer to the burning at the final judgment, Miller concluded that Jesus' Second Advent was to take place at the end of the 2,300 days. Except for his rejection of the belief that the Jews would be restored to Palestine and his assertion that Jesus would return about 1843, Miller's interpretation of the prophecies was similar to that of the British premillennialists.

Not wanting to present his startling conclusions prematurely to the public, Miller continued to study. Finally, in 1831 he gave his first public lecture in nearby Dresden, where he sparked a revival. Soon he began receiving invitations from elsewhere in New York and New England, and despite being over fifty years of age and by his own admission a poor speaker, he became a full-time lecturer. In 1832 Miller published a series of sixteen articles in the *Vermont Telegraph* that he combined the next year into a sixty-four-page pamphlet, "Evidences from Scripture & History of the Second Coming of Christ about the Year CE 1843." He later expanded this pamphlet into a similarly titled book, which was published in 1836.

### Joshua V. Himes and the Emergence of a Movement

Speaking mostly in small towns, Miller to this point was not well-known. In 1839, however, he gave a lecture series at Exeter, New Hampshire, where he made the acquaintance of Joshua V. Himes (1805–1895), a Christian Connection minister from Boston. Himes invited Miller to speak at his Chardon Street Chapel, where he drew large crowds during two series of meetings in late 1839 and early 1840. Himes had been active in both the New England Anti-Slavery Society and the New England Nonresistance Society and soon was using the publicity techniques learned in those causes on behalf of Miller. In March 1840 Himes began publishing a biweekly paper, the *Signs of the Times,* promoting the imminent return of Christ according to the biblical prophecies as interpreted by Miller. By the end of the year, the *Signs* had 1,500 subscribers.

Himes quickly became Miller's publicist and chief organizer. As interest in Miller's views developed, Himes and several other ministers announced in the *Signs* that a general conference of those believing that Christ's coming was near at hand would meet in Boston beginning on October 14, 1840. Because of illness, Miller was unable to attend the conference at Himes's church. But two hundred did attend the event. Among the major speakers were Henry Dana Ward, a Congregationalist, Josiah Litch, a Methodist, and Henry Jones, a Presbyterian, which suggests the interdenominational appeal of Miller's message. A second conference, held in Lowell, Massachusetts, in June 1841, established committees to raise money, publish papers, and organize future conferences.

Although three more conferences were held in 1841, the meeting that took place in Boston in May 1842 proved pivotal. This conference passed a resolution that for the first time clearly defined the movement's articles of faith. The articles rejected belief in the restoration of the Jews to Palestine and postmillennialism and affirmed that Jesus would return in 1843. In response to this emphasis on a specific time, some early leaders in the movement, particularly Jones and Dana, who had never adopted the specifics of Miller's prophetic interpretation, began playing less visible roles. The conference also appointed a committee to organize camp meetings as a means of promoting the message of Christ's soon return. Finally, the conference voted to print three hundred copies of a pictorial chart interpreting the prophecies of Daniel and Revelation. These charts became a standard feature of adventist preaching.

From this point on, the movement gained momentum and visibility. The first Millerite camp meeting took place in Canada, at Hatley, Quebec, in June 1842. The first meeting in the United States was held later that same month in East Kingston, New Hampshire (poet and essayist John Greenleaf Whittier attended the meeting and later described it). The East Kingston meeting raised money to purchase a large tent that was used the following month at Concord. The "Great Tent" itself, reportedly the largest in America, became a means of publicity and was used seven more times that year. Even though the tent was severely damaged by winds in 1843, camp meetings, tent or no tent, became an increasingly important element of the movement, and the number of meetings grew from 31 in 1842, to 40 in 1843, to 125 in 1844.

Publications were even more important than camp meetings. Himes expanded circulation of the *Signs of the Times* by hiring agents who received a commission for each subscription sold. By early 1842 the paper was able to claim five thousand subscribers, and in April Himes moved to weekly publication. That same year he developed the strategy of establishing temporary papers to accompany specific evangelistic campaigns and provide the opportunity for regional variety and closer support for new believers. In November 1842, Himes and Nathaniel Southard, formerly an antislavery activist, started the first of these papers, the *Midnight Cry,* in New York City, where they printed ten thousand copies each, of twenty-four issues. The paper's popularity led to its continuation as a weekly. More than forty papers were eventually published, among them the *Trumpet of Alarm* (Philadelphia), *Second Advent of Christ* (Cleveland), *Voice of Elijah* (Montreal), and *Western Midnight Cry* (Cincinnati). In addition to these regional publications, the *Advent Message to the Daughters of Zion* addressed women, and the *Advent Shield,* a quarterly, provided a scholarly exposition of Millerite interpretations.

Beginning as early as 1840, the adventists began issuing tracts and pamphlets. Among these was a series entitled "Words of Warning," which included brief discourses on topics such as "The Last Days," "The End of Time," and "How Awful to Meet an Angry God." Himes also created the "Second Advent Library," which eventually ran to nearly fifty volumes; these varied in size from a few pages to more than two hundred pages. To support the camp meetings and other

gatherings, Himes published *Millennial Harp, or Second Advent Hymns* (in 1842), a collection of both traditional and new songs related to the Second Coming of Christ.

Although Miller provided the movement's message and Himes its organizational and publicity direction, other individuals also emerged into prominence. Josiah Litch (1809–1886), a Methodist minister, adopted Miller's interpretations in 1838, and in June of that year he published *The Probability of the Second Coming of Christ about the Year 1843.* By 1841 he had left his ministerial appointment to become a full-time adventist lecturer. Charles Fitch (1805–1844), a minister and antislavery activist associated with William Lloyd Garrison, adopted Miller's ideas in 1838, but because of criticism from his Presbyterian colleagues abandoned those ideas a short time later. In 1841, however, he left the Presbyterian ministry because of the denomination's opposition to his advocacy of Oberlin Holiness theology. Shortly thereafter, Litch encouraged him to restudy Miller's prophetic interpretation, which he once again adopted. The following year, Fitch and Apollos Hale created the pictorial chart that played such an important role in adventist preaching. Joseph Marsh (1802–1863), a Christian Connection minister, accepted Miller's message in 1843 and the following year began publishing the *Voice of Truth* in Rochester, New York. A few women, among them Lucy Maria Hersey, Olive Maria Rice, and Elvira Fasset, also preached for the adventists. Although the number of adventist lecturers is unknown, in the spring of 1844 the *Midnight Cry* claimed that between fifteen hundred and two thousand men and women were preaching the message. It appears that the majority of the preachers were Methodists or Baptists.

## The Year 1843

As 1843 approached, under Himes's direction the adventists intensified their efforts, moving around the country much like a military campaign. They especially concentrated on major cities such as New York City in late 1842 and Philadelphia in early 1843. Fitch visited Oberlin College in the fall of 1842 and a short time later established a headquarters in Cleveland. In the spring of 1843 the movement gained the support of biblical scholar N. N. Whiting and prominent Baptist ministers Elon Galusha, F. G. Brown, and J. B. Cook. Cook soon went to Cincinnati to direct efforts in southern Ohio. In June, Himes and George Storrs (1796–1879), a Christian Connection minister, took the Great Tent first to Rochester, New York, and later in the summer west to Buffalo and south to Cincinnati, Ohio. Storrs stayed in

Cincinnati so Cook could move northeast to Pittsburgh, Pennsylvania. Some speakers traveled as far west as Indiana and Illinois, and Fitch held a campaign in Detroit, Michigan. Although Millerism was primarily a northern movement, some speakers went as far south as the Carolinas, and Litch held successful meetings in Baltimore, Maryland.

Although Miller had always spoken of Christ's coming in "about" the year 1843, his followers began pressing for greater specificity. At the same time, newspapers were erroneously attributing to Miller various dates for the Second Advent. To clarify his position, Miller wrote a "New Year's Address to Second Advent Believers," which was published in the *Signs of the Times* in January 1843. Using the Jewish lunar calendar rather than Gregorian calendar, he declared that Christ would come between March 21, 1843, and March 21, 1844, observing that no prophetic period extended beyond 1843. Not everyone in the movement agreed with Miller, for even though Jones, Ward, and Whiting believed that Jesus would return soon, they refused to identify a specific year. Some adventists, however, did not hesitate to name specific dates, among them February 10 (forty-five years after the French capture of Rome), February 15 (the anniversary of the establishment of the Roman Republic), and April 14 (Passover, in 1843).

As the adventist movement intensified, it faced increasing criticism. Newspapers published stories asserting that Himes and Miller were growing rich, and that they were hypocrites who did not live as if they soon expected the end of the world. Rumors passed from one publication to another of Millerites going insane or donning white ascension robes in preparation for meeting their Lord—accusations consistently rebutted by the adventist papers.

More significant, as the adventists aggressively pushed their message the denominations began to close their doors to them. Whereas previously Millerite preachers had been valued because they stimulated revival, the increased specificity by both leaders and followers on the time of Christ's coming and their expectation that everyone would agree with them frequently made adventist believers a disruptive force within the churches to which they belonged. By August 1842 Himes was reporting that churches were not allowing adventists to hold meetings within their buildings, a problem that increased over the next two years. Furthermore, denominations began revoking the licenses of any of their preachers who had accepted adventism or pressured them to leave their employment. In 1843, for example, Congregational ministers in Vermont passed a resolution that

prohibited anyone within their ranks from teaching about the coming Second Advent. That same year Marsh lost his position as editor of *The Christian Palladium,* a Christian Connection journal, and in 1844 Galusha tendered his resignation as a Baptist minister because he was unwilling to curtail his preaching of Christ's soon return. Finally, individual Millerite believers were increasingly prevented from speaking of their beliefs within their local churches, a situation that frequently led to cessation of their attendance and sometimes to their expulsion. One example was the Harmon family in Portland, Maine, in 1843.

Partly as a result of their own internal dynamic and partly in response to these increasing external pressures, the adventists moved in a sect-like trajectory. Although in their early conferences they had declared that they sought to work within the churches and had no desire to initiate conflict, their very actions in organizing conferences, publishing papers, and aggressively pressing their doctrine established a degree of independence from the start. In 1842 they had organized a Second Advent Association in New York, which collected funds and organized Sunday afternoon meetings; similar associations were formed elsewhere. Another sign of separation was the building of Millerite tabernacles, the first of which was erected in Boston in 1843. It offered a place for large numbers of adventists to meet on a regular basis.

By mid-1843 the tension between the adventists and organized Christianity apparently reached a breaking point. In July Fitch preached a sermon entitled "Come Out of Here, My People," based on Revelation 14:8 and 18:1–5. Whereas at this time Protestants generally and most Millerites applied the term *Babylon* to the Roman Catholic Church, Fitch now argued that Babylon included anyone who opposed adventist teaching. Therefore, he urged those who looked forward to Christ's return to separate themselves from the existing churches.

Fitch's sermon appeared in his own publication, *Second Advent of Christ,* in July, and in September it was reprinted in the *Midnight Cry,* although accompanied by a statement from Himes indicating his disagreement. It also appeared as a pamphlet that achieved wide distribution. Even though Miller, Himes, and Litch did not immediately accept Fitch's position, emerging figures such as Storrs and Marsh picked up the theme, and by early 1844 it pervaded the movement. As thousands of Millerites left their churches, they were taking on the very sect-like characteristics they had earlier disavowed.

The reason Millerism appealed to so many people during this period has never been fully understood. There does not seem to have been many social and economic differences between those who were attracted to the movement and those who rejected it. The fact that Millerism arose during and contributed to a major religious revival was probably the key element in its popularity. Also, it shared the biblicism common to American culture at the time, combining it with a commonsense rationalism that made its references to historical events and chronological calculations seem reasonable. Furthermore, during a time when a variety of reform movements had emerged, it offered the ultimate reform: the immediate cleansing of the earth from sin and the establishment of Christ's kingdom.

## Disappointment and the Seventh-Month Movement

Looking toward the end of all things in just a few months, Himes, Miller, and Litch organized major campaigns in northeastern cities for early 1844. Between January and March, Miller preached in Boston, Philadelphia, and Washington, among other places, before returning home on March 14 to await his Lord. After March 21 passed uneventfully, however, he admitted his error and expressed his continuing conviction in Christ's soon return, a belief reiterated by Himes and others. Although the leaders were clearly disoriented for several weeks, in April the *Advent Herald* connected Habakkuk 2:2–3, which spoke of an "appointed time . . . though it tarry," with the parable of the ten virgins in Matthew 5, which referred to the bridegroom tarrying. Thus, the article concluded, earth was in a "tarrying time" of unspecified length prior to Christ's return. With this explanation of their experience at hand, Himes and his colleagues gained renewed focus, and by early summer they were once again organizing camp meetings and distributing their papers.

By August the movement's activity had picked up, although without a designated time for the Second Coming it lacked its earlier intensity. But this situation changed drastically in August at the Exeter, New Hampshire, camp meeting. There, Samuel S. Snow (1806–1870), a religious skeptic before converting to Adventism, asserted that the Old Testament festivals were symbols of Christ's ministry and that the Day of Atonement, the "tenth day of the seventh month," was the only festival that had not yet been fulfilled. He argued that this festival, understood in relation to Daniel 8:14, indicated the specific day of Christ's Second Advent, which, as determined by study of the Jewish calendar, fell on October 22, 1844.

Reportedly, Snow's ideas swept through the camp meeting like wildfire. A few days later, Snow began publishing his own paper, the *True Midnight Cry,* and by September Storrs was espousing the new view. Although the "seventh month" interpretation spread quickly among the adventist believers, leaders were slow to accept it. In late September, however, Marsh and Southard gave the support of their papers to the October 22 date, followed by both Himes and Miller on October 6 and Litch on October 12. Meanwhile, Fitch, who had become seriously ill after baptizing believers in frigid Lake Erie, accepted the seventh-month teaching a few days before he died on October 14. By mid-October, it appears, virtually all of the major Millerite leaders were looking forward to Christ's coming on October 22.

As the day of expectation approached, excitement built up among the adventist believers. Miller and the *Signs of the Times* counseled their followers to continue to fulfill their family and economic responsibilities, whereas others took more radical positions that more fully carried out the implications of their millennial expectations. Marsh advised believers to give away all property not used for present needs, while Storrs urged that they rid themselves of every material possession and leave their crops standing in the fields. Anecdotal evidence suggests a wide variety of responses to this conflicting advice, ranging from continuation of one's business to the closing of shops, the giving away of property, and decisions not to harvest. Adventists continued to hold meetings, both to offer the world a final warning and to provide spiritual and social support to one another as the division between themselves and unbelievers became starkly apparent. Mob violence against the adventists, which forced the closure of meetings in cities such as New York, Boston, and Philadelphia, must have reinforced the Millerite sense of alienation. As October 22 dawned, the adventist believers, who Miller later estimated to number about fifty thousand, gathered in homes and meeting houses to await Christ's coming. Himes, rather than staying in Boston where his tabernacle was filled with believers, traveled to Low Hampton to be with Miller.

But October 22 passed uneventfully, in time becoming known to adventists as the "Great Disappointment." In contrast to the spring disappointment, believers reported deep feelings of despair over their loss of hope and anxiety about their future as they faced the ridicule of an unbelieving public. Almost immediately Himes set to work to address the situation, putting forth a plan to aid destitute adventists who no longer had property and restarting the publication of the

*Midnight Cry* and *Advent Herald.* Some of the adventist preachers resumed their travels, meeting with groups of believers to provide consolation and encouragement

Beyond their immediate physical and emotional needs, the adventists also had to address the problem of what had gone wrong. There was, however, considerable confusion and difference of opinion. On October 24 Southard declared that the leadership must simply admit that it had been wrong, but on October 30 the *Advent Herald* argued that the October 22 date was correct and that Jesus would return within a few days. By mid-November, however, both the *Herald* and the *Midnight Cry,* along with Himes, had admitted their error, but they continued to assert that God had been in their movement. It took Litch until May 1845 to fully reject the seventh-month interpretation, while Miller moved slowly from admitting that his calculations may have been off by a few years to recognizing by September 1845 that October 22 had no prophetic significance at all.

But the seventh-month movement had not originated with these leaders, and, not surprisingly, other adventists were not so willing to give up their belief. They proposed a variety of solutions to their dilemma. In January 1845 Joseph Turner and Apollos Hale put forth the "shut door" theory, stating that the opportunity for unbelievers to accept Jesus had ended on October 22 when Christ had returned spiritually as bridegroom. Hiram Edson and O. R. L. Crosier argued that Jesus had entered the Most Holy Place of the heavenly sanctuary on that date to begin the work of judgment that must precede his Second Advent. Others set new dates, a practice that continued to affect adventism for the next two decades. In addition to reinterpreting their beliefs about the Second Coming, in the months after the Disappointment some adventists began pursuing a variety of other doctrinal innovations, including the seventh-day Sabbath and conditional immortality (also known as "soul sleep") that previously had played a minor role in the movement. Many believers simply left adventism to rejoin their previous churches, while others lost their Christian faith. A few, such as Enoch Jacobs, found a temporary spiritual home with the Shakers.

With their movement fragmenting, the adventist leaders called for a meeting in Albany on April 29, 1845. The Mutual Conference of Adventists, which drew representation from what might be called mainstream adventism, reaffirmed its belief in the coming of Jesus without making any reference to time, developed a plan for further evangelism, and condemned what it regarded as extreme views—among

them the seventh-day Sabbath, foot washing, and the "Holy Kiss." From this point on, the adventist movement was divided between a mainstream that differed from its Protestant environment only in its emphasis on the premillennial Second Advent and a radical fringe that continued to experiment with new doctrines and practices.

## Adventist Churches

The failure of the Millerite predictions in 1844 appeared to bring premillennialist interpretation of the Bible into disrepute. Nonetheless, the movement spawned several denominations, most of which developed around influential publications. Shaped by Himes's *Advent Herald,* the mainstream adventism of the Albany conference evolved into a movement that established a formal church organization in 1858, the American Evangelical Advent Conference. By the 1920s, however, the Evangelical Adventists, as they were known, had lost their distinctiveness and were absorbed into fundamentalist Christianity.

From the more radical wing of adventism arose the Advent Christian Church, formed largely around Miles Grant's *World's Crisis,* which combined Miller's historicist prophetic interpretation with a belief in conditional immortality. Like other Millerite groups, this denomination was slow to organize, establishing publishing and missionary societies in the 1860s and a general conference in 1893.

Drawing on Marsh's *Advent Harbinger and Bible Advocate,* the Church of God of the Abrahamic Faith adopted the belief that some who had not accepted Christ would be spared destruction at his coming and have a second chance at salvation during an "age to come." Although this movement formed some regional conferences in the 1850s, it did not adopt a name until 1888 or fully establish a general conference until 1921.

One of the smallest of the radical adventist groups ultimately became the largest denomination to arise out of the movement. It adopted the seventh-day Sabbath, the interpretation that Jesus had entered the heavenly sanctuary on October 22, 1844, conditional immortality, and the divine origins of the visions of Ellen G. (née Harmon) White, a young adventist in Maine. The Sabbatarian adventists began publishing the *Second Advent Review and Sabbath Herald* in 1850 and formed the General Conference of Seventh-day Adventists in 1863. This new denomination combined historicist premillennialism with publishing, health, and educational institutions that established its presence in American society and provided the basis for a worldwide missionary outreach. By the early twenty-first century, it had about a million members in the United States and from twelve to fifteen million abroad.

## The Rise of Dispensationalism

Apart from these adventist groups, premillennialism went into eclipse for the next quarter-century. Meanwhile, the "futurist" version that had developed earlier in Great Britain gained some credence because it rejected historicism and held that the last days prophecies would be fulfilled during a short period prior to Christ's Second Coming. John Nelson Darby's version of futurism was called "dispensationalism," because it divided history into eras or "dispensations"; during each dispensation God dealt with sin in a different way. Darby asserted that God had one plan for Israel and another for the Christian church. He therefore anticipated two events. First, God would secretly take his saints to heaven (the "rapture"), after which a great tribulation would occur on earth and the prophecies for Israel would be fulfilled. Then, the Second Coming would take place as Jesus and the saints returned to earth to destroy the armies gathering for the battle of Armageddon, to throw Satan into the bottomless pit, and to establish Christ's rule for a thousand years. At the close of this millennium, Satan would rebel once more and be defeated, the dead would be resurrected, and the Last Judgment would take place, after which God would create a new heaven and a new earth.

Darby visited North America seven times between 1859 and 1874, spreading this dispensationalist theology and influencing Dwight L. Moody, among others. The Niagara Bible Conferences (1875–1897) soon adopted premillenialism, whereas the dispensationalist version dominated the American Bible and Prophetic Conferences (1878–1918). Dispensationalism gradually won a large following. Charles I. Scofield's *Reference Bible* (1909), influential pastors such as James H. Brookes and A. J. Gordon, and training schools such as the Moody Bible Institute convinced many within the conservative Christian community that it was the correct interpretation of the scripture. Indeed, world events such as the emergence of Zionism and World War I seemed to confirm the dispensationalist position. By the 1920s it had become the dominant form of premillennialism and was strongly associated with fundamentalism. Lewis Sperry Chafer, John F. Walvoord, and Charles C. Ryrie became major dispensationist theologians, but the belief system gained popular attention with Hal Lindsey's *The Late Great Planet Earth* (1970) and Jerry Jenkins and Tim LaHaye's sixteen *Left Behind* novels (1995–2007), which sold millions of copies. Dispensationalist premillennialism remained a major force within American Protestantism.

**See also** *Adventist and Millennialist Denominational Families; Apocalypticism; Bible entries; Evangelicals entries; Fundamentalism; Great Awakening(s); Independent Bible and Community Churches; Jehovah's Witnesses; Latter-day Saints; Seventh-day Adventists; Shakers.*

Gary Land

## BIBLIOGRAPHY

Barkun, Michael. *Crucible of the Millennium: The Burned-Over District of New York in the 1840s.* Syracuse, N.Y.: Syracuse University Press, 1986.

Bliss, Sylvester. *Memoirs of William Miller Generally Known as a Lecturer on the Prophecies and the Second Coming of Christ.* Boston: Joshua V. Himes, 1853. Reprint, with "Historical Introduction" by Merlin D. Burt. Berrien Springs, Mich.: Andrews University Press, 2005.

Bloch, Ruth H. *Visionary Republic: Millennial Themes in American Thought, 1756–1800.* New York: Cambridge University Press, 1985.

Boyer, Paul S. *When Time Shall Be No More: Prophecy Belief in Modern American Culture.* Cambridge, Mass.: Belknap Press of Harvard University Press, 1992.

Carwardine, Richard. *Transatlantic Revivalism: Popular Evangelicalism in Britain and America, 1790–1865.* Westport, Conn.: Greenwood Press, 1978.

Cross, Whitney R. *The Burned-Over District: The Social and Intellectual History of Enthusiastic Religion in Western New York, 1800–1850.* Ithaca, N.Y.: Cornell University Press, 1950.

Dick, Everett N. *William Miller and the Advent Crisis, 1831–1844.* Foreword and Historiographical Essay by Gary Land. Berrien Springs, Mich.: Andrews University Press, 1994.

Doan, Ruth Alden. *The Miller Heresy, Millennialism, and American Culture.* Philadelphia: Temple University Press, 1987.

Gaustad, Edwin, ed. *The Rise of Adventism: Religion and Society in Mid-Nineteenth Century America.* New York: Harper and Row, 1975.

Harrison, J. F. C. *The Second Coming: Popular Millenarianism, 1780–1950.* New Brunswick, N.J.: Rutgers University Press, 1979.

Hewitt, Clyde. *Midnight and Morning.* Charlotte, N.C.: Venture Books, 1983.

Knight, George R. *Millennial Fever and the End of the World: A Study of Millerite Adventism.* Boise, Idaho: Pacific Press, 1993.

Nichol, Francis D. *The Midnight Cry.* Washington, D.C.: Review and Herald, 1947.

Numbers, Ronald L., and Jonathan M. Butler, eds. *The Disappointed: Millerism and Millenarianism in the Nineteenth Century.* Bloomington: Indiana University Press, 1987.

Rowe, David L. *God's Strange Work: William Miller and the End of the World.* Grand Rapids, Mich.: William B. Eerdmans, 2008.

———. *Thunder and Trumpets: Millerites and Dissenting Religion in Upstate New York, 1800–1850.* Chico, Calif.: Scholars Press, 1985.

Sandeen, Ernest R. *The Roots of Fundamentalism: British and American Millenarianism, 1800–1930.* Chicago: University of Chicago Press, 1970.

Thomas, N. Gordon. *The Millennial Impulse in Michigan, 1830–1860: The Second Coming in the Third New England.* Lewiston, N.Y.: Edward Mellen Press, 1989.

Weber, Timothy P. *Living in the Shadow of the Second Coming: American Premillennialism, 1875–1982.* Enlarged ed. Grand Rapids, Mich.: Academie Books, 1983.

Wellcome, Isaac C. *History of the Second Advent Message and Mission, Doctrine and People.* Yarmouth, Maine: Isaac C. Wellcome, 1874. Reprint, with "Historical Introduction" by Gary Land. Berrien Springs, Mich.: Andrews University Press, 2008.

# Adventist and Millennialist Denominational Families

The central doctrinal affirmation of adventist and millennial groups is the Second Advent of Christ. Although they may differ from each other, these groups share that doctrine.

The adventist groups examined here took root in the advent movement of the 1840s that received its inspiration from William Miller (1782–1849), a Baptist layperson. The 2007 *Yearbook of American and Canadian Churches* lists four "Adventist Bodies": the Advent Christian Church, the Church of God General Conference (Oregon, Illinois, and Morrow, Georgia), the Primitive Advent Christian Church, and the Seventh-day Adventist Church. That list should have included the Church of God (Seventh Day). Two other denominations once were in this family but no longer exist: the American Evangelical Adventist Conference and the Life and Advent Union.

## Millerite Adventism

In 1818 William Miller came to the conclusion from a study of Daniel's time prophecies that Christ would return "about the year 1843." Because Christ's teaching implied that no person will know the exact time, Miller had no desire to set a specific date.

Indeed, fearing he might be wrong, he continued to study the prophecies for the next fifteen years without saying much in public. But by the late 1830s he had attracted some very skilled pastors into what was becoming a movement. Especially important was Joshua V. Himes (1805–1895), an influential Christian Connection leader and a confidant of abolitionist William Lloyd Garrison. Himes, who was one of the public relations experts of his day, put Millerism on the American religious map. The movement grew rapidly throughout the northern states in the early 1840s. It recruited from among the social reformers of the day several active clergy who perceived the Second Advent

as the ultimate reform that would transform the very climate that bred social injustice.

Miller's theology focused on two points: salvation in Christ and the premillennial Second Advent. The leaders in the movement that formed around his leadership sought to avoid other theological issues that would prove to be divisive to its growth across denominational lines. All their energy was put into the urgency of preparing for the return of Christ. It was never their intention to form a denomination. Miller himself was convinced that all Christians would be more than eager to rally around the return of their Lord.

Millennial interest permeated the American Christianity of the time, and so it was an invasive challenge to preach premillennialism (the belief that Christ would return at the beginning of the millennium) in a context in which the vast majority of the population was postmillennialist (that is, they believed that Christ would return at the end of the millennium, during which social conditions would continue to improve until the kingdom of God was established on earth). By mid-1843 the confrontation of millennial ideologies had set the stage for the expulsion of those Millerite preachers and members from several denominations who would not keep quiet about the topic closest to their hearts. In that context, Charles Fitch (1805–1844), a Congregational pastor who had been closely aligned with Charles G. Finney (1792–1875), an 1821 convert who became the most famous of the Second Great Awakening preachers, sounded the call to "come out of Babylon." Thus the stage was set for the rise of a distinctive adventist body.

The Second Advent, of course, did not take place in 1843. The Millerite adventists, following the lead of Samuel S. Snow (1806–1870), a Methodist pastor, eventually came to believe through a series of calculations based on the book of Daniel that Christ would return on October 22, 1844. His nonappearance became known as the "Great Disappointment" and led to the dissolution of adventism as a unified movement.

## Postdisappointment Transitions

It is impossible to give a completely accurate picture of the disappointed Millerites, but it is probable that the majority abandoned their advent faith and either went back to their previous churches or drifted into secular unbelief.

The remaining believers divided themselves into two main orientations toward the fulfillment of the prophecy in October 1844. One group, following Himes, claimed that nothing had happened and that adventists needed to continue to warn the world of the pending advent. The other group held that the prophecy had definitely been fulfilled in October, but they split over exactly what had happened. The larger segment held that Christ had indeed returned, but spiritually in their hearts rather than physically in the clouds of heaven. The smaller segment held that the fulfillment signaled the movement of Christ into his final work in the heavenly sanctuary depicted in the book of Hebrews.

By early 1845 those adventists who believed that Christ had come spiritually into their hearts and that, as a result, they were now in the millennial period, proved to be the most active. Unfortunately, the "Spiritualizers," as they were called, stimulated fanatical excesses. Their spiritualizing approach destroyed the calm hermeneutical controls of the earlier Millerite movement, and so things rapidly spun out of control in a segment of adventism that would self-destruct by the end of the 1840s.

Meanwhile, Himes and Miller, fearing the destruction of a religious understanding in which they firmly believed, called for an adventist convention in Albany, New York, in April 1845 to counteract the excesses of the Spiritualizers and to establish post-1844 adventism on a firm basis.

The Albany meeting stabilized the vast majority of believers in the advent by establishing a congregational system of church governance that would be held together by periodicals and periodic meetings of the movement's pastors and leading laity, by certifying "trustworthy" pastors, and by setting forth a rudimentary doctrinal platform largely emphasizing items related to the advent and salvation. The convention specifically rejected the "anti-Scriptural" post-millennial doctrine that the world would be converted to Christ and the teaching that held that the Jews would be restored as a nation. They also resolved to have no fellowship with adventism's fanatical wing and those who had adopted new tests of fellowship beyond the acceptance of Christ and a belief that he would soon reappear.

Unfortunately, the very actions of the Albany conference split the moderates, because many of them, with their fresh memories of their recent bad experiences with the denominations that had expelled them, had come to believe that to authorize any organization was to return to an oppressive Babylon. Some were against organization even at the congregational level. That anti-organizational mentality influenced all the developing adventist groups to some extent, and made it almost impossible for them to organize as religious bodies until the late 1850s and early 1860s.

But formal church organization would eventually come in some fashion to the remaining advent believers. The nineteenth century would see four denominations grow out of the Albany orientation, and two out of those believers who at first came to focus on the heavenly ministry of Christ since 1844 eventually observed the seventh-day Sabbath. The Spiritualizer segment produced no religious movements that existed beyond 1850.

## American Evangelical Adventist Conference

The Albany orientation was the major visible adventist presence during the late 1840s and most of the 1850s. But definite moves toward concrete denominational formation were hindered by the ongoing antipathy toward organization by the vast majority of adventists. Thus the Albany adventists continued to be held together by a shared interest in the Second Advent promoted by their major periodical, the *Advent Herald.*

But theological harmony was not achieved easily. The major dividing force in the 1850s was the teaching of conditionalism—the belief that people are not born immortal, but receive immortality as a gift at the Second Advent through their faith in Christ—and annihilationism—the belief that because the wicked are not innately immortal, they cannot burn perpetually but will be eternally destroyed.

Those teachings had entered Millerite adventism in the early 1840s through George Storrs, who had been a Methodist minister. Himes and Miller had been able to stem the force of those teachings before 1844, but afterward they would gain increasing influence.

By 1858 those who accepted and those who rejected conditionalism and annihilationism among the Albany party had come to an impasse. Thus in May 1858 the rejecters, who controlled the *Advent Herald,* formed the American Evangelical Adventist Conference to disseminate "original" adventism as defined in 1845 at Albany. In November 1858 the Evangelical Adventists approved a constitution and elected a slate of officers. Therefore the most powerful of the Albany groups had formed the first adventist denomination.

But it would not be a lasting one. With only the premillennial advent to separate it from the general Christian populace, Evangelical Adventism lost its reason for a separate existence when a large share of conservative Protestants also adopted forms of premillennialism in the decades after the Civil War. By 1890 its membership had shrunk to 1,147, and it disappeared in the early twentieth century.

## Advent Christian Association

Meanwhile, back in 1858 the conditionalist segment of Albany adventism was horrified by the move of the Evangelical Adventists to organize. This group, which had been shut out of the pages of the *Advent Herald,* solidified around the *World's Crisis,* a periodical that set forth its views of both the advent and conditionalism.

Gradually and reluctantly the *Crisis* adventists drifted toward formalizing a church organization. In July 1860 they formed the Christian Association to support the formation of a publication society, to organize local congregations, and to aid in certifying and supporting an efficient gospel ministry. In October the Christian Association was renamed the Advent Christian Association. Thus was born a second adventist denomination, although because of the strong antidenominational feelings of many of its members it was called an association rather than a church.

Even though the Advent Christians had organized, their administrative structure was extremely weak. Clyde E. Hewitt, the most recent historian of the movement, claims that it never overcame that weakness, which has contributed to the denomination's lack of growth.

Throughout the mid- to late nineteenth century the Advent Christians continued to gain influence over the ever-shrinking Evangelical Adventists. According to the 1890 census, there were 25,816 Advent Christians at the time. Their rallying point had become their firm belief in conditionalism and annihilationism, which had overtaken even their ongoing belief in the Second Advent as the doctrinal center of the movement.

The Advent Christians sponsored a very modest mission outreach program, but by 2004 the denomination had a mere 24,182 members in the United States, worshiping in 304 congregations. Hewitt attributes their lack of growth to a lack of evangelism, insufficient organization, and "smallness in vision."

Over the years the Advent Christians sponsored some educational work, of which Aurora College in Illinois was the center. But they gave up control of that institution in the late twentieth century, even though Aurora's library still contains one of the finest collections of Millerite documents in existence.

Today, the denomination's general conference is located in Charlotte, North Carolina. Doctrinally, it upholds the Bible as the only rule of faith and practice and believes that salvation is free to all on the condition of repentance, faith, and faithfulness to God. It holds that the only ordinances of the church are the Lord's Supper and baptism, which is always by immersion. The Advent Christians maintain doctrinal distinction in the areas of conditional immortality, the sleep of the dead until the return of Christ, and establishment of the kingdom of God on the earth made new.

## Life and Advent Union

The Life and Advent Union grew out of an internal squabble among the Advent Christians soon after their founding. A significant minority of Advent Christians had begun to teach that God would not raise the wicked dead from their unconscious sleep only to resentence them to eternal death. In 1863 the majority, holding that the Bible taught the resurrection of both the righteous and the wicked, would not allow the group espousing the nonresurrection of the wicked to publish their views in the *World's Crisis.* In response, the smaller group established the Life and Advent Union on August 3, 1863, as well as the *Herald of Life and the Coming Kingdom* to publish their views.

The "Life" adventists aggressively evangelized in the 1870s and 1880s and had a membership of 1,018 in 1890, but by 1926 that figure had fallen to 535. In 1957 only three congregations remained, and in 1964 the denomination merged back into the Advent Christian group.

## Primitive Advent Christian Church

The Primitive Advent Christian Church grew out of a twentieth-century rupture with its parent body over foot washing and the rebaptism of backsliders who return to fellowship. The original Advent Christians reject both teachings.

Located entirely in West Virginia, as of 2005 the Primitive Advent Christians reported 76 churches with 3,965 communicants. Their doctrinal platform reflects that of the parent church in terms of salvational issues and the role of the Bible as the only rule of faith and practice. But they have expanded the number of ordinances to three, adding the saints' washing of one another's feet to baptism by immersion and the Lord's Supper. They also differ from the Advent Christians in that they hold firmly to noncombatant principles, whereas the Advent Christians, while holding that war is contrary to the teachings of Christ, leave the arms-bearing issue up to the discretion of the individual conscience.

## Church of God General Conference

The small family of denominations that grew out of the Evangelical and Advent Christian movements was directly related to the Albany meetings. The Church of God General Conference, although in general theological harmony with the Albany adherents, disagreed with them over the steps they had taken to organize. Thus, although the Church of God cohort originated in the same adventist population pool, it was in essence a reaction, under the leadership of Joseph Marsh and his *Voice of Truth,* to Albany rather than an outgrowth of it.

Early on, this sector of adventism taught that the Jews would return to Israel and that individuals would have a second chance to be saved during the millennium or the "Age to Come." Such positions were closer to those of the British premillennial literalists than they were to Millerite adventism, which had rejected the positions in 1840 at its first "general conference" meeting.

During the 1850s there was a great deal of interaction between the Age to Come believers and those evolving into the Advent Christians. But after the latter organized, the two groups drifted apart.

From its position at the extreme edge of the antiorganizational wing of adventism, the Age to Comers found it next to impossible to organize as a denomination. By the 1880s several streams had fed into the movement, and they organized in 1888 as the Church of God in Jesus Christ. But because of strong convictions about congregational rights, the 1888 organization soon ceased to function. In 1921 the present general conference was organized as the Church of God of the Abrahamic Faith, with its headquarters in Oregon, Illinois. In 1991 it moved its headquarters and training school to Morrow, Georgia, where the school became the Atlanta Bible College. In 1890 the Church of God had a membership of 2,872, and as of 2004 it reported eighty-nine congregations and 3,860 members.

Central to its doctrinal affirmations is the teaching that the kingdom of God will begin in Jerusalem at the return of Christ and be extended to all nations. Thus the promises of God to Abraham will be literally fulfilled. The church also affirms the creatorship of God, with Jesus not existing prior to his birth in Bethlehem. Baptism of believers is by immersion.

## Seventh-day Adventist Church

Unlike the five religious movements just described, Seventh-day Adventism did not originate among those adventists who held that no prophecy had been fulfilled in October 1844. To the contrary, Seventh-day Adventists believed that prophecy had been fulfilled; that fulfillment, however, was

not the Second Advent but the inauguration of Christ's final work in heaven before returning to earth.

The primary founders of the movement were Joseph Bates (1792–1872), James White (1821–1881), and Ellen G. White (1827–1915). By 1848 the Sabbatarian adventists were advocating not only the nearness of the Second Advent, but also the seventh-day Sabbath, the role of Christ in the heavenly sanctuary, and conditionalism and annihilationism. Beyond that, they held that Ellen White had a genuine prophetic gift.

The Sabbatarians aggressively evangelized from 1848 onward, using literature and traveling evangelists to great advantage. They eventually came to believe on the basis of Revelation 14:6–12 that they had a message the whole world needed to hear before the return of Christ pictured in Revelation 14:14–20. By 1890 they had become the largest adventist church, with membership in North America of 28,991. The twentieth century saw rapid and continual growth, with the denomination having at the beginning of 2007 over one million members in North America and over fifteen million worldwide.

Part of its success can be attributed to a worldwide organization designed to facilitate mission. That organization, however, got off to a rather slow start. After all, the members of this denomination were members of the group that by adventist tradition opposed any organization. But by 1861 they had formed their first state conference, and 1863 witnessed the formation of the General Conference of Seventh-day Adventists to coordinate the efforts of the state conferences. Unlike the congregational structures in the other adventist denominations, not only did the Seventh-day Adventists develop a layered structure, but each level in the Seventh-day Adventist structure had very definite administrative authority.

## Church of God (Seventh Day)

Owing to their Millerite heritage, not all of the Sabbatarian adventists appreciated the movement's drift toward organized status under the guidance of James White. Not only did the Sabbatarian dissidents balk at White's growing authority, but they also rejected and resented the visions and writings of his wife, Ellen.

Beginning in the 1860s, Sabbatarian groups in Michigan and Iowa united in their opposition to Seventh-day Adventism. In 1863 they united to publish the *Hope of Israel,* which eventually became the *Bible Advocate,* the movement's current publication. The General Conference of the Church of God was formed in 1864, and "(Seventh Day)" was added to its name in 1923. Its denominational headquarters was in Stanberry, Missouri, from 1888 to 1950, when it moved to Denver.

The church's doctrinal distinctives include an understanding of the perpetuity of the Ten Commandments (including the seventh-day Sabbath), conditionalism and annihilationism, and an earthly millennium following the Second Advent, at the end of which the wicked will be resurrected. Salvation is a gift, but one that results in a changed life. The two ordinances of the denomination are baptism by immersion and an annual communion service accompanied by foot washing.

The Church of God (Seventh Day) has never been a large denomination. It had 647 members in 1890 and reported 9,000 members in the United States in 2001. Schism has plagued its history. Thus in 1933 a section of its membership split off to form the Church of God (Seventh Day), headquartered in Salem, West Virginia. A similar body is the General Council of the Churches of God, Seventh Day, located in Meridian, Idaho. Because of possible confusion over the name, the original Sabbatarian Church of God is sometimes identified as the Church of God (Seventh Day), Denver, Colorado.

### Christadelphians

The Christadelphians arose in 1848 under the leadership of John Thomas (1805–1871). Although they were a restorationist body that looked forward to the return of Christ in power to set up a visible worldwide theocracy, they appear to have had no direct connection with the Millerite denominations discussed earlier. They did, however, share several doctrinal positions espoused by some of the Millerite denominations, including conditional immortality, annihilationism, and immersion as the only form of baptism.

**See also** *Adventism and Millennialism; Apocalypticism; Evangelicals entries; Fundamentalism; Independent Bible and Community Churches; Jehovah's Witnesses; Seventh-day Adventists.*

George R. Knight

#### BIBLIOGRAPHY

Arthur, David T. "'Come Out of Babylon': A Study of Millerite Separatism and Denominationalism, 1840–1865." PhD dissertation, University of Rochester, 1970.

Gaustad, Edwin S., ed. *The Rise of Adventism.* New York: Harper and Row, 1974.

Hewitt, Clyde E. *Devotion and Development.* Charlotte, N.C.: Venture Books, 1990.

———. *Historical Waymarks of the Church of God.* Oregon, Ill.: Church of God General Conference, 1976.

———. *Midnight and Morning: An Account of the Advent Awakening and the Founding of the Advent Christian Denomination, 1831–1860.* Charlotte, N.C.: Venture Books, 1983.

———. *Responsibility and Response.* Charlotte, N.C.: Venture Books, 1986.

Knight, George R. *A Brief History of Seventh-day Adventists,* 2nd ed. Hagerstown, Md.: Review and Herald, 2004.

———. *Millennial Fever and the End of the World: A Study of Millerite Adventism.* Boise, Idaho: Pacific Press, 1993.

Nickels, Richard C. "History of the Seventh Day Church of God." http://www.giveshare.org/churchhistory/historysdcog.

Numbers, Ronald L., and Jonathan M. Butler, eds. *The Disappointed: Millerism and Millenarianism in the Nineteenth Century.* Bloomington: Indiana University Press, 1987.

Wellcome, Isaac C. *History of the Second Advent Message and Mission, Doctrine and People.* Yarmouth, Maine: Isaac C. Wellcome, 1874. Reprint, with "Historical Introduction" by Gary Land. Berrien Springs, Mich.: Andrews University Press, 2008.

# African American Baptists

See *Baptists: African American.*

# African American Methodists

See *Methodists: African American.*

# African American Music

See *Music: African American; Music: African American Gospel; Music: African American Spirituals.*

# African American Pentecostals

See *Pentecostals: African American.*

# African American Religion: Colonial Era through the Civil War

It is tempting to take advantage of simple chronology and concrete origin and begin a study of African American religion during the colonial era at the moment and place that people of African descent initially set foot in the "New

World." Thus the investigation might start in 1619, when Africans arrived as indentured servants in Jamestown on the banks of the James River sixty miles from the mouth of the Chesapeake Bay. Founded a decade earlier by Virginia Company explorers operating under the charter of the British Crown, Jamestown marked the establishment of the first permanent English colony, Virginia. Another, more sophisticated option for selecting a starting point emerges if the term *New World* is defined more broadly to include the earliest years of European imperial contact with the Western Hemisphere. In this framework, one might assume the year of beginning to be 1502, when the first ship of African slaves landed on the Spanish-controlled island of Hispaniola in the Caribbean.

## Origins

But both approaches pose a similar analytical risk, one that has limited the explanatory scope of the literature on African American religion for generations: the neglect of the world left behind by the native-born Africans forcibly transported across the Atlantic. Too often the dating and examination of the sacred history of black Americans commences with the physical introduction of their ancestors to the New World—however interpreted—and its trajectory is drawn without a full consideration of the influence of traditional African beliefs. Older investigations routinely cast aside the matter of the African character of African American religion or focused on the question of to what extent, if any, "Africanisms" survived the Middle Passage. Frequently missing was a thoughtful analysis of the shifting and malleable interaction of the past and the present, of the symbiosis between religious cultures formed in Africa and ones developing in newer environments.

More recently, scholars have rightly stressed that the roots of African American religion stretch back to the native cultures of Africa itself. Well before Portuguese soldiers of the military Order of Christ first descended on West African villages in the fifteenth century, Africans were a religious people. The estimated ten to twelve million Africans shipped as human cargo to the Western Hemisphere over the next 350 years arrived at their destinations not lacking a rich sense of the sacred. Over the course of centuries in Africa, they had created worlds of gods and spirits that lent meaning to their lives, even if their spiritual precepts and practices were dismissed as primitive and offensive by Christian missionaries and slavers. Although some Africans were Muslim or Christian, the great majority practiced traditional beliefs.

## The Memoir of Olaudah Equiano

Olaudah Equiano made the case for the rich religious background of native-born Africans in his memoir, published first in England in 1789 and in America two years later. Born in 1745 to a large, prosperous, Ibo-speaking family in what is now eastern Nigeria, Equiano was stolen from his home at age eleven, sold to white slave traders, and eventually purchased by the captain of an English merchant ship in Virginia. He worked as a slave in the Caribbean, England, and Philadelphia until he purchased his own freedom in 1766.

Although he converted to Protestant Christianity as an adult, Equiano keenly recalled the complex spiritual culture of his early African boyhood. Many "believe in the transmigration of souls to a certain degree. Those spirits, which are not transmigrated, such as their dear friends or relations, they believe they always attend them, and guard them from the bad spirits of their foes." He noted rituals designed to appease these spirits and ceremonies that marked the New Year or burial of leading citizens, in which "most of their implements and things of value were interred along with them." He wrote, too, of his community's "priests and magicians" who served as doctors and "were very successful in healing wounds and expelling poisons."

Equiano's account identifies some of the core dimensions of conventional African religion that Africans transported to the New World and relied on to explain and confront their new lives. In particular, he evoked the common African conviction that honoring the spirits and ancestors through prayer and sacrifice promised a good life, whereas ignoring or angering them brought evil and ill fortune into the world. Spirits, though invisible, could take human or animal form, come alive through a ceremonial mask or specially concocted medicine, and communicate with worshippers through dancing, drumming, chanting, and spiritual trances. Equiano also indicated how Africans celebrated turning points in life and practiced rituals that helped them manage unpleasant or traumatic turns in life such accidents, disease, sickness, and death.

## Under Slavery: Hybrid Faiths and the Great Awakening

Africans and their descendants blended their traditional sacred lives with the pressures and constraints of slavery. In Catholic communities throughout North America, for example, they viewed the saints as similar to African spirits in terms of their special powers and spheres of interest. They took advantage of the overlaps between Catholicism and the religions of Africa to give birth to hybrid faiths. In Brazil, Africans and their descendants created Candomble; in Cuba, Santería; and in Haiti, vodou or voodoo. Central to them was African-styled worship services featuring energetic dances, communal song, powerful traditional rhythms banged out on drums, and spiritual visions.

In British North America slaves only slowly converted to Protestant Christianity. Much of this was of the white missionaries' own doing. Before the early eighteenth century British clerics often refused to school slaves in the history of their faith or even to baptize them for fear that such a formal statement of Christian identification might lead to their emancipation under British law or upset hierarchies of social order. Instead, they preached that slaves should obey their masters. To be sure, white Protestants organized missionary societies, such as the Society for the Propagation of the Gospel in Foreign Parts, which underwrote the efforts of English clergy to labor in the colonies. But various factors greatly limited the society's success, most especially the fear among whites that Christian slaves were fundamentally disobedient slaves. As a result, missionaries struggled to gain permission from masters to visit their bond servants. Even when they did, slaves infrequently took to their preaching. Sometimes the issue was language: native-born African slaves struggled to understand missionaries. But even English-speaking slaves often made poor candidates for conversion because many simply rejected Christianity as the faith of their oppressors.

The interest of slaves in Christianity changed dramatically beginning in the 1730s, when a series of religious revivals rolled across the colonies in what was dubbed the Great Awakening. In lengthy public meetings aimed at saving as many souls as possible, preachers whipped up popular enthusiasm through fiery sermons. They made a special point of inviting blacks and including them as speakers, prayer leaders, and singers. Some slaves gained permission to attend from sympathetic masters, while others stole away to the gatherings. They then converted to Christianity in unprecedented numbers largely because of the revivalists' egalitarian ethos and particularly their concentration on the experience of individual conversion as the central requirement for Christian membership.

Revivalist ministers such as William Tennent and George Whitefield called men and women, rich and poor, free and slave, to experience God's saving grace. Gone was any prerequisite literacy, mastery of scripture, or social rank. They preached excitedly, voices soaring and bodies jumping. Biracial audiences responded with equal fervor; caught up in the excitement of the moment, many entered spiritual trances while others wept openly, shouted, waved their arms in the air, danced, fell to the ground, or simply collapsed. Clergy and laypeople alike understood that these behaviors were vital components of worship and individual spiritual growth. People simply communicated the intensity of their emotions, the powerful experiences of conversion, and the presence of the Holy Spirit through physical means. In these meetings, slaves finally experienced a type of Protestant Christian worship that resembled their own African traditions, which, in turn, led them to better understand Christianity and convert.

The pattern of slaves converting to Christianity continued throughout the eighteenth and early nineteenth centuries. The success of the American Revolution further threw into doubt the moral claims of slavery and accentuated the democratic impulse unleashed by the revivals. Antislavery petitions grew among some denominational groups. In the late 1700s, Baptist and Methodist ministers pushed the boundaries separating blacks from fully fledged leadership in their churches by licensing African Americans, free and slave, to preach to fellow blacks. Some become part of white churches, while others formed the first generation of all-black houses of worship and took critical steps toward making Christianity fit with the experiences and stresses of black life in America.

## Institutions

Although most African Americans living during times of slavery practiced their religion away from any black-led church, this was not always the case.

### Southern Independent Black Churches

In the South and particularly in the North, blacks founded and controlled their own houses of worship. One of the first efforts to organize a black church in the South was spearheaded in the late eighteenth century by David George in Silver Bluff, South Carolina. George, born in the mid-eighteenth century to African parents in Essex County, Virginia, spent much of his young life as a runaway seeking shelter among the Creek and Natchez Indians. He eventually joined a plantation owned by an Indian agent for South Carolina, George Galphin, who lived in Silver Bluff, and there David George apparently helped build the Negro Baptist Church.

During the Revolutionary War, Pastor George and fifty members of his congregation relocated to Savannah, Georgia. His church grew and became part of a fledgling African American Baptist community led by a slave, Andrew Bryan. For years Bryan had defied local authorities and gathered blacks to worship, sometimes paying a price measured in lashes. Eventually officials determined that Bryan posed no direct threat to the social order and permitted him to host open meetings, but never at night. By 1790 Bryan was presiding over a sizable Baptist congregation that boasted a membership of 225 communicants and hundreds more not yet fully accepted. It became the African Baptist Church of Savannah and quickly spawned offshoots: in 1803 the Second African Baptist Church was created, and several years later the Third African Baptist Church took shape. Bryan tapped a former slave and a close friend, Henry Francis, from Silver Bluff, to lead the Third Baptist church. Literate and possessing eighteen years of experience as a minister, the fifty-two-year-old Francis was well suited to the task.

The success of the African Baptist Church of Savannah, however, was unusual in the South before the Civil War. Slaves and freed people seeking to worship independently confronted whites eager to control their movements and behavior, especially during times when fears of slave revolts ran high. Still, a small number of southern blacks formed houses of worship and thus created an important counterpoint to the more prevalent pattern of southern blacks attending white-run churches, sitting in segregated quarters, and hearing about their supposed social and intellectual inferiority.

## Northern Independent Black Churches

The story of independent black churches was very different in the North, where multiple denominations emerged, drawing thousands of African American congregants by the eve of the Civil War. There, the leveling impulse unleashed by the Revolutionary War, the slow eradication of slavery, and the legal separation of church combined to generate greater freedom of assembly. Less constrained by laws and customs designed to tightly manage their whereabouts and activities, northern blacks enjoyed wider public opportunities to articulate the meaning of their spiritual lives. Beginning in the late 1800s those who were part of the traditional white-run denominations increasingly sought improved status as members, access to sacramental privileges, and prospects for liturgical leadership. When their requests were ignored, many formed their own churches.

Such was famously the case in the founding in 1794 of Bethel Methodist Episcopal Church in Philadelphia by Richard Allen. Born the slave of a Quaker in the City of Brotherly Love in 1760, Allen eventually became the property of a Methodist living outside of Dover, Delaware. At seventeen he converted to Methodism. Soon thereafter he bought his freedom, became a Methodist exhorter, and returned to Philadelphia in 1786. Joining the white-led St. George's Methodist Church, Allen and other blacks worshipped for years through the scrim of racial segregation. Although permitted to form their own private prayer groups, they were forced to sit in black-only pews and lacked their own church. But during one Sunday service at St. George's, the matter of black religion and the color line came to a head. As Allen recounted in his autobiography, he and fellow black members entered the church, placed themselves in a white-only section, and joined in the prayer being led by the presiding Elder. "We had not been long upon our knees before I heard considerable scuffling and low talking. I raised my head up and saw one of the trustees, H—M—, having hold of the Rev. Absalom Jones, pulling him up off his knees, and saying 'You must get up—you must not kneel here.' Mr. Jones replied, 'Wait until prayer is over.' Mr. H—M—said 'No, you must get up now, or I will call for aid and force you away.'" In quick succession, Jones refused to move, the trustee called for aid, and he and two other white men ejected Jones. In response, Allen and every other black member immediately "went out of the church, and they were no more plagued with us in the church. . . . But my dear Lord was with us, and we were filled with fresh vigor to get a house erected to worship God in." Allen then spearheaded a successful effort to build Bethel Methodist Episcopal Church.

In the subsequent fight for ecclesiastical and legal control of Bethel, one made curious by the fact that blacks owned the very property on which their church sat, Allen squared off against white Methodist clerics and pursued the matter to the Pennsylvania Supreme Court, which ultimately ruled in his favor. The predatory efforts by the white Methodists prompted Allen to gather black Methodists from the region in 1816 to discuss the issue of their religious autonomy. The result was the creation of the African Methodist Episcopal Church and the election of Allen as its first bishop. Other black Methodist groups quickly followed suit. In 1815 Peter Spencer founded the Union Church of Africans in Wilmington, Delaware; six years later, under the guidance of Peter Williams, the African Methodist Episcopal Zion

Church—which added "Zion" to its title as a way to distinguish itself from Allen's denomination—took root in New York City and elected James Varick as its bishop. Though eager to differentiate his church from other black Methodist churches, Varick echoed Allen when recounting its early history. He described the relationship between white and black Methodists as controversial at times, indicating that "as the whites increased very fast the Africans were pressed back; therefore it was thought essentially necessary for them to have meeting-houses of their own . . . in order to invite their coloured brethren yet out of the ark of safety to come in."

Black Christians founded other types of African American churches as well. For example, in 1794, the same year he was rousted from St. George's, Absalom Jones became founding pastor of St. Thomas African Episcopal Church in Philadelphia. Nearby was the first African Presbyterian Church, organized in 1807 by John Gloucester. Thomas Paul established independent black Baptist churches: the African Baptist Church in Boston in 1804 and Abyssinian Baptist Church in New York City four years later. Taken collectively, the new black churches formed the nexus of northern black religious life through which African American ideas about religion and society developed.

**Antislavery Words and Deeds**

Uniting the different northern black churches was their shared revulsion of slavery and segregation. Northern white denominations typically offered only muted criticism of the peculiar institution, but African American leaders loudly proclaimed it as the main bane of the nation's history. On July 4, 1827, as part of an Emancipation Day celebration honoring the twentieth-eighth anniversary of the abolition of slavery in the state of New York, Rev. Nathaniel Paul, pastor of Hamilton Street Baptist Church in Albany, devoted the occasion to detailing the evils of slavery. "Slavery . . . is but a hateful monster, the very demon of avarice and oppression, from its first introduction to the present time; it has been among all nations the scourge of heaven and the curse of earth."

Most blacks shared the notion that slavery was a blight on American civilization, but a few spokesmen took it one step further and suggested that, at some near point in the future, those who sanctioned bondage would pay dearly for their deeds. One such person was David Walker. Walker, born of a slave father and free mother in Wilmington, North Carolina, in 1785, settled in Boston at the turn of the century and

became active in abolitionism and church life. He published a fiery pamphlet, *Appeal,* in 1829, which heavily criticized slavery and included a dramatic twist that excited southern state legislators to ban black residents from ever reading it. In a view that eerily forecast the outbreak of the Civil War, Walker argued that America's sordid history as a slave nation not only angered God but also promised its eventual ruin. "Perhaps they will laugh at, or make light of this; but I tell you Americans! That unless you speedily alter your course, *you* and *your Country* are gone!!!!!! For God Almighty will tear up the very face of the earth!!!!" He then concluded, "I call God—I call angels—I call men, to witness, that your DESTRUCTION *is at hand,* and will be speedily consummated unless you repent."

In addition to preaching an antislavery message, black church and public leaders took more concrete steps toward accomplishing their goal. Many made their houses of worship into stops on the Underground Railroad. They hosted political conventions to organize support for abolition. They formed self-help societies in the strong conviction that raising the general levels of moral character and living conditions was a vital means of strengthening their communities and combating negative stereotypes. One example of a self-help organization was the Free African Society of Philadelphia, organized by Richard Allen and Absalom Jones shortly after they parted ways with St. George's Methodist Church. They built this club to encourage blacks to live orderly lives, avoid alcohol, support the sick, and contribute monthly dues for the purpose of providing financial support to widows and orphans.

Central to the self-help efforts was the rise of black fraternal orders. Closely partnered with churches and often sharing members with them, fraternal orders reinforced the disciplinary codes taught by preachers and offered a world of rituals that celebrated black achievement. In 1785 Prince Hall, an African American from Boston, took matters into his own hands soon after his bid to join a white Masonic lodge was rejected because of his skin color. He founded the all-black Prince Hall Masons, which offered members a series of rituals loosely based on white Masonry and a vow to help them financially during times of need. The group taught members about a glorious African past in which black men were political leaders, hosted marching drills and parades, required that blacks follow a strict moral code of conduct that avoided drinking spirits, and adhere to the precepts of the Bible. It spread rapidly across the North and triggered the growth of other black fraternal orders.

Although their many labors minimized the brutality of slavery, northern blacks still confronted vexing questions about the religious meaning of slavery for African Americans. What was God's purpose in allowing blacks to be enslaved for centuries? Clergymen were quick to argue that God did not will such a course of history, but instead permitted it to happen for reasons of his own design. The most common explanation offered was that slavery brought native-born Africans and their progeny into direct contact with the message of the gospel and thus made possible their conversion to Christianity. In turn, black Methodists and Baptists could bring their newly discovered faith back to Africa as missionaries and spread the "Good News." As early as 1792 Rev. David George of Savannah, Georgia, established a Baptist church in Sierra Leone on the west coast of Africa. By the time Alexander Crummell, a black Episcopal priest, arrived in Liberia in 1853 to begin a twenty-year endeavor to "redeem" Africa, more than eight thousand black Americans were already living in the city. Crummell framed his efforts as a way of seeing good come from the horrors of slavery. As he wrote, the "EVANGELIZATION OF AFRICA" was "the end, and aim, and object of that divine will and providence which the Almighty has been working out by the means of institutions and governments, by afflictions and sufferings, and even oppressions, during the course of centuries."

Northern blacks also used the history of slavery to fashion a radically different understanding of the relationship between divine providence and America. For many white Americans, their nation was a "promised land" of economic and social opportunity, where the yoke of past oppression was thrown off and freedom enjoyed by all. God amply blessed America and intended it to act as a beacon of liberty and democracy for the world. The meaning of America was more ambiguous for blacks. For them, the country was no promised land of freedom but more akin to Egypt of the Old Testament, where the ancient Israelites, God's favored race, endured generations of bondage before being emancipated. Black leaders also pointed out the serious shortcomings of white Americans who professed to be Christian yet practiced slavery. Frederick Douglass put the matter vividly in his 1834 autobiography: "I . . . hate the corrupt, slaveholding, women-whipping, cradle-plundering, partial and hypocritical Christianity of this land. Indeed, I can see no reason, but the most deceitful one, for calling the religion of this land Christianity. I look upon it as the climax of all misnomers, the boldest of all frauds, and the grossest of all libels."

## Struggles of Radical African American Women

At the same time that black churches were publicly campaigning for African American freedom, they were also stymieing attempts by women to serve as religious leaders. Like white clerics, black preachers widely banned female congregants from ordination and from obtaining a license to preach and often required them to seek special permission to serve as class and prayer leaders. No black denomination formally recognized a woman as a cleric until the African Methodist Episcopal Church ordained Julia Foote in 1895. Still, black women sought to preach during the colonial and antebellum eras. Among the first was Jarena Lee, born free in 1783 in Cape May, New Jersey. As a twenty-one-year-old woman then living in Philadelphia, she preached in public with such verve and passion that she earned an invitation from Rev. Richard Allen to speak at his church. Yet few other ministers welcomed her, which Lee struggled to understand theologically. As she argued in 1833, "If the man may preach, because the Savior died for him, why not the women, seeing he died for her also? Is he not a whole Savior, instead of a half one, as those who hold it wrong for a woman to preach, would seem to make it appear? Did not Mary *first* preach the risen Savior? Then did not Mary, a woman, preach the gospel?"

A more radical contemporary of Lee's was Rebecca Cox Jackson. Growing up as a free woman in Philadelphia during the early 1800s, she lived much of her life with her brother, Joseph Cox, an African Methodist Episcopal (AME) minister. Following instructions given to her by a heavenly spirit in 1830, Jackson began to host prayer meetings that quickly surged in popularity. She stirred controversy by tossing aside convention and inviting men and women to worship side by side. She earned a temporary reprieve, however, after a visit by Morris Brown, who succeeded Richard Allen as bishop of the AME Church. Brown came to one of Jackson's meetings with the idea of silencing her, but left thoroughly impressed by her preaching and ordered that she be left alone. In 1833 Jackson embarked on a preaching tour outside of Philadelphia but met with new and greater resistance. Her insistence on her right to preach, open refusal to join a church, and radical views on sexuality that included celibacy within marriage angered area clerics and, Jackson claimed, motivated some to assault her. Eventually she broke ranks with the free black church movement and joined a Shaker group in Watervliet, New York. In 1851 she returned to Philadelphia and founded a Shaker community composed mainly of black women.

Lee and Jackson rejected the limitations placed on their preaching because of their sex. Like others black women, they found confirmation for their efforts not in any church rule or clerical pronouncement but through their personal interpretation of the Bible and, more important, an unflagging conviction that God had called them to preach. Though denied official recognition as preachers, they still touched the lives of many and represented a vital dimension of the religious lives of northern blacks.

While rarely acting as preachers to a slave community, black women served as spiritual leaders in other ways. As mothers and grandmothers, they introduced children to the precepts of their faith and passed on traditions through story and song. Many earned the respect of their peers by exercising skills as midwives, folk healers, and comforters of the sick and dying. A few gained popularity as wise and trusted counselors able to interpret strange dreams and forecast the future. Although without large followings or the same degree of influence as male preachers, black women in the South, as in the North, influenced the evolution of African American sacred life.

## Beyond the Master's Eye

Although African Americans built their own churches, denominations, self-help societies, and fraternal orders during slavery, most did not participate in these institutions. This was especially true in the South, where the overwhelming majority of slaves and freed people lived and had little direct access to black churches or even white ones. They often lived too far from any kind of house of worship to participate in its life on a regular basis and were lucky to receive visits from itinerant preachers or even hear their masters read from scripture.

This is not to say, however, that southern blacks failed to create and sustain a religious identity. The truth was just the opposite. They developed a dense sacred life outside of the walls of any church and far beyond the master's eye, one that integrated themes and practices of Christianity with the realities of their existence as bond servants and their African traditions. Eager to push beyond the banal platitudes issued by white clerics about willfully and cheerfully accepting their lowly status, slaves gathered and nurtured an alternative spiritual community. At night, in fields, brush harbors, thickets, and secret meeting places, they probed their place in God's unfolding plan for humanity and created their own sermons, visions, dreams, and performance styles.

In contrast to the servile messages promoted by white clergymen, blacks stressed their special value in the eyes of God, especially through their distinctive interpretation of the book of Exodus. They saw in the story of Exodus a map for their history: like the Hebrews, they were God's chosen children, suffering in bondage but destined to be freed and taken to the Promised Land. Their conviction came to life during their secret rendezvous and praise services, when they commemorated through dance and song the act of slipping Pharaoh's grasp and crossing the Red Sea to freedom. Transforming biblical history into a lived reality, if only for a few moments, slaves refreshed their identification as a just people blessed by God, who would eventually emancipate them. This identification, in turn, helped them to deflect white claims that God preordained blacks for lives of forced labor.

## Power of Preaching and Song

The leader of the slave religious community was the slave preacher. Though sometimes illiterate, the preacher earned his status by employing a dramatic style of communicating that consisted of biblical verses, gestures, and stories committed to memory and expressed through repetition and parallelism. Often called the chanted sermon, it followed a common pattern, beginning with spoken prose but swiftly moving to a rhythmic cadence punctuated by cries of encouragement from the audience. It typically climaxed in a near tonal chant, when the preacher brought his listeners to their feet, singing and swaying with him.

A central part of slave religious life was song. Frequently limited by law and custom from leaning how to read and write, slaves turned to song as a powerful way of expressing themselves. Integrating African-influenced cadences with Protestant hymns and Bible verses, they fashioned their spirituals, a particular type of sacred music sung alone or in groups, in the fields or their homes. In the spirituals, they blended hopes for freedom with the pain and suffering of everyday life. For example:

> Oh, that I had a bosom friend,
> To tell my secrets to,
> One always to depend upon
> In everything I do!
>
> How I do wander, up and down!
> I seem a stranger, quite undone;
> None to lend an ear to my complaint,
> No one to cheer me, though I faint.

At other times the spirituals concentrated explicitly on the promise of freedom and rang with biblical references about emancipation, in this case reaching the Jordan River that separated the Israelites from the Promised Land.

> Jordan River, I'm bound to go,
> Bound to go, bound to go,—Jordan River,
>    I'm bound to go,
> And bid 'em fare ye well.

## Alternatives to Protestant Christianity

Although most slaves practiced a form of Christianity, some were Muslim. Indeed, Islam was the religion of choice for a small minority of slaves, perhaps as high as 10 percent. Omar ibn Said, who authored the only surviving North American slave narrative in Arabic, was a member of a wealthy family from Futa Turo in West Africa. He was born about 1773. Captured by international slave traders, he arrived in South Carolina in chains in 1807 and remained there in bondage until his death in 1864. He recalled his early Islamic upbringing as a follower of "Mohammed, the Apostle of God," and his routines of praying throughout the day, tithing, making pilgrimages to Mecca, and joining yearly "holy wars against the infidels." As he explains in his autobiography, Said, like other Muslim slaves, confronted masters impatient with his faith.

Some slaves were also Roman Catholic, especially in national centers of Catholicism such as Maryland and Louisiana. In 1783 the bishop of Maryland estimated that about one-fifth, or three thousand, of all slaves in the state were Catholic. Two orders of black nuns formed in the first half of the nineteenth century. Mother Mary Lange, a free black woman originally from Haiti, began the Oblate Sisters of Providence in 1829 in Baltimore. And a free woman of African descent, Henriette Delille, began the Sisters of the Holy Family in New Orleans in 1842. These orders cared for the black population. No black priests were ordained in America until after the Civil War.

More popular among slaves as an alternative to Protestant Christianity was conjure, a mix of magic, medicine, spiritual beliefs, folklore, and African traditions that stressed the conjurer's healing abilities. It promised ways to bring good or harm to people, to tell the future, and to cure the sick. Through spells, chants, songs, and potions composed of roots and herbs, conjurers offered a different pathway to understanding and confronting the challenges of daily life. They typically enjoyed high status among blacks and many whites, especially if they were effective in their work. Though slaves might doubt conjure as a dependable defense against slavery's evils, many still resorted to it during moments of crisis. Henry Bibb, born in bondage in 1815 in Shelby County, Kentucky, but who eventually escaped to freedom in Canada, recalled that many slaves "believe in what they call 'conjuration,' tricking, and witchcraft; and some of them pretend to understand the art, and say that by it they can prevent their masters from exercising their will over the slaves." Bibb himself was skeptical of conjure, though he benefited from it on occasion. Facing a near-certain flogging by his master for breaking a rule, he desperately sought out a conjurer for help. "After I paid him, he mixed up some alum, salt, and other stuff into a powder, and said I must sprinkle it about my master, if he should offer to strike me; this would prevent him. He also gave me some kind of bitter root to chew, and spit towards him, which would certainly prevent my being flogged." Bibb did as he was told and escaped punishment.

## Beyond Slavery

Black Americans greeted the outbreak of the Civil War with a mix of hope and skepticism. Many prayed that the conflict would finally end the peculiar institution of slavery and interpreted it as God's punishment meted out upon the entire nation for its slave history. Not long after northern troops fired on Fort Sumter in South Carolina, northern blacks rushed to join the Union Army, while southern blacks fled for Yankee encampments to escape slavery. Independent black churches organized relief efforts for black soldiers and the runaways, providing food, shelter, and basic literary training. Others, however, were only guardedly optimistic about the lasting meaning of the Civil War. Even if the war broke the chains of bondage, they worried that racism's poison, so long pumping through the heart of the nation, would limit any permanent change to the citizenship rights of African Americans. These anxieties proved to be well founded. For although the war broke slavery's back, it failed to uproot national ideas about racial hierarchy or check the customs and laws of segregation that came into being during the 1880s and 1890s and defined race relations for generations. To be sure, the war's conclusion made possible an explosive growth of black churches and denominations, fraternal orders, religious schools, and seminaries. But it also bore witness to a sadder truth—that even though African Americans were no longer slaves, they were still not free. Their historical identification with the ancient Hebrews in the book of Exodus as they journeyed from slavery to freedom would persist, only now focused on the process of seeking the promised land of liberty.

**See also** *Abolitionism and Antislavery; African American Religion entries; African Traditional Religions; Great Awakening(s); Invisible Institution; Literature: African American; Missions: Foreign; Music: African American; Roman Catholicism: African American Catholics.*

John M. Giggie

## BIBLIOGRAPHY

Allen, Rt. Rev. Richard. *The Life, Experience, and Gospel Labours of the Rt. Rev. Richard Allen. To Which Is Annexed the Rise and Progress of the African Methodist Episcopal Church in the United States of America. Containing a Narrative of the Yellow Fever in the Year of Our Lord 1793: With an Address to the People of Colour in the United States.* Philadelphia: Martin and Boden, Printers, 1833.

Bibb, Henry. *Narrative of the Life and Adventures of Henry Bibb, An American Slave, Written by Himself.* New York: Author, 1849.

Chreau, Yvonne. *Black Magic: Religion and the African American Conjuring Tradition.* Berkeley: University of California Press, 2003.

Crummell, Alexander. "The Regeneration of Africa." In *African American Religious History: A Documentary Witness,* 2nd ed., edited by Milton Sernett. Durham, N.C.: Duke University Press, 1999.

Davis, Cyprian. *The History of Black Catholics in the United States.* New York: Crossroads, 1990.

Douglass, Frederick. *Narrative of the Life of Frederick Douglass, an American Slave.* New York: Dover Publications, 1995.

Du Bois, W. E. B. *The Souls of Black Folk,* edited by David W. Blight and Robert Gooding-Williams. Boston: Bedford, 1999.

Equiano, Olaudah. 1789. *The Interesting Narrative of the Life of Olaudah Equiano, or Gustavus Vassa, the African. Written by Himself.* 2 vols. London: Author.

Lee, Jarena. "Life and Experience." In *African American Religious History: A Documentary Witness,* 2nd ed., edited by Milton Sernett. Durham, N.C.: Duke University Press, 1999.

Levine, Lawrence W. *Black Culture and Black Consciousness: Afro-American Folk Thought from Slavery to Freedom.* New York: Oxford University Press, 1978.

Mathews, Donald. *Religion in the Old South.* Chicago: University of Chicago Press, 1977.

Newman, Richard. *Freedom's Prophet: Bishop Richard Allen, the AME Church, and the Black Founding Fathers.* New York: New York University Press, 2008.

Paul, Nathaniel. "Address." In *African American Religious History: A Documentary Witness,* 2nd ed., edited by Milton Sernett. Durham, N.C.: Duke University Press, 1999.

Price, Richard. *Alabi's World.* Baltimore: Johns Hopkins University Press, 1990.

Raboteau, Albert J. *Canaan Land: A Religious History of African Americans.* New York: Oxford University Press, 2001.

———. *Slave Religion: The "Invisible Institution" in the Antebellum South.* New York: Oxford University Press, 1978.

Said, Omar ibn. *Autobiography,* 1831, http://docsouth.unc.edu/nc/omarsaid/menu.html.

Sernett, Milton C. *Afro-American Religious History: A Documentary Witness.* 2nd ed. Durham, N.C.: Duke University Press, 1999.

Sobel, Mechal. *The World They Made Together: Black and White Values in Eighteenth Century Virginia.* Princeton, N.J.: Princeton University Press, 1987.

Washington, James Melvin. *Frustrated Fellowship: The Black Baptist Quest for Social Power.* Macon, Ga.: Mercer University Press, 1985.

West, Cornell, and Glaude, Eddie, Jr. *African American Religious Thought: An Anthology.* Louisville, Ky.: Westminster John Knox Press, 2003.

Woodson, Carter G. *The History of the Negro Church.* 3rd ed. Washington, D.C.: Associated Publishers, 1972.

# African American Religion: From the Civil War to Civil Rights

Black churches became the most dominant and stable institutional area to emerge from slavery largely because of the great ambivalence of most white Christians and slave masters toward freedom of religion and the conversion of enslaved Africans.

Although white missionaries and slave owners made many attempts to control slaves' religious lives and to produce obedient and docile servants, the Africans often held their own religious services with their own leaders in the backwoods and bayous of plantations and used a syncretism of Christianity and African traditions as a form of resistance. Sociologist E. Franklin Frazier has called this phenomenon "invisible religion." Gradually, slaves' invisible religion, or what others have called the "invisible institution," was transformed into visible independent black churches and denominations as more Africans gained their freedom starting in the mid-eighteenth century.

As a result of their dominance and independence in black communities, black churches often functioned as more than worship centers because they also participated in all aspects of people's lives, including communal and personal morality, politics, economics, education, music, and artistic activities. Sociologist C. Eric Lincoln found that the onerous pilgrimage of the black man and woman in early America was eased somewhat by their religion. According to Lincoln, "It was the peculiar sustaining force which gave him the strength to endure when endurance gave no promise, and the courage to be creative in the face of his own dehumanization."

## African American Churches from the Civil War to the End of the Nineteenth Century

The clergy who led the established northern black denominations—the African Methodist Episcopal Church (AME Church) and the African Methodist Episcopal Zion

The Rev. Hiram Revels, an AME clergyman from Mississippi, became the first African American citizen and senator elected to Congress in 1870.

Church—took advantage of the chaos caused by the Civil War to recruit new members among the enslaved Africans in southern states. Even before the Emancipation Proclamation of 1863, both denominations sent numerous missionaries into the South, following the advance of the Union armies. Thousands of new members were recruited from the "invisible institution," and there were massive defections from the black constituency of the Methodist Episcopal Church, South. They flocked to the black denominations where they found an unaccustomed dignity and a sense of self-worth. Enslaved Africans who attended white church services with their masters were often relegated to an upstairs balcony or seated at the rear of the church. Sometimes they even had to sit outside by the window to hear the sermon, prayers, and hymns.

The inclusion of newly emancipated black southerners led to enormous growth in the black denominations. The membership of the AME Church grew from a modest 20,000 members before the Civil War to more than 400,000 by 1884. Although the denomination was established in Philadelphia, South Carolina became its strongest demographic region. A similar phenomenon occurred with the New York–based AME Zion Church, which had 4,600 members in 1860. Its membership grew to 300,000 by 1884. The state of North Carolina emerged as the Zion Church's largest area in terms of members and numbers of churches.

The third black Methodist denomination, the Colored (later Christian) Methodist Episcopal Church (CME Church), was established on December 15, 1870, in Jackson, Tennessee. It grew more slowly than the African churches; it had 103,000 members, 75 percent of whom were located in Alabama, Georgia, Mississippi, and Tennessee. The CME Church has remained the smallest of the three black Methodist denominations.

Independent black Baptist churches were the earliest black institutions, created between 1750 and 1775. However, the black Baptist denominations were not organized until the late nineteenth and early twentieth centuries. At a meeting in Atlanta on September 28, 1895, the National Baptist Convention U.S.A., Inc. was established, and Rev. E. C. Morris was elected as the first president of the new convention. Black Baptist churches constituted the largest sector of the black church population, with twenty thousand churches and three million members in the late nineteenth century.

## Re-enslavement and Lynching

The period after the Civil War was characterized by several events: the rising violence of the Ku Klux Klan and the development of a more rigid system of segregation in the South; the establishment of black educational institutions by black churches and the American Missionary Association; the collapse of the Freedman's Savings Bank and the need for black banks and life insurance companies; and the emergence of the Holiness-Pentecostal movement.

In 1865 two groups were formed to oppose the Reconstruction efforts of the Union and to intimidate the recently freed African Americans through acts of violence and vigilante terrorism: the Ku Klux Klan, a white supremacist organization founded by Confederate veterans, and the southern Convict Lease System. The Thirteenth Amendment to the Constitution (1865), which freed the slaves, contained a proviso that made prison labor the only form of legal slavery or involuntary servitude permissible in the United States. The southern Convict Lease System, which was based on this amendment, was used to re-enslave thousands of African Americans who were imprisoned for often petty charges such as vagrancy. Ninety percent of the convicts were African Americans, who were leased out by local sheriffs at cheap rates to plantation owners and farmers.

Because the former slave owners were no longer responsible for the health and well-being of their laborers, untold thousands died under the Convict Lease System.

The deadlocked presidential election of 1876 led to a compromise by the eventual winner, Rutherford B. Hayes, who promised to withdraw the Union Army from the southern states if southern politicians gave him their electoral votes. The subsequent withdrawal of the Union Army from the South in 1877 unleashed a wave of violence and lynching that continued into the first decades of the twentieth century. Laws passed by southern states eventually eliminated the rights of African Americans to vote, and the 1896 U.S. Supreme Court decision in *Plessy v. Ferguson* legitimated racial segregation laws in public accommodations throughout the South.

Black churches and their clergy attempted to oppose this climate of violence and intimidation. Some black clergy preached against the violence and acts of discrimination that their members were suffering, while others were intimidated by the attacks on black churches, which included gunfire, burnings, and bombings. Ida B. Wells, a former newspaper editor, led an antilynching crusade after witnessing the hanging of three successful black grocery store owners in Memphis in 1892. Most of Wells's public speeches against lynching were given in AME churches.

## Civil Rights Act of 1867

The Civil Rights Act of 1867 passed during the Reconstruction era conferred on former slaves in the South and other black people in the North the right to vote. These black voters succeeded in electing twenty black representatives and two black senators. In 1870 Rev. Hiram Revels, an AME clergyman from Mississippi, became the first black citizen and the first black senator elected to Congress. Another AME clergyman, Rev. Richard H. Cain of Georgia, was elected to the House of Representatives in 1873. Both Revels and Cain established the tradition of the clergy-politician in black communities, a pattern that would be revived in the mid-twentieth century. President Hayes's southern compromise and the withdrawal of Union troops in 1877 led gradually to the elimination of black voting rights in southern states before the end of the nineteenth century. Thus blacks were limited to voting in their churches—for their pastors, bishops, and convention presidents, and for their deacons, stewards, and members of their boards of trustees, including the leaders of women's conventions, missionary societies, and ushers and nurses. Because for almost a century black people could vote only in their churches, black church politics at the local, state, and national levels steadily became a highly competitive and contested terrain.

## Sunday Schools, Music, Black Colleges, and Banks

The Sunday schools of black churches often fulfilled the rudimentary task of teaching adults and children reading and writing skills. In many southern states it was illegal to teach an enslaved person how to read and write. When freedom came, the pent-up demand for education was overwhelming. Every school that opened in Savannah, Georgia, after the Civil War was deluged by blacks of all ages who wanted to learn how to read and write in spite of the fact that an education would not lead to a job in the devastated southern economy. A primary motivation for most black people to become literate was so they could read God's Word for themselves. Their belief in a transcendent God had enabled them to survive the brutalities, deaths, and horrors of the slave system.

Music in black churches during the postbellum period consisted of a mixture of Negro spirituals, Isaac Watts's hymns, and locally developed songs. Bishop Richard Allen, the founding pastor of the Mother Bethel AME Church in Philadelphia, developed the first collection of Negro spirituals—songs created by enslaved Africans about their lives, faith, and hopes. Because many black Christians were illiterate at the time, the hymn lining tradition became prevalent—a leader would call out the line to be sung, and it would be repeated by the congregation. Much of the music at this time was a cappella, accompanied by hand clapping and foot stomping. To move to a more formal worship style that emphasized "order and decorum," Bishop Daniel Payne introduced the use of an organ at the Bethel AME Church in Baltimore in 1847.

Black churches independently, and sometimes in cooperation with the northern American Missionary Association, helped to turn the schools established in church basements into the first black colleges and universities. Bishop Payne of the Bethel AME Church, who had a reputation for promoting education, paved the way by founding in 1856 the first African American institution of higher learning, Wilberforce University in Ohio. Six other AME-sponsored colleges followed. Morehouse College grew out of a school of the Springfield Baptist Church in Augusta, Georgia, and it later moved to Atlanta. Spelman College was founded in the basement of Atlanta's Friendship Baptist Church. The Tuskegee Institute received its start in the basement of an AME Zion Church in Tuskegee, Alabama. Often called the "black Harvard," Fisk University was established by the American Missionary Association in 1866. It became famous for the Jubilee Singers and for the undergraduate training of well-known scholars such as W. E. B. Du Bois and John Hope Franklin. Howard University, the "black Yale," was established by private benefactors in 1867 and has received funds from the federal government as most colleges do.

The Freedman's Savings and Trust Bank, established by Congress in 1865 to provide banking services for the newly freed people, collapsed in 1874 because of the financial recession of 1873 and the bank's mismanagement by white overseers. This bank held the cash bounties that thousands of black soldiers received for joining the Union Army during the Civil War and the funds of many black churches, fraternal lodges, and mutual aid and beneficial societies. The collapse left black people without any banking services because white banks refused to serve them. As Du Bois noted in 1907, the study of "economic cooperation among Negroes must begin with the Church group." In 1888 the fraternal lodges and black churches helped to capitalize black banks such as the True Reformers' Bank in Richmond, Virginia, and the Capital Savings Bank in Washington, D.C. In the late nineteenth century the Sixteenth Street Baptist Church of Birmingham established the Penny Savers Bank for its members. The bank's first president was the church's pastor. About a dozen black banks were created in the years that followed, but most of them collapsed during the Great Depression. Black churches and lodges also helped to capitalize the first black-owned life insurance companies, North Carolina Mutual in 1898, the Afro-American Industrial Insurance Society of Jacksonville in 1901, and Atlanta Life Insurance in 1905. The Afro-American Industrial Insurance Society began as a mutual benefit society in Rev. J. Milton Waldron's Baptist church in Jacksonville.

## Holiness Movement and Pentecostalism

During the post–Civil War period, the Holiness movement developed from its roots in the Second Great Awakening and became highly influential among black churches. The concept of an experience of sanctification by the Holy Spirit, of living a holier life, originated in John Wesley's belief that spiritual perfection in this life was possible. The first national camp meeting of the movement was held in Vineland, New Jersey, in 1867, and the movement began to spread to the camp meetings of other black and white Christians, who in the beginning were largely Methodists but later hailed from other denominations. Black Holiness churches developed in small rural towns in the South and spread widely in urban storefront churches in northern cities during the great migrations. Holiness members believed in a second blessing of the Holy Spirit or a religious experience of sanctification beyond the first blessing of personal salvation or "being saved." Women in black Holiness churches wore long white dresses, head coverings, and gloves as symbols of sanctification. In the 1890s and early twentieth century the Holiness movement began to be blended with Pentecostalism. Pentecostalists believed in a third blessing of the Holy Spirit as manifested in gifts of the Spirit such as "speaking in tongues," interpretation of tongues, and healing.

The blending of the Holiness-Pentecostal movement is illustrated by the life of Bishop Charles H. Mason, the founder of the Church of God in Christ, the largest black Pentecostal denomination. This Baptist minister in Arkansas experienced sanctification at a revival in Mississippi. He was eventually ousted from the Baptist association, but as a Holiness preacher he attracted many followers. His first church, which he called the Church of God in Christ, was established in a former cotton gin house in Lexington, Mississippi. In 1907 he attended the Azusa Street revival, an international phenomenon that spanned 1906–1909 in Los Angeles, and was led by a black Holiness preacher, Elder William Joseph Seymour. Like the thousands of black and white attendees, Mason experienced the blessing of the Holy Spirit and began speaking in tongues. He returned to Memphis and organized other clergy into a Pentecostal denomination.

As the first Pentecostal bishop, Mason ordained both black and white clergy. However, the biracial character of Pentecostalism in the United States was short-lived, because the white clergy eventually split off and in 1914 established their own Pentecostal denomination, the Assemblies of God. The northern urban migrations proved to be beneficial to the rapid growth of the Church of God in Christ, as it developed from a handful of rural southern clergy and churches to the second largest black denominational group after the Baptists.

## African American Churches, the Great Migrations, and the Great Depression

In 1890 about 90 percent of the black population of the United States resided in the South, and about 80 percent of African Americans lived in the southern rural counties from Virginia to Mississippi called the "Black Belt," because of the demographic predominance of black people living in the rural areas of these states. By the end of the civil rights era in 1968, only 51 percent of the total U.S. black population remained in the South. Many African Americans had joined others in the largest internal migrations the country has ever seen. From 1870 to 1970 about seven million people left the rural South for northern and western urban areas. Many of those who remained in the South also began moving to its urban areas. Thus a largely rural population became in the late twentieth century one of the most highly urbanized. The vast migrations were clustered around the periods of the two World Wars and the Korean War, transforming the demographic landscape as millions of African Americans relocated in search of jobs and a better life.

Employment was the primary reason for migration, but other factors also spurred black people to move: the mechanization of agriculture in the South, the lynching and violence of a rigid system of Jim Crow segregation, the long-term decline of sharecropping and individual black-owned farms, and the need for cheap labor in northern factories and industries. Near-starvation forced some church congregations and whole sections of black towns to leave. People wanted to get out of "this land of sufring" and seek the promised land elsewhere.

## Urbanization and the Black Pastorate

Since their beginnings in the mid-eighteenth century, the majority of black churches in the South have been rural institutions. The major effect of the migrations was to produce a largely "absentee pastorate" among these churches. One pastor typically cared for three or four rural churches, preaching at each one once a month. The automobile and the growth of highways made this monthly circuit possible. The absentee pastorate meant that the pastor no longer resided in the rural area where the churches were located but usually in a nearby city. It also meant that rural church members had to be self-sufficient, carrying on activities such as weekly prayer meetings and Bible study without the guidance of their pastors. Meeting once a month also produced the phenomenon among some black church members in urban areas of preferring to attend church on the "first Sunday," "second Sunday," or "third Sunday," and still considering themselves to be faithful Christians.

Although the migrations depleted rural congregations in the South, it was extremely difficult to close a rural church. Part of the reason for the high levels of loyalty was found in the cemeteries of these churches. Enduring segregation from birth to death, generations of black families traced their roots to these rural church cemeteries, and some family clans made annual pilgrimages to these churches.

To encourage the migration of black laborers, northern companies advertised in black newspapers, and railroad companies gave steep discounts on train tickets to black clergy and their families if they moved north with members of their congregations. The net result was the tremendous growth of urban black churches in the twentieth century. The established black churches in cities such as Chicago or New York City were overwhelmed by the needs of black migrants not only for worship services but also for social services, such as help in finding housing and jobs, and, for the poorer migrants, clothing and food. As the membership of these established urban congregations swelled, some of the migrants who felt uncomfortable in the environs of black middle-class churches began to start their own churches, often in storefronts in the poorest sections of the city. If a preacher was not available to lead them, they called those from their rural churches.

Urban areas also provided a level of anonymity and freedom for religious experimentation that was unavailable in rural areas, where people's behavior and moral reputation were closely scrutinized by church deacons and clergy. Breaking the moral code often led to social isolation and excommunication from the church community. The migrants reveled in their newfound freedom in cities, and some of them began their individual quests for meaning in adopting new identities and joining new movements, such as Marcus Garvey's United Negro Improvement Association, black nationalism, Noble Drew Ali's Moorish Science Temple, and Master Fard and Elijah Muhammad's Nation of Islam. Other popular charismatic religious leaders of large national urban religious movements were Father Divine, Daddy Grace, and Rabbi Cherry.

One of the fruits of urbanism was the elevation of black women to the ranks of the clergy. Although there has been a long tradition of black preaching women, some of whom wanted to be ordained, such as Jarena Lee, from the days of slavery onward African American women often met strong resistance from black male clergy. The African Methodist Episcopal Zion Church became the first denomination, black or white, to raise women to the clerical ranks. At the urging of a group of feminist Zion bishops, Bishop James Walker Hood ordained Julia A. Foote, a conference missionary, as a deacon on May 19, 1894, at the Catherine Street AME Zion Church in Poughkeepsie, New York. Bishop Alexander Walters ordained Mary J. Small, the wife of Bishop John B. Small, as a deacon in Philadelphia in 1895. In 1898 Bishop Calvin Pettey ordained Mary Small as an elder in the Philadelphia-Baltimore conference. Julia Foote was also ordained as an elder by Bishop Alexander Walters in 1900. Both Small and Foote were the first women to achieve the rights of full ordination to the ministry by any Methodist denomination.

The AME Zion Church's ordination of women preceded similar action by other black or white Methodist denominations by half a century. And yet women in the black Baptist denominations have struggled to be ordained as clergy. The Church of God in Christ, the largest black Pentecostal body, still prohibits the ordination of women.

Because urban politics and economics were often more complex than the politics and economics normally faced by rural pastors, the migrant clergy had to adjust their leadership styles and become less autocratic in their relationships with their congregations and local communities. Some of the leading black clergy in urban areas realized the need to create secular, broad-based civil rights organizations. Clergymen such as Rev. Reverdy Ransom and Rev. J. Milton Waldron were influential members of W. E. B. Du Bois's Niagara Movement, which preceded the founding of the interracial National Association for the Advancement of Colored People (NAACP) in 1909 as the guardian and advocate for black rights in the political arena. In 1911 the National Urban League was created through the influence of black educator and leader Booker T. Washington to help black people improve their employment and economic opportunities. Both organizations found their primary black support in black churches, and many local chapters were led by black clergy.

In 1915 the National Baptist Convention, U.S.A., experienced a schism over ownership of its publishing house in Nashville. The dispute erupted between the "Boyd faction," led by Rev. R. H. Boyd, secretary of the Publishing Board, and the "Morris faction," led by Rev. E. C. Morris, president of the convention. Clergy in the Boyd faction withdrew and set up their own Baptist denomination, taking the name National Baptist Convention of America. Because a long time passed before it was legally incorporated, this group was often referred to as the "unincorporated" convention, and the original body was called the "incorporated" convention. The original denomination began to emphasize this aspect in its name, the National Baptist Convention, U.S.A., Inc.

## From War to Depression and Back Again

Black veterans returning from World War I experienced high levels of racial discrimination in their search for employment in both the North and the South. In the summer of 1919 a

series of bloody racial riots broke out in twenty-five cities, largely instigated by whites who were reacting to the large numbers of African Americans migrating to these areas and competing for jobs. Black people were attacked in the streets, and some were lynched, and black neighborhoods were burned. More riots occurred during the "Bloody Summer of 1919" than during any other period until the racial conflagrations of the late 1960s. The Ku Klux Klan, which had its headquarters in Indianapolis, expanded its membership nationwide to two million in the 1920s. Thousands of Klan members also held a march on Washington.

In the 1920s the migrations of blacks to urban areas prompted a creative outburst of exceptional talent by African American artists, writers, poets, intellectuals, and musicians. The Harlem Renaissance, as it was called, spread from Harlem in New York City to other urban centers. Although it has not been fully studied the impact of the Renaissance on black churches and clergy, the one tangible area of change was in the music of black churches. Thomas "Georgia Tom" Dorsey, a blues nightclub musician who learned his music in church, returned to the church to combine blues music with Charles Tindley's hymns to produce what he called "Gospel songs." Because of its association with nightclubs and houses of prostitution, blues was often called the "Devil's music" by black church members. However, the simple but livelier gospel music with its compelling imagery gradually spread to black churches, especially influencing their choirs from the 1930s to mid-1960s. After Dorsey's wife and child died tragically, he wrote "Precious Lord, Take My Hand," which Elvis Presley made famous.

The Great Depression was devastating to black communities and churches, as unemployment and poverty levels rose throughout the 1930s. However, the churches and clergy continued to participate in local urban politics during the interwar years, primarily as mobilizers of the black vote in cities such as Chicago, where African Americans played a significant role in Big Bill Thompson's Republican political machine. The majority of black voters were staunch members of the Republican Party, the party of Lincoln the Emancipator, from the Civil War until the middle of the Great Depression, when President Franklin D. Roosevelt's liberal social welfare policies convinced many of them to join the Democratic Party. In Chicago, black clergy such as Archibald Carey and some secular black leaders became part of the "client-patron" politics, in which African Americans became clients of white political patrons such as Thompson and later Mayor Richard J. Daley. The ongoing arrival of large numbers of rural migrants and the devastating economic conditions pushed many black churches into a conservative political stance. Gayraud Wilmore has described the interwar period as the "deradicalization of the Black Church." Sociological studies by Benjamin Mays and Joseph Nicholson, St. Clair Drake and Horace Cayton, and Gunnar Myrdal detected a robust conservative stance among some black clergy and churches, a withdrawal from the political and social involvement in their communities, and a strong tendency toward assimilation into the mainstream white culture.

Some black churches, however, were moving in the opposite direction—toward greater political activism. Rev. Martin Luther King Sr., pastor of the Ebenezer Baptist Church in Atlanta, led members of his congregation to city hall to attempt to register to vote in 1935, when black disenfranchisement was the order of the day in southern states. Many large black churches in major cities such as New York, Baltimore, and Chicago allowed A. Phillip Randolph to hold organizing and recruitment meetings for his fledgling black labor union, the Brotherhood of Sleeping Car Porters. Staunch laywomen such as Mary McLeod Bethune and Nannie Helen Burroughs were active on the national political scene, as well as in the women's conventions of their denominations. Bethune reached national prominence as a member of the Roosevelt administration in part because of her close friendship with First Lady Eleanor Roosevelt.

In the late 1930s Rev. Adam Clayton Powell Jr., pastor of the eight-thousand-member Abyssinian Baptist Church in Harlem, called for protests in the streets on economic issues. He also organized the Greater New York Coordinating Committee to focus attention on job discrimination. Later, he broadened the committee to include other religious and secular groups, and eventually it became the political instrument that broke the power of New York's Tammany Hall political organization in Harlem. In 1944 Powell was elected to the U.S. House of Representatives, the first black politician from the east to serve in Congress. He revived the tradition of the black preacher/politician. Flamboyant, outspoken, and controversial, Powell became chairman of the House Committee on Education and Labor and made major legislative contributions that led to the rise of the civil rights movement.

In 1934 AME bishop Reverdy Ransom established the Fraternal Council of Churches, composed of largely progressive black Methodist and Baptist churches. From the mid-1930s to the 1950s, the council lobbied in Washington on civil rights issues such as antilynching legislation and desegregation of the armed forces. President Harry S. Truman signed the antilynching legislation in 1946 and desegregated the armed forces in 1947. Father Divine's Peace Mission was also a major force in the antilynching campaign, begun by Ida Wells in the late nineteenth century.

After years of negotiation, a plan was finally adopted in 1939 to unify the major white Methodist bodies—the Methodist Episcopal Church, the Methodist Episcopal Church, South, and the Methodist Protestant Church—that had split over the issue of slavery in 1844. However, the price of union was the creation of a separate black jurisdiction within the newly unified church. The new Methodist Church was organized into five geographical regions or jurisdictions. A sixth entity, called the Central Jurisdiction, consisted of all the black conferences and missions in the United States, which encompassed 315,000 black Methodists. Although the Central Jurisdiction participated equally with the others at the national level of the church, at all other levels blacks were officially segregated. They could elect their own black bishops, but those bishops could function only as bishops of black Methodists; they had no authority over white Methodists. The result was to institutionalize a black Methodist church, which literally was a church within a church. It was not until the pressures and agitation of the civil rights movement and the merger with the Evangelical United Brethren Church that the Central Jurisdiction was abolished in 1966. The new entity was called the United Methodist Church.

## World War II and the Postwar Period

As economic historians have pointed out, the Great Depression ended only after the economic stimulus provided by the country's involvement in World War II took effect. Fought on two fronts, Europe and the Pacific, World War II surpassed World War I in providing job opportunities for black men and women in northern factories and industries. These jobs, combined with the opening of labor union membership to blacks, served as the economic foundation for a growing black middle class. As in past wars, black soldiers, sailors, and pilots served in segregated military units commanded by white officers. However, these travels abroad and the experiences gained in other countries broadened the horizons of the African American soldiers. Although they encountered some racial discrimination from fellow white soldiers, their experiences in combat also taught them that friendships could be forged across racial barriers. They also saw that other countries had no rigid segregation laws.

However, upon returning to the United States many of these black veterans encountered the same hostility and racial discrimination in employment that black veterans had experienced after the end of World War I. Thus, although they had served in segregated units, the black war veterans were able to form a broad support group that had the leadership experience needed for the agitation and changes that the civil rights movement would bring.

## Foundations of the Civil Rights Movement

Several other events or actions also laid the foundations for the emergence of the civil rights movement. The first was President Truman's order to desegregate the military. It ensured that blacks who fought in the Korean War and future wars would serve in integrated units. It also opened upward mobility for African Americans to become officers, even generals.

The second was the 1954 U.S. Supreme Court decision in *Brown v. Board of Education of Topeka*, which declared segregated education in public schools illegal. In this case, Rev. Oliver Leon Brown of St. Mark's AME Church in Topeka, Kansas, with the support of the NAACP Legal Defense Fund, sued the Board of Education on behalf of his nine-year-old daughter, Linda Brown, and all other black children similarly injured by segregation in the public schools. NAACP attorney Thurgood Marshall, supported by the psychological studies of the effects of segregation on young black children conducted by Kenneth and Mamie Clark, argued the case and won. The Supreme Court's *Brown* decision provided the legal legitimacy for the attempts of the civil rights movement to desegregate public transportation and public accommodations throughout America.

The third was the lynching of Emmett Till, a fourteen-year-old teenager from Chicago who was visiting his uncle in the rural delta town of Money, Mississippi, in August 1955. After buying candy and soda at a grocery store, Till allegedly flirted with the white woman clerk. Unknowingly, he had broken one of the oldest southern taboos against interracial relationships, which placed the purity of white women on a pedestal. Several days later, Till was taken from his uncle's home at night by the clerk's husband, Roy Bryant, and half-brother, J. W. Milam. Till was then brutally beaten to death, and his body was thrown into the Tallahatchie River. In the ensuing trial the alleged perpetrators, Bryant and Milam, were found innocent. Till's mother, Mamie Till Bradley, held a funeral for her son in her church in Chicago. The open casket revealed her son's smashed head and disfigured face. Photos in *Jet* magazine and black newspapers aroused the conscience and emotions of the national black community.

During the decades of the 1940s and 1950s, sociological studies found that the earlier trend of upwardly mobile African Americans joining white church denominations was continuing. According to the eminent black sociologist of Howard University E. Franklin Frazier, the "Negro Church" was a stumbling block in the attempts of black people to assimilate into mainstream American society.

## African American Churches and the Rise of the Civil Rights Movement

In 1955 in Montgomery, Alabama, E. D. Nixon, president of the local chapter of the NAACP and a member of the Brotherhood of Sleeping Car Porters, was preparing to challenge segregation on the city's public buses. Nixon and several members of the NAACP, such as chapter secretary and seamstress Rosa Parks, had been trained in the tactics of nonviolent protest at the Highlander Folk School in Tennessee. On Thursday, December 1, 1955, Parks was arrested for refusing to give up her seat to a white man on a crowded bus. That evening Jo Ann Robinson of the Women's Political Council printed and circulated a flyer calling for the black community to stay off the buses when Parks's case came up for trial on the following Monday. At a meeting of local leaders, Rev. Dr. Martin Luther King Jr., the newly arrived pastor of the Dexter Street Baptist Church, was elected as the leader of the bus boycott by the recently formed Montgomery Improvement Association. Nixon had chosen the twenty-six-year-old King to be leader of the recently formed association because he was new, young, and "untouched" by the intimidation of white political leaders. The mass meeting held on Saturday, December 3, at a black church was overflowing with enthusiastic supporters. Plans were made for carpooling, walking, and riding bicycles, and black cab drivers were to charge the same fare as the city buses.

The one-day Montgomery boycott was so successful that plans were made to continue it until the white leaders agreed to black demands to desegregate the buses. Accompanied by numerous mass meetings at black churches, sometimes held almost nightly, the boycotters carried on the struggle in the face of threats by white employers, beatings, and intimidation by imprisonment. King was arrested and spent two weeks in jail. Bayard Rustin from the War Resisters League advised King and the Montgomery movement on the philosophy and strategy of Gandhian nonviolence. The boycott was supported by legal rulings from a federal district judge and the U.S. Supreme Court that Alabama's racial segregation laws for buses were unconstitutional. After 381 days, the boycott officially ended on December 20, 1956, when the city of Montgomery ruled that black passengers on buses could sit wherever they wanted.

The success of the Montgomery bus boycott inspired many other African Americans to begin protesting and attacking de jure and de facto segregation throughout the country. Although boycotts of public transportation had been led by black clergy in the 1920s and 1930s, the Montgomery event succeeded where the others had failed.

### Southern Christian Leadership Conference and Student Nonviolent Coordinating Committee

Buoyed by the success of Montgomery, King and other black Baptist leaders formed the Southern Christian Leadership Conference (SCLC) in 1957, in order to continue to protest the segregation of public facilities in southern states. In 1959 Rev. James Lawson, another disciple of Gandhian nonviolence and organizer for the Fellowship of Reconciliation, moved to Nashville and began teaching students at Fisk and Vanderbilt Universities about the tactics of nonviolent protest. His efforts led to sit-ins at lunch counters and protests at segregated downtown stores in February 1960. The Nashville movement was led primarily by students, such as future ministers Bernard Lafayette and John Lewis, and the president of the Fisk student body, Diane Nash.

About the same time, four African American students from North Carolina A&T State University in Greensboro held a sit-in at a Woolworth's lunch counter. Throughout the South other college and university students became involved in local civil rights protests. In April 1960, Ella Baker, national secretary of the SCLC, led a broad coalition of the students in a conference at Shaw University in Raleigh, North Carolina. She advised them to form their own independent student group instead of becoming a youth branch of the SCLC, as Reverend King wanted. They followed her advice and formed the Student Nonviolent Coordinating Committee (SNCC), which focused on civil rights protests, voter registration and education, and community organizing at the grassroots level. Baptist seminarian John Lewis became the first chair of SNCC, and its organizers spread throughout the rural South. SNCC had major roles in the sit-ins, freedom rides, March on Washington, Mississippi Freedom Summer, Mississippi Freedom

Democratic Party, and movements in Albany, Georgia, and Birmingham, Alabama.

According to sociologist Aldon Morris, throughout the protests and demonstrations of the civil rights movement, black churches provided the mobilizing foreground. They also provided many of the leaders and bodies that became the frontline troops for the movement. In rural and urban areas many mass meetings were held in black churches, because they were the only facilities large enough to accommodate the crowds of several hundred to more than a thousand protestors in a segregated South. Not all black clergy and church members participated in the civil rights movement because of the violence and intimidation they would face, but enough of them did so to the credit of this institution. In addition to meeting places, leaders, and followers, the rituals and songs of the churches provided a sustaining and inspirational force for the civil rights movement. Indeed, a genre of music called "Civil Rights Hymnody" emerged. SNCC Freedom Singers from Albany, Georgia, toured the country, holding fund-raising concerts and singing freedom songs. Evidence of the significance of black churches in the freedom movement was the many black churches that were shot at, bombed, or burned—some three hundred churches in Mississippi alone from 1960 to 1965. Probably the worst bombing was of the Sixteenth Street Baptist Church in Birmingham, where four young girls attending Sunday school were killed.

Although Rev. Martin Luther King and other major figures of the Southern Christian Leadership Conference were Baptists, the president of the National Baptist Convention, U.S.A., Inc., Rev. Joseph H. Jackson, refused to support the civil rights movement. The authoritarian Jackson, who wanted to be president for life, was challenged by the King faction, which was led by the outstanding orator Rev. Dr. Gardner C. Taylor, who ran for the presidency at the Philadelphia convention in 1960. However, Jackson won, and his faction refused to let the "Taylor team" into the convention held in Kansas City the following year. After they were finally admitted, the Taylor delegates approached the elevated stage to speak, but fisticuffs erupted on the floor of the convention. In November 1961 the King faction formed the Progressive National Baptist Convention, Inc., at the Zion Baptist Church in Cincinnati.

The civil rights movement's largest gathering was the highly successful March on Washington held in August 1963. More than 250,000 people attended, the largest assembly in Washington, D.C., up to that point. Martin Luther King's "I have a dream" speech became a riveting classic. Less than a month later, the Sixteenth Street Baptist Church was bombed. That bombing and the death of three civil rights workers—Michael Schwerner, James Chaney, and Andrew Goodman—in Mississippi, in 1964, brought pressure on Congress to pass and President Lyndon B. Johnson to sign the Civil Rights Act of 1964. Likewise, the brutal beatings and tear gassing of civil rights marchers on the Edmund Pettus Bridge in Selma, Alabama, and King's speech on the steps of the state capitol in Montgomery led to passage of the Voting Rights Act of 1965. Both acts formed the basis for public policies that removed many of the barriers to racial equality in politics, employment, housing, education, and public accommodations. They provided the legal basis for the rise of a viable black middle class. Women of all colors used the Civil Rights Act to open the doors of opportunity for themselves. And other racial minorities such as Native Americans, Latinos, and Asians sought legal protection under this act.

In an attempt to move the civil rights movement toward attacking de facto racial segregation in housing in the north, King spent some months in the Chicago area in 1966. However, his protests and demonstrations failed because they encountered fierce resistance.

## Black Power and Black Liberation Theology

The assassination of Rev. Martin Luther King on April 4, 1968, at the Lorraine Motel in Memphis, Tennessee, is sometimes regarded as the formal end of the civil rights period. The death of this nonviolent warrior led to some 450 urban rebellions across the country as black people expressed their rage, anger, and sorrow in the streets in the weeks and months after the assassination. America was literally burning. Militant black students on college campuses began occupying buildings and demanding more black faculty and black studies programs and departments. The Black Power and Black Consciousness movements swept the country as similar movements took root in South Africa and elsewhere. Black people began demanding a place at the table in all areas of life. In black and white church denominations, the clergy formed separate black caucuses. In 1969 James Cone of the Union Theological Seminary produced a genre of theological reflection called black liberation theology. His black women doctoral candidates, Katie Cannon and Jacqueline Grant, developed a womanist theology, a black feminist version of the liberation theology of the late 1960s and 1970s. Both theologies have been highly influential in the education of black clergy.

The Black Consciousness era produced a new and greater appreciation of the historical role of black churches in the struggle for equality and justice in all areas of life for black people. It also stemmed the earlier tide of blacks joining white denominations. Members of the new black middle class became staunch supporters of black churches.

**See also** *Abolitionism and Antislavery; African American Religion* entries; *African Traditional Religions; Baptists: African American; Great Awakening(s); Invisible Institution; Literature: African American; Methodists: African American; Music: African American; Religious Thought: Womanist; Roman Catholicism: African American Catholics; South as Region.*

Lawrence H. Mamiya

## BIBLIOGRAPHY

Cannon, Katie. *Black Womanist Ethics.* Atlanta: Scholars Press, 1988.
Cone, James. *Black Theology and Black Power.* New York: Seabury, 1969.
———. *A Black Theology of Liberation.* Philadelphia: Lippincott, 1970.
Drake, St. Clair, and Horace Cayton. *Black Metropolis: A Study of Negro Life in the North.* Rev., 2 vols. New York: Harper and Row, 1962.
Du Bois, W. E. B. *Economic Cooperation among Negro Americans.* Atlanta: Atlanta University Press, 1907.
———, ed. *The Negro Church.* Atlanta: Atlanta University Press, 1901.
Frazier, E. Franklin. *The Negro Church in America.* New York: Schocken Books, 1964.
Jones, Jacqueline. "To Get Out of 'This Land of Sufring': Black Migrant Women, Work and Family in Northern Cities," 1900–1910." Working Paper No. 91, Wellesley College Center for Research on Women, Wellesley, Mass., 1982.
Hurston, Zora Neale. *The Sanctified Church.* Berkeley, Calif.: Turtle Island, 1983.
Lincoln, C. Eric, ed. *The Black Experience in Religion.* Garden City, N.Y.: Doubleday, 1974.
Lincoln, C. Eric, and Lawrence H. Mamiya. *The Black Church in the African American Experience.* Durham, N.C.: Duke University Press, 1990.
Mays, Benjamin, and Joseph Nicholson. *The Negro's Church.* New York: Russell and Russell, 1969.
Morris, Aldon. *The Origins of the Civil Rights Movement: Black Communities Organizing for Change.* New York: Free Press, 1984.
Myrdal, Gunnar. *An American Dilemma: The Negro Problem and Modern Democracy.* 2 vols. New York: Harper and Row, 1964.
Nelsen, Hart M., and Anne Kusener Nelsen. *Black Church in the Sixties.* Lexington: University of Kentucky Press, 1975.
Southern, Eileen. *The Music of Black Americans: A History.* 2nd ed. New York: W. W. Norton, 1983.
Washington, James Melvin. *Frustrated Fellowship: The Black Baptist Quest for Social Power.* Macon, Ga.: Mercer University Press, 1986.
———, ed. *A Testament of Hope: The Essential Writings of Martin Luther King, Jr.* San Francisco: Harper and Row, 1986.
Wells, Ida B. *On Lynchings: Southern Horrors; A Red Record; Mob Rule in New Orleans.* New York: Arno, 1969.
Wilmore, Gayraud. *Black Religion and Black Radicalism: An Interpretation of the Religious History of Afro-American People.* 2nd ed. Maryknoll, N.Y.: Orbis, 1983.

# African American Religion: Post–Civil Rights Era

African American religion is perhaps best understood to be an arrangement of competing and overlapping faith claims present in African American communities from the period of enslavement to the present. All these claims were forged in an effort to help African Americans form life meaning and a strong sense of place in the world in spite of the oppressive forces imposed by slavery and the discrimination that followed. Over the centuries, race and racism would serve as the issue most consistently addressed within the context of African American religion. While response to issues of race and racism would continue to mark African American religion during the post–civil rights era, it was matched by concern about a variety of other issues, along with the accompanying transformations of the nature of African American religion itself.

## Religion and the Web of Oppression

Before the onset of the civil rights movement, scholars discussed African American religious activism almost exclusively in terms of the struggle against oppression in the form of racism, and in that context they highlighted black churches as the most visible and systemically organized brand of African American religion. But within the context of the civil rights movement and during the post–civil rights discourse, a preoccupation with race and racism was challenged, for example, by African American women, who sought to bring the critique of sexism found within feminist thought into the struggle for liberation within African American communities. This greater attention to the problem of sexism within African American religious communities pointed out the large numbers of women involved in African American religious communities and the awkward nature of such large laity numbers in view of the very small number of women who exercised substantive leadership, including pastors. Indeed, although women represented some 70 percent of the membership, they represented roughly 5 percent of the leadership within the seven largest African American denominations.

This challenge to patriarchy within Christian organizations has met with some success. For example, in the African Methodist Episcopal Church, several women now exercise authority as bishops. The first was Rev. Vashti Murphy McKenzie, who in 2000 became the first woman

to serve as a bishop. In this position, she and the others who followed have a share of the most powerful position within the organization, helping to establish and monitor the workings of the church on the local, regional, national, and international levels. Pentecostal denominations and Baptist conventions have not made as much progress on this front, although some women are serving as church pastors. In many of these cases, they gained the leadership of particular churches after the death of their husbands. Within some Baptist circles there has been some forward movement, such as the late twentieth century pastor Suzan Johnson Cook, who in 1983 became the first woman to serve as senior pastor of a church within the American Baptist Churches of the USA. In addition, she was the first woman to head the Hampton University Ministers' Conference, which is one of the most significant gatherings of African American preachers in the country. African American women in majority-white denominations also made progress on this issue. For example, in 1989 Barbara Harris became the first African American woman to serve as a bishop in the Anglican Church; she became assistant bishop of the Episcopal Diocese of Massachusetts. As early as 1956 the General Conference of the Methodist Church granted women full ministerial rights, and currently more than ten thousand women serve in all leadership capacities of the church. However, it was not until 1984 that Leontine T. C. Kelly became the first African American woman to serve as a bishop within this denomination, three years after the first woman was elevated to this office. In addition, in 1974 Katie G. Cannon became the first African American woman ordained within the United Presbyterian Church (USA).

Even though outside the context of Christian institutions some instances of sexism have arisen, generally there is still greater openness to leadership regardless of gender within African-based traditions. For example, within Santería women have been initiated into the priesthood associated with particular deities, and in that capacity they head a community or house of practitioners. In fact, in 1961 the first African American woman was initiated as a priestess—two years after the first African American male.

## Disillusionment and the Changing Function of Black Churches

The assassinations of activists Martin Luther King Jr. and Malcolm X marked a decline in the optimism and reach of the civil rights movement. Claims that greater commitment to an active faith would result in the transformation of life circumstances in the United States seemed to falter. The optimism generated by religious commitment seemed out of step with the continuing struggle, and theology was challenged by the secular ideology of more radical and more nationalistic organizations. Black churches were the primary target of this pessimism in large part because they had greater numbers of adherents and they had received most of the popular and scholarly attention up to this point. Although the majority of African Americans when polled confessed belief in God and commitment to religion, black churches lost much of their luster, and some African Americans during the 1970s and 1980s shifted their personal allegiance away from these churches.

Declining membership within some of the major African American denominations—although there were increases within some others—spoke to the disillusionment some experienced. Further complicating this situation was the growing number of African American youth with little or no knowledge of black church tradition. Born after the glory days of the civil rights movement and the death of its most celebrated leadership, these young people had no ties to black churches and what they represented. Talk of "tradition" failed to motivate this population as it might have inspired their parents and grandparents. Drawing from different cultural resources and frustrated by the ongoing oppression the civil rights movement fought against, some of these young people critiqued black church tradition and called into question its theological assumptions, as opposed to what they saw as the realities of life. Their absence within black churches has spurred many African American ministers to develop creative ways of reaching out to this population. Many of these strategies have involved rethinking church liturgy and ritual structures in ways that incorporate the cultural realities and views of young people. From the perspective of some church leaders, recruiting this population is required if churches are to thrive and maintain connection to African American communities.

Within two decades of the civil rights struggle, some members of the African American middle class were disillusioned with life in the suburbs, the struggle for material success, and the setbacks in trying to break through the "glass ceiling"—that is, discrimination within the United States continued to shape and frame life options. Because of this situation, the story does not end with the decline of the black church's reputation and population. In fact, the 1990s marked a return to black churches by members of the African American middle class and others whose disillusionment with the socioeconomic and political shape of life overshadowed their difficulties with those churches. In the last decade of the twentieth century religious commitment seemed an answer to life struggles. After all, religion provided order, life structure, and the framework for hope. In search of stability, clear identity, understanding, and a basis for hope, some returned to black churches for grounding faith and community as well as the centering effects of religion. According to sociologist C. Eric Lincoln, during this period roughly 78 percent of African Americans claimed church membership. Although this percentage is difficult to verify, black churches by the end of the 1990s reported increasingly impressive numbers—over twenty million members spread across more than fifty thousand local congregations

The return to black churches forced changes in the nature and arrangements of church leadership. It had long been assumed for good reason that the church minister was the most educated and politically connected person within the church culture. However, with the influx of members of the African American middle class laity had as much if not more educational training, experience, and political know-how than their ministers. Church leadership for so long premised on the status of the pastor had to shift to recognize and include the talents and capabilities of professional church members. In response, some churches developed a community responsibility model in which the abilities of those within the church, not the assumed expertise of the pastor, determined patterns of authority. This model amounted to synergy between pastoral leadership and lay leadership. New models of leadership also included a determination to creatively incorporate the interests and concerns of young African Americans.

The new "look" of black churches as a result of this influx of middle-class African Americans was at times matched by a renewed call for community activism to respond to the conservative political policies that restricted assistance to the most economically challenged citizens. Churches were taking some ownership of the problems plaguing the communities in which they were located—that is, those churches that did not move to suburban communities during the period of decline in the inner cities. Outreach strategies including living out religious commitment in ways that maximized the talents of church members and allowed for partnerships with secular community organizations that otherwise might not cooperate with churches. Churches with political connections were able to receive local governmental assistance with the development of low-cost housing. This development seemed to cut across regions. For example, First AME Church in Los Angeles, Windsor Village United Methodist Church in Houston, and Concord Baptist Church in Brooklyn, New York, all partnered with secular community organizations and local government in order to advance development projects.

Financing these and other outreach programs (often in the form of community development corporations) has grown to involve more than the resources available through member contributions—tithing and targeted giving opportunities. More and more churches are looking to the federal government for the financial resources needed to start and maintain community initiatives. Perhaps the most widely known and most controversial form of government assistance has been the faith-based initiative program associated with the presidency of George W. Bush. Bush argued that religious communities can serve as effective ways to get resources into communities without the degree of red tape government agencies would require.

Based on "Charitable Choice" from 1996, the Office of Faith-Based Initiatives at the White House was meant to encourage and enable faith communities of all kinds to play a role in the socioeconomic transformation of communities. Successful applicants received federal funding for outreach programs that addressed community needs without requiring those receiving assistance to embrace the theological teachings of that particular religious community.

In 2009 newly elected president Barack Obama announced that his administration would continue this initiative, renamed the Faith-based and Neighborhood Partnerships program. Over the years the work of this office has met with mixed reviews. Some question whether it is constitutionally viable for the government to partner with religious organizations and in essence privilege them with respect to government funds. Others argue that this initiative might in fact be a political ploy to secure the all-important African American vote by appealing to the dominant religious organization and its leadership. And these funds, while useful on a certain level, might foster an unhealthy relationship between politics and the ministry of churches that compromises the latter for the sake of the former. Others have raised questions about whether most churches are administratively prepared and equipped to manage government funds. In addition, they point to the small number of churches (typically with large memberships) receiving these funds. Some suggest that

churches do not necessarily separate their theological commitments from access to their social service programs. Finally, critics note the failure of this office to provide funds to non-Christian organizations.

Those in favor of this program and who make use of such funding argue that it is a vital way to ensure that organizations committed to the welfare of African American communities are given the materials required to meet the needs of those communities. After all, black churches have remained the central organization within black communities; they have easy access to large groups of African Americans and the ability to quickly disseminate information and resources. By way of illustration, supporters of faith-based initiatives point to the civil rights movement and the key role in it played by churches. More recently, it has been suggested that the centrality of black churches is evident in the ability of these churches to effectively address issues of voter registration and provide relief during natural disasters such as Hurricanes Katrina (2005) and Ike (2008).

## Challenge to the Status Quo in Majority-White Denominations

African Americans have never limited their involvement in the Christian community to predominately African American denominations such as the African Methodist Episcopal Church, Church of God in Christ, or National Baptist Convention, USA. For centuries majority-white denominations have also been home to African American Christians. And although the presence of African Americans has raised the challenge of social discrimination and the proper Christian response, the presence of discrimination within these churches was put into graphic relief during the civil rights movement. For example, the "Black Manifesto" read in 1969 by James Forman at Riverside Church in New York City called upon majority-white denominations to recognize the racism embedded within their leadership structures and that undergirded their financial resources. It demanded that these churches surrender some of their money to the cause of African American liberation. This event caught the attention of many majority-white churches and forced them to wrestle with their internal race-based flaws. However, it was not simply external pressure that required this reevaluation; African American members during this period also critiqued their church homes and called for substantial change.

Organizations such as the National Black Presbyterian Caucus were organized as a way to centralize African

American concerns and unify their voices. African Americans argued that such issue-oriented committees and caucuses provided an opportunity to think through ways to create greater diversity in leadership. In some instances this push resulted in ordinations and other shifts in church authority. In general, however, substantial roles for blacks in white-majority church governance are still slow in coming and continue to be a source of tension in the twenty-first century.

The push by African Americans for a greater presence in predominately white churches was not limited to administrative and pastoral roles—the form and content of worship were a concern as well. For example, many churches altered artwork, songs, and other elements of worship in order to represent the cultural heritage of their diverse membership. For example, late in the twentieth century Saint Alphonsus Liguori Catholic Church in St. Louis, Missouri, changed its worship as its membership changed. The church, under the leadership of Rev. Maurice J. Nutt, gained an Afrocentric approach to worship and aesthetics, which included the use of gospel music and artwork that reflected African-styled carvings.

## Megachurches and Prosperity Gospel

As noted, the 1990s marked an increase in the stature of black churches that fostered a general trend toward growth in membership and programming. Many of these churches—both denominational and nondenominational, suburban and urban—constitute the corpus of what is now commonly known as megachurches. These churches are often defined as those who attract several thousand congregants each Sunday. And according to available accounts, as of the early 1990s fewer than fifty churches in the United States had memberships exceeding five thousand. Most churches were rather modest in size. More recent estimates suggest that more than thirty African American churches have memberships over the five thousand mark. These churches, pastored by ministers such as T. D. Jakes and, Creflo Dollar have in recent years not only established themselves as a religious force but also gained political influence through personal connections to major political leaders.

Marked by the emergence of ministries such as Fred Price's Crenshaw Christian Center (Los Angeles,) in the late 1960s, these churches use technology to minister to a follower base that includes not only those who physically attend the church but also the millions who consider themselves members via television programming, Web sites, CDs, and DVDs. These churches tend to lack the traditional iconography and structure suggestive of a traditional church building, opting instead for the look of stadiums or auditoriums. Worship within these churches involves a mix of preaching, singing, and other activities meant to please the senses with less emphasis on the harder theological questions. Some scholars refer to this approach as "religio-tainment."

Many of these churches and their leaders are known not only for their size but also for the theology they preach. Often referred to as the "Prosperity Gospel," this message seeks to balance material success and spiritual growth. It tends to downplay the importance of social critique and rarely challenges the political establishment. It suggests that God wants humans to be successful; in fact, material success can be a sign of a proper relationship with God. Understanding and living the Bible—particularly the New Testament—result in blessings, and traditional theological vocabulary and grammar are at times replaced with the language of corporate America.

Critics charge that the Prosperity Gospel simply offers a religious justification for a form of crude materialism. Rather than offering African Americans substantial ways to approach and address the issues in their personal lives, it poses the answer in terms of greater participation in a problematic economic system. Championed in this context is radical individualism, a religious justification for the "American Dream." The critique continues by suggesting that Prosperity Gospel preachers offer their followers nothing of lasting worth—no response to controversial issues. Thus this brand of message paints the minister as a motivational speaker rather than a prophetic representative of the social gospel—the commodification of spirituality. In response, many of these churches argue they do not offer material goods as the end point or as the purpose of religious commitment. Instead, they see their function as encouraging and guiding a proper relationship with God; economic benefit is simply a consequence of the primary objective—a personal relationship with God and with humanity.

The success of these churches raises questions and challenges for churches that do not have large memberships or do not preach the Prosperity Gospel. They may critique the megachurch and its brand of theology, but traditional churches are also pushed to respond in ways that allow them to maintain their viability. In the twenty-first century, a response to the megachurch phenomenon (complete with its theology) is unavoidable.

## *The Appeal of Non-Christian Religious Traditions*

The religious landscape of African American communities from the earliest presence of people of African descent in the Americas to the present has been marked by religious pluralism beyond various Christian denominations. Although always present, it was not until the second half of the twentieth century that these traditions and their adherents challenged the authority of black churches and entered the popular imagination of the United States.

## Islam

Drawing on the disillusionment of black nationalists, former Christians, and others, Islam provided a new context for life by connecting African Americans to a world community. It gave balance and purpose to the "me generation" and urged connection to others within a context marked by global conflict and a general ethos defining a sociopolitical and cultural nadir.

For some African Americans, the Nation of Islam provided a more compelling explanation of and response to oppression in the United States than did the black church and other religious orientations. However, the nature of the Nation of Islam changed during the post–civil rights era, first through the death of its leader, Elijah Muhammad, in 1975. This development was followed by a surprise move as Wallace Muhammad (Warith Deen Muhammad as of 1980), Elijah Muhammad's sometimes rebellious son, became the new leader of the movement. Warith worked to bring the Nation of Islam in line with the world community of Islam by changing its teachings and the aesthetics of its practices and by dismantling other elements inconsistent with Sunni Islam. Three years after Warith Deen Muhammad became leader, Minister Louis Farrakhan broke away and reconstituted the Nation of Islam under the original teachings of Elijah Muhammad.

Even though it is difficult to gauge with any accuracy the membership of the Nation of Islam, it is clear that some African Americans have continued to find it a more compelling response to spiritual desire. Maintaining the essence of the original teachings, Farrakhan with time suggested that the more controversial teachings, such as the demonic nature of white Americans were to be understood in symbolic terms. For example, white Americans were not demons; rather, white supremacy was demonic behavior. Farrakhan also opened the Nation of Islam to other people of color willing to abide by its teachings. This

new policy was in fact consistent with Elijah Muhammad's understanding of Latinos, Native Americans and, other "people of color" as part of the "Original People"—that is, those people created by God to rule the earth. Because of Farrakhan's health challenges, the nature of leadership within the Nation of Islam is under review, and more authority is being given to a governing group as opposed to a strict reliance on a single charismatic figure. Under Farrakhan's leadership, members of the Nation have also been encouraged to become politically involved, which marks a shift from the early separatist stance of Elijah Muhammad.

Farrakhan's relationship with the U.S. government has been tense at times, but he has exhibited an ability to capture the imagination and commitment of large numbers of African Americans. The "Million Man March" he organized in 1995 in Washington, D.C., was a symbolic gathering of African American men meant to suggest their renewed embrace of their responsibilities to themselves, their families, and their communities. In the post–civil rights era, the Nation of Islam continues to secure the allegiance of many African Americans because it provides life structure, a strong religious and racial identity extending beyond the borders of the United States, and straightforward explanations of historical developments. The Nation of Islam also provides its members with a sense of hopefulness and certainty in a world marked by turmoil.

The same can be said about the appeal of Warith Deen Muhammad's push for an African American Islam consistent with the beliefs and practices of the world community of Islam. Shortly after taking control of the organization once led by his father, Warith Deen Muhammad renamed the organization the World Community of Al-Islam in the West. In 1980 the name was changed again to the American Muslim Mission, and yet again in the 1990s to the Muslim American Community. Each name change was meant to represent the growth of an African American Muslim community consistent in all respects with Sunni Islam as practiced elsewhere in the world. Furthermore, these changes represented an effort to connect with the roots of Sunni Islam within African American communities, first represented, by the Islamic Mission of America Inc., founded by Shakyhk Dauod Ahmed Faisal in 1924, and the First Mosque of Pittsburgh.

The successful transition from the teachings of Warith Deen Muhammad's father to Sunni Islam is expressed not only in the development of a strong community represented by over two million African American Muslims, with schools and mosques across the country, but also in Muhammad's stature. For example, he is a member of the World Mission Council of Imam Administrators, and he is of undeniable importance to any Muslim in the United States wishing to undertake the pilgrimage to Mecca (one of the five pillars of the faith) because he provides the necessary certification. Muhammad's organization now represents the dominant expression of Sunni Islam within African American communities. These African American Sunni Muslims are connected to the world community of Islam and practice the faith in a way that would be recognizable to Muslims across the globe. Although many mosques tend to be tied to particular racial or ethnic groups, many of whom have immigrated to the United States, African American Sunni Muslims are found in a variety of cities and within mosques that are racially and ethnically diverse.

### African-Based Traditions

The years following the heyday of the civil rights struggle were marked by a reevaluation of African American identity. The continuing sting of discrimination in all areas of life stoked the suspicions of some African Americans that they would never be fully integrated into U.S. society. Their sense of self and community therefore had to extend beyond the cultural and social arrangements that defined the majority community. For those with this perspective, a cultural and spiritual connection to Africa was often vital, and African-based religiosity provided an answer.

The influx of immigrants from the Caribbean provided the injection of ritual expertise and cosmological knowledge needed to supplement a rather thin adherence to the African ways. African American involvement in traditions such as Santería thus increased during the post–civil rights era, its rituals protected by the Constitution, with African Americans developing "houses" of their own. In addition, the Oyotunji African Village, founded shortly after the assassination of Martin Luther King Jr., continues in Sheldon, South Carolina, as a religiocultural connection to African practices. This village, founded by the first African American initiated into Santería, in 1959, commits itself to the preservation of Yoruba tradition in the United States. Although the number of adherents actually living in the village has fallen over the last several decades, it remains a point of orientation and allegiance for many living elsewhere in the United States who seek the counsel of the village elders on issues of personal struggle and initiation into the priesthood.

Elsewhere, movement between Haiti and the United States during the twentieth century served to keep voodoo present and vital. And it would remain a religious option for African Americans committed to a faith tradition consistent with their perception of African heritage. Although voodoo lacks a standard doctrine, the late twentieth-century immigration of Haitians served to advance the tradition by an influx of ritual expertise. However, in some instances the substance of the tradition has been lost and what remains involves peddling to (for financial gain) the stereotypical assumptions of tourists, who buy voodoo dolls and other trinkets. For those who maintain allegiance to voodoo as a complex and rich tradition, general suspicion about it and other African-based traditions continue to call for secrecy. Scholars and popular outlets have helped to advance the interest in voodoo beyond the stereotypical depictions found in popular films. Examples are ethnographic discussions of particular voodoo leaders, such as Alourdes Margaux (Mama Lola) in New York City and Ava Kay Jones in New Orleans, and their work.

### Buddhism

Americans' embrace of the new age movement during the late twentieth century included African Americans as well. A feeling that life in the United States was empty inspired a turn toward the East for guidance and new ways of living. One manifestation of this search for life balance was the interest in Buddhism. Although present to some degree in the United States in the 1800s through missionary efforts and the writings of D. T. Suzuki, it was not until the 1960s with the proselytizing efforts of Soka Gakkai International-USA that African Americans began to embrace Buddhism in noteworthy numbers. Eventually African Americans would constitute more than 20 percent (twenty thousand) of Soka Gakkai's total membership and would hold positions of authority within the organization such as serving as district leaders and as vice general director.

Part of the appeal of Buddhism for African Americans stemmed from its commitment to equality and mutuality. In this way, African Americans felt free to embrace their heritage as people of African descent, denounce discrimination, and do so within the context of religious commitment. Furthermore, Buddhism has provided some African Americans with a sense of balance and serenity within a country marked by discord. There is within Soka Gakkai, according to some, opportunity for self-improvement and freedom to rethink the context and terms of life.

## Humanism

Since the period of slavery, some African Americans have rejected theistic orientations and have instead embraced various forms of humanism. Denouncing supernaturalism, these African Americans have preferred religious naturalism in which ethics trumps notions of the divine, and humans are understood to be accountable for the problems plaguing them as well as responsible for solving these problems. During the twentieth century African American humanism often revolved around an embrace of the Communist Party because of the perceived inability of Christian churches to address adequately the issues facing African Americans. During the civil rights movement some African Americans maintained this humanistic orientation through a rejection of the theological assumptions of leaders such as Martin Luther King Jr. Instead, they worked with organizations such as the Student Nonviolent Coordinating Committee (SNCC), as well as the Black Panther Party, both of which were disillusioned with the Christian ethos of the dominant civil rights struggle. Shifting to a human-centered framework was thought to be a more effective way of addressing the ills facing African Americans, in that it removed the possibility of divine sanction for oppression and allowed for a strong sense of human worth and hope generated by a sense of control over one's destiny. Today, many African Americans who continue to maintain this perspective and want to do so within the context of community join organizations such as the Unitarian Universalist Association, a no-creed religious denomination.

## Black and Womanist Theologies

In the1960s a group of progressive religious leaders and academics attempted to express a radical form of the social gospel meant to directly respond to racism and discrimination. In essence they sought to wed theologically black power and the Christian faith. This group, known as the National Council of Negro Churchmen (later the National Council of Black Churchmen), published statements on the religious import of black power and the obligation of Christians to seek freedom for the oppressed. Some of the early work in this area was carried out by Rev. Albert Cleage (*The Black Messiah,* 1968) who argued that God was black and Jesus was a black revolutionary whose activities pointed toward the liberation of oppressed African Americans. Yet it was with the publication of *Black Power and Black Theology* (1969) by James H. Cone that academic black theology

assumed its current structure and expression. Cone argued for an intimate connection between God and the struggle for liberation. In fact, he argued, God, in keeping with the biblical story of the Jews, sided with the oppressed and worked for their liberation. The mode of this struggle and partnership did not exclude, from Cone's perspective, the use of violence. In framing this agenda, black theology argued the meaning of oppression in the United States in terms of the plight of African Americans. The next year Cone published *A Black Theology of Liberation* (1970), in which he extended his earlier reflections. For example, Cone argued that God's connection to the oppressed in the United States (that is, African Americans) is so strong that God must be understood as black, or as ontologically black. With its commitment to the best of the Christian faith and the ability of that faith to promote healthy life options, black theology became a Christian theology.

Roughly three generations of black theologians are committed to the agenda initiated some forty years ago by Cone and others such as J. Deotis Roberts. They have expanded its attention to African American cultural materials and altered it in other ways while maintaining an allegiance to its fundamental structure and purpose. Some African American academics have challenged black theology to include more sophisticated social theory and analysis and to provide more rigorous attention to its reading of scripture and history. Others have pushed for better recognition of religious pluralism in the theology (including its nontheistic orientation). Furthermore, a small group, inspired by William R. Jones's 1973 book *Is God a White Racist? A Preamble to Black Theology,* has called into question the manner in which black theological discussions tend to understand human suffering as having some type of benefit in the struggle for liberation.

Amid the disagreements on the scope, framing, and articulation of black theology was an underlying problem that was not addressed in a systematic manner until the late 1970s. African American women academics pointed out the unchallenged sexism framing black theology and the teachings and practices of Christian churches. In the mid-1980s, a small group of African American women in ethics and theology added to a centuries-old critique of black churches a constructive element, womanist thought. This new theological paradigm critiqued the racism of many feminist thinkers and the sexism of many African American thinkers. The notion of "womanish" offered by novelist Alice Walker in her book *In Search of Our Mothers' Gardens* (1982) provided both a new methodology for the study of African American religion as well as new source material for understanding the development of that religion. Katie G. Cannon and Delores Williams, who are credited with naming this new mode of religious analysis, argued that a proper theological and ethical thinking capable of transforming life for the most oppressed must recognize the ways in which African American women were suffering because of oppression's triadic structure—racism, sexism, and classism.

The only way, these scholars argued, to develop sensitivity to and a critique of racism, sexism, and classism as they function in African American communities was to pay attention to the voices of African American women who were suffering from this web of oppression. Thus the literature and other materials that chronicled the concerns and experiences of women began to draw attention. And the perspective of women emerging from these materials was used to rethink the Christian faith. For example, Delores Williams in *Sisters in the Wilderness* (1993) used the challenges faced by African American women during slavery and freedom to interrogate traditional thinking on theories of the Atonement. Rather than embracing suffering as the central mark of the Atonement, Williams argued that not the death but the ministry of Christ was the most important: people should behave in the world in ways consistent with the teachings and practices of Christ. Williams was not the first to challenge traditional thinking about the Christ Event. In 1979 Jacqueline Grant (*Black Woman's Jesus, White Woman's Christ*) pushed both black theologians and feminist scholars by suggesting that African American women and white women have very different perceptions of Christology based on the modalities of oppression experienced by African American women. In terms of ethics, Katie Cannon in *Womanist Ethics* (1988) used the work of African American writer Zora Neale Hurston to think through the ethical lessons one can learn from the manner in which African American women have responded to oppression.

In addition to identifying the triadic structure of oppression as a way to reformulate African American religious thought and practice, womanist thinkers have also pushed African American Christians to address homophobia within African American churches, as well as the more general lack of attention to issues of sexuality. From the perspective of womanist scholars, African American Christians have had a troubled relationship with the human body. According to womanist theologian Kelly Brown Douglas (*Sexuality and the Black Church*, 1999, and *What's Love Got to Do With It?*

2005), this troubled relationship with the body stems from Christianity's platonic privileging of the spirit over the flesh. To overcome this dualism, Douglas argued for a theologically informed regard for the body, stemming from an appreciation of the Christ Event as the perfect union of God and humanity in relation to the body—that is, the body is not seen as a barrier to proper relationship with God, but rather as the vehicle through which God is made manifest in the world. This new attitude toward the body, then, allowed African American Christians to understand a full range of relationships—including sexual relationships— as of profound value.

As for homophobia, womanist scholars challenge the assumed biblical basis for this form of discrimination. For African American Christians to discriminate against homosexuals runs contrary to the deep love and respect for all highlighted in the ministry of Christ. The underlying assumption present in womanist scholarship is recognition of the manner in which people are both oppressed and oppressing, participating in a complex system of interactions that privilege some and harm others. And liberation must involve recognition of the web-like nature of oppression and the effort to work in solidarity with all living creatures.

Finally, it is only within womanist scholarship over the last several years that destruction of the environment has been understood to be a religious issue that should be addressed by African American Christians. Drawing again on the pattern of commitments and relationships present in the Bible, scholars such as Emilie Townes (*Breaking the Fine Rain of Death*) argue that liberation must also involve a proper relationship with the earth.

**See also** *African American Religion* entries; *Faith-based Community Organizations; Faith-based Initiatives; Gender; Islam in North America; Literature: African American; Megachurches; Music: African American Gospel; Nation(s) of Islam; New Religious Movements: Black Nationalist Movements; Race and Racism; Religious Thought: Womanist; Santería; Voodoo; Women.*

Anthony B. Pinn

## BIBLIOGRAPHY

Cone, James H., and Gayraud Wilmore, eds. *Black Theology: A Documentary History*. 2 vols. Maryknoll, N.Y.: Orbis Books, 1992.
Harris, Frederick C. *Something Within: Religion in African-American Political Activism*. New York: Oxford University Press, 1999.
Pinn, Anthony B. *Varieties of African American Religious Experience*. Minneapolis: Fortress Press, 1998.
Raboteau, Albert. *Slave Religion: The 'Invisible Institution' in the Antebellum South*. New York: Oxford University Press, 1978.

Smith, Drew R. *Long March Ahead: African American Churches and Public Policy in Post–Civil Rights America.* Durham, N.C.: Duke University Press, 2004.

Walton, Jonathan. *Watch This! The Ethics and Aesthetics of Black Televangelism.* New York: New York University Press, 2009.

Wilmore, Gayraud S. *Black Religion and Black Radicalism: An Interpretation of the Religious History of Afro-American People.* Maryknoll, N.Y.: Orbis Books, 1983.

# African American Religious Thought

See *Religious Thought: African American*

# African American Roman Catholics

See *Roman Catholicism: African American Catholics*

# African Traditional Religions

Written accounts of African traditional religions first appeared in the nineteenth and twentieth centuries and resulted from Westerners' contact with Africans during colonization and the slave trade. Prior to this time, there were some accounts written by missionaries or traders, but their contact was often extremely limited, and their ability to converse in local languages calls into question their ability to understand local customs. In addition to these written sources, scholars have utilized oral sources, although their reliability is also questionable, since most were recorded generations after colonization and it is impossible to know how contact may have influenced them. Archeological findings, such as rock paintings, have also been utilized by researchers, although they require a great deal of interpretation, which is difficult considering the lack of supporting historical sources. Although there has been an increased interest in studying African traditional religions, much of the older scholarship is based in a Eurocentric, racist understanding of African culture, and this has inevitably affected modern scholarship.

Though at present westerners know little about African traditional religions prior to Western contact, it is clear that the practices of African traditional religions have been in decline. Prior to 1900, the practice of indigenous religions was almost universal in sub-Saharan, non-Muslim Africa. By the turn of the twenty-first century, however, the percentage of Africans practicing traditional religions decreased dramatically. The majority of Africans were either Christian or Muslim, with only about 25 percent considering themselves members of traditional religions.

## The Supernatural in Africa

African traditional religions generally focus on this world, and as a result, practitioners' interactions with the supernatural realm tend to be instrumentalist. This means that they appeal to divinities, spirits, and ancestors in hope of gaining their help in this world, rather than simply worshipping them to show their devotion or to gain personal salvation. Religion is more about maintaining order and creating systems of support in which community identity is key, and issues of personal devotion and salvation are not primary. Furthermore, religion is not considered a distinct sphere within traditional African culture. Rather, it is intertwined with other aspects of life much more so than in the West. Prior to Western contact, there was not a sense that religion was distinct, and this makes it difficult to distinguish what is and is not "religious" within African culture. Because practitioners do not make such distinctions, one must recognize that outsiders impose such categorizations upon traditional African ways of life.

Although it is difficult to generalize about African traditional religions, most include a concept of a supreme being, or god, who is eternal and omniscient. They also involve myths about the divine origins of life, suffering, disease, and death as well as a belief in lesser deities and spirits that are active in the world in both positive and negative ways. A belief in the evil power of witches is also common, especially in societies where status is earned rather than ascribed.

The supreme being, or high god, is often associated with the sun or sky, though the nature of these beings differs between religions and cultures. Some of these deities are male, others female, and still others are androgynous and are understood as neither male nor female. In addition to different personifications of these supreme beings, the roles that they play in this world also differ among traditions. For example, creation myths in different cultures describe the supreme being's involvement in the creation of the world in various ways. The Yoruba tradition of Nigeria and Benin, for example, maintains that their supreme being, known as Olodumare, delegated the creation of the world to lesser beings, known as *orisha*. Similarly, the Dogon of Mali believe that their high god, Amma, began the creation of the world but had lesser spirits, known as *Nummo*, complete the process. In contrast, the Nuer and Dinka of southern Sudan, the BaMbuti of the Congo, and the Kboisan of South African believe that their supreme being was the sole creator of the universe.

In addition to different myths about the creation of the world, African traditional religions also have different conceptions of how their supreme being interacts with this world. Yoruba tradition understands the high god as a distant ruler, in a category distinct from other, lesser deities. Like Yoruba kings, who rule from afar and have very little interaction with their people, one does not appeal to this high power for assistance but instead petitions lesser deities and spirits for their help. As a result, many regions do not have shrines to their supreme being or artwork depicting the high god, but only lesser beings. The highest god also tends not to be involved in rituals of spirit possession. This has often been understood by outsiders to be evidence that the highest being is not central to African traditional religions, but in fact, the lack of shrines or presence during ritual is because the supreme being is considered too distant and powerful to be bothered with everyday concerns. This is not universal, however, and among the Igbo, for example, the high god, Chukwu, has shrines in his honor and has been known to speak to his people through an oracle. Rather than being a distant figure, Chukwu communicates with the Igbo people and directly affects their lives.

Although the supreme being is generally not the focus of ritual appeals, many traditions maintain that he is active in the most critical issues of this world. In many cultures he is central to birth and death. For example, the Dogon tradition maintains that pregnancy is the result of the supreme being's allowing a birth force to enter a woman's womb. Similarly, Yoruba custom says that Olodumare allows the spirits of ancestors to enter a woman's body in order to be reborn. The highest god is also commonly thought to judge people after death and assign them to an afterlife or reincarnation depending on the lives they led. It should be noted that reincarnation is not seen as negative in most African cultures, as it is in Asian religions. Instead, it is an expected outcome of living a good life. Other traditions also believe that the supreme being is in control of the rain. This is especially true in regions where rain is scarce and droughts are a serious threat to communities' survival.

As mentioned above, in addition to the supreme beings that are found in nearly all African traditional religions, most traditions also believe in the power of lesser deities and spirits. Like those of the high gods, the natures and powers of these lesser beings also differ among traditions. For example, the Nuer of Sudan believe that lesser deities are emanations of the supreme being, so a strict distinction between the higher and lower beings is not made. They are seen as part of one whole. Among the Yoruba, however, there are thought to be hundreds of distinct lesser deities, known as orisha. Each orisha is independent from the high god, Olodumare, and has his or her own history, myths, personality, and rituals associated with him or her. Specific deities are also commonly associated with certain professions. For example, in Yoruba culture, blacksmiths and hunters are associated with Ogun, the god of iron and war. The belief that lesser deities are autonomous is common among other West African groups as well, especially among groups with strict sociopolitical hierarchies, such as the Yoruba or the Akan of Ghana. Most African traditional religions also involve a belief in a god or goddess of water. They are particularly important in the Igbo culture and tend to be the dominant local divinity in this region. To the Igbo, the goddesses of water are stern rulers who are quick to punish but are also devoted to the protection of their people. In contrast, the Ijo people found in the Niger Delta have a different understanding of water deities. They believe in a society of male and female spirits that live beneath the waterways and communally control only the water.

In addition to lesser deities, ancestors are also important among many practitioners of African traditional religions. Bantu-speaking peoples of Equatorial, East, and South Africa, for example, focus a great deal on their ancestors. These are people who died a good death, lived to an appropriate age, and had proper burial rites performed on their behalf. After passing into the afterlife, they continue to influence this world and the lives of their descendants by punishing, rewarding, and protecting them. Ancestor cults tend to look back four to five generations. These people's names, stories, and histories are still remembered, and they are thought to be closer to those still living than people who passed away longer ago. Similarly, the elderly are often revered in these societies because they are closer to the afterlife and therefore to the ancestors. Although most ancestors can only affect the lives of their progeny, after death sacred rulers can influence the lives of all the people living in their territories, just as they could while living. Shrines and rituals devoted to ancestors and deceased rulers are common in many African traditions, even among those who have converted to Islam and Christianity. Yoruba and Igbo traditions have also focused on ancestors, in addition to the lesser deities mentioned above. They believe that ancestors are active in the world and that they become physically present during ritual masking dances.

Among the people of Central and West Africa, fetish cults are often even more important than ancestors. Although these cults were more important and prominent prior to the twentieth century, they are still a part of some religious practice. The Kongo people from the Republic of the Congo, the Democratic Republic of Congo, and Angola are examples of groups that participate in fetish cults. In these traditions, spirits are associated with sacred objects, known as *minkisi*. Minkisi are often bundles or sculptures that are extremely powerful because of their connection to spirits and the supernatural realm.

Although there is no strict dualism between good and evil in most African traditional religions, and gods, spirits, and deities both help and harm people, evil forces are often associated with witches. In most cultures, witches' supernatural powers can only be used for evil, although Yoruba culture teaches that they can also bring about positive ends, if they are placated. Witches are generally thought to be older women who survive by stealing the life force of living things, although the Chewa believe they can be male or female. Witchcraft can either be inherited, learned, or can result from a woman's consuming human flesh, which requires her to repay a supernatural debt. The relationship of witches to the natural world is inverted, and they are seen as more closely connected to the animal world and are often assumed to be shape-shifters. Unlike people, who eat animals and make companions of humans, witches feed on humans and develop close relationships with animals. In many cultures the presence of witches and their power is taken for granted, and witchcraft is often used as an explanation for sickness or unfortunate accidents. Although not all misfortune is attributed to witchcraft, as gods and ancestors are also capable of causing people harm, witches are often blamed when something bad and unexpected happens. Rituals are often utilized to counteract the power of witches.

A final group of supernatural beings found in many African traditional religions are *tricksters*, and these beings are especially common in West African traditions. They love to create confusion and chaos in supernatural and natural realms. They often tempt humans to act impulsively, hoping to create unexpected chaos. Tricksters are also commonly portrayed as messengers who intentionally manipulate their messages to cause confusion. For example, among the Yoruba, Eshu is a trickster who is responsible for calling together other orisha for rituals. He intentionally leaves out or changes part of his messages, however, which causes confusion among the other orisha and makes rituals fail. Although many westerners have understood tricksters to be evil beings and have tended to associate them with Satan, this dualistic view of good and evil is not found in most African traditional religions, and tricksters and other deities are not seen as strictly good or evil but as part of a more complicated system of interaction between the supernatural and natural realms.

## Rituals in Africa

Ritual practices are also an integral part of African traditional religions, although many rituals have died out or changed dramatically in the recent past. There are multiple reasons for these changes. With the appearance of colonial powers, many cultures changed dramatically, and traditions such as religious rituals were no longer seen as necessary. Also, many colonizers and missionaries restricted or outlawed indigenous religious rituals, making it difficult for the traditions to continue on.

Rituals are commonly performed among adherents to African traditional religions to encourage fertility, bring about rain, heal the sick, and protect the community, and they often take the form of prayer, animal sacrifice, or offerings of food or beverages. These behaviors are set apart as distinct from everyday activities, which is what makes them powerful. Because rituals must be distinct from daily life, specific instruments are used. Special bottles and bowls hold sacrificial food and libations, special tools are used for killing and the preparation of sacrificial meals, and certain dress is often required for rituals to take place.

Sacrifice and bloodless offerings are common in African traditional religions. They are generally understood as a form of communication between supernatural beings and humans. By offering sustenance, believers nourish the deity or ancestor, and in return they are assisted in the natural world. These forms of sacrifice tend to also nourish the believers, who often consume the sacrificial food and drink as part of the ritual. The more important the object being offered is to the community, the more significant the sacrifice. For example, the Nuer, Dinka, and Masai people traditionally raised cattle, which were essential to their survival. This made the offering of a bull or a cow a supreme sacrifice.

Prior to contact with Europeans, human sacrifices were also a part of some African traditional religions' ritual practices. For example, in the late nineteenth century, the Igbo of Niger still sacrificed slaves when a titled man was initiated into his position and when he died. In other instances, humans were sacrificed to atone for the community's sins or to appease natural forces, such as the ocean. Most human sacrifices ceased after colonization, however. Though blood sacrifices of animals or humans have been common in African traditional religions, not all cultures perform animal sacrifices, and some specific deities do not require blood offerings.

In addition to offering sacrifices, it is also common for adherents to African traditional religions to take part in rituals when they transition between life stages. For example, when a member is born or dies, is named, goes through puberty, gets married, or is installed into office, it is common for a ritual to be performed. There are often three stages to these rituals. During the first stage, the initiate is removed from his or her familiar life. He may be removed from his home or separated from his family or community. During the next phase, he enters a liminal stage, where he is between life stages and is no longer a part of the previous stage but has not yet entered the next. At this time, members are often subjected to physical suffering as well as made to feel helpless, while they are also taught their new responsibilities. The final step is for the initiate to be reintegrated into his community with new responsibilities based on his new status.

Masking cults and spirit possession are also common to many African traditional religions, and some cultural regions recognize thousands of named masks. These tend to be male-dominated secret societies, and members perform rituals in order to receive the presence of deities, spirits, or ancestors. Spirits may be part of the natural world—an animal or a more general natural force—or spirits of deceased relatives. Unlike other forms of spirit possession, which tend to focus on healing, masking cults are more concerned with social order and control and are thought to counteract the power of witches. Although elaborate costumes are required for these rituals, the supernatural being is not within the material of the costume; rather, the ritual dress allows these beings access to the practitioners.

Divination is also a common ritual practice among many members of African traditional religions. Divining is the art of foretelling the future or gaining insight into a situation by accessing supernatural knowledge through the performance of rituals or the interpretation of omens. Trained men generally perform divination to find meaning in people's daily lives and to find cures for afflictions. Though divination is widespread in African traditions, the practices and purposes of divining vary dramatically. The Dogan of South Mali, for example, lure desert foxes with nuts and then look at their footprints and interpret their meaning. Among these people it is believed that foxes could once speak, but now they can only communicate through diviners. Another widespread tradition is Ifa, which is the dominant divining tradition of the Yoruba region. This tradition centers on the collection and recitation of oral poetry. Diviners memorize hundreds of poems, which are then randomly selected when a believer comes for assistance. After the poem is determined, the diviner recites it, and it directs the seeker. Afa is another common divination practice among the Igbo, although there are regional differences even among the Igbo, and northern and southern versions of Afa differ. In the north, diviners cast seed pods and read their positions as a secret language, which provides guidance. In the south, however, twenty symbolic objects are cast, and the positions in which they fall are interpreted. Other groups read the behavior of animals or interpret their deaths or look to their entrails for direction. As with most traditional rituals, divination is becoming less and less common, but politicians and leaders are still known to rely on traditional divining for guidance, even today.

Christian missionary efforts in Africa, as well as the colonization of the continent by Christian nations, have led to a dramatic decrease in the number of adherents to traditional religions. Although not as common as they used to be, these traditions are still practiced by a large portion of the African population. In addition to the influence that African traditional religions have had on African cultures, their influence has also spread through the African diaspora. As African slaves were taken from their homelands and sold around the world, their religions spread. This was particularly true in North and South America and the Caribbean, as this is where the majority of slaves ended their journey.

## African Traditional Religions in the "New World"

Any time religions and cultures are transplanted from one area to another, they are bound to change, and this was particularly true of African traditional religion in the so-called New World. African traditional religions came to the Americas during the slave trade, when Africans transplanted their indigenous religious beliefs and practices after being taken from their homelands. There has been a long-standing debate among scholars about the extent to which African slaves were able to maintain and preserve aspects of their religion and culture while enslaved and, consequently, the extent to which African culture has influenced African American religious life in the twentieth and twenty-first centuries. Melville Herskovits and E. Franklin Frazier are two of the most well-known scholars who engaged in this debate, with Frazier arguing that the institution of slavery stripped Africans entirely of their native religions and cultures. According to Frazier, this meant that twentieth-century African American culture had no meaningful connection to traditions of Africa. Herskovits, on the other hand, maintained that enslaved Africans were able to preserve many aspects of their cultures, including aspects of their religions, and as a result, the influence of African traditions could still be seen in twentieth-century American black culture.

Late-twentieth and early-twenty-first century scholars have stressed a middle ground between Herskovits and Frazier. Although slave masters worked diligently to erase African culture from the lives of their slaves, Africans and their descendents fought just as hard to maintain aspects of their past. Recent research indicates that although African slaves were forced to give up a great deal of their religious lives, they were nonetheless able to preserve much of their culture during slavery. African folklore, music, language, and ritual actions all remained a part of many slaves' religious lives, even though they changed in order to accommodate a new setting and the institution of slavery. Beliefs in the power of spirits to control and animate the natural world remained important to transplanted Africans, as did the role of spirit possession in religious ritual. Fetishes, which tended to be in the form of amulets or charms, also remained important for protecting against illness, misfortune, and witchcraft in the New World, and slaves continued to utilize divination techniques to predict the fate of people or to know the will of ancestors and gods. Finally, religious dancing, drumming, and singing, all of which were integral to the religious lives of many West Africans, remained important within slave communities. As mentioned above, although these African traditions were transplanted into a slave context, there were necessarily changes that occurred. Many slave owners banned the use of drums, so slaves began replacing drumming with rhythmic clapping, foot tapping, preaching, and call-and-response singing. These new practices were related to spirit possession among African Americans and accomplished what drumming had in Africa by calling spirits to possess their believers. While drumming was no longer an option, African slaves invented new systems for accomplishing what drumming had contributed.

Although Christianity and Islam were present on the African continent before the slave trade began, most slaves were believers in African traditional religions. Africans brought to the Americas tended to be from West Africa and the Congo-Angola region, where traditional religions were still the dominant religious force. This having been said, slaves came from a variety of tribes, nations, and language groups, and traders often went out of their way to separate Africans based on their backgrounds, so as to weaken the ties to their past. This made it nearly impossible for African slaves to maintain their religions and cultures intact, requiring them to build communities that incorporated their diverse backgrounds. Slave communities often combined the beliefs and practices of their various traditional beliefs, while also incorporating aspects of Christianity and Native American religions. This, combined with their new environment and their experience as slaves, resulted in many new, syncretic religious traditions among slaves in the Americas.

## Afro-Caribbean Religions

In areas of the Caribbean where Catholicism dominated, such as Haiti and Cuba, African slaves developed religious traditions that were syncretic alternatives to Catholicism and Christianity. They formed distinct rituals, which occasionally corresponded with Catholic traditions but were in many ways distinct. In regions where Protestantism was prominent, such as Jamaica and Trinidad, Africans often created alternate forms of Christianity by interpreting Christianity and the Bible in Afrocentric ways.

Caribbean traditions such as vaudou (also spelled vodou or voodoo), shango, and Santería conflated African gods and Catholic saints. This worked well for a number of reasons. First, Catholic emphasis on the cult of saints allowed African slaves to disguise the worship of their gods in the guise of Catholicism. Similarly, the intercession of saints on behalf of Catholic believers was reminiscent of the African system of lesser deities acting as intermediaries between the supreme god and human beings. Finally, it was common among African religious believers to accept the gods of other African groups. As cultures intermingled in Africa because of marriage or warfare, Africans were typically willing to shift devotion from one god to another, making syncretism more palatable to African slaves than Europeans.

One of the most well-known instances of African traditional religions influencing religious culture in the Caribbean is found in Haiti. Haitian vaudou is most commonly associated with Dahomey culture, although it was influenced by cultures from Senegal to Congo and all over West Africa. Practitioners of Haitian vaudou believe in a supreme being, known as Gran-Met. Although Gran-Met is the highest god, like many African traditions, vaudou has a pantheon of lesser deities, known as *loa*. Similarly, these lesser gods tend to be the focus of vaudou rituals because they are the ones involved in human affairs, while Gran-Met is distant and removed from daily life. Another similarity between Haitian vaudou and traditional religions as found in Africa is the emphasis placed on possession. Practitioners of vaudou perform rituals that allow lesser deities to possess their bodies, providing direct contact with the supernatural realm, and the behaviors of the possessed believer allow others to identity which loa is present. This is similar to possession in much of Africa.

Many of the major Yoruba and Dahomean gods are also worshipped by name among the Shango cult of Trinidad, though they are in many ways actually more local than African. Eshu, Ogun, Yemanja, and Shango are worshipped by name, but the myths associated with these gods have been replaced. Rather than having African myths associated with them, they now have Catholic hagiographies.

Combinations of African traditional religions and Catholicism also characterize Cuban Santería. Again, Yoruba influences are significant, but the tradition is clearly infused with Catholic traditions and beliefs as well. Practitioners of Santería refer to themselves as Lucumi, taken from the Yoruba greeting *Oluki mi*, which means "my friend." Many Yoruba gods also became identified with the saints and were worshipped as such. Also, spirit possession, animal sacrifice, Ifa divination, drumming, and singing are all very reminiscent of Yoruba traditions, with Ifa divination being almost identical in Cuba and Africa.

Possession is also important to many Jamaican religious groups. Revival and Pocomania are two religious communities that have melded Protestant theology with African styles of possession. Like so many African and syncretic traditions, these groups emphasize the importance of spirit possession. Unlike traditional African possession, however, these believers are thought to be possessed by Christian figures, rather than African gods or ancestors. They connect with Old Testament prophets, the twelve apostles, archangels, and the Holy Spirit.

The Convince cult and Cumina are other Jamaican traditions that incorporate West African theology, although they too no longer refer to African gods or spirits by name. Members of the Convince cult are called *Bongo men* and trace their roots to a group of runaway slaves. These slaves escaped to the mountains and fought against the British until they were eventually granted their independence in 1739 by a treaty. Unlike traditional religions, which tend to focus on recently deceased ancestors, Bongo men venerate older ancestors, who died in Africa, and Jamaican slaves. They also offer animal sacrifices, like practitioners of African traditional religions. In language similar to African tradition, spirits are said to "mount" believers and ride them like horses. Cumina believers worship Shango, the Yoruba god of thunders, although he is the only African god that remains a part of the tradition. Although Shango is the only African god, practitioners also venerate spirits of the sky and earth and the ancestors, with gods of the sky being the highest and ancestors the least powerful. This is similar to many African traditional practitioners, who assume that there are spirits associated with each of these realms, although they are often given names and distinguished one from another, rather than worshipped as a whole. Also similar to African traditional religions, the spirits connected with these realms have certain food preferences, drum rhythms, and dance styles that are associated with them and determine the ritual behavior of followers.

## Afro-Brazilian Religions

The Candomblé tradition is found primarily in Brazil and was heavily influenced by Yoruba culture and also emphasizes the importance of sacrifice, drumming, singing, and possession. Similar to the Yoruba tradition, Candomblé has multiple deities with unique personalities and histories, although unlike Yoruba traditions, there is more of a focus on the relationship between practitioners and their personal deity, known as their *Orixá*. Priests and priestesses, known as *paes* or *maes de santo*, have a special devotion to their deity and are in charge of maintaining their temple, organizing worship, and training other devotees. By providing their personal Orixá with the appropriate sacrifices and by observing their deity's commands, believers are able to receive magical powers, known as *axé*. Candomblé also places a special emphasis on the importance of trances, which allow practitioners to directly connect with their Orixá and act as mediums between the supernatural and natural realms.

Umbanda is another syncretic religion found in Brazil, and it was heavily influenced by the religion and culture of the West African Bantu people and spiritualism. It developed later than many other syncretic traditions, beginning at the end of the nineteenth century. Umbanda cults were found primarily within urban areas, although Umbanda never gained much of a following in the northeast, and it was especially popular in Rio de Janeiro and São Paulo. Umbanda groups are self-governing, with each high priest, or *Pai de santo*, being relatively autonomous. This has led to little consistency among groups and has resulted in different doctrines and rituals in different regions.

## North America

African traditional religions surely influenced African North American as well as South American cultures, especially during slavery, although the theology and practices associated with African traditional religions did not survive in North America to the same degree as they did in the Caribbean and Latin America. There are a number of reasons why this was the case. First, some scholars have argued that Catholicism, with its focus on ritual action and the saints, was more conducive to the survival of traditional religions. African slaves were able to incorporate aspects of their traditional behavior into Catholic ritual and were able to replace their worship of traditional gods with devotion to Catholic saints. This was less the case within Protestant settings, as Protestants tended to downplay the importance of ritual and focused rather on inward contemplation and individual experience. Consequently, slaves were able to transfer and therefore maintain their devotion to traditional gods and rituals less easily when placed within a Protestant setting. Because Catholicism was much more influential in the Caribbean and Latin America than in North America, African traditional religions were able to survive more clearly there. Second, there were fewer slaves imported to North America than other regions of the New World. By the time of North American emancipation in 1863, there were more than four million slaves in the United States. This is ten times the number of slaves that were brought into the country. In the Caribbean and South America, however, the number of emancipated slaves was consistently less than the number of slaves imported. This is to say, by emancipation, most slaves in the United States were native-born and were born into slavery. Their connections to the African continent were often generations removed, which weakened their ties to traditional religion and culture. In other regions, however, where slaves were consistently imported and recent arrivals made up the majority of the enslaved population, there was a more direct connection to Africa, and traditional rituals and beliefs were constantly being reintroduced and reinforced.

Although it was difficult for slaves in the United States to maintain much of their traditional cultures, there are clear ways in which African traditional religions influenced American religious practices. The ring shout is one of the most obvious instances of African influence in North America. During this ritual, slaves danced in a circle as part of their religious worship. Although the name implies ritual shouting of some kind, this was not essential to the practice. During the ring shout, rhythmic clapping, singing, and dancing continued to call for spirit possession, but these were no longer the spirits of ancestors or African gods but of the Christian Holy Spirit. Though the theology behind possession changed, the behaviors were similar and were recognizably African. Slaves' ecstatic behavior, although inspired by a different religious view, nonetheless included behaviors that pointed to the influence of their African heritage on New World religion. Ecstatic religious practices borrowed from African traditional religions not only influenced African American religions but also affected the religious lives of whites. This was particularly evidenced in the camp revival meetings of the Second Great Awakening. Again, rather than being possessed by gods or ancestors, white Protestants were overwhelmed by the power of the Holy Spirit and participated in clapping, dancing, and singing in order to bring about these ecstatic states.

In addition to these general trends in slave religions in North America, there are also instances of specific communities on which African traditional religions had a particularly notable influence. One example is a community that flourished until the nineteenth century in New Orleans, Louisiana. This group practiced voodoo, which was related to Haitian vaudou but should not be confused with it. The beginnings of the voodoo tradition in New Orleans were associated with slaves from the French West Indies, but voodoo grew as a result of an influx of slaves and freed blacks who left Saint-Domingue during the Haitian Revolution. Believers in voodoo centered their worship around a snake god, although there are aspects of other traditional gods and goddesses also present in the tradition. Like so many other traditions with African influences, voodoo practitioners integrated drumming, dancing, singing, spirit possession, and animal sacrifices into their religious lives. They similarly used charms, amulets, and potions to predict the future as well as affect the present. Voodoo practitioners in New Orleans became quite successful and gained influence and prestige among both white and black Louisianans. Although this community was fairly confined to the New Orleans area, voodoo came to be associated more generally with conjuring in the United States, regardless of its connection or relationship to Haitian vaudou or African traditional religions. Though much of the theological backing is removed from modern forms of voodoo, many of the folk practices remain to this day.

Although the influence of African traditional religions has continued into the present, there are not many practitioners of African traditional religions in America today. Though the number of African immigrants into North America has been increasing in the past few decades, most of these immigrants are Christians and Muslims. Even so, the increase in the African-born American population that resulted from the 1990 Immigration Act has meant that practitioners of African traditional religions are more common in the United States than they have been since slavery. There are a few men and women who associate with African traditions and have followings in the United States, but their followings tend to be small. They generally come from the priestly class of West African diviners, known as *babalawos*, and divination is often their only African-influenced practice. There has also been an increase in the popularity of African traditional religions among African Americans in recent years. Most of these practitioners are American-born, however, and are self-consciously seeking to reconnect with their African heritage through religious devotion and ritual.

The Christianization of Africa since colonial times has led many scholars to overlook African traditional religions on the African continent as well as in the so-called New World. The efforts of missionaries and colonizers to silence traditional beliefs and end indigenous practices were often quite successful, which has caused problems for researchers who seek to understand Africa's indigenous cultures and religions. This problem was further exacerbated by the fact that many Christian and Muslim Africans understand traditional beliefs to be nothing but superstition, which has also led African scholars to de-emphasize the importance and influence of African indigenous religions.

**See also** *African American Religion* entries; *Santería; Voodoo.*

Monica Reed

**BIBLIOGRAPHY**

Ayorinde, Christine. *Afro-Cuban Religiosity, Revolution, and National Identity.* Gainesville: University Press of Florida, 2004.
Bellegarde-Smith, Patrick, ed. *Fragments of Bone: Neo-African Religions in a New World.* Chicago: University of Illinois Press, 2005.
Brown, Karen McCarthy. *Mama Lola: A Vodou Priestess in Brooklyn.* Berkeley: University of California Press, 2001.
Clarke, Peter Bernard. *New Trends and Developments in African Religions.* Santa Barbara, Calif.: Greenwood, 1998.
Frazier, E. Franklin. *The Negro Church in America.* New York: Schocken, 1964.
Griffith, R. Marie, and Barbara Dianne Savage, eds. *Women and Religion in the African Diaspora: Knowledge, Power, and Performance.* Baltimore: Johns Hopkins University Press, 2006.
Herskovits, Melville. *The Myth of the Negro Past.* New York: Harper, 1941.
Isichei, Elizabeth. *The Religious Traditions of Africa: A History.* Westport, Conn.: Praeger, 2004.
Mbiti, John S. *Introduction to African Religion.* Portsmouth, N.H.: Heinemann, 1991.
Murphy, Joseph M. *Santería: An African Religion in America.* Boston: Beacon, 1988.
Olupona, Jacob K., and Regina Gemignani, eds. *African Immigrant Religions in America.* New York: New York University Press, 2007.
Raboteau, Albert J. *Slave Religion: The "Invisible Institution" in the Antebellum South.* New York: Oxford University Press, 1978.
Thomas, Douglas E. *African Traditional Religion in the Modern World.* Jefferson, N.C.: McFarland, 2005.
Trost, Theodore Louis, ed. *The African Diaspora and the Study of Religion.* New York: Palgrave Macmillan, 2007.
Young, Jason R. *Rituals of Resistance: African Atlantic Religion in Kongo and the Lowcountry South in the Era of Slavery.* Baton Rouge: Louisiana State University Press, 2007.

# Amana Communities

The seven villages of the Amana Colonies, Iowa, were founded in 1855 by a German religious group known as the Community of True Inspiration. Formed under the leadership of Eberhard Ludwig Gruber (1655–1728) and Johann Friedrich Rock (1678–1749) in 1714 in the Wetterau region of Germany, the Community of True Inspiration had its roots in the German Pietism movement of the late seventeenth and early eighteenth centuries. Like other Pietist groups, the Inspirationists emphasized a pious, personal religious experience outside of the established church, advocating humility, quiet reflection, prayer, and Bible study. Their belief that God still communicated directly to people just as to the prophets of the Old Testament set the Community of True Inspiration apart from other Pietist groups. In the history of the community, several women and men have been recognized as instruments of the Lord, or *Werkzeuge*, who delivered divine pronouncements. Scribes wrote down these pronouncements, or testimonies, as they were spoken. Many were printed and disseminated.

In the first half of the eighteenth century, the group flourished, and Inspirationist communities could be found

The Amana Colonies in Iowa, founded in 1855, developed a communal economy based on manufacturing and agriculture.

in dozens of towns in southwestern Germany, Switzerland, and Alsace. After the death of Rock in 1749, the movement experienced a general decline.

### Emigration to Ebenezer, New York

In the 1820s, under the leadership of a new Werkzeug, Christian Metz (1793–1867), the Community of True Inspiration was revitalized. Its growth and enthusiasm, however, caused it to come under closer scrutiny by religious and secular authorities. In the 1830s, Inspirationist families and congregations throughout southern Germany, Switzerland, and Alsace left their homes to avoid persecution for their beliefs. Many came to live on large estates leased by the community in Hesse, one of the more tolerant German provinces. Hesse, however, offered only a temporary respite for the Community of True Inspiration. Religious and civil authorities grew less tolerant of religious separatists. Depressed economic conditions also weighed heavily on the community. Finally, an inspired pronouncement through Christian Metz determined that the community should move to America.

The Inspirationists decided to settle in America in a community of their own, separate from the rest of the world. In 1842 they pooled their money to buy land and pay passage for those members who could not afford it themselves.

They called their new home near Buffalo, New York, "Ebenezer." By 1845, more than seven hundred members of the Community of True Inspiration had immigrated to Ebenezer, where they had purchased more than five thousand acres and built six villages, constructed textile factories and craft shops, and cleared land for their agricultural endeavors. Here they created a communal economic and social system that remained essentially unchanged for eighty-nine years. All land and buildings were owned by the community; families were provided with living quarters and household necessities; communal kitchen houses prepared meals for all members; and each adult worked without wages at assigned tasks in the kitchens, fields, factories, or shops.

### Move to Amana, Iowa

Despite their prosperity in Ebenezer, the Inspirationists faced problems that caused them to move again. By 1854, the population had grown to more than a thousand members, but land prices had increased dramatically, and the Inspirationists could not afford to purchase additional land. Also, Metz and the community elders were concerned about the growth of the city of Buffalo, which they felt threatened the community's separation from the sinful world. The community looked to the Midwest to find a more suitable place to settle. Along the Iowa River about twenty miles west of the Iowa state capitol, Iowa City, they found an ideal place that had all the requisite resources: fertile land available at a reasonable price; water that could be used to power their mills; and abundant timber, stone, and clay for construction. Of equal importance in their decision to move to Iowa was the fact that the exploring party reported that they "felt at home" there.

The Inspirationists started buying land and began construction of the first village in 1855. They called their new home "Amana," a biblical name that signifies "remain true." They incorporated as a religious organization, the Amana Society, retaining communal property ownership. Their new constitution declared that their purpose was to serve God and seek salvation and that "the foundation of our civil organization is and shall remain forever God, the Lord, and the faith which He worked in us according to his grace and mercy."

Over a period of eight years, the community sold the Ebenezer villages and the members relocated to the new Iowa site, which came to include more than twenty-six thousand acres of farm and timber land and seven villages: Amana, Middle, East, High, West, South, and Homestead. Each village had its own church, trade shops, and farm. The economy of Amana, like Ebenezer, was based on manufacturing and agriculture. The farms and flour mills sold goods to the outside market. Two woolen mills and a calico factory sold textiles nationwide. Membership reached eighteen hundred people in the last decades of the nineteenth century.

## Life in Nineteenth-Century Amana

Although the demands of providing for the economic vitality and material needs of the community played a large part in the lives of its residents, for the most part daily life in communal Amana was based on religion. To assist them in leading pious and humble lives, the Inspirationists attended eleven regular church services a week: every evening; Wednesday, Saturday, and Sunday mornings; and Sunday afternoon. The community also observed Easter, Christmas, and other Christian holidays. In addition, the Inspirationists in communal Amana held several special services during the year. Of these, the *Bundesschliessung*, an annual renewal of the covenant between each member and the community, and *Liebesmahl* (Holy Communion) were the most important. Bundesschliessung occurred on Thanksgiving and began as a response to Lincoln's Civil War declaration to hold a day of fast and repentance. Liebesmahl was held only at times

determined through inspiration until the death of Christian Metz in 1867 and thereafter usually every other year. An *Unterredung* or yearly spiritual examination was held over several months, with the elders visiting each village in turn. Each member of the community came before the elders and was questioned regarding his or her spiritual condition and admonished to lead a more pious life.

The church elders, always men, constituted the leadership in the community. During the time of the Werkzeuge, elders were chosen through divine testimony. After the death in 1883 of the last Werkzeug, Barbara Heinemann Landmann (1795–1883), elders were chosen by the Great Council. The control and management of all the affairs of the Amana Society, both religious and secular, was vested in a thirteen-member Great Council that was elected annually from among the elders. The council made decisions regarding not only religious matters of the community but also business operations, admission of new members, and members' spending allowances and job assignments. For more than a generation after Landmann's death, the elders were able to show sufficient flexibility and compromise in their leadership to allow the Inspirationists to become one of America's longest-lived communal organizations.

## The "Great Change"

Nevertheless, by the early twentieth century, the communal system in Amana had generated stresses that the leadership could not resolve. Many community members found the rules associated with communal living to be petty and overly restrictive. Families wanted to eat together at home rather than in the communal kitchen dining rooms. Some members were frustrated by their inability to enjoy more material goods. Some did not do their share of the work. Increasingly the elders were unable to enforce the rules. In short, for many members, communalism was no longer a tenet of faith.

In 1932 the elders presented the membership of the community with a choice to return to a more austere and disciplined life or to abandon the communal system. Significantly, dissolution of the church was not considered. The members elected to retain the traditional church as it was and to create a joint-stock company for the business enterprises to be operated for profit by a board of directors. Each member of the communal society received stock in this new corporation. The separation of the church from the economic and social functions of the community—the abandonment of communalism—is referred to by Amana residents as "the Great Change."

## Contemporary Beliefs and Practices

In twenty-first-century America, the Amana Church still is defined by its Inspirationist beliefs and traditions, acknowledging a Profession of Faith formulated by the Inspirationist leadership in 1839. The tenets include these three central beliefs:

• Baptism. "We hold that baptism of the Holy Spirit is the essence of this sacrament. By not giving undue importance to water baptism, the spiritual baptism can take place uninterruptedly. It is only by baptism of the Holy Spirit that we can obtain forgiveness and salvation."

• Communion. "We believe in the Communion or the Lord's Feast of Love and observe it exactly as instituted and ordained by the Lord. It is an extremely important and holy act."

• Inspiration. This term is understood to be a presentation and influence or vitalization of the Holy Spirit as one of the gifts that God promised the people and that was already given them in the Old Covenant and through all time up to the present. It serves next after the Holy Scriptures as a guide and course toward salvation.

The Amana church buildings are little changed since they were built in the mid-nineteenth century. The building exteriors are unpretentious: no steeple or colored-glass windows declare that the edifice is a house of God. Inside, the unfinished wood floors, plain pine benches, and unadorned walls echo the tradition of humility and piety. Men enter and sit on one side of a central aisle; women, many dressed in traditional black shawl, apron, and cap, sit on the other. The elders, all lay members of the church, sit in front facing the congregation. Worshippers come early for quiet contemplation.

English-language services were introduced in 1960, but in both German and English services the order of worship remains very traditional: a reading of a testimony from one of the inspired Werkzeuge; a prayer while kneeling; a reading from scripture; and hymns sung a cappella from the church's own hymnal, the *Psalter-Spiel*, that would be recognized by a congregation of a century earlier. The presiding elder comments on the readings and exhorts all to have faith in Christ, believe in the word of God, strive for peace and humility, and "remain true." Just as the church buildings and order of worship have changed little, the cemeteries in the seven Amana villages continue to express the Inspirationist ethos of equality, humility, and simplicity. As they have been for more than 150 years, members are buried in order of death with plain, uniform headstones.

The Amana Church Society has experienced some change. Perhaps most notably, the role of women in the church was expanded to include serving as elders; currently, of the ten church elders, four are women. A Church Guild was organized to provide an opportunity for social involvement for members. Although the Unterredung was discontinued after 1932, the Amana Church continued to emphasize a personal examination of one's spiritual condition. There has also been a reemphasis on the Covenant service for members to affirm their devotion to God and the community. Communion is now an annual service. As fewer members remained fluent in German, a translation committee has worked to translate the fundamental documents of the tradition into English.

Life in the Amana villages still is shaped in part by the community's religious, communal, and German heritage. In 1965, the twenty-six thousand acres and seven villages of the Amana Colonies were designated a National Historic Landmark, and the villages have become a major tourist destination in the state of Iowa. Several local organizations, including the Amana Heritage Society, actively work to preserve the buildings, landscape, and cultural heritage of the community. The Amana Society, Inc. still owns the agricultural land of the former communal society and plays a major role in the economic and social life of the community. Amana Appliances, founded by Amana people soon after the end of the communal system, is a major employer and markets home appliances around the world. The Amana Church Society, as the Community of True Inspiration now calls itself, with a membership of four hundred adults, continues as the religious foundation of the Amanas.

**See also** *Anabaptist Denominational Family; Anabaptists; Great Plains Region; Moravians; Oneida Community; Pietism; Shakers; Utopian and Communitarian Experiments.*

Lanny Haldy

## BIBLIOGRAPHY

Andelson, Jonathan G. "The Community of True Inspiration from Germany to the Amana Colonies." In *America's Communal Utopias*, edited by Donald E. Pitzer. Chapel Hill: University of North Carolina Press, 1997.

DuVal, Francis Alan. *Christian Metz: German-American Religious Leader and Pioneer.* Edited by Peter Hoehnle. Iowa City: Penfield Books, 2005.

Grossmann, Walter. "The Origins of the True Inspired of Amana." *Communal Societies* 4 (1984): 133–149.

Hoehnle, Peter A. *The Amana People: The History of a Religious Community.* Iowa City: Penfield Books, 2003.

Liffring-Zug, Joan. *The Amanas Yesterday: A Religious Communal Society.* Iowa City: Penfield Press, 1975.

Nordhoff, Charles. *The Communistic Societies of the United States: From Personal Observations.* 1875. Reprint, New York: Dover, 1966.

Rettig, Lawrence L. *Amana Today: A History of the Amana Colonies from 1932 to the Present.* Amana, Iowa: Amana Society, 1975.

Shambaugh, Bertha M. H. *Amana: The Community of True Inspiration.* Iowa City: State Historical Society of Iowa, 1908.

# America, Religious Interpretations of

The United States of America is a continental nation-state, but this has not always been the case. Beginning with a revolution waged against its mother country, England, in the late eighteenth century, the nation, set between the Atlantic and Pacific Oceans, evolved over the next two centuries. Bordered on the north by Canada and on the south by Mexico, two noncontiguous territories, Alaska and Hawaii, eventually completed it as a nation containing fifty states. This nation-state, with the exception of Hawaii, is contained within North America, which is a part of the Western Hemisphere, the landmass west of Europe across the Atlantic, which also contains the territories and states of Central and South America. These simple facts form the bases for considering a meaning of religion within the temporal-geographical area referred to as *America*. While this essay is centered upon the political entity of the United States of America, contextual considerations warrant attention to the broader meanings evoked by the appearance of America and the Americas on the world scene. There are certain modes of "the given" and the "a priori" nature occasioned by the name and meaning of this space. These modes serve as background and evoke the deeper structures of the cultures of this space where human actions have taken place.

## Introduction: Orientation and Beginnings

Fernand Braudel, in *The Mediterranean and the Mediterranean World in the Age of Philip II* (1972), introduced the notion of three temporal rhythms as history. There is an environmental geography of time that is slow-moving and repetitious replete with seasonal cycles, mountains, terrain, waters, rivers, and so forth. This is history as the *longue duree*. There is then history as the time of groups and groupings—a social history of collective life that moves in a rhythm faster than the *longue duree* but is still at a slow tempo; this is history as *conjuncture*. And finally, there is the fast-moving history of events. This is "a history of brief nervous fluctuations, by

definition ultra sensitive; the least tremor set all antennae quivering." Braudel calls this layer of history *evenementielle* (vol. I, pp. 20–21). These layers of time are easy to locate in the Mediterranean, for it has been the locale of many and diverse human passages for more than three millennia. As Charles H. Long wrote in "Passage and Prayer: The Origin of Religion in the Atlantic World" (1999: 15), "it is also a womb for the gestation and birth of gods—from the Ancient Egyptians through the Jews and Christians to the Mithra, Zoroaster, and Islam." By way of contrast,

> The Atlantic world introduces us to the globalization of humanity. . . . The Atlantic is, however, not a revealer of deities, seers, and prophets; it is not under the sign of revelation but of freedom, civilizations, and rational orders. It manifests no regard for the layered thickness of time. It is a world justified by the epistemologies of Descartes and Kant, the English empiricists, and the ethical economies of Adam Smith and Karl Marx. (P. 15)

In spite of these major dissimilarities, certain hints may be derived from Braudel that help to decipher a distinctive meaning of a religious orientation arising from the Atlantic world in North America. Though America does not appear in Mediterranean guise, its spatial geography fails to express a homogeneous meaning in relationship to the spatial and temporal orders of the peoples, cultures, or land. D. W. Meinig's four-volume *The Shaping of America: A Geographical Perspective on 500 Years of History* (1986–2004) takes up Braudellian hints in the understanding of American religious orientation. These volumes offer the most comprehensive historical cultural geography of the United States.

The religious issue here is not so much one of transcendence but rather an awareness of those unchanging or ever so slowly changing realities of the created order out of which human societies emerge and upon which they are dependent. These given orders of creation not only undergird and sustain but are equally reflected and refracted in the symbolic and imaginative structures of human communities.

In this essay, religion is defined as orientation. *Orientation* refers to the manner in which a culture, society, or person becomes aware of its place in the temporal spatial order of things. Implied in the term is a recognition of the powers that accrue to the specificities of the modes of being that are coincidental to this situation. Orientation expresses creativity and critique in the face of the given orders of creation. This is not a simple task; it is by its very nature a dialectical process, for it is precisely in the act of creating one's world that the world is understood as having been already given. More specifically, orientation as religion is most appropriate to the situation of the Americas. To use the language of Gerardus van der Leeuw in his *Religion in Essence and Manifestation* (1938),

> Religion . . . in other terms, is concerned with a "Somewhat." But this assertion often means no more than this "Somewhat" is merely a vague "something"; and in order that man may be able to make more significant statements about this "Somewhat," it must force itself upon him, must oppose itself to him as being "Something Other." (P. 24)

What better way to speak of the voyages of Columbus and most of the later "explorers" and "discoverers"? Though Columbus made land in a territory after months of travel on the western ocean and presumed he knew where he was, he had indeed confronted a type of "vague Somewhat." It was given to Amerigo Vespucci to make known that he had blundered into a landmass that was totally unknown to any of the heirs of European traditions. Europeans did not know the land and were thus alien to this land. European knowledge of the "lands across the Atlantic," the Americas, combined the precision of a kind of empirical and scientific discourse of navigation and cartography with a vague speculative sense of the unknown and the mysterious. They were both fascinated and frightened by the land. In "The Earliest Accounts of the New World," Antonelli Gerbi (1976: 37) remarks, "It must be remembered, however, that America (apart from the fact that it was long believed to be a peninsula of Asia), exercised its perplexing impact well before 12 October 1492."

Edmundo O'Gorman adds to this ambiguity about America in *The Invention of America* (1961) by questioning the logical and philosophical legitimacy of the "language of discovery" that becomes synonymous with the European meanings of America. Stated succinctly, O'Gorman makes the point that because Europeans did not know of the existence of America, it would be impossible to discover it since one cannot discover something that did not exist. Instead of "discovering America," O'Gorman tells us that America was, rather, "invented" by the Europeans and that the ambiguity of this meaning has permeated all European discussions about the "lands across the Atlantic." Henri Baudet extends this discussion in *Paradise on Earth: Some Thoughts on European Images of Non-European Man* (1988). On the one hand,

Europeans have a knowledge of non-European peoples gained from concrete and direct relationships with them. On the other hand, Baudet describes a European "knowledge" of non-Europeans that is a product of their imagination of the otherness of non-Europeans. He goes on to explain that the knowledge gained from concrete empirical relationships hardly ever changes the myth-like imagination that constitutes the other pole of their knowledge and subsequent relationships. Such notions were not simply ideational and ideological; they find expression in practice and in the establishment of institutions, thus becoming basic ingredients in the cultures of contact in North America.

With the coming of the Europeans, a massive reorientation on the part of all the participants took place among the three major cultures—the indigenous aborigines, the Europeans, and later the Africans who were brought into these lands as enslaved persons from various cultures. The meaning and orientation of religion now takes place within a "contact zone." As opposed to those narratives that tacitly imply that the Europeans "knew who they were," whereas the original inhabitants of the indigenous cultures were ignorant or debased, orientation within a contact zone provides the basis for creativity and critique on the part of all parties within it. Marcel Mauss's notion of total prestations, outlined in his essay *The Gift, the Form and Reason for Exchange in Archaic Societies* (1990), provides a structure for the range of relationships and exchanges that take place within the contact zones of the Americas. Mauss's understanding of the reciprocity of exchanges as a specification of the ongoing relationships between groups that were originally geographically and historically separated allows for a methodological orientation that is adequate to the historical cultural situation of America—a meaning of religion that takes into account the deeper order and structures of temporality as well as the materiality of the things exchanged and the attendant symbolic modalities of these exchanges. This meaning of religion is capable of dealing with the unique orientation of the religion of the "three races," especially as each is related to the geographical space that they occupy together; but simultaneously, and equally important, it provides a way of understanding a meaning of religion that emerges from the relationship and exchanges among and between these three cultures that inhabit the territory of the United States. While several groups of people from various cultural backgrounds now occupy the space of the United States, the "three races" express the original constitutive founding groups of an American culture. From this perspective, America from its beginnings has been an Aboriginal-Euro-African culture.

In addition, precisely because the nation is a political entity, some understanding of those peoples and cultures that lie within its boundaries but were not always considered citizens of the political community must be achieved. And finally, the issue of the very nature of the founding of the political nation-state of the United States within this geographical space must be considered. Given the variety of aboriginal cultures, the several and different origins of the European immigrants who came to inhabit the land, and the Africans who were brought as enslaved persons from Africa, one finds little unity among and between the three groups except that imposed by political or other forms of domination, including violence. To be sure, Europeans had in most cases come from cultures that practiced some form of Christianity, and even if they denied a religious sentiment, it was a denial based upon a Christian understanding of the nature and meaning of religion. From this perspective there has never been an American religion, per se—that is, a single explicit tradition with common rituals, deities, a cosmology, and so forth.

While there has been no "American religion" in the strict sense, but only several religious traditions that are expressed in the country, there have been modes and meanings that identify essential elements of another religious orientation. From time to time, these modes come to the surface and are expressed in religious language, symbols, and styles.

Chapter 10 of part II of Alexis de Tocqueville's *Democracy in America* is entitled, "Some Considerations Concerning the Present State and Probable Future of the Three Races That Inhabit the Territory of the United States." De Tocqueville's work, written in the middle of the nineteenth century, acknowledges the structural presence of the "three races": the aboriginal cultures, the European immigrants (primarily English), and the enslaved Africans.

If de Tocqueville is taken seriously, one must acknowledge that American history and culture have been since the first European settlements a vast "contact zone." The term *contact zone* has received academic parlance through the work of Mary Louise Pratt, who, in *Imperial Eyes* (1992), describes a contact zone as a "space of colonial encounters, the space which peoples geographically and historically separated come into contact with each other and establish on-going relations, usually involving conditions of coercion, radical inequality, and intractable conflict" (p. 6).

## The Three Races That Occupy the Land

The land as geographical space has been the constant ingredient shared by all the collectivities. Each group possessed a different perception of and use for the land. For the aboriginal populations, the land expressed not only their livelihood but also their identity. As a place for human habitation it had been given to them by a creator or other divine beings. The original inhabitants of the lands, known by another misconceived misnomer as "Indians," had already been in this land for more than a thousand years when the first Europeans arrived. The land was held in common by the entire group in the culture of the specific aboriginal society. The land was not possessed as real estate and thus could not be bought or sold. The aboriginal cultures possessed both tacit and empirical knowledge of the land. Such knowledge was not only expressed in rituals and beliefs but was a pervasive aspect of their everyday existence. For the aboriginal populations the land performed a mutual orientation—it oriented them to their world, and they in turn served the land through the preservation of its orientation in space.

Beginning as a series of English colonial settlements dating from the early seventeenth century, the colonies became independent through a revolution in the latter part of the eighteenth century, and the United States has since become a nation of immigrants, primarily from Europe. In the Middle Colonies, primarily Virginia and the Carolinas, through the activities of Richard Hakluyt, whose writings about North America can be described as combining travel literature with real estate promotion urging investment in charter companies promoting ventures in Virginia and the Carolinas, the land is portrayed as paradisial. As Bernard Sheehan put it in *Savagism & Civility* (1980) in regard to Hakluyt's rhetoric, "the effulgence of the rhetoric and the prediction that wealth would be obtained, 'with or without art or man's help' contained profound paradisiacal implications." Sheehan continues with a comment about Hakluyt's collaborator, Samuel Purchas: "He had traveled on three continents but held Virginia 'by the naturall endowments, the fittest place for an earthly paradise'" (p. 12).

In *Wilderness and the American Mind*, Roderick Nash relates how William Bradford stepped off the *Mayflower* into what he called a "hideous and dangerous wilderness" (p. 23). From the time of Bradford to the present, the wilderness theme has been a feature of American culture, of its practices and rhetoric. The wilderness is an example of the New World as both threatening and sinister on the one hand

and fascinating on the other. One of the most influential books on American culture and religion was Perry Miller's *Errand into the Wilderness*. Miller's book initiated a renaissance in the study of the religious meaning of American culture. Since the aboriginal populations were not a part of the city traditions of the European immigrants, they were identified with the wilderness, threatening realities to be avoided or overcome. The European metaphorical expressions ranged from wilderness to virgin to paradise. In spite of the force of these metaphors, it is clear that the English settlers in New England and the Middle Colonies were able to work out a way of understanding and cooperating. Indeed, the colonists were dependent upon the native populations for long periods of time.

Francis Jennings had already made use of the term *invasion* to describe the landing and settlements of the English in his 1975 work *The Invasion of America: Indians, Colonialism, and the Cant of Conquest*. Jennings's study is important because of its focus on the meaning and nature of the aboriginal populations at the time of the English arrival, and it discusses in detail the inner structure of their relationships over a period of time. It also erases the mild or neutral language of "pilgrimage" and the search for religious freedom that had defined the American rhetoric of the Massachusetts settlements. Jennings continued to debunk the other American shibboleths the land as "virgin" or "wilderness." As Jennings put it, from a metaphoric point of view, the Europeans occupied a "widowed land":

> European explorers and invaders discovered an inhabited land. Had it been pristine wilderness, it would possibly be so still today, for neither the technology nor social organization of Europe in the sixteenth and seventeenth centuries had the capacity to maintain, of its own resources, outpost colonies thousands of miles from home. . . . They did not settle a virgin land. They invaded and displaced a resident population. (p. 15)

The scholarship on the colonial period over the past few decades has gone far to emphasize two major factors that had not been put to the fore in previous works—the structure and periods of relationships of accommodation and the violence waged by the English populations against the original inhabitants of the land. The fact that accommodations were possible did not erase the European imaginings of these inhabitants of the land as savages. Given the several concrete relationships that the English experienced with the aboriginal populations, Bernard Sheehan mused over

> the profound inability of the reigning . . . European ideas to offer even a glimmer of truth about the meeting of white and Indian in America. Englishmen certainly behaved toward Indians in certain ways because they believed them to be savages, but more important was the irony that they continued to believe them savage even when circumstances inspired an utterly different relationship. Because the English were trapped by the disjunction between savagism and civility, they could never grasp the reality of their dealings with the native inhabitants of America. (pp. x–xi)

In his novel *The Confidence Man*, Herman Melville coined the phrase, "the metaphysics of Indian-hating." It is clear that many observers equate the violence against those of non-European racial groups to the experience of the English of the colonial period. One example is Richard Drinnon's *Facing West: The Metaphysics of Indian-Hating and Empire Building* (1980). Ralph Slotkin in a series of studies has taken up the theme of violence from the colonial period through the twentieth century as one of the basic ingredients in the formation of Anglo-American culture. Violence is not discussed as simply physical acts of harm but the rhetoric and language of many American institutions and practices.

In 1619 a Dutch ship arrived in Jamestown, Virginia, with twenty African persons aboard, including men, women, and children. They were sold as indentured servants, but this initial form of limited servitude of Africans opened the door to the full-fledged enslavement of millions of Africans imported into the colonies from Africa. The Africans in America constitute an "involuntary presence" in the land. Of the "three races of people," they are the one group of people who did not wish to be here and who were brought to the country bound and in chains. From the small band of indentured servants, the African slave population grew to approximately three million by 1850, most enslaved on plantations in the Chesapeake region, the Carolinas, Georgia, Alabama, Mississippi, and Louisiana. Some form of slavery existed in every part of the country, however, with the largest slave port north of Charleston, South Carolina, located in Providence, Rhode Island. No person of African descent was, or could become, a citizen of the United States until after the American Civil War. Europeans coveted the land inhabited by the indigenous peoples and their ability to trap furs and utilize other resources of the land for the international market. It was the bodies of Africans that were desired and coveted by Europeans. The Africans, themselves, became commodities in an international market participated in by all the European maritime nations. The enslaved African was the major source of agrarian labor throughout the eighteenth and most of the nineteenth centuries.

The enslaved Africans worked land that was neither their own nor the lands of those who had enslaved them. Their relationship to the land was highly ambiguous, being at once the reality that opposed them in the act of labor and at the same time allowing for a direct relationship with a form of the irreducible reality of this labor that defied the intervention of their owners. Through solitary and communal labor they were inspired with a notion of freedom that was not conveyed through the language and practice of their owners and other slaveholders.

In addition and as corollary to the economic value of the institution of slavery were the symbolic and political effects of its existence in the colonies and later the United States. With the legitimation of slavery by the Constitution of the United States at the founding of the American republic, the values consistent with those of the slave system were destined to permeate the nation. Ira Berlin remarked in his book *Many Thousands Gone: The First Two Centuries of Slavery in North America* (1998) that there are "societies with slaves" and "slave societies." What distinguishes them is that "in societies with slaves," the enslaved are marginal to the central productive processes. In "societies with slaves," no one presumed the master-slave relationship to be the social exemplar. In "slave societies," slavery stood at the center of economic production, and the master-slave relationship provided the model for all social relations: husband and wife, parent and child, employer and employee, teacher and student. From the most intimate to the most public relationship, the archetype of slavery reigned; no relationship lay outside this group.

While the three constitutive races of American culture have been in constant relationship since coming to share the same geographical and human spaces, their relationships have seldom been peaceful. This is characteristic of the tensions involved in contact zones. The American historian Stephen Saunders Webb points to the year 1676 as crucial with respect to the possibility of the three races forming an expression of the American reality, embodying the cultural symbols and languages that gave authentic expression to their cultural beginnings. In his book *1676: The End of American Independence* (1985), Webb interprets Bacon's revolt in Virginia as a turning point in the colonial determination of cultural and economic destiny. This revolt involved Bacon and his followers against the English Crown's representatives and the Iroquois League against the Susquehanna, who supported the Crown. Africans formed a significant cohort in Bacon's ranks. The other event of this time was King Philip's War in Massachusetts. The colonists were too weak after these conflicts to cohere as a possible united force to work out their own destinies and, according to Webb, fell into a purely Anglophone mode of understanding themselves as colonials. Though they would wage a revolution against the Crown a century later, this revolution was not fought in the terms of the new and creative forms of the three races sharing the land but in terms consistent with those of a purely Anglophone polity.

## Civil Religion: Founding and Orientation

Sidney E. Mead published his essay "The American People: Their Space, Time, and Religion" in 1954 in the *Journal of Religion*, it was later included in a group of his essays published as *The Lively Experiment, The Shaping of Christianity in America* (1963). A long history of books and articles have been devoted to American identity or character, from Hector St. John Crevecoeur's *Letters from an American Farmer* (1904), through Alexis de Tocqueville's *Democracy in America*, to Robert Bellah's and Sidney Mead's own studies of the 1960s and 1970s. Mead's essay is one of the few that employs a geographical historical perspective; there are echoes of Frederick Jackson Turner's "frontier thesis" running through the essay. Turner's thesis, initially delivered as a lecture at the World Columbian Exposition in Chicago (the Chicago World's Fair) in 1893, was expanded into a book, *The Significance of the Frontier in American History* (1920). Turner's thesis presents the Americans as a people who moved across the land from one frontier to the next—from the Atlantic to the Pacific, occupying the continent. At each frontier the American pioneer, as bearer of civilization, touches primitive forces of wilderness and its inhabitants. In an agonistic conflict these primal energies provide the power to overcome the frontier and move on to the next.

Mead's essay, while paralleling Turner, adds the pathos of religious sentiment to this pilgrimage across the land. Mead mentions the Indian indigenous population only in passing and the Africans not at all. In the last analysis, the American is a person of European descent moving across and taking possession of a vast territory. The land and other inhabitants of the territory are not presented within any real space and time; they are real to the extent that they become aspects and dimensions of the inner consciousness of the Europeans.

In 1975 Mead published another group of essays entitled *A Nation with the Soul of a Church*. In these lectures Mead was able to comment on the programmatic essay of Robert Bellah, "Civil Religion in America," published in the journal *Daedalus* in 1967. Bellah's essay begins as a commentary on the election of the first Roman Catholic president, John F. Kennedy. From this point of view it might be seen as a fulfillment of Will Herberg's formula for American religious identity set forth in his *Protestant, Catholic, Jew* (1955). Herberg was attempting to give substance to the notion that American civil or secular religion was an ill-defined, "American way of life." President Eisenhower had memorialized this notion in the statement, "Our government makes no sense unless it is founded in a deeply felt religious faith—and I don't care what it is."

The context for most discussions of civil religion in America is strictly circumscribed as a negotiation about the proper accommodation of persons of European descent within the American republic. No mention is made of the Supreme Court decision of 1954 outlawing segregation in public education, nor is any reference given to the monumental study of race relations in America edited by Gunnar Myrdal and published as *An American Dilemma* in 1944. As a matter of fact, very little attention is given to the other "two races" that have inhabited the land since the beginnings. None of these studies deal with the debates of the abolitionists, nor do we hear anything of a specific nature regarding the "Trail of Tears" or the negotiation or adjudication of aboriginal native lands. Given the critical tone of these works, they are nevertheless suffused with a sense of optimism. In the words of Mead, what Americans had accomplished was done in a *very short time*. Maybe in time, Americans might achieve a tragic sense of life and express the maturity of the founding documents of the republic. If one takes seriously the existence of the three races, the tragedy might be situated at the founding, and if not there then at the end of the Civil War.

All discussions of civil religion deal extensively with the founding documents and the founders, their beliefs, and their faiths. Very few raise the religious meaning of founding itself. Catherine Albanese's *Sons of the Fathers: Civil Religion in the Revolution* (1976) details the importance of the Roman model and the rituals and pageants that accompanied the inauguration of George Washington as the first president. The nature and meaning of foundings and beginnings as basic modes of orientation for cultural life are discussed in the many writings of Mircea Eliade, especially in his *Patterns in Comparative Religion* (1958), and in Joseph Rykwert's *The Idea of a Town: The Anthropology of Urban Form in Rome, Italy and the Ancient World* (1976). To date, only in the work of Hannah Arendt, *On Revolution* (1963), is there a thorough philosophical discussion of founding in general and the descriptive critical discussion of the specific founding of the United States.

Arendt shows that the American and French revolutions differed from other radical and violent upheavals. While other upheavals had changed the ruling class, they had not changed the "nature of things"; the general hierarchy remained: some would always be rich, others poor; some always rulers, the others ruled. While the "actors" changed, the drama remained the same. The American Revolution intended to create a new drama; it was a revolution in the name of freedom. And this freedom was based on the idea that all persons could take part in their governance. Arendt notes that the possibility for a new drama of freedom was undergirded by the great economic wealth of the colonies. She points out that Europeans marveled at the wealth of the colonies, and Benjamin Franklin and other American colonists were amazed by the poverty that was pervasive in European societies. The wealth of the colonists was dependent upon the acquisition and exploitation of indigenous lands, the involvement of aboriginal populations in the international fur trade, and the labor of the enslaved Africans. In *Slave Counterpoint* (1998), Philip D. Morgan noted,

> From 1700 to 1780, about twice as many Africans as Europeans crossed the Atlantic to the Chesapeake and Lowcountry. Much of the wealth of early America derived from slave-produced commodities. Between 1768 and 1772, the Chesapeake and Lowcountry generated about two-thirds of the average annual value of the mainland's commodity exports. Slavery defined the structure of these British American regions, underpinning not just their economies but their social, political, and ideological systems. (p. xv)

Arendt discussed the philosophical meaning of the American founding. The men of the American Revolution knew that they were founders, and they perceived that their founding must have a model. They knew of two models of founding: that of the Hebrews' escape from the Egyptians and the story of Aeneas from Virgil's *Eclogues*. They chose the Roman model, for it hinted at the establishment of political instruments for governance. They chose as their motto for founding part of a line from the beginning of the Fourth Eclogue, *magnus ab integro saeculum nascitur ordo*. This can be translated, "The great order of the ages is born afresh." The American version reads as follows: *novus ordo saeculum*, which in translation is "a new order begins." The American motto implies that they created *ex nihilo*, that there is no past and that nothing occurred in the land before their Constitution. The Roman formula knew that every new creation must recognize a past, and thus their creation is a renewal and continuation of other past creations.

A revolution breaks into and disrupts the old order so that a new order might begin. There is a moment in revolutionary temporality when the old order is *no longer* but the new order is *not yet*; this is a moment that allows for new forms of thought, new interpretations of the past, and heretofore unknown meanings and imaginations to enter into the new formulations of the new order. It is at this point that a meaning of the eternal as the absolute of all time presides over and permeates the meaning of this in-between time of the revolution. At this point of hiatus, the novel meanings, imaginations, and actions of "the three races that inhabit the territory" and their understanding of what freedom could be in this land should have been injected. Instead the American notion of "pursuit of happiness" fell back into the various older forms of mercantilism, and with the continuation and legitimating of the institution of slavery, the idolatry of race gained a hold on the American nation and the American republic continued its invasion of aboriginal lands. The eternal as a normal part of the ordinariness of common life became an abstract political symbol upholding in most cases the tyranny of the majority.

**See also** *Abolitionism and Antislavery; African American Religion* entries; *American Revolution; Atlantic World; Civil Religion in the United States; Civil War; Frontier and Borderlands; Geographical Approaches; History of Religions, Approaches; Immigration* entries; *Native American Religions: Post-Contact; Pledge of Allegiance; Pluralism; Race and Racism; World War I; World War II.*

Charles H. Long

## BIBLIOGRAPHY

Albanese, Catherine L. *American Religious History: A Bibliographical Essay*. Washington, D.C.: Department of State Bureau of Educational and Cultural Affairs, Office of Academic Programs, 2002.

———. *Sons of the Fathers: Civil Religion in the Revolution*. Philadelphia: Temple University Press, 1976.

Arendt, Hannah. *On Revolution*. New York: Viking, 1963.

Axtell, James. *The Invasion Within: The Contest of Cultures in Colonial North America*. New York: Oxford University Press, 1985.

Baudet, Henri. *Paradise on Earth: Some Thoughts on European Images of Non-European Man*. Middletown, Conn.: Wesleyan University Press, 1988.

Bellah, Robert N. "Civil Religion in America." *Daedalus* 96, no. 1 (Winter 1967): 1–21.

Berlin, Ira. *Many Thousand Gone: The First Two Centuries of Slavery in North America*. Cambridge, Mass.: Harvard University Press, 1998.

Braudel, Fernand. *The Mediterranean and the Mediterranean World in the Age of Philip II*, 2 vols., translated by Sian Reynolds. New York: Harper and Row, 1972.

Chidester, David, and Edward Linenthal. *American Sacred Space*. Bloomington: Indiana University Press, 1995.

de Tocqueville, Alexis. *Democracy in America*. Edited by J. P. Mayer. Garden City, N.Y.: Doubleday, 1969.

Drinnon, Richard. *Facing West: The Metaphysics of Indian-Hating and Empire Building*. New York: New American Library, 1980.

Eliade, Mircea. *Patterns in Comparative Religion*. Translated by Rosemary Sheed. New York: Sheed and Ward, 1958.

Gerbi, Antonelli. *The Dispute about the New World: The History of a Polemic, 1750–1900*. Pittsburgh, Penn.: University of Pittsburgh Press, 1979.

———. "The Earliest Accounts of the New World." In *The First Images of America*, vol. I, edited by Fredi Chappelli. Los Angeles: University of California Press, 1976.

Herberg, Will. *Protestant, Catholic, Jew: An Essay in American Religious Sociology*. Garden City, N.Y.: Doubleday, 1955.

Jennings, Francis. *The Invasion of America: Indians, Colonialism, and the Cant of Conquest*. Chapel Hill: University of North Carolina Press, 1975.

Kupperman, Karen. *Settling with the Indians: The Meeting of English and Indian Culture in America, 1580–1640*. Totowa, N.J.: Rowman and Littlefield, 1966.

Long, Charles H. "Civil Rights—Civil Religion: Visible People and Invisible Religion." In *American Civil Religion*, edited by Russell E. Richey and Donald G. Jones. New York: Harper and Row, 1974.

———. "Passage and Prayer: The Origin of Religion in the Atlantic World." In *The Courage to Hope*, edited by Quinton Hosford Dixie and Cornel West. Boston: Beacon, 1999.

Mauss, Marcel. *The Gift, the Form and Reason for Exchange in Archaic Societies*. Translated by W. D. Hall. New York: Norton, 1990.

Mead, Sidney E. *The Lively Experiment, the Shaping of Christianity in America*. New York: Harper and Row, 1963.

———. *A Nation with the Soul of a Church*. New York: Harper and Row, 1975.

Meinig, D. W. *The Shaping of America: A Geographical Perspective on 500 Years of History*. 4 vols. New Haven, Conn.: Yale University Press, 1986–2004.

Miller, Perry. *Errand into the Wilderness*. Cambridge, Mass.: Harvard University Press, 1978.

Morgan, Philip D. *Slave Counterpoint: Black Culture in the Eighteenth-Century Chesapeake and Lowcountry*. Chapel Hill: University of North Carolina Press, 1998.

Nash, Roderick. *Wilderness in the American Mind*. New Haven, Conn.: Yale University Press, 1967.

O'Gorman, Edmundo. *The Invention of America*. Bloomington: Indiana University Press, 1961.

Pratt, Mary Louise. *Imperial Eyes, Travel Writing and Transculturation*. New York: Routledge, 1992.

Rykwert, Joseph. *The Idea of a Town: The Anthropology of Urban Form in Rome, Italy and the Ancient World.* Princeton, N.J.: Princeton University Press, 1976.

Sheehan, Bernard. *Savagism & Civility: Indian and Englishmen in Colonial Virginia.* Cambridge: Cambridge University Press, 1980.

Slotkin, Ralph. *The Fatal Environment: Myth of the Frontier in the Age of Industrialization.* New York: Henry Holt, 1991.

———. *Gunfighter Nation: Myth of the Frontier in Twentieth Century America.* New York: Harper, 1993.

———. *Regeneration through Violence 1600–1800.* Middletown, Conn.: Wesleyan University Press. 1993.

van der Leeuw, G. *Religion in Essence and Manifestation.* London: Allen & Unwin, 1938.

Webb, Stephen Saunders. *1676: The End of American Independence.* Cambridge, Mass.: Harvard University Press, 1985.

# American Revolution

The American Revolution (1775–1783) was a war that disrupted religious practice in North America, and it was a transformative era (from roughly 1760 to the early nineteenth century) that reshaped the social and cultural practices of religious organizations and practitioners. The American Revolution transformed religious structures, practices, and beliefs throughout North America. The religious changes were fitful and incomplete, much like the broader influences of the Revolution itself. Sharing in the social and physical upheaval that went along with the challenges to traditional authority and practices, religions and the religious joined in the tearing down of an old social and political order and the exploration of novel ideas and structural arrangements; and, through all the changes and the experimentation, they regularly employed governance and ideas that had unintended consequences and did not entirely eschew the past.

## Neutral Individuals and Groups

For individuals and for religious institutions, the Revolution was disruptive. The strains, struggles, and threats were not only things to endure, they were also dangerous and destructive to congregations. The physical violence destroyed churches, disrupted services, and scattered participants. Church members and organizations who chose sides faced reprisals from their foes. Neutrals garnered double the scorn and worse. Methodist Francis Asbury (1745–1816) became such a target. He asserted that his Methodism and its intensely spiritual focus transcended the worldly distraction and corruption that disputes over money and power caused. Partisans on both sides disagreed, forcing Asbury into hiding, his purity and balancing act made ever more precarious

when his supervisor, the English leader of Methodism, John Wesley (1703–1791), published a shrill condemnation scorning American complaints about taxes. Moravians in North America chose neutrality, as the Asbury had done, and they added to the principled reasons some pragmatic justification for their stance. Moravians in North Carolina had little complaint against a colonial government that had helped them carve out an exceptional presence in the backcountry—their tract of land called Wachovia—but they were partially surrounded by partisans who urged them toward the cause of independence. As armies and militias ranged about, the Moravians held their principled and practical neutrality by supplying goods to all visitors, while trying to shield their young men from on-the-spot recruitments. Members of the Society of Friends, too, generally maintained their pacifism against the pressures of their neighbors on both sides of the conflict, but individuals such as General Nathaniel Greene (1742–1786) and a faction labeling itself the "Free Quakers" chose to break from their brethren and join the battle against the British.

## Deism and Rationalism

The physical disruptions were matched by less tangible dangers. Threatening voices, such as that of Thomas Paine (1737–1809), whispered and then began to shout that religion was as corrupt and antiquated as the monarchical order that Americans were beginning to leave behind. Paine was simply the most vocal among many who perceived in traditional religion too many irrationalities—ancient stories filled with misrepresentations and lies about miracles and divinities designed to deceive gullible people. Paine and a cohort of freethinkers asserted that religious irrationalities were wedded to political ones, priesthoods paralleled presumed aristocratic bloodlines, and all religious belief represented a soon-to-be bygone era of superstition. A new enlightened "age of reason" would prevail over the centuries of myth and manipulation that had propped up both church and kingdom. Faced with such criticisms and associations, Christian apologists wrote and spoke to distinguish their traditions from those targeted by the political revolutionaries, and through their writings and sermons, they strove to carve out a compatible place for Christianity in the emerging order.

Many other revolutionaries embraced some form of deism, a more modest but sufficiently threatening challenge to Christianity. Leaders such as George Washington (1732–1799) spoke of a divine being and creator who impersonally managed the universe after having created it; Jesus was simply a very wise teacher—not divine—in this formulation. Washington spoke in vague terms of a creator and did not mention the name of Jesus, and Thomas Jefferson (1743–1826) was so agitated by the ideas of miracles and divinity on earth that he clipped all such references out of his Bible to create a palatable testament. Jefferson valued the teachings of Joseph Priestley (1733–1804), who in his Unitarianism denied the doctrine of the trinity, the divinity of Jesus, the efficacy of sacraments, and a host of other corruptions of Christianity that generations of misguided believers had imposed on the ethical teachings of the human Jesus. These thinkers were ready to redefine religion in a way that fit the new, rational world America was creating, a faith that would be distinctly different from traditional Christianity and its continued adherence to the trinity and miracles. The Revolution, with its appeal to natural law and reason, seemed to favor religious experiments and usher in a new era that would favor a realistic form of devotion to better principles. The nation and its citizens would exemplify the highest ethics associated with verifiable and reasonable truth.

## Freethinking and 'Dissenting' Alliance for Disestablishment

Christians often labeled freethinkers and deists their enemies, and the latter regularly criticized the naiveté of the churchgoers; but in the revolutionary age, the groups found a shared complaint. For a moment, they found a common enemy in the established church—the Church of England that was by law the single official religion that encompassed all subjects of the kingdom—and a common cause in the movement for religious choice and disestablishment. Freethinkers relished the prospect of being at liberty to pursue their heterodoxies safe from stigma and attacks originating with the traditional and unreasonable. For their part, many Christian groups, including Baptists, Presbyterians, and Friends, chafed against the classification as "dissenters" to the established Church of England, a status that effectively prevented them from functioning without oversight and limits. Dissenters paid taxes in mandatory support of the "One" church while making offerings in voluntary support of the several they claimed as their own. Ministers were restricted from violating parish boundaries in some regions, had to register, and could not perform marriage ceremonies. Dissenters, those groups that had fought the two-hundred-year-long quest to garner the role as substitute for the medieval Roman Catholic Church, continued to assert complaints and to criticize, even as they

conceded that their very presence at least could be tolerated by the Church of England. Dissenters defensively feared encroachments on their hard-won opportunities, however, sometimes trying to carve out for themselves geographic niches, territories where they could implement their religious designs, as the Puritans strove to do in Massachusetts Bay. There, distant from the established church, they tasted an exclusive freedom they would try to retain through the Revolution.

On the eve of the war, disputes over the presence of an Anglican bishop in North America rankled dissenting church members, who feared a possible bolstering of the establishment. In southern colonies, members of the Church of England themselves resisted such plans, fearing that such an authority in America could diminish the strong control local vestries often exercised over parish matters, including the direct criticism of parishioners' behaviors, and especially control over the levels of clerical salaries, paid out of required fees. In New England, the Quebec Act (1774), which permitted Roman Catholics to worship in the territories transferred from France to England after 1763, irritated and threatened Protestant colonists. Seeing parallels between the current dispute with England and the longstanding religious complaints against establishment, ministers such as the Presbyterians James Caldwell (1734–1781) and John Witherspoon (1723–1794) became aggressive and outspoken in their support of the revolutionary cause. Some clergy, such as the liberal Congregationalist Jonathan Mayhew (1720–1766), added loud voices of criticism over the Stamp Act as the revolutionary crisis developed; others served as chaplains and even volunteered for direct military service, such as the Lutheran minister Peter Muhlenberg (1746–1807), who served in the Virginia militia.

## Preaching and Rallying for or against the Revolution

Preachers advocated their causes in print and pulpit, spreading their ideas of patriotism, loyalty, or neutrality. Mayhew preached and published *A Discourse Concerning Unlimited Submission and Non-Resistance to High Powers* in 1750—the anniversary of the killing of Charles I (1600–1649; ruled 1625–1649). Mayhew urged Christians as a matter of duty to challenge tyrants, and his views set a pattern for sermons favoring the patriot cause during the Revolution. Ministers regularly harmonized Christian beliefs with notions of rights and resistance developed during the English Civil War (1640s and early 1650s), when

Parliament challenged, deposed, and killed the king; the Restoration of the monarchy (1660), when England called Charles II (1630–1685; ruled 1660–1685) back to the throne, investing him with largely symbolic powers; and the Glorious Revolution (1688), when Parliament invited William and Mary (ruled 1689–1702) to take the throne. Religious leaders equated and mixed these political events that strengthened England's parliament and reduced the powers of the monarchy with the religious legacy of Protestant protests against Catholic monopoly. In the sermons' formulation, believers and subjects had the right to challenge tyrannical leaders who might oppress or misguide their people. The Americans' complaints represented another step in the path toward liberty of person and conscience. That step, however, would be an enormous stride, for the results of the American efforts could be transformative: the Revolution could be the beginning of a new era—a golden age, equated in religious terms with the millennium, that thousand-year period anticipating the return of Jesus.

People living in the revolutionary era employed new forms of communication and social interaction in their religious and political efforts. Patriot leaders such as Patrick Henry (1736–1799) adapted tactics of traveling preachers such as the famous George Whitefield (1714–1770), who spoke extemporaneously and dramatized his messages with emotionally charged inflections and sharpened vocabulary as he toured England, Ireland, Scotland, and the American colonies in the mid-1700s. Henry and other organizers became evangelists for their political cause, much the way dissenting preachers had employed those tools to challenge the established authority of an established church and the decorum that came with presumed status. Similarities compounded as many political rallies and speeches spilled out of buildings into streets and open fields, the very places New Light ministers had claimed when expelled from established churches and parishes. Evangelistic and patriot efforts—encouraging of the spontaneous expressions of the seemingly unqualified and performed in prominent places—implicitly threatened the staid and structured systems of monarchy and establishment.

## Impact on Women

Revolutionary disruptions spread throughout the societies being recreated in the thirteen colonies. During the upheaval and experimentation, when militias and churches struggled to fill ranks, pews, and pulpits, some religious groups accepted the leadership of women. Often, the roles were auxiliary, reinforcing the long-standing reliance on women to support functions by cooking, nursing, tending, and simply populating meetings. But on occasion during the revolutionary moment, women soldiered, exhorted, and preached. Their experiences became standards for their hearers, leading to new public appreciation for their religiosity and new causes they advocated. Ann Lee (1736–1784), who endured the devastating loss of eight children—four stillborn and four dying before age seven—advocated sexual abstinence. She also promoted women's equality with men, affirmed by her discovery of the perfect attributes of God in her female self. The "Shakers" who followed Lee's teachings would attract women and men committed to celibacy and some measure of equality between men and women.

## Impact on Native Americans

The Revolution transformed relations between settlers and Native Americans. The interactions between the two were complex from the start, but lurking behind the many conflicts had been a tacit hope that cooperation could prevail. Trade offered the greatest potential, but Christians hoped that Native Americans might convert to their beliefs, and Native Americans found ways to fit the arrival of strange people into their beliefs and prophecies. Hope quickly soured, with Native Americans turning away from Europeans whose notions of cooperation had taken the form of missions and schools designed more to enforce cultural conformity than anything else. By the time of the Revolution, hopes for cooperation were replaced by expectations that Native Americans and settlers would live in irreconcilable worlds and would hold incompatible beliefs. American militia attacked Native Americans vigorously, accelerating the pace at which Native Americans were being eliminated from lands between the Appalachians and the Mississippi River—a less organized anticipation of President Andrew Jackson's (1767–1845) official policy of Native American removal just a few decades later.

These changes affected the religious landscape, removing many Native Americans from sacred sites and killing many people who held the oral traditions handed down through generations. Some of the remaining missionaries began to rework their previous roles, functioning as defenders of Native Americans out of moderate (and often condescending) sympathy for people they had come to respect. By the time President Jackson committed the resources of the federal government to Native American removal, a handful of missionaries were the most vocal critics of the new assault. In the meantime, Native Americans were open to the ideas of prophets such as the Delaware Neolin (c.1725–c.1775), who called for the rejection of European influences in all aspects of Native American life, and a return to a purer set of practices and beliefs untainted by the newcomers. The aggression so violently applied to Native Americans was part of an unleashing of energies, expectations, and designs for an emerging country. As Americans emerged from the years of struggle against the British, they began to celebrate their opportunities. Taking land from Native Americans and dismissing them at a more rapid pace was one success, they thought. The elimination of religious establishment was another.

## Filling the Void of Disestablishing the Church of England

As independence became a reality, real detachment from the Anglican Church and the long fought battle for recognition also dawned on Americans. Their first response was mixed, for although many Americans wanted the destruction of the establishment, they disagreed about what should fill the void. State by state they debated their particular opportunities, with some stronger denominations plotting to take their rightful place as substitutes—either alone or in conjunction with other groups. Several states, including Massachusetts and Connecticut, continued to require citizens to pay taxes for the support of a church, but they allowed for the choice of religion. Virginians considered multiple establishments briefly before rejecting both establishment and general assessment. Instead, through the operations of Jefferson and James Madison (1751–1836), and the support of numerous dissenting groups, Virginia introduced the broad concept of free religious choice based on conscience by passing Jefferson's Act for Establishing Religious Freedom (drafted 1779; passed 1786). This more liberal concept of religious freedom grew in influence and respect, and its core assumption helped shape the results for the new U.S. Constitution, which did not mention God, religion, support, or tests; instead, the new document included the First Amendment that barred establishment and guaranteed free exercise of religion.

## Immigration and Migration Westward

Religiously free Americans poured out into the new country, freely exercising their right to pursue what their consciences told them, happily free to try telling others what their consciences should tell them, and finding new places to spread their many visions of God, the devil, and the other characters in their spiritual dramas. The Revolution and its new notion of citizenship confirmed what the religious dynamism of the eighteenth century had offered—that people were free to think and choose for themselves. The United States became a hotbed of religious innovation in the nineteenth century, with flourishing churches, spiritually aware citizens, and a host of new religious beliefs and organizations, including the Latter-day Saints, who celebrated the vision of Joseph Smith (1805–1844) of an American scripture and holy people. Although Smith and the Mormons tapped into religious strains that had roots in medieval times, the newly created United States figured prominently in their religious hopes and in the designs of many others. Some thought that the creation of the new nation held profound symbolic significance, perhaps ushering in a millennial era, a thousand years of improvement that would advance the world toward the culminating return of Jesus. Others assumed that the nation itself represented a truth that, mixed with proper religion, would create a civic religion focusing faith on the promise of the benefits that the nation would bring.

Missionaries hailed the opportunity to pursue settlers beyond the Appalachian Mountains into the Ohio River Valley and further. Not only did they feel the lure of potential new converts, missionaries also sensed their alienation from the populated areas of the east coast. Both the Revolution and the religious revivals of the eighteenth century had taught them their responsibility to throw off corruption from the past, evils that had infiltrated America and remained, despite the efforts during the 1700s. The West became a place to find the promise of America and Christianity, an area where hard-working preachers met challenging but open people. There could be nurtured a religion of common sense, free from the elitism of cities and too much education. There, too, could flourish a religion that could skip over human inventions and returned to the purity of its origins; in the Christian tradition, that meant the model of the early church described in the New Testament. Western preachers such as Alexander Campbell (1788–1866), Lorenzo Dow (1777–1834), and Peter Cartwright (1785–1872) lauded the virtues of the expansive lands, and they attempted to recreate a purer religiosity that linked Ohio, Kentucky, and Tennessee directly back to the natural ancestors in Ephesus and Philippi.

## Renewal of Religious Competition and Sectarianism

The many efforts to make America and its religions anew did not always produce the intended results. The experiments to create a pure, universal Christianity in the new American lands steadily added new churches to the existing multiplicity already littering the religious landscape. The religious freedom created by the Revolution brought into the open the many competing sects that had proliferated since the Reformation and accelerated the pace of their multiplication. On occasion formerly competitive groups combined efforts to address the growing need for ministers and churches; the cooperative union between many Presbyterians and Congregationalists from New England exemplified this spirit, but it did garner some criticism and opposition. The many religious groups could not divorce themselves from their past assumptions. Lurking in their designs for conversion, cooperation, and growth was the ultimate goal that one truth would overwhelm the competing messages of the competition. Charismatic and sometimes authoritative leaders regularly led upstart and splinter groups and became the focus of their growth and legacy. Religious proliferation and freedom were built on the strengthening of religious organizations and their influential leaders. Baptists, for example, who had defined themselves in part by their practice of congregational independence and autonomy, began to create local associations, and regional and national organizations through the revolutionary era into the nineteenth century.

Increasingly concerned with their influence in society, the various sects strove, like the competing political leaders, to build their parties and legitimate themselves, and they struggled against each other with conflicting views of the proper paths to take. Steadily churches began to restrict the leadership roles of women, excluding them from ministry and even delimiting their roles as exhorters. As an alternative, one that fit neatly with selected principles from the Revolution and the assumptions long ingrained, notions of republican motherhood became the celebrated paradigm. Women would be important, even vital to the success of the nation, but they could best contribute by maintaining homes that nurtured children who might grow up to be capable and respected citizens, and supporting husbands who could contribute to the public life of the country. The Revolution's disruption of some traditions had introduced alternatives that would not be forgotten; steadily into the nineteenth century, women would claim moral authority as protectors of household and families and through such assertions steadily increase the boundaries of their domestic responsibilities. Through voluntary religious organizations—so vital in a religiously free nation—women helped lead several reformist causes in the nineteenth century,

addressing issues such as temperance, mental health, and abolition.

## Impact of the Revolution on the Institution of Slavery

"Freedom" and "liberty" had been the mottos of the revolutionary cause, and "slavery" the term used to describe British mistreatment of colonists. For a moment, some Americans applied these ideas broadly by releasing enslaved African Americans, outlawing slavery in newly forming states, and accepting African Americans into religious fellowships. Religious groups had been at the vanguard of such efforts. Participants in the meetings of the Society of Friends regularly spoke out against slavery, and they were sometimes joined by a smattering of Baptists and Methodists, who occasionally expressed their shock at the mistreatment of the enslaved in the American South. Most would compromise quickly, however, backing away from broad critiques of the morality of slavery, and instead calling for limited reform that could improve the relative treatment of the enslaved within the practices of slavery. The altered approach opened a few more doors, although slaveholders were more amenable to hearing calls for their slaves' obedience than criticisms of their own vices. African Americans who converted to Christianity were selective, weeding out calls for their submissiveness and instead celebrating the stories of Exodus and release from captivity. Some were able, despite separation from land, relatives, and others who shared their traditions, to continue practicing strands of African religions, including some elements of music and burial practices. A few continued to practice the Islamic faith that had been theirs in Africa. White Christians rarely accommodated African American sensibilities, and steadily, black participants were relegated to balconies in mixed services, and whites tried to supervise the independent meetings that African American worshippers tried to carve out for themselves. Many of these gatherings took place at night, secreted away in woods. Some few, however, developed in the open atmosphere that larger port cities supplied. Richard Allen (1760–1831) was quite successful in Philadelphia, developing a fellowship and eventually the African Methodist Episcopal Church—a reflection of both opportunity and nonacceptance by white Americans after the Revolution.

## Religious Freedom

Religious freedom answered the mutual needs of the two most aggressive religious participants in the revolutionary era. Dissenting Christians and freethinkers awarded themselves the opportunity to pursue their religious interests. These two groups could agree that the new country held promise in its religious experimentation, and that promise took on its own life. Americans celebrated the success of their Revolution, their leaders, and their freedoms in ways that echoed the trappings of religiosity. This "civic" religion, exercised in the veneration of Washington, in anthems and poems, and on a series of holidays (including, over time, the 4th of July), celebrated the success of the Revolution and the values, variously interpreted, of the Founders. Through the nineteenth century and especially in the twentieth century, Americans of various religions have shared an appreciation of the generic values associated with revolutionary freedoms. They have also attached portions of their religious faiths to the success of the American experiment to justify their beliefs and add a triumphal sensibility to their faith. Their collective efforts have led to strains of religion, usually versions of Christianity, that link the United States to dreams of divine plans or a chosen nation. Reflexively these faithful distort the role of Christianity in history, superimposing a flattened, ahistorical concept of Christianity on the revolutionary era and especially its leaders. The effect has been counter to the trajectory during the revolutionary age. Instead of furthering religious freedom, the insistence on a "Christian nation" has ascribed to the Founders some particular contemporary beliefs.

Many Americans in the revolutionary era hesitated to extend religious freedoms. It was sufficient to have thrown off the formal demands and structure of one group—the Church of England—and to have replaced it with the informal influences of a host of local fellowships. Technically, there would be no restrictions, but in practice, many people were reluctant to admit Jews, Muslims, and even Roman Catholics into full participation in the Republic, especially as participants in political leadership. Many Jews who had carved out local acceptance and quiet tolerance under the earlier system now struggled in the seemingly freer world after the Revolution, when a spotlight of attention illuminated their presence in the competitive religious world. The mutuality of dissent gave way; informally, most Americans assumed—or required—a tacit acknowledgment of Protestant Christianity as the nation's religion. Particular Protestant groups vied for priority of place, and they closed ranks only to stave off newcomers, such as the homegrown Latter-day Saints or the immigrant Roman Catholics in the nineteenth century. The broad language used to guarantee Protestant pluralism, however, held the potential for broader inclusion in the future—slowly

opening American religious freedom to other groups in the nineteenth century and eventually to individuals and individual consciences in the twentieth. Revolutionary freedom of religion continues to struggle against notions of establishment, but the Revolution itself ended the institutional presence of religious establishments, shifting only a portion of the remnant to the new political entity itself.

**See also** *African American Religion: Colonial Era through the Civil War; Anglicans in Colonial and Revolutionary America; Church and State: Revolutionary Period and Early Republic; Civil War; Deism; Methodists: Through the Nineteenth Century; Moravians; Pacifism and Conscientious Objection; Roman Catholicism: Catholics in the Atlantic Colonies.*

Philip N. Mulder

## BIBLIOGRAPHY

Albanese, Catherine L. *Sons of the Fathers: The Civil Religion of the American Revolution.* Philadelphia: Temple University Press, 1976.
Bloch, Ruth H. *Visionary Republic: Millennial Themes in American Thought, 1765–1800.* New York: Cambridge University Press, 1985.
Bonomi, Patricia U. *Under the Cope of Heaven: Religion, Society, and Politics in Colonial America.* New York: Oxford University Press, 1986.
Buckley, Thomas E., S.J. *Church and State in Revolutionary Virginia, 1776–1787.* Charlottesville: University Press of Virginia, 1977.
Butler, Jon. *Awash in a Sea of Faith: Christianizing the American People.* Cambridge, Mass.: Harvard University Press, 1990.
Curry, Thomas J. *The First Freedoms: Church and State in America to the Passage of the First Amendment.* New York: Oxford University Press, 1986.
Frey, Sylvia R. *Water from the Rock: Black Resistance in a Revolutionary Age.* Princeton, N.J.: Princeton University Press, 1991.
Hatch, Nathan O. *The Democratization of American Christianity.* New Haven, Conn.: Yale University Press, 1989.
———. *The Sacred Cause of Liberty: Republican Thought and the Millennium in Revolutionary New England.* New Haven, Conn.: Yale University Press, 1977.
Heimert, Alan. *Religion and the American Mind, from the Great Awakening to the Revolution.* Cambridge, Mass.: Harvard University Press, 1966.
Hoffman, Ronald, and Peter J. Albert, eds. *Religion in a Revolutionary Age.* Charlottesville: University Press of Virginia for the United States Capitol Historical Society, 1994.
Isaac, Rhys. *The Transformation of Virginia, 1740–1790.* Chapel Hill: University of North Carolina Press for the Institute of Early American History and Culture, 1982.
Lambert, Frank. *The Founding Fathers and the Place of Religion in America.* Princeton, N.J.: Princeton University Press, 2003.
Morgan, Edmund S. "The American Revolution Considered as an Intellectual Movement." In *Paths of American Thought*, edited by Arthur M. Schlesinger Jr. and Morton White. Boston: Houghton Mifflin, 1963.
Wood, Gordon S. "Religion and the American Revolution." In *New Directions in American Religious History*, edited by Harry S. Stout and D. G. Hart. New York: Oxford University Press, 1997.

# Anabaptist Denominational Family

Anabaptism first appeared as an inchoate movement during the Protestant Reformation, but although a unified organization or a formal set of shared beliefs never materialized, believer's baptism nevertheless became nearly universal among Anabaptists. *Anabaptism* means "to baptize again"; the first generation as children had experienced baptism by the established churches, and baptism as adults was their second.

Anabaptist groups that survived the Reformation era developed a system in which the faith community imitated the New Testament church by separating itself from the sinful world and becoming an alternative community with its own relationships and rules. Consequently, obedience to the scriptures, or discipleship, became critical to membership in God's kingdom, but unity within the faith community about the characteristics of discipleship was also vital. The fellowship's collective discernment of the Bible, considered superior to individual insight, delineated the specifics of the restored New Testament Church. Anabaptists, then, were nonconformists (to the larger society), who ideally conformed to God's will as determined by the faith community.

Past scholars anointed Conrad Grebel (1498?–1526) in 1525 as the first Anabaptist, but current thinking stresses several spontaneous sources of origins, that is, polygenesis. Grebel's failure to persuade Ulrich Zwingli in Zurich, Switzerland, to endorse believers' baptism marked the birth of Anabaptism there. But in other parts of central Europe other Anabaptist groups also appeared. In south Germany Anabaptism was a legacy of the Peasants War (1525), a broad uprising of commoners linked to the Protestant Reformation. After authorities crushed the rebellion, some reformers adopted community of goods, as practiced by the New Testament church, and this laid the groundwork for nascent Anabaptism in that region. In the north German city of Münster, millennial reformers calling themselves Anabaptists gained political control through legal, due process and adopted community of goods and polygamy. After a bitter siege authorities regained power and killed most of the inhabitants, but the radical Münsterites had stamped Anabaptism with fanaticism, an image that lasted for centuries, and widespread persecution resulted. Anabaptist martyrs were burned at the stake, drowned, tortured, imprisoned, or exiled. A Dutch priest, Menno Simons (1496–1561), brought order to this scattered, persecuted movement. Menno, as his

subsequent followers refer to him, emphasized inner change and nonresistance (refusal to serve in the military and non-retaliation in personal life), far different from the revolutionary and violent call for social reform at Münster. Under his influence the movement acquired its emphasis on separation and unity, and he also stressed church discipline through the ban, sometimes called "shunning," which mandates avoidance of excommunicated members in many social settings. Traveling from group to group, mostly in north Germany, Menno created enough organization that some Anabaptists adopted his name, calling themselves "Mennonites." The Anabaptist family tree, however, has several trunks—North German/Dutch Mennonites, South German/Swiss Mennonites, Hutterites, Amish, Brethren, and Brethren in Christ (in approximate chronological order).

In the late seventeenth century Anabaptists began migrating to North America, a movement that continued into the twentieth century. Eighteenth- and nineteenth-century North American Anabaptists usually shared several beliefs and practices besides believers' baptism. Generally, they practiced nonresistance; humility; non–swearing of oaths; and plainness, especially in dress but also in material goods. Congregations chose ministers who had no formal training and served without pay. Women voted and perhaps spoke in congregational councils but did not hold leadership positions other than deaconess. North American Anabaptists worshipped either in homes or in very simple, unadorned meetinghouses. They did not serve in public office and did not own slaves. They expelled members particularly resistant to the fellowship's guidance about avoiding the sinful world. Amish and Brethren men wore untrimmed beards.

But despite these common threads, Anabaptists have suffered persistent disagreements over the application of discipleship, especially in separating from the larger culture. Furthermore, like many minority immigrant religious groups in North America, Anabaptists confronted Americanization, which threatened to assimilate their vision of the restored, unified, countercultural church, and much of American Anabaptist history reflects this tension, especially beginning with late-nineteenth-century industrialization when conservatives, called "Old Orders," resisted change and "fast" progressives more willingly accepted it. Consequently, today Anabaptism is a multihued continuum that ranges from horse-and-buggy Old Orders to progressives who have abandoned much of the tradition and resemble mainstream Protestants more than their conservative Anabaptist cousins.

## Mennonites

The first permanent Anabaptist settlement in North American began in 1683 when Dutch and North German Mennonites settled in Pennsylvania, but the lower Rhine never generated a steady flow of immigrants. In the early eighteenth century, however, Palatine and Swiss/South German Mennonites arrived, the first of many from that source. Economic opportunity strongly motivated their transatlantic odyssey despite the heritage of Anabaptist persecution, and the patterns of arrival and settlement of South German Mennonites resembles that of other eighteenth-century German immigrants. They located initially in Germantown, outside of Philadelphia, and then in the rich farmland of southeast Pennsylvania, expanding into western Maryland and Virginia's Shenandoah Valley prior to the American Revolution. After the Revolution they followed frontier migration west into Ohio, Indiana, and Illinois, and others went north into Ontario; later generations put down roots in Kansas and Nebraska. Eventually Mennonites descended from eighteenth- and early-nineteenth-century immigrants followed larger population movement patterns to the West Coast, particularly Oregon.

The descendents of Swiss/South German Mennonites defined Mennonite life until after the Civil War. They baptized by pouring, and worship was in German although English made gradual inroads. Mennonites gathered in homes or in plain meetinghouses for sermons, prayer, and hymns. Men and women sat separately, and the preachers faced them from behind a simple table. Ministers were chosen from among the fellowship, and they served without pay, received no special training, and remained in their secular occupation, usually farming. Candidates for the ministry received nomination from the membership, but casting lots determined the final selection. Each nominee received a book, usually a Bible or hymnal, one of which had a slip of paper inside. The books were shuffled, and the candidate who received the book with the paper was God's choice. Usually several ministers served several congregations, which limited the accumulation of power by individual preachers. Mennonites preserved unity by expelling, but they preferred to maintain conformity through gentle persuasion and role models, especially ministers. A member who violated custom might receive a quiet visit from a preacher. Although they believed in salvation by faith, early American Mennonites emphasized that faith without works is dead and stressed discipleship—that is, that believers should obey the Bible's directives for daily life.

Additionally, Continental Pietism (the doctrine that believers can receive forgiveness for their sins, and experience an intimate relationship with Christ and salvation by voluntarily accepting Christ's lordship—called "Continental" for the European continent) heavily influenced early American Mennonites. Menno had not taught heartfelt faith, and, in fact, he predated Pietism by more than a century. Mennonites typically favored orderly worship, such as camp meetings, and revivalism's penchant for personal testimony and counting converts struck many as excessive individualism and a prideful emphasis on numbers rather than biblical humility. But the Dutch priest had stressed a changed life, including spiritual rebirth, repentance, and conversion, and born-again religion merged comfortably with Anabaptism. By the mid-eighteenth century many North American Mennonites embraced moderate Pietism, and late-eighteenth and early-nineteenth-century revivalism attracted Mennonite participants, although the most enthusiastic revivalists tended towards the fringes rather than the core of Mennonite society. Eastern North American descendants of Swiss/South Germans, then, crafted a form of Anabaptism based on discipleship, a unified faith community, and the new birth.

In the 1870s a new stream of Anabaptism imported by Russian Mennonites arrived on the Great Plains, with different ideas about how to maintain fellowship and avoid the world. The newcomers were the progeny of Dutch/North German Mennonites who had migrated into east Europe and Russia. In Russia Mennonites retained German folkways, and they lived in ethnic islands separate from the larger society. Consequently, they saw their distinctiveness in language, customs, and hymns rather than plainness, especially in dress. Some were Mennonite Brethren. They practiced footwashing, a ritual performed by various but not all eastern Mennonites, and their mode of baptism by immersion, one time backward, was a clear marker between themselves and other Mennonites. They clung to German-language worship, but they did not choose leaders by lot. Finally, Mennonite Brethren fused evangelicalism with Anabaptism, and although generations of eastern Mennonites had been Pietists, Mennonite Brethren made experiential conversion and mission central to their message. As a result, humility, nonconformity, nonresistance, and plain dress, though present, became less essential than in the east.

In the late nineteenth century the pace of change for Mennonites accelerated. Mission, for example, received attention from progressive Mennonites. In 1880 Samuel and

Susannah Haury established the first North American Mennonite mission when they moved to Indian Territory (Oklahoma) and lived among the Arapahoes. In 1889 the first overseas missionaries went to India. Also, revivalism became popular. Led by John S. Coffman (1848–1899), Mennonite revivalists bent the methods of mainstream tent preachers to Mennonite customs. Coffman, for example, preached the classic evangelical message of salvation, but he spoke in a conversational style between the singsong of traditional Mennonite preachers and the extroverted pulpit pounding of tent revivalists. Protracted meetings were an especially controversial symbol, and when local sentiment opposed them, Coffman announced services one by one. The methods of Coffman and other Mennonite revivalists won much favor, and by the early twentieth century altar calls reaped a bountiful harvest of young Mennonite converts.

Growing acceptance of higher education represented a further transformation of Mennonites. Between 1893 and 1917 Mennonites opened seven colleges: Bethel (Kansas, 1893), Goshen (Indiana, 1903), Bluffton (Ohio, 1914), Freeman (South Dakota, 1903; closed 1987), Tabor (Kansas, 1908), Hesston (Kansas, 1909), and Eastern Mennonite (Virginia, 1917). Typically these campuses became centers of Mennonite scholarship, but higher education also often pushed the envelope against traditionalism. Conservatives deeply distrusted the liberal influence of Mennonite higher education, and the most conservative Mennonites considered higher education as anathema.

Ironically, revivalism, another change and clearly an outside influence, sparked renewed interest in traditional Mennonitism, especially dress. Garb was always important for Mennonites because it encouraged nonconformity in daily life, but although early American Mennonites had dressed plainly, they had not adopted uniform dress. But the intensity brought by revivalism inspired greater interest in modesty and consistency in dress, and the resulting trend was towards formal, written codes. Many men, including John Coffman, wore plain coats without a collar and lapel and cast aside neckwear. Women adopted a shapeless dress with an especially modest cape covering the upper torso. The New Testament instruction for women to cover their heads received special attention, and female Mennonites set aside fashionable bonnets and hats for prayer caps, a simple head covering worn at all times. When outdoors, they added a plain, black bonnet that fit over the prayer cap. Because Mennonites remained decentralized, specifics on dress fell to districts and congregations, with considerable variation.

Some districts, for example, permitted bowties, and a few still allowed neckties. Similarly, headwear for women varied in shape, material, and color of the strings, which could be tied or loose. To an extent the new standards of plainness replaced the German language as a sharp line of distinction between Mennonites and the American mainstream, but plain dress also divided conservative from progressive Mennonites, who kept the dress codes at arm's length.

By the 1890s four groupings dominated American Mennonitism: Old or Mennonite Church Mennonites, General Conference Mennonites, Old Orders, and Mennonite Brethren (described above). Old Mennonites, later called Mennonite Church Mennonites, descended from the Swiss/South German trunk, and "Old" distinguished them from fellowships that had splintered away throughout the nineteenth century (for instance, Reformed Mennonites, Mennonite Brethren in Christ, and East Pennsylvania Mennonite Conference). Strong bishops with authority over several congregations gave Old Mennonites top-down leadership, a departure from past practice. Old Mennonites, still swimming hard against the mainstream, dressed plainly and only slowly accepted publications, education, missions, and associations with other Protestants. Old Mennonites considered themselves the Mennonite mainstream between the progressives and Old Orders.

General Conference Mennonites were a progressive association that included both Dutch/Russian descendants on the Plains and Swiss/South German descendants east of the Mississippi. More willing, or "faster," than most Mennonites to discard nonconformity, they hoped to persuade conservative Mennonites to abandon alleged cultural backwardness and adopt education and mission. In the nineteenth century they stopped dressing plainly, a concession to individualism, and in the 1920s they adopted English worship. They also hoped to unite all Mennonites under one large pan-Mennonite organization, and their adherence to congregational authority gave them flexibility that facilitated their vision. Most other Mennonite conferences, however, eventually adopted education and mission on their own terms rather than merge with the General Conference. Nevertheless, in 1920, various Mennonite groups, including the General Conference Mennonites, Mennonite Brethren, and Mennonite Church Mennonites, organized the Mennonite Central Committee, an umbrella organization that assisted resettlement of Russian Mennonites fleeing the Soviet Union and, when that task ended, devoted itself to international relief, development, and peace work.

On the Mennonite right wing was a third group, the Old Orders. As progressive Mennonites increasingly assimilated into the American Protestant mainstream, Old Order objections arose. Revivalism, with its testimonies, unrestrained emotion, and convert-counting still looked to most conservatives as awash with individualism and juxtaposed to humility. Sunday schools, another mainstream practice increasingly popular with progressives, were too ecumenical for Old Orders, who suspected that non-Mennonite influences jeopardized nonresistance and nonconformity. Higher education, foreign missions, and English-language worship were other dangerous intrusions of the world. On another level, Old Orders resisted the modern rationalism adopted by many other Mennonites with the coming of the industrial age. Progressives, for example, held spirited debates and maintained detailed minutes, but Old Orders cherished unity through consensus and kept barebones records. Old Orders never created institutions that connected their scattered communities, another rejection of modern rationalism, but they communicated closely and visited one another, an informal system more compatible with a premodern outlook. But beyond all the specifics, Old Orders felt that change should come slowly, and now it was coming quickly.

In the early decades of the twentieth century, technology and fundamentalism raised more questions about how the faith community should relate to the world and provided new ways to tear at the Mennonite fabric. For conservatives the new technology endangered the faith community by closing the distance between it and the larger society. Accordingly, Old Orders were standoffish towards electricity and telephones, but they disagreed over the automobile. The most conservative remained "team" or "horse-and-buggy" Mennonites, but other Old Orders accepted the horseless carriage.

Fundamentalism was also disruptive. The old-time religion of mainstream Protestants with its lists of fundamentals easily merged with conservative Mennonitism and its tendency towards detailed discipleship in daily life. Fundamentalism, then, influenced all branches of Mennonites, although the Old Orders, who remained more aloof from larger Protestantism, felt its impact less directly. Dispensationalism and premillennialism became especially popular, and the Scofield Bible and the *Sunday School Times* enjoyed wide Mennonite readerships. As in broader Protestantism, denominational colleges and seminaries became battlegrounds. Between 1913 and 1951 fundamentalism influenced the resignation of seven Mennonite college presidents,

and Goshen College (Indiana) closed for the 1923–1924 academic year because its board suspected that modernism had infected the campus. In truth, few Mennonites were modernists, but fundamentalists nonetheless flung the charge of liberal or modernist at those unenthusiastic about premillennialism and at progressives refusing to wear the plain coat. Like revivalism, fundamentalism reinforced traditional Mennonite norms, but technology and fundamentalism both provided new opportunities for assimilation into the Protestant mainstream and stoked new tensions within the faith community.

By the late twentieth century, nonconformity and unity remained important Mennonite themes. At this point only Old Orders defined nonconformity in terms of dress, and many Mennonites expressed their relationship to the world through peace work, social activism, and a simple lifestyle. During the peak of the Vietnam War, Mennonite theologian John Howard Yoder published *The Politics of Jesus* to reassure a young generation of Anabaptist activists that they could simultaneously belong to the set-apart Kingdom of God and the wider peace and civil rights movements. Yoder's book achieved wide circulation beyond Anabaptist circles. And Mennonites took a step towards unity when in 1989 the General Conference and the Old Mennonite Church combined into the Mennonite Church USA, the largest current Mennonite organization with approximately one hundred thousand members.

Currently, assimilated Mennonites, especially the Mennonite Church USA, suffer a membership decline similar to the mainline denominations. Racial/ethnic Mennonites (Asian, Hispanic/Latino, African American, Native American), however, are a growth edge for the denomination and may represent as much as 15 percent of its membership, much higher than for other U.S. denominations that are historically European. Old Orders are less than 10 percent of U.S. Mennonites, but their strong, clear boundaries against the larger society result in higher retention rates than for progressives. The Old Order disdain for organization and fondness for specific lines against the world in daily life encourage variety. Stauffer Mennonites, for example, dress very plainly and use horses and buggies. Wenger Mennonites are also horse-and-buggy Mennonites but are somewhat less plain than the Stauffers; they use tractors, albeit with steel wheels rather than rubber tires. Horning Mennonites, slightly more progressive but still Old Order, occupy yet another position in the range of plainness; they own automobiles but require them to be black and ministers to strip them of chrome. For non–Old

Order Mennonites the current debate over how to reconstruct the New Testament Church focuses on divorce, military service, the ordination of women, and homosexuality. Meanwhile, the Mennonite Central Committee continues as a large and effective service organization. Unity over how to separate from the world still eludes North America's spiritual descendents of Menno Simons.

## Hutterites

Hutterites, another Anabaptist stem with roots in the Reformation era, trace their origins to 1528 when a small group in Moravia, led by Jakob Hutter (d. 1536), began to hold property in common, making them the most direct Anabaptist link to the Peasants War. They survived European persecution and poverty, and in the 1870s approximately twelve hundred migrated to the Dakota Territory. The majority of the immigrants, called *Prarieleut* (Prairie People) abandoned communal living and drifted into Mennonite congregations. The minority retained goods in common and established three branches: *Schmiedleut, Dariusleut,* and *Lehrerleut,* each named for its founder. Although the three groups share many beliefs, they function independently and rarely intermarry. Like many Anabaptists, Hutterites stress that true faithfulness comes by surrendering the self to God and to a faith community set apart from the larger world, but for Hutterites this means that individuals have no private property except for a few personal items, such as clothing and books. They work without pay for the community, or "colony," which functions as a legal corporation. The colony aims for self-sufficiency but buys and sells with the outside world, usually in large quantities. Continued use of German also distinguishes Hutterites from the larger society.

Hutterite socialization depends upon education. At age three children enter a nursery and come under the supervision of the colony. At six they eat in the children's dining hall rather than with their parents, and six-year-olds also enter school, where they learn both English and German. The English and German schools meet within the colony rather than off-premises. A non-Hutterite hired by the local school district teaches the English school, but a member of the colony leads the German school. The German teacher is an unquestioned moral authority who emphasizes Hutterite heritage, habits, and beliefs.

Worship further reinforces norms. Services consist of singing, preaching, and prayer in a simply furnished room. Worshippers file in and sit according to rank based on age and gender. The oldest sit in the back, enter last, and leave first, and men precede women. Seating also is segregated by gender, and the oldest woman follows behind the youngest boy.

During World War I Hutterites, like all German-speaking, nonviolent, U.S. Anabaptists, suffered persecution at the hands of authorities. Some were imprisoned and mistreated, and two young Hutterites died while in detention at Fort Leavenworth. Consequently, many Hutterites moved to Canada, but as militant patriotism subsided in the 1930s a few returned. In 2000, Hutterites had 425 colonies with approximately ninety members each. Approximately 75 percent are in Canada, especially Alberta, Manitoba, and Saskatchewan, and the remainder are in the United States, mostly in South Dakota and Montana. Hutterites are the oldest communal society in North America.

## Amish

The Amish version of Anabaptism emerged from a dispute among South German/Swiss Mennonites in Europe. In 1693 the dispute grew into a schism, and the dissenters, led by Jakob Amman (1656?–before 1730?), became known as "Amish." They came to North America in two waves in the mid-1700s and early 1800s. The first immigrants settled in southeastern Pennsylvania, then followed the Pennsylvania German diaspora into the Midwest (but not the Virginia backcountry). The nineteenth-century group moved immediately to the Midwest.

In the late nineteenth century the Amish turned to Old Orderism. Progressive Amish, known as Amish Mennonites, assimilated into Mennonite fellowships, but the Old Order Amish resolutely spurned many aspects of modernization, especially telephones, electricity, and automobiles. Amish memory is uncertain about the reason for banning telephone ownership except that the new communications technology led to gossip and was generally worldly. In 1919 high-voltage electricity became off-limits when the Amish agreed to permit energy from 12-volt batteries rather than public utilities. Although unknown at the time, the ban on alternating current from power lines became a high wall against the larger society because most appliances required 110 volts. Automobiles similarly became forbidden for their potential to bring the outside world to Amish doorsteps. Horse-and-buggy transportation and field work forced a slower pace of life and naturally limited contact with the larger society. These and other restrictions on technology erected particularly effective boundaries that isolated the Amish from the larger world.

Old Order Amish, however, do not flatly ban all forms of technology and modernity but rather adopt them at their own pace and control their growth within the community. (The same is true for Old Order Mennonites.) The rule against telephones, for example, forbids ownership but not usage, and telephones lurk around the fringes of Amish society. Phone shanties, which first appeared during the 1930s, are small hut-like buildings at the end of farm lanes that contain phones shared by several families, mostly for outgoing calls for appointments and farm business. Many Amish borrow phones or use those belonging to neighbors, and sometimes phones are in barns and shops. At this writing, easily concealable cell phones are under discussion in many Amish communities. Likewise, the Amish limit electricity rather than avoid it completely. When in the sixties horse-drawn farm implements declined in availability, they began to use portable gas-powered welding equipment to adapt tractor-drawn equipment for their teams. Soon, however, some plugged their generators into other electrical devices, such as freezers or even lightbulbs in barns. Faced with this new threat, the Amish permitted generators only for welding equipment, which allowed them to continue to farm without tractors, a vital part of their life. Just a few years later milk dealers required storage in cooled, stainless steel tanks, which the Amish powered with diesel engines and stirred with generators connected to twelve-volt batteries. But the basic ban against electricity drawn from power lines remains. Most Amish kitchens and bathrooms use bottled gas to heat water and operate stoves and refrigerators, and gas-pressured lanterns illuminate homes, barns, and shops. Amish farmsteads remain readily recognizable by the absence of wires running from the road.

In addition to limits on technology, the Amish observe nonconformity in many other aspects of daily life. Amish garb is more than plain and distinctive; most Amish groups limit buttons and prohibit belts. Dresses are gray, green, purple, blue, or wine; and the men wear black with green, purple, blue, or wine dress shirts. Women wear a prayer cap at all times, and vests, black felt hats, and untrimmed beards are mandatory for men. Most Amish speak a Pennsylvania German dialect. Religious services, held in homes, are a mix of dialect and formal German and consist of congregational singing, prayer, and two extemporaneous sermons. Absent are organs, offerings, flowers, crosses, choirs, litanies, and robes. Hymns come from the *Ausbund*, a sixteenth-century book in German without musical notation. The slow tempos can stretch a hymn to more than twenty minutes.

Additionally, the Amish do not participate in the Social Security program. In 1965 they secured exemption from self-employed social security taxes—they hold that the body of believers should care for the elderly—and in 1988 the exemption extended to Amish employed in Amish businesses. As a consequence, they do not qualify for Social Security, Medicare, or Medicaid. Currently, most Amish operate their own eighth-grade education system in one-room facilities. The Amish participated in public education when it consisted primarily of one-room schools, but consolidation and pressure to attend high school created tension with authorities. In 1972 a landmark Supreme Court decision (*Wisconsin v. Yoder*) provided exemption from compulsory education laws. In brief, despite considerable variation on details of nonconformity, such as gas refrigerators or mechanical hay balers pulled by horses, and despite hundreds of congregations spread across twenty-five states and the absence of anything close to a central organization, remarkable uniformity characterizes the Amish method of separating from the world.

In 2000 the Old Order Amish included more than 180,000 adults and children, mostly in Indiana, Ohio, and Pennsylvania. With high birth rates and strong retention, their population doubles every twenty years. On the other hand, the high cost of land pressures Amish off the farm and into small businesses and wage employment, which brings them into greater contact with the larger society and provides new strain on their system of nonconformity.

Since 1927 a smaller and loosely organized group popularly known as the Beachy Amish (named for an early leader, Moses Beachy) has also existed in North America. The Beachy Amish dress quite plainly and reject certain aspects of modern technology, particularly entertainment technology such as television and movies. However, they drive cars, use English, and engage in vigorous evangelism.

### Brethren

The Brethren trunk of Anabaptism grew out of the moment in 1708 when Alexander Mack (1679–1735) and seven others baptized themselves in a central German stream. Brethren have long pondered whether Anabaptism or Radical Pietism came first to their tradition, but the latest scholarship argues that Mack's movement materialized from a swirl of ideas that included both. From Radical Pietism Mack embraced a personal relationship with Christ and the fear that religious institutions, especially the established churches, could impede this. But he also concluded that the

New Testament emphasized the body of believers. Mack thought that Mennonites came closest to the New Testament model of the church, but he criticized them as lifeless, no doubt inaccurately, as many Mennonites had discovered Pietism. Mack and his followers, then, created their own fellowship. In 1719 the first Brethren arrived in Pennsylvania, and within a generation the entire fellowship had been transplanted to North America. They followed the larger settlement patterns into the southern backcountry, the Midwest, the Plains, and eventually the West Coast.

Like the other Anabaptist groups, the Brethren developed several distinctive ways of restoring the New Testament Church. Worship, for example, resembled the practice of other Anabaptist groups, and it included a sermon, exhortations or short comments on the sermon, prayer, and a few hymns. Brethren baptism was especially unusual: full immersion three times, once for each member of the trinity. This mode gave them a nickname, "Dunkers," widely used by others prior to the Civil War (other variations include "Dunkards" and "Tunkers"), although Mack's followers preferred simply "the Brethren." (The official name through the nineteenth century was German Baptist Brethren.) Another distinctive Brethren practice was their interpretation of Love Feast, which included feetwashing, a holy meal, and communion. Unlike the other early Anabaptist groups, the Brethren developed a strong denominational structure with an annual meeting that provided common policy as the fellowship grew geographically and numerically. These yearly gatherings began in the late eighteenth century and in the next century responded to the market revolution with large and small lines against the world, including sanctions on wallpaper, fancy furniture, sleigh bells, and hoop skirts, as well as and other fashionable clothing.

The first Brethren schism came in 1728 when Conrad Beissel broke with the fellowship, and four years later he and his followers created the Ephrata Society on the Pennsylvania frontier. The core of Beissel's followers were communal with a Spartan, monastic, celibate lifestyle. Married "householders" resided in the surrounding neighborhood, and the fellowship met for worship on the Sabbath, that is, Saturday. Ephrata developed a flourishing printing operation, which issued a fifteen-hundred-page chronicle of martyrdom for Mennonites. After Beissel's death in 1768, the Society's membership aged and struggled to recruit new members. Ephrata also suffered heavily from its use as a military hospital during the American Revolution. The last celibate died in 1813, but married members maintained the Society until

1941, and a spin-off congregation in central Pennsylvania still survives.

After the Civil War more serious division came to the Brethren as progressives advocated admitting the Protestant mainstream, especially revivalism, into the fellowship. For progressives soul-winning now trumped separation from the world, and a message of salvation replaced nonconformity. Plain dress, denominational publications, missions, higher education, and Sunday schools were other points of controversy. In the late nineteenth century the Brethren opened more than twenty academies and colleges. Most failed, but the survivors are Ashland (Ohio, 1897), Bridgewater (Virginia, 1880), McPherson (Kansas, 1888), La Verne (California, 1981), Manchester (Indiana, 1895), and Elizabethtown (Pennsylvania, 1899). In 1880 Old Orders angry that the German Baptist Brethren had accepted too many modern innovations started the process of withdrawal, which led to the formation of the Old German Baptist Brethren. In 1882 the denomination disfellowshipped (that is, excommunicated) progressive leader Henry R. Holsinger (1833–1905), who was impatient with the pace of change, and the next year his followers founded the Brethren Church. What remained, the middle and the largest of the Brethren branches, still had progressives and conservatives and in 1908 changed its name to Church of the Brethren.

In the 1920s Alexander Mack's movement further divided. In the previous decade the Church of the Brethren had abandoned plain dress as a test of membership, and in the 1920s an Old Order faction formed the Dunkard Brethren Church. Aside from dress, they also complained about bobbed hair on women, church picnics, Sunday schools, pianos and organs in worship, membership in secret societies (labor unions), and paid pastors, all departures from the tradition.

The Brethren Church also suffered division during the twenties when fundamentalists detected liberalism and argued with nonfundamentalists over the need for discipleship, which fundamentalists associated with legalism. Led by Alva J. McClain (1888–1968), in 1930 Brethren Church fundamentalists organized a seminary for their denomination, but conflict ensued. In 1937 two fundamentalist professors, McClain and Herman A. Hoyt, were dismissed from the seminary, and they launched a rival institution. In 1939 schism resulted, and the fundamentalists formed their own denomination, the Fellowship of Grace Brethren Churches. Once independent, the Grace Brethren continued towards fundamentalism, emphasizing dispensationalism and replacing traditional Brethren nonconformity with a fundamentalist-like relationship with the larger society.

In the post–World War II era the three largest Brethren groups made different choices about their relationship with the Protestant mainstream. The Church of the Brethren abandoned many traditional Anabaptist practices, such as plain dress and unpaid ministers, and became heavily ecumenical and service-oriented. During World War II it joined with the Mennonite Central Committee and the Society of Friends to negotiate with the federal government for alternative service for conscientious objectors, which resulted in Civilian Public Service. In 1942 the Church of the Brethren founded Heifer Project, a plan to improve the breeding of farm animals overseas by donating genetically superior stock. The idea came from Dan West, appalled by the starvation he witnessed in the Spanish Civil War. In 1953 Heifer Project became an independent organization. The Brethren Church, often called "Ashland Brethren" for its headquarters in Ashland, Ohio, remained heavily evangelical, now placing these former progressives to the right of the Church of the Brethren. Both the Church of the Brethren and the Brethren Church suffered serious membership losses after the mid-twentieth century. Meanwhile, the Grace Brethren abandoned nonresistance and added typical fundamentalist causes, including support for capital punishment and opposition to feminism and abortion. In 1948 it founded Grace College (Ohio) to implement an evangelical version of higher education.

In 1992 the Grace Brethren fractured over several traditional Brethren rituals. In a running argument during the last half of the twentieth century, strong evangelicals favored allowing adults from denominations without adult baptism to transfer membership without undergoing the ceremony. Also debated was whether communion could be practiced separately from Love Feast. Conservatives favored the "closed" position that required adult baptism and restricted communion to the threefold service, that is, feetwashing, the holy meal, and communion. Dissenters also complained of growing denominationalism and loss of congregational independence. In 1992 traditionalists departed, forming the Conservative Grace Brethren Churches International Fellowship.

Today, with progressives, Old Orders, and evangelicals, the Brethren family of denominations resembles the Mennonite spectrum. The spiritual descendents of Alexander Mack are just as divided as those tracing their lineage to Menno Simons.

## Brethren in Christ

The most recent species of Anabaptism is the Brethren in Christ, who are distinctive for their combination of an Anabaptist understanding of nonconformity and unity with an emotional variety of Pietism similar to Wesleyanism. Originally called "River Brethren," for their location near the Susquehanna River in Lancaster County, Pennsylvania, they were the product of an awakening among Pennsylvania Germans in the late eighteenth century, the same revival that created the United Brethren and the Evangelical Association, both ethnic German. This made River Brethren more revivalistic than most North American Anabaptists at that time. Unlike the United Brethren and Evangelical Association, however, the River Brethren combined their new birth enthusiasm with an Anabaptist understanding of the church that included discipleship, nonresistance, avoidance of politics, non–swearing of oaths, plain dress, and use of the ban in congregational discipline. From the Dunkers, specifically, they adopted trine immersion baptism, beards on men, and Love Feast, including feetwashing. River Brethren also worshipped in homes rather than in meetinghouses. In 1864 they took the name Brethren in Christ.

In the late nineteenth century some Brethren in Christ, like progressive Brethren and Mennonites, adopted innovations from larger Protestantism, including revivalism, missions, Sunday schools, and higher education. In 1909 Messiah College (Pennsylvania) opened its doors. Those objecting to this trend became Wengerites, Old Order River Brethren (Yorkers), and the United Zion Children. Also during this period Wesleyan holiness grew in popularity among the Brethren in Christ. By the first half of the twentieth century the Brethren in Christ were firmly in the evangelical mainstream with a large mission program, revivals, and popular holiness camp meetings. Nevertheless, in 1939 they adopted the plain coat for men and the cape dress for women, similar to other Old Order Anabaptists. During the two world wars the Brethren in Christ reaffirmed nonviolence, and in 1940 they joined the Mennonite Central Committee. In the 1950s they became more evangelical and less Anabaptist, repealing dress rules, permitting musical instruments in worship services, and affiliating with the National Association of Evangelicals and the Christian Holiness Association. At this writing the Brethren in Christ are a tripartite combination of Anabaptism, evangelicalism, and fundamentalism experiencing small growth in membership.

Anabaptists today are probably best known for their Old Orders, especially the Amish, and for their contributions to the historic peace church movement. The Anabaptist route to outsiderness, particularly through equine transportation, plain dress, and nonresistance, makes them conspicuous; and their countercultural behavior, usually but not universally accepted, testifies to tolerance amidst diversity in American religion and to the guarantee of religious freedom in the U.S. Constitution. But Anabaptists have also felt the power of Americanization, and while some contemporary progressive Anabaptists may consider service as an acceptable replacement for lost traditions, reconstructing the New Testament Church through separation and unity is a declining concept among them.

**See also** *Anabaptists; Fundamentalism; Moravians; Pietism; Revivalism: Nineteenth Century; Social Ethics.*

Stephen Longenecker

## BIBLIOGRAPHY

Bach, Jeff. *Voices of the Turtledoves: The Sacred World of Ephrata.* University Park: Pennsylvania State University Press, 2003.

Bender, Harold S., et al., eds. *The Mennonite Encyclopedia.* 4 vols. Scottdale, Pa. Herald Press, 1955–1959.

Bowman, Carl Desportes. *Portrait of a People: The Church of the Brethren at 300.* Elgin, Ill.: Brethren Press, 2008.

Bowman, Carl F. *Brethren Society: The Cultural Transformation of a Peculiar People.* Baltimore: Johns Hopkins University Press, 1995.

Durnbaugh, Donald F. *Fruit of the Vine: A History of the Brethren, 1708–1995.* Elgin, Ill.: Brethren Press, 1997.

———. ed. *The Brethren Encyclopedia.* 4 vols. Philadelphia, Pa., and Oak Brook, Ill.: The Brethren Encyclopedia, Inc., 1983 and 2005.

Juhnke, James C. *Vision, Doctrine, War: Mennonite Identity and Organization in America, 1890–1930.* Vol. 3 of *The Mennonite Experience in America.* Scottdale, Pa.: Herald Press, 1989.

Kanagy, Conrad L. *Road Signs for the Journey: A Profile of Mennonite Church USA.* Scottdale, Pa.: Herald Press, 2007.

Kraybill, Donald B. *The Riddle of Amish Culture.* Baltimore: Johns Hopkins University Press, 1989.

Kraybill, Donald B., and Carl F. Bowman. *On the Backroad to Heaven: Old Order Hutterites, Mennonites, Amish, and Brethren.* Baltimore: Johns Hopkins University Press, 2001.

Kraybill, Donald B., and James P. Hurd. *Horse and Buggy Mennonites: Hoofbeats of Humility in a Postmodern World.* University Park: Pennsylvania State University Press, 2006.

MacMaster, Richard K. *Land, Piety, Peoplehood: The Establishment of Mennonite Communities in America, 1683–1790.* Vol. 1 of *The Mennonite Experience in America.* Scottdale, Pa.: Herald Press, 1985.

Schlabach, Theron F. *Peace, Faith, Nation: Mennonites and Amish in Nineteenth-Century America.* Vol. 2 of *The Mennonite Experience in America.* Scottdale, Pa.: Herald Press, 1988.

Stayer, James M. *The German Peasants' War and Anabaptist Community of Goods.* Montreal, Canada: McGill-Queen's University Press, 1991.

Toews, Paul. *Mennonites in American Society, 1930–1970: Modernity and the Persistence of Religious Community.* Vol. 4 of *The Mennonite Experience in America.* Scottdale, Pa.: Herald Press, 1996.

Yoder, John Howard. *The Politics of Jesus: Vicit Agnus Noster.* Grand Rapids, Mich.: Wm. B. Eerdmans, 1972.

# Anabaptists

The term *Anabaptists*, meaning "rebaptizers," refers to persons and groups that, in the context of the Protestant Reformation, advocated radical ecclesiastical reform measures, including adult baptism. Initially a derogatory label fashioned by the radicals' opponents, the term *Anabaptists* was eventually embraced by groups that found adult baptism (or "believers baptism") theologically superior to infant baptism. Although significant diversity existed within early Anabaptism, historians have nonetheless documented widely shared, if not consensual, emphases beyond believers baptism, including commitments to disciplined Christian living, nonresistance (pacifism), and other forms of social nonconformity. These emphases continue today in a host of North American religious groups, including Amish, Brethren, Mennonite, and Hutterite groups, that trace their roots to the sixteenth-century Anabaptist movement.

## Anabaptist Origins

As with many religious traditions, the question of origins is contested with respect to the Anabaptist tradition. One prominent school of thought has focused on the followers of Ulrich Zwingli (1484–1531), the Protestant reformer who assumed a preaching post in Zurich, Switzerland, in 1519. Zwingli's reform agenda, driven by the principle of *sola scriptura*, eventually included a proposal to abolish the Catholic mass. In 1523, the Zurich city council considered this idea and demurred, not because it disagreed with Zwingli's reasoning but because it feared the idea was too radical for immediate implementation. Zwingli affirmed the council's right to decide the pace of reform, a decision that alienated some of his young disciples, including Conrad Grebel (c. 1498–1526) and Felix Mantz (or Manz, c. 1498–1527). According to his disenchanted followers, the Bible's teachings, not the council's political calculus, should take priority in matters of ecclesiastical reform.

Charging Zwingli with "false forbearance," these radicals soon began to advocate more drastic reforms, including the rejection of infant baptism. Earlier, Zwingli had demonstrated some openness to this idea, but he had since backed off. On January 21, 1525, the radicals decided they would wait no longer for Zwingli or the city council to endorse their ideas. They took it upon themselves to baptize one another, a practice they considered their first true baptism (although to others it appeared to be a second baptism, that is, a rebaptism). For some mid-twentieth-century Anabaptist historians, and certainly in the historical imagination of contemporary Anabaptist churches, this act of baptismal defiance constituted *the* formal beginning of the Anabaptist movement.

Other historians, however, have contested this simple, normative account of Anabaptist origins. To these later-twentieth-century historians, many of whom were unconcerned about identifying a useable Anabaptist past, the "monogenesis" account of Anabaptist origins ignored the complex realities of the radical Reformation. They advocated instead a "polygenesis" account that highlighted numerous people who pushed beyond the strictures of state-sponsored churches and advocated adult baptism as one facet of their reform. According to polygenesis historians, the Anabaptist movement is best conceived as originating in several geographically disparate places. One particularly influential argument noted that in addition to the Mantz-Grebel circle of Anabaptists in Zurich, two other influential circles emerged quite independently at about the same time: one in south Germany, led by the mystics Hans Hut (d. 1527) and Hans Denck (c. 1500–1527), and one in the Low Countries (north Germany and Holland), led by the apocalyptically inclined Melchior Hoffman (c. 1495–1544?). Over time these different Anabaptisms grew, merged, migrated, and declined, producing an ever-changing mélange of European Anabaptist expressions. The polygenesis historians, who gave priority to social history over ecclesiastical and intellectual history, underscored not only the diversity of Anabaptist expressions but also the importance of their social contexts in shaping diverse reform agendas. In some cases, they noted, early Anabaptists rejected what is today often seen as a normative, consensual Anabaptist value: pacifism.

In many respects, polygenesis became in the 1970s and 1980s the reigning paradigm for delineating Anabaptist origins. More recently, however, some scholars have sought to temper the diversity suggested by the polygenesis account. More specifically, these scholars have suggested that an overemphasis on historical *origins* has come at the expense of recognizing the ways the different geographical centers influenced one another and moved toward various points of consensus. "What we see in early Anabaptism," writes historian Arnold Snyder in "Beyond Polygenesis," "is a movement with significant internal theological agreement and coherence that, in early stages of development, could and did overlook many implications which later would become divisive issues" (p. 3). So, for instance, in addition to affirming the broad outlines of historic Christian doctrine, as well as embracing particular emphases of the Protestant reformers (for example, *sola scriptura* and salvation by faith through grace), Anabaptist groups shared many other ideas in common with each other beyond their commitment to believers baptism (for example, the anthropological doctrine of free will, a soteriology that stressed the centrality of discipleship, a view of the visible church that placed Christians in tension with the larger world, and an openness to the revelatory power of the Holy Spirit). In this regard, Snyder and other scholars contend that one can rightly talk about an Anabaptist movement with an Anabaptist theology (singular), albeit with varying places of origin and different practical emphases.

## Early Emphases and Expressions

One of the earliest events aimed at defining Anabaptism occurred in 1527, when Swiss Anabaptist leaders gathered near the town of Schleitheim. Overseen by Michael Sattler (d. 1527), the gathering produced a seven-article manifesto known as the Schleitheim Confession that delineates the key elements of Swiss Anabaptism: adult baptism; stringent church discipline ("the ban"); the breaking of bread as a communal act; separation from worldly evils; the importance of a faithful, congregationally chosen ministry; the rejection of the sword; and the refusal to swear oaths. One mid-twentieth-century Mennonite scholar notes that, taken together, these seven articles point to the essential concerns of early Anabaptism: "the nature of Christian obedience, the idea of the gathered people of God, and the way of Christian love." With these words in his Introduction to *The Schleitheim Confession*, John Howard Yoder corroborated the work of his mentor, Harold Bender, who had posited an "Anabaptist vision" of three distinct emphases: *discipleship*, in which one's life is patterned after the life of Jesus Christ; *a voluntary church* consisting of a converted membership; and *an ethic of love and nonresistance.*

The Anabaptists' separatist ecclesiology had clear political implications. First and foremost, their views spawned persecution at the hands of the state. Civil authorities considered the Anabaptists both heretical and seditious; indeed, in an age when tax roles and military conscription were based on infant baptismal records, Anabaptist theology spawned fears of anarchy—and quick and brutal repression. This state-sponsored persecution, which began almost immediately, redoubled the early Anabaptists' sense of pessimism toward the social order that, according to the Schleitheim Confession, was beholden to "the evil one." A logical corollary to this pessimistic view of the world, at least in the case of Swiss

Anabaptism, was pacifism. According to the Schleitheim confession, the sword was "an ordering of God outside the perfection of Christ"; as an instrument of the world it was not to be wielded by Christians. Although some historians have suggested that pacifism was merely a way for Anabaptists to make a virtue of their victimization, the Schleitheim Confession reveals a deeply principled commitment to pacifism based on a dualistic understanding of the church and world.

Not all the early Anabaptists were pacifists, however. The most dramatic instance of Anabaptists taking up the sword occurred in the northern German city of Münster in 1534. Captivated by the apocalyptic visions of German Anabaptist Melchior Hoffman, a Dutch Anabaptist named Jan Matthijs (or Matthys, d. 1534) sought to hasten that end in Münster. Hoffman had preached that God would pave the way for Christ's return by destroying the ungodly; Matthijs modified that message to say that individual Christians could help prepare for Christ's return by annihilating the wicked. When Matthijs declared Münster the New Jerusalem—and forced unconverted citizens to leave the city in anticipation of Christ's return—the Catholic bishop of Münster rallied an army to retake the city. In the end, Matthijs and many other Anabaptists died in a lengthy siege. For centuries thereafter the term *Anabaptists* was used to denote dangerously misguided revolutionaries.

Although Münster loomed large in the minds of the Anabaptists' detractors, still other forms of Anabaptism took hold in the 1520s and 1530s that diverged sharply from the violent Anabaptism that characterized Münster. Perhaps most significant in this regard was a smattering of individuals and groups that historians often lump together under the label "South German Anabaptism." Some South German Anabaptists (Hans Hut, for instance) manifested an apocalyptic interest akin to the Münsterites (but without the violence), an interest that helps to explain Hut's disinterest in founding churches that would outlive him. Like Hut, other South German Anabaptists showed more interest in the regeneration of individuals and, in some cases, mystical encounters with Christ, than in starting and maintaining church communities.

In Moravia, however, a group of Anabaptist refugees seeking safe haven from persecution created an alternative community that, rather surprisingly, has survived to the present: the Hutterites. First gathering in Nickolsburg in 1527, and shortly thereafter migrating to Austerlitz, these Moravian Anabaptists began practicing a communal sharing of goods as outlined in the New Testament book of Acts. In 1529, an Anabaptist pastor named Jacob Hutter (d. 1536) began visiting the Austerlitz refugees to provide counsel and receive encouragement. In time, Hutter became the group's leader, and the group eventually took the name *Hutterites*. Although Hutter was captured and put to death in 1536, the Hutterites survived. They continue today as a distinct North American Anabaptist group, located primarily in Canada.

## Persecution and Survival

The martyrdom of Jacob Hutter was hardly unique. Over the course of the sixteenth and early seventeenth centuries, at least twenty-five hundred Anabaptist men and women lost their lives on account of their faith. Thousands of others were arrested or otherwise harassed. In response, many early Anabaptists worshipped in secret, and still others migrated in search of more hospitable environments. Persecution not only reaffirmed the Anabaptists' dualistic, good-versus-evil view of the world, but it also shaped their identity as faithful disciples sharing in Christ's suffering. Nowhere was this claim more apparent than in *Martyrs Mirrors*, a compilation of Anabaptist martyr accounts assembled by Dutchman Thieleman J. van Braght (1625–1664) and published in 1660. Even today this large tome can be found in many Anabaptist church libraries and in some members' homes. The 1685 edition included copper etchings that illustrated the martyrs' experiences, sometimes quite graphically. One etching in particular, depicting the Anabaptist Dirk Willems rescuing his would-be captor from an icy pond, has achieved nearly iconic status in some twenty-first-century Anabaptist communities.

Despite many sources of persecution, and despite the public relations disaster at Münster, the Anabaptist movement survived. In part, this survival can be attributed to effective leaders who, in the aftermath of Münster, helped to define Anabaptism in more moderate terms. No leader was more important in this regard than the Dutch Anabaptist Menno Simons (1496–1561). By 1544, just eight years after Menno's conversion from Catholicism, the term *Mennist* appeared in a letter to refer to the Dutch Anabaptists. Today, the most common label for North American Anabaptists is *Mennonite*.

Another factor that contributed to the survival of Anabaptism was the Anabaptists' ability to find out-of-the-way places where they could live in peace. In the sixteenth century, some Swiss Anabaptists migrated to Moravia for this reason; a century later, others made their way to the Alsace region in present-day France. Dutch Mennonites, on the other hand, made their way to the Vistula Delta along the Baltic Sea, and from there, in the eighteenth century, moved on to Russia. In many of these places, Anabaptist refugees found welcome due to their expert farming practices; they were allowed to worship freely as long as they contributed to the region's economic well-being and resisted the temptation to proselytize. For this reason, some Anabaptist groups, particularly those of Swiss origin, developed a reputation for quietism. Russian Mennonite groups, on the other hand, assumed a more politically engaged posture, in part because they were given administrative oversight of the large colonies they created.

## The Amish-Mennonite Division of 1693

As noted, one place where early Anabaptists found sanctuary from persecution was the Alsace region of present-day France. Migrating there from Switzerland in the mid- and late seventeenth century, these Swiss-Alsatian Anabaptists nonetheless maintained fellowship with other Swiss Anabaptist churches, at least for a time. Under the leadership of Jacob Amman (1656?–before 1730?), however, some chose to break from the more established Swiss Anabaptist churches in 1693, citing Swiss church leaders' lack of faithfulness to the original Anabaptist vision. In particular, Amman and his faction complained that Swiss Anabaptists had become lax on a variety of lifestyle and ecclesiastical issues, most significantly their commitment to church discipline. Invoking earlier Anabaptist precedents for shunning wayward church members, the Ammanists demanded a reinvigoration of this potent form of church discipline.

When Swiss Anabaptist leaders rejected the Ammanists' demand, the Amish church was born. Henceforth the Swiss Anabaptism movement would be characterized by two dominant streams: the more strictly disciplined Amish stream and a more world-embracing stream that assumed the Mennonite moniker. In twentieth-century America, the Amish would become renowned for their steadfast commitment to an agrarian lifestyle and their selective use of modern technology, a visually potent combination that has spawned a thriving Amish-themed tourist industry in some Amish regions. By contemporary standards, however, the sociological differences between the seventeenth-century Amish and their European neighbors was slight; indeed, most of the distinctions that are so apparent today did not emerge until the late nineteenth and twentieth centuries, long after the Amish had migrated to North America. Nonetheless, the die had been cast in 1693 for ecclesiastical

categories—Amish and Mennonite—that survived the Anabaptists' migration to North America, categories that continue to be used today.

## Migration to North America

The dispersion of Anabaptists across Europe, and the conditions they experienced in their adopted homes, shaped their decisions about migrating to North America. In the case of Swiss-German Anabaptists, this decision first came in the late 1600s. The first Mennonites arrived in Philadelphia in 1683, settling in what is now Germantown. About fifty years later, in 1737, Amish immigrants arrived aboard the ship *Charming Nancy*, which also docked in Philadelphia. Indeed, Philadelphia became the favored port of entry in the ensuing decades for most Amish and Mennonites. Correspondingly, Mennonites and Amish first settled in Pennsylvania before continuing their migrations westward (to Ohio and Indiana), northward (to New York and Ontario), and southward (to Maryland and Virginia). In the eighteenth century, Amish and Mennonite immigrants, almost all of them farmers, established a Pennsylvania German ethnic identity, one element of which was a dialect known as Pennsylvania Dutch, from Deutsch, meaning German. Some observers found these Pennsylvania Dutch citizens to be "dull and ignorant boors," but other observers highlighted more positive traits: agricultural proficiency, a willingness to work hard, honesty, and piety.

In addition to the Amish and Mennonites, another German Anabaptist group—the Brethren—began emigrating to North America in the early 1700s. The Brethren had not been in Europe long. In fact, the roots of the Brethren movement stretched back only a few years prior to their North American migration, to the development of radical Pietism in late-seventeenth-century Germany. Disenchanted with the spiritual state of Germany's Lutheran and Reformed churches, some Pietists adopted the beliefs and practices they saw in early Anabaptism, including adult baptism, pacifism, and strict modes of church discipline. In 1708, eight adults were baptized in the Eder River near Schwarzenau, Germany. Eleven years later, in 1719, the first Brethren migrated to North America. In eighteenth- and nineteenth-century America, these Brethren were called German Baptist Brethren or "Dunkers," the latter term owing to their practice of baptism by immersion.

The Anabaptist groups that had journeyed eastward in Europe—the Hutterites in Moravia and the Dutch Mennonites in Russia—migrated to the New World much later than the Swiss-German Anabaptists, first arriving in North

America in the 1870s. Rather than settling in Pennsylvania, the Hutterites and Russian Mennonites settled further west; the Hutterites initially made their homes in the Dakota Territory, whereas the Russian Mennonites put down roots in a variety of upper midwestern states (Kansas and Nebraska, for example) and Manitoba, Canada. As was their earliest pattern in Europe, some Hutterites created colonies that practiced the communal sharing of goods. In fact, the Hutterites remain the only North American Anabaptist group that lives in cloistered, communally owned colonies separate from the larger society. The Russian Mennonites, like their Swiss-German counterparts, settled largely as independent farmers, having brought with them a variety of red winter wheat that flourished in the prairie states' climate.

## The North American Anabaptist Mosaic

In many respects the Old World experiences and the subsequent migration patterns of Europe's Anabaptists created the contours for Anabaptism in North America. Scholars of North American Anabaptism have frequently noted the ethnic divide between Swiss-German Anabaptists, who first migrated to America in 1683, and Dutch-Russian Anabaptists, who immigrated to America almost two hundred years later. This ethnic divide does not tell the full story, however, for within these two ethnic camps one can find significant ecclesiastical diversity. For instance, the Swiss-German ethnic family includes a variety of Mennonite, Amish, and Brethren groups; likewise, the Dutch-Russian family boasts a variety of Mennonite-related groups. Moreover, one Mennonite denomination, the now-defunct General Conference Mennonite Church, was founded by Swiss-German Mennonites but was quickly populated by immigrating Dutch-Russian Mennonites.

Perhaps the most common way to think about the diversity of Anabaptist expression in North America is by denominational family, or what Donald B. Kraybill and C. Nelson Hostetter call Anabaptist "tribes." In this organizational scheme, four tribes—Amish, Brethren, Hutterite, and Mennonite—comprise the hundreds of churches and denominations that exist in actual practice. Of course, even then it is not always clear into which family a particular church or denomination falls. For instance, the Brethren in Christ Church was likely founded by Mennonites, but the fledgling church also appears to have been influenced by German Baptist Brethren.

A different way to categorize the variety of Anabaptist churches in North America places greater emphasis on sociological features than organic historical connections. In addition to their tribal paradigm, Kraybill and Hostetter divide Anabaptist groups into three categories based on their degree of assimilation to the larger culture. The *traditional* groups, often known as Old Orders, use horse-drawn transportation, dress plainly, speak a distinct dialect, and use technology very selectively. At the other end of the spectrum, the *transformational* groups value higher education, hold professional jobs, use a wide range of technology, and participate in most mainstream cultural and recreational activities. In between these two extremes lie the *transitional* groups that continue to wear plain clothing and often reject some technologies (such as television) but nonetheless engage the larger world more assertively than the traditional groups (by engaging in evangelistic practices, for example).

Some observers mistakenly believe that the Amish and Hutterites make up the traditional category and that Mennonites and Brethren make up the other two categories. Generally speaking, that is the case, but a closer look reveals a more complicated reality. For instance, the Beachy Amish are a good example of a transitional Anabaptist group; moreover, Old Order Mennonite and Old Order Brethren groups are rightly located on the traditional end of the spectrum. Indeed, Mennonite and Brethren groups can be found in all three sociological categories, and Amish and Hutterite groups can be found in two. And while it is more likely for an Anabaptist person or group to migrate from the unassimilated end of the spectrum toward the more assimilated end than vice versa, some people, and even some groups, have sought not simply to slow but to reverse the trend toward assimilation to the larger culture.

## The Demographics and Significance of North American Anabaptism

From a numerical standpoint, North American Anabaptists constitute a small percentage of North American Christianity. Although precise numbers are hard to find, one recent count of Anabaptist church membership estimated 540,000 members (if children and other nonmember participants are included, the North American Anabaptist population rises to about 860,000). Of those 540,000 members, 43 percent belong to the Mennonite tribe, 39 percent to the Brethren tribe, 16 percent to the Amish tribe, and less than 2 percent to the Hutterite tribe. Using the other categorization scheme outlined above, 67 percent of the 540,000 North American members belong to transformational churches, 13 percent to transitional churches, and 20 percent to traditional churches.

Given the greater likelihood of Anabaptist individuals and groups to move toward increased assimilation, one might conclude that the proportion of Anabaptists in the more assimilated (transformational) churches will increase over time. But that assumption fails to account for two things that traditional Anabaptist churches do better than transformational churches. First, they procreate at a higher rate; for instance, the typical Old Order Amish woman in Lancaster County, Pennsylvania, gives birth to seven children over her lifetime, four more than the average non-Amish woman in Lancaster County. Not only do Old Order families produce more children, their children are more likely to join their birth churches. In fact, many Old Order Amish communities retain 85 to 95 percent of their children.

These two factors—high birth rates and successful retention—have led to growth rates in traditional and transitional Anabaptist churches that, from 1950 to the present, have far exceeded those of most transformational Anabaptist churches. One relatively recent study charting membership changes showed that Old Order Amish churches had doubled their membership over a fifteen-year period, the Beachy Amish church had grown by 76 percent, and Old Order Mennonite churches had grown by 51 percent. Contrast this to 9 percent growth over fifteen years for the Mennonite Church and −3 percent growth for the General Conference Mennonite Church, the two largest transformational Mennonite denominations (these denominations have since reorganized to form the Mennonite Church USA and the Mennonite Church Canada). Another recent study indicated that only 30 percent of Mennonite Church USA members are under the age of forty-five, a striking contrast to the Old Order Amish of Lancaster County, in which 82 percent of the population is under the age of forty-five.

Of course, one area in which the more assimilated North American Anabaptist churches have grown and the less assimilated Anabaptist churches have not is in the realm of ethnic diversity. The traditional and transitional churches continue to be overwhelmingly Euro-American and largely Swiss-German. On the other hand, almost 25 percent of the new members who joined the Mennonite Church USA from 2001–2006 were African American, Latino, Native American, or Asian.

Whether traditional or transformational in orientation to the larger culture, Anabaptists have arguably demonstrated a significance in North America that outpaces their relatively modest numbers. On the traditional end of the spectrum, groups like the Old Order Amish have generated significant public interest for their disarmingly alternative lifestyle. Although few outsiders opt to undertake an Old Order lifestyle, the way of life the Old Order Amish represent has catalyzed significant soul-searching among those who observe it. Indeed, the Old Order Amish function as something of a religious Rorschach test for many Americans, who find various (and sometimes contradictory) meanings embedded in the Old Order lifestyle.

As for the transformational Anabaptists, their significance owes less to their visual distinctiveness than to their theological vision. In an age when many North American Christians cobble together their religious commitments, Anabaptist emphases on nonresistance, radical discipleship, simple living, and community have found a broad resonance. Moreover, socially engaged Anabaptists, drawing on long-standing Anabaptist values, have made important contributions to the emerging fields of conflict transformation and restorative justice. In some cases, transformational Anabaptists have even undertaken political advocacy, particularly with respect to war, poverty, and hunger. In these and other ways, transformational Anabaptists are challenging the dualistic assumptions that track a long history in Anabaptist life. To be sure, many North American Anabaptists continue to live as "the quiet in the land." At the same time, Anabaptists on the transformational end of the spectrum have effectively complicated the notion that quietism is an essential Anabaptist trait.

**See also** *Anabaptist Denominational Family; Moravians; Pietism; Social Ethics.*

David L. Weaver-Zercher

## BIBLIOGRAPHY

Bender, Harold S. "The Anabaptist Vision." *Mennonite Quarterly Review* 18 (1944): 67–88.

Driedger, Leo, and Donald B. Kraybill. *Mennonite Peacemaking: From Quietism to Activism.* Scottdale, Pa.: Herald Press, 1994.

Kraybill, Donald B., and C. Nelson Hostetter. *Anabaptist World USA.* Scottdale, Pa.: Herald Press, 2001.

Nolt, Steven M. *A History of the Amish.* Rev. ed. Intercourse, Pa.: Good Books, 2003.

———. "The Mennonite Eclipse." *Festival Quarterly* 19, no. 2 (Summer 1992): 8–12.

Roth, John D., and James M. Stayer, eds. *A Companion to Anabaptism and Spiritualism, 1521–1700.* Boston: Brill, 2007.

Sawatsky, Rodney James. *History and Ideology: American Mennonite Identity Definition through History.* Kitchener, Ontario, Canada: Pandora Press, 2005.

Snyder, Arnold C. *Anabaptist History and Theology: An Introduction.* Kitchener, Ontario, Canada: Pandora Press, 1995.

———. "Beyond Polygenesis: Recovering the Unity and Diversity of Anabaptist Theology." In *Essays in Anabaptist Theology*, edited by

H. Wayne Pipken, 1–33. Elkhart, Ind.: Institute of Mennonite Studies, 1994.

Stayer, James M., Werner O. Packull, and Klaus Depperman. "From Monogenesis to Polygenesis: The Historical Discussion of Anabaptist Origins." *Mennonite Quarterly Review* 49 (1975): 83–121.

van Braght, Thieleman J. *The Bloody Theatre; or, Martyrs Mirror.* 14th ed. Scottdale, Pa.: Mennonite Publishing House, 1985. First published 1660 (in Dutch).

Weaver-Zercher, David. *The Amish in the American Imagination.* Baltimore: Johns Hopkins University Press, 2001.

Yoder, John Howard. Introduction. In *The Schleitheim Confession,* edited and translated by John Howard Yoder. Scottdale, Pa.: Herald Press, 1977.

# Angels

An unorganized religion of angels, shaped by commercial and cultural forces, emerged in the United States during the twentieth century and continues into the twenty-first. Anchoring this religion is a network of about six thousand Hallmark stores and innumerable independent shops that sell angel statues, pins, ornaments, and cards in dozens of forms. Above these material angels soar angels of popular culture, literature, and art, appearing in the scores of television shows, movies, songs, books, and paintings featuring angels that have proliferated since the 1930s.

Meanwhile, the organized religions of America also emphasize angels in their own ways. Millions of evangelicals take part in spiritual warfare, in which human prayer aids Michael and his angels against Satan and his demons. New Age believers read books and attend workshops on talking with angels and take advice from those who channel angels. Mormons credit the beginning of their movement to the angel Moroni, who brought revelation to Prophet Joseph Smith and whose statue stands atop each of their temples.

All of these versions of angels share in an American tendency to see angels less as servants of God than as natural, even bodily creatures who serve humanity. Because God tends to disappear in all of these angel stories and symbols, theories, and practices, American angels exemplify the trend toward a type of faith called *transtheism*. Transtheistic faith provisionally accepts many sources of spiritual power, with a sense that some unity (which may be impersonal, as in Love or Awareness or the Force) underlies everything. The hunger for objects of transtheistic faith is so acute in the United States that Americans are constantly inventing new objects, such as the Care Bears of children's cartoons (who descend in the manner of angels from their heavenly Care-A-Lot to solve the world's problems) and superheroes such as Superman, whose powers have grown until they equal those of an angel.

A transtheistic faith in angels suits American tendencies toward pluralism and optimism. In American visions of the future, from *Star Trek* to the *Left Behind* novels, many different kinds of humans are usually pictured living on a par with angels. Statements of human equality with angels occurred in the writings and sermons of English Puritans and Spanish Conquistadors, long before there was a United States.

## From Colonial Men to Victorian Women

According to Jorge Cañizares-Esguerra in *Puritan Conquistadors* (2006), the Spanish invasions of the Americas produced accounts of war with Satan that were translated into English, and this "satanic epic" influenced English literature. The prominent roles John Milton gave to Satan, to Raphael, to Michael, and to many other angels in *Paradise Lost* reflected widespread interest among philosophers and theologians. One Milton scholar counted several dozen "substantial works" in English dealing with angels between 1640 and 1665.

In the English colonies in America, interactions between humans and angels tended to be as intimate as the scene from *Paradise Lost* in which Raphael blushed while describing angelic sex. Increase Mather's (1639–1723) *Angelographia* (1696) reported a man cured of disease by an angel who gave him a potion of "Blood wort and Red sage, steeped in small beer." Eleven years earlier, in 1685, Mather's son, Cotton Mather (1663–1728), had recorded in his diary a visit to his study by an angel. Both Mathers reported that angels and demons attended church services, helping the prayers of human saints and distracting the damned.

Though the eighteenth century brought a turn toward rationalism and the dominance of secular leaders over the clergy, angels remained prominent in service to humanity. Jonathan Edwards (1703–1758), the revivalist and theologian, wrote that the angels are "made inferior to the saints in honour" because they were created for us. Edwards also agreed with Milton in seeing the creation of humanity and the plan of the Incarnation as the reason for Satan's rebellion and added that good angels were not confirmed in their salvation until Jesus ascended to Heaven in a glorified human body.

The primary contribution of the eighteenth century to American angelology came from the Swedish mystic Emanuel Swedenborg (1688–1772), who conversed with angels in visions and recorded his findings in *Heaven and Hell* (1758). For Swedenborg, angels and demons were former humans, and their opposed influences on humanity opened the way for human freedom. He described heaven as a place with houses and people marrying each other and working, while hell was filled with mobs, slums, and brothels. Though denounced by many, Swedenborg was also widely read. His doctrines were spread across America by missionaries, including John Chapman (1774–1845), also known as "Johnny Appleseed," who distributed Swedenborgian tracts as he planted apple trees. Those who accepted Swedenborg's visions as revelation were limited to the tiny Church of the New Jerusalem, but his picture of heaven as a replica of earth prefigured that of Elizabeth Stuart Phelps in the best-selling *The Gates Ajar* (1868). The Swedenborgian idea that angels are former humans appeared both in Mormon doctrine and in the popular culture through films like *It's a Wonderful Life* (1946) and *Angels in the Outfield* (1951, 1994).

In the era from the 1800s through the 1920s, America witnessed a triumph of angels in visual art. Angels had been an exception to the rule against making graven images since biblical times, and even the Puritans put heads with wings on their tombstones. After George Washington's death in 1799, lithographs showing Washington borne into heaven by angels were reproduced for display in thousands of homes. American sculptures of angels began with marble cherubs and male youths by Horatio Greenough in the 1830s and proceeded through the massive, bronze, female *Angel of the Waters* in Central Park, New York, by Emma Stebbins (1873). Around the turn of the century, winged figures by Augustus Saint-Gaudens and Daniel Chester French created public sacred places in American cities. In the park-like cemeteries that replaced churchyards, starting with Mount Auburn in Cambridge, Massachusetts, in 1831, angels became part of the standard decoration for tombs. The trend toward monumental angels reached one of its greatest expressions in the rotunda of the Capitol at Washington, D.C., in 1865, where Constantino Brumidi painted Washington surrounded by angels as he looked down from the dome. By 1905, the Presbyterians of Pittsburgh were worshipping in a downtown church that featured eleven Tiffany windows of angels.

Angels dominated the Women's Building of the 1893 Columbian Exhibition in Chicago, where a student from the San Francisco School of Design named Alice Rideout made twelve-foot bronze female angels of Enlightenment and Innocence to set upon the roof. Inside that building, Dora Wheeler Keith painted an angel called Imagination raising her gorgeous, multicolored wings. Until the

Renaissance, when a few female angels appeared, angels in painting and sculpture had always been male, but by the late nineteenth century they had become predominantly female.

This change in the sex of angels reflected a rise of the feminine throughout the Christian world. Male artists shared and eventually took over the trend toward female angels. The thirteen angels painted by Brumidi in the Capitol dome are female. Abbott Thayer (1849–1921), a reclusive Yankee, painted his daughter Mary as an angel for the first time in 1889, probably in response to the death of his wife. The portrait, called *Angel*, has appeared on many cards and book covers, and Thayer painted Mary with wings at least twelve more times. Looking at *Angel*, one can see the same aesthetic that appears in the lingerie fashion shows that the Victoria's Secret company has broadcast since 1999, in which supermodels called Victoria's Secret Angels combine sensuality with magic, spirituality, and innocence as they walk the runway with huge wings. Daniel Chester French, the sculptor of the Lincoln Memorial, the *Minuteman* of Concord, and the John Harvard statue in Harvard Yard, made many large female angels. Ironically, the female artists who helped to make angels female, such as Emma Stebbins and Alice Rideout, were largely forgotten during the twentieth century.

Several major American writers of Victorian times wrote about angels, especially when they dealt with the problem of evil. Ralph Waldo Emerson's "Uriel," a poem of 1846, made the traditional angel of the sun his spokesman for an assertion that evil cannot be separated from good. For Edgar Allan Poe, the envy of angels explained the death of his child bride in "Annabel Lee" (1849). Herman Melville ended the sinking of the *Pequod* in *Moby Dick* (1851) with the image of a "bird of heaven" tangled with the ship and sinking "with archangelic shrieks," an evocation of Michael in his contest with Satan. In that same year, Henry Wadsworth Longfellow brought the seven angels of the planets—two of whom later observed Satan—to the birth of Jesus in a narrative poem, "The Golden Legend." Walt Whitman wrote defiant lines for Satan in "Chanting the Square Deific" (1865).

Just before his death, Mark Twain (1835–1910) wrote *Extract from Captain Stormfield's Visit to Heaven*, a satire of the heavenly vision genre that descended from Swedenborg through Victorian spiritualists. Twain's protagonist found that wings were more of a hindrance than a help, so that angels used them only on ceremonial occasions. He also discovered that angels he might glimpse at a ceremony had little interest in talking with humans who had just died. In a posthumously published work, *The Mysterious Stranger*, which Twain wrote in three different versions that were combined by an editor, a son of Satan tried to make up for the damage his father had done but ended by destroying human faith. Psychologist and philosopher William James wrote of the Earth as "our guardian angel," one among many spiritual forces, in *A Pluralistic Universe* (1909). As the age of high literature ended, the poet known as H.D. (Hilda Doolittle) wrote *A Tribute to the Angels* (1944), in which angels became explicitly transtheistic, because each angel was identified with at least one ancient god. H.D. equated Michael with Thoth, an Egyptian judge of the dead; Uriel with Zeus; and Annael (the angel of Venus) with Aphrodite and Astarte.

## Breakthrough of an Angel Religion into Mass Culture

Through three iconic works, angels descended from their dignified places on memorials and in literature to enter American mass culture. *The Littlest Angel*, written in 1939 for a radio broadcast, turned into a children's book with a Christmas market, as well as two cartoon versions and a television musical. Walt Disney's *Fantasia* (1940) presented a transtheistic universe in which Satan was the most vibrant presence. Frank Capra's *It's a Wonderful Life* (1946) set the pattern for angel therapists.

*The Littlest Angel* was written by Charles Tazewell, a descendent of Puritans who moved to Hollywood. In this story, a boy dies at four and a half and has a hard time adjusting to heaven. He causes the gatekeeper to blot his page; comes late to choir; sings off-key; and is generally disruptive until he is asked what could make him happy, and requests that a box containing his old dog's collar, a dead butterfly, a robin's egg, and two white stones be fetched from under his bed. Having this box makes him content, until he hears the news that Jesus is to be born on earth as God's son, and the angels begin to create gifts for the child. The littlest angel finds that he has no skill to make a gift. At the last moment, he is inspired to give Jesus his box, which he sets before God's throne. After God looks over the gifts the angels have made, God picks out the box and asks who has given this. Terrified, the littlest angel steps before God, certain that his shabby box has been found unworthy. God says that this box pleases him more than all the other gifts, since his son will be born as a human and learn to love such things. God then sends the box into the heavens and transforms it into the Star of Bethlehem.

Illogical as the story may appear, *The Littlest Angel* confirmed and extended the roles played by angels in America since colonial times. Angels lived to exalt the material world and to serve humanity. Making gifts for the human Jesus was the most important activity of their lives.

Through Walt Disney's *Fantasia*, Satan became a cartoon star. In the final sequence of the film, Modest Moussorgorsky's *Night on Bald Mountain* begins with the mountain of the title turning into an enormous creature with leathery, bat-like wings and yellow glowing eyes, black skin, and a muscular chest and abdomen. This figure raises souls out of a village graveyard, makes them dance, crushes them into flames, and watches as they writhe and combine with each other in more frenzied dancing. Just when it seems that the world will be swallowed into the maw of hell, dawn breaks, and each tolling of a church bell causes the Satanic figure to flinch and recoil from the light, until he wraps his wings around himself and turns again into the mountain. Without a break, the last notes of Moussorgorsky's piece blend into the opening of Franz Schubert's hymn, *Ave Maria*. The dawn mist is punctuated by a line of candles carried by white-robed figures who may be angels like the worshipful bands disrupted by the littlest angel. The procession enters a gate to a garden (that might also be a cemetery) and disappears in a golden sunrise.

According to the official Disney history of *Fantasia*, Walt Disney intended to juxtapose good and evil and to create a movie that worked on the level of fairy tales and myths. Before Satan, the damned souls, and the angels appeared, the movie had featured a sorcerer and his apprentice; magical brooms with arms and legs; Greek and Roman gods from Bacchus to Zeus, Vulcan, and Apollo; male and female centaurs; and many winged cherubs or Cupids. *Fantasia* contributed more than any film before *Star Wars* to the transtheism that underlies the religion of angels.

*It's a Wonderful Life* established the model of angels as therapists. In the story written by the filmmaker Frank Capra, a small-town banker named George Bailey, faced with a scandal and prosecution because of a shortage of funds, is about to kill himself when an old man falls from the bridge from which Bailey intended to jump. After rescuing the man, Bailey discovers that the man is an angel, sent to show Bailey what the world would have been like if he had never lived. When Bailey finds his town turned into a den of vice, abandoned homes, and slums, he resolves to go back and face whatever will happen. Bailey's neighbors rally to his side, contributing to make up for the shortage at the bank.

The angel, Clarence, who had been trying for two hundred years to earn his wings, finally succeeds.

Though *It's a Wonderful Life* was the greatest example, this pattern of angels helping people to understand themselves appeared in many films, including *Here Comes Mr. Jordan* (1941) and the remake, *Heaven Can Wait* (1978), *The Bishop's Wife* (1947) and its remake, *The Preacher's Wife* (1997), *Angels in the Outfield* (1951, 1994), and *Michael* (1996). The British reaction to *It's a Wonderful Life* showed how American it was to depict an angel in this way. One British critic called it "an embarrassment to both flesh and spirit," while another said it was "a very good film—for Americans" (Jeanine Basinger, *The It's a Wonderful Life Book*, p. 66). Beyond bad reviews, the movie had great difficulty being shown in Britain because of censorship. Censors apparently concerned with theology demanded that Capra remove all references to Jesus and Mary, all discussion of first- and second-class angels, and even the word *wings*. To illustrate the difference that had grown up between American and English sensibilities on angels, one might consider the "space trilogy" (*Out of the Silent Planet, Perelandra*, and *That Hideous Strength*) written by C. S. Lewis between 1938 and 1945, which featured angels. Whenever an angel spoke with a human in the Lewis books, the human perceived the world reeling at an angle while the angel stood straight.

### Therapy, Sex, and War in the Angel Craze of the Twentieth Century

The most therapeutic angels in American culture appeared in two television shows, Michael Landon's *Highway to Heaven*, which had a successful run from 1984 to 1989, and *Touched by an Angel*, the creation of Martha Williamson, which posted consistently high ratings between 1994 and 2003. Landon's character was a former human, a lawyer who had died young and been sent back to Earth to earn his status as an angel. Traveling with a human, a former policeman who knew his identity, "Jonathan Smith" took jobs in nursing homes, brought homeless people to protest to city government, and generally worked as a community organizer. In *Touched by an Angel*, the theologically aware, born-again Methodist producer Martha Williamson did not depict her female angels, a "case worker" and her apprentice, as former humans. These angels worked more often with personal and family problems than with social issues, although the series did touch on slavery in Sudan and terrorism. While Landon's climaxes sometimes showed villains punished for their sins, Williamson's plots usually drove toward

the moment when everyone saw that God loved them more than they could possibly know and that they should let go of whatever fear or hatred was distorting their lives. Though both shows could be offered as proof of the statement by Marx that religion is "the opium of the people," they interjected a message that God sides with those who are poor and suffering into a medium that normally celebrates violence, sexual imagery, and materialism.

While therapeutic fictions skirted the subject of angels and sex (suggested at times in *The Bishop's Wife* and *Touched by an Angel*), this ancient taboo (dating from Genesis 6) was broken in the last half of the twentieth century. A precursor appeared in 1923, when Daniel Chester French made a male angel as part of an alarmingly sexual couple in a work called *The Sons of God Saw the Daughters of Men That They Were Fair*. A few English writers and artists, particularly Edward Bourne-Jones, had sexualized angels in the nineteenth century, but in the United States angelic sex emerged as a theme of popular culture.

The theme first proliferated in popular music. Romantic songs like "Earth Angel" (black version 1954, white cover 1955), "My Special Angel" (1957, remade often), and "Teen Angel" (1960) accustomed audiences to language that made human lovers into angels. The trend continued with Bobby Vee's "Devil or Angel?" (1960), Curtis Lee's driving "Pretty Little Angel Eyes" (1961), and Shelley Fabares's longing ballad "Johnny Angel" (1962). Neil Sedaka brought angels to doo-wop with "Right Next Door to an Angel" (1962) before the innocent phase of the sixties ended. After a few years in which the Beatles, the Rolling Stones, and Bob Dylan made songs too real to be populated by angels, the metaphor returned with "Angel of the Morning" (1968), a ballad about losing virginity, and Karen Carpenter's "Close to You" (1970), which cast angels as the creators of a human lover. Then came the very first popular song celebrating a sexual relationship between a human and a real angel: "Angel" by Jimi Hendrix, released in 1971.

Two movies that included sex with demons rocked the nation. In *Rosemary's Baby* (1968), Mia Farrow played a heroine impregnated by Satan at a Black Mass. This fiction overlapped with the actual practice of Satanism, because the role of the Devil went to Anton LaVey, a Satanist leader, and the director Roman Polanski lost his wife Sharon Tate to the Satanist Manson "family" cult shortly after the film was completed. Five years later, just before the end of 1973, *The Exorcist* broke all box office records for horror films with its tale of a young girl's possession, with grossly sexual overtones. Eleven years later, sex between Satan and women moved into the realm of cultural satire with John Updike's novel *The Witches of Eastwick*, which became a 1987 movie. A human male and an angel female became a couple in a minor comedy, *Date with an Angel*, also in 1987. In Germany, 1987 brought *Wings of Desire*, a film by Wim Wenders that was remade in America as *City of Angels* (1998). In the soundtrack for *City of Angels*, musicians including the Goo Goo Dolls, Sarah McLachlan, and U2 performed songs about humans and angels that became popular hits.

Angels and sex dominated Broadway in 1993 and 1994, when Tony Kushner's two-part *Angels in America: A Gay Fantasia on National Themes* won the Tony award for Best Play. Here the Continental Principality of America, a creature with eight vaginas and a "bouquet of phalli," brought both a gay prophet and a Mormon mother to orgasm as moments in a healing ritual for the plague of AIDS. The play marked the arrival of gay men at the center of American culture, a center marked by the statue of the Angel of the Waters in New York's Central Park.

Tens of millions among Christian believers did not acknowledge that center, however. Even as *Angels in America* played Broadway and the spirits of *Touched by an Angel* began their multicultural healing ministry, many evangelicals, especially in the Pentecostal churches identified with the Third Wave or the Vineyard movement, saw angels as soldiers in a spiritual war. According to Third Wave theorists such as George C. Otis and C. Peter Wagner, fallen angels occupied many places on the Earth, especially in a rectangular "window" between 10 and 40 degrees above the equator that extended from West Africa through the Middle East and Central Asia to Japan, impeding the Christian gospel and keeping billions of souls in darkness. Angels called the "Prince of Persia" and the "Prince of Greece" in the book of Daniel still prowled the world today, possessing the leaders of Iran and inspiring hatred in Lebanon's Bekaa Valley. Because Daniel described Gabriel and Michael fighting these fallen angels, one could imagine good angels continuing their battles. Christians who adopted this worldview practiced "spiritual warfare," a kind of prayer aimed at helping the fight. In 2002, as American troops invaded Afghanistan, which is located in the "10/40 Window"—the predominantly non-Christian countries in the Eastern Hemisphere—Lieutenant General William Boykin, a founder of the Army's Delta Force, was wearing his Army uniform while showing pictures of fallen angels and giving talks on spiritual warfare at American churches.

Meanwhile, bookstores everywhere stocked spiritual warfare fiction. Frank Peretti's novel *This Present Darkness* (1986), pitting American humans and multicultural good angels against demons led by Rafar, the Prince of Babylon, sold 2.8 million copies in its first decade. Twelve novels under the title *Left Behind*, by Tim LaHaye and Jerry Jenkins, sold 60 million copies between 1995 and 2004. They did not focus on angels as much as Peretti, but they did conclude with the battle between Michael and Satan.

By the twenty-first century, angels in the United States reached a status worthy of religious symbols about which Jews, Christians, and Muslims could agree. *Crash*, the movie that won the Academy Award for Best Picture of 2004, featured a spirit that a Latino called a fairy and a Persian called a *favrashi*, or guardian angel. Advertising for the movie *Superman Returns* (2006) showed Superman in an angelic light. In virtual settings such as Second Life and World of Warcraft, Americans made winged, flying avatars for themselves. Angel channelers and therapists continued to run workshops. Books on animal angels were sold at the National Cathedral in Washington, D.C. Hallmark stores offered Willow Tree angels, Precious Moments angels, and dozens of others. American angel theorists, from William James to Mortimer Adler in *The Angels and Us* (1982), had seen their countrymen aspiring to angelhood, and they were right.

See also *Film; Literature* entries; *Popular Religion and Popular Culture* entries; *Sexuality and Sexual Identity; Visual Culture* entries.

Peter Gardella

## BIBLIOGRAPHY

Basinger, Jeanine. *The It's a Wonderful Life Book.* New York: Alfred A. Knopf, 1986.

Davidson, Gustav. *A Dictionary of Angels: Including the Fallen Angels.* New York: Free Press, 1967.

Gardella, Peter. *American Angels: Useful Spirits in the Material World.* Lawrence: University Press of Kansas, 2007.

MacGregor, Geddes. *Angels: Ministers of Grace.* New York: Paragon House, 1988.

# Anglican Tradition and Heritage

Anglicanism is the religious tradition that emerged out of the Reformation of the sixteenth century in England. It has often been something of a puzzle to outsiders (and not a few insiders). It has claimed itself to be both a Reformation and a pre-Reformation church and to embrace both Protestantism and Catholicism. Indeed, even its name is problematic. Although the term *Anglican* is universally used to refer to the movement, the name itself did not appear until the 1830s, over three hundred years after the beginnings of the English Reformation, and it reflected a distinctive development. Anglican history has been shaped by these paradoxes.

## Sixteenth and Seventeenth Centuries: Henry VIII to the Book of Common Prayer

The religious policies of Henry VIII (1491–1547) set the pattern. Although personally conservative on religious matters—he received the title "Defender of the Faith" from the pope for his treatise defending the seven sacraments—Henry's religious policies were shaped by dynastic concerns. Fearing that his Tudor dynasty could be maintained only through a male heir, by the late 1520s he recognized that such was no longer possible through his wife, Catherine of Aragon. The reason for this crisis, he came to believe, was that his marriage stood condemned since it had violated the scriptural injunction against a man wedding his brother's wife (Lev. 18:16). Catherine had earlier been betrothed to Henry's older brother, Arthur, and subsequently was permitted to marry Henry only thorough a papal dispensation. Henry sought a further papal dispensation to annul his marriage and wed Anne Boleyn. When such a dispensation was not forthcoming, Henry, through Parliament, separated the English church from Rome and declared that he was the "Supreme Head of the Church of England." Neither liturgy nor doctrine was changed, and the hierarchy of bishops and archbishops was untouched, but through a series of parliamentary acts, the English church began to go its own way. The medieval monastic houses were suppressed, with their wealth going to the Crown and Henry's supporters.

Although in no way a Protestant movement like those of the Continent, Henry's actions did provide an opportunity for those who were sympathetic with continental reform movements. Thomas Cranmer (1489–1556), archbishop of Canterbury, and others were surreptitious forces for a more Protestantized Church of England. Henry's policy was to have as advisers both conservatives and Protestants, carefully balanced, each having voice, largely for international political reasons.

Religious policy was to be reconceived after Henry's death in 1547. His first successor was his son, Edward VI. Hailed as the "new Josiah" (in reference to the Old Testament king who cleansed the Temple), Edward did attempt to push the English church in a Protestant direction. This was most dramatically seen in the reform of the liturgy, which was largely the work of Cranmer. During Edward's reign two Prayer Books were issued. The 1549 edition, while in English and having a Protestant subtext, was traditional in its form and usage. The 1552 edition, however, was more strongly Protestant. Traditional practices and beliefs were rejected, including the real presence of Christ in the Eucharist. Edward's religious policy also called for the elimination of much of the medieval fabric of the church. The marriage of clergy was permitted, and a set of Articles of Religion were drawn up, reflecting a decidedly Protestant point of view.

Edward's death in 1553 led to the accession of his half-sister, Mary Tudor. Daughter of Catherine of Aragon, Mary was dedicated to restoring the old religion. The Latin liturgy was revived, the religious orders (suppressed by her father) were reestablished, and papal authority restored. The success of Mary's campaign has been a source of debate, but two of the side effects of her actions would have a lasting impact. For many, her use of force to establish religious uniformity would link the old religion to a spirit of persecution and, in contrast, associate Protestantism with liberty. Likewise her marriage to Phillip II of Spain would tar the old religion with the mark of foreignness, while linking the new with English nationalism. The accession of Mary led a number of English men and women (the "Marian exiles") to take residence on the Continent in Rhineland cities such as Frankfurt and Geneva. There they encountered a much more rigorous form of Reformed Protestantism, which they would bring back to England with their return.

Mary's death in 1558 brought her half-sister, Elizabeth, to the throne. Elizabeth's religious policy was firmly Protestant—as the daughter of Henry and Anne Boleyn she was viewed by the papacy as illegitimate—but sought to create a national church broad enough to include sympathizers of both the old religion and the new. She combined firmly Protestant theological statements such as the Articles of Religion (revised in 1566 and published in 1572), with a liturgy that retreated from the radical Protestantism of the book of 1552. The Eucharistic office was recast to allow for, but not necessitate, a belief in the real presence. Traditional practices and vestments were emphasized to enforce continuity with the past. Lastly Elizabeth was insistent that unity was to come from common prayer and not from complete unity in doctrinal matters. Her church was to be marked by orthopraxis, not rigid orthodoxy. As she famously claimed, "I do not wish to make windows in the souls of my subjects."

This policy has been called the "Elizabethan compromise," and for the rest of the century it put the Church of England in a unique position. On the one hand the church was part of the great world of international Protestantism, participating in its struggles with Rome. Yet on the other hand the church seemed only partially reformed, clinging to many older practices. In the short run the compromise was accepted as a political necessity, but by the late 1560s some voices demanded further reformation. They called for a pruning of nonscriptural practices from the Prayer Book (for example, the ring at weddings), stripping away trappings that emphasized continuity with the past (for example, clerical vestments), and revising church discipline to resemble that found in the Reformed churches on the continent. The movement became known as Puritanism. By the 1580s these critics also advocated a rejection of the episcopate, the ruling body of bishops, in favor of the biblical polity of Presbyterianism. Among the churches breaking from Rome, England was unique in preserving an unbroken chain of bishops. (England's reformation was not limited to England itself. In Wales and Ireland the official church was also reshaped along English lines, though it never was as popular in either land, and in the latter was at best a religion of a small Anglo-Irish minority.)

In response to critics an apologetic emerged that argued for the superiority of the Elizabethan compromise. Richard Hooker, in his *Laws of Ecclesiastical Polity* (1593), challenged the narrow scripturalism of Puritan critics and called for a wide engagement with human culture. "The general and perpetual view of man," he wrote, "is as the sentence of God himself." In addition Hooker offered a defense of the piety of the Prayer Book, which emphasized the value of set prayers and aspects of worship besides merely the preaching of sermons. Others took up this defense. Lancelot Andrewes called not for the further purging of traditional practices but the restoration of them. Richard Bancroft argued that it was episcopacy and not presbyterianism that was to be found in scripture, and a true church must have a succession of bishops back to the apostles (apostolic succession). Finally William Laud, supported by King Charles I, attempted to impose these new ideas upon the larger church, along with an Arminian theology that rejected the reigning Calvinism. As a result of Laud's policy, tens of thousands of Puritans fled to the New World.

By 1637 Laud attempted to introduce his vision to Scotland. Through the influence of Charles's father, James I, episcopacy had been introduced into the Church of

Scotland, and since then episcopacy and presbyterianism had existed in uneasy tension in the Scottish church. Laud's decision in 1637 to introduce the Prayer Book into Scotland (and indeed one modeled in key ways after the more traditional 1549 edition) resulted in disruption and war between Scotland and England. This led to the rejection of Laudian policy, and eventually to the English Civil Wars, pitting king and those loyal to the church of the Elizabethan compromise against Parliament and its Puritan supporters.

The defeat of the king led to the rule of the Commonwealth, and the formal rejection of Anglicanism along with its bishops and Book of Common Prayer. Anglicanism continued nonetheless, practiced surreptitiously in England and among the exiles abroad. With the end of the Commonwealth and the restoration of the monarchy in 1660 with Charles II, Anglicanism once again became the established religion of the realm. Those who would not conform to it (Nonconformists) were ejected from their churches and denied full participation in the society. In 1662 a revision of the Book of Common Prayer was issued that not only rejected the earlier Puritan objections but strengthened sacramental practices.

Restoration Anglicanism became marked by a number of factors. The movement away from Calvinism continued, and the emphasis upon the way of salvation through the living of the Christian life was stressed. The idea that Anglicanism was a *via media,* or a middle path, between the excesses of Protestantism and Roman Catholicism was exalted, and along with it was the central importance of the episcopal succession. Finally the importance of Anglicanism as the national established religion was highlighted. To receive Communion one passed under the old medieval rood screen, but now it was topped not with a crucifix but with the symbol of the Crown. The Articles of Religion were seen as the safeguard against the entry of Nonconformists or Roman Catholics into the halls of power. The elaborate marriage of Crown and altar has been called by some scholars the "confessional state."

By the 1680s the English church began to be divided between those who took an elevated view of bishops and king (High Church), and those who took a more moderate view (Low Church). Politics again played a great role as High Church and Low Church divided as to whether one could accept James II, the Roman Catholic brother of Charles II. The Glorious Revolution of 1688 replaced James with the Protestant monarchs William and Mary. The unwillingness of many High Church clergy to affirm loyalty to William and Mary meant that these clergy were exiled, and they became known as the "nonjurors." This led to the withdrawal of support of episcopacy in Scotland, and finally, in 1715 (because of their continuing support for the exiled Stuarts), the church became subject to the Penal Laws, which imposed severe limitations on nonjuring clergy.

### Seventeenth and Eighteenth Centuries: Exporting Anglicanism to the Colonies

This convoluted history would be transported across the Atlantic as the English began to found their empire. Although Anglican chaplains undoubtedly performed on earlier exploratory expeditions, continuous services began with the founding of the English colonies. An American branch of the English church was established in Virginia in 1607, in Maryland in 1702, in South Carolina in 1704, and eventually also in North Carolina and Georgia. In some ways the colonial establishments mirrored English practices. The various colonies were divided into parishes, and ministers were paid, churches built, and glebes (farms to support the church) established, all through public funds. But the absence of an episcopate created a power vacuum, and lay governing boards, or vestries, exercised far greater control than they had in England.

By the end of the seventeenth century Anglican life in the American colonies began to become more organized. In 1689 Henry Compton, bishop of London, appointed James Blair as his personal representative, or commissary, to the church in Virginia. The commissary was to provide episcopal oversight for the clergy, yet he possessed neither episcopal sacramental powers nor any authority over laity. Eventually commissaries were active in nine of the thirteen colonies. At the same time royal governors in places such as Massachusetts and New York began to act as patrons to the church, giving it support. Finally, one of the early commissaries, Thomas Bray, on his return to England, founded two organizations that did much to quicken the life of colonial Anglicanism. In 1698 he organized the Society for Promoting Christian Knowledge, which was dedicated to founding libraries in the colonies. In 1701 he founded the Society for the Propagation of the Gospel in Foreign Parts. The SPG, as it came to be known, was the first Anglican missionary society, and it provided educated clergy for the English colonies, as well as missionaries to Native Americans. As a result of the SPG, Anglicanism took on a new vigor, particularly in areas such as the middle colonies and New England, where it previously had had little impact.

Still another source of vitality was converts. SPG missionaries such as George Keith actively promoted Anglicanism to the non-Anglican public. The most dramatic event, however, was in 1722, when Timothy Cutler, rector of Yale College; Daniel Brown, a tutor; and several other Congregational ministers, including Samuel Johnson, shocked the Congregationalist establishment by announcing their plans to seek episcopal ordination. Known as the Yale apostates, these men traveled to England, received ordination, and returned. Cutler and Johnson were particularly active as SPG missionaries, the former in Massachusetts and the latter in Connecticut. Johnson would also be appointed the first president of King's College (now Columbia University), in 1754.

Anglicanism also entered into Canada through English colonization. Explorers brought their religion from the Old World, and indeed the first service from the Book of Common Prayer on American soil was a celebration of Holy Communion at Frobisher Bay in 1578. The first Anglican church in what is now Canada was a garrison chapel at St. John's Fort, Newfoundland, sometime before 1698. The capture of Nova Scotia in 1710 led to the establishment of another Anglican center at Annapolis Royale.

The events of the middle decades of the eighteenth century would leave a marked influence on both American and Canadian Anglicanism. The religious excitement of the 1740s and 1750s, known as the Great Awakening, introduced a conversion-oriented piety to the North American scene and a distinctive religious understanding known as evangelicalism, which challenged earlier religious patterns. In the northern colonies the disruptions led many to seek Anglican churches as havens of peace in a sea of controversy. If in the northern and middle colonies the Awakening proved a boon to Anglicans, in the southern colonies it was the reverse. The conversion-oriented piety and strict biblical morality challenged the Anglican establishments and proved attractive to many. Furthermore, Baptists (leading proponents of the Awakening in the South) were critical of the very idea of an established church and labored to undermine it. Although some Anglicans, such as Devereux Jarratt, attempted to harness the new evangelical spirit for Anglicanism, and Methodist societies (at the time still formally connected to the church) tried to hold the two together, the new evangelicalism proved a challenge to the southern Anglican order.

Political developments as well would have their impact. The decades-long struggle for empire between Britain and France reached its final chapter in the conflict known in

Europe as the Seven Years' War, and in America as the French and Indian War. The result was a triumph for the British and the incorporation of French Canada into the British Empire. In 1755 British administrators ordered the evacuation of the Acadians from Nova Scotia, and in 1758 the Church of England was made the established religion. With complete victory in 1763 the formal British goal was "Anglicization," or bringing Canadian practices in line with those of Britain, and this in turn involved a privileged status for the Anglican Church. In practice, however, British governors attempted to placate the French population and its church. A formal British policy was finally established in the Quebec Act (1774). The act granted Catholics free exercise of religion, recognized the church's hierarchy, and its right to receive customary dues. It also affirmed the property rights of Catholic institutions.

## Eighteenth Century: Anglicization and the American Revolution

In what is now the United States, the end of the war left the British government with a disjointed empire that had evolved with little thought, as well as massive debt. A similar policy of Anglicization was instituted. For religious Anglicans such a policy needed to include the strengthening of the English church through the establishment of an American episcopate. Although the idea of a colonial episcopate had been floated earlier at a number times, in the 1750s and 1760s it became a leading cause for many colonial Anglicans. Throughout the northern and middle colonies a vigorous campaign for an American episcopate was launched. Leaders such as Thomas Bradbury Chandler argued against the unfairness of forcing colonials to make the dangerous Atlantic sea crossing to attain ordination.

For the descendents of the Puritans, who had been forced out of England more than a century earlier, such a campaign for episcopacy was not an issue of justice but a threat to religious liberty. Despite Chandler's insistence that all that was desired was a primitive episcopacy (that is, with none of the political powers of established English bishops), the children of the Puritans feared the episcopal persecution, from which their forefathers and mothers had fled. Opposition to bishops, along with opposition to taxes that Parliament had enacted to pay its debt, created a sense of mistrust between many non-Anglican colonists and the mother country. The passage of the Quebec Act, which granted to Roman Catholics not merely political rights but also extended the border of Canada down to the Ohio River, was a further indication

that Parliament was intent upon undermining Protestant religious liberty. Thus, as relations between Britain and the American colonies began to deteriorate, northern and middle colony Anglicans found themselves defending the Crown while their non-Anglican neighbors opposed it.

The situation was different in the southern colonies. There, enthusiasm for bishops was far less intense and almost exclusively limited to small pockets of clergy. Indeed the Virginia House of Burgesses publicly rebuked the campaign for episcopacy and its few clerical supporters. There were also signs that the Anglican churches of the southern colonies were losing support. The growing popularity of evangelicalism, on one side, and of deism, or a confidence in a religion based on reason rather than revelation, on the other, sapped lay support. In places like Virginia the reputation of the established clergy suffered from a perception of avarice. In the late 1750s some Virginia clergy had sued in order to protect their salaries, and the failure of the "Parson's Cause" weakened their reputation.

All of these tensions came to a boil with the Revolution, with northern clergy, many of whom had been shaped in the High Church theology of the SPG, lined up behind Britain. For them the Revolution was but a new phase of the seventeenth-century English Civil War, in which Puritans attacked both church and Crown, and threatened to overthrow the very order of society. A High Church cleric, Samuel Seabury, became one of the most powerful pamphleteers for the pro-British side. For others it was a matter of oaths. At ordination clergy had sworn to obey the Crown, and to faithfully use the Book of Common Prayer with its many prayers for the king. To fail to do so was to violate a sacred oath. Clergy in New England closed their churches rather than either deny their oaths or face angry patriotic crowds. Still others fled to British-occupied areas, and, in 1776, when the British reoccupied the city, New York became the center of Anglicanism in the northern colonies.

A handful of northern clergy did side with the revolutionists, and none was as important as William White. Minister of the United Parishes of Christ Church and St. Peter's Church in Philadelphia, White served as chaplain to the Continental Congress from 1777 to 1789, and he continued to be chaplain to the national Congress until it moved from Philadelphia in 1800. In contrast to the High Church northern clergy, for whom Anglicanism was an inseparable part of the British union of church and state, White believed that Anglicanism could be adapted to republican institutions.

Nowhere was Anglicanism more affected by the Revolution than in the southern colonies. The old Anglican establishments were all eliminated through an alliance of evangelicals and deists. The effects were particularly dramatic in Virginia. There, the privileged status of the colonial church was removed by degree between 1776 and 1785. With the withdrawal of public support many clergy left and the church largely collapsed, shrinking from over ninety clergy to thirteen. If this were not enough, by the 1790s the state claimed that the properties of the once-established church now belonged to the Commonwealth and not the reconstituted church.

## Eighteenth Century: After the Revolution

The two years after the British were defeated at Yorktown, Virginia, in 1781 were an uneasy time. The British controlled a few port cities such as New York; the revolutionaries possessed the rest of the colonies; and neither side could budge the other. In this stalemate two schemes for moving forward emerged among colonial Anglicans. William White's *The Case of the Episcopal Churches Considered* (1782) called for the organization of an American Episcopal Church, even if temporarily without bishops, along republican political principles. In contrast, Connecticut Anglicans believed that episcopacy was essential for any true church. Accordingly, in 1783 Connecticut Anglican clergy selected Samuel Seabury to travel to England to receive episcopal consecration. He encountered opposition there, both because of concerns about Seabury's Connecticut support and an unwillingness to ordain anyone without the oath of allegiance to the British Crown. Although having been both a defender of the British and a chaplain to a Loyalist regiment, Seabury recognized that any such oath would make an American ministry impossible. After eighteen months of frustration, he turned to the nonjuring Scottish Episcopal Church, which had been legally proscribed since the early part of the century. On November 14, 1784, Seabury was consecrated by Scottish bishops. He also signed a concordat accepting the Scottish communion office (which was more in keeping with the service of 1549), and other points. The concordat between Seabury and the Scottish bishops was momentous in the self-understanding of Anglicanism. It was the first time an "Anglican" agreement was reached without the involvement of the Church of England.

Seabury returned to Connecticut in 1785, wearing perhaps the only mitre (the ceremonial head gear of a bishop) in the Anglican world, and attempted to impose his High Church vision of Anglicanism upon the American scene. While he was doing so in New England, southern and middle state churches in 1785 organized a Protestant Episcopal Church along the principles of William White's *Case of the Episcopal Churches Considered*. Laity were included in governance, republican principles were assumed, and the power of bishops (still absent) was circumscribed. The Book of Common Prayer was also adapted for American use. Although the preface to the proposed book of 1786 stated, "this church is far from intending to depart from the Church of England in any essential point of doctrine, discipline or worship," it did take a free hand at modifying the liturgy. Two of the historic creeds were removed, key changes were made in the services of baptism and matrimony, and traditional priestly authority was modified. Many of the more radical changes did not sit well with the bishops of the Church of England and were subsequently modified. White (who had been elected bishop of Pennsylvania) and Samuel Provoost (of New York) traveled to England in 1787 and received episcopal consecration (now permissible, since Parliament had passed the Consecration of Bishops Abroad Act in 1786). Finally in 1789 Seabury came to the General Convention, and there compromises were made to unite the two wings of the American church. A separate House of Bishops (ensuring episcopal authority) was created to meet alongside a House of Deputies (containing clerical and lay members). Also, the communion office Seabury had received in Scotland was accepted. In the organization of the Protestant Episcopal Church something new entered Anglicanism—a church liturgically and theologically in continuity with the English church, but politically independent. It would be an anomaly almost unique until the twentieth century.

The disruption of the American Revolution led many Loyalists, including many Anglicans, to seek refuge in Canada. Convinced that the problems of the Thirteen Colonies had stemmed from an inadequate linking of church and empire, the British Crown took steps to put the Church of England on a firm legal footing in English-speaking Canada. Charles Inglis, one of the exiled Loyalists, was appointed bishop of Nova Scotia in 1787, and in 1791 the British Parliament secured the Church of England in British Canada. The Constitutional Act of 1791, while not establishing the Church of England, did endow it. Some individuals, such as the bishop of Nova Scotia, were paid directly by Parliament, but in addition 675,000 acres of property were set aside as a "Clergy Reserve" to support "Protestant"—that is Anglican—clergy.

## Nineteenth Century: Evangelicalism, Wesleyanism, and the Oxford Movement

Anglicanism was greatly transformed in the course of the nineteenth century. Political, imperial, theological, and social factors all contributed to reshaping the tradition. The old idea of the established church being one of the foundations of the confessional state began to weaken in the early decades of the nineteenth century. As Britain became more religiously and socially complex, the idea of the realm being held together by an established church began to be questioned. Beginning in the 1820s a series of parliamentary acts were passed granting more privileges to Roman Catholics and Protestant Nonconformists. The Test Acts were repealed, Parliament began to include non-Anglicans, and eventually the universities of Oxford and Cambridge became open to non-Anglicans. The Reform Act of 1832, which increased suffrage, created a Parliament less sympathetic to the church than ever before, and some saw the ending of the establishment. The established position of the Church of England remained (though not that of the Church of Ireland and Wales), but Anglicanism was far less central to the social and political order in 1850 than it had been earlier. The confessional state had given way to a world where religion was becoming an individual concern.

The passing of the confessional state inevitably led to a discussion of what was the nature of Anglicanism. Two theological movements within Anglicanism attempted to provide an answer. The first was evangelicalism. The interest in a conversion-oriented piety, coupled with strict personal morality first emerged in the Church of England through John Wesley. Challenged by his experience of German Pietism (in Georgia, in the American colonies, where he briefly and unsuccessfully ministered), Wesley became a fervent advocate of the religion of the heart. His Methodist movement achieved great popularity but gained little support from the powers of the Church of England. Although his societies were supposed to be fellowships within the church, official opposition was so great that by the time of Wesley's death in 1791 they had become independent churches (the split occurred earlier in America, in 1784). Others, however, attempted to encourage the evangelical spirit within the confines of the church. Anglican evangelicals such as Charles Simeon, William Wilberforce, and Hannah More argued that heart religion and biblical morality were at the core of the religion of the English Reformation. They insisted upon a seriousness of religious and moral purpose not usually characteristic of eighteenth-century Anglicanism.

Anglican evangelicals, although a minority in the church, quickly made their influence felt both in the church and the nation. They advocated reforms in manners and morals among both the high and the low of society. They actively worked to distribute Bibles to the multitudes and in doing so cooperated with non-Anglican evangelicals. They were on the forefront of missions, and the Church Missionary Society, founded in 1798, became the chief vehicle for spreading Anglican evangelicalism around the world. Finally, through the work of people like Wilberforce, they led the campaign to abolish slavery in the British Empire.

Another solution to the changing place of the Church of England was to reassert its Catholic nature. Since the end of the seventeenth century there had been a "High Church" party that had emphasized the importance of both bishops and kings. But by the early 1830s some in the High Church party took a radical turn. In the face of Parliament's attempt to reform the church (and in the case of Ireland to eliminate bishoprics), John Henry Newman, John Keble, Edward Bouverie Pusey, and others claimed that Parliament had no right to reform the church because the church was not theirs to reform. The Church of England was in fact a branch of the traditional Catholic Church and was loyal to it alone. This movement, known as the Oxford Movement, or Tractarian movement, not only opposed state dominion of the church but called for the restoration of many Catholic beliefs and practices that had slipped out of Anglicanism over the course of time. Apostolic succession, a concern for sacramentalism, and an emphasis on holiness became the hallmarks of the movement. In stressing the Catholic nature of Anglicanism, leaders of the movement ran into problems with the Protestant heritage of the English Reformation. Newman, in his *Tract XC* (1841), argued that the Articles of Religion were not Protestant as they seemed, but when read "properly" allowed for prayers for the dead, the complete sacramental system, and other Roman Catholic practices. Although Newman's tract caused an uproar (as a result of which he eventually converted to Roman Catholicism), later Anglo-Catholics—as those in the movement came to be known—continued the reincorporation of Catholic practices, such as advanced ceremonialism, and the revival of the religious orders that had been suppressed by Henry VIII.

The battle over "churchmanship" would affect the larger Anglican world. American Episcopalians recognized even earlier than their English coreligionists that such a reconceptualization was necessary if Anglicanism were to flourish in the Republic. Evangelical leaders, like Charles P.

McIlvaine, emphasized the evangelical nature of the church, while High Church leaders, such as John Henry Hobart, stressed that the church was in continuity with the primitive church of the earliest centuries.

Newman's *Tract XC,* although controversial, raised a serious question for Anglicans: What was the authority of the Articles of Religion? The Articles—a product of the Reformation era and deeply influenced by the continental Reformation—already by the seventeenth century did not reflect actual Anglican belief and practice. Their teaching on predestination was increasingly an embarrassment for most Anglicans. But the Articles were nonetheless seen as a bulwark, defending the established church, and effectively keeping out those of heterodox belief. During the eighteenth century attempts to liberalize them had been beaten back, but by the middle of the nineteenth century their role in defining Anglicanism theologically was being challenged. This was particularly the case with those who argued that Anglicanism needed to be flexible enough to respond to the changing intellectual and social world. These advocates called not for a church rigidly defined by evangelical piety, nor by a Catholic ministry, but one broad enough to include diverse opinions. In contrast to the High Church (or Catholic) vision, and the Low Church (or evangelical) vision, theirs was a vision of a broad church.

Moral uplift, intellectual openness, and a de-emphasis on doctrine characterized the Broad Church party. Its openness to new intellectual trends was reflected in the 1860 publication of *Essays and Reviews,* which introduced the English public to the new German biblical criticism that questioned not only the veracity of the literal text but also such traditional religious categories as the miraculous. Likewise, in persons such as Frederick Denison Maurice, one saw an interest in Christianity addressing the social questions of the day. The Industrial Revolution had created great disparities in wealth among the rich and the poor, creating a class antagonism that threatened the social peace. Maurice called for the church to respond with a "Christian Socialism." As Maurice famously explained, Christian socialism stood against "Unsocial Christians and Unchristian Socialists." Maurice's influence would transcend the confines of the Broad Church party and would lead many Anglicans to emphasize the role of the church in achieving a just society.

## Nineteenth Century: Worldwide Expansion

If all of these changes were not enough, the nineteenth century saw the expansion of Anglicanism into a worldwide

religion. Scholars speak of the British imperial expansion of the nineteenth century as the Second British Empire, and as the empire expanded so did Anglicanism. In places like South Africa, Australia, and New Zealand, it followed the pattern already established in North America, taking root principally within the European population. Although never a majority in these colonies, its attachment to the imperial government gave it a privileged status. But Anglicanism also expanded through its growth among indigenous populations. This kind of expansion involved controversy. The British East India Company, which governed India until the 1850s, forbad any missionary activities with the native populations, fearing such actions would create social strife and conflict that would be financially hurtful. It was not until 1813—through pressure from evangelicals led by William Wilberforce—that Parliament changed the company's charter to secure a place for missionaries.

The first five decades of the nineteenth century saw Anglicanism becoming organized in India (including in Sri Lanka and the East Indies), Australia, New Zealand, and South Africa. One factor that would be important in the later Anglican Communion was that the vast majority of those who took up the missionary cause in these decades were evangelicals. The Church Missionary Society was perhaps the most important vehicle for evangelical missions. Evangelicals were not, however, alone. A significant minority of the missions were inspired by the High Church vision of the Oxford Movement. George Selwyn, the first missionary bishop to New Zealand, for example, brought Tractarian theology to that area. In 1857 the (Anglican) University Mission to Central Africa was founded, and it became the favored missionary society among Catholic-leaning Anglicans. The High Church/Low Church divide was transferred to the colonial churches.

It was during this period that the term *Anglicanism* (and still later *Anglican Communion*) came into use. The former term, which apparently first appeared in 1838, reflected a belief that the movement growing out of the Reformation in England had evolved into something more complex than simply the Church of England. It was both less, since by 1850 barely half of English Christians continued to identify with it, and more, since it could now be found in many places in addition to the British Isles. Indeed, for a person such as John Henry Newman (who was an early advocate of the term), it was more accurately found outside England, since the continued trappings of establishment veiled its true nature. The term *Anglican Communion* was first used by an

American missionary bishop, Horatio Southgate, in 1847 to describe the worldwide spread of Anglicanism.

The complexities of this emerging communion required adaptation. It was not until 1840, through the Scottish Episcopal and Other Clergy Act, that American and Scottish clergy could legally minister in England. But the great innovation was the establishment of a meeting of the worldwide Anglican bishops. Although such a meeting had been suggested as early as 1851, by the American bishop John Henry Hopkins, its origins can be traced to the request of a synod of Canadian Anglicans to the archbishop of Canterbury, C. T. Longley. Canadian bishops were upset at the trends of modern biblical criticism, not only by the 1860 publication of *Essays and Reviews,* but also more pointedly by the publication of a work by J. W. Colenso, bishop of Natal in South Africa, questioning the Mosaic authorship of the Pentateuch. Canadians and Americans both hoped for a great legislative gathering that would authorize and define doctrine, but instead, the archbishop of Canterbury invited the bishops around the world, "not only the Home and Colonial Bishops, but all who are avowedly in communion with our Church," for united worship and common council. It was not to be a legislative session. "Such a meeting would not be competent to make declarations or lay down definitions on points of doctrine." Seventy-six bishops accepted the invitation, and in 1867 the first Lambeth Conference was held, named for the London palace of the archbishop, where the meeting took place.

By the 1880s the Lambeth Conference, and Anglicanism generally, had become involved in a new concern—church unity. An American Episcopal priest, William Reed Huntington, had published in 1870 *The Church-Idea,* calling for the uniting of American Protestantism on the basis of scripture, the sacraments of baptism and the Eucharist, the Apostolic and Nicene Creeds, and the historic episcopate. Huntington, however, had another goal in addition to church unity. These four principles, he claimed, lay at the core of Anglicanism; they were its uniting essence. Older theological statements, such as the Articles of Religion and even the Cranmerian Prayer Book, itself were of lesser importance. Huntington's four principles were taken up by the General Convention of the American Episcopal Church in its Chicago meeting of 1886. Two years later, in 1888, they were approved by the Lambeth Conference. The Chicago–Lambeth Quadrilateral, as the document came to be called, remains the official ecumenical document of the Anglican Communion, and also the boldest attempt by Anglicanism to define itself in light of its changed environment. The Lambeth Conference would continue to express interest in church unity, most particularly in its 1920 statement, an "Appeal to All Christian People."

## Twentieth Century: Ecumenical Movement and Demographic Shifts

A concern for church unity led some to go further. In the early years of the twentieth century Protestant Christians in India desired to establish a united church that would still reflect the different traditions. By the 1920s Anglicans, inspired both by the Lambeth Quadrilateral and the "Appeal to All Christian People," were participants in this plan. Although the organization of the Church of South India, in 1947, called for the introduction of an episcopate in historic succession, the decision to recognize the validity of all the ministries (and not just those who had been episcopally ordained) was a point of controversy within the Anglican Communion, and the Church of South India was admitted into full membership in the Communion only when all of its clergy had episcopal ordination.

Still another concern that began to surface was liturgical reform. With the exception of the United States and Scotland, most of the Anglican world was tied to the 1662 Book of Common Prayer, a liturgy that was neither flexible nor modern. Many could point to its problems. Anglo-Catholics found the Eucharistic service incomplete and interpolated prayers into it. Broad church clergy chafed at the picture of God found in some of the Psalms and other theological elements out of keeping with modern sensitivities. Evangelicals found the lack of venue for extemporaneous prayer frustrating. Yet to change the Prayer Book was a momentous thing. Since Anglicanism did not possess a historic confession, such as those of other churches of the sixteenth-century Reformation, the Prayer Book united them not only liturgically but theologically as well. *Lex orandi, lex credendi* (the law of prayer shapes the law of belief) was a deeply held principle. The liturgical revisions that began in the late nineteenth century and continued into the early twentieth century (America, 1892, 1928; Ireland 1878, 1928; Scotland, 1912, 1929; Canada, 1922; and so on) were conservative in nature, and attempted to preserve the Cranmerian language and structure. But, still, Prayer Book revision was controversial. After years of preparation, the revision of the 1662 Book of Common Prayer by the Church of England was rejected by Parliament, in part because of Protestant (and to a lesser extent Anglo-Catholic) objections.

Until the middle of the twentieth century the Anglican Communion, though evolving, was stable. Since most of its communicant churches were still part of the British Empire, its shape was still largely assured. Although having little actual authority, the archbishop of Canterbury was assumed to have primacy. Englishness, the Cranmerian Prayer Book, and an ethos of reasonable moderation seemed to characterize the church. A distinctive Anglican theology had emerged by the end of the nineteenth century that stood in marked contrast to a Protestantism being racked by conservative-modernist divisions and a Roman Catholicism emphasizing papal infallibility and rejecting modernism. Anglicans stressed the importance of the Incarnation, a sacramental vision of the universe, and an attempt to balance reason and faith. Theologians such as Charles Gore and William Temple demonstrated how an Anglican sense of balance and modesty, anchored in prayer, could hold the faith in changing times.

By 1945 forces were afoot that were to lead to changes in world of Anglicanism. The interest in international organizations of cooperation, such as the United Nations, in the wake of the Second World War had ecclesiastical ramifications. Many recognized that the Anglican Communion needed to be better organized if it were to be an effective force on the world scene. In 1958 Lambeth called for an executive officer to coordinate the various international efforts. In 1968 the Anglican Consultative Council was organized with representatives from every province to share information and resources. Finally, in 1978, a "Primates Meeting" was established so that the chief bishops of each province could gather for prayer and discussion. These last two organizations, along with the archbishop of Canterbury and the Lambeth Conference, would become known as the instruments of unity and would give to international Anglicanism far more structure than it had earlier. The new structure gave increased visibility to the international Anglican Communion, which by the latter part of the twentieth century was seen as the third-largest worldwide Christian body.

At the same time there were political shifts as well. The decline of British preeminence in the years after the Second World War and the ending of the British Empire were to have their impact upon Anglicanism. Anglicanism had always been held together by the solid center of the Church of England, the oldest, largest, and wealthiest of the churches of the Anglican Communion. Although in age and tradition it continued to be preeminent, the wealth and activism of the Anglican churches in North America began to shift the balance of power. It is significant that the first executive

officer chosen for the Communion, Stephen Bayne, was an American. In 1955 Canadian Anglicans formally changed the name of their church from the Church of England in Canada to the Anglican Church of Canada. At a number of key points American bishops stated they would not be subservient to the Church of England. While this was happening, the colonial churches, particularly in Africa, having become independent of England, began to grow at very rapid rates. Over the course of the twentieth century Anglicans in Uganda increased 140-fold, while Anglicans in Nigeria increased almost 700-fold. The demographic center of the Anglican world was moving south. This was occurring at a time when Anglicanism in Britain and North America was declining in membership.

These institutional and demographic changes have occurred at the same time that there has been a theological shift within Anglicanism. For centuries a key point of division was churchmanship—or whether Anglicanism was a Catholic church or a Protestant church. In the early decades of the twentieth century the vigor of the Anglo-Catholic party waxed strong, but by midcentury it had peaked; and particularly in the wake of the changes in Roman Catholicism instituted by the Second Vatican Council, Anglo-Catholics have been somewhat adrift, and questions of churchmanship have waned. But in their place have emerged issues arising from new attitudes concerning race, gender, and sexuality that came out of the 1960s.

## Twentieth and Twenty-First Centuries: Divisive Controversy over Gender Issues

Anglicanism had always had a male-only ordained ministry, and when Protestant churches first began to recognize women clergy, Anglicans refused. But by the 1960s the question of women's ministry reemerged. The Lambeth Conference of 1968 stated that there were "no conclusive theological reasons for withholding priesthood from women," a statement Catholic Anglicans would have challenged. Difficult debates occurred over the next three decades, but between 1970 and 1990 Anglicans in the United States, Canada, New Zealand, Brazil, Kenya, and Uganda all accepted the ordination of women to the priesthood. And in 1993 the Church of England did likewise. The opening of the office of the episcopate occurred more slowly. Barbara Harris became the first woman bishop in the Anglican Communion in 1989, when she was consecrated a bishop of the diocese of Massachusetts. By the end of the first decade of the twenty-first century, women bishops could be found in the churches in the United States, Canada, New Zealand, Australia, and Cuba. In 2008 the Church of England itself took decisive steps toward allowing women into the episcopate. Such decisions, however, alienated many traditionalists and pointed to a new liberal–conservative split that was replacing the older issues of churchmanship.

Despite the divisions the Anglican Communion weathered the question of the ordination of women. The Lambeth Conference of 1988 resolved that "each province respects the decision and attitudes of other provinces in the ordination or consecration of women to the episcopate," though adding that respect did not necessitate agreement. The issue of sexuality proved more difficult. From the late 1970s many Anglicans in Europe and North America began to participate in a large-scale reassessment of the traditional taboos against homosexual activities. This decision not only further exacerbated the frustrations of the conservative members in many churches, but it also provoked anger in many parts of the growing Anglican community in the Southern Hemisphere. Many of these churches had been shaped by the conservative evangelical teachings of the Church Missionary Society. Others, such as the church in Kuala Lumpur, were influenced by the charismatic renewal. Many Anglicans from the global south were critical of the apparent ease with which northern Anglicans could dispose of traditional biblical mores. In addition, many African Anglicans shared an African distaste for homosexuality. These factors erupted in the 1998 meeting of the Lambeth Conference. The conference went on record to proclaim that "homosexual practice is incompatible with Scripture." For one of the first times in its history, the Lambeth Conference spoke out against the autonomy of provinces. When, in 2003, the General Convention of the Episcopal Church affirmed the election of V. Gene Robinson (divorced, gay, and noncelibate) as bishop of New Hampshire, and when, in 2002, the Canadian Anglican diocese of New Westminster voted to permit the blessing of same-sex unions, the stage was set for a crisis within Anglicanism. What was to give way: the long cherished idea of autonomous national churches or the idea of an international Anglican Communion?

The growing concept of an international Anglican community would contribute one more aspect to the crisis. Dissident conservative congregations in the United States and Canada have attempted to disassociate from their national churches and in turn to affiliate with more conservative churches in Asia, Africa, and South America. The Anglican Church of Nigeria established a Convocation of Anglicans, an ecclesial body offering a home for conservative North American Anglicans. In 2007 the American diocese of San Joaquin (California) attempted to leave the Episcopal Church and join the province of the Southern Cone (which was made up of Anglican churches from a number of South American nations). Such actions challenged the long-honored Anglican view that there should be one church within one nation.

To address these issues the archbishop of Canterbury, Rowan Williams, established a commission, which in 2004 issued its report. The Windsor Report criticized both the churches in North America for their unilateral actions and the churches of the Southern Hemisphere for their violation of diocesan boundaries. In 2008 work began on a proposed covenant that would limit the autonomy of the individual provinces and give more coherence to the Communion. The fate of such a covenant remains unclear.

The crisis in the eighty-million-member Anglican Communion in the twenty-first century, allegedly about sexuality, is actually about the nature of Anglicanism, as the Windsor Report concluded. Can its noncreedal fellowship of churches, sharing a common liturgical structure and an English heritage, survive in a world far different from that which gave it birth?

**See also** *Anglicans in Colonial and Revolutionary America; Canada: Anglicans; Caribbean Religious Culture and Influence; Episcopalians* entries; *Gender; Latino American Religion: Mainline Protestants; Literature: Colonial; Mainline Protestants; Methodists: Tradition and Heritage; Worship: Anglican.*

Robert Bruce Mullin

### BIBLIOGRAPHY

Avis, Paul. *Anglicanism and the Christian Church: Theological Resources in Historical Perspective.* 2nd ed. London: T & T Clark, 2002.

Bernard, G. W. *The King's Reformation: Henry VIII and the Remaking of the English Church.* New Haven, Conn.: Yale University Press, 2005.

Bosher, Robert S. *The Making of the Restoration Settlement: The Influence of the Laudians, 1649–1662.* Westminster, UK: Dacre Press, 1951.

Brown, Stewart J. *The National Churches of England, Ireland, and Scotland 1801–1846.* New York: Oxford University Press, 2001.

Chadwick, Owen. *The Victorian Church.* 2 vols. New York: Oxford University Press, 1966–1970.

Chapman, Mark. *Anglicanism: A Very Short Introduction.* New York: Oxford University Press, 2006.

Doll, Peter M. *Revolution, Religion and National Identity: Imperial Anglicanism in British North America, 1745–1795.* Madison, N.J.: Fairleigh Dickinson University Press, 2000.

Hassett, Miranda K. *Anglican Communion in Crisis: How Episcopal Dissidents and Their African Allies Are Reshaping Anglicanism.* Princeton, N.J.: Princeton University Press, 2007.

Hastings, Adrian. *A History of English Christianity, 1920–1990*. 3rd ed. London: SCM Press, 1991.

Hayes, Alan L. *Anglicans in Canada: Controversies and Identity in Historical Perspective*. Urbana: University of Illinois Press, 2004.

Hylson-Smith, Kenneth. *Evangelicals in the Church of England, 1734–1984*. Edinburgh: T & T Clark, 1989.

Jacobs, W. M. *The Making of the Anglican Church Worldwide*. London: SPCK, 1997.

Lake, Peter. *Anglicans and Puritans? Presbyterianism and English Conformist Thought from Whitgift to Hooker*. London: Unwin Hyman, 1988.

MacCulloch, Diarmaid. *Thomas Cranmer*. New Haven, Conn.: Yale University Press, 1996.

Mullin, Robert Bruce. *Episcopal Vision/American Reality: High Church Theology and Social Thought in Evangelical America*. New Haven, Conn.: Yale University Press, 1986.

Platten, Stephen, ed. *Anglicanism and the Western Christian Tradition: Continuity, Change, and the Search for Communion*. Norwich, UK: Canterbury Press, 2003.

Prichard, Robert. *A History of the Episcopal Church*. Rev. ed. Harrisburg, Pa.: Morehouse, 1999.

Sachs, William L. *The Transformation of Anglicanism: From State Church to Global Communion*. Cambridge: Cambridge University Press, 1993.

Spurr, John. *The Restoration Church of England, 1646–1689*. New Haven, Conn.: Yale University Press, 1991.

Strong, Rowan. *Anglicanism and the British Empire, c1700–1850*. New York: Oxford University Press, 2007.

Sykes, Stephen, and John Booty. *The Study of Anglicanism*. Rev. ed. London: SPCK, 1998.

Ward, Kevin. *A History of Global Anglicanism*. Cambridge: Cambridge University Press, 2006.

# Anglican Worship

See *Worship: Anglican*

# Anglicans in Colonial and Revolutionary America

When English settlers began traveling to North America in the late sixteenth and early seventeenth centuries to establish colonies, they carried with them their religion—a Protestantism born of the English Reformation. Many, but by no means all, of these men and women followed the religion of England's established church, the Church of England. A hybrid creation blending reformed Protestantism and Roman Catholicism, the Anglican Church combined reformed theology with an episcopal form of church government, that is, a church governed by bishops. Some of England's North American colonies were founded by its adherents; others were founded by members of dissenting persuasions. As a result, the status of the Church of England varied from colony to colony. The Church of England in colonial North America, in fact, is best understood not as a single institution but rather as a series of institutions, each born out of the adaptation of England's established church to a variety of circumstances peculiar to the mother country's numerous Atlantic seaboard colonies.

The Church of England became the established church in several colonies, particularly those in the South. It was established by law in Virginia (by 1619), Maryland (1702), South Carolina (1706), North Carolina (1715), Georgia (1758), and in the four lower counties of New York (1693). In the other colonies it remained a dissenting faith.

## Early Seventeenth Century

The Church of England was first established in North America in Virginia, where it had been the religion of most of the settlers for over a decade before establishment. Imbued with both militant Protestantism and a firm belief that English colonization of North America had been foreordained by God, English settlers sent by the Virginia Company of London established a colony at Jamestown in April 1607. The company's charter, like the charters issued to previous colonization ventures, directed the settlers to follow the practices of the Church of England "in all fundamentall pointes." Company leaders took this charge seriously, and until its dissolution in 1624 the Virginia Company emphasized the place of religion in the colony's life. Ministers who wanted to serve in the colony had to pass a rigorous selection process, the highlight of which was a trial sermon preached before members of the company; only the most qualified ministers were accepted. Despite the rigors of this screening process, the Virginia Company nonetheless maintained a sizable number of clergy in Virginia (it sent at least twenty-two ministers between 1607 and 1624) who served the settlers' pastoral needs.

This promising start collapsed when Virginia became a royal colony, and by the end of the 1620s North America had become a missionary field for the Church of England. For much of the seventeenth century the English Church took little interest in the spiritual lives of English men and women in the colonies, and the church suffered. Too few ministers served a growing population. Colonial men who wished to become priests had to journey to England to be ordained and then back to North America. During the eighteenth century, one of every five or six postulants who made the trip died before returning to the colonies.

In the South, parishes were far larger than those in England, and ministers found it difficult to serve their widely dispersed congregations. In the middle colonies and New

England, members of the Church of England were largely dependent on the High Church–leaning Society for the Propagation of the Gospel in Foreign Parts (SPG), founded in 1701 by Maryland's commissary, Thomas Bray (1656–1730), to supply them with clergy. And while settlers may have successfully planted the Church of England's form of worship in the New World, its administrative structure was another matter. Absent guidance and support from the church's hierarchy, colonists created a hodgepodge of different forms of ecclesiastical organization for the Church of England in North America. The one common denominator was the rise of lay power over both the church and the clergy.

## Mid- to Late Seventeenth Century

By the early 1660s Virginia's General Assembly had passed laws establishing parish vestry, setting their size (twelve men), and outlining their duties. The vestries, the group of men who made decisions for the parish, and wardens, the two officers who generally carried out the vestry's duties, engaged in a number of secular and religious tasks: They chose the minister; they collected tithes to pay the minister, care for the poor, educate orphaned children, and construct or maintain church buildings; they presented moral offenders to the county courts; they maintained roads and ferries; they oversaw the processioning of lands [or "going round . . . the bounds of every person's land" in the parish at periodic intervals, usually every three or four years, and renewing the marks that separated one person's property from that of another]. Parish freeholders elected each parish's original vestry, but the vestries soon became largely closed corporations, and when vacancies arose, the vestrymen themselves rather than the parish chose a replacement. In Maryland a different system emerged. The vestries did not become closed institutions as in Virginia, but vestrymen also held far fewer powers. There the governor appointed and removed clergy, the local sheriff collected a tobacco tax that paid clergy salaries, vestries reported moral offenders, and the county courts provided for poor people. Anglican ministers in South Carolina were paid from the colony's general treasury.

In New England and the middle colonies, where the church was established only in the four lower counties of New York, the Church of England was a dissenting religion and was supported by voluntary contributions in the form of pew rents, lotteries, or subscriptions, and in some cases by funds donated by the SPG. Vestries in these areas had tremendous power over the clergy since the Church of England was not a governmental institution.

Conditions improved somewhat for the colonial Church of England in the 1670s, when Henry Compton became the bishop of London. Although the bishop of London nominally had charge of the church in the colonies, most previous incumbents of the see had done little to advance the mission of the church abroad. Compton, however, took the North American portion of his jurisdiction seriously, even calling himself the colonies' "diocesan" at one point, and introduced measures that helped increase both the quantity and the quality of men serving colonial cures. He issued instructions to colonial governors asking that they allow no minister to serve a parish without presenting a letter testifying to the parson's fitness signed either by Compton or by another English bishop.

Compton also introduced the commissary system to the church in North America. An office peculiarly suited to the administrative necessities of the medieval church, the position was fading from use in seventeenth-century England. Bishop Compton, however, recognized the utility of having commissaries (or representatives) in the colonies who could oversee the clergy and act as advocates for the church. A deputy of the bishop who acted on his behalf, a commissary could "summon the clergy, conduct visitations, administer oaths customary in ecclesiastical courts, and administer discipline to wayward clergy either by admonition, suspension or excommunication." Men appointed to the position—like James Blair of Virginia, Thomas Bray of Maryland, and Alexander Garden of South Carolina—helped to expand and strengthen the church, attract worthy ministers to the colonies, and raise clergy salaries to adequate levels. Yet since they were not bishops, they could not do the one thing that would have helped the colonial Church of England most: they could not ordain men to the priesthood. Frustrated by this enduring problem, Thomas Sherlock (bishop of London, 1748–1761) stopped appointing commissaries for colonies other than Virginia in an attempt to force Parliament to appoint a bishop for North America.

## Colonial Anglican Worship

The men and women who worshiped in the Church of England in colonial America came from all segments of society, from slaves (who often worshiped in segregated galleries or at a separate service) and indentured servants to members of elite families. They worshiped in church buildings often constructed near rivers or crossroads in an effort to facilitate attendance. In particularly large parishes, especially in the southern colonies, vestries may have had smaller chapels of ease built at convenient spots so that parishioners would not have to travel so far to attend church. In these circumstances ministers served the mother church and chapels in rotation on successive Sundays or occasionally during the week. The Reverend James Maury of Virginia referred dismissively to all the traveling his vocation required as "a post-boy's life."

The church building itself would likely have been a rectangular or cruciform edifice constructed in the Georgian style. Steeples were rare. In the rural South church buildings often resembled tobacco warehouses. In the interior of the building (particularly after the wave of religious revivals known as the First Great Awakening in the 1730s and 1740s), a two- or three-decker pulpit would have been the dominant feature and center of attention in most Anglican churches. The parish clerk used the lowest level as a reading desk from which he led the congregational responses. The minister read the lessons for the day and led the service from the second level; he preached from the third or highest level. In the sanctuary, behind and to the sides of the holy table (adorned with neither flowers nor candles), panels on the wall contained the texts of the Ten Commandments, the Lord's Prayer, the Apostles' Creed, and in some cases the Royal Arms. Parishioners sat in box-style pews, those closest to the front indicating the wealth and status of the owner.

A typical Sunday worship service in colonial America followed the Book of Common Prayer and included Morning Prayer, the Great Litany, Ante-Communion (or the Communion service through the prayer for the church militant), and a sermon. Anglican ministers generally celebrated Communion about four times each year (often on or near the three principal festivals of the church: Christmas, Easter, and Ascension), although some clergy claimed to have celebrated the sacrament six or eight times a year. Divine service lasted about ninety minutes, although some historians have suggested they lasted twice as long. The sermon, usually read from a prepared text, was often modeled on the discourses of John Tillotson, archbishop of Canterbury, 1691–1694, whose pulpit oratory shaped the Anglican sermon for decades. Colonial parsons borrowed liberally from Tillotson's published works (as well as from those of other English divines), sometimes transcribing lengthy passages from the archbishop's discourses to intersperse with their own original work. And like their model, Anglican sermons often explicated a single verse of scripture, most frequently on the one taken from the New Testament. Colonial laypeople enjoyed a good sermon and often stayed

at home on Sunday if the minister, who alone could preach an original discourse, was officiating at one of the parish's other churches or chapels of ease. Nor were parishioners reluctant to comment on the quality of sermons they heard. William Byrd II of Virginia once confided to his diary that the minister had "preached the congregation into a lethargy." Ministers sometimes commented on what they considered the inattention of their congregations as well. One Anglican minister condemned his parishioners' frequent talking, claiming that they seemed to have news "of such importance & necessity to be communicated immediately that even the duties of hearkening to God's word in the lessons & singing his praises in the Psalms must give way."

Until the advent of the Great Awakening, singing in the Church of England was largely limited to metrical Psalms, usually by 1700 to a setting in Nahum Tate and Nicholas Brady's popular "New Version" of the Psalms. In some parishes, conflict erupted when congregations and their ministers disagreed about which version to use.

In public as well as in private, the Book of Common Prayer was the single greatest influence shaping the devotional lives of colonial Anglicans; only the Bible surpassed it as the book most commonly appearing in the colonists' libraries. Its liturgy repeated weekly at public worship and read each day privately by many individuals provided a constant source of structure for the spiritual life. Congregations and individual worshippers in private repeated the Apostles' Creed and the Lord's Prayer at each office, and in the lessons appointed for each day the Bible was read through in the course of each year. Anglican liturgy, in fact, echoed the Bible, with many of its prayers crafted from the words of Holy Scripture. Day after day, week after week, the Book of Common Prayer gave voice to the same themes in the same words that called the faithful to repentance at every office and offered them the means of grace. By repeating the same words at each office and by using the same words week after week, the set liturgies in the Book of Common Prayer were intended to work a gradual transformation in the lives of the faithful. Unlike the evangelicals of the Great Awakening, Anglicans placed little emphasis on conversion and their style of worship reflected this difference. Both as a devotional work and as a service book, the Book of Common Prayer aimed less at conversion than at assisting individuals already presumed to be Christians to maintain and deepen their faith. It served as the liturgy for a people thought to be Christian by virtue of their membership in the English Commonwealth.

## Eighteenth Century

### The Great Awakening

Not everyone found this quiet and reflective liturgy a suitable means of expressing the Christian faith. Adherents of a trans-Atlantic revival movement known as the Great Awakening opposed the Church of England as well as other established churches as too formal and spiritually dead for the vital task of spreading the gospel. Rather than an enlightened religion that emphasized intellectual assent to the idea of justification by faith, the Awakening was more subjective, appealed to the emotions, and asked that believers feel within themselves the immediacy of justification by faith alone. This evangelical movement was dominated by an itinerant Church of England minister, the Reverend George Whitefield, from 1739–1740, when he made his first trip to North America, until his death in 1770. Whitefield was a tremendous orator and organizer who relied upon a dramatic style of preaching to communicate his Calvinist message. Rather than following the set liturgies in the Book of Common Prayer, he prayed extemporaneously. In addition, he emphasized the importance of the conversion experience (or "new birth") to salvation and denounced both the Church of England's episcopal form of church government and the widely popular writings of John Tillotson. With the notable exception of Virginia's commissary James Blair (c. 1655–1743), few Anglican ministers allowed Whitefield to preach from their pulpits. South Carolina's commissary, Alexander Garden (1685–1756), brought Whitefield up on charges of heresy.

The Great Awakening had a profound effect on the colonial Church of England. In the South, great numbers of people joined dissenting churches led by itinerant preachers, denounced by Anglican clergy as "strolling pretended ministers." In New England, on the other hand, some residents had grown weary of Calvinism and distrusted the Awakeners' "enthusiastical" preaching. As a result the church in New England gained members. The Reverend Timothy Cutler of Massachusetts explained: "Enthusiasm has had a long Run . . . so that many are tired of it, and if the Door were open would take Refuge in our Church from Error and Disorder." By the early 1760s another change had taken place: Some younger Anglican clergy began to accept Whitefield's preaching style, which emphasized the affections rather than logical assent to theological principles, all the while rejecting his theology. A small but influential evangelical movement that included Devereux Jarratt

(1733–1801) and Charles Clay (1745–1820) of Virginia, Samuel Peters (1735–1826) of Connecticut, Samuel Magaw (1735–1812) of Delaware, and William McClenachan (d. 1766 or 1767) of Pennsylvania thus emerged within the colonial church. Many of these men were sympathetic to the Methodist (or Wesleyan phase) of the Awakening that emerged after Whitefield's death. Like Jarratt, they were just as likely to feel betrayed when Methodists in the United States split from the Church of England in 1784.

The Great Awakening had an impact on Anglican worship in other ways as well. To emphasize the importance of the sermon, pulpits became even more important than before as church leaders had large pulpits constructed in the center-front of the church rather than to the side; sometimes the pulpit obscured the holy table from view. Hymns, although in limited numbers and hindered by the occasional arrest of ministers who allowed them, also came to the Church of England as a result of the Great Awakening.

Anglicans also established colleges to help combat the Calvinism and enthusiasm of the Great Awakening. The College of William and Mary had been founded in Virginia in 1693, in part to train colonial men to serve as Church of England ministers, but Anglican education in the middle and New England colonies lagged behind. In 1753, however, a group comprising mainly members of the Church of England founded King's College (later Columbia) in New York City on land donated by Trinity Church, Wall Street. Another majority Anglican group started the College of Philadelphia. So many students from Yale converted to Anglicanism in the 1750s that the school's president forbade students from attending the nearby Church of England parish.

### Relationships to Slaves and Native Americans

Both prior to and after the Great Awakening, individuals, rather than the institutional church, shaped Anglican efforts to Christianize African and African American slaves. Slaveholders in the seventeenth century opposed the clergy's efforts to proselytize to their chattel, convinced that slaves who received the sacrament of baptism would be freed. Indeed, a series of court cases in Virginia in the 1700s granted freedom to slaves who could prove they were Christians, thereby affirming the commonly accepted notion that Christians should not own other Christians as slaves. Ministers concerned about slaves' spiritual salvation, ironically, worked to remove this impediment to conversion, thus helping to create a pro-slavery Christianity. (Very few Anglican clergy, in fact, opposed the institution of slavery itself.) The legislatures of both Maryland and Virginia passed statutes declaring that baptism did not change a slave's civil status, and Edmund Gibson, the bishop of London, issued a pastoral letter in the 1720s further stating the sacrament's irrelevance to whether a black person was bond or free.

Nonetheless, the belief that conversion equated with freedom would not die. As late as the 1730s some colonial church leaders echoed these fears of earlier slaveholding generations, claiming that slave converts were largely insincere and that the hope of freedom was all that motivated their embrace of Christianity. Continued resistance by slave owners to Christianizing their bondmen and women meant the Church of England had a very mixed record when it came to spreading the gospel in the slave quarters. Ministers who insisted on this work were sometimes denounced as "Negro Parsons." Slaveholders argued that baptism only made slaves feel proud and that Christian slaves were less likely to work hard than others. Ministers countered this argument by claiming that Christianized slaves became better slaves, more likely to obey their earthly masters. To appease planter fears, the Reverend Francis Le Jau (1665–1717) of Goose Creek Parish in South Carolina introduced a ritual to baptisms in which slaves announced before their masters that they did not seek the sacrament in order to claim their freedom.

Anglican clergy who tried to spread the message of the gospel to Virginia's slave population received support from the Associates of Dr. Bray, a group formed in 1723–1724 to help educate and Christianize blacks in the colonies. They sent books to colonial ministers for this purpose and established schools for blacks in Philadelphia (1758); New York (1760); Williamsburg (1760); Newport, Rhode Island (1762); and Fredericksburg, Virginia (1765). The onset of the American Revolution, however, led to the collapse of this initiative.

Attempts to evangelize slaves were as individual as the relationships among particular slaves, particular masters, and particular ministers. Some masters took the duty more seriously than others, just as some slaves no doubt desired to become Christians more than others, and just as some ministers pressed the work more vigorously than others.

Anglican efforts to Christianize Native Americans ended with even more disappointing results, hampered in part by an English belief that natives should be "civilized" before they could become Christians. Despite the occasional spectacular conversion, like that of Pocahontas, daughter of the head of the Powhatan Confederacy, near the English settlement in Virginia, this harvest of souls was meager. The College of

William and Mary accepted a bequest from the will of renowned chemist Robert Boyle (1627–1691) that was intended to support Indian education, but the college's Indian school taught few native people. Perhaps the high point of missionary work among North America's indigenous people came with the career of the Reverend Henry Barclay, a missionary in the 1730s who worked among the Mohawk in New York. He learned the Mohawks' language and translated the Book of Common Prayer; he also established a series of chapels for the Indians in central New York. Barclay, however, soon became rector of Trinity Church, Wall Street, and his missionary work did not survive this change in vocations.

## Episcopacy Controversy

In the decade preceding the American Revolution no issue caused the Church of England more difficulty or revealed more clearly the varying emphases of the church in different regions of British North America than did the so-called episcopacy controversy of 1766–1767. Attempts to establish a bishop in colonial North America were not new. Archbishop William Laud had tried to settle a bishop in New England in 1638 (albeit to keep an eye on Puritans more than to help Anglicans), and the process of sending a bishop to the colonies had advanced so far in the 1670s that a charter creating a bishopric in Virginia was written. There was even some talk in the 1710s of making Commissary James Blair a suffragan bishop (a bishop without political powers).

By the 1760s frustrated clergy in the northern colonies, where the Church of England held a High Church outlook, began holding conventions to petition for the introduction of a bishop to North America. (High Church in the eighteenth and nineteenth centuries did not refer to a particular style of worship but to an emphasis on episcopacy and the necessity of the apostolic succession to a true church.) Why, they asked, could Moravians in Pennsylvania and Roman Catholics in British Quebec have bishops when members of the mother country's established church could not complete its own traditional ecclesiastical hierarchy? Members of other denominations viewed these efforts to introduce a bishop to North America in the context of the hated Stamp Act of 1765: An Anglican bishop would not only be an innovation in North America but also might introduce a form of tyranny that could threaten the civil liberties of religious dissenters. Bishops had exercised both ecclesiastical and civil powers in Great Britain for so long that opponents could simply not conceive of a bishop who exercised his authority only over members of the Church of England.

Southerners held different opinions about episcopacy as well as churchmanship. Lay vestries in the South had traditionally exercised great power over the church, and laypeople there were reluctant to concede authority to a resident bishop. Absent a bishop, the laity could continue to dominate the church; a bishop would only threaten the laity's entrenched authority. Episcopacy remained important to their understanding of Anglican identity; they just did not want a bishop in the colonies. The inconvenience of sending postulants across the Atlantic Ocean for ordination was far less important to them than was protecting the laity's control of the church.

Southern clergy also questioned the wisdom of sending a bishop to America and criticized northern clergy who asked for a bishop when northern laity offered only lukewarm support for the plan. Northern clergy in turn tarred southern ministers as unworthy men afraid that inspection by a bishop would reveal their numerous shortcomings. Ironically, support for a resident bishop was lowest in those southern colonies where the Church of England had long been the established church. Even there opponents of episcopacy sometimes viewed bishops through the lens of the Stamp Act. A South Carolina minister, for example, warned in 1765 that "it would be as unsafe for an American Bishop (if such should be appointed) to come hither, as it is at present for a distributor of the Stamps." In the end, the petitions of northern clergy and the concerns of southern laypeople meant little to the debate. After the crisis brought on by the Stamp Act, imperial authorities back in Great Britain came to believe that introducing a bishop to the North American colonies ran too great a risk of angering the colonial public and thus creating yet another crisis.

## Revolutionary War

The Church of England grew tremendously during the eighteenth century. In 1700 there were 111 Anglican parishes in colonial North America; in 1780 that number had risen to 440 parishes. The number of ministers available to serve these parishes was increasing as well. Between 1745 and the onset of the American Revolution in 1776, the bishop of London licensed just over four hundred ministers to serve colonial parishes. Colonial vocations were on the rise also. By the 1740s nearly 25 percent of Anglican clergy in the colonies had been born in North America. Despite this impressive growth, however, the Church of England was actually losing ground. In the decades after 1700, Congregationalists had increased their numbers more than five times. The increase for Baptists and Presbyterians was even greater, fourteen and seventeen times, respectively. And by percentage far fewer people worshiped in the Church of England than at the turn of the century. In 1700 approximately one-quarter of all Americans considered themselves members of Great Britain's established church; by 1775 the figure had fallen to one-ninth of the population.

Despite the ambiguous conclusions suggested by these figures, the colonial Church of England was arguably at its strongest point in the mid-1770s. The Revolutionary War, however, confronted the church with unprecedented challenges and made even more apparent the sectional divisions revealed a decade earlier during the episcopacy controversy. Clergy, for instance, found themselves in an awkward position. At their ordinations they had sworn allegiance to the king. In addition, the Act of Uniformity of 1662 required them to use the Book of Common Prayer at worship service—including its prayers for Parliament, the royal family, and the king. This obligation presented scrupulous clergy with a grave dilemma: Their ordination vows required them to pray for the king, but after the adoption of the Declaration of Independence to pray for the king as their vows demanded was to commit treason. Many southern ministers addressed this dilemma shrewdly. When southern legislatures ordered clergy not to pray for the king, many ministers resolved the question by arguing that the king deserved their prayers and allegiance only when he ruled justly.

With no bishop in North America, the Church of England in the new United States, especially in the southern states, also faced the problem of finding additional clergy to replace those who died, quit, or fled during the war. Once war formally broke out, English bishops refused to ordain men they considered rebels, thus making it even more difficult for colonial parishes to secure ministers.

Although the majority of Anglican laypeople supported the patriot cause, clergy sympathies were another matter and broke sharply along sectional lines. In New England and New York (where the vast majority of Anglican clergy were SPG missionaries) and the middle colonies, most ministers were Loyalists. One account, in fact, suggests that in the northern colonies nearly 80 percent of all clergy considered themselves Loyalists. Many received support not from their congregations but from Great Britain's Society for the Propagation of the Gospel (SPG), and those guidelines stated that ministers could be dismissed for disloyalty, thus linking clergy salaries to the British cause. Given this dilemma many northern clergy suspended services or allowed lay readers (who had not taken vows of allegiance to the king) to lead services.

According to some estimates by the end of 1776 only a handful of Anglican churches remained open in Pennsylvania, New York, Connecticut, and New Jersey. The Reverend Charles Inglis of Trinity Church in New York City wrote proudly in 1776 of the SPG missionaries in New England and the middle colonies, claiming that they "have proved themselves faithful, loyal subjects in these trying times." Churches in New England and the middle colonies did not begin to open again until 1779, after the SPG had given its missionaries tacit permission to drop prayers for the king, asking only that they not pray for the American Congress.

Southern clergy offered a more ambiguous response to the Revolution than did the Anglican clergy in New England. In Virginia and South Carolina most supported the patriot cause, while majorities in Maryland and North Carolina were Loyalists. No matter where they lived, many Loyalist ministers were persecuted by state and local committees of safety. The Reverend Jonathan Boucher of Maryland, a Loyalist, felt concerned enough to take two pistols with him when he conducted services. In Massachusetts the legislature threatened Loyalist parsons by passing legislation that made it a crime punishable by a fifty-pound fine (the approximate value of a New England minister's yearly stipend) to preach anything that might weaken support for the war. Throughout the United States approximately thirty-five ministers who supported the British cause were forced from their cures during the American Revolution. Others had their churches or rectories burned. Some, like Charles Inglis of Trinity Church, who later became the first bishop of Nova Scotia, fled the country for Canada or Great Britain. A number of ministers, patriots as well as Loyalists, served as chaplains to American and British soldiers.

One of the greatest challenges to the Church of England during the Revolutionary War came from disestablishment in those states where the church had been established before the war, primarily in the South and in New York. In some places the process was swift; in New York the legislature simply repealed the legislation that had granted the Church of England partial establishment. In other states, such as Virginia, the process was a protracted one that took the better part of thirty years to complete, ending there in the early 1800s with the partial confiscation of church property. Anglican ministers suffered financially from disestablishment: In each state where the church had been established, the legislatures voted between 1776 and 1778 to end tax support for clergy salaries. In short, disestablishment meant that in New York City and in the southern states the new

Episcopal Church would have to find a way to function as a voluntary association lacking state support. Full recovery took decades in states like Virginia and North Carolina.

## Anglicanism after the Revolution

The American Revolution also broke any remaining ties between the Church of England and the Episcopal Church and forced church leaders to create a new institutional structure to govern the Protestant Episcopal Church in the United States. (The term *Protestant Episcopal Church* had first been used in Maryland in the early 1780s.) Regional factions reflecting the church's varying theological and institutional development during the colonial period quickly emerged. A High Church party that emphasized clergy leadership and the absolute necessity of episcopacy to a "true" church led by the Reverend Samuel Seabury (1729–1796) developed in New England, while a group with a more pragmatic focus led by the Reverend William White (1748–1836) of Pennsylvania emerged in the middle states. The middle state faction (which was also supported by what remained of the church in the South) granted the laity a greater role in church governance and conceded that although episcopacy was desirable, the Episcopal Church might have to be led by "presiding clergy" elected by state conventions or "general vestries" who would carry out some episcopal duties until they could find English or Scottish bishops willing to consecrate a bishop for the United States. White suggested a three-level system of church governance in which laity and clergy shared decision-making powers at the local, regional, and national levels. The New Englanders and Seabury, who was consecrated bishop by Scottish nonjurors in 1784, objected to this form of organization, complaining that it differed little from Congregationalism, and refused to attend the General Conventions held in 1785 and 1786.

While Seabury set about organizing the church in New England, delegations from the Episcopal Church in the middle states, Virginia, and South Carolina met in Philadelphia in 1785. Led by White, the delegates drafted a constitution and an American version of the Book of Common Prayer; they sent letters to the archbishop of Canterbury and the archbishop of York asking the two prelates to consider consecrating American bishops so that the Episcopal Church could maintain the apostolic succession. In 1786 Parliament agreed to allow English bishops to consecrate men who were not British, and in response the General Convention gave White and Samuel Provoost (1742–1815) of New York permission to seek consecration as bishops. Yet even after White and Provoost returned from Great Britain, having been elevated to the episcopate in February 1787, creating a single Episcopal Church in the United States from the competing regional institutions remained a vexing challenge. The various regional churches disagreed not only on what constituted proper church polity but also about the language of the creeds and which creeds should be included in the Book of Common Prayer. The General Convention, in fact, had refused to accept the validity of Seabury's consecration to the episcopate; in at least one case, an Episcopal minister in Pennsylvania refused to open his pulpit to a minister ordained by Seabury.

At the General Convention of 1789 (the first session of which the New Englanders refused to attend), the Episcopal Church in the United States successfully crafted a degree of institutional unity. Delegates from the southern and middle states agreed to accept Seabury's consecration as valid. They also introduced a House of Bishops that would sit independently from the House of Deputies and would hold some degree of veto power over that body of clerical and lay delegates. Pleased with these and other concessions, the New Englanders attended most of the convention's second session at which the church factions came to agreement on what would become the 1789 Book of Common Prayer, the first American prayer book. The new prayer book shortened some services, agreed to retain the Nicene Creed (although some clergy complained that it included a "mystery beyond human comprehension" and the use of "regeneration" in the baptismal liturgy), retained language about Christ's descent into hell in the Apostles' Creed, and deleted the Athanasian Creed and its condemnatory language.

Although the 1789 General Convention created institutional unity for the church that allowed factions to continue their battle over the meaning of the English Reformation as members of the same church, the Episcopal Church in the United States did not achieve complete independence from the Church of England until 1792. Bishops White and Provoost had made concessions to English church leaders about the validity of Seabury's consecration and agreed not to consecrate another American bishop until a third American bishop had been consecrated in England, an event that took place in 1790, when English bishops consecrated James Madison (1749–1812) as bishop of Virginia. (Bishop Madison was a cousin of the president of the same name.) Two years later the four American bishops consecrated the first bishop of Maryland, Thomas Claggett (1743–1816), thus giving the American church full independence. It was at that time a church of about ten thousand Americans, and it faced an uncertain future.

See also *American Revolution; Anglican Tradition and Heritage; Architecture: Early America; Canada: Anglicans; Episcopalians* entries; *Establishment, Religious; Great Awakening(s); Worship: Anglican.*

Edward L. Bond

## BIBLIOGRAPHY

Anderson, Owanah. *400 Years: Anglican/Episcopal Mission among American Indians.* Cincinnati: Forward Movement Publications, 1997.

Beasley, Nicholas M. *Christian Ritual and the Creation of British Slave Societies, 1650–1780.* Athens: University of Georgia Press, 2009.

Bolton, Charles S. *Southern Anglicanism: The Church of England in Colonial South Carolina.* Westport, Conn.: Greenwood Press, 1982.

Bond, Edward L., and Joan R. Gundersen. "The Episcopal Church in Virginia, 1607–2007." *Virginia Magazine of History and Biography* 115 (2007): 164–215.

Doll, Peter M. *Revolution, Religion, and National Identity: Imperial Anglicanism in British North America, 1745–1795.* Madison, N.J.: Fairleigh Dickinson University Press, 2000.

Hatchett, Marion J. *The Making of the First American Book of Common Prayer, 1776–1789.* New York: Seabury Press, 1982.

Hein, David, and Gardiner H. Shattuck Jr. *The Episcopalians.* New York: Church Publishing, 2004.

Holmes, David L. "The Episcopal Church and the American Revolution." *Historical Magazine of the Protestant Episcopal Church* 47 (1978): 261–291.

Laing, Annette. "'Heathens and Infidels'? African Christianization and Anglicanism in the South Carolina Low Country, 1700–1750." *Religion and American Culture* 12 (2002): 197–228.

Loveland, Clara O. *The Critical Years: The Reconstitution of the Anglican Church in the United States of America, 1780–1789.* Greenwich, Conn.: Seabury Press, 1956.

Nelson, John K. *A Blessed Company: Parishes, Parsons, and Parishioners in Anglican Virginia, 1690–1776.* Chapel Hill: University of North Carolina Press, 2001.

Nelson, Louis. *The Beauty of Holiness: Anglicanism and Architecture in Colonial South Carolina.* Chapel Hill: University of North Carolina Press, 2009.

Pointer, Richard W. *Protestant Pluralism and the New York Experience.* Bloomington: Indiana University Press, 1988.

Prichard, Robert W. *A History of the Episcopal Church.* Harrisburg, Pa.: Morehouse, 1999.

Rhoden, Nancy L. *Revolutionary Anglicanism: The Colonial Church of England Clergy during the American Revolution.* New York: New York University Press, 1999.

Steiner, Bruce E. "New England Anglicanism: A Genteel Faith?" *William and Mary Quarterly* 3d ser. 27 (1970): 122–135.

Van Horne, John C., ed. *Religious Philanthropy and Colonial Slavery: The American Correspondence of the Associates of Dr. Bray, 1717–1777.* Urbana: University of Illinois Press, 1987.

White, William. *Memoirs of the Protestant Episcopal Church in the United States of America.* New York: Swords, Stanford, 1836.

Woolverton, John Frederick. *Colonial Anglicanism in North America.* Detroit: Wayne State University Press, 1984.

# Anti-Catholicism

In a speech delivered to the Greater Houston Ministerial Association on September 12, 1960, John F. Kennedy insisted, "Contrary to common newspaper usage, I am not the Catholic candidate for President. I am the Democratic Party's candidate for President who happens also to be a Catholic. I do not speak for my church on public matters—and the church does not speak for me." Kennedy's advisers hoped this speech would assuage fears among Protestant voters that were he to become president, he would be obligated to enforce Vatican edicts rather than U.S. laws. Questions about the Catholic Kennedy's loyalty to the nation loomed throughout his presidential campaign. From the moment he won the Democratic Party's nomination until he narrowly defeated Richard Nixon in November, Kennedy struggled to prove that he was a patriotic citizen committed to the separation of church and state. Both during and after the election, Nixon would insist that it was Kennedy himself who made Catholicism and religious tolerance a campaign issue. While it is true that Kennedy supporters, especially former president Harry Truman, often accused his opponents of being anti-Catholic, it is also true that Kennedy faced serious opposition from Protestants who argued that no Catholic could be trusted to hold the nation's highest executive office. In September of 1960, the National Association of Evangelicals (NAE), with the support of prominent minister Norman Vincent Peale, sponsored a conference aimed at generating antipathy toward the Catholic candidate. The conference's organizers compared Kennedy to Nikita Khrushchev in a front-page *New York Times* article, in which they also declared that the "actions and policies of the Catholic Church have given Protestants legitimate grounds for concern about having a Catholic in the White House." Even the Reverend Billy Graham, a public proponent of religious tolerance who avoided the NAE's convention and advised Nixon to keep the religion question at bay, expressed concern that a Catholic president could become a papal puppet. Kennedy's speech to the Houston ministers was thus designed to present him as a privately religious man who could maintain secular public commitments—something many Protestant Americans believed no Catholic capable of doing.

Kennedy's election to the presidency in some ways marked a turning point in U.S. political and public culture. After all, not only was Kennedy the first Catholic to win a presidential election, he was also only the second Catholic to capture a major party's nomination. But anti-Catholicism in the United States certainly did not originate with the Kennedy campaign, nor did it fully abate once that election cycle was complete. Indeed, anti-Catholicism took root in North America long before the formation of the United States, and it has long played an integral role in the shaping of U.S. culture.

## British Roots

Anti-Catholicism was, in many respects, a European and particularly British import to the Americas. In the wake of the Reformation, many colonists brought with them a deep distrust of Rome and its religion. Englishmen arriving in seventeenth-century North America were particularly invested in anti-Catholicism, in part because British Catholics and Protestants had been fighting each other since Henry VIII broke with the Church in 1533. To many English Protestants, national history since Henry's formation of the Church of England was marked by Catholic designs on English liberty. The five-year reign of Henry's Catholic daughter Mary I—or "Bloody Mary," as the Protestants called her—had brought with it not only the restoration of English ties to Rome but also the persecution and execution of many English Protestants. Fear of Catholicism's influence persisted even when Mary's Protestant sister Elizabeth I succeeded her in 1558. In 1559, English lawmakers passed the Acts of Supremacy and Uniformity, which banished priests, excluded Catholics from public employment, and made attendance at Church of England services compulsory. Protestant suspicions about Catholicism seemed only to be confirmed by rumors that Mary Stuart, the Queen of Scots and Elizabeth's Catholic cousin, held designs on the English throne. When Elizabeth had Mary beheaded in 1587, Catholic Spain retaliated with its Armada. The surprise victory of England's navy over the Armada in 1588 stood in the minds of many Englishmen as proof of Protestantism's assured ascendency. Even so, English Protestants continued to fear Catholic designs on their nation. And when Catholic revolutionaries led by Guy Fawkes were arrested in 1605 for attempting to blow up Parliament, those fears seemed less irrational paranoia than justifiable suspicion. Throughout the sixteenth and seventeenth centuries, Anglo-Protestants came to view Catholicism as a threat not only to their new system of belief but also to the sovereignty of the English nation-state.

## Colonial Anti-Catholicism

It was out of this cultural climate that the English colonists to the Americas emerged. Although those colonists often violently disagreed with each other on theological matters, Low and High Church Protestants alike feared that Catholic France or Spain would build an empire in the Western Hemisphere. Distrust of Catholics not only unified members of divergent Protestant denominations within the Americas, but it also created a link between the colonies and their home government, as the American territories largely reproduced English laws prohibiting Catholic practice. By 1700, Rhode Island was the only colony to officially afford Catholic residents full equal rights. Massachusetts passed perhaps the most aggressive anti-Catholic legislation, decreeing in 1647 that all Jesuits would be banished or, if they refused to leave, executed. Virginia officially disenfranchised its Catholics in 1642; New Hampshire enfranchised only Anglo-Protestant men; in both North and South Carolina "papists" were refused the right of "liberty of conscience"; and in even tolerant Pennsylvania Catholics were excluded from public office. Although Maryland had been founded by the Roman Catholic Lord Baltimore, it repealed its own Toleration Act in 1654 and passed a law denying Catholics legal protection in the colony. In the aftermath of the Glorious Revolution of 1688, England's new Protestant monarchs William and Mary revoked Maryland's charter altogether and established Anglicanism as the colony's official religion. Thus the thirteen colonies that would become the United States, in many respects replicated the situation in England: colonial governments and Protestant citizens viewed Catholics as a threat not only to the religious but also the political order.

## Anti-Catholicism as a Source for Revolution

Although anti-Catholicism linked England to her colonies for more than a century, in the late eighteenth century it ultimately became a source of tension between them. In June of 1774, King George III signed the Quebec Act, which legalized the practice of Roman Catholicism in the formerly French colony. The act essentially fulfilled conditions already laid out in the 1763 Treaty of Paris, which George had signed when Louis XV surrendered all Canadian territories to England at the close of the Seven Years War. But though it merely codified a decade-old promise between monarchs, the Quebec Act triggered a flurry of anti-Catholic activity. On the eve of the bill's signing, an anonymous vandal blackened the bust of George III that stood in Montreal's Place d'Arms and around its neck hung a rosary made of potatoes and bearing the inscription, "*Voilá le Pape du Canada, ou le sot Anglois*" (Behold the Pope of Canada, or the English fool). In more official channels, the

Continental Congress denounced the Quebec Act not only as "dangerous in an extreme degree to the Protestant religion," but also as threatening "the civil rights and liberties of all America." To many colonists, the King's apparent collusion with the French Catholics was just one more illustration of his disdain for the thirteen colonies. And when Thomas Jefferson drafted the Declaration of Independence in 1776, he included among the colonists' list of grievances an item accusing the crown of "abolishing the free System of English Laws in a neighbouring Province, establishing therein an Arbitrary government, and enlarging its Boundaries so as to render it at once an example and fit instrument for introducing the same absolute rule into these Colonies." The incorporation of Catholic Quebec into the English empire thus became one more reason for Protestant colonists to revolt.

## Rise of "Nativism"

In the aftermath of the Revolution, the ratification of the Constitution and Bill of Rights largely eliminated official federal persecution of and discrimination against Catholic U.S. citizens. And despite the fact that some states maintained official church establishment into the nineteenth century (Massachusetts was the last to disestablish in 1833), Catholics were increasingly granted—in theory if not always in practice—equal rights of citizenship in individual states. Suspicion of the Catholic presence in the new nation, however, did not suddenly dissipate. Although numerous Catholics joined the U.S. Army to fight against Britain in the War of 1812, Protestants retained their concern that Catholics threatened both religious liberty and national sovereignty because they would always remain primarily loyal to the Church. Thus when immigrants from "Catholic" nations such as Ireland and Germany began arriving in the Unites States in the 1820s and 1830s, the rhetoric of nativism became linked to a narrative of Catholic encroachment on the "American way of life," and the nation's long-standing but simmering anti-Catholicism resurfaced in public culture. In 1834, nativist activist Samuel F. B. Morse (coinventor of the telegraph and Morse code) published a series of letters accusing Europe's monarchs of colluding with the Catholic Church in an effort to stymie the spread of democracy in the Americas. That same year, following a series of lectures in which Lyman Beecher—famed Presbyterian clergyman and father of Harriet Beecher Stowe—claimed that the western frontier was being overrun with despotic Catholics, mob violence broke out in Charleston, Massachusetts, and resulted in the burning of an Ursuline convent. Despite the violence that his anti-Catholic invective inspired, Beecher published *A Plea for the West*, a digest of his lectures, the following year. Tales of the abuse of young girls in Catholic convents also became popular in the 1830s. In 1834, Rebecca Reed published *Six Months in a Convent*, a supposed exposé of the terrible treatment she, a Protestant, had been subjected to while a novitiate. Two years later, Maria Monk published *Awful Disclosures of the Hotel Dieu Nunnery of Montreal*, in which she claimed to have been sexually abused by priests. Although Monk's story was ultimately discredited, her book sold more copies than any other in America (besides the Bible) until the publication of *Uncle Tom's Cabin* in 1853.

## Mexican War and Italian Rebellion

Anti-Catholicism was never merely a domestic question in the United States, and in the 1840s two major events generated concern among Anglo-Protestant Americans. The first was the Mexican War (1846–1848). A complicated conflict that generated much controversy in the United States because it seemed to many an illegal war designed to increase the country's slaveholding territories, the Mexican War also reminded the American public that the nation with which it shared its southern border was populated mainly by Catholics. While some Protestants viewed the war as an opportunity to spread Protestantism into the southern parts of the hemisphere—the writer George Lippard even referred to it as "the new crusade"—others bristled at the thought of incorporating the Catholics living in northern Mexico into the United States. At the same time that the nation's southern boundary was being violently reordered, many Americans were also looking to Europe, where the protracted battle for Italian unification, or *Risorgimento*, was under way. At the heart of the Risorgimento conflict was the question of whether the pope should remain the head of the Italian states or relinquish state power to a secular authority. In a series of dispatches written from Rome for Horace Greeley's *New York Tribune*, the prominent transcendentalist thinker and women's rights advocate Margaret Fuller compared Italy's revolution against papal power to the emancipation of slaves. "I listen to the same arguments against the emancipation of Italy, that are used against the emancipation of our blacks," she wrote in 1848, "the same arguments in favor of the spoliation of Poland as for the conquest of Mexico. I find the cause of tyranny and wrong everywhere the same." Although Protestants in the United States generally supported the Italian revolutionaries, many U.S. Catholics believed that the

pope should retain civil authority. Pope Pius IX's efforts to quash the European revolutions of 1848, and the perceived support for Roman rule among American Catholics further convinced Anglo-Protestants that Catholics could never fully assimilate into secular democracy.

## Know-Nothing Party

Concern over Catholicism eventually translated into political organization. In 1843, anti-Catholic nativists formed the American Republican Party, the platform of which included a call for a twenty-one-year naturalization period for all immigrants, a banning of foreign-born citizens from public office, and mandatory reading of the King James Bible in public schools. As the Whig Party split itself apart because of slavery, and as Democrats and Republicans battled over it, the American Republican Party began to emerge as a viable third party in 1854. The party renamed itself the American Party, but critics and opponents referred to it as the Know-Nothing Party. The precise origin of the title "Know Nothing" is itself unknown, but it seems to have derived from the members' commitment to anonymity. The party drew most of its membership from two nativist organizations: Charles B. Allen's secret society the Order of the Star Spangled Banner (OSSB) and the older but less secretive Order of United Americans, which merged with the OSSB in 1852. In 1854, the Know-Nothings engineered surprise electoral victories in numerous state and local elections. The care with which the party guarded the identity of its members has made it difficult to determine precisely how many candidates it actually placed in office, but two of its biggest victories were in Maine, where the declared Know-Nothing candidate Anson Morrill won the gubernatorial seat, and Philadelphia, where the winner of the mayoral race, Robert T. Conrad, turned out to be a Know-Nothing in Whig's clothing. But the Know-Nothings' greatest achievement that year may have been architectural rather than electoral. On March 6, vandals who were likely party members stole the block of marble that Pope Pius IX had donated for the Washington Monument's interior wall. The stone, which had once been part of the Temple of Concord in Rome, was never recovered—perhaps because it ended up at the bottom of the Potomac River. Although the stone itself had enraged Protestants who believed that the secular monument should not contain stone imported from a Catholic space, its disappearance angered both Catholics and Protestants, and private donations for the monument's construction evaporated when the stone could not be recovered. Construction on the monument all but ceased until the Know-Nothing Party disappeared from the U.S. political stage four years later.

## Millard Fillmore: Know-Nothing Candidate for President

In 1856 the Know-Nothing Party made its only bid for the presidency, nominating former president Millard Fillmore to head the ticket with Andrew Jackson Donelson, nephew of Andrew Jackson, as his running mate. Fillmore was, in some respects, an odd choice for the party. For one thing, he had never actually won a presidential election: having finished out Zachary Taylor's term following his sudden death in 1850, Fillmore failed to win the Whig nomination when he came up for reelection. Even more problematic, he was not particularly sympathetic to nativist and anti-Catholic causes. The Unitarian Fillmore had enrolled his daughter in Catholic school, and in the past he had donated funds for the building of Catholic churches. The Know-Nothings chose Fillmore, however, because of his commitment to the preservation of the union and his noncommittal stance on slavery. As the Republican Party built its abolitionist platform, and as the Democrats prepared to run pro-slavery candidates, many Know-Nothings believed that Fillmore's aversion to sectionalism would resonate with voters on both sides of the Mason-Dixon Line. That year, Fillmore and Donelson ran with posters boasting the somewhat redundant slogan, "I know nothing but my country, my whole country, and nothing but my country." His campaign also attempted to damage the reputation of Republican candidate John C. Frémont by spreading rumors that he was a Catholic. Although Fillmore won 21.6 percent of the popular vote—the largest share any third-party candidate has ever received—he and Frémont both lost to Democrat James Buchanan. Following the 1856 election, the Know-Nothing Party faded from the political landscape and was essentially defunct by 1859. Most of Fillmore's supporters migrated to the Republican Party.

## Civil War

Anti-Catholicism at the national level declined substantially in the years leading up to and during the Civil War. This was partly because many northerners who had been suspicious of foreign and Catholic influence in the United States now came to see slavery as the real threat to U.S. republican principles. Also, because both the northern and southern armies required large numbers of soldiers, they simply could not afford to discriminate against Catholics. This is not to say

that religious tension entirely subsided in this period. In July of 1863, for example, a three-day riot broke out in New York City in part as a response to Congress's institution of a Union Army draft. The rioters were mainly poor and Irish men who had recently arrived in the United States. They attacked not only those running the draft itself but also wealthy New Yorkers—who could buy out of the draft—and African Americans—whom they incorrectly blamed for the war itself. To many Protestant northerners, the draft riots stood as an emblem not only of the Catholic foreigner's violent tendencies but also of his inability to integrate into the nation. Still, in general, anti-Catholic sentiment waned in this period, as attention focused increasingly on the possibility of national division.

## Republican Anti-Catholicism and the A.P.A.

In the aftermath of the war and Reconstruction, anti-Catholicism did revive in the United States, though it was not as vehement as it had been in previous decades. At the end of the 1860s, Catholic organizations suggested that the reading of the King James Bible in public schools promoted Protestantism, and they demanded that Catholic parochial schools receive a share of state funds. At the same time, Catholic charitable organizations made the case that they should be eligible for as much state aid as their Protestant counterparts. Such demands revived fears of Roman designs on the state and its resources. The Republican Party, which had absorbed many of the former Know-Nothings, took up the anti-Catholic banner and attempted to convince constituents that only it stood between the nation and Rome. Republicans as prominent as Ulysses S. Grant and Rutherford B. Hayes accused their Democratic opponents of pandering to Catholic interests and placing public education at risk. Through the 1890s anti-Catholicism remained at the center of nativist complaints, and anti-Catholic committees, fraternal organizations, and secret societies continued to flourish. Perhaps the most powerful of these groups was the American Protective Association (A.P.A), founded by Henry F. Bowers in 1891. Drawing strength from the class conflict arising from the depression of 1893, the A.P.A. instructed its members never to vote for Catholic candidates for public office and to boycott Catholic businesses and labor. It is important to note, though, that during this period anti-Catholicism both fed into and stemmed from a larger climate of nativism. If in earlier decades the figures of priest and pope represented the great threat to "American" life and politics, at the end of the nineteenth century it was the immigrant—understood in terms broader than simply Catholicism—who posed a threat to national stability. At the same time, the question of race began in many ways to supplant the question of religion in conversations about what it meant to be "American," and whiteness became an even more salient social category than Protestantism.

## Early Twentieth Century: Al Smith for President

In the early decades of the twentieth century, Catholics still often appeared to their Protestant neighbors as papal subjects ill-suited for U.S. democracy. The second, 1915 incarnation of the Ku Klux Klan—the first manifestation of which had declined in the 1870s—included Catholicism along with immigration, Judaism, and racial difference in its list of perceived threats to Americanism. Catholicism, Klansmen argued, was antithetical to American democracy, because the Catholic Church not only promoted hierarchy in its theology but also materially supported a number of monarchies in Europe. Still, in the 1920s many Protestant Americans found themselves on the same side of a political divide as their Catholic neighbors, because members of both religious groups opposed the rise of communism. It was partly this emerging sense of Catholicism as anti-communist that made it possible for Alfred E. Smith, governor of New York, to become the first Catholic to win a major party's presidential nomination, when he ran as a Democrat against Republican Herbert Hoover in 1928. Smith's candidacy inspired immediate religious controversy. Early in the campaign, Charles G. Marshall, a Protestant lawyer from New York, wrote an open letter to Smith that appeared in the *Atlantic Monthly*. The letter asked Smith to respond to charges that a Catholic president would be unable to both maintain his allegiance to the Church and uphold the Constitution's separation of church and state. In his own letter to the *Atlantic*, Smith refuted Marshall's claim, asserting that he believed in the liberty of conscience and the principles of religious liberty that the Constitution promoted. In the end, however, Smith's Catholicism—along with his opposition to Prohibition—stymied his campaign, and he lost to Hoover by the largest electoral margin in U.S. history. Three decades would pass before another Catholic, Kennedy, would represent a major party on the presidential ballot.

## Anti-Catholicism after the Second Vatican Council

Anti-Catholicism did not disappear from the American landscape in the aftermath of Kennedy's presidency and assassination, but it did cease to be a prime motivator of social and political organization. Pope John XXIII's 1962 opening of the Second Vatican Council, in which the Church adopted numerous reforms including a greater recognition of liberty of conscience and religious diversity, indicated to many Americans that Catholicism was not at odds with liberal politics. Still, in the later twentieth century, the battles that candidates for office such as Geraldine Ferraro and John Kerry have fought with the Church over issues including abortion and gay rights have given some Protestant voters pause over the Vatican's influence on Catholic politicians. When he ran for president as a Democrat in 2004, Kerry responded to questions about his faith by asserting that, like Kennedy, he would be "a president who happens to be Catholic, not a Catholic president"; but unlike Smith and Kennedy, Kerry never was asked to give a serious accounting of how his Catholicism might affect his presidency. In the end, however, the decline of organized anti-Catholicism within the American landscape in the latter part of the twentieth century may have more to do with the emergence of anti-Islamism in the aftermath of the terrorist attacks of September 11, 2001. In recent years, Islam seems to have replaced Catholicism as the dangerous religious Other in U.S. culture, and Catholicism has become increasingly aligned with Protestantism as yet another sect of Christianity.

**See also** *Anti-Semitism; Ethnicity; Immigration* entries*; Politics: Nineteenth Century; Religious Prejudice; Roman Catholicism* entries.

Elizabeth Fenton

## BIBLIOGRAPHY

Anbinder, Tyler. *Nativism and Slavery: The Northern Know Nothings and the Politics of the 1850s.* Oxford: Oxford University Press, 1992.

Billington, Ray Allen. *The Protestant Crusade 1800–1880.* New York: Macmillan, 1938.

Carty, Thomas. *A Catholic in the White House? Religion, Politics, and John F. Kennedy's Presidential Campaign.* New York: Palgrave, 2004.

Cogliano, Francis. *No King, No Popery: Anti-Catholicism in Revolutionary New England.* Westport, Conn.: Greenwood, 1995.

D'Agostino, Peter. *Rome in America: Transnational Catholic Identity from the Risorgimento to Fascism.* Chapel Hill: University of North Carolina Press, 2004.

Franchot, Jenny. *Roads to Rome: The Antebellum Protestant Encounter with the Catholic.* Berkeley: University of California Press, 1994.

Gillis, Chester. *Roman Catholicism in America.* New York: Columbia University Press, 1999.

Griffin, Susan. *Anti-Catholicism and Nineteenth-Century Fiction.* Cambridge: Cambridge University Press, 2004.

# Antinomian Controversy

"Antinomian Controversy" conventionally designates an incident in the Massachusetts Bay Colony in 1636 to 1638 about assurance of personal justification before God as a qualification for church membership. The English Puritans who settled Massachusetts in the 1630s sought to create congregations of truly godly Christians, "sifted" out from worldly people, who could commune together with Christ in the sacrament of the Lord's Supper purely. The controversy concerned the basis for sifting. "Antinomian" ("against the law"), in Christianity, refers to the perfectionist view that the moral law revealed in the Bible is irrelevant to true Christians. Few people in early Massachusetts acted on this view, though the teaching of one party suggested it. The controversy embroiled the government of the Bay, and the laity and clergy of its churches, and threatened the colony.

## Persons

The controversy centered on the Boston church and four people associated with it: John Cotton, Anne Hutchinson, Henry Vane, and John Wheelwright. Cotton (1584–1652), a prominent Puritan minister in Boston, Lincolnshire, came to Massachusetts in June 1633 and was appointed teacher of the Boston church, alongside John Wilson (c. 1591–1667), the pastor. His preaching produced a surge of new members. His views about assurance and the nature of personal conversion, and Hutchinson's version of them, became a focus of the controversy. Hutchinson (c. 1591–1643) came from Lincolnshire in May 1634 and, with her merchant husband, joined the Boston church. She believed that the Holy Spirit had taught her to distinguish true ministers of the gospel from false, so she could only hear Cotton and her brother-in-law, Wheelwright. Of godly character and a persuasive interpreter of scripture, she became sought-after in Boston for counsel about people's spiritual condition. With Cotton's approval and Vane's encouragement, she held meetings of lay people ("conventicles," an established Puritan practice) in her home to interpret Cotton's sermons. She considered herself a godly prophetess.

Vane (1613–1662), son of a prominent member of Charles I's Privy Council, arrived in October 1635, joined the Boston church, and lived with Cotton. He was made governor in March 1636 because of his English connections. He shared with Hutchinson unusual views about the "legal" character of the "letter" (verbal meaning) of scripture, of moral and pious actions considered in themselves, and the nature of Christ's union with believers. Wheelwright (c. 1592–1679), also from Lincolnshire, arrived in May 1636. He was a proponent of "free grace" and the Spirit's special witness to personal godliness. Some in the Boston congregation wished to appoint him coteacher with Cotton. John Winthrop (1588–1649), recently governor, leading citizen, and Wilson's friend, blocked it because Wheelwright's doctrine seemed odd.

In the spring of 1636, Thomas Shepard (1604–1649), pastor at Newtown (Cambridge) called Cotton's attention to questionable opinions circulating in Boston. Shepard and other ministers conferred with Cotton, Wheelwright, and Hutchinson in October and December and found Hutchinson and Wheelwright provocative. Contention became public and parties formed. Cotton, Hutchinson, Wheelwright, Vane, and their adherents in Boston distinguished themselves from Shepard, Wilson, the other ministers, Winthrop, and most of the magistrates in the General Court. The issues were whether sanctification could be evidence to a person of justification, whether created graces were active in believers, whether the Holy Spirit witnessed by means of scripture or independently, and whether the ministers were preaching a covenant of works or of grace.

## Ideas

Massachusetts Puritans made personal conversion the defining event in Christian life, generally understanding it in terms formulated by the English Puritan theologian William Ames (1576–1633). God made a "covenant of works" with Adam, whereby, if he obeyed the moral law, he would attain eternal blessedness. Adam failed to obey, fell into sinfulness, and, with his descendants, became liable to God's punishment. Before time, God elected some persons for blessedness. For their sake, he made a "covenant of grace" with Adam, whereby those who receive Christ in faith as savior attain blessedness. Faith in Christ is a divine gift, freely bestowed. In conversion ("effectual calling"), the covenant of grace becomes effective for individuals. The Holy Spirit infuses new spiritual power into the soul, freeing it from bondage to sin, enabling it to know God truly and love him as the highest good. The soul is turned from attachment to self and world toward God and holy things and is enlivened to seek these. This transformation is manifest in the act of faith, wherein the individual, abandoning attempts to earn God's reward by personal obedience, receives and wholly relies on Christ as savior. It is also manifest in personal "sanctification," that is, in God-directed actions in daily life, including

Christian "duties." Under the covenant of grace, God "justi-fies" those who take Christ in faith (accounts them forgiven and free of punishment for sin). Gracious conversion is real, but not dramatically unmistakable or complete. The con-verted struggle with sin's remnants; strength and vividness of faith vary. If genuine, faith endures, and the converted grow in grace until perfected in Heaven.

Assurance that conversion is real became an issue in Mas-sachusetts in the 1630s; and "hypocrisy"—pretending, or naively assuming, that one is actually gracious, a member of Christ, and a candidate for church membership—was a con-cern on both sides. Misplaced confidence could be eternally fatal for individuals; undiscovered, it threatened the purity of "sifted" congregations. Around 1636, Massachusetts churches began requiring candidates for membership to give a plau-sible account of the "work of grace" in themselves, and ministers preached about the marks of graciousness and the mistakes of hypocrites.

Shepard and his associates in the controversy maintained that hypocrisy could be discerned, and graciousness con-firmed, by examining one's actions in relation to motives, with guidance from the clergy. Election and justification are in God's mind, not directly knowable; but holiness is in a person as infused grace, which expresses itself. Confidence and zeal for duties change, but gracious disposition persists. The mind, by reflection, can know whether, in efforts at godliness, it truly rests on Christ for salvation and seeks to do his will out of love for God—or not. In scripture, in so-called conditional promises, God indicates that acts of faith and love characterize the blessed. Taking act, motive, and promise together, one has evidence that one's calling is "effectual" and that God accounts one justified.

Cotton drew a sharp distinction between actions of the gracious soul, as a mere creature, and the animating and revealing activity of Christ and the Holy Spirit. In conver-sion, the soul is passive. Grace empties the soul of self-righteousness; faith is a capacity of receiving Christ as savior. After receipt, the Spirit "witnesses" to the soul, in an "abso-lute promise," that it is beloved by God and justified, where-upon the person believes that this is so. This happens when a scripture verse, in which God offers grace without condi-tions, forcefully occurs to one's mind as directed to oneself. Sanctification cannot be evidence of justification, or a basis for assurance, unless one first "sees" one's justification by the Spirit's witness and knows thereby that one's sanctification is genuine. In conversion, Cotton insisted, works and grace are mutually exclusive. Sanctification involves acts of obedience.

Though gracious, these acts of a fallible creature; inferences from them are acts of created reason. As "creatures," both are insufficient apart from the Spirit's confirming testimony, above and independent of human acts and reasoning. People who, without this "seal of the Spirit," derive assurance of justification from their sanctification wrongly "go aside to" a covenant of works; their assurance is false. Those who assume that God justifies them because of their sanctifica-tion "go on in" the covenant of works. The former may be converted, but do not know; the latter are not.

## Contention

At a special court in December 1636, Governor Vane tried to resign, lest the colony's dissension incur divine judgment. The court refused and summoned the ministers for advice. Vane objected to an independent meeting of ministers to investigate Cotton's teachings. One told Vane bluntly that he was the cause of the trouble. Wilson blamed it on the new opinions in Boston, for which the Boston church formally admonished him. The court appointed January 19, 1637, as a day of fasting and humiliation.

On that day, Wheelwright preached at Boston. The only reason to fast, he declared, is Christ's absence from the churches, which occurs because his true children fail to fight his enemies. There are two kinds of professing Christians: those who belong to Christ, are under a covenant of grace, and take their assurance of justification from Christ's direct revelation of himself; and those who belong to Antichrist, are under a covenant of works, and derive assurance from works of sanctification. The former must battle the latter with the fire of the gospel. Christ's enemies are the greatest enemies of the state, so the resulting upheaval in church and com-monwealth is warranted. He cautioned those under a cove-nant of grace to preserve unity in love, deal correctly with opponents in ordinary business, and not give occasion for charges of antinomianism and libertinism. The caution reflected divergence in the Boston group between Cotton's version of "free grace" and Spirit's "witness" and more radical versions. Despite the caution, the godly at Boston, including Vane, demonstrated their opposition to "legalists"—boycotting ordinations, abstaining from militia duty, and questioning ministers' legitimacy after sermons. In public affairs, people distinguished each other as under covenants of works or grace and behaved accordingly. The Boston church refused admission to any who would not renounce their sanctification and wait for the Spirit's revelation and dispar-aged admitted members who would not do so.

Wheelwright raised the temperature. The court in March, for the safety of the state, summoned him, pressed him on his teaching about evidencing justification (Cotton defended him), and judged him guilty of sedition and contempt, for stoking contention on an occasion intended for reconciliation and for maligning the ministers. The proceeding was contentious, and the court moved the May meeting, for election of a new government, to Newtown, away from Boston. The controversy was now fully politicized. At the election meeting, Governor Vane refused to proceed without hearing a Boston petition against Wheelwright's conviction. A wrangle ensued; Winthrop led the freemen to one side and held the election. He was made governor, and the Boston faction was omitted. On a rumor that English sectaries were about to arrive, the court limited new arrivals to a three-week stay without its approval. Winthrop and Vane conducted pamphlet warfare over the court's actions and threats to appeal to the king. Cotton contemplated leaving the colony with part of his congregation. Instead, Vane, in August, returned to England, to the Boston faction's disappointment and their opponents' relief. The court, led by Winthrop, set about restoring order.

In August, the ministers met in synod for three weeks at Newtown to discuss and confute the "erroneous opinions" underlying the contention. One set of these opinions, concerning the soul's passivity in conversion and the relation of faith, justification, sanctification, and the Spirit's witness, derived from Cotton's and Wheelwright's preaching, extended by Hutchinson and her associates. Another set, reflecting Hutchinson's more radical teaching, made faith and sanctification the activity of Christ and the Spirit in the soul and assimilated sanctification, holy duties, and scripture commands to the covenant of works. Outward accommodation was achieved with Cotton.

At the November court, Wheelwright declined responsibility for public consequences of his sermon (Christ was the cause of them, he said) and refused to stop preaching. He was banished from the colony with two of his principal supporters. Hutchinson was summoned to answer the charge that she said the ministers preached a covenant of works and were not able ministers of the gospel. She dismissed the ministers' method of evidencing justification as a way to hell and explained how Christ, in scripture verses, by an "immediate" voice, had taught her how to distinguish his voice in sermons from Antichrist's. In the same way, he showed her that she must go to New England, be afflicted there, and be delivered providentially, to the ruin of the court. The court found her

the source of the troubles, convicted her of slander, and banished her. Fearing violence, it removed the colony's munitions from Boston and disarmed Wheelwright's supporters.

The controversy now wound down. The ministers visited Hutchinson, held in a private house, in hope of recovering her. She became more explicit. The consensus that had sustained the Boston congregation's sense of superior godliness collapsed. In March, the church summoned Hutchinson to revoke her errors, including that the soul is mortal; there is no resurrection of the body; resurrection is union with Christ in conversion; and there are no graces of faith or sanctification inherent in the converted, but only in Christ who acts them. The libertine and fundamentally un-Christian implications of these ideas were pointed out to her. Cotton (who supported her in court and church) formally admonished her for recalcitrance. Then she claimed, contrary to public knowledge, that she had not held these views before her house arrest. The church excommunicated her for lying. Shortly, she joined some of her associates in Rhode Island.

## Contexts

Since the late nineteenth century, the Antinomian Controversy has been a periodic topic for scholars, who tend to find in it issues current in their own times. Regarding the event in its contemporary context, the following may be noted.

Puritans held the conventional hierarchical assumptions of their time about social status and gender roles. Those assumptions allowed scope for lay activist public godliness by men and women. Hutchinson's conventicles were mostly uncontroversial until attendees challenged the spiritual character of church members and ministers. Hutchinson had active support from women. Serious sanctions—disfranchisement, disarmament, banishment, excommunication—fell principally on men. Wheelwright's and Hutchinson's main support lay among fairly prosperous, respectable people in and around Boston—freemen, officeholders, merchants. Most of them had arrived before 1634, many from Lincolnshire. "Antinomian" agitation was localized in Boston and neighboring Roxbury. Elsewhere in the Bay, clergy and laity united fairly quickly to oppose it. On both sides, laity, in churches and the General Court, was prominent in challenge and defense.

The Massachusetts group comprised the first Puritans to enjoy political power and the opportunity of actualizing the godly church in a Puritan society. How godly might it be? They arrived intending to enjoy "Christ's ordinances" free of human corruption and regarded the gathered congregation as the form of the true church. In the mid-1630s, they took the further step toward a "sifted" congregation of the inwardly godly. The Boston church, stimulated by Cotton's teaching about grace versus works and the Spirit's special witness, drew the circle of godliness very tightly, to the point of challenging the legitimacy of other congregations. Cotton was not a separatist, but after they lost the political contest, Hutchinson's prominent supporters fairly readily removed to Rhode Island to enjoy godly purity. One result of the controversy was the organization, and containment, of the sectarian urge for purity in a combination of government supervision of churches, mutual consultations of ministers, and lay control of church membership based on personal profession of inward godliness. With variations, this combination became "the New England way" of congregational church polity into the next century.

English Puritans, in the 1620s, had an "antinomian controversy" of their own. Preachers in London and elsewhere propagated a gospel of "free justification" without works, personal "union with Christ," and relief from pious moral scrupulosity. Puritan polemicists called them "antinomians" and "familists" (alluding to the Family of Love, a sixteenth-century Dutch sect). These terms together covered a loose set of propositions distinguishing sharply between covenants of works and grace, subordinating human activity to divine, and rejecting "legal" obedience. Vane's and Hutchinson's more striking notions, and Wheelwright's more excited ones, belonged to this set. Cotton's teaching tended toward it and stimulated local variants. Winthrop, Shepard, and Cotton knew people on the radical side in England. When Shepard sounded Cotton, in 1636, about strange notions at Boston, he did so with such a sense of recognition and of puzzlement that Cotton seemed not to notice them. The Massachusetts incident echoed this preexistent intra- and semi-Puritan religious radicalism.

Around 1600, Puritan pastors worked out a program of introspective disciplinary piety, propagated in handbooks and organized in rituals of self-examination. Their aim was God-directed living, as application of biblical precepts to Christian life, by means of deliberate resistance to worldliness and sensuality and carefulness about thoughts and acts. This intensive piety defined conduct for the Puritan subculture and defined the content of inward godliness. In relation to the doctrine of divine election, it was a source of both assurance and anxiety. In England in the 1620s, it stimulated an "antinomian" reaction, in the name of "free justification" by Christ's righteousness, independent of "legal" efforts at personal obedience. The Massachusetts incident was part of this reaction. Tell us not of graces, duties, and meditation (said some in Cotton's congregation), but tell us of Christ! That the incident centered in and around Boston, and was transient, suggests that the pious program worked relatively well for others in the colony.

Massachusetts Puritans believed that God truly regenerates individuals, in conversion, and works in harmony with their created natures. Infused grace restores the "image of God" in which Adam was created, as deliberate agent, enlightening understanding and liberating will, to take Christ and obey his commands. Original nature is not replaced but reborn in its essential character. Conversion is God's work, but the content of it is in the person, as a new disposition, a real moral renewal. "Antinomians" talked of direct acts of the Trinity, independent of regenerate mind and of radical newness different from created nature. The "new creature" is not Adam's image renovated (which the unconverted may have and perish) but Christ personally indwelling. Cotton and Wheelwright held that graces of faith and holiness inhere in the regenerate; but only the Spirit's testimony, revealing free pardon immediately, "above" any creature, can certify both. No, said Shepard: Christ's greatest work is to change the hearts of the converted, not just their acts, and created minds can know it. "Antinomians" seemed to deny that God regenerates *persons* and therein to invoke a different model of God's relation to created souls than the conventional Puritan one. That the conventional model was a social idealization, imposed on ordinary mental and social life, ensured that it was experienced ambiguously. "Antinomian" responses to the ambiguity pressed the edge of a widely held Puritan and reformed Protestant worldview.

**See also** *Calvinist/Reformed Tradition and Heritage; Congregationalists; Establishment, Religious; Presbyterians* entries*; Puritans; Reformed Denominational Family; Religious Thought: Reformed Protestant.*

William K. B. Stoever

## BIBLIOGRAPHY

Bozeman, Theodore D. *The Precisionist Strain: Disciplinary Religion and Antinomian Backlash in Puritanism to 1638.* Chapel Hill: University of North Carolina Press, 2004.

Como, David R. *Blown by the Spirit: Puritanism and the Emergence of an Antinomian Underground in pre-Civil-War England.* Stanford, Calif.: Stanford University Press, 2004.

Foster, Stephen. *The Long Argument: English Puritanism and the Shaping of New England Culture, 1570–1700.* Chapel Hill: University of North Carolina Press, 1991.

Gura, Philip F. *A Glimpse of Sion's Glory: Puritan Radicalism in New England, 1620–1660.* Middletown, Conn.: Wesleyan University Press, 1984.

Hall, David D., ed. *The Antinomian Controversy, 1636–1638: A Documentary History.* Middletown, Conn.: Wesleyan University Press, 1968.

Stoever, William K. B. *"A Faire and Easie Way to Heaven": Covenant Theology and Antinomianism in Early Massachusetts.* Middletown, Conn.: Wesleyan University Press, 1978.

Winship, Michael P. *Making Heretics: Militant Protestantism and Free Grace in Massachusetts, 1636–1641.* Princeton, N.J.: Princeton University Press, 2002.

# Anti-Semitism

Anti-Semitism refers to an act, feeling, or idea that displays aversion or animosity towards Jews solely on the basis of religion or ethnicity. Anti-Semitism is rooted in, and gives rise to, religious intolerance or racial persecution, legal discrimination or casual disdain, political division or theological dispute. Its proponents ascribe negative motives to Jews, fear incursion of Jews into the Christian domain, blame Jews for suffering that is not fully comprehended, and attribute a menacing quality to the survival of Jews. Prejudicial attitudes toward Jewish individuals have sometimes included stereotypes that Jews are greedy, clannish, and demonic. Less poisonous than its counterparts elsewhere, American anti-Semitism has nonetheless found favor over the years with political groups ranging from right- to left-wing, with ethnic groups from Anglo-Saxon Protestant to African American, with organizations ranging from country clubs to labor unions, and with religious organizations from Southern Baptists to the Nation of Islam.

Economic competition and resentment have stirred antagonism toward Jews and included charges that Jews are communist or capitalist exploiters. However, several factors have diminished the potency of American anti-Semitism. Jews acquired equal rights under the law—albeit unevenly—alongside white (Caucasian) ethnicities. The constitutional clause prohibiting the establishment of religion by the federal government fostered a pluralism of religious association. Social patterns in the United States are crosscut with so many ethnic, national, and religious differences that Jews do not stand out particularly; and the congregational decentralization of Judaism fits as comfortably into a predominantly Protestant landscape as either Catholicism or Mormonism.

Anti-Semitism has two sides, approaching Jews in two related but distinct ways: it places Jews within a shared social framework but outside the powerful classes, an ethnocentric view; and it places Jews outside society as an external threat, a xenophobic view. While the ethnocentric view has taken precedence over the course of U.S. history, during periods of social disruption, such as wartime, the xenophobic view has sometimes come to dominate.

## Historical Dimensions

In the late nineteenth century, the German term *Antisemitismus* was coined to give a more "objective" ring to hatred of Jews than the Greek *judaeophobia*. Whether feeling or principle, and having an ancient tradition with a record of evidence in Egypt and Rome, anti-Semitism was shaped by Christian belief over many centuries before Jews landed on North American soil. While some Christian tradition identifies the Romans under Pontius Pilate as responsible for Christ's Crucifixion, other traditions believed Jews were guilty, which meant that Jews could justifiably suffer punishments in the form of special taxes, restrictions, execution, or expulsion. In medieval Europe, Jews were accused of ritual murder (the blood libel), host piercing, and well poisoning. The sixteenth century marked a dividing point: the Spanish doctrine of blood purity subordinated Jews to Christian rule, whereas freedom to reside and worship was offered in the Netherlands and England. The historical consensus is that the modern period in Europe was characterized by the expectation that in exchange for rights under the law, Jews would reject at least some aspects of their Jewishness; the dynamic of Jewish emancipation did not proceed without anti-Semitism.

### From Settlements to States

Signals were mixed from the start about how to identify Jews amidst the early European settlers of the New World. On the one hand, Jews were never targets of genocidal policies or slavery. On the other hand, Jews did not adopt Christianity as had many Native Americans and African Americans. Upon the 1654 arrival of twenty-three Portuguese Jews to New Netherland, a Dutch West India Company enterprise, Governor Peter Stuyvesant requested expelling "the deceitful race—such hateful enemies and blasphemers in the name of Christ," because they would open doors to Lutherans and Papists; but company directors under pressure from Amsterdam Jews lifted restrictions on Jewish settlement and trade. Divines condemned Jews for deviousness and Catholics condemned Jews for their devilishness. In the only recorded legal case involving religious discrimination, the state of Maryland charged but did not convict a Jew for the crime of blasphemy in 1658. However,

British and Dutch territories relieved Jews of the many restrictions that were placed on them in Europe. In a sign of appreciation that paradoxically rendered the Jews archaic, and silent, Puritan leaders of New England romanticized the ancient Israelites. The Jews were seen as outsiders from American society who posed a modest threat to Christian purity, but even so, they were beneficial interlopers whose trading networks extended widely.

When England granted conditional citizenship to colonial Jews in 1740, the colonies differed in their treatment of these citizens; political enfranchisement of the Jews was slow, if steady. Soon after the ratification of the Constitution, Delaware, Georgia, Pennsylvania, and South Carolina allowed Jews to vote. Yet many of the states had religious tests for holding public office. Connecticut, Maryland, Massachusetts, New Hampshire, and South Carolina maintained state-established churches. Not until New Hampshire lifted restrictions in 1877 could Jews vote in every state of the union. Allowance for Jews to serve in public office followed a slow path, including a protracted contest over the "Jew Bill" Maryland passed in 1826, finally allowing Jews to hold office in that state.

By 1790, fewer than two thousand Jews (of roughly four million worldwide) resided in the United States, mostly in Charleston, New York, Philadelphia, and Newport. Perhaps because of the small size and productivity of the Jewish population, ideas broadcast through newspapers about Jewish institutions were not particularly unwelcoming. Nevertheless, discrimination against Jews did surface in commercial suits. Also, ministers and politicians occasionally displayed their distrust of Jews, mainly on the basis of their outsider status.

## The Early Republic

The early Republic witnessed a shift in which Jews came to be viewed less as outsiders than as a distinctive group within American society; however, they were perceived as a threat to social and religious cohesion. George Washington honored synagogues with visits; Presidents John and John Quincy Adams expressed mixed feelings about Jews; Thomas Jefferson maligned the Jews. Whereas laws eradicated oaths testing the faith of political officeholders, Jews were commonly associated with internal and external plots (for example, Jacobin, Jeffersonian, Federalist) to undermine the states. Although every state eventually disestablished its church, revivalists of the Second Great Awakening actively sought Jews to convert. Journalism traded in stock figures of the Jewish usurer and peddler, and yet President Fillmore defended equal treatment of Jews under the law. In short, as Frederic Cople Jaher puts

it in *A Scapegoat in the New Wilderness*, Jews, though "insulted," were scarcely "assaulted" (p. 169). Shakespeare's Shylock was performed sympathetically onstage.

## The Nineteenth Century

From 1830 to 1860, mass migration increased the number of Jews, especially from Germany (often industrious and skilled), and fostered a new wave of anti-Jewish prejudice. Jews played prominent roles on both sides of the Civil War: for example, the politician Judah P. Benjamin served as Confederate Secretary of War and then State, and the banker Joseph Seligman prominently helped finance the Union effort. Each side disdained Jews for some reason and charged them with having the stereotypical traits of the *parvenu*, moneylender, or pawnbroker. In one of the few anti-Semitic acts of the Union, Ulysses S. Grant's Order #11 expelled the Jews from Kentucky, Tennessee, and Mississippi, ostensibly on the grounds of illegal trading; however, Lincoln, on the argument that the Constitution prohibited singling out a group for collective guilt without a trial, commanded the order rescinded. Nevertheless, commercial discrimination was widespread, bursting into occasional violence. The worsening economy and a religious revival provided a context for accusations of ritual murder and deicide to take hold. Slanders were printed in newspapers, which conjured the phrase "to out-Jew the Jew" and the verb "to jew." While anti-Semitic allusions appeared in popular writings of Nathaniel Hawthorne and Mark Twain, it was perhaps Hermann Melville who gave voice to an ironic strain of anti-Semitism that praised the diversity of America's *non-Jewish* population ("Englishman, Frenchman, German, Dane, or Scot") precisely because "[w]e are not a narrow tribe of men, with a bigoted Hebrew nationality." Just as laws of political equality began to achieve some parity, in short, resistance rose against Jewish social assimilation. In the crucible of this discord, says Jaher, "was forged modern American anti-Semitism" (p. 170), insofar as dependence on the talent and wealth of many individuals and institutions was detested on the grounds that Jews were neither Christian nor Anglo-Saxon, one or the other of which trait virtually every other resident (including most African Americans and many Native Americans, but excepting most Asian residents) obtained.

During the Gilded Age and Progressive Era generally, discrimination against Jewish American citizens became less defensible on constitutional grounds of liberty; but a certain social disdain for Jews, and anxieties about their rising numbers due to immigration patterns, grew vocal and visible.

When Grant was president, he offered the post of Treasury secretary to Joseph Seligman, who declined the offer but whose prominence turned the denial of his admittance into the Grand Union Hotel in Sarasota Springs, New York, into a cause célèbre of 1877. Oliver Wendell Holmes recorded overcoming his personal aversion toward Jews. Yet following the influx of new arrivals from Russia after 1880, Congress passed the 1891 Immigration Act limiting entry. In 1884 the poet, critic, and diplomat James Russell Lowell associated "Jewish blood" with the "ignobler scepter of finance." The man of letters Henry Adams wrote of the Jews who were held responsible for an economic crisis in 1892, "I live only and solely with the hope of seeing their demise." A currency crisis surrounding the 1896 presidential election stirred an agrarian campaign against Jewish bankers who were seen to sell out national interest for the gain of their "race." Massachusetts Senator Henry Cabot Lodge proposed a literacy restriction on immigration to include only those who spoke either English or the language of a native country, which by excluding Yiddish was a thinly veiled effort to curb Jewish immigration.

The firestorm over Jewish immigration was reignited by a 1911 report by Congress, which firmly rejected preferential treatment of older ethnic groups over newer arrivals in 1917. In this less religious atmosphere, anti-Semitism targeted Jewish race more than religion. However, Congress and many Jews rebuffed other Jews' efforts to define "Hebrew" as a race in the National Census. With millions of new arrivals from 1881 to 1930, the Jewish portion of the U.S. population swelled from less than 1 percent to more than 3 percent. With an increasingly prominent role in major cities, especially, Jews were called depraved and avaricious in muckraking journals, which fantasized about Jewish economic domination, although most Jews lived at the edge of poverty. Meanwhile Boston Brahmins claiming hereditary descent from the city's Protestant founders resisted the 1916 appointment by Woodrow Wilson of the public advocate Louis Brandeis as the first Jewish Supreme Court Justice. While influential books were published detailing how Jews were invaders who could never assimilate, rare physical assaults of Jews occurred spontaneously.

## The Leo Frank Case

The most vicious anti-Semitic incident in American history began with the 1913 conviction in Atlanta of New York transplant Leo Frank for the murder of Mary Phagan, a young Christian girl in the employ of Frank's factory.

A populist newspaperman and would-be politician Tom Watson, to whom Georgia subsequently gave a U.S. Senate seat in 1920, constantly hounded the "filthy perverted Jew from New York" whose only defenders conspired for a "Parasite Race." Using potently sacrificial language, Phagan's pastor called for "a victim worthy to pay for the crime." After an eyewitness's deathbed confession exonerated Frank and his sentence was commuted by Georgia's governor, a group of prominent citizens of Phagan's hometown, including a minister and a sheriff, murdered Frank near Marietta, Georgia, in the sole lynching of a Jew on American soil. It resulted in the creation of the American Jewish Committee and the Anti-Defamation League of B'nai Brith.

## Shifting Color Lines

Following World War I and the Bolshevik Revolution, anti-Semites charged Jews with allegiance to socialism and communism, as well as with control of international finance. Jews, though comprising less than 3 percent of the total U.S. population but 5 percent of the soldiers, were again labeled "war profiteers." The industrialist Henry Ford accused "German-Jewish bankers" of waging "subversive warfare upon Christian society"; his paper *The Dearborn Independent* headlined "The International Jew" in 1920, summarizing the forged *Protocols of the Elders of Zion*. Harvard University proposed, after its Jewish proportion of students rose from 6 percent in 1908 to 22 percent in 1922, to restrict admissions. Its president, Abbott Lawrence Lowell, argued the move would help the fewer Jews admitted in the long run because, unlike the perceived degradation of Columbia University into a school for Jews, Harvard would retain the exclusivity of a patrician establishment. However, the faculty rebuffed him. Nevertheless, versions of the *numerus clausus* (the medieval prohibition against Jews' partaking of higher education) were imposed at other private colleges and professional schools; for instance, Cornell Medical School's Jewish population went from 40 percent before 1922 to less than 4 percent after 1940. Likewise, job discrimination was rampant. Capping waves of new arrivals from Russia, Congress passed the Immigration Act of 1924 (the Johnson-Reed Act) and restricted entry into the United States by a system of quotas. In the first half of the decade Jews amounted to roughly 10 percent of immigrants; the proportion shrunk to 3 percent in the second half. Private restrictions on Jewish life were endemic: neighborhood covenants prohibited selling Jews a home, and some clubs and private vacation areas barred Jews; in response, Jews established parallel institutions, following the example of Seligman, who ultimately purchased the hotel that had denied him admittance.

To combat this increase in anti-Semitism, which seemed to occur within the bounds of legal consensus during the era before civil rights (when racism against blacks was still legal), different, sometimes competing, but constructive organizations were established, including the Anti-Defamation League, the American Jewish Committee, and the American Jewish Congress. Louis Marshall, head of the American Jewish Committee, notably brokered a deal with Ford to recant his endorsement of "the International Jew" (although in 1940 Ford came to blame Jews for causing the war).

At the same time, a revived Ku Klux Klan ignored Jews from Western Europe, and even sought their support. Following the wave of Jewish immigrants from Eastern Europe, a class line of sorts divided those Yiddish-speaking Jews from the German and Sephardic Jews who had settled decades earlier. The ethnic slur "kike" circulated amongst Jews to designate Eastern European Jews before non-Jews adopted it to designate any Jew. With debates over whether *Jewish* meant religious, racial, or ethnic raging in 1925, the Yiddish poet I. J. Schwarz dubbed Jews a "white race of another kind."

## Great Depression to World War II

Violent anti-Semitic incidents may have decreased in number as the Great Depression took its toll, but fantastic ideas about a Jewish scourge seemed to grow with the prominence of Jews in business and government. Franklin Delano Roosevelt's employment of many Jews, mostly from New York and Boston, including the 1934–1945 secretary of Treasury, Henry Morgenthau Jr., and Abe Fortas, legal counsel of the Public Works Administration (later tapped by his friend Lyndon B. Johnson in 1965 for the Supreme Court), prompted critics to caricature the administration's "Jew Deal." In 1936, after reporting that more than 50 percent of the nation approved Germany's treatment of the Jews or expressed indifference to their plight, *Fortune* magazine dismissed the "suggestion that Jews monopolize U.S. business" but declared "the apprehensiveness of American Jews" a major influence on society. Allegations of Jewish control over the Hollywood Empire notably accompanied praise of Jewish progress through the same. The journalist and popular commentator, the "Sage of Baltimore," H. L. Mencken, displayed ambivalence, repeating slurs against Jews while defending their rights against the Nazi menace.

As World War II approached, anti-Semites critical of Jewish presence in the United States had tremendous effects on European Jewry. In print and on radio, with millions tuning in weekly, the Catholic priest, Father Charles Coughlin, spread the German National-Socialist message, cresting days after *Kristallnacht* (the "Night of Crystal") in 1938, but his affiliation with the Christian Front led to conspiracy charges by the FBI in 1940 and silencing by his Detroit bishop after the tragedy at Pearl Harbor. The Disciples of Christ minister Gerald L. K. Smith followed suit. Urban working-class Irish and Jews occasionally brawled. Nearly 80 percent of Americans polled in 1938 did not want quotas lifted for war refugees. In an effort to show that no Western country would willingly accept Jews who were obviously seeking political asylum, the Nazis had devised a propaganda campaign by setting more than nine hundred Jews to sail in May 1939 with tourist visas aboard the German cruise ship the *St. Louis*. Upon arrival in Cuba, its passengers were refused entry; on June 4, under pressure from Cordell Hull and southern Democrats, President Roosevelt denied the ship's passengers permission to disembark in Florida. Against the advice of Jewish administration officials fearful of raising the Jewish profile, Roosevelt replaced the late Benjamin Cardozo with Felix Frankfurter to serve on the Supreme Court bench alongside Justice Louis Brandeis. Majorities of the population seemed to feel that Jews held "too much power," were "different and should be restricted," and were a "menace."

When, in September 1941, flying hero Charles A. Lindbergh spoke about the "danger" of Jewish "influence" before the America First Committee, founded in 1940 to keep the United States from entering World War II, he was denounced in every public quarter. Nevertheless, official or semiofficial anti-Semitism persisted more subtly. Not until March 1944 did President Roosevelt publicly discuss the Nazi genocide. Henry Morgenthau's Treasury Department titled its audit of the State Department's suppressing evidence of genocide, "Report to the Secretary on the Acquiescence of This Government in the Murder of the Jews." In these years the United States did not even fill quotas, admitting many fewer refugee children than did Great Britain, several Western European nations, and Shanghai, China. A June 1945 poll indicated that Jews were considered a more dangerous threat than German or Japanese descendents. The information about the Nazi genocide released by the U.S. press was paltry and minimized. Although not disenfranchised (like African Americans), ghettoized (Mexicans), or interned

(Japanese), Jews were subject to harsh recriminations due as much to their recent advancement as their persistent segregation. Marking the anti-Semitism of this period were the thousands of name changes officially registered by Jews; even greater numbers probably converted to Christianity.

## Post–World War II

Alongside other Americans of various ethnic groups, Jews individually and collectively advanced rapidly in the decades after 1945; many of the social and economic programs geared towards the white males who had served in the military (for instance, the G.I. Bill and home-loan programs) redounded directly to the benefit of Jewish men, but not to African Americans or women. Alongside a kind of mainstreaming effect, the institutional-political energy the Jewish community marshaled to protect itself against another Holocaust increasingly rallied around generic efforts to oppose hatred and intolerance. Overt expressions of anti-Semitism declined in the United States as never before. Soldiers returning from war and the military itself opted to lift boundaries, although prejudices remained entrenched in some quarters. Thanks to legal measures instituted by states, residential and job discrimination broadly decreased, except in the cases of social restrictions (for instance, country clubs and corporate boards in heavy industries and utilities). How Jewish and non-Jewish coworkers parted ways outside work was depicted in *Gentlemen's Agreement*, awarded an Academy Award for Best Motion Picture in 1947. Anti-Semitic groups diminished in number, though sporadic vandalism desecrated synagogues, correlating with the growth of suburban Jewish populations. The Catholic Church began, under Pope John XXIII, to thaw relations with Jews, and Jewish communities began to meet formally with evangelical Protestants in the mid-1960s.

## Quiescence

While overt and orchestrated anti-Semitism fell out of public favor after World War II, a quiet bigotry pervaded the upper and lower classes, whether because upwardly mobile Jews were encroaching on scarce territory or stepping over those less fortunate. Surveys taken in 1964 and 1981 indicated a downward trend of attributions to Jews of characteristics such as loyalty to their own, excessive control over financial sectors, and other familiar charges. According to *Time* magazine in 1965, "anti-Semitism is at an all-time low and publicly out of fashion."

There were still contrary indications of anti-Semitism. School board member Newt Miller of Wayne, New Jersey,

opposed electing two more Jews in addition to another on the board because, he claimed, "we lose what is left of Christ in our Christmas celebrations." While political leaders and the press denounced that precedent, the Jewish candidates lost by a landslide, one resident commenting, "It was a terrible shame that the Jews caused all this trouble." Anti-Semitism beneath the surface only awaited the opportunity to arise. The South witnessed some violent expressions of anti-Semitism, including a spate of temple bombings; in response, U.S. Jews divided between the northern elements directly confronting prejudice and southern elements preferring not to highlight their distinctiveness. In 1964 two white civil rights workers in Mississippi murdered alongside an African American were, not coincidentally, Jewish.

## African Americans and Anti-Semitism

The Christian heritage of anti-Semitism has sometimes infected African American culture. Also, as the diplomat and Nobel Peace Prize winner Ralph Bunche observed, "it is safe to scorn the Jew" because this was a white group ostracized by other whites. Many African Americans denounced their prior anti-Semitic sentiments, such as W. E. B. Du Bois in a 1936 essay. Adam Clayton Powell Jr., who represented Manhattan in the House of Representatives (1945–1971), called anti-Semitism "a deadly virus of the American bloodstream," countering more popular African American voices such as the Chicago newspaper that declared, "What America needs is a Hitler." Anti-Jewish riots took place during summer 1943 in Detroit and Brooklyn. Jewish institutions, opting to fight bigotry in general rather than isolate Jews for defense, were prominent supporters of the civil rights movement and were praised by leaders such as Martin Luther King Jr. However, small, loose organizations (for example, neighborhood papers) denounced Jewish exploitation of the inner-city poor, including blacks; a peak of animosity was reached in 1968–1969 with riotous protests in a few cities. James Baldwin's 1967 *New York Times Magazine* article put his anti-Semitism ironically: "The Negro is really condemning the Jew for having become an American white man" hindering African Americans.

Occasional incidents at the end of the century revealed a specific brand of ethnocentric animosity. Jesse Jackson caused a flap in his 1984 Democratic primary campaign when he admitted having called New York City "Hymietown." A spokesperson for Louis Farrakhan applied the long-standing charge of "bloodsuckers" against Jewish bankers to shop owners and landlords. Black scholars repudiated Leonard

Jeffries's canard that Jews had directed the slave trade. Many factors contributed to anti-Semitism among African Americans, including Christian influences, making Jews a scapegoat for mistreatment of African descendants in America, suspicion of negotiating with Jews, and perhaps taking revenge on a white outsider (a Jew) by aligning with a more socially dominant white person (an anti-Semite). These factors probably incited three days of African Americans' looting and damaging Jewish property and marching with anti-Semitic signs and chanting "Whose streets? Our streets" in Crown Heights, Brooklyn (New York), following the death of a Guyanese child accidentally struck by a Jewish driver on August 19, 1991. During the event Yankel Rosenbaum, an orthodox Jewish student visiting from Australia, was killed by a group of African Americans, including Lemrick Nelson Jr., who, acquitted for murder and then convicted of violating his victim's civil rights, admitted to stabbing the victim.

### End of the Millennium

Anti-Semitism from the 1970s through the 1990s took on a less virulent tone but simmered in small events. On the one hand, Jewish organizations were reaching consensus that under no historical circumstances had modern Jews suffered less violent forms of anti-Semitism. Various, and variously reliable, polls generally confirmed a measurable decline in anti-Semitic feelings or judgments. On the other hand, minor incidents occurred, ranging from occasional synagogue and gravestone desecrations; to a few instances of political indiscretion; to a heavily publicized and protested request by neo-Nazis to march in Skokie, a Chicago suburb, in 1977–1978; to campus bigotry of every stripe. Statistically, Jewish presence grew in business, university, and public life. Christians have criticized their own past anti-Semitism. The popular evangelical reverend Billy Graham expressly recanted the derogatory remarks he made in the Oval Office while counseling Richard Nixon. Indicating decreased intensity or reach of anti-Semitism is the exponential rise of intermarriages. About 10 percent of U.S. Jews married non-Jews in 1965, but by 1990 this figure was closer to 50 percent.

Criticism of U.S. foreign policy in the Middle East provoked a January 1993 *New York Magazine* cover to warn of "The New Anti-Semitism." Some evangelical Christian and Jewish groups united to support Zionism and set a new stage. On the other hand, we cannot simply equate anti-Zionism and anti-Semitism: criticizing specific policies in the state of Israel is different from ascribing U.S. foreign policy in the Middle East to the so-called Israel lobby.

## Critical Assessment

Perhaps anti-Semitism is best specified in terms of aversion, antipathy, and indifference to Jews. Also a blurry distinction remains between anti-Semitism and philosemitism, or a special fondness for Jews. The stated belief that Jews hold too much power in the United States, for instance, may represent an attitude of resentment or envy, blame or praise. A lingering question is how much distance separates an insult or personal affront, such as the Church of Jesus Christ of Latter-day Saints purporting to convert deceased Jews, from killing Jews or otherwise threatening their worldly lives. Perhaps it is because Jews are a small minority of the U.S. population whose cultural and political prominence and visibility overshadows even larger minority populations that anti-Semitism has manifested so weakly and yet been subject to a vociferous reaction; a prominent African American organization in the United States *promotes advancement* and a prominent Jewish organization *opposes defamation.*

## Current Status

In the early twenty-first century, U.S. anti-Semitism and philosemitism center on a few issues: religion, Israel, the media, and the economy. Surveys conducted in 2002, as reported by Robert Michael in *A Concise History of American Antisemitism*, indicate that millions of Americans believe Jews killed Christ as well as control the media and Wall Street (p. 210). American Defamation League surveys in 2002 and 2005 show that around 30 percent believe the Jews killed Christ, 30 percent believe Jews are more loyal to Israel than the United States, and 15 percent believe that Jews have too much power in the United States. The *American Jewish Yearbook* of 2006 reported 6.5 million Jews in the United States, while the Jewish percentage of the total population dropped from around 3.5 percent (from 1937 through the 1960s) to 2 percent. November 2006 saw the election of forty-three Jewish members of Congress (or 12 percent), a record. Numerous factors contributed to the sharp decline of discrimination and, though harder to quantify, perhaps prejudices against Jews as well: advocacy and education; public trials of Holocaust perpetrators; occupational and geographical mobility leading to increased social interaction and intermarriage; law enforcement; and the civil rights movement. Nevertheless, the idea held onto by some that Jews are not fully American persists: having called U.S. Senator Charles Schumer (New York) "that Jew" in May 2009, Arkansas State Senator Kim Hendren apologized, explaining how he had meant it to indicate someone who does not "believe in traditional values."

Just as the line between what Jews find anti-Semitic and what non-Jews find anti-Semitic is unclear, so too is the line between what one Jew finds anti-Semitic and another Jew does not. Mel Gibson's 2004 film *The Passion of the Christ* was praised by Christian ministers and church leaders despite being denounced by many Jews as disingenuously anti-Semitic; however, a tape of Gibson spewing anti-Semitic slurs upon his 2006 arrest for drunk driving in Malibu, California, was released to a chorus of scorn. Meanwhile, in September 2002, the president of Harvard University, Lawrence Summers, crystallized a contentious debate within the American Jewish community by warning that critics of Israel risk expressing views that are "anti-Semitic in their effect if not in their intent." The question of what counts as anti-Semitism in the United States remains complicated by historical, cultural, political, and religious factors.

**See also** *Anti-Catholicism; Ethnicity; Film; Holocaust; Judaism* entries; *Race and Racism; Religious Prejudice; Zionism.*

Gregory Kaplan

## BIBLIOGRAPHY

Almog, Shmuel, ed. *Antisemitism through the Ages.* New York: Oxford University Press, 1988.

Blakeslee, Spencer. *The Death of Antisemitism.* Westport, Conn.: Praeger, 2000.

Carr, Steven Alan. *Hollywood and Antisemitism: A Cultural History up to World War II.* New York: Cambridge University Press, 2001.

Dinnerstein, Leonard. *Anti-Semitism in America.* New York: Oxford University Press, 1994.

Garber, David A., ed. *Anti-Semitism in American History.* Champaign: University of Illinois Press, 1986.

Goldstein, Eric L. *The Price of Whiteness: Jews, Race, and American Identity.* Princeton, N.J.: Princeton University Press, 2006.

Gurock, Jeffrey, ed. *American Jewish History: Antisemitism in America.* New York: Routledge, 1998.

Jaher, Frederic Cople. *A Scapegoat in the New Wilderness: The Origins and Rise of Anti-Semitism in America.* Cambridge, Mass.: Harvard University Press, 1994.

Leff, Laurel. *Buried by the Times: The Holocaust and America's Most Important Newspaper.* New York: Cambridge University Press, 2006.

Michael, Robert. *A Concise History of American Antisemitism.* Lanham, Md.: Rowman and Littlefield, 2005.

Rosenbaum, Ron, ed. *Those Who Forget the Past: The Question of Anti-Semitism.* New York: Random House, 2004.

# Apocalypticism

In 1987, the American alternative rock band R.E.M. produced an apocalyptic-themed song entitled "It's the End of the World as We Know It (I feel fine)." Fourteen years later, the terrorist attacks on September 11, 2001, instilled the song with new meaning. R.E.M.'s song described a series of catastrophic events associated with the end of the world: "earthquake, . . . birds and snakes, . . . aeroplane, . . . hurricane, . . . fire, . . . that low plane, . . . rapture, . . . foreign tower, . . . book burning, . . . bloodletting, . . . continental drift divide." The song also revealed conditions that hid the impending destruction, things like "games, . . . government, . . . reporters baffled, . . . save yourself, . . . serve yourself, . . . six o'clock-TV hour, . . . a tournament of lies, . . . birthday party, cheesecake, jelly bean, boom!" (lyrics by Berry et al.). The song warns against feeling fine since no one is safe and anyone who thinks she or he is safe is being deceived.

On one level the song provided an ironic commentary on the idea of an apocalyptic end to the world. However, since September 11, 2001, the song can be interpreted as creating a strong apocalyptic message to heed the warning and wake up before it is too late. Following 9/11, it was too late and nobody, at least nobody living in twenty-first-century America, felt fine. The term *apocalyptic* in American culture has come to mean some kind of earth-shattering, cataclysmic event, although in the original Greek the term simply referred to a revelation or an uncovering of something hidden.

John J. Collins is one of the most distinguished scholars among those who have attempted to define apocalyptic literature. In *The Apocalyptic Imagination*, he claims that apocalypses have two distinguishing characteristics. First is an angelic guide who uncovers the symbolically hidden divine message. Second is a message of glorious salvation for God's people and retribution for God's enemies. This divine punishment will continue beyond death, and it is often joyfully anticipated by God's people (pp. 5–6). This genre of literature also raises questions about terms like the millennium and the timing of Christ's Second Coming. A millennium is simply a thousand years, and the millennium referred to in the apocalyptic Book of Revelation is the thousand years of peace and holiness when Jesus's followers rule the earth. In particular, Protestants in America have had a lively debate about the time of Christ's Second Coming. Those theological positions that claim Christ will return before the start of the millennium are referred to as *premillennialists*, and those who believe Christ will return after the millennium are *postmillennialists*.

## Seventeenth-Century Puritan Apocalypticism

Traveling back to the beginning of the seventeenth century, Puritans in England began to feel less fine as the sting of political uncertainty and persecution brought the world as they knew it to a close. First they fled to Holland and then to Plymouth in order to build a new colony in what was to them a new world. These English travelers set sail in a time of political and religious volatility. Their worldview had been influenced by two pieces of apocalyptic literature written during times of crisis. They were canonical books produced by Jewish writers during times of oppression. First was the Book of Daniel, a text produced by Jews facing persecution under the Seleucid King Antiochus IV Epiphanes (175–164 BCE). Second was the Book of Revelation written by Jewish followers of Jesus facing persecution from the Roman Emperor Domitian (81–96 CE). Those two apocalyptic texts and the theological commentaries written about them influenced the English Puritans.

The settlers of North America in general and of New England in particular were significantly influenced by the apocalyptic narratives of Daniel and Revelation. Their numerous journals, letters, and sermons displayed evidence of a worldview that was shaped by many apocalyptic assumptions. Their apocalyptic outlook could be discerned by the ease with which they equated the French and their Indian allies with God's enemies, and their long-held belief that the Catholic Pope was the antichrist.

The Puritans' sense of "mission," which has so often been written about since Perry Miller's groundbreaking 1952 essay "Errand into the Wilderness," was not in itself a demonstration of the influence of apocalypticism on their worldview. Yet much of their "mission" does appear to have been driven and justified by an apocalyptic perspective. Furthermore, it was not that their original "errand" was a divinely sanctioned part of God's millennial plan for the world that made their "mission" apocalyptic since, as J. J. Collins points out, there were many Hebrew prophets of old who believed they were living in the last days prior to God's judgment. Rather, the apocalyptic influence became clear through the Puritans' interpretation of history as a supernatural revealing of biblical signs proving the French and their native allies were indeed God's enemies and as such deserved total destruction.

John Winthrop's sermon on the Arbella, in which he evokes the image of the new settlers creating a holy commonwealth which would be a model or a "City upon a Hill" for all of Old England to copy, lacked a clear apocalyptic motif. In his sermon, apocalyptic themes and images were also lacking. Even if Winthrop did believe this "City" would help to usher in the end of time and Christ's millennial reign, an apocalyptic tune was absent. Stephen Stein in his article "American Millennial Visions" makes the distinction between the apocalyptic, world-transforming motives of the "crusading" Christopher Columbus as compared to the "metaphorical" apocalypticism in the background of the Puritans who were seeking a better life (p. 193). But once Winthrop's millennial vision became situated within a framework of isolation and unpredictable external attacks, the early Puritans' sentiments quickly turned apocalyptic and the settlers' adversaries become equated with God's enemies who must be destroyed.

Neither the small group of Separatist Puritans who settled at Plymouth nor the larger group of Puritans hoping to reform the Church of England who settled at Massachusetts Bay formulated their apocalyptic ideas on their oceanic voyage or during their confrontations with the natives. Rather, their apocalyptic imagination, as John Collins has so aptly named this worldview, was shaped in England. As Reiner Smolinski points out in "Apocalypticism in Colonial North America," English Reformation theologians since the early part of the sixteenth century had been examining Revelation and Daniel in order to decipher those books' mysterious end-of-the-world scenarios (pp. 36–42). The writings of English theologians such as John Bale (1495–1563), John Foxe (1516–1587), and Thomas Brightman (1562–1607) all contributed to Congregationalists in England perceiving themselves as God's chosen millennial people who were still trying to figure out when and if the millennium had started.

Bale dated the millennium in the distant past, beginning with Christ's Resurrection, and interpreted Christ's rule as a spiritual reign in the hearts of his followers. Foxe followed Bale's scheme; however, Brightman's commentary on Revelation published in 1609 dated the millennial reign as a present reality that began in the middle 1300s with the dissent of John Wyclif (1330–1384), who was England's "morning star" of the Reformation. However, the traditional preterist approach of interpreting apocalyptic literatures' end-of-the-world scenarios as allegorical events that were fulfilled in the past or were being fulfilled in the present would soon be challenged. The voice of dissent came from the German theologian Johann Heinrich Alsted (1588–1638). In 1627, he published a tract on Revelation in which he proposed that the start of the millennial reign of Christ would come in the future. Smolinski finds the roots of Cotton Mather's (1663–1728) later and more literal premillennial eschatology in Alsted, while the majority of eighteenth-century American theologians such as Daniel Whitby (1638–1726), Jonathan Edwards (1703–1758), and Samuel Hopkins (1721–1803) remained in the traditionalist camp, interpreting Christ's millennial reign allegorically (pp. 39–40). Their allegorical thinking held the millennium was symbolic of a spiritual truth that may have been a past or present reality rather than a literal future event.

An English theologian who impacted the Puritan travelers' apocalyptic outlook was Joseph Mede (1586–1638), who published a commentary on Revelation. In his commentary, he placed Christ's millennial reign in the future. In addition, he determined that the time of Christ's millennial reign could be calculated based on the 1,260-year reign of the antichrist, the beginning of which he placed on one of two possible dates in the fifth century. These two potential dates situated the demise of the antichrist and the start of Christ's millennial rule in either 1716 or 1736.

One reason for Mede's influence on the English settlers in New England stemmed from his association with John Cotton (1584–1652). In 1633, Cotton traveled to New England where he became pastor of the First Church in Boston. In 1639 Cotton's interpretation of Revelation followed many of the same conclusions as Mede. However, according to Cotton's historical calculations, 1655 was the year that marked the fall of the antichrist and the beginning of Christ's millennial rule. As Smolinski notes, Cotton's interpretation of Revelation also served an important pastoral role as he bound the covenant, individual salvation, and church membership with the visible church's role in the downfall of the antichrist (pp. 41–43).

The Protestant and Catholic wars during the sixteenth and seventeenth century helped to shape the Puritan outlook, which only intensified the "end of the world" scenarios. These future apocalyptic scenarios were produced by calculating past events as a timeline from biblical texts (usually Daniel and Revelation), which were interpreted as revealing a definitive starting time for Christ's millennial reign. The English Protestant millennial expectations set the stage for the apocalyptic worldview that would justify the violence done to the French and their native allies, as well as provide a rationale validating both the War for Independence with England and the Civil War that violently tore the nation apart.

The Puritans living in seventeenth-century New England, as Amanda Porterfield has pointed out in *The Protestant Experience in America*, were a fairly insulated and isolated group (p. 30). While their leaders still had some communication with England and Europe, the Atlantic made communication difficult and slow. Therefore, the Puritans' self-identity was influenced by how they differentiated themselves from outsiders: the Roman Catholics and the native peoples. Since Catholics were the religious "other" and native peoples were the cultural "other," both groups were easy to conceptualize as the enemy within a worldview that was shaped by both a Calvinistic dualism, separating people into God's chosen versus God's rejected, along with an apocalyptic dualism where the godly were relentlessly struggling against the forces of evil.

By 1637 the increase in Puritan migration to the Massachusetts Bay colony created a tenuous situation with the surrounding native peoples whose lands were disappearing. In May, the settlers' fear of native attacks led to military action. They sent a militia along with a Connecticut militia to attack a Pequot fortified village near Mystic. The militias set fire to the village and it was consumed in minutes, killing men, women, and children. The inferno was described in apocalyptic terms by the militias' leaders. Porterfield quotes the Connecticut leader, "Such dreadful Terror did the ALMIGHTY let fall upon their Spirits, that they would fly from us and run into the very Flames [that consumed them all]" (p. 31).

The village's destruction was interpreted by the leaders as God's restoration of a time of peace and freedom granted to God's people, who had been held captive by the threat of future Indian attacks. Accordingly, as quoted in Porterfield, "the LORD turned the Captivity of his People, and turned the Wheel upon their Enemies; we were like Men in a Dream; then was our mouth filled with laughter, and our tongues with Singing; thus we may say the LORD has done great things for us among the Heathen" (p. 31). Porterfield connects these statements to the biblical prophets as a common theme of the English settlers, who justified war based on a biblical precedent where the settlers were the New Israel taking the new Promised Land by driving out the Canaanites. Yet within these statements there is also a clear indication of apocalyptic influence, justifying the settlers' perception of the natives as evil enemies of God's people who need to be destroyed. In addition, their conclusion that the fiery death of women and children would be their salvation plus their joy at the complete annihilation of their foe conveys a significant degree of apocalyptic influence on their actions.

## Eighteenth-Century Apocalypticism

Like the sixteenth- and seventeenth-century millennial debates that influenced the English settlers' apocalyptic rhetoric justifying violence against their enemies, so too would the eighteenth-century theological debates concerning Revelation's millennial vision shape the apocalyptic rhetoric during the colonial push for independence. The colonist apocalyptic outlook easily found a new enemy once the French and their native allies had been defeated. The millennial views of two prominent eighteenth-century theologians will provide a useful background to the colonial apocalyptic rhetoric justifying violence against their present enemy.

Cotton Mather and Jonathan Edwards were two of the most influential early-eighteenth-century Puritan pastors, and their ideas concerning the millennium demonstrate the influence of apocalypticism within the New England colonies. In 1703 Cotton Mather expressed his views on the millennium in the published tract *Problema Theologicum*. According to this tract, Cotton Mather clearly agreed with the preterist position of his father, Increase Mather. However, by 1720 Cotton Mather's views had shifted and his interpretation of Revelation took a sharp antiallegorical stance. In that year he published a new literalist interpretation of Revelation in an article entitled "Triparadisus." In this work, he predicted Christ's literal appearing at both the beginning and end of the millennium. Thus, his text indicated that both resurrections depicted in Revelation should be interpreted as literal historical and future events. The first resurrection, according to Cotton Mather, was symbolic neither of the spiritual conversion of individual Christians nor of the Reformation of the Church. His revised opinion did not diminish the importance of individual salvation and church reformation; rather his changing perspective actually strengthened his resolve that the church militant here on earth be faithful in order not to be cut off from the future, literal millennial reign of Christ.

Jonathan Edwards's Reformed orthodoxy would not be swayed by the new literalist interpretation of apocalyptic texts in general or the Book of Revelation in particular. In Edwards's faithfulness to the allegorical tradition of interpreting apocalyptic literature, he anticipated a new awakening of God's spirit within his own Northampton congregation during the "last days." The church in Northampton had experienced at least seven revivalistic periods under Solomon Stoddard prior to Edwards's taking over as pastor. Edwards as a young pastor of twenty-six thrived in his authoritative position, and as he developed as a pastor he began to trumpet the call for bigger and better awakenings of God's spirit. While the reasons for his revivalistic determination were many, perhaps the most obvious was his ambitious drive to do great deeds for the worldwide kingdom of God. Too often, however, commentators on Edwards's thought point to his millennial outlook and his passing remark concerning the possibility of America being the place where Christ would inaugurate his millennial reign.

Jonathan was the only male heir to Timothy Edwards, and he was raised knowing the family's name was his legacy. Perhaps this is what influenced his expectation that the current revivals in America could spark the millennial reign of Christ. However, the vast majority of his millennial views remained traditional, allegorical, and, as classified today, postmillennial. His postmillennialism, however, was not the tame, waiting for the world to improve so Christ could return variety. Within Edwards's writings, the historical demise of the antichrist, as Smolinski keenly observes, included enough global warfare, horror, and gore to compete with all the visions of Christ's supernatural destruction of the antichrist postulated by Cotton Mather and other premillennialists of that time (p. 59).

In 1739, Edwards preached a series of sermons entitled "A History of the Work of Redemption" in which he highlighted Christ's love as being the central focus of God's dealings with creation throughout history. Edwards was convinced that the 1734–1735 revival in his church at Northampton was an historical manifestation of Christ's redeeming love that would ultimately triumph. However, in keeping with his traditional Reformed doctrine, he also believed Christ's ultimate redemption would occur gradually throughout history in successive cycles of good and evil that would eventually establish the Kingdom of God at the end of time. Therefore, according to Edwards's sermons, the apocalyptic texts of Daniel and Revelation were useful guides to indicate the timing of Christ's victory over Satan.

In Edwards's "Notes on the Apocalypse," a kind of informal commentary on Revelation written over thirty-five years (1723–1758), he directed his rhetoric of violence towards the Roman Catholic Church, the primary enemy of Protestants throughout the seventeenth and eighteenth centuries. In these "Notes" he speculates that the antichrist's reign began in 606 and would be ended around the year 1866. Even at the present time, however, there were growing signs of the antichrist's weakening power. Thus, any event that weakened the Pope or diminished the Catholic Church's wealth was viewed by Edwards as a fulfillment of Revelation's prediction that the antichrist would be defeated with the drying up of the Euphrates. The Reformation in 1517 along with all the seventeenth- and early-eighteenth-century wars that drained away wealth from Spain and France all contributed to the weakening of the Catholic antichrist. Yet Edwards believed that the antichrist would make a final stand in which terrible devastation would ensue, so that only the faithful would survive.

In 1757, James Cogswell wrote a tract to spur on the colonists in their fight against the French—it was the same apocalyptic rhetoric justifying war that would be used in less than ten years to spur the colonists to unite against the evil English empire. He wrote to his fellow countrymen, "Endeavor to stand as Guardians of the Religion and Liberties of *America;* to oppose Antichrist . . . [as] the art of War becomes a Part of our Religion" (quoted in Smolinski, p. 67). Following the defeat of the French in 1763, England sought ways to increase tax revenue to pay for the extended war with the French, passing the Sugar Act in 1764 and the Stamp Act in 1765. By the time Parliament had passed the Quebec Act (1774) granting freedom of religion to the Catholics in the conquered French territory, the colonists had ample time to figure out their new enemy. The old apocalyptic rhetoric that fit so well on the French, the Roman Catholic Church, and the Pope was quickly reassembled to fit Great Britain, the Anglican Church, and especially King George.

The tribulation that the colonists faced now was interpreted as coming directly from the oppressive tax and pro-Catholic policies of England. The new colonial symbol of the antichrist was King George III, who, if not the antichrist himself, was at least viewed as in collusion with the Catholic antichrist to do the work of Satan by oppressing the chosen people of God. Thus, the strong desire for political independence from the beast of British power, and religious freedom from the antichrist who headed the Roman Catholic Church, brought forth an intense apocalyptic rhetoric that fueled the violent fight for independence. Once the Revolutionary War era was over the American fascination with apocalyptic images and debates about the beginning of the millennium would continue, and by the mid-nineteenth century the apocalypticism of war would once again pit enemy against enemy in the lead-up to the American Civil War. In this conflict, however, the Roman Catholic Church was not the symbolic antichrist doing the work of Satan; rather, it was Northern and Southern Protestant cultures demonizing each other.

## Early Nineteenth-Century and Antebellum Apocalypticism

In the early nineteenth century Jonathan Edwards's theological ideas became known as postmillennialism and were widely accepted by Protestant denominations. The idea of postmillennialism, at this time, took on some of the more progressive characteristics of the Protestants who held this theological belief. Therefore, it became associated with an optimistic worldview that anticipated and strived for improving society as a way to initiate the Kingdom of God. This eschatological system was influenced by scientific and technological advances, along with a growing faith that education could solve society's problems. Postmillennialism became an undergirding support for the revivalistic spirit in America in the early nineteenth century. This revivalistic movement became known as the Second Great Awakening (1790s–1850s), as it produced enthusiastic conversions that drew comparisons to the 1740s Great Awakening. In addition to emphasizing personal salvation, this revivalistic movement focused on evangelical outreach programs, societies for social improvement, and world missions. While the revivalistic spirit and personal conversions waned after the 1850s with the country's preparation for war, the Second Great Awakening in many important ways prepared the way for a movement that arose in the early twentieth century, a theological movement known as the "Social Gospel." The Social Gospel was encapsulated in the preaching, social outreach ministries, and theological writings of Walter Rauschenbusch. Thus, throughout the nineteenth century, even during the horror of the Civil War, most mainline Protestants believed the apocalyptic images in scripture to be symbolic and allegorical, representing historical cycles of violence that were necessary to rid the world of evil before Christ would return. During this time, America produced and became home to numerous new religious movements, many of which held worldviews based on interpretations of apocalyptic texts.

As a representative of mainline Protestantism at this time, Lyman Beecher (1775–1863) wrote *A Plea for the West,* in which he attempted to prove America's central place within God's millennial plans by citing Jonathan Edwards. Quoting Edwards was a favorite activity of nineteenth-century revivalists, as they attempted to justify their revivalistic efforts to inaugurate the Kingdom of God by pointing back to earlier revivals in the eighteenth century. While the dominant

Protestant force in America perceived a threat in the large number of immigrating Catholics, there were several religious groups in America that either sought cultural isolation or faced real ridicule and often relentless oppression that actually intensified their apocalyptic outlook. The two religious groups used as examples here were chosen from a multitude of religious and political movements influenced by apocalypticism. While this type of apocalyptic worldview was not limited to Protestant religious groups, in America during the nineteenth century, Protestant groups were still numerically dominant, and within this religious majority many became fascinated with prophecy and a literal interpretation of Revelation.

During the antebellum years in America, Cotton Mather's literal and premillennial doctrine did not disappear. And as the Civil War loomed closer, more and more religious groups embraced the supernatural apocalyptic visions of Christ's imminent return prior to the millennium. The Millerite Adventist religious movement was one such group. It was a religious movement that started from the teachings of William Miller (1782–1849), a self-taught biblical student fascinated with prophecy, who in the early 1830s began preaching in upstate New York. He was a self-proclaimed Baptist preacher who began to teach that Christ's Second Coming would take place sometime around 1843–1844. His prediction was based on his interpretation of biblical apocalyptic texts, especially Daniel, and his calculation of the start of the millennial reign of Christ was determined by using the date of the rebuilding of the Hebrew temple. His premillennial preaching spurred conferences, camp meetings, and a newspaper entitled *The Midnight Cry*. By the start of the 1840s, his followers pushed for a more exact date and he essentially complied. He identified Christ's return as coming between March 21, 1843, and March 21, 1844. When the predicted dates passed, social persecution and ridicule were intense; however, a revised calculation of October 22, 1844, was suggested by some Adventist leaders. William Miller eventually concurred, although by this time, he was becoming doubtful that the imminent return of Christ could be calculated. When Christ did not return on October 22, most Adventists were devastated, and the failure was dubbed the "Great Disappointment." Out of the Adventist ashes, however, Ellen White resurrected a movement with millennial hopes that has refused to predict future events while interpreting apocalyptic literature. Yet these Adventist members still look in earnest for signs of Christ's Second Coming in power and glory.

Another religious movement that enjoyed its climax of popularity in antebellum America was a group that came from England in the 1790s. The movement's name reveals much of its millennial hopes: The United Society of Believers in Christ's Second Appearing, or The Millennial Church. However, most people recognize them by their more common name: the Shakers. The movement originated in England in 1747 and was founded by James and Jane Ward. They were superseded by Ann Lee, who was regarded as "Mother Ann" and accepted as the fulfillment of the Second Coming of Christ. She was revered as the "female Christ principle" in the same way that Jesus was revered as the "male Christ principle." In 1774 she brought to America her group of dedicated followers, who soon founded other Shaker communities. The Shakers' more common name was a result of the "shaking" and "quaking" that ensued while members were being filled and possessed with God's spirit during "the last days." In addition to a belief in spirit possession and in Mother Ann's millennial fulfillment of Christ's Second Coming, the movement also practiced a strict communal disciplinary regimen to ensure holiness. Most important to this communal holiness was the aspect of complete celibacy and total marriage to the Christ principle. Within the apocalyptic spiritual milieu that was America during the antebellum years, the Shakers' message found some fertile ground, and by 1840 the movement peeked with just over six thousand members. By the late twentieth century, however, the movement had all but disappeared.

## Apocalypticism from the Civil War to the Early Twentieth Century

War and apocalyptic influence and imagery are closely connected, and the Civil War era in America was no exception. Abolitionists found motivation in apocalyptic imagery that they interpreted as supporting abolition as the fastest way to establish Christ's millennial reign. Apocalyptic hopes and nightmares filled the imagination of most Americans living through the Civil War years. Terrie Dopp Aamodt traces the apocalyptic images of this era in both its religious and secular forms in her text entitled *Righteous Armies, Holy Cause: Apocalyptic Imagery and the Civil War*.

Following the Civil War, many new religious groups that were influenced by apocalypticism came to the forefront within the United States. During this time, premillennialism enjoyed a new and continuing popularity, while many postmillennialist Protestants who hoped that the church would partner with science and technology to progressively improve society began leaving the church, taking their liberalism in a more secular direction. As more mainline Protestants began to disregard biblical apocalyptic texts, the door was opened for premillennialists, dispensationalists, and fundamentalists to articulate and propagate their interpretations of apocalyptic passages in scripture. Dispensationalism is the interpretation of history as a series of divinely sanctioned periods of time. Christian theological proponents of this interpretation usually view apocalyptic scripture as literal and hold to a premillennialist view of Christ's return. Fundamentalism, as used here, refers to a Protestant movement that reacted against modernism by asserting the Bible is both infallible as a guide to faith and literally true as a historical record.

Paul Boyer, in *When Time Shall Be No More*, traces the rise of fundamentalist dispensationalism in the work of John Nelson Darby (1800–1882) and Cyrus Scofield (1843–1921). John Darby was a founder of the more radical wing of the English Plymouth Brethren, and by the year 1837 he started taking extensive preaching tours. In 1859 he traveled to America, where he became perhaps the most prominent promoter of a premillennialism based on fundamentalist dispensationalism (p. 87). Darby's system used charts and timelines to demonstrate the ever-closer hour of Christ's return and the church's Rapture.

He also learned a lesson from William Miller, as he avoided predictions of an exact time in the future for Christ's return. Darby's system of dispensationalism divided history into time periods, in which God dealt with humanity (or the chosen people) through a series of covenants in which salvation could be achieved through various means. According to this literalist approach to scripture, the present covenant is the "church age," which will end with the Rapture of the church. This will throw the rest of the world into a seven-year period of terrible tribulation. At the end of the tribulation, Christ will return with his saints to overthrow the antichrist and bind Satan for a thousand years, inaugurating his millennial reign. Darby's system was supported through the *Scofield Reference Bible,* published in 1909. Scofield applied a dispensationalist interpretation upon the entire Bible, making it appear to readers that dispensationalist's categories were an actual part of the scriptural text. This bible is still popular today within conservative evangelical circles and has sold more than twelve million copies.

The early twentieth century in America was a time of increasing racial violence and division; however, one apocalyptic religious movement used the biblical imagery of the "last days" as a time when "God's spirit would be poured out upon all flesh" to overcome racists' bigotry, at least for a few years. While the theological doctrines that gave rise to the Pentecostal Movement were diverse and historians of religion and America debate their origins, most scholars point to the 1906 Azusa Street revival as the birth of the modern Pentecostal movement.

William J. Seymour, a black holiness preacher, led the revival that broke down racial and gender distinctions as people flocked to Los Angeles, California, to witness the emotional revival. The revival also drew from the many Baptist, Methodist, and Holiness churches in the area as fellow believers came to hear the emotionally charged message of God's baptism with power. The primary distinction within this Pentecostal revival was the literal biblical theme that speaking with other tongues was the physical evidence of God's spirit being poured out, just like it was back in the first century, when the disciples were baptized in God's spirit and empowered for missionary service. Thus, this twentieth-century revival combined a simplistic, literalistic reading of prophetic and apocalyptic texts with a very modern evidentiary proof that this spiritual revival was real. For the first three years of the revival, the missionary power of spirit baptism could not be denied as Pentecostal missionaries from Los Angeles traveled throughout America and the world. The Pentecostal revival incorporated women, African Americans, and Hispanics in leadership roles, as all who were spiritually baptized could pray, preach, and teach during any worship service.

After a few years the revival lost its ability to quell racial bias and bigotry to such a degree that the movement split down racial lines. The racial division convinced William Seymour that speaking with other tongues was not evidence of baptism in God's spirit; rather, for him, the true evidence of spiritual baptism was the ability to love brothers and sisters of other races. Just as the power of God's spirit convinced Peter to love and preach to the gentiles, so the proof of God's spirit being poured out in the "last days" before the Rapture should be a spiritual love between all of God's children, regardless of race.

## Mid- to Late-Twentieth-Century Apocalypticism

By the mid-twentieth century, America was a triumphant world force, having just defeated Imperial Japan and the Nazi military machine that had threatened all of Europe. However, Seymour's vision for American racial reconciliation was becoming less of a reality, as southern evangelicals armed with premillennial dispensationalism began to ignore racial inequality in America, while pushing for a new aggressive message of American nationalism. Billy Graham's preaching tours expanded into great crusades, the likes of which had not been seen since the days of George Whitefield's revivalistic tours during what is now referred to as the Great Awakening. Graham's premillennial message of the need for salvation before the coming tribulation was grounded in Darby's system and set the stage for a literary explosion that took America by storm in the 1970s and turned Hal Lindsey into a literary star in fundamentalist and conservative circles. Hal Lindsey cowrote *The Late Great Planet Earth* in 1970 with Carol C. Carlson. The book combined the narrative styles of catastrophic science fiction with a premillennial approach to apocalyptic narratives, which were interpreted as providing a literal timeline of horror that would follow the Rapture of the church. The book claimed to point out the fulfillment of apocalyptic biblical passages in Daniel, Ezekiel, and Revelation, and it captured the imagination of the growing number of Christians who were expecting the Rapture. As a book with fantastic descriptions of the horrors that awaited the earth, it caught the attention of a secular press and became the "non-fiction" best seller of the 1970s, selling more than nine million copies by 1978. Future editions of the book had to be revised and updated to take into account changing geopolitical conditions that made earlier editions inaccurate.

The literary model of *The Late Great Planet Earth* was continued when a politically active conservative evangelical minister in the 1990s wrote a series of novels based on the apocalyptic horrors that non-Christians would face following the Rapture. In 1995, Tim LaHaye cowrote *Left Behind* with Jerry B. Jenkins, and the book's popularity spurred a Left Behind series containing twelve volumes. Seven of these volumes became best sellers, and series total sales have topped sixty-five million copies.

The success of both the Left Behind series and the earlier *Late Great Planet Earth* points to the fascination Americans have always had with apocalyptic scenarios of future destruction of one's enemies. This has been true from the English settlers' first violent encounter with natives, who had aligned themselves with the Roman Catholic antichrist by their association with the French, up through the current generation of conservative evangelical Christians anticipating a rapturous escape from the coming horrors that non-Christians will suffer.

## Connection between Apocalypticism and War

This American fascination with apocalypticism relates to an American fascination with war. Some used these terms about the United States war effort to liberate Iraq (first from Saddam Hussein and then from the terrorists); but each American generation has had a violent fight in which it has been able to identify some evil enemy who could be connected to the enemies of God. There are the terrorists now as there were the communists in the Vietnam era, the communists in the cold war period, the Nazis in WWII, the Kaiser in WWI, the Protestant demonizing of each other during the Civil War, King George and taxes in the Revolutionary era, and the Roman Catholic Church with native tribal collaborators. War has a way of bringing out the best in a nation's "apocalyptic imagination," and the American people's fascination with apocalyptic themes has a way of being expressed in their music.

In 1861, at the start of the Civil War, Julia Ward Howe heard Union soldiers marching to the song "John's Brown's Body," a popular tune in the North written for a Northern martyr. John Brown was executed shortly after his raid on the military arsenal at Harpers Ferry during a slave insurrection he organized. Howe became inspired by the soldiers and wrote the words to the "Battle Hymn of the Republic." The first and third verses demonstrate the power of the apocalyptic influence upon Northern culture. She began by writing about the Lord's coming with vengeance: "Mine eyes have seen the glory of the coming of the Lord; He is trampling out the vintage where the grapes of wrath are stored; He has loosed the fateful lightning of his terrible swift sword; His truth is marching on." By the third verse the judgment of God has arrived and the feet of Northerners rejoice: "He has sounded forth the trumpet that shall never call retreat; He is sifting out the hearts of men before his judgment seat; Oh, be swift, my soul, to answer Him! be jubilant, my feet; Our God is marching on." Julia Howe's apocalyptic images are completely grounded in the scriptural idea of a wrathful God's judgment upon the enemy. This theme fills her lyrics with expectations that God will fight for the Northern cause and ensure its victory. Just as the Lord's coming would ensure Northerners' military victory, it would also ensure the end of the world as they knew it while still allowing them to feel fine. One hundred twenty-seven years later in America, R.E.M. was once again writing lyrics, albeit more secular in nature, with the end of the world in sight while still trying to feel fine.

**See also** *Adventism and Millennialism; Adventist and Millennialist Denominational Families; Bible* entries; *Civil War; Evangelicals* entries; *Fundamentalism; Great Awakening(s); Jehovah's Witnesses; Pentecostals; Puritans; Seventh-day Adventists; Shakers; Social Gospel.*

Robert Britt-Mills

## BIBLIOGRAPHY

Aamodt, Terrie Dopp. *Righteous Armies, Holy Cause: Apocalyptic Imagery and the Civil War*. Macon, Ga.: Mercer University Press, 2002.

Amanat, Abbas, and Magnus T. Bernhardsson, eds. *Imagining the End: Visions of Apocalypse from the Ancient Middle East to Modern America*. New York: I.B. Tauris, 2002.

Berry, Bill, Peter Buck, Mike Mills, and Michael Stipe. "It's the End of the World as We Know It (I Feel Fine)." Lyrics. *Document*. I.R.S Records, 1987.

Boyer, Paul S. *When Time Shall Be No More: Prophecy Belief in Modern American Culture*. Cambridge, Mass.: Belknap Press of Harvard University Press, 1992.

Collins, John Joseph. *The Apocalyptic Imagination: An Introduction to Jewish Apocalyptic Literature*. Grand Rapids, Mich.: William B. Eerdmans, 1984.

———. *Apocalypticism in the Dead Sea Scrolls*. New York: Routledge, 2002.

Collins, John Joseph, Bernard McGinn, and Stephen J. Stein. *The Encyclopedia of Apocalypticism*. Vol. III. New York: Continuum, 1998.

Haldeman, Bonnie, and Catherine L. Wessinger. *Memories of the Branch Davidians: The Autobiography of David Koresh's Mother*. Waco, Tex.: Baylor University Press, 2007.

Johns, Loren L. *Apocalypticism and Millennialism: Shaping a Believers Church Eschatology for the Twenty-First Century*. Kitchener, Ontario, Canada: Pandora Press, 2000.

Moorhead, James H. "Apocalyptism in Mainstream Protestantism, 1880 to the Present." In *The Encyclopedia of Apocalypticism*, 72–107. New York: Continuum, 1998.

Porterfield, Amanda. *The Protestant Experience in America*. Westport, Conn.: Greenwood, 2006.

Smolinski, Reiner. "Apocalypticism in Colonial North America." In *The Encyclopedia of Apocalypticism*, 36–71. New York: Continuum, 1998.

Stein, Stephen J. "Apocalypticism outside the Mainstream in the United States." In *The Encyclopedia of Apocalypticism*, 108–139. New York: Continuum, 1998.

———. "American Millennial Visions: Towards Construction of a New Architectonic of American Apocalypticism." In *Imagining the End: Visions of Apocalypse from the Ancient Middle East to Modern America*, edited by Abbas Amanat and Magnus T. Bernhardsson, 187–211. New York: I.B. Tauris, 2002.

Wessinger, Catherine Lowman. *Millennialism, Persecution, and Violence: Historical Cases*. Syracuse, N.Y.: Syracuse University Press, 2000.

# Appalachian Mountain Religion

Appalachian mountain religion has been observed only in recent decades as a regional American religion in its own right. Virtually all Protestant denominations and many sects, as well as Catholicism and non-Christian religions, are represented in the region, although that which characterizes mountain religion is native and distinct by its emphasis on autonomy, spiritual worship, and the importance of personal religious experience. Religion is a deep and abiding concern for Appalachians, even for many who may not confess to being religious. Influenced by the landscape and culture, Appalachian mountain religion represents a rich diversity of traditions that are not fatalistic—as some have claimed—but purposeful and meaningful in the daily life of those who call the region home.

## The Region and Culture

Since the Appalachian landscape has influenced its cultural development, the religion cannot be understood apart from the region itself. The mountains and their valleys stretch along the eastern United States, traversing thirteen states, including northeastern Mississippi; the northern reaches of Alabama and Georgia; the western regions of South Carolina, North Carolina, and Virginia; the eastern parts of Tennessee, Kentucky, and Ohio; all of West Virginia; western Maryland; northern and western Pennsylvania; and southern New York. This area accounts for some 205,000 of the 3,537,438 square miles of U.S. land and about 23.6 million of the 300 million people living in the United States as of 2009. The core region looks to the north and west from the Allegheny/Cumberland Mountains and reaches toward the east from the Blue Ridge Mountains; these majestic terrains and the fertile Great Valley, nestled between them, occupy the six states of Georgia, North Carolina, Tennessee, Kentucky, Virginia, and West Virginia. It is the upper regions of this area, known as the southern "highlands," that most often are associated with native mountain religion, although mainline denominations in the area also have been influenced to some degree by the mountain culture.

During its settlement, this rugged wilderness met European immigrants—mostly English, Scots-Irish, and Germans—with a challenging life involving danger, harsh conditions, and isolation. It was survival in this environment that influenced the development of an Appalachian culture, with values reminiscent of an earlier America that persist to the present day. Such values include independence and self-reliance, two of the most basic and proudest Appalachian traits that have been passed down through generations, from pioneers who learned to survive wilderness life by doing for themselves. A common tendency toward neighborliness and hospitality can be traced to the frontier need for cooperation with others, in such things as house and barn "raisings" and the harvesting of crops. The emphasis on family is another important value rooted in the need to "stick together"—particularly in the face of hardship or misfortune—and to provide for relatives, sometimes by "taking them in" until a crisis has passed. Also linked to wilderness survival, personalism involves the ability to relate easily to those of familiar acquaintance and also the penchant to maintain distance from others who are less known; it further involves the tendency to be agreeable with another—even though one actually disagrees—for the sake of avoiding offence. The culture also has fostered a general sense of modesty—one that cautions to not "get above your raising"—that affords a fair self-estimate of one's own abilities. A sense of place has developed over generations and describes a rootedness in the mountains and belongingness that often lure out-migrants back for periodic "homecomings." Other values include a sense of beauty that appreciates nature as well as fine craftsmanship, and a sense of humor that "pokes fun" at self and at others to sometimes break the somberness of life. Perhaps the most important value passed down in Appalachian culture is that of religion, which has helped generations to transcend the stark challenges of their environment and to make sense of their lives. Influenced by the landscape, mountain religion continues to be of great importance in Appalachia and reflects many of the above qualities.

## Mountain Religion Spirituality

Mainly Protestant, mountain religion itself is diverse and complex; however, some commonalities of highlander spirituality may provide an understanding of the world it affords. In general, Calvinism has contributed to the belief that all of humanity is limited by sin and depravity, thus projecting a duality of the world in terms of the natural and the spiritual, which are always in conflict. Although larger society generally sees itself on a road toward progress, mountain people may interpret daily events from a spiritual context, sometimes as a regression that is moving the world toward the end times. This situation leaves one helpless and in need of God's indwelling power, not only for salvation but also for combating the evil that is resident in the world. If not persuaded by an election to salvation, one must trust in grace and pursue holiness to be ready in the last days; regardless, the imminence of the end-times allows little concern for improving social conditions in the ephemeral world and gives focus to more important matters of spirituality. As much as anyone, highland Christians are well aware of the hardships of life and the reality of death. However, they find in religion the power of transcendence such that "death is swallowed up in victory"—whether at the Resurrection or the Second Coming. Heaven will be a place of happiness

and freedom from the sorrows, disappointments, and pain of earthly life.

Among many highlanders, God is the creator of the universe and reigns in sovereign power and majesty; however, his only abode is the human heart. Whether faith involves the Arminian idea of seeking salvation, or the Calvinist belief of being awakened to salvation, many believe God dwells in the hearts of all who are aware that they need him, and they know experientially when he takes residence, from the sense of peace, joy, and spiritual power that provides affirmation. For most, God is triune and expressed in the Father, Son, and Holy Ghost, although some hold fast to the Oneness concept in which Jesus is the name for all members of the so-called Trinity. Although seldom mentioned among mainline churches, Satan is a reality in the lives of some highlanders. A fallen angel, he desires to thwart God's plan and purpose in the world. As the Evil One, he ever lurks behind the scenes to tempt the righteous with worldliness, the lust of the flesh, and sin; furthermore, everyday misfortune and calamity are products of his handiwork. Straying from close communion with God makes one vulnerable to Satan's devices—thus behooving the righteous to stay on guard.

Of utmost concern to many highland believers is salvation, although how it is obtained depends upon the specific tradition to which one belongs. For many, salvation begins with God working in the heart to bring forth conviction or remorse for sins, leading to godly sorrow and repentance. Subsequently, the grace of God acts upon the heart to regenerate new life through spiritual rebirth—as God's spirit takes residence. For Calvinists and Arminians, God's grace plays a central role in the experience, both in awakening the heart to the call of repentance and in providing meaning in the midst of life's hardships and suffering. Some traditions of mountain religion require immersion baptism after conversion in obedience to the Bible; converts may be immersed once or even "dipped" three times—depending on tradition—as a symbol of the spiritual resurrection that has taken place. The sacrament of the Lord's Supper is practiced with variable frequency according to tradition, followed by some with footwashing; the former represents the vertical relationship between the believer and God, whereas the latter illustrates humility and servanthood in the horizontal relationship between believers.

There are other aspects of salvation. Although many highland Christians speak of the Holy Spirit as a presence in conversion and in daily life, holiness Pentecostals describe an experience beyond conversion as the baptism of the Holy Ghost, evidenced by speaking in tongues; this indwelling of the Holy Ghost is believed to provide super-natural power for overcoming Satan and living a successful Christian life. What salvation means may differ among mountain religions: Calvinists believe in the guarantee of eternal security, which means that one cannot fall from grace or lose salvation; Arminians believe that one can fall from grace after salvation through backsliding and be eternally lost, unless one repents to receive salvation once again. According to the latter, the best safeguard against backsliding is to experience a second work of grace called sanctification, through which the sin nature is eradicated by the blood of Christ, leaving unhindered the regenerated heart to live holy and free from sin. To the Calvinist, however, sanctification means being set apart from the world by one's "position" of righteousness in the family of God, which is made possible through new birth; one's "condition" of living imperfectly in the sinful world is nullified by virtue of that position, which is based on the imputed righteousness of Christ. Many of the mountain religious believe that salvation saves one from hell, a place of unspeakable punishment and pain, and allows for entrance into heaven, a place of beauty, peace, and relief from troubles of earthly life. Heaven is sometimes described as including mansions not made with hands, streets paved with gold, a crystal river, angelic harps and choirs, reunion with loved ones, and constant companionship with Jesus and the patriarchs of old. Not all mountain Christians, however, believe in eternal hell as a punishment for sin. The "No-Hellers," a small group among Primitive Baptists, believe that because of Christ's atonement all of humanity is predestined for heaven—regardless of how that earthly life is lived; accordingly, hell is experienced only in this life, in terms of the hardships and unhappiness brought on by sinful living. The ultimate concern of salvation for highlanders is transcendence of death and eternity with God.

Other aspects of mountain spirituality are found in worship practices. Of primary importance for many is prayer as direct communication with God not only as the sovereign, but also as a father; it serves as a medium for praise, thanksgiving, and petition in time of need. A special time for personal testimonies is common in many services and provides an opportunity for any to offer thanksgiving for salvation, prayers answered, and blessings received; depending on the tradition, it also allows for women to participate in services, even though they may not be allowed to preach. The tenor of testimonies sometimes may rise to passionate exhortations that move and strengthen the faith of hearers. As in most religious traditions, music plays a significant role in mountain religion. Set to melodies that evoke deep emotion, the lyrics, in both hymns and gospel songs, can communicate such themes as redemption in the blood of Jesus, the trials of pilgrim-believers, the faithfulness and peace of God, and the hope and beauty of heaven. For some, the message in a song can be more moving than that conveyed through a sermon. There is little concern for elegance in voice, for the song is offered not for show but as worship unto God; singing is something that all believers can do as an act of praise.

The above characteristics can be considered only as general aspects of mountain religion and spirituality. They may vary among specific faith traditions, sometimes being more or less pronounced. Although they may offer some insight into highland spirituality, there always is hazard in providing such basic descriptions as these—as should be noted.

## Roots of Mountain Religion

Appalachian religion and spirituality evolved largely from three religious traditions brought from Europe to the mountains by early settlers and ministers: the Presbyterians, Baptists, and Methodists. The Scots-Irish of Northern Ireland began a major migration to America in the early 1700s and populated regions in southeastern Pennsylvania, western Virginia, and the Piedmont of the Carolinas. The vast majority of these were Ulster Presbyterians who embraced Calvinism and the practice of a rich tradition of annual sacramental meetings known to promote spirituality and piety. A reaction against the Catholic Eucharist, these meetings emerged in post-Reformation Scotland and emphasized the mystery of Christ's presence around a Communion table where believers partook of the Lord's Supper; the touching and tasting of the bread and wine often led to ecstatic experiences that many counted as their day of conversion. These sacramental meetings—which included days of exhortation, thanksgiving, and celebration—became immensely popular as a time for evangelism and spiritual renewal; they eventually were exported to colonial America, where they afforded traditional and new religious meaning in the face of opportunity and challenge. As the first Great Awakening (circa 1726–1745) swept the eastern seaboard, these meetings drew hundreds to thousands among not only Scots-Irish Presbyterians but also Anglicans, English dissenters, and even slaves. By the late 1700s, the Scots-Irish had pressed westward into the mountains in search of land and opportunity, taking with them their religion and sacramental practices. Their pietism, revivalism, and religious fervor would come to serve mountain religion in a profound and meaningful way.

During the Great Awakening, New England Baptists—mostly Calvinists—were awakened from slumber as entire congregations of Separatists, who rejected the union of church and state, joined their ranks. The Baptists themselves had taken exception to this alliance a century earlier under the leadership of Roger Williams, who feared the corruption of the church by the state; furthermore, they distrusted central forms of government, favoring local autonomy. These Separate Baptists came late to the revival but appreciated the fervor and spontaneity of meetings, in contrast to Regular Baptists, who favored more orderly and formal worship. Particularly in Tidewater, Virginia, the Separate Baptists found themselves in growing dispute with the American-established Church of England and its aristocracy, not only for religious but also social and political reasons. The foundation of their protest was based on the democratic notion that individuals, regardless of status, wealth, or education, should have the right to think for themselves in matters of religion and practice. Their tendency to be vocal led to persecution and sometimes imprisonment—which only added to their mission and numbers. By the nineteenth century, this maltreatment led as many as one-fourth of Virginia Baptists on an exodus into the mountains of eastern Kentucky where they could breathe more freely. Their religious values on individual conscientiousness and local autonomy followed them into the mountains, where they would help shape what mountain religion would become.

Led by Anglican John Wesley, Methodism began as a rejection of Calvinism for the Arminian belief that Christ died not only for the elect but for all of humanity. Unlike predestination, salvation in Arminianism could be known for certain because of a "heartfelt" crisis conversion. Furthermore, salvation could be followed by another crisis experience known as sanctification, through which one might be "cured" of the sin nature, overcome temptation, and live a life of perfection. A major key to the success of Methodism was Wesley's "method" of organizing small groups that met in homes for Bible study, prayer, and worship. After migration from England, Methodists formed such groups in the middle colonies of Maryland, New York, and Pennsylvania in the 1760s but realized little growth until after the war. Wesley sent ministers for assistance, of whom the most effective was Francis Asbury who, from 1800 to 1813, rode a circuit on horseback from Maine to Georgia and back to New York on a yearly basis. His visits to the highlands were especially important, since ministers of any denomination in those regions were in short supply. It was Asbury and his circuit riders who spread Methodism and its emphasis on holiness in the highlands and who modeled an itinerant type of ministry that continues in mountain religion today.

A convergence of the Presbyterian, Baptist, and Methodist traditions came about on the Appalachian frontier at the onset of the Second Great Awakening (circa 1790–1840). With rich valley land taken by planters, "plain-folk" settlers pushed into the highlands where they cleared small plots of less fertile farmland. Life in such a dangerous and rugged environment cultivated need for a sense of control over one's life—and the type of religion experienced at the 1801 Cane Ridge revival, in Kentucky, afforded such control through a transformed worldview that managed relationships and a disciplined approach to life. The event itself was begun by Presbyterian ministers as an August sacramental meeting and was later joined by both Methodist and Baptist preachers. About a thousand came forward to sit at communion tables, while tens of thousands came to participate in other revival activities or simply to observe, scoff, socialize, or carouse. Peter W. Williams noted in *America's Religions* that skeptics of the event speculated that "more souls were conceived than saved during the proceedings" (p. 188). History reports some of the most ecstatic displays of emotion on record in American religious history. Participants danced, jerked, swooned, barked, expelled "holy" laughter, and fell into trances—all of which were perceived as manifestations of God's power. From meetings such as this, Baptists and Methodists gained in number as the camp-meeting format was more conducive to their experiential type of worship. Since Presbyterians had fewer ministers serving the highlands, their denomination began to decline as members left to join ranks with the better-supplied Baptists and Methodists: Baptist preachers were self-supporting farmers of the area, and Methodist preachers were appointed and supported by their denomination.

From camp-meeting experiences, pioneers not only perceived heartfelt encounters directly with God, they also benefited from a transformed worldview. The subsequent taboo of vices, such as drinking and gambling, demonstrated in everyday life their rejection of the world and the force of their beliefs in an intellectual, disciplined, and concrete way. Contentment of salvation in the present world, and hope in the next, mitigated the frustration from economic ambitions linked with unlikely success in a planter society. Furthermore, the fellowship of believers fostered a vital sense of cooperation that tempered the proud and sometimes costly individualism of frontier life. In general, camp-meeting religion provided a transformed view of self and the world through participation in a divine order.

## The Emergence of Mountain Religion

Certain factors pertaining to denominationalism and economic development are important in understanding the social psychology of how mountain religion evolved and came to be defined; they also are important for observing how mountain religion came to understand itself as a coffer of spiritual meaning. After Cane Ridge, the frequency and intensity of frontier camp-meeting revivals waned, and camp meetings lapsed from national attention by the 1840s. Led mostly by frontier plain-folk preachers, they were never fully embraced by the leadership of denominations represented among them. Both Baptists and Methodists were becoming more successful as denominations and leaning toward an educated clergy, as evidenced by the founding of several Bible colleges in Appalachia during the 1800s. Furthermore, they were becoming more successful as landowners and coming to appreciate the values of an affluent and elite Southern culture, including the institution of slavery. Losing appeal among mainstream denominations, camp meetings remained an important influence, however, in the spiritual life of Appalachia.

Deborah McCauley has marked the growth of the Baptist and Methodist denominations, from 1800 to 1840, as the beginning of mountain religion in a regional sense, for it was during this time that concerns shifted toward national prominence and political influence. Leaving concern for "vital" religion, they focused instead on developing highly complex and centralized organizations that were committed to education, missions, and social issues—which birthed an era of American benevolence and concern for Christianizing America. Development of this ambitious agenda required a transfer of finance and responsibility from local congregations into the hands of a few who would act by proxy for their denominational membership. Many autonomous and self-reliant churches of Appalachia took great exception to this move.

Particularly among Baptists, the notion of a mission board at a national office offended good theology and gave rise to an Appalachian antimission sentiment. From a Calvinist perspective, the mission effort was misguided and without biblical basis, particularly since people had within them either the seed of regeneration—as the elect—or the seed of damnation. Thus, any global attempt to Christianize an entire nation was a lost cause and misuse of money. Other issues

were more broadly defined. For example, such a mission effort would devalue the work already being done by frontier churches; a centralized office would undermine local autonomy and pave the way for an aristocracy; the practice would subject financially dependent missionaries to political influence from their national office; and the required training would promote ministry as a chosen profession rather than an ordained calling by God. All this, and the constant plea for finances, made the centralized form of denominational leadership offensive to many highlanders and drove a wedge between congregations and their denomination.

The 1800s also found Presbyterian and Methodist denominations losing influence in the highlands. Presbyterians, who required a college-educated clergy, lost ground after the frontier revival for lack of qualified ministers to fill their pulpits; few educated men would make the sacrifice of relocating to the difficult wilderness environment. Furthermore, before the mid-1800s, the denomination had taken a more rational and less intense approach to worship, which resulted in a push from leadership to replace the annual, regional, outside sacramental meetings—sometimes creating a carnival-like atmosphere—with a more frequent, orderly practice of sacrament inside the local church. The nonrational, emotional type of religion still practiced by highlanders came to be viewed as disorderly and improper.

It was much the same for Methodists. Throughout the mid-1800s, and by the 1890s, both factions of the Methodist Episcopal Church, which split in the 1840s over slavery, distanced themselves from the "frenzied" worship so common in the early years of Methodist revivalism. Furthermore, they had compromised their stance on sanctification as a second immediate work of grace with subsequent "sinless perfection" for one that was gradual and progressive. The Holiness doctrine and its associated heartfelt worship, however, had rung a bell in the wilderness frontier and found practical use in guiding life in a region where vices such as drinking, gambling, and fighting were common. The allegiance of frontier churches to this type of faith made them different from an aspiring denomination that preferred an approach to religion more appealing to mainstream America.

The relationship between mountain religion and major denominations also was affected by socioeconomic factors. Toward the end of the nineteenth and into the twentieth century, America was fast becoming an industrial world leader, which brought pressure to rural Appalachia in the harvesting of its natural resources of iron, coal, and timber. The social and economic changes that followed were profound for a region that largely had been isolated from much of America since 1850, when settlers began using alternate routes around the mountains. Industrialization not only changed the landscape of the region, it also transformed the face of a culture that at one time had been proudly independent and self-reliant, leaving many in poverty with little more than their religion to assist them in their social and economic adjustment.

It was during this time, from 1880 to 1930, that mountain religion gained further definition, as major denominations and various home missions boards took notice of Appalachia as a field in great need of American benevolence and evangelism. Despite the Christian and deep spiritual nature of Appalachia, the denominations often viewed the region as largely "unchurched" or, at best, considered mountain religion as an "otherness"—an aberration of true Christianity in need of correction. Therefore, various denominational churches were organized to evangelize the region and address the problem. In many respects, denominational as well as independent home missions boards were helpful in establishing agencies, clinics, and schools, which provided not only basic education for mountain children but also domestic and vocational training; some also were successful in establishing colleges and universities in central Appalachia for training in ministry and professional careers. On the religious front, however, denominations met with limited success, for though mountain people did change over time in response to the social efforts, the essence of mountain religion remained important for highlanders. They tended to abstain from denominational religion, which appeared too formal and tepid for their needs, in preference to their own, which afforded a more meaningful way of experiencing God. Ironically, the denominational interventions in Appalachia helped to distinguish more clearly what came to be seen as a regional Christian religion in its own right.

## Appalachian Religious Groups

Non-Christian religions, Catholicism, and virtually all Protestant denominations and sects are represented in Appalachia, although that which is characterized as mountain religion is predominantly Protestant. Bill J. Leonard has proposed a useful typology of four Christian groups that cover the landscape of Appalachia: (1) mainline churches, (2) evangelical churches, (3) Pentecostal churches, and (4) mountain churches. This categorization can serve to highlight religion in Appalachia today and distinguish basic groups that are unique to mountain religion.

Mainline churches include the Roman Catholic Church and major Protestant denominations found in the region. The Presbyterian, American Baptist (USA), and United Methodist Churches, as well as the Lutheran and Episcopal Churches, all have congregations in Appalachia, as does the United Church of Christ. The Christian Church (Disciples of Christ) also is represented and has roots in the Stone-Campbell traditions, which were birthed and joined following the 1801 Cane Ridge revival; these traditions were restorative in nature but eventually separated into three groups: the Christian Churches (Disciples of Christ), the Churches of Christ, and the "independent" Christian churches, which are undenominational. The Cumberland Presbyterian Church also emerged from the Cane Ridge revival and separated from the Presbyterian denomination in 1810 over the requirement that ministers be college-educated; by relaxing that condition on the frontier, Cumberland Presbyterians experienced marked growth in the years that followed. Today, however, commonly found among all mainline churches are an educated clergy, a formal worship liturgy, and an emphasis on social action regarding cultural and political issues.

Evangelical churches of Appalachia are less formal and are centered on the need for spreading the gospel to the unconverted. Among these are different Baptist and Nazarene congregations, Churches of Christ, and a host of independent churches that are nondenominational and non-Pentecostal; even among churches that are denominationally affiliated, there is great emphasis on local autonomy and other values embraced by mountain religion. Fundamentalist groups are represented here, as well as an emphasis by all on the Bible as the word of God. Ministers of these churches may or may not have college or seminary training and are less likely to be paid full-time, if at all. Their worship includes gospel or contemporary worship music, Bible sermons, and prayer time at the end of service. Depending upon the church tradition, conversion experiences may be either sudden or gradual, although emphasis is given to personal salvation in Jesus Christ. In general, concern for addressing social problems is supplanted by stress on moral issues in relation to social and private life.

Pentecostal churches are represented by denominations such as the Church of God (Cleveland, Tennessee), Church of God of Prophecy, International Pentecostal Holiness Church, Church of God Mountain Assembly, and Assemblies of God, as well as numerous independent Pentecostal groups with no denominational affiliation. Like the Church of God Mountain Assembly, the Church of God is a denomination indigenous to Appalachia that emerged from the Holiness revival that swept the region in the late nineteenth century; it split in 1923 over leadership issues to become the Church of God (Cleveland, Tennessee) and what would become the Church of God of Prophecy. Common to all mountain Pentecostal groups is an emphasis on spirit-filled worship, spontaneous preaching, Spirit baptism with tongues-speaking, and the exercise of various charismatic demonstrations such as healing and prophesying. The clergy may or may not be educated or compensated for services they provide. Any emphasis on ministry for improving society is minimized by concern for living in a holy manner in the present world as a prerequisite for heaven in the next.

The last group, mountain churches, is indigenous particularly to central Appalachia; these churches have no denominational ties, hold fiercely to local autonomy, and practice particular rituals associated with Appalachia. Among them are a variety of Baptist churches, a variety of independent Holiness traditions, and Holiness-Pentecostal serpent-handling sects. All embrace the Bible—mostly the King James Version—as the inerrant word of God and stake its claim as the final authority on all matters pertaining to religion and life.

Because of its predominance, the Baptist church historically has been viewed as the prototypical native mountain church, which is characterized by immersion baptism after conversion. Among the multitudes of different Baptist churches in Appalachia, Howard Dorgan identified six groups that are concentrated particularly in the highlands and are representative of mountain religion: Primitives, Old Regulars, Regulars, Union, Free Will, and Missionary Baptists. Among these groups, there is a range in beliefs and practices. Some (Primitives and Old Regulars) are more strongly Calvinist, rejecting Sunday school and revival campaigns, whereas others (Missionary and Free Will) are more clearly Arminian and thus mission- and evangelism-oriented. The tenor of worship ranges from the formality and reserve of Primitives to the weeping and shouting of Old Regulars. With the exception of the Free Will Baptists, all these groups—as descendents from pioneer Separates and Regulars—are indigenous to the mountains and properly known as "Old-Time Baptists."

Although differing in some beliefs and customs, the Old-Time label fits these groups because all preserve at least some of the following features of mountain religion: (1) a capella lined-singing, extemporaneous preaching, shouting, and emotional worship; (2) living water (creek) baptism by immersion and footwashing; (3) practice of old-time biblical mandates regarding gender and dress; (4) prohibitions against divorce and "double-marriage"; and (5) practice of a particular worship protocol common to them all. Most Missionary and United Baptists no longer adhere to some of these practices, although a few still practice them all.

Mountain churches also are represented by many small, independent Holiness churches scattered across the highlands. All have roots in Methodism that spread throughout the mountains in the wake of the Great Revival. As such, they continue to practice the same experiential worship (sometimes with tongues-speaking) and emphasize piety as a way of life; however, what constitutes the specifics of holiness may differ among groups. Also indigenous to the mountains—and most often misunderstood and unappreciated—are the Holiness-Pentecostal sects that practice serpent handling in obedience to a perceived commandment of Jesus in Mark 16:17–18. Little in their beliefs and worship practices varies from other Holiness-Pentecostal churches, except for the occasional handling of venomous serpents. Some handlers are of Oneness persuasion, which rejects the doctrine of the Trinity for belief in Jesus as the name of the one God, although the majority are Trinitarians.

In general, mountain church preachers may have limited theological or formal education and emphasize that preaching is not a chosen vocation but a calling from God. Their preaching is typically impassioned, sometimes extemporaneous, and "Spirit-led," offered in a chanted, cadenced, musical pitch. Sometimes unpaid, they offer their ministry to the church and community as a sacrifice of love for God. As Leonard observed in *Christianity in Appalachia*, "They are linked to the mountain culture in powerful ways, through grassroots constituency and kinship, as well as a pervasive piety and spirituality" (p. xxii). As for mountain churches in general, belief in salvation by grace and the practice of heartfelt worship are appreciated not only among Old-Time Baptists but by all who embrace mountain religion itself.

Mountain religion and spirituality have persisted over generations largely because of oral tradition. Within the context of a worship service, oral tradition facilitates the transmission of beliefs, behaviors, practices, and rituals through verbal communication and their performance according to rules of the tradition. Such rules are used implicitly by the audience to approve (or disapprove) of a specific performance, as given by one who prays, testifies, sings, preaches, and so forth; audience approval takes form in behavioral responses to the performance, such as singing with the singer, shouting, dancing, or interacting with the preacher, as the case may be. Accordingly, audience participation in mountain religion is an important factor not only in its spirituality but also in the very survival of its traditions.

As a regional phenomenon, Appalachian mountain religion must be understood within its cultural and geographical context. For a people whose history has involved numerous challenges, religion has played no small role in providing spiritual meaning at moments of grave circumstance in life and the hope of heaven when life is done. This type of religion often is misconstrued as fatalistic or compensatory, when in reality it is best understood as a culture attempting to understand its world and make sense of its experiences. As found in mountain religion, the perception of the world as a realm of supernatural power provides a way in which to understand how the forces of good and evil are part of everyday life—be it Baptist Calvinists who are called to election and enabled by divine power to live godly in an evil world or Holiness-Pentecostals who are infused through Spirit baptism with power to overcome evil surrounding them. It is in the hope of heaven that believers gain a different perspective on the tribulations of everyday life, for as they perceive the manifestation of God's presence and power in the midst of calamity, they see spiritual evidence of a world yet to come—one in which troubles, trials, and even death have no part. Their abstentions from worldliness and the practice of sin enable them to avoid struggles between good and evil, which bear witness that they are not of this world, but already part of the one to come. Mountain religion of Appalachia, then, is undeserving of the fatalist and compensatory labels that many have used to describe it. It seems best understood as a religion based on belief in spiritual power that transforms and makes life meaningful in a unique region of America.

**See also** *Baptists: Sectarian; Camp Meetings; Holiness Movement; Missions: Domestic; Music: Appalachian Religious; Revivalism: Nineteenth Century; Serpent Handlers; South as Region.*

W. Paul Williamson

**BIBLIOGRAPHY**

Appalachian Region Commission. "Counties in Appalachia." 2009. www.arc.gov/index.do?nodeId=27.

Campbell, John C. *The Southern Highlander and His Homeland.* Lexington: University Press of Kentucky, 1969. (Orig. pub. 1921.)

Dickson, Bruce D., Jr. *And They All Sang Hallelujah: Plain-Folk Camp-Meeting Religion, 1800–1845.* Knoxville: University of Tennessee Press, 1974.

Dorgan, Howard. *Giving Glory to God in Appalachia: Worship Practices of Six Baptist Subdenominations.* Knoxville: University of Tennessee Press, 1987.

———. "Old-Time Baptists of Central Appalachia." In *Christianity in Appalachia: Profiles in Regional Pluralism,* edited by Bill J. Leonard, 117–137. Knoxville: University of Tennessee Press, 1999.

Evans, Mari-Lynn, Holly George-Warren, Robert Santelli, and Tom Robertson. *The Appalachians: America's First and Last Frontier.* New York: Random House, 2004.

Henry, George W. *Shouting.* Oneida, N.Y.: G. W. Henry, 1859.

Hood, R. W., Jr., and W. Paul Williamson. *Them That Believe: The Power and Meaning of the Christian Serpent Handling Tradition.* Berkeley: University of California Press, 2008.

Jones, Loyal. *Appalachian Values.* Ashland, Ky.: The Jesse Stuart Foundation, 1994.

———. *Faith and Meaning in the Southern Highlands.* Urbana: University of Illinois Press, 1999.

Lawless, Elaine J. *God's Peculiar People: Women's Voices and Fold Tradition in a Pentecostal Church.* Lexington: University Press of Kentucky, 1988.

Leonard, Bill J. *Baptists in America.* New York: Columbia University Press, 2005.

———, ed. *Christianity in Appalachia: Profiles in Regional Pluralism.* Knoxville: University of Tennessee Press, 1999.

Lippy, Charles H. "Popular Religiosity in Central Appalachia." In *Christianity in Appalachia: Profiles in Regional Pluralism,* edited by Bill J. Leonard, 40–51. Knoxville: University of Tennessee Press, 1999.

McCauley, Deborah V. *Appalachian Mountain Religion: A History.* Urbana: University of Illinois Press, 1995.

Schmidt, Leigh E. *Holy Fairs.* Princeton, N.J.: Princeton University Press, 1989.

Synan, Vinson. *The Holiness-Pentecostal tradition: Charismatic Movements in the Twentieth Century.* Grand Rapids, Mich.: Eerdmans, 1997.

Wacker, Grant. *Heaven Below: Early Pentecostals and American Culture.* Cambridge, Mass.: Harvard University Press, 2003.

Williams, John A. *Appalachia: A History.* Chapel Hill: University of North Carolina Press, 2002.

Williams, Peter W. *America's Religions: From Their Origins to the Twenty-First Century.* 3rd ed. Urbana: University of Illinois Press, 2008.

# Appalachian Religious Music

See *Music: Appalachian Religious*

# Architecture

Religious architecture refers to physical structures conceived, designed, and erected for religious uses, especially worship. It is part of the broader built environment of religion and is closely related to religious landscape, which it helps shape. It is also part of the material culture of religion, which includes the entire range of physical objects employed for religious purposes. In North America, which is characterized by extensive religious pluralism and populated with religious cultures that often have been imported from Europe, Asia, or elsewhere, religious architecture is manifold, complex, and highly revealing of the broader contours of the American religious and social experience.

## Religious Architecture and Sacred Space

The terms "religious architecture" and "sacred space" are clearly related to one another but are by no means identical. The primary function of religious architecture is to house and otherwise accommodate the performance of ritual, which is an essential characteristic of religion. Ritual, however, may be performed without any human-built structures, as in the Sun Dance of the Plains Indians and many other rites of native peoples. Many contemporary followers of "New Age" religion, some of whom find inspiration in what they interpret as the spirituality of native peoples, regard the realm of nature as the most appropriate setting for their own private meditations or collective ceremonies. On the other hand, the New England Puritans of the seventeenth century deliberately instituted a new form of religious building, namely, the meetinghouse. Both the name and the structure itself were intended to provide a suitable physical backdrop for the proclamation of the Word of God, the central ritual in their worship. These Puritans, however, were adamant that the meetinghouse was not in itself sacred—that is, possessed of divine power—since such a belief would have compromised their Calvinistic premise that only God (and, by extension, the Word of God) was in any sense sacred. The invention of the meetinghouse and the theology behind it were the continuation of an argument that had originated in the European Reformation and would be continued vigorously in the New World context.

## Church versus Meetinghouse

The conflict, implicit or otherwise, that characterized much of the religious argument that informed colonial American religious life can be summarized as church versus meetinghouse. "Church" is a term that originally referred to a congregation of worshippers but later came to refer to the structure in which they assembled for worship as well. Early Christian churches were often erected on sites associated with the martyrdom of saints and thereby took on an aura of sacred power. By the time of the Reformation, the term "church" had acquired a multiplicity of meanings: a building for worship; a congregation of worshippers; the institution, national or international, to which individual churches (or parishes) belonged and by which they were controlled; or, most cosmically, the entire assemblage of believers, past, present, and future, who constituted the "church invisible." Both the Roman Catholic Church and the various national churches that arose in the wake of Luther's reforms claimed the title of "church," with the implications of power over earthly conduct that the term had acquired, and which was embodied in the multiplicity of individual church buildings that shaped the religious landscape of Europe. These individual churches, for Eastern Orthodox and Roman Catholics and in varying degrees for the new Protestant groups, were places where sacramental worship could be conducted efficaciously because the buildings themselves had been consecrated as sites of sacred power.

The various groups that colonized the Atlantic seaboard during the colonial era reflected the entire range of European opinion on these issues, with some twists of their own. The dominant institutional presence in the English-speaking colonies was the Church of England, whose parish churches were designed for the peculiar mixture of Catholic and Protestant worship that had come to characterize the emergent Anglican tradition, and which also stood as reminders of royal authority in a colonial arc that swept from the maritime provinces of Canada through the British West Indies. Structures such as King's Chapel in Boston, Bruton Parish Church in Williamsburg, and St. Michael's in Charleston were often the largest, most conspicuous, and most centrally located structures in colonial cities and were outward and visible signs of Establishment—that is, the Church of England as the official ecclesiastical arm of the British Empire.

Although other state churches of Europe, such as the Roman Catholic and the Swedish Lutheran, had outposts in the Atlantic colonies, they had no legal status and, in the case of Maryland Catholics, had to worship inconspicuously in private homes after that colony's original Catholic founders had to yield power to Anglicans (that is, members of the Church of England). The real contest took place in colonies where groups of English dissenters—Puritan Congregationalists in most of New England, the Society of Friends (Quakers) in Pennsylvania, and a loose alliance of Baptists and Quakers in Rhode Island—all challenged the Church of England not only politically and theologically but visually and materially in their propensity for erecting meetinghouses rather than churches. Despite the considerable differences among themselves—especially between Quakers and Puritans—their common rejection of the notion that sacred

Bruton Parish Church in Williamsburg, Virginia, reflected the peculiar mixture of Catholic and Protestant worship that had come to characterize the emergent Anglican tradition. Such edifices also stood as reminders of British royal authority in the colonies.

power could be embedded in worldly structures was a radical challenge to the orthodoxy represented by the "church" form of religious building. For Puritans and their Baptist offshoots, the meetinghouse framed the preaching of the divine Word; for Quakers, it was a convenient but simple structure in which the testimonies of the Inner Light could be heard and witnessed. For none was it a place designed primarily for sacramental worship.

## Pluralism, Fashion, and Ideology

The earliest Puritan meetinghouses embodied the same aesthetic exemplified in Puritan sermons: the "plain style." These meetinghouses, best represented today in Old Ship (1681) in Hingham, Massachusetts, were deliberately designed on the model of private homes, village guild halls, or other "secular" structures rather than traditional churches. Instead of an altar, the pulpit was the visual focus of the interior, and communion was served occasionally from a hinged board or movable table. These meetinghouses could also be used for legitimate secular purposes such as town meetings, school classes, or defense against native attacks, without compromising their religious character—which was never defined as in any way embodying the "sacred."

Other than occasional nonfigurative wood carving, these structures were unornamented and intentionally lacked any visual or material representations of the divinity.

With the passage of generations and the loss of Puritan dominance, however, the meetinghouse began to morph into something new—or, rather, something older. Although it retained some of the basic structural features of older structures of the sort, such as a central pulpit and the main entrance on one of the long rather than short sides, Boston's Old South Meetinghouse of 1729 boasted a very unpuritanical steeple and other neoclassical stylistic features popularized by Sir Christopher Wren and his successor, Sir James Gibbs, in the rebuilding of London's "churchscape" following the Great Fire of 1666. The meetinghouse, in short, now resembled nothing so much as an Anglican church. Although Quakers continued to resist this appeal of fashion, at least in the Philadelphia area, Baptists and others followed the Puritan/Congregational lead in abandoning the plain style of the founders in favor of what the Quakers deemed the "fancy" mode of the pacesetters of ecclesiastical as well as architectural fashion. By the nineteenth century, the term "meetinghouse" itself had largely yielded to the more generic "church."

With the loss of Puritan dominance, buildings such as Boston's Old South Meetinghouse of 1729 began to resemble traditional Anglican churches.

By the 1820s, the Wren-Gibbs neoclassical mode had largely given way to a newer form of classicism, namely, the Greek revival. Although ancient in inspiration, this mode evoked for Americans highly resonant associations with ancient Athenian democracy, and before long not only government buildings and private homes but religious buildings of all sorts—from Roman Catholic to Reform Jewish to Episcopal to Swedenborgian—now took on the aspect of "pagan" temples, as each denomination vied to assert its loyalty to American republican values. (The custom of displaying American flags in churches that began during World War I and diminished after the Vietnam conflict is a latter-day corollary.) The proliferation of both governmental buildings and memorials to wars and heroes in classical form

along the mall in the nation's capital is also a good example of the deliberate invocation of sacred allusions in structures not designed for explicit religious worship but that collectively do in fact invoke the patriotic cultus sometimes deemed the American "civil religion."

## Medieval Revivals

A major influence on Victorian American church design was the Cambridge Movement, a corollary of the better-known Oxford Movement that promoted a revival of emphasis on sacramental worship and the historic church among Anglicans on both sides of the Atlantic. The Cambridge Camden Society—also known as the Ecclesiologists—insisted that medieval Gothic was the only appropriate style for Christian sacramental worship and began to provide designs for model churches based on medieval prototypes. In the United States, such churches began to appear among Episcopalians by the mid-1840s, most notably Richard Upjohn's Trinity Church at Wall Street and Broadway in Manhattan. Upjohn, an English expatriate, also invented a new and distinctively American form, namely, "carpenter Gothic," an adaptation of some of the most distinctive features of that style reduced to their essentials and easily built in "board and batten" form from wooden planks and simple tools. As Americans of all denominations began to settle the prairies, Great Plains, and mountain west, they brought this style with them, and it proliferated until it took on iconic dimensions for artists and photographers.

Although Episcopalians, particularly those of "High Church" or "Ritualist" inclinations, readily took to the Gothic revival, it was resisted by some of their "Low Church" coreligionists, as well as many evangelical Protestants with whom the latter identified. These latter, however, found an appropriate medieval style in the Romanesque revival, exemplified in H. H. Richardson's Trinity (Episcopal) Church in Boston's new Copley Square (1877.) The Romanesque, associated by some with the early Christian centuries rather than the later Middle Ages dominated by Roman Catholicism, was adapted by Richardson and his eclectic imitators into Victorian preaching halls for "princes of the pulpit," such as Trinity's Phillips Brooks. Both Gothic and Romanesque revival churches, often massive in scale, became fundamental markers of the Victorian American urban landscape.

## Identity and Adaptation

Although American Protestant churches of a range of denominations proliferated during the great age of urbanization

Richard Upjohn's Trinity Church at Wall Street and Broadway in Manhattan (New York City) reflected the insistence of the Cambridge Camden Society (the Ecclesiologists) that medieval Gothic was the only appropriate style for Christian sacramental worship.

that spanned the decades between the Civil War and the Great Depression, Americans of other backgrounds found themselves in need of adapting to the new situations in which they found themselves through immigration from Europe or in-migration from rural and small-town America. Prominent among the latter were African Americans, who fled north and west in vast numbers in the wake of segregation and peonage. Black slaves had worshipped as they could, in secluded outdoor "hush harbors" or in segregated galleries in white churches. Free blacks often erected modest rural churches in the Greek revival mode, creating a style as iconic as the carpenter Gothic of their western white counterparts. Those newly arrived in Chicago and other northern

cities did what they could, worshipping in storefronts or, if they ascended into the middle classes, either taking over former white churches or building their own, often in the Romanesque revival style. The distinctiveness of their worship was found not in their architecture, an arena in which they lacked economic resources to compete, but rather in their expressive manner of preaching and music.

Those coming from Europe as part of the "New Immigration"—primarily from eastern, central, and southern parts of the continent—were more likely than not to carry with them the Eastern Orthodox, Jewish, or Roman Catholic traditions, and found themselves in the industrial centers of the Northeast and Great Lakes trying to create, or recreate, a suitable environment for worship with limited resources. Eastern Orthodox were perhaps the most traditional, using local materials to build sacrament-centered churches marked by the round domes characteristic of the Greeks and the onion domes of the Russians and other Slavs. Jews, on the other hand, had few distinctive traditions, having adapted those of their host cultures over millennia of diaspora. Touro Synagogue in Newport, Rhode Island (1763), the oldest surviving Jewish house of worship in the nation, is distinctive in its lack of distinctiveness, since it was designed to resemble the houses of the wealthy merchants among which it was situated. By the Victorian era, a new, eclectic urban style had emerged, fusing elements of the medieval revivals found in Christian churches with stylistic aspects of Moorish (Mediterranean Islamic) architecture, as a historical reference to the long association of Jews and Muslims in Iberia prior to the Reconquest of 1492. Exemplified in Cincinnati's Plum Street Temple (1865) and New York's Central Synagogue (1872), as well as in more modest versions in many small towns across the nation, this "Jewish Victorian" style represented active participation in the American civic scene while asserting a note of individuality.

During the early twentieth century a distinctively Jewish American genre emerged: the synagogue-center, which incorporated recreational and educational facilities with worship space to accommodate the needs of a community desirous of maintaining a religious and ethnic identity while conforming to the broader norms of American society.

Roman Catholics, more ethnically diverse and numerous, brought with them an elaborate liturgy and a variety of architectural traditions, many of which were adapted for American use. Patrick Keeley, a prolific Irish-American architect, favored the French Gothic style that appealed to his fellow Irish Catholics, and hundreds of his churches helped form the massive institutional infrastructure that became characteristic of American Catholicism. American Catholics also utilized a variety of styles with historical associations, such as German and Italian Romanesque and Spanish mission, the latter of which emerged during the colonization of northern California during the late eighteenth century by Franciscan missionaries. Although the Catholic immigrant community lacked the resources of many American Protestant denominations, the accumulated small contributions of unnumbered working-class families made possible the erection of such architectural monuments as St. Patrick's Cathedral on Manhattan's Fifth Avenue in 1879. Catholic parishes—the geographical units into which dioceses are subdivided—throughout the nation consisted not only of houses of worship in various revival styles but also of parochial schools, rectories, and convents, while dioceses sponsored high schools and colleges, hospitals, orphanages, cemeteries, shelters for young single people, and other structures designed to mediate life transitions under church supervision.

Protestants also acknowledged the new demands of the pluralistic city with their own adaptations. In addition to a multitude of neighborhood churches built by all denominations, some new forms emerged as distinctive to the American urban context. Episcopalians vied with Roman Catholics in erecting cathedrals and churches, usually large ones, that were designated as the ecclesiastical "seats" of bishops in their dioceses. Cathedrals were intended to be impressive material symbols of the presence of the church in the city, just as they had been in medieval Europe, and often housed lavish collections of art. Some of the latter, which could also be found in wealthier urban churches, consisted of paintings and sculpture collected and donated for the purpose, while other art objects, such as stained glass windows and reredoses (altarpieces), were built into the fabric of the cathedral itself. Cathedrals could also be expressions of aspirations towards religious dominance, as in the (Episcopal) National Cathedral that overlooks the nation's capital.

Cathedrals had social as well as liturgical and political functions and were parts of administrative complexes from which the activities of a diocese, including outreach to the poor, could be coordinated. Evangelical denominations such as the Salvation Army or entrepreneurial preachers also established urban missions, usually nondescript buildings where the poor would be welcomed for shelter, meals, and exposure to a religious message. "Mainline" churches also founded missions where the immigrant poor could worship and receive aid without intruding on the decorous English-language worship of the middle classes. An important innovation of the era was the "institutional church," which often occupied an entire city block and consisted of worship space—often a large Gothic revival church—together with a physical plant housing educational and recreational facilities, including parlors, Sunday school rooms, bowling alleys, basketball courts, and libraries and reading rooms. Such amenities were often aimed not so much at the Episcopalians, Presbyterians, or Congregationalists who were already members but rather at young people recently arrived in the city from farms and small towns who might drift off into the pathways of urban vice if left without wholesome alternatives. (The YMCA and YWCA movements were similar evangelical responses.) Roman Catholic parishes at times offered similar facilities and programs, as did the Jewish synagogue-center.

## Postwar Patterns

Religious building came nearly to a stop during the years of the Depression and world wars, but it revived in the late 1940s as the rush to the suburbs again transformed the geographical and demographic shape of American life. New churches and synagogues proliferated, sometimes in stylized versions of established modes—the colonial revival had patriotic resonances during the cold war era—and others that incorporated the design elements generated by the modernist movement in Europe and by the liturgical revival that originated in Benedictine monasticism and received a major impetus from the reforms of Vatican II. Instead of hierarchically arranged worship spaces, with a processional aisle leading up to the high altar, churches now were frequently designed in semicircular configurations with an altar-table centrally located amidst the congregation, whom the priest now faced. American Lutherans, whose order of worship closely resembled that of Roman Catholics and Anglicans, quickly joined their liturgical bedfellows in creatively adopting these architectural forms.

The evangelical revival that began in the 1970s also ushered in a new era of religious design and building, now situated primarily in the far suburbs and exurbs that grew up around the rapidly expanding conurbations of the Sunbelt. Although such churches began with domestic-like structures that resembled ranch houses, the distinctive new building form was the "megachurch." Megachurches are usually defined as churches with membership of more than two thousand, sometimes exceeding the fifteen thousand mark. Usually but not always evangelical in tone, such churches are in some ways the heirs of the institutional church movement of the era of urbanization. Vast in scale, eclectic in style, and designed to provide both auditorium-style space for preaching and high-tech facilities for any number of other group activities, megachurches target uprooted and unchurched suburbanites as their potential clientele.

Whereas the megachurch was the continuation of a long tradition of Anglo-American preaching-centered evangelicalism, another new feature of the late-twentieth-century American "churchscape" was the proliferation of houses of worship of religions beyond the Jewish-Christian spectrum. The result in large part of the Hart-Cellar Immigration Act of 1965, which facilitated the settlement especially of professionals from Asia and the Middle East, these newcomers brought with them the Buddhist, Hindu, and Muslim traditions. Their often high income levels enabled them to construct appropriate places for worship, often in affluent suburban locales with easy access to interstate highways. Such structures were frequently not simply replicas of prototypes in the home nations of these immigrants but rather adaptations to American circumstances similar to those created by earlier waves of European immigrants when confronted with the new social realities of the American city. Where mosques are a common feature of the urban landscape of Arab countries, for example, American Muslims have been concerned not simply with securing places of worship but also with preserving and transmitting their religious cultures to American-born generations, issues with no relevance in countries where Muslims predominate. The result was the Islamic center, much like the older Jewish synagogue-center, which combined educational and recreational with worship facilities and brokered the cultural differences of the many national groups represented in nascent American Muslim communities. Hindu temples in America similarly reflected new social realities such as changing gender roles, ethnic differences, and the universal immigrant problem of cultural transmission.

## Religious Architecture and the American Landscape

The story of American religious architecture is in many ways the story of American religion and, more broadly, of America itself. The clues offered by such architecture can be a valuable addition to other sorts of evidence for interpreting those stories. The following are some general themes illustrated in the preceding narrative.

*Ritual.* Although ritual is a universal constituent of religion, the ways in which it is enacted are as diverse as religion itself. Religious architecture is, first and foremost, a material backdrop for worship, and the study of worship is inseparable from that of its backdrop. Ritual, though often tradition-bound, is seldom static, and changes in belief and worship frequently exist in dialectical tension.

*Expanded Religious Functions.* In a new society in which many social functions provided by traditional communities no longer existed, religious organizations by some mixture of choice and necessity began to take them up. The result was the erection under religious auspices of programs and physical facilities for recreation, education, and the care of the ill and the indigent.

*Pluralism.* The enormous variety of religious building, past and present, in the United States is reflective of the diversity of religious adherence that has been fundamental and distinctive in America's religious composition.

*Political Presence.* Religious buildings are visible markers of a religious body's presence in a community and may be assertions of civic participation or political influence.

*Immigration and Ethnicity.* The major source of U.S. diversity has historically been immigration, from virtually every part of the world, an immigration predating the arrival of Europeans as indigenous peoples arrived from Siberia (and perhaps other locales) and spread throughout the American continents. One of the primary components of the cultural baggage of immigrants is their religion, and with it the remembered physical settings for the performance of that religion.

*Adaptation.* Although immigrants often seek to replicate the built environment, religious and otherwise, of their homelands, they almost inevitably find themselves having to adapt and innovate as well, incorporating new raw materials and building techniques as well as devising new sorts of structures to meet needs that had never existed in the lands whence they came.

*Demographic Change.* In addition to immigration, the patterns of American life have been historically affected deeply by in-migration, the movement of populations within the boundaries of the nation. As the focus of American settlement shifted from farm to city to suburb to exurb, religious building, as well as other types, have adapted in scale, siting, and structure to the needs presented by continually shifting patterns of settlement. Where the Anglican churches of colonial Virginia, for example, were sited for access from scattered plantations by horse or boat, the megachurches of the early twenty-first century must have easy interstate access and vast parking facilities.

*Economic and Social Status.* Building costs money. The scale, siting, and style of religious buildings are primary evidence of the social status of a congregation, as reflected in the financial resources it can muster for its building.

*Fashion.* In addition to money, fashion is another marker of social status, and religion and its built environment are by no means exempt from its call. Fashion in religious building may result, as it did in medieval Europe, from the primacy of religious institutions and leaders as shapers of fashion (hence Gothic); from the dominant role of governmental institutions, as in the Roman Empire (Romanesque); from a privileged aristocracy, as in Georgian England (neoclassicism); or, as in the United States, the prestige of commercial culture, which has been cited as an explanation for the putative resemblance of megachurches to shopping malls or corporate headquarters.

The built environment of American religion is, in short, not only diverse but as complicated in its forms, functions, and sources as the religious traditions that have produced it within the context of a broader society, the character of which it reflects and by which it has been shaped.

**See also** *Architecture* entries; *Immigration* entries; *Liturgical Arts; Megachurches; Music* entries; *Worship* entries.

Peter W. Williams

**BIBLIOGRAPHY**

Buggeln, Gretchen T. *Temples of Grace: The Material Transformation of Connecticut's Churches, 1790–1840.* Hanover, N.H.: University Press of New England, 2003.

Chidester, David, and Edward T. Linenthal, eds. *American Sacred Space.* Bloomington: Indiana University Press, 1995.

Goldman, Karla. *Beyond the Synagogue Gallery: Finding a Place for Women in American Judaism.* Cambridge, Mass.: Harvard University Press, 2000.

Ivey, Paul Eli. *Prayers in Stone: Christian Science Architecture in the United States.* Urbana: University of Illinois Press, 1999.

Kaufman, David. *Shul with a Pool: The "Synagogue-Center" in American Jewish History.* Hanover, N.H.: University Press of New England, 1999.

Kilde, Jeanne Halgren. *When Church Became Theatre: The Transformation of Evangelical Architecture and Worship in Nineteenth Century America.* New York: Oxford University Press, 2002.

Nelson, Louis, ed. *American Sanctuary: Understanding Sacred Spaces.* Bloomington: Indiana University Press, 2006.

White, James F. *Protestant Worship and Church Architecture.* New York: Oxford University Press, 1964.

Williams, Peter W. *Houses of God: Region, Religion and Architecture in the United States.* Urbana: University of Illinois Press, 1997.

# Architecture: Asian Religions

Architecture of Asian religious traditions in the United States includes temples, churches, and *Gurdwaras* used by Hindu, Buddhist, Sikh, Jain, and Shinto congregations. The internal diversity within the immigrant groups, the existence of religious subcultures, and practice of congregational and noncongregational services influence the kinds of structures built to house these traditions.

## Buddhist Architecture

Buddhist traditions in America include Theravada, Mahayana, and Vajrayana schools of Buddhism. Paul Numrich argues that there are two parallel congregations in American Buddhist temples: the immigrant/Asian American congregation and the non-Asian, native-born (often white) American congregation.

The Japanese brought Mahayana practices to the United States between 1868 and 1912. Buddhist temples in America did not carry the architectural characters of temples and monasteries (*vihara*) in Japan (such as landscaped courtyards, pagoda roofs, and grottos). Instead, the immigrants modified existing buildings by adding decorative motifs such as the dharma wheel and lotus symbols on the walls. They re-created temple altars (*butsudan*) to hold statues of the Buddha and *bodhisattavas* (divine beings and incarnations of Buddha).

Sociologist Tetsuden Kashima argues that Buddhist temples in Japan were primarily places of worship and spiritual development, while in America they became religious and social spaces that sustained ethnic communities. Many of the immigrants practiced Jodo Shinshu, a denomination of Amida Buddhism. The main temple of this sect is Hongwanji-Ha in Kyoto. The 1898 Bukkyo Seinen Kai Buddhist organization (also known as Young Men's Buddhist

Association) met in the home of one Dr. Katsugoro Haidu in San Francisco. Within a few months, the congregation met in the Pythian Castle Auditorium (909 Market Street) and within a year moved to a building in Mason Street. After moving about in multiple locations, in 1905, the Buddhist Church of San Francisco was reestablished at 1880 Pine Street. After major rebuilding in 1935, the new three-storied structure looked like a Western church with arches and pediments. However, external architectural motifs such as the lotus on the doorway and a domed roof with a pagoda finial mark this as a Buddhist building. Internally, it had a *hondo* (worship sanctuary), a *stupa* (Buddhist reliquary), food and incense offerings area, a gymnasium, and office spaces.

After the Japanese internment during World War II, freed prisoners spread out across the United States carrying their religious beliefs. The Midwest Buddhist Temple and Buddhist Temple of Chicago opened in 1944. Buddhist churches and meeting places across the country doubled up as community centers. For instance, in 1945, returning internees found sanctuary in temporary prefab houses built on the grounds of the Arizona Buddhist Church.

Zen is a practice within Mahayana traditions. The Buddhist Society of America opened in New York City in 1931 to popularize Zen meditation. Zen teacher Nyogen Senzaki opened Zen centers in San Francisco and Los Angeles during this decade. By the late 1950s Zen was popular among the predominantly Anglo-American congregations of the Beat Generation, and by the mid-1960s centers opened in New York, Rochester, Boston, Philadelphia, Washington, D.C., Chicago, Los Angeles, San Francisco, and Hawaii to cater to a mixed native-born, Anglo, and Asian congregation.

The Buddhism practiced by the Chinese incorporates deities originating from Taoism and Confucianism. The main architectural elements in a Taoist/Buddhist temple, popularly called Joss Houses, are (1) a sloping roofed structure with a front porch; (2) altars, food offering tables, bells, and gongs; and (3) wall inscriptions and tapestries. In the United States, a Joss House has come to stand for a Chinese shrine. The origins of this term can be traced back to joss sticks, or incense sticks that are burnt in this space. Temple layout, based on Chinese rules of geomancy, includes a single room with an altar and screens to channel good spirits. Often rooms are added on either side or at the back of the main room to house a storeroom, a kitchen, or a priest's living quarters.

The Kong Chow Temple of San Francisco (1853, rebuilt after 1909), Oroville's Moon Temple (wooden structure in 1850s, rebuilt in 1863), the Mo Dai Miu temple in Mendocino, and the Bok Kai Miu Temple in Marysville (1854) are early examples of Taoist temples. According to the Pluralism Project, by the end of the nineteenth century, there were four hundred Chinese temples on the West Coast and in the Rocky Mountain frontier states.

The Weaverville Joss House Temple, built in 1874 (first built in 1852 and rebuilt three times), is a typical Taoist temple located in a wooded site. The building is a wooden structure with a porch and two parallel gables. In China, temples are built of stone and tile. In the New World, immigrants used wood, but they painted the wooden façade to resemble sky-blue tiles with pearl white mortar. The porch has a cedar gate with golden Chinese inscriptions hung over it. Symbols of a lotus flower, dragon fish, and dragons embellish the rooftop. Ornate cornices transform this ordinary building into a temple. A bright red screen near the entrance door guards against evil spirits. The inside room is dimly lit and fragrant due to burning incense. The floor is made of cedar and the altar has a railing. Silk

Storefront Taoist/Buddhist temple in New York City dedicated to Guan Gong.

tapestry banners, embroidered and stitched scrolls, and King's umbrellas embellish the walls. In addition to deities, brass inscribed tablets and ceremonial objects such as oracle books, incense burners, and divination sticks are placed on the altar. An offering stand holds fruits, candy, or incense.

A study of the Guan Gong temple (294 Broome Street, New York) conducted by this author and his students, shows that recent Taoist/Buddhist storefront temples resemble the interior layouts of their twentieth-century predecessors. This temple is one of many set up by the recent Fuzhounese immigrants in New York. Like the older Joss Houses, these storefront temples include a central hall with multiple altars, a platform for offerings, wall tapestries and scrolls, and incense and offerings. In addition, back rooms serve as kitchens, storerooms, and living spaces.

Theravada Buddhist places of worship appeared in the American continent after 1965 with the coming of new immigrants and refugees from Thailand, Laos, Cambodia, Sri Lanka, and Vietnam. New Theravada temples built since the 1990s follow the architectural details of temples in Asia. Examples include the Buddhist Vihara (1966) and the Dharma Vijaya Buddhist Vihara (1980) for Sri Lankan immigrants in Washington, D.C.; Wat Thai Temple in Los Angeles for Thai worshippers (1972); and Wat Lao Phouthavong Temple in Catlett, Virginia, for Laotians (1979). The temples double as social spaces catering to immigrants. Theravada worship involves ritual chanting on a raised platform and sacred enclosure (*mandapaya*) next to the altar. The main prayer hall is called a *sala*. Many new temples have accommodations for the monks in the temple precincts. In Wat Promkunaram, a Thai temple in Waddell, Arizona, living quarters for the monks, a library, and offices are tucked behind the prayer hall. A larger community hall with a kitchen and dining space is built separately in the site to accommodate social events and ceremonies. In addition, temples are festooned with brightly colored flags.

Tibetan Vajrayana Buddhist centers include the Land of Compassion Buddha in West Covina, California, ongoing building projects of the United Trungram Buddhist Fellowship (Sankhu Monastery, Mahamudra Hermitage, Trungram International Academy), and the Drepung Loseling Monastery in Atlanta, Georgia.

In general, buildings used by Asian Buddhist congregations can be categorized into two types: (1) preexisting structures reused as religious spaces, often indistinguishable from surrounding secular buildings; and (2) new custom-built structures set apart from the surrounding landscape by their

The Fresno Betsuin Buddhist temple, located at 1340 Kern Street, belongs to the Jodo Shinshu (Pure Land) denomination of Buddhism.

scale, architectural form, and building materials. The first kind, popular in the early years of the twentieth century, comprised buildings that reused local materials and structures but added symbolic elements and inscriptions to the façade and painted the buildings in ways that made them resemble structures back home. Recurring elements such as lotus flowers, dharma wheels, and post and lintel gates were often added so that the buildings were identifiable from outside. Immigrants often transformed these buildings by creating an appropriate ambience through ephemeral and sensory modifications to the environment. As a result, most changes occur in the interior of the buildings, including smells, sounds, and haptic choreographing of access into the shrine. Newer buildings, especially those built since the 1980s by recent immigrants, are more ostentatious, their external façades resembling temples in Asia. High plinths and pagoda roofs (Hsi Lai Temple, Hacienda Heights, California), elaborate sculptural gates and landscaping (Wat Promkunaram, Waddell, Arizona), replicas of temples in Asia (Wat Florida Dhammaram, Kissimmee) and signage in Asian languages make these temples stand out in the American landscape.

## Shinto Architecture

The architectural layout of Shinto shrines includes a main hall for worshipping (*haiden*) and a smaller hall for the deity (*honden*). In more elaborate temples, one may find a room between the *haiden* and the *honden*. Called *heiden*, these rooms offer spaces accessible to the priests only. The sacred precinct of the temple is delineated by a ceremonial gate called the *torii*. These gates, generally made of wood, have straight or curved lintels. The path and landscape leading to the shrine via the *torii* is decorated with stone lanterns and lion statues (*komainu*). The eaves of shrine roofs sometimes have carvings of mythical beasts. The temple walls have strips of white paper (*gohei*) and sacred plaited ropes (*shimenawa*). Since ablutions are necessary during prayer, shrines also have a tub for washing the face and hands. The Tsubaki Grand Shrine erected in Stockton, California, in 1987 is the first documented Shinto shrine within the U.S. mainland. Earlier temples exist in Hawaii (such as the Hawaii Kotohira Jinsha started in 1920).

## Hindu Religious Architecture

Hinduism is a complex tradition with many subgroups with diverse local languages, practices, and deities. Hindu religious spaces are of two types: shrines and consecrated temples. Because Hindu worship need not be congregational, Hindu shrines appear in homes, businesses, and places of work. These shrines, housed in elaborate cabinets, are sometimes located in rooms set aside for worship or placed on shelves and china cabinets.

Hindu temple building in the United States has increased since the 1970s. Two kinds of temples appear in the American landscape: spaces where practice is primarily congregational and temples where ritual practice is common. According to John Y. Fenton, consecrating a temple is a symbolic act during which the site of the temple becomes part of a larger sacred landscape. Diana Eck refers to the notion of pilgrimage in order to understand the social reproduction of Hindu sacred geography in the United States. Some temple compounds literally re-create temples and landscapes from India (for example, Shiva Vishnu Temple in Lanham, Maryland, the Divya Dham Temple in Queens, New York, and the Shri Venkateshwara temples in multiple American cities).

The term "Missionary Hinduism" describes an intellectual Hinduism that has appealed to American converts since the nineteenth century. The interior architecture of Missionary Hinduism buildings primarily caters to congregational practices. Examples include temples for Vedanta Societies (started in 1900), Self-Realization Fellowship (started in 1920), and International Society for Krishna Consciousness (established in 1966). The opulent International Society for Krishna Consciousness temple designed in New Vrindaban, West Virginia, contains multiple temples built in eclectic Rajput architectural styles resembling palaces and temples in the Indian state of Rajasthan.

A prominent example of a building for congregational worship is the Vedanta Temple of San Francisco, known as the first Hindu temple of the West (built in 1906, added to and completed in 1908). The San Francisco temple served a largely Anglo congregation during a time of popular anti-Asian sentiments and negative perceptions of Hindu and Oriental religions. The architectural style of this building is eclectic, with elements borrowed from Islamic mausoleum domes, Hindu temple towers from Bengal and North India, Moorish arches, onion domes, battlemented parapets of European castles, and bay windows akin to those found in neighboring Victorian homes in the upscale Filmore neighborhood where the temple is located. Foliated arches over the windows, lotus-petal canopy protruding over a marble-mosaic doorway, and a Taj Mahal dome are architectural elements that refer to its exotic eastern origins. The building layout is not so "exotic": it has a congregational prayer hall, a rectory, and a series of terrace-top chapels. Men and women sat in separate chairs across the central aisle during "vesper" services on the weekends and evenings. The monk stood on the elevated wooden dais on the altar platform to give a sermon to his seated congregation. Hindu practices were mixed with Christian ones, creating a hybrid behavior in this space. The building was designed by Joseph Leonard, an architect and developer from the Bay Area.

Another good example is the Vedanta Temple of Berkeley, California, built in 1939. Designed by Henry Higby Gutterson (1884–1954), a prominent Bay Area architect who worked with John Galen Howard (1864–1931) and Bernard Maybeck (1862–1957), the temple is designed to look like a church.

Raymond Williams argues that immigrant Hindu temples in America put aside internal differences, creating a pan-Hindu ecumenical order. In these temples we find an attempt to accommodate diverse deities, practices, and architectural styles in ways that are not found in India. Nonecumenical temples catering to specialized traditions exist. Examples are the Swaminarayan temples and the Pushtimarga temples (Vraj, Pennsylvania; Sayreville, New Jersey) built by Gujarati

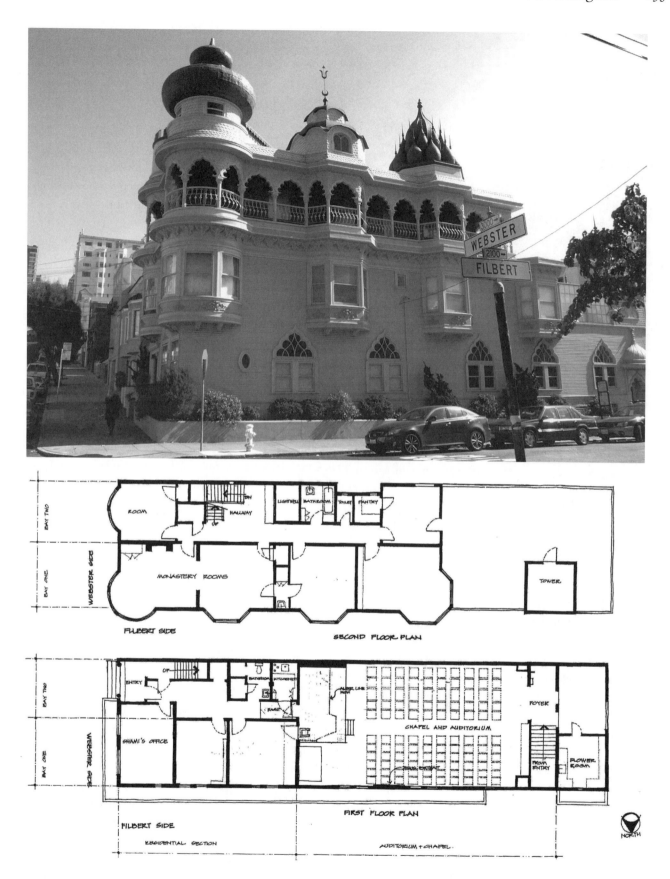

The Vedanta Temple in San Francisco. Plan and Elevation. The temple was built in 1906 and completed in 1908. Vedanta practice emerged from Hinduism.

The Hindu Temple Society of North America, Ganesh Temple, Flushing, New York.

Fremont Hindu Temple in California; and in the faux relief on the façade of the Vaikunth Hindu-Jain Temple of South Jersey in New Jersey.

In contrast, the South Indian style is identifiable by a pyramid-shaped tower gate (*gopuram*), with smaller stepped stories containing pavilions and carved statuettes. Examples of temples built in the South Indian style include Shri Venkateshwara Temple, Pittsburgh; Ganesh Temple, Flushing, New York; Meenakshi Temple, Houston; Shri Venkateshwara Temple, Los Angeles; Shri Vishwanatha Temple, Flint, Michigan; Rama Temple, Lemont, Illinois; Shri Venkateshwara Temple, Aurora, Illinois; and Shiva-Vishnu Temple, San Francisco.

The Hindu Temple of Greater Chicago is an example of the two variations built side by side. The Rama Temple with its towering South Indian–style *gopuram* is flanked by the shorter North Indian–style *shikhara* of the Ganesh-Shiva-Durga Temple. However, these "styles" are monikers that stand for complex politics of temple building and the differences between immigrant subgroups. Major regional and historical variations within these styles can be easily missed by following the simplistic binary nomenclature. Students of Indian temples should therefore carefully examine the details of the temple before using existing categories to describe temple architecture.

*immigrants*, Venkateswara temples (Pittsburgh, Chicago, and other locations) built by Tamils and Telegu-speaking groups, and Kali Temple (New York) or Ananda Mandir (Somerset, New Jersey) by Bengali-speaking immigrants. Indo-Caribbean Hindus (American Sevashram Sangha, Jamaica, New York; Sri Ram Mandir, Cyprus Hill, Brooklyn, New York) have also built temples in recent times.

The basic layout of a Hindu temple includes one or more sanctum areas. Variations of these spaces (called *garbha griha* in Sanskrit or *grabhagraham* in Tamil) include a separate room or an area delineated within a larger space by a canopied platform (*mandapam* or *mandap*) or a simple raised dais. The sanctum area is not accessible to lay worshippers and is only entered by officiating priests. Worshippers circumambulate the sanctum.

Scholars categorize Hindu temples under North Indian and South Indian styles. The North Indian style, also known as the *Nagara* style, is loosely characterized by the presence of a beehive-shaped tower (*shikhara*) made in multiple overlapping layers and tipped by a round, flattened element called the *amalaka*. Examples of North Indian temple architecture can be seen in temples such as the Hindu-Jain Temple in Monroeville, Pennsylvania; the Hindu Temple of metropolitan Washington; Sunnyvale Hindu Temple and

## Jain Architecture

Jainism is a distinct religion popular in India. Jain temples in the United States share premises with Hindu temples (for example, Hindu-Jain Temple, Monroeville, Pennsylvania; Samarpan Hindu Temple, Philadelphia). Some are located in the same grounds as Hindu temples (for example, Jain Religion Center of Wisconsin, Pewaukee). Since the late 1990s, new temples dedicated to Jain worship have appeared (for example, Jain Center of Northern California, Milpitas; Jain Center of Southern California at Buena Park). Nevertheless, a majority of contemporary Jain centers are located in existing buildings and rented halls. Architecturally, the new Jain temples resemble North and West Indian temples. The sanctum houses deities of Mahavira, the founder of the religion, and twenty-four *tirthankaras* (enlightened liberated souls).

## Sikh Architecture

The Sikh place of worship is called a *Gurdwara* (literally a doorway to the guru). A typical layout of a Sikh *Gurdwara* consists of a rectangular room to house the sacred scriptures called the *Guru Granth Sahib*. The sacred scripture is placed on a raised platform with a covering canopy. The room can be entered from all four sides. Men and women traditionally sit in separate aisles. The central hall is designed for circumambulation of the sacred scriptures. Sometimes a ribbed dome with ornamental toppings crowns this room, and arched copings and architectural kiosks are attached to this structure. A saffron or blue flag called *Nishan Sahib* is flown atop the *Gurdwara* to mark the sacred domain. A *Gurdwara* also includes a public meeting place, an educational institution, a service space for the community, and a communal kitchen (*langar*).

The first *Gurdwara* in the United States was established in Stockton, California. The *Gurdwara* began in a small frame house in 1912. The November 22, 1915, issue of the *Stockton Record* newspaper reported the opening of the Stockton *Gurdwara* on 1936 South Grant Street. The article described the worship ceremonies in this two-storied building. The sanctum was on the second floor while the first floor acted as a public meeting room. In 1929, the old structure was moved, and a new imposing brick building with a large arched entrance portal was built in the same location. In addition to being religious spaces, twentieth-century *Gurdwaras* along the Pacific Rim became sites of nationalist activism against British rule in India and meeting places for Indian immigrants from all religious persuasions.

A new wave of Sikh immigrants came to the United States after 1965 and again in the mid-1980s. Many of them came to the borough of Queens, New York. After using the basement of St. Michael's school in Flushing as a Sunday meeting and worship space, the first *Gurdwara* on the East Coast was built in Richmond Hill in 1972. This *Gurdwara* catered to a large community: the community kitchen fed more than five thousand men and women during festivals. The 1970s saw a spurt in the number of *Gurdwaras* across the country. While many of them are housed in temporary spaces, churches, basements, preexisting buildings, and warehouses (Millis, Massachusetts; Denver; Bridgewater, New Jersey; Hayward, California), there are new ostentatiously built structures such

as the ones in California, including El Sobrante (1970s), Yuba City (1969), Fremont (1978), and Sacramento (1983); and in Durham, North Carolina (1985). These new buildings are often bigger to accommodate larger and richer congregations. They are built in the Indo-Persian style of architecture, resembling the main Sikh shrine of Harimandar Sahib in Amritsar. Fluted and solid domes, multifoil arches, decorated panels and pilasters, and variations of trefoil arches are architectural elements used in these buildings. However, building such large and architecturally significant structures is also fraught with political resistance from local communities, as seen in the controversy surrounding the design and building of a $10 million Sikh *Gurdwara* on a forty-acre property in the Evergreen Hills neighborhood of San Jose, California, in 1997. The Pluralism Project at Harvard University lists 251 religious centers related to Sikhism in its 2008 database.

## Conclusion

A point to keep in mind while studying Asian religious architecture in the United States is that cultural forms are translated and interpreted differently in new contexts. Theories of cultural diffusion focus on the retention and reuse of material and visual forms, symbolic details, interior layout, and architectural styles in buildings. Indeed, due to their visual alterity, stylistic and formal features such as the dharma wheel, temple towers, gates, and signage take precedence over less apparent spatial characteristics such as the processional layout, forms of access and territories, sensory ambience, and conflicting user interpretations of these spaces. These visual forms are therefore the first identifiable features that distinguish religious buildings. However, for Asian religious architecture, theories of hybridity, performance, and translation offer a better framework of analysis. An interpretive framework that relates the building to its social, economic, and political context allows us to see how these architectural forms are tempered and construed as a response to local government, communities, media, and other forms of authorship.

Buildings housing Asian religions in the United States fall under a continuum of architectural marking strategies used by their builders to relate to the larger cultural landscape—from camouflaging, or erasing all signs of difference from the exterior form, on the one hand, to accentuating visible difference through exotic architectural forms, on the other. Buildings are marked by using a bank of symbolic forms and details that reproduce social and spatial boundaries and distinguish these buildings from the surrounding landscape. Semifixed and impermanent features such as flags, posters, and signage are easy to tack on and can be a quick and easy way to demarcate religious territories. Fixed features such as towers, lintel detailing, and structural features are more expensive and difficult to build and hence require a larger and politically sustainable congregation, as well as amenable social, political, and economic circumstances. Hence we find that at different historical periods these strategies varied with demographics and the acceptability of these religions within American society.

Boundary maintenance and marking processes occur in the interior of buildings, too. Manipulation of visual and physical access, interior layout and use, creation of processional movement spaces, controlling smells and sounds, and home behavior are tactics that are ephemeral, performative, and dependant on the user. Different users experience and interpret these tactics differently, making it necessary to situate these spaces within social and spatial contexts.

See also *Architecture* entries; *Bahá'í*; *Buddhism in North America*; *Buddhist Tradition and Heritage*; *Canada: Pluralism*; *Hindu Tradition and Heritage*; *Hinduism in North America*; *Jainism*; *Sikhs*; *Zen Buddhism*.

Arijit H. Sen

## BIBLIOGRAPHY

Carnes, Tony, and Fenggang Yang. *Asian American Religions: The Making and Remaking of Borders and Boundaries*. New York: New York University Press, 2004.

Chace, Paul G. "The Oldest Chinese Temples in California: A Landmarks Tour." *Gum Saan Journal: Chinese Historical Society of Southern California* 14 (June 1991): 1–19.

Eck, Diana, ed. *On Common Ground: World Religions in America*. CD-ROM. New York: Columbia University Press, 1997.

Fenton, John Y. *Transplanting Religious Traditions: Asian Indians in America*. New York: Praeger, 1988.

Mann, Gurinder Singh, Paul David Numrich, and Raymond Brady Williams. *Buddhists, Hindus and Sikhs in America*. Religion in America Series. New York: Oxford University Press, 2001.

Munekata, Ryo, ed. *Buddhist Churches of America*. Vol. 1, *75 Year History, 1899–1974*. Chicago: Nobart, 1974.

National Park Service. "A History of Japanese Americans in California: Organizations and Religious Practices." In *Five Views: An Ethnic Historic Site Survey for California*, November 17, 2004. www.cr.nps.gov/history/online_books/5views/5views4c.htm.

Numrich, Paul David. *Old Wisdom in the New World: Americanization in Two Immigrant Theravada Buddhist Temples*. Knoxville: University of Tennessee Press, 1996.

Prentiss, Karen Pechilis. "The Pattern of Hinduism and Hindu Temple Building in the U.S." The Pluralism Project at Harvard University, 1997–2008. www.pluralism.org.

Sen, Arijit. Mapping Transnational Boundaries: Urban Cultural Landscapes of South Asian Immigrants in San Francisco and Berkeley, 1900–2000. Unpublished dissertation, University of California, Berkeley, 2002.

# Architecture: Early America

As many historians have noted, religion in colonial America was pluralistic from the beginning. The varied religious denominations transplanted by colonists were a reflection of their ethnic and geographical origins, which in turn influenced their respective modes of worship and the buildings they constructed. However, out of necessity, in the early years of settlement all colonists worshipped in temporary structures or in buildings constructed for other purposes. Later, as communities grew and colonists became more settled, worshippers began to erect more permanent and impressive buildings of enduring indigenous materials. In some cases, forms such as the Congregational meetinghouse type were adopted by other Protestant denominations in the colonies. Increasingly throughout the eighteenth century, architectural style and taste from England began to influence the design of colonial religious buildings, providing a greater aesthetic unity across denominations.

## Anglican Churches in Virginia

The earliest English settlement on the eastern seaboard was in the Virginia colony. In 1607, colonists established the first permanent English settlement, which they named Jamestown. These Virginia colonists, distinguished from colonists in New England who sought religious freedom, were instead motivated by economic independence. Despite the reason for their emigration, the Jamestown colonists were not without faith and appear to have held worship services immediately upon arrival in their new home. Their leader Captain John Smith wrote of their early experience,

> I well remember wee did hang an awning (which is an old saile) to three or foure trees to shadow us from the Sunne, our walles were rales of wood, our seats unhewed trees till we cut plankes, our pulpit a bar of wood nailed to two neighbouring trees. In foule weather we shifted into an old rotten tent; for we had few better....

It was in such a primitive worship space that these colonists recited from the *Book of Common Prayer* two times a day and held Sunday service. Later, a more permanent wood structure was built. This edifice was probably of earthfast construction, where wooden posts providing the structural support for the building were set directly into the ground. After this church burned in 1608, colonists replaced it with another structure approximately thirty feet by twenty-four feet, also of wood. A third church built in 1617 likewise was of wood, but it was set upon a stone and brick foundation, an enhancement that extended its life. However, it was not until 1639 that colonists began construction of a truly permanent church of brick—a project that took them until 1647 to complete.

The importance placed on building worship space at Jamestown was not completely driven by the colonists' own piety. The charter authorizing the Virginia settlement declared the Anglican or Church of England the official church, which in turn was supported by public monies. Gradually, legislation further defined the role of the Anglican Church, directed its physical development, and regulated colonists' participation. Within two years, the Virginia Company Council dictated that three settlements would be established and each would have a church. By 1624, acknowledging both the rural quality of the colony and its system of plantations, the General Assembly ordered that every plantation should have a room or a building in which to worship. As a practical matter, the organization of the Anglican Church in Virginia was based on parishes, which ranged in size from a single plantation to a county or larger. In the 1630s, a law was passed mandating Communion three times a year and authorizing the imposition of a fine for an unexcused absence from worship service.

According to architectural historian Dell Upton, most of Virginia's churches of the colonial period were wood and, accordingly, do not survive. One of the earliest examples for which there is documentation is the nonextant Poplar Spring Church of 1677 in Gloucester County. Probably of earthfast construction, its interior belied its crude construction and exterior. With paneled pews, a chancel screen, and a pulpit that rose three levels, it also reportedly had painted cherubim. Typical of these early wood churches, its construction necessitated its replacement by 1723. Throughout the eighteenth century, a majority of churches continued to be built of wood. Two notable wooden churches that survive are Slash Church (1730) in Hanover County and Tillotson Parish Church (c. 1760) in Buckingham County. These rectangular buildings have entrances directly into the long sanctuary. A gallery at the west end provided additional seating.

A seventeenth-century brick church known as St. Luke's, in Isle of Wight County, Virginia (c. 1680), survives as Virginia's oldest church and is today considered by many to be the quintessential church of colonial Virginia. Stylistically, the exterior is an amalgam of several European influences. The tall entrance tower, buttresses, and pointed arched windows with tracery reference the Gothic style—a late survivor of this medieval style. The crow-stepped gable at the east end shows a Flemish influence. Details such as the quoin and applied pediment over the entrance exhibit an awareness of classical architecture on the part of the building's unknown designer. Inside is the long nave with center aisle but without a separate chancel. This interior arrangement was derived from the rectangular room or auditory churches of rural England that began to emerge in the early seventeenth century. A related church is St. Peter's Parish Church in New Kent County, Virginia, of 1701–1703. Obvious similarities between these two churches include the use of brick, the Flemish curvilinear parapet gables at the east and west ends, and the rectangular nave. The tall tower of St. Peter's was added forty years after the initial construction as an embellishment, as the congregation grew more settled and affluent.

Other colonial churches in Virginia include Bruton Parish Church erected on Duke of Gloucester Street in the colonial capital of Williamsburg. This church, the third iteration on this site, was built between 1710 and 1715 and was designed by colonial Governor Alexander Spotswood. Although its cruciform shape is a medieval form, its proportions and detailing are classical. Indeed, Bruton Parish is the first colonial church influenced by Christopher Wren, the architect hired to design fifty-one churches in London following the disastrous fire of 1666. Similarly, Christ Church in Lancaster County of 1732 is cruciform in plan but with classical references, including round-headed windows with keystones and an arched pediment and classical pilasters at the entrance. A three-tiered pulpit, classical altar, and paneled box pews finished the interior. This building was financed by wealthy plantation owner Robert "King" Carter, who wrote, "The more [God] lends us, the larger accounts he expects from us." Christ Church served as the model for a number of other Virginia parish churches well into the third quarter of the eighteenth century.

In the mid-eighteenth century, classicism continued to dominate the design of Anglican churches in Virginia. Aquia Church of 1751–1755 in Stafford County is a Greek cross-plan church with a tower and cupola over its west arm. The church is built of brick laid in Flemish bond (an expensive embellishment) and with quoins and keystones of local Aquia sandstone. The three entrances have door architraves taken from Batty Langley's *Builder's and Workman's Treasury of Designs* (1750), a remarkably swift transmission of an

St. James Church at Goose Creek near Charleston (built 1713–1719) is a rural parish church set in one of nine parishes established by South Carolina's General Assembly in 1706.

a Baroque painted reredos with the Ten Commandments and the Lord's Prayer. The royal coat of arms of George I featuring a lion and unicorn hanging over the pulpit was a physical reminder to worshippers of the dependence of the colony and the church on England and the Church of England.

St. Michael's Church in Charleston, South Carolina, marks an important departure in the design of Anglican churches in the South. This monumental building erected by Irish-born architect Samuel Cardy in 1761 was based on James Gibbs's innovative design for St. Martin-in-the-Fields (1722–1726) in London. Built of brick but covered with stucco, perhaps the most impressive feature is this building's two-story Doric portico topped with a five-story steeple. The interior and the sacraments practiced within similarly displayed new ideas that represented important shifts in Anglican theology. Historian Louis P. Nelson has noted that the use of a tray ceiling in the sanctuary instead of the more commonly used celestial-inspired barrel vault signaled an acceptance of empiricism and a rejection of the supernatural. Cherubs and other supernatural forms were supplanted by a "theology of aesthetics"—a set of values that privileged reason and beauty over mystery. With the design of this church, the vestry made conscious choices to adopt the latest architectural styles from abroad and to change the way in which Anglican beliefs were expressed in iconography and liturgy.

architectural idea given that Aquia Church was completed just five years after publication. A focal point of the interior is an elaborate altarpiece with Ionic pilasters and pediment. Mounted on the altar are four tablets on which are inscribed the Lord's Prayer, Ten Commandments, and Apostles' Creed.

## Anglican Churches in South Carolina

Outside of the Virginia colony is St. James Church at Goose Creek, near Charleston. It was built from 1713 to 1719, and its construction was partially funded by the Society for the Propagation of the Gospel in Foreign Parts. This one-story brick building, covered with stucco in the nineteenth century, is a rural parish church set in one of nine parishes established by South Carolina's General Assembly in 1706. The main entrance is framed with Doric pilasters, and the pediment above holds a stucco relief of a pelican piercing her breast with her beak to feed her young—a Christian symbol adopted by the Society of the Propagation of the Gospel in Foreign Parts. In the interior, a center aisle and two flanking aisles separate the box pews. A gallery across the rear of the sanctuary and supported with Ionic columns provides additional seating. At the east end, a curving staircase leads to the elevated pulpit, which is situated in front of

## Congregationalist Meetinghouses in New England

To the north, the Puritans or English Separatists first arrived in the New World in 1620, but it was ten years later when the great Puritan migration took place with the establishment of the Massachusetts Bay Company in 1630. These colonists were in search of religious freedom for themselves, and as William Bradford, governor of Plymouth, declared, they were committed to the task of "propagating and advancing the gospel of the kingdom of Christ in those remote parts of the world." The Puritans' earliest worship services took place in temporary structures hastily erected, in colonists' homes, or in the parsonage. It was the meetinghouse form, however, that came to epitomize early Protestant protected from the elements by clapboard on the exterior. Typically, these buildings were one-and-a-half stories, with the entrance on one of the long sides, small casement windows with diamond-shaped panes of glass, and thatched roofs. These plain buildings served the strict functional purpose of providing a gathering space and deliberately avoided overt religious symbolism such as an altar. Puritan worshippers instead focused their attention on proclamation and preaching. Accordingly, the arrangement of benches on which the worshippers sat and the prominence of the pulpit facilitated that emphasis. Communion, using plain vessels and plates, was offered occasionally throughout the year in the meetinghouse, but baptisms typically took place in private homes.

The next generation of meetinghouses in New England was distinguished by an increase in scale. Old Ship Meeting House in Hingham, Massachusetts, is the earliest surviving example of this type. Originally built in 1681, it was forty-five feet by fifty-five feet in plan but was altered in the eighteenth century: its floor plan was expanded to seventy-three feet by fifty-five feet and a cupola was added. The building is heavy timber frame covered with clapboard on the exterior but with its structural system, including the cruck frame (naturally curving timbers supporting the roof), exposed on the interior. With more windows and larger ones at that, the interior of Old Ship was better illuminated than its more humble antecedents. However, continuing the tradition of the New England meetinghouse, the pulpit was located opposite the main entrance. Pews on the main floor and on three sides in the balcony provided sightlines to the pulpit and auditory advantage.

Throughout the eighteenth century, the internal arrangement of meetinghouses continued to maintain their focus on the spoken Word but also began to exhibit a knowledge of up-to-date architectural trends in England, transmitted to colonial America largely through the increased availability of books and prints. Georgian architecture, named after England's ruling monarchs beginning with George I in 1714, appeared in the colonies by the third decade of the eighteenth century. Georgian order expressed through strict symmetry, classical proportions, and classical ornament showed increasing architectural sophistication in the colonies. An example is the Congregational Old South Meetinghouse in Boston of 1729. Designed by Robert Twelves, this building is rectangular in plan with a tall tower topped by a cupola and spire (added in the 1770s), with its entrance on one of the long sides—a holdover from earlier meetinghouses. The largest building in Boston at the time, this

ST. MICHAEL'S CHURCH.

St. Michael's Church in Charleston, South Carolina, reflects a significant departure in the design of Anglican churches in the South, including the adoption of the latest architectural styles from abroad. The design represented a change in the way in which Anglican beliefs were expressed in iconography and liturgy.

worship space in New England in the colonial period. These Congregational meetinghouses were usually constructed and supported with public money and owned by the town. In addition to serving as the community's worship space, they were also the places where civic meetings of all types took place in the early years of the colonies. Literally and figuratively, the meetinghouse was centrally located usually in the town green and symbolically represented both the civic and religious life of the community.

The first meetinghouses to be constructed, such as those in Sudbury and Dedham, Massachusetts, date from the early seventeenth century. Small in scale, these rectangular wooden buildings resembled domestic buildings and were undistinguished from the homes of the more well-to-do colonists. These meetinghouses were of heavy timber frame construction infilled with wattle and daub, which in turn was impressive brick structure has tall round-head arched windows, a molded cornice, and moderately classical details on its interior. In keeping with the dual function of the New England meetinghouse, this building was the home of a radical congregation and was the site of politically charged meetings leading up to the American Revolution.

## Anglican Churches in New England

Anglican churches in New England, even more so than Congregational examples, reflected architectural trends from abroad and, in particular, showed an awareness of the church designs of Christopher Wren. Boston's Old North Church (also known as Christ Church) of 1723 was built as an Anglican church and is the earliest example in New England to show the influence of Wren. Boston print dealer William Price designed the church and probably was inspired by engravings of Wren's churches in London, which he handled in his gallery. Old North Church is composed of a brick rectangular block for the sanctuary, with a brick entrance tower modeled after Wren's St. Garlickhythe (c. 1680) in London. The wood steeple rises 175 feet in the air (where, in April 1775, illuminated lanterns signaled to Paul Revere the approach of British troops). The interior is filled with box pews, and a balcony on the second level has additional seating. A vaulted plaster ceiling and sounding board above the pulpit helped amplify the service for the congregation. Two years later, craftsman Richard Munday designed Trinity Church in Newport (1725–1726), based on Old North Church but rendered in wood rather than brick. Originally, the Newport church was nearly square in proportions, but it was lengthened in 1762. The steeple with clock also resembles that of Old North and was completed in 1741. On the interior, the wineglass pulpit projects into the sanctuary, making the preacher visible. A sounding board suspended over the pulpit reflected his voice towards the congregation, making him easily understood.

King's Chapel (1749–1750), built in Boston of Quincy granite by Newport architect Peter Harrison, is distinguished as the first American church built of stone. For the design of this church, Harrison likely was inspired by church designs by Christopher Wren published in James Gibbs's *Book of Architecture* of 1728. King's Chapel is rectangular in plan with a hipped roof. Its first-floor segmental arched windows surmounted by round-topped windows on the second floor are inspired by Marybone Chapel by Gibbs. The interior has elegant classical details including Corinthian columns supporting the gallery and a Palladian window in the apse.

It was the influence of James Gibbs's church designs that began to supplant Wren in the colonies. According to architectural historian William Pierson, Gibbs's St. Martin-in-the-Fields Church (1722–1726) in London was the most influential and most commonly imitated church, particularly after the mid-eighteenth century. The first church in the colonies to show the influence of Gibbs was Philadelphia's notable

King's Chapel (built 1749–1750) in Boston is distinguished as the first American church constructed of stone. Rectangular in plan with a hipped roof, its interior has elegant classical details including Corinthian columns supporting the gallery.

Anglican Christ Church. Gentleman architect John Kearsley designed Christ Church in 1727, and its construction was completed in 1744. A large brick church with Palladian windows, the building also has a simplified interior based on that of St. Martin. In New York, Thomas McBean, a student of Gibbs in London, constructed St. Paul's (1764–1766) in New York, which is also a close copy of St. Martin.

## Churches of Other Denominations

### Dutch Reformed

In addition to the Congregationalists and Anglicans, other denominations settled in the colonies and established their own traditions. The Dutch Reformed Church, a Calvinistic denomination that was a result of a split from Catholicism, took hold in New Amsterdam. Like the Puritans, the Dutch Reformed congregants eschewed what they termed the excesses of Catholicism and a hierarchical church organization. As a result, their Dutch Reformed church buildings were simple and placed a special emphasis on the pulpit. An unusual octagonal form inspired by similar worship space in the Netherlands was adopted for a number of churches and gave no one person, minister or laity, special status. One such example is a nonextant, but documented, stone octagonal church with a steep roof constructed in Bergen, New Jersey, around 1680. Other Dutch Reformed churches were more similar to those of other Protestant denominations in the colonies, rectangular in plan but with Dutch gambrel roofs and simple ornamentation. In 1679, the Dutch constructed a stone church approximately sixty by forty-five feet in plan near the tip of Manhattan. This building had a tall tower topped with a bell and a gambrel roof. In Albany, the Protestant Dutch Church was erected of stone in 1715. This building had a steeply sloped hipped roof topped with a cupola and bell. Access into the building was through an attached vestibule, called a *doop huys*.

### Society of Friends

The Society of Friends or Quakers settled throughout the colonies of Massachusetts, Connecticut, New Jersey, New Hampshire, and Rhode Island, but the largest concentration was in Pennsylvania. Of Welsh, Irish, English, and German extraction, their earliest services were held in private homes, but by the end of the seventeenth century they began building meetinghouses, first in wood and later in brick. Similar to Puritan meetinghouses, these buildings were plain on the exterior and interior with no obvious religious references;

however, Quaker meetinghouses had separate doors for men and women who sat segregated on plain benches. By the mid-eighteenth century, approximately 250 Quaker meetinghouses had been constructed in the colonies. The Great Meeting House in Philadelphia was a building fifty feet square topped with a cupola that illuminated the interior. This meetinghouse was replaced in the mid-eighteenth century by a two-and-a-half-story brick building that was simple in detail like its predecessor.

### Lutherans

Swedish Lutherans first settled in the Delaware River Valley in the seventeenth century. They constructed their earliest church buildings of horizontal logs, a building tradition the Swedes brought with them. One of their earliest churches was in fact a converted log blockhouse constructed circa 1666 in modern-day Philadelphia. For its first decade, the structure served as both fortress and church. In 1677, the blockhouse was completely taken over for sacred purposes, and to mark that conversion, parishioners added a roof and small spire. This building served as a church until circa 1700, when the Lutherans replaced it with a brick building named Old Swedes' Church, a cruciform-plan church adorned with an altar painting by noted portrait artist Gustaf Hesselius. In Delaware, Lutherans first worshiped in Fort Christiana, but in 1699, colonists decided to erect a separate building on a hill opposite the fort. This church, Holy Trinity Church (Old Swedes' Church), in Wilmington, Delaware, is the oldest Lutheran church in America. Built by stonemason John Yard and his three sons of dark granite cut into irregularly shaped blocks of native stone, its original entrances were located in the middle of the two long sides of the building. Round arched windows illuminated a plain interior with low arched ceiling. Lutherans elsewhere appropriated and modified the meetinghouse form of the Congregationalists. For example, just prior to the American Revolution, Lutherans in Waldoboro, Maine, constructed a New England meetinghouse but located the building's main entrance on the gable end.

### Presbyterians

Missionary Francis Makemie, who arrived in Maryland in the 1680s, brought Presbyterianism to the American colonies. However, it was in the eighteenth century, when immigrants from Scotland and Northern Ireland came in larger numbers, that Presbyterians began to shape the built environment. First Presbyterian Church in Philadelphia was erected in 1704. In the 1740s, swept up in the religious fervor of the Great Awakening, an alternate Presbyterian congregation split off from this conservative church and built for themselves a more elaborate brick church. Leading Philadelphia architect and builder Robert Smith constructed the Georgian-style Second Presbyterian with a pedimented façade, arched windows, Palladian window on the façade's second story, and urns mounted on the gabled roof. In 1761, the congregation added a tall steeple that brought them ridicule for its perceived excess.

## Baptists

The Baptists established themselves in the colony of Rhode Island led by Roger Williams, who founded the first Baptist church in Providence. For the first sixty years of settlement, these worshipers met in private homes. Their first purpose-built church was constructed circa 1700. Later in the eighteenth century, the congregation constructed the First Baptist Meetinghouse in Providence, in 1774–1775. This frame building nearly eighty feet square with entrance doors on all four sides was designed by Brown University professor, mathematician, and astronomer Joseph Brown. The two-story building has numerous classical details including quoining, a Palladian window, a bold pediment with brackets, and round-headed windows with keystones that Brown appears to have taken out of James Gibbs's *Book of Architecture* (1728). The tower of First Baptist is a nearly literal copy of a rejected design by Gibbs for St. Martin-in-the-Field that Gibbs illustrated in his book. The nave has a barrel-arched sanctuary with two side aisles. Brown carried the classicism of the exterior through to the interior with the addition of fluted Doric columns.

## Methodists

As with the Baptists, Methodism in colonial America was slow to take hold, but New York, Pennsylvania, Delaware, and Maryland were among the colonies with Methodist settlements in the eighteenth century. Most early Methodist services took place outdoors or were held in whatever building was available. St. George's Methodist congregation in Philadelphia appropriated a German Reformed Church, where they began holding services in 1769. In New York, a fledging Methodist congregation worshiped in private homes and in a sail loft until they built Wesleyan Chapel in 1768 on John Street. This plain two-and-a-half-story meetinghouse, probably of stone, was indistinguishable from its New England counterpart except that the main entrance

was located in the gable end rather than on the long side of the building. Just prior to Independence, approximately half of the Methodists in America resided in Maryland. In Baltimore, Methodists erected a stone meetinghouse called the Lovely Lane Meetinghouse (nonextant) in 1774, where ten years later the Methodist Episcopal Church was organized. Today that congregation claims to be the "Mother Church of American Methodism."

## Conclusion

Colonists who emigrated to America beginning in the seventeenth century sought both economic independence and religious freedom. Upon arrival, they struggled to build shelter and establish a livelihood while at the same time practicing the religious faith they brought from their homeland. What distinguished these colonists were their individual worship practices and how these religious differences were manifested in the designs of their churches and meetinghouses. Congregationalists in New England emphasized hearing the Word, which led to the development of meetinghouses and interior spaces where the congregation could see and hear the preacher. Anglicans in the southern colonies were politically, culturally, and economically connected to England and made this association with their mother county visible in their churches. Quakers emphasized the equality of men and women and constructed buildings of simplicity and plainness. Yet despite these differences, there were also important similarities, particularly in the widespread adoption of the meetinghouse form in the northern and mid-Atlantic colonies by denominations other than the Congregationalists. It was in the eighteenth century, however, when the architectural taste of these Protestant denominations north and south grew closer together. With some exceptions, Protestant colonists began to adopt a more sophisticated classical architectural expression for their worship buildings. Ironically, the most important architectural influence came from England through the designs of architects Christopher Wren and James Gibbs. Transmitted to the colonies through the greater availability of books, these English ideas profoundly shaped the physical development of a colony on the verge of political independence.

**See also** *Anglicans in Colonial and Revolutionary America; Architecture entries; Congregationalists; Dutch Reformed; Lutheran Churches; Methodists: Through the Nineteenth Century; Presbyterians: Colonial; Puritans; Quakers: Through the Nineteenth Century; Worship: Anglican; Worship: Protestant.*

Paula A. Mohr

**BIBLIOGRAPHY**

Benes, Peter, ed. *New England Meeting House and Church, 1630–1850.* Boston: Boston University Press, 1979.

Brownell, Charles E., et al. *The Making of Virginia Architecture.* Richmond: Virginia Museum of Fine Arts, 1992.

Howe, Jeffery. *Houses of Worship.* San Diego, Calif.: Thunder Bay Press, 2003.

Kennedy, Roger G. *American Churches.* New York: Stewart, Tabori & Chang, 1982.

Nelson, Louis P. *The Beauty of Holiness: Anglicanism & Architecture in Colonial South Carolina.* Chapel Hill: University of North Carolina Press, 2008.

Pierson, William H., Jr. *American Buildings and Their Architects: The Colonial and Neoclassical Styles.* Vol. I. Garden City, N.Y.: Doubleday & Company, 1970.

Upton, Dell. *Holy Things and Profane: Anglican Parish Churches in Colonial Virginia.* New Haven, Conn.: Yale University Press, 1986.

Williams, Peter W. *Houses of God: Region, Religion, and Architecture in the United States.* Urbana: University of Illinois Press, 1997.

# Architecture: The European Protestant Background

To understand the development of Protestant religious architecture in the United States requires an understanding of the development of the built environment of Protestantism in Europe, from which so much American ecclesiastical design is derived. Just as the Protestant Reformation and the traditions that emerged from it were multiple, rather than unified, so has been the architecture that has come to constitute the built environment of Protestantism. Since this latter term has been taken to include everything from Quakers to Old Order Amish to Anglo-Catholics, caution is required in suggesting that there is any particular sort of architecture that is distinctively, uniquely, or essentially "Protestant." To be sure, there are some unifying themes. Just as biblical restorationism—the goal of restoring contemporary religious life to that of apostolic times—informed the visions of virtually all of the early reformers, so has the idea of returning to the norms and practices of the early church been a common theme in liturgical reform and its architectural expression. On the whole, though, it is more useful to think about religious architecture in terms of a range of typologies, each of which reflects certain assumptions about theology, worship, and polity—remembering, all the while, that in the messiness of actual experience, it is vain to look always for precise correspondences between any one ideal type and the experience and practice of a particular community.

## Typologies

The architectural baseline for understanding Protestant architectural theory and practice was the Gothic of the later Middle Ages, which had evolved ultimately from the Roman basilica as a public, rectangular, processional space in which the focus of attention was on the ultimate authority—in this case, God, and the hierarchy and clergy instituted to carry out his worship. Such architecture was at once *hierarchical*, in that it emphasized distinctions of sacrality and authority in its internal arrangements, and *sacramental*, in that its primary purpose was the provision of a suitable place for the celebration of the Eucharist, as well as the other sacraments, in which humanity came into direct contact with the divine through the mediation of the Church. Most of the material fabric of religious life in which the Reformation arose was either in this mode or that of the earlier Romanesque, a style fundamentally similar in plan if not in structural and decorative detail. Emergent Protestant communities therefore had either to adapt such churches for their own uses or, when enabled or compelled by circumstance, to create new forms.

The creation of such new forms or the radical modification of the old often brought with it a new nomenclature: instead of "church," which implied for some the earthly presence of the sacred in material form, "temple," "tabernacle," or "meetinghouse" became distinctly Protestant alternatives. A new emphasis on preaching—foreshadowed by later medieval religious orders such as the Franciscans and Dominicans, who themselves had built new structures, such as the "hall church," for this function—was common among those who were called Protestants. Those such as Calvin and his followers, however, who particularly focused on the proclaimed Word, were most inclined to shape their houses of worship around this practice. The *preaching hall*, in which elaborate sacramental apparatus and depictions of sacred personae were minimized or eliminated and the authoritative role of the minister as preacher took material shape in a central, dominant pulpit, emerged as a major alternative to the *sacramental/hierarchical church.*

Among the more radical communities engendered by the Reformation, though, still another model emerged to reflect a different and still less hierarchical self-understanding. The Radical Reformation (Anabaptists) and later groups such as the Friends (Quakers) rejected the authority of clergy as well as bishops and saw the primary, local community as the locus of religious experience and authority. Such buildings were generally austere, and their interior arrangements minimized clergy-lay distinctions. The testimony and sometimes the immediate experience of the assembled community could now play out in this even more egalitarian structure, which we might call the "assembly house," the external shape of which was frequently domestic in scale and style.

A final model suggests itself in the ecumenical liturgical convergence that has characterized twentieth-century experience, in which the polarity of Catholic/Protestant began to erode, even as differences among those who had traditionally called themselves "Protestant" began to increase. Here clergy and laity interact in a differentiated but no longer sharply divided manner, echoing themes of earliest Christianity, the early Reformation, and the Roman Catholic ecumenical council Vatican II. We might call this model that of the *renewal church*, in which sacrament, Word, and community all receive significant emphasis. The external style here might vary, but it is frequently modernist in conception and circular or polygonal in shape, minimizing hierarchical distinctions.

These models, which arise out of particular theological moments, do not describe experienced reality exhaustively. Early Lutherans, for example, can probably be placed somewhere between the sacramental/hierarchical and preaching hall models; Pentecostals fall between the latter and the community house in their actual practice; while Anglo-Catholics, as their name suggests, have embraced the sacramental/hierarchical church perhaps even more avidly than many of their Roman Catholic contemporaries, who have embraced the renewal church. What we call "Protestantism" has always been and still continues to be polymorphic and protean.

## Lutherans

The attitude of Martin Luther and his early followers towards religious building was consistent with the broader religious culture that Luther's movement generated. Compared with Reformed and Anabaptist theologians, Luther followed a comparatively moderate, pragmatic, even mediating course between Catholic practice and more extreme Protestant biblical restorationism. Luther's concern was not with the wholesale revocation of the medieval past but rather with the adaptation of existing space to the needs of proper liturgical performance. As a result, little new religious building took place during the early decades of reformation in the German-speaking states. Extant churches were not destroyed but retrofitted with galleries and elevated pulpits better suited to an emphasis on the proclaimed Word; similarly, side altars dedicated to the Virgin Mary and

other saints were often eliminated. Preaching, and sometimes the entire service, was frequently conducted in the nave alone. During the mid-sixteenth century, new building was confined to a handful of princely chapels, such as the small hall church erected for the Elector Johann Friedrich at Torgau in 1543–1544.

By the later sixteenth century, new building, mainly in the late Gothic style, began to take place. By the following century, new models began to develop such as the hall (preaching-oriented) church, L-plan churches, or multigalleried chapels. Jakob Wurstmann's 1618 Zum Heiligen Geist (Holy Ghost) church at Nidda in Hesse, essentially a rectangular meetinghouse with a square or pentagonal apse, was an early and influential example of a plan that persisted both in Europe and North America into the subsequent century. The baroque style, so successfully employed by the Jesuit order that arose in the service of the Catholic Reformation, or Counter-Reformation, was also adopted by German and Scandinavian Lutherans for their own purposes. The centralizing and dramatizing devices of the baroque, such as highly focused lighting, found a Lutheran focus in the *Prinzipalstück*, a new concept in liturgical furnishings in which altar, pulpit, and often the baptismal font were combined. A prime example of Lutheran baroque was Georg Bähr's Frauenkirche (Church of the Virgin Mary), built in 1725–1743, in Dresden, destroyed by Allied bombing during World War II, and restored and reopened in 2005. Capped by an oval dome and resembling a grand opera house, it was circular in form and included five tiers of galleries. By the eighteenth century a number of forms had come into use, including other circular plans as well as rectangles, polygons, and L shapes. Similar developments were also characteristic in the Scandinavian lands during the early centuries; by the later nineteenth century, however, a widespread romantic nationalism aimed at recapturing the historic genius of particular peoples affected all aspects of Scandinavian design and resulted in Lutheran churches based on motifs derived from traditional folk building styles.

## Continental Reformed

John Calvin and Huldreich Zwingli, usually regarded as the founders of the Reformed tradition, were more radical than Luther in their iconoclastic rejection of the arts and distrust of the notion that sacred space could be embodied in earthly vehicles. Nevertheless, little in the way of an architectural program emerged in the first generation of Swiss reform; rather, Calvin's stripping of Geneva's cathedral church of St. Pierre of its Catholic religious art and liturgical furnishings in favor of a dominant pulpit was a typical combination of ideology and pragmatism designed to highlight the centrality of the preached Word.

In France, Huguenots engaged in limited but significant building from the mid-1500s until their expulsion with the revocation of the Edict of Nantes in 1685. Many of the leading architects of the period were Calvinists in the employ of Catholic rules; as Catharine Randall provocatively argues, they made their faith known obliquely through a strategy of subverting and distorting the absolutist political and religious purposes their patrons envisioned by employing such devices as grotesque or excessive ornamentation. Prior to the Edict of Nantes, they had been obliged to worship in adapted Catholic churches or secular structures such as barns. The earliest known example of a public structure for Calvinist worship was the Temple de Paradis attributed to Jean Perrissin, built at Nantes in 1564. Other major examples were Philibert de l'Orme's octagonal temple at La Rochelle in 1577 and Salomon de Brosse's temple at Charenton in 1606. These Huguenot "temples"—a term presumably chosen to avoid the sacral connotations of "church/*église*"— were severely plain in design and large in scale, accommodating up to six thousand worshippers after the Edict of Nantes imposed a limit on the number of such structures. Designed to facilitate the hearing of the preached Word, they featured central pulpits and multiple galleries to concentrate seating close to the pulpit. In many cases the temples were situated within a walled enclosure that also included a concierge's house, parish house, cemetery, dining hall, and other amenities. All were destroyed with the revocation of the Edict, after which exiled Huguenots generally blended into other congregations in the Netherlands, Britain, and the North American colonies. A handful of structures were designed specifically for Huguenot congregations in diaspora, such as the centrally planned building at Church

Georg Bähr's *Frauenkirche* (Church of the Virgin Mary), built from 1725 to 1743, in Dresden, is a prime example of Lutheran Baroque architecture.

Street, Spitalfields, in London (1743), and the Gothic revival Huguenot church in Charleston, South Carolina, built in 1845 for a congregation established in 1681.

The pattern of retrofitting medieval churches according to Reformed usage characterized the early years of Calvinist development in the Netherlands, which was preoccupied with its struggle for independence from Spain until well into the seventeenth century. The emergent Reformed pattern of a preaching house featuring an octagonal shape, galleries, round-headed windows, and prominent pulpit on a side wall characterized the earliest Dutch Reformed house of worship, that built at Willemstad by Prince Maurice in 1596. The Zuiderkerk in Amsterdam, designed by Hendrik de Keyser—the architect of the only three churches erected in that city during its "boom" years—and built in 1603–1611, was more conservative in pattern, modifying Gothic form with classical detail for Protestant liturgical usage. A Greek cross form was the basis for churches built in the early seventeenth century in Blokzijl, Amsterdam, and Maasluis, which exemplified Dutch classicism in style and lacked chancels with altars.

## Anabaptist

The Anabaptist—Amish, Hutterite, Mennonite—tradition of religious building was shaped both by the constraints of official persecution and by the theological imperative of rejecting the notion of sacred space in favor of a gathering of the faithful, whose very act of coming together evoked the sacred. Two roughly synonymous terms were utilized by early Anabaptists to describe this space: *Bethaus* ("house of prayer") in Eastern Europe and *Versammlungshaus* ("meeting house") in German-speaking lands. The internal configurations of these structures resembled those of Anglo-American Quakers in their patterns of face-to-face seating, with the collective leadership on a bench or behind a table along one of the building's long walls, with a modest pulpit; seating divided along gender lines; minimal interior ornamentation except for scripture verses and floral motifs; and a functional exterior. When necessary, barns or other secular structures were utilized for worship; and some groups, such as the communal-dwelling Hutterites, and Old Order and other extremely conservative Amish, continued to reject any specialized structure for worship, regarding the entire complex of landscape in which a godly life is enacted as sacred. With minor variations, this pattern diffused with the diaspora of Anabaptists across Central and Eastern Europe and through parts of North and South America. Changes began to take place on a significant scale first in the nineteenth century, when toleration and prosperity led to the erosion of the notion of worship as subsisting in the gathered congregation in favor of the erection of buildings that for the first time took on the name of *Kirche* ("church"). This onset of "worldliness" accelerated the process of schism that had long been latent in the movement. Whatever the degree of acculturation, however, Anabaptists have always expressed an affinity for the notion of the house of worship as first and foremost an *assembly house*.

## Anglican

After Henry VIII's break with papal authority, little changed in England for the remainder of his lengthy reign with

James Gibbs's St. Martin-in-the-Fields Church (built 1722 to 1726) in London was the most influential and most frequently imitated church, particularly after the mid-eighteenth century.

regard to worship or its physical setting, other than the purging of many churches of "popish" art and furnishings. Although various experiments with the interior setting of worship took place with the introduction of the *Book of Common Prayer* in 1559, and the emergent Puritan party began to demand more drastic change, the first major paradigm shift to take place in the fabric of worship for the Church of England was occasioned by natural rather than human causes. The Great Fire of London of 1666 destroyed a considerable number of that city's multitudinous houses of worship, and it fell to Sir Christopher Wren to replace them. The fifty-one churches designed by Wren, together with the elaborations on his architectural themes by successors such as James Gibbs and Nicholas Hawksmoor, constituted a new chapter in Protestant architecture in which neoclassicism became explicitly linked with the notion of the church as a preaching house, an essentially rectangular structure with clear glass windows and no chancels. While no Anglican church could be conceived without provision for the administration of the sacraments as well, Wren was explicit in designating churches of his design as *auditories*—buildings in which all could clearly hear the preached Word—in contrast with the "larger Churches . . . [of] the Romanists . . . [where] it is enough if they hear the murmur of the Mass." Although a number of Wren's city churches were destroyed during World War II bombing or through other causes, those that remain continue to constitute a distinctive feature of London's cityscape, and they provided the prototypes for provincial adaptations in North America and elsewhere in subsequent generations. What has subsequently become known as the "Wren Baroque" or "Wren-Gibbs" style, modified in the direction of a purer classicism, remained normative in England until the advent of the Gothic revival in the 1840s.

## British Nonconformist and Wesleyan

The English Calvinists—Puritans—who took exception to the usages of the Church of England under Elizabeth I and the early Stuarts were forced, as many Continental dissidents had been earlier, to worship covertly and haphazardly, in the private chapels of the elite or in private homes, barns, guild halls, or other secular structures. The Interregnum period of the 1640s and 1650s saw considerable destruction wrought on medieval Anglican property by the troops of Oliver Cromwell, who saw only idolatry in the sacred figures displayed in statuary and stained glass, but little if any new building. It was during this period that the Westminster Confession (1646), a major articulation of Reformed principles in English, gave classic expression to the Reformed attitude towards the issue of sacred space: "[n]either prayer nor any part of religious worship is now under the gospel, either tied unto or made more acceptable by any place in which it is performed, or towards which it is directed." The Toleration Act of 1689 made possible for the first time the widespread buildings of Dissenting houses of worship. After this date, Baptists, Independents, Presbyterians, Quakers, and, several decades later, Methodists, began to cover the landscape with thousands of preaching houses featuring central pulpits, galleries, and box pews or benches designed to maximize exposure to the preached Word.

Although rectangular forms were most common, the octagon, of which John Wesley himself had spoken favorably,

also found numerous manifestations. Many early Dissenting buildings were modifications of extant churches or modest in scale and design. By the eighteenth century, when Wesley and his movement as well as other Dissenting groups began to gain momentum and respectability, more monumental structures, such as the Presbyterians' Octagon Chapel at Norwich (1754–1756) and Wesley's Chapel at City Road, London (1777–1778), were somewhat more sophisticated— usually neoclassical—in design; the latter, for example, was a brick building with two stories, or round-headed, a five-bay façade, and a three-bay pediment. As Methodism broke from the Church of England and established its own sacramental practices, its chapels began to feature communion tables as well as pulpits. The rapid urbanization and new iron construction technology of the nineteenth century resulted in the erection of huge tabernacles for preachers such as the eminent Baptist Charles Haddon Spurgeon; the latter's Metropolitan Tabernacle in London (1859–1861) possessed two tiers of galleries and could seat five thousand. Although the rage for such buildings rapidly spread across urban Britain, many have subsequently been demolished.

## Medieval Revivals

By the 1840s, a convergence of demographic change, taste, and theological principle brought about a major paradigm shift in religious design, especially in the Anglo-American realm, though not without parallels elsewhere. The rapid growth of urban population, first in Britain and then in North America, necessitated a vast new program of church building. The English Parliament's establishment of a Church Building Commission in 1818 was to be the last major program of governmentally funded religious building in that country; the thirty-five or so neoclassical Commissioners' Churches that resulted were displaced by the privately financed Metropolis Churches Extension Fund of 1836, which launched a massive building campaign throughout England during the next several decades (3,765 Church of England churches were built or restored during the years 1835–1875). The architectural theology of this explosive new campaign was provided by the Cambridge Movement, the name given to the work of the Cambridge Camden Society (founded in 1839), also known as the Ecclesiologists, which served as a counterpart to the Oxford Movement that was simultaneously reviving an emphasis on church and sacraments in historical tradition. Promoting their views through *The Ecclesiologist* (begun 1841), the Cambridge Movement insisted that the only proper style for sacramental Christian worship was the "English decorated" form of Gothic that had flourished in the early fourteenth century, in which every detail was laden with profound Christian symbolic import. In addition to the building of countless new churches, the Movement also inspired and attempted to control the restoration of many medieval churches, by advocating that they be brought into the conformity with the style of the period they regarded as normative. Although Anglo-Catholic ritualism was the major force shaping Victorian church design, Roman Catholic convert Augustus Welby Pugin's architectural designs and critique of contemporary society and critic John Ruskin's promotion of Venetian Gothic as an eminently "moral" style, reflecting the wholesomely organic character of the society that had produced it and compatible with Protestant values, contributed to the popularity of the mode in the United States as well as in Britain.

## Twentieth-Century Liturgical and Architectural Reform

By early in the twentieth century, the enthusiasm for medieval revival styles that had consumed groups as disparate as British Anglo-Catholics, American Unitarians, and German Lutherans began to yield to a combination of economic, theological, and architectural forces that rendered them virtually obsolete by the onset of World War II. The Great Depression of the 1930s brought the construction of new churches to a virtual halt, and the war itself decimated a considerable amount of the ecclesiastical fabric of Britain and the Continent. Even before this enforced hiatus in church design, though, other new forces conspired to bring about a new era. From various national directions, but epitomized in Germany's *Bauhaus*, the movement of modernism in architecture declared war on the principles of romantic revivalism that the medieval styles had represented. Frank Lloyd Wright in the United States, Walter Gropius and Mies van der Rohe in Germany (and later the United States as well), and Le Corbusier in France were among the leading names in this loosely knit movement, although these particular figures only occasionally turned their hands to religious design. Modernism embraced new techniques of construction, such as the use of structural steel, and an aesthetic that condemned any decoration not intrinsic to a building's structure. It rejected the revival of historical styles outright in favor of a new, international mode based on the beauty of unadorned materials and their textures, simple geometrical forms, and the play of light and shade.

A similar recall to fundamentals informed the liturgical movement within Christianity, which found early exposition among French and American Benedictines and eventually received normative status within Roman Catholic circles as a result of Vatican II. Informed by a desire to return to the forms of worship that had characterized the earliest Christian community (and, by implication, rejecting medieval practice as normative), this movement soon permeated the architectural thought of many Protestants, particularly those in traditions such as the Anglican and Lutheran that emphasized more formal and elaborate liturgical practice. (The impact of the ecumenical movement and the convergence of liturgical practice encouraged this coming together of architectural mode as well.) The desire for simplicity and authenticity that had informed architectural modernism was central to the liturgical movement and what we earlier called its resultant "renewal church" as well. The early emergence of European Catholic church architects such as Domenikus Böhm and Rudolf Schwarz established a vocabulary of ecclesiastical design that was rapidly appropriated by both Protestant and Catholic, as the massive program of rebuilding that followed World War II provided the opportunity, yet again, for reconstructing the Continent's ecclesiastical fabric literally from the ground up. It was here that the "renewal church" paradigm of sacramental but nonhierarchical worship space began to be realized on a grand and ecumenical scale.

To speak of Protestant architecture, then, is as problematic as speaking of Protestantism. Although the general tendency among the new movements of the Reformation era was to simplify worship along the perceived lines of biblical practice and to adapt or invent religious architecture towards this end, disagreement in both theory and practice was the rule, as competing and contrasting traditions within the realm of Protestantism took shape. Although biblical worship as a guiding principle never disappeared, periodic rediscoveries of the sacramental ideal gave rise to architectural revivalism along medieval lines. During the twentieth century, the whole notion of a Protestant worship and architecture that was essentially distinct from that of Roman Catholicism began to erode rapidly, as Christian ecumenism and architectural modernism converged to shape a renewed Christian paradigm that transcended and rendered obsolete traditional Catholic/Protestant distinctions and rivalries. And, as in Europe, these processes would express themselves in the United States as well.

**See also** *Anabaptists; Anglican Tradition and Heritage; Architecture* entries; *Calvinist/Reformed Tradition and Heritage; Lutheran Tradition and Heritage; Methodists: Tradition and Heritage; Worship: Protestant.*

Peter W. Williams

**BIBLIOGRAPHY**

Addleshaw, G. W. O., and Frederick Etchells. *The Architectural Setting of Anglican Worship*. London: Faber and Faber, 1948/1956.

Davies, Horton. *Worship and Theology in England*. 5 vols. Princeton, N.J.: Princeton University Press, 1965–1970.

Finney, Paul Corby, ed. *Seeing beyond the Word: Visual Arts and the Calvinist Tradition*. Grand Rapids, Mich.: Eerdmans, 1999.

Heathcote, Edwin, and Iona Spens. *Church Builders*. Chichester, UK: Academy Editions, 1997.

Jeffrey, Paul. *The City Churches of Sir Christopher Wren*. Rio Grande, Ohio: Hambledon Press, 1996.

Kieckhefer, Richard. *Theology in Stone: Church Architecture from Byzantium to Berkeley*. New York: Oxford University Press, 2004.

Randall, Catharine. *Building Codes: The Aesthetics of Calvinism in Early Modern Europe*. Philadelphia: University of Pennsylvania Press, 1999.

Roth, John D., ed. "Anabaptist-Mennonite Spaces and Places of Worship." Special issue, *Mennonite Quarterly Review* 73, no. 2 (1999).

Turner, Harold W. *From Temple to Meeting House*. New York: Mouton, 1979.

White, James E. *The Cambridge Movement*. New York: Cambridge University Press, 1962.

———. *Protestant Worship and Church Architecture*. New York: Oxford University Press, 1964.

# Architecture: Jewish

For nearly three centuries, synagogue architecture in the United States has both reflected its environment and evolved an aesthetic of its own. As the public face of American Judaism, the synagogue edifice is shaped by the key tension of *assimilation/survival*, the powerful impulse for modern Jews to integrate socially and assimilate culturally versus the persistent desire to set themselves apart from Christianity and thus preserve Judaism as an independent faith community. On the interior, the synagogue sanctuary plays out the tension between *tradition/modernity*, the ongoing conflict between historical norms of the Jewish tradition and contemporary norms of modern civilization. In sum, the architecture of the synagogue may offer some resolution to these tensions, often by splitting such social and symbolic functions between the building's exterior and interior. All such design solutions are subject to religious custom regarding the synagogue layout, while allowing for flexibility given the lack of historical style for the synagogue, as well as the relative dearth of *halachic* (Jewish legal) guidelines for its architecture. Important precedents in Western Europe offer useful illustration of these principles. Amsterdam's Sephardic "Esnoga" synagogue of 1675 is a hip-roofed, monumental structure meant to echo the ancient Temple of Jerusalem; and London's Bevis Marks synagogue of 1701 is similarly a boxy brick building contrasting with neighboring churches yet comfortable in its urban milieu. Both buildings managed to simultaneously represent Jews as being a part of their social context while remaining religiously apart. On the interior, both influential synagogues had the traditional arrangement with its three primary elements: (1) the *Aron ha-Kodesh*—the holy Ark on the east wall, orienting prayer toward Jerusalem; (2) the *bimah*—the Torah reading platform located prominently in the center of the sanctuary; and (3) the *ezrat nashim*—the raised gallery for the separate seating of women. In a sign of modernization, however, the galleries were now enclosed by open balustrades, allowing the women to better see and be seen. Beginning in the eighteenth century, Jewish women at prayer would become ever more included in the service. Similarly, other elements of the synagogue would evolve in response to changing social mores, and hence synagogue design will be seen to be reflective of Jews' relation to society at large.

## *The "Synagogue-Community"*

The earliest Jewish settlers in North America were Sephardic refugees from Brazil who landed in New Amsterdam in 1654. They formed a congregation sometime after their arrival and managed to build their own synagogue structure by 1730. The Mill Street Synagogue of Shearith Israel (Hebrew, "remnant of Israel") was a modest stone building in vernacular style that would serve New York Jews for a century as the sole center of Jewish life, a "synagogue-community." Though the building has not survived, its traditional interior layout has been preserved in a small sanctuary within the current structure, the congregation's fourth. The second synagogue in colonial America would arise in Newport, Rhode Island—the Touro Synagogue of 1763, today the country's oldest standing synagogue. The upwardly mobile Jews of Newport's Jeshuat Israel hired a prominent architect, Peter Harrison, to design a fashionable Georgian structure; like its most obvious model, Bevis Marks in London, it was a two-storied meeting hall with the traditional interior arrangement. The exterior only betrayed itself as a synagogue in subtle ways, as by its orientation: set at an awkward angle to the street, the building faces in the traditional eastward direction. Likewise, the 1794 steepled synagogue of Charleston, South Carolina's Beth Elohim, looked very much like a church on the exterior but once again maintained the traditional Jewish arrangement within. Early American Jews had two priorities, both met by their synagogue structures: to establish themselves as good neighbors

The Touro Synagogue of 1763 is the country's oldest standing synagogue. The upwardly mobile Jews of Newport, Rhode Island's Jeshuat Israel hired architect Peter Harrison to design a fashionable Georgian structure.

in the eyes of their fellow Americans and to preserve Judaism as best they could at the same time. Both goals remain in place in the twenty-first century.

## The "Rite Congregation"

A new wave of Jewish immigration from Central Europe ensued in the early nineteenth century, and the monolithic synagogue community soon broke up into a pluralistic "community of synagogues"—multiple congregations distinguished by their *minhag*, or "rite," and variant liturgical traditions based on place of origin. The new diversity in American Judaism would be reflected by a new eclecticism in synagogue architecture. Philadelphia's Mikveh Israel, for example, hired architect Thomas Strickland to design their new synagogue of 1825, and he gave them an Egyptian Revival façade together with a sky-lit oval interior; like its contemporary in Vienna, the Seitenstettengasse "Tempel" of 1826, the design was both modern in conception while retaining its distinctiveness as a synagogue. The choice of Egyptian Revival, an early use of the style, may have been intended to signal both the ancient roots of Judaism as well as the non-Christian identity of the congregation. Another Egyptian Revival synagogue was built in Philadelphia in 1849 for Beth Israel, but far more often in the antebellum period, Greek Revival would be the preferred style for new synagogues—again signifying the classicism of Jewish

tradition, but now adding the association of American democracy. In 1834, Shearith Israel constructed its second synagogue building—in the neoclassical mode. Other Greek Revival synagogues, all with classical temple fronts and traditional Jewish interiors, included Cincinnati's Bene Israel of 1836, Charleston's Beth Elohim of 1841 (built to replace the earlier structure destroyed by fire in 1838), and the Baltimore Hebrew Congregation of 1845—the latter two are today the second and third oldest standing synagogues in the United States. The trend toward historical eclecticism would continue with synagogues in the Gothic style—for example, Cincinnati's B'nai Yeshurun of 1848; New York's Anshe Chesed of 1850 and B'nai Jeshurun of 1851; and San Francisco's Emanu-El and Sherith Israel, both of 1854. Somewhat more commonly, American synagogues of the mid-nineteenth century were built in Romanesque Revival, a style attaining popularity in Central Europe at the same time. The round-arched style was often adopted, therefore, by American Jewish congregations of German background—for example, New York's Shaaray Tefila of 1847, designed by the country's first Jewish architect, Leopold Eidlitz; Baltimore's Har Sinai of 1849; and New York's Rodeph Shalom of 1853. In 1860, the original Sephardic congregations of New York and Philadelphia dedicated new synagogue buildings. Philadelphia's Mikveh Israel was built in the new Romanesque style, whereas New York's Shearith Israel erected its third building in a neoclassical Baroque style. Rather than following the prevailing trends, the architect, Robert Mook, had looked carefully at the previous building of 1834 before presenting his plans.

The antebellum period also saw the modernization of the synagogue interior, by a process Leon Jick called "the Americanization of the Synagogue." The first major change was the inclusion of an organ in Charleston's new synagogue of 1841. As was the case in Europe, the addition of organ and/or choral music to the synagogue service—innovations derived from Christian practice—often signified religious liberalization and the advent of "Reform" Judaism. Not yet Reform but progressive nonetheless, Baltimore's 1845 synagogue offered two new features: expanded seating through the elimination of the central *bimah* in favor of a simpler reading desk next to the Ark and the novelty of stained-glass windows, one in the form of a Star of David—the six-pointed star would become the principal symbol of the synagogue until the mid-twentieth century (when the newly founded state of Israel adapted the symbol). All synagogues, both traditional and Reform, would soon adopt another church practice, as American rabbis began offering regular sermons around midcentury—and thus the addition of a preacher's pulpit became common in the 1850s. The change was momentous, as the elimination of the central *bimah* in favor of a frontal pulpit and reader's desk meant a transformation in the Jewish experience of worship. Intended to promote decorum, the rearrangement of

Philadelphia's Rodeph Shalom of 1870, designed by American architect Frank Furness in an eclectic picturesque style, is an example of the "Reform Temple" which came to predominate American Judaism after the Civil War.

the synagogue sanctuary would turn the liturgical leader around to face the congregants and render them a passive audience. Yet the most controversial change would be the installation of family pews in lieu of the separate women's gallery. Its first appearance was in the Albany congregation of Rabbi Isaac Mayer Wise in 1851. It was, at first, a matter of expediency—Wise's congregation, Anshe Emeth, had purchased a former Baptist church and rather than alter the floorplan chose to preserve its family seating and allow the innovation in synagogue practice. What began as a practical decision to adopt the American mode of worshipping as a family would later be ideologically justified by arguing for the more equal status of women in the synagogue. The separation of women in prayer had long occasioned negative comment on the part of both acculturated Jews and non-Jewish visitors. Now the criticism would be answered by the leap to mixed seating; and it, in turn, became the principal sign of a Reform congregation.

## The "Reform Temple"

Following the Civil War, as American Jews attained greater affluence and social status, Reform synagogues came to predominate in American Judaism—and were now most often called "temples" to differentiate them from the traditional synagogue. Their architecture set them apart as well, as the new temples were built in monumental form in the

most opulent fashion. Intriguingly, the earlier division between Americanized exterior and Judaized interior was now reversed, as the new reforms were institutionalized inside the sanctuary and architects designed exotic-looking edifices, most commonly in Islamic Revival style. The first of these were built in 1866 in Cincinnati and San Francisco for congregations B'nai Yeshurun (better known as the Plum Street Temple or the Isaac Mayer Wise Temple) and Emanu-El, respectively. Both were twin-towered cathedrals, highly conspicuous on the cityscape, and both were designed in Islamic or "Moorish" style to accentuate the non-Christian, unabashedly Jewish identity of their Reform congregations. New York's Temple Emanu-El followed suit in 1868 with a Moorish cathedral on Fifth Avenue—billed as the world's largest synagogue—codesigned by Leopold Eidlitz and fellow Jewish architect Henry Fernbach. Fernbach would later design other prominent New York synagogues, including Shaaray Tefila in 1869 and Ahavath Chesed in 1872. The latter, now known as the Central Synagogue, recently underwent extensive restoration reviving its original nineteenth-century magnificence. Other such opulent and exotic synagogues of the time include Philadelphia's Rodeph Shalom of 1870, designed by American architect Frank Furness in an eclectic picturesque style; Portland's San Francisco–inspired Beth Israel of 1888; New York's Beth El of 1891, by Arnold Brunner—the first

American-born Jewish architect—in a striking Byzantine style; and Chicago's Anshe Maarivin, in 1891, by the firm of (Dankmar) Adler and (Louis) Sullivan in the American style of the "Chicago School." Following the Chicago Columbian Exposition of 1893, and perhaps in response to the arrival of East European Jews, a new neoclassical trend took hold—for example, Brunner's Renaissance palazzo design (albeit with Moorish arcades) for New York's West End Synagogue (Shaaray Tefila) in 1894 and, three years later, a new Shearith Israel by the same architect in Roman Corinthian style. Though the latter had retained its identity as a Sephardic Orthodox synagogue, the trend toward Reform was otherwise so pervasive that even when congregations could not build anew, they often renovated their interiors to conform to the new religious style—for example, Charleston's historic Beth Elohim, which eliminated its central *bimah*, added a preacher's pulpit, and installed family pews in 1879.

### The Orthodox Shul

Between 1880 and 1915, more than two million Jews from Russia, Poland, and elsewhere in Eastern Europe immigrated to the United States. The immigrant synagogue of this era would be Orthodox in orientation and called simply, in Yiddish, *shul*. Its characteristic building would fall into one of three architectural categories: (1) the adaptation of an existing structure, (2) modest synagogues built on the narrow footprint of the urban tenement, and (3) grand synagogues built to rival the Reform temples of uptown Jewry. In the first case, the largely impoverished immigrants often made do with any prayer space they could afford. Thus, the earlist *shuls* were makeshift operations holding services in rented storefronts and converted apartments. Moving into older city neighborhoods, immigrant Jews also acquired the habit of purchasing and converting former church buildings for use as synagogues. American synagogues had taken over church buildings before, but the phenomenon had special resonance for a group that had originated in lands where the spheres of church and synagogue were strictly separated. The fact that in America, a church could actually become a synagogue (and later, the opposite case would be just as common) offered a powerful demonstration of social and religious equality in the new land. Sometimes the "church" acquired was a former Reform temple. As the earlier Jewish immigrants from Central Europe moved uptown they left their synagogue buildings behind, and those passed down to the new immigrant community included New York's Anshe Chesed and Rodeph Shalom, which were taken over by Anshe Slonim and Chatam Sopher, respectively. In Baltimore, no fewer than four nineteenth-century synagogues were recycled by the East European immigrant community. Whether converting a church or a temple, the immigrant congregation typically would modify the building to transform it into an Orthodox synagogue. This might entail adding exotic ornament on the exterior and Hebraic mural art on the interior to "Judaize" the building—especially common for a former church, as at Beth Hamedrash Hagodol in New York—and furthermore adding a central *bimah*, removing or concealing the organ, and if necessary building a new women's gallery.

Once on their feet economically, immigrant congregations were able to build their own synagogues, whose architecture would reflect many aspects of immigrant Jewish life. For example, the "tenement *shul*"—the smaller-scale synagogue built in the tight space between neighboring tenement buildings—clearly indicated how immigrant Judaism was adapted to and subsumed within the socio-economic realities of the immigrant ghetto. Such *shuls* proliferated in the immigrant communities and were most often constructed by a *landsmanshaft*, a mutual aid society of immigrants from the same hometown; the *landsmanshaft shul* thus served social as well as religious functions. It was, in effect, a home away from home, and like a multistoried house, the interior was divided between a well-appointed sanctuary on the upper floors and a daily prayer/study hall and communal meeting place below. Their exterior façades were of the same dimensions as the tenements on either side but were given far more decorative treatment. Whether in neoclassical or Moorish Revival mode, their message was the same—that despite their humble circumstances, immigrant Jews aspired to the same level of social acceptance and religious propriety as their uptown brethren. The larger, "great synagogues" of the immigrant community made this point all the more emphatically. The first such grand structure was built in New York in 1886 by Congregation Khal Adas Jeshurun, creating a landmark synagogue better known as the Eldridge Street Shul. Though inconspicuously located on a side street, Eldridge Street's ornate façade boldly announced the arrival of downtown Jewry. Clearly derived from the Moorish temples of uptown Jews, the design of the new *shul* expressed both the immigrants' ties to other Jews and their shared portion of the American dream. Similarly, the Renaissance Revival design of the 1903 Kalvarier Shul, located a few blocks from Eldridge Street, was a direct imitation of the 1902 uptown *shul* of Kehilath Jeshurun, itself inspired by the West End Synagogue of 1894. In Boston, no fewer than four immigrant synagogues borrowed their *Rundbogenstil* design from the leading Reform synagogue of the city, Temple Israel. All these new constructions included intricately carved arks and *bimahs* on the interior, as well as painted murals and other lavish decoration. In all, the grandness of the grand synagogues, both inside and out, was the concrete realization of the East European Jewish immigrants' dream of finding a home in America, both for themselves and for their faith.

## The "Synagogue-Center"

As the children of the immigrants joined the middle class, they moved to better neighborhoods and built new synagogues to suit. Following WWI, and for the better part of the twentieth century, the characteristic American synagogue would be the large, multipurpose complex called a "synagogue-center." The synagogue-center concept was to some degree inspired by the precedent of the institutional church, but it had its more direct origins in the earlier functional expansions of both the Reform temple and Orthodox *shul*. The rabbi most closely identified with the new institutional form was Mordecai M. Kaplan, who founded the Jewish Center on Manhattan's Upper West Side in 1918. The building was designed by architect Louis Allen Abramson, who was also involved in the construction of the Young Women's Hebrew Association of the same year. Like the YWHA, the new synagogue would include a swimming pool, gymnasium, auditorium, library, and rooms for the manifold functions of such an all-purpose Jewish institution. Two years later, Abramson also designed the Brooklyn Jewish Center, which, like its predecessor, was situated on a broad avenue and resembled a grand apartment house far more than a traditional house of worship. Such multiuse synagogues were soon built throughout the New York City boroughs and in other cities as well. Most would be affiliated with the

burgeoning Conservative movement, but some were Orthodox and Reform as well—for example, Baltimore's Beth Tfiloh synagogue and center of 1925–1927 and Brooklyn's Union Temple, designed by the firm of Arnold Brunner in 1926–1929. Though not all included the amenities described above, the general idea of a combined synagogue and community center, fondly called a "*shul* with a pool," had won the day. As the trend spread across the country, the architectural style most often chosen for the monumental new structures was Byzantine Revival, characterized by a centralized sanctuary topped by a massive dome. In 1925, eminent urban historian Lewis Mumford advocated the application of the Byzantine style to the "Modern Synagog" so as to "recognize the reintegration of the Jewish culture and Jewish civilization." The central dome had been used in synagogues before but would now be intended to symbolically unify the spiritual, cultural, communal, and social functions of Jewish life. Such monumental domed synagogue-centers were built throughout the 1920s in every major Jewish community, such as Boston (Ohabei Shalom), Chicago (Isaiah Temple), Cleveland (The Temple), Newark (B'nai Jeshurun), San Francisco (Temple Emanu-El), and many others. The monumental synagogue-center also institutionalized the use of representative art on the interior, a

Affluent post–World War II suburban Jewish congregations sometimes hired famous architects to create striking, sculptural designs, such as Frank Lloyd Wright's 1957 Beth Sholom Synagogue, located in Elkins Park, Pennsylvania.

trend begun by the first Reconstructionist synagogue (Mordecai Kaplan's second congregation), the Society for the Advancement of Judaism, founded in 1922. It featured a wall mural designed by artist Temima Gezari, depicting scenes from Jewish history; and a similar artistic scheme was used in a mural encircling the sanctuary of Los Angeles's Wilshire Boulevard Temple of 1929.

Following WWII, the synagogue-center idea was transferred to suburbia. But rather than evoking the former urban monumentality and picturesque decor, the new structures reflected the sprawling informality of suburban life and the stark aesthetic of modernism. Perhaps the most conspicuous new feature was the spacious parking lot surrounding the complex of low buildings. Of the buildings, the synagogue sanctuary often received artistic treatment in a modern mode, and a more prosaic wing housed the religious school. Modernist architects adorned the new Jewish centers with symbols celebrating the arrival of Judaism in American suburbia, often an abstracted version of the *menorah* (candelabrum) of the ancient Temple in Jerusalem (replacing the Jewish star in popularity). The sanctuary interior betrayed a lack of such reverence, however, as a "flexible plan" was adopted wherein the sanctuary could be expanded into a larger space, usually the adjoining social hall, to provide for the overflow crowds on the high holidays. During the rest of the year, the sanctuary was more than adequate to house the dwindling numbers of worshippers. But another constituency did come more regularly—youth. Though the concept of an all-purpose synagogue was still in effect, the suburban synagogue had become a child-centered institution, and hence the school facility often became the hub of greatest activity. Nevertheless, suburban Jewish congregations sought attention for their new edifices, and the more affluent hired well-known architects to create striking sculptural designs. Prominent examples of the postwar suburban synagogue include St. Louis' parabola-roofed B'nai Amoona of 1949 and Cleveland's domed Park Synagogue of 1953, both designed by noted German Jewish architect Eric Mendelsohn; Providence's 1954 Temple Beth El and Miami Beach's 1956 Temple Beth Sholom, both by American Jewish architect Percival Goodman, responsible for more than fifty modern synagogues; Port Chester's (suburban New York) 1956 Kneses Tifereth Israel, by Philip Johnson; Elkins Park's (suburban Philadelphia) 1957 Beth Sholom Synagogue, by Frank Lloyd Wright; Baltimore's 1960 Temple Oheb Shalom, by Walter Gropius; Glencoe's (suburban Chicago) 1964 North Shore Congregation Israel, by Minoru Yamasaki; and Buffalo's 1967 Temple Beth Zion, by Harrison & Abramovitz.

## The Synagogue "Havurah"

In the late twentieth century, following the social upheavals of the 1960s, the synagogue turned inward. Many young Jews abandoned the synagogue altogether during those years, but a select few reacted to the large, impersonal synagogues of their childhoods by creating a new style of Jewish religious community, the *havurah*. *Havurah* Jews aspired to greater intimacy, communality, and spirituality and eschewed professional leadership and the usual bureaucratic trappings of a synagogue—their motto was "do-it-yourself Judaism." They had no rabbi, and neither did they require a synagogue building. Instead, apartments and houses were converted to use as *havurot* (pl.), and, as at Havurat Shalom in Somerville, Massachusetts (founded 1968), the living room was used as the prayer hall, with pillows spread around the floor for seating. In the years since, the *havurah* movement has had a profound effect on the mainstream synagogue and its architecture. Synagogues have begun to downplay their role as public monuments to Judaism in favor of more user-friendly private spaces conducive to Jewish learning and living. In fact, many contemporary synagogues have added such subsidiary spaces to their existing complexes. For example, in 1979, North Shore Congregation Israel added a chapel to its landmark Yamasaki structure; and in 1988, Temple Oheb Shalom of Baltimore commissioned the firm of Levin/ Brown to add a separate chapel to the earlier Gropius design—such chapels, often called in Hebrew *bet midrash*, are now *de rigueur* in contemporary synagogue design. In a variation on the theme, Scarsdale's Westchester Reform Temple added a congregational "living room" for small informal events and study sessions. The interiors of all these spaces, as well as of the contemporary sanctuary, are characterized by warm-toned wood surfaces and have large windows and skylights allowing natural light to pour in. Some have eliminated fixed seating in the sanctuary in favor of *havurah*-style informality and nonhierarchal community. Yet others have begun to reintroduce the central *bimah*, both to reclaim a sense of Jewish authenticity and to reemphasize the participatory nature of Jewish worship. The general effect replicates the homey ambience of the *havurah*—warm, hospitable, inviting, and spiritually uplifting. Many suburban and rural synagogues have even adopted the look of domestic architecture, taking literally the Hebrew term for synagogue, *bet k'nesset*, "house of assembly." At the same time, many post-1960s Jews have returned to the city center, and so we have seen the return of the urban synagogue, though now with the modernism of suburbia and the intimacy of the *havurah* combined. Wherever synagogues are built and in whichever style, they continue to display the twin imperatives of American Jewish life: to be a part of America and to remain apart as Jews at one and the same time.

**See also** *Architecture* entries; *Judaism: Conservative; Judaism: Orthodox; Judaism: Reconstructionist; Judaism: Reform; Music: Jewish; Women: Jewish; Worship: Jewish.*

David E. Kaufman

**BIBLIOGRAPHY**

Goldman, Karla. *Beyond the Synagogue Gallery: Finding a Place for Women in American Judaism.* Cambridge, Mass.: Harvard University Press, 2000.

Gruber, Samuel. *American Synagogues: A Century of Architecture and Jewish Community.* New York: Rizzoli, 2003.

Jick, Leon. *The Americanization of the Synagogue, 1820–1870.* Hanover, N.H.: University Press of New England, 1976.

Kampf, Avram. *Contemporary Synagogue Art: Developments in the United States, 1945–1965.* Philadelphia: The Jewish Publication Society of America, 1966.

Kaufman, David E. *Shul with a Pool: The "Synagogue-Center" in American Jewish History.* Hanover, N.H.: University Press of New England, 1999.

Wertheimer, Jack, ed. *The American Synagogue: A Sanctuary Transformed.* Hanover, N.H.: University Press of New England, 1987.

Wischnitzer, Rachel. *Synagogue Architecture in the United States: History and Interpretation.* Philadelphia: The Jewish Publication Society of America, 1955.

# Architecture: Muslim

The presence of Muslims in antebellum America is central to the understanding of the development of the first American Muslim communities. Some sources estimate that the transatlantic slave trade brought up to 12 million West Africans to North and South America between the seventeenth and nineteenth centuries, with an estimated 645,000 to the United States. By 1860, according to the census, the slave population in the United States had grown to 4 million.

That Islam did not survive in the antebellum era as an organized practice among Muslim captives does not mean that it did not flourish in some rebellious form during slavery. Indeed, the African Muslim community succeeded in following the precepts of their faith. Several of these captives stood out as men of education and knowledge, for example, Omar ibn Said (1770–1864)—after whom a mosque at Fayetteville, North Carolina, is named.

Thus far, researchers have been unable to identify the earliest established mosque in the United States with any degree of certainty. In the early 1920s a Muslim community was established in Ross, North Dakota, and a mosque was built there around 1928. Another community was established during the 1930s in Rapid City, South Dakota. In 1934, Lebanese immigrants built a mosque in Cedar Rapids, Iowa; this building is popularly referred to as the oldest mosque in America. In 1930, African American Muslims established the First Muslim Mosque in Pittsburgh, Pennsylvania.

A Cleveland, Ohio, mosque founded in 1932 by al-Hajj Wali Akram is now the oldest continuously running indigenous Muslim institution in America. During the Great Depression (1929–1945), Professor Muhammad Ezaldeen established the Ad-Deen Allah Universal Arabic Association in Jabal Arabiyya, a Muslim village at Buffalo, New York. Professor Ezaldeen was an African American who had studied in Cairo from 1931 to 1935 and was knowledgeable in both Arabic and Islamic studies. In the 1930s Malcolm Bell Jr. (1913–2001) photographed and interviewed many coastal Georgia blacks as part of a Works Progress Administration program; this project was published in 1940 and entitled *Drums and Shadows: Survival Studies among the Coastal Georgia Negroes.* Bell interviewed a number of coastal Georgia blacks who were descendants of Muslim slaves; they described the daily ritual prayer that was still being performed at the time of the interview. One interview mentions a building that a slave master had ordered to be torn down; from the description it appears to have been a place for Muslim worship (*musalla*) rather than a domicile. The *musalla* is the most common type of building used for communal worship because adapting an existing structure is far less costly than constructing a new building. However, two approaches have their parallels in the aesthetics of the urban mosque. One views fragments of aesthetics as precedent handed down through history, independent of meaning or time. Another quotes the formal elements, devoid of any meaning. What differentiates these approaches is a fundamentally spatial form with many types of corresponding modes of creative expression. But the picture is more complex: besides communal worship, there exists a ghostly residue of emotional and cultural feeling attached to the image of the edifice that causes a most intractable aesthetic problem for an untrained architect, who may not be familiar with the planning of this type of structure. In Europe and America there are four or more stages in the development of the urban mosque and Islamic center: (1) an early period dating to the turn of the twentieth century, including such examples as the Mosquee de Paris built in 1926; (2) a second period epitomized by the Islamic Center of Washington, D.C., built in 1957; (3) a third period witnessing the proliferation of mosques in the West, such as the London Central Mosque completed in 1977, up to the 1990s and the Islamic Cultural Center of New York; and (4) the period from 2000 to the present day, including the Islamic Cultural Center of Boston and al-Farooq Masjid Atlanta, both completed in 2008. The idea of using the term "Islamic center" gained legitimacy in the early 1960s when a host of ancillary functions were added to the typical edifice (mosque) simply built or modified for communal worship; these ancillary functions now include education, socializing, recreation, and civic activities for the entire urban or suburban community. The terms "Islamic center" and "mosque" are often used interchangeably.

## The Formation of the Urban Mosque (Masjid)

The pious saying (hadith) "the whole world is a mosque ..." sanctions the injunction of public worship anywhere in the world. Today there are between fifteen hundred and three thousand mosques in the United States; the vast majority of these buildings exist in urban communities. *The Mosque in America: A National Portrait*, by Ihsan Bagby, Paul M. Perl, and Bryan T. Froehle (2001), estimated the total number of Muslims living in the United States as between six and seven million. African Americans were reported to make up 42 percent of the total, 24.4 percent were Indo-Pakistani, 12.4 percent were Arabs, 5.2 percent were Africans, 3.6 percent were Iranian, 2.4 percent were Turks, 2 percent were from Southeast Asia, 1.6 percent were white Americans, 3.2 percent were Albanians, and all other groups constituted 5.6 percent. The same study estimated that the majority of existing mosques (87 percent) had been founded since 1970. Likewise, approximately 64 percent of all mosques are located in urban areas, while 36 percent are established in rural or suburban locations.

Urban mosques can be found in Brooklyn, New York; Newark, New Jersey; Philadelphia; Boston; Los Angeles; Houston; Chicago; Detroit; and elsewhere. A kaleidoscope of ethnic Muslim groups have settled in the aforementioned urban locales over the past fifty years; however, the latest wave of immigration is distinct in two ways. First, new Muslim immigrants tend to reside where there are established Muslim communities; second, recent arrivals are more likely to live in ethnic suburban enclaves, with other ethnic Muslims from the same country. Until the early 1970s, the most prominent ethnic group of Muslim immigrants in Brooklyn, New York, and Detroit, Michigan, had come from Yemen in the 1950s and 1960s. Since the 1970s this group has increased to include immigrants from Lebanon and the rest of the Middle East. After 1980 many Iranian immigrants also settled in Los Angeles, California.

In inner-city neighborhoods all across America, the urban mosque represents an edifice dedicated to communal worship, education, and social activities. Three prominent examples include the Islamic Center of Washington, D.C. (1957); the Islamic Cultural Center of New York (1991); and the Islamic Cultural Center of Boston, Roxbury (2007).

Social and religious practice undoubtedly influences the desire for communal worship and is rooted in a long tradition of public gathering, especially on Fridays and for important religious events. Urban and rural mosques usually differ only in size and ancillary function; however, these differences can be the result of construction costs or the availability of land. While no prescriptive form for the urban mosque occurs in the Qur'an, the need for communal worship among immigrants and indigenous Muslims has led to the development of a particular American plan for these buildings.

Differing in more than just outward appearance, the North American mosque gives priority to a balanced mix of functions and innovative aesthetic features. Because many cultural and religious traditions persist, immigrant mosques in North America have a two-tiered identity, which may differ according to the cultural interaction of the émigré. First, "diaspora aesthetics," cultural sentiments informed by nostalgia, a host of customs, traditions, and present-day beliefs, associate the mosque with memory and as such a style adapted from far-away foreign places. Stylistically the design of a mosque falls within three common genres: first, a strict adherence to an aesthetic tradition influenced by sign, symbol, and building convention; second, an attempt at design interpretation employing experimental and popular ideas and resulting in a hybrid image; and finally, a faithful attempt to understand modernity, tradition, and urbanism.

In North America the urban mosque operates under unique existing site constraints. Among these constraints is the qiblah, the need for Muslim worshippers to face Makkah (Mecca). The edifice must, therefore, conform to this canonical requirement. Architects and designers have sought to preserve meaning, religious practice, and social interaction in new ways. But the difficulty lies in deciding what to select from a particular vocabulary of an émigré's place or history, and this kind of aesthetic profile in short accounts for the vast majority of stylistic variations that exist today. Appropriation of space must also consider religious values to adequately explain design strategy. Conversely, it could be argued that while architecture differs from the literal exegesis (commentary) of the Qur'an, architecture is nonetheless a by-product of religious belief and practice.

### Aesthetics and Religious Values

A mosque is primarily a place of spiritual repose, a spiritual sanctuary. Mosques are not built according to divine patterns; the two main religious texts for Muslims, the Qur'an and the *hadith* (writings that recount the statements or actions of Muhammad), provide no clear rules as to what a mosque should look like. However, the Qur'an does stress the value of the edifice as a place for the remembrance of God, and the *hadith* prescribe lists of profane actions that are not allowed to take place in a mosque. The essence of sacred art remains always reflective, contemplative, and theocentric; the acceptance of revealed truths requires a keen intellect (*al-aql*), purity of heart (*qalb*), and piety of soul (*ruh*).

All mosques can be traced to a valued origin with an affinity to the first *masjid*—the Prophet's mosque built at Madinah (Medina), Arabia, in the seventh century CE. The first edifice was originally a simple demarked orthogonal walled space, with an open courtyard and two or three doors and a shaded rectangular portico (*musalla*) to one end facing Makkah. The portico was supported by columns, which were spaced at regular intervals to support the roof structure. This simple structure became the paradigm for all buildings built following the expansion of Islam in the first century after the death of the Prophet Muhammad. The American mosque demonstrates a regional development and refinement and a modern expression; likewise, in North America, regional building traditions may have a direct influence on the aesthetics of the edifice.

The development of the first prototype and its later variations were generally sustained via a commonly understood cosmological order. That order can be defined by five themes: *belief, order, space, materials,* and *symbols*. These themes find their primordial origin in rational sciences (geometry, for example), which were engaged as means of expressing the idiosyncratic aesthetic themes. In the development of the American *masjid* (urban mosque), the use of rational science as an aesthetic device, like the absence of iconography in any place of Muslim worship, is a universal tenet. This tenet is as fundamental a principle of Muslim belief as *tauheed* or monotheism. *Tauheed* in Muslim aesthetics is related to the power of *shari'ah* (sacred law). Muslim religious aesthetics is therefore a theocentered epistemology. It has no associated symbolic form, only the primary act of individual submission and, as such, a reluctance to directly invest an edifice with any symbolic connotation. The ultimate principle of monotheism is the rejection of idolatry. The individual act of submission is paired with the physical experience; thus, the cognitive rule of facing toward the *kabah*, a stone building at the center of the Great Mosque in Makkah, can be explained as the axis of prayer (*qiblah*), which is the universal axis for Muslims anywhere on the planet. An important injunction in the Qur'an (3:36) states that the believer should face Makkah while performing the ritual prayer. This means that mosques must have a wall 90 degrees to the direction of Makkah; this is commonly called the *qiblah* wall, which is laid out transversely to the correct prayer direction. Muslims refer to this as the wall facing Makkah or the axis of prayer. Owing to the importance of calculating the direction of the *qiblah* when the site of a mosque is established, various methods were firmly incorporated to determine its accuracy, as well as that of the placement of the *mihrab*, a niche in the wall facing Makkah.

Congregational prayer is governed by this rule, which also affects the orientation of the prayer space toward the *kabah* in Makkah. This idea, the orientation of the prayer space toward the *kabah*, reveals an architectural condition that imparts a control over the space and building in terms of the physical and the conceptual. The axis of prayer (*qiblah*), or direction to Makkah, recognizes that the term mosque (*masjid*) is related to both a place of prostration and the act of prostration (*sa-ja-da*, to prostrate); the *qiblah* is therefore vital with regards to the performance of individual and communal prayer.

### The American Mosque since 1950

Because Islam is often imbedded in a transnational identity, the collective activity of worship treats the mosque as a reflection of the diaspora community; yet the belief system cannot be ignored, and as such the types of aesthetics that we find in American mosques span a range of cultural nuances, modern schemes, and traditional or hybrid styles, which have power over the image of the edifice. It is important to realize that both architect and client face two related design choices. First, the approach must attempt to interpret and bring critical analysis to bear on space, form, symbol and order. Second, differing in more than just outward appearance, the hybrid model gives priority to an unbalanced mix of functions and aesthetic features. The North American mosque displays a wide variety of styles based on this broad interpretation of aesthetic vocabulary and the need to meet liturgical requirements. However, the plan of a mosque's fellowship hall for men and women is a fundamental criterion: it is primarily governed by the liturgical axis towards Makkah.

In Muslim aesthetics the *shari'ah* has dominated the written and spoken word, often altering the relationship of faith to aesthetics. Historically three kinds of visual patterns can be found among a myriad of examples in North America: (1) designs derived from plant life, often called *arabesque* in the West; (2) Arabic calligraphy, which is the most revered art form in Islam because it is believed to convey the word of God; and (3) tessellation, or the repetitive "ordering" of a geometric pattern.

In general, these three are not common to all North American mosques, although isolated examples of their occurrence do exist. There are no formal design standards for an American mosque; it was only recently that *masjid* standards were included in the religious building section of the *Architectural Graphic Standards*, which is consulted by professional architects and architectural students. A second text, *Design Criteria for Mosques and Islamic Centers: Art, Architecture and Worship*, was published in 2007.

American architects have to deal with a set of unique design problems when planning a *masjid* because adequate design standards have not been formally established. In their absence, American architects who have been commissioned to design mosques have exercised absolute freedom in interpreting planning prerequisites to meet American code requirements.

The forces that shape the American mosque are therefore complex and at the same time unique in sociohistorical terms. Three examples present an interesting overview of the architectural complexity of American mosques. The Islamic Center of Washington, D.C. (1957) includes various motifs from the Muslim world, primarily Egypt. The Dar al Islam (abode of tranquility) at Abiquiu, New Mexico (1980), is built primarily of adobe construction; it also employs several traditional methods and crafts from ancient Nubia, in what is now Egypt. Another approach is a modern interpretation of belief, order, space, materials, and symbols; this can be seen in the Manhattan *masjid* and Islamic center in New York designed by Skidmore, Owings and Merrill (1990).

## The Islamic Center of Washington, D.C.

The cornerstone of the Islamic Center Washington, D.C. was laid in 1949, and President Eisenhower formally inaugurated it in 1957. It was built primarily for the diplomatic community. The first major Islamic religious edifice to be built in a major American city, the Washington building, like the Regent's Park Mosque in London and the Grand Mosque of Paris, employs a unique aesthetic vocabulary. The architect Abdur Rahman Rossi reproduced several Egyptian mosque motifs, which can best be understood by studying the inscriptions, which depict both meaning and style. While each inscription is primarily intended to further the knowledge of the community, deciphering the text of the inscription is an overwhelming task for anyone who is not adept in reading Arabic. Several verses of the Qur'an have been arranged in a symmetrical configuration and in various patterns on the interior walls and ceilings of the primary prayer hall. The divine names of Allah (*Al-Asma Allah Al-Husna*) and several familiar and often-quoted

Built primarily for the diplomatic community, the Islamic Center of Washington, D.C. (1957) was the first large Islamic religious edifice to be built in a major U.S. city. The architect, Abdur Rahman Rossi, reproduced several Egyptian mosque motifs whose inscriptions are intended to further the knowledge of the community.

verses from the Qur'an, such as *Al-Alaq* 96:1–5, are inscribed in large framed borders of Arabic (*thuluth*) script, with smaller framed panels of ornamental Kufic script.

Two inscription bands run horizontally across the face of the prayer niche (*mihrab*). The upper band reads, "Verily we have seen the turning of your face to the heaven . . . ," and the lower band says, " . . . surely we shall turn you to a *qiblah* that shall please you" (*Al-Baqara* 2:144). The *mihrab's* decorative treatment follows the Iznik and Bursa tradition of using glazed tiles—blue, red, and green—which are commonly found in Ottoman Turkish buildings.

The plan of the building contains three halls (*iwan*) framed by an exterior double arcade (*riwaq*), which serves as an *extra muros* space or *ziyada*. The orthogonal arcade remains perpendicular to the street, but the *masjid* is set out at a tangent to conform to the *qiblah* axis, which has been calculated on the basis of the great circle: the shortest distance when facing Makkah. In the building there is a small court (*sahn*) open to the sky, but the whole central space of the *masjid* is covered with a modest clerestory dome. An arcade (*riwaq*) consisting of five contiguous arches serves as an entry portal and a key part of the façade.

The entry portal runs parallel to the street, and for added emphasis it has an inscription band of Kufic script at the upper part of the façade, which reads, "In houses of worship which Allah has permitted to be raised so that His name be remembered, in them, there [are such as] extol His limitless glory at morning and evening" (*Al-Nur* 24:36). The *masjid's* composition epitomizes an array of Muslim aesthetic themes; the overall *image* the inscriptions evoke is significant in regard to the use of epigraphy (calligraphy—pious verses from the Qur'an) from two aspects: first as a devotional theme and second as an emotional device with symbolic meaning that satisfies a quiet devotional disposition. With regards to art and worship, epigraphy has both essence and appearance: it is self-evident, it has meaning when it is read, and even when it is rendered in a highly stylized manner it evokes delight. Calligraphy is a composition that transmits a message. For example, when seen as art, it exhibits beauty and meaning; its communicative power exists because

of its syntactical structure. In terms of syntax, the development of epigraphy was more systematized and controlled than building structures, simply because it is essential that the meaning of a text be understood.

### Dar al-Islam, Abiquiu, New Mexico

In 1980, Hassan Fathy (d. 1989) was commissioned to design the master plan for a Muslim village in Abiquiu, New Mexico. The mesa site is framed by surrounding arid hills and several snow-capped mountains that are visible in the distance. At the top, one can expect to experience the reflective aura of the mosque and the *madrassa* (school). The Abiquiu site shares an empathic relationship with Fathy's theory of creativity, and a balanced spiritual awareness of a sense of unity between building, landscape, and user imposes an intangible order on the building and the site.

The idea of the Dar al-Islam (Abode of Islam) village was the dream of an American-born Muslim and an American-educated Saudi industrialist who met at Mecca in the late 1970s. The original idea was to establish a Muslim village, the largest and most comprehensive of its kind in America. Today, the Dar al-Islam organization emphasizes education first, and the site provides a quiet retreat as sacred site.

Abiquiu, the Chama Valley, and their immediate surroundings were populated before the arrival of the Spanish by several Native American peoples. Spanish settlers arrived

In 1980 Hassan Fathy (d. 1989) was commissioned to design the master plan for a Muslim village in Abiquiu, New Mexico. The site reflects a sense of unity among building, landscape, and user.

The Islamic Cultural Center of Manhattan (1990) explores the use of modern technology, and geometric themes are employed as a unifying element throughout the interior and exterior.

in 1598. The harsh environmental conditions at Abiquiu provided an ideal setting for using adobe construction. In making use of adobe, Hassan Fathy remained faithful to a long-established building tradition endorsing the notion that "small is beautiful." As Fathy put it, "Tradition is a key element of culture . . . when the craftsman was responsible for much of the work of building, traditional art came out of the subconscious of the community . . . it is held together by an accumulated culture, rather than by one individual's idea of harmony." The traditional Nubian building technique worked well for the choice of site and the project itself. Not only can the site be considered in terms of its psychological impulse, but it is, in a manner of speaking, a spiritual place: a container that naturally embodies physical space.

### The Islamic Cultural Center of New York

The Islamic Cultural Center of New York (1990, by Skidmore, Owings and Merrill) explores the use of modern technology as a compositional device. The *masjid* confronts both tradition and modernity, seeking to reinterpret various aesthetic themes associated with extant models found in the Muslim world. First, the surface motifs reflect geometric themes, which are employed as a unifying element throughout the *masjid*'s interior and exterior. These motifs can be seen primarily on the carpet where worshippers assemble for prayer in horizontal and parallel rows facing the *qiblah*.

They also appear in the surface treatment of the *minbar*, the exterior façade, and several other interior elements as well. Geometry is a fundamental theme in Muslim cosmology, but in this instance it comes closer to a modernist, secular interpretation than a traditional, cosmological one.

The inscriptions, which are included in the decorative features of the *masjid*'s interior, are rendered in a geometric Kufic style. They are set in straight, horizontal, and vertical arrangements to accommodate a modernist concept of order. For instance, around the *mihrab* the geometric Kufic script reads, "Allah is the Light of the Heavens and the Earth."

Admittedly, the use of traditional inscriptions as a decorative element is in some respects incongruent with the idea of a secular, modernist interpretation of surface treatment. Using geometry as a spatial theme, with the aid of a corresponding angular Kufic inscription, provides visual affinity; a less complementary script would have put the theme of composition and "order" at risk. The aesthetic treatment of the interior of the dome over the central prayer hall further illustrates this point. The dome's structural ribs have been left bare and rudimentary, which provides a bold geometric texture to the dome's inner face when seen from below. The inner drum of the dome is covered with a band of angular Kufic inscription, but the pattern of concentric ribs clearly dominates the composition, especially since the text of the band is largely unreadable from the main prayer hall below. Both compositional elements—epigraphy and geometry—were clearly intended by the architect to be operative aesthetic devices.

### *Summary*

The design conceptualization of a mosque and its aesthetics supports two primary themes. First, it preserves the identity of the various forms that constitute the elements of a religious edifice for men and women and the relationship between spiritual repose and aesthetics. Second, religious practice and the *shari'ah* have traditionally been the major factors organizing the human space of the mosque. Furthermore, there is a common consensus that Muslim religious aesthetics is a theocentric dogma. In a conceptual framework, one must also consider the unique aesthetic language that explains the elements employed in spatial treatment within a mosque. From a historical point of view, there are exhaustive categories of types and subtypes of mosque, yet in its simplest function the mosque is a space for contemplation, repose, and communal worship. In the West this formula holds true, with the added proviso that the North American urban context has no parallel to the Muslim world. In the Muslim world, Islamic law (*shari'ah*) has substantive meaning for the study of urbanism in the *madinah* or the pre-modern Islamic city. The *shari'ah* is a commonly accepted means of adjudication in habitat disputes; it is therefore a reasonable criterion for the "ordering" of habitat, which forms the corpus of building ordinances.

See also *Architecture* entries; *Islam in North America; Islam Tradition and Heritage; Nation(s) of Islam; Qur'an; Women: Muslim; Worship: Muslim.*

Akel Ismail Kahera

**BIBLIOGRAPHY**

Bagby, Ihsan, Paul M. Perl, and Bryan T. Froehle. *The Mosque in America: A National Portrait.* Washington, D.C.: Council on American Relations, 2001.

Darsh, S. M. *Islamic Essays.* London: Islamic Cultural Center, 1979.

Hakim, Jameela A. *History of the First Muslim Mosque in Pittsburgh, Pennsylvania.* N.p., 1979.

Kahera, Akel Ismail. *Deconstructing the American Mosque: Space, Gender & Aesthetics.* Austin: University of Texas Press, 2002.

———. "Gardens of the Righteous: Sacred Space in Judaism, Christianity and Islam." *CrossCurrents* 52 (Fall 2002): 304–311.

———. "Two Muslim Communities: Two Disparate Ways of Islamizing Public Spaces." *Space and Culture* 10, no. 4 (2007): 384–396.

———. "Urban Enclaves, Muslim Identity and the Urban Mosque in America." *Journal of Muslim Minority Affairs* 22, no. 2 (2002): 369–380.

———. "The Urban Mosque: Urban Islam, Activism & the Reconstruction of the Ghetto." *Studies in Contemporary Islam* 3, no. 2 (2001): 42–55.

Metcalf, Barbara, ed. *Making Muslim Space in North America and Europe.* Berkeley: University of California Press, 1996.

Sayeed, Asma. "Early Sunni Discourses on Women's Mosque Attendance." *International Institute for the Study of Islam in the Modern World NewsLetter* 7, no. 1 (March 2001). www.isim.nl.

# Architecture: New Religious Movements

The United States has provided a fertile environment for a broad range of spiritual organizations and religiously based utopian settlements. Some of these groups, such as the Shakers, Quakers, and Swedenborgians, were founded in Europe, and the Vedantists in India, but all found a following and made important contributions to the religious built environment of America. Other groups, such as the Christian Scientists, Theosophists, and the Latter-day Saints, the largest of America's new religions, were indigenous groups from the nineteenth century that grew rapidly in the United States and spread their influence across the globe.

## Early Communal Impulses

One of the earliest successful utopian groups was the celibate United Society of Believers in Christ's Second Appearing, or Shakers, who founded their first community at Hancock, Massachusetts, in 1790. By the 1820s, the Shakers developed a systematic planning of villages, usually surrounding a centralized meetinghouse. At one time they had twenty-two communities in New York, New England, Kentucky, Ohio, and Indiana with six thousand members scattered across the eastern United States. In these villages the Shakers developed a distinct style of architecture that emphasized simplicity and functionality. Shaker religious architecture emphasized the separation of the sexes and therefore was built to allow minimal contact between men and women. Meetinghouses had three entrances, one for each sex and one for the ministry, with interiors that consisted primarily of unadorned and unimpeded spaces for the ecstatic dancing that was part of the religious rituals of the group. Today there are fifteen Shaker villages and museums that celebrate their innovative architecture, design, agriculture, and industry. The National Park Service provides the Shaker Historic Trail, a travel itinerary of the National Register of Historic Places.

The Religious Society of Friends, or Quakers, a Puritan group that emerged in seventeenth-century Britain, developed a set of quite diverse worship styles over the past four hundred years in America, which is reflected in their historical and current architecture. The Friends General Conference supports unprogrammed worship, consisting of the congregants waiting in silence, much like original Quaker colonists, while the Friends United Meeting has semiprogrammed worship with clergy. The Evangelical Friends Church International services and architecture more closely resemble other forms of Protestantism. The earliest forms of the meetinghouse, emerging in a building boom in the late eighteenth century, were generally vernacular, south-facing, one- or two-story wood, brick, or stone buildings without stained glass or steeples. Exemplary was the popular early Quaker plan, such as the one in Buckingham, Pennsylvania

(1768), that consisted of domestically scaled, plain, symmetrical, rectangular buildings. The buildings were generally end-gabled, with six-bay façades, consisting of separate entrances for men and women between two windows on either side of each door. Interiors were simple, unornamented, and austere and contained long benches for seating arranged in varying ways on either side of the worship space, one side reserved for women and one side for men. Worship consisted of waiting to be moved by the voice of God within: there was little ritual and no need for a pulpit or other hierarchical or liturgical arrangements. Either a permanent or movable partition was placed between men and women for conducting separate business meetings and sometimes even for worship. As other forms of worship emerged, different bays, openings, and orientations were needed for new functions, such as preaching from a fixed pulpit. A particularly beautiful example of a modern meetinghouse based on the earlier Quaker plan is architect Leslie Elkin's gray-clapboard Live Oak Friends Meeting House (2001) in Houston, Texas, with its multiple bay doors and seating arranged in a hollow square for unprogrammed worship. It features one of artist James Turrell's "Skyspaces" in the vaulted ceiling, which encourages contemplation of the framed sky and passing clouds as a metaphor for seeking the "inner light."

The Mother Church of Christian Science was a small Romanesque revival edifice when first built (1894). A monumental extension (1906) was designed in the Renaissance classical style, inspired by the 1893 Exposition in Chicago, the center of the Christian Science movement.

## Metaphysical Groups

The first Swedenborgian church was formed in Baltimore in 1792, with a General Convention of the New Jerusalem in the United States established in 1817. An institutional break occurred in 1890, resulting in the creation of a more conservative General Church of the New Jerusalem, now known commonly as the General or New Church, headquartered in Bryn Athyn, Pennsylvania. This body emerged from the General Convention of the New Jerusalem in North America, now known as the Swedenborgian Church, headquartered in Newtonville, Massachusetts.

The early Swedenborgian church built several significant buildings in the Gothic style. An early example is the Gothic-revival Cambridge Swedenborg Chapel built in 1901, designed by H. Langford Warren, an important Arts and Crafts architect and founder of the architectural curriculum at Harvard University. The Swedenborgian Church of San Francisco opened its doors for worship in 1895 and was designed by a distinguished group of architects, including the celebrated Bernard Maybeck. Its founding

pastor, Rev. Joseph Worcester, encouraged rustic Arts and Crafts principles in the church design, integrating natural materials that were simply and honestly expressed in the structure. A more recent innovative example is Frank Lloyd Wright's organic 1951 Wayfarer's Chapel in Rancho Palos Verdes, California, a redwood and glass structure integrated with trees and panoramic views, reflecting the correspondences between the inner and outer world so important to the seer and prophet of the group, Emanuel Swedenborg. The use of natural materials and open glass expanses is also apparent in several new designs, such as the Church of the Open Word Garden Chapel, built in 1957 in St. Louis.

The New Church's headquarters at Bryn Athyn, outside Philadelphia, is a stunning Gothic-inspired cathedral.

Erected in 1913 and dedicated in 1919, a Romanesque council hall was completed by 1926 and a choir hall added in 1928. Initially designed by famous Gothicist Ralph Adams Cram, the church building was supervised by church member Raymond Pitcairn, who wanted to create a unique organic structure built through communal effort. The building was continually altered by the draftsmen and builders during the course of construction. Pitcairn encouraged the use of local materials and had his artisans create working models derived from his collection of medieval and antique examples.

The Mother Church of Christian Science was built in Boston in 1894, a small Romanesque revival edifice, later abutted by a monumental extension in 1906 designed in the Renaissance classical style. Aside from Bernard Maybeck's Arts and Crafts masterpiece, First Church of Christ, Scientist, Berkeley, California (1911), Christian Scientists generally chose a monumental classical style with Greek pediments and Roman domes for their unornamented urban edifices. This was the result of the growth of the movement in Chicago around the time of the 1893 Exposition, when Chicago stood at the geographical and demographic center of the Christian Science movement. Between 1896 and 1910 eight edifices were built in Chicago, each seating between one thousand and fifteen hundred people. These were all classical edifices, built of stone, and inspired by the example of the "White City" of the World's Columbian Exposition. The Exposition both launched Christian Science into the limelight of public respectability and provided a model for the architectural style of its new edifices. Subsequently, well over a thousand edifices were designed in the classical style, often with elaborate art glass domes featuring unimpeded open worship spaces where congregations were led by two lay readers, usually a man and a woman. Through architects such as Chicago-based Solon Beman and Leon Stanhope, the classical style was defended in the press and debated with architects such as Elmer Grey, who argued for a more broadly historical and site-specific approach. The cult of the colonial dominated new suburban branch church designs after 1950, with some significant modern designs, such as architect Paul Rudolph's now-razed brutalist Christian Science Organization Building at the University of Illinois (1962); Harry Weese's Seventeenth Church of Christ, Scientist, Chicago (1968); Araldo Cossutta's reinforced concrete Christian Science Center in Boston (1968–1974); and Cossutta's brutalist Third Church of Christ, Scientist, Washington, D.C. (1971).

## Mormon Restorationism
### Nineteenth Century

This covenant-based group of denominations, the largest of which is the Church of Jesus Christ of Latter-day Saints, was first founded by Joseph Smith in 1830 in upstate New York. Envisioning a "city of Zion" in the west near Independence, Missouri, many of his followers attempted settlement in the area, organizing their first community in Kirtland, Ohio, between 1831 and 1838, when they were forcibly removed and settled on the banks of the Mississippi river at Nauvoo, Missouri. Continued altercations with non-Mormons resulted in the murder of Joseph Smith, and a succession crisis ensued. Brigham Young led the adherents from Nauvoo in 1846 to the Great Basin in Utah and legally founded the church in 1850 in the new territory of Utah. Urban planning resulted in distinctive geometric city and town patterns.

The first Mormon architecture, the Kirtland, Ohio Temple (1833–1836), was designed by Joseph Smith. It was a simple rectangle with pointed roof and tower at its east end, like a typical New England meetinghouse. The neoclassical Nauvoo Temple (1841–1845) was like the Ohio Temple. Though it burned down in the hostile environment of 1848, a faithful reproduction was erected in 2002. Both of these two-story structures were primarily assembly rooms, reflecting a time before temples were deemed the place of the holiest of holies and before temple ordinances had been fully developed. The lower hall was used for public worship, while the upper hall was used for instruction in the Aaronic and Melchisidek priesthoods. Unique were the series of pulpits on each end of the hall, tailored to the needs of whichever priesthood was in session.

The more intimidating castellation of Mormon temples indicated a shift of emphasis, borrowed from Masonic rites, of secret rituals and initiations that were not open to the public. By the rise of the intentional settlements in Utah, temple rituals were well established. In these temples, worthy members obtained instruction; carried out initiation rituals; and received their endowment to participate in sacred ordinances, including baptisms by proxy of family members and others who were dead before the restoration of the gospel, as well as sealing ceremonies of eternal marriage for couples and families that ensured their connection into eternity. Subsequent temples contained progressive ordinance rooms, often with murals, and some were situated for live-action endowment ceremonies and later film

The Church of Jesus Christ of Latter-day Saints' Temple Square in Salt Lake City, Utah, is based on a sketch by Brigham Young that informed Truman Angell's design. The style of the building is a mix of Romanesque and Gothic.

viewing. The first functioning temple in Utah was the Gothic-style temple at St. George (1871–1877), similar to the Nauvoo Temple. Soon after, temples were built in Logan (1877–1884) and Manti (1877–1888), the latter designed by William Folsom in a French Renaissance style.

Brigham Young chose Temple Square immediately after arriving in the Great Basin in 1847. At ten acres it paralleled the ten-acre block system provided for Salt Lake City. His 1853 sketch informed Truman Angell's design for the temple that was finally completed in 1893 of local granite. The style of the building is a mix between Romanesque and Gothic, with tower groupings in threes and of different sizes indicating the organization and powers invested in the two priesthoods. This six-tower model inspired a number of more contemporary temples, such as

the Washington, D.C., temple (1968–1974); the Boise, Idaho Temple (1982–1984); and several others that used a simplified modern architectural style with a gabled roof, similar to many meetinghouses and stake centers built during this era.

## Twentieth Century

The Laie Hawaii Temple (1915–1919) and the Mesa Arizona Temple (1921–1922) were both modified classical designs reminiscent of pre-Columbian temples. The early Cardston, Alberta Temple (1913–1923), with its Aztec influences, designed by important church architects Hyrum C. Pope and Harold W. Burton, showed the influence of Frank Lloyd Wright. Wright's influence also marked meetinghouses and tabernacles during this period, designed by them and by Wright renderer Taylor Woolley: together they produced a Wright-inspired "Mormon style." The pyramidal single-spired Art Deco Idaho Falls Temple (1939–1945) subsequently inspired a number of single-spire examples, including the church's then-largest Los Angeles Temple (1951–1956).

The responsibility for the architecture of the church has generally been centralized. Truman Angell was the first official architect for the church after it arrived in Utah, and he designed the homes of his brother-in-law and leader of the church, Brigham Young, as well as the St. George Temple and the Salt Lake City Temple. Brigham Young's son, Joseph Don Carlos Young, studied architecture at the Rensselaer Polytechnic Institute in New York and was then appointed church architect.

Standardization of the meetinghouse/stake center ensued under Young to create a utilitarian and recognizable Mormon form. At first, only simple, functional buildings were built for worship. By the early twentieth century, these structures were supplemented by buildings for auxiliary meetings and recreation, often built in the colonial style, designed by the church architectural department. These were usually connected by a foyer through the 1940s and then became integrated into a single structure in the 1950s.

During the first half of the twentieth century, the church was responsible for more than one thousand buildings. Today the Mormons have 128 operating sacred temples, dedicated as houses of the Lord Jesus Christ, open only to members in good standing, with 17 in various phases of realization. Of these, 127 were built after 1980.

More recently a centralized church building committee has functioned to create uniform and affordable accommodations for the movement. These more standardized plans began with Emil Fetzer's modern Ogden Temple (1969–1972) and Provo Temple (1969–1971) and continued with a series of temples designed with long, low roofs and single dramatic towers. A particularly exceptional design, conceived outside the church's official architectural office, was the double-towered San Diego Temple (1988–1993), designed by William S. Lewis Jr. and Dennis and Shelly Hyndman.

Meetinghouses, like larger stake centers, usually consist of a chapel accommodating between two hundred and four hundred worshippers, mirrored by a multipurpose "cultural hall" auditorium/gym, surrounded on three sides by a large kitchen, baptismal font room, classrooms, and other office spaces. Other large stake center projects are increasingly moving to urban cores with new modified colonial structures, similar to those built in the 1920s, such as the Cambridge, Massachusetts Stake Center (2009).

Mormon meetinghouses or stake centers are organized geographically and are used by several congregations called branches or wards that make up the stake (diocese), depending on membership density. Tabernacles are built for stake conferences. The most famous is the Mormon Tabernacle at Temple Square, Salt Lake City, erected between 1864 and 1867 to seat eight thousand. The elliptical building with elongated dome was an engineering and acoustic marvel, designed by civil engineer Henry Grow and Angell using Ithiel Town's lattice truss system.

The second largest Mormon group, with 250,000 members, is the Community of Christ, until 2001 known as the Reorganized Church of Jesus Christ of Latter-day Saints, founded in 1860 during the crisis of succession after Joseph Smith's death. The church recently built a stunning nautilus-shaped world headquarters in Independence, Missouri, erected between 1990 and 1994, designed by Gyo Obata.

## East Meets West

With immigration from Asia in the last half of the nineteenth century, many missions were established that ministered to new workers in the American West. Aside from groups that ministered directly to their constituencies from China and Japan, such as the Jodo Shinshu sect of Buddhism known as the Buddhist Churches of America, several Eastern groups made inroads into mainstream society through their active teaching to Anglo audiences.

Swami Vivekananda, for example, represented Hinduism at the World's Parliaments of Religions, an auxiliary Congress of the World's Columbian Exposition held in Chicago in 1893. He opened several centers and was instrumental in

solidifying Hindu teachings in the United States, through support of the Sri Ramakrishna sect in India (now the largest Hindu body in India). The first Vedanta Hindu Temple in America was built in San Francisco by Swami Trigunatita in 1906, with windows and moldings in the Moorish style. At first simply a Victorian house, the elaborate upper-third-story veranda was added in 1908. Four metal towers crown the structure, copied from the styles of several Indian temples, including one sacred to Shiva in Bengal. This combination of architectural features was designed to symbolize the harmony of East and West. A later temple, designed by Henry Gutterson and built in 1959, serves as the headquarters of the society in San Francisco, and Gutterson built another fine example of Spanish Romanesque architecture in his Berkeley Vedanta temple, constructed in 1939.

The Vedanta Society in Southern California built a small Taj Mahal–inspired temple in the Hollywood Hills in 1938. By 1942, a beautiful country estate in the Santa Barbara hills was given to the Vedanta Society and in 1946 became a convent. In 1956 the devotees hired Lutah Maria Riggs. Riggs was inspired by traditional Indian temples and built a superb wooden structure that won an award that year for the best new civic building in Santa Barbara.

The Theosophical Society, founded by Helena Petrovna Blavatsky and Henry Steel Olcott in New York in 1875, soon relocated to Adyar (now Chennai), India, in 1879. Theosophical writings brought ancient esoteric wisdom, based in both Eastern and Western theologies and philosophies, to the West. The American Section of the Society was led by William Quan Judge. After Judge's death in 1896, the American Section had leadership challenges, and several new groups emerged.

One institution still loyal to Adyar was the Krotona Institute of Theosophy, founded as a utopian outpost and built in the Hollywood Hills in 1912. A grand organizational headquarters was planned, but only a court and temple, research building, and several houses with Eastern and esoteric ornaments were constructed. The group sold the property in 1924 and moved to Ojai Valley, California, where a school of theosophy still functions. This school and grounds were designed by esoteric architect Robert Stacy-Judd in the Pueblo/Spanish tradition in the late 1920s. The American Section continues to be the largest group, with its headquarters in Wheaton, Illinois, designed by the important Chicago architectural firm Pond and Pond, Martin and Lloyd, erected in 1927. An Egyptian pylon portal gate designed by theosophical architect Claude Bragdon marks its entrance.

One group that claimed leadership after Judge's death was led by Katherine Tingley. She founded the Raja Yoga Academy at Point Loma, California, and became the controversial leader of the Universal Brotherhood and Theosophical Society, founded to promote world brotherhood and the use of the arts in religion and education. "Lomaland" was founded in 1897 and buildings began to be erected in 1898, many after Tingley's own designs. By 1900 an aquamarine-domed hotel sanatorium was converted for the group's use, and a purple-domed circular Aryan Memorial Temple was completed. A school that numbered almost three hundred by 1910 was established. Students and teachers lived together in round cottages with skylights. Children were schooled, worked in the elaborate gardens, practiced music, and worked on Pont Loma's often grandiose dramatic presentations, held in the first Greek amphitheater built in the United States, erected in 1901. Since 1972 the site has been home to Point Loma Nazarene University, and only several original buildings remain, including an octagonal house, festooned with esoteric and symbolist architectural ornaments designed and executed by Tingley's British follower Reginald Machell.

The Temple of the People, founded by Dr. William H. Dower and Francia La Due in Syracuse, New York in 1898, moved to the central coast of California in 1903. Seeing themselves as Judge's true successors, the temple founders joined other theosophical groups who moved to California but were unique in their commitment to communitarian economic ideals and in their desire to build a city as a physical manifestation of the New Jerusalem. The group built a thirty-seven pillared, three-sided temple, designed by Los Angeles architect Theodore Eisen and Dower. A memorial to Francia La Due, the Blue Star Memorial Temple (1924), was built on lines of mathematical and geometrical symbolism.

Originally theosophical, the Rosicrucian Fellowship in Oceanside, California, was founded by Max Heindel and emphasized spiritual healing and astrology. Their concrete Ecclesia Temple was built between 1914 and 1920. Highly symbolic, the temple is twelve-sided, to conform to the twelve signs of the zodiac, which the Rosicrucians believe directly influences the restoration and maintenance of health. Inside is an array of symbolic stained glass and mural art. The door contains carved panels representing Leo and Aquarius. Those admitted sit in places ordained by their zodiacal sign.

## Conclusion

Alternative religious architecture in the United States demonstrates the tendency of new groups to choose forms of architecture that not only serve the functional aspects of their rituals but solidify and publicize their theological teachings in built forms often quite distinct from traditional and historical Judeo-Christian architectural styles. From the simple Quaker meetinghouse to the monumental Bahá'í or Mormon Temple, these buildings make important contributions to the built environment of a religiously pluralistic America.

**See also** *Architecture* entries; *Christian Science; Harmonialism and Metaphysical Religion; Hinduism in North America; Latter-day Saints; Quakers* entries; *Shakers.*

Paul Eli Ivey

BIBLIOGRAPHY

Andrew, Laurel B. *The Early Temples of the Mormons: The Architecture of the Millennial Kingdom in the American West.* Albany: State University of New York Press, 1978.
Ashcroft, W. Michael. *The Dawn of the New Cycle: Point Loma Theosophists and American Culture.* Knoxville: University of Tennessee Press, 2002.
Glenn, E. Bruce. *Bryn Athyn Cathedral: The Building of a Church.* New York: C. Harrison Conroy Co., 1971.
Hamilton, C. Mark. *Nineteenth-Century Mormon Architecture and City Planning.* New York: Oxford University Press, 1995.
Hayden, Dolores. *Seven American Utopias: The Architecture of Communitarian Socialism, 1790–1975.* Cambridge, Mass.: MIT Press, 1976.
Ivey, Paul E. *Prayers in Stone: Christian Science Architecture in the United States, 1894–1930.* Urbana: University of Illinois Press, 1999.
Jackson, Carl T. *Vedanta for the West: The Ramakrishna Movement in the United States.* Bloomington: University of Indiana Press, 1994.
Lapsansky, Emma Jones, and Anne A. Verplanck, eds. *Quaker Aesthetics: Reflections on a Quaker Ethic in American Design, 1720–1920.* Philadelphia: University of Pennsylvania Press, 2002.
Nicoletta, Julie. *Architecture of the Shakers.* Woodstock, Vt.: Countryman Press, 2000.
Ross, Joseph E. *Krotona of Old Hollywood, 1866–1913.* Santa Barbara, Calif.: El Montecito Oaks Press, 1989.
Williams, Peter W. *Houses of God: Region, Religions and Architecture in the United States.* Urbana: University of Illinois Press, 1997.

# Architecture: Protestant, from the Nineteenth Century to the Present

Protestants have designed their religious buildings to provide environments for worship, education, service, and fellowship and to express their message and social position. Interior arrangements have responded to changing theologies of worship, standards of comfort, and communication technologies. Congregations have employed classical, medieval, and modern styles to embrace changing aesthetic standards, create an atmosphere conductive to worship, and project a prominent and relevant image of churches' roles in society. The surrounding environment has also shaped buildings as Protestants have responded to the particular demands of urban, rural, and suburban neighborhoods and reflected regional architectural practices.

## Vernacular and Professional Architecture

Many church buildings are vernacular in character. They reflect local customs of construction and lay understandings of appropriate styles. Similar vernacular traditions have shaped the adaptive reuse of storefronts and other structures. Other congregations, especially in cities and wealthy suburbs, have employed expensive, high-style architects to design buildings that display their refined taste and assert their prominence.

Beginning in the mid-nineteenth century, denominations and architects sought to provide professional guidance on a mass scale. Denominations published plan books and mail order plans to facilitate uniformity and quality control in buildings erected with denominations' church extension funds. Some architectural firms began to specialize in churches, erecting similar churches throughout whole regions. Between 1915 and 1924, major denominations established architectural bureaus that provided centralized guidance. They also assisted congregations in hiring architects to design buildings for specific sites. While the Great Depression caused the elimination or consolidation of these bureaus, a boom in church construction following World War II combined with increasing architectural professionalization to support an enduring industry of advice and expertise.

## Denominational Characteristics

The succession of styles and interior arrangements discussed below has had a broad impact across denominations. However, a few denominational characteristics should be noted. The strong influence of Reformed theology caused many denominations to favor a plain worship space devoid of pictorial decoration. Anglicans took the lead in incorporating decoration, but by the late nineteenth century, changing aesthetic standards made visual images, particularly stained glass windows, more a sign of style and class than of denomination.

Anglicans, and to a lesser degree Lutherans, constitute a special case because of their enthusiasm for altar-centered chancels. These were practically universal in their churches by the end of the nineteenth century. Later this arrangement also became very popular among Presbyterians, Congregationalists, and especially Methodists. Baptists and Pentecostals have been more consistently inclined toward pulpit-centered spaces. These and other evangelical groups have often been satisfied with simple vernacular structures. The unprogrammed worship of the Quaker tradition is distinctive for meetinghouses without pulpits where the worshippers are arranged facing one another.

Until at least the late twentieth century, Anglicans, Methodists, and Lutherans placed kneeling rails before their altars or communion tables. Other denominations served communion in the pews. These groups also preferred a freestanding communion table, a feature the more liturgical denominations have also adopted since the 1970s. Churches where the Lord's Supper was infrequent sometimes had no permanent table. Baptists and others requiring believers' baptism by immersion initially did this outdoors. By the late nineteenth century, however, they commonly provided a baptismal pool within the church.

## Federal Churches

In the decades following the Revolutionary War, Congregationalist churches throughout New England replaced their colonial meetinghouses with elegant churches in what was later termed the Federal style. Inspired by the designs for churches in London, England, by Christopher Wren and James Gibbs, these churches typically combined a multilevel steeple with a rectangular building and classical details. Frequently, as at Center Church, New Haven, Connecticut (completed 1814), a large porch stood at the entrance. Unlike earlier meetinghouses, the interiors of these churches were arranged longitudinally. The pulpit was placed on the short wall opposite the steeple. Slip pews (that is, benches often seen in churches today) replaced box pews. These were typically sold or rented to worshippers to help finance the building. Seating for worship enacted the social hierarchy.

The high tub pulpit characteristic of colonial churches soon yielded to a large desk at a slightly lower level that sometimes resembled a judge's bench. The communion table sat in front of it on the floor. Pipe organs became increasingly common and were placed in a rear gallery. Church interiors were sometimes fitted with rich details such as Corinthian columns. They were also increasingly used exclusively for religious services. In sum, these buildings appeared more churchly than their predecessors. Abandoning Puritan language, worshippers began to refer to them not as meetinghouses but as churches.

Whether constructed of brick, wood, or stone, the Federal church, especially the Wren-Gibbs spire, was popular

In the late eighteenth and early nineteenth century, Congregationalist churches throughout New England replaced their colonial meetinghouses with elegant structures that were recognizable as churches. Center Church in New Haven, Connecticut (completed 1814), typified this design and construction, later termed the Federal style.

## Evangelical Revivalism and the Greek Revival

Until the mid-nineteenth century, with a few exceptions, growing evangelical denominations such as Baptists and Methodists did not employ high-style architects. They preferred vernacular structures focused on a preaching stand. Pews were not rented, and men and women often sat on opposite sides of the church. African Americans were frequently restricted to special sections.

Evangelicals' outdoor camp meetings produced another type of worship space. In the typical arrangement, a platform for the preachers faced a natural amphitheatre surrounded by tents. In later decades, this arrangement took more permanent form in some places such as Oak Bluffs, Massachusetts. A large wooden or steel structure, often called a tabernacle, provided shelter for the worshippers, and the tents were replaced by wooden cottages. Similar tabernacles would be built in later years for urban evangelists such as Charles Finney and Dwight Moody.

When evangelical groups began to erect more sophisticated churches, they often built in the style of the Greek Revival. Popular from 1820 to 1850, it employed simpler lines than the Federal style while retaining the classical aesthetic. The front of churches typically resembled a Greek temple with a porch supported by columns, topped by a triangular pediment, as at First Baptist in Charleston, South Carolina (1822). Other churches included a central tower above the porch, such as Saint Paul's Episcopal, Richmond, Virginia (1845), or used a recessed portico as at Government Street Presbyterian in Mobile, Alabama (1837). To finance these urban churches, even Baptists and Methodists began to rent pews. A national style, the Greek Revival was particularly popular in the South and among Presbyterians, Methodists, and Baptists. It was widely adopted into wooden vernacular buildings. Many historians have argued for a strong association between the Greek Revival and democratic ideology and an emphasis on reason. More recently, others have contended that it was more simply a fashion and popular for its affordability and its chaste lines that bespoke middle-class respectability.

## Nineteenth-Century Gothic Revival

While classical styles were often seen as modern, the Gothic Revival was seen as distinctly traditional. Most closely associated with the Anglican tradition and its emphasis on historical continuity, it was also utilized by other Protestants. While Gothic came to the forefront in the 1840s, the earliest examples are from the beginning of the century. In plan,

among many denominations. It was erected in the western towns, such as the 1826 Congregationalist Church in Tallmadge, Ohio, as well as in southern cities such as Charleston and Savannah. During the twentieth century, and especially during World War II, these buildings became icons of America. They served as the models for many so-called colonial revival churches. Imitations of their spires made even the most nondescript buildings recognizable as churches.

churches such as Trinity Church, New Haven, Connecticut (1815), were very similar to Federal churches. They were rectangular with a tower centered above the entrance. In some cases there was even a central pulpit above the communion table. Yet the buildings were constructed of roughly laid stone, incorporated pointed windows and castellated roof lines, and were often finished to provide the illusion of vaulting in the interior.

In the 1840s, the influence of a more academically correct Gothic Revival movement appeared. In England, the Cambridge Camden Society formulated laws of church building by studying medieval churches. Along with other writers such as A.N.W. Pugin and John Ruskin, these "Ecclesiologists" promoted the idea that Gothic was the true Christian style. It expressed Romantic sensibility by evoking transcendent mystery, unbroken tradition, and unity with nature. Churches often exhibited picturesque qualities including construction from fieldstone in a random pattern, asymmetrical exteriors, and a rural setting.

The first American church erected according to designs furnished by the Ecclesiologists was St. James the Less (Episcopal) (1848), in what is now Philadelphia, Pennsylvania. Churches such as St. James featured a chancel whose lower roof line made it visibly distinct from the nave where the congregation sat. The altar was placed against the far wall of the chancel. A pulpit for preaching and a lectern for reading scripture lessons faced the congregation from either side of the chancel steps. Between the steps and the altar, stalls for clergy and sometimes the choir were arranged facing each other. By the end of the century, this arrangement, often referred to as a "split" or "divided" chancel, would be ubiquitous in Anglican and Episcopal churches. The altar was often fitted with a cross and candlesticks, and interiors were decorated with stained glass and carvings in stone and wood.

The Gothic Revival was extended into wooden structures that emphasized verticality with tall pointed gables, elaborate spires, and vertical board-and-batten siding. This so-called carpenter Gothic was frequently used in rural settings. It was given particular distinction in a popular plan book by Richard Upjohn. He also designed many stone churches, such as Trinity Church on Wall Street in New York City (1846).

Gothic designs were not limited to Episcopal churches but were also adopted by other Protestants, particularly those populated by a similarly high social class such as Unitarians, Congregationalists, and Presbyterians. In the nineteenth century, however, these denominations almost never adopted a divided chancel. As at Upjohn's First Parish Church in Brunswick, Maine (1845), the focal point of the church remained the large desk or pulpit from which the preacher led the service. Lutherans made the altar the focus but used a shallow chancel to keep it close to the congregation, an expression of their belief in the priesthood of the people.

## Romanesque and Other Revival Styles

Another style with medieval associations was the Romanesque Revival. It appeared first in Germany, where it was known as the *Rundbogenstil* or "round-arch style." Kathleen Curran has argued that this style was associated with the undivided Christianity of late antiquity, as well as the Early Middle Ages, and was chosen as a sign of ecumenical Christianity. It is unclear to what extent this association was operative in the many urban American congregations that built in this style from the 1840s to the 1870s. What is known is that it was accepted as a distinctly Christian style that was not Gothic, supported fashionable decoration, and worked well in brick and stone.

In the 1870s, the Romanesque was transformed by Henry Hobson Richardson, particularly in his design for Trinity Church (Episcopal) in Boston, Massachusetts. Richardson distinguished Trinity not with a tall spire but with a massive tower over the nave. He also used wide, heavy arches and stone of contrasting colors. Richardsonian Romanesque was popular for more than thirty years. It provided monumentality and associations with nature and tradition. It was also adaptable to a variety of interior plans, particularly those that were broad rather than long.

In the nineteenth century's eclectic architectural environment, some churches were also built in nearly every other available style. Classical associations extended into an Egyptian revival, for example First (now Downtown) Presbyterian, Nashville, Tennessee (1851). A few domed structures were Roman in their associations such as First Unitarian Church, Baltimore, Maryland (1818). Gothic Revival extended into many forms including the colorful High Victorian Gothic and combinations with Tudor and Stick styles. The Shingle Style provided wooden buildings with some of the design features of Richardsonian Romanesque. It also, along with Queen Anne, gave churches a rather domestic exterior.

## Auditorium Churches

Revivalist Charles Finney had built a circular auditorium for his Broadway Tabernacle in New York City in 1836, but in the tense decades that led to the Civil War this innovative arrangement found few imitators. From the 1870s to the

1900s, however, auditorium churches were very popular among Baptists, Methodists, and other evangelical Protestants. Designed to provide a comfortable and acoustically successful space for worship, they used sloping floors and rear and side galleries to arrange worshippers in curved, cushioned pews around the speaker's platform. Here a large speaker's desk served as the pulpit. The open platform drew attention to the preacher or song leader as a personality, not simply a voice. Music also received a prominent place. Behind and above the platform was a choir loft and above it organ pipes.

Such spaces shaped worshippers in two opposing ways. The visibility of the congregation to one another increased a sense of egalitarian community and facilitated participation in worship. The circular arrangement undercut social hierarchy, and partly for this reason pew rental was gradually abolished. On the other hand, auditorium churches suggested that the congregation's primary role was to be a passive audience for the preacher's message and the beautiful music offered by organist and choir.

Erected throughout the country, auditorium churches often commanded street corners in burgeoning streetcar suburbs. Richardsonian Romanesque was particularly suited to these innovative square-planned churches, but they also appeared in a variety of Gothic, Shingle, and classical styles. Examples include Trinity Methodist Episcopal in Denver, Colorado (1887); Pilgrim Congregational, Cleveland, Ohio (1894); and Sixteenth Street Baptist Church, Birmingham, Alabama (1911).

The color and furnishing of these novel worship spaces helped sacralize them by linking them to the sacred sphere of the Victorian home. Church buildings increasingly incorporated domestic spaces such as parlors and kitchens. The pictorial stained glass windows, designed by Lewis C. Tiffany and other artists, that became common around the turn of the century continued the domestic association by depicting sentimental scenes, such as Jesus the Good Shepherd, the Great Consoler, or praying in Gethsemane.

## Sunday School Architecture

Closely associated with auditorium churches was the Akron Plan Sunday School. Developed at First Methodist Church in Akron, Ohio, in 1869, the Akron Plan provided a large, typically semicircular "rotunda" for Sunday schools' opening and closing exercises. Surrounding this space, on two levels, were smaller rooms that were closed off by sliding or rolling partitions for individual classes. Frequently the rotunda was connected to the main auditorium by another sliding partition, enabling the capacity of the auditorium to be nearly doubled. For this reason, "Akron Plan" was sometimes used to designate this combination arrangement or auditorium churches generally.

The Akron Plan was designed to support a curriculum where all ages studied the same Bible passage. In the early twentieth century, many churches adopted graded curriculums in which different ages studied passages appropriate to their developmental stage. Sunday schools were reorganized into age-level departments with distinct classrooms. These were often placed in a building that was visibly distinct from the church proper. Increasingly built for "seven-days-a-week" ministry, churches' expanded buildings often included gyms and film projection booths, and sometimes swimming pools and bowling alleys. These developments were strongly supported by denominations' newly formed architecture bureaus. They were also made possible by the larger lots churches occupied in new automobile suburbs.

## Beaux-Arts Classicism and the Late Gothic Revival

From the 1890s to the 1920s, Beaux-Arts Classicism made a strong claim to be America's national style. Solidly supported by the architectural profession, many churches were built in this academically correct and often elaborate style, especially among southern evangelicals. Some structures had domes and retained the square plan of earlier auditorium churches. Others styled after Greek temples took a more rectangular shape, while retaining the typical platform of auditorium churches. These rectangular spaces were promoted as having better acoustics.

Enthusiasm for classical styles, however, was tempered by a renewed enthusiasm for Gothic. The buildings designed and promoted by Ralph Adams Cram and others were at once more academically correct than those of the High Victorian era and more modern in their clear massing and restrained decoration. Cram's very faithful Perpendicular Gothic chapel for Princeton University (1928) and the more modern Rockefeller Chapel at the University of Chicago by Bertram Goodhue (1928) illustrate the tendencies. Cram and his colleagues insisted on approving a unified scheme of decoration for each church. In stained glass, large images copied from popular paintings yielded to intricate mosaic designs. These harmonized with the architecture but were more apt to be filled with small medallions than easily legible images.

Whereas in the nineteenth century only Anglicans and Lutherans had commonly made an altar the focal point of their churches, by the 1920s most Protestants placed divided chancels in their new Gothic Revival churches. This altar-centered arrangement was valued not primarily because of an increased focus on the Eucharist but, rather, because it provided a symbolic focus and created a distinctly religious space that encouraged the sense of transcendence and tradition that many Protestants valued in Episcopal and Catholic churches. With strong support from architecture bureaus and experts on worship, from the mid-1920s to the mid-1960s, divided chancels were introduced in churches of all styles. Many older churches with auditorium or center-pulpit arrangements were renovated to include divided chancels. Methodists embraced the divided chancel most widely, but it was adopted by Presbyterians and other Reformed denominations and even some Baptists.

Given the understanding of the worship space expressed by the divided chancel, "auditorium" now seemed too secular a term. Most Protestants, however, were not inclined to distinguish between church and parish house as Episcopalians commonly did. Thus, "sanctuary" became widely used to designate the room built for public worship.

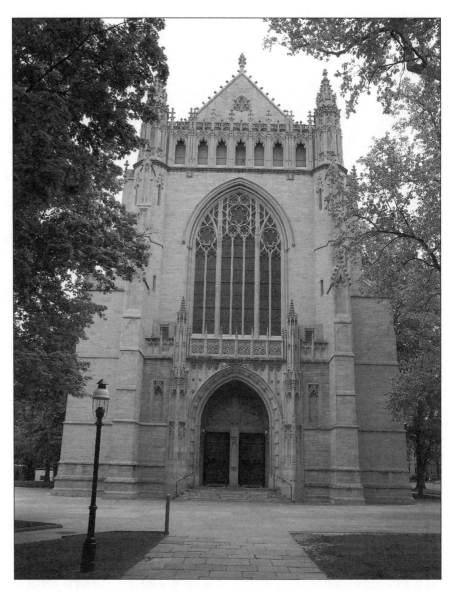

A renewed enthusiasm for the Gothic style was evident in Ralph Adams Cram's Perpendicular Gothic chapel for Princeton University (1928).

## Colonial Revivals and Modernism

In the 1920s, among congregations unwilling to embrace or finance Gothic, Beaux-Arts Classicism gave way to structures with Georgian or Federal references, usually understood as colonial revival and often associated with the vigor of patriots and pioneers. These red brick structures were more economical than stone Gothic ones and could be combined pleasingly with simple educational buildings. Such churches became ubiquitous in some eastern states after World War II, but churches evoking Bruton Parish Church, Williamsburg, Virginia, or a Federal meetinghouse could also be found in other regions. In some cases, particularly in states once ruled by Spain, this revival took a Spanish form, whether with elaborate baroque details or the simplicity of an adobe mission.

The twentieth century also saw new churches free of stylistic precedent. First among these was Frank Lloyd Wright's Unity Temple in Oak Park, Illinois (1906). Built of concrete, in a square configuration, the space drew the congregation close to the pulpit. A few modern churches were built in the Art Moderne style (frequently called Art Deco), such as Boston Avenue Methodist Episcopal Church in Tulsa, Oklahoma (1929). Far more churches in modern styles were built after 1950. Many employed modern materials but with

Frank Lloyd Wright's Unity Temple in Oak Park, Illinois (1906), among the first twentieth-century churches whose design did not reflect a stylistic precedent, was built of concrete in a square configuration.

traditional, even Gothic, arrangement and massing. These include the numerous A-frame churches built after the pioneering example of Eero Saarinen's chapel for the Concordia Seminary campus in Fort Wayne, Indiana (1953–1958). Churches in modern design were more common in the West and Midwest, where the colonial revival was weaker.

The liturgical renewal that reshaped the interiors of Catholic churches since the 1960s also affected mainline Protestants. The central idea was to emphasize the participation of the congregation in the actions of worship, particularly by arranging them around a freestanding communion table. Designers sought to avoid hierarchical separations between nave and chancel and between choir and congregation. They emphasized God's presence in the gathered assembly. Some, especially in the 1960s, sought to avoid exterior forms that were distinctively churchly. Most churches embodying this approach were modest in size. Trinity United Methodist Church, Charles City, Iowa (1972), is one example by Edward A. Sövik, an architect particularly associated with this approach.

## New Auditorium Churches

The most prominent churches employing modern designs belong to the megachurches that came to prominence at the end of the twentieth century. Churches such as Willow Creek Community Church in South Barrington, Illinois,

take the form of a large complex of modern buildings, often devoid of religious decoration. Occupying their own suburban campuses, they aim to provide an environment for church activities that is as comfortable and fashionable as commercial establishments. Campuses often include a food court, coffee bar, small meeting rooms, a large informal lobby, and thematically designed spaces for children and youth, along with a large auditorium often equipped with theatre-style chairs.

The basic concept of what is often called the "worship center" is similar to earlier auditorium churches, except that if the house lights are dimmed, worshippers are not visible to one another. The arrangement of the stage area is shaped by the type of music that predominates. Many focus on a large choir loft. In others that use rock-style music, worship leaders lead or perform from a stage with professional-quality lights, sound equipment, and instruments. Large screens display the words of songs and, frequently, images of the preacher. They have become as characteristic of Protestant worship space as organ pipes once were. Screens and stages are also found in smaller churches where contemporary worship music is used. This has become the typical arrangement of evangelical and Pentecostal churches.

## Twenty-First Century

Many recent buildings incorporate large, flexible gathering spaces and, in most mainline churches, adaptable liturgical arrangements shaped by twentieth-century liturgical renewal. Some of the worship services in evangelical churches often labeled "emergent" have employed similar spaces. Others, in a postmodern embrace of plurality, arrange spaces that allow individuals in the same worship service to choose between different simultaneous activities, such as corporate song or individual Communion. These and other congregations often place an emphasis on adaptive reuse of existing buildings or seek to meet in secular spaces such as nightclubs or coffee houses.

Churches of recent decades have often displayed postmodern architecture's openness to the innovative adaptation

Willow Creek Community Church in South Barrington, Illinois, is often cited as an example of the "megachurch." Consisting of a large complex of modern buildings situated on suburban campuses, these churches aim to provide an environment that is comfortable and fashionable—akin to that of commercial establishments.

of historic styles. Some Charismatic churches have placed particular emphasis on their buildings as signs of God's blessings, occasionally employing historical styles as a sign of their authenticity, such as the Cathedral of the Holy Spirit in suburban Atlanta, Georgia (1991). Some large modern auditorium churches affiliated with Southern Baptists and other traditional denominations are also apt to incorporate spires and stained glass. The seemingly secular designs of many evangelical church auditoriums were shaped in part by the desire of baby boomers for a church unencumbered by tradition. Recent studies indicate that younger generations prefer churches that evoke a sense of mystery and beauty. This could yield another permutation of revival styles.

**See also** *Architecture* entries; *Canada: Protestants and the United Church of Canada; Congregationalists; Education: Sunday Schools; Episcopalians: The Gilded Age and Progressive Eras; Evangelicals* entries; *Liturgical Arts; Megachurches; Revivalism* entries; *Visual Culture; Worship* entries.

David R. Bains

## BIBLIOGRAPHY

Buggeln, Gretchen Townsend. *Temples of Grace: The Material Transformation of Connecticut's Churches, 1790–1840.* Hanover, N.H.: University Press of New England, 2003.

Curran, Kathleen. *The Romanesque Revival: Religion, Politics, and Transnational Exchange.* University Park: Pennsylvania State University Press, 2003.

Howe, Jeffery W. *Houses of Worship: An Identification Guide to the History and Styles of American Religious Architecture.* San Diego, Calif.: Thunder Bay Press, 2003.

Kilde, Jeanne Halgern. *When Church Became Theatre: The Transformation of Evangelical Architecture and Worship in Nineteenth-Century America.* New York: Oxford University Press, 2002.

Loveland, Anne C., and Otis B. Wheeler. *From Meetinghouse to Megachurch: A Material and Cultural History.* Columbia: University of Missouri Press, 2003.

Raguin, Virginia Chieffo, ed. *Sacred Spaces: Building and Remembering Sites of Worship in the Nineteenth Century.* Worcester, Mass.: College of the Holy Cross and the American Antiquarian Society, 2002.

Shand-Tucci, Douglas. *Ralph Adams Cram: An Architect's Four Quests— Medieval, Modernist, American, Ecumenical.* Amherst: University of Massachusetts Press, 2005.

Smith, Ryan K. *Gothic Arches, Latin Crosses: Anti-Catholicism and American Church Designs in the Nineteenth Century*. Chapel Hill: University of North Carolina Press, 2006.

Torgerson, Mark Allen. *An Architecture of Immanence: Architecture for Worship and Ministry Today*. Grand Rapids, Mich.: Eerdmans, 2007.

Vergara, Camilo J. *How the Other Half Worships*. New Brunswick, N.J.: Rutgers University Press, 2005.

Williams, Peter. *Houses of God: Region, Religion, and Architecture in the United States*. Urbana: University of Illinois Press, 1997.

# Architecture: Roman Catholic

The architecture of Roman Catholicism in North America encompasses a broad range of buildings and features that have shaped the religious and social life of Americans from European contact to the present. Beyond cathedrals and churches, Roman Catholic architecture also includes shrines, convents, monasteries, schools, colleges, charitable buildings, cemeteries, and other constructions. Two major themes have consistently animated this varied Catholic landscape: (1) the primacy of the pope and the Church's hierarchical organization, and (2) the centrality of the Eucharist as the literal reenactment of Christ's sacrifice. These have combined to produce an approach to the material world in which sacred space is clearly identified and distinguished from secular space. Nevertheless, alongside these themes and this approach, Roman Catholic architecture has expressed a great deal of diversity, maintaining a close relationship with place and time.

## The European Heritage and Spanish Colonization

Roman Catholic architecture in the Western Hemisphere began with the earliest colonial settlements. Christopher Columbus apparently did not bring any priests with him as part of his first, risky voyage. However, at least a dozen Catholic clergy accompanied him on his second, larger expedition in 1493, reflecting the explorer's religious zeal and that of his Castilian sponsors. In late 1493 and early 1494, the Franciscans Juan Pérez and Bernaldo Buil and others celebrated the first mass in the Western Hemisphere and built a rough church in the new settlement of La Isabela on the island they called Hispaniola. Made of stone, earth, and other local materials, the church also housed a bell and other religious implements sent from Spain expressly for this construction, to benefit the settlers and the local Taino Indians.

At the time the little church was built, there was no single model for Roman Catholic architecture from which the early colonizers might draw. The Catholic architectural heritage in Europe ranged from rural shrines, to imposing monasteries and universities, to ancient basilicas—rectangular halls adopted from Roman legal traditions—and to soaring new cathedrals, all more reflective of their region, patrons, and era than of any single Roman Catholic mode. The nearest thing to an ideal Catholic space appeared a generation after Columbus's voyages, with the beginnings of the reconstruction of St. Peter's Basilica in Rome. The resulting Renaissance wonder, based on studious humanistic planning and designs, took more than one hundred years to complete. With its enormous size, triumphant central dome, and rich decoration, it presented an inspiring though rarefied focal point for the faith.

Still, there were commonalities shared by the array of Catholic buildings. All church property was vested in the name of the Church, rather than in that of nobility, congregations, or states. And that property was intended for the benefit of the whole fabric of society, rather than select groups of believers or social classes. Furthermore, the Church was tied together, in bonds sometimes more and sometimes less steady, by the authority of the pope, the bishop of Rome, seen as Christ's representative on Earth. Beneath the pope, a carefully guarded hierarchy, made up of properly ordained cardinals, bishops, and priests, conducted sacraments in the various facilities. And reflecting the needs of the Eucharist, the primary sacrament, all churches required a properly consecrated and dressed altar, at which the host bread and wine during the mass transformed into the actual body and blood of Jesus Christ, in the presence of the clergy and congregants. This miracle helped dictate the Catholic definition of sacred space, in which buildings and burial grounds could be irrevocably "consecrated," dedicated to sacred purposes, and in which worshippers' senses encountered the divine.

Another common factor that shaped Catholic architecture emerged after 1517, when German monk Martin Luther famously protested against existing Church policies. The ensuing Protestant Reformation, which followed Luther's excommunication in 1521, irrevocably changed the Catholic landscape in Europe as well as the New World. In Europe, old cathedrals, churches, convents, and schools—centuries of wealth accumulated in the treasury of the Church—were desecrated, seized, and refashioned by successful new reforming groups in the northern and western portions of the continent. The primary Protestant objections involved what the reformers saw as corruption within the Church's ranks and,

Construction of the Metropolitan Cathedral in Mexico City began in the late 1500s, and continued until its substantial completion around 1813. The commanding structure illustrates the hallmarks of aggressive, Counter-Reformation Catholicism and would remain the largest church space in the Western Hemisphere for centuries.

even more importantly, the correct relationship of believers to God. Protestants emphasized direct access to God through the scriptures, and therefore they grew wary of the artistic equipage that accompanied priestly intervention in this divine relationship.

The official Roman Catholic response to the Protestant Reformation became known as the Counter-Reformation, or the Catholic Reformation. Its policies were formalized at the Council of Trent held in northern Italy between 1545 and 1563, which developed in step with the Spanish conquest of the mainland west of the Caribbean after 1519. During the council, the Church revised and standardized the Latin mass, strengthened the pope's leadership, confirmed the role of visual arts as essential aids to devotion, and reemphasized the sacrificial importance of the Eucharist.

With this broad backdrop, the Spanish conquered much of Central and South America. The island of Hispaniola served as the initial disembarkation point, and its capital,

Santo Domingo, boasted a noteworthy cathedral, literally the bishop's seat and diocesan center, by 1541. Santa María de La Encarnación Cathedral was built of stone with an intricate Plateresque façade, reflecting an emerging Spanish architectural style in which carved surfaces resembled the decorative work of contemporary Iberian silversmiths. The cathedral's interior was vaulted, with plain walls and few windows.

The primacy of Hispaniola was soon overshadowed by developments in Mexico City, both politically and ecclesiastically. The very first church in Mexico City was fairly rough, like the church built at La Isabela, though it was built symbolically on the foundations of the great Aztec temple. In the 1570s, however, initial designs for a massive rectangular cathedral were sent from Spain, and work continued in successive waves until its substantial completion around 1813. It was dedicated to the Assumption of the Virgin Mary in 1656 and consecrated eleven years later. The Spanish colonial system depended upon heavy, forced Indian labor, and the construction of the cathedral by Indian masons, carpenters, and artists reflected this practice. The building illustrates the hallmarks of aggressive, Counter-Reformation Catholicism, equally suited to impress doubting Indians and the European atmosphere of Protestant detractions. The building commanded the Zócalo, the city's huge plaza, and it would remain the largest church space in the Western Hemisphere for centuries.

This complex sandstone building mingled baroque and more severely classical features, two primary streams of Renaissance and post-Renaissance design. Classicism involved the precise, geometrical orders resurrected from ancient Greece and Rome, while the baroque indicated a more vibrant, sculptural approach to surfaces and spaces. The cathedral's creative mixture of the two was probably the product of several successive archbishops and architects, with most attribution given to Spanish architect and sculptor Claudio de Arciniega. Twin bell towers and a central dome were added in the eighteenth century, as was the adjoining side chapel, the Sagrario Metropolitano. The cathedral's interior featured double aisles to the chancel. Art crowded the walls and interior spaces, with dozens of paintings, altarpieces, and statues, yet the central focal point remained the high altar. The cathedral also accumulated a rich inventory of communion vessels, vestments, censers, and other furnishings.

Catholic architecture in New Spain radiated outward from Mexico City. The Church was the largest landholder in the colony, and it developed an impressive system of convents, shrines, schools, hospitals, and missions throughout the varied geography of the lower portion of the North American continent. In 1573, Philip II attempted to order the landscape by decreeing a grid plan for new towns, with a central plaza featuring public buildings and the church or cathedral. Also, the Church and crown remained committed to the conversion of indigenous peoples, much of the work of which was performed by Franciscans, Augustinians, Dominicans, and members of other religious orders. At Tepeaca, Franciscans built a representative monastery in the sixteenth century with a decidedly fortified character. This set of austere buildings was surrounded by three roads, sentry boxes, battlements, and embrasures. It also promoted interplay between the shelters and the outdoor spaces, with walled atria and open-air chapels for the Indians' worship, an arrangement congenial to the racial views of the colonizers and the pre-Hispanic traditions of the colonized. Another example of a fortified, multiuse Franciscan convent can be seen in the 1678 complex at Churubusco.

As the colony spread north into the borderlands of Florida, Texas, New Mexico, and California, churches became simpler than those to the south. Missionaries adopted more indigenous and domestic building traditions, with coquina shell stone and wood in the east and mud-brick adobe and wood in the west. The missions achieved conversions, but they also inspired fierce reactions. Among the Pueblo Indians on the Rio Grande, Franciscan authorities had to contend with well-defined, pre-Conquest ritual centers called *kivas*—circular, subterranean, windowless rooms covered with earth or adobe—that still nurtured indigenous religion. Missionaries attempted to forcibly redirect Pueblo attention to their newly constructed churches, also made of adobe, and their altars inside. The tensions inherent in these two competing ritual spaces erupted during the Pueblo Revolt of 1680, in which the bulk of the

Spaniards and Franciscans were driven from the Rio Grande area in the Pueblo Revolt of 1680, but they reestablished missions by 1700 and built the comparatively vernacular cathedral of Saint Francis in Santa Fe in 1713.

Indians conducted a well-orchestrated uprising against Spanish rule, temporarily driving the colonists and their few Indian sympathizers entirely out of the province. During the revolt, the rebels tortured and killed a high proportion of the colony's missionaries and desecrated Catholic symbols—spreading excrement on statues and altars, destroying crucifixes and chalices, and shattering bells. Yet the Spanish and the Franciscans would return by 1700 to reestablish missions and then construct the comparatively vernacular cathedral of Saint Francis at Santa Fe in 1713. At the same time in the east, armed English incursions and Indian depopulation forced the Franciscans to abandon their line of sixty working missions stretching from the St. Johns River to present-day Alabama. The California mission complexes lining the West Coast reflect the latest phase of Spanish settlement, begun after 1769. By the time of their construction, monumental Catholic projects in the cities to the south had absorbed another expressive Spanish architectural style—the Churrigueresque, in which florid stucco sculpture was used to enhance surfaces, as at the Sagrario Metropolitano in Mexico City.

## French Colonization

Simultaneously, a very different sort of Catholic landscape was developing in the upper reaches of the continent. In New France—on the northern Atlantic coast, along waterways of the St. Lawrence River valley, around the Great Lakes, and down the Mississippi River—French priests, nuns, and brothers attempted to minister to highly mobile colonists and convert the region's Algonquian and Iroquois Indians. As in New Spain, members of religious orders provided much of this labor, though the particular orders differed in the predominance of Jesuits and Ursulines. The city of Quebec, founded in 1608, provided the central rallying point for their efforts. From there, individual Jesuits or small groups undertook "flying missions" along with traveling Indians or fur trappers, gathering a vast amount of knowledge about the Indians' lives but leaving few permanent constructions in their wake.

Catholic institutions in the cities of New France proved much more substantial. Quebec, Trois Rivières (founded 1634), and Montreal (founded 1642) housed Catholic institutions that rivaled those of New Spain by the early eighteenth century. Naturally, French religious facilities reflected a different culture. French colonial architecture blended medieval craft traditions with academic trends, especially with the growing importance of the Italian-inspired

classicism in the seventeenth century. French constructions drew less upon Indian labor and art than the Spanish examples, and they were less forceful in terms of visual expression. Educational institutions were prominent, including the châteaux-style Jesuit College built in Quebec in 1666; the Congregation of Notre Dame's numerous schools in Montreal; and the Ursuline school for girls in Trois Rivières, which occupied a solid two-story mansion previously used as a governor's residence.

Many of these Catholic structures were multifunctional, with portions of the buildings used for care of the sick or indigent. The notable Hôtel-Dieu was founded by Jeanne Mance in a small building inside the fort at Montreal in 1644, with two sick wards and scanty service areas. In the 1690s, the building was replaced by a more substantial stone structure, constructed under the direction of Paris-born architect François de la Joue. At this point, it housed a chapel and other sanctuary spaces. Later, such convents developed a common architectural program, usually made up of an H- or E-shaped plan with a central chapel.

Due to building fires, Indian wars, and English raids, there was no designated cathedral in New France until a papal bull recognized Quebec's parish church of Notre-Dame-de-la-Paix as such in 1674. The stone church had a plan in the form of a Latin cross, with a semicircular apse facing east. In the next decade, this structure was enlarged under the direction of architect Claude Baillif, and a bell tower was added. Baillif also built the city's lavish but unfinished Episcopal Palace in 1693. Outside the major cities, parish facilities tended to cluster in their villages, with church, rectory, and cemetery occupying single enclosures. But many major French fortification sites in the interior and along the Gulf Coast had no dedicated religious structures.

At the mouth of the Mississippi River, the city of New Orleans offered a more semitropical contrast to the Canadian scene. Founded late (by colonial standards) in 1718, and planned by Louisiana's engineer-in-chief, Le Blond de La Tour, New Orleans boasted a prominent central Place d'Armes fronted by a notable church site. This site saw the construction of the substantial, classical parish church dedicated to Saint Louis in 1727, which served the city's French, Spanish, and African residents until its ultimate replacement in 1794 with the neoclassical cathedral building still standing today (though altered in the nineteenth century). In keeping with Catholic tradition and canon law, a consecrated burial site was also established in the 1720s with

St. Peter Street Cemetery, which ultimately led to the city's unique above-ground necropolises by the early 1800s. This tradition officially excluded the burial of deceased Protestants and unbaptized residents in Catholic ground, thereby reinforcing the Church's concept of sacralization.

Catholic female orders were active in Louisiana as they were in Canada, and the Ursulines completed an impressive new convent on Chartres Street in 1753. This two-story building presented a classically balanced façade with a hipped roof and dormer windows. Offering female-directed space for the successful convent, school, and orphanage, the building's plan nevertheless reflected the hierarchical organization of nuns, novitiates, and students, all of whom depended on male priests for practice of the sacraments.

## British Colonization and American Independence

After the founding of Jamestown in 1607, the British colonies occupying North America's Atlantic coast between the French and Spanish Catholic empires defined themselves as vigorously Protestant. The Reformation in Great Britain had been a fluid yet intense affair, and by 1607, animosity towards the Roman Catholic Church characterized the nation's identity. Yet upper-class Catholics, even after lamenting the outlawing of their faith and the seizure of their church property, could still find rare opportunities for religious expression. This was the case with Lord Baltimore's Maryland, and when English Catholics founded St. Mary's City in 1634, one of their first construction projects included the church building. Jesuits served as the principal religious leaders, but since many of the original colonists were Protestant, and those numbers continued to swell in the coming decades, the proprietors urged restraint in the public expression of Roman Catholic worship. Restraint proved even more necessary after the colony's Catholic leadership was displaced during England's Civil War and then after its Glorious Revolution, and Catholic worship in the colony retreated to discreet domestic settings and private chapels. The Jesuits initiated missions to the area's Indians, but these too proved ephemeral. Still, Maryland retained a unique Catholic presence that would reemerge and coalesce around Baltimore in the next century. Elsewhere in the British colonies, the pattern of discreet private worship among the few scattered Catholics in coastal cities held sway, with the exception of Quaker Philadelphia, where St. Mary's Church opened its doors in 1734.

The American Revolution changed this situation dramatically. The language of liberty, the assistance of the French, and

John Carroll, the first Catholic bishop in the United States, oversaw construction of British America's first cathedral in Baltimore, Maryland, between 1805 and 1821.

the patriotic ardor of Maryland Catholics culminated in new public freedoms and the consecration of John Carroll as the first Catholic bishop in the United States in 1790, seated in the Diocese of Baltimore. Bishop Carroll oversaw the gradual construction of new churches and schools northward, southward, and westward in the vast reaches of his diocese. His cathedral, constructed between 1805 and 1821, the first in British America, provided the Church's most important architectural statement. Carroll worked closely with British-born architect Benjamin Henry Latrobe, who was schooled in classicism and had a hand in the design of the U.S. Capitol. The men selected a prominent hilltop site, and Latrobe presented Carroll with two different designs from which to choose— one Gothic and one neoclassical. He suggested that the Gothic was relevant because of its historic associations and its grandeur. Carroll made the neoclassical choice, explicitly aligning his faith with the image and ideals of the young nation. The resulting building featured a Latin cross plan with a great coffered dome and oculus over the crossing and twin bell towers at the western, Greek-detailed portico. The building was spacious inside, with white marble floors and clear glass windows. Despite its general harmony with national designs, no one would have mistaken the cathedral for a Protestant structure.

Nearby, the bishop helped found socially and architecturally important colleges and seminaries. Earlier, in 1789, Carroll and other former Jesuits created an academy at Georgetown, which developed into the nation's first Catholic university by 1815. Back in Baltimore, members of the Society of Saint-Sulpice founded St. Mary's Seminary in 1791. By the early 1800s, the seminary had expanded into a quadrangle of institutional buildings, and campus leaders engaged French architect Maximilian Godefroy to design the seminary chapel. Finished in 1808 as the city's cathedral was still taking shape, Godefroy's chapel displayed a bold, early example of the Gothic Revival, with pointed windows, flying buttresses, and a vaulted roof.

As Catholic leaders took satisfaction from new civil rights and construction projects, they also wrestled with peculiarly American struggles over ownership of church property. In a series of bitter battles that came to be known as "trusteeism," various new congregations and their lay trustees claimed the right to control their church buildings independently of the Catholic hierarchy and to appoint or dismiss their own priests (rights most Protestants practiced within their own denominations). The struggle began when a splinter group of German-born Catholics in Philadelphia founded and ran Holy Trinity Church in 1787 until reconciled to official church leadership in 1802. Similar problems surfaced among different ethnic congregations in New Orleans, Charleston, Norfolk, and Buffalo, and continued without complete resolution until the Civil War in the 1860s.

Throughout this era, French dominance in the hierarchy eventually gave way to the Irish. St. Joseph's, built in Bardstown, Kentucky, between 1816 and 1819 as the first cathedral in the United States west of the Allegheny Mountains, reflected this early French influence. When Bishop Benedict Joseph Flaget arrived in the state in 1811, he found twenty-four stations, ten log churches, and one brick church. The bishop secured some local Protestant funds for his cathedral project, and he contracted with Baltimore architect John Rogers to design the structure. The cathedral presented an elegant neoclassical façade, and its interior displayed fine paintings of the crucifixion and other scenes, as well as gold candlesticks and a carved tabernacle, all gifts from Pope Leo XII and European royalty. The structure lost its diocesan position when Flaget shifted his seat to Louisville twenty years later, but it remains a beloved landmark of its era.

Still, the material presence of Roman Catholicism in the young republic remained slight. As late as 1820, only about 124 Catholic churches could be found from the Atlantic coast to the Mississippi River, and these generally clustered around Baltimore and New Orleans—Maryland and Louisiana held almost half of the nation's total number. A significant portion of the nation's 195,000 Catholics still conducted their lives beyond the shadow of a consecrated sanctuary. In contrast, American Baptists and Methodists each occupied about 2,700 meetinghouses, distributed across the country. Even the modest Quakers held 350 meetinghouses, more than doubling Catholic holdings.

## Nineteenth-Century Immigration and Revival Styles

The story of national independence played out differently in the Caribbean, Mexico, and Canada. But Canada and the United States did share in two major developments in the nineteenth century: the spike in European immigration and the flowering of revival styles.

The first development changed the landscape by the sheer number of new Catholic churches and other facilities built to serve the unprecedented flood of Irish and German immigrants into the United States and Upper Canada. From 1820 to 1850, American Catholics built more than one thousand new churches throughout the United States, outpacing the rate of construction of every other denomination and establishing a Catholic footing for the very first time in hundreds of new communities. In New Jersey, Catholic churches increased from 3 in 1820 to 23 by 1850. The handful of early Catholic congregations in Ohio grew to include 130 church buildings by midcentury. And New England's 6 Catholic churches increased to at least 82, with the Boston area accounting for only about 9 of these. In Canada, Irish Catholics built churches in the English-speaking Maritime Provinces and in Ontario, breaking ground far beyond the traditional French/Catholic enclave around Quebec. A corresponding number of schools and cemeteries accompanied this growth.

Irish-born architect Patrick Keely stood at the unofficial helm of this new construction. He is estimated to have helped produce more than seven hundred religious buildings over the course of his career, ranging from Nova Scotia westward to Wisconsin and southward to the Gulf of Mexico. He designed cathedrals, such as St. Michael's in New Brunswick and Holy Cross in Boston, as well as parish churches, such as Sts. Peter and Paul in Brooklyn and

St. John the Baptist in Manayunk, Pennsylvania. He was also an accomplished woodcarver and integrated his handiwork into many of his buildings, as with the wood reredos—the customary, decorative screen behind an altar—at Sts. Peter and Paul Church.

Most of Keely's churches drew upon the Gothic or the Romanesque revival styles, both of which were becoming the preeminent choices for church construction of all denominations. The use of the Gothic involved an array of pointed arches, stained glass, window tracery, towers, vertical lines, and exterior buttresses intended to evoke late medieval designs, while the Romanesque featured the round arches and heavier masses that had preceded the Gothic era. As with other revival styles popular in the nineteenth century, the Gothic and the Romanesque revivals reflected attempts to capture the mood of historic architectural traditions without adhering to original engineering techniques or archaeological accuracy. These attempts meshed with the era's broad intellectual romanticism and theories of the picturesque. For Christian congregations, the Gothic held special appeal, with its celebrated connections to memorable cathedrals, abbeys, and parish churches and its explicit Christian symbolism. Religious congregations of all stripes turned from Enlightenment classicism to embrace the mysterious light and shadows cast by forceful medieval architecture.

Catholic architects, builders, and theorists worked to distinguish their Church's use of the Gothic from the attempts by all other denominations. In particular, A.W.N. Pugin, England's strident convert to Catholicism and a design prodigy, published his arguments widely and aggressively. Pugin held that Roman Catholicism was the only true heir to Gothic designs; that the Church had orchestrated an organic, moral society during the Middle Ages; and that medieval architecture properly reflected that morality and Christian spirit. Therefore, he recommended the Gothic for Catholic churches above all other styles. Other Anglican critics made variations on these claims for their own Church's Gothic Revival. But Roman Catholics in North America indeed did apply the Gothic differently from Protestants. Their designs made room for multiple interior chapels; they made sure that the high altar was dramatically visible; they included more representational art in sculpture, painting, and window designs; and they looked to continental models of Gothic architecture in addition to English examples.

The crowning achievement of these trends came with the construction of St. Patrick's Cathedral in New York City (1853–1879). This monumental structure was designed by Episcopalian architect James Renwick Jr. at the behest of Archbishop John Hughes. It indirectly followed in the footsteps of the Cathedral of Notre Dame (1824–1843) in Montreal. Notre Dame was enormous, with twin west towers, triple central doorways with triple statuary niches high above, and a double tier of galleries inside. Yet St. Patrick's was built in the gaze of a skeptical or hostile Protestant community in upper Manhattan. Renwick took designs and inspiration from Cologne Cathedral, and when finished, his gleaming, twin-towered, white marble structure occupied nearly an entire city block. It attracted throngs of curious, approving spectators and was proclaimed the largest ecclesiastical edifice in America. Remarkably, it had only been a generation since a Protestant mob had burned a stately convent of Ursulines on a Charlestown, Massachusetts, hilltop and nativists had demolished Catholic churches and other buildings in riots across Philadelphia and Louisville.

At the same time, the patterns of immigration were shifting again. From the 1880s through the 1920s, Roman Catholics from southern and central Europe came in even larger waves to the United States and Canada, increasing the faith's ethnic complexity. Immigrant groups settled in dense urban areas, establishing fortress-like enclaves where language-based parishes served more than religious needs. The Catholic sacred landscape became more varied, as urban grottoes, statuary, cemeteries, and streets became sites for feasts, processions, and miracle stories. The Irish hierarchy and its embrace of the Gothic and Romanesque (as well as the later Byzantine and Renaissance revivals) could not fully contain immigrant worship. However, church leaders did succeed in establishing a nationwide system of parochial schools.

The revival styles also proved important in Texas, on the West Coast, and even in Mexico towards the end of the century. In the 1880s, church leaders at San Miguel de Allende moved to update their seventeenth-century sanctuary, built with Indian labor, that sat on the city's main square. *Indígena* mason Cerefino Gutiérrez oversaw the addition of a pink Gothic façade and tower that remains a curiosity today. Our Lady of Guadalupe Cathedral in Michoacan, begun in 1898, presented a more complete, if structurally unfinished, Gothic Revival statement. New churches in Mexico continued to be built in the baroque and neoclassical styles as well. But the tensions between opulent sanctuaries and humble farms, and between liberal new governments and conservative reactions, resulting in liberal victories and the loss of the mandatory tithe as well as some church properties, significantly slowed the Church's progress.

## The Twentieth Century—Old and New

When the twentieth century opened on North America and Europe, Catholic architecture pulled in two directions. It looked to the past and the future simultaneously. These tensions drew from several sources, but one contributing factor grew out of nineteenth-century Europe, where small pockets of monastics and scholars had began to reconsider the original sources of Christian scripture, worship, art, and life. In France, the Benedictines conducted fruitful research into early Christian liturgies and music, and by the early twentieth century, the movement had gone so far as to reconsider the very nature of the Eucharist. Official encouragement of this general movement, which would be known as the liturgical movement, came in 1903 with the election of Pope Pius X, who called a conference to explore the nature of the liturgy and encouraged more frequent Communion by the faithful. All of this historical investigation led to a greater emphasis on congregational participation in worship and laid a basis for ecumenical comparisons across denominations and even across religions. It also prompted architectural changes in Catholic sanctuaries, with critics recommending the dismantling of superstructures built high over altars and their tabernacles in an effort to simplify spaces that had grown confused with Victorian stuffing and multiple, competing devotions. A model of this liturgical work, and indeed a landmark project, resulted from the call of Baldwin Dworschak, head of St. John's Benedictine Abbey and University in Collegeville, Minnesota, in 1950, for a new building program on his campus. A Hungarian architect and former member of the Bauhaus in Germany, Marcel Breuer, was chosen, and he completed construction of the Abbey Church of Saint John the Baptist in 1961, in addition to several other campus buildings. Breuer's monumental concrete design for the church, with a 112-foot, trapezoidal bell tower standing in front of the honeycombed sanctuary wall, invited worshippers in past a flowing frontal baptistry to a central altar underneath a simple baldachin. The Benedictines expressed a kinship with the utopian goals and honest use of materials that infused such modern designs.

Both the impulse to involve congregations in worship and the impulse to engage modernist architecture found a forceful voice through the Second Vatican Ecumenical Council, held from 1962 to 1965 and known as Vatican II. Scholars disagree about whether Vatican II prompted new devotional and artistic changes in itself or merely confirmed the trends brewing since earlier in the century, but there is no question that Catholic spaces around the world changed dramatically in the decades afterwards. Cathedrals and parish churches everywhere were remodeled; altars were pushed forward into the congregations, statuary was removed, and the laity assumed a greater role in services—leading prayers, reading from scriptures, and even distributing the holy elements during the Eucharist. And priests had the freedom, even the directive, to recite the mass in vernacular languages rather than in Latin.

In this spirit, earlier experiments with modernist designs gave way to full-blown postmodern fantasies, in an attempt to engage the spirit of the age. Central and circular plans took the place of older, longitudinal plans. Examples abound, from Precious Blood Church in Winnipeg, Manitoba (1969), to Saint Mary's Cathedral in San Francisco, California (1970), to Our Lady of the Angels Cathedral in Los Angeles, California (2002). The change was wrenching for some and inspired a conservative reaction to perceived coldness in the new designs—witness the title of Michael S. Rose's 2001 *Ugly as Sin: Why They Changed Our Churches from Sacred Places to Meeting Spaces and How We Can Change Them Back Again.* A particularly bitter battle between proponents and opponents of the innovations took place at St. Martin of Tours Church, Cheviot, Ohio, where organized lay opponents submitted a formal petition against the proposed renovation of their sanctuary to the Vatican in 1999. During these same decades, older buildings in urban areas weathered changing demographic circumstances due to suburban flight and new immigration. And church scandals, along with a decline in the relative number of clergy and the loss of groups of traditional members, have recently suggested a trend toward the closure and abandonment of some historic church locations.

Thus, the nature of the Roman Catholic architectural heritage remains in dispute. Ideals involving the earliest Christian worship are intertwined with radical new designs, which also share the public stage with historic sanctuaries. In North America, the past four centuries of Catholic settlement may mix most poignantly just north of Mexico City, at the Basílica de Nuestra Señora de Guadalupe, one of the most popular pilgrimage sites in the world. Finished in 1976, the basilica showcases the original image of the Virgin of Guadalupe, said to have imprinted on the cloak of the poor Indian Juan Diego in 1531. The new basilica stands on the Aztec sacred site of Tepeyac, where Juan Diego is said to have received his visions, and the sanctuary grounds still hold the original seventeenth-century Capilla del Cerrito, or "hill chapel," as well as the successive basilica built in 1709.

The 1976 basilica, designed by Pedro Ramirez Vasquez, has a tent-shaped roof and circular floor plan, allowing views of the image from anywhere inside. And moving walkways transport visitors back and forth under its frame hanging above the main altar. The basilica also houses two chapels on the main floor, nine chapels on the upper floor, and crypts underground. The front walls of the basilica, facing the Plaza of the Americas, can be rolled up to involve hundreds of thousands more pilgrims outside. Masses are celebrated there almost every hour, every day; hundreds of baptisms, weddings, and confirmations take place each week; and confessions are heard regularly. Although the Virgin of Guadalupe has served as a Mexican national symbol, her devotion and arts have transcended political boundaries, with churches and shrines dedicated to her throughout the United States and Latin America, along with countless private spaces. She has been proclaimed Patron of the Americas, and indeed, the fervent activity that engulfs her seventeenth-, eighteenth-, and twentieth-century spaces at the basilica, with official and folk devotions intertwining atop the one-time Aztec hill temple, reveals to us the power and paradoxes of the continent's built Roman Catholic heritage.

**See also** *Architecture* entries; *Canada: Catholics; Mexico: Colonial Era; Mexico: Twentieth Century; Roman Catholicism* entries; *Suburbanization; Worship: Roman Catholic.*

Ryan K. Smith

## BIBLIOGRAPHY

Baird, Joseph Armstrong, and Hugo Rudinger. *The Churches of Mexico, 1530–1810.* Berkeley: University of California Press, 1962.

Berger, Teresa. *Women's Ways of Worship: Gender Analysis and Liturgical History.* Collegeville, Minn.: Liturgical Press, 1999.

Carey, Patrick. *People, Priests and Prelates: Ecclesiastical Democracy and the Tensions of Trusteeism.* Notre Dame, Ind.: University of Notre Dame Press, 1987.

Crews, Clyde F. *Presence and Possibility: Louisville Catholicism and Its Cathedral: An Historical Sketch of the Louisville Catholic Experience as Seen through the Cathedral of the Assumption.* Louisville, Ky.: n.p., 1973.

Decker, Kevin Frederic. "Grand and Godly Proportions: Roman Catholic Cathedral Churches of the Northeast, 1840–1900." PhD diss., State University of New York at Albany, 2000.

DeSanctis, Michael E. *Building from Belief: Advance, Retreat, and Compromise in the Remaking of Catholic Church Architecture.* Collegeville, Minn.: Liturgical Press, 2002.

Farnsworth, Jean M., Carmen R. Croce, and Joseph F. Chorpenning. *Stained Glass in Catholic Philadelphia.* Philadelphia: St. Joseph's University Press, 2002.

Gaustad, Edwin S., Philip L. Barlow, and Richard W. Dishno. *New Historical Atlas of Religion in America.* New York: Oxford University Press, 2001.

Giffords, Gloria Fraser. *Sanctuaries of Earth, Stone, and Light: The Churches of Northern New Spain, 1530–1821.* Tucson: University of Arizona Press, 2007.

Gowans, Alan. *Church Architecture in New France.* New Brunswick, N.J.: Rutgers University Press, 1955.

Kane, Paula M. *Separatism and Subculture: Boston Catholicism, 1900–1920.* Chapel Hill: University of North Carolina Press, 1994.

Kervick, Francis William Wynn. *Architects in America of Catholic Tradition.* Rutland, Vt.: C.E. Tuttle Co., 1962.

MacRae, Marion, Anthony Adamson, and Page Toles. *Hallowed Walls: Church Architecture of Upper Canada.* Toronto, Canada: Clarke, Irwin, 1975.

Martin, Tania. "Housing the Grey Nuns: Power, Religion, and Women in Fin-de-Siècle Montréal." *Perspectives in Vernacular Architecture* 7 (1997): 212–229.

McDannell, Colleen. *Material Christianity: Religion and Popular Culture in America.* New Haven, Conn.: Yale University Press, 1995.

O'Connell, J. B. *Church Building and Furnishing: The Church's Way, a Study in Liturgical Law.* Notre Dame, Ind.: University of Notre Dame Press, 1955.

Peterson, Fred W. *Building Community, Keeping the Faith: German Catholic Vernacular Architecture in a Rural Minnesota Parish.* St. Paul: Minnesota Historical Society Press, 1998.

Reed, Henry Hope. "In the Shadow of St. Barbara and St. Thomas: Catholic Church Architecture in America." *Thought: Fordham University Quarterly* 31 (Autumn 1956): 326–349.

Rose, Michael S. *Ugly as Sin: Why They Changed Our Churches from Sacred Places to Meeting Spaces and How We Can Change Them Back Again.* Manchester, N.H.: Sophia Institute Press, 2001.

Smith, Ryan K. *Gothic Arches, Latin Crosses: Anti-Catholicism and American Church Designs in the Nineteenth Century.* Chapel Hill: University of North Carolina Press, 2006.

Springer, Annemarie. *Nineteenth Century German-American Church Artists: Old World Traditions and New World Innovations.* New York: Peter Lang, 2000.

Treib, Marc. *Sanctuaries of Spanish New Mexico.* Berkeley: University of California Press, 1993.

Tweed, Thomas A. *Our Lady of the Exile: Diasporic Religion at a Cuban Catholic Shrine in Miami.* New York: Oxford University Press, 1997.

White, James F. *Roman Catholic Worship: Trent to Today.* New York: Paulist Press, 1995.

White, Susan J. *Art, Architecture, and Liturgical Reform: The Liturgical Arts Society, 1928–1972.* New York: Pueblo Publishing, 1990.

Williams, Peter W. *Houses of God: Region, Religion, and Architecture in the United States.* Urbana: University of Illinois Press, 1997.

Wilson, Samuel, Jr. "Religious Architecture in French Colonial Louisiana." *Winterthur Portfolio* 8 (1973): 63–106.

# Atheism, Agnosticism, and Disbelief

Proclaiming faith in religious beliefs—particularly Christian beliefs—is common in American society. From an intellectual standpoint, however, there is nothing common about religious faith. Religious beliefs go well beyond everyday experience by affirming such things as the existence of unseen beings, the divine authority of ancient books, or the causal efficacy of prayer and ritual action. In every other area of life we are encouraged to question authority, demand observable evidence, and evaluate competing ideas by how well they square with ongoing experience. Yet in the case of religion we are asked to suspend our usual cognitive standards and instead comply with authority or tradition. It is thus understandable that there are always some persons who cannot in good intellectual conscience endorse their society's religious beliefs.

Over the course of American history there have been almost as many kinds of disbelief as there have been kinds of belief. Some forms of disbelief emphasize the value of living "without God" and are thus literally forms of a-theism. Since the word *theism* represents the beliefs and practices (*ism*) based on belief in a god (*theos*), the word *atheism* simply means a philosophy without a god. As far back as the fifth century BCE, however, atheism has commonly been understood as a more intentional position based on cognitive certainty that there is no God or supreme being. Other forms of disbelief are more accurately defined as agnostic (that is, without certain knowledge) in that they proclaim that human reason is not capable of ascertaining whether a god does or does not exist. Like atheism, agnosticism represents a philosophy without a god. Unlike atheism, agnosticism is defined more by its stance toward the nature and limits of human rationality than by certainty about the nonexistence of supernatural beings.

Distinguishing between atheism and agnosticism is only the first step toward appreciating the many varieties of American disbelief. Even more important is identifying the personal and philosophical motives that lead people to think in nonreligious ways. Many of these motives are secular or this-worldly. Persons might, for example, be committed to the intellectual methods found in the natural sciences and therefore oppose the way religions proclaim truth for methodological reasons. Other persons might be suspicious of religious claims concerning "absolute truth" because they are aware of how such claims appear from the wider perspective of historical and cultural relativism. There are even religious reasons why some Americans are counted among the unbelievers. Anyone who embraces a religion other than Christianity appears an unbeliever in some American communities. Jews, Muslims, Hindus, and Buddhists are nonbelievers from the standpoint of many among America's Christian majority. Christians, however, are viewed by some as nonbelievers in India or Saudi Arabia. And, too, many Americans have developed religious philosophies that substitute monistic or pantheistic conceptions of god for belief in the personal God of the Western biblical tradition. Their religious beliefs, while often the culmination of a long spiritual journey, make them unbelievers in the eyes of those who hold more conventional views.

The sheer variety of disbelief in American history alerts us to an important point. We need to focus less on what "unbelievers" are *against* and instead concentrate on what they are *for*. Atheism, agnosticism, and other forms of disbelief are usually motivated by more than the desire to expose believers' intellectual errors. Proponents of disbelief are often champions of a worldview that they believe has more long-term value than the religious systems they reject. They, too, often seek converts. They hope to persuade others to abandon seemingly outmoded ways of thinking and to embrace a new worldview that might better affirm humanity's highest powers and potentials. The history of American disbelief is thus simultaneously the history of faith in reason to lead humanity to a better future. Although self-identified nonbelievers have been a minority in American history, they have exerted considerable influence in shaping the basic structure of American government, securing constitutional protections of religious liberty, forming social reform movements, creating research universities that pursue knowledge without fixed religious conclusions, and championing the cause of individualism rather than conformity to societal norms.

## The Colonial Era

The history textbooks used in American classrooms present a highly selective version of the nation's origins. The story of the Pilgrims at Plymouth gives the impression that the colonies were made up of pious Bible-believers, while obscuring the real social and cultural history of the nation's founding. Many of the Europeans who ventured across the Atlantic did so to seek economic opportunities or to escape criminal punishment (at least sixty-five thousand criminals were forcibly ordered by English and Irish courts to be transported to the colonies). Relatively few came for religious reasons.

Indeed, only about one in five persons throughout the colonial period would have considered herself or himself very religious. Drunken revelry, barroom brawling, gambling, and extramarital sex were all more prevalent in early America than attending church. As the Frenchman Hector St. John de Crevecoeur observed in *Letters from an American Farmer*, "Religious indifference is imperceptibly disseminated from one end of the continent to another, which is at present one of the strongest characteristics of the American people" (p. 76). In a statistical sense, then, disbelief was America's original cultural heritage. It rarely seems this way, however, because the ministers who served the 15 or 20 percent of the population that did belong to a church wrote sermons and books that disproportionately represent their views in the historical record.

The churchgoing segment of the colonial population was overwhelmingly Protestant Christian. Their theological orientation is typically designated as Puritan, indicating that religion to them was less about participating in rituals than holding Bible-based beliefs. Colonial Puritanism was, however, more than a set of theological creeds. It was also a program for organizing society. While the religious segment of early American society had come to the New World for their own religious freedom, they had no intention of granting such liberty to others. They believed that uniformity in religion was the only proper foundation for a moral society. One of the principal functions of religion in any society is to establish clear-cut tribal boundaries. Commitment to religious beliefs is, after all, a conscious act of conformity. Declaring faith in religious beliefs therefore signals who are loyal members of the tribe—and who are outsiders or rebels who refuse to submit to authority. Colonial Puritans were therefore hyperalert to those who dared transgress doctrinal boundaries. Salem Village in colonial Massachusetts, for example, labeled its dissenters "witches" and promptly executed them for undermining the theological foundations of their righteous community. Authorities of the Massachusetts Bay Colony put Anne Hutchinson on trial for pointing out that the local ministers blatantly twisted the Bible to support their efforts to control people's lives. It was clear throughout the trial that Hutchinson was better-versed in scripture and intellectually quicker than her accusers. But the court nonetheless found her guilty of holding "strange opinions" and concluded that her failure to conform to the colony's male authorities made her unfit for their righteous community. She was forcibly banished.

Throughout the American colonial period European intellectuals participated in a philosophical movement known as the Enlightenment. Scientific discoveries in the late seventeenth and early eighteenth centuries led to a newfound confidence in the power of human reason. Perhaps no era in human history has witnessed greater faith in humanity's ability to discern the lawful principles governing the universe. The Enlightenment, or Age of Reason, was an era that focused attention on human abilities, this world, and the scientific method that moves gradually from observed data to universal laws or principles. It was, in other words, an age eager to replace Bible-based religion with both humanism and rationalism.

A few Americans such as Thomas Paine, Benjamin Franklin, and Thomas Jefferson would become self-appointed spokespersons for the Enlightenment outlook. But many others absorbed Enlightenment thought piecemeal and mediated through other cultural forms. One such cultural form was the rapid growth of Freemasonry in the colonies. Freemasonry originated in Europe, probably emerging from periodic gatherings of the stonemasons who built churches and cathedrals in England. What was first an association concerned with the occupational development of stonemasons eventually developed an interest in ancient wisdom, particularly as promulgated in contemporary esoteric philosophies such as Rosicrucianism. The tools of masonry (the square and compass) became symbols for building moral and spiritual character. By the early eighteenth century, the movement began to organize into "lodges" that were responsible for recruiting, initiating, and educating new members. The movement spread to France, Scotland, and eventually colonial North America, where more than forty lodges had been established by the time of the American Revolution.

Freemasons used symbol-laden ceremonies to initiate new members and to mark their progress through successive levels of character development. Freemasonry encouraged new members to reinterpret religion from the perspective of Enlightenment rationality. Masons were taught, for example, to view God in the era's rational categories as the impersonal "grand architect" of the natural order. Masons were, furthermore, taught that it is possible to distinguish the core concepts thought to be universal elements of all world religions from the culturally embellished beliefs that separate them. In this way Masons were trained to abandon blind faith in various denominational theologies and instead to build an eclectic, consciously chosen religious outlook. At least nine, and perhaps as many as thirty, of the fifty-six gentlemen who signed the Declaration of Independence were Freemasons. It thus appears that by the end of the colonial period, it was fashionable to be intellectually adventurous when it came to religion.

## The Founders

Even in the twenty-first century, it is common for some Americans to suggest that the "founding fathers" established the United States on Bible-based religious beliefs. Myths persist, it seems, despite all evidence to the contrary. Ethan Allen, Thomas Paine, Benjamin Franklin, and Thomas Jefferson were as pivotal in shaping the early republic as any four persons could have been. All were deists, meaning that their religious views conformed as closely as possible to what can be affirmed on the basis of reason alone. Deists, therefore, believe in God, but only insofar as reason can infer the existence of a first cause behind the elaborate workings of nature. Deists typically referred to God as the impersonal "architect" of the universe, while insisting that this architect no longer intervenes in the lawful operations of nature. The rational underpinnings of the deist outlook made it impossible for them to believe in the divinity of Jesus, the special authority of the Bible, or the whole notion of supernatural miracles.

Deism, not Christianity, was thus the religious outlook of such founding fathers as Allen, Paine, Franklin, and Jefferson. James Madison, the principal architect of the Constitution, was also a staunch advocate of Enlightenment ideas about religion, if perhaps a bit more discreet than a Paine or Jefferson. Similarly, John Adams and George Washington were at best mild adherents of conventional Christian beliefs and interjected a great deal of Enlightenment humanism into their general philosophical outlook. The founders, it seems, were secular humanists who wished to keep biblical religion outside the public sphere.

Thomas Paine (1737–1809) was perhaps the most provocative rationalist of the Revolutionary era. His *Common Sense* (1776) was the first public call for American independence and marked him as the era's most adventurous patriot. Yet his later work, *The Age of Reason* (1795), provoked the churchgoing population to vilify him as an infidel. Paine was, however, no infidel. He was an impassioned rationalist who developed an intellectually sophisticated belief in God as the "great mechanic" underlying nature. Paine's deistic conceptions of God led him to conclude that many conventional Christian beliefs were irrational. He wrote, for example, that no rational person should be expected to accept the Bible on authority. Belief in miracles, he argued, violates the

lawful order we observe in nature and portrays God as some kind of "show-man," who performs stunning acts to amuse us. He further maintained that Christianity is an inferior source of moral guidance. Morality, he argued, should be based on our rational knowledge of justice and how we might best make our fellow creatures happy. Even though Paine's rational humanism led him to denounce many of the religious ideas that prevailed in American society, he was in reality a deeply religious thinker. His message was that we might best understand God by studying nature. He was the revolutionary voice of a religious style based on his credo that "My own mind is my own church."

Ethan Allen (1738–1789) is usually remembered as a Revolutionary War hero. He first fought in the French and Indian War and later for a local militia, where he rose to the rank of "colonel commandant" of the Green Mountain Boys. Allen became a symbol of Revolutionary bravery when his troops captured Fort Ticonderoga in 1775. This patriotic icon, however, was also the author of several pamphlets that championed deism over and against biblical supernaturalism. Allen's most famous tract, *Reason the Only Oracle of Man* (1784), maintained that the rational investigation of nature yields all the philosophical principles required for philosophy and ethics. He argued that the existence of God is perfectly rational insofar as the vast system of cause and effect found in nature surely points to a first cause from which the universe derives its constancy, uniformity, and regularity. Allen deduced that the laws of nature are themselves God's revelation. For this reason humans best revere God by thinking and acting in rational harmony with natural law. Allen's unflinching devotion to reason did, of course, render him an unbeliever from the standpoint of conventional Christianity. From Allen's point of view, it was utterly irrational to believe in either the divinity of Jesus or that the Bible is a direct revelation from God. Reason, he showed, is the only oracle of truth and therefore the only trustworthy guide to moral living.

What Americans most admire about Benjamin Franklin (1706–1790) is his witty advocacy of "common sense." Often overlooked is the fact that it was precisely this common sense that prompted Franklin to deem Christianity both unintelligible and doubtful. In its place he substituted a largely deistic philosophy that reduced religion to a few moral principles. Franklin's intellectual pilgrimage away from Christian belief began with his birth into a pious Puritan household. By his teenage years Franklin came to view church attendance as an unpleasant duty. Bible-based religion preyed on the emotions of guilt and fear so thoroughly that he deemed it inherently incapable of cultivating our highest potentials. The young Franklin was an avid reader. He studied Isaac Newton's scientific treatises and John Locke's social philosophy. Such Enlightenment works confirmed his rational objections to Christianity and strengthened his resolve to replace it with a more rational and practical religious philosophy.

In later life Franklin sought to separate what he considered "the essentials of every religion" from irrational ideas found in specific religions such as Christianity. The first of these essentials was belief in the existence of the deity, assuming that this term connoted not the vain being depicted in the Bible but rather the grand architect who established the system of physical laws that govern our universe. Franklin's conception of deity led him to conclude that the most acceptable service of God is not worship but, rather, the doing of good to our fellow human beings. And to underscore this emphasis on moral duty, he added that the essentials of religion also include belief in the immortality of the soul, as well as future reward or punishment for our worldly behavior. It seems, then, that the very commitment to common sense that led Franklin to reject Christian beliefs simultaneously led him to affirm religious beliefs he deemed consistent with the virtuous living necessary to a democratic society.

Thomas Jefferson (1743–1826) authored the Declaration of Independence. He served with John Adams and Benjamin Franklin as America's ambassadors to European governments. He then became the nation's second vice president before being elected to two terms as the nation's third president. Throughout all of this he was an inventor, scholar, farmer, architect, and man of letters. He was, however, also reviled by his era's churchmen because of his forthright religious opinions. Newspapers, political pamphlets, and Sunday sermons alike smeared his reputation by labeling him a "French infidel and atheist." Clergy warned that, if elected president, Jefferson would overthrow all churches and have every Bible in the country destroyed. Jefferson was certainly an unbeliever if by that we mean he was not a Christian. But he was no atheist. In fact, Jefferson is clearly the most philosophically sophisticated religious thinker ever to be elected president of the United States.

Jefferson received the finest education the colonies could provide. In his youth he was trained in the classics, giving him a thorough background in rationalist and humanist moral philosophy. He later graduated from the College of William and Mary before taking up the study of law. Through all of this, Thomas Jefferson picked up the excitement being

generated by European proponents of Enlightenment thought. He developed an abiding faith that reason was the greatest gift that God had imparted into creation. Loyalty to reason, then, was humanity's most important religious obligation.

Like other deists, Jefferson rejected traditional conceptions of God as a father sitting on a heavenly throne in favor of such impersonal categories as "infinite power," "giver of life," "ulterior cause," or "intelligent and powerful agent." Unlike most deists, Jefferson devoted a great deal of his life to the study of the Bible. Few of his contemporaries could claim that they had studied it more systematically. Indeed, Jefferson was a pioneer of what in the late nineteenth and early twentieth centuries would evolve into the scholarly exegesis of the Bible. He devised an intricate theoretical framework that allowed him to see the Bible as a humanly constructed text (as opposed to a text delivered once and for all through divine revelation). He reasoned that nothing truly grounded in divine reality could be irrational, for this would be contrary to the very order and design God imparted to the universe. Jefferson then went through the Bible identifying those passages that to a scientifically educated reader were blatant nonsense. Jefferson concluded that in addition to many lofty ethical principles, the Bible also contained ignorance, absurdity, untruth, and charlatanism.

Jefferson's exegetical method was designed to differentiate between the sound ethical principles contained in scripture and "vulgar ignorance and superstition." The application of this method became most controversial when it came to New Testament attestations concerning the divinity of Jesus. Many deists dismissed Jesus altogether, viewing him as deluded in his claim to be the divine son of God. Jefferson, however, remained a serious student of Jesus all of his adult life. He was convinced that Jesus had been a sublime moral teacher. He saw in Jesus' teaching the three main principles of a rational religion: (1) that there is one God, and that he is all-perfect; (2) that there is a future state of rewards and punishments; and (3) that we should love our neighbors as ourselves. The problem, in Jefferson's view, was that Jesus' original ethical teachings were later transmitted by unlettered and ignorant men. He singled out Paul in particular as having corrupted the teachings of Jesus. Jefferson's point was that Jesus' moral insights over time degenerated into irrational and superstitious beliefs. Jefferson's rationalism caused him to reject such traditional Christian beliefs as the virgin birth, miracle stories, the resurrection, and the atoning sacrifice. As he wrote to John Adams about the virgin birth, "The day will come when the mystical generation of Jesus, by the

Supreme Being as his father, in the womb of a virgin, will be classed with the fable of the generation of Minerva in the brain of Jupiter" (letter to John Adams, April 11, 1823).

Of particular interest is the fact that Jefferson used a pair of scissors to edit his copy of the New Testament. Jefferson carefully cut out all of Jesus' moral teachings, omitting all references to his supposed divinity, miracles, and so forth. Jefferson's intention was to strip away the supernatural elements of the New Testament and to emphasize, instead, the simple moral teachings that he thought comprised the real basis of Jesus' life and teachings. This text, commonly known as the "Jefferson Bible," still resides in the Smithsonian Museum in Washington, D.C.

Jefferson's friend and fellow Virginian James Madison was another of the era's Enlightenment rationalists. It was Madison more than any other "founding father" who oversaw the writing of the U.S. Constitution. Madison and Jefferson collaborated in ensuring the passage of first the Virginia Act for Establishing Religious Freedom and then the First Amendment to the Constitution of the United States declaring that "Congress shall make no law respecting an establishment of religion or prohibiting the free exercise thereof." It is important to note that the desire for freedom *from* religion even more than freedom *of* religion animated Madison and Jefferson to construct the constitutional wall of separation between church and state. Disbelief, it turns out, is greatly responsible for the nation's fundamental religious liberties. Freethinkers such as Franklin, Washington, Adams, Jefferson, and Madison distanced themselves from the era's conventional religious life and created a governmental structure that would both protect freedom of religious belief and prevent religious groups from imposing their beliefs on the nation's legal process.

## The Great Agnostic

The nineteenth century witnessed an explosion in church membership. Revival-based Protestantism spurred commitment to Bible-based beliefs. While most of the century's religious enthusiasm reinforced Protestant Christianity's central tenets, there were several countervailing movements that appealed to people who styled themselves to be progressive or independent thinkers. Transcendentalism, Swedenborgianism, mesmerism, and spiritualism all attracted sizeable numbers of middle-class followers who had grown indifferent to biblical religion. Spokespersons for all four of these esoteric or metaphysical systems disputed the literal truth of the Bible, expressed disbelief in the special divinity

of Jesus, and rejected the spiritual value of conventional Christian worship or ritual. From a Christian standpoint, they were fomenters of unbelief. They were, however, deeply interested in spiritual matters. They unquestionably believed in the existence of higher spiritual dimensions of reality. They also believed that every human being has within himself or herself the ability to connect inwardly with the spiritual powers emanating from these higher realms. What made them appear unbelievers to some, then, was their unabashed desire to proclaim a spiritually and intellectually satisfying alternative to the faith of the churches.

The late nineteenth century also witnessed the astonishing career of the nation's most eloquent agnostic, Robert Ingersoll (1833–1899). Oddly enough, Ingersoll was the son of a Presbyterian minister who adhered to a strict Bible-based faith. It is, in fact, quite possible that it was precisely Robert Ingersoll's prolonged exposure to theological rants concerning human depravity, the blood sacrifice of Christ, and the necessity of thoroughgoing repentance that turned him instead to rational humanism. Ingersoll was deeply committed to personal and intellectual honesty. Such honesty and openness, he thought, were the bedrocks of America's democratic government. Deeply committed to civil liberties and progressive political causes, Ingersoll devoted his life to urging fellow citizens to follow truth wherever it leads—even if this means abandoning authoritarian religious beliefs and authoritarian social values.

Ingersoll became a successful attorney in Peoria, Illinois, and even served a term as the state's attorney general before finding his calling as a professional agnostic. He was portly and rather unassuming in his physical appearance. But the nation may have never had a greater orator than Robert Ingersoll. Mixing warm humor with obvious passion and energy, the "great agnostic" charmed his audiences even while he hammered home a message most thought blasphemous. His fame as an eloquent provocateur spread rapidly though the country. By the 1880s and 1890s, he was receiving invitations to speak in hundred of cities a year. Ingersoll turned his lectures into books such as *The Gods* (1872), *Some Mistakes of Moses* (1879), and *Why I Am an Agnostic* (1896) that extended the reach of his attack on Christian faith. Suffused throughout his lambasting of institutional religion was his own faith in reason and human nature. He explained to his audiences that humanism, too, has a valuable creed based on cherishing human happiness in the here and now.

Ingersoll charged large sums of money for his public lectures. Audiences consequently paid dearly for the right to have their beliefs satirized by the great agnostic. Ingersoll poked fun of typical Sunday worship services where parishioners must endure lengthy sermons and be accused of every imaginable kind of sin. He measured out equal amounts of humor and sarcasm to force audiences to reconsider how they had come to profess faith in Christianity's extraordinary beliefs. One newspaper recorded that those who had come for evening entertainment actually hissed at the great infidel preacher. A few surely did hiss. Most, however, laughed occasionally to relieve the uncomfortable feelings that inevitably arose as they found themselves examining previously unquestioned dogmas. It seems unlikely that many in his audiences were ever moved to denounce religion and become converts to secular humanism. Ministers typically used Ingersoll's visits to their communities as an occasion to intensify their preaching and to alert parishioners to the danger of entertaining doubt. Within days of his lectures, most in his audience went right back to accustomed forms of believing. But it is also possible that some had been gently coaxed into becoming more flexible in their religious thinking.

Ingersoll's career was both cause and symptom of a fairly widespread sensitivity to "freethought" in the realm of religion. Freethought represents the intellectual viewpoint that holds that our beliefs should conform to both scientific knowledge and logical principles. A few freethinking periodicals such as *Truth Seeker, Free-Thought Ideal*, and *Iconoclast* emerged to advocate the maxim that it is always wrong to believe anything without sufficient evidence. Neither Ingersoll's meteoric career nor the short-lived agnostic movement of the era had a long-lasting influence on American thought. Yet all the while throughout the 1880s and 1890s, a more pervasive cultural movement was emerging that was to give disbelief an enduring place in American life and thought—modernism.

## The Rise of Modernism

The late nineteenth century was a tumultuous period in American life. Social and intellectual change outpaced cultural innovation. Immigration and urbanization combined to erode Protestantism's ability to transmit its beliefs through accustomed socialization processes. From 1865 to 1900, more than thirteen million immigrants arrived on American shores. A large number of these had languages, customs, and religious affiliations that differed from their Protestant Yankee "hosts." By the first decade of the twentieth century, one out of every three church members in the country was Catholic. And while there were only 250,000 Jews in the United States in 1880, that number increased almost tenfold in the span of just three decades. The increasingly pluralistic character of American society made it startlingly clear that religion was an "accident of birth," not a universal truth. What is more, most of the immigrants who arrived on American shores headed straight for the cities. As virtually every American city along the nation's eastern seaboard tripled in size during the 1880s and 1890s, Protestantism found it increasingly difficult to impose its patterns on American life.

Even as social changes displaced Protestantism from the nation's cultural center, a new intellectual climate rapidly altered the way that educated people thought about their lives. Science enjoyed newfound cultural prestige. The scientific method demonstrated its superiority over competing intellectual systems on an almost daily basis. The technological advances ushered in through scientific achievement gave humans control over areas of life that were formerly thought to be governed by fate or by the whims of God. Religion appeared increasingly anemic. The scientific method focuses upon the observable laws of cause and effect; it has no room for ideas that cannot lend themselves to empirical confirmation. Belief in miracles or supernatural intervention seemed the stuff of ancient folklore.

Darwin's eloquent explanation of biological evolution became the focal point of the cultural clash between science and religion. In the academic world, Darwin emerged victorious. By 1880 virtually every important scientist in the United States had been converted to the new worldview. Biological evolution does not invalidate the possibility of taking a religious perspective upon the world. But it does invalidate the Bible as a source of factual information. Although the academic world had quickly embraced evolutionary science, it was the infamous Scopes trial in 1925 that focused public attention to the shift occurring in American culture. John Scopes, a young substitute biology teacher, was charged with violating Tennessee's statute making it illegal to teach a theory that denies the divine creation of man as taught in the Bible. The "Scopes Monkey Trial" attracted worldwide attention from the press. Scopes's guilt should have taken only a minute or two to ascertain as he had clearly attempted to teach modern science to his students. Instead, the trial lasted eleven days and featured the impassioned orations of the opposing attorneys (William Jennings Bryan assisting the prosecution and the famed agnostic criminal lawyer Clarence Darrow heading up the defense). Scopes was eventually found guilty and fined $100, but public sentiment went resoundingly against the biblical fundamentalists, who came across to the nation as backward and intolerant.

The challenges that science presented to religious belief were matched by those emerging from the field of modern biblical scholarship. Academic scholars began using the techniques of scientific history and careful literary analysis to examine the origins and authorship of Jewish and Christian texts. Their sophisticated analyses established beyond scholarly dispute that the Bible was the work of numerous authors who collected, edited, and arranged their narratives according to their own conceptions of religious truth. Modern scholarship therefore made it impossible to view the Bible as a "delivered once and for all" revelation from God. The Bible was instead now seen to be a collection of ancient writings whose original purpose was to witness to their authors' personal faith, not to convey factual information.

By the dawn of the twentieth century, the university had replaced the church as the source from which Americans would expect to find reliable knowledge. The disbelief generated by a skeptic such as Robert Ingersoll was limited to the power and reach of his personal orations. Agnosticism and disbelief were consequently limited in range of scope or influence. With the onset of modernism, however, American universities would provide a stable institutional base for the kind of empirical and inductive reasoning processes that undermine the credulity of religious belief. Henceforward philosophical examinations of religion would be greatly influenced by the natural and social sciences. Thus, for example, both Thomas Huxley and Herbert Spencer became effective popularizers of Darwin's ideas. Both of these British authors extended Darwin's core insights into full-blown philosophical positions that left no room for traditional religion. Most American readers were not capable of distinguishing between the scientific principles and the unscientific ideology mingled together in their writings. The general effect of such manifestos of modernist thought was thus to convince the general public that science leads inexorably away from religion. Even those who continued to profess conventional religious beliefs nonetheless used science-based technology on a daily basis. As a consequence, religious persons have been forced to compartmentalize their religious beliefs in ways that isolate them from the kinds of thinking that otherwise dominate modern life.

New academic disciplines such as sociology and psychology were also carriers of modernism's secularist tendencies. Although Karl Marx and Sigmund Freud were European thinkers, their views were avidly debated by American professors interested in aligning sociology and psychology with the newest intellectual trends. Karl Marx, an economic historian and early sociological thinker, argued that religion is the opiate of the masses. Marx's point was that religious beliefs divert our attention from the real causes of human happiness or suffering. Instead of actually demanding changes in the social and economic forces that affect the quality of life, religion comforts people in their misery by reassuring them that they will be compensated for their suffering when they reach heaven. Marx argued that religious beliefs, like opium, provide an illusory feeling of well-being but do absolutely nothing to improve the conditions that actually cause this misery. Marx's humanistic message was clear. If we wish to better the human condition, we must first give up the unproductive kinds of thinking fostered by religion and instead tackle our problems in a rational, technical manner.

Sigmund Freud also viewed religious belief as a misguided form of thinking. A medical doctor and the founder of modern psychotherapy, Freud's confidence that reason and science can lead us to a better future predisposed him to conclude that religion has no constructive role in modern life. Freud began his classic critique of religion, *The Future of an Illusion*, by acknowledging that life is hard to endure. We are powerless in the face of natural disasters, accidents, disease, and death. The prototypical human response to our fundamental weakness is "to humanize nature"—to envision supernatural beings who have the power to help and protect us if they are so inclined. Once we believe the world to be governed by beings similar to ourselves, we are no longer entirely helpless. We can hope to gain at least some control by attempting to bribe, appease, or cajole these supernatural beings much the way we would human beings. Freud further observed that we tend to visualize these supernatural beings in the image of a father figure who can be implored to watch out for and protect his family. We thus find ourselves yearning for a heavenly father who will protect us if we beg and flatter (i.e., pray and worship). The idea of God, then, is not based upon any empirical evidence or rational process. Instead, the idea of God originates in the human wish for protection against the dangers of existence. Freud argued that a belief held only because we want it to be true is an illusion. Religious beliefs, like illusions, rest on nothing more than wishful thinking. Freud thus used modern psychology to portray religion as a form of psychological weakness. Religion, though an understandable coping device, stands in the way of our taking a more rational, problem-solving approach to life. Freud believed that we cannot become fully mature persons until we abandon the illusion of religion and face life in a realistic and rational manner.

Many of the pioneering psychologists and sociologists turned their academic tools to the study of religion. James Leuba, George Coe, Edwin Starbuck, William James, and John Dewey were among those who showed how the new social sciences could explain the "real" forces shaping religion, leaving no doubt that religion was a human-made set of beliefs that lacked the kind of intellectual authority of modern science. Even when these new academic disciplines did not specifically address religion, their efforts to explain "the good person" and "the good society" without explicit reference to revealed religion were alone sufficient to carry the banner of humanistic philosophy. John Dewey, for example, never attacked religion per se, but he did inject American life with a new confidence in reason and the democratic process. His well-known *A Common Faith* (1934) ignored organized religion and instead celebrated the public virtues that emerge from social processes alone. All the while, social reformers such as Jane Addams demonstrated how charitable social activities can steadily uplift human lives with no connection to biblical religion.

## Humanist and Atheistic Organizations

The ongoing tradition of disbelief mostly consists of a series of individual writers such as Thomas Paine, Thomas Jefferson, Ethan Allen, and Robert Ingersoll. We might add to this group the agnostic sentiments found in the writings of Samuel Clemens (Mark Twain), Sinclair Lewis, and Baltimore journalist Henry Louis Mencken. Their solo voices have emboldened a small but continuing minority of Americans to resist social pressure and instead maintain a wholly nonreligious outlook on life. However, none of these impassioned humanists gave rise to anything resembling an organization that might disseminate disbelief on a broader scale.

As early as 1826 the Welsh industrialist Robert Owen organized a community of freethinkers in New Harmony, Indiana. Owen was convinced that the social environment plays a determining role in the development of personal character. This philosophical commitment had already prompted him to establish a model factory town in New Lanark, Scotland, that was founded on the principles of communal living and mutual support. Owen passionately believed that an ethical community could evolve new social forms that would replace traditional economic and religious practices. Those who gathered in New Harmony not only ignored biblical religion, they expressly opposed it. What

attracted them to this communal endeavor were their shared commitments to education, freethinking, and the construction of a moral community. These commitments, however, proved insufficient for sustaining an entire economic system. Other opportunities, the era's individualistic spirit, and the lack of an effective governing structure prompted the community to dissolve a year later.

Shortly after the Civil War a group of humanistic Unitarians decided that their liberal denomination still harbored a residual trace of religiosity. Under the leadership of Octavius Brooks Frothingham, they broke away from the Unitarians and established the Free Religious Association to promote the principles of free thought and moral philosophy without any reference to Christianity. The movement struggled to gain a core constituency partly because the Unitarians already had a long tradition of attracting the nation's freethinkers and partly because a similar organization, Ethical Culture, emerged and successfully competed for new adherents. Ethical Culture was organized by Felix Adler. A Reform Jewish rabbi, Adler was deeply steeped in the tradition of combining progressive rationality with moral concern. Ethical Culture's main purpose was to use religious-like ceremonies and lectures to promote ethical commitment with no reference to the Bible, God, or the supernatural. Adler eventually severed his ties with Reform Judaism and instead redirected the kind of ethical impulse found in Jewish prophetic tradition to contemporary social causes such as education, medical care, and the rights of labor.

Many of the immigrants who came to the United States in the last few decades of the nineteenth century or the first few decades of the twentieth century had secularist leanings. Severed from the religious institutions of their homelands and eager for economic prosperity, they put their energies into any number of freethinking and moral causes. Finnish, Czech, German, and Jewish freethinkers put their faith in this-worldly reforms and sought to counter the moral tenor of the entrenched Protestant population. Because many freethinkers were vociferous advocates of labor unions and other "radical" social causes, the nation's Protestant majority often viewed freethinking with great suspicion.

Several freethinking periodicals such as *Truth Seeker*, *Free-Thought Ideal*, and *Iconoclast* were launched about the turn of the twentieth century. The editor of the *Iconoclast*, William Cowper Brann, published his journal from Texas, square in the middle of conservative Baptist territory. Brann gained national attention not only for his raging criticisms of biblical religion but also for his claims that morality can be fashioned on a wholly rational basis apart from religious beliefs. Another freethought leader was Joseph Lewis. From 1915 until his death in 1968, Lewis served as president of the Freethinkers of America. Lewis had been deeply influenced by the writings of Thomas Paine and Robert Ingersoll. Through a steady stream of publications including *The Bible Unmasked* (1926) and *An Atheist Manifesto* (1951), Lewis offered the semblance of national organization for the otherwise disconnected proponents of disbelief in America.

There were numerous organizations founded throughout the twentieth century to disseminate freethinking principles, including the American Humanist Association and the American Association for the Advancement of Atheism. The most widely known organization, however, was the American Atheists founded by Madalyn Murray O'Hair. O'Hair was something of a natural-born agitator. She first gained attention when, in 1960, she filed a lawsuit against the Baltimore City Public Schools claiming that it was unconstitutional for the public schools to force her son Bill to participate in Bible readings. Her suit was eventually consolidated with a similar dispute, *School District of Abington v. Schempp* (1963), and reached the United States Supreme Court, which voted 8–1 in O'Hair's favor, thereby making it illegal for public schools in the United States to include the Bible in their curriculum.

Although O'Hair's organization probably never had more than a thousand members, she became the public face of atheism in America during the 1960s and 1970s. She was constantly invited to appear on television shows and to debate Christian ministers in large public forums. Her advocacy of atheism was complicated by her endorsement of other provocative causes such as "sexual liberation." O'Hair was not herself an original thinker, nor did her confrontational style help her attract a more philosophically sophisticated core of supporters. She succeeded, however, in generating considerable publicity for both the separation of church and state and the civil rights of nonbelievers. The greed and deceit surrounding her murder in 1995 by an associate within the American Atheists cast further suspicion on her philosophical beliefs, as did her son's conversion to evangelical Christianity.

## Theologies of Disbelief

Intellectuals in the twentieth century found it increasingly hard to articulate belief in God without appearing philosophically naïve. Modernism had gradually turned the tables; the burden of proof was now on those who proposed belief

in God rather than on those who found no warrant for such belief. Two quite different philosophical currents contributed to this philosophical assault on religious ideas. First, the epistemological methods utilized by science gave rise to a fully modern philosophical position known as logical positivism. Logical positivism focused attention on the empirical basis for claims to knowledge. Bertrand Russell, A. J. Ayer, and Anthony Flew were among the many notable philosophers who concluded that religious statements were literally nonsense—that is, religious beliefs did not signify anything in our world of sensory experience and therefore had no credible content. The era's most dominant philosophical trend thus deemed religion utterly lacking in cognitive significance.

A second important philosophical current, existentialism, also rejected the significance of religion, but for very different reasons. Based in part on the work of the German philosopher Friedrich Nietzsche and propounded by the French writers Jean Paul Sartre and Albert Camus, existentialism voiced the era's profound suspicion of those who profess to know absolute truths. For Nietzsche, the end of theism was simultaneously the beginning of a new era of humanism. His pronouncement that "God is dead" was simultaneously a celebration of the fact that humans have the power to transform themselves into whatever they desire. Sartre and Camus voiced a more somber despair with notes of anomie and nihilism. Although there are many versions of existentialism, all deny the existence of any transcendent, universal essences (truths). All we have is what we make of our own existence. Existentialists deem religious orientations to life to be "inauthentic" insofar as they avoid taking full responsibility for determining our own lives and values. Authenticity, they contend, requires a willingness to face life with brutal honesty and without the false securities of religion.

By the 1960s these philosophical trends found their way into liberal Protestant thought. The German theologian Dietrich Bonhoeffer, for example, declared that modern people can no longer be religious. Although Bonhoeffer continued to believe in God and in the basic authority of scripture, he nonetheless ceased identifying religion with belief and instead equated it with service to our fellow humans. More daring still was the thought of Paul Tillich. Tillich asserted that educated persons could no longer intellectually affirm scripture or traditional church doctrines. Tillich even went so far as to declare that he did not believe in a supreme being, if by that we mean believing in the existence of some supernatural entity. According to Tillich, what distinguishes thought or action as religious is not that it intends some object referred to as "God." Instead, thought or action becomes religious to the extent we seek to connect with the "ground" or "depth" of life. Tillich's definition of religion as "ultimate concern" implied that there is nothing intrinsically religious about what transpires in a church. Tillich's final legacy was that he encouraged persons to distance themselves intellectually from biblical religion and instead to find ways of being "ultimately concerned" outside of institutional churches.

Another theological expression of the 1960s was "the death of God" theology. William Hamilton, Paul van Buren, Thomas Altizer, and Richard Rubenstein were among the most prominent of those theologians who agreed with Nietzsche's dictum that "God is dead" and that it is time for humans to abandon supernaturalist modes of thought. For some, the "death of God" was primarily a sociological statement meant to draw attention to the fact that modern culture no longer thought in supernatural categories and hence traditional religion was irrelevant to contemporary moral reflection. For others, the "death of God" was an actual metaphysical pronouncement that humans are alone in this universe. The "death of God" theology thus represented a radical departure even from the positions taken by the era's most liberal Christian thinkers such as Tillich. Whereas liberal theology accepts the basic authority of the Bible but tries to reinterpret its message in modern ways, the "death of God" theology rejects the Bible altogether as it represents a mode of thinking no longer credible to the modern educated person. And whereas liberal theology represented an attempt to rethink the nature of God in ways that spoke more directly to modern persons, the "death of God" theology expressed radical doubt about the very existence of God.

Though there was great diversity in the views of the era's "death of God" theologians, they shared at least two important commitments. First, as a group, they held up the man Jesus as the normative model for human life. Although they rejected the traditional Christian formulas concerning the divinity of Jesus, they embraced Jesus as "the man for others." Indeed, they maintained that the death of God must be accompanied by the birth of humanistic commitment, and for this reason Jesus represented a life devoted to our neighbors and the world. Second, their message was not one of existentialist despair or nihilism. It combined self-conscious declaration of the death of God with a positive affirmation of human life. Death of God theologies celebrated humans as free and morally responsible agents. Denying the existence of

God simultaneously affirmed the significance of this world. By acknowledging that we can no longer expect supernatural assistance, we accept responsibility for living fully and ethically in the concrete world of human relationships.

These theologies of disbelief had limited impact on Americans' religious outlooks. The death of God movement was especially short-lived. Even though the movement made for spicy media coverage including the cover of *Time* magazine during Easter week of 1966, it was all but forgotten by the end of the decade. The liberal Protestant views popularized by Paul Tillich, John Robinson, and Harvey Cox have had a longer influence. Rather than revitalizing Christian thought, these daring views may have encouraged some to drift away from institutional religion altogether. Ironically, these liberal theological ideas siphoned away potential members of theologically moderate Protestant denominations and thereby accentuated the relative dominance of theologically conservative churches in the last decades of the twentieth century.

## "Nones" in the Twenty-First Century

It is extremely difficult to estimate the number of atheists, agnostics, or other kinds of nonbelievers in the United States. People are usually guarded when responding to opinion surveys and often comply with what they perceive as polite protocol. There is also the problem of what criteria should be used to classify persons as religious or nonreligious: membership in an organization, attendance at weekly services, or a professed sense of affiliation even without attendance or membership? Taking all these methodological difficulties into account, recent social surveys indicate that the percentage of nonbelievers is growing in the twenty-first century. When asked, "What is your religion, if any?" more than 14 percent of respondents answer "none."

Most scholars agree that the percentage of "nones" in the United States population is substantial and has been growing since the 1990s. Less certain, however, is whether this figure of 14 percent is a reasonably accurate estimate or whether the actual number is a little higher. It seems likely, for example, that 46 percent of American adults regard themselves to be members of a religious organization. This leaves 54 percent in the category of religiously unaffiliated. Some of these unaffiliated Americans have clearly defined religious beliefs. But the rest can be arranged along a scale that includes being religiously indifferent, holding nontraditional religious views, agnosticism, and atheism. A tentative estimate is that the number of "nones" in America is somewhere between 14 and 20 percent of the population depending on research methodology and definitions.

We know a little bit about who these "nones" are. Males outnumber females, perhaps accounting for 60 percent of those who have no religious affiliation. Younger Americans outnumber older Americans, with the highest percentage being in the age category of eighteen to thirty-five years. The western states of Colorado, Idaho, California, Washington, and Oregon have the highest concentration of nonbelievers. We also know that "nones" are more likely to have higher levels of education and more income. Persons of Asian ethnicity are also more likely to have no religious affiliation.

Less certain is just where these persons range along the scale from holding nontraditional religious beliefs to being wholly secular. Surely some are simply indifferent to metaphysical questions or concerns. Others are more self-consciously opposed to supernatural ideas. In the first decade of the twentieth century, several prominent scholars published books that pointed out both the intellectual flaws and disastrous cultural consequences of religious belief. Richard Dawkins's *The God Delusion* (2006), Sam Harris's *Letter to a Christian Nation* (2006), and Christopher Hitchens's *God Is Not Great* (2007) were among the many books that boldly articulated reasons for rejecting religious belief. Importantly, however, American nonbelievers remain more interested in what ideals or values they seek to promote rather than what they find themselves opposing. For this reason nonbelievers use a variety of terms to describe themselves: naturalist, rationalist, humanist, freethinker, or empiricist. Many are quick to point out that they seek to move beyond the tribal mentality so often associated with religion and embrace a more universal, even cosmic view of how human life fits into the larger scheme of things.

The 14 to 20 percent of younger Americans who proclaim no religious affiliation thus join a long American tradition of disbelief. Biblical religion has held no monopoly on American moral philosophy. Colonial settlers, founding fathers, and humanist philosophers alike have espoused moral outlooks based on reason alone. The nation's deepest political values, indeed even its explicit provisions for individual liberties and religious liberty, are largely the product of those who placed their confidence in human rationality rather than institutional religion. Atheists, agnostics, and nonbelievers of many varieties have not only sought to expose the limitations of views that fly under the banner of faith but have also championed alternative visions of how Americans might best realize their personal and national potentials.

**See also** *American Revolution; Church and State: Revolutionary Period and Early Republic; Death of God Theology; Deism; Enlightenment; Evolution, Creation Science, and Intelligent Design; Humanistic Traditions and Movements; Puritans; Transcendentalism; Unaffiliated.*

Robert C. Fuller

## BIBLIOGRAPHY

Buckley, Michael. *At the Origins of Modern Atheism*. New Haven, Conn.: Yale University Press, 1987.

Crevecoeur, Hector St. John de. *Letters from an American Farmer*. Edited by Albert Stone. New York: Penguin, 1981.

Fuller, Robert. *Religious Revolutionaries: The Rebels Who Reshaped American Religion*. New York: Palgrave Macmillan, 2004.

Jacoby, Susan. *Freethinkers: A History of American Secularism*. New York: Metropolitan Books, 2004.

Marty, Martin. *Varieties of Unbelief*. New York: Holt, Rinehart, and Winston, 1964.

Persons, Stow. *Free Religion: An American Faith*. New Haven, Conn.: Yale University Press, 1947.

Stein, Gordon, ed. *An Anthology of Atheism and Rationalism*. Buffalo, N.Y.: Prometheus Books, 1980.

Turner, James. *Without God, without Creed: The Origins of Unbelief in America*. Baltimore: Johns Hopkins University Press, 1985.

# Atlantic World

Expansion of Europe into the Atlantic basin beginning in the fifteenth century eventually carved up the Americas into colonial zones. By 1660 parts of North America were variously claimed by the French, English, Dutch, and Spanish. While these European powers would be entirely removed in the nineteenth century, the legacy of their presence, their faiths, and their policies shaped religion in North America. The Atlantic world brought together Europeans, Africans, and Native Americas in an encounter that affected the various faiths and traditions involved. Europeans drew upon their common religious heritage to justify expansion and various colonialist practices, especially enslavement. Tensions within the European community also shaped the Atlantic world, and from the English perspective no tensions were more important than the Catholic-Protestant divide. Anti-Catholicism first fueled expansion and then influenced relations among the various colonizing states. For their part, British Protestants found it difficult to transfer their religious institutions to a New World setting while at the same time welcoming adherents to a variety of alternative Protestant traditions from Europe, who found in the British Atlantic a refuge. Diversity challenged assumptions about the necessity of religious uniformity, creating a situation conducive to the exploration of religious liberty. After 1800, by which time the British Atlantic world had been torn in two, a common religious culture continued to connect that world.

## Encounter

Europeans moving into the Atlantic necessarily encountered people with faith traditions different from their own. First encounters brought together explorers and native inhabitants. Early meetings along the coast introduced unknown disease pathogens into the North American environment, sparking epidemics that severely reduced populations and challenged religious beliefs.

Meeting the natives of the Americas, Christian Europeans categorized them as "pagans." They understood pagans to be those people outside of the three great monotheistic traditions of the Mediterranean world—Judaism, Christianity, and Islam. Christians assumed such people either had no religion or adhered to a false belief system based on superstitions and that as a result they would be ripe for conversion. Although conversion of native peoples was considered an imperative, many early encounters did not involve aggressive proselytizing but rather exploratory conversations in which Europeans and Native Americans sought information about the other's belief system. The English looked for evidence that natives had some inkling of the truth, by which they meant ideas similar to their own. European sojourners thought Native Americans who knew of a supreme deity or life after death were ripe for conversion to Christianity. Europe's growing reading audience enjoyed perusing their reports of native belief systems and cultural practices.

The Atlantic world hosted many other encounters, beyond those between Europeans and Native Americans. New peoples and their religious traditions were added to the mix by trading voyages to coastal Africa and by the sale of captive Africans in the Americas. Europeans generally viewed these people as pagans. A majority were polytheists, adhering to traditional West African beliefs, but a few were Roman Catholics, converted by Portuguese missions in the region around the Congo River, or Muslims, converted via trading ties with North Africa. The movement of peoples that this era of expansion brought created new opportunities for interactions among those from different traditions who haled from the same broad geographical region. English Christians met European Jews in the Americas, for instance, at a time when Jews encountered discrimination in England itself. The circulation of peoples brought increased exposure to a variety of faiths and traditions.

## Religion's Role in Colonialism

In confronting non-Christian peoples in Africa and the Americas, European Christians drew upon ideas that facilitated the settlement of new lands and the expropriation of labor. Europeans understood the biblical injunction to "fill the earth and subdue it" (Genesis 1:28) as an endorsement of their own modes of agricultural use. In this view, the seasonal migration, hunting, gathering, and limited agriculture of the peoples of the eastern seaboard of North America did not constitute appropriate use, and the native failure to subdue the earth justified European land claims.

Such ideas worked in conjunction with the demographic catastrophe that witnessed the near collapse of native populations in some areas. Early English settlers cited the high incidence of epidemic disease to support their claims, noting that God had prepared the way for the arrival of Christian settlers by providentially destroying the native population. Such conceptions made it easier for Europeans to justify land seizures to critics of the violence and exploitation that accompanied colonization.

The enslavement of Africans as well as the treatment of Native Americans were justified in part using religious ideas. European slavery, to the extent that it was still practiced, usually involved persons of a different faith, such as pagans or Muslims. The word *slave* came from *Slavs*, as pagan Slavs had been enslaved in Europe in an earlier era using this justification. African and Native American pagans qualified as persons who could be enslaved. This construction, however, raised the prospect that once converted to Christianity, the individual might become free. Slave masters worried over this issue, opposing missions among their slaves in part to circumvent this possibility. Eventually colonies that relied heavily on slave labor passed laws stating that conversion had no impact on a slave's status.

## Catholic-Protestant Tensions

English expansion was launched at a time of religious polarization in Europe. By the late sixteenth century, the Protestant Reformation had divided Western Europe between Protestant and Catholic. England and Scotland both embraced Protestantism, the former erecting a Church of England with the monarch as its head and an episcopal hierarchy, and the latter creating a Presbyterian state church. Ireland remained largely Roman Catholic, although the English imposed a legally established Protestant church on the country that had a small membership and a disproportionate share of authority. With Scotland and England both including a residual population of Catholics, not one of those kingdoms was religiously uniform at the time that English expansion began. Europe was similarly divided, with the Scandinavian countries, the United Provinces, and some German states becoming Protestant; portions of the populations of some Catholic countries, such as France, also converted to the new faith. This religious bifurcation sparked many decades of war, until finally the Treaty of Westphalia (1648) enshrined the principle that the religious identity of a state should follow that of its ruler and no outside power would attempt to change that by force.

The first English colonies were founded at the height of these religious conflicts. The English launched their colonies partly as an effort to reduce the power and wealth of Spain, which had already successfully conquered much of the Americas and Caribbean. They declared that they would convert Native Americans to Protestantism and thereby prevent the Spanish from wining more souls and from extracting wealth that could support Catholic causes. Puritans were especially suspicious of Catholicism. Their tendency to think of the Church of England as flirting with "popery" created distrust among English Protestants at various key moments.

Anti-Catholic rhetoric was a regular refrain in the English colonies. The Glorious Revolution of 1688–1689 witnessed the ouster of James II, who was unacceptable to his subjects on both sides of the Atlantic for his Catholicism. Denunciations of James cited his religion and equated it with abuse of authority. With the mainland colonies eventually hemmed in by Catholic settlement to the north (New France) and the south (Florida), border wars had a religious component. Intermittent warfare on the northern border caused clashes in which not only the French soldiers but also their Native American allies might be Catholic. When captive English settlers occasionally converted, their Protestant relations expressed dismay. A particularly infamous case involved the young daughter of a Massachusetts minister. The government of Spanish Florida offered freedom to any runaway slave who would convert to Catholicism, outraging English masters and attracting enough ex-slaves to create a town of their own. In places like New York City, too, colonists feared that Jesuit priests in disguise were fomenting slave uprisings. When the British government did not outlaw Catholicism among the French population in the newly conquered Canada, colonists, parliamentarians, and London crowds all protested. They again equated Catholicism with an attack on the liberties of English men. Suspicion and outright hostility to Catholics was common throughout the British Atlantic.

## Institutional Expansion

In colonizing the Americas, European states expected to transfer their religious institutions to their distant dominions. The Spanish, Portuguese, and French intended to transplant Roman Catholicism, bringing priests, friars, and nuns and establishing churches, convents, and schools. Swedish settlers along the Delaware River brought the Lutheran Church with them, and the Dutch West India Company that founded New Netherland and other colonies established the Dutch Reformed Church as the official religious institution. Similarly the English monarchs expected their colonies to create Church of England religious establishments, with state support for the ministry and church buildings. Colonial charters included provisions for the supply of ministers, and churches were the first public buildings erected in most colonies. Governments developed funding schemes to support the church. To provide local governance of the church, colonies such as Virginia expanded the role of the vestry into a board made up of local elites who oversaw the workings of the church, hiring ministers, collecting their salaries, and caring for church buildings.

Transferring religious institutions proved a difficult task, especially in the Protestant churches with institutional hierarchies that were less developed than those bolstering the spread of Catholicism. English colonial promoters usually had difficulty recruiting ministers willing to sojourn to colonies. Initially high death rates indiscriminately killed clergymen along with settlers. The church did not send a bishop to the colonies before 1800, which meant that the institutional hierarchy in America was only an attenuated version of that in England and Wales. In practical terms it also meant that any colonial man who sought ordination had to go to London, where the bishop would perform the service. This hurtle effectively reduced the number of colonists who became clergymen in the Church of England. Even after the College of William and Mary was founded in 1693 to train men for the ministry, few such ordinations occurred. Recruitment of ministers for the colonies improved only in the eighteenth century when new missionary societies such as the Society for the Propagation of the Gospel in Foreign Parts (SPG) worked to locate and finance clergy for the American churches. While about 80 percent of the English population belonged to the Church of England in the mid-eighteenth century, only about 30 percent of the North

American colonial population did. Still, the Church of England had a presence in the thirteen colonies by the eve of the American Revolution, and it was established in more than half of all colonies throughout the British Atlantic world, ranging from Nova Scotia to Barbados.

Attempting to transplant the Church of England faced more than just institutional challenges, however, because the religious complexity of the three kingdoms ruled by the early Stuarts meant that many migrants from Britain and Ireland were not members of the state church. In colonial New England, the proportion of the ministers in the migrating population was high, but the clergymen who went in such large numbers were critics of the established church. They used their migration as a means to create a new church order, which would come to be known as Congregationalism. They also quickly founded Harvard College to train the next generation of ministers, thereby eliminating the need to rely on Oxford and Cambridge graduates who might support the Church of England. The first two colleges founded (Harvard, 1636, and Yale, 1701) trained ministers not for the Church of England but for the Congregational alternative.

Congregationalism, while dominant in colonial New England, was not the only option arising in the British Isles that increased colonial complexity right away. Other migrants were adherents to Presbyterianism, which was the established church in Scotland and also claimed adherents in England, Wales, and Ireland. Some Catholics from England and Ireland migrated as well, especially to the early colony of Maryland, owned by a Catholic proprietor. Over the course of the seventeenth century, too, the religious landscape in Britain and Ireland became more complex, with new religious movements, such as the Quakers, emerging and older sects, such as the Baptists, increasing their numbers. Colonies included adherents to all these faiths, which made it difficult to create an Anglican establishment. The Stuart realms were diverse, which immediately foiled the goal of religious uniformity in the colonies.

The Stuarts and their successors came to doubt their ability to achieve this institutional uniformity, although they never abandoned the idea of an established church for their colonies. As England became more diverse and as Britain and Ireland became refuges for displaced Protestants from the Continent, the government eventually came to tolerate dissenting views within certain limits.

In the Atlantic world, the situation for dissenters had always been better. With the exception of New England's execution of four Quaker missionaries between 1659 and 1661, no government had responded more harshly to dissent than England did routinely. The mechanisms for suppression were less well developed initially, and later, toleration became official policy in various locations. By the mid-eighteenth century, about half of the colonies had a Church of England establishment, but its weak institutional base limited its ability to squash dissent. In colonies without an official establishment, toleration was officially the order of the day: such was the case in most New England colonies once the Congregational establishment was pulled down by the British government (1680s), but it was also true in Pennsylvania, Georgia, and, for much of its history, North Carolina.

Authorities sometimes considered colonies as potential receptacles for dissenters, raising this to the level of policy when chartering Maryland to a Catholic proprietor or West Jersey and Pennsylvania to Quakers. As their thinking turned increasingly into these tracks, officials worked against their own assumption that an established church was necessary to support loyalty and promote social and political stability.

## Protestant Refuge

The British Atlantic immediately re-created and even exacerbated the religious complexity of the Stuart kingdoms, and diversity then increased further as a result of migration from other parts of Europe. Britain and Ireland received refugee populations from the Continent when Protestants were displaced by war or changes in religious policy. Huguenots (French Protestants), left France in large numbers from 1685. In that year, the king revoked a 1598 royal edict that had permitted Protestants to remain in their predominantly Catholic country. What had been a small-scale emigration then turned into a flood, as perhaps half a million Protestants departed. They went in large numbers to Britain, Ireland, or the colonies. These refugees were Calvinists, so they shared much in common with many English and Scottish Protestants. Some, especially members of the elite, were quickly absorbed into the Church of England, but others established separate French churches in various locations.

Protestants also came from German-speaking parts of Europe where economic hardship and wars made life difficult. The German states included a wide variety of Christian churches and sects, besides the dominant Lutheran tradition. Much of that diversity was re-created in the North American Middle Colonies, especially in Pennsylvania. William Penn's colony received a large proportion of German migrants because he recruited heavily in that region. Eager to attract settlers and able to offer religious liberty, Penn sought settlers widely, sparking a sustained migration from Central Europe and welcoming many Presbyterian Scots Irish settlers as well. Even Catholics—German, Irish, and others—were welcomed in Penn's colony. Moravian missionaries, who launched a worldwide evangelical effort in the 1730s, would include many British colonies in their efforts, further enhancing the available religious options.

As the British Atlantic became a destination for Protestant migrants, the diversity there rose sharply. By the late colonial period, the area hosted adherents of all the variations on Christianity present in Britain and Ireland as well as every major alternative—and many minor ones—within Western Europe. Adding to that the traditional faiths of West African slaves, the spirituality of Native Americans, and the Islamic beliefs of some captive Africans, the religious landscape in the British Atlantic was as varied and as complex as any of its day.

## Evangelical Religion

In theory, colonial government and the Church of England establishment supported missions, although these were late in developing and slow to reach beyond the non-European populations. Early efforts were modest, such as fund-raising for a never-founded Indian school in Virginia and a Jesuit mission in Maryland, both in the respective colonies' first decades. Massachusetts, working with Parliament while it temporarily ruled England during the Commonwealth period (1649–1653), launched a mission that resulted in the establishment of Praying Indian Villages and the translation of the Bible into an Algonquian dialect. At its height, this effort involved a few thousand native converts, before violence and prejudice weakened it severely during King Philip's War (1675–1676). After 1700, the Church of England engaged in missionary work, especially under the auspices of its SPG (founded in 1701). The organization had a dual mission with regard to the colonies: to bolster the Church of England among the settler population by providing ministers and to evangelize among the Native American population. Its success in both areas was uneven, although a mission to the Mohawks in northern New York was particularly robust. Other churches organized missions in the eighteenth century, with the Moravians offering one far-flung example.

Religious revival in the late 1730s and early 1740s affected churches and individual believers on both sides of the Atlantic and laid groundwork for later evangelical growth among enslaved Africans. Periodic revivals had occurred in individual churches around the Atlantic basin before Jonathan Edwards oversaw one in his Northampton, Massachusetts, church in 1736. Many parishioners underwent emotional conversion experiences and joined the church as full members. Edwards subsequently published accounts that primed ministers elsewhere to watch for signs of revival in their own flocks. When George Whitefield, the famed "boy preacher," began touring the American colonies to raise money for a Georgia orphanage, he spoke at mass meetings up and down the coast starting in 1739. Other itinerates soon followed. Many individuals experienced conversion, joined churches, or started informal meetings for worship. The Great Awakening, as the resulting intensive period of revivalism came to be known, had its greatest effect in New England, followed by the Middle Colonies; revivalism was also common in England, Wales, and to a lesser extent Scotland and Ireland in this era. It ultimately gave rise to new churches, including many Baptist congregations, and energized older churches, such as the Middle Colony Presbyterians. Members of both communities would later proselytize in the southern colonies, among the enslaved as well as the settler populations. Midcentury revivals created transatlantic networks of evangelicals anxious for news of God's work in various locations. It helped to knit the Atlantic together, even as it caused divisions in some communities and churches.

## Religious Liberty

That people of such diverse faith traditions could live together peaceably seemed highly unlikely to Western Europeans, but the reality of the situation within the British Atlantic world challenged that assumption. Europeans had long believed that religious uniformity was necessary to social and political harmony, and it was a view that many thought was proven by the wars and other difficulties that a religiously divided Europe had experienced since the Reformation. Diversity in the colonies in particular seemed potentially dangerous, as critics cited the weak institutional structure supporting many churches; they tended to see colonists as lacking religion altogether, if they did not have the full panoply of supports for their faith that many in Europe enjoyed. The varied religious scene and the relative weakness of transplanted churches caused alarm to conservative observers.

Even though the British Atlantic could be taken to prove the need for stronger churches and more rigorous policies to eliminate religious dissent, at the same time the Atlantic setting furthered the opportunities for dialogue around the issues of toleration and liberty of conscience. From the very first, some colonies had permitted greater freedoms. Maryland, founded by a Catholic proprietor who wanted to protect the liberty of his coreligionists, had created no establishment and had tolerated all Christians. Religious tensions had been rife there in the seventeenth century. Rhode Island, settled largely by individuals who disagreed with the emerging church establishment in Massachusetts Bay, enacted religious liberty immediately. Later codifications of that practice clarified that the colony welcomed all Christians, although Jewish migrants from Brazil also made a home there. In Pennsylvania, the Quaker commitment to allowing each individual to follow his or her conscience led proprietor William Penn to enshrine religious liberty as government policy. Other colonies founded in the later seventeenth century, such as the Carolinas, created loose establishments that permitted a degree of freedom. For practical or principled reasons, diversity and religious freedoms moved forward together.

Ideas about supporting religious liberty circulated in the Atlantic, gaining support from the colonial context while at the same time shaping it. The earliest idea in this vein was toleration. A fairly limited idea, toleration assumed that divergence from the accepted way might in some cases be permitted. The freedom granted through toleration was grudging and often provisional. A more expansive idea was that of liberty of conscience, which suggested that each individual should make up his or her own mind on matters of faith. Often associated with radicals in the seventeenth century, the idea became more commonplace with time. Roger Williams, an early colonial leader, supported this idea, but he did so because he believed that the faithful few needed freedom to purse the truth unmolested by others. By the late seventeenth century, some religious thinkers suggested that certain differences among Christian churches were incidental matters and should not block ecumenical cooperation. This thinking fostered acceptance of difference. As Christian leaders began to fear irreligion more than religious difference, cooperation among Christians received more support. Gradually the reality of diversity and changing views of religious difference created an atmosphere in which cooperation and accommodation became possible.

## Common Religious Culture

The transatlantic community forged in the two centuries after England began colonizing the Americas was pulled apart politically with the American Revolution. Political revolution created two separate polities, but it could not sunder the shared religious culture that had been created since 1600. Great Britain, its remaining Atlantic colonies, and the new United States continued to have many ties and developed in some similar ways after 1800. The major churches of the early United States all had British roots, whether they were the Episcopal, Methodist, Baptist, Presbyterian, or Congregational churches. The evangelical connection that linked together Christians throughout the British Atlantic operated despite the altered political context after the Revolution. Conversion of captive Africans, which had made large strides only in the years just before the Revolution, would proceed apace in both the British Caribbean and the new United States, and the circulation of Christian slaves and former slaves that the Revolution sparked would bring evangelical preaching to a number of African communities that had not previously seen many conversions. The burgeoning of missionary organizations, tract societies, and Sunday school movements in the United States had their British counterparts and were usually based on British models. Even the religious impulse to found an African colony that would serve as a new home to ex-slaves who were expected to evangelize the native population started with the British (Sierra Leone, 1787) and spread to the Americans (Liberia, 1815). When the United States gave rise to perhaps its first indigenous religious movements in the Church of Jesus Christ of Latter-day Saints, large numbers of the first generation of converts who journeyed to Utah had been converted in Britain. The anti-Catholicism that had so shaped expansion continued, affecting the reception of the Irish immigrants who would later travel to the United States. That they would remake once-Puritan and vehemently anti-Catholic Boston as a Catholic city would be a great irony. Transatlantic connections also continued into the nineteenth century, in revivalism, missionary outreach, and other areas. The groundwork for much of the religious culture of the early United States had been laid in the British Atlantic world.

**See also** *Anglicans in Colonial and Revolutionary America; Anti-Catholicism; Benevolent Empire; Evangelicals: Colonial America; Freedom, Religious; Native American Religions: Post-Contact; New England Region; Quakers entries; Roman Catholicism: Catholics in the Atlantic Colonies; South as Region.*

Carla Gardina Pestana

## BIBLIOGRAPHY

Bonomi, Patricia U. *Under the Cope of Heaven: Religion, Society, and Politics in Colonial America.* New York: Oxford University Press, 1986. (Rev. ed. 2003.)

Bross, Kristina. *Dry Bones and Indian Sermons: Praying Indians in Colonial America.* Ithaca, N.Y.: Cornell University Press, 2004.

Butler, Jon. *Awash in a Sea of Faith: Christianizing the American People.* Cambridge, Mass.: Harvard University Press, 1990.

Frey, Sylvia R., and Betty Wood. *Come Shouting to Zion: African American Protestantism in the American South and British Caribbean to 1830.* Chapel Hill: University of North Carolina Press, 1998.

Holifield, E. Brooks. *Era of Persuasion: American Thought and Culture, 1521–1680.* Boston: Twayne, 1989.

Lambert, Frank. *The Founding Fathers and the Place of Religion in America.* Princeton, N.J.: Princeton University Press, 2003.

Pestana, Carla Gardina. *Religion in the British Atlantic, 1500–1830.* Philadelphia: University of Pennsylvania Press, 2009.

Pybus, Cassandra. *Epic Journeys of Freedom: Runaway Slaves of the American Revolution and Their Global Quest for Liberty.* Boston: Beacon, 2006.

Silverman, David J. *Faith and Boundaries: Colonists, Christianity and Community among the Wampanoag Indians of Martha's Vineyard, 1600–1871.* New York: Cambridge University Press, 2005.

Ward, W. R. *Early Evangelicalism: A Global Intellectual History, 1670–1789.* New York: Cambridge University Press, 2006.

# Bahá'í

The Bahá'í faith was born in nineteenth-century Iran but has rapidly spread to many parts of the world, including America. The faith began when an Iranian reformer and prophet named Ali Muhammad (1819–1850) or "the Bab" (Arabic: doorway or gate) claimed to possess a new message from God. A crucial part of his message was that a greater messenger or manifestation of God was to arrive soon, regenerating the world and ushering in a new, millennial age. Because most Muslims believed Muhammad was the last prophet, the Bab and his followers were persecuted. Just six years after making his radical claim, the Bab himself was shot by firing squad in a public square. After his death, the Bab's followers were in disarray, though in time one of them, Mirza Husayn Ali (1817–1892), assumed the title "Bahá'u'lláh" (Arabic: Glory of God) and claimed to be the divine messenger anticipated by the Bab. Most of the Bab's followers embraced Bahá'u'lláh, but though he consolidated and unified the community, the persecutions did not abate. Bahá'u'lláh himself was tortured, imprisoned, and finally exiled with his family and some followers from Iran to Iraq; Turkey; and, in 1868, the penal colony at Akka, in Ottoman Palestine, where he lived under house arrest until his death in 1892. Bahá'u'lláh's many letters, books, and other writings constitute the core of Bahá'í scripture. They also delineate the elected and appointed administrative bodies that today govern the Bahá'í world community.

The American history of this faith is linked to its Middle Eastern origins. Starting in 1892, several Middle Eastern Bahá'í teachers came to America, converting about fifteen hundred Americans of evangelical and liberal Protestant background before 1899. Figures from the 1890s in America and Canada show that converts came from a range of Christian denominations, with large numbers of Methodists and religious liberals in particular. Many saw this faith as the fulfillment of biblical prophecies about the "end times"; some could conjure memories of great millennial disappointments at midcentury and see the Bab's prophetic proclamation in 1844 as a sign that they had been right all along. For these believers, there was no disappointment after all. Some Americans, learning from Eastern teachers about this *great new day of God,* wished to journey themselves to the Holy Land, to Ottoman Palestine, and those with means did so starting in 1898. There they met Bahá'u'lláh's family and especially his appointed successor, his eldest son, 'Abdu'l-Bahá (1844–1921), whom many of them saw as a divine figure, a "return" of Christ. ('Abdu'l-Bahá rejected these notions and insisted that such titles belonged only to Bahá'u'lláh.) A number of Bahá'í pilgrims to Palestine were wealthy religious seekers, people such as Phoebe Hearst, the widowed wife of Senator George Hearst (and mother of William Randolph Hearst). Hearst brought her African American butler along on the trip, a man named Robert Turner, and he became the first African American convert.

What was the substance of the Bahá'í message? Bahá'u'lláh taught that each of the world's religions had been part of God's plan to educate and uplift all the peoples and cultures in the world. His revelation was the most recent divine installment, an update of earlier ethical and social teachings and a restatement of earlier religious emphases on daily worship, devotion to God, and service to all people. All religions, Bahá'u'lláh said, have two different aspects, spiritual and social. In their spiritual aspect, religions reveal God to human beings and prescribe ways of worshipping him. In this aspect they are all similar. In their social aspect, on the other hand, religions are different because urgent communal and ethical problems are different in each age and culture. God sends different messengers to different people to offer different solutions, insights, and moral emphases. So the world's religions, though differing in many ways, are from the same transcendent source. Bahá'u'lláh insisted that the crucial problem facing the world today was living as a single global community, and his key social teachings therefore focus on such things as overcoming national, racial, and religious prejudices; appreciating cultural and religious differences; and finding new global systems of communication and governance. He prophesied the eventual development of a worldwide community of federated states. He also emphasized the equality of men and women, universal education, the importance of eliminating extremes of wealth and poverty, and the importance of seeing science and faith as complementary.

## American Converts

In the early twentieth century, the ecumenical ideas contained in Bahá'í teaching appealed to a range of educated, cosmopolitan Americans. The World's Parliament of Religions in Chicago in 1893 marked a moment of widening interest in foreign religions, and the vibrations emanating outward from that event stimulated new religious thoughts, wanderings, and conversions. Some spiritual wanderers journeyed into the Bahá'í fold. One place where many learned about the new "Persian Revelation" was Sarah Farmer's Green Acre community in Eliot, Maine, an eclectic retreat center founded in 1894 for Emersonians; freethinkers; theosophists; and visiting Buddhist, Bahá'í, and Hindu teachers. Its founder, Sarah Farmer, brought to Green Acre eminent American religious liberals such as Edward Everett Hale, Henry Wood, Ralph Waldo Trine, Annie Besant, Paul Carus, D. T. Suzuki, and W. E. B. Du Bois, as well as foreign teachers such as the Hindu guru Swami Vivekananda and 'Abdu'l-Bahá. Farmer was less interested in dispassionate study than she was in spiritual improvement, and eventually she found that the best way to do this was by embracing the Bahá'í faith. The Green Acre retreat center continued introducing Americans to comparative religions and Bahá'í teachings in the early decades of the twentieth century, and it still functions today as a Bahá'í retreat center and school.

But if Bahá'í ecumenism and cosmopolitanism attracted liberal believers early in the century, Bahá'í emphases on overcoming prejudice and racism drew in more Americans, of different varieties, throughout the century. In 1912, when 'Abdu'l-Bahá made a nine-month missionary trip to America, he talked about racism in America as a crucial issue and confronted the problem by hosting mixed-race meetings and seating African Americans next to himself and white Americans. This caused a stir, especially in places that had very clear race protocols, such as Washington, D.C. 'Abdu'l-Bahá frequently spoke to Americans about the dangers of racism and encouraged interracial friendships and marriages. This was at a time, of course, when Jim Crow laws separated the races and interracial marriage was illegal in more than half of the American states. 'Abdu'l-Bahá also spoke about race unity to the fourth annual meeting of the NAACP. After 'Abdu'l-Bahá's departure, the community continued to sponsor "race amity" conferences, especially in the Northeast. As the American Bahá'í community grew around the middle decades of the twentieth century, its message of race unity attracted a large number of converts, especially in the South, where there is today a strong African American community. Though the evidence is impressionistic, rates of interracial marriage among Bahá'ís today seem to be significantly above the national average.

In the early twentieth century, Bahá'í growth was slow but steady: in 1936 there were 2,584 American Bahá'ís; in 1944 there were 4,800; in 1956 there were 7,000. But in the 1960s the growth curve spiked. There were 18,000 American Bahá'ís by 1970 and 60,000 by 1974. As Robert Stockman remarked in *The Bahá'í Faith in America*, older Bahá'í families and conservative Iranian Bahá'í immigrants suddenly had to adjust to a Bahá'í community "filled with persons with long hair, dirty clothing, and youthful enthusiasm." Of course, other alternative and new religions also did well in this period, and others also experienced the inevitable strains of such dramatic growth. In the Bahá'í case, the community suddenly was filled with believers who knew little about basic Bahá'í beliefs or practices; some of them eventually withdrew from the religion. Others who stayed brought different personal styles and religious and ethnic backgrounds to the community, and individual Bahá'ís had to find ways to make good on promises to embrace difference. They were not always successful, and some disaffected Bahá'ís left the community precisely because they felt their different perspectives were not valued. The remarkable growth of the community beginning in the 1960s continued, however, sustained not just by youthful converts but also by systematic teaching efforts that led to large numbers of African American conversions, especially in South Carolina and other parts of the rural South.

The American Bahá'í community today is diverse and growing. In 2008, the total number of American Baha'is was about 157,000. Though precise demographics are hard to come by (the community does not ask converts about ethnicity), African Americans probably account for about 10 to 15 percent. Hispanic and Native American peoples also have converted in significant numbers, and there are about 12,000 Iranians and a smaller number of Southeast Asians. Surveys of the American Bahá'í community indicate that it is slightly more educated than the American population as a whole and that Bahá'ís are of average income. There are Bahá'í centers in most major American cities and smaller Bahá'í communities in most other cities and towns. The community is widely but thinly spread, though there are larger concentrations in southern towns (such as Atlanta) and in California. The American Bahá'í national center is in Wilmette, Illinois, where, on the shores of Lake Michigan, there is also a large Bahá'í temple, the first Bahá'í temple in North America.

## Community Life

What are the daily religious practices of American Bahá'ís? It should not be forgotten in any survey of this community that the Bahá'í religion, like most religions, is fundamentally about an inner, spiritual transformation pursued through practices such as prayer, meditation, fasting, and sacrificial service. First of all, it is almost impossible to overstate the importance of prayer. Bahá'u'lláh instructed believers to pray every day and wrote several special, daily prayers that emphasize God's love and mercy, human dependence, and the power that comes with submitting oneself to the divine will. Unlike the ritual prayers (*Salat*) in Islam, these daily prayers are said in solitude. Bahá'u'lláh and 'Abdu'l-Bahá composed prayers with many different themes and for all occasions. Daily prayer, however, is only one of several key Bahá'í practices. There also is a month of fasting, during which believers cultivate self-restraint and thankfulness by abstaining from food and drink during daylight hours. This is considered a sacred time of reflection, prayer, and meditation. The Bahá'í fast occupies the last month of the Bahá'í calendar, which is a solar calendar that consists of nineteen months of nineteen days' duration. The final month, the month of the fast, corresponds to March 2–20; and March 21st the first day of spring, is new year's day (*Naw Ruz*).

There also are nine holy days during the year during which work is suspended, days that commemorate key events in the early history of the religion, including Bahá'u'lláh's birth and death and his April 1863 announcement of his prophetic mission. An important devotional practice worth mentioning here is service, and specifically service that is sacrificial and that benefits other people or advances a worthy humanitarian cause. Typical Bahá'í forms of service include interfaith activities; social work; education; social or economic development projects in developing countries; and missionary activities, or "teaching" the religion to others.

What are some critical issues and tensions in this community? First is a set of tensions that arise when Bahá'ís think about how precisely to teach the religion to others and consolidate them into the Bahá'í community. Bahá'u'lláh spoke of the importance both of sharing his good news and avoiding aggressive proselytizing. How exactly to balance these prescriptions has led to an ongoing and sometimes difficult conversation about the appropriate ways to share the Bahá'í faith with others. Making this conversation more urgent have been ongoing encouragements from national and international bodies that call Bahá'ís to carry Bahá'u'lláh's message to more and more people. The result has been a kind of experimental attitude in which teaching the faith is cautious in some contexts and bold and assertive in others. A second pressing issue is creating more cohesive Bahá'í communities that allow Bahá'í families (and especially children) to develop Bahá'í identities. Bahá'ís do not drink alcohol; they do not believe in sexual relations before marriage; they have regular worship and prayer practices that set them apart; they have a series of holy days that are virtually unknown to non-Bahá'ís. How might American Bahá'ís develop strong Bahá'í identities given these facts and given that their numbers are quite small relative to the population? The small size of the Bahá'í community is a crucial issue that it will have to face. Third and finally, though the faith embraces the intellectual life and scientific inquiry in particular, Bahá'ís themselves have not yet developed a cadre of historians and religious studies scholars. The result has been that scholarly conversations about Bahá'í history and theology have proceeded slowly, an unfortunate development both for Bahá'ís and for scholars of religion and history. Were these conversations developed in new ways, they would surely help Bahá'ís understand better their history and unique religious perspectives. They also would tell historians and other academics important things about new religious movements; religious transnationalism and cosmopolitanism; American religious seekers and converts to other religions; and religion, modernity, and reform in the Middle East and America.

**See also** *Islam Tradition and Heritage; New Religious Movements.*

Christopher White

## BIBLIOGRAPHY

Hollinger, Richard, ed. *Studies in the Babi and Bahá'í Religions: Community Histories.* Los Angeles: Kalimat Press, 1992.

McMullen, Michael. *The Bahá'í: The Religious Construction of a Global Identity.* New Brunswick, N.J.: Rutgers University Press, 2000.

Schmidt, Leigh. *Restless Souls: The Making of American Spirituality.* San Francisco: Harpers San Francisco, 2005.

Smith, Peter. *An Introduction to the Bahá'í Faith.* Cambridge: Cambridge University Press, 2008.

Stockman, Robert. *The Bahá'í Faith in America.* Vol. 1, *Origins 1892–1900.* Wilmette, Ill.: Bahá'í Publishing Trust, 1985.

———. *The Bahá'í Faith in America.* Vol. 2, *Early Expansion, 1900–1912.* Wilmette, Ill: Bahá'í Publishing Trust, 1995.

———. "The Bahá'í Faith in America: One Hundred Years." *World Order* 25, no. 3 (Spring 1994): 9–23.

# Baptists: African American

Many African American denominations have flourished in the United States. Although some black congregations existed as early as the latter half of the 1700s, the first permanent black Baptist denomination did not form until the late 1800s. Yet in the context of Baptist denominations, white and black, the late emergence of the first enduring black Baptist group, the National Baptist Convention, in 1895, was not as anomalous as it might appear initially. The mainly white Triennial Baptist Convention began in 1814, but it did not survive beyond 1845, the year the Southern Baptist Convention was founded. The National Baptist Convention (NBC) preceded the formation of the Northern Baptist Convention (currently the American Baptist Churches, U.S.A.) by a decade.

Black Baptists, then, were being true to Baptist tradition in their slow march to organized denominationalism. Like white Baptists, they jealously guarded the principle of congregational autonomy, arguing that the true definition of church includes the preeminence of the local congregation and its autonomy from coercive control by other bodies. They insisted that each congregation was a democratic polity, establishing its own rules and selecting its own leaders. Believers regarded the Bible as the authoritative word of God and the sole reliable guide for doctrine, church

governance, and personal behavior. Black Baptists, like their white counterparts, firmly believed that conscious, voluntary Christian conversion must precede any valid baptism, and they held an unshakeable conviction that the only biblically mandated and acceptable form of baptism is by total immersion in water.

Although black and nonblack Baptists shared the long march to denominational unity and organization, doctrines, rituals, and polity, separate, independent black denominations continue to exist. These include the National Baptist Convention, USA, Inc. (NBCI); the National Baptist Convention of America (NBCA); the Progressive National Baptist Convention (PNBC); and the National Missionary Baptist Convention (NMBC). In addition, there are smaller bodies, such as the Lott Carey Baptist Convention (LCC), the National Primitive Baptist Convention (NPBC), and the United American Free Will Baptist Church (UAF-WBC). Among the reasons for this division are the desire of black Baptists to escape racial discrimination in church life; the opportunity for blacks to participate more fully in leadership; the struggle against slavery, segregation, and social injustice; a belief that black organizations under black leadership could more effectively pursue missions and benevolent enterprises at home and abroad; and what today we would call "racial identity" but that in the nineteenth century was termed the search for racial "manhood." Coupled with these reasons for black separation from whites was whites' discomfort with the presence of blacks, especially when blacks actively sought equality and justice within the church and society.

## Early Black Congregations and Regional Organizations

The move to form independent black organizations dates back to the eighteenth century and sometimes enlisted the support of white sympathizers. Black involvement in Christianity in the English North American colonies manifested itself as early as the first decades of the seventeenth century. It was with the advent of the First Great Awakening, a period of religious revival that lasted from the 1730s until about 1760, that significant numbers of Africans embraced the Christian faith and affiliated mainly with the Baptists, the evangelical forerunners of the Methodists, and the Presbyterians. In the context of this evangelical movement the earliest congregations of black Baptists arose. Among them were the Silver Bluff Baptist Church in South Carolina, near Augusta, Georgia, in the mid-1770s; the

Springfield Baptist Church in Augusta, in the 1770s or early 1780s; the First African and First Bryan Baptist Churches in Savannah, Georgia, officially organized after 1780; and the Bluestone Baptist Church in the area of Mecklenburg, Virginia, in the late 1750s.

Although church people and scholars might differ regarding the identity of the first black Baptist church, there is consensus on some points. First, the rise of these southern congregations reflects a desire for independence that manifested itself in other places and other denominations. Second, especially in the South, separate black congregations did not mean the termination of racially mixed, though white-controlled, congregations in which the black membership in some areas was more than quadruple that of white membership. Third, these earliest churches were part of an international Baptist movement. During the 1780s and 1790s, David George, a black Baptist minister active in the Silver Bluff church, and others journeyed from Savannah to Nova Scotia, eventually settling in Sierra Leone in West Africa. David Liele, also a minister from Silver Bluff, and some others ventured to the Caribbean area and there founded the first Baptist churches, white or black.

A second important stage in the denomination-forming process was the creation of regional Baptist associations. It was in the midwestern region of Illinois, Ohio, and Michigan that we find the earliest black Baptist associations, in the 1830s, 1840s, and 1850s, including Wood River, in Illinois; Union, in Ohio; and Amherstburg, in Ontario, Canada. In the 1850s the Western Colored Baptist Convention, which developed from the Wood River Association, seems to have been a move toward forming a national convention. In the Northeast, in 1840, there emerged among black Baptists the American Baptist Missionary Convention, which included in its memberships the renowned Abyssinian Baptist Church membership in New York City. Although this convention aspired to be a national body concerned with domestic and foreign missions, various factors, including the difficulty of any independent black group to expand into slave territory, essentially confined it, like the Western Colored Baptist Convention, to one region.

## Civil War and Reconstruction

The advent of the Civil War, in 1861, and the Reconstruction era that followed occasioned heightened efforts to achieve black denominational unity. These African American exslaves, and the few and severely restricted southern free people, now had occasion to select and govern their own religious organizations on a mass scale with historically unparalleled freedom. Northerners, white and black, had new opportunities to conduct religious and humanitarian work in the South. As a result, new congregations appeared, and black Baptists in practically every state with a sizable black population formed state conventions to pursue missions and education, with Virginia, North Carolina, and South Carolina leading the way in the South.

Southern blacks united forces with northern blacks, and sometimes northern whites, to establish new Baptist regional associations and merge with existing ones, as well as aspiring national conventions, producing groups such as the Northwestern and Southern Baptist Convention, or NSBC (1864), encompassing eight southern and midwestern states; the Consolidated American Baptist Missionary Convention (1866), which merged the American Baptist Missionary Convention with the NSBC; the Southwestern and Southern Missionary Baptist Convention (1875); the Baptist Foreign Mission Convention, or BFMC (1880), which focused on African missions; and the American National Baptist Convention, or ANBC (1886), a strong attempt by the Kentucky Baptist William J. Simmons to unite all black Baptists in the face of growing racial reaction in the South; and the Baptist National Education Convention, or BNEC (1893).

Because approximately 90 percent of blacks in the United States were concentrated in the South, most new associations and conventions had southern bases or headquarters or had large southern memberships. Yet some conventions and associations operated mainly as nonsouthern groups in terms of headquarters and governance. They include the Baptist General Association of Western States and Territories, founded in 1873, and the New England Baptist Missionary Convention, established in 1874.

All of these groups played important roles in uniting Baptists across state and regional lines, conducting missionary and educational work, pursuing overseas missions (especially in Africa), supporting local churches, and demonstrating the abilities, commitments, endurance, and progress of a people who only recently had been slaves and for whom some whites had predicted extinction. A national organization of Baptist forces proved elusive for more than twenty-five years after the end of the Civil War. Yet prior to 1895 no Baptist group of significant size, black or white, had attained the stature of a national organization reminiscent of or approaching that of the defunct Baptist Triennial Convention. The white-controlled Southern Baptist Convention (SBC), formed in 1845, was by far the most successfully organized Baptist denomination, a model that subsequent national bodies, white and black, would emulate. Nonetheless, during this era it was essentially a southern regional organization. The northern white-controlled groups had followed the society model and focused their multiple institutions on specific fields of endeavor (foreign missions, domestic work, and religious literature and education), rather than subsuming all their efforts under the single umbrella of a convention, as did the SBC. Their work among, and in cooperation with, black and white southerners notwithstanding, these northern Baptists were also essentially regional. It would not be until the first decade of the twentieth century, about ten years after the founding of the black National Baptist Convention, that the northern Baptists would organize and consolidate their activities into a national convention model.

Therefore black Baptists, like their white counterparts, found it difficult to organize and maintain a national convention or denomination because of issues surrounding polity and congregational autonomy, as well as because of tensions between Baptists of different geographical sections. To be sure, the controversy over slavery that divided the country, the Civil War, and Reconstruction ultimately brought together black Baptists across geographical lines, while these factors divided Northern and Southern white Baptists. Indeed, many of the blacks in the North at the time of the Civil War still had relatives, friends, and other intimate connections in the South, because a significant number of Northern blacks themselves had once been Southern slaves before escaping or by some other means obtaining freedom. Although absent the same level of rancor and hostility existing between Northern and Southern whites, blacks nonetheless also experienced conflicts reflecting the sectional divide. Black Northerners and even some nonabolitionist white Northerners believed that Southern white religion had become a false, heretical brand of the faith since it had been corrupted by cooperation with, and approbation of, slavery.

Likewise, these Northerners tended to believe that enslaved blacks had been taught a defective form of Christianity by white Southern heretics, and hence the black people themselves held a corrupted form of the faith. These northerners apparently were unaware that most blacks received the faith through other blacks, not from whites. Additionally, many Southern blacks did in fact practice aspects of the faith that differed from whites and Northern blacks. In some areas in the South, the performance of a sacred dance known as the ring shout and a reliance on

visions, dreams, and strongly emotional spiritual experiences (even in comparison with other evangelicals) caused some dismay among outsiders. To a considerable extent these emphases reflected continuations and influences of traditional African religions. Other factors that contributed to sectional tensions were the impoverishment of former slaves, the gap in literacy levels between Northern missionaries and local blacks, and the financial and transportation difficulties in attending meetings in distant places for people, North and South, who for the most part were poor.

## Formation of the National Baptist Convention

In 1895, in Atlanta, Georgia, these and other impediments were overcome with the formation of the first national, enduring denomination of African American Baptists. The desire for Christian unity, union of forces for religious work, greater institutional racial unity occasioned by increasing levels of "legal" acts of racial discrimination (such as segregation and voting disfranchisement), and violent acts (such as lynching) propelled black Baptists to form the National Baptist Convention. The founding meeting, in September 1895, arose from an earlier proposal, the Tripartite Union, which was revived by Albert W. Pegues of North Carolina and William J. Simmons of Kentucky. This proposal called for the union of three black denominations: the Baptist Foreign Mission Convention (1880), the American National Baptist Convention (1886), and the National Baptist Education Convention (1893). Henceforth, the work of foreign missions, domestic missions, and education would fall under the auspices of one convention, as was then the case with the practically all-white Southern Baptist Convention. Within a decade the National Baptist Convention had formed a number of important boards to deal with pressing denominational business: foreign and home missions, publications, Sunday schools, and youth work. A number of commissions were formed, including those devoted to rural life, evangelism, business, race relations, ecumenism, and engagement with the international Baptist community.

An important development was the formation, in 1900, of the Woman's Auxiliary to the convention; it was led by dynamic personalities including Nannie Helen Burroughs (1879–1961), an educator, social activist, and denominational organizer. The members of the auxiliary were also members of the convention, but they fought successfully to retain their autonomy in governance and operations. The establishment of the auxiliary represented the desire of women to exercise more openly leadership roles within the convention. Of course, women traditionally had engaged in home and foreign mission work, education, and prayer groups, and often, if not usually, they led the way in raising funds for various enterprises and functions of Baptist organizations of all types and at all levels—local, regional, national, and international. In addition to Burroughs, a number of other black women had a tremendous impact in Baptist and wider circles. A few, such as Virginia Broughton, who advocated a holiness theology, even preached, though it appears that unlike some of their Methodist counterparts none of these women actually sought ordination or "full" ministerial rights (this would include pastoring churches and officially performing central rituals of baptism, Communion, or weddings). Emma B. DeLaney, a graduate of Spelman College, journeyed to southern and western Africa during the first two decades of the twentieth century, as a missionary and, unusuall for the time, was unaccompanied by a husband, father, or other male relative. Lucie Campbell Williams, who composed classic hymns during the first half of the 1900s, was a leader in the popularization and acceptance of the new gospel music.

Another trait of the National Baptist Convention—which became the National Baptist Convention, USA, Inc. (NBCI), about the time of the division in the NBC ranks in 1915–1916—has been the longevity of presidential leadership, which resulted in both positive and negative developments. The first president, Elias C. Morris, served from 1895 until his death in 1922. Morris was an outspoken advocate for racial justice, denominational and racial unity, and domestic and foreign missions. He was succeeded by Lacey Kirk Williams, who served approximately eighteen years, and David V. Jemison, who served approximately thirteen years. The longest tenure as president belongs to Joseph H. Jackson, pastor of Olivet Baptist Church in Chicago, who served from 1953 to 1982. Jackson's term witnessed internal disputes regarding convention governance and the relationship of the convention to the civil rights movement of the 1950s and 1960s, eventually resulting in a serious schism. A damaging blow came to the organization with the presidency of Henry J. Lyons in the 1990s. Along with the public disclosure of Lyons's marital problems, there came to light financial irregularities connected with his leadership that resulted in his imprisonment in a federal facility. The episode also revealed that the reported NBCI membership number of approximately seven million was probably inaccurate and in fact was lower. The fact that neither the governing board nor the convention repudiated Lyons did not serve the reputation of the national body well.

The missteps of Lyons notwithstanding, since the 1980s the convention has sought to involve itself more actively in issues of social justice, cooperated with other black Baptist groups, and continued ecumenical dialogue with predominantly black groups as well as predominantly white groups. The convention contributes to the support of a number of educational institutions, including the American Baptist Theological Seminary, in Nashville, and the Morehouse School of Religion, in Atlanta (which is separate from Morehouse College). It also continues mission work in the Caribbean and in western and southern Africa. Some estimate the membership of the NBC to be approximately five million members, extending to almost all areas of the United States and to the Caribbean and Africa.

## Divisions within the National Baptist Groups

All of the major black Baptist denominations and some of the minor ones have their origins in divisions or secessions from the National Baptist Convention or National Baptist Convention, USA, Inc. (NBCI). The first significant division occurred in 1897. The Lott Carey Baptist Foreign Mission Convention (LCC), later the Lott Carey Baptist Convention, with leaders such as Calvin S. Brown of North Carolina, formed because of disagreements over cooperation with white Baptists and the conduct of foreign missions. The Lott Carey Convention has received its greatest support from the states of the upper Atlantic South and mid-Atlantic region, including the District of Columbia, Virginia, North Carolina, and Maryland. This new convention, in addition to sensing that some of the central leaders and states in the foreign mission enterprise had not been respected and had been marginalized in the operations of the new NBC, believed that the mother group had been too inflexible in making cooperative arrangements with white Baptist groups, especially those in the North. The NBC, for its part, accused the LCC of being so eager for interracial cooperation in ventures like foreign missions and publication that it was willing to accept a subordinate rather than an equal role in pursuit of these efforts.

The LCC soon found that it was not as easy to establish acceptable terms with the Baptists of the North in the conduct of foreign missions as they had envisioned. After the failure of a cooperative alignment with the NBC, beginning in 1905, the LCC in 1924 established a cooperative arrangement to conduct foreign missions on behalf of the National

Baptist Convention of America (which had separated from the NBC). In the long run this second arrangement also failed to meet the original expectations of either group, and each began conducting its own mission enterprises. Led by Wendell C. Somerville, the LCC experienced a revival of its mission programs in the 1940s. By the early twenty-first century, the LCC had members in sixteen states and the District of Columbia and sponsored more than one hundred missionaries in West Africa, India, and Guyana. It has promoted education and evangelism, worked to combat hunger, cared for lepers, and established hospitals. The LCC has established departments that are concerned with women and youth.

The second major division in the NBC, which occurred in 1915, produced the National Baptist Convention of America (NBCA) under the leadership of Richard Boyd. The principal issue behind the split was the control of the publishing house. Soon after the founding of the original NBC, the convention had established a publishing house so that black Baptists could produce their own literature rather than relying on the white American Baptist Publication Society. In 1899 E. C. Morris, then the NBC president, had unsuccessfully attempted to establish greater control by the convention over the venture. The publishing house, however, was incorporated under Tennessee law in the name of Richard Boyd, not the NBC. Boyd, therefore, was successful in thwarting efforts of the NBC to secure greater funding from the prosperous publishing house and refused to abide by aspects of the convention charter. When the NBC sought to press its case with greater fervor in 1915, the NBCA broke ranks. With a membership of approximately four million, the NBCA's greatest strength is in the southern states of North Carolina, South Carolina, Mississippi, Louisiana, and Texas.

In 1961 the third major black Baptist division occurred when the Progressive National Baptist Convention (PNBC) withdrew from the NBCI. The separation was occasioned by two principal issues: the length of tenure of the convention president and the most effective way in which to pursue civil rights for African Americans. Joseph H. Jackson assumed the presidency in 1953, accepting the idea of term limits on holders of the office. According to a 1952 amendment passed by the NBCI, persons who wanted a fifth term as president must let one year intervene after they had served four consecutive terms. When Jackson decided to seek a fifth consecutive term, the law was challenged in federal court and judged to have been passed improperly. Linked with the tenure issue was a disagreement between

Jackson and his critics over civil rights. Jackson argued for an approach to civil rights for African Americans that emphasized legal challenges, pursued economic development, and generally avoided civil disobedience and mass protests, the latter two being hallmark strategies of Martin Luther King Jr. After attempts to unseat Jackson failed, dissidents, including L. Venchael Booth of Ohio and Gardner Taylor of New York, met in 1961 to form the Progressive National Baptist Convention, which would be committed to term limits and to a more direct, activist approach to civil rights and economic justice. The PNBC has supported traditional civil rights organizations in the United States and opposed apartheid in South Africa. With a membership of approximately two million, it supports a number of schools, including the Morehouse School of Religion and Shaw University's Divinity School, in Raleigh, North Carolina.

In 1988 a fourth major division occurred with the secession of the National Missionary Baptist Convention from the National Baptist Convention of America. The NBCA attempted to have a Sunday school congress and publishing house on the model of other conventions. Approximately one-fourth of the membership supported the Boyd family, which still controlled the publishing house, and at that point those members withdrew and formed the new convention. By 2000 the NMBC had a membership of approximately 2.3 million.

## Non-National Baptist Denominations

In addition to the National Baptist conventions, there are several smaller, lesser known black Baptist denominations. Two examples illustrate what in many ways are the opposite sides of a theological spectrum in religious life. Adhering to an Arminian theology, the first group, the United American Free Will Baptist Church (UAFWBC), organized its first general conference in 1901. The Free Will Baptist movement traces its origins to the 1700s, when it rejected what at that time was perhaps the majority view in Baptist theology: strict Calvinism, including the acceptance of predestination. After the Civil War, black Free Will Baptists began to separate from their white counterparts in the South, forming their first congregation as early as 1867, calling an annual meeting in 1887, and following that up with a general conference fourteen years later. Arminian theology rejects historic Calvinist ideas such as unconditional predestination, perseverance of the righteous ("once saved, always saved"), total human depravity that erases human free will in matters of salvation, and the extension of God's grace to the sinner. Not only do the Free Will Baptists share the Arminian theology of Methodists but they have also appropriated the Methodist form of governance. The UAFWBC has conferences at the local, regional, and national levels, and the conference leader is known as "senior bishop." It supports a Bible college in Kinston, North Carolina, and a newspaper, the *Free Will Baptist Advocate*. With at least 100,000 members, the UAFWBC has its greatest strength in North Carolina, Georgia, Florida, Louisiana, Mississippi, and Texas.

Second, the National Primitive Baptist Convention of the United States of America (NPBC), a Calvinist body, was founded in 1907 in Huntsville, Alabama, a part of the larger Primitive Baptist movement. As early as the late 1820s some Baptists, especially in southern and border areas, began separating from the Baptist Triennial Convention and certain national societies that promoted missions, the distribution of Bibles, and seminaries. Primitive Baptists believed that these organizations above the levels of the local church and associations were non–biblically based entities started by human beings rather than by God. They referred to themselves as "primitive" because they were attempting to reestablish the first, pure, original, and, therefore, authentic God-willed ways of conducting the church. Blacks were also members of these early Primitive churches and associations, and they faced the same racial discrimination and segregation as non-Primitive African American Baptists. As the Civil War ended, blacks in these churches organized their own independent churches and associations. Among the earliest was the Indian Creek Association, formed in 1869 in northern Alabama.

As 1900 approached there was growing interest in establishing national, institutional unity among African American Primitive Baptists. This is a significant difference between white and black Primitive groups of the time. Whites adhered to the principle that there should be no organizations above the association level. But black Primitive Baptists, evidently motivated by the same concerns as the National Baptists, believed their interests would be served by forming a convention or national group. Led by Clarence Francis Sams, James H. Carey, and George S. Crawford, most of the participants in the formation of the convention were from the South. E. J. Barry, in the 1850s, established a Primitive Baptist Publishing House in North Carolina. Primitive Baptists share many Baptist doctrines, but they are Calvinist in their views of predestination and other matters relating to salvation. They practice closed Communion; that is, they do not share the sacred ritual with persons outside the local congregation. In addition to the two Baptist ordinances of baptism and the Lord's Supper, Primitive Baptists also practice foot washing and retain a strong emphasis on congregational polity and independence. Some estimates of the membership range up to 250,000.

In the early twenty-first century, Baptist churches and denominations have continued to play a leading role in the lives of African Americans and the nation. Constituting a majority of black religious adherents, the Baptists, especially those of the National Baptist family, in recent decades have shown through dialogue and collaboration among themselves, other black denominations, and other religious bodies that they wish to make an even greater organized contribution to religious and civic society in the present and future.

**See also** *African American* entries; *Baptists* entries; *Evangelicals* entries; *South as Region.*

Sandy Dwayne Martin

## BIBLIOGRAPHY

Fitts, Leroy. *A History of Black Baptists.* Nashville: Broadman Press, 1985.

Higginbotham, Evelyn Brooks. *Righteous Discontent: The Women's Movement in the Black Baptist Church, 1880–1920.* Cambridge, Mass.: Harvard University Press, 1993.

Lincoln, C. Eric, and Lawrence H. Mamiya. *The Black Church in the African American Experience.* Durham, N.C.: Duke University Press, 1990.

Mamiya, Lawrence H. "National Baptist Convention of America." In *Encyclopedia of African and African-American Religions,* ed. Stephen D. Glazier, 208–210. New York: Routledge, 2001.

———. "National Baptist Convention, USA, Inc." In *Encyclopedia of African and African-American Religions,* ed. Stephen D. Glazier, 210–212. New York: Routledge, 2001.

Martin, Sandy D. *Black Baptists and African Missions: The Origins of a Movement.* Macon, Ga.: Mercer University Press, 1989.

McBeth, H. Leon. *A Sourcebook for Baptist Heritage.* Nashville: Broadman Press, 1990.

Newsome, Clarence G. "A Synoptic Survey of the History of African American Baptists." In *Dictionary of African American Religious Bodies.* 2nd ed., ed. Wardell J. Payne, 20–31. Washington, D.C.: Howard University Press, 1995.

Pelt, Michael R. "Baptists, Free Will." In *Encyclopedia of Religion in the South.* 2nd ed., ed. Samuel S. Hill, Charles H. Lippy, and Charles Reagan Wilson, 104–106. Macon, Ga.: Mercer University Press, 2005.

Washington, James Melvin. *Frustrated Fellowship: The Black Baptist Quest for Social Power.* Macon, Ga.: Mercer University Press, 1985.

Williams, L. H. "United American Free Will Baptist Church." In *Dictionary of Baptists in America,* ed. Bill J. Leonard. Downers Grove, Ill.: InterVarsity Press, 1994.

# Baptists: Denominations

More than fifty distinct groups in the United States claim the name Baptist in some form or another. Of the approximately 42 million Baptists worldwide, some 30 million reside in North America, congregating in over 100,000 churches. These groups span the nation, though they have particular numerical strength in the South and Southwest. Theologically they include fundamentalists and liberals, Calvinists and Arminians, and denominationalists and antidenominationalists.

Amid their differences Baptists share a variety of beliefs and practices that, while not necessarily unique to their particular form of Protestantism, become distinctively Baptist when combined in specific ways. These include a strong commitment to biblical authority as the primary guide for faith and practice, an ecclesiology centered in the concept of a believer's church comprising those who claim a personal experience of God's grace through faith in Jesus Christ, and immersion as the normative mode of baptism for those who have professed faith. Baptism and the Lord's Supper (sometimes called Holy Communion) are the two sacraments, or ordinances, of the church. Some Baptists add a third sacrament, the washing of feet as practiced by Jesus and his disciples prior to his crucifixion. Baptists also maintain that local congregations of believers are autonomous and that the authority of Christ mediated through the community of believers fosters congregational church polity. Other beliefs are liberty of conscience in the interpretation of scripture, the Reformation principle of the priesthood of all believers, associational fellowship between churches "of like faith and order," and a historic concern for religious liberty and the separation of church and state.

Beyond these standard beliefs Baptists disagree over many issues, including the meaning of church–state separation, evangelism and missions, predestination and free will, the role of women in the church and its ministry, denominational affiliation and associational relationships, open or closed baptism and Communion, and ecumenical relations with other denominations.

## Theological Differences: General and Particular Baptists

From the early days of their movement, Baptist denominations covered a theological spectrum that reflects historic differences born of seventeenth-century Arminianism and Calvinism. These distinctive positions revolved around questions of free will, election, predestination, and the nature of salvation. Some Baptists—General and Free Will groups—solidly support Arminian views, while others—Primitive and Old Regular Baptists—are staunchly Calvinist in their theological orientation. Still others reflect a blend of the two views, drawing on both traditions to create a more moderate theological system.

General Baptists, the first of the Baptist communions, were formed about 1609 by a group of English Separatist exiles in Amsterdam, some of whom returned to London in 1612. These Baptists, who wished to separate from the Church of England, were influenced by the work of a Dutch theologian, Jacob Arminius, and his response to Reformed theology, especially the ideas of divine sovereignty and the nature of Christ's atoning death. They believed that although human beings were tainted by original sin, they retained the free will to accept or reject God's grace. Prevenient (enabling) grace "cooperated" with God's saving grace to accomplish salvation. All persons potentially could be elected to salvation, but only those who came on the terms of election—repentance and faith—could actually claim such grace. Christ's death on the cross was a general atonement, efficacious for the sins of the entire world (hence the name General Baptists). If individuals had the free will to accept Christ, they also had the free will to reject him along the way; therefore, "falling from grace" was a distinct possibility.

By the 1630s another group of Baptists had appeared on the English scene. Many were Puritan Congregationalists (independents) who accepted the practice of infant baptism. These Particular, or Calvinist, Baptists organized around the theology of the Geneva reformer, John Calvin. They believed that all persons were depraved and thus had no inherent free will whereby they might move toward salvation. Redemption was possible only through the infusion of grace given unconditionally by God to those elected to salvation before the foundation of the world. Christ's death was limited in its application only to the elect. The elect might resist grace for a time, but ultimately it would overwhelm them, bringing the regeneration that produced the necessary repentance and faith. The elect would be kept by divine grace, persevering in Christian living until the end.

## The Colonial Period: Regular and Separate Baptists

These differing Arminian and Calvinist positions have shaped the theology of various Baptist groups from the first colonial Baptist churches founded in Rhode Island in the 1630s to the present day. These early churches included General, Particular, Seventh Day, and other groups of Baptists. By the 1700s, as the fervor of the First Great Awakening moved through the American colonies, Baptists, like other Protestant denominations, divided over support of revival theology and methodology. The name Regular Baptist was given to those who, while affirming the need for conversion, shied away from the exuberance of revivalist methods. They favored orderly worship and erudite sermons, sang the Psalms as the only divinely inspired hymnody, encouraged an educated ministry, and discouraged "enthusiastical" conversion.

Separate Baptists were Calvinists who modified their theology, preaching as if everyone could be saved while insisting that God would use such preaching to awaken the elect. Their services were characterized by powerful preaching and emotional conversions. Many feared that education, especially in ministers, would contribute to a lifeless dogmatism that stifled the Holy Spirit. The influence of Regular and Separate Baptists remains evident in various Baptist subdenominations across the United States.

## General Baptists

General Baptists came to America in the 1600s and were present in many of the earliest colonial Baptist churches, including the First Baptist Church of Providence, Rhode Island, the original Baptist congregation in America. They struggled, however, because of problems in organization, clarity of theological views, and scarcity of church buildings. Many moved toward Calvinism or entered other Arminian-oriented Protestant communions. Some eventually became part of the Free Will Baptist tradition. By 1800 General Baptists were in sharp decline.

In 1823 an Indiana preacher named Benoni Stinson (1798–1869) founded a new General Baptist church in Evansville, Indiana, and began a movement to revive Arminian views. In 1824 he helped establish the Liberty Baptist Association in Indiana, a new gathering of General Baptist churches. In 1870 the General Association of General Baptists was established with the assertion that "Christ tasted death" for everyone through his general atonement for the sins of the world. General Baptists stress the need for salvation and the possibility that all persons may choose grace by faith in Christ. They practice baptism by immersion, celebrate the Lord's Supper, and share in the washing of feet. General Baptists support Oakland City College, an undergraduate school in Indiana. Their publishing house, Stinson Press, is housed at the national headquarters in Poplar Bluff, Missouri. They claim about 70,000 members from churches located largely in the South and Midwest, including Tennessee, Missouri, Illinois, Arkansas, Michigan, and Kentucky.

## American Baptist Churches in the United States

The group known as the American Baptist Churches in the USA (ABCUSA) traces its roots to the earliest Baptist congregations in the colonies, including the First Baptist Churches of Providence and Newport, Rhode Island. These churches helped to form the General Missionary Convention of the Baptist Denomination in the United States, in 1814, for the purpose of funding missionary activity at home and abroad. Known as the Triennial Convention because it met every three years, the organization was a clearinghouse for a variety of independent societies established to fund home and foreign missions, education, publishing and other benevolent endeavors. These included the American Baptist Home Mission Society, the American Baptist Foreign Mission Society, and the American Baptist Publication Society. When the Triennial Convention split in 1845 over the question of slavery, the southerners formed the Southern Baptist Convention and the northerners continued to work through diverse benevolent societies. By the 1870s women's missionary organizations had also been established.

The need for greater denominational efficiency led, in 1907, to the formation of the Northern Baptist Convention, a denominational mechanism for raising funds, conducting business, and strengthening organizations that conducted certain types of ministry. The American Baptist Home Mission Society worked diligently during these years to respond to the social and physical needs of people, many of whom had no previous Baptist experience.

Throughout much of the twentieth century, a controversy between fundamentalists and liberals brought numerous debates and divisions into the Northern Baptist Convention. From the 1920s to the 1940s conservative leaders tried unsuccessfully to reform the denomination in more specifically fundamentalist directions. The resulting schisms led to the founding of new Baptist groups, such as the Conservative Baptist Association of America, established in 1947 by individuals and churches that came out of the Northern Baptist Convention.

In 1950 the denomination was renamed the American Baptist Convention, and efforts were begun to extend connections between the various societies. In 1955 the women's mission societies were united administratively with the foreign and home mission agencies. By the 1960s connections had developed between societies such as the American Baptist Historical Society, the Ministers and Missionaries Benefit Board, and the American Board of Education and Publication. Judson Press remains the longtime publishing arm of the ABCUSA, offering resources for churches as well as texts in history, theology, and preaching. In 1972 a new organizational plan was approved, and the denomination's name was changed to the American Baptist Churches in the USA. The General Board of the denomination, with approximately two hundred members, encourages participation at every level of church and denominational life. Efforts are also made to make meetings and boards within the convention racially and ethnically diverse and inclusive. As a result of these efforts, the ABCUSA has become one of the most racially diverse denominations in the United States.

The ABCUSA is a diverse communion of Baptist congregations spanning theological positions from liberal to conservative, Calvinist to Arminian. It maintains membership in the National Council of Churches of Christ, the World Council of Churches, and the Baptist World Alliance. It has historic connections with Andover Newton, Colgate Rochester Crozier, Northern and Central Baptist Theological Seminaries, as well as the Baptist Seminary of the West. Many of its churches ordain women and call them as pastors. During the early years of the twenty-first century, the ABCUSA encountered significant controversy over homosexuality, specifically related to ordination, same-sex unions, and member churches that are "open and affirming" in their reception of gay members. The denomination numbers a little over one million members.

## Seventh Day Baptists

Seventh Day Baptists began in England in the 1650s. These Baptists practiced baptism by immersion, the laying on of hands, foot washing, and congregational polity, within the context of a believers' church. They also insisted that certain laws set forth in the Hebrew scriptures were not negated by the coming of Christ, chief among them being the Ten Commandments. They refused to substitute the first day of the week as the Lord's Day and called all Christians to return to the Sabbath as God's day of rest and worship.

Seventh Day Baptists were present in the First Baptist Churches of Providence and Newport, Rhode Island, by the late 1600s. Ultimately, these groups of "Sabbatarians" departed those churches to found their own congregations built around the basic teachings of Jesus and the Ten Commandments. New England and Pennsylvania were early centers of Seventh Day Baptist church life, and in 1801 the General Conference of Seventh Day Baptists was founded in Rhode Island. By the 1840s the denomination had formed mission societies for ministry at home and abroad. Many of the early Sabbatarians opposed slavery, secret lodges (Masons), and excessive use of alcohol. During the twentieth century they were among the earliest Baptist participants in the World and National Council of Churches, the Baptist World Alliance, and other ecumenical groups.

## Appalachian Baptist Groups

The Appalachian region was an early seedbed of Baptist influence, producing some of the most distinctive members of the Baptist groups. These "mountain churches" share numerous characteristics that include fierce independence, staunch theological and ethical conservatism, a strong sense of family and community, suspicion of broad denominational alliances, and a desire to preserve the "primitive" traditions of Christian origins as evidenced in their historic Baptist practices. Many of these churches developed limited denominational identities as a result of controversies over missions and mission boards, revivals, worship, and certain theological differences. Their churches often reject any translation of the Bible apart from the King James Version, and their preachers are generally "bivocational," with little or no salary from their churches. They have often been looked down on by members of certain larger and more regionally diverse Baptist groups, some of whom gave these mountain churches the pejorative label of "hyper-Calvinist." Some Baptist denominations sent missionaries into Appalachia, often implying that no appropriate Baptist presence had been present in the region.

## Primitive Baptists

Although Primitive Baptist churches exist outside Appalachia, their strongest presence is found inside the region. Many of their practices reflect the traditionalism of old-line mountain churches. Their earliest organizational alliance began in 1826, with the decision of the strict Calvinist Kehukee Association in North Carolina to oppose formation of mission societies, theological seminaries, and denominational systems that were outside local churches or regional church fellowships. These Baptists insisted that the "primitive" (meaning the earliest and most biblically orthodox) churches knew nothing of mission societies or denominational agencies. Their leaders also declared that sending missionaries, holding revivals, and establishing Sunday schools ultimately undermined orthodox (Calvinist) theology by implying that all persons could be saved (not simply the elect) and offering a "works-righteousness" approach to salvation grounded in human behavior rather than in divine sovereignty and predestination.

Primitive Baptists cultivated a distinct worship style that often included outdoor baptisms; the Lord's Supper and foot washing; shaped-note or plainsong hymnody unaccompanied by musical instruments; bivocational pastors given to sing-song preaching ("the holy whine"); and close associational relationships between churches, many of which were located in rural areas deep in the mountains of Appalachia.

During the nineteenth century Primitive Baptists led in the "antimission" movement that divided Baptist churches, especially in the South. Churches and associations that previously had been in fellowship with one another split over the biblical, theological, and practical implications of missionary endeavors.

Primitive Baptists maintain a loose fellowship of churches with no elaborate denominational organization. More recently, certain congregations have developed a more intentional evangelicalism in their efforts to proclaim the gospel. Some even fund various types of ministries that could be considered missionary endeavors developed for local churches. Many remain rural, "stem family churches" composed of a few core families who have intermarried over the years.

## Old Regular Baptists

Old Regular Baptists began in 1825 with the founding of the New Salem Association in Kentucky. The association and succeeding churches affirmed many of the same doctrines held by the Primitive Baptists, with some significant distinctions. Old Regulars softened the doctrine of election with their suggestion of "election by grace," the belief that salvation by grace may be sought by anyone and is both the process for and the conclusion of election. Sinners may pursue salvation that only God can bestow. Free will is thus possible even as election determines the recipients of God's grace.

Old Regulars are antimission Baptists who reject Sunday schools, religious radio broadcasts, and revivals or other forms of evangelistic outreach. Their preaching and worship

often reflect greater emotional enthusiasm than their Primitive Baptist counterparts. They wash feet and celebrate the Lord's Supper and baptismal immersion. Many observe the Lord's Supper only once a year. Their ministers often appear to chant the gospel and preach in a distinctive sing-song manner. Their annual associational meetings (homecomings) include business meetings, preaching services, and memorials to members who died in the past year. Many practice particular dress codes aimed at contributing to the modesty of men and women. Their "holiness code" discourages divorce, prohibits musical instruments in church, and limits discussion of church business to men. Old Regulars claim approximately 19,000 members in 326 congregations located in states that include Arizona, Florida, and Maryland, as well as the District of Columbia.

## United Baptists

United Baptists began in the late 1700s and early 1800s, especially in Kentucky, as a result of efforts on the frontier to bring together Regular and Separate Baptists. Many of the beliefs and practices of the United Baptists parallel those of the Old Regulars. They insist that salvation comes only from grace but is conditioned on fulfilling other biblical mandates related to repentance and faith. They believe that foreign missions have no place in a New Testament–based church, even as they urge their bivocational ministers to preach the gospel wherever they live and work. They refuse to support formal ministerial training and insist that women must not occupy any leadership roles in the congregation. They practice immersion following a confession of faith, share yearly communion, and wash feet as a sign of true Christian community. They report more than 75,000 members in almost 500 churches in over 100 counties, largely in Kentucky, Virginia, and Tennessee.

## Regular Baptists

Regular Baptists trace their origins to the colonial Regular Baptists of the 1700s. They share common doctrines with other Appalachian Baptist groups with an emphasis on such Primitive Baptist dogmas as divine sovereignty, unconditional election, and Christ's limited atonement. However, like the Old Regular Baptists, they favor the idea of election by grace and often seem more classically evangelistic, allowing churches to conduct Sunday schools and revival meetings. Some Regular Baptist churches also utilize a more contemporary style of gospel music in their services, but they generally reject the use of musical instruments in worship. They have a very small membership, perhaps fewer than 500 people, with churches in three North Carolina associations known as Little Valley, Mountain Union, and Little River.

## Union Baptists

Union Baptists grew out of a dispute over support for the North during the Civil War. By 1867 the Silas Creek fellowship in Ashe County, North Carolina, was formed by churches that had supported the Union during the war. Four associations remain active today: the Mountain Union Association, the Union Baptist Association, the Primitive (Union) Baptist Association, and the Friendship Association, all in North Carolina. Union Baptists reflect a greater appreciation for evangelism than some of their counterparts through Sunday schools and revivals, with an emphasis on election by grace. They allow members to broadcast music and preaching on local radio stations as a witness for Christ. Members are also permitted to attend services in other types of Baptist churches, a practice sometimes discouraged by other mountain congregations. Most churches reject the use of musical instruments, choirs, and other formal singing groups. Some churches continue to "line out" the hymns with the leader singing a phrase that is repeated by the worshiping congregation.

## Duck River and Kindred Baptists

The Duck River and Kindred Baptists group, often called the General Association, is located primarily in counties in Georgia, Kentucky, Tennessee, and Alabama, and has more than 10,000 members. The movement seems to have come from a group of Baptists in the Elk River Association in Tennessee, founded in the early nineteenth century. The new Duck River Association was composed of persons who reacted against the strict Calvinism of the region. Members affirmed the role of free will and human choice in the process of salvation. As "liberal" or modified Calvinists, the Duck River and Kindred Baptists used the terminology of Calvinism but restated it in terms of revivalistic conversionism and human free will. They practice three ordinances: the baptism of believers, the annual observance of the Lord's Supper, and foot washing.

## Free Will Baptists

Free Will Baptists are not exclusive to the Appalachian region and reflect a wide swath of churches and ministries across the United States. They represent the largest of the Arminian Baptist groups. "Free-willers" trace their origins to two individuals: Paul Palmer, who started a church in North Carolina in 1727, and Benjamin Randall, who founded a Free Will Baptist Church in New Hampshire in 1780. Segments of those two groups came together in 1935 as the National Association of Free Will Baptists, but they split in 1962 with the founding of the General Conference of Original Free Will Baptists in Ayden, North Carolina. Randall, who was converted through the influence of colonial revivalist George Whitefield, led his segment of the Free Will tradition in a variety of progressive endeavors that permitted women to preach and exercise church leadership, opposed slavery, and admitted blacks to membership. Some of these New England churches merged with the Northern Baptist Convention in 1911.

From the beginning these subdenominations offered a response to the majority Calvinism while practicing open Communion and foot washing. The latter rite is understood to be of sacramental value and a continued reminder of Christian humility. Free Will Baptists maintain a membership of approximately 250,000, with almost 300 churches.

## Ethnic Baptist Groups

The Baptist presence in America has included a variety of groups that were related to ethnic groups who brought their Baptist identity with them or discovered it on arrival. Among these are Romanian, Hungarian, Polish, and Scandinavian Baptists, as well as several Asian Baptist communities. The Swedish and German conferences reflect the diversity of ethnically based Baptists but are not definitive.

The Swedish Baptist presence in the United States began with the arrival of Gustavus W. Schroeder, a Swede converted on a trip to America, baptized in New York, and nurtured by German Baptists on his return to Europe. Schroeder helped convert Frederick O. Nilsson, who was baptized by German Baptists and commissioned to return to the United States as a missionary. In 1848 Nilsson formed the first Swedish Baptist church in America. Greatly influenced by German Pietism, the Swedish Baptists thrived in the United States, and a General Conference was established in Illinois in 1879. The Swedish Baptist General Conference continues with more than 100,000 members. A theological seminary was founded in Chicago in 1871, and in time it became Bethel Seminary, and, since 1914, has been located in St. Paul, Minnesota.

German Baptist churches began in the United States by 1843, with the founding of the first congregations. The first

General Conference, which was established in 1851, eventually became the North American Baptist Conference (NABC). It exists today with a membership of more than 60,000, with almost 400 member churches. The Rauschenbusch family is one of the most well-known families in early German Baptist life in America. August Rauschenbusch and his son Walter (1861–1918) were teachers and pastors in German Baptist life. Walter Rauschenbusch's days as a pastor in Hell's Kitchen, an impoverished section of New York City, convinced him of the social implications of the gospel and the need for "Christianizing the Social Order." From his position as professor of church history at the Rochester Theological Seminary, Rauschenbusch became the "father of the Social Gospel in America." The German Baptists have held triennial meetings since 1865, and the denomination holds a variety of regional conferences across the United States. In 1944 the seminary was renamed the North American Baptist Theological Seminary, and in 1949 it was moved to Sioux Falls, South Dakota.

## Landmark Baptist Groups

The Old Landmarkism was a successionist movement that began in the South in the 1850s, with an effort by Baptist ministers J. R. Graves (1820–1893) and J. M. Pendleton (1811–1891) to establish the "marks" of the true New Testament church. In a treatise called *An Old Landmark Re-Set,* Pendleton, pastor of the First Baptist Church, in Bowling Green, Kentucky, gave the movement its name, which was based on Proverbs 22:28: "Remove not the ancient landmark, which thy fathers have set." Pendleton believed that a series of dissenting churches—Montanists, Donatists, Cathari, Waldensians, Anabaptists, and Baptists—moved through the centuries from the time of the New Testament and were "Baptists in everything but name." Graves, a longtime member of the First Baptist Church in Nashville, Tennessee, delineated the "marks" of the true church. These included the primacy of the local congregation of believers; the inability of nonimmersed (pedo-Baptist) ministers to participate in Baptist worship; and the beliefs that Baptist churches are the only churches to exist from New Testament times and that they are the only true churches remaining in the world. Because Baptists alone adhered to the true New Testament form of baptism, rebaptism was required of all who had not previously received Baptist-based immersion, no matter how long they had professed the Christian faith. The Lord's Supper was entirely a local church ordinance to be received only by members of the specific congregation in which it was celebrated.

## Baptist Missionary Association

Formed in Texas in 1900, the Baptist Missionary Association (BMA) took shape in the 1840s with a group of conservatives who opposed the formation of the Baptist General Convention of Texas because it usurped authority that belonged only to local churches. Denominational formation of missionary boards and agencies contradicted the New Testament model of missionary work through local congregations. In 1879 a group of Landmark Baptists, expelled from the First Baptist Church, Dallas, for their divisive actions, formed the Live Oak Baptist Church, and in 1883 the church called Samuel A. Hayden (1839–1918), a prominent Landmark preacher, editor, and controversialist, as pastor. Hayden led the church to reunite with First Baptist, but he continued to publish attacks on convention leaders, charging them with heresy and dishonesty. Disciplined by the convention, for sowing "discord," Hayden brought suit against numerous Baptist leaders in 1898, a case that was finally concluded with an out-of-court settlement. Continued defeat in the Baptist State Convention of Texas led other Landmarkists to the founding of the Baptist Missionary Association. Although small, the BMA continues to promote fundamentalist and Landmark theology, send out missionaries funded only by local churches, and promote the "independence" of local Baptist churches free from denominational "hierarchy." It also promotes Landmark doctrines of Baptist successionism, closed Communion, and baptismal immersion, rejecting the validity of "alien immersion," administered in non-Landmark churches.

## American Baptist Association

The American Baptist Association (ABA) is another fundamentalist and Landmark group. Founded in 1905 as the Baptist General Association, it was renamed in 1924. Ben Bogard (1868–1951), a proponent of J. R. Graves's Landmark views, led in founding the ABA in opposition to state Baptist conventions in Arkansas and Texas. Churches affirm their independence from denominational alliances, their call to send out their own missionaries without the help of denominational boards, and the fundamentals of orthodox faith including biblical inerrancy, Christ's virgin birth, substitutionary atonement, and bodily resurrection. Its Landmark positions led the ABA to insist that Baptists are the only true church existing in an unbroken line of churches from the New Testament era. In spite of its suspicion of denominationalism, the ABA maintains a headquarters and publishing house in Texarkana, Arkansas. Its total membership in 2008 was approximately 800,000.

## Fundamentalist Baptist Groups

Although theological and ethical conservatism is imbedded in many Baptist groups in the United States, there are numerous groups that grew out of historic debates related to fundamentalism and liberalism during the twentieth century. These Baptist communions affirm the need for orthodoxy at every level of church life. Although the dogmas of fundamentalism are many, several of these groups give particular emphasis to the classic "Five Points," which include biblical inerrancy, the virgin birth of Christ, his substitutionary atonement, bodily resurrection, and literal Second Coming (premillennialism). Some are separatist fundamentalists who warn that any connection to liberal denominations or individuals is a compromise of the faith. Many were born of schisms that divided existing Baptist denominations. These included congregations such as Highland Park Baptist Church in Chattanooga, Tennessee.

## General Association of Regular Baptist Churches

The General Association of Regular Baptist Churches (GARBC) began as a response to what some felt was the liberal drift of the Northern Baptist Convention. In 1920 conservatives founded the Fundamental Fellowship of the Northern Baptist Convention, an organization that worked inside the convention for more than twenty-five years to create strategies for moving it in fundamentalist directions. Although many of its members wanted to remain in the Northern Baptist Convention and change the convention from within, others, insisting that it could not be changed, demanded separation from all signs of liberalism.

Separatists led by W. B. Riley (1861–1947), J. Frank Norris (1887–1952), and T. T. Shields (1873–1955) organized the Baptist Bible Union in 1922, and the group mounted strenuous attacks on the policies of the Northern Baptist Convention. The Baptist Bible Union formed Sunday school and mission programs, and acquired a Bible school in Des Moines, Iowa. The school soon went bankrupt after students rioted when trustees fired faculty and administrators. The General Association of Regular Baptist Churches officially began in 1933 as the successor to the Baptist Bible Union. Its leaders continued to promote fundamentalism as

the doctrinal center of the movement. They also developed a mission society called Baptist Mid-missions that became a clearinghouse for funds used by independent congregations to send missionaries around the world. The denomination, strongest in the South and Southwest, claims about 250,000 members. It continues to assert fundamentalist doctrines and practices.

## Conservative Baptist Association of America

The Conservative Baptist Association of America (CBAA) was founded in 1947 by a group of conservative–fundamentalists in the Northern Baptist Convention. Somewhat more "moderate" in their fundamentalism, many hoped to influence the NBC toward more conservative agendas, especially in the appointment of conservative missionaries and seminary professors. When it became clear that these changes would not occur, the group formed the Conservative Baptist Foreign Mission Society in 1943. Although members of the group requested recognition by the Northern Baptist Convention, it was not granted, and thus funds given to the new society would not count toward voting membership in the NBC. A formal division occurred in 1947, as NBC loyalists acknowledged it was time for the dissidents to go and the fundamentalists acknowledged that their views would not prevail in the parent denomination.

The new denomination founded a Home Mission Society and, in 1950, organized the Conservative Baptist Theological Seminary in Denver, Colorado. In 1951 members gained another seminary in Portland, Oregon, a school originally founded in 1927. At first, many of the CBAA churches retained "dual alignment" with the NBC, but those connections declined over time. Firmly fundamentalist in theology, the leaders of the new group preferred the designation "conservative" for their theological position. Promoting the well-known Five Points of orthodox dogma, they nonetheless experienced some division over premillennialism and specific details of Christ's return. In many churches, a thoroughgoing premillennial eschatology, or concern with the end of the world, prevailed. The CBAA continues to maintain strong connections to its seminaries and its missionary origins. It claims approximately 400,000 members in some 1,500 churches.

## Baptist Bible Fellowship

The Baptist Bible Fellowship (BBF) is among the strongest of a collection of fundamentalist fellowships born of controversies developing in the early to mid-twentieth century. These churches are unashamedly, often militantly fundamentalist in their orientation, promoting orthodox dogmas as nonnegotiable for those who would claim to be genuinely "born again" Christians. They are highly evangelistic in orientation, conducting seasonal revivals, warning unbelievers of "the wrath that is to come," and anticipating the premillennial return of Christ at any time. Many are separatist fundamentalists, rejecting any fellowship with those whose Christianity is deemed to be tainted by the world. They preach from the King James Bible, send out their own local church-funded missionaries, and denounce worldliness and secularism as evidence of the moral collapse of human society.

The Baptist Bible Fellowship began as a result of a schism in the fundamentalist ranks when a group of leaders in the First Baptist Church, Fort Worth, Texas, rejected the authoritarian leadership of the pastor, J. Frank Norris. Known as the "Texas Tornado," Norris was an early leader in Baptist fundamentalism, attacking the Baptist General Convention of Texas and the Southern Baptist Convention as requiring an organizational conformity that denied the authority of local congregations. Norris's efforts to control both the First Baptist Church and the church-owned Baptist Bible Seminary brought him into conflict with many leaders of the congregation. Various attempts to fire the faculty resulted in a schism in which his closest associates, Louis Entzminger (1878–1956) and G. Beauchamp Vick (1901–1975), moved to Springfield, Missouri, where in 1950 they founded the Baptist Bible Fellowship. They also organized a new Baptist Bible College and a periodical called the *Baptist Bible Tribune*. Both the school and the journal became important vehicles for extending Baptist fundamentalism throughout the twentieth century. The *Tribune* has long published scathing commentaries on the evils of liberalism in the church and in the larger society, attacking the civil rights movement and denouncing Martin Luther King Jr. (1929–1968) as un-Christian, fretting about liberalism at Texas-based Baylor University and other schools of Baptist origin, and promoting crusades for school prayer and against abortion, communism, and the ecumenical movement. Largely Landmark in its understanding of the church, the BBF is not considered a denomination by its adherents but a loose gathering of pastors who serve fundamentalist Baptist churches. Many BBF-related congregations were among the first "megachurches" in the United States, developing a variety of marketing techniques for attracting and evangelizing large numbers of people.

## Newer Baptist Groups

The Alliance of Baptists was founded in 1986 by a group of Southern Baptists distressed by the continuing controversy between "moderates" and "conservatives" in the denomination. Originally called the Southern Baptist Alliance, it was established as a way of reasserting Baptist principles of local autonomy, soul competency, and religious liberty that founders felt were being negated in the Southern Baptist Convention debates. Based in Washington, D.C., the alliance holds an annual national conference and facilitates missionary and social endeavors among member churches. Member churches are more likely than most Baptists to support women in the ministry and to be "open and affirming" in matters related to gender and sexuality. The group also partners with other denominations, such as the Progressive National Baptists and the United Church of Christ, in various ministry actions.

The Cooperative Baptist Fellowship (CBF) is a configuration of "moderate" Baptist churches and individuals, many of whom came out of the Southern Baptist Convention after decades of denominational controversy. The group was founded in 1991 and maintains offices in Atlanta, Georgia. CBF member churches contribute funds that are used in its global missions program, fund a variety of related seminaries and divinity schools, and offer aid to Baptist-related groups such as the Baptist Joint Committee on Religious Liberty, Associated Baptist Press, and the Baptist Center for Ethics. Several state groups have developed their own networks for regional ministry and fellowship. CBF-related churches are often positive in their response to women in ministry and ecumenical engagement. In recent years the CBF has engaged in dialogue and cooperative efforts with a variety of Baptist and other Protestant communions.

Reformed Baptists are represented in various loose networks of churches, developed since the 1960s and reasserting principles of Calvinist theology in local congregations and interchurch fellowships. These congregations are often organized around certain seventeenth-century Particular Baptist doctrinal statements, such as the First and Second London Confessions of Faith. They emphasize divine sovereignty, election, predestination, and other Calvinist dogmas within the context of the believers' church, immersion, and local church autonomy. Various associations of Reformed churches across the United States maintain varying degrees of fellowship, some founding their own Bible schools and seminaries, often in local congregations. Some insist that Reformed theology is the only viable theological foundation for historic Baptist identity.

## Multiplication by Division

The diversity of Baptists was evident from the beginning across a spectrum that included Calvinists and Arminians, proponents of open and closed Communion, and advocates of congregational autonomy. Later Baptists divided over theories of biblical inspiration, the relationship between church and state, and issues related to regionalism, gender, and race. Yet they are unified around commitment to concepts of a believers' church, believers' immersion, associational relationships, congregational polity, and the priesthood of all believers. A concern for the centrality of the local church has led many Baptists to be wary of denominational systems or "top down" authority. Yet commitments to organizational and communal relationships continue to create a need for denominations in some form or another.

See also *Appalachian Mountain Religion; Baptists entries; Baptists: Tradition and Heritage; Fundamentalism; Latino American Religion: Mainline Protestants; Missions: Domestic.*

Bill J. Leonard

### BIBLIOGRAPHY

Dorgan, Howard. *Giving Glory to God in Appalachia: Worship Practices of Six Baptist Subdenominations.* Knoxville: University of Tennessee Press, 1987.

Grammich, Clifford, Jr. *Local Baptists, Local Politics: Churches and Communities in the Middle and Uplands South.* Knoxville: University of Tennessee Press, 1999.

Jonas, W. Glenn, ed. *The Baptist River: Essays on Many Tributaries of a Diverse Tradition.* Macon, Ga.: Mercer University Press, 2006.

Leonard, Bill J. *Baptists in America.* New York: Columbia University Press, 2005.

———. *Baptist Ways: A History.* Valley Forge, Pa.: Judson Press, 2003.

———. "Independent Baptists: From Sectarian Minority to 'Moral Majority,'" *Church History* (December 1987).

———. "A Theology for Racism: Southern Fundamentalists and the Civil Rights Movement." In *Southern Landscapes,* ed. Tony Badger et al. Tübingen, Germany: Stauffenburg Verlag, 1996.

McBeth, H. Leon. *The Baptist Heritage.* Nashville: Broadman Press, 1987.

Mead, Frank S., Samuel S. Hill, and Craig Atwood, eds. *Handbook of Denominations in the United States.* 12th ed. Nashville: Abingdon Press, 2005.

Shurden, Walter B. *The Struggle for the Soul of the SBC: Moderate Responses to the Fundamentalist Movement.* Macon, Ga.: Mercer University Press, 1993.

# Baptists: Sectarian

Baptists are usually described as independent, congregational people. Precisely what it means to be a Baptist varies from interpreter to interpreter. However, one may find several common characteristics, including acceptance of the Bible as authoritative in matters of faith and practice; a polity that stresses the independence and autonomy of each congregation as well as congregational rule; church membership only for believers baptized by immersion, thus resulting in a "believers' church"; and a symbolic rather than sacramental understanding of the ordinances. Baptists have adopted numerous confessions of faith that articulate their theological preferences, but they share no common creed and recognize no ecclesiastical authority beyond the local church. They also support religious liberty and the separation of church and state.

Defining Baptist sectarianism is not an easy task. For some the words *Baptist* and *sectarian* may seem synonymous. After all, Baptist and sectarian doctrinal stances on regenerate church membership and baptism by immersion for believers only, coupled with their free church and antiauthoritarian tendencies, do not lend themselves to ecumenism. Even so, defining *sectarianism* is not easy. Scholars are divided over whether the word *sect* stems from the Latin *secare,* "to cut," or *sequi,* "to follow." Assuming the latter, one may infer that in the broadest sense *sect* describes those who leave an established religious body to form a new one. As such, sects are voluntary organizations that do not conform to mainline norms with respect to doctrine, practice, or both. Sect leaders usually promise their followers a clear, "true" representation of biblical doctrine, while sect members tend to be fervent, devoted, and especially zealous for the sect's truth claims that separate them from everyone else.

If defining sectarianism is difficult, identifying the sectarians in Baptist ranks is equally so. Sects often reject mainline or traditional sources of authority such as the Bible, creeds, and church council decisions, but most sectarian Baptists remain staunchly committed to biblical authority in matters of faith and practice. Historically, some may be classified as sectarian because they differ from the established church on polity, points of theology, and hermeneutics (interpretations of texts). Some are sectarian because they differ from other Baptists over procedural issues. Further, throughout their history some Baptists have displayed more sectarian tendencies than have others. Over time a number of splinter groups emerged who espoused certain doctrines that dramatically distinguished them from the groups they had left. Thus, while retaining aspects of more "mainline" Baptists, these groups usually positioned themselves as more "pure" than their parent group. Even though sectarian Baptists foster exclusivism in the sense of their being outside the religious mainstream, they are open to receiving new recruits provided that the newcomers agree with the sect's doctrine and polity.

## Early Baptist History

Early American Baptists resembled their spiritual kin in England. Beginning in the late sixteenth and early seventeenth centuries English churches faced religious turmoil, much of which centered on the relative purity of the Anglican Church. Puritans claimed that the Church of England retained too many vestiges of Roman Catholicism. In addition to the Puritans, a host of dissenting groups and independents openly longed for a "pure" church, free from secular and sacral corruption.

Early British Baptists were among those who wanted purity among churches. The earliest modern-era Baptists were identified according to their understanding of Christ's atonement. General Baptists held to the idea of a "general atonement" in which Christ died for everyone without exception. One need only repent and believe for salvation. General Baptists also maintained that if faith was voluntary, individuals could renounce their faith and "fall away from grace." By contrast, the Particular Baptists were Calvinistic. They held to a "particular atonement" in which Christ died for a specific, unalterable number of people chosen by God before creation.

As seventeenth-century England lurched toward civil war, many came to North America to escape religious persecution and seek new opportunities. Roger Williams (1603–1683) was among the earliest colonists in North America. Ordained as an Anglican priest in 1627, Williams turned to Puritanism in 1629. He came to America in 1631 and soon ran afoul of the Puritan establishment for openly advocating freedom of conscience and criticizing Massachusetts Bay Colony leaders, who in his estimation were exploiting Native Americans. He was exiled from the colony in 1635, whereupon he turned to the Narragansetts, purchased a tract of land, and established Providence Plantation in what is now Rhode Island.

Williams's nonconforming tendencies led him to be a Baptist for a time. It is difficult to say with certainty, but it appears that he established a Baptist church in Providence in either 1638 or 1639. Soon afterward, John Clarke (1609–1676), also a religious exile from England, established a Baptist church in Newport. Despite the fact that Williams and Clarke had Calvinistic leanings, both Providence and Newport churches were likely mixed congregations of both Calvinist members, who believed that people were predestined for salvation, and Arminian members, who insisted that individuals accept God's offer of salvation of their own free will.

General and Particular Baptists had scarcely gained a toehold in North America before both faced a challenge from the Seventh Day Baptists. Like other early Baptists the Seventh Day Baptists searched for a pure church, and they turned to the Bible for direction. Unlike their fellow Baptists, however, their study of the scriptures led them to conclude that nothing about Jesus' life or ministry cancelled the Jewish Sabbath. Thus they adopted Saturday, the "seventh day," as the proper day for worship.

The Seventh Day Baptists appeared in America as early as 1665. Stephen Mumford, a recent immigrant to colonial North America and sympathetic to the Seventh Day doctrine, raised the issue of Sabbath observance in Newport. Soon a number of Newport's church members had openly embraced Sabbatarianism, the belief that the Old Testament's Sabbath was binding on New Testament Christians. The issue festered until 1671, when a group left the church to form the first Seventh Day Baptist church in the North American colonies. Although they never rose to the prominence of either the General or the Particular Baptists, the Seventh Day Baptists became a regular feature of North American religious life, leaving Baptists with three branches in its young family tree.

## Associationalism and the Great Awakening

Regardless of their doctrinal convictions, Baptists were not very strong in the American colonies. Roger Williams's *The Bloudy Tenent of Persecution* (1644), and *The Bloudy Tenent Yet More Bloudy* (1652), and John Clarke's *Ill Newes from New England, or a Narrative of New England's Persecutions* recounted numerous tales of mistreatment at the hands of colonial governments. Churches were small; converts few. Dogged by persecution and indifference, seventeenth-century Baptists struggled to survive. The eighteenth century, however, witnessed at least two noteworthy changes.

The General, Particular, and Seventh Day Baptists all practiced congregational polity, and each followed British precedent in creating associations whereby like-minded congregations met periodically and voluntarily for fellowship and mutual assistance. In 1707 a group of seven churches near Philadelphia formed the Philadelphia Association. America's middle colonies, especially Pennsylvania and New Jersey, tended to be more religiously tolerant and diverse than the other colonies, thus offering Nonconformists a relatively safe haven. Over time the Philadelphia Association proved to be the most successful Baptist Association in early America.

Theologically Calvinistic, the Philadelphia Association grew steadily throughout the eighteenth century. The association corresponded with churches along the eastern seaboard and helped create several new associations, including the Charleston Association in South Carolina and the Warren Association in New England. In 1742 they produced their own confession of faith, the Philadelphia Confession of Faith, styled after the Second London Confession with additional provisions for hymn singing and "laying on of hands." They also promoted literacy and education, as well as limited missionary work.

As the Philadelphia Association was gaining strength, a series of revivals commonly known as the Great Awakening triggered dissent within Congregational and Presbyterian churches. These revivals featured intense emotional conversion experiences along with a host of zealous converts. Not everyone rejoiced over the awakening or its fruit. The so-called Old Lights objected to the revival and its emotionalism, while the New Lights welcomed the new burst of religious enthusiasm and piety. The rift between those supporting the Great Awakening and those opposing it led to numerous schisms. Many New Lights left their churches to form new, pro-revival congregations, and others left to join Baptist churches.

Baptists were not the Awakening's most vociferous supporters, but they gladly added many of its converts to their numbers. By the mid-eighteenth century the Particular Baptists had come to be known as Regular Baptists, thanks in part to the Philadelphia Association's shaping of normative practices for its associating churches, as well as its reluctance to embrace some of the Awakening's perceived irregularities. That is, Regular Baptists welcomed the conversion of sinners, but they disapproved of the emotionalism and spontaneity associated with revivalism. The Awakening's sharp distinction between pro- and anti-revival camps and its subsequent transdenominational realignment led to the formation of a new group of pro-revival Baptists, the Separate Baptists.

Shubal Stearns (1706–1771) and Isaac Backus (1724–1806) numbered among the early converts to the Separate Baptists. Both Backus and Stearns played important roles in shaping religious life in America. Backus remains one of America's most prolific Baptist authors. A leading voice of the Warren Association, he along with John Leland (1754–1841), a Regular Baptist from Virginia, argued tirelessly for the separation of church and state. However, Stearns may be the most celebrated of all Separate Baptists.

Unlike Backus, Stearns apparently wrote nothing. Yet under Stearns's leadership Separate Baptist influence moved south from his native Connecticut, stopping briefly in Virginia, and eventually settling in North Carolina. There, in 1755, Stearns and his brother-in-law, Daniel Marshall, established the Sandy Creek Baptist Church in Liberty in what was then Guilford County. Stearns enjoyed a reputation for persuasive oratory, and the Sandy Creek Baptists quickly began spreading the message of Christ with revivalistic fervor. The Separate Baptists enjoyed considerable success, especially in the South. Within seventeen years of its establishment the Sandy Creek Church spawned as many as forty-two new churches. In 1760 Marshall and his wife, Martha, moved to South Carolina, where they labored for about a decade before relocating to Georgia. In both cases the Marshalls reportedly shared the Separate Baptist message with great passion.

Primary documents on the Sandy Creek Church and the Sandy Creek Association are scant at best. Theologically, the Separate Baptists were Calvinistic, but they shunned formal statements of faith. The first official, written statement of the Sandy Creek Association's beliefs came in 1816, forty-five years after Stearns's death. In reality, Separate and Regular Baptists differed more in style than in theology, with the Separates preferring emotional, freewheeling services over the more staid, formal services of the Regulars. In 1787 Virginia's Separate and Regular Baptists laid their differences aside and formed a new group called the United Baptists. Other states soon followed suit. In the early nineteenth century most United Baptists joined forces with the emerging missionary movement.

### Free Will Baptists

The Separates were not the only Baptists who originated in eighteenth-century American revivalism. The Free Will

Baptists are also rooted in the Great Awakening. Free Will Baptists stem from two different sources. In the early 1700s North Carolina claimed a small group of General Baptists. As early as 1727 Paul Palmer established a church in Chowan, in eastern North Carolina. Palmer's wife, Joanna, was the stepdaughter of a noted British General Baptist, Benjamin Laker. Palmer's persistent preaching of "free salvation" earned him and his followers the nickname "freewillers," hence, Free Will Baptist, or as some preferred, "free Baptists." Palmer managed to attract a number of followers in scattered North Carolina congregations, but most of these churches became Calvinistic in the 1750s as a revival of Calvinism swept the South.

Not all Free Will churches converted to Calvinism. Those churches who remained Free Will regrouped in the early nineteenth century, and by 1830 they had experienced a comeback. They were organized into quarterly meetings, and they affirmed an adaptation of the Standard Confession of English General Baptists titled, "An Abstract of the Former Articles of Faith Confessed by the Original Baptist Church Holding the Doctrine of General Provision with a Proper Code of Discipline."

Meanwhile, in New Hampshire Benjamin Randall (1749–1808) provided the second source of Free Will Baptists. Apparently converted about 1770, Randall briefly united with a Congregational church before joining a Baptist church in 1776. He chafed under Calvinism, however, and in 1779 a local council declared they could no longer continue in fellowship with him. In response to this indignity, Randall allegedly quipped that as long as Jesus owned him it didn't matter who disowned him. Like Palmer, Randall preached "free salvation" and openly accepted the descriptor "Free Will." Randall and his associates spread their teachings throughout New England, and by 1808 Free Will Baptists in New England numbered about six thousand.

Throughout the nineteenth century both the Palmer and Randall branches of Free Will Baptist life faced the challenges associated with denominational organization, not to mention internal squabbling. By the twentieth century a number of Free Will Baptists affiliated with the newly formed Northern Baptist Convention. Others refused to unite with the NBC and chose rather to form the Cooperative General Association of Free Will Baptists, in 1916. Meanwhile, Free Will Baptists in the South regrouped to form a General Conference in 1921. These two groups merged in 1935 and located their headquarters in Nashville, Tennessee.

## The Nineteenth Century and the Modern Mission Movement

The dawning of the nineteenth century and the rise of the modern mission movement was a crucial time for Baptists in America. The guarantee of religious freedom, along with the western expansion and revivalistic fervor, promised new opportunities for Baptists. Organized missionary activity captured the Baptist imagination more than anything else during this time. If the nation saw a "Manifest Destiny" in western expansion, Baptists saw it too and added their own spiritual twist to the mix.

In the early nineteenth century many Baptists embraced organized international mission work when Luther Rice (1783–1836) and Adoniram Judson (1788–1850) joined their ranks. Rice and Judson had sailed for India as Congregational missionaries under the sponsorship of the American Board of Commissioners for Foreign Missions. En route to the field, both decided to become Baptists. Judson stayed in India, while Rice returned to America to inform the board of commissioners of their defection to the Baptists and to solicit financial support from their new brethren.

On May 18, 1814, Rice met with interested parties in Philadelphia and formed the General Missionary Convention of the Baptist Denomination in the United States of America for Foreign Missions. Also known as the Triennial Convention because it met every three years, this body was open to a variety of missionary opportunities. The Triennial Convention encouraged the creation of education and publication societies, which most Baptists quickly embraced as reasonable missionary ventures.

With the new opportunities, however, came questions regarding missionary activity. Some wondered if churches should shoulder the responsibility for building schools and producing religious literature. Others claimed that the New Testament did not sanction organization for religious work beyond individual churches. Hence, critics claimed the newly forming mission organizations were both unnecessary and unbiblical, as were their non–biblically sanctioned administrators.

Three names are especially prominent among early missionary critics. Daniel Parker first gained notoriety among Baptists with a booklet titled "A Public Address to the

Baptist Society, and Friends of Religion in General, on the Principle and Practice of the Baptist Board of Foreign Missions for the United States of America" (1820). In this booklet Parker questioned the scriptural legitimacy of missionary societies and organizations. In a similar vein, John Taylor suggested that organized missionary work might infringe on republican values. His now famous broadside, "Thoughts on Missions" (1819), was also a polemic against Rice for what Taylor perceived to be disreputable means in raising money for missions. Finally, Alexander Campbell claimed that the New Testament did not sanction missionary organizations. Campbell ultimately left the Baptist ranks to restore what he called "the ancient order" of things, particularly regarding baptism, thereby launching the Restoration Movement. It is important to note that Taylor, Parker, and Campbell did not oppose evangelizing the unconverted. All three, however, opposed the expansion of missionary organizations beyond individual churches.

## Primitive Baptists

Primitive Baptists are among the most sectarian of all Baptist groups. They are a diverse lot, but their roots are in the antimission movement of the early nineteenth century. They are fiercely independent and noted for their extreme Calvinism. They also claim a unique worship style that features a cappella singing. Primitive Baptists shun Sunday schools and mission organizations, claiming they are man-made institutions and unnecessary. In addition to baptism and the Lord's Supper, most Primitive Baptists also practice foot washing as a church ordinance.

Unlike most Baptist sects, the Primitive Baptists did not have a single recognized voice for the movement in its earliest phases. As the concept of "missions" expanded, some Baptists argued that *they* followed an ancient way and that their doctrine and practice mirrored New Testament teachings. Hence, they styled themselves Primitive Baptists and rejected organized missionary activity and everything associated with it. The movement gained momentum through the 1820s and 1830s as churches and associations wrestled with the organizational shifts Baptists were initiating to fulfill their mandate for missions. Those who disagreed with mission work and its associated agencies and boards cited "Thoughts on Missions" (1819) and "A Public Address to the Baptist Society" (1820), along with "The Black Rock Address" (1832), named for Black Rock, Maryland, where those adopting it met, and other treatises, until Joshua Lawrence (1778–1843, a Baptist preacher in North Carolina, emerged in the 1840s as the leading voice for Primitive Baptists. Thus, in the case of the Primitive Baptists, the sect was formed before it had a recognized leader.

It was not long before the Primitive Baptists faced internal strife over points of doctrine and interpretation. Broadly considered, Primitive Baptists fall into either one of three categories. One group maintains that God has absolutely predestined all things. A second group maintains that God has predestined all things pertaining to the elect and their salvation, but not anything else. A third group, the so-called Progressive Primitives, are theologically Calvinistic, but they have adopted many trappings of more mainline Baptist churches, including Sunday schools, the use of musical instruments in worship services, and paid ministers.

## Two-Seed-in-the-Spirit Baptists

The Two-Seed-in-the-Spirit Baptists are arguably the most sectarian of all Baptist groups. Much like the Primitive Baptists, they came into existence during the antimission controversy of the early nineteenth century. Their founder, Daniel Parker, was born in Virginia, reared in Georgia, and moved to Illinois in 1817. He received a limited education, mostly from his mother, but he managed to attract a following among Baptists on the American frontier, first by opposing mission organizations and organized missionary activity and then by introducing his now famous doctrine of the "two seeds." In 1833 he established the Pilgrim Predestinarian Regular Baptist Church and then promptly relocated to Texas.

Parker had gained notoriety with a work titled "A Public Address to the Baptist Society" (1820) that questioned the legitimacy of newly formed missionary organizations. Six years later he published another work, "Views on the Two Seeds," in which he articulated his understanding of the "two seeds in the spirit." Parker argued that Genesis 3:15 describes "two seeds," one of the woman, the other of the serpent. These seeds are spread throughout all humanity. The woman's seed represents the elect, while the serpent's seed represents everyone else. Some have seen Parker's Two Seedism as an extreme form of Calvinism, but it may be more accurate to say that it represents Manichean tendencies among a small segment of Baptists, especially in stressing the difference between good and evil as found in the two seeds. What is not clear is whether Parker formulated his theology to buttress his strident antimissionism, or if his antimissionism stemmed from his two-seed theology.

## Landmark Baptists

Landmark Baptists follow a strict form of local church ecclesiology. The term *Landmark* comes from two biblical injunctions, Proverbs 22:28, "Remove not the ancient landmark, which thy fathers have set," and Job 24:2, "Some remove the landmarks. . . ." They share certain features with the Primitive Baptists; among them are the rejection of any ecclesiastical authority beyond individual churches, including mission boards and other "sending agencies." But unlike the Primitive Baptists, Landmarkers support missionary ventures and Sunday schools.

To understand Landmarkism, it is helpful to understand the impact of the Restoration Movement on Baptist life. The movement quickly gained headway among nineteenth-century Baptist churches under Campbell's leadership. The Restorationists, sometimes pejoratively called Campbellites, emphasized a "common sense" approach to biblical interpretation. They preached baptism by immersion for believers. Moreover, they claimed to practice a form of Christianity that mirrored the purest form of New Testament faith, thereby restoring the Bible's "ancient order." Baptists listened closely to Campbell's claims that contemporary Christianity had drifted from its first-century moorings. Many Baptists left their churches to follow Campbell. Others rejected Restorationist teachings, but the mission movement had raised questions of biblical propriety and the limits of ecclesiastical authority that they could not ignore.

Landmarkism became a regular feature of Baptist life in the South in the middle of the nineteenth century. Early Landmarkers claimed three leaders: A. C. Dayton (1813–1865) was a dentist by trade, but his novel *Theodosia Ernest* (1857) served as an excellent means of articulating Landmark sentiments through the eyes of a young girl on a spiritual quest to find the "true church." James Madison Pendleton (1811–1891), one of the most respected preachers and educators in the South, served as the second member of the "Landmark Triumvirate." Finally, James Robinson Graves (1820–1893), generally recognized as the father of "Old Landmarkism," served as the movement's most outspoken advocate.

A renowned controversialist, Graves served as editor of *The Baptist,* later renamed *The Tennessee Baptist,* from 1846 until his death in 1893. Graves claimed that Baptist churches were the only true churches; all others were merely "religious societies." In 1851 Graves and other like-minded Baptists affirmed the basic tenets of Landmarkism in what came to be known as the Cotton Grove Resolutions. The meeting posed a series of five questions: (1) Can Baptists, consistently with their principles or the scriptures, recognize those societies not organized according to the pattern of the Jerusalem church, but possessing different governments, different officers, a different class of members, and different ordinances, doctrines, and practices, as churches of Christ? (2) Ought they to be called gospel churches, or churches in a religious sense? (3) Can Baptists recognize the ministers of such irregular and unscriptural bodies as gospel ministers? (4) Is it not virtually recognizing them as official ministers to invite them into Baptist pulpits, or by any other act that would or could be construed into such a recognition? (5) Can Baptists consistently address as *brethren* those professing Christianity, who not only have not the doctrine of Christ and walk not according to his commandments, but are arrayed in direct and bitter opposition to them? Although Graves affirmed only Baptist churches as genuine Christian churches, he did not suggest that Baptists were the only redeemed individuals on Earth. Neither did all subsequent Landmarkers assign equal significance to each particular question posed by the Cotton Grove Resolutions. Thus Landmarkers tend to agree that there is no universal church, and there is no warrant for organizations beyond local churches.

Graves never left the Southern Baptist ranks, and Landmarkism did not cause a schism until the early twentieth century. In 1905 Benjamin Marcus Bogard and a number of Landmarkers formed the General Association of Baptists, renamed the American Baptist Association in 1924. In 1950 a group of individuals left the American Baptist Association and formed the North American Baptist Association, changing their name to the Baptist Missionary Association of America in 1968 to avoid confusion with the other group. Although some Landmarkers prefer to remain officially unaffiliated, they generally form voluntary associations for fellowship.

Landmarkism remains one of the most significant features of Baptist life, particularly in the South. In addition to fueling sectarian tendencies, Landmarkism provided mid-nineteenth-century Baptists with a polemical platform for countering Restorationist claims to biblical and historical authenticity. Graves and his followers claimed they were not restoring an ancient way. Rather, they maintained they were the legitimate heirs to New Testament Christianity. Additionally, Graves used his resources as a publisher to promote G. H. Orchard's *A Concise History of the Baptists* (1838).

Relying on Orchard, Graves claimed that Baptists could trace their lineage back to the New Testament era, thus legitimizing Baptist faith and practice. Following Graves's logic, sound hermeneutics and knowledge of history were all anyone needed to make a case for Baptist legitimacy.

## Other Sectarian Baptists

Certain Baptist sects are found mostly, though not exclusively, in the Appalachian region. The Primitive Baptist Universalists are among the more enigmatic of these sects. This sect originated in 1924, when the Washington District Association of Primitive Baptists divided over the issue of eternal damnation. Sometimes known as "no-hellers," Primitive Baptist Universalists share some beliefs and practices with the Primitive Baptists, including elements of worship style. They differ markedly from other Primitive Baptists in that they reject the Calvinistic doctrine of limited atonement whereby Christ died for the elect only, choosing rather to believe in universal redemption where everyone without exception is ultimately reconciled to God. Their designation "no-hellers" is misleading in that the Primitive Baptist Universalists believe individuals suffer their own hells on earth prior to death because of their separation from God.

The Old Regular Baptists are located primarily in Appalachia. They identify with an 1801 melding of the Elkhorn and South Kentucky Associations that brought the Commonwealth's Separate Baptists and Regular Baptists together as United Baptists. Eventually, this group experienced schisms, and those who remained gradually became identified as Old Regular Baptists. Theologically they tend to be Calvinistic, but they neither espouse individual election to salvation nor Arminianism, per se. Old Regular Baptists teach that Christ's atonement produces a call to individuals. This call leads to a personal awakening to one's own sinfulness, which in turn begins a spiritual odyssey to ultimate repentance and faith. Old Regular Baptists continue certain practices including an unpaid clergy, "lined singing," annual foot-washing ceremonies, and gender-segregated congregations. They shun Sunday schools, and they prefer to baptize individuals in running streams.

The United Baptists trace their origins to the late eighteenth and early nineteenth centuries. The main distinction between the Separates and the Regular Baptists amounted to worship style, not doctrine. Ultimately, these groups began laying aside their differences and seeking union. The Kehukee Association (Regular) and the Sandy Creek Association (Separates) in North Carolina entered into discussions as early as 1772, the year after Shubal Stearns's death. In 1787 the Ketocton Association (Regular) and the Separate Baptists of Virginia united; they were followed by the Elkhorn Association (Regular) and the South Kentucky Association (Separate), who united in 1801. Having laid aside their differences, they became known as United Baptists.

Because of their missionary enthusiasm, many United Baptists joined forces with larger missionary groups like the Southern Baptists. Those who remained United Baptists are diverse in their views. Some are theological Arminians; some are Calvinists. Some United Baptists correspond with Free Will groups. They are located primarily east of the Rocky Mountains and in the southeastern United States, but they can be found in Arkansas and as far north as Michigan.

## Interpretive Constructs

If modern Baptists emerged from conflict, perhaps it is not surprising that conflict became a way of life for them. Their devotion to a "free church" combined with local church independence and the lack of any centralized authority has both helped and hindered Baptist development. On the one hand, Baptist polity is flexible, and this flexibility enabled them to adapt to changing social and cultural norms, especially in North America. On the other hand, Baptist polity has traditionally fostered political and ecclesiastical antiauthoritarianism, thereby facilitating schism and the proliferation of various sects.

Baptist ecclesiology by definition furnishes its followers with sectarian tendencies. Their insistence on a gathered church of baptized believers and their insistence on freedom of conscience marked them as radically different from the colonies' established churches. Moreover, America's earliest Baptists tended to carry over theological and polity issues from Britain, thus reinforcing arguments by late-twentieth-century social historians that American colonists tended to see themselves as British, not distinctly American. If early American Baptists tended to see themselves as British, they also tended to replicate those ecclesiastical structures with which they were most familiar, reinforcing an emerging consensus that American religious practices, at least through the eighteenth century, were neither exceptional nor uniquely American.

The early nineteenth century marked a dramatic shift for Baptists in America. Religious liberty as guaranteed by the First Amendment teamed with revivalistic fervor to create new opportunities for religious expression. Baptists used their newfound liberty to their best advantage. Their rapid growth merged them into America's religious mainstream, and they were no longer "outsiders." Earlier generations had gauged orthodoxy by doctrinal or polity standards, and although subsequent generations did not abandon their pursuit of doctrinal purity, missions opened new doors for cooperation and controversy.

The rise of the modern mission movement marked a dramatic shift in Baptist thinking about polity, procedure, and large-scale organization. The resources necessary for intercontinental mission work demanded new organizational structures previously unknown among Baptists. Some embraced these new structures, while others did not. Once missions came to dominate Baptist thinking, defining what constituted sectarianism became largely a matter of how or if sects related to missionary activity.

Missions also shaped denominationalism for Baptists. Prior to the nineteenth century Baptists were at best on America's religious periphery. Religious liberty, as well as the organizational impetus missions provided, helped create a denominational identity for Baptists by which non-missionary Baptists would appear sectarian. Consequently, Seventh Day and Free Will Baptists, two of America's earliest sects, quickly became non–sect like as they organized missionary boards and eased into the religious mainstream. Others, however, like the Two Seeders and the Primitives, demonstrated no desire to win the world to their viewpoint or their doctrinal convictions and remained on the fringe.

Organized mission work and the specific organizational structures Americans created to evangelize the world may have widened the gap between American and British Baptists. Granted, the American and British experiences had never been identical. Still, they shared many similarities at least throughout the colonial era. They continue to share certain doctrinal similarities. However, organized missionary activity accentuated existing differences and likely created new ones.

Baptist sects were often born in controversy. Early sects were born in the struggle for religious liberty, a struggle that migrated to America from England. Later controversies led to schisms that led to new sects. Most Baptist sects formed because of disputes over fine points of doctrine. Once formed, however, many sects faced further schism, with some opting to cooperate with other Baptist networks and others choosing to remain sectarian for cultural rather than doctrinal reasons.

## Contributions

Sectarian Baptists have enriched the American social, political, and religious landscape even though they may be the last ones to acknowledge it. For example, by defining themselves against prevailing norms whether doctrinal or organizational, sectarian Baptists helped affirm dissent as a Baptist hallmark. For better or worse, dissent and its consequences have played crucial roles in shaping the American Baptist experience. Baptist sects also demonstrate that there is more than one way to be Baptist.

As dissenting sectarians, Baptists helped secure religious freedom. They were not single-handedly responsible for religious liberty, but they were among its most outspoken advocates. Further, their continuing legacy of maintaining the separation of church and state remains one of their enduring contributions to American society.

By dissenting among themselves, sectarian Baptists have proved to be invaluable for Baptist self-definition. Sectarians pushed the bounds of acceptable doctrinal belief and ecclesiastical practice. In other words, Baptist sects have helped "mainline" Baptist groups define themselves in terms both positive and negative.

Yet sectarian Baptists have done more than simply perpetuate dissent. Some Baptist sects have helped preserve worship styles and musical forms from bygone eras. They serve as a reminder that some among the faithful find comfort and identity in the "old ways" rather than in the most recent theological trends. Because Baptists insist that religious worship be a voluntary act, sect members follow the old ways by choice, not from coercion.

Finally, sectarian Baptists contributed to religious journalism, especially in the nineteenth century. Sectarians used newspapers, magazines, and books toward hortatory and didactic ends. Daniel Parker, James Robinson Graves, John Taylor, and others offered both a voice of dissent for their followers and a means of spreading their particular messages. In addition, many sectarian groups tended to promote their views aggressively, and their journalistic contributions forced all Baptists to consider their arguments carefully.

At the end of the twentieth century an estimated 90 percent of the world's Baptists lived in the United States. They have overcome persecution and animosity to become mainstays on America's religious scene. Ironically, as Baptists became more denominational and made the transition from despised sect to social acceptability, they retained certain sectarian impulses. These quarrelsome tendencies may be an important feature of their dynamism.

**See also** *Baptists: Tradition and Heritage; Baptists* entries; *Church and State: Revolutionary Period and Early Republic; Great Awakening(s); Missions* entries; *Stone-Campbell Movement.*

Keith Harper

## BIBLIOGRAPHY

Brown, Candy Gunther. *The Word in the World: Evangelical Writing, Publishing, and Reading in America, 1789–1880.* Chapel Hill: University of North Carolina Press, 2004.

Crowley, John G. *The Primitive Baptists of the Wiregrass South: 1815 to the Present.* Gainesville: University Press of Florida, 1998.

Dorgan, Howard. *In the Hands of a Happy God: The "No-Hellers" of Central Appalachia.* Knoxville: University of Tennessee Press, 1997.

———. *The Old Regular Baptists of Central Appalachia: Brothers and Sisters in Hope.* Knoxville: University of Tennessee Press, 1989.

Gardner, Robert G. *Baptists of Early America: A Statistical History, 1639–1790.* Atlanta: Georgia Baptist Historical Society, 1983.

Goen, C. C. *Revivalism and Separatism: Strict Congregationalists and Separate Baptists in the Great Awakening.* Middletown, Conn.: Wesleyan University Press, 1987.

Graves, James Robinson. *Old Landmarkism: What Is It?* Memphis: Baptist Book House, 1881.

Hassell, Cushing Biggs. *History of the Church of God.* Revised and completed by Sylvester Hassell. Atlanta: T. Lassiter, 1948.

Leonard, Bill J. *Baptists in America.* New York: Columbia University Press, 2005.

———. *Baptist Ways: A History.* Valley Forge, Pa.: Judson Press, 2003.

Lumpkin, William L. *Baptist Confessions of Faith.* Valley Forge, Pa.: Judson Press, 1969.

Mathis, James R. *The Making of the Primitive Baptists: A Cultural and Intellectual History of the Antimission Movement, 1800–1840.* New York: Routledge, 2004.

McCauley, Deborah Vansau. *Appalachian Mountain Religion: A History.* Urbana: University of Illinois Press, 1995.

Mead, Frank S., Samuel S. Hill, and Craig D. Atwood. *Handbook of Denominations in the United States,* 12th ed. Nashville: Abingdon Press, 2005.

Parker, Daniel. *A Public Address to the Baptist Society, and Friends of Religion in General, on the Principle and Practice of the Baptist Board of Foreign Missions for the United States of America. Views on the Two Seeds Taken from Genesis 3d Chapter, and Part of the 15th Verse.* Vandalia, Ill.: Robert Blackwell, 1826.

———. *The Second Dose of Doctrine on the Two Seeds.* Vincennes, Ind.: Elihu Stout, 1826.

Pelt, Michael R. *A History of Original Free Will Baptists.* Mount Olive, N.C.: Mount Olive College Press, 1996.

Sacks, Francis. *The Philadelphia Baptist Tradition of Church and Church Authority: An Ecumenical Analysis and Theological Interpretation.* Lewiston, N.Y.: Edwin Mellen Press, 1989.

Tull, James. *A History of Southern Baptist Landmarkism in the Light of Historical Baptist Ecclesiology.* New York: Arno Press, 1980.

# Baptists: Southern

The Southern Baptist Convention (SBC) is the largest Protestant denomination in the United States. Founded in 1845 because of divisions among Baptists over slavery and home and foreign missions, the convention developed an extensive network of local, regional, state, and national connections, inculcating a powerful sense of identity in generations of adherents. Characterized by strong evangelistic and missionary efforts, it weathered a controversy between fundamentalists and liberals in the 1920s, but encountered serious divisions over doctrine and ethics during the later twentieth century. Throughout much of its history, denominational unity was supported by a common southern culture, a strong sense of loyalty to the convention, theological conservatism, and evangelistic zeal.

Although the SBC maintains a national presence, the primary constituency of the denomination lives in the American South and Southwest. By the early twenty-first century, the SBC had experienced numerical declines and other demographic influences that mirrored those of other traditional American denominations. Controversies over theology and ethics led to significant changes in the organization and constituency of the convention. The history of the denomination is characterized by great numerical success within the context of southern culture and a wide array of public controversies and internal debates.

## Southern Baptist Beliefs

Theologically, Southern Baptists generally affirm classic doctrines associated with Christian orthodoxy and broader Baptist traditions. They affirm a belief in the authority of Old and New Testament scriptures along with the freedom of conscience that enables Christian believers, under God, to read and interpret the scriptures for themselves. Throughout the twentieth century Southern Baptists struggled with particular theories of biblical inspiration, especially those concerning the doctrine of inerrancy, a belief that the Bible is without error in every topic it discusses, as revealed in the original manuscripts of the biblical text. Debates over biblical inerrancy have caused great controversy in the ranks of the SBC. These debates were especially sharp in the 1980s and 1990s, leading to an exodus of many lifelong Southern Baptists who rejected attempts to make inerrancy the only viable method of biblical inspiration appropriate to the convention and its member churches.

Southern Baptists also insist that the true church on earth is to be composed of "believers only," those who testify to a work of divine grace in their hearts and receive baptism by immersion as a sign of that grace. Baptism and the Lord's Supper (Communion) are considered "ordinances" established by Christ for his church. Baptism is given to those who confess faith in Christ and request membership in the church. The normative mode of baptism is immersion, dipping the entire body in a pool of water inside the church or outside in a river, creek, or stream. Baptism is given to both adults and children, and some congregations permit the baptism of children during the preschool age. In certain SBC-related churches baptism is sometimes repeated for those who say they were not truly "saved" at the time of their original immersion. Indeed, the phenomenon of the rebaptism of Southern Baptist church members increased significantly throughout the late twentieth century.

Most Southern Baptists believe that the Lord's Supper is a symbol of Christ's death, to be taken in memory of him. Others affirm Christ's spiritual presence in the Supper. Churches generally celebrate the Supper monthly or quarterly, using unleavened bread and the "fruit of the vine," normally unfermented grape juice, a practice that developed with the rise of the temperance movement in the nineteenth century. A small number of Southern Baptist churches continue to use wine in the observance of the Supper.

Congregational polity is the normative form of government in Southern Baptist churches. Such congregationalism is grounded in the belief that the authority of Christ is mediated through the congregation of believers who vote on issues related to the calling and ordination of ministers and deacons, and the administration of church business financially and corporately. Southern Baptists place great emphasis on the autonomy of the local congregation as the basic source of authority for Baptist ecclesiastical life. Each congregation therefore is free under God to set its own bylaws, develop its own ministries, and promote its particular approach to Baptist theology and practice.

Local congregations may also choose to participate in regional Baptist associations, cooperating with other churches for collective ministry, fellowship, and mutual encouragement. State conventions link churches in a larger geographic region, often supporting Baptist colleges, children's homes, campgrounds, and other benevolent and evangelical efforts that one congregation may not be able to accomplish on its own. The Southern Baptist Convention system allows churches to join in funding theological education, missions, and a variety of other social, educational, and missionary endeavors. Member churches may send "messengers" to the annual meeting each June. Those messengers are full members of participating churches, charged to vote their consciences in matters that come before the convention.

Southern Baptists also affirm the priesthood of the laity even as they ordain persons for professional ministry, or the "ministry of the word." The two officers of the church are pastors and deacons. Pastors "preach the word," offer the "care of souls," and lead the church spiritually and administratively. Deacons are lay members of the church who serve the community of faith in a variety of spiritual and practical ways. Southern Baptists ordain both pastors and deacons with a service that involves the laying on of hands, thereby setting them aside for special service to the church. More recently some Southern Baptist churches have limited the role of the congregation in the fiscal and administrative activities of the church, utilizing business managers or committees of "elders" who represent the congregation in these matters. The congregational system represents a kind of overarching democracy in which many persons may participate in the overall life of the church in very direct ways.

At its best the priesthood of the laity and the work of the (ordained) ministry complement each other in extending the church's witness and teaching the faithful. Yet this democratic ideal often creates tensions related to the authority of pastors and congregational leaders. Indeed, clergy–laity conflicts are not uncommon in Southern Baptist life and can revolve around issues as varied as determining the nature of scripture or doctrine, where to build a new building, or what color to paint the church kitchen.

Southern Baptists have also given great attention to the divine imperative for evangelization, working to bring all persons to a "saving knowledge of Jesus Christ." Across the years SBC churches and individuals have established ways of "witnessing" to the lost, those who have never received a "personal experience" of grace through Jesus Christ. "Soul winning" classes, revival services, and other evangelistic campaigns have long been a part of Southern Baptist efforts to evangelize the nation and the world. These endeavors have been a major source of numerical growth for the denomination and its churches.

As in other Baptist groups, a concern for religious liberty has also characterized much Southern Baptist rhetoric and shaped certain practices. Although religious liberty was a hallmark of seventeenth-century Baptist religious dissent in England and America, much of that emphasis was lost or at least minimized in the late nineteenth and early twentieth centuries simply because Southern Baptists were the majority religious group in the South, a region dominated by Protestantism and, with a few exceptions, a region with limited religious pluralism. With the rise of the Roman Catholic influence in the South and Southwest in the post–World War II era, Southern Baptists again reasserted the separation of church and state, often out of concern that Catholics would succeed in their demands for state aid to parochial schools and other state-funded religious prerogatives. Through the Baptist Joint Committee on Public Affairs, founded in 1946, Southern Baptists joined other Baptist denominations in opposing what they termed "parochaid," the appointment of a U.S. ambassador to the Vatican, and other perceived encroachments on religious liberty. They also divided over U.S. Supreme Court rulings regarding prayer in schools, abortion, and the use of funds for "faith-based" programs. These divisions led the convention to sever its ties with the Baptist Joint Committee and, in 1988, establish its own Washington, D.C.–based office called the Ethics and Religious Liberty Commission.

## Beginnings of the Convention

Baptists in the North and the South were drawn together in cooperative endeavor in the early 1800s through efforts to fund missionary programs at home and abroad. The most explicit project began in 1812, when Adoniram Judson, Ann Hasseltine Judson, and Luther Rice accepted Baptist views while on their way to India as missionaries of the Congregational church. Realizing that they could no longer accept funds from the Congregationalists, they sent Rice back to the United States to seek Baptist support. In response, mission-minded Baptists formed the General Missionary Convention of the Baptist Denomination in the United States of America for Foreign Missions, in May 1814. Known as the Triennial Convention because its national meetings were held every three years, the organization became a clearinghouse for multiple "societies" that enabled Baptist individuals, congregations, or regional associations to pool their funds to support home and foreign missions, education, publications (a "tract" society), and other activities. Each of these societies was independent of the other, maintaining its own officers and board of directors. The "society method" allowed Baptists to carry out national and international ministries efficiently but within a context that was not hierarchical, given Baptist mistrust of ecclesiastical authorities that could undermine the sovereign autonomy of local congregations.

The Triennial Convention was the first truly national denominational experience for Baptists in America. Funds were raised and missionaries were sent to Burma, the Caribbean, and ultimately to China. The American Baptist Home Mission Society also sent out missionaries, such as John Mason Peck and his wife, Sally, who, in 1817, traveled west to the Missouri Territory to work with Native Americans and settlers. A Tract Society published materials for use in evangelization, as well as for biblical and doctrinal instruction.

With the rise of abolitionism, evident in the development of various abolitionist Baptist churches and associations, tensions arose over the issue of slavery, sanction (the idea that the New Testament in several places seems to sanction or approve of slavery), and ultimately the appointment of slaveholders as missionaries funded by the missionary societies. Many Baptist leaders in both the North and the South worked diligently to moderate the issue, keep it from dividing the Triennial Convention, and avoid denominational schism. In 1844, as abolitionists pressed their case, members of the Georgia State Baptist Convention requested that the American Baptist Home Mission Society appoint James Reeve, a southerner and known slave owner, to the society. When the society refused to respond to the request, Georgia Baptists cut off funds to the missionary society and appointed Reeve themselves, demanding that Baptists in the South convene a gathering that would found a new Baptist denomination.

The result was the formation of the Southern Baptist Convention at the First Baptist Church, Augusta, Georgia, in May 1845. The founders stated that the new convention was established to fulfill the church's missionary imperative, now impeded by the mission society's refusal to appoint duly called and certified southern (slaveholding) missionaries. The convention's organizational structure grew out of a plan offered by South Carolina pastor William B. Johnson (1782–1862) that involved greater connectional or "associational" cooperation between churches and denominational agencies. Instead of maintaining the loose cooperation evident in autonomous societies, Johnson proposed a more extensive connectionalism that linked local churches, regional associations, and state conventions with the national denomination in providing a variety of programs that could be coordinated more efficiently than those of the autonomous societies. These connectional relationships made possible more centralized administrative efforts and anticipated the growth of a powerful sense of "Baptistness" among clergy and laity alike. Indeed, after the defeat of the South in the Civil War, this denominational program combined with elements of southern culture to inculcate a profound theological and regional identity in SBC churches and members.

## The Development of Convention Agencies

The newly formed denomination soon set about forming its own agencies for accomplishing various benevolent and evangelical tasks at home and abroad. A Foreign Mission Board (now the International Mission Board) was founded in 1845, with headquarters in Richmond, Virginia. Funds came gradually, but before the Civil War the first wave of Southern Baptist missionaries were sent to such places as China, Liberia, Nigeria, and Brazil. The early China missionaries were a tough group that included Matthew and Eliza Yates, J. Lewis Shuck, T. P. Crawford, and Charlotte Diggs (Lottie) Moon (1840–1912). Lottie Moon's work was so exemplary that she became one of the Southern Baptists' best-known missionaries, an iconic exemplar of sacrifice and commitment. Teaching and preaching widely, Moon worked in several remote provinces of China, where she exhausted herself for the work of the mission, dying off the Japanese coast on her final journey to America. In response to her sacrifice, the Woman's Missionary Union (founded in 1888) named their annual foreign missions offering in her honor. Following the Civil War, the Foreign Mission Board expanded slowly but persistently, ultimately sending missionaries worldwide and establishing the largest missionary task force of any American Protestant denomination.

The Home Mission Board (now the North American Mission Board) was also established in 1845, with headquarters in Marion, Alabama, where it remained until 1892, when it was moved to Atlanta. The earliest Baptist home missionaries were charged with founding new churches, working with slaves (later with freed blacks), and Native Americans. Many SBC home missionaries ministered to soldiers during the Civil War. After the war ended in 1865, defeat left the board in such dire financial straits that it was almost abandoned by the convention. In 1882 the

appointment of Isaac T. Tichenor as corresponding secretary (director) led to a renewed effort to establish distinct Southern Baptist ministries, improve publications, and delineate regions of service from those covered by the American Baptist Home Mission Society (Northern). A conference held at Fortress Monroe, Virginia, in 1894, led to an agreement for mutual ministries to freed blacks, including educational opportunities, and terms for avoiding overlapping ministries in new home mission "fields." Work with African Americans may not have been as extensive as early reports from the board implied, however.

By the twentieth century, the Home Mission Board worked to establish new churches, provide varied social ministries in rural and urban areas, and offer cooperative endeavors with a variety of ethnic and immigrant groups. During the latter half of the century, Home Mission Board literature and action reflected some of the most progressive attitudes toward racial equality and reconciliation of any of the SBC agencies.

The Sunday School Board of the SBC took longer to develop, since many southern churches had no Sunday school at all, and many of those that did continued to use the American Baptist Publication Society (Northern) for their instructional literature. Early attempts at founding publication societies in the South failed on at least four occasions, until 1892, when, through the work of J. M Frost, the Southern Baptist Sunday School Board was established in Nashville to produce literature for the denomination and its churches.

With the growth of Sunday schools as a mainstay of Baptist biblical studies and weekly programs, the publication of Baptist-friendly literature became extremely important. The Sunday School Board thus accepted its role as the chief publishing arm of the denomination, developing a huge circulation for its products, and forming a large network of writers including clergy and laity and professors and students at Baptist schools. For many years the board utilized the Uniform Series of biblical studies, a lectionary of common scripture texts used Sunday to Sunday by a variety of Protestant groups. Gradually, Sunday evening study programs, such as the Baptist Young People's Union (BYPU), provided instruction in ethics, church history, and Christian living. A publishing house, known as Broadman Press (now Broadman and Holman), produced books on theology, doctrine, biblical studies, and discipleship, much of which was written by Baptist authors.

## Educational Institutions

Many of the earliest Baptist educational institutions in the South predated the founding of the SBC. These colleges were developed not by the national denomination but by specific state conventions that established varying degrees of charter relationships, appointed trustees, and provided funding for students and general operations. Such schools included Mississippi College (1826), Furman University (South Carolina, 1826), the University of Richmond (Virginia, 1832), Mercer University (Georgia, 1833), Wake Forest University (North Carolina, 1834), Howard College (now Samford University, Alabama, 1844), Baylor University (Texas, 1846), Stetson University (Florida, 1882), and numerous others. These schools struggled financially throughout much of their early history, but they provided undergraduate education for generations of young people who came from Baptist churches and often remained within the SBC system for the rest of their lives. Schools offered a basic liberal arts education, provided religion majors with preparation for the seminary and Baptist ministry, and extended Christian education by requiring Bible classes, mandating weekly chapel attendance, and offering a variety of religious activities—from religious emphasis week to campus revivals and summer mission trips. Baptist colleges and universities were major sources for inculcating Baptist identity into a new generation of young people, many of whom were the first generation of their family to enter college.

Southern Baptists began to establish their own seminaries in 1859 with the creation of the Southern Baptist Theological Seminary on the campus of Furman University in Greenville, South Carolina. In 1877 the school was moved to Louisville, Kentucky, a region less devastated by the Civil War. The seminary closed during the war and reopened after the conflict with one student and four faculty members. Firmly anchored in reformed theology the seminary founders required that all faculty members subscribe to the Abstract of Principles, a basic statement of Baptist doctrine. Faculty members are still required to sign the document. Five other denominationally owned seminaries were founded by the SBC during the twentieth century: Southwestern Baptist Seminary (Fort Worth, Texas), New Orleans Baptist Seminary, Midwestern Baptist Seminary (Kansas City, Missouri), Southeastern Baptist Seminary (Wake Forest, North Carolina), and Golden Gate Seminary (Mill Valley, California). They remain among the largest theological schools in the United States. Some estimates suggest that one in five American seminarians attends a Southern Baptist seminary.

To this day many Southern Baptists demonstrate something of a love-hate relationship with their educational institutions, strongly recognizing the need to provide a liberal arts education that opens intellectual, spiritual, and financial doors to southern youth, while also fearful that such schools will "steal the faith" of the young, introducing ideas that lead them to challenge traditional religious dogmas and cultural norms. Throughout the history of the SBC controversies large and small frequently descended upon the biology and religion departments of Baptist colleges over the use of certain textbooks, the historical-critical method of biblical studies, the teaching of evolution, and the role of women and African Americans in southern society. Disputes related to fundamentalist, conservative, progressive, and liberal approaches to biblical and theological studies have long characterized Southern Baptist seminaries.

## The Cooperative Program

The development of a collective giving program known as the Cooperative Program, approved in 1925, was an important illustration of the growth of the Southern Baptist Convention and its plans for the future. The program linked churches, state Baptist conventions, and the national denomination in common funding relationships. Churches sent funds to their respective state conventions that then forwarded a percentage directly to the denomination. Each state was permitted to determine the percentage of funds to be divided between the national and state conventions. Although it took many years for churches to come to full acceptance of the plan, the Cooperative Program ultimately became the lifeline of funding for collective endeavors undertaken by the denomination. Indeed, participation in the Cooperative Program became a major sign of denominational commitment for churches and individuals. Throughout the twentieth century, those who differed with denominational policies often withheld funds or simply complained about the financial uniformity demanded by denominational leaders.

In 1927 the Executive Committee of the SBC was linked to the Cooperative Program with the committee charged with managing the finances of the denomination, establishing funding agreements with the state conventions, and allocating the specific percentages received by denominational agencies. These efforts served to extend the connectional centralization of the denominational organization.

## A Confession of Faith

Although many of the early Southern Baptist churches were constituted around a confession of faith that laid out specific dogmas, the denomination itself had no official doctrinal statement until 1925, when the convention set forth its own confession of faith, entitled the Baptist Faith and Message. Its approval was due, at least in part, to the impact of the fundamentalist–liberal disputes that were dividing large segments of American Protestantism in the 1920s. The Baptist Faith and Message is based on an earlier document known as the New Hampshire Confession of Faith, first compiled in the 1830s as a modified Calvinist response to Baptists' increasing emphasis on free will, the general atonement (Christ's death for the entire world), and the imperative for world evangelization. The document touches on basic beliefs related to scripture, the nature of God, the Trinity, election, salvation, baptism, the Lord's Supper, the priesthood of all believers, church polity, academic freedom, clergy and laity, church and state, and "end times." The Baptist Faith and Message was revised in 1963, in response to controversies regarding the Bible and the rights of professors in Baptist schools. It was revised again in 2000, with particular attention given to a new entry noting that women are not to receive ordination to the pastoral office in a local congregation. The new edition addresses the need for opposition to such issues as racism, adultery, homosexuality, and pornography. Reference is also made to marriage as a divinely intended union between a man and a woman.

Although Southern Baptists are not required to subscribe to the Baptist Faith and Message in order to belong to a Southern Baptist church, most denominational employees—seminary professors, missionaries, writers, and trustees—are asked to make such a commitment. In recent years the denominational leadership has expressed concern that the SBC affirm and maintain a strong confessional identity, grounded in the orthodox doctrines of the official confession of faith.

## SBC Controversies

Southern Baptists are never without controversy on issues related to race, the Bible, denominational control, and innumerable doctrinal differences. Some of the most divisive debates include the following.

### Landmarkism

Old Landmarkism was a movement that developed in the 1850s, in an effort to trace Baptists in an unbroken succession back to the New Testament church and establish Baptist identity as the source of the true church. Landmarkists envisioned a "trail of blood" and martyrs who constituted the true New Testament church in every age and were Baptist in everything but name. These included Montanists, Donatists, Cathari, Waldensians, Anabaptists, and Baptists. Although this view of Baptist history was not new, it became more pronounced in Landmarkism. One of the early controversies related to the movement involved the question of whether pedo-baptist (one baptized as an infant) clergy could preach in a Baptist pulpit. It was concluded that they could not do so since they were not members of the true church and did not have a true New Testament baptism.

J. R. Graves (1820–1893) and J. M. Pendleton (1811–1891) were Baptist ministers who led the early Landmark movement, writing numerous works that delineated its doctrines. Pendleton's treatise, *An Old Landmark Re-Set,* gave the group its name; it was based in a statement from Proverbs 22:28: "Remove not the ancient landmark, which thy fathers have set." It was also an attempt to discern the marks of the true church in ways that identified Baptists as the clearest recipients of the biblical authority and churchly practice. Graves's views were published in 1880 in a work entitled *Old Landmarkism: What Is It?* In it he proclaimed that Baptists were the only true church, and that such a church was found only in the local congregation. Non-Baptist pastors could not share Baptist pulpits since their communions were mere "societies." Contemporary Baptist churches could be traced in an unbroken succession to Jesus and the early church; thus Baptists alone retained the authority to baptize and celebrate the Lord's Supper. Only Baptist immersions were valid; even those who had had a non-Baptist "alien immersion" were required to have a Baptist baptism. Only members of each individual church could participate in the congregation's celebration of the Lord's Supper. Since the local congregation was the only source of authority for the church, many Landmark leaders were critical of what they believed to be the hierarchical practices evident in Southern Baptist denominationalism. Some rejected the use of mission boards as unscriptural and insisted that missionaries should be supported directly from local churches.

Although Landmarkists sought to impose their views on the entire convention prior to the Civil War, their efforts were largely unsuccessful. However, their views live on in those congregations that require immersion of people who join their churches and had been baptized as infants. Thus many Southern Baptist churches require the immersion of new converts and old believers who have never received baptism by immersion. Although many Southern Baptist churches practice open Communion—inviting all baptized persons to the table—others continue to practice closed Communion, restricting participation to members of the specific congregation or those who affirm orthodox Baptist doctrines. One of the best-known controversies related to nineteenth-century Landmarkism occurred in the 1890s at the Southern Baptist Theological Seminary, in Louisville, when William H. Whitsitt, the seminary's president and professor of church history, published a book entitled *A Question in Baptist History,* suggesting that the earliest English Baptists had not practiced immersion until some thirty years after the movement began in 1609. Whitsitt's findings, now fully accepted by most Baptist historians, were a powerful threat to Landmark claims that Baptists preserved immersion in an unbroken tradition as established by Jesus in the river Jordan. Landmark denunciation of Whitsitt's views led to his resignation in 1899.

## Racial Issues

Born of the national schism over slavery, the SBC became the largest Protestant denomination in the segregated South, a racial position supported by a majority of convention members throughout much of the twentieth century. Integration of SBC-related colleges, universities, and seminaries did not begin until the 1960s, in many cases brought to a head over the admission of students from Africa, who had been evangelized by Baptists on the mission field. Many local churches were torn asunder over the admission of African American members, and pastors who stood against racist cultural norms were often summarily dismissed. Although many denominational publications promoted progressive views on race, some denominational leaders held membership in the Ku Klux Klan. Not until 1995 did the SBC apologize for its failures in the slaveholding and Jim Crow–based societies of the South.

## The Fundamentalism–Liberalism Divide

Debates between fundamentalists and liberals divided American Protestant denominations throughout the twentieth century, and Southern Baptists were no exception. During the 1920s and 1930s the Southern Baptist Convention weathered a challenge from fundamentalists, many of whom instituted what became known as the Independent Baptist movement. Denominationalists, already committed to theological and social conservatism, successfully resisted efforts by fundamentalists such as J. Frank Norris (1877–1952) to impose the classic "Five Points" of fundamentalism (the inerrancy of the Bible; the virgin birth of Christ; Christ's substitutionary atonement, through which he died for the sins of individual human sinners who believed; his bodily resurrection; and his literal Second Coming) as litmus tests for all denominational employees, schools, and member churches. Norris, sometimes known as "the Texas Tornado," was pastor of First Baptist Church, Fort Worth, and a frequent critic of Baptist seminary and college professors, denominational "lackeys," and what he saw as efforts by the convention to usurp the authority of local congregations. Norris's outlandish behavior and fundamentalist diatribes led to the expulsion of his church from the Baptist General Convention of Texas in 1924. In response, he helped begin a new group of Independent Baptists, identified by their fundamentalist views, evangelistic zeal, and congregational autonomy, loosely connected to the Baptist Bible Union and the World's Christian Fundamentals Association. A schism between Norris and some of his followers led to the founding of the Baptist Bible Fellowship, one of the largest groups of Independent Fundamentalist Baptist churches in the United States.

The Southern Baptist Convention managed to avoid a major schism by reasserting its doctrinal orthodoxy, its commitment to world mission and evangelism, and the need for denominational unity to accomplish these evangelistic tasks.

Following World War II, concerns again arose among many SBC conservatives regarding the "liberal drift" of the denomination, evident in such things as the use of the historical-critical method of biblical studies in college and seminary classes, social progressivism promoted by certain denominational agencies such as the Home Mission Board and the Christian Life Commission, Broadman Press's publication of books promoting liberal theology, and the support for Supreme Court rulings on prayer in public schools by the Baptist Joint Committee on Public Affairs. These concerns became full-blown controversies in the 1960s and 1970s related to the publication of various books by the denominational press. The publication of *The Message of Genesis* by Ralph H. Elliott, a professor at Midwestern Seminary, in 1961, led to a firestorm of opposition against his use of historical-critical methodology and its impact on doctrines of biblical infallibility. In response, Broadman Press refused to approve a second printing of the book. Although seminary trustees initially supported Elliott, his decision to have the text republished by another company led to his dismissal in 1962. Similar concerns developed in 1970, when the first volume of the Broadman Bible Commentary series was rescinded because its use of historical-critical methodology was thought to undermine the historicity of the Genesis accounts.

In 1979, in an effort to stem the tide of what they felt to be a rapidly developing liberalism in the SBC, a group of conservatives began a concerted effort to promote conservative–fundamentalist ideology at every level of the denominational system. Led by longtime conservative pastors Adrian Rogers of Memphis and W. A. Criswell of Dallas, as well as Houston Appeals Court judge Paul Pressler and Criswell College president Paige Patterson, the group determined that by electing a succession of SBC presidents and using their appointive powers to change the boards of trustees at each denominational institution, they could achieve a needed "course correction" against liberalism. The litmus test for those appointees was their commitment to the doctrine of biblical inerrancy and their desire to require that view of biblical inspiration of all denominational employees. Adrian Rogers's election as SBC president in 1979 marked the official beginnings of their efforts. Moderate Baptists soon responded, asserting their conservative credentials but resisting what they perceived to be a "takeover movement" on the part of the Religious Right. These political machinations brought huge numbers of "messengers" to the annual June meeting of the Southern Baptist Convention. Although many of the votes were close, the conservatives were able to win every presidential election and, over a decade (1980–1990), succeeded in appointing to each convention agency a majority of trustees who shared their views and their agenda for denominational change. By the mid-1990s conservatives were in firm control of the national denomination, extending the confessional requirements for denominational employees by revising the Baptist Faith and Message, and replacing large numbers of seminary faculty, missionaries, and other denominational employees who would not support the changes.

At the same time, new divisions erupted in state Baptist conventions, in Baptist-related colleges and universities, and among those moderate Baptists who moved slowly to found new organizations, schools, and programs. The Alliance of Baptists was founded in 1986 by a group of churches and individuals who desired to move beyond the SBC controversy in order to direct their energies in more positive

directions. They encouraged the establishment of a new theological seminary, Baptist Theological Seminary, in Richmond, Virginia, founded in 1991 as an alternative for moderate Baptist ministers. In 1991 a larger group of moderate Baptists came together in Atlanta to found the Cooperative Baptist Fellowship, a society of churches joining together for fellowship, encouragement, and common support for projects related to the church's mission in the world. State Baptist conventions also divided along conservative and moderate lines, with South Carolina, Georgia, and Florida drawn into the conservative camp and Virginia and Texas moving toward the moderates. Other conventions such as Alabama and Mississippi have been less divisive, while Kentucky and North Carolina continue to move between the various factions. Although some state Baptist colleges and universities remain under control of their respective state conventions, others have severed those ties in favor of self-perpetuating trustee boards and formal breaks with their parent bodies. Schools such as Meredith College (North Carolina), the University of Richmond, Wake Forest, Furman, Mercer, Stetson, Belmont, Samford, and Baylor now control their own boards of trustees. Some continue to receive funds from the state conventions, though most do not. Other schools such as Louisiana College, Shorter College (Georgia), and Union University (Tennessee) remain firmly connected to conservatives in their state conventions. Still others continue a traditional yet tenuous connection with their parent Baptist bodies. New divinity schools and seminaries with varying connections to the SBC controversy have also been established at Campbell, Gardner Webb, Mercer, Baylor, Hardin-Simmons, and Samford Universities. Baptist houses or programs have also been established inside divinity schools at Duke, Emory, Wake Forest, and Texas Christian Universities. The SBC continues to experience realignments and disconnections some thirty years after the original "course correction/ takeover" movement began. Although the departure of moderates did not immediately take large numbers of churches from the SBC, it did serve to deprive the convention of some of its oldest and most active congregations. The overall effect of these departures on the convention remains to be seen.

## Continuing Issues

At the beginning of the twenty-first century, as conservatives settled into leadership of the SBC, certain actions were taken to increase the doctrinal uniformity of all member churches. As membership statistics declined, the denomination renewed its commitment to evangelism and church growth, with particular efforts to increase the presence of African Americans in the SBC. The convention also continued to oppose a variety of religio-political issues including abortion, homosexuality, euthanasia, and the ordination of women for the pastorate of Baptist churches. Some fretted over the rising influence of Calvinism, the increasing debates over church–state relationships, prayer in public schools, and relationships between Christian and non-Christian communities. Discussion of these issues inside the denomination and in its pronouncements in the public square has had a significant impact on the way many Americans understand the nature of the Southern Baptist Convention and the way in which Southern Baptists' conservative theology has carried them into a variety of responses toward the culture.

Perhaps there is no clearer illustration of the nature of Southern Baptists' varied responses to political activity than in the attitude of the SBC leadership to the presidential candidacies of Baptist Democrats, from Harry Truman in 1948 to Jimmy Carter (1976 and 1980), Bill Clinton (1992 and 1996), and Al Gore (2000). All of these lifelong Baptists were essentially rejected in their bids for the White House by many in the SBC because of their liberal views on a number of social, economic, and political issues. At the same time, divisions of opinion have also arisen over the way in which SBC-related laity and clergy have related to the Republican Party. Conservatives also modified the rules for determining "messengers," representatives from member congregations to the annual convention meetings, amending the by-laws accordingly. They retained the earlier guidelines that churches in "friendly cooperation" with the convention are able to send up to ten messengers to the meeting, with one messenger for every 250 members or for every $250 contributed to the convention during the past fiscal year. However, since 1992 the convention states that no churches can claim friendly cooperation that "affirm, approve or endorse homosexual behavior." Churches must certify each messenger with a letter presented at convention registration.

In 2008 the SBC reported declines in both membership and baptisms. Membership statistics were posted at 16,266,920, a 0.24 percent decline since the previous year. Baptisms dropped by 5 percent, the seventh decline in baptisms in eight years. The number of SBC-related churches was listed at 44,696.

See also *Appalachian Mountain Religion; Baptists* entries; *Baptists: Tradition and Heritage; Fundamentalism; Religious Right; South as Region.*

Bill J. Leonard

## BIBLIOGRAPHY

Baker, Robert. *The Southern Baptist Convention and Its People, 1607–1972.* Nashville: Broadman Press, 1974.

Campbell, Will D. *The Stem of Jesse.* Macon, Ga.: Mercer University Press, 1995.

Fletcher, Jesse C. *The Southern Baptist Convention: A Sesquicentennial History.* Nashville: Broadman and Holman, 1994.

Garrett, James Leo, Jr., E. Glenn Hinson, and James E. Tull. *Are Southern Baptists "Evangelicals"?* Macon, Ga.: Mercer University Press, 1993.

Hankins, Barry. *Uneasy in Babylon: Southern Baptist Conservatives and American Culture.* Tuscaloosa: University of Alabama Press, 2002.

Harvey, Paul. *Redeeming the South: Religious Cultures and Racial Identities among Southern Baptists, 1896–1925.* Chapel Hill: University of North Carolina Press, 1997.

Leonard, Bill J. *Baptist Ways: A History.* Valley Forge, Pa.: Judson Press, 2003.

———. *Baptists in America.* New York: Columbia University Press, 2005.

———, ed. *Dictionary of Baptists in America.* Downers Grove, Ill.: InterVarsity Press, 1994.

———. *God's Last and Only Hope: The Fragmentation of the Southern Baptist Convention.* Grand Rapids: Eerdmans, 1990.

McBeth, H. Leon. *The Baptist Heritage.* Nashville: Broadman Press, 1987.

Pressler, Paul. *A Hill on Which to Die: One Southern Baptist's Journey.* Nashville: Broadman and Holman, 1999.

Wills, Gregory A. *Democratic Religion: Freedom, Authority, and Church Discipline in the Baptist South, 1785–1900.* New York: Oxford University Press, 1996.

# Baptists: Tradition and Heritage

Baptist churches, part of the diverse Protestant tradition, originated in seventeenth-century England and are most clearly identified with the practice of the baptism of believers by immersion. Baptists are the largest Protestant group in the United States, in 2008 representing 17.1 percent of the adult population. In 2008 the Southern Baptist Convention alone represented 6.7 percent of adults, a larger percentage than that of any other Protestant tradition. In comparison, all Methodist groups represented 6.3 percent of adults, followed by all denominations classified as Lutheran (4.6 percent), Pentecostal (4.3 percent), Presbyterian (2.7 percent), and Episcopalian (1.7 percent). Moreover, most African American Protestants are Baptists, with 4.4 percent of the overall population listed as members of historically black Baptist churches. Baptists achieved such numerical success in several phases. Beginning as a minority group in the seventeenth century, Baptists grew exponentially through revivals in the eighteenth and nineteenth centuries and maintained their expansion through a succession of organizations and divisions.

Most Baptists believe that the Bible is the highest religious authority. Church traditions and confessions are helpful records of Christian experience and beliefs in particular times and places, but creeds are problematic because they can be improperly elevated to rival scriptural authority. Baptism is reserved for believers who have testified to an experience of conversion and have voluntarily sought membership in the church. Baptism and the Lord's Supper (Communion) are not "sacraments," which confer grace, but are "ordinances" or "memorials," which are outward signs of discipleship. In church governance the local church has full authority over its own worship, theology, and witness. Ministers are ordained for ministerial work, but ministry is not limited to a clerical office; all believers are called to serve the church. Furthermore, believers are their own priests in that they can approach God directly, with no human intermediary. Finally, all people can claim the religious liberty to follow the convictions of their consciences without interference from any human authority; only God judges the soul.

## Origins of the Baptist Tradition

Although most historians trace Baptist beginnings to seventeenth-century England, many Baptists have disagreed on the origins of the movement. Three main theories have emerged on the question of Baptist origins, each connected to particular claims for Baptist identity and witness.

First, the *successionist* view claims that the Baptist church originated with the New Testament church and has continued in a line of succession to modern times. Advocates of this theory admit that this church, founded on the baptism of believers, has been known by various names over the centuries, including Donatist, Anabaptist, and finally Baptist, but the substance of the church has remained constant. This view was influential in a nineteenth-century movement called Landmarkism, where it was used to defend the claim that the Baptist church was the one true church in the face of much denominational competition. Most modern historians reject this perspective, but its persistence throughout Baptist history indicates the strength of Baptist convictions for biblical authority and local autonomy. That is, advocates of the successionist view claimed that Baptists were the most primitive, and the most biblical people, since the

Baptist church was linked directly to the church of the New Testament. And since the Baptists were the most biblical people, they were to protect their autonomy, refusing to taint themselves by forming unbiblical associations with other denominations and churches.

Second, the *Anabaptist influence* view is understood in different ways: Some claim that Baptists emerged directly from Anabaptist communities, while others argue that Anabaptists influenced certain Baptist characteristics, including believers' baptism by immersion and convictions concerning religious liberty. Although Anabaptists may have influenced early Baptists to some degree, most historians deny a direct line of succession from the Anabaptist movement to Baptist churches. There were major disagreements between Anabaptists and Baptists, especially regarding participation in war. (Most Anabaptists were pacifist; most Baptists were not.) Moreover, many seventeenth-century Baptists denied any connection with Anabaptists. And yet this view of Baptist origins has persisted throughout history, especially among those who find in the Baptist heritage a witness for peacemaking and the separation of church and state.

Third, the *English Separatist* view, which most historians support, claims that the Baptist movement originated in seventeenth-century English Puritanism. Puritans believed that the Church of England needed to be purified of unbiblical elements in doctrine and worship. Aside from this common goal, however, Puritanism was a diverse, even conflicted, movement. Although some believed that the Church of England could be reformed, others concluded that it was so corrupt that believers should abandon it. These radical Puritan "Separatists" split from the Church of England to start new congregations and then faced persecution for rejecting the official Anglican Church. To escape, many Separatists fled—some to Holland and others to North America (as in the case of the "Pilgrims" aboard the *Mayflower*). The Baptist movement arose among a group of Separatists in Amsterdam. Their leader, John Smyth (c. 1570–1612), renounced his baptism, which had been administered by the Church of England, in favor of a new baptism—one that would restore the biblical practice of believer's baptism. Smyth baptized himself and then his followers, thereby forming the first Baptist church in 1609. When Smyth later sought to join the Mennonites, some in his church retuned to England to form a Baptist congregation led by Thomas Helwys (c.1550–c.1615). Back in England, Helwys and other Baptists were imprisoned for their faith, and several responded by publishing defenses of religious liberty. Among these was Helwys's *Mistery of Iniquity* (1612).

Historians labeled the Smyth and Helwys group as General Baptists because they believed that Christ's salvation was "general" or offered to everyone; salvation was not limited to a particular group of "elect" that God had predestined for grace. The term for this view, Arminianism, was taken from the name of Dutch theologian Jacobus Arminius (1560–1609), who defended human freedom in salvation in opposition to traditional Calvinist views of predestination. Another group of Baptists emerged in the 1630s and were called Particular Baptists because they were more traditionally Calvinist, believing that Christ's salvation was "particular"—available only for the elect. Like their General Baptists predecessors, Particular Baptists began as Puritan Separatists. Although the General Baptists emerged first, the Particular Baptists were much more influential in North America, a development that accounts for the strong Calvinist tradition among most Baptist groups in the United States.

## Colonial North America

Baptists in the English colonies suffered persecution, especially in New England, where Puritans had formed alliances of church and state and dealt harshly with any unauthorized churches. In reaction, colonial Baptists followed their English Baptist predecessors in becoming advocates for religious liberty. They protested colonial taxes to support "official" churches, and they defended the authority of local churches to direct their own theology and worship without interference from the state. In the colonial period, therefore, Baptists were among the first advocates of religious liberty. Although Baptists often disagreed on the definition and extent of religious liberty, the idea remained central to the Baptist heritage, even when Baptists were no longer the persecuted minority. And that dramatic shift from a small, besieged movement to a major denominational force occurred through two major events of colonial America: a succession of revivals called the Great Awakening and the American Revolution.

### Persecution in New England

The first advocate of religious liberty in colonial America was also the founder of America's first Baptist church, Roger Williams (1603–1683). Born in England, Williams and his wife, Mary Barnard Williams, joined other Puritan migrants to the Massachusetts Bay Colony. Soon after arriving in Massachusetts in 1631, Williams surprised his Puritan colleagues by declaring Separatist views, and then disputing repeatedly with Massachusetts's leaders until they finally banished him in 1635. Banishment was serious but necessary, Puritan leaders believed, because Williams was guilty of spreading dangerous ideas. Not only was he a Separatist, but he also rejected the alliance that Puritans had formed between church and state. After the Israel of the Old Testament, Williams argued, there were no Christian nations, only a Christian church, and any government that claimed to be Christian perverted true Christianity rather than supporting it. The implications were serious and even affected colonialists' rights to American lands. After all, Williams reasoned, the English king, Charles I, had no right to bequeath the land to the English because he did not own it; the Native Americans did. The king's claim to the land was based on illegitimate "rights" as a Christian ruler over heathen peoples—a distinction that held no value because Christ had no kings, only churches. Alliances of church with state, therefore, were not Christian but "Christendom," a coercive, political enterprise that Christ never endorsed. True Christianity, in contrast, required that persons freely accept (or freely reject) the gospel. After his banishment for these radical ideas, Williams headed south from Massachusetts, negotiated with Narragansett sachems (rulers) for a place to live, and in 1638 established North America's first Baptist church in the settlement he called Providence.

Williams did not remain Baptist for long. Eventually he determined that all churches were corrupt, along with their baptisms, and only a new influx of Christ's apostles could reestablish the true, primitive faith. Even so, Williams continued to quote Baptist authors in his writings, and in turn Baptists throughout history cited Williams as a pioneer of Baptist principles. As first governor of the new colony of Providence Plantations (later Rhode Island) Williams launched a society with religious liberty as a central principle. Afterward Rhode Island became a haven for dissenters, including Baptists and Quakers. More important than Williams for ongoing efforts to promote the Baptist faith was John Clarke (1609–1676), who led a Baptist church at Newport and took over from Williams the leading role in securing the final charter for Rhode Island in 1663. Like Williams, Clarke faced persecution firsthand. He and other Baptists, including Obadiah Holmes, were arrested for their illegal worship in Massachusetts. After Puritan leaders punished Holmes by flogging, Clarke narrated the episode as an account of religious persecution for English readers, *Ill*

*Newes from New England* (1652). This narrative joined Williams's *Bloudy Tenet of Persecution* (1644) and other works in defending religious liberty and exposing New England's persecutions to an English audience.

## The Philadelphia Baptist Association

While early Baptists struggled in New England, they prospered in the middle colonies. The center of Baptist strength was Pennsylvania, where there was no established church to force religious taxation or to interfere with Baptist worship and organization. In Pennsylvania, therefore, Baptists were not a harassed minority; they were a respected group with the freedom to organize the influential Philadelphia Baptist Association (PBA) in 1707.

Although the PBA did not impinge upon the autonomy of local churches, it fostered cooperation and advised Baptists on doctrine, missions, and education. In pursuit of such goals, the PBA helped to establish a Baptist school that later became Brown University, and it approved a confession of faith in 1742. The Philadelphia Confession was, essentially, the Second London Confession that Particular Baptists approved in 1677, but with the addition of two articles—one to allow hymn singing and the other to condone a ceremony of laying hands on the baptized. Through this confession alone, the PBA's influence was extensive. Baptist associations from South Carolina to Rhode Island adopted the Philadelphia Confession and its Calvinist theology. In addition, the PBA published materials on polity, a hymnal, a catechism, and a two-volume history of Baptists written by Morgan Edwards (1722–1795), a tireless advocate of the PBA. Through these and other efforts, the PBA became the center of a broadly Calvinist tradition that became known as Regular Baptist.

## The Great Awakening

The revivals of the mid- to late eighteenth century, often called the Great Awakening, moved many Congregationalists to join Baptist ranks. Baptist churches more than doubled during the prime revival years, from 47 to 101 churches. Most revival preachers were not Baptists—most famously, George Whitefield (1714–1770) was Anglican, and Jonathan Edwards (1703–1758) was an heir to the Puritan tradition in New England. Even so, disputes over revivals divided Congregationalists and Presbyterians, and Baptists benefited from the divisions. Specifically, pro-revival Congregationalists often formed separate congregations that embraced revival piety. These Congregationalist "Separates" often moved one step further to become Baptists, convinced that

believer's baptism was both more scriptural than infant baptism and more supportive of a pure church comprising those who had experienced true conversion.

These Separate Congregationalists who became Separate Baptists dramatically increased the Baptist ranks in the colonies. Influential among Separate Baptists were Martha Stearns Marshall (1726–c.1793), her brother, Shubal Stearns (1706–1771), and her husband, Daniel Marshall (1706–1784)—New Englanders whose revival zeal inspired a missionary enterprise to the South in 1755. They eventually settled in the Piedmont area of North Carolina and established the Sandy Creek Baptist Church. With Stearns serving as first pastor of this church, the Marshalls founded another church, thereby setting the pattern through which Sandy Creek launched more than forty additional Separate Baptist congregations in the South. The leadership of Martha Marshall demonstrates the Separate Baptist openness to women in the ministry. Women's ministerial activity was but one of several points of contention between the pro-revival Separate Baptists and the Regular Baptists who rejected revivalist emotionalism in favor of a dignified worship style and a professional, educated clergy.

## The American Revolution

Early in the Revolutionary period, in the last half of the eighteenth century, Baptists were on both sides of the dispute between the colonies and Britain. Some Baptists even looked to the king of England for support against colonial governments that forced Baptists to pay taxes to support the established churches. Eventually, however, most Baptists concluded that religious and political liberties were inseparable. Tyranny was the enemy, whether in the form of a British king or through forced taxation in support of an "official" church. A key figure in crafting the Baptist legacy for religious liberty in the Revolutionary era was Isaac Backus (1724–1806), a minister in the Puritan tradition who embraced Baptist views in 1756. Backus believed that religious liberty was crucial both to Baptist identity and to the political responsibility of Baptists in America. In defense of this view, he wrote a history of Baptists in New England, represented the Warren Association of Baptists in defending religious liberty before the Continental Congress, and published *An Appeal to the Public for Religious Liberty against the Oppression of the Present Day* (1773).

Joining Backus in representing Baptists in revolutionary times was John Leland (1754–1841), who, like Backus, was born a Congregationalist in Massachusetts before adopting the Baptist faith. Leland's early influence was in the South, specifically in Virginia, where Leland opposed the government's alliance with the Anglican Church. When the states began the process of ratifying the new Constitution, in 1787, Backus supported it, while Leland demurred. Backus was satisfied with the Constitution because it opposed religious tests for political offices, but Leland wanted a clearer statement in support of religious liberty. Leland's opposition to the Constitution was serious because of his strong influence in Virginia. Legend has it that James Madison negotiated a deal in which Leland agreed to support ratification in exchange for Madison's promise to secure religious liberty in a future constitutional amendment. The story is plausible because Leland was influential, and Baptist votes were essential to the Constitution's success in Virginia.

The combination of political democracy and evangelical revival sparked exponential growth for Baptists from the revolutionary period through the end of the eighteenth century. In fact, the number of Baptists grew even more dramatically during the revolutionary era than they had during the revivals, from 254 churches and 13,817 members in 1770 to 978 churches and 67,320 members in 1790.

## The Nineteenth Century

The nineteenth century was a time of transformation for Baptists. As the new nation expanded into the frontier, Baptists flourished. By 1850 Baptist church membership was 715,500—an increase of more than 600,000 members in sixty years. At least four factors contributed to Baptist growth. First, while other denominations required ministers to be theologically educated and officially ordained before venturing out on the frontier, most Baptists required neither. Baptist ministers were often "farmer–preachers," or bivocational pastors who had secular employment and accepted little or no money for their ministry. For many Baptists, the farmer–preacher model was a necessary and even desirable alterative to "professional" ministers who could be accused of entering God's service for worldly gain. Second, any group of willing believers could start a Baptist church, without approval from any higher denominational authority. Third, Baptists were uniquely positioned to succeed in the political ethos of the new nation. Baptists had struggled against church–state establishments long before the First Amendment (ratified in 1791), which meant that they had already shaped their identity around the idea of liberty, just as the new nation was doing the same. Fourth, Baptists' voluntary church membership, which required individuals to join the church rather than being born into it, fit perfectly with democratic self-reliance and individual freedom. Likewise, Baptist convictions for the independence of each church meshed perfectly with a democratic frontier where local authority was as sacred as scripture.

### Cooperation for Missions

In the religious landscape of the new nation, a competitive situation developed. Churches could not rely on state support; they had to vie with other denominations for members. The number of converts became the measure of success for Protestants, and revival became the chief means of achieving it. The early-nineteenth-century revivals known as the Second Great Awakening had both commonalities and contrasts with the revivals of the previous century. The latter revivals took various new forms, including camp meetings on the frontier, most famously the revival at Cane Ridge, Kentucky, in 1801, and the innovative revivalist techniques ("New Measures") of Charles Finney (1792–1875), the era's premier evangelist. As in the first Great Awakening, the most prominent leaders of these revivals were not Baptists, but Baptists were among the revivals' chief beneficiaries.

Revivals often inspired missions, and that was especially the case with most Baptists. The support for missions was clearly revealed in the name of the first national Baptist organization, the General Missionary Convention of the Baptist Denomination in the United States for Foreign Missions (known as the "Triennial Convention"). The convention was founded in May 1814 in Philadelphia, in part due to the efforts of Luther Rice (1783–1836), whose conversion to the Baptist faith became missionary lore. Two years before helping to found the Triennial Convention, Rice was a Congregationalist missionary on his way to India with Adoniram Judson (1788–1850) and Judson's wife, Ann Hasseltine Judson (1789–1826). While aboard ship, all three missionaries decided that infant baptism was unbiblical. Soon after arriving in Calcutta, therefore, they sought baptism by immersion, administered by Baptists from Britain, and later resigned their positions with the Congregationalist missionary board. Rice then returned to America to seek support from Baptists—support that resulted in the Triennial Convention.

In addition to this new national convention, state conventions emerged, along with two national societies, the Baptist General Tract Society (1824) and the American Baptist Home Missionary Society (1832). In forming a society devoted to home missions, Baptists competed with other denominations in the expanding frontiers of the West and Southwest. By the late eighteenth century Baptists were in Tennessee and Kentucky and had clashed with Spanish Roman Catholics in the Mississippi and Louisiana territories. When President Andrew Jackson's Indian Removal Act (1830) forced Native Americans westward, Baptist home missionaries moved west as well. Among the leading missionaries in this effort was John Davis, a Creek Indian who converted to the Baptist faith in the Southeast, moved west with the Creeks, helped to found the first Baptist Church in Oklahoma in 1832, and translated part of the New Testament into Creek. By midcentury the American Baptist Home Mission Society was substantially invested in the West. In 1840 American Baptist home missionaries Osgood and Elizabeth Wheeler were in San Francisco, where they founded the First Baptist Church of the city and baptized converts in the San Francisco Bay.

Education was essential to building a national denomination. Baptists organized Sunday schools to educate children, especially in frontier locations in which schools were scarce or nonexistent. While Sunday schools provided a needed resource, they also spread churches and strengthened denominational identity. Further educational interests led Baptists to form several institutions before the Civil War, including Andover-Newton Theological Seminary (in Massachusetts), and Furman (South Carolina), Baylor (Texas), Wake Forest (North Carolina), and Mercer (Georgia) Universities.

Although many Baptists believed that missionary conventions and educational institutions were necessary, others were suspicious. Early on, John Leland distrusted denominational systems and professional ministers who cared more for money, prestige, and advanced degrees than for saving souls. Leland was present at the first meeting of the Triennial Convention, but he warned against missionary societies and the power struggles and bureaucracy that accompanied them. Others who shared Leland's opposition to missionary societies included Daniel Parker (1781–1844), who was born in Virginia and became a state senator in Illinois before establishing an early Baptist church in Texas. A devoted Calvinist, Parker founded the Two-Seed-in-the-Spirit Predestinarian Baptists and concluded that all missions were human attempts to interfere with God's election of souls.

With few tax-supported churches in the states, and no official church for the new nation, denominations competed for members and funding. Baptists faced off against Presbyterians, Methodists, Congregationalists, Episcopalians, and new religious movements such as the Church of Jesus Christ of Latter-day Saints. Americans had a bewildering array of religious options, which left many people asking which among the many churches was the most authentically Christian.

A major defense of the Baptist church as the only true faith came from Landmarkism, a movement that gained popularity through the influence of James Robinson Graves (1820–1893), a Tennessee preacher and journalist. Graves spread Landmarkist views as editor of *The Tennessee Baptist* (circulation 13,000 in 1859) and as an author (*Old Landmarkism: What Is It?*, published in 1880). According to the Landmarkist argument, the Baptists were not only the most faithful to biblical practices, the Baptist church was in the Bible. The church of the New Testament shared all the ancient "landmarks" of the Baptists, especially believer's baptism, and it was the one true church that survived to modern times, though often under different names. Moreover, the only authentic form of the church was the local community. Christ established a local fellowship, not a universal church (in the Catholic model) and not a national church (as in many Protestant models). Church membership, discipline, and rights to baptism and Communion were locally authorized and controlled. On this basis, Landmarkists believed in closed Communion—the Lord's Supper was open only to members in good standing in their local congregations. Communion required discipline, Landmarkists reasoned, and each church could know and discipline only its own members. This ecclesiology had obvious appeal for evangelicals who honored biblical authority while defending their independence.

## Slavery and Schism

In the nineteenth century slavery divided the United States—racially, regionally, and politically, but also religiously. Such divisions resulted from fissures that were present a century earlier. Amid the celebration of liberty at the nation's founding, slavery was the glaring obstacle that separated rhetoric from reality. Some Baptists, including Leland, recognized the vast contradiction between slavery and a free nation, but most were as divided over slavery as the rest of the nation. Later, conflicts over slavery escalated into violent uprisings, often with religious motivations. Baptists played central roles in two famous slave revolts—an attempted insurrection in South Carolina initiated by Denmark Vesey (1767–1822), in 1822, and a bloody rebellion led by a Virginia slave, Nat Turner (1800–1831), in 1831. Turner's insurgency, sparked by apocalyptic visions of godly violence against evil, was explicitly biblical in its justification. Both revolts ignited a fear of slave insurrection that lasted for years to come.

In large part because of conflicts over slavery, the three major Protestant denominations divided into northern and southern factions—Presbyterians in 1837, Methodists in 1844, and Baptists in 1845. These divisions were a portent of the looming national crisis. Not only did the churches fail to unite the nation, but religious arguments on both sides of the slavery controversy fueled the fires of war, providing theological justification for sectional division and violence.

Unlike Presbyterian and Methodist denominations, which reunited after the Civil War, the Baptist rupture created a permanent institution: the Southern Baptist Convention (SBC), formed in May 1845. Although the conflict over slavery was the major reason that southerners established the SBC, a disagreement about missions was also involved. Many asked the controversial question: Were Baptists who owned slaves qualified to be missionaries? Georgia Baptists forced the issue by recommending James Reeve, a slave owner, for assignment with the American Baptist Home Mission Society. When the society rejected Reeve, southerners protested, asserting that slavery was a secular issue that should not invade missionary work. Southern representatives met in Augusta, Georgia, to develop plans for the SBC. Unlike the Triennial Convention, which operated under a "society" approach, allowing its agencies much autonomy, the SBC developed a "convention" strategy that more tightly controlled its various activities.

## Organization for Mission and Publication

Despite their contrasting organizations, Baptists in both North and South shared similar objectives, namely missions and publications. In the North the Triennial Convention marked its division from southern Baptists by changing its name to the American Baptist Missionary Union (ABMU). The name both communicated the society-based approach to a single cause (foreign missions) and defied southern claims to sovereignty—the *American* Baptist Missionary Union would represent all Baptists in America. In the South the convention-based approach communicated a broader institution with boards for both home and international missions, but in reality foreign missions were the driving force, just as in the North.

International missions involved women as organizers, educators, and missionaries. Women's leadership in missions was not new, however. A combination of Baptist and Congregationalist women founded the Boston Female Society for Missionary Purposes in 1800. In the same city in 1871 the Woman's Baptist Foreign Mission Society was formed to send women to the mission field under the authority of the ABMU. A similar group formed that same year in Chicago—the Woman's Baptist Missionary Society of the West—and three years later a San Francisco–based group emerged, the Woman's Baptist Foreign Missionary Society of the Pacific Coast.

For Southern Baptists the place of women in missions achieved legendary status with Charlotte ("Lottie") Diggs Moon (1840–1912). Born and educated in Virginia, Moon pursued a teaching career before entering missionary service. In 1873 the Foreign Mission Board sent her to China, where she served nearly forty years. Not only was she a tireless missionary in the field, Moon was an effective fundraiser. She called for a Christmas offering to fund missionaries and was especially successful in persuading Baptist women to give. Moon died on Christmas Eve of 1912, in part from malnutrition. For Southern Baptists, Moon's death was characteristic of her sacrificial life for Christ. Five years later the offering she inspired became the Lottie Moon Christmas Offering for Foreign Missions. In 2008 the SBC goal for the Lottie Moon offering was $170 million.

In home missions, fierce rivalries developed between North and South. During the Civil War, the North's War Department gave the Home Mission Society (HMS) permission to take over any Southern church unless its minister claimed loyalty to the Northern cause. Since very few Southern churches fit that description, the Home Mission Board (HMB) could confiscate church buildings and disperse congregations at will. Although the HMB rarely acted on this authority, the few instances in which churches were overtaken and Southern pastors were arrested aroused the resentment of Southern Baptists. In reaction to such Northern encroachment, the SBC asserted the traditional Baptist conviction for religious liberty. The state should not interfere with the church, they claimed, which was exactly what happened when a Northern government claimed the authority to subdue Southern churches. The resentment continued after the war as the Home Mission Society continued working in the South in defiance of the SBC's Board of Domestic Missions (renamed the Home Mission Board in 1875). Northern Baptists justified their work in the South as an effort toward reunification after the war. The nation had reunited, they reasoned, as had other denominations, and Baptists should do

Charlotte "Lottie" Diggs Moon served nearly forty years as a missionary in China. Her service and fundraising inspired the Lottie Moon Christmas Offering for Foreign Missions.

likewise. And some reunification had taken place; several state Baptist conventions in the South aligned with the HMS. On the whole, however, Southern Baptists resisted realignment.

Despite much division, there was one area in which unity prevailed after the Civil War: publications. The American Baptist Publication Society (ABPS) greatly influenced Baptist education. Working through traveling colporteurs, this Philadelphia-based society distributed Bibles, confessions, hymnals, and especially Sunday school literature throughout the nation. The ABPS ignored the schisms over slavery and the Civil War, arguing that the North–South division centered on the missionary societies and had nothing to do with publications. Many southern Baptists agreed, continuing to use literature from the northern ABPS for decades after founding the SBC. In 1891 the SBC finally launched its own publishing enterprise, the Sunday School Board, which eventually overtook the ABPS in the South. Ironically, the Sunday School Board, which was late in coming

for the SBC, became the most influential bond of unity for the convention.

## African American Baptist Autonomy

Most African Americans in the early nineteenth century encountered Christianity as slaves. The alignment between Christianity and slavery was deliberate. From the beginning of the slave trade in the Atlantic world, slavery was justified as a means of Christianizing slaves. Although many slaves rejected Christianity as a religion of bondage, others reshaped it to resonate with the experiences of slavery. When slaves accepted Christianity, they usually did so in evangelical communities, especially Baptist and Methodist churches. Unlike more liturgically formal denominations, Baptists and Methodists stressed revival experience that resonated with some African religious forms, especially experiences of ecstasy in worship and spirit possession.

The Baptist emphasis on local control allowed the possibility of independent congregations for slaves. A pioneer in this effort was George Liele (c.1750–1820), a Georgia slave who preached in the Savannah area. Liele influenced the early ministries of two slave preachers who then founded two of the earliest black Baptist congregations: David George (c.1742–1810), who helped to form the Silver Bluff church, in South Carolina, no later than 1775, and Andrew Bryan (1737–1812), who cofounded the First African Baptist Church, in Savannah, in 1788. The ministries of Liele, George, and Bryan were innovative and controversial. In most cases, however, slaves who accepted Christianity worshiped either in white-controlled congregations, which relegated slaves to separate seating and marginalized their status, or in secret worship services conducted by and for slaves.

In the North, African Americans founded churches, established associations, and pursued a variety of objectives in education and missions. Early northern churches included Boston's Joy Street Baptist Church (from 1804) and New York's Abyssinian Baptist Church, both founded in part by Thomas Paul (1773–1831), who was pastor at Joy Street for more than two decades. Racial prejudice and abolition influenced the formation of black Baptist churches and associations, including Providence Baptist Association and the Union Association, both in Ohio (1836), and the Colored Baptist Association and Friends to Humanity (1939), in Illinois, which was renamed Wood River Association in 1852. This associational zeal reached a zenith in 1840, when representatives met at Abyssinian Baptist Church to form the American Baptist Missionary Convention, which was a forerunner to the National Baptist Convention.

## Theological Developments

Academic theology was a point of contention among Baptists. While some advocated theological education, others worried that doctrinal systems complicated the simple message of scripture and, in so doing, removed theology from the control of the people. John Leland was one of the strongest opponents of academic theologies. He associated doctrinal systems with a professionalized ministry that commandeered theology for the educated elite. Other Baptists disagreed, however. Brown University, which Baptists founded as the College of Rhode Island in 1764, trained theologians in the revivalist Calvinism of the Jonathan Edwards tradition, and several other Baptist colleges were formed to promote an educated ministry. These two strains of Baptist theology, populist and academic, coexisted in the nineteenth century. Some Baptists defended the necessity of theological education for ministers, while others adopted the virtues of the farmer–preacher model out of fears that doctrinal training would deflect attention from a plain reading of scripture.

Most Baptist theology in the nineteenth century represented some variety of Calvinism. But Arminianism never disappeared from Baptist life and was represented by many groups, including the Free Will Baptist Church, founded in 1780 by former Congregationalist lay preacher Benjamin Randall (1749–1808). The great majority of Baptists, however, adopted a moderate Calvinist theology that called everyone to repentance and made extensive use of revivals. Among the leading theologians in the Baptist tradition was John Leadley Dagg (1794–1884), professor and president of Mercer University, whose *Manual of Theology* of 1857 represented a strong Calvinist tradition. Dagg and other Baptist theologians claimed an explicitly biblical theology that resonated with deep currents in Baptist life. And yet Baptist theologians, like most other academic theologians in the nineteenth century, supported their claims for biblical authority with external proofs, especially drawn from the philosophical tradition of Scottish Common Sense Realism.

## Immigration

The staggering growth of Baptist churches convinced many American Baptists that their denomination was uniquely suited to the United States. Baptists, they concluded, had a democratic church polity that best supported democracy and a tradition for religious liberty that best resembled the independent ethos of the nation. In his scathing attack on Methodism, for instance, J. R. Graves argued that the Methodist system closely resembled Roman Catholicism, which he believed directly opposed American democracy. But the America that Baptists identified with changed rapidly as waves of immigration brought millions of Europeans to the country in the nineteenth century. Baptists responded in a variety of ways, including nativist reactions, especially against Catholic immigrants. Institutionally, however, Baptists seized upon the new immigrant population as an opportunity for home missions.

Included among the immigrants were Swedish and German Baptists, and their arrival prompted the American Baptist Home Mission Society and the Home Mission Board of the SBC to expand their efforts to support the new communities. There were 324 Swedish congregations by the beginning of the nineteenth century, most of which belonged to the Swedish Baptist General Conference, which formed in 1879. In 1945 the conference changed its name to the Baptist General Conference to represent the rise of non-Swedish members.

The first German Baptist church in America was founded in 1843 in Philadelphia. The church's pastor, Konrad Fleischmann (1812–1867), was instrumental in forming the General Conference of German Baptist Churches in North America, which was later renamed the North American Baptist Conference. The center of German Baptist education was the Rochester Theological Seminary, where August Rauschenbusch founded an area of German studies. It was while teaching at Rochester that August's son, Walter Rauschenbusch (1861–1918), profoundly influenced theological ethics and societal reform through his leadership in the Social Gospel movement. The department that August Rauschenbusch founded moved to Sioux Falls, South Dakota, in the late 1940s, to become the freestanding North American Baptist Seminary, a name that it kept until 2007, when it took on the nondenominational name Sioux Falls Seminary.

Missions among Spanish-speaking people developed after the United States gained control over Texas territories in the Mexican-American War, with Baptist home missionaries from both major conventions increasing their work in Texas. And after the Spanish-American War, the American Baptist Home Mission Society led missionary efforts in Cuba and Puerto Rico. As a result of home missions, Mexican Baptist churches arose in San Antonio and El Paso in the 1880s and 1890s, and the Mexican Baptist Convention of Texas was founded by 1910. In the early twentieth century Spanish-speaking people were a small percentage of

Baptists in the United States. That would change dramatically with the rise of Spanish-speaking immigrants in the late twentieth century.

## The Twentieth Century

By the early twentieth century Baptists were one of the two largest Protestant groups in America, totaling over four million members. Their challenge, therefore, was not how to survive in the American religious landscape but how best to shape it. On this question there was great disagreement. Baptists were on both sides of nearly every major debate over theology, economics, social justice, and race. In all Baptist communities, the affinity for local church authority remained strong, though Baptists continued to seek cooperation. In 1905 Baptists from around the world sought international unity in founding the Baptist World Alliance (BWA). Despite the global witness of the BWA, complete unity among Baptists remained elusive, primarily because of the traditional Baptist conviction for local autonomy.

### From "Northern" Baptists to "American" Baptists

Although northern Baptists traditionally resisted centralized authority, by the end of the nineteenth century they also recognized the difficulties of a denomination composed of autonomous agencies. Moreover, northern Baptists observed the success of the SBC, and they longed for a convention that would bring efficiency and unity to Baptist life in the North. When the Northern Baptist Convention began in 1907, it combined American Baptist organizations for missions and publications. The convention safeguarded the autonomy of the societies, each of which kept its own governing board and budget (though with the convention's oversight). In 1950 the Northern Baptist Convention became the American Baptist Convention. Several agendas marked this transition: to recognize the convention's reach across all regions of the nation, to expand through connections with other groups, and to reinvigorate Baptist life through ecumenical outreach and renewed efforts to honor Baptist history and identity. The convention changed its name again in 1972, becoming the American Baptist Churches in the USA. The shift from "Convention" to "Churches" in the name indicated the transition to a more flexible, less centralized structure that sought alignment with various Baptist groups. In the shifts between these three organizations, northern Baptists wrestled with the longstanding Baptist tensions of autonomy versus cooperation and society versus convention.

### Poverty, Wealth, and the Gospel

The United States changed dramatically in the late nineteenth century. The rise of industry, combined with the arrival of millions of European immigrants, caused unprecedented growth in the cities. These social and economic changes pressured Baptists and other Protestants. Not only were many immigrants Jewish and Catholic, and thus a challenge for missions, but many of them were poor, and their struggles to eke out a living in the cities forced churches to face issues involving economic justice. Although industrialism brought great wealth to some, many, including children, toiled in sweatshops and endured extreme poverty.

Northern Baptists approached these new realities differently. One response came from Philadelphia minister Russell Conwell (1843–1925), whose book *Acres of Diamonds* (1915) asserted that wealth was a Christian virtue. Conwell emphasized the responsibilities as well as the rewards of wealth—the rich should use their money for God's kingdom—and his philanthropic theology retained a self-help emphasis, which called on individuals to improve their own situations. This perspective conflicted with the Social Gospel movement, which recognized that individual effort alone could not solve social crises. Instead, entire economic systems needed transformation; systemic injustices demanded systemic corrections, and the traditional Christian gospel of individual conversion was inadequate when society itself needed renewal. The most prominent theologian of the Social Gospel was Walter Rauschenbusch, who discovered his academic vocation while pastoring in the poverty-stricken Hell's Kitchen area of New York City. Rauschenbusch crafted a theology for societal reform in books entitled *Christianity and the Social Crisis* (1907), *Christianizing the Social Order* (1912), and *A Theology for the Social Gospel* (1917). Rauschenbusch's theology was optimistic, influential, and Baptist. In a series of articles entitled "Why I am a Baptist" (1905–1906), Rauschenbusch praised Baptists for elevating personal experience above creeds, honoring democratic polity instead of loyalty to bishops, and prioritizing Christ-centered morality over ritualistic formality in faith and worship.

### Theological Controversy: Fundamentalism versus Modernism

Rauschenbusch's vision for a Social Gospel was part of a larger movement called Protestant liberalism (or "modernism"). The modernist movement met strong resistance from fundamentalism, a movement comprising evangelicals who believed that modernism threatened true Christianity at its biblical foundations. Although the modernist–fundamentalist crisis was broad, covering several denominations, it especially divided Baptists and Presbyterians.

Protestant modernism arose out of a concern that traditional Christianity was irrelevant in the modern world. Not only did the gospel need to meet the social needs of the city, modernists believed, it also needed to meet the intellectual needs of a scientifically literate society. Of specific concern were recent challenges to scripture, especially Charles Darwin's theory of the evolutionary development of life, which seemed to contradict the biblical explanation of creation, and the rise of historical-critical methods of interpreting texts, through which modern interpreters questioned the historical accuracy of the Bible. Protestant modernists responded to these challenges. Evolution was compatible with Christianity, they argued, because God worked within the natural process of evolution. This view of God and history was optimistic. Sin could be overcome through human effort. Gone was a view of Christ's atonement as a sacrifice for sin; instead, Jesus was a moral example, demonstrating human potential for good. And scriptures, along with doctrines and creeds, were vital but fallible records of human experience that needed revision as people evolved into clearer understandings of God.

Several modernist leaders were Baptists, including Shailer Mathews (1863–1941), dean of the University of Chicago Divinity School, and Harry Emerson Fosdick (1878–1969), prominent New York minister and professor at Union Theological Seminary. In 1922 Fosdick preached his famous sermon "Shall the Fundamentalists Win?"—a widely published foray into the controversy between modernists and fundamentalists. In opposition to fundamentalism, Fosdick asserted several traditional Baptist convictions that fit well with modernism, especially religious liberty, the priority of individual experience, and the rejection of authoritarian creeds.

But Baptist convictions could also support fundamentalism. It was probably a Baptist who first used the term *fundamentalist*—Curtis Lee Laws (1868–1946), editor of the popular newspaper the *Watchman-Examiner*. Several Baptists led the movement, including Amzi Clarence Dixon (1854–1925), who edited an influential series called *The Fundamentals,* and William Bell Riley (1861–1947), a Minneapolis pastor who opposed liberalism in education by founding several schools, including Northwestern Evangelical

Seminary (1935). Riley became the founding member of the World's Christian Fundamentals Association (WCFA, 1919), which entered the fray against evolutionism on the nation's most visible stage—the famous Scopes Trial of 1925. The WCFA chose William Jennings Bryan to prosecute the case against John Scopes, a biology teacher accused of illegally teaching evolution to high school students in Dayton, Tennessee. Although Bryan and the state won the trial, the media spectacle branded fundamentalism as a hick theology, hopelessly out of place in a progressive, modern nation.

Although fundamentalism lost its voice in much of the Northern Baptist Convention, it developed strength through other networks, especially the Independent Baptist movement, which began as a reaction to modernist strength in the Northern Baptist Convention, though the movement was never limited to the North. Early Independent Baptists included J. Frank Norris (1877–1952), an influential pastor in Forth Worth, Texas. The title of Norris's latest biography described him as "God's Rascal"; others called him the "Texas Tornado," a moniker he earned from confrontational rampages against alcohol, liberalism, and Catholicism. Norris's Forth Worth congregation grew to fifteen thousand, and for thirteen years he simultaneously pastored Temple Baptist in Detroit, Michigan, which had a membership of ten thousand. Moreover, Norris expanded his influence by editing several newspapers, including *The Baptist Standard* and *The Fundamentalist*. One of the most influential Independent Baptists of the twentieth century was Jerry Falwell (1933–2007), pastor of Thomas Road Baptist Church in Lynchburg, Virginia, and founder of the Moral Majority in 1979. Falwell used the mass media to wage crusades against abortion, homosexuality, and the Equal Rights Amendment.

## Growth and Division in the Southern Baptist Convention

The SBC is the largest Protestant denomination in the United States, growing in membership from 3.6 million members in 1925 to 15.9 million in 2000. This growth has been achieved in spite of—or perhaps because of—much controversy, including rifts that centered on central Baptist convictions, especially the authority of scripture, religious liberty, and local autonomy in relation to centralized denominational institutions. Although each of these convictions was important to nearly every controversy, the rhetoric of the debates usually fixated on the integrity of the Bible. Similar to the debates that fragmented Northern

Baptists in the 1920s, a series of controversies over biblical inerrancy raged among Southern Baptists, beginning in the 1960s.

When Baptists debated the Bible, women's ordination was usually a divisive issue. Since the beginnings of the Baptist movement, women have had a prominent place in church life, though most often not in positions of leadership over men. Lottie Moon's tenacity as a missionary pushed the limits of Southern Baptist acceptance of women in religious leadership, though Moon never sought ordination. Women had more opportunities in the North, where some Baptist churches ordained women to preach. The first ordained woman was probably Frances Townsley (1849–1909) of Massachusetts, who was ordained in 1885. In 1921 the Northern Baptist Convention selected the first woman ever to lead a denomination, Helen B. Montgomery (1861–1934). A biblical scholar, Montgomery published the first translation of the New Testament by a woman. Montgomery was also socially progressive, an advocate of suffrage and a colleague of Frances Willard, a well-known reformer. Montgomery's legacy thrived among Northern Baptists: the ABC officially advocated women's full equality in ministry in 1965.

The response to women's ordination was much different in the South, however. A woman was not elected as a convention officer until 1963—forty-two years after Montgomery's presidency in the northern convention—and a woman has never served as president of the SBC. The first woman ordained to the ministry in the SBC was Addie Davis (1917–2005), in August 1964, and that action by Watts Street Baptist Church in Durham, North Carolina, stirred controversy. In 1973 the SBC issued a statement opposing women's liberation movements and advocating traditionally subordinate roles for women. In the early 1980s the SBC opposed the Equal Rights Amendment and stated that women had the same "worth" as men, though they had different responsibilities. These resolutions did not speak for the entire convention, however. Conferences were held to discuss women's activity in ministry in the 1970s and 1980s, and by the mid-1980s both Southern and Southeastern Baptist Theological Seminaries voiced support for women in pastoral ministry. This shift in support of women's ordination in the seminaries contributed to the perception among conservatives that the SBC needed a change in direction. Just as the seminaries began to support women as ministers, the SBC affirmed an official statement against women's ordination in 1984.

These disputes were elements of a broader controversy, as conservatives in the denomination attempted to reverse what they perceived as a trend toward liberalism. By the late 1970s conservative leaders developed a strategy for overtaking the SBC. The plan was to elect a series of conservative presidents who would appoint only conservatives in leadership positions, allowing them to control all areas of the SBC. Those who devised this strategy included Paige Patterson, head of the Criswell Center for Biblical Studies in Dallas, Texas, and Adrian Rogers (1931–2005), pastor of Bellevue Baptist Church in Memphis, Tennessee. The election of Rogers to the presidency in 1979 started the process for conservative control. Over the next eleven years, each meeting of the convention was a struggle between conservatives and self-proclaimed "moderates," with each side calling itself defenders of authentic Baptist identity. Conservatives argued that the moderates threatened the conservative doctrinal and biblical foundations that Baptists had always supported. Most critically, conservatives claimed, liberalism in seminaries undermined the authority of scripture and threatened to populate churches with ministers who doubted biblical truth. Moderates countered that the conservatives' drive for doctrinal uniformity conflicted with cherished Baptist convictions for liberty of conscience. Baptists had never agreed on doctrinal issues, moderates pointed out, and to force conformity in an authoritative convention was decidedly non-Baptist. By 1990 conservatives had gained control of the convention. In response, moderates formed two new groups, the Cooperative Baptist Fellowship and the Alliance of Baptists, and established new divinity schools at Baylor, Mercer, Gardner-Webb, and other universities, along with seminaries such as the Baptist Theological Seminary in Richmond, Virginia.

**African American Baptist Conventions**

At the end of the twentieth century the largest African American denomination in America was the National Baptist Convention, USA, Inc., with 3.5 million members. The NBC was formed in 1895, when representatives from three African American Baptist conventions—all formed in the 1880s—united to establish a new organization, national in scope and focused on missions and education. The first president was Elias Camp Morris (1855–1922), an Arkansas minister who was born a slave in Georgia. During Morris's presidency, the convention divided over the ownership of its publication board, which had become enormously successful under the leadership of Richard Henry Boyd

(1843–1922). When Morris pushed for the NBC's control of the board, a lawsuit ensued that favored Boyd's ownership. Boyd and his followers subsequently withdrew from the NBC in 1915, forming the National Baptist Convention of America.

The next major division of the NBC involved the civil rights movement. With the leadership of Martin Luther King Jr. (1929–1968), the drive for civil rights was intimately connected with Baptist communities. King was a Baptist minister, as were his father and grandfather. While working on his PhD dissertation at Boston University, King accepted the call to the pastorate of Dexter Avenue Baptist Church in Montgomery, Alabama. After the Montgomery bus boycott in 1955 launched King into the national consciousness, his prophetic message for justice and nonviolent resistance received much attention—not only for its effectiveness and the heated reactions that ensued, but also for its call to religious communities to take up the struggle. Although nearly all African American Baptists agreed with King's goals, some rejected his methods. Perhaps the most prominent opponent of King's use of civil disobedience was Joseph H. Jackson (1900–1990), president of the NBC for nearly thirty years. King intended for civil disobedience to be peaceful, Christian, and effective, but Jackson called it criminal, disruptive, and unpatriotic. Jackson preferred more gradual approaches, including cooperation with the NAACP, and an emphasis on education, including religious instruction to expose racism as a spiritual disease. Many of those supportive of King opposed Jackson, not only for his distaste for civil rights but also for his domineering leadership style. Those critical of Jackson formed a new convention in 1961, the Progressive National Baptist Convention. By the mid-1990s the PNBC claimed 2.5 million members and 2,000 churches, some of which were dually aligned with the American Baptist Convention.

## Twenty-first Century Trends

At the beginning of the twenty-first century at least three realities forced Baptists to reassess their identity: the success of nondenominationalism, a resurgence of Calvinist evangelicalism, and new strategies for cooperation.

### Baptists in a Postdenominational Religious Culture

Membership in nondenominational churches increased dramatically at the beginning of the twenty-first century. The popularity of these churches created an increasingly postdenominational religious culture that challenged traditional churches. In order to connect with the appeal of nondenominational communities, some churches maintained partnerships with denominations but without advertising denominational affiliations in the names of their churches. For example, the Saddleback Church in Lake Forest, California, formed multiple congregations and partnered with the SBC, though without identifying itself exclusively as a Baptist church. Saddleback's pastor, Rick Warren, reached a level of fame far beyond denominational boundaries, selling millions of copies of his books, including *The Purpose Driven Life* (2002), and offering the invocation at President Barack Obama's inauguration in 2009. On his Web site, Warren claimed to teach "theology without using theological terms and telling people it is theology"— an educational strategy that attempted to address human needs with nontraditional and nondenominational methods. This trend has led some churches to drop the name "Baptist" in favor of brands that communicate a positive, spiritual message, while casting aside traditional labels that some perceive as outdated and legalistic. In probably the most visible example, the Southern Baptist Convention changed the name of its Baptist bookstores to LifeWay Christian Stores, and even changed the name of the Sunday School Board to LifeWay Christian Resources. The nondenominational movement has influenced the American religious landscape with its megachurches and bestselling authors. But perhaps more prominently, the success of unaffiliated churches has influenced traditional denominations to rethink their identities.

### The Perseverance of Calvinism

The debate between Calvinism and Arminianism has always engaged Baptists. Weary of theological quarrels, John Leland asserted that preachers should be Calvinist in proclaiming God's sovereignty and Arminian in asserting human freedom. Much Baptist theology has pursued this moderately Calvinist position, retaining a sense of God's authority without sacrificing human agency. But that balance has been difficult to achieve. At the start of the twenty-first century, evangelical Calvinism surged in Baptist denominations. With the downfall of the moderate movement in the SBC, the convention moved in a more Calvinist direction with leaders such as Albert Mohler, president of Southern Seminary. Perhaps the most prominent Calvinist thinker among Baptists was John Piper, bestselling author and pastor of Bethlehem Baptist Church in Minneapolis, Minnesota. The central thrust of the renewed popularity of Calvinism among Baptists seemed to be a hunger for doctrinal depth in what some perceived to be a shallow religious culture.

## The Quest for Unity

Baptist history is a narrative of conflict. Despite their passion for independence, Baptists have always sought cooperation, though most efforts toward unity have caused further divisions. In the early twenty-first century, Baptists made significant moves toward reconciliation. In January 2005 the four predominantly African American Baptist denominations cooperated in a historic meeting in Nashville, Tennessee. These denominations—the National Baptist Convention, USA, Inc., the National Baptist Convention of America, Inc., the Progressive National Baptist Convention, Inc., and the National Missionary Baptist Convention of America— met not only to signify their ecclesial unity, they also issued statements calling for an end to the war in Iraq and opposing several domestic policies of President George W. Bush's administration.

Just over a year later, former president Jimmy Carter convened a group of Baptists to represent the vast diversity of Baptist life, moving across geographical, racial, theological, and cultural differences. These representatives produced a "North American Baptist Covenant," which stressed social justice on behalf of the poor and advocated "religious liberty and respect for religious diversity." A meeting of this New Baptist Covenant in early 2008 included over thirty Baptist groups. Noticeably absent was the Southern Baptist Convention, and many conservatives viewed the covenant as a politically liberal response to the politically conservative agendas of the SBC, which had long affiliated with the Republican Party and the Religious Right. In contrast, supporters of the New Baptist Covenant included not only Carter but also other prominent Democrats, including former president Bill Clinton and former vice president Al Gore. The formation of the New Baptist Covenant, and the reaction against it, demonstrated how thoroughly Baptist identity had become politicized—an ironic development for a tradition noted for advocating religious liberty and the separation of church and state.

## Conclusion

Although the Baptist denomination has a global presence, 75 percent of the world's Baptists live in the United States. Several factors account for Baptist success in North America. Theologically, most Baptists have resisted creeds, allowing for much diversity in doctrinal convictions. This flexibility has allowed Baptists to expand their reach across the theological spectrum. Baptists have been leading liberal theologians, such as Walter Rauschenbusch, and prominent fundamentalists, such as Jerry Falwell. Even with this theological diversity, most Baptists have advocated three convictions that have been enormously successful in populating the American religious landscape: the importance of revivalism, the necessity of missionary zeal (both at home and abroad), and ultimate allegiance to the Bible in theology and practice. Clearly Baptists have disagreed on these issues. They have debated revivalist theologies and strategies, argued over whether missionary societies were an asset to missions or their downfall, and divided over the inerrancy of scripture. But even divisions on these points have furthered Baptist growth, allowing for a variety of communities that claim the name Baptist. Because of their conviction for local church autonomy, theological divisions have pushed Baptists outward, allowing them to reinvent themselves in different locations to reach diverse communities. This conviction for autonomy has never eclipsed Baptists' desire for unity, but Baptist organizations have always been tenuous. In Baptist life, commitments to autonomy and independence have both stimulated Baptist growth and imperiled large-scale Baptist cooperation.

*See also* *Anabaptists; Baptists* entries; *Bible: Interpretation of; Calvinist/Reformed Tradition and Heritage; Canada: Protestants and the United Church of Canada; Fundamentalism; Latino American Religion; Mainline Protestants; Missions* entries; *Revivalism* entries.

James P. Byrd

## BIBLIOGRAPHY

Ammerman, Nancy Tatom. *Baptist Battles: Social Change and Religious Conflict in the Southern Baptist Convention.* New Brunswick, N.J.: Rutgers University Press, 1990.

Backus, Isaac. *Isaac Backus on Church, State and Calvinism: Pamphlets, 1754–1789.* Cambridge, Mass.: Harvard University Press, 1968.

Brackney, William H. *Baptists in North America: An Historical Perspective.* Malden, Mass.: Blackwell Publishing, 2006.

———. *A Genetic History of Baptist Thought.* Macon, Ga.: Mercer University Press, 2004.

Byrd, James P. *The Challenges of Roger Williams: Religious Liberty, Violent Persecution, and the Bible.* Macon, Ga.: Mercer University Press, 2002.

Dawson, Joseph Martin. *Baptists and the American Republic.* Nashville: Broadman Press, 1956.

Durso, Pamela, and Keith Durso. *The Story of Baptists in the United States.* Brentwood, Tenn.: Baptist History and Heritage Society, 2006.

Ernst, Eldon G. "The Baptists." In *Encyclopedia of the American Religious Experience: Studies of Traditions and Movements,* ed. Charles H. Lippy and Peter W. Williams, 555–577. New York: Scribner, 1988.

Evans, Christopher Hodge. *The Kingdom Is Always but Coming: A Life of Walter Rauschenbusch.* Grand Rapids, Mich.: Eerdmans, 2004.

Flynt, Wayne. *Alabama Baptists: Southern Baptists in the Heart of Dixie.* Tuscaloosa: University of Alabama Press, 1998.

Gardner, Robert C. *Baptists of Early America: A Statistical History, 1639–1790.* Atlanta: Georgia Baptist Historical Society, 1983.

Gaustad, Edwin S. *Liberty of Conscience: Roger Williams in America,* Grand Rapids, Mich.: Eerdmans, 1991.

Gaustad, Edwin S., and Bill J. Leonard. "Baptist Churches." In *Encyclopedia of Religion,* 2nd ed., ed. Lindsay Jones. Detroit: Macmillan Reference USA, 2005.

Goen, C. C. *Broken Churches, Broken Nation: Denominational Schisms and the Coming of the American Civil War.* Macon, Ga.: Mercer University Press, 1985.

———. *Revivalism and Separatism in New England, 1740–1800: Strict Congregationalists and Separate Baptists in the Great Awakening.* Middletown, Conn.: Wesleyan University Press, 1987.

Hankins, Barry. *God's Rascal: J. Frank Norris and the Beginnings of Southern Fundamentalism.* Lexington: University Press of Kentucky, 1996.

———. *Uneasy in Babylon: Southern Baptist Conservatives and American Culture.* Tuscaloosa: University of Alabama Press, 2002.

Harvey, Paul. *Redeeming the South: Religious Cultures and Racial Identities among Southern Baptists, 1865–1925.* Chapel Hill: University of North Carolina Press, 1997.

Hatch, Nathan O. *The Democratization of American Christianity.* New Haven, Conn.: Yale University Press, 1991.

Higginbotham, Evelyn Brooks. *Righteous Discontent: The Women's Movement in the Black Baptist Church, 1880–1920.* Cambridge, Mass.: Harvard University Press, 1993.

Holifield, E. Brooks. *Theology in America: Christian Thought from the Age of the Puritans to the Civil War.* New Haven, Conn.: Yale University Press, 2003.

Leland, John, and L. F. Greene. *The Writings of John Leland.* New York: Arno Press, 1969.

Leonard, Bill J. *Baptists in America.* New York: Columbia University Press, 2005.

———. *Baptist Ways: A History.* Valley Forge, Pa.: Judson Press, 2003.

Leonard, Bill, ed. *Dictionary of Baptists in America.* Downers Grove, Ill.: InterVarsity Press, 1994.

McLoughlin, William G. *New England Dissent, 1630–1833: The Baptists and the Separation of Church and State,* 2 vols. Cambridge, Mass.: Harvard University Press, 1971.

———. *Soul Liberty: The Baptists' Struggle in New England, 1630–1833.* Hanover, New Hampshire: University Press of New England, 1991.

Moon, Lottie, and Keith Harper. *Send the Light: Lottie Moon's Letters and Other Writings.* Macon, Ga.: Mercer University Press, 2002.

Newman, Mark. *Getting Right with God: Southern Baptists and Desegregation, 1945–1995.* Tuscaloosa, University of Alabama Press, 2001.

Noll, Mark A. *America's God: From Jonathan Edwards to Abraham Lincoln.* New York: Oxford University Press, 2002.

———. *The Civil War as a Theological Crisis.* Chapel Hill: University of North Carolina Press, 2006.

PEW Forum on Religion and Public Life. *U.S. Religious Landscape Survey,* February, 2008, http://religions.pewforum.org.

Pitts, Walter F. *Old Ship of Zion: The Afro-Baptist Ritual in the African Diaspora.* New York: Oxford University Press, 1993.

Rauschenbusch, Walter. *Christianity and the Social Crisis.* Louisville, Ky.: Westminster/John Knox Press, 1991.

Shurden, Walter B. *Associationalism among Baptists in America, 1707–1814.* New York: Arno Press, 1980.

———. *Not a Silent People: Controversies That Have Shaped Southern Baptists.* Macon, Ga.: Smyth and Helwys, 1995.

Shurden, Walter B., and Randy Shepley. *Going for the Jugular: A Documentary History of the SBC Holy War.* Macon, Ga.: Mercer University Press, 1996.

Spain, Rufus B., and Samuel S. Hill. *At Ease in Zion: A Social History of Southern Baptists, 1865–1900.* Tuscaloosa: University of Alabama Press, 2003.

Willis, Alan Scot. *All According to God's Plan: Southern Baptist Missions and Race, 1945–1970.* Lexington: University Press of Kentucky, 2005.

Wilson, Charles Reagan. *Baptized in Blood: The Religion of the Lost Cause, 1865–1920.* Athens: University of Georgia Press, 1980.

# Benevolent Empire

The Benevolent Empire was a name given to a group of interrelated organizations born of revivalism and Protestant evangelicalism in the first part of the nineteenth century in the United States. These groups included missionary societies, Bible and tract societies, and educational and Sunday school societies that eventually became national presences. They laid the foundations for a variety of later reform organizations, some religious and some secular, including those associated with temperance, antislavery, and women's rights. Also known as the Evangelical United Front, the Benevolent Empire was an interdenominational movement that used new organizational means associated with the growth of market capitalism to create communities of like-minded Christians, harnessing their energies in nationally oriented evangelical and reform causes. In addition, Benevolent Empire organizations tried to extend the reach of evangelical Christianity to include non-Christian peoples, both foreign and domestic. In the process of using new measures—including interlocking organizational directorates, mass communications, and nationally coordinated fundraising—the Benevolent Empire helped to transform the relationship between Protestantism and American society.

The major Benevolent Empire organizations included the American Board of Commissioners for Foreign Missions (chartered in 1812), the American Bible Society (1816), the American Sunday School Union (1824), and the American Tract Society (1825), with the American Education Society (1815) and the American Home Missionary Society (1826) also a part of the united effort. A generation after they began to flourish, these organizations spawned a second wave of reform that took on a life of its own outside the Protestant evangelical establishment. Of these, the American Temperance Society (1826) and the American Anti-Slavery Society (1833) both had significant and long-lasting effects on American civic and political life, although their rise to visibility also spelled the end of the Benevolent Empire model of cooperative evangelical effort that gave rise to them.

## Benevolent Origins: Ideological and Denominational Roots

Evangelically driven reform societies were a presence in much of the English-speaking world in the nineteenth century. Those that grew and flourished in the first half of the century in the United States and that came to make up the Benevolent Empire resembled those elsewhere dedicated to spreading a particular, theologically driven vision of individual behavior and cultural values through the use of sophisticated organizational and marketing techniques. American Benevolent Empire organizations with national aspirations arose in the northeastern part of the United States between about 1790 and 1830. These organizations nearly always were patterned after, and sometimes directly linked to, similar organizations among British dissenting groups. They were part of a transatlantic impulse in which religiously motivated people organized into voluntary associations to evangelize, using both modern techniques of business management and mass media as means to their goal.

### Theological and Organizational Roots

In the United States several ideological factors converged to give rise to the missionary, education, and tract organizations that arose in the last decade of the eighteenth century and the first decade of the nineteenth and that became the regional prototypes for Benevolent Empire associations. These included a Neo-Calvinist theology that emphasized self-abnegation and disinterested service to others; transatlantic connections with dissenter groups, who themselves were energized by opposition to the French Revolution to increase evangelical outreach; and an internal denominational split between theologically conservative Congregationalist and Presbyterian elites, on the one hand, and liberal rationalists from the same traditions, on the other.

Most Benevolent Empire organizations had common theological roots in the Hopkinsian Calvinist tradition, the "New Divinity," that arose in Congregational New

England and Presbyterian New York and New Jersey between about 1760 and 1790. The Reverend Samuel Hopkins (1721–1803), pastor of the First Congregational Church in Newport, Rhode Island, and one of the principal proponents of this theology, claimed the spiritual mantle of the renowned Jonathan Edwards. Their theology focused on the concept of *disinterested benevolence,* or the willingness to seek the good of the whole as decreed by God's plan and to abandon selfishness, the source of all sin. Or, as Hopkins put it,

> No man can know that he loves God until he does really love him; that is, until he does seek his glory above all things, and is disposed to say, "Let God be glorified, whatever may be necessary in order to it," without making any exception; and this is to be willing to be damned, if this be necessary for the glory of God. (*The Works of Samuel Hopkins, D.D.,* 148.)

The philosophy of turning away from self and toward work for the good of all became the underpinning of a movement that lasted several generations. Organizations formed on Hopkinsian principles had in common the belief that Christian individuals were called to work for the good of all.

At about the time the New Divinity gained adherents among the conservative elite Calvinist ministry in the Northeast, Protestant dissenters in Britain, including mainly Presbyterians, Baptists, and Congregationalists, formed organizations designed to evangelize, both within Britain and in parts of the world that were becoming parts of its empire. American Calvinists and British Nonconformists had long enjoyed a correspondence with one another. Major developments among the one group were readily known by the other. Jonathan Edwards's 1747 plea for corporate concerts of prayer for the revival of religion around the world was a shared project for both. During the last third of the eighteenth century, as British Nonconformists began to rely on printed materials to extend the reach of evangelization efforts to the poor, to the unchurched, and to non-Christians in foreign parts, American Calvinist ministers quickly became aware of those efforts. A growing British evangelical press supported the extension of missionary and tract organizations whose goal, in an era of revolution on the Continent, was to maintain and to extend religious values that would make for a well-ordered society.

The Society for Promoting Religious Knowledge among the Poor, founded in 1750, was the first of Britain's tract societies in which the distribution of printed literature became a major vehicle for evangelization. A Sunday School Society, organized in London in 1785, brought institutional advocacy to the spread of Sabbath schools. By the 1790s efforts to use mass forms of communication to spread religious values picked up speed with the founding of missionary societies that relied on print to recruit supporters and attract funding. These organizations included the London Missionary Society (founded in 1794 by British Baptists), the Religious Tract Society (founded by Hannah More in 1799), and the British and Foreign Bible Society (1804).

The earliest American evangelical organizers knew of British efforts—their goals, their methods, and their organizational practices. The books, journals, and society reports used by the British to publicize their efforts provided prototypes for would-be local organizers, who, by the late 1790s, began to form home-grown groups in the United States. Once print became a major factor in generating membership and sustaining the identification of members with new geographically dispersed organizations, it was only a matter of time before economies of scale led to the mergers of the smaller organizations into larger umbrella groups that could handle recruitment, fundraising and expenditures, and print dissemination more efficiently from centralized locations such as New York, Philadelphia, and Boston.

## The Second Great Awakening and University Politics

Although the theology of evangelical benevolence and the example of British organizations provided important preconditions for the rise of evangelical organizations in the American Northeast during this period, their appearance on the scene has been most strongly associated with what has been called the Second Great Awakening. Beginning in the late 1790s and continuing through the mid-1830s, an orientation toward revival became a marker of evangelical identity among many associated with the Calvinist tradition in the United States. This revivalism, both as a shared practice and as a sign of a distinct theological orientation, sparked a widening split between orthodox and rationalist elements of the New England Congregationalist establishment. By the 1820s the movement resulted in a full-fledged schism between orthodox Congregationalists and Unitarians, with complete religious disestablishment an accomplished fact everywhere in the region by 1833.

With disestablishment, the role of religion in society was transformed. In the new religiously pluralist environment, denominations now competed with each other for adherents and resources. As evangelical activism and outreach received new emphasis, affiliated parachurch organizations sprang up to organize adherents in new ways to maintain religious identity. Distinctive theological differences and competition for confessional loyalty played a larger role in New England in the earliest stages of Benevolent Empire organization than it did in New York, Pennsylvania, or New Jersey, where disestablishment was already the rule and where there was less at stake in terms of competition for real property or civic influence. By the 1820s and 1830s, however, competition for communicants had become the common rule there, with the revivals of Charles Grandison Finney (1792–1875)—a New York Presbyterian and lawyer turned preacher—playing a particularly visible role. What was to be the relationship between religious and civic values in a nation where religious establishments would no longer serve as a formal pillar of social authority and order? The sociologist Michael P. Young has argued (in *Bearing Witness against Sin,* 2006, p.49) that the Second Great Awakening was less important in effecting direct change in actual religious practice among Americans than in establishing "religious competition among evangelical Protestants [that] created a national religious audience before there was a truly national economic market or a national electorate." Although religious awakening was the governing metaphor of the time, what may really have been at stake was an organizational revolution sparked by shifting local and translocal realignments and power shifts.

New England's Old Calvinists, who had the most to lose through erosion of their power, by the 1790s called for a new wave of revivals, which they linked explicitly with Edwards's 1747 call for prayer for the revival of true religion. Connecticut's Yale University, under the leadership of President Timothy Dwight (a grandson of Edwards), became the training grounds for those advocating revival-inspired conversion. Massachusetts's Harvard University, in contrast, served as the seminary of choice for the portion of the establishment that had adopted rationalist and gradualist approaches to both religion and life. The Yale group had strong links to Presbyterian and Dutch Reformed groups in New York and New Jersey; the Harvard-trained ministry, cosmopolitan and market-oriented, dominated mainly Boston and its environs.

Dwight, the president of Yale, was concerned not only about right theology but also about cultural changes he feared might transform a milieu dominated by the Congregational (and Federalist) elite into at best a democratic anarchy and at worst a clergy-killing mirror of the atheistic French. Jedidiah Morse, who was perhaps the most prominent of Massachusetts's conservative clergy, took the lead in denouncing liberalism as the road to atheism. He turned to the press to combat the forces of irreligion, denouncing a purported international conspiracy against religion led by a group of European atheists, the Bavarian Illuminati. Alarms about a rising tide of religious disaffection combined with calls for religious revivals, which were formally advocated by the Connecticut General Association of Ministers in 1798. In response to attacks on Calvinist Christianity, the threat of disestablishment, and a rising tide of irreligion, the orthodox clergy preached a renewed attention to conversion, as well as to the biblical Great Commission (Matthew 28: 16–20), in which Jesus exhorts his followers to spread the gospel.

By 1805 the appointment of liberal minister Henry Ware to the Hollis Professorship of Divinity at Harvard signaled to the more conservative and moderate Calvinist faction the institutional triumph of liberalism. With their control of the religious establishment slipping, "orthodox Calvinists" entered into battles with the liberals over the control of Massachusetts's Congregational churches. In the process they came increasingly to emphasize their theological distinctiveness, which consisted in their orientation to revivals and religious conversions, a theology based in benevolence, and an emphasis on evangelization. To realize their newly articulated objectives, they founded an institution dedicated to educating an evangelical ministry, Andover Seminary (1807), which over time became a headquarters for Benevolent Empire activity and a training ground for its clerical leadership. In addition, in the year of Ware's appointment as Hollis Professor, the conservatives began to use the press in systematic ways to yoke missionary organization and extension with the antiliberal cause. The *Panoplist,* a magazine of Christian biography and missionary work published by the Massachusetts Missionary Society and edited by Morse, fused benevolent causes and antiliberal theology, in the process helping to create a new evangelical audience for religious literature in the Northeast.

These factors—evangelical impulse, British models, the theology of benevolence, and the culture of revivalism—provided rationales for organizations that brought together geographically dispersed devotees into a united effort.

Although the initial efforts were locally organized and managed, they had in common governing boards that included prominent ministers and laypeople; a need for fundraising on a larger scale than before; the production of either journals or annual reports to give heightened visibility to organizations; and the necessity to engage in public relations, both as an evangelical imperative and as a practical matter of economic survival. In the early days of their existence, ministerial associations tended to be the driving force behind many of these organizations, with women often a strong behind-the-scenes force. Over time, however, the functions of these organizations necessitated separate incorporation as legal entities and the inclusion of lay directors, executive secretaries, or other officers. Organizational boards often read like a list of the most prominent evangelical civic leaders of the new market-driven Northeast, with bankers, lawyers, and merchants presiding over well-organized and integrated initiatives.

## Benevolence Abroad: Foreign Missions

Evangelicals first organized in major ways around missionary endeavors. Missions had existed in New England and the Atlantic states since European settlement began. But evangelical ferment, sparked by British precedent and a desire to differentiate the religion of the converted from the religion of the complacent, led to the formation of missionary organizations such as the New York Missionary Society (1796), the Northern (New York) Missionary Society (1797), the Missionary Society of Connecticut (1798), and the Massachusetts Missionary Society (1799), among others. Oriented not only to evangelization as a general goal but to the distinctive experience of the converted and their need to promulgate their own social values, these organizations were intended to support conversion of the "heathen," to spread revivals, and to ensure that the sons and daughters of the Yankee exodus continued to be churched in the ways of their fathers and mothers.

Churches had a long history of sponsoring missionary efforts in New England and New York aimed at the conversion of Indians. The British- and Anglican-based Society for the Propagation of the Gospel in Foreign Parts, for example, played a major role in helping to fund the Congregational mission to the Indians it set up in Stockbridge, Massachusetts, in 1734. Efforts to Christianize Indians in New York and New Jersey proceeded throughout this period as well. (By "conversion," missionaries meant not only adoption of Christian beliefs and religious practices but also of values associated with settled agriculture and literacy—a set of goals that would carry over into work with non-Christians in foreign lands.) By the last third of the eighteenth century, the increasing flow of out-migrants to new white settlements in remote areas led to concern among the established clergy of New England and among mid-Atlantic Presbyterians that missionary efforts ought to focus not only on conversion of the Indians but also on the religious needs of those moving to far-flung regions in search of land. By 1797 the Connecticut General Association, in consultation with the local ministerial associations of the state, determined to constitute a state missionary society, whose aims would be "to Christianize the heathen in North America and to support and promote Christian knowledge in the new settlements within the United States."

Presbyterians and Congregationalists of Massachusetts, New York, New Hampshire, and Vermont quickly followed suit with the incorporation of similar state organizations, and Baptists in many locations formed organizations of their own as well. The larger organizations published their own missionary magazines to disseminate news of evangelical progress to large groups of people, to raise funds for continuing efforts, and to provide godly reading material, particularly for those in newly settled areas without the services of regular pastors. The *Connecticut Evangelical Magazine* and the *New York Missionary Magazine* began publication in 1800, the *Massachusetts Missionary Magazine* and the *Baptist Missionary Magazine* in 1803. Women's missionary organizations and charitable "cent societies," whose institutional structures nearly always remained local, contributed to these efforts as well.

## The Haystack Revival and the Rise of National Organizations

Just as the desire to expand missionary activity produced the first evangelically inspired local organizations, they also produced the first Benevolent Empire organization with national aspirations. Inspired by the example of the British Baptist missionary William Carey and his *Particular Baptist Society for Propagating the Gospel Among the Heathen* (1792), five earnest young men from Williams College, who were converted in the so-called Haystack Revival in 1806, lobbied the orthodox wing of the established Massachusetts ministry until, in 1810, they gained support for their own missionary project. The first foreign missionary association in the United States, the American Board of Commissioners for Foreign Missions (ABCFM), proposed to send evangelists to foreign nations to convert non-Christians. Samuel Mills, the leader of the Williams group (and a future founder of the American Bible Society as well as the ABCFM), spearheaded the effort to persuade the established Congregational clergy to support the first foreign effort, a mission to south Asia along the lines of those of Carey and the Baptists.

With the ABCFM, evangelical benevolent organizations began to aspire to a larger reach and scope. The desire to extend the geographic reach of the new missionary effort led to an invitation by the Massachusetts General Association of Ministers to the General Association of Connecticut, requesting that they send representatives to a governing board. With the addition of four representatives from Connecticut to five from Massachusetts, the American Board came into existence as a foreign missionary organization that its founders hoped would mirror the aspirations and successes of its British counterpart. Its constitution specified that at least one-third of the membership of the board would consist of laypeople and at least one-third of clergy, with the remaining one-third to be drawn from either group. When formally incorporated as a legal entity in 1812, however, the American Board became separate from the organizations from which it sprang, with four designated fields of missionary endeavor: people of ancient civilizations, primitive cultures, the ancient Christian churches, and Islam. The Presbyterian General Assembly endorsed the efforts of the ABCFM, but the New York Presbyterians and Dutch Reformed organized their own foreign mission association in 1817. In 1826, however, the two groups merged into one under the ABCFM designation, with membership drawn not only from much of New England but also from much of New York, New Jersey, and eastern Pennsylvania. The American Baptist Foreign Mission Society (ABFMS), born of the conversion of American Board missionaries Adoniram and Ann Hasseltine Judson to the Baptist faith while on mission in Burma in 1814, and similar in aim and organization to the Congregational and Presbyterian Societies, always remained a separate and parallel effort.

## American Board Missionaries

The American Board sent its first delegation of missionaries to Marathi, British India, in 1813. In the next quarter-century its agents established foreign missions in fourteen locations in China, Asia Minor, south Asia, Africa, and the Pacific Islands. Beginning in 1817, home missions to the Cherokee, the Chickasaw, the Choctaw, and the Osage Indian peoples were established. Wherever American Board missions were planted, they had a common agenda: cultivating native evangelists, opening schools to teach literacy skills, translating the Bible into local languages, and inculcating a set of cultural values related to family and work that would integrate the evangelized groups into the Euro-American cultural orbit. Young men who aspired to missionary work were required to be married—in part to allow for a stable family existence in a foreign environment, in part to head off any tendency unattached men might have to marry local women. For the first time, women might take on the work of missionaries as well by marrying young men bound for foreign evangelization. Women were active partners in the missionary endeavor. They were charged not only with making homes and families for male missionaries, but also with the specific work of evangelizing women and children. Often a particular concern, not only for the women missionaries but for readers following mission efforts back home, was finding ways to raise the status of women in "foreign" cultures.

Missionary exploits received significant coverage in the newly prominent religious press of the period. The American Board's *Panoplist and Missionary Magazine,* successor to the *Massachusetts Missionary Magazine,* thrived under the editorship of Jeremiah Evarts, later the corresponding secretary of the organization. The periodical became an all-purpose missionary organ conveying information on evangelism efforts, both foreign and domestic, and represented a new mass medium that served as an alternative to the secular press for many of the pious. Read by women as well as by men, missionary periodicals fueled the formation of evangelical communities of identity and common purpose—a national "virtual community" in a country where organizations of other types with national reach were still weak or nonexistent. The print media provided stories of revivals and missionary exploits, advice, pious meditation, and scriptural commentary that gave its readers a common vocabulary and universe of discourse.

## Benevolence at Home: The Benevolent Empire and Print Evangelization

In contrast to the foreign mission effort, which had its strongest American roots in New England Congregationalism, the work of Bible production, distribution, and dissemination began largely in the Middle Atlantic states, particularly among Presbyterians of New Jersey and Philadelphia. The city, a major center of commercial activity and print production in the early Republic, was a prime location for an evangelical ministry that focused, as its primary activity, on dissemination of the Word of God "without note or commentary." Although this region gave rise to the first local American Bible societies, these groups quickly spread to other areas dominated by educated and well-capitalized religious elites. Modeled on the British and Foreign Bible Society, founded in 1804, Bible societies formed quickly in 1808 and 1809 in Pennsylvania, Connecticut, Massachusetts, New Jersey, and New York. Twenty-eight local and regional societies existed in the Northeast by 1816, with nearly a hundred nationwide. These bodies organized to raise money to purchase Bibles and to find ways to distribute them to the needy. Since the principle of *sola scriptura*—the sufficiency of the Bible alone—lay at the heart of the Calvinist tradition, knowledge of true religion required direct access to scripture by literate individuals. In a world where literacy was tied to religious responsibility, access to the Bible meant not only the ability to know the sacred, it also implied the ability to read in general.

### Nationalization of Bible Societies

As with missionary societies, Bible societies first existed as independent or loosely affiliated organizations headed by wealthy laymen, mainly merchants and local professionals, as well as by clergy. They formed nerve centers for the collection of funds and the distribution of Bibles to the poor and indigent within their respective geographic areas. However, a report in 1813 by ABCFM missionary Samuel Mills, who had toured the West with fellow missionary J. F. Schermerhorn, triggered an effort at national organization linked to the needs of that newly expanding realm of missionary activity. Mills, a Connecticut Congregationalist minister who had been a leader in the Williams College Haystack prayer group and was one of the major organizers of the American Board, went on a missionary journey to the Mississippi Valley in 1812. On his return, he spoke with urgency to the problem of supplying white settlers there, and the unchurched everywhere, with appropriate religious materials—an effort that might require up to half a million Bibles. Not coincidentally, his pleas took on added force because many of those without Bibles in the West were Roman Catholic and perceived as a threat to the good order of Protestant America—a Benevolent Empire theme that would grow in importance as time went on. "The existing societies are not able to do this work," Mills wrote. "They want union; they want cooperation; they want resources. If a National

Institution cannot be formed, application ought to be made immediately to the British and Foreign Bible Society for aid." (*The Centennial History of the American Bible Society,* 15.)

Mills's cry of alarm found a response in both the Philadelphia Bible Society, which began a massive effort to coordinate the supply of the needed materials, and in Elias Boudinot, a prominent New Jersey Presbyterian layman who had served in the Continental and U.S. Congresses, as a Princeton University trustee, and as president of the New Jersey Bible Society. Boudinot, like Morse and his Connecticut theocrat colleagues, had since Thomas Paine's *The Age of Reason* (1795) feared the inroads of deism and rationalism on American life. Boudinot promoted Mills's plan for a national organization. After considerable effort and some opposition from the stronger local societies (including Philadelphia's), he succeeded in forming a national organization for the distribution of Bibles that included six different denominations. The emphasis on the mutual cooperation of geographically dispersed and confessionally different groups to promote a common evangelical Christian agenda became an important hallmark of Benevolent Empire organizations. For the American Bible Society (ABS), it was also the source of the stipulation that the Bibles distributed be "without note or commentary."

Under Boudinot's leadership, the American Bible Society was established in New York in 1816 to coordinate the efforts of numerous local Bible societies (auxiliaries) under the umbrella of an organization capable of large-scale reach and productivity. The agreement of Congregationalist leaders Lyman Beecher and Jedidiah Morse, who served on the executive committee of the New York Bible Society, was important to bridging differences and creating the multidenominational organization. Like most other Benevolent Empire societies, it was controlled by a lay board with business expertise and, as Peter Wosh noted (in *The Bible Business in Nineteenth-Century America,* 1994, p. 39–40), it was possessed of "a broad cosmopolitan outlook and extensive participation in a transatlantic, Anglo-American world of business, benevolence, and intellectual life." Called forth by Mills's missionary rhetoric, the society formed at a time when new technologies made an economy of scale in printing and distribution a real possibility. Consolidation of capital and the introduction of business management techniques proved vital to the success of these new large-scale and print-based endeavors. The new stereotype technology for printing, along with the use of steam power, made possible production in bulk. A national pooling of capital for mass production of Bibles and Testaments made not only good religious sense but good business sense as well.

## The American Bible Society

At first the goal of the American Bible Society (ABS) was solely to ensure that Bibles were placed into the hands of Americans who could not afford them. The national organization relied heavily on local auxiliaries to gauge need in their local regions, to raise funds, and to distribute the Bibles and cheap Testaments that were the stock in trade of the society. In exchange for returning to the national body any surplus of funds, auxiliaries would receive Bibles at 5 percent below cost and would have voting rights at the national level. As time went on, major alterations took place in the relationship between locals and the national coordinating body. First, it rapidly became clear that auxiliaries could not predictably provide the cash to ensure continuous production. The ABS began to hire agents of its own—up to forty in the 1820s—to raise money and distribute Bibles as a supplement to the efforts of the auxiliaries. These agents were generally seminary students or trained ministers who abandoned settled pastorates for a while to undertake the distribution of the Word in printed form as their calling. In addition, the ABS grappled with the problem of funding the production and distribution of Bibles using only a charitable model. Over time the group moved to a system of production of Bibles for sale, with a system of differential pricing requiring recipients to pay what they could afford. Middle-class demand for elaborate Bibles led to an increase of production for the market. It also, however, produced protests from commercial book publishers and sellers who saw a staple of their own businesses produced at lower cost.

ABS receipts more than tripled in the 1820s, in part because of these innovations in business structure and production and in part because of a major campaign to ensure that every family in the United States had a Bible by 1831. Although the latter campaign met with considerable success, it had lost steam by 1833 and was revived on an even larger scale with a campaign to supply the entire world with Bibles within twenty years. The ABS thereby expanded its mission to include the world and began to invest in the translation of the Bible into various languages.

## The American Tract Society

Like many other of the Benevolent Empire organizations, the American Tract Society resulted from a merger of New

England and New York–based societies. As early as 1802, in imitation of the new British tract societies, Jedidiah Morse had promoted an early effort in Massachusetts to promote the production and distribution of tracts, chiefly for distribution in newer settlements. By 1814 a more ambitious regional effort, the New England Tract Society, had arisen out of the same Andover Seminary nexus that gave rise to the ABCFM. The Reverend Justin Edwards, later of temperance reform fame, took the lead in encouraging the collection of funds to publish Christian exhortations. The New England organization, formed explicitly to supply local societies with materials for distribution rather than to distribute those materials itself, was patterned on the work of the Bible societies. Tracts, upwards of four pages in length, commonly contained readable and homely stories about everyday behavior. As time went on, tracts also frequently contained woodcut illustrations. They were distributed at cost to regional depositories and local auxiliaries. By 1821 the New England society boasted relationships with seventy-one depositories nationwide, and in 1823 it legally changed its name to the American Tract Society.

Like the American Bible Society, the American Tract Society (ATS) was primarily a charitable venture organized to print material to give away. In a country flooded with print of various sorts, its goal was to compete in the marketplace of ideas and to establish an evangelical Christian presence, thereby ensuring the availability of popular reading material that inculcated godly attitudes and behavior. Like the American Bible Society, the ATS also relied on local auxiliaries, technologies for the mass production of print, governing boards comprising rich and well-connected businessmen and professionals, and regional depositories. And like the ABS the ATS was deliberately and explicitly interdenominational, its work premised on the belief that "the great body of evangelical Christians were agreed in all that truth which the Bible makes essential to vital godliness and salvation, and also in that which would promote sound morality." (*Letters to Members, Patrons, and Friends of the Branch American Tract Society in Boston, Instituted 1814; and to Those of the National Society in New York, Instituted 1825,* 8.) The multidenominational board charged with approving tracts for production guarded against publications that might promote particular theological tenets.

Although the first tract society with national aspirations grew from evangelical Congregational soil, tract societies were not exclusively—or especially—New England phenomena. Societies formed in New York (1812),

Philadelphia (1815), Baltimore (1816), and Hartford (1816), locations where a strong tradition of an educated Calvinist ministry and an accumulation of capital resources existed. Several of these produced extraordinary numbers of tracts for distribution. Although the New England–based American Tract Society signaled through its name its hopes of extending its national dominance, it was not to be. New York was clearly becoming the center of operations for most Benevolent Empire organizations. Increasingly important as national capital, commercial, and communication center, New York became the home of an expanded—and interdenominational—American Tract Society in 1825, with the Boston branch continuing to exist as an independent subsidiary of the national organization. The work of the new society received substantial underwriting from prominent merchant and reform benefactor Arthur Tappan, who, with his brother Lewis, later became central figures in the antislavery movement.

By the mid-1820s many tracts were mass-produced using stereotype technology. The efforts of the ATS to produce and distribute tracts mirrored closely those of the ABS, with an initiative to provide a "general supply" of tracts to all families in the United States through systematic monthly distribution beginning in 1829. Organizers hoped to disseminate the same tract everywhere to create a coordinated evangelical theme of the month. This effort had modest success, particularly in well-financed efforts in eastern cities. But as with the Bible initiative, tract distribution fell substantially short of aspirations, especially in the West. Where tracts circulated abundantly and freely, however, they became an especially important way for bringing home the lessons of scripture to young learners. In addition, they became a staple of Sunday schools as networks of the latter began to be established.

The ATS ran into problems of financing, with auxiliaries seldom remitting the required 25 percent of their annual receipts to the national organization. Beginning in 1827, the organization began to publish full-length books for sale to help offset the costs of production of tracts for charity distribution. Traveling agents were employed directly to address distribution problems in remote areas, but with mixed results. By 1841 the American Tract Society made a decision to professionalize, hiring salaried administrators, managers, and colporteurs. The result—an explosion in the number of books sold, tracts distributed, and territory covered—made the society a prominent force in antebellum America, not only in the spreading of evangelical Christianity but also in establishing a common canon of popular reading.

## The American Sunday School Union

The third major evangelical disseminator of print in the Benevolent Empire was the American Sunday School Union, founded in Philadelphia in 1824. Like other Benevolent Empire organizations, it was modeled on British practice dating from the 1780s. Although the first Sunday school in the United States began in Philadelphia in 1791 under the direction of the First Day Society, New York merchant Divie Bethune and his wife, Joanna (who in 1816 founded the Female Union for the Promotion of Sabbath Schools), were major forces in promoting American Sabbath schools, beginning with the school held in their home in 1803. Bethune, a Scottish immigrant, merchant, and one of the founders of Princeton Theological Seminary, was, according to observers of the time, not especially religious but exceedingly disturbed at the rising tide of profanity and vice around him. As in Britain, the very first Sunday schools were largely urban phenomena, as much concerned with teaching basic moral and cultural values of order as in raising literacy levels among children and adults. Over time, the population they served included significant numbers of African Americans, women, western residents, and children of the poor for whom no significant literacy alternatives existed.

The process and timing of Sabbath school development paralleled that of other Benevolent Empire societies: first, contemporaneous development of local and regional societies in urban commercial centers, such as Boston, Hartford, New York, New Haven, and Philadelphia; second, large-scale regional production of printed materials (books, pamphlets, and periodicals) designed for free dissemination, in this case through the libraries that became one of the chief attractions of the Sabbath schools; third, combination into an interdenominational national organization (including Congregationalists, Presbyterians, Baptists, Methodists, Episcopalians, Lutherans, and Reformed Dutch) designed to enlarge the project to a national scope and to increase its effectiveness by using economies of scale. The American Sunday School Union utilized the same relationship between auxiliaries and the national organization as that used by the ABS and the ATS. Like the ABS, it took on the role of publisher of books for the middle class, in part to help finance its charity ventures. It too embarked on an initiative to extend Sunday schools to unserved areas, chiefly in the West, and moved to partial reliance on paid iterant missionaries

and agents to do the job. Between 1824 and 1837 the number of children who attended Sunday schools increased from about fifty thousand to about a million.

## Other Organizations

The American Bible Society, the American Tract Society, and the American Sunday School Union were the major domestic evangelical arms of the Benevolent Empire. All had in common an emphasis on dissemination of a message of morality and salvation broadly acceptable to major evangelical denominations of the period through mass dissemination of the printed word. A number of other organizations also existed primarily for domestic evangelization purposes, especially among indigent and unchurched populations in the western United States. The most important of these included the American Education Society (1815), originally the American Society for Educating Pious Youth for the Gospel Ministry, established to provide funds to poor young men wishing to study for the evangelical ministry, and the American Home Missionary Society (1826), founded to evangelize sparsely settled areas, particularly in the West. As the Benevolent Empire grew in organization and power, campaigns increasingly were geared toward areas of newer settlement. The formal merger of the Presbyterian and Dutch Reformed missionary efforts with the (largely Congregationalist) ABCFM in 1826 ignited hope that a similar united effort might be mounted with regard to domestic missionary work as well. Societies from the three denominations combined to form the American Home Missionary Society, whose goal was to unite in an effort to bring evangelization and civilization to remote areas. By supporting new and feeble churches in newer and sparsely settled sections of the country, the organization would ensure the perpetuation of evangelical Christian values among those unable to support a settled pastor and the extension of those values to immigrant populations.

The specter of illiteracy and disorder as well as the perceived threat of Roman Catholicism to Protestant "civilization" evoked extraordinary efforts and new means to find ways to meet the challenge of growing populations dispersed over large geographical areas. By 1830 these organizations had raised more than $2.8 million for their charitable work. What had begun primarily as urban efforts by these groups expanded to take on the responsibility of service to vast reaches of the Republic without the capital or resources to found similar organizations or auxiliaries on their own. Western efforts sponsored by the Benevolent

Empire reached their apex in the early 1830s. By 1835, however, the evangelist Lyman Beecher, who had moved from New England to Ohio, called for a significant shift in tactics. Itinerants and Bibles from the East were no longer enough, he proclaimed in *A Plea for the West* (1835): It was time for the West to train its own ministry and erect its own institutions. In essence, Beecher's sermon made a case for the West as something other than missionary territory. Culture and institutions, he argued, must reach a stage where they were not sustained by national evangelization efforts but produced their own. Such institutions, he maintained, would bring on the millennium, which was America's role to herald.

## The Age of Reform: Perfectionism, Temperance, and Antislavery

A theology of benevolence, modeled by British organizations and picked up by educated American clergy in the Calvinist tradition, set off the waves of evangelical organization that began in the 1790s. The first phase of benevolent reform involved widespread agreement among evangelical Protestants—mainly Presbyterians, Congregationalists, Baptists, and Dutch Reformed, but also sometimes Methodists, Episcopalians, and Lutherans—on the importance of disseminating sacred scripture, making available moral reading, and providing instruction in evangelical values. Although governing boards of the major Benevolent Empire organizations were controlled largely by prominent laypeople, these engines of evangelization were also closely tied to the denominations that gave rise to them, and publication boards with varied denominational representation exercised control over the organizations' publications. By the late 1820s and early 1830s the organizational model was well established, and in a form that could be reproduced endlessly by new organizations: a central governing board supported by local auxiliaries that acted as the "hands and feet" of the national group; an emphasis on the use of printed media to create an identity of interest and sentiment among adherents and to raise funds for further extension of the organization; and an emphasis on interdenominational cooperation rather than competition in the support of common evangelical goals.

### Rise of Perfectionism

By the 1820s, however, the well-established Benevolent Empire began to experience shifts in tone and operation. These would lead within a decade to reform activity taking on a life of its own apart from its evangelical denominational base. First, organizations of a new type arose—groups such as the Prison Discipline Society (1825), the American Seamen's Friend Society (1826), the General Union for the Promotion of the Observance of the Sabbath (1828), the American Peace Society (1828), and Magdalen societies for the redemption of prostitutes in Philadelphia (1826) and New York (1829). Their efforts, while based on the benevolent organization model, more narrowly focused on eradicating particular sins or on outreach to particular groups. In addition, by the late 1820s and early 1830s even mainline benevolent organizations had also begun to turn to paid agents and managers to realize their aims, creating a group of ministers and employees tied to the particular cause of the organization rather than to general evangelical work. This group of agents who saw themselves tied to particular reforms first and the general cause of evangelicalism second caused a change in the rhetoric surrounding reform. Perhaps most important, "perfectionism," a new theology emphasizing individual choice in conversion and establishing the eradication of sin as an ideal, began to displace Hopkinsian benevolence among a new generation of evangelicals oriented to possibility.

These factors created a shift in cultural climate and led to a new wave of reform. In many ways, the new type of reform efforts shared much in common organizationally and operationally with first-wave benevolent organizations. But a philosophy of social purification and focus on the eradication of sin eventually set several key new organizations at odds with both the organized churches and the Benevolent Empire apparatus on which it was modeled. Two organizations in particular took on special importance: the American Temperance Society (formed in 1826; renamed the American Temperance Union in 1835) and the American Anti-Slavery Society (1833).

Perfectionism as a theology originated with the Methodist founder John Wesley (1703–1791). Christians were called to a state of sinlessness—perhaps not as a matter of likely achievement during this life but as a matter of aspiration and as an ideal. Such a theology ran at odds with Old Calvinism, which emphasized human inability to choose the good and the right apart from the arbitrary and unmerited grace of God. Perfectionism made a rather uneasy marriage with the Calvinist tradition, chiefly in the work of Charles Grandison Finney. Between 1825 and 1837 Finney used emotional techniques, or "new measures," to induce revivals upon which Calvinist traditionalists looked askance. In Finney's theology, not only could individuals be led to conversion by special methods, they could will and choose their own conversions. In addition, according to Finney, true Christianity required of its adherents "perfect obedience to the law of God," which he held to be possible in this world. The eschewal of sin in all its forms meant for many a willingness to abandon any compromise as an unacceptable alternative.

Initially, considerable friction existed between Finneyite revivalism, with its emphasis on "new measures" and emotional appeals, and orthodox Congregationalism. Congregationalists and Presbyterians had been allied in a formal way since 1801, when a Plan of Union united the two denominations in an effort to evangelize the West. But the advent of Finney's new measures and of his perfectionist theology threatened to drive the two groups apart. Lyman Beecher, perhaps the most prominent of the New England evangelical faction at the time, met with Finney in New Lebanon, Connecticut, in 1827, where the two achieved an uneasy truce. But by the next year, even at Yale University, the citadel of New England evangelicalism, a "New School" of theologians began to emphasize freedom of the will. Nathaniel William Taylor's watershed *Concio ad Clerum* (Advice to the Clergy), a sermon delivered in the Yale chapel in 1828, denied that human depravity consisted in an innately warped nature. Taylor instead defined depravity as a human ability and willingness to sin, something that individuals could avoid if they wished to do so. In a nation where individual capability was increasingly being celebrated and the self-made man increasingly an ideal, a theology where *should* implied *could* was popular. Where perfectionism dominated, organizations became less oriented toward general evangelization and conversion and more oriented to self-improvement and to the absolute eradication of particular sins. Such a shift did not take place in every organization. But where it did, it often ended up blasting apart the consensus on means and ends that had existed for a generation among Benevolent Empire organizations.

## The American Temperance Society

Formal temperance organization, the effort to reduce or eliminate the consumption of alcoholic beverages, began in the United States with the Massachusetts Society for the Suppression of Intemperance, organized in 1813. For once the American organized effort preceded that in Great Britain. As with other reforms, prior to regional and national organization, local societies sprang up, especially in New York and New England. Their objective usually was to advocate for liquor license restriction as a way of curtailing the use of ardent spirits. Temperance originated with Presbyterian and Congregational clergy and remained a cause largely dominated by those denominations, despite the usual benevolent aspiration toward multidenominationalism. In 1826 the American Temperance Society was organized in Boston under the leadership of Justin Edwards—the same person who had been instrumental in organizing the American Tract Society, which by this time was distributing popular reading matter on sin and moral failing in bulk. Perhaps not coincidentally, the temperance organization took shape just as the American Tract Society headquarters moved from Boston to New York, leaving the now affiliated but still relatively autonomous New England body with a niche to fill and a challenge to its preeminence. Lyman Beecher, the powerful Congregationalist evangelist, preached a series of six sermons on intemperance in 1825, and they formed the substance of one of the first publications disseminated by the new organization in the tract tradition. Beecher denounced alcohol use as a sin to be avoided at all costs, a snare that would inevitably lead imbibers on a downward spiral and to damnation.

The founding of the American Temperance Association marked a new phase in the temperance campaign: Alcohol use was not only a social evil; it was a sin. Within five years, the group moved from advocating against the consumption of distilled spirits as a cause of alcohol abuse to a campaign that urged Christians to take the pledge—to forswear the use of *any* alcohol as a sin against God. Temperance was the first single-cause reform to attract a significant number of national adherents: It claimed about a million and a half members by 1835. Using auxiliaries, hired agents, lecturers, and publications, the organization advocated against the consumption of alcohol in any form and had striking success in decreasing domestic consumption over the quarter-century period when it relied primarily upon "moral suasion." In addition, it began to outdistance other Evangelical United Front organizations in its membership, numbers of auxiliaries, and geographic reach.

By 1840 the Washingtonians, a largely working-class temperance organization without ties to the Benevolent Empire, provided a challenge to the reform leadership of the American Temperance Union by appealing to a new and independent constituency. The appearance of this group marked the beginning of a proliferation of organizations with similar instrumental goals but with very different ideological roots and assumptions. With the fragmentation of a unified national movement for temperance of which evangelicals could claim ownership, temperance became a goal to be achieved by multiple organizations and people, and increasingly through statutory means. As time went on, the cause was only marginally identified with either evangelical culture or Benevolent Empire leadership. Having taken on a life of its own as an independent reform cause, it broke any potential Benevolent Empire monopoly in this realm of American life.

## The American Anti-Slavery Society

The American Anti-Slavery Society followed a similar path of development and distancing from the evangelical core of the Benevolent Empire. Although it had fewer members and auxiliaries than did the American Temperance Society, with somewhere between 150,000 and 250,000 members by 1840, it may have had the greater impact on American life and politics through its relentless agitation for abolition. Born in Philadelphia in 1833 of the merger of the New England Anti-Slavery Society (founded in Boston by William Lloyd Garrison in 1831) and of the New York Anti-Slavery Society (founded by Arthur and Lewis Tappan in the same year), the organization advocated for the immediate and unconditional abolition of slavery, which it branded without qualification as sin. The American Anti-Slavery Society used the now-common organizational template of national organization: lay board of governors, local auxiliaries, mass print dissemination of message through journals and tracts, and hired agents and speakers. However, far from encouraging cooperation among evangelicals, antislavery brought a sword that not only divided denomination from denomination but that produced schism within individual denominations themselves. It provoked mob attack in the North and barring of printed materials and tracts from the mail in the South (which had never been much of a Benevolent Empire stronghold to begin with). More than any other force, the divisiveness produced by the antislavery impulse destroyed the ground on which a common evangelical project for the promotion of civic morality had grown. Without the possibility of widespread agreement on the parameters of benevolent reform, the Benevolent Empire by the 1840s fragmented and lost significant ground as a unified moral and civic force.

Although the temperance movement was perhaps the first to develop a distinct culture based on a reform cause, replete with a literature, a tradition of melodrama, and a well-developed network of associated women's organizations with it, Anti-Slavery grew into a genuine countercultural movement. For many, it became a self-conscious alternative to both American market-oriented culture and the evangelical culture of benevolence. "A clergy independent of the Churches, an itinerating clergy," the Reverend Leonard Bacon of New Haven warned in 1837,

—a clergy distributed into various orders, each charged with its single topic of instruction or agitation, is making its appearance among us. . . . One class of itinerants preaches temperance, according to the *latest discoveries*. Another is determined to know nothing but anti-slavery. . . . What surer method can be devised to make him [the lecturer] a flaming enthusiast? (*New York Evangelist*, April 29, 1837: 69, quoted in Michael P. Young, *Bearing Witness against Sin*, 2006, p. 7.)

Antislavery clergy and agents more than any other came to hold as their first allegiance the antislavery cause. Where churches admitted slaveholders as members or allowed congress with them in any way, it was the churches that became expendable.

Nowhere did the antislavery cause raise the specter of revolution more strongly than in its potential to catalyze women into radical action. Although women had been deeply involved in Benevolent Empire causes since the very beginning—as contributors to the larger organizations, as founders of societies for orphans and widows, as missionaries, as authors of pious texts, and as founders and operators of independent female auxiliaries—female antislavery activists were now claiming as their moral right the right to speak out in public, and in mixed assemblies of women and men, against sin. In 1837 Angelina and Sarah Grimké, sisters from a South Carolina slaveholding family and Quakers, elicited a sharp rebuke for their public antislavery activities from the evangelical establishment of Massachusetts in a *Pastoral Letter of the General Association of Massachusetts to the Congregational Churches Under Their Care*. The ministers denounced women reformers who, fired by passion against a sin with which they believed no compromise was possible, stepped out of the roles deemed appropriate for them. "We appreciate the unostentatious prayers and efforts of woman, in advancing the cause of religion at home and abroad," the ministers wrote:

—in Sabbath schools, in leading religious inquirers to their pastor for instruction, and in all such associated effort as becomes the modesty of her sex; and earnestly hope that she may abound more and more in these labours of piety and love. But when she assumes the place and tone of a man as a public reformer, our care and protection of her seem unnecessary, we put ourselves in self defence against her, she yields the power which God has given her for protection, and her character becomes unnatural.

Women had spent two generations as powerful partners in benevolent activities, but within strictly defined parameters. Work was often undertaken in a largely anonymous way, or it was confined to an all-female sphere or to work with children, or it was framed as supportive of the major organizational efforts of husbands or male clergy. The "woman question" within antislavery efforts proved so contentious that it occasioned a split in 1840 between those who continued to favor more traditional roles for women (including prominent Benevolent Empire benefactors Arthur and Lewis Tappan) and more radical reformers (including William Lloyd Garrison and Frederick Douglass). After the split, the Tappan brothers took leadership of the new American and Foreign Anti-Slavery Society, which began to adopt political means for achieving its goals and which did not allow women full membership. The American Anti-Slavery Society, headed by Garrison, allowed women full membership. Under Garrison's leadership, it also advocated for nonresistance to and noncooperation with any bodies, whether ecclesiastical or civil, that condoned slavery—including the United States. But not only did the "woman question" divide antislavery forces, it also led to a new movement agitating for women's rights and equality, a movement that conservative evangelicals saw as a major threat to the divinely decreed order of things.

## The Waning of the Benevolent Empire and Its Legacy

By 1840, even within abolitionism, adherents were forced to choose between a more conservative version of reform that maintained its ties with the evangelical elite and a more radical version that promised to rearrange gender, racial, and class hierarchies in the name of the eradication of sin. But antislavery had begun to unravel the generation-long alliance between Protestant evangelicals in other ways as well. The denominations involved in United Front activity had already begun to splinter and fragment over the slavery question. In 1837 the Presbyterian denomination, one of the major pillars of Benevolent Empire efforts, split. An Old School faction ("consistent Calvinists") abrogated the 1801 Plan of Union with the Congregationalists and expelled from fellowship a New School faction, defined largely by Taylorist theological views, Finneyite revivalism, and support for antislavery. In 1844 the Methodist Episcopal Church also split, this time explicitly over the slavery issue, as did the Triennial Convention

union of Baptists, from which the Southern Baptist Convention split in 1845.

As Old School Presbyterians withdrew from denominational union, they set up new versions of the older Benevolent Empire efforts, including their own Board of Foreign Missions. After the Presbyterian split, the American Education Society largely reverted to its Congregational roots and became an arm of that denomination, despite retaining its more inclusive name. Other major Benevolent Empire organizations—the American Board, the American Bible Society, the American Tract Society, and the American Home Missionary Society (AHMS)—survived, sometimes in attenuated form but registering the strains of the national divide over the slavery issue nonetheless. The American Bible Society suffered the withdrawal of a number of abolitionists in the mid-1830s and the Baptists in 1836. Throughout the 1840s and 1850s abolitionists agitated for a commitment by the national organization to supply Bibles to African Americans. The ABS resisted, in deference to its auxiliaries, who maintained local autonomy in the work of Bible distribution. Abolitionists similarly urged the American Tract Society, which had produced materials on every other kind of sin, to distribute materials on the sin of slavery as well. The ATS resisted for two decades because its interdenominational board, which had the right of veto over materials produced, regularly vetoed antislavery materials. The American Home Missionary Society, because it continued to admit slaveholders as members, saw its abolitionist members depart in 1846 to form a new society willing to bar slaveholders and to include evangelization of African Americans among its goals. Led and financed by the Tappan brothers, the new American Missionary Society siphoned off funds that had gone to the AHMS.

Benevolent Empire organizations continued to exist well into the latter part of the century, some with new names and denominational identities and some still relatively intact today. But by 1840 no new organizations formed along the lines of the original evangelical cooperative template. By that time, new political parties, ready and willing to take on the national organizing functions that the Benevolent Empire had pioneered, translated the old evangelical cultural agenda into a political one. New streams of popular literature from commercial presses built on the audiences established by the evangelical press, and in many instances commercial sentimental novels and periodicals, supplanted the influence of the evangelical presses with a new generation of readers.

The Benevolent Empire left a significant legacy. A rich and varied historiography has attempted over the course of a number of generations to describe its meaning and significance. It points to the role of these organizations in dealing with the status anxiety of old elites threatened by the decline of their power in the early American Republic; in linking dispersed new elites into larger national organizations, capable of harnessing capital and exerting control over national attitudes through moral suasion; in promoting nationwide literacy and the birth of a new popular mass medium of communication; in catalyzing groups of women into civic activism and a quest for public power; in providing religious sanction for a wave of reform that was both reaction to and promoter of a new market-oriented culture of individual possibility; and in developing strategies, technologies, and prototypes for mass movements of reform.

The French visitor to the United States, Alexis de Tocqueville, wrote in 1840, in *Democracy in America,* "In democratic countries, the knowledge of how to form associations is the mother of all knowledge since the success of all the others depends on it" (p. 600). The Benevolent Empire was perhaps the major nursery where this knowledge was developed and perfected.

**See also** *Abolitionism and Antislavery; Bible: As Sacred Text, Translations, Cultural Role; Education* entries; *Evangelicals: Nineteenth Century; Great Awakening(s); Missions: Domestic; Missions: Foreign.*

Mary Kupiec Cayton

**BIBLIOGRAPHY**

Abzug, Robert H. *Cosmos Crumbling: American Reform and the Religious Imagination.* New York: Oxford University Press, 1994.

Banner, Lois W. "Religious Benevolence as Social Control: A Critique of an Interpretation." *Journal of American History* 60 (June 1973): 23–41.

Bliss, Seth. *Letters to Members, Patrons, and Friends of the Branch American Tract Society in Boston, Instituted 1814; and to Those of the National Society in New York, Instituted 1825,* 3rd ed. Boston: Crocker and Brewster, 1858.

Blocker, Jack S., Jr. *American Temperance Movements: Cycles of Reform.* Boston: Twayne Publishers, 1989.

Bodo, John R. *The Protestant Clergy and Public Issues, 1812–1848.* Princeton, N.J.: Princeton University Press, 1954.

Boyer, Paul. *Urban Masses and Moral Order in America, 1820–1920.* Cambridge, Mass.: Harvard University Press, 1978.

Boylan, Anne M. *The Origins of Women's Activism: New York and Boston, 1797–1840.* Chapel Hill: University of North Carolina Press, 2002.

———. *Sunday School: The Formation of an American Institution, 1790–1880.* New Haven, Conn.: Yale University Press, 1988.

Dwight, Henry Otis. *The Centennial History of the American Bible Society.* Vol. 1. New York: Macmillan, 1916.

Foster, Charles I. *An Errand of Mercy: The Evangelical United Front, 1790–1837.* Chapel Hill: University of North Carolina Press, 1960.

Friedman, Lawrence J. "Confidence and Pertinacity in Evangelical Abolitionism: Lewis Tappan's Circle," *American Quarterly* 31 (1979): 81–106.

Griffin, Clifford S. "The Abolitionists and the Benevolent Societies, 1831–1861," *Journal of Negro History* 44 (1959): 195–216.

———. *Their Brothers' Keepers: Moral Stewardship in the United States, 1800–1865.* New Brunswick, N.J.: Rutgers University Press, 1960.

Hirrel, Leo P. *Children of Wrath: New School Calvinism and Antebellum Reform.* Lexington: University Press of Kentucky, 1998.

Howe, Daniel Walker. *What Hath God Wrought: The Transformation of America, 1815–1848.* New York: Oxford University Press, 2007.

Kilsdonk, Edward. "Religious Groups, Benevolent Organizations, and American Pluralism." American Religious Experience Web site, http://are.as.wvu.edu/kilsdonk.htm.

Mintz, Steven. *Moralists and Modernizers: America's Pre–Civil War Reformers.* Baltimore: Johns Hopkins University Press, 1995.

Nord, David Paul. *Faith in Reading: Religious Publishing and the Birth of Mass Media in America.* New York: Oxford University Press, 2004.

Tocqueville, Alexis de. *Democracy in America.* New York: Penguin, 2003.

Walters, Ronald G. *American Reformers, 1815–1860.* New York: Hill and Wang, 1978.

*The Works of Samuel Hopkins, D.D.,* Vol. 3. Boston: Doctrinal Tract and Book Society, 1852.

Wosh, Peter J. *The Bible Business in Nineteenth-Century America.* Ithaca, N.Y.: Cornell University Press, 1994.

Young, Michael P. *Bearing Witness against Sin: The Evangelical Birth of the American Social Movement.* Chicago: University of Chicago Press, 2006.

# Bible: As Sacred Text, Translations, Cultural Role

The Bible, in both Jewish and Christian formats, is the most influential book in American history. No text has been more frequently translated, printed, studied, debated, revered, or exploited. Although originally written in Hebrew and Greek in distant ancient contexts, the Bible's stories, translated into English in classics such as the King James Version, tell of characters who became like family members to many devoutly religious Americans. In the early American Republic, after the disestablishment of the former state churches, the Bible inspired a welter of upstart groups, from Methodists to Mormons, who honed in on its passages as doctrinal touchstones.

Writers and artists, meanwhile, found in the Bible a wellspring of images and idioms, making scripture the great subtext of the American literary and artistic canon. Even persons less familiar with the Bible's stories often treated the book itself as sacrosanct, using it in courtrooms to swear oaths, displaying it in salesrooms to prove financial probity, or invoking it in classrooms as the rock of American civilization. Yet though the Bible served as a unifying talisman, it also loomed at the center of some of the most bitter conflicts in U.S. history, from the battle over slavery during the Civil War to struggles over sexuality and gay rights. Any exploration of the Bible as America's central sacred text must therefore examine not only the English translations through which most people encountered scripture, but also the disparate arenas of cultural change and conflict driven by Holy Writ.

## The Idea of Vernacular Scripture

From their beginnings the three Abrahamic faiths—Judaism, Christianity, and Islam—were religions of the book. All three traditions assumed that God spoke to humans through direct revelations, which were subsequently recorded as holy scripture (from the Latin *scriptura,* or "writing"). Yet whereas Muslims had a revelation uniquely their own (the Qur'an), Jews and Christians shared a sacred text: the book that Jews often call *Tanakh,* an acronym derived from the Hebrew names for the Bible's three parts (Torah, prophets, and writings). In Christianity, this Bible became the "Old Testament" after Christians had added their own body of sacred texts, the New Testament. Written in Greek in the Roman Empire during the first and second centuries, the New Testament often quoted the Old and reinterpreted the Bible's prophetic books as pointing forward to Jesus. Although Jews accused the early Christians of perverting Hebrew scripture's original meaning, the Christian canon of the Old and New Testaments was destined to become the most common form of the Bible in the United States.

In the Western Christian tradition (Roman Catholic and Protestant, as opposed to Eastern Orthodox), the Latin translation of the Bible known as the Vulgate was for centuries the ecclesiastical standard. Long after the death of the Roman Empire, bishops and scholars retained Latin as a means of unifying the disparate national traditions within the Catholic Church. Although Protestant apologists would later accuse Catholic prelates of deliberately hiding the Bible from the laypeople (most of whom knew no Latin anyway), the medieval church in fact taught biblical stories through other media: visual art (statues, frescoes, stained glass windows), preaching (which was often catechetical in its function), and drama (passion plays and even the Eucharist

itself). It is also untrue that the Catholic hierarchy showed no interest in the original Greek and Hebrew of scripture. After the advent of printing in the mid-fifteenth century, Cardinal Francisco Ximénez, archbishop of Toledo in Spain, sponsored the Complutensian Polyglot (1514–1517), the first multilingual printed edition of the entire Bible, which became an important tool for scholars of biblical languages. In the same era the Catholic humanist Erasmus of Rotterdam published a Greek–Latin parallel edition of the New Testament (1516; second edition, 1519), which sold some 3,300 copies.

Yet it was the early Protestants, particularly Martin Luther in Germany and William Tyndale in England, who insisted on translating the Bible from the original Greek and Hebrew into the languages of the people. Luther and Tyndale consulted Erasmus's Greek edition as a basis for their translations of the New Testament into German (1522) and English (1526, 1534), respectively. Similarly, Luther and Tyndale based their versions of the Old Testament on the Hebrew Masoretic text (produced by the medieval Jewish scholars known as the Masoretes). No less important than actual translations was the Protestant ideology that supported them. The Protestant slogan of "scripture alone" reversed the traditional Catholic priority of the institutional church over the book and made the Bible the measure of all belief and practice. Vernacular scripture, moreover, cut out churchly intermediaries, making the Bible in theory accessible to any literate person. Early Protestants frequently spoke of the "priesthood of all believers" and claimed that the Bible was self-authenticating (2 Timothy 3:16: "All scripture is given by inspiration of God") and self-interpreting (meaning that the average reader could deduce the meaning of obscure verses by comparing them with easier passages). Such commonsense interpretation was said to require no bishop or pope for guidance. Unlike the Catholic Church's Latin Bible and liturgy, which were shrouded in sacred mystery, the vernacular Bible promoted the idea—so influential in U.S. history—that ordinary people had unmediated access to the very words of God.

The English Bible thus became for many American Protestants the icon of a word-centered piety that supposedly transcended Catholic "superstition" and built religion on solid empirical foundations. Although English Catholics produced a vernacular Bible of their own—the Douay-Rheims Version (1582–1609), translated by British exiles in France and Flanders—Latin would remain the official language of Catholic worship until the reforms of the Second

Vatican Council (1962–1965). The corporate piety of Catholics centered on the ritual of the Mass, with its mystical idea of communion with Christ's true body, while Protestant piety centered on biblical exposition through preaching. Likewise, whereas individual piety among Catholics centered on the rosary, novenas, and other devotions, the most common devotional practice among Protestant laypeople was private Bible reading.

## Protestant Translations: The First Three Centuries

The most zealous Bible readers in early America were the Puritans, whose emphasis on the supposedly pure standard of scripture, uncorrupted by human invention, contributed to much higher rates of literacy in the New England colonies than in any other part of British America or most of England. The Puritans' own edition of scripture was the Geneva Bible (1560, with various revisions thereafter), which was heavily dependent on Tyndale's translation and whose copious marginalia were laced with anti-Catholicism, as at Revelation 17:4, where the note identified the Whore of Babylon as "the Antichrist, that is, the Pope." Yet with its doctrinaire annotations, the Geneva Bible seemed particularly time-bound; it was produced by Puritan exiles in Geneva, Switzerland, during the reign of England's Catholic queen Mary Tudor. It was eventually superseded, even among the Puritans, by the King James, or Authorized, Version (1611), which lacked doctrinal marginalia (though some early editions of the new translation appeared with notes from the Geneva Bible).

The diction of the King James Version soon became the native religious language of clergy and laypeople alike. Colonial intellectuals pored over every word of scripture, composing massive commentaries that rivaled the output of English exegetes such as Matthew Poole and Matthew Henry. Boston minister Cotton Mather's commentary, which he dubbed his Biblia Americana, extended over 4,500 manuscript pages in six folio volumes. Mather's younger contemporary Jonathan Edwards kept a 910-page notebook, interleaved with pages of a small King James Bible, in which he penned in minuscule handwriting his annotations to every scriptural page. Clergy such as Mather and Edwards were also assiduous commentators from the pulpit. The typical Sunday sermon consisted of elaborately drawn-out moral lessons extracted from a single verse or two of scripture. Laypeople took these lessons to heart, or at least internalized the Bible's language. In the midst of life's daily hardships and occasional calamities, people fell back on

biblical verses to make sense of their experiences. Such was the case with Massachusetts colonist Mary Rowlandson, whose narrative of her Indian captivity, *The Sovereignty and Goodness of God* (1682), overflows with biblical citations designed to show the hand of Providence amid her suffering. Laypeople also quoted freely from the Bible in the conversion relations, or accounts of their turning to Christ, that New England pastors typically required as a condition of full church membership.

The zeal of New Englanders for the Bible was equally evident in their missionary endeavors among the Native Americans. In 1663, after more than a decade of study with Native tutors, Puritan minister John Eliot translated the Bible into Massachusett, an Algonquian language of southern New England. A group of ministers, including Eliot, had earlier produced the Bay Psalm Book (1640), the first English volume published in the colonies and the first American translation of any portion of the Bible. But Eliot's Indian Bible, as it became known, was the first American edition of the entire Bible and the first translation of the scriptures in a Native American vernacular. Eliot took certain liberties to make the book more understandable to Native American readers: He changed the ten virgins in the parable of the wise and foolish virgins (Matthew 25:1–13) to men because of the high premium on male chastity in Massachusett culture. Yet by the early eighteenth century, such attempts at linguistic and cultural translation would be eclipsed as Cotton Mather and others insisted that missionaries must anglicize the Indians and teach them the Bible in the English of King James.

The King James Version (KJV) reigned supreme throughout the colonial period and early American Republic, despite a few attempts to dethrone it. One notable insurgent was the politician Charles Thomson, who served as secretary of the Continental Congress from 1774 to 1789. After suffering a forced retirement at the hands of his political opponents, Thomson returned to his estate near Philadelphia and began translating the whole Bible—the New Testament from the original Greek and the Old Testament from the Septuagint (the Hellenistic Jewish translation of Hebrew scripture into Greek). Two decades later, in 1808, Thomson published his work in four octavo volumes. Although it was the first American translation of the whole Bible into English, it quickly fell into obscurity, a victim of the KJV's much greater esteem and affordability among the general public. The development of cheap printing technology in the antebellum period made the KJV readily available, as did the well-orchestrated efforts of the American Bible Society

(ABS). Founded in 1816 by the consolidation of more than a hundred local societies, the ABS distributed millions of Bibles in successive campaigns to put a copy of the KJV in every American home.

The ABS campaigns did not deter a variety of individuals in the nineteenth century from seeking to improve on the KJV. Some, such as the lexicographer Noah Webster, tried to make the Bible's English more delicate, as when he changed "not one that pisseth against a wall" (1 Kings 16:11) to "not one male." Other individuals modified the Bible for theological reasons. Alexander Campbell, the founder of the Disciples of Christ, retranslated the New Testament from the Greek, rendering the verb *baptizō* as "immerse," a change hailed by advocates of believers' (adult) baptism. (The KJV had simply transliterated the term as "baptize.") The resistance of the ABS to the publication of an "immersion" version led a group of Baptists to form the rival American Bible Union in 1850. Among the group's leaders was the biblical scholar Thomas Jefferson Conant, whose 1860 version of the Gospel of Matthew was published with a 107-page appendix defending "immerse" as the most correct translation. Although the American Bible Union published a complete revision of the New Testament in 1864, no new translation garnered widespread public notice until the discovery of additional ancient manuscripts ushered in the modern age of Bible translation in the 1880s.

### Protestant Translations and Editions after 1881

The first major new Bible translation to reflect modern textual scholarship was a joint British–American project, the Revised Version (1881–1885). In the decades leading up to the new Bible's publication, biblical scholarship had developed on two fronts. Higher (or historical) criticism attempted to separate fact from fiction in the biblical narratives and questioned traditional assumptions about biblical authorship (for example, that Moses wrote the Pentateuch, the first five books of the Old Testament). Lower (or textual) criticism attempted to reconstruct the original Hebrew and Greek texts of scripture from the immense array of surviving manuscript variants. Although higher critics often grabbed headlines, as when the Presbyterian biblical scholar Charles Augustus Briggs denied the Mosaic authorship of the Pentateuch in his inaugural address at New York's Union Seminary in 1891, lower criticism proved more important as a basis for new English translations.

A major turning point occurred in 1859, when the German biblical scholar Constantin von Tischendorf discovered

the fourth-century Codex Sinaiticus—the oldest complete manuscript of the New Testament ever uncovered—at the Monastery of St. Catherine on Mount Sinai. Together with the Codex Vaticanus (made public in the same era by the Vatican Library), the Codex Sinaiticus became the basis for the New Testament portion of the Revised Version. Published amid great excitement—the *Chicago Tribune* printed a pilfered copy of the entire New Testament in its Sunday edition of May 22, 1881—the project was a triumph for the American committee of translators, a group of Protestant scholars headed by the Union Seminary professor and Swiss immigrant Philip Schaff. But the new Bible also sparked considerable controversy because of the doubt it cast on the authenticity of certain biblical passages—for example, the Longer Ending of the Gospel of Mark (16:9–20), which was set apart with a marginal explanation noting the passage's absence from codices Sinaiticus and Vaticanus.

The Revised Version was slow to win converts among average churchgoers, and a modest recension of the text, dubbed the American Standard Version (1901), was widely panned for its wooden, literal renditions. Calls for a completely new American translation resulted in the formation of a thirty-two-member committee chaired by Luther Weigle, dean of Yale Divinity School. In a major ecumenical milestone, Weigle and his colleagues invited a Jewish scholar, Harry M. Orlinsky of the Hebrew Union College–Jewish Institute of Religion in New York, to join the committee—the first instance of official Jewish–Christian cooperation in the history of the English Bible. The new translation was sponsored by the National Council of Churches, a federation of liberal Protestant bodies, which hoped to replace the KJV with a Bible cast in less archaic idiom that would become the new standard for Christian education and worship.

A huge publicity blitz heralded the new Bible, known as the Revised Standard Version (RSV), in September 1952. At the White House, President Harry Truman received a leather-bound copy from Weigle, and newspapers across the country ran front-page stories celebrating the event. The celebration abruptly ended, however, when conservative Protestants discovered that the RSV had changed the "virgin" in the King James reading of Isaiah 7:14 (traditionally seen by Christians as a prophecy of the virgin birth of Christ) to "young woman" (a more accurate rendering of the original Hebrew word). To many conservatives, this smelled of a liberal plot to discredit the doctrine of Jesus' miraculous birth and even to deny the whole idea of predictive prophecy. Intense controversy ensued. Fundamentalist preachers burned the RSV before cheering congregations; pamphleteers denounced it as modernist and communist; and even the U.S. Air Force Reserve, in a spectacular breach of church–state separation, urged recruits to avoid it. Only when the firestorm died down did cooler heads realize the RSV's significance as the first Christian translation to attempt to read the Old Testament on its own terms as a Jewish document.

In the wake of the RSV controversy, Bible translation among American Protestants became increasingly polarized between conservatives and liberals. The New International Version (NIV, 1978), born of conservative opposition to the RSV, restored the virgin of Isaiah 7:14 and became a favorite among evangelical readers. (Scholars on the NIV committee were required to sign a statement attesting to their belief that the Bible was "inerrant" in its long-lost original manuscripts.) Similarly, the English Standard Version (2001), an evangelical revision of the RSV, reverted to "virgin" even while translating other passages more literally. Meanwhile, liberal Protestants issued the New Revised Standard Version (1989), which updated the RSV to include more gender-inclusive language. Not to be outdone, conservatives unveiled Today's New International Version (TNIV, 2002), which split the evangelical community over its own use of gender-neutral terminology. Several popular evangelical apologists, including Bill Hybels and Lee Strobel, endorsed the TNIV, while the nation's largest Protestant denomination, the Southern Baptist Convention, passed a resolution against it.

The proliferation of Bibles was also market driven. By the turn of the twenty-first century, niche study Bibles had become a mainstay of religious publishing. A forerunner of the genre was the *Scofield Reference Bible* (1909), which popularized a dispensational premillennialist scheme dividing history into seven dispensations that would be followed by the Rapture, the Great Tribulation, and the Second Coming. In the later twentieth century, with the rise of evangelical powerhouse publishers such as Zondervan the number of special-interest Bibles rapidly proliferated. The decade of the 1990s alone brought the publication of, among others, the *NIV Women's Devotional Bible* (1990), the *NIV Men's Devotional Bible* (1993), the *Recovery Devotional Bible* (1993), and the *New Believer's Bible* (1996). Study Bibles catering to particular denominational or ethnic traditions also gained popularity. African American Protestants could explore Afrocentric interpretations in the *Original African Heritage Study Bible* (1993) or read African American

Baptist perspectives in the *African-American Devotional Bible* (1997); conservative Calvinists could peruse predestinarian glosses on Paul's epistles in the *New Geneva Study Bible* (1995) or the *Reformation Study Bible* (2005); United Methodists could find an index of Wesleyan terminology in the *Wesley Study Bible* (2009); and mainline Lutherans could consult historical articles and timelines on Martin Luther in the *Lutheran Study Bible* (2009). Bible publishing even merged with youth culture in editions such as *Revolve* (2003), which took the form of a glossy fashion magazine for teenage girls, and the *Manga Bible* (2007), which imitated the distinctive style of Japanese comic books.

## Jewish and Catholic Translations

Although the Bible marketplace for Jews and Catholics was, by the turn of the twenty-first century, beginning to resemble that for Protestants—with titles such as the *Jewish Study Bible* (2004) and the *Catholic Study Bible* (1990)—non-Protestant communities had long resisted vernacular scripture for liturgical reasons. Jews, like Muslims, traditionally regarded translations of scripture as having no authority. Biblical Hebrew was regarded as God's sacred tongue—the "language spoken by the angels," as one Mishnaic tractate put it. Consequently, coming-of-age rites (bar mitzvah for boys; bat mitzvah for girls) required the initiate to read aloud in Hebrew the portion of the Torah and prophets appointed for the day's worship. Jewish Kabbalah invested the Hebrew alphabet with mystical significance, and many Protestants, from Jonathan Edwards to University of Chicago founder William Rainey Harper, were enamored of ancient Hebraic wisdom. (Yale University, from which Harper received his PhD at age nineteen, embodied this Protestant Hebraism: The university seal, designed by president Ezra Stiles, bears an open book with the Hebrew words *Urim and Thummim,* the sacred oracles associated with the breastplate of the biblical high priest.)

Jewish leaders in the United States nevertheless recognized early on the utility of English translations and worried that Jews were being misled by the King James Version. Isaac Leeser, the *hazan* (cantor) of Philadelphia's Mikveh Israel, was particularly distressed that copies of the KJV distributed by the American Bible Society had chapter headings and other elements reinforcing a Christian interpretation of the Old Testament books. Leeser, who knew that most American Jews actually understood little Hebrew, in 1838 began his own translation of the Bible into English. Published in 1853, it included the Hebrew and a literal English translation on facing pages. The edition also eliminated the KJV's

Christianization of key passages, substituting "young woman" for "virgin" in Isaiah 7:14 and lowercasing "son" in Psalm 2.

Dissatisfaction with the cost and wooden style of Leeser's Bible led to periodic calls for an alternative, and in 1895 work began on the first committee-based Jewish translation. The project's sponsor was the Jewish Publication Society (JPS), founded in 1888. The editor in chief was Max Margolis, an immigrant from eastern Europe who prepared himself for the task of translation by perusing the classic literature of Elizabethan and Restoration England. When the new Bible appeared in 1917, its preface declared Jewish independence from the Christian translation tradition: "The Jew cannot afford to have his Bible translation prepared for him by others." Yet some critics faulted the JPS Bible for sticking too closely to the Protestants' Revised Version. Further developments in biblical scholarship, along with the rapid professionalization of the field after World War II, led the JPS to appoint a new translation committee, headed by RSV veteran Harry Orlinsky, which began its work in 1955. In addition to its professional scholarly members, the committee also included rabbis from Judaism's three major branches (Orthodox, Conservative, and Reform). After the initial work on the Torah and prophets, a new committee, whose members included the novelist Chaim Potok, began translating the third section of the Old Testament, the writings. All three parts appeared under the title *Tanakh* in 1985. A second edition appeared in 1999, and Oxford University Press published an annotated edition in 2004.

Although *Tanakh* (also known as the New JPS translation) became the standard English Bible among American Jews, it did not stop individual scholars from producing alternatives. Among the most significant was the 1995 edition of the Torah by Clark University professor Everett Fox, who followed the philosophy of the German scholars Martin Buber and Franz Rosenzweig in preserving the idiom and poetic structure of the original Hebrew as much as possible. Fox also used the Hebrew forms of biblical names (*Moshe* for Moses, *Yitzhak* for Isaac, *Rivka* for Rebecca), and retained the tetragrammaton, YHWH, where other translations typically substituted "the Lord" for God's unutterable sacred name. The purpose behind the translation was to recover the Bible's sacred strangeness, which Fox believed had been sacrificed in the modern rush to cast scripture in contemporary idiom.

A similar reverence for the power of ancient language characterized traditional Catholic attitudes toward the Latin

Mass and the Vulgate (the ancient Latin translation of the Bible originating with St. Jerome). In the face of the Protestants' insistence on vernacular translation from the original Greek and Hebrew, the Council of Trent in 1546 declared the Vulgate the only authentic version for public reading and theological debate. For unofficial use, however, the Douay-Rheims version, as revised and annotated in the 1740s by London bishop Richard Challoner, became the standard Bible for American Catholics until the twentieth century. The marginal glosses occasionally lapsed into polemic, as at the account of the Last Supper in Matthew 26:26, where the note attacked many Protestants' denial of the real presence in the Eucharist: "*This is my body. He does not say, This is the figure of my body.*" In 1790 the Irish Catholic printer Matthew Carey printed the first American edition of Douay-Rheims, but disappointing profits eventually led him to print the KJV for Protestant readers instead.

In the antebellum Republic, as new Catholic immigrants crowded rapidly into eastern U.S. cities, controversy exploded over which Bible—Catholic or Protestant—would be read in the public schools. In 1843 Philadelphia bishop Francis Kenrick successfully petitioned the local school board to excuse Catholic children from reading the King James Bible. The fact that the KJV was not based on the Vulgate was just one reason Catholics rejected it. American editions of the KJV invariably appeared without the Apocrypha, the fifteen additional biblical books accepted by Catholics and many Anglicans. (Most Protestants rejected the Apocrypha because it contained, among other things, the key proof text for the doctrine of purgatory.) The exemption obtained by Kenrick was a fleeting triumph, for Protestant nativists regarded it as a plot to remove the Bible entirely from the schools. Ethnic and religious tensions eventually escalated into a citywide riot in 1844 that killed at least thirteen people. Kenrick, meanwhile, had begun work on his own revision of Douay-Rheims, a project he continued after becoming archbishop of Baltimore in 1851. Although Kenrick never published a complete edition of the Bible, his version was the most important American Catholic translation before the twentieth century.

Between the two world wars, Catholic biblical scholarship rapidly professionalized, as is evident in the founding of the Catholic Biblical Association in 1936. The group's first major project was a revision of Douay-Rheims, the New American Bible (NAB), which published with the New Testament in 1941. Sponsored by the Confraternity of Christian Doctrine (the apostolate responsible for the religious education of youth), the NAB was based on the Vulgate, as church regulation required, but it took account of the Greek in the footnotes. Then, in 1943, Pope Pius XII issued a major encyclical, *Divino Afflante Spiritu,* fully sanctioning the translation of vernacular Bibles from the original Greek and Hebrew. This forced an overhaul—much welcomed by scholars—of the NAB project and delayed its completion until 1970, when the full Bible appeared. Along the way, the Second Vatican Council contributed greatly to the new era of openness in Catholic scholarship. The council also allowed for ecumenical cooperation between Catholics and Protestants in the translation of scripture. The first fruits of this cooperation appeared in 1966 with the RSV Catholic Edition, which integrated a small number of Catholic textual preferences, chiefly in the New Testament. As a gesture of appreciation, Pope Paul VI awarded RSV chairman Luther Weigle (himself a Congregationalist) the papal knighthood of St. Gregory the Great.

## The Bible and New Denominations

For all the varied editions of scripture on the market, no version exerted greater cultural influence than the King James Bible. Particularly in the nineteenth century, after the First Amendment created a free marketplace of religious sects, various upstart brands of Protestantism looked to the Bible as their founding charter. Some groups focused on a particular passage, even a single verse, of the KJV as the interpretive key for unlocking everything else. Other groups appealed to the Bible more generally as a document that supposedly transcended merely human doctrines and customs. Common to all these groups was the notion that the Bible, like the U.S. Constitution, broke the monarchial authority of inherited traditions. This idea of starting afresh was expressed in the new nation's Great Seal, designed by Bible translator Charles Thomson, which included the Latin motto *Novus Ordo Seclorum* (New Order of the Ages). For many Americans, this new order entailed a return to something ancient—the allegedly pure standard of scripture.

Ironically, in New England, where the back-to-the-Bible emphasis had been particularly strong, this biblical primitivism planted the seeds of Puritanism's own demise, as many onetime Puritans embraced Universalism or Unitarianism. Universalists, who were so named because of their doctrine that universal salvation was God's ultimate purpose, found inspiration in KJV verses such as Luke 3:6 ("all flesh shall see the salvation of God") and 1 Timothy 2:4 ("Who will have all men to be saved"). Unitarians, meanwhile, argued that

scripture nowhere spelled out the doctrine of the Trinity, a metaphysical invention they believed was at odds with the biblical picture of Jesus as the savior empowered by the Father (who alone was fully God) to work miracles and teach moral lessons. In discounting the Trinity, some Unitarians noted that the doctrine's chief proof-text, 1 John 5:7 ("the Father, the Word, and the Holy Ghost: and these three are one") was not found in the most ancient Greek manuscripts. Unitarian scholars regarded this textual intrusion, which had been pointed out as early as the sixteenth century by the humanistic scholar Erasmus, as a flaw in the otherwise revered KJV.

As Unitarianism thrived in the early nineteenth century in liberal bastions such as Harvard, more populist movements such as Methodism were also appealing to scripture in combating the older Calvinist message that God intended to save only an elect few. In camp meetings on the frontier, Methodist circuit riders repeated biblical refrains of "whosoever" ("whosoever believeth in him," John 3:16; "Whosoever shall confess me before men," Luke 12:8) as evidence that God gave humans the ability to choose between life and death. Other frontier groups, such as the followers of Alexander Campbell and Barton Stone, echoed the same freewill line in proclaiming their independence from all "man-made" doctrinal systems. Campbell, who began his career as a Presbyterian in Ulster, in Ireland, declared "Bibleism" his only theology. The phrase "no creed but the Bible" likewise became a rallying cry for Campbellites and Stoneites as they worked to unlearn the "speech of Ashdod" (Nehemiah 13:24)—the language of Philistines, which was Campbell's name for invented human dogmas.

"Bibleism" always involved selective appropriation of scripture, however, and some groups read the Bible more selectively than did others. Among the more unusual sects were the Millerites, led by the onetime deist William Miller, who found in scripture the key to the end of time. Miller foreshadowed Cyrus I. Scofield, editor of the famous reference Bible, in scouring the KJV for numerical clues to the date of Christ's Second Coming. After reading through the entire Bible, Miller singled out Daniel 8:14 ("Unto two thousand and three hundred days; then shall the sanctuary be cleansed"). He interpreted this as 2,300 years from the "seventy weeks" (Daniel 9:24), which some biblical chronologies dated from 457 BCE. Thus, by Miller's calculation, the Second Coming (which he equated with the cleansing of the sanctuary) would happen 2,300 years from 457 BCE, or in the year 1843. Miller made his prediction in 1816, which gave his followers twenty-seven years to build up expectations. As the date drew near, some Millerites sold their farms or gave up other worldly attachments. But when 1843 came and went, and Miller's revised date of 1844 also failed to bring Christ's return, his movement suffered what came to be known as the Great Disappointment. The Millerites' later successors, the Seventh-day Adventists, took the perils of precise date setting to heart and maintained a more general sense of the imminent end. Other apocalyptic groups, such as the Jehovah's Witnesses, boldly proclaimed new dates, each time revising their predictions based on supposedly better understandings of the biblical "facts."

No less striking than apocalyptic readings of scripture were interpretations focused on the powers given to Christ's followers in the here and now. For Mary Baker Eddy, the founder of Christian Science, the key to scripture was Matthew 9:1–8, the story of Jesus healing a man with palsy. Eddy discovered the passage, which affirmed that God "had given such power unto men" (Matthew 9:8), from her sickbed in 1866 and subsequently experienced a remarkable recovery. A decade later, she published *Science and Health with Key to the Scriptures* (1875), her manifesto of mental healing, in which she reinterpreted the Bible through a metaphysical lens. For Eddy, the key to scripture was in understanding that the material world is an illusion. Sickness and death do not truly exist because only mind is real, and it is immortal. In summing up her view, she quoted Romans 8:7: "The carnal mind is enmity against God." This passage revealed that the "central fact of the Bible," as she put it, "is the superiority of spiritual over physical power."

Eddy was hardly the only American to find in scripture a paradigm for healing. Some other groups, most notably Pentecostal Christians, regarded divine healing as one of the miraculous gifts of the Holy Spirit that would be given to the faithful in the last days. For Pentecostals, the key to scripture was the New Testament account of the outpouring of the Spirit on Jesus' disciples, when they miraculously spoke in other tongues "as the Spirit gave them utterance" (Acts 2:4). Pentecostals connected this passage with the Old Testament prophecy of the "former rain" and the "latter rain" (Joel 2:23). The former rain was the first Pentecost experience of the disciples in Jerusalem. The latter rain was the modern revival of charismatic practices—speaking in tongues, divine healing, casting out demons—in the birth of the Pentecostal movement. This modern revival neatly coincided with the turn of the twentieth century when Agnes Ozman, a follower of the former Methodist preacher

Charles Fox Parham, spoke in tongues at Parham's Bible school in Topeka, Kansas. From there, the movement spread rapidly, especially after the African American preacher William J. Seymour initiated the more famous revival at Azusa Street in Los Angeles.

## The American Religious Text: The Book of Mormon

The most dramatic restoration of biblical paradigms came in the Church of Jesus Christ of Latter-day Saints (LDS), better known as the Mormon tradition. Mormonism's logic was compellingly simple: If God imparted direct revelations in apostolic times, why could he not reveal things directly to people today? Ongoing revelation, in other words, was Mormonism's key, not only in the emergence of new scriptures (the Book of Mormon) but also for the interpretation of old ones. The revelations to Mormon founder Joseph Smith Jr. began in 1820, when Smith was only fourteen. He learned in a vision that all the existing sects were wrong and that all their creeds were an abomination in God's sight. Eventually he was directed to a hillside near his home in upstate New York, where he found a buried trove of ancient writings engraved on gold plates. These plates became in translation the Book of Mormon (1830), a text immediately assailed as a forgery by critics but hailed as a divine revelation by the Mormon faithful.

For historians of American religion, the Book of Mormon's authenticity is beside the point. What matters is its cultural significance as a uniquely American bible—a continuation of the Bible's story on American soil. The doctrine of ongoing revelation meant, moreover, that even the Book of Mormon could be supplemented by later disclosures. Such is the purpose of Mormonism's open-ended Doctrine and Covenants, a compilation of later revelations imparted to Smith and his successors as prophets of the church. Smith also received revelations correcting or clarifying certain passages in the Bible itself. The revised KJV text became known as the Joseph Smith Translation. (Modern editions of the KJV published by the LDS Church include Smith's minor textual modifications in footnotes and print the longer ones in an appendix.)

Direct revelation was just one of the biblical practices restored by Smith and his successors, beginning with Brigham Young. The Latter-day Saints regarded their westward trek to Utah as a replication of the Israelites' journey from bondage in Egypt to the freedom of the Promised Land. Like the Israelites, the Mormons built a great temple, and they restored Israel's patriarchal offices of leadership, which they dubbed the Aaronic and Melchizedek priesthoods. The Latter-day Saints also restored New Testament practices such as divine healing, typically through the anointing of the sick with oil and the laying on of hands by an elder. Most controversially, the early Mormons restored the biblical practice of plural marriage, which, in conjunction with their doctrine of eternal families, was seen as a way of enlarging the eventual company of heaven by sealing women to the men of the priesthood. Although the church renounced polygamy in 1890 as a condition of Utah statehood, Mormons retained their underlying zeal for the restoration of Zion—the new Jerusalem.

Indeed, the Book of Mormon tells the story of a group of Israelites who fled old Jerusalem in 600 BCE, before its destruction by the Babylonians. They traveled by ship to America, where they split into two rival tribes, the Nephites and the Lamanites, who remained in conflict for centuries. After Jesus was crucified and raised from the dead, he appeared in America and shared his teachings with the inhabitants. Eventually, in the fourth century the Lamanites defeated the Nephites, whose last survivor, Moroni, buried an account of the events on the gold plates found by Smith some 1,400 years later. The Lamanites, meanwhile, became the ancestors of the Native Americans, who, according to the Book of Mormon, would eventually turn to Christ and thereby usher in the Second Coming. Mormons consequently took a missionary interest in the conversion of Native peoples, who became pivotal players in the restoration of the biblical drama on the North American continent.

### The Bible, Race, and Slavery

Mormons resembled many other Americans in reading scripture for clues about the origins and destinies of particular peoples. The original edition of the Book of Mormon prophesied that at the last day, the descendants of the dark-skinned Lamanites would become "white and delightsome" (2 Nephi 30:6). (The modern edition of the text changed the wording to "pure and delightsome.") The Mormons' teaching about the Lamanites' Israelite origins, moreover, partook of a long tradition of American speculation about the ancient Hebrew tribes and their possible connections to the indigenous peoples of America. The Puritan Roger Williams, in *A Key to the Language of America* (1643), cited what he thought were resemblances between the Hebrew and Narragansett languages and religious practices to bolster his theory that the Indians were the descendants of the ten "lost tribes" of Israel (the tribes that never returned to Jerusalem after the Assyrian-Babylonian exile). Williams's contemporary, the Bible translator John Eliot, hazarded a similar hypothesis in a letter printed in *Jews in America* (1660) by the English Puritan divine Thomas Thorowgood. More often than not, however, Puritan writers equated Native peoples not with the Hebrews but with the Canaanites—the indigenous inhabitants of Canaan who had to be defeated before Israel could take possession of the land.

The dispossession and even extermination of Native Americans thus seemed to some English colonists to have a clear biblical warrant. Like the Canaanites, the Indians seemed given to idolatry. The cultivation of multiple spirits in Native rituals seemed, to English eyes, little different from the cults of Baal and other Canaanite gods. The English conquest of early America could therefore be read as a latter-day struggle to vanquish the idols and establish the exclusive worship of the God of Israel.

An equally fateful reading of scripture occurred with the rise of the Atlantic slave trade, as Europeans turned to the Bible to explain the origins of African peoples. By the nineteenth century, it had become commonplace among slaveholders in the American South to justify the subjugation of Africans by appeal to the so-called curse of Ham. Ham was the son of Noah who, unlike his obedient brothers Shem and Japheth, "saw the nakedness of his father" (Genesis 9:22), who was lying drunken and uncovered in his tent. Because of this transgression (the exact nature of which has always been debated), Noah cursed Ham's progeny, namely his son Canaan: "Cursed be Canaan; a servant of servants shall he be unto his brethren" (Genesis 9:25). The story of Ham is followed in Genesis 10 by a table of nations listing the descendants of Noah's three sons. Ham's descendants include Cush (Ethiopia), a connection used in nineteenth-century pseudo-scientific racial theories as evidence that the "Hamitic" line consisted of dark-skinned peoples condemned to perpetual servitude. As the prominent Southern Presbyterian minister Benjamin Palmer declared in an 1861 sermon in New Orleans soon after the outbreak of the Civil War, "We find in Noah's prophetic utterances to his three sons, the fortunes of mankind presented in perfect outline."

Yet even as many white southerners used the Bible to justify the notion of black inferiority, African Americans found scripture equally fruitful as a document of liberation. Although the Bible presupposed slavery as an institution, it also contained the Exodus narrative in which the Israelites, through God's providential assistance, escaped enslavement in Egypt for the freedom of the Promised Land. In retellings by African Americans as well as by white abolitionists, the biblical crossing of the Red Sea foreshadowed the bloody Civil War, which delivered the United States from the sin of slavery. Slave spirituals likewise repeated the Exodus story in song, as in the famous lines, "Go Down, Moses, / Way down in Egypt land, / Tell old Pharaoh, / Let my people go." A century later, leading figures of the civil rights movement invoked the same motif in exhorting the nation to live up to its constitutional ideal of liberty for all. In his last sermon on the eve of his assassination, Martin Luther King Jr. alluded to the dying Moses gazing out at Canaan from atop Mount Pisgah: "I've been to the mountaintop. . . . And I've seen the Promised Land. And I may not get there with you. But I want you to know tonight that we as a people will get to the Promised Land."

African American laypeople, no less than clergy, turned to biblical narratives for solace amid their suffering and for the courage to confront injustice. Jarena Lee, a domestic servant born to free black parents in New Jersey in 1783, experienced an ecstatic conversion that she compared to the "third heaven" spoken of by the apostle Paul (2 Corinthians 12:2). Later, when she appealed to Richard Allen, founder of the African Methodist Episcopal Church, for the right to be ordained as a woman preacher, she invoked the vision of the last days in Joel 2:28 ("your sons and your daughters shall prophesy"). She also pointed out that it was a woman, Mary Magdalene, who first witnessed the Resurrection and proclaimed the good news to Jesus' disciples (John 20:18). A century later, after the sharecropper and civil rights activist Fannie Lou Hamer was savagely beaten in a Winona, Mississippi, jail, she witnessed to the jailer's wife by quoting Acts 17:26 ("And hath made of one blood all nations of men")—a verse that subverted the separate and unequal races that segregationists had tried to prove by appeal to Noah's sons.

However discredited the notion of inferior bloodlines had become by the last half of the twentieth century, the questions of slavery and race had opened up a wider crisis of biblical interpretation that would have ongoing implications for the Bible's relevance in the culture. Protestants in particular, who before the Civil War had been united in their conviction that the Bible was uniformly unambiguous and authoritative for moral guidance, came to blows over whose cause—the North's or the South's—enjoyed a preponderance of scriptural support. No one better expressed

the tragic irony of the two sides than Abraham Lincoln in his second inaugural: "Both read the same Bible and pray to the same God, and each invokes His aid against the other."

### The Bible as "Great Code": Arts and Letters

The tragedies and triumphs, as well as the relentless ambiguities, of the American affair with scripture have always been especially vivid in the nation's arts and letters. The English poet William Blake once commented that the Old and New Testaments were the "great code" of art, and this would also describe the Bible's role in the American imagination. Quite apart from debates over the historical accuracy or moral applicability of particular scriptural passages, the Bible as a *literary* source typically functioned as a seamless narrative, a grand epic running from the world's creation to its end. This epic told the history of salvation, and it was populated with characters both noble and flawed. Thus the Bible became the lens through which many writers, such as the twentieth-century African American novelist James Baldwin, viewed the world. Baldwin's *Go Tell It on the Mountain* (1952) contains numerous biblical allusions. The leading characters—Gabriel, Deborah, Elizabeth, and John—are namesakes, respectively, of the biblical archangel, the Israelite judge, the mother of John the Baptist, and John the Baptist himself. Many of the novel's scenes also recapitulate biblical stories, from John's gazing out over Manhattan from atop a hill in Central Park (an allusion to the temptation of Christ by Satan on the mountaintop in Matthew 4) to John's wrestling with the boy-preacher Elisha (an allusion to Jacob's wrestling with the angel of the Lord in Genesis 32). Midway through the novel, Deborah tells her husband, Gabriel (a lay preacher): "ain't no shelter against the Word of God, is there, Reverend? You is just got to be in it, that's all." To "be in it": This epitomizes the Bible's role as the imaginative universe inhabited by some of America's greatest writers and artists.

Some writers in American history succeeded in mass-marketing biblical themes. The first American literary blockbuster was the Puritan minister Michael Wigglesworth's long poem *The Day of Doom* (1662), which recreates in lurid detail the Last Judgment scene in Matthew 25. The scenario unfolds when a light breaks forth at midnight, causing sinners to awake in terror. Some people vainly try to escape by drowning themselves, but there is no getting away as Christ commences to separate the sheep from the goats. Such popular literature found its twentieth-century equivalent in

Left Behind, a series of sixteen novels published between 1995 and 2007 by the dispensational premillennialists Tim LaHaye and Jerry Jenkins. The series describes the travails of persons left on earth after Christ's faithful ones vanish in the Rapture.

Between the bookends of *The Day of Doom* and Left Behind, which both broke publishing records for their times, an array of other popular works appeared, including novels based on the life of Jesus. A best seller of this genre was the Episcopal priest Joseph Holt Ingraham's *The Prince of the House of David* (1855), an epistolary novel written from the perspective of Adina, a fictional first-century Jewish girl who witnesses the key events of Jesus' ministry. Another successful venture was Elizabeth Stuart Phelps's *A Singular Life* (1894), which narrates the tale of Emanuel Bayard, a renegade New England minister. A thinly veiled Christ figure, Bayard—whose parents' names are Mary and Joseph—bucks the Congregational establishment and sets up his own ministry to fishermen in a seaside town. He is ultimately stoned to death by henchmen of the local saloonkeeper, who is angry about the loss of his customers. Phelps, whose father was a professor at the Congregational seminary at Andover, Massachusetts, epitomized the spirit of the Social Gospel movement, which stressed the countercultural aspect of Jesus' ministry. Jesus appeared in her fiction, as he did in Ingraham's novel and in many lesser-known works, as the great mirror reflecting the anxieties and aspirations of each new era in U.S. history.

Popular literature, of course, always coexisted with the more sophisticated works judged canonical by the academic arbiters of America's literary output. Here the Bible's influence was often more subtle but no less pervasive. Herman Melville's monumental classic *Moby-Dick* (1851) is so full of biblical names and tropes that scholars have produced concordances of all the references. From the biblical names of the characters (Ishmael, Ahab, Elijah) to Melville's complex play on themes from the book of Jonah (whose protagonist, unlike Captain Ahab, yields to God's will in the end), *Moby-Dick* can scarcely be understood apart from its scriptural underpinnings. Similarly, the Bible forms the substructure of the fiction of Nathaniel Hawthorne, who, like Melville, wrestled with scriptural preoccupations inherited from the Calvinist–Puritan tradition. The theme of sin looms throughout Hawthorne's great novel *The Scarlet Letter* (1850), including the tapestry depicting the adulterers David and Bathsheba that hangs in the Reverend Arthur Dimmesdale's study.

The Bible continued to be the great repository of figures for twentieth-century fiction writers and essayists. The titles alone of many works are either full or partial quotations of biblical phrases: James Agee's *Let Us Now Praise Famous Men* (1941), William Faulkner's *Absalom, Absalom!* (1936), Ernest J. Gaines's *In My Father's House* (1978), Shirley Ann Grau's *The Keepers of the House* (1964), Ernest Hemmingway's *The Garden of Eden* (published posthumously, 1986), Toni Morrison's *Song of Solomon* (1977), Katherine Anne Porter's *Pale Horse, Pale Rider* (1939), Marilynne Robinson's *Gilead* (2004), O. E. Rölvaag's *Giants in the Earth* (1927), and John Steinbeck's *East of Eden* (1952).

The Bible's ubiquity in American literature is rivaled only by its influence in the visual arts and music. In visual art, this influence extends as far back as colonial New England, despite the Puritans' iconoclasm. In England, Puritanism had inspired waves of iconoclastic destruction as zealous mobs, in obedience to the biblical prohibition against graven images, smashed the statues and stained glass that adorned many medieval churches. The Puritans brought this iconoclastic zeal to the New World, where a typical New England meetinghouse was furnished with not so much as a simple cross. Yet steeped as they were in the literary figures of scripture, Puritan artisans soon developed their own traditions of biblically inspired folk art, most notably the carved headstones still visible in many New England cemeteries. Juxtaposed with the familiar skulls and mottoes of mortality (*fugit hora*: the hour is fleeting) were stylized renditions of women's breasts, which were based on Christian readings of the Song of Solomon (the breast as a type of the life-giving power and maternal care of Christ the redeemer). By the nineteenth century, the iconoclastic aesthetic of the Puritan meetinghouse, which had influenced not only Puritans but also many other colonial Protestants, began to give way to the neo-medieval sensibilities of architects such as Richard Upjohn and Ralph Adams Cram, who designed Gothic revival churches replete with biblical epics set in stained glass. Early American painters such as the colonial-era master John Singleton Copley also belied New England's iconoclastic tradition. In addition to painting portraits of Boston's elite, Copley is also known for *The Ascension* (1775), a dramatic depiction of the astonished apostles watching as Christ is lifted up to heaven.

Copley's incorporation of Renaissance and Baroque elements lent his work a European flavor, but distinctively American traditions of biblical depiction emerged, as in the decidedly vernacular Millerite prophecy charts, reprinted by

Bible: As Sacred Text, Translations, Cultural Role

the thousands in the antebellum republic. On these appeared the apparitions of the apocalypse: the "great image" with a golden head and feet of clay (Daniel 2), the five-horned sheep (Daniel 8), the seven trumpets (Revelation 8–11), and the seven-headed dragon (Revelation 12). Equally influential on the popular imagination were illustrated editions of scripture, such as Harper and Brothers' highly successful *Illuminated Bible* (1844), which included 1,600 engravings of biblical scenes. Visual representations of biblical scenes also permeated the world of popular devotional publishing, as in John Cameron's 1849 lithographs of the Crucifixion and Resurrection, which were widely distributed by the American Tract Society, and Warner Sallman's 1941 painting *Head of Christ,* which was reprinted more than five hundred million times, thus becoming the most recognizable image of Jesus in the culture.

Music was another important medium through which Americans experienced the Bible. In colonial America, Puritan worship typically included the singing of metrical psalms, usually without accompaniment. Over time, other biblical texts, retold in verse by writers such as the English Nonconformist Isaac Watts, were set to hymn tunes for congregational singing. With the publication in 1844 of *The Sacred Harp* by Benjamin Franklin White and Elisha J. King, a distinctively American genre came into its own: sacred harp or "shape note" hymnody (so named for the distinctively shaped musical notations used to aid untrained singers). Sung a cappella in four-part harmony, the sacred harp combined haunting melodies with rhymed stanzas, as in the tune *Windham* (with text based on Matthew 7:13–14): "Broad is the road that leads to death / And thousands walk together there; / But wisdom shows a narrow path, / With here and there a traveler." Although biblical texts formed the basis for a variety of more complicated works by later American composers—from Leonard Bernstein's first symphony, *Jeremiah* (1942), to Carlisle Floyd's opera *Susannah* (1955)—the stark hymns of the sacred harp, sung in frontier meetinghouses and revival tents, best captured the biblical worldview that animated countless ordinary people.

## The Bible as Contested Book: Religious and Secular Politics

The Bible's tremendous influence on American habits of mind is owed in no small part to the widespread belief in the book's literal veracity. In polls between 1991 and 2007, for example, the Gallup organization found that 31 percent

of Americans, on average, believed that the Bible is the actual word of God and is to be taken literally. Another segment of the population, hovering near 50 percent, accepted the Bible as the inspired word of God but believed that not everything in it should be taken literally. The combined percentages therefore indicated that roughly four of five Americans at the turn of the twenty-first century regarded the Bible as in some sense the word of God. Although other polls have indicated a gradual upward trend in the number of religious skeptics, the United States remains unique among Western industrialized societies in the extent of its biblicism.

The nation's presidents are well aware of the Bible's legitimating potential and routinely quote scripture in their oratory to lend gravity or provide comfort, especially in times of crisis. Presidential use of scripture is bipartisan. On the night after the September 11, 2001, attack, which killed nearly three thousand people, George W. Bush invoked Psalm 23 ("Even though I walk through the valley of the shadow of death, I fear no evil"). In repudiating some past policies and the unwillingness to address certain problems, President Barack Obama, in his inaugural address, paraphrased 1 Corinthians 13:11 ("the time has come to set aside childish things").

Yet the bipartisan rhetorical use of scripture belies the fact that the Bible remains the most divisive book in American history. Its divisiveness stems from two factors external to scripture itself. The first, and more basic, issue is the modern manner of reading the text that has dominated since the eighteenth-century Enlightenment. Modern readers tend to judge the text based on its perceived degree of correspondence to historical, factual reality. Many conservative Christians presume a complete correspondence—hence the modern doctrine of "inerrancy" (the notion that the Bible lacks any error, whether historical, scientific, or theological). Liberal Christians presume that the Bible is a mixture of authoritative material and ancient legend, a view shared by critical biblical scholars. The divisiveness arises when the two sides clash over the extent of the Bible's normative status. In 1993, for example, a group of liberal scholars known as the Jesus Seminar made waves with *The Five Gospels,* a new edition of the four New Testament Gospels along with the noncanonical Gospel of Thomas, in which every verse is color-coded according to how reliable the committee judged it to be. Conservative scholars condemned the project and appealed to the favorite proof text of inerrantists, 2 Timothy 3:16 ("All scripture is given by inspiration of God"). Such controversies continue to reinforce a conservative–liberal divide even as the most strident voices on the two sides inevitably drown out the less polarized perspectives of other scholars and many average people.

The second source of the Bible's divisiveness concerns the particular passages judged authoritative by different constituencies and how those passages should be applied to ethical issues of modern times. In the nineteenth century, the burning question was slavery and whether the biblical passages that presumed the institution should be relativized. In the early twentieth century, especially in the famous Scopes "Monkey" Trial of 1925, the issue was the teaching of evolution in the public schools. Creationists feared that the Darwinists' rejection of a literal reading of Genesis would imperil the whole providential view of history in which God planned all things, from the creation to the end of the world. By the turn of the twenty-first century, controversy centered on homosexuality, specifically the question of whether passages such as Leviticus 18:22 ("Thou shalt not lie with mankind, as with womankind") are timeless ethical verities or time-bound products of an ancient culture that lacked nuanced understandings of sexual and gender differences. For Christians, the homosexuality debate is made all the more divisive by the complicated issues of Bible translation surrounding passages such as 1 Corinthians 6:9, in which one of the disputed Greek words has been variously rendered as "effeminate," "homosexuals," and "sexual perverts," among other readings. Such exegetical debates are far from idle, for they relate to hotly contested questions in the political realm. When Massachusetts became the first state to legalize same-sex marriage in 2004, activists on both sides of the issue redoubled their efforts to claim the Bible for their respective causes.

The Bible, in other words, seems destined to remain a politically contested book, at least in the short term. The long-term outcome of the contemporary culture wars is less clear. Will battle fatigue over sexuality ultimately help weaken the Bible's hold over the lives of many Americans? Or will a majority continue to find ways to Americanize the ancient text and make it relevant to new contexts? History would seem to favor the latter, for as the Bible itself attests (Ecclesiastes 12:12), "of making many books there is no end."

**See also** *Benevolent Empire; Bible, Interpretation of; Book of Mormon; Qur'an; Religious Thought* entries; *Torah.*

Peter J. Thuesen

## BIBLIOGRAPHY

Amory, Hugh, and David D. Hall, eds. *A History of the Book in America,* Vol. 1, *The Colonial Book in the Atlantic World.* Cambridge: Cambridge University Press, 2000.

Barlow, Philip L. *Mormons and the Bible: The Place of the Latter-day Saints in American Religion.* New York: Oxford University Press, 1991.

Brown, Jerry Wayne. *The Rise of Biblical Criticism in America, 1800–1870: The New England Scholars.* Middletown, Conn.: Wesleyan University Press, 1969.

Curtis, Susan. *A Consuming Faith: The Social Gospel and Modern American Culture.* Baltimore: Johns Hopkins University Press, 1991.

Daniel, David. *The Bible in English: Its History and Influence.* New Haven, Conn.: Yale University Press, 2003.

Faulring, Scott H., Kent P. Jackson, and Robert J. Matthews, eds. *Joseph Smith's New Translation of the Bible: Original Manuscripts.* Provo, Utah: Religious Studies Center, Brigham Young University, 2004.

Fogarty, Gerald P. *American Catholic Biblical Scholarship: A History from the Early Republic to Vatican II.* San Francisco: Harper and Row, 1989.

Gaustad, Edwin S., and Walter Harrelson, eds. *The Bible in American Culture.* 6 vols. Philadelphia: Fortress Press, 1982–1985.

Goldman, Shalom. *God's Sacred Tongue: Hebrew and the American Imagination.* Chapel Hill: University of North Carolina Press, 2004.

Gordis, Lisa M. *Opening Scripture: Bible Reading and Interpretive Authority in Puritan New England.* Chicago: University of Chicago Press, 2003.

Gutjahr, Paul C. *An American Bible: A History of the Good Book in the United States, 1777–1880.* Stanford, Calif.: Stanford University Press, 1999.

Hatch, Nathan O., and Mark A. Noll, eds. *The Bible in America: Essays in Cultural History.* New York: Oxford University Press, 1982.

Haynes, Stephen R. *Noah's Curse: The Biblical Justification of American Slavery.* New York: Oxford University Press, 2002.

Hills, Margaret T. ed. *The English Bible in America: A Bibliography of Editions of the Bible and the New Testament Published in America, 1777–1957.* New York: American Bible Society and New York Public Library, 1961.

Johnson, Sylvester A. *The Myth of Ham in Nineteenth-Century American Christianity: Race, Heathens, and the People of God.* New York: Palgrave Macmillan, 2004.

Marsh, Charles. *God's Long Summer: Stories of Faith and Civil Rights.* Princeton, N.J.: Princeton University Press, 1997.

Morgan, David. *Protestants and Pictures: Religion, Visual Culture, and the Age of American Mass Production.* New York: Oxford University Press, 1999.

Noll, Mark A. *Between Faith and Criticism: Evangelicals, Scholarship, and the Bible in America.* San Francisco: Harper and Row, 1986.

———. *The Civil War as a Theological Crisis.* Chapel Hill: University of North Carolina Press, 2006.

———. *God and Race in American Politics: A Short History.* Princeton, N.J.: Princeton University Press, 2008.

Orlinsky, Harry M., and Robert G. Bratcher. *A History of Bible Translation and the North American Contribution.* Atlanta: Scholars Press, 1991.

Raboteau, Albert J. *A Fire in the Bones: Reflections on African-American Religious History.* Boston: Beacon Press, 1995.

Sperling, S. David, Baruch A. Levine, and B. Barry Levy. *Students of the Covenant: A History of Jewish Biblical Scholarship in North America.* Atlanta: Scholars Press, 1992.

Thuesen, Peter J. *In Discordance with the Scriptures: American Protestant Battles over Translating the Bible.* New York: Oxford University Press, 1999.

Wimbush, Vincent L., ed. *African Americans and the Bible: Sacred Texts and Social Textures.* New York: Continuum, 2000.

Wosh, Peter J. *Spreading the Word: The Bible Business in Nineteenth-Century America.* Ithaca, N.Y.: Cornell University Press, 1994.

# Bible: Interpretation of

The Bible has played an important role in the religious life of North American Christians and has been interpreted in a number of different ways. The academic study of the scriptures has been a primary focus for seminaries throughout the United States and Canada. Preaching and teaching the Bible has been a central task of churches in a variety of ways, both formally and informally. Millions of Christians in their own personal and devotional interactions with the Bible have studied and interpreted scripture since the earliest days of Christianity in North America. Likewise, Jewish readers have studied the Hebrew Bible and related materials, keeping alive a centuries-old tradition of scriptural study and interpretation.

There are two dimensions to any consideration of the Bible. First, it is inevitable that a view about the nature of scripture is held or will be developed. One studies the scriptures in a variety of ways and does so out of convictions about what the Bible is. These convictions may be explicit or implicit. But interaction with the Bible leads to a view or is occasioned by a view of what kind of book the Bible is. Among other viewpoints, the Bible may be considered as a book of inerrant facts; as a medium through which one is in contact with the divine; as a record of the religious experiences of ancient peoples; or as a book of morals or source of wisdom for daily living.

A second factor is that the Bible is interpreted. Whenever the scriptures are read and comments are made, biblical interpretation is occurring. Declarations about "what the Bible says" are always interpretive acts. In both formal and informal ways, one interprets the scripture when its verses are read, pondered, or discussed. This has been the case throughout the history of the Christian church. Biblical scholars and theologians have developed highly structured methods of biblical interpretation. But the interpretative process is also a part of what ordinary Christian believers have done and do on a regular basis. Likewise, interpretation is involved for those many people who study the Bible for a number of reasons or do not operate from explicitly religious convictions. Interpretive judgments emerge no matter from what perspective readers approach their study of the Bible.

The interpretation of the Bible in North America has been intimately tied into the culture of the United States and Canada. This is true in relation to the kinds of concerns biblical interpretation has addressed, as well as the ways in which descriptions of the nature of scripture and the means of its appropriate interpretation are articulated. Events in American culture in both social and personal arenas have elicited comments from religious people about what they interpret the Bible to teach and its relation to certain issues. A "religious interpretation" of American history, for example, is often predicated on specific interpretations of biblical passages that relate to how "God" and a "nation" should interact. Prominent political figures often cite—and thus interpret—the Bible in their rhetoric and speeches. So biblical interpretation in North America has not been an isolated event or a private endeavor. The Bible has held a prominent place in the "marketplace," and its significance has been ongoing into contemporary times.

Views about the nature of scripture and the means to interpret it are related in many and often subtle ways. What one believes about what the Bible is will influence what methods one employs to interpret it. When one is committed to a basic interpretive approach to scripture, one's views about what the Bible is can be reinforced or altered. This is true if one adopts the approach of literalism, in which texts are interpreted at their face value, or literally; or if one looks at the Bible as allegorism, which establishes a set of hidden meanings for which the words of the text are a code; or if one uses critical methods, in which the text is examined rationally for a number of features, such as its language, context, or impact upon its readers. There is an interplay between "theoretical constructs" and "interpretive practices" or between views of the nature of scripture and the ways one believes it should be interpreted

The views discussed in the following section have been prominent in North America. A short description of each viewpoint's concept of the nature of scripture is followed by comments about interpretive practices and leading practitioners.

## *The Nature of Scripture and Its Interpretation*
### Roman Catholicism

North American Roman Catholics have adhered to the traditional position that the Bible is God's revelation and is to be interpreted through the work of the *magisterium,* or authority, of the Roman Catholic Church. The church is the guarantor of the correct interpretation of Scripture. This view has been expressed in the tradition of the Roman church and its official pronouncements, so the church's tradition is the means by which the true interpretation of the Bible has been expressed. Thus scripture and tradition serve as dual sources of God's revelation.

Until the Second Vatican Council (Vatican II), 1962–1965, methods and results of biblical interpretation for Roman Catholic theologians had to coincide with the church's teachings. Use of emerging critical methods of studying the Bible was forbidden. (The Catholic Biblical Association of America, founded in 1936, had begun publishing the *Catholic Biblical Quarterly* for the scholarly study of scripture in 1939.) With the approval of the Constitution on Divine Revelation (*Dei Verbum*), in 1965, a number of Roman Catholic scripture scholars became prominent figures. Among them were Roland Murphy (1917–2002), Raymond E. Brown (1928–1998), and Joseph A. Fitzmyer (1920–). By the 1970s the doors had been opened for important Roman Catholic scholars to adopt most of the scholarly consensus on most issues of biblical interpretation. For example, Fitzmyer argued against the traditional viewpoint but in line with other New Testament scholars, that the apostle Paul did not write the pastoral letters (1 and 2 Timothy and Titus, which traditionally had been attributed to him). Brown, who had argued that the apostle John wrote the Gospel according to John, later rejected this position. These are indications of the ways Roman Catholic scholars, while remaining loyal to church dogma and tradition, were able to employ contemporary methods of scholarship used by non-Catholic biblical scholars as well. Examples of Catholic contributions to biblical studies currently abound in the number of high-level biblical commentaries and specialized studies produced by Roman Catholic exegetes.

## Liberal Theology

Liberal theology in the eighteenth and nineteenth centuries emerged at the time when biblical scholars were increasingly employing a number of new forms of analysis in their study of the scriptures. These included scientific, sociological, economic, and psychological approaches. Overall, what became known as historical criticism, or the historical-critical method, became prominent. This was the attempt to understand ancient texts in relation to their historical origins, the time and place in which they were written, the sources that informed them, and the dates, events, places, persons, and things (including customs) that are mentioned or implied in the texts. Basic presuppositions of this approach include the convictions that ancient reality is accessible to investigation by the use of human reason and that the contemporary experience of humanity can indicate the objective criteria by which to determine what could or could not have happened in the past. Liberal theology embraced the historical-critical method as the means of interpreting biblical texts and for understanding the nature of the Bible.

The liberal theology of eighteenth- and nineteenth-century European Protestants, including Friedrich Schleiermacher, Albrecht Ritschl, and Adolf von Harnack, was expressed in North America by a number of interpreters. Prominent figures were William Adams Brown, Harry Emerson Fosdick, Walter Rauschenbusch, and Shailer Mathews. They viewed the Bible as the record of the religious experiences of ancient peoples, written by fallible human authors, that nonetheless could inspire contemporary readers with its great beauty, power, and dignity. The Bible's authority was in its power to evoke religious experience through the ancient writings and to confront readers with the great questions of human existence. Fosdick spoke of the Bible as presenting "abiding experiences and changing categories."

Liberal theology embraced the emerging critical study of the Bible as compatible with its desire to separate the Bible's "religious" understandings from the social and cultural contexts in which these were presented in the scriptures. A full range of critical methods and schools of interpretation can be applied to biblical interpretation in order to separate the husk from the kernel—the historical, sociological, and cultural backgrounds of biblical texts from their religious meanings. Liberal theologians sought to communicate the experience of the biblical writers ("abiding experiences") in the contemporary thought forms and language of their own times ("changing categories").

The impact of critical biblical scholarship, especially as developed in Germany, on Americans has been substantial. This can be seen in the number of American scholars who studied in Germany. In most years in the 1890s, more than four hundred American students were enrolled in German theological faculties. After World War II a number of prominent Continental biblical scholars assumed teaching posts at major North American theological institutions.

## Neo-Orthodox Theology

The Swiss theologian Karl Barth (1886–1968) was the leading Protestant theologian of the twentieth century. Barth had been a student of leading German liberal theologians, including Adolf von Harnack. But when he saw his former professors supporting the kaiser's war policies at the start of World War I, Barth rejected liberal theology and began his own study of scripture.

For Barth and those who followed him (often labeled "neo-orthodox"), the Bible was "witness." As such, the category of "inerrancy" and the demands for "factual accuracy" were not a set of concerns. Barth "returned" to the Bible, and, along with colleagues such as Emil Brunner, developed a "dialectical" approach to scripture. This viewpoint stressed the great contrast between God and humanity, between the transcendent and holy God and finite and sinful human beings. In Jesus Christ, who was truly divine and truly human, as the ancient church affirmed, God has been revealed fully and finally, as "the Word made flesh." In Jesus Christ, God has bridged the gap between the divine and human by the divine "Word," which for Barth took three forms: the Word revealed (Jesus Christ); the Word proclaimed (preaching); and the Word written (scripture). The Bible "becomes" God's Word when through preaching Jesus Christ is proclaimed. The scriptures are our only source of knowledge of Jesus Christ and are the divine witness to the Word made flesh. Biblical writers were "inspired" but were still fallible humans recording in words their witness to what they had seen and heard. These writers and words had the "capacity for errors"; yet they were used by God through the Holy Spirit to point to the central character of scripture, Jesus Christ, and to accomplish God's divine purposes in the world. Scripture's "authority" arose when the Holy Spirit took the words of human witnesses and through this witness brought faith and obedience to Jesus Christ. Whatever "discrepancies" or "difficulties" or perceived "errors" in the biblical text may be found do not at all diminish what God is doing in and through the Bible by providing a "witness" to the greatest news in the universe: "The Word became flesh and lived among us" (John 1:14).

Barth did not find much of the work of his contemporaries in historical-critical studies of the Bible to be useful for enabling the theological meanings of the biblical texts to emerge. He did careful exegesis, but he always regarded that work as a prelude to the task of the "theological exegesis" of scripture in which the primary focus was on hearing and understanding what the biblical texts were pointing toward in terms of God's revelation in Jesus Christ. Some critics thought Barth's Christological focus was detrimental to exegesis because his Christocentric theology was always looking for how texts (even in the Old Testament) were pointing toward Jesus Christ. The Bible was authoritative for Barth insofar as its writers were used by God's Holy Spirit as witnesses to God's Word in Jesus Christ. The Bible was to be interpreted with this focus.

Those who adopted this neo-orthodox approach to the nature and interpretation of the Bible were not drawn in to the arguments around inerrancy that were to rage among other American Protestants. Among academic theologians and some biblical scholars, Barth's influence in the 1950s and 1960s was pervasive. It also reached wider audiences in some churches through preachers trained under neo-orthodox American seminary professors and also through church school curricula that adopted this approach to the Bible and its interpretation.

## Fundamentalism

A strong reaction to the liberal and later the neo-orthodox views of the nature of scripture and its appropriate interpretation is evident in the development of American fundamentalism. This movement got its name from the writing project called The Fundamentals: A Testimony of the Truth, a series of twelve paperback books published between 1910 and 1915, that sought to answer the charges of liberalism in terms of the nature of scripture and its appropriate interpretation. Approximately three million copies of these books were distributed free to Christian leaders throughout the world.

Fundamentalist theology was attractive to evangelical Protestant Christians who came out of the revivalist tradition of American religion and in the twentieth century sought to oppose the "modernism" of liberal theology and the cultural changes that this theology endorsed. The fundamentalist movement was composed of people from a number of related traditions and began to take on its own identity. Fundamentalist theology viewed the Bible as containing divinely inspired and "inerrant" propositions that were directly revealed by God to human writers who recorded God's "Word" in all their words without error. The entire (Protestant) canon of scripture is thus inspired ("plenary inspiration") and is inspired "verbally," in every word. Since God is "true" (Romans 3:4) and God has "inspired" the scripture (2 Timothy 3:16), the Bible must be true and without error in all that it teaches. This truth is revealed in the propositions of the Bible that by the direct inspiration of God stand as God's Word, which is true in all senses—not only "religiously" or theologically, but also historically and scientifically.

The fundamentalist view of scripture is tied primarily to a literalist hermeneutic, or approach to interpreting biblical texts. This means that biblical passages are interpreted in their plain, literal, or "historical" sense unless there is a pronounced clarity indicating that some other method of understanding should be used. (For example, Jesus' parables of the New Testament do not have to be read as literal or historically accurate stories.) The results of this emphasis on literal Biblical interpretation are seen most clearly in the interpretation of the first eleven chapters of Genesis as literal history. The biblical accounts of creation—of the universe and of humanity—are understood to be historically accurate, literal accounts of how the universe came into existence and how humans were created by the direct action of God. The most highly publicized example of fundamentalist theology on display was the famous Scopes "Monkey" Trial in 1925, in Dayton, Tennessee, when John Scopes, a high school biology teacher, was charged with violating Tennessee law by teaching Darwinism and the theory of evolution.

Today, the viewpoint known as creationism is a restatement of the fundamentalist view of how the opening chapters of Genesis should be interpreted in a literal way. The fundamentalist approach to biblical interpretation can also be found in some "pro-life" arguments in North American religious life about abortion as well as capital punishment. Leading fundamentalist leaders have included John R. Rice, Charles C. Ryrie, Jerry Falwell, and Pat Robertson. Also prominent was C. I. Scofield, whose *Scofield Reference Bible*, first published in 1909, is still widely used. The Scofield Bible popularized the approach to biblical interpretation known as dispensationalism, in which God is seen as dealing with the people of God in different ways during different biblical "dispensations," or periods.

An expression of Scofield's dispensationalism as applied to eschatology, or the doctrine of the "last things," is in the popular Left Behind series of fiction books by Tim LaHaye and Jerry B. Jenkins. These are narratives that express a particular reading of apocalyptic biblical passages, particularly from the book of Revelation. Emphasis is on the Second Coming of Jesus Christ, which, according to this way of interpreting scripture, is to occur prior to the thousand-year reign of Christ known as the millennium. This view is called

premillennialism. It features the "rapture" of believers (based on 1 Thessalonians 4:13–18), the appearance of the "Beast" whose "number" is 666, the Antichrist, and the vanquishing of Satan. The phenomenal sales of the Left Behind series, along with a resurgent fundamentalism throughout American culture, have established an appeal for the literal hermeneutic of fundamentalism in relation to speculations about the end of the world and its time frame—which adherents believe will be able to be seen as coming to pass within the events of current history. Overall, this effect of fundamentalist views of biblical interpretation continues to play a part in popular interpretation of the Bible among many people in the United States.

## Protestant Scholastic Theology

The emphasis on the nature of scripture and its literal interpretation are also found in an important viewpoint that continues to find expression in American religious life and that is associated with seventeenth-century Calvinism: Protestant scholastic theology. It is the approach of prominent theologians of Princeton Seminary, in New Jersey, in the nineteenth and early twentieth centuries, in which scripture is understood as doctrine. Archibald Alexander, Charles Hodge, Archibald Alexander Hodge, Benjamin B. Warfield, and the New Testament scholar J. Gresham Machen continued the tradition of seventeenth-century Reformed orthodoxy and developed a view that saw the Bible as authoritative because it was verbally inspired by God.

Since divinely inspired writers cannot err (under the influence of the Holy Spirit), the Bible must convey inerrant truths in all dimensions of what it teaches, including areas of history, science, and all issues of fact. A. A. Hodge and Warfield wrote an essay on "Inspiration," in 1881, in which they argued that this inerrancy pertains directly to the "original autographs"—the original documents of scripture. These, they claimed, were "absolutely infallible when interpreted in the sense intended." To disprove this view, they said, it would have to be shown that two apparently "discrepant" passages of the Bible existed in the original autographs (which are no longer extant); that the interpretation of the apparent discrepancy is the interpretation intended by the passage; and that the true sense of the text in the autograph of scripture is "directly and necessarily inconsistent with some certainly known act of history, or truth of science, or some other statement of Scripture certainly ascertained and interpreted." One comes to recognize the inerrancy of scripture by the acquiescing of the mind to the truths of scripture as found through the powers and processes of human reason, under the influence of the Holy Spirit. Scripture presents "doctrines" to be believed—a view that fit well into the confessional Calvinism of the "Old Princeton" theologians, in which subscription to a confession of faith (the Westminster Confession of 1646) was an important act of faith.

The sophisticated doctrine of the inerrancy of scripture was developed by the Princeton school in the light of the attacks of nineteenth-century "higher critics"—those who used the historical-critical method—on the veracity and accuracy of the Bible. The Princeton view of scripture was appropriated by a number of fundamentalists, and Princeton Seminary professor Benjamin B. Warfield wrote the article on the Bible for *The Fundamentals*. The transdenominational and breadth of the fundamentalist-scholastic approach of inerrancy is crystallized in that fact, since others who wrote for the series would not agree with Warfield's Calvinism or with his specific views on issues such as election and predestination or the millennium. The Princeton tradition maintained this view of the Bible's verbal inspiration, and thus authority, as well as the view that the inerrancy of scripture had been the church's historic view through the ages.

The contention that the "inerrancy view" had been the church's historic position was challenged in the nineteenth century by the Presbyterian Charles Augustus Briggs, an Old Testament scholar at Union Theological Seminary in New York City. Briggs had studied in Germany and became proficient in biblical criticism. He challenged the Hodge-Warfield formulation, this "scholastic view," as being an expression of seventeenth-century Reformed theologians who came after the time of Calvin. Briggs claimed the inerrancy view was not the viewpoint of Calvin and the Reformation confessions of faith. Briggs pointed out that none of the official confessions of the period had stated that the words of the original autographs of scripture were without error and also that the great reformers recognized errors in scripture and did not hold to the inerrancy of the original autographs. Briggs believed minor errors in detail did not destroy the Bible's credibility and its trustworthiness as the revelation of God. In Briggs's view, credibility was to be distinguished from infallibility.

Briggs's views led to his ecclesiastical trial within the Presbyterian Church in 1892. By then a majority of Presbyterian ministers and through them church members had been educated in the scholastic theology of Hodge and Warfield in the Old Princeton tradition. In 1893 Briggs was convicted of denying the Bible's authority. He lost his

ordination in the Presbyterian Church and later became ordained in the Episcopal Church. In the same year the General Assembly of the Presbyterian Church acted to make the Hodge-Warfield theory of inerrancy the correct interpretation of the Westminster Confession for American Presbyterians. This was not modified until 1927, when a special theological commission was appointed in the church to deal with the continuing polarization of views over issues of biblical criticism and evolution. The General Assembly ruled that no body, even a General Assembly itself, could prescribe binding interpretation of the Westminster standards.

The view of the nature of the Bible as presenting doctrines to be believed, as well as an authoritative source of information on all it affirms, had many implications for biblical interpretation. Under divine inspiration, in this view, the biblical writers perfectly portrayed that which they were inspired to write, based on what they saw and heard. In interpretation, the interpreter sought through rigorous study of the biblical text, using the original languages of Hebrew and Greek, to find the established usage for the words in the text, and in so doing could be brought into direct contact with the event conveyed in scripture. This process enabled interpreters to encounter the biblical event as if they had been present and had personal experience. The testimony of others, as "witnesses," could also mediate historical events with veracity and accuracy. Thus miracles, for example, could be considered as true when they were established by the testimony of credible witnesses. The testimony of credible witnesses made an event every bit as "true" as if one had had the experience of being present at the original event. The logical meanings of statements were most important, and by induction (the influence of Francis Bacon), one could construct a "systematic" theology from the biblical texts. The influence of Scottish "common sense" realism was strong in the Princeton School. It enabled an essential confidence in the abilities of readers to interpret the biblical text in a straightforward manner and to enter into the "world of the Bible" with confident assurance that human powers of reasoning, along with the work of the Holy Spirit, would lead one to the right interpretation of biblical texts

## Neo-Evangelical Theology

Reactions to the fundamentalist and scholastic views of the inerrancy of the Bible in the wake of many American denominational splits over the nature of scripture led Harold John Ockenga, pastor of Park Street Church, Boston, in 1948, to call for a "new evangelicalism." This was to distinguish "evangelicals" from "fundamentalists," especially in calling for more social involvement by Christians in the nation's problems. In 1942 Ockenga and others had formed the National Association of Evangelicals. Since that time, evangelicalism has become a visible and potent factor in American religious life. There are today various streams or strands of the American evangelical movement with differing relationships to the fundamentalist theology from which they wish to distinguish themselves.

At the same time, the Reformed theological tradition, and particularly the Presbyterian tradition, which had produced the Old Princeton stress on the inerrancy of the Bible, has also evolved. Over the past sixty years, new Presbyterian churches have been formed, and in 1983 the two main bodies of American Presbyterians—the Presbyterian Church in the United States of America and the United Presbyterian Church of North America—merged to become the Presbyterian Church (U.S.A.).

Evangelicalism and Presbyterianism are two groupings in American religious life that have produced some who adhere to a view of the nature of scripture that is neither fundamentalist nor scholastic but that wants to hold to the Bible as God's authoritative Word and wants to be open to different means of biblical interpretation, using a variety of scholarly tools. This viewpoint may be labeled neo-evangelical, though the term is not used as much as it was in the past. Yet the viewpoint, which is held by many who call themselves evangelical, or who are part of mainstream Protestant churches through which they have their theological identity, has enduring importance as what might be described as a centrist position. A primary concern of evangelicals is that a person's relationship with Jesus Christ by faith is what makes one a Christian. It is through the Bible that Christ becomes known and present. An emphasis on religious conversion has been prominent among leading evangelicals (such as Billy Graham). The Bible functions as the means by which religious conversion can be effected.

Scripture, in this view, may be regarded as "message." A distinction is made between the words *infallibility* and *inerrancy*. In fundamentalist and scholastic theology, the Bible was considered verbally inspired by God and therefore logically had to produce an "inerrant" (original) text. In this sense, the Bible is true. In neo-evangelical theology, *infallibility* is regarded as the more appropriate term, with the emphasis being on the Bible as God's revelation, which is true in the sense that it will not lead one astray and is completely trustworthy for the purposes for which it is written.

The primary purpose is to guide people to faith in Jesus Christ and allow them to have eternal life in his name (John 20:31). In this view the Bible is authoritative because it is centered in Jesus Christ and it conveys the truth of Jesus Christ to those who believe, by the work of the Holy Spirit. Scripture *is* the Word of God because it is God's divine revelation, which has been conveyed through the inspired writers of the Bible. But in this view the central purpose of scripture is to convey the divine message of salvation, which comes from God, who uses limited, fallible human writers to present this message. The biblical writers were inspired by God, but this inspiration emerges in and through their personalities and does not exempt them from the limits of their own humanity and their time and place and cultures. The purpose of the scriptures is a theological one—proclaiming the message of salvation in Jesus Christ—and this does not entail the need for the Bible to be an inerrant book in the sense of providing exactly accurate information on all topics about which it speaks. Scripture is infallible in accomplishing its purpose, but infallibility does not imply a necessary inerrancy.

The neo-evangelical viewpoint has drawn on European predecessors, especially in regard to challenging the Old Princeton view of inerrancy as the historic position of Christian churches and as being the view of Calvin and the Reformation leaders. Those who critiqued the inerrancy view and who believed *infallibility* was a better term to describe the nature of scripture were Thomas Lindley and James Orr, in Scotland, in the nineteenth and early twentieth centuries, and Abraham Kuyper and Herman Bavinck, at the same time, in the Netherlands. In the mid-twentieth century, the Dutch theologian G. C. Berkouwer played an important role in helping to establish this view of scripture as a responsible "evangelical" viewpoint. Other important voices in the United States have been Donald Bloesch and Jack Rogers.

A neo-evangelical view of scripture that speaks of the "divine message expressed in human thought forms" is open to a variety of methods of biblical interpretation. Both "lower" criticism (study of the biblical texts) and "higher" criticism (all other forms of biblical criticism) can be used for interpreting biblical texts, as well as in other interpretive approaches. This openness is possible because of the view that the divine message is expressed through human writers who lived and wrote in ancient cultures. The more we can understand their backgrounds, languages, and all other dimensions of their cultures, the more fully we can understand what message the writers are trying to convey. The

Word of God comes through human writers whose own limitations—by the contemporary standards typically employed in the fields of history, sociology, and the sciences—are not barriers to hearing scripture's message. This is why, in this view, a comprehensive scientific accuracy is not required of the biblical text. God's message is given in the midst of the human domain. Any "findings" by biblical critics of seeming problems with the biblical stories or texts do not detract from the Bible's functioning as the Word of God, which was given to proclaim the message of salvation in Jesus Christ. Since the Bible's primary purpose is theological, the findings of history or science do not jeopardize the Bible's authority. So while the linguistic distinction between "inerrancy" and "infallibility" may seem small, the distinction is crucial and has had tremendous implications for the religious lives of millions of American Christians.

This divide was expressed memorably in "the battle for the Bible" controversies that were prominent on the evangelical landscape from the mid-1970s onward. The continuing influence of the cultural changes of the 1960s and early 1970s surely played a role in the need felt by some to focus on the Bible's divine and absolute authority. In a time when many felt that North American culture was "adrift," when older cultural norms and practices were under attack and breaking down, and when "authority" was questioned through many voices, a need to reassert the unchanging authority of the Bible was appealing to many conservative Christians. Besieged by events of the day, such as the war in Vietnam, women's liberation, and the emerging drug culture, many conservatives felt compelled to defend biblical authority in the face of "attacks."

In 1976 the evangelical leader Harold Lindsell published *The Battle for the Bible*. In it, he expressed the belief that no one who did not adhere to his view of the inerrancy of the Bible could rightly claim the name "evangelical." Lindsell's book threatened to divide American evangelicals, all the more so since those who did not agree with his views of biblical interpretation on issues such as the role of women or the relation of science and scripture were said to deny the authority of the Bible. In particular, Lindsell took aim at Fuller Theological Seminary, an institution with which he had been associated.

In 1978 the International Council on Biblical Inerrancy (ICBI) was formed. Its purpose was to establish a ten-year initiative to "win back" those in churches who had drifted away from the position of inerrancy. In the literature that followed, it was the scholastic theology of the Hodge–Warfield view of inerrancy that was considered by proponents as the only historically and theologically sound approach to biblical authority and interpretation.

The Chicago Statement on Biblical Inerrancy, drafted by a coalition of fundamentalist and Protestant scholastic theologians and endorsed by many others, affirmed the importance of the theory of inerrancy. The statement maintained that while God caused the biblical writers to write the words that God chose, this did not mean that he overrode their individual personalities. A shorthand expression for the view was, "What scripture says, God says." Another article in the statement issued qualifications about what the theory of inerrancy did not mean—apparently to provide biblical scholars with measures of freedom in which to work. These qualifications included the denial that inerrancy was negated by "lack of modern technical precision," the "reporting of falsehoods," the "topical arrangement of material," and the "use of free citations," among other items.

This tension between the theory of biblical authority and the practice of biblical interpreters who dealt with the "phenomenon" of scripture continued to be a source of difficulty for American evangelicals. For some, "inerrancy" was a way of affirming the Bible's truth and trustworthiness as God's revelation—similar to what may be meant by "infallibility." For others, it was an absolute necessity to affirm how the Bible was true and the nature of this truth—thus, "inerrancy."

In 1979 Jack B. Rogers (of Fuller Seminary) and Donald K. McKim published *The Authority and Interpretation of the Bible: An Historical Approach*. In this book the authors argued that the central tradition of the church through the centuries had been to see the scriptures as focused on presenting the story of salvation, culminating in Jesus Christ, and that the church's main theologians—in particular, Calvin and Luther—did not hold to what later became the inerrancy view of the Old Princeton theology. Rogers and McKim traced the beginnings of the inerrancy theory to post-Reformation scholasticism and its development in America at Princeton Seminary, where, for its first sixty years (1812–1872), the primary theology textbook was not Calvin's *Institutes* (1536) but the *Institutes* of a later Geneva theologian, Francis Turretin, published in 1679–1685. Turretin's theological method was opposite to that of Calvin, and he was instrumental in developing the view that the autographs of scripture were inerrant. (Turretin's text was replaced at Princeton in 1872 with Charles Hodge's *Systematic Theology*.) The significance of this fact, maintained Rogers and

McKim, was that those who were taught the "Princeton theology," including inerrancy, thought they were learning the views of the Westminster Confession and Calvinist theology when, in fact, they were learning the post-Reformation scholasticism of Turretin and his successors. These scholars and students were facing the beginnings (and later the development) of scientific criticism of the Bible and sought to ensure the Bible's authority with a theory of scripture's inerrancy. Correlatively, according to Rogers and McKim, some of the important features of the church's central teaching about the authority and interpretation of the Bible (such as Chrysostom's, Augustine's, and Calvin's concept of "accommodation") had been lost.

The publication of the Rogers and McKim volume evoked a number of responses. Many evangelicals and those in mainstream churches found the work liberating in freeing them from having to adopt an inerrantist viewpoint. Those to the left of Rogers and McKim on the theological spectrum said the book was merely saying what had been known for years and that fundamentalists and inerrantists should be ignored. Some saw the book as irrelevant to the real concerns of the church. For some (a bit to the right of Rogers and McKim on the theological spectrum), the real problem with biblical authority was with liberal theology in mainstream churches, and it is these views that must be criticized.

In the 1980s the lines hardened even more among American evangelicals. The political expression of evangelicalism with Jerry Falwell's Moral Majority, founded in 1979, and the rise of the new Religious Right during Ronald Reagan's presidency (1981–1989) gave prominence to the "evangelical presence" in American religious life and to questions about the distinctiveness of evangelicalism in relation to fundamentalism. While all fundamentalists may be evangelicals, not all evangelicals would consider themselves fundamentalists.

Harold Lindsell's sequel, *The Bible in the Balance* (1979), focused on even more people and institutions that he saw as having abandoned historical evangelicalism. A 1982 volume by John Woodbridge, *Biblical Authority: A Critique of the Rogers/McKim Proposal,* questioned Rogers and McKim's reading of church history and maintained that the biblical writers wrote inerrantly "not only for matters of faith and practice, but also in making incidental affirmations concerning history, geography and the natural world." The term *inerrancy* had become a battle cry and a term that measured the fidelity of evangelicals.

The issues raised by the inerrancy debate have continued. Political and social events and ethos in American religious life have ensured that differences over biblical interpretation predicated on views of the nature of scripture have continued to have relevance. It is realistic to think that the controversies will continue, both in academic terms among scholars as well as in the day-to-day lives of American Christians as they consider their own cultural attitudes and theological commitments.

## Other Contemporary Views

Other viewpoints about the nature of the Bible and its appropriate interpretation have also played a role in considering biblical interpretation in America on both the academic side and on more popular levels.

Existential theology is associated with the theology of the German thinker Paul Tillich (1886–1965). The emphasis here is on scripture as "living encounter." The scriptures comprise religious symbols through which readers can encounter "God" as the "ground of being" and enter into the power of the original revelatory events, and encounter the supreme symbol, "Jesus the Christ." The religious symbols of the Bible link contemporary individuals to Jesus Christ and to the power to make each a "new being." As one reads and interprets the Bible, healing events of "salvation" are mediated as the power of being rescues those who are living an estranged existence, cut off from the "ground of being." This is a personally transformative experience mediated through a "holy object"—the scriptures.

Process theology is associated with the American theologians John Cobb and David Ray Griffin. Scripture is perceived as "unfolding action," as it describes the actions of God in leading the world to what it can be and in presenting possibilities for life that go beyond the ordinary, to open new perspectives as God and the world are evolving and are "in process" of "becoming." As one reads and interprets the Bible, one finds experience confirmed or enlarged, and thus discovers a way God can be known. Scripture provides insight and inspiration, a way to new possibilities of experience for readers.

Liberation theologies are found in American religious life in terms of African American theology, feminist theology, and womanist theologies. In these, scripture is the source of the stories that provide for liberation, freedom, and emancipatory praxis. Overcoming oppressions of racism and sexism are possible through the biblical accounts that show God's "preferential option" for the poor, and God's desire for persons to be free from both personal and corporate forms of sinfulness, expressed through oppression. Biblical stories such as the Exodus are paradigms of God's work to free those enslaved and to aid oppressed minorities, including women and people of color. The Bible can provide a new vision of the reality of life and society as God desires them to be and is to be interpreted in ways that bring liberation to persons enslaved in all forms of oppression. The story of the Exodus of the people of Israel from oppression in Egypt, the cry of the Hebrew prophets for social justice, and the way of Jesus as he related to women and to those rejected by society are all biblical models that provide a vision of emancipatory possibilities.

## Conclusion

There are many approaches to reading the history of biblical interpretation in North America. One could focus, for example, on the biblical interpreters themselves, the exegetes, those who wrote biblical commentaries. One could also focus on the various interpretive methods that have won the allegiance of scholars and have been used in many ways to interpret biblical texts.

The story throughout is plurality. There is no single method or approach that can be used to discover the meaning or meanings of this sacred text. The variety of approaches indicates that the Bible is richly faceted and can be approached from a number of different angles. The reason so much attention and energy has been expended on interpreting the Bible is that it continues to be the basic source for knowledge in the Christian religion and for Christian theology. As biblical scholars and theologians continue their work, they will keep turning to the Bible with new and old interpretive tools and methods.

**See also** *Adventism and Millennialism; Evangelicals* entries; *Fundamentalism* entries; *Liberation Theology; Neo-Orthodoxy; Protestant Liberalism; Religious Thought* entries; *Roman Catholicism* entries; *Scriptures: American Texts.*

Donald K. McKim

### BIBLIOGRAPHY

Dulles, Avery. *Models of Revelation.* New York: Orbis Books, 1992.
Geisler, Norman L. ed. *Inerrancy.* Grand Rapids: Zondervan, 1979.
Goldingay, John. *Models for Interpretation of Scripture.* Grand Rapids: Eerdmans, 1994.
———. *Models for Scripture.* Grand Rapids: Eerdmans, 1994.
Hatch, Nathan O., and Mark A. Noll, eds. *The Bible in America: Essays in Cultural History.* New York: Oxford University Press, 1982.
Holcomb, Justin S., ed. *Christian Theologies of Scripture: A Comparative Introduction.* New York: New York University Press, 2006.
Kelsey, David H. *The Uses of Scripture in Recent Theology.* Philadelphia: Fortress Press, 1975.
Lindsell, Harold. *The Battle for the Bible.* Grand Rapids: Zondervan, 1976.
———. *The Bible in the Balance.* Grand Rapids: Zondervan, 1979.
Marsden, George M. *Fundamentalism and American Culture: The Shaping of Twentieth-Century Evangelicalism, 1870–1925.* New York: Oxford University Press, 1980.
McKim, Donald K. *The Bible in Theology and Preaching: How Preachers Use Scripture.* Nashville: Abingdon Press, 1993.
———, ed. *Dictionary of Major Biblical Interpreters.* Downers Grove, Ill.: InterVarsity Press, 2007.
———, ed. *A Guide to Contemporary Hermeneutics.* Grand Rapids: Eerdmans, 1986.
Noll, Mark A., "Biblical Interpretation." In *Dictionary of Christianity in America,* ed. Daniel G. Reid et al. Downers Grove, Ill.: InterVarsity Press, 1990.
Rogers, Jack B., and Donald K. McKim. *The Authority and Interpretation of the Bible: An Historical Approach.* 1979. Reprint, Eugene, Oregon: Wipf and Stock, 1999.
Woodbridge, John D. *Biblical Authority: A Critique of the Rogers/McKim Proposal.* Grand Rapids: Zondervan, 1982.

# Bioethics

Bioethics is the study of ethical issues that arise in the settings of healthcare and medical research. Ethical concern about medical practice is perhaps as old as medical practice itself. The Hippocratic oath, which dates back to the time of its originator, the Greek physician Hippocrates (fifth century BCE), and which doctors still sometimes recite upon graduation from medical school, reads in part: "I will use treatment to help the sick according to my ability and judgment, but never with a view to injury or wrongdoing." Yet even with medicine's long-standing tradition of ethical concern, bioethics would never have become the public morality phenomenon that it is today without the multitude of scientific and technological breakthroughs that have occurred since the 1960s. Since that time we have come to understand the structure of human genes, developed mechanical ventilators and dialysis machines, performed organ transplants, and created human embryos in a petri dish. Despite the benefits that these developments have brought to humanity, they have also created unprecedented ethical dilemmas.

## Methodology in Bioethics

In addition to discussing particular issues in bioethics, such as embryonic stem cell research and euthanasia, bioethicists

have engaged in much reflection on the proper moral standards to employ to resolve these issues. When an ethicist
attempts to resolve a bioethical dilemma, she must offer a
principled moral justification for her solution, a justification
that is presumably open to public scrutiny. But to what sort
of moral standard should she appeal? Discussions of this
question among bioethicists have often been fraught with as
much controversy as the discussions of the bioethical issues
themselves.

One methodological approach is to employ a general
normative theory, such as utilitarianism (as employed in
bioethics by Joseph Fletcher, R. M. Hare, and Peter Singer,
among others), to justify decisions in particular cases. Utilitarianism maintains that an act is right if and only if it is the
one that will result in the most good for the most people. If
we wished to determine whether stem cell research, for
example, were morally right, we would examine the goods
and evils that might result for all those affected by the
research. If conducting the research appeared on the whole
to maximize the good, then it would be right to engage in
it. Utilitarianism is a controversial view, however, and many
ethicists reject it. Many have complained, for instance, that
utilitarianism sometimes requires the basic rights of an individual to be sacrificed for the general good of society, and
that this is never acceptable. There are certainly other general normative theories besides utilitarianism that have been
applied by their adherents to resolve medical ethics dilemmas (for example, Kantian theories, which require that
people always be treated as ends in themselves, and divine
command theories, which define right in terms of what
God commands). Like utilitarianism, though, these views
face serious challenges from their critics. Of course, this is
not to say that they are false. Rather, the controversy surrounding all of these general theories renders attempts to
resolve bioethics dilemmas by facile applications of them
suspect.

Others have chosen a more particularized, case-driven
approach. Casuistic approaches have been defended as a
method for adjudicating bioethical conflicts by ethicists such
as Stephen Toulmin and Albert Jonsen. Casuistry involves
using settled paradigm cases to arrive at values or principles
that can be employed to decide unsettled cases. The goal
is to determine which of the paradigm cases the disputed
case most closely resembles and then resolve it accordingly.
Yet most ethicists have found casuistry too unstructured
and unprincipled to be an acceptable methodology for
bioethics.

A third approach to method in bioethics purports to
incorporate elements of both of the foregoing approaches.
This method is known as the principles approach, or, simply,
principlism. The most sustained and influential expression of
principlism is that found in *Principles of Biomedical Ethics* (first
published in 1979) by Tom Beauchamp and James Childress.
Indeed, many would say that this book is the most important general work on bioethics ever written. At the heart of
Beauchamp and Childress's method are four principles:
respect for autonomy (that is, a concern to respect a person's
right to determine his or her own destiny); beneficence (a
duty to promote the well-being of others); non-maleficence
(a duty not to harm others); and justice (a duty to distribute
goods fairly). These are midlevel principles. That is, they are
not as general as the basic claims of normative theories like
utilitarianism, but they are not as specific as the particular
judgments about paradigm cases emphasized by casuists.
One of the benefits claimed by those who favor the principles approach is that it can bypass the controversies concerning which normative theory is correct. For whether
one is a utilitarian, a divine command theorist, or a casuist,
one will presumably find the four principles intuitively
appealing. It is thus at least possible to justify resolutions of
bioethical dilemmas by appeal to standards that virtually
anyone would accept. Principlism, too, has had its detractors,
but it continues to have broad appeal, so much so that the
principles approach is today the most widely used method
among both bioethicists and healthcare professionals.

In recent years, however, alternatives to the aforementioned approaches to bioethical decision making have
emerged. Chief among these are virtue ethics and care ethics.
Virtue ethics concerns itself less with what acts should be
done and more with the character traits and motives of the
people doing the acts. Acts are right when the people performing them are acting from virtuous dispositions. Care
ethics, which is largely an outgrowth of feminist philosophy,
also downplays the importance of assessing actions against
the backdrop of moral rules and principles. Instead, it
focuses upon the importance of interpersonal relationships
and the virtue of sympathy in healthcare contexts. To opponents of these approaches, though, both virtue and care
ethics have seemed inadequate as a means of resolving bioethical issues, for such resolutions frequently require a statement of what we should do, not how we should be. This
difficulty seems especially pressing when the public policy
dimensions of many bioethics issues are kept in view. Nevertheless, even some critics of virtue and care ethics have

allowed that these views can serve as useful supplements to act-oriented ethics. In particular, many feel that the ethics training of prospective healthcare providers should include more than abstract considerations of moral theories and principles; it should also stress the importance of becoming virtuous, caring professionals.

## Issues in Medical Research

Cases of grossly unethical medical research have played a large role in bringing the field of bioethics to the fore of public attention. These cases have prompted many to reflect on the conditions under which it can be morally acceptable to use human (and other sentient) beings to advance medical knowledge. Among the most horrific examples of unethical research are the experiments performed by Nazi doctors, such as Joseph Mengele, on concentration camp inmates during World War II. Some inmates were forced to sit in vats of ice-cold water until they developed hypothermia, so the efficacy of various hypothermia treatments could be tested. Others were deliberately infected with malaria, so treatments for malaria could be studied. Still others were cut on their bodies and then the wounds were purposely infected with bacteria, wood shavings, and specks of glass, in order to test the efficacy of infection-treating drugs. Many of the subjects suffered and died during the course of these nightmarish experiments, and those mentioned represent only a small sample of the Nazi experiments. In 1947, at the Nuremberg Trials, fifteen of the Nazi doctors were convicted of crimes against humanity, and several were executed. But from the Nuremberg proceedings came the Nuremberg Code, the first international code of ethics for research on humans. Chief among the code's requirements wass that research on a human could be done only with the subject's informed consent. Issues of informed consent have since dominated the ethics of medical research.

Doctors in the United States, some of whom were working under the direct supervision of the federal government, conducted research on subjects where consent was not sufficiently informed or was lacking altogether. During the Cold War between the United States and the former Soviet Union, nuclear war seemed a very real possibility. It thus seemed crucial to study the effects of radiation on humans and the measures for treating those effects. Thus various groups, including such vulnerable populations as pregnant women, prison inmates, and mentally retarded children, were exposed to radiation. In some cases, they were exposed without their consent; in others, they consented but without

being told of all the risks involved. Some involved in carrying out the research justified it by likening it to the draft. In a time of war the government could draft a young man and place his life on the line in battle, even if he did not want to be so placed and had very little understanding of why he was there. Why could not other people be "drafted" into becoming medical research subjects during the Cold War?

Many other instances of unethical research in the United States could be cited, but perhaps the most infamous case of all is the Tuskegee syphilis study, which was conducted by the U.S. Public Health Service in Tuskegee, Alabama, from 1932 to 1972. The Tuskegee experiment was designed to be a study of the natural course of syphilis if left untreated. The study's subjects were 399 African American men, all of whom had syphilis. None of the men were told that they had syphilis, nor were any of them treated (even after penicillin, the most effective treatment for syphilis, became widely available in the mid 1940s). The men instead were told that they had "bad blood" and were given only placebos for treatment. Finally, in 1972, Peter Buxtun, an official at the U.S. Centers for Disease Control, after trying unsuccessfully to have the study stopped, revealed details of the study to the press.

Of the many things that occurred in the aftermath of the revelation, the passage of the National Research Act of 1974 has greatly impacted medical research ethics in the United States. This act mandates that every institution which receives federal funding for its research must establish an institutional review board to ensure that its research is conducted in an ethical manner. The act also created the National Commission for the Protection of Human Subjects of Biomedical and Behavioral Research. The commission was given the task of identifying the core principles of ethical research on humans. The commission, whose findings were published in the so-called Belmont Report, identified three core principles: respect for persons (which, among other things, requires that informed consent always be obtained from research subjects), beneficence, and justice.

Medical experimentation in the United States involving nonhuman animals also experienced a watershed event. Neurologist Thomas Gennarelli was doing research to understand brain injury in humans by inflicting serious brain injuries upon monkeys and baboons. Gennarelli videotaped his procedures, and in May of 1984 some members of the Animal Liberation Front, an animal rights group, broke into his lab and stole a number of these tapes. The tapes showed many abuses of the animals: animals that were not properly anesthetized before being injured, animals that were injured repeatedly, and researchers who were laughing at and joking about the animals' injuries. Edited versions of the tapes were shown to members of the U.S. Congress and were aired on the television newsmagazine *20/20*. Many were outraged over what the tapes revealed, and in 1985 Congress, largely in response to the revelation, passed an amendment to the Animal Welfare Act of 1966. The new act, known as the Improved Standards for Laboratory Animals Act (analogous to the National Research Act), requires that every institution engaged in federally funded research must empanel an institutional animal care and use committee (IACUC) to ensure that the institution's animal research complies with federal regulations on the humane treatment of laboratory animals. IACUCs, like institutional review boards, are now a fixture of ethical research practice in the United States.

Some believe, however, that federal regulations and IACUCs do not go far enough to protect animals. Philosopher Peter Singer, for example, has argued, on utilitarian grounds, that since animals are sentient creatures with as much capacity to feel pain as does a mentally handicapped human baby, we should not perform any experiment on an animal that we would not be willing to perform on a mentally handicapped human baby. Other philosophers, such as Tom Regan, have argued on more deontological grounds (an approach emphasizing acts rather than consequences and regarding the goodness of an act as self-evident) that animals have rights akin to those of humans and that animal research should simply be abolished. For thinkers like Singer and Regan, therefore, mere guidelines for humane animal research, IACUCs, and so forth, fall terribly short of what morality requires of humans in regard to their treatment of animals.

The foregoing discussion represents some of the pivotal cases and events that gave rise to the field of research ethics. Researchers struggle with many other issues today. There are the frequent financial conflicts of interest that arise from the fact that private drug companies fund most new drug research and also give doctors and researchers involved in the research indirect payments and other "perks." These financial inducements can tempt researchers to cut ethical corners on informed-consent requirements and to be less than forthright about negative results in the research. Another issue is what to do with the data collected in immoral experiments. There was, for instance, much discussion in medical ethics literature in the late 1980s and early 1990s about whether it was ethically permissible to use the data from Nazi experiments in current research. Would citing it somehow legitimize the evil of the experiments? Would not citing it mean that the victims had suffered in vain? Such issues, along with many others, make the field of research ethics the important area of bioethics that it is.

## Assisted Reproduction

One of the most rapidly developing areas of both medical practice and bioethical discussion is that of assisted reproduction. In assisted reproduction, technologies such as in vitro fertilization and artificial insemination are employed to help people have children who could not otherwise have them. The drive to bear children is one of the deepest and most profound of all human inclinations. Indeed, this fact is the basis of the primary argument for using these technologies. Since the drive to reproduce is so basic, some feel that there is actually a right to reproduce, a right that would include the freedom to use assisted-reproduction technologies when necessary.

A variety of means exist to aid reproduction today. In vitro fertilization (IVF) involves placing a man's sperm and a woman's egg in a petri dish to allow fertilization and the formation of an embryo to occur. Generally, several eggs (as many as twenty) from the woman will be fertilized in this way. Some of the fertilized eggs are then placed into the woman's uterus in the hope that one will implant, grow to term, and be born a healthy baby. Thus prospective parents who, for various reasons (for example, low motility in the man's sperm), are unable to conceive a child by natural means are given a chance to have children by means of IVF. IVF was first used successfully in 1978 in England to bring about the birth of Louise Brown, whom the press dubbed as the world's first "test tube baby." In many cases, not all of the created embryos end up being needed. Between four and eight of the embryos are placed at one time in the woman's uterus (which sometimes results in multiple births—twins, triplets, quadruplets—and the attendant health complications for the children). If the first attempt results in a successful pregnancy, the remaining embryos are kept frozen until such time as they may be needed. Sometimes, for various reasons, couples never use their other frozen embryos. As will be discussed below, these unused embryos are the ones that would typically be used in embryonic stem cell research.

Also prevalent is the practice of artificial insemination (AI), in which sperm from a woman's husband, partner, or an anonymous donor is injected through a catheter-like tube directly into the woman's uterus. AI can increase the chances of conception when the man's sperm count is low or when the woman's vaginal environment is chemically hostile to sperm. Of course, AI is also used by women who have no male partner but who simply wish to have a baby. The female analogue of AI is ova donation (OD). In OD, eggs are taken from a woman (usually an anonymous donor), fertilized with the sperm of the intended father by means of IVF, and then implanted in another woman, either a gestational surrogate (discussed below) or the woman who intends to be the resulting child's mother. Unlike sperm donors, who generally receive only $50–$200 for their services, ova donors can receive as much as $5,000 for their eggs, and they can donate multiple times (though current guidelines recommend no more than six times). And stories abound of even higher payments than this. OD is a moderately demanding procedure that requires the donor to undergo strong hormone injections (to stimulate ovulation) and a minor surgical procedure to extract the eggs. In AI and OD, when anonymous donors are used, though the identity of the donor is concealed, characteristics of the donor, such as hair and eye color, race, height, athletic ability, and various intellectual attributes (for example, that the donor has artistic ability, that the donor is a medical school student, and even that the donor has high SAT scores), are revealed. And people choose donors largely on the basis of these features. This fact has led some to charge that there is a subtle form of eugenics at work in these practices.

Another assisted-reproduction practice that has been the subject of considerable legal and ethical discussion is surrogacy, in which a woman gestates a baby for another woman for the nine months of pregnancy and then gives the baby to the other woman to be raised by her (and frequently her spouse or partner). There are two types of surrogacy: surrogate mothering, where the surrogate also furnishes the egg from which the baby will come, and gestational surrogacy, where the surrogate carries a baby for another couple but is not biologically related to it. In both types, IVF is used to create the embryo that the surrogate carries. In most instances a contract is drawn between the surrogate and the intended parents. Under the contract, the surrogate, who, as the one who gives birth to the child, will be, in most states, the legal mother of the child, agrees to surrender custody of the child to the intended parents. The intended parents agree to pay the surrogate for her services. Amounts vary, but they usually lie between $10,000 and $25,000. Not

surprisingly, these arrangements have sometimes gone awry, as surrogates have occasionally changed their minds about giving up the babies. The first such case, *In the Matter of Baby M* (1988), arose in New Jersey and brought surrogacy to national attention. The New Jersey Supreme Court, though it essentially awarded custody of the child, Baby M, to the intended parents (because the surrogate was emotionally unstable), held that surrogacy arrangements were too close to baby selling to be upheld. The Supreme Court of California, on the other hand, in *Calvert v. Johnson* (1993), upheld surrogacy contracts on the ground that the money paid to the surrogate is for her time and trouble, not the baby, and so is not against public policy.

The foregoing assisted-reproduction practices raise a host of ethical issues. First, there are concerns about potential harm to the children born of these practices. For example, some studies have suggested that children conceived through IVF are about twice as likely as naturally conceived children to be born with certain birth defects and other health complications. In addition, some have feared psychological harm to children born through AI (from a donor) or OD, as, for example, such children may have identity problems arising from never knowing one of their biological parents. Second, all of these technologies involve reproduction without sexual intercourse. This fact has been a primary reason for the Roman Catholic Church's opposition to most forms of assisted reproduction. The children of assisted reproduction do not result from the two becoming one flesh, and thus such reproduction, even when it is between a husband and wife, departs from God's design for procreation. Third, some have raised the worry that AI (where the sperm comes from a donor), OD, and surrogacy involve adultery, or some other impermissible encroachment upon the sanctity of marriage, as these technologies bring in a third party to the very private and intimate realm of marital procreation. Fourth, many have been concerned that these technologies might further contribute to the breakdown of the traditional family. AI allows single women to have children purposely without a father's involvement in raising the children. Lesbian couples can also have children by AI, and gay couples can have children by means of OD and surrogacy. In these cases, and unlike those in which an already living child is adopted, a child is intentionally conceived to be, in some sense, the fruit of the two lovers' union (in the case of homosexuals) or the fruit of the single woman's genes. The traditional norm of the family unit as consisting of a man and woman who are married to each other, and who bear children that are the fruit of their union, has thus seemed under siege to those (for example, the Catholic Church, officially, and most evangelical Christians) who hold it as the ideal. Lastly, some have expressed concern that OD and surrogacy may perpetuate the objectification of women. These technologies could, it is argued, cause some women to be seen as mere medical supply cabinets (in the case of OD), or incubators (in the case of surrogacy), and not as persons with rights equal to those of men. These are not the only moral worries raised by assisted reproduction, but they are some of the most commonly asserted ones.

Assisted-reproduction practices have also given rise to many novel and unprecedented court cases in the United States. The surrogacy cases mentioned previously are prime examples, but there are many others. The Tennessee case of *Davis v. Davis* (1992) involved a divorcing couple's custody battle over seven embryos they had in frozen storage. The husband wanted the embryos destroyed, but the wife wanted them to be donated to a couple who could not have their own children. The Tennessee Supreme Court ruled in favor of the husband. In *Buzzanca v. Buzzanca* (California, 1998), a couple who had received an embryo created from the gametes of two unknown donors had arranged for the embryo to be carried by a surrogate. Thus no fewer than five people were involved in bringing the child into the world. During the pregnancy, however, the couple decided to divorce, and neither the husband nor the wife, nor the surrogate, had any interest in raising the child. The California appeals court held that the Buzzancas were the legally responsible parents of the child because they were the ones who had intended to bring about the birth of the child. Since, as a result of these new reproductive practices, biological parentage (that is, being a person from whose sperm or egg a child has come) is no longer always the clearly relevant one, many jurisdictions in the United States are now, like California, moving toward the concept of parentage by intent. It is fair to say, then, that new reproductive technologies are profoundly affecting many people's understanding of the nature and ethics of the family and parentage.

## Embryonic Stem Cell Research

The issue of embryonic stem cell research is yet another controversial outgrowth of assisted-reproduction technology. After an ovum is fertilized, it begins dividing, and after a few divisions have occurred, a cluster of cells results. These cells are what are referred to as embryonic stem cells. They

are unspecialized cells that have the potential to develop into any type of cell in the body (brain cell, bone cell, and so on). As the embryo develops, instructions in its genetic code essentially tell the cells what form to take, and a human body, with all of its many and diverse parts, is formed. In 1998 researchers announced that they had isolated and cultured these cells from early-stage embryos, and this development opened up the possibility for therapeutic uses of the cells. If, for example, someone had suffered a spinal cord injury, then, in principle, embryonic stem cells could be introduced at the injury site, and these cells would then specialize into new spinal cord tissue and heal the injury. Similar uses of the cells to treat diabetes, Parkinson's disease, heart damage, and many other afflictions have been suggested. Although such therapeutic uses for the cells remain largely conjectural, the possibility of such applications is real. Yet a great many different embryonic cell lines would have to be created in order to provide close tissue matches to all of the different people who might be treated. Thus a very large number of embryos would be needed. This is where assisted reproduction enters the picture. At present, there are thousands of unused frozen embryos in fertility clinics across the United States. These embryos were created for couples who were trying to have a baby via IVF, but who no longer need or want the embryos. These embryos would be the primary supply for embryonic stem cell research.

The controversy over stem cell research arises because the embryos are destroyed when the stem cells are removed from the embryos. For those, such as conservative evangelicals and the Catholic Church, who take the view that human personhood begins at the moment of conception, this process would mean that the research requires the killing of many human persons. It is not permissible, they maintain, to kill an innocent person deliberately in order to save others. Those who support the research are unwilling to ascribe personhood to a small cluster of cells and so feel no moral trepidation about destroying the embryos, if so doing could help someone suffering from a serious affliction. Thus, driven as it is by clashing perspectives on the personhood status of embryos, the stem cell debate in the United States greatly resembles the abortion debate and will likely prove to be just as intractable.

At present the research is legal, though President George W. Bush signed an executive order that banned federal funding for any stem cell lines developed after August 2001. (The order allowed such funding for lines developed before that time.) Despite multiple attempts by Congress to enact legislation overriding Bush's order, the ban remained in effect throughout Bush's presidency. In 2009 President Barack Obama issued another executive order that rescinded the Bush policy and opened new opportunities for stem cell research. Yet in response to the earlier federal ban, some states such as California with its Proposition 71 (approved in November 2004) have passed their own funding initiatives for stem cell research. In addition to private funding, then, stem cell researchers can seek state funding for their studies.

## Euthanasia and Physician-Assisted Suicide

Bioethicists, as the discussion of assisted reproduction and stem cell research illustrates, have been greatly concerned with ethical questions that surround the beginning of life. But they are equally concerned with ethical issues that pertain to the end of life. Foremost among end-of-life concerns are those pertaining to euthanasia. In its origins from the Greek, the word *euthanasia* expresses the idea of a good or easy death. As understood today by ethicists and healthcare providers, euthanasia comes in two forms: active euthanasia, which involves intentionally administering some means (for instance, a lethal injection) to hasten the end of an already dying person's life, and passive euthanasia, in which life-sustaining treatments (for instance, ventilators, CPR, antibiotics) are simply withheld or withdrawn from a dying person. In the latter case, it is the underlying illness that kills the person, while in the former, though there is an underlying terminal affliction, it is whatever lethal means that are administered to the person that kills him. What ethicists refer to as physician-assisted suicide (PAS) falls under the heading of active euthanasia, as it involves physicians actively administering or at least providing the means to bring about the death of a patient. At the present, many take the position that passive euthanasia is morally permissible, while at the same time asserting that active euthanasia is wrong. This, for example, is the current position of the American Medical Association (AMA). Some believe that the moral distinction between the two forms of euthanasia is not always clear, however.

The most widely discussed cases of passive euthanasia are those concerning patients in deeply unconscious and generally irreversible comas known as persistent vegetative states (PVSs). Patients in a PVS have lost all brain functions involving consciousness; typically only their brain stem, which controls basic bodily functions, such as heartbeat and respiration, remains operative. They generally must be fed through nasogastric feeding tubes, their bodies shrivel into rigid fetal positions, and they sometimes even need the assistance of ventilators to breathe. What is worst of all, for many, is that they can go on for many years in this state before dying, all the while with virtually no prospect for recovery.

As with many of the prominent issues in bioethics, ethical consideration of these cases has been framed against the backdrop of nationally publicized legal disputes. The first such dispute was *In The Matter of Quinlan* (New Jersey, 1976), in which the parents of Karen Ann Quinlan sought to have their daughter's ventilator removed so that she could be free to die. The New Jersey Supreme Court ruled in favor of the parents, finding that the personal liberties guaranteed by the U.S. Constitution included a right to be free from unwanted medical treatment. The next major case was *Cruzan v. Director, Missouri Department of Health,* a 1990 decision of the U.S. Supreme Court. Like *Quinlan, Cruzan* involved parents of a PVS patient (Nancy Cruzan) who wanted life-prolonging measures for their daughter, in this case nutrition and hydration through a tube, stopped. Although the Court, because of particular issues surrounding the Missouri law in question, ruled against the parents, it did recognize a basic right to die founded upon the Constitution's Fourteenth Amendment and its protection of personal liberty from state interference.

The two chief arguments for allowing passive euthanasia arise from the principles of respect for autonomy and beneficence. The courts in the Quinlan and Cruzan cases both essentially held that being free from unwanted medical treatment is a basic aspect of personal liberty, and this is nothing less than respect for autonomy expressed in the language of constitutional jurisprudence. What could be more basic to personal autonomy than having some control over the timing and manner of one's own death? The other argument is that allowing people who are suffering with grave terminal conditions to die is an act of mercy and is thus required by the principle of beneficence. We are actually conferring good upon them by not prolonging their suffering with further life-sustaining medical care. A principal argument against passive euthanasia, advanced by both Catholic and theologically conservative Protestant ethicists (though not endorsed by all of them), is that human life, being made in the image of God, is intrinsically valuable and worth preserving, no matter what its condition. Another argument against passive euthanasia is that it is contrary to the purposes of medicine. Doctors and other healthcare providers exist to preserve the lives of their patients, and passive euthanasia seems at odds with this directive. Lastly, many opponents of passive euthanasia fear that allowing it will lead to descent down a moral slippery slope. That is, if passive euthanasia is allowed, then once people have become accustomed to it, active euthanasia will be allowed, and soon the government will begin determining what sorts of lives are worth living and even require euthanasia for those lives that fall short of the standard, as occurred in Nazi Germany. As healthcare costs spiral out of control, actively euthanizing the very sick may come to be seen as an efficient cost-saving measure.

Active euthanasia in the form of physician-assisted suicide has also been a subject of national attention. Dr. Jack Kevorkian, who, from 1989 until his conviction for the crime of PAS in 1998, actively euthanized more than one hundred people, was a primary catalyst for this debate in the United States. Some states, such as Kevorkian's home state of Michigan, have enacted specific laws banning PAS, and most states have more general prohibitions barring anyone from assisting in the suicide of another. The U.S. Supreme Court, in the cases of *Washington v. Glucksberg* and *Vacco v. Quill* (both decided in 1997), has ruled that such laws do not violate the liberty interests protected by the Constitution. It is consistent with these cases, however, for a state to allow PAS, and that is what the states of Oregon and Washington have done with their Death with Dignity legislation (Oregon in 1994 and Washington in 2008). These laws allow physicians to write a prescription for a lethal dosage of barbiturates for patients who have six months or less to live, as certified by their physician and a consulting physician. The patients administer the drugs to themselves, but physicians provide the drugs with a full knowledge of what they will be used for.

The moral arguments for and against PAS and active euthanasia are essentially the same as those for passive euthanasia. Considerations of autonomy and beneficence are still the primary reasons for permitting PAS, and worries about devaluing human life, flouting the basic purposes of medicine, and sliding down a slippery slope are what lead many to oppose it. This fact illustrates why the position that passive euthanasia is morally acceptable while active euthanasia is not strikes some as rather tenuous. On the other hand, if we were to allow PAS in the name of autonomy and beneficence, then why should it be available only to those with six months or less to live? Why not allow it for those with a year to live, or even for those with conditions they judge to be

unbearable but that are not necessarily terminal? Is it because the government has made an implicit quality of life judgment, to the effect that people with six months or less to live no longer have a life worth saving, but those with more life left do? Do we want the government making such judgments? The unsettled nature of these questions suggests that the euthanasia debate will continue to be at the fore of public concern for a great while to come—as will a host of other fascinating questions of bioethics.

**See also** *Environment and Ecology: Current Ethical Issues; Health, Disease, and Medicine; Religious Thought* entries; *Social Ethics.*

Dennis Plaisted

## BIBLIOGRAPHY

Beauchamp, Tom L., and James F. Childress. *Principles of Biomedical Ethics.* 6th ed. New York: Oxford University Press, 2009.
Callahan, Daniel. "When Self-Determination Runs Amok." *Hastings Center Report* 22 (1992): 52–55.
Caplan, Arthur L. *When Medicine Went Mad: Bioethics and the Holocaust.* Totowa, N.J.: Humana Press, 1992.
Cohen, Cynthia. "'Give Me Children or I Shall Die!' New Reproductive Technologies and Harm to Children." *Hastings Center Report* 26 (1996): 19–27.
Congregation for the Doctrine of the Faith. "Instruction *Dignitas Personae:* On Certain Bioethical Questions." December 8, 2008, www.vatican.va/roman_curia/congregations/cfaith/documents/rc_con_cfaith_doc_0081208_dignitas-personae_en.html.
Glannon, Walter. *Biomedical Ethics.* New York: Oxford University Press, 2005.
Hanscombe, Gillian. "The Right to Lesbian Parenthood." *Journal of Medical Ethics* 9 (1983): 133–135.
Holland, Suzanne, et al. *The Human Embryonic Stem Cell Debate: Science, Ethics and Public Policy.* Cambridge, Mass.: Bradford/MIT Press, 2001.
Jonsen, Albert R. *A Short History of Medical Ethics.* New York: Oxford University Press, 2000.
Kuhse, Helga, and Peter Singer, eds. *A Companion to Bioethics.* Malden, Mass.: Blackwell Publishing, 2001.
Munson, Ronald. *Intervention and Reflection: Basic Issues in Medical Ethics.* 8th ed. Belmont, Calif.: Thomson Wadsworth, 2008.
Pence, Gregory E. *Medical Ethics: Accounts of the Cases that Shaped and Define Medical Ethics.* 5th ed. New York: McGraw-Hill, 2008.
Rachels, James. "Active and Passive Euthanasia." *New England Journal of Medicine* 292 (1975): 78–80.
Regan, Tom. *The Case for Animal Rights.* Berkeley: University of California Press, 2004.
Reich, W.T., ed. *Encyclopedia of Bioethics.* London: Simon and Schuster and Prentice Hall International, 1995.
Shapiro, Michael H., et al., eds. *Bioethics and Law: Cases, Materials and Problems.* 2nd ed. St. Paul: Thomson West, 2003.
Singer, Peter. *Animal Liberation.* San Francisco: Harper Perennial, 2001.
Steinbock, Bonnie. "Surrogate Motherhood as Prenatal Adoption." *Law Medicine and Health Care* 16 (1988): 44–50.

# Black Nationalist Movements

See *New Religious Movements: Black Nationalist Movements.*

# Book of Mormon

On the March 26, 1830, the *Wayne Sentinel,* the village newspaper of Palmyra, New York, printed an advertisement under the heading "The Book of Mormon." The advertisement reproduced the title page of the book in question, which had created a considerable stir in the area months before its publication, followed by a simple announcement: "The above work, containing about 600 pages, large Duo-decimo, is now for sale, whole-sale and retail, at the Palmyra Bookstore, by HOWARD & GRANDIN." This announcement heralded the publication of what would become the most widely distributed book in American history, save only the Bible. And that publication was the immediate prelude to the organization of the Church of Jesus Christ of Latter-day Saints, organized on April 6. That same church has consistently relied, from the day of its founding to the present, on the Book of Mormon as the principal agent of conversion to the gospel it preached.

Joseph Smith, the founder of the Mormon religion, said he experienced a personal visitation of God the Father and Jesus Christ in 1820, at the age of fourteen. Subsequent visions revealed to him the location, near his New York home, of engraved golden plates, which he translated into the Book of Mormon.

### An Ancient American Epic

The Book of Mormon could be said to have two points of origin, each setting in motion events that would converge on the March day of publication when a new "American Bible" altered the face of American religious history. The point of first origin is described by the record itself as a year of turbulence in the ancient city of Jerusalem. A man named Lehi is called by God to preach repentance to a rebellious populace. The people reject him, God commands him to flee with his family, and Lehi and his clan escape both the anger of the crowd and the ensuing Babylonian bondage (c. 600 BCE). After some years in the wilderness, Lehi's group migrates, by ship, to the New World, where his son Nephi assumes the leadership and begins to maintain a record of his people on metal plates. Essentially a tribal history, the record is kept by Nephi and his descendents for the next thousand years, chronicling the rise and collapse of a civilization of Nephites, who are plagued with recurrent internal strife, cycles of prosperity and spiritually debilitating pride, and warfare with a dissenting branch called Lamanites.

The record also details the religion of these people, who follow the Mosaic law, even as they anticipate the coming of

a Messiah they refer to by name as Jesus Christ. After his death and resurrection in the Old World, the record claims, this same Christ appears to a group of righteous Nephites, preaches his gospel, and organizes a church—all along the pattern detailed in the New Testament—before departing into heaven and leaving his New World disciples to enjoy several generations of utopian peace, before the descent into their final cataclysm begins. In the early fifth century, after witnessing the utter destruction of his people, Moroni, a Nephite general and the last record keeper of the plates, seals up his record and buries it in the earth.

### Joseph Smith

The modern history of the Book of Mormon could be said to begin in 1820. That was the year that a young Joseph Smith (1805–1844), one of thousands of seekers searching out true religion in the era of the Second Awakening, claimed to have experienced a personal visitation of God the Father and Jesus Christ in response to his earnest entreaties for spiritual guidance. Although Smith depicted this visitation at the time and apparently ever after as largely a personal conversion narrative, the experience ushered him into a career of epiphanies and angelic visitations. In 1823 the same Moroni who had buried the sacred record in the fifth century appeared to Smith as a resurrected being, relating to him the history of the Nephites and the buried plates. After four years of tutelage, Smith was permitted to retrieve the plates from a repository he was directed to, in a hillside near his home in Palmyra, New York. Along with the plates, he found an instrument called "interpreters," which consisted of two clear stones in a silver setting, that functioned for him as seer stones and that enabled him to translate the writing on the plates.

Slowed by his own intractable poverty, encumbered with supporting a new family, and distracted by the curiosity and harassment of outsiders that at times became violent, Smith made slow progress with the translation. The first portion of 116 pages was stolen in the summer of 1828, and he began the process again. The arrival of Oliver Cowdery, a young schoolteacher, who volunteered to serve as scribe, initiated a burst of productivity in the spring of 1829, and in June of that year Smith completed the work. That same month, Cowdery and ten others were shown the plates, which until then Smith alone had been permitted to see and handle. In their published testimony, the first three witnesses describe how the plates were laid before their eyes by "an angel of God [who] came down from heaven." Although they were close enough to the relics to see "the engravings thereon," as they twice tell us, they neither touched nor handled them for themselves. The other eight witnesses, on the other hand, were allowed to handle the plates and draw their own conclusions. The plates, they write, did indeed have "the appearance of gold," and the engravings had "the appearance of an ancient work," for "we did handle [them] with our hands."

## Old Wine in New Bottles?

The content of the Book of Mormon is a striking mix of the familiar and the unexpected. Beginning as it does in a scene of Jerusalem prophets, it invites immediate comparison with the Judeo-Christian scriptures. The notion of ancient Israelites in the New World is patently strange, as is the idea of people worshipping a Christ whose coming is hundreds of years in the future. At the same time, the "doctrine of Christ" taught by Book of Mormon prophets was both familiar and appealing, especially in an age full of restorationists and primitivists (religious seekers who craved a return to the Christianity described by the New Testament). Faith in Jesus Christ, repentance, baptism for the remission of sins, and the gift of the Holy Ghost are all affirmed as core principles. One striking departure from orthodox teachings is the Book of Mormon's repudiation of the doctrine of original sin, and the recasting of the biblical Eden story as a "fortunate fall":

> And now, behold, if Adam had not transgressed he would not have fallen, but he would have remained in the garden of Eden. And all things which were created must have remained in the same state in which they were after they were created; and they must have remained forever, and had no end. And they would have had no children; wherefore they would have remained in a state of innocence, having no joy, for they knew no misery; doing no good, for they knew no sin. But behold, all things have been done in the wisdom of him who knoweth all things. Adam fell that men might be; and men are, that they might have joy. (2 Nephi 2:23–25)

Another motif in the Book of Mormon is even more fundamental to the religion the scripture launched. That is the principle of individual, dialogic revelation. Like the Old Testament deity, the God of the Book of Mormon engages in frequent interaction with prophets—directing, counseling, and commanding. The Book of Mormon God, however, extends those acts of literal communication and interaction to a new level. God directs inquiring generals where to attack and hungry patriarchs where to hunt, provides doctrinal understanding to the piously curious on issues from infant baptism to the spirit world, reassures anxious parents about their children, or directs high priests in how to resolve ecclesiastical conundrums. Time and again, "the voice of the Lord" is heard, at times repeatedly and insistently, in the face of resistance or spiritual obtuseness. No vague intimations, these, but articulate, conversational episodes fill the pages of the Book of Mormon, making God's interaction at the level of personal concern a dominant leitmotif.

Other themes are similarly adaptations or modifications of familiar biblical ones. God's covenant with Israel is almost as central a topic here as in the Old Testament, with the additional urgency that it would naturally have to a people dispossessed and a hemisphere away from the promised land. And that promised land itself proves to be a highly portable concept, shifting from Jerusalem to the New World, and through successive phases of habitation and divinely directed resettlement, as war and dissension drive the people of God deeper and deeper into an alien wilderness. Scripture proves to be of such consummate value that lives are hazarded and even taken to preserve it. And reinforcing the splintering and expansion of the Christian canon that the Book of Mormon physically embodies, the record emphasizes the endless proliferation of scripture: "for behold, I shall speak unto the Jews and they shall write it; and I shall also speak unto the Nephites and they shall write it; and I shall also speak unto the other tribes of the house of Israel, which I have led away, and they shall write it; and I shall also speak unto all nations of the earth and they shall write it" ( Nephi 29:12).

## Debates and Reception

The claims made by the Book of Mormon were at the same time occasion for both eager anticipation and vehement denunciation. Even before the book was published and available, reports of a new record purporting to be scripture inflamed public opinion. For many who had been anxiously expecting marvelous works and signs in evidence of a Christian renewal presided over by God's spirit, the Book of Mormon was the "marvelous work and a wonder," the "ensign to the nations" foreseen by the prophet Isaiah. But for more of the public, its very existence was a blasphemous affront to a Christianity believing its canon to be closed and its Bible solely sufficient. That fact, and the sheer unlikelihood of its two stories—the one involving seafaring Israelites and the other gold plates and angels—meant that few investigations into Book of Mormon historicity rose to the level of actual analysis of the evidence. Proponents appealed to spiritual confirmation—a witness "borne of the spirit"—and opponents dismissed it on prima facie grounds.

The earliest support mustered for the Book of Mormon was in the form of affidavits from the eleven witnesses who testified they had seen the plates, published in every copy of the Book of Mormon from 1830 to the present. With the discovery of impressive ruins, including temple complexes and magnificent remains in Central America, popularized by John Lloyd Stephens in the 1840s, Mormons gained confidence that archaeology supported their view of the Book of Mormon as a record of now vanished civilizations. By the 1920s, however, the first real difficulties with the Book of

Mormon were coming to the fore. Principal among these were the variety of American Indian languages, which could hardly have evolved from a Hebraic precursor, especially in the short span of two millennia, and the mention in the Book of Mormon of apparent anachronisms, including the horse, steel, and silk. Environmental explanations that trace the Book of Mormon to nineteenth-century contexts have largely displaced early attempts to link its authorship to works by two nineteenth-century figures, Solomon Spaulding or Ethan Smith. This kind of criticism, first begun in 1830 and continuing to the present, draws attention to parallels between elements of the Book of Mormon and environmental influences of the period. These included doctrinal preoccupations such as infant baptism and universalism, secret oaths and "combinations" of malevolent groups (reminiscent, to some, of Masons), anti-Catholic intimations, and emotional behavior consistent with nineteenth-century revivalism. Most recently, critics have appealed to DNA evidence for lack of a connection between modern Native Americans and Israelite lines.

Each onslaught has been met by Mormon-mustered evidence and counterarguments, at times attaining a high level of sophistication. Scholars have found parallels between Book of Mormon accounts and Israelite coronation rituals, numerous examples of ancient writing on metal—even gold—plates, etymologies that tie Book of Mormon names to Egyptian and Asiatic derivatives, and chiastic structures— a kind of reverse parallelism typical of ancient Hebrew poetry and quite prevalent in the Book of Mormon. The DNA approach has been largely discredited as misapplied science, especially in light of ungrounded assumptions about the ethnic purity of Book of Mormon peoples and descendents. Finally, dramatic evidence surfaced in Yemen, on the Arabian Peninsula, in the 1990s of stone altars inscribed with the name NHM, apparently corroborating a Book of Mormon place name situated in that same area by the narrative's early pages. Book of Mormon apologists have also reconstructed a historically plausible exodus route for Lehi's trail, and others appeal to the growing group of diffusionists, who argue for multiple sources of New World settlement.

With the growth of Mormonism undiminished at the beginning of the twenty-first century, and the Book of Mormon still featuring prominently as the principal tool of missionary efforts, the influence of the naysayers appears to be negligible. The work of the apologists may be said, in this regard, to have successfully countered the attacks of the critics. More likely, scientific and archaeological approaches tend to confirm both believers and doubters, who have already drawn their conclusions on the basis of prayerful inquiry or religious presuppositions, as might be said of the Bible's believers and critics. In addition to the Book of Mormon, Smith produced two other works that consisted of revelations and purported translations of ancient texts, bringing to four the number of scriptures in the Mormon canon: the Holy Bible, the Book of Mormon, the Doctrine and Covenants, and the Pearl of Great Price.

See also *Bible* entries; *Great Awakening(s); Latter-day Saints.*

Terryl L. Givens

## BIBLIOGRAPHY

Bushman, Richard L. *Mormonism: A Very Short Introduction.* New York: Oxford University Press, 2008.

Givens, Terryl L. *The Book of Mormon: A Very Short Introduction.* New York: Oxford University Press, 2009.

———. *By the Hand of Mormon: The American Scripture that Launched a New World Religion.* New York: Oxford University Press, 2002.

Hardy, Grant, ed. *The Book of Mormon: A Reader's Edition.* Urbana: University of Illinois Press, 2003.

Metcalfe, Brent Lee. *New Approaches to the Book of Mormon: Explorations in Critical Methodology.* Salt Lake City: Signature Books, 1993.

Parry, Donald W., Daniel C. Peterson, and John W. Welch. *Echoes and Evidences of the Book of Mormon.* Provo, Utah: Foundation for Ancient Research and Mormon Studies, 2002.

Vogel, Dan, and Brent Lee Metcalfe. *American Apocrypha: Essays on the Book of Mormon.* Salt Lake City: Signature, 2002.

# Buddhism, Zen

See *Zen Buddhism.*

# Buddhism in North America

The term *Buddhism* is used to denote a highly diverse collection of religious traditions that developed in south, central, and eastern Asia. Although Buddhist schools of thought vary widely in specialized doctrine, praxis, and organization, they share a common origin that they trace back to a single man, Siddhartha Gautama. According to traditional narratives, Gautama was born into a noble family in what is now southern Nepal but was then northern India. His exact dates are uncertain, but recent scholarship puts his birth at approximately 485 BCE and his death about 405 BCE. Dissatisfied with the royal life, Gautama went off into the wilderness to find a way to end suffering; at the age of thirty-five, after six years of searching, he achieved a breakthrough that brought him the peace he sought. He began to teach his insights to others, and a community formed around him. In time he came to be called Buddha, meaning "the Awakened One."

At the heart of the Buddha's teaching was a cosmology that divided the world into several different realms, into which living beings are repeatedly born; these realms range from hellish places of punishment, through the domains of animals and humans, and finally to the heavenly lands. An impersonal natural force known as karma controls where a being will be reborn: Good actions lead to relatively pleasant rebirth, bad actions lead to undesirable new births. All beings—whether humans, animals, gods, or ghosts—eventually die and are reborn, and even the most fortunate life contains elements of suffering. Therefore the goal of Buddhism is to escape from the endlessly cycling wheel of birth and death. One accomplishes this through a process of self-cultivation, resulting in insight into the true nature of reality. This leads to permanent dwelling in the peaceful state of nirvana beyond the sorrows of mortal life. Both the exact process of achieving this awakening and particular interpretations of what exactly nirvana constitutes differ among the various schools of Buddhism.

Buddhism spread throughout the Indian Subcontinent, and under the Buddhist emperor Asoka (c. 272–c. 231 BCE) it extended into southeast Asia. It reached China around the first century BCE, Korea by the fourth century BCE, Japan in the sixth century, and Tibet in the seventh century. Naturally, the doctrines, beliefs, and practices of Buddhism changed considerably over such a large period, both within India and in other parts of Asia. In many cases, Buddhism was far more than just a religion: It carried medical and scientific knowledge, alphabets and literature, music and cuisine, social theories and moral proscriptions, altering each new society it encountered. Overall, Buddhism's dissemination was peaceful, growing from the activities of pious merchants traveling along the Silk Road as well as from monks and nuns sent abroad to bring the Buddha's teachings to the world. It stimulated changes in the religions it encountered, sometimes being copied or partially assimilated with other religions, sometimes prompting backlash and anti-Buddhist revivalism.

## Buddhist Groups in America

From humble beginnings the American Buddhist community has come a long way: Virtually every form of Buddhism has some representation in the United States. There are too many different sects of Buddhism to treat here, but it is important to touch on some of the broader categories that have significant numbers of adherents in the United States.

## Theravada Buddhism

Theravada ("Teaching of the Elders") Buddhism is primarily represented in America by Thai, Sri Lankan, Burmese, Cambodian, and Laotian immigrants and their descendants. This is the oldest surviving form of Buddhism, though like all religious traditions it has undergone significant changes over the centuries. This conservative form of Buddhism has a strong focus on the original Buddha Gautama and his immediate disciples, though various other saints, deities, and spirits also receive veneration in popular practice. Monks are usually held to a strict interpretation of the monastic rules, necessitating their reliance on the laity in most cases for food, clothing, transportation, and other needs. This strict practice has complicated matters in America, where differences in climate and culture have sometimes led to creative reinterpretations of the rules. For example, monks traditionally are expected to go barefoot, but in cold American regions some have taken to wearing socks and shoes dyed the color of monastic robes. Major Theravada temples in American include the New York Buddhist Vihara, Wat Thai in Los Angeles, and the Bhavana Society in West Virginia.

The twentieth century saw the rise of a subtradition within Theravada, known as the Vipassana movement. Named after a popular form of meditation, this reformist movement has placed meditation practice at the center of Buddhist life, often removing the more ceremonial and communal aspects of Theravada. This pared-down form of Buddhism has attracted many Euro-Americans, in part because it is less ethnically based and thus more accessible to individual American converts. Also known as Insight Meditation, the Vipassana community has created an influential network of practice centers across the country. The most notable Vipassana centers in the United States are the Insight Meditation Society (based in Barre, Massachusetts) and Spirit Rock Mediation Center in northern California.

## Mahayana: Pure Land, Zen, and Nichiren Buddhism

While Theravada is a relatively unified tradition, Mahayana ("Great Vehicle") Buddhism is a riot of different sects stressing many and various scriptures and venerating a greatly expanded pantheon of cosmic Buddhas and bodhisattvas (Buddhas in training). Perhaps the prototypical form of Mahayana Buddhism in the modern world is Pure Land Buddhism, which focuses on the salvific power of Amitabha Buddha. Devotion to Amitabha through such common practices as chanting his name results in rebirth in the Buddha's pure land, where it is easy to become a Buddha oneself.

Pure Land ideas and motifs are widely diffused throughout Buddhism, found in some manner within virtually all Buddhist sects other than Theravada. Although arguably the most widespread form of Buddhism in Asia, this is the only major Buddhist tradition that has failed to attract significant numbers of American converts, both because it resembles Christianity in some ways (a religion that many of its converts wish to renounce) and because in America it has been associated with ethnically based temple organizations. The most important Pure Land organization in the United States is the Buddhist Churches of America. A second significant group is the Amitabha Buddhist Society, whose American headquarters is in Sunnyvale, California. This organization mainly attracts Chinese Americans.

Another type of Mahayana Buddhism is Chan, more familiar to Americans by the Japanese name "Zen." Central to this tradition is an emphasis on specific lineages of semi-mythical awakened patriarchs who embody a penetrating insight into reality passed down from the original Buddha. Although frequently portrayed as a meditation-oriented tradition, actual Chan meditation in Asia is uncommon. Rather, Chan activities for the average layperson tend to include heavy amounts of Pure Land–type devotion and ancestor veneration. This makes it hard to categorize the average Chinese temple as simply Chan, Pure Land, Tantric, or any other specific tradition. A good example of this mixture is Fo Guang Shan, a large Taiwan-based international organization whose American headquarters are located at the Hsi Lai Temple outside Los Angeles.

Chinese Chan and its Korean (Son) and Vietnamese (Thien) versions are primarily practiced by Asian Americans in the United States. However, Zen presents an interesting exception to this trend. Never enjoying particularly large representation within the immigrant Japanese population, Zen was spread instead by the missionary efforts of Westernized Asian Zen teachers who portrayed Zen as a timeless, intuitive spiritual tradition focused on silent meditation and relatively unadorned with ritualistic trappings. This modern reformist Zen appealed to many Euro-Americans and, by the 1960s, resulted in the first significant groups of American Buddhist converts. Major centers include the San Francisco Zen Center, representing the Soto

Dancers at the San Fernando Valley Hongwanji Buddhist Temple summer Obon festival in California. Japanese Pure Land temples such as this one provide not only a religious home, but also a place to maintain Asian cultural traditions and convey them to the next generation. Amid the participants in traditional costumes are those dressed in ordinary street clothes, and some of the popular folk dances are original creations, originating in North America.

Zen sect, and Dai Bosatsu Zendo Kongo-ji in upstate New York, a member of the Rinzai Zen sect. A few convert-oriented versions of Son and Thien, often simply labeled "Zen," have also enjoyed considerable popularity since the 1970s. The most prominent ones are the Korean-derived Kwan Um School and the Vietnamese teacher Thich Nhat Hanh's (1926–) Community of Mindful Living.

A third form of Mahayana is Nichiren Buddhism. This is a highly fractious form of Buddhism containing a great many sects that all trace their teachings back to the Japanese monk Nichiren (1222–1282), who advocated complete reliance on the Lotus Sutra scripture and the chanting of the title of the sutra as the ultimate practice. Although a tiny portion of worldwide Buddhists, Nichiren Buddhist groups are often highly missionary in orientation and have successfully brought their understanding of the dharma to other countries in recent decades. In America the most significant of these is Soka Gakkai. Characterized by sometimes aggressive proselytization efforts and a belief that chanting can have material as well as spiritual rewards, Soka Gakkai is somewhat unusual in its declaration that Nichiren was the true Buddha for our age. This sect has grown to be one of the single largest Buddhist groups operating in the United States due to a successful recruitment of non-Japanese. Other Nichiren groups that are present but less popular are the mainstream Nichiren Shu and the liberal Rissho Koseikai.

## Vajrayana, or Tantric, Buddhism

The third and final broad type of Buddhism is Vajrayana ("Diamond Vehicle"), or Tantric, Buddhism. This outgrowth of the Mahayana tradition includes an even larger pantheon of deities and awakened beings, often manifesting both peaceful and wrathful forms. Vajrayana Buddhism includes additional scriptures known as tantras, often couched in esoteric and highly symbolic language requiring special initiations to understand. The master–disciple relationship is particularly central to Tantric Buddhism, which claims to be able to help one become a Buddha within a single lifetime. Vajrayana Buddhist immigrants come mainly from Tibet, Mongolia, Nepal, and the small Caucasian state Kalmykia, none of which have very large populations in America. An even smaller number of Japanese Americans and Chinese Americans practice in tantric lineages such as Shingon or Tendai, though tantric influences are common in many Mahayana Buddhist traditions.

So-called Tibetan Buddhism in America is in fact dominated by Euro-American converts, who easily outnumber the small numbers of Asian American practitioners. Fueled in part by positive Hollywood portrayals and the international charisma of the Dalai Lama (1935–), but also by dynamic and highly trained teachers who have set up shop in the United States, Tibetan Buddhism has blossomed since the 1980s and has overtaken Zen as the most visible form of

Buddhism. This type of Vajrayana includes a belief in *tulkus,* wise teachers who deliberately reincarnate life after life in order to continue teaching unawakened beings. The Dalai Lama, currently in his fourteenth incarnation, is the most famous example of this. He belongs to the Gelug sect, represented in America by such centers as Namgyal Monastery in Ithaca, New York, and Jewel Heart in Ann Arbor, Michigan. Probably the most important Tibetan-based Buddhist organization in North America is Shambhala, based in Nova Scotia and with dozens of centers in the United States. Founded by the flamboyant Tibetan missionary Chogyam Trungpa (1939–1987), this eclectic lineage includes elements of the Kagyu and Nyingma sects.

## Early History in America

Information on Buddhism began trickling into America via trade ties and European scholarship, but sustained contact with Buddhism did not develop until the mid-nineteenth century. Buddhist studies in America began in 1842, when the American Oriental Society was convened. At the first meeting, Edward Elbridge Salisbury (1814–1901) delivered a breakthrough lecture entitled "Memoir on the History of Buddhism." This was also the year in which Americans first began to display an interest in Buddhism for its potential spiritual resources, a development signaled by the first English-language publication from a Buddhist scripture. The excerpt, entitled "The Preaching of the Buddha," appeared in the Transcendentalist journal *The Dial.* Transcendentalism—made famous by such figures as Ralph Waldo Emerson (1803–1882) and Henry David Thoreau (1817–1862)—was an outgrowth of Unitarian Christianity and the first American religious movement to take Asian traditions seriously as a possible source of spiritual insight.

The California gold rush was touched off in 1848, and soon people from all over the world were streaming into California. Within a few years tens of thousands of Chinese had arrived. In 1853 the Sze Yap Company established America's first temple. Located in San Francisco's Chinatown, it provided a mixture of Pure Land Buddhism and other Chinese religious elements. But the Chinese were resented for doing work that might go to Americans, and they were seen as invaders from a foreign racial stock practicing an alien religion. In 1854 the California Supreme Court ruled that Chinese people in America could not serve as witnesses in criminal cases and essentially had no rights. As the Chinese moved up and down the West Coast, carrying Buddhism with them, they encountered ever more discrimination. Finally, in 1880,

Congress passed the Chinese Exclusion Act, banning most Chinese immigration.

A complicated mix of scholarly interest, exotic attraction, half-informed speculation, and anxiety defined American attitudes toward Buddhism. For many Christians, Buddhism was dismissed out of hand as heathenism. Yet there was also a vigorous discussion among liberals and scholars over the nature of Buddhism. Most authors approached their subject with assumptions derived from Protestantism. They believed that the Buddhism of the Buddha should be seen as the truest Buddhism, the only authentic expression of the Buddhist impulse. Later developments in Buddhism were viewed as degradations. They sought this original Buddhism almost exclusively through texts—the older the better—which could be appropriated and employed by Western scholars and critics. Buddhist practices of Pure Land worship or monastic asceticism seemed strange to them, but the Buddha himself came to be widely admired as a virtuous role model.

As the century drew toward a close, American interest in Buddhism developed even further, as a trickle of Euro-Americans began to turn from talking about Buddhism to identifying themselves as Buddhists. In 1880, during a Theravadin ceremony in Ceylon (later, Sri Lanka), Henry Steel Olcott (1832–1907) and Helena Blavatsky (1831–1891), a naturalized citizen of the United States, become the first Americans to formally pledge their allegiance to Buddhism. Olcott and Blavatsky were the founders of Theosophy, an eclectic religious movement that incorporated Hinduism and Buddhism into its beliefs. Even after their vows, their understanding of Buddhism was heavily influenced by Theosophical ideas. But the same cannot be said of Ernest Fenollosa (1853–1908) and William Sturgis Bigelow (1850–1926), who in 1885 took the Tendai precepts and began practicing Shingon meditation practices in Japan.

It was 1893 that proved to be a watershed year in the history of Buddhism in America. This was the year that the World's Parliament of Religions was held in Chicago. The parliament brought together representatives of religions from around the world, and popular speeches were delivered by representatives from many Buddhist sects. It was one of the few instances of Buddhists being able to represent themselves, rather than being represented by others, often unsympathetic Christian Americans.

An important interpreter of Buddhism during this time was Paul Carus (1852–1919). A German immigrant, Carus identified Buddhism as one of the closest approximations to his vision of a rational, investigative approach to universal spirituality. In 1894 he published *The Gospel of Buddha, According to Old Records,* a popular book that helped to introduce Buddhism and the life of the Buddha to a general audience.

The end of the nineteenth century seemed to herald a bright future for Buddhism in the United States. Hawaii was already home to 25,000 Japanese Buddhists when the United States annexed it in 1898. Furthermore, the Japanese had begun to immigrate to the mainland. The result was the creation of the Buddhist Mission of North America in 1899 in San Francisco. And yet Buddhism had still only barely penetrated America's diverse but often contentious religious landscape. A handful of converts and a marginalized collection of Chinese and Japanese communities did not add up to a mass movement. In fact, it would be another two generations before Buddhism began to make major inroads into the American consciousness and attract significant numbers of followers.

## The Twentieth Century

During the first five decades of the twentieth century Buddhism in America was dominated by Japanese traditions. Japanese Buddhist sects founded many of their first American temples during this time, including Nichiren Shu, Shingon, Soto Zen, and Jodo Shu. The primary form of Buddhism in the United States, the Japanese-derived Jodo Shinshu Pure Land school, continued its rapid expansion during this time period. Already by 1900 English-language study groups and periodicals were appearing. Nevertheless, Jodo Shinshu remained a heavily Japanese American form of Buddhism, as temples continued to be founded wherever Japanese immigrants went throughout Hawaii and the West Coast.

But hard times loomed for the Japanese Americans. The Immigration Act of 1924 virtually eliminated Japanese immigration. With the flow of Japanese immigrants cut off, Pure Land Buddhism's growth slowed, and few other sects experienced further development. The day after the Japanese attack on Pearl Harbor on December 7, 1941, federal agents began to detain Buddhist priests and other community leaders. By 1942 more than 120,000 Japanese Americans and immigrants had been forced from their homes into internment camps because of suspicion of their loyalties. Temples were ransacked during the process, and many families lost their homes and land. In the camps, makeshift Buddhist centers formed, and the younger generation began to push for adaptations that would make Buddhism seem more "American." Among the results was the reorganization of the Buddhist Mission of North America into the Buddhist Churches of America, the widespread use of English in services and publications, and the adoption of Christianized terms such as *minister* and *bishop*.

Although these fifty years of American Buddhism largely belong to Japanese Americans, a few notable milestones were achieved by others as well. In 1927 Walter Yeeling Evans-Wentz (1878–1965) produced one of the most famous American Buddhist texts, a translation and commentary of the *Bardo Thodol* entitled *The Tibetan Book of the Dead.* A second classic of American Buddhism was published by Dwight Goddard (1861–1939) in 1932. Goddard's *Buddhist Bible* was a large collection of sutras and other traditional materials in translation, the first easily accessible volume of such texts available to the English-speaking world.

In the 1950s a new cycle of non-Asian interest in Buddhism began to appear. Most visible was the rise of the Beats, a loose collection of avant-garde literary pioneers who explored Asian traditions in an effort to find meaningful art and spirituality. Buddhism played a large part in these explorations. Probably the most famous of the explicitly Buddhist-related works produced by the Beats was Jack Kerouac's 1958 novel, *The Dharma Bums,* in which Kerouac (1922–1969) gave a semifictional account of hitchhiking literary Buddhist wanderers roaming the highways of Eisenhower's America. The Beats and later converts were influenced by D.T. Suzuki (1870–1966), who had worked with Carus in Chicago and returned to the United States in 1949 to teach on Buddhism, especially Zen. Suzuki's university lessons, which stressed the value of spontaneity, playfulness, simplicity, and mystic wisdom in Zen, caught the imagination of the developing counterculture and led to profiles of him in major magazines and television appearances. Although his interpretation of Zen was highly idiosyncratic, he was a talented teacher and his presentation of Zen as an unfettered, ineffable, experiential core of religion indelibly stamped American attitudes toward Zen.

While the 1950s began to heat up interest in Buddhism once again, the 1960s were the breakout decade for American Buddhism. In 1960 Daisaku Ikeda (1928–), the leader of the Japanese Buddhist new religious movement Soka Gakkai, visited the United States for the first time. An American Soka Gakkai organization was quickly established, and Soka Gakkai Buddhism began to spread. A number of new Zen missionaries were offering Zen practice as well. Significantly, these Zen teachers included not only Asian immigrants but also non-Asian Americans. Both types of Zen missionaries tended to focus their efforts specifically on non-Asians.

Their approach contrasted with that of a new generation of Chinese teachers and promoters, such as Hsuan Hua (1918–1995), who directed their energies toward Chinese Americans and non-Asians alike, and included not only Zen-type Chan Buddhism but Pure Land, Tantric, and scholastic Buddhism as well. In 1969 five of Hsuan Hua's students became the first fully ordained American-born monastics.

The most important event of the 1960s for American Buddhism was the passing of the Immigration Act of 1965. This legislation lifted the racist immigration laws that had helped to choke off Buddhism's growth, allowing a new tide of Asian immigrants to reach the United States. The Chinese came again, as did the Japanese (though in smaller numbers), and they were joined by Sri Lankans, Koreans, and Vietnamese. These newcomers brought new forms of Buddhism, either as beliefs to be transplanted along with their lives, or as religious commodities to market to a new mission field in America. In the wake of this revitalization of American Buddhism, the first Theravada temple in North America was founded, in 1965, in Washington D.C.

The first trickle of Tibetans into America also began during this period. A Vajrayana temple in a Tibetan lineage, the Lamaist Buddhist Monastery of America, had already been founded quietly in New Jersey in 1955. In 1965 Robert Thurman (1941–) became the first Westerner ordained as a Tibetan monk, taking the lower ordination in a ceremony presided over by the Dalai Lama in India. In 1969 Tarthang Tulku (1934–) founded the Tibetan Nyingma Meditation Center in Berkeley, California, the first temple in the Nyingma tradition, the oldest of Tibet's sects. This is also the year that Shambhala Publications, the first large Buddhist press in the United States, was established.

A perception of Buddhism as ancient, wise, peaceful, and esoteric pervaded the counterculture of the 1960s and 1970s, with concepts like karma and reincarnation reigning side by side with free love and widespread drug use in the growing network of new-convert Buddhist centers. Some missionaries did little to discourage these combinations. One example of this is Chogyam Trungpa, a Tibetan guru who founded the Tail of the Tiger practice center in Vermont in 1970. Charismatic, insightful, traditionally trained, sexually promiscuous, and alcoholic, Trungpa embodied a form of "crazy wisdom" highly compelling to the baby boomer seekers investigating Buddhism and other Asian religions.

Not all Buddhist teachers, Tibetan or otherwise, were as flamboyant as Trungpa. The 1970s saw a steady increase of Tibetan monks who attracted small bands of followers, such as Kalu Rinpoche (1905–1989) and Dudjom Rinpoche (1904–1987). Another form of Buddhism, the lay-oriented Vipassana meditation movement, also reached America during this time. It was led by American laypeople who had trained in Asian Theravadin countries, such as Jack Kornfield (1945–) and Joseph Goldstein (1944–), who founded the Insight Meditation Society in Massachusetts in 1975. And the flow of immigrants continued, bringing the first Thai (1971), Korean (1973), and Cambodian (1979) temples.

The counterculture began to wane in the 1980s, as the baby boomers aged and the country, under President Ronald Reagan, shifted in a more conservative direction. Nonetheless, Buddhism continued to expand in America during the Reagan years and President George H.W. Bush's presidency, largely along the same established trajectories: more Zen, more Tibetan, and more Vipassana Buddhism, as well as many more Asian immigrants and their ethnic forms of Buddhism.

In some ways the 1980s was the golden era of women's Buddhism in America. In 1987 the Theravada nuns' order was resurrected, revived at the Dharma Vijaya Buddhist Vihara in Los Angeles. The same year Jetsunma Ahkon Lhamo (1949–) was recognized as the first Western female reincarnate lama. Less positive in its genesis but ultimately of equal significance was the development of greater democracy and awareness of the need for inclusion of women teachers in convert Buddhist centers, sparked in part by a series of sex scandals involving prominent male Buddhist teachers.

Buddhism once more became trendy in the 1990s, with major movies (including *Little Buddha,* 1993, and *Kundun,* 1997), bestselling books such as Lama Surya Das's *Awakening the Buddha Within* (1997), and seemingly endless amounts of media buzz, especially around famous converts such as film star Richard Gere, who began to turn toward Buddhism following a trip to Nepal in 1978. The first major English-language Buddhist magazine, *Tricycle: The Buddhist Review,* appeared in 1991, oriented toward elite Buddhist converts involved in Tibetan, Zen, and Vipassana Buddhism. The same year, Soka Gakkai, which by then boasted tens of thousands of members in America, was summarily excommunicated by its parent Nichiren Shoshu organization. Soka Gakkai was only temporarily slowed down by this debacle, quickly regrouping and seeming to thrive without the guidance of the traditional priesthood. The network of temples and centers founded by Chogyam Trungpa likewise rebounded after a period of scandal and decline, reorganizing as Shambhala International, which continues to be a major force in American Buddhism.

As the millennium turned, Buddhism seemed at last to have made itself comfortable in America. By the end of President George W. Bush's second term, in 2009, American-trained teachers led most of the convert-oriented temples and meditation centers founded in the previous four decades, and groups affiliated with major lineages were operating in every part of the country. Relationships between cutting-edge brain sciences and Buddhism seemed to herald a new era in Western cognitive and therapeutic concepts, and meditation was becoming widely accepted as a technique for managing stress and pain. An impressive secondary literature on Buddhism's many American manifestations had appeared as American Buddhism became a legitimate subfield of academic research.

## Early Twenty-First-Century Issues

One question that often confounds researchers is the deceptively simple issue of "who is a Buddhist?" Because Buddhism is largely noncreedal in nature and most Asian temples do not have formal members, there can be significant difficulty in determining what constitutes legitimate Buddhist identity. Is someone who reads several books on Buddhism a year and likes its philosophy a Buddhist? What about someone who meditates and occasionally attends Buddhist events, but doesn't believe in reincarnation or karma? Obviously, such behaviors make it difficult to quantify the number of Buddhists in America, an issue made even harder by the persistent tendency of surveys (which undercount non-English speakers) to overlook segments of the American Buddhist community.

A possible solution lies in the attempt to measure Buddhist *influence,* rather than simply numbers. Although scholars have speculated that the number of Buddhists in America ranges anywhere from 1.4 million to 4 million adults, a 2004 study by religion scholars Robert Wuthnow and Wendy Cadge demonstrated that one in seven Americans has had contact with Buddhism and one in eight believes Buddhism has had a measurable impact on their religious life. That's 12.5 percent, a percentage far above the actual representation of fully identified Buddhists in the population. Thus Buddhism's contribution to American religious culture may lie less in its ability to obtain converts or nurture immigrant communities and more in the way that Buddhist

ideas, practices, and motifs have successfully made their way into the culture at large.

Perhaps the most obvious issue involving the Buddhist communities in America is the racial homogeneity of so many temples and meditation groups. Although not a universal phenomenon, most Buddhist groups are overwhelmingly composed of a single ethnic group, and Buddhism overall can be loosely grouped into Asian American and (mainly Caucasian) convert types. While instances of cross-racial cooperation and appreciation do occur, more common are misconceptions and even prejudices about the ways the other racial group is believed to practice Buddhism. This racializing of American Buddhism is not necessarily a conscious phenomenon, but it arises in part because immigrant groups may have significantly different community and religious needs from those of native-born converts to Buddhism.

Meanwhile, African Americans often feel particularly marginalized in American Buddhism, lost in a sea of nonblack faces wherever they go. The only significant exception to these segregating trends is Soka Gakkai, which is probably one of the most integrated religious organizations in the country, including significant numbers of all racial groups. This multiethnic phenomenon is the result of Soka Gakkai's evangelical approach to spreading Buddhism and serves as a point of pride that manifests the sect's belief that all people possess Buddha-nature.

A second issue is gender. In North America, there has been a push by women for greater responsibility and recognition, in some cases fueled by sexual inappropriateness on the part of male teachers. Euro-American groups in particular have often made efforts to develop more female-affirmative Buddhist ideals, and a growing number of women teachers and abbesses have appeared in the past twenty years. Less recognized are the contributions made by Asian American women; their labor and donations are often the backbone of their communities, and they also frequently play important organizational and spiritual roles in their temples.

The emergence of stronger positions for women within American Buddhism is partially the result of another issue: the lack of monks. Traditionally, the monastic orders have played a key role in the maintenance of teaching, guidance, and morality in Buddhist communities. Furthermore, the monks (and, in those fewer countries that have them, nuns) acted as fields of merit, engines for generating good karma, which could be tapped into by the laity through the traditional lay roles of providers and disciples. But celibacy and renunciation have had a difficult time in America. Asian American youth and young adults are more likely to pursue a high-paying career over the life of a religious beggar, and Euro-Americans seem disinclined to consider full-blown monasticism as an option. For Asian American communities, this has often meant the importation of foreign monks and nuns with Old World cultural and religious assumptions and weak English skills. Operating in a strange culture, these monks often stay for only a few years, meaning that there is a constant turnover of foreign leaders that retards the development of many communities and can lead to friction with the Americanized laity. Meanwhile, many Euro-American groups have elevated laypeople into the roles traditionally played by dedicated monastics, often with only a partial understanding of how Buddhist clergy are trained and expected to act in Asia.

Another issue is the unusual way in which Euro-American groups tend to conceive of proper Buddhist activities. Meditation is central to most Euro-American Buddhists, for leaders and laypeople alike. This is a startling contrast to historical Asian Buddhism, where meditation has always been a relatively uncommon practice engaged in by a small number of elites, usually monks. This strange positioning of converts, neither really monk nor layperson, is reshaping Buddhism. Many profess to find this combination liberating; it remains to be seen, however, whether laypeople entangled in families and jobs can carry on strenuous monastic-type practices over decades and pass on strong traditions to new generations.

One conflict that Buddhist temples have had to face is discrimination from non-Buddhists. The Chinese and Japanese first confronted prejudice in America in the nineteenth century, and though religious tolerance has grown considerably since those first problems, Asian American Buddhists continue to encounter difficulties in many places. Race complicates the attempt to classify vandalism of temples and harassment of monks as specifically ethnic or religious bigotry, but clearly Buddhism's non-Christian status is one significant contributing factor to marginalization. Besides having to deal with outright confrontations, Buddhists often find themselves unable to build temples because of restrictive zoning laws that in some cases are enforced by local communities specifically to keep Buddhists out.

But not all interactions with non-Buddhists are negative. In fact, many of the people attending Buddhist centers

identify themselves as Christians or Jews. In some cases, this is part of a dual religious identity, while for others Buddhism is approached as a technique or a philosophy, not as a religion per se, and thus offers no particular threat to more traditional American religion.

## Developments and Trends

Where is Buddhism going in the twenty-first century? Predictions are always a tricky business, but some general trends can be pointed to. First, as important as the American context is for Buddhism in the United States, it is developments in Asia that will have the largest effect on American Buddhism. Buddhist immigration has always been tied to conditions in Asia, whether caused by political conflict, economic depression, or missionary zeal. Unforeseeable events will continually reshape the American Buddhist landscape as new wars and other factors push various Asian groups to seek a better life in the United States. Even established Buddhist groups are likely to remain at least somewhat porous to new ideas and practices developed first in Asia.

A second development counter to the first is the expansion of American Buddhist missionary programs to other countries. Despite its relatively young status among the nations of the world, the United States has long been a launching pad for foreign missionary endeavors. As Americanized forms of Buddhism continue to evolve, the unparalleled status the United States enjoys as a rich, technologically sophisticated, and militarily powerful country will likely facilitate the spread of Buddhism from America to newer pastures, such as Latin America. Thus while the United States will remain an importer of Buddhism, it will be a significant exporter of Buddhism as well.

This raises the issue of exactly what "American Buddhism," rather than "Japanese Buddhism" or "Tibetan Buddhism," might be. Many Buddhist groups themselves have wrestled with this question, some attracted to the idea of a uniquely American expression of Buddhism, others fearful that American materialism and ignorance will devolve the dharma. America is so large, so diverse, and already host to so many forms of Buddhism that the future will probably be ever-increasing pluralism, rather than a united or definitive form of American Buddhism. One source of diversity within American Buddhism is likely to be the encounter with non-Buddhist religions. Buddhism has been continually impacted by other religions it interacted with in its spread across Asia, such as Daoism and Shinto. Exchanges and conflicts with various forms of Christianity, Judaism, and New Age paths, as well as Western secularism, scientific materialism, and psychology, will surely lead to a multiplicity of responses and new developments within Buddhism.

A final issue confronting Buddhism's future in America is the difficulty of transmitting the tradition to younger generations in a meaningful way. The Buddhist Churches of America has declined to a mere seventeen thousand families, down from a high of approximately fifty thousand in 1960. The problem has come especially from out-marriage and conversion to Christianity among the newer generations, as well as the low rate of Japanese immigration to replace aging members. Other primarily Asian American Buddhist groups face similar problems as many of their young people seek to leave Buddhism behind in their ongoing assimilation process to mainstream American culture. On the other hand, Euro-American groups are experiencing a graying effect as well because of the tendency to emphasize meditation—an activity that typically excludes unruly youngsters—and the lack of effective children's programs at convert temples. Although Buddhism will surely continue in some fashion, the specific organizations that currently dominate the scene may fail to survive these processes of attrition.

See also *Architecture: Asian Religions; Buddhist Tradition and Heritage; California and the Pacific Rim Region; Canada: Pluralism; Celebrity Culture; Devotionalism; Zen Buddhism.*

Jeff Wilson

## BIBLIOGRAPHY

Cadge, Wendy. *Heartwood: The First Generation of Theravada Buddhism in America.* Chicago: University of Chicago Press, 2004.

Coleman, James William. *The New Buddhism: The Western Transformation of an Ancient Tradition.* New York: Oxford University Press, 2001.

Gregory, Peter N., and Susanne Mrozik. *Women Practicing Buddhism: American Experiences.* Boston: Wisdom Publications, 2008.

Hammond, Phillip, and David Machacek. *Soka Gakkai in America: Accommodation and Conversion.* New York: Oxford University Press, 1999.

Hunter, Louise H. *Buddhism in Hawaii.* Honolulu: University of Hawaii Press, 1971.

Kashima, Tetsuden. *Buddhism in America: The Social Organization of an Ethnic Religious Organization.* Westport, Conn.: Greenwood Press, 1977.

Paine, Jeffrey. *Re-Enchantment: Tibetan Buddhism Comes to the West.* New York: W.W. Norton, 2004.

Prebish, Charles, and Martin Baumann, eds. *Westward Dharma: Buddhism Beyond Asia.* Berkeley: University of California Press, 2002.

Prebish, Charles, and Kenneth Tanaka, eds. *The Faces of Buddhism in America.* Berkeley: University of California Press, 1998.

Prothero, Stephen. *The White Buddhist: The Asian Odyssey of Henry Steel Olcott.* Bloomington: Indiana University Press, 1996.

Snodgrass, Judith. *Presenting Japanese Buddhism to the West.* Chapel Hill: University of North Carolina Press, 2003.

Suh, Sharon. *Being Buddhist in a Christian World: Gender and Community in a Korean American Temple.* Seattle: University of Washington Press, 2004.

Tweed, Thomas A. *The American Encounter with Buddhism, 1844–1912.* Chapel Hill: University of North Carolina Press, 2000.

Williams, Duncan Ryuken, and Christopher Queen, eds. *American Buddhism: Methods and Findings in Recent Scholarship.* Richmond, Surrey, UK: Curzon Press, 1999.

Wuthnow, Robert, and Wendy Cadge. "Buddhists and Buddhism in the United States: The Scope of Influence." *Journal for the Scientific Study of Religion* 43 (Sept. 2004): 363–380.

# Buddhist Tradition and Heritage

Buddhism originated in northeastern India in the sixth century BCE with the teachings of a former prince named Siddhartha Gautama. It draws upon ancient ritual language associated with the religious tradition Brahmanism, although the ideas about salvation, or soteriology, of Buddhism differ significantly from those expressed by the Brahman priests of ancient India. Expanding rapidly throughout Asia, Buddhism was a missionizing religion that developed into various forms, many of which have successfully established themselves in Europe and in North America. In fact, some demographic studies identify Buddhism as the fastest growing religion in places like Western Europe because of the large number of Westerners claiming loyalty to the religion (whether as active practitioners or as "bookstore Buddhists" whose adherence takes an intellectual form).

## Life of the Buddha

The life experiences of the founder played a decisive role in the formation of the Buddhist religion. Born in the Lumbini area (in what is today southern Nepal) to a royal family known as the Shakyas, Siddhartha Gautama earned the epithet Buddha ("the Awakened One") in later life, after a breakthrough experience that occurred while he was meditating under a tree. He is also known as Shakyamuni (literally "Sage of the Shakya Clan"). The details of Siddhartha's birth are indicative of his special status and potential. His mother conceived the child while she was dreaming of a white elephant, a symbol of royalty. Legendary accounts say that she gave birth without pain, with the child emerging bloodlessly from her side. The child was born amidst a rain of flowers and auspicious earthquakes. Immediately after taking birth, Siddhartha reportedly ascended to the top of the universe and declared that this would be his final rebirth: He would attain Buddhahood and experience no more rebirth. The baby's mother died within a week of giving birth, assuring that the vessel that bore this *bodhisattva* (a being destined to awaken to the truth of the Buddhist teachings, or *dharma*) would not be "sullied" by subsequent sexual and gestational activity.

The child's body was unusual, with a number of odd features, such as webbed hands and special marks on his feet. His father invited soothsayers to interpret the marks and was told that the boy would grow up to be a great king or a great spiritual ruler. From that time on, the bodhisattva's father deliberately sheltered his son from the sight of all suffering, in an attempt to ensure that the prediction about the child growing up to take a spiritual path would not come true. The boy's father provided the child with the choicest of luxuries, and as he came of age his father provided him with a bevy of royal brides and consorts and also surrounded him with guards. Despite all the efforts made by the bodhisattva's father to bind his son with chains of pleasure, the bodhisattva had some dramatic experiences in his late twenties that shook him, causing him to leave his family behind and embark on a search for a path leading beyond birth and death. According to legends the young man obtained permission to go on an excursion, and his father arranged to have all poor people, old people, and people suffering from disease removed from the path. The deities conspired to see that the bodhisattva nevertheless encountered an old person, a diseased person, and a dead person. Next, he encountered a renouncer who inspired him to leave home. The quest for a path beyond birth and death was not easy and did not yield fruit immediately. After six years of extreme asceticism, the bodhisattva reportedly discovered the middle way between asceticism and hedonism. He moderated his ascetic lifestyle, began to eat normally, achieved awakening, and earned the epithet "Buddha."

## Teachings of the Buddha

Buddhist tradition indicates that the Buddha was hesitant to teach, believing that the insights he had achieved would be difficult for ordinary beings to comprehend. Nevertheless, a deity convinced the Buddha to teach what he had learned for the benefit of those few who were ready for such advanced ideas. At his first teaching, the Buddha is said to have set forth four propositions known as the Four Noble Truths. First, life is dissatisfying. Second, life is dissatisfying because of craving or "thirst." Third, life doesn't have to be dissatisfying; dissatisfaction can end. And, fourth, there is a path that leads to the end of dissatisfaction.

This fundamental teaching is often compared to a medical diagnosis in which the Buddha (often referred to as the Great Physician in Buddhist literature) identifies the malady at the heart of the human condition and prescribes a cure. In the scriptural languages in which the Four Noble Truths are preserved, the term used to characterize the ills of life (Sanskrit, *duhkha;* Pali, *dukkha*) is a word that means suffering, discomfort, dissatisfaction, or unsatisfactoriness. Linguistically, this term is the opposite of a term meaning ease, satisfaction, or pleasure. Hence the term can be translated literally as "dis-ease." This is the condition that plagues all sentient beings; this is the ailment or syndrome that Buddhism cures. According to the second noble truth, the source of this state of dissatisfaction, or dis-ease, is craving or thirst. Although often translated as "desire," the term that is rendered in English as "craving" or "thirst" is more narrow in meaning than the English "desire," referring more specifically to desire that is in some sense distorted, excessive, or misdirected. Sometimes the term is translated as "egoistic grasping" because it refers to ego-driven craving. Craving or thirst appears in three forms: first, craving for sensual pleasure, or pleasure derived from taste, touch, and other sensory experiences; second, craving for renewed existence; and, finally, craving for the nonexistence of those things and beings that disturb us or craving for our own nonexistence when we are feeling unhappy.

All three forms of craving lead to rebirth—even a person who craves nonexistence and commits suicide will be born again—and rebirth is considered by Buddhists to be a source of pain. To those with little background in Buddhist teachings, rebirth or transmigration may sound quite pleasant. Since it entails the experience of life in some other form after death, rebirth thus seems to promise novelty and excitement as well as extended life. But none of the various forms of rebirth that Buddhists might envisage, including extremely pleasant forms of life as a deity, offer the possibility of endless life. Those who take birth in various hells (or who are born as insects or other sentient beings with limited faculties) because of their lack of virtue in their present lives will experience tremendous discomfort. Even those who, having performed meritorious deeds in their present lives, enjoy tremendous ease and satisfaction of physical needs by taking rebirth as gods and goddesses, will eventually die. Rebirth is inherently dissatisfying because life must end, and at the end of each life one not only endures the breakdown of one's body and the pain of saying good-bye to life, but one must also separate from loved ones. This dissatisfying cycle of rebirth is driven by *karma,* a term that refers to the effects of our actions: Our actions bear fruit for us, with results that we will experience either later in this life or in future lives.

Craving is a source of bondage, according to the teaching of the Four Noble Truths, which keeps one bound to repeated sufferings and dissatisfactions in the cycle of birth and death. Craving or thirst is said to be like a fire: the more you feed it, the more powerful it becomes. Once one's cravings are gratified, one begins to crave more. Because one can never satisfy craving once and for all, it is a source of pain. It is especially difficult to satisfy craving when, according to Buddhist teaching, everything that exists is impermanent. Everything changes, and what satisfies one's cravings today will not be there tomorrow. We are always hankering after things that do not last; whenever we get comfortable with a situation, it changes, constant change being the only thing that stays the same in this world of transient phenomena.

So to sum up the second noble truth, craving or thirst leads to dissatisfaction or dis-ease. But the third noble truth asserts that there is an optimistic prognosis for someone who finds life unsatisfactory. This malady caused by craving is curable. If the craving ceases, dissatisfaction ends. Nirvana is the state that one experiences when the fire of craving that feeds on the fuel of ignorance is put out. The fourth noble truth summarizes the path by which one experiences *nirvana,* the state of awakening.

In terms of the medical model, the fourth noble truth lays down a treatment plan. The path has eight elements, each described as correct or proper, and hence is known as the eightfold path. The first of these eight elements is proper understanding, a frame of mind, which comes from experientially, or existentially, understanding the Four Noble Truths. The second element of the path is proper intention, which entails cultivating thoughts free from sensuality, malice, and cruelty. Proper speech, most importantly avoiding dishonesty and harmful speech such as gossip or slander, is the third element of the path. The fourth element is proper action. The key aspects of Buddhist morality that guide proper action are encoded in the five precepts that laypeople undertake to follow at all times; these require refraining

from killing, stealing, inappropriate sexual conduct, lying, and the use of intoxicants. In addition to the five precepts, monks and nuns cultivate proper action by following a code of conduct contained in the monastic rule of their order. The fifth element of the path is proper livelihood, or avoiding occupations that would violate the precepts, such as butchering animals or battlefield military duty. The sixth element of the path is proper effort: being energetic and vigilant in monitoring one's thoughts, trying to cultivate pure and compassionate thoughts. The seventh element is proper mindfulness, which refers to the practice of insight meditation. The point of this kind of meditation is to cultivate mindful awareness (sometimes called "bare awareness"). It can be done while sitting, while walking, or while engaged in any number of mundane activities. While so engaged, one focuses one's attention on the body, following the breath while in seated meditation or noting the feeling of one's feet against the ground while walking. Proper concentration is the eighth element of the path. The ideal is a state of objectless awareness often described as "going into a trance" where one has no awareness of self or other, no sense of such mundane details as the passage of time. Thus when one achieves perfect concentration, there is nothing to apprehend and no one there doing the apprehending. Practicing proper concentration is thus an excellent way to experientially realize the central Buddhist doctrine that an eternal soul or abiding self does not exist—a doctrine that distinguished the Buddha as a religious teacher from other religious teachers of his day.

The path eventually came to be condensed into three elements: morality, meditation, and wisdom. Each element is considered necessary for the next. Thus only a person practicing a morally disciplined life can succeed in meditation, and meditation is a prerequisite for the cultivation of wisdom.

## Cultural Context

Buddhism arose at a time in Indian history when the idea of the autonomous individual was emerging. Challenging prevalent notions of salvation as a family affair in which family members would enjoy (or suffer) afterlife destinies achieved by the ritual activities of the head of the household, Buddhists articulated a religious ideal of individualism whereby a person stands apart from his or her family and determines an individual destiny for him or herself as an independent religious actor (by performing meritorious deeds or by failing to act meritoriously). In the criticism of family life and the praise heaped upon the unfettered existence of the religious wanderer in early scriptural texts, one can see a valorization of the individual who stands apart from family as the sole shaper of his or her own fate. Celebrations of the holy wanderer equate the homeless life of the religious nomad with the exercise of religious autonomy. The Buddha and his followers lived a peripatetic lifestyle, traveling about nine months a year. Monks who followed the Buddha left their families and jobs behind and lived off the generosity of lay supporters, who provided food, clothing, and other necessities. Late in life, the Buddha agreed to accept women into the monastic order and established a separate order for nuns.

The young religion appealed to all classes of Indian society, but it was especially successful with merchants and other members of the commercial classes. From its beginnings in northeastern India, Buddhism began to spread throughout India. By the third century BCE, missionary efforts led to Buddhism taking hold in Sri Lanka, Burma (Myanmar), Thailand, and other countries of southeastern Asia. The religion also moved northward into the region of the Himalayas (present-day Sikkim, Bhutan, and Nepal), into Tibet, Mongolia, and other parts of central Asia, and also into China, Korea, and Japan.

## Organization of the Religion

As Buddhism developed in India, it did not develop a centralized ecclesiastic authority. When the Buddha was dying, he instructed his community that he would not appoint a successor: His teachings (the dharma) would stand in the place of a single leader of the community. Thus no religious leader dictates ecclesiastical policy for Buddhists in a manner comparable to, for example, the functions of the pope for Roman Catholics. Perhaps inevitably differences of practice and interpretation arose within a few centuries of the death of the Buddha. A division occurred at the second council at which all members of the entire far-flung monastic community came together to communally recite the Buddha's teachings, as recollected by different memory specialists. The two groups that emerged from this council at a later time divided into additional factions.

As Buddhism spread throughout Asia, different denominations came to dominate in different areas. Theravada, the predominant Buddhist tradition today in Sri Lanka, Burma (Myanmar), Thailand, Cambodia, and Laos, once competed with other Buddhist denominations in these places. Vestiges of religious polemics between Theravada Buddhists and

those who competed with them for dominance have left a trail of problematic terminology and claims to leadership in the secondary literature on Buddhism. For instance, the term "Hinayana," meaning "the Inferior Vehicle" or "the lesser path," is a pejorative term used by other Buddhists to characterize Theravada Buddhists. Although the term is still sometimes used by scholars, it has polemical connotations that render it unsuitable in academic discourse. In addition, readers should be aware that the claim that Theravada Buddhism preserves the original teachings of the Buddha is a sectarian claim with which most current scholars of Buddhism take issue. Theravada Buddhists rely on a canon that was redacted several centuries after the death of the Buddha. While there are some very ancient materials in this corpus of the literature, the same can be said of the canons of other denominations.

Theravada Buddhists place a high premium on the virtues of monasticism, with its opportunities for education and meditation. In Theravada circles, the laity supports monastic renouncers of the cycle of production and reproduction with gifts of food, clothing, shelter, and sons to serve as novice monks. Laypeople donate their material goods and symbolically "donate" their offspring in this life to help establish good roots for future flourishing, by which they might achieve awakening themselves as renouncers in future lives. The path to nirvana begins with the recognition that the Four Noble Truths accurately describe the human condition (and indeed the condition of all sentient beings, for no Buddhist is concerned only with the well-being of humans). The person who achieves this recognition is known in the Pali liturgical language of the Theravada denomination as a "stream enterer." Such a person can expect to achieve enlightenment or awakening in no more than seven subsequent human births. At a more advanced stage, according to the Theravada typology of stages of the path, a person wins the status of a "once returner" who will be born only once more as a human before achieving awakening. The "nonreturner" will not be born as a human being but will achieve awakening in one of the many subtle spheres of existence known as the Pure Abodes. The *arhat* (Pali, *arahant*) is a person who has awakened to the truth of the dharma in the fullest sense and is liberated from the cycle of reincarnation entirely.

The form of Buddhism that is dominant today in Vietnam, China, Korea, and Japan (and is also present in Tibet and Mongolia) is called Mahayana, or "the Great Vehicle." Advocates of the Mahayana questioned the sharp division between laity and monastics characterizing those rival sects that the Mahayanists called Hinayana (of which the only denomination surviving today is the Theravada, "Way of the Elders," that is predominant in southeast Asia and in Sri Lanka). The Mahayana presents itself in its scriptures as an inclusive path open to all, rather than an exclusive or narrow path in which one can enter nirvana only through the gateway of the monastery. One of the other doctrinal developments that set the Mahayana apart from rival schools was a new conception of the goal of the religion. Advocates of the Mahayana presented their ideal as the aspiration to the full and complete awakening of the Buddha, a larger goal than that of passing away from the realm of birth and death in that it includes the aspiration to bring all sentient beings to awakening.

Mahayana texts problematize the goal of escaping the realm of birth and death from moral and philosophical viewpoints. In its sutras (the *sutra* form in a genre of Buddhist text that represents a particular occasion in which the Buddha taught a lesson), the Buddha is shown to interpret in significantly different ways what he is said to have taught in the sutras of other Buddhist traditions; where new viewpoints are presented, they are explained as secret teachings that the Buddha taught to bodies of advanced beings, such as bodhisattvas, in private settings. To focus on eliminating one's own craving and hence alleviating one's own dissatisfaction is to ignore the needs of others and thus is morally questionable. But to emphasize the idea of a self on whom one focuses one's practice is to show flawed thinking from a philosophical point of view, for no such entity exists. Human beings (and other sentient beings as well) are compound entities consisting of physical and psychic elements. We are combinations or aggregates of component parts, and there is no empirical evidence accepted by Buddhists for a soul or self that dwells within. Hence one cannot alleviate one's own suffering without also alleviating the suffering of others.

The Mahayana ideal of the bodhisattva is derived from earlier usages of the term, but it has the technical meaning of an aspirant to Buddhahood who remains within the realm of birth and death. The Mahayana bodhisattva is thus a type of saint; the term derives from earlier usages of the term *bodhisattva,* which refer to the former lives of the Buddha when he aspired to the future state of Buddhahood. But the term takes on new meaning in Mahayana contexts, as the primary expression of what it means to focus on the needs of all sentient beings. Part of the grandness of this Mahayana vision of salvation is that to aspire to become a bodhisattva requires both the courage to suffer within *samsara* (the cycle of reincarnation) and the wisdom to see that nirvana is already achieved. According to the doctrine of emptiness, a philosophical orientation that is systematically expressed by Mahayana philosophers such as Nagarjuna (c. 150–250 CE) but is also articulated in other Mahayana texts, each form that one takes within the realm of birth and death is empty of enduring essence. Each of the component parts that together compose the human being (including the physical organs of the body as well as sensations, perceptions, volition, and consciousness itself) is a transient phenomenon that arises and ceases through a combination of various factors. Neither the component parts nor the human being they make up can be said to have any enduring reality.

One of the most compact of all the Mahayana sutras is the Heart Sutra. In it, the bodhisattva Avalokiteshvara surveys the world from the perspective of perfect wisdom and finds no suffering, no cause of suffering, no extinction of suffering, and no path that leads to the extinction of suffering. All components of the human being, Avalokiteshvara declares, are empty. The eye, the ear, the nose, and the tongue, as well as the sights, sounds, smells, and tastes that these organs apprehend, are empty of own-being, or essence. We cannot say of these organs (or of the sights, sounds, smells, and tastes they bring us) that they come into existence and pass away, or that they may be characterized by suffering or dissatisfaction. When seen from the perspective of perfect wisdom, eyes, ears, noses, mouths, sights, sounds, smells, and tastes do not arise and do not cease.

It is natural to assume that for Mahayana Buddhists, emptiness is something like what God is for Jews, Muslims, and Christians, or that emptiness is something like what Hindu philosophers call *brahman*—that ultimate reality from which all things emerge and to which all things will return. Were this the case, exponents of the way of emptiness would have us look beyond the empirical world to find the ultimate reality that is its source. But as Avalokiteshvara goes on to observe in the course of the Heart Sutra, emptiness is not a separate existence or reality but is just "form" itself. The physical forms that we take, with their eyes and other sense organs, are empty of enduring essence, and emptiness is none other than physical form itself. It is none other than our eyes and the sights we see—not something that we will know when our sense organs have ceased to function. Apart from form, there is no emptiness and no alleviation of suffering. Apart from samsara, there is no nirvana. Given this nondifference, the unsatisfactoriness of life is ultimately nothing to fear. By virtue of the nature of the cycle of birth and death (when properly understood with the eyes of perfect wisdom), nirvana is already attained. Hence one need not renounce domestic life and seek to eradicate craving. Craving, when properly understood, is nirvana itself.

Vajrayana Buddhism is the dominant form of the tradition in Tibet, Mongolia, and elsewhere in central Asia. With the rise of Vajrayana Buddhism (or "the Way of the Thunderbolt") in India and south Asia from about the seventh century of the common era, Mahayana insights into the indistinguishability of samsara and nirvana were set forth in a thunderbolt-fast path, promising the experience of nirvana in this very lifetime. Also known as Tantric Buddhism (from *tantra,* the Sanskrit term for "weave" that denotes a body of esoteric scriptures), the Vajrayana shares many of the presuppositions of Hindu tantric texts, including the importance of ritual as a means of breaking down false distinctions that make salvation well-nigh impossible in this present degenerate age. The Vajrayana offers esoteric methods (taught only to initiates) for transforming the three poisons of attraction, revulsion, and ignorance into positive forces, requisites for the experience of nirvana. The poisons can thus become nectars of immortality when properly handled in ritually controlled environments. Male Vajrayana saints practiced ritualized forms of sexual union with their wives and spiritual consorts and did not follow the celibate path of monastic Buddhism. For example, Padmasambhava, who established Buddhism in eighth-century Tibet, had two principal wives. The eleventh-century translator Marpa was married and had eight other spiritual consorts.

## Expansion of Buddhism in the West

During the age of exploration and colonial interventions in Asia, Western observers saw the practice of Buddhism first-hand. So diverse were the practices of Buddhists in Japan and Sri Lanka that the first Western observers did not recognize these practices as belonging to the same religion. Civil servants and other representatives of Western nations traveling and living in Asia expressed interest in the forms of Buddhism they witnessed during the early modern period. Because of such cultural exchanges, the study and dissemination of Asian religious texts has contributed to the development of European and American philosophical discourses. Such cultural exchanges have also contributed to the development of new forms of modern Buddhism. In mid-nineteenth-century colonial Sri Lanka (Ceylon, at the time), Mohottivatte Gunananda and Anagarika Dharmapala combined forces with one of America's first Buddhists, a man named Henry Steel Olcott, to combat the spread of Christianity and the decline of Buddhism in Ceylon. The resulting synthesis of Protestant reliance on the inward and suspicion of ritual forms with Buddhist claims about supernormal powers resulted in what many scholars have termed "Protestant Buddhism." Stephen Prothero's *The White Buddhist: The Asian Odyssey of Henry Steel Olcott* (1996) gives an account of the fascinating life of Olcott. Similarly, modern forms of Buddhism have developed wherever Buddhism's wide swath of dissemination has placed Buddhists in dialogue with practitioners of other religions in a modern setting.

Buddhism began to appeal to a wide spectrum of subcultures in Europe and America during the twentieth century and continued to appear frequently in census data drawn in the twenty-first century. Census data in 2001 indicated, for example, that Buddhism was the fastest growing religion in Britain. Buddhism has been of interest to Americans for some time now. Jan Nattier, in "Buddhism Comes to Main Street" (1997), speaks of the "Buddhism boom" of Victorian America, when references to Buddhism began to appear frequently in mass media outlets. And because of high levels of education and income of many who identify as Buddhist in America, as well as many celebrity Buddhists, Buddhism even has adherents on Wall Street. One of the noteworthy things about contemporary Buddhism in the West is that its influence exceeds the numbers of practitioners; this phenomenon is due to the highly influential film directors, songwriters, musicians, artists, and the like who have adopted Buddhism. Indeed, one sees references to Buddhism throughout popular culture. The Dalai Lama (the official leader of the Tibetan government-in-exile and a religious leader in the Gelug school of Tibetan Buddhism) has lent his face to the marketers of Apple computers. Tibetan prayer flags are used to sell all sorts of services and products. Buddhist monks of vaguely Himalayan origin ride around in Subaru Foresters and send each other dharma lectures and jokes by computer. Late capitalism has clearly embraced the message of a man who left his kingdom and wealth behind and lived six austere years in the forest.

## Issues and Concerns

Questions about practice, sexuality, and gender are among the most interesting issues that contemporary Buddhists face as they work to realize the dharma in their lives as modern persons. A number of Buddhist communities in North America and Europe have split into factions over allegations that their leaders and other high-ranked teachers committed sexual improprieties or engaged in systematic sexual abuse. The controversies raised by these "sex scandals" have led to some useful dialogue about what is permissible in student–teacher relationships, and what kinds of expectations Buddhists bring when they enter the door of an American or European dharma center with regard to the sexual conduct of their leaders. By convening interdenominational Buddhist conferences and meetings with such figures as the Dalai Lama, gay, lesbian, and transgendered Buddhist practitioners in the West have raised the issue of sexual orientation as a topic worthy of exploration at the highest levels of Buddhist ecclesiastical discussion.

Another issue that has been raised to a high level of visibility is the provision by Buddhist priests in Japan of mourning services for aborted fetuses. Reliance on abortion as a means of family planning is widespread in contemporary Japan. Mourning services for aborted or stillborn fetuses (known as *mizuko*, or "water babies") did not exist prior to the 1960s and have been the subject of considerable controversy. Media exposés in Japan have focused on the profits Buddhist temples stand to gain by promoting these memorial services. Feminist analysts lament the social conditions that lead so many Japanese women to seek abortions, having few alternatives to abortion as a means of family planning.

As a religion originally centered on a core community of celibate monastics, Buddhists have tended to place religious value on the freedom from those domestic entanglements that follow from heterosexual activity in the absence of modern forms of birth control and abortion (at least for the select group of those who seek to put an end to dissatisfaction in this life). As we have seen, some Mahayana and Vajrayana Buddhists regard sex as a potential means of progress on the Buddhist path. Some (at least in theory) regard lay practice as equal to monastic practice. Those Buddhists, like Buddhists in Japan who have abolished the requirement of clerical celibacy, have moved away from the tendency to consider those committed to the practice of celibacy as superior to those who are sexually active. Western Buddhists have also placed less emphasis on celibacy than did their early Indian coreligionists by creating monastic or quasi-monastic roles for noncelibate practitioners.

As effective means of contraception and abortion become more widely available to contemporary Buddhists, and sex is thereby separated more and more from procreation, it is possible that some Asian Buddhists (such as Theravadins) who have traditionally maintained a clear division between monastic and lay paths will create quasi-monastic or interstitial roles that enable sexually active people to take ordination and pursue higher levels of path attainment. It is equally possible, though, that Buddhists in Asia will respond to these developments by identifying such innovations as signs of moral decay, especially given scriptural predictions about the inevitable decline of the dharma. Any shift in ecclesiastical stances toward celibacy (for example, the creation of monastic roles for noncelibate persons) might be viewed as a sign of encroachment by or thoughtless imitation of looser Western standards of sexual conduct. Concerns about Western sexual "promiscuity" might be expected most especially in postcolonial nations of Asia, where Buddhists have sought to recover and articulate what they regard as traditional practices untainted by the cultural influence of former colonial powers.

Buddhism has proved to be a highly adaptive religious tradition that has taken root in a wide variety of cultural contexts. Its insistence that the truth of the Buddhist dharma transcends concrete manifestations such as deities, spirits, and local heroes has helped to ensure that wherever Buddhists go, they can effectively join forces with many of those who would see the sacred manifest in local goddesses, gods, and demons. Such beings have their place, and the religion can flourish in almost any cultural environment. It is a religion well suited to flourish in settings such as North America and Europe, and it has made significant inroads in these places.

**See also** *Architecture: Asian Religions; Buddhism in North America; Celebrity Culture; Devotionalism; Hindu Tradition and Heritage; Zen Buddhism.*

Elizabeth Wilson

## BIBLIOGRAPHY

Coleman, James William. *The New Buddhism: The Western Transformation of an Ancient Tradition.* New York: Oxford University Press, 2001.

Eckel, Malcolm David. *Buddhism: Origins, Beliefs, Practices, Holy Texts, Sacred Places.* New York: Oxford University Press, 2002.

Fields, Rick. *How the Swans Came to the Lake: A Narrative History of Buddhism in America*. 3rd ed. Boulder: Shambhala Publications, 1992.

Harvey, Peter. *An Introduction to Buddhism: Teachings, History, and Practices*. New York: Cambridge University Press, 1990.

Lopez, Donald S. *The Story of Buddhism: A Concise Guide to Its History and Teachings*. San Francisco: Harper San Francisco, 2001.

Nattier, Jan, "Buddhism Comes to Main Street." *Wilson Quarterly* 21 (Spring 1997): 72.

Prebish, Charles S. *Luminous Passage: The Practice and Study of Buddhism in America*. Berkeley: University of California Press, 1999.

Prothero, Stephen. *The White Buddhist: The Asian Odyssey of Henry Steel Olcott*. Bloomington: Indiana University Press, 1996.

Reynolds, Frank, and Jason A. Carbine. *The Life of Buddhism*. Berkeley: University of California Press, 2000.

Seager, Richard Hugh. *Buddhism in America*. New York: Columbia University Press, 1999.

Trainor, Kevin. *Buddhism: The Illustrated Guide*. New York: Oxford University Press, 2001.

Tweed, Thomas A. *The American Encounter with Buddhism: 1844–1912*. Bloomington: Indiana University Press, 1992.

Williams, Duncan Ryuken, and Christopher S. Queen, eds. *American Buddhism: Methods and Findings in Recent Scholarship*. Richmond, UK: Curzon Press, 1999.

# California and the Pacific Rim Region

People have practiced a multitude of religions in the vast geographical area of California and the American Pacific rim region for thousands of years. This layered complex history and the resulting contemporary diversity serves as a crucible for religious innovation. Cultural diversity, an environment of great natural beauty, and its situation in the borderland regions between the United States and Mexico and the United States and the Pacific have had important roles in shaping the religious characteristics of the region. The religious character and history of the Pacific rim region of America are understandably focused on California, but its delineation needs to account for the whole Pacific coast region, from the Alaska coast and the Pacific Northwest, to the coast of the Mexico-U.S. borderlands of Baja, California, and it will also encompass Hawaii.

## *Native Religious Traditions*

Hundreds of communities existed along the Pacific coast of North America and in Hawaii before any European or Asian people were here. Most migrated into the region from other parts of North America and the Pacific. The Native American cultures were characterized by a great many small localized societies, many closely related but different languages, and a shared larger regional economy with common cultural characteristics. These communities shared an economy based in the sea, the rivers, and the coastal scrub or forests. The oldest of these religious traditions are difficult to

describe, partly because little evidence of their presence remains except for shell mounds, burial artifacts, and oral traditions, whose religious purpose and import is probable but not specifically discernable, and partly because many of their descendants do not believe it is appropriate to discuss these religious matters with outsiders or because they no longer know what the older traditions were. The Spanish were the first Europeans to arrive in the area. They were more interested in converting the Native Americans to Christianity than making note of the religion they already practiced, though Spanish accounts of their observations provide important though limited sources of information. The older traditions persisted, even when European missionaries called on colonial military power to enforce their conversion efforts.

From these traditions, explained in contemporary Native American writings, recorded by interested observers, or contained in the complaints of Christian missionaries, it is known that the native religions fostered a close connection between people and the land, looked to the leadership of wise elders or healers, or shamans, and that their ceremonies were performed for blessing, healing, or to create relationships or to ease tensions between scattered small groups. Native American religious leaders had knowledge of ceremonies and medicines used for healing and gaining spiritual power. Many native people shared cosmological and moral beliefs with each other and with European and Asian immigrants into their areas. The Pacific Island religious traditions contained elements that supported the nineteenth-century embrace of Christianity in Hawaii and Samoa and other Pacific Islands under the influence of the United States. Like other Native American traditions, Pacific Island religions also focused on the natural world, the sea, and the sky. Chiefs and shamans represented the divine. European encounters with these native traditions initiated a competition of spiritual powers.

The European arrival precipitated a sharp decline in Native American populations and traditions. Disease, cultural and economic disruption, and persistent European efforts to eliminate them as enemies combined to create a demographic disaster. Nonetheless, these native communities and traditions still exist and is some places are recovering their numbers and reviving their languages and religions, though often in the face of continued suppression and poverty. Anthropology and new age religious movements have fostered interest in Native American traditions among nonnative people. This outside interest draws a mixed reception from native people and complicates the effort to understand these religions. While outsiders often publish a great deal about Native American religions, it is important to be aware of possible misunderstandings and missing information in such accounts. Religion in native societies tends to be tribally based and its traditions embedded in an oral tradition and practice rather than in written texts, though such written texts exist.

## Colonial Introduction of Christianity

The Pacific region was touched by competing European colonial empires long before any of them settled in the region. In the sixteenth century a few European ships, Spanish and English, touched the Pacific coast of the Americas and stopped in Hawaii on the way from Mexico to the Philippines. Visits from Asian groups were not out of the question. These chance encounters did not result in religious exchange at first. The introduction of Christianity into the Pacific rim region began in the late eighteenth century. The Russians began to expand their colonial empire across the Bering Strait in 1794, down the Alaska coast, reaching the Pacific Northwest and California by the mid-nineteenth century. Russian Orthodox missionaries accompanied the commercial colonial project although the Russian Orthodox missionary activity with California Native Americans was carried out by Native Alaskan Orthodox Christians more than by Russian missionaries. Today Alaska is the center of Russian Orthodox population in the region and the majority of the Orthodox adherents are Native American. In California, Russian and Greek Orthodox immigration increased in the twentieth century.

The Spanish colonies to the south in Mexico and the expansion of the French fur trade into the Pacific Northwest brought Catholic missionaries into the region by the end of the eighteenth century as well. French Jesuit missionaries from Canada served a small population of Catholics related to the fur trade in the Rocky Mountains. The majority of the Catholic Christian expansion in the Pacific Region was related to the Spanish colonies. Anxious about the Russian expansion southward, the Spanish established a series of presidios and Franciscan missions along the coast of California beginning in 1769, meeting the southernmost Russian outpost at Ft. Ross (1812) with the establishment of the Sonoma mission and presidio (1824). Two distinctive but related Catholic communities developed on the Pacific coast: Franciscan missions in California focused on the conversion of the native people to Christianity and European ways of life, and the Catholic parishes serving the Spanish and Mexican colonists living in and around the presidios and on land grants. The Franciscan missions established by Father Junipero Serra (1713–1784) sought to encourage the native people to give up their particular way of life and live communally in the mission, learning to be Christians and members of Spanish colonial society. While the invitation to join the mission at first seemed voluntary and was actually attractive to many Native Americans, the Franciscans were willing to use coercion and violence with the support of the troops at the presidio to enforce discipline on the newly converted, and the Spanish colonial authorities often used coercion to force conversions to Christianity. In native Christian communities, whether converted by force or by choice, people blended older native traditions and beliefs with newer ones from Christianity. The resulting mission culture was shaped both by Spanish and native interests. The missions, with their close living quarters, became places where disease spread rapidly and the population of mission residents declined rapidly. As in other parts of the northernmost Spanish colonies, support for both the missions and the parish churches was thin, connections to the oversight of bishops was weak, and the result was a strong tradition of lay piety and independence. In 1836, soon after Mexico gained its independence (1821), the Franciscan missions were secularized and the Franciscan missionaries were recalled to Spain. Though a few survived as parish churches, the missions were left to decay until they were rebuilt by later arrivals, especially American Catholics with a romantic interest in the Spanish colonial period.

Because the Philippines were for a short time being considered as an American colony, from after the Spanish American War in 1898 until 1904, the meeting of Spanish Catholicism, an older Muslim religious presence, and American Protestantism should be noted. Both Muslims and Catholics vied for the attention of the native Filipino people, some of whom successfully resisted conversion by either of the traditions. In the Pacific Islands, Christianity became the predominant religion, blending native traditions with the new religion in a synthesis. In most cases, particularly Hawaii and Samoa, conversion to Christianity was instigated by social elites. In Hawaii, Kaahumanu, the queen mother, encouraged Christianity in the 1830s. In Samoa, with its system of local independent extended families, the conversion of the high chiefs resulted in the conversion of the people.

## U.S. Era and Religious Developments

The Overland Trail brought immigrants from the United States into the Pacific rim region beginning in the mid-nineteenth century. Most of these immigrants claimed adherence to some Christian denomination or Jewish community.

As the United States solidified its control of the Pacific coast in the wake of the Mexican War (1848) and the California gold rush (1849) until World War II (1942–1945), Protestant and Catholic Christians from the United States, Jews, and a few new religious movements, most notably the Latter-day Saints, or Mormons, began to establish institutional presence and worshiping communities in the region. In addition, European and African American Protestants and Catholics, Asian peoples of many religions, and Latin Americans, mostly Roman Catholic, joined the earlier Native American traditions and Spanish/Mexican Catholic layers.

Religious practice thinned out with the move east or west or north into the region. The establishment of religious institutions was slow and many people dropped their religious practice, at least in an organized form. Many others changed religious identities with a change of residence. Because the "world rushed in" to a relatively confined space in the California gold rush, people encountered many alternative religious traditions and were aware of choices not available to them before. In the transitions of the overland trail, the Pacific voyage, or the journey north or south, the commonly expected Protestant establishment characteristic of the rest of the United States broke down. By the time the Pacific region had achieved statehood, California, Oregon, and Washington—and later Hawaii and Alaska—shared with the Pacific Northwest the twin characteristics of being on the one hand the most religiously diverse regions of the United States and also the least formally affiliated population. Recent publications have referred to the Pacific Northwest region as the "none zone," but the term could apply as well to California.

From the gold rush to the world wars, California was one of the few places in the United States where the Protestants were not the dominant tradition. With a few local exceptions, the Pacific region is characterized by the lack of a dominant religious group. The characteristic Protestant establishment of the rest of the country did not materialize, even with significant immigration from heavily Protestant regions such as the Midwest and South.

Throughout the twentieth century, Catholics and Jews represented the first and second largest religious groups in California; both Catholics and Jews found better opportunities for political office than in other parts of the country. The Pacific coast cities of San Francisco and Los Angeles became the largest centers of American Jewish presence outside of New York. Jewish communities in the Pacific region were characterized by ethnic differences—German, Polish, Turkish, and Russian predominantly—each group establishing its own synagogues. In addition, Judaism was divided into Reform, Conservative, and Orthodox branches theologically. Catholicism remained a significant presence due to the Catholic immigrants from Mexico, Ireland, Italy, Germany, and the Philippines, and later from China and Vietnam.

During the twentieth century, immigrants from Asia who were already Christian also formed congregations based on their previous church ties. Until after World War II, these racially or ethnically based missions formed subgroups within the white denominations. Historically African American churches, Baptist and Methodist, also started churches in the Pacific region as blacks moved west in increasing numbers. They remained among the dominant traditions in the African American communities of the region. The Catholic Church, as the jurisdiction changed from the Mexican to the U.S. branch of the Catholic hierarchy, also fostered the development of ethnic congregations. All of the mainline Protestant and Catholic churches in this period encouraged the use of the English language, many opened schools for immigrants and for American children as well to teach English and to provide a general education from their particular religious points of view. As in other areas of the United States, in the Pacific region the prevailing ethos of the public schools was nonsectarian by policy but Protestant in unspoken ways, and Catholics tended to start their own parish school systems. Perhaps the most influential legacy of these Protestant churches is the many colleges and universities they started. The University of California had some of its roots in a Protestant college established in the 1860s.

## Religious Diversity in the Region

As a total group, Protestants outnumber other religious traditions in the region; however, no single Protestant denomination attracted enough members to become a dominant group. All of the mainline Protestant traditions (Baptist, Congregational, Disciples of Christ, Episcopalian, Lutheran, Methodist, Presbyterian, and Reformed) established a presence in both rural and urban areas of the West in the post–Civil War era, competing with one another for the sparse rural population and increasingly disinterested urban population. Their home missionary societies cultivated new congregations and slowly organized the denominational structures over the course of this period. Smaller but well-established Protestant, Quaker, and Mennonite churches, as well as newer Protestant-related churches such as the Unitarian Universalists, the Seventh-day Adventists, and the Church of Christ, Scientist did well in California.

Protestantism cultivated these congregations along racial and ethnic lines. The first such efforts in the region were the mission of the American Board of Commissioners of Foreign Missions to Hawaii and the mission of the London Missionary Society in Samoa. In California, the home missionary societies of the white denominations focused most of their work on the English-speaking, mostly European-descended immigrants from other parts of the United States. In addition they formed congregations of European immigrants based on language and ethnicity. Various "foreign" missionary societies developed congregations among the former Mexican population, attempting to convert them from Catholicism. They also began mission work among the Chinese, Japanese, and later Filipino and Korean immigrants in the Pacific region, especially in Hawaii. Many of these ethnic and racial divisions in the Protestant churches were also characterized by denominational divisions because the larger Protestant churches cooperated with each other and divided up the mission work into territories to minimize their competition with each other.

In the special case of the Japanese Americans during World War II, religious communities were strained by the internment resulting from Executive Order 9066, February 14, 1942. Japanese Americans, regardless of religion, were forcibly removed from the Pacific coast areas of North America after the Japanese attack on Pearl Harbor. From 1942 until 1946, they lived for the most part in scattered internment camps in remote desert areas of the western states such as Mazanar, California; Topaz, Utah; Poston, Arizona; and Heart Mountain, Wyoming. Religious leaders were especially suspected of being possible collaborators with the Japanese government in their war against the United States and were removed from their communities. Without leaders, many Japanese religious groups had a hard time surviving. After the war, Japanese Americans' survival was further jeopardized by the appropriation of their property by others while they were gone. The Buddhist Churches of America, many Christian congregations and some smaller sects such as Tenrikyo, survived the internment and formed the nucleus of postwar growth for these groups. In Hawaii, the state governor successfully resisted the internment of the Japanese Americans in his state, allowing the religious institutions to remain in place.

Mormonism also grew significantly in the region during the mid-nineteenth century. San Francisco was an entry point for Mormons migrating to Utah. With the establishment of outposts in San Bernardino and other places in California, they hoped to improve their access to transportation and supplies for the Utah Mormon communities. In the early years the Reorganized Church, a minority tradition within Mormonism, represented the largest group of Mormons in the Pacific region, but their numbers have been eclipsed by the more mainstream Mormons based in Utah. Mormons, early in their history, engaged in missions to the Pacific Islands. Mormonism grew in Samoa as well as Hawaii, rivaling the success of the Protestants. A century later, half a million Mormons lived in the Pacific rim region representing 20 percent of the U.S. Mormon population.

Because California receives the majority of the immigrants to the United States from Asia and the Pacific Islands, Asian religions are well represented even during the eras when Asian immigration was suppressed. Before World War II, Buddhism was represented in two forms: Mahayana (from China, Japan, and Korea) and Theravada (from Southeast Asia). The Japanese-based Buddhist Churches of America borrowed institutional forms from American Protestantism. Zen Buddhism, introduced to the United States during the World Parliament of Religions in 1893, attracted American adherents in California. Confucianism, as well as Daoism, traveled with Chinese immigrants throughout the region beginning with the gold rush. Hindu and Sikh communities were present in California by the early twentieth century; the oldest Sikh *gurdwara* in the United States was established in Stockton, California, in the early twentieth century. Some forms of Hindu belief and practice also attracted American adherents outside of the immigrant communities, particularly after the World's Parliament of Religions in 1893. Muslim immigrants from the Middle East, Africa, and Southeast Asia were present in the Pacific region. Islam also appealed to many African Americans in California urban areas who joined the African American Nation of Islam or attended more mainstream mosques.

## New Religious Movements

Perhaps because of the sheer number of diverse religious groups gathered together during this period, the Pacific region, particularly California, became a crucible of religious creativity. The fastest growing form of Christianity in the world by the end of the twentieth century, Pentecostalism, while not founded in California, got its most spectacular start at the Azusa Street Revival of 1906 in Los Angeles. By the end of the twentieth century, Pentecostal adherents outnumbered mainline Protestant adherents in the region. The third largest of these Pentecostal denominations, the International Church of the Foursquare Gospel, originated with Aimee Semple McPherson (1890–1944) in Los Angeles in 1927 and initiated another creative approach by California religionists in the adoption of electronic mass media to proclaim its message and further its cause. Radio in the 1920s and 1930s and television in the 1950s and 1960s became favorite tools of Pentecostal preachers and evangelists as a result of McPherson's innovation. Pentecostalism has developed particularly strongly among marginalized and minority populations, shows great ethnic and racial diversity, and is often found in smaller, store-front churches in urban areas, or in rural areas serving migrant populations and working-class people. One of the largest African American Pentecostal denominations, the Church of God in Christ, traces its founding to Los Angeles's Azusa Street revival.

California served as the birthplace of hybrid religious movements. Nature played a role in the development of a regional sense of spirituality. John Muir (1838–1914) argued that nature was a place of spiritual renewal, that the presence of wilderness was necessary for a health society. The development of national parks fostered this sense of spiritual connection with nature, as well as ethical trends toward the preservation of the environment. A relationship developed between this sense of nature spirituality and Native American traditions, particularly notable among artists and writers, and deeply connected to the nineteenth-century Romantic Movement in the broader culture. The diversity of American religious cultures drew from many a desire to find a unified way that all people could follow. Many branches of Christianity—including Mormonism—and Islam took an exclusive view as did some Buddhist traditions. Others sought to create new religions that would provide such unity. The Bahá'í faith, representing a nineteenth-century Persian effort to unite Hinduism, Judaism, Buddhism, and Islam, attracted interest in the Pacific Region after the World Parliament of Religion. A branch of the Theosophical Society, founded in New York, but settled in California at Pt. Loma, San Diego, blended Asian mysticism with interest in healing and in the universal unity of humanity. Established religions with a more liberal or open attitude allowed their adherents to import practices from other traditions or to practice more than one tradition. Thus many Jews were drawn to Buddhist traditions such as Zen. Unitarian Universalists also sought to express unity by allowing many religious practices to coexist in one church.

Finally, the most steadily growing religious group in the region was that of the unaffiliated. It is characteristic of the region that people tend to be less religious, fewer participate in organized religious activities, and fewer consider themselves to be adherents of any particular religion. An exception to this trend are recent immigrants because religion serves as a bridge linking their past identity to their future identity and as a social support system, but the second generation often declines to participate in the churches.

After World War II, the region entered into what one historian characterized as an era of fluid identities. From the bedrock layers of Native American traditions to the new immigrant traditions, the complex layers of religious history and tradition bleed through into one another and people frequently change religious affiliations and combine older commitments with new practices in different communities. The changes in the immigration laws in the 1960s allowed increasing numbers of immigrants from Asia and the Pacific Islands, multiplying the presence of Asian religious traditions, increasing the numbers within each one already present, and contributing to a large array of choices for people increasingly inclined to seek out a religious tradition to meet their needs and interests.

## The Post–World War II Era

The period after World War II saw enormous changes in American culture: the civil rights movements, being especially strong in the African American, Chicano, and Native American communities; women's liberation; movements to increase acceptance and equality for gay, lesbian, or transgendered people; and movements galvanized by these changes, such as the antiabortion effort, opposition to the war in Vietnam, movements opposed to the inclusion and increasing openness to leadership from women or gay, lesbian, or transgendered people in religious organizations and society, and eventually the environmental movement. In the 1960s and 1970s, many religious traditions became politically active. African American churches and new movements in the black community such as the Nation of Islam supported the civil rights movement, though they did not always agree on the means. Many white churches joined the effort toward civil rights, or opened their doors to women's leadership for the first time, or became activists in opposition to the Vietnam War. Churches divided sharply over abortion, what should or should not be taught in public schools, the Vietnam War, and the role of women or those of minority sexual orientations in society. Debate about these issues characterized the post–World War II era and greatly weakened the mainline Protestant churches in particular. Popular religiosity and spirituality shaped more by video media and music than by religious institutions grew at a rapid pace. Religious motifs in rock music, popular films, and literature joined traditional scriptures, practices, and holy sites and objects in informing people's religious beliefs and practice. Rapid decline in participation in institutional religion began with the "baby boom" generation (those born 1946–1964) and intensified with their children, though the diffuse but popular hippie movement and later nondenominational megachurches enjoyed local growth and influence. Though not unique to California and the Pacific region, many of these churches were started in California. Examples include the Crystal Cathedral in Garden Grove, California, which started in a drive-in movie theater; Glide Memorial United Methodist Church in San Francisco, which grew by inviting a racially inclusive group of people to worship and serve the marginalized people of the city in what had once been a declining middle-class church; and Saddleback Community Church in Orange County, California, which began by building a basketball court. The megachurches claimed up to 20 percent of religious adherents by the end of the twentieth century. They tend to fall into the conservative evangelical theological spectrum, though Glide Memorial is liberal, and to be pioneers in using electronic media for religious purposes.

Recent passage of the Native American Freedom of Religion Act (1978) granted Native American tribes a measure of freedom to practice their religions after centuries of repression. Many small groups in California and the Pacific rim region failed to receive recognition and can still be harassed for ceremonies in which otherwise illegal substances played a sacramental part or using sacred places that have been appropriated by the dominant society.

Native American traditions along with Asian religious traditions have become popular in the mainstream culture. The commoditization of religious symbols and literature resulted in the proliferation of bookstores and other shops dedicated to resources for spiritual practice on a do-it-yourself model. Practices that in their traditions would be communal and done with oversight from designated religious leaders are offered by individuals for purchase. The state of California recognized a mail-order form of ordination as authorization to perform marriages.

## General Trends of Religion in the Pacific Rim Region

Despite the proliferation of new religious movements and the relative decline of mainline religious traditions, the persistence of Catholic, Jewish, Protestant, and Mormon congregations indicates an ongoing interest in these traditions. In the same way traditional Native American and Asian religious traditions persist even in the face of suppression or decline. Most of the religious traditions of the region are imported from elsewhere. This immigrant quality of all but the Native American traditions shapes the ethos of these religions. They exhibit a paradoxical independence and dependence in relation to their centers. For the most part, these religious traditions are centered a long way away from the Pacific region. This distance weakens the supervision of the center for its marginalized constituency. The religious history of California is filled with stories of maverick religious leaders taking their people outside the boundaries of their traditions general practice, sometimes dangerously. An example was Jim Jones, a pastor ordained in a mainline Protestant denomination, who founded the Peoples Temple in California that came to an end in Jonestown, British Guiana, in 1978 as he led the community in a mass suicide. On the other hand, in the Pacific region, most religious communities depend on the main body of their tradition for support in their early years. Since religious institutions in the region tend to be weak, this state of dependency can last a long time. These communities may never be granted enough resources to become strong institutions. While denominational identity can be strong, denominational loyalty suffered from this lack of support and from the distance most religious organizations were from the center of their tradition.

The Pacific rim region, in which most religious traditions were marginal to their cultural centers, fostered individual religious independence as well and a self-help religious style. Individuals found ways to practice their religions, or chose new ways of practicing religion that did not depend on support from the institutional authorities. The Pacific rim region is characterized by a high degree of individual or community experimentation with religion and religious practices.

The diversity of religion in California and Hawaii is such that there has never been a dominant tradition, unless the growing number of religiously unaffiliated people constitutes one. Where at least half of the population has no particular religious commitment, it is possible to curb public efforts by religiously motivated people to shape society. Diversity has its challenges also. Many of these traditions are historically hostile to one another, yet in the Pacific rim region are living closely together. Interreligious tension is present in the public arena in debates over public policy regarding marriage, education, and health care.

## Religious Trends in California

The continued development of new religious movements is also characteristic of the region, especially of California. The freedom from establishment allows for change and experimentation without risking the disapproval of religious authority. Three compelling interests combine to encourage this experimentation, interest in healing, desire for a sense of identity, and freedom from established norms, particularly the freedom to be curious about unusual or supernatural phenomena. Spiritualism, mesmerism, Pentecostalism, Christian and Religious Science, Swedenborgian mysticism, Seventh-day Adventists, and recently New Age spiritualities promote mental and physical healing as an outcome of religious practices. Traditions of Yoga, Zen meditation, and Hare Krishna chanting used physical practices to create health and healing as well as spiritual enlightenment. The California dream of paradise, made possible by mild weather and spectacular natural scenery, as well as by the extraordinary human effort of moving the necessary extra water from the rivers and lakes to the cities, creating inexpensive electricity along the way, provoked certain religious impulses. The self-help character of New Age traditions built upon the California idea that human beings could almost create a paradise. Neo-Pagan traditions have found a home in California, seeking to recover European nature-based religious practices and borrowing from other earth-centered religions of the world. The rise of the environmental movements in the twentieth century have been secular expressions of the same desire to be at home in nature.

Religion still plays an important role in creating a sense of identity for immigrants from east and west, north and south. In a culture in the United States that inevitably assigns people identities based on skin color, gender, culture, and language, religion has provided a place for immigrant people to find a sense of their own identity apart from those assigned to them. Religious community and practice allows the development of hybrid and fluid personal identity. Immigrants are often more religious than the general culture. Religious institutions provide social services, community based on language and a sense of connection to one's country of origin. Not only immigrants but many people who feel lost in the urban sprawl of the Pacific region cities are attracted to religions such as Pentecostalism, Evangelical Protestantism, or Mormonism because they are characterized by the giving of an individual name, a personal connection to both the divine and to the community. The megachurches of the new evangelical movement provide another avenue of self-help style religious life and belief. These churches offer to the individuals who agree to join a sense of personal purpose connected with divine purpose, and a sense that by deciding to join, one can fulfill this purpose.

## Religious Trends in the Pacific Islands

In the Pacific rim region, especially in Hawaii but also to some degree in the southern Pacific Islands, each island is a microcosm of the whole Pacific region. Because the islands are open on all sides to newcomers, encounters between people of different cultures are a regular part of island life. Mormons and Buddhists began their Pacific Island missions very early. Jodo Shinshu was established in Hawaii in the nineteenth century. The first Mormon temple outside of Utah was built in Hawaii in 1919. By the end of the twentieth century, the Latter-day Saints had changed their theological interpretation of the gathering of the Saints in Zion, largely because of their Pacific experience. Instead of one temple there are now hundreds. Protestant and Catholic Christianity also developed trans-Pacific communities during the twentieth century. In California and Hawaii the Roman Catholic Mass is celebrated in many Asian languages. Protestant denominations from Asia now have congregations in North America. The multireligious world is represented and concentrated in California and Hawaii.

## Borderland Religions

California not only shares a borderland quality with the Pacific region as a whole, it is part of a significant international borderland between the United States and Mexico. Because it was, until the mid-nineteenth century, part of the Spanish colonial empire and the Republic of Mexico, the region continues to share economic and cultural ties with Mexico and Latin America. Los Angeles is said to be the largest Mexican city outside of Mexico. Roman Catholicism, particularly incorporating the bicultural icon of the Virgin de Guadalupe, provides continuity of religious identity as people move back and forth across the border. This Catholicism is also shaped by Native American religions rooted in the desert environment. The New Age religious movements of the late twentieth century have been intrigued by this hybrid desert spirituality. Carlos Castaneda's *Teachings of Don Juan* (1968) inspired interest in shamanism and for some served as a guide to drug-induced religious experience. The borderlands magical realism genre of literature also conveys interest in spiritual powers associated with the land. For more than a century Anglo Protestants also sent missionaries into the borderlands area and converted a small percentage of the Latino population to mainline forms of Protestantism. In the twentieth century, Pentecostalism became the fastest growing religious tradition in the region.

## Role of Religious Influence on Society and Public Life

Unlike other regions of the United States, this region never had a history of Protestant establishment or even quasi-establishment. It is the home of strong centers of minority traditions such as Judaism, Buddhism, and other world religions. In addition, Native American traditions persist and hare reemerged in the twenty-first century after years of suppression, though native people still face enormous difficulties in regaining their right to practice their religion. Religion has been a factor in shaping public education. In the nineteenth century, public schools often taught a Protestant

Christian ethos without specific reference to any particular church. However this "nonsectarian" ethos did not include Roman Catholics or Jews and actively worked against Native American and Asian religious traditions. Roman Catholics responded by developing their parish school systems. Controversies persist today when religious groups complain about the presence or absence of particular religious practices, such as prayer or particular content such as the Bible or recognition of religious holidays, in public schools or public life in general. Conservative forms of Christianity are often associated with conservative political parties and policies. Conflict about personal moral choices such as marriage or abortion, often based in particular religious beliefs, permeate the political life of the region. The increasingly important environmental issues facing California and the Pacific rim region also create opportunities for religiously committed people to express their views about public policy. New religious movements such as the neo-pagan traditions join the Native American traditions, those sharing the nineteenth-century and early-twentieth-century sense of wilderness as a sacred reality necessary to the health of society, and the concerns of many religious about fairness and sustainability in supporting public policies that foster environmental health.

Demographic trends in the region indicate that the diversity of religion will persist. It will continue to be a crucible for creating new religious movements; however, the persistent trend of decline in interest in organized forms of religious life will probably continue.

**See also** *Buddhism in North America; Eastern Orthodox Tradition and Heritage; Frontier and Borderlands; Geographical Approaches; Great Lakes Region; Great Plains Region; Latino American Religion: Catholics, Colonial Origins; Latter-day Saints; Missions: Domestic; Mountain West and Prairie Region; Native American Religions entries; Neo-Paganism; New England Region; New Religious Movements entries; Pacific Northwest Region; Pentecostals; Sexuality and Sexual Identity; South as Region; Southwest as Region; Zen Buddhism.*

Randi Jones Walker

## BIBLIOGRAPHY

Arrington, Leonard J., and Davis Bitton. *The Mormon Experience: A History of the Latter-day Saints.* New York: Knopf, 1971.

Engh, Michael E. *Frontier Faiths: Church, Temple, and Synagogue in Los Angeles, 1846–1888.* Albuquerque: University of New Mexico Press, 1992.

Ernst, Eldon G., with Douglas Firth Anderson. *Pilgrim Progression: The Protestant Experience in California.* Santa Barbara, Calif.: Fithian Press, 1993.

Forbes, Jack D. *Native Americans of California and Nevada: A Handbook,* Healdsburg, Calif.: Naturegraph, 1969.

Frankiel, Sandra Sizer. *California's Spiritual Frontiers: Religious Alternatives in Anglo-Protestantism, 1850–1910.* Berkeley: University of California Press, 1988.

Hardwick, Susan Wiley. *Russian Refuge: Religion, Migration, and Settlement on the North American Pacific Rim.* Chicago: University of Chicago Press, 1993.

Iwamura, Jane Naomi, and Paul Spickard. *Revealing the Sacred in Asian and Pacific America.* New York: Routledge, 2004.

León, Luis D. *La Llorona's Children: Religion, Life, and Death in the U.S.-Mexican Borderlands.* Berkeley: University of California Press, 2004.

Maffly-Kipp, Laurie F. *Religion and Society in Frontier California.* New Haven, Conn.: Yale University Press, 1994.

Maffly-Kipp, Laurie, and Reid Neilson, eds. *Proclamation to the People: Nineteenth-century Mormonism and the Pacific Basin Frontier.* Salt Lake City: University of Utah Press, 2008.

Richardson, E. Allen. *East Comes West: Asian Religions and Cultures in North America.* New York: Pilgrim Press, 1985.

Roof, Wade Clark, and Mark Silk. *Religion and Public Life in The Pacific Region: Fluid Identities.* Walnut Creek, Calif.: AltaMira Press, 2005.

Rosenbaum, Fred. *Visions of Reform: Congregation Emanu-El and the Jews of San Francisco, 1849–1999.* Berkeley, Calif.: Judah L. Magnes Museum, 2000.

Sandos, James A. *Converting California: Indians and Franciscans in the Missions.* New Haven: Yale University Press, 2004.

Sarris, Greg. *Keeping Slug Woman Alive: A Holistic Approach to American Indian Texts.* Berkeley: University of California Press, 1993.

# Calvinist/Reformed Tradition and Heritage

The Reformed Tradition, of which Calvinism has been a shaping and distinguishing theology, originated in the sixteenth-century Protestant Reformation in Europe. Calvinist theology is characterized by a focus on the absolute sovereignty of God. This focus informs the other aspects for which Calvinism is best known, particularly the doctrines of human depravity, predestination, and a limited atonement. What belief in these doctrines has meant, for individual believers and societies influenced by the Reformed Tradition over time, is a rich subject of inquiry. Some have argued that election was a source of comfort for those who felt their human weaknesses deeply, while others have suggested that election created undue anxiety about salvation and damnation that led to a softening of Calvinist theology by the mid-nineteenth century. Still others have suggested that a this-worldly asceticism developed from Calvinism, in which believers focused on work and on reform of the world as a sign of favor for the next, and as a means

of fulfilling God's plan for history. The denominational, theological, and cultural heritage of the Reformed Tradition has been varied and far from static, suggesting the tradition's adaptability to different geographical and historical circumstances, as well as its continued vitality.

## Background of the Reformed Tradition in the Reformation Era

The Reformed Tradition refers to that branch of the Protestant Reformation that grew out of the reforms of Ulrich (Huldreich) Zwingli in Zurich (1484–1531) and John Calvin (Jean Cauvin) in Geneva (1509–1564). Although some scholars have argued that "Calvinist" is too narrow a term for the tradition, others have used the terms "Reformed" and "Calvinist" interchangeably. The "Reformed Tradition" is a more inclusive term than "Calvinism," since Calvinism often refers to a particular set of beliefs to which Reformed theologians and churches have not always adhered over time. This article will use the term "Reformed Tradition" to refer to those groups and denominations whose lineage is rooted in the reforms of Zwingli and Calvin during the Reformation, and "Calvinism" to refer to the theology specifically identified with Calvin and referred to as such by its practitioners.

Zwingli initiated his reforms in Zurich, Switzerland, in the early 1520s. Abuses of the indulgence system were common in Switzerland as in Martin Luther's (1483–1546) Germany. Although traditionally sold as pardons for the remission of temporal punishments due to sins, some in the medieval Roman Catholic Church had also begun selling indulgences for the remittance of punishments in purgatory, for the living and for their deceased relatives. Mercenary activity was also rampant, as Swiss troops fought for European monarchs and the pope in exchange for pensions and gifts that often enriched captains while killing scores of ordinary soldiers. Zwingli began his attacks on the existing leadership with criticisms of this mercenary activity. His decisive break with Rome came in the early 1520s. Though he always took care to differentiate himself from Luther and to suggest that he had developed his ideas separately, Zwingli was nevertheless aware of Luther's writings, admired his courage, and condemned what he saw as the church's persecution of the man, leading ultimately to his own decisive break with Rome. Zwingli attacked, as did Luther, the idea that works and money could buy salvation, and emphasized justification by faith alone. However, he went beyond Luther's magisterial reformation by arguing that the religious celebration of the mass was a mere remembrance of

The Reformed Tradition refers to that branch of the Protestant Reformation that grew out of reforms initiated by Ulrich Zwingli and John Calvin, pictured. Calvin was influenced by humanism and the Renaissance-era turn toward the classics as an ideal to be recaptured. His arrival in 1536 helped transform Geneva, Switzerland, into a vibrant center of the Reformed Tradition.

biographical evidence about how Calvin's experiences shaped his theology is sparse, especially compared to the evidence that exists for Luther, as a student Calvin was influenced by humanism, the Renaissance-era turn toward the classics as an ideal to be recaptured by the present age. Zwingli, too, had found humanism compelling, and both his and Calvin's emphasis on ancient biblical examples as representing the best models for life and for the church reflect their humanistic education. During this period Lutheran ideas and works circulated among Calvin and his peers, and Calvin himself left Paris at the end of 1533 because of suspicion that he was a Lutheran. In late 1534, he moved to Basel, Switzerland, where he wrote the first edition of the *Institutes of the Christian Religion*. In 1536 he came to Geneva, which he would transform, despite some internal conflict and a brief interlude in Strasbourg, France, into a vibrant center of the Reformed Tradition.

In Calvin's Geneva, church and state had separate, though often overlapping, jurisdictions. The church focused on spiritual affairs, while the secular government focused on external behavior. Yet the Consistory, the disciplinary arm of the church, would often turn violators of church discipline or morality over to the secular government to be punished. The Protestant belief in the priesthood of all believers under God meant that the church in Geneva was less hierarchical than the Roman Catholic Church, yet the Consistory's oversight into the lives and affairs of Genevan residents was more rigorous than they had previously experienced. Calvin's theology, in which God was so "other" from humanity as to prevent his being captured in symbol or statuary, also imparted a typically Reformed iconoclasm to Geneva, as had been the case in Zurich.

Though some Genevan residents chafed under the oversight of the Consistory and its partnership with civil magistrates in punishing people for spiritual and moral matters, Geneva became a magnet for persecuted Protestants, not only because of its reputation for success in reforming church and society, but also because of its academy. The Reformed Tradition began to spread rapidly in the second half of the sixteenth century, as Protestant exiles from other European countries came to Zurich and Geneva and then brought Reformed ideas back to their respective countries and beyond. John Knox (1514–1571) carried Reformed ideas to Scotland. Reformed Protestants in France, known as Huguenots, fought for legal toleration, which they eventually won after much persecution and years of forced exile. After similar struggles, Reformed churches eventually

Christ's sacrifice, in which Christ was present spiritually but not physically, and by replacing the liturgy with a preaching service focused on the word of God. Zwingli also focused his energies on the moral reform of society, instituting a civic morals court in Zurich. In addition, he attacked the trappings of what he believed were false worship practices much more vehemently than did Luther, imparting an iconoclastic spirit to his reforms in Zurich.

Zwingli fell on the battlefield in 1531. Because of his untimely death, he did not exert as profound an influence on the Reformed Tradition as Calvin. He lived to see the Reformation in much of Switzerland, but it was Calvin who contributed a theological basis to the tradition, and important ideas about church polity, that gave the movement the vitality and adaptability to spread throughout Europe and across the Atlantic.

Calvin received his education in the cities of Paris and Orléans in France, where he studied the law. Though dominated the northern provinces of the Netherlands, and the Reformed Tradition even spread to Hungary and the Polish-Lithuanian Commonwealth. Reformed Protestants also brought their faith to the New World. French Huguenots who settled in Brazil, for instance, performed the first Reformed service in the Americas in 1557. Huguenots also participated in the settling of Port Royal (Parris Island, South Carolina) in 1562.

In England, Henry VIII (r. 1509–1547) had only partially shorn the church of its Catholic roots; Reformed ideas exercised much more influence under his son, Edward VI (r. 1547–1553). During Edward's reign, publication of books by Protestant reformers, which had previously been suppressed by long-standing medieval-era statutes, burgeoned, including those written by Calvin and his followers. Calvin's ideas also spread when Reformed exiles from other countries came to England during Edward's reign. Edward's sister and successor, Mary I (r. 1553–1558), was a Catholic, however, and Reformed Protestants fleeing persecution under her reign went to Switzerland, where they were further exposed to Reformed theology and church polity. Upon their return after the ascension of Elizabeth I (r. 1558–1603), Reformed theology lived, though often uneasily, within the Church of England.

In the early seventeenth century, Puritan dissenters began to criticize the Church of England for losing its theological and ethical rigor. Calvinists were among the first settlers in Jamestown, Virginia. Separatist dissenters, known as the Pilgrims, who felt that the church could not be reformed, settled in Plymouth in 1620, while Puritan nonseparatists, who believed they could create a model society in the New World as an example for the Church of England to emulate, began immigrating to Massachusetts Bay in 1628. Eventually almost 20,000 English Puritans would make their way to Massachusetts between 1620 and 1640, establishing the first permanent Reformed settlements in the New World. Particular Baptists who immigrated to America from England also subscribed to Calvinist principles (that is, "particular" election), adopting a modified version of the Westminster Confession of Faith in a 1742 convention in Philadelphia.

Reformed Protestants also came to North America from the Netherlands, as Dutch Protestants settled New York (then New Amsterdam) as early as 1623. Scots and Scots-Irish Presbyterians immigrated to North America in large numbers in the early eighteenth century and beyond, settling in the piedmont regions of the Carolinas and Georgia, the Hudson valley, western Pennsylvania, and Virginia.

Reformed Protestants from Germany also came to America beginning in the late seventeenth century, many of them settling in Pennsylvania as well.

## Characteristic Beliefs

The Reformed Tradition has its theological basis in Calvin's *Institutes of the Christian Religion* (first edition 1536), and in the classic confessions of the tradition: the First Helvetic Confession (1536), the Belgic Confession (1561), the Heidelberg Catechism (1563), the Thirty-Nine Articles of the Church of England (1563), the Second Helvetic Confession (1566), the Canons of the Synod of Dort (1618–1619), and the Westminster Confession of Faith (1647).

The central identifying characteristic of the Reformed Tradition is belief in the absolute sovereignty, majesty, and "otherness" of God. From this central belief emerges the other doctrines for which Calvinism is best known (codified by the Synod of Dort, and commonly given by the acronym TULIP):

- Total depravity: humans cannot save themselves;
- Unconditional election: God alone acts in salvation, and predestines whom he will save independently of humankind's good works;
- Limited atonement: Christ's sacrifice on the cross saves only those whom God predestined for salvation (as opposed to making salvation available to all humankind);
- Irresistible grace: the elect cannot resist salvation; and
- Perseverance of the saints: the elect can never fall from grace.

Rather than representing unchanging ideas to which those in the Reformed Tradition have unquestioningly hewed through the ages, these beliefs have existed in creative tension with each other and with others and have been modified, explained, developed, and contested by theologians and laypeople in the Reformed Tradition over time.

### Calvin's Theology

In fact, though Calvinism is perhaps best known for the doctrine of predestination, and though that doctrine is the one that opponents most frequently seized on in criticizing the theological tradition, Calvin himself had not intended predestination to be a central, terror-inducing, or unifying principle. Rather, he saw it as one of many mysteries with which humans have to contend, such as why some suffer or prosper in this life while others do not, and why some reject the gospel while others embrace it. Calvin believed that election should be a source of comfort to the saints, much as Luther's emphasis on justification by grace alone was supposed to alleviate the anxieties of having to work for or purchase salvation within the Roman Catholic Church. If God alone took care of matters of salvation or damnation, human beings simply had to submit themselves to his will and work for his glory rather than subsume themselves in self-interested worry about their eternal welfare. Calvin's emphasis on the sovereignty of God was meant to take human beings' focus away from themselves and toward God, whose will for the world, regardless of the outcomes of individual sinners, was good and desirable. The doctrine of the perseverance of the saints provided additional comfort to the elect: if they could never fall from grace, they could devote their energies to serving others and God without worrying about themselves.

Calvin's theological writings also covered much more than the doctrine of predestination. He devoted much thought, for instance, to the problem of how fallen humans can know anything of God. He suggested that all humans can obtain a general knowledge of God by studying the Creation, though only the scripture reveals God's plan of salvation. Calvin's belief that the Creation manifests the glory of God, and that pondering the Creation enhances worship of its creator, meant that he was far from opposed to the study of the natural sciences, though some historians have accused him of such. Others have argued that Calvin's appreciation of the natural world fostered a spirit of scientific enquiry in those countries most influenced by the Reformed Tradition.

Though Calvin believed that study of the Creation was important, he also emphasized the importance of studying the scripture as a guide to the life of the individual and the church. Though God in his absolute power was unknowable, Calvin argued that God accommodated himself to mankind through the revealed Word. This focus on the Word informed Reformed worship, as often-lengthy sermons took center stage, rather than the mass or the liturgy. Theological education was also centrally important to Calvin, and the founding of seminaries and colleges has been an important characteristic of the Reformed Tradition in general. Calvin established an academy in Geneva in 1559, which contributed to the city's international reputation. More academies were founded as the Reformed Tradition spread throughout Europe, and then in the New World.

Calvin also believed in the importance of organizing the church according to God's revealed Word. Whereas Luther felt that church organization depended on historical context, Calvin argued that church polity should have a theological basis. Ironically, Calvin's emphasis on biblically correct church polity had to do with the historical context in which the Reformed Tradition developed. Unlike Lutheranism, which had the support of the state in much of Germany, Reformed Christians often faced hostility and outright persecution from Catholic governments, such as in France and in Marian England. A strong and independent church structure, which could cooperate with the state when possible (as in Geneva, when the Consistory and civil magistrates worked together to punish immorality and the like), or which could function on its own when not, was vital to the continuance and geographical spread of the tradition. Geneva represented the working out in practice of Calvin's ideas, summarized in his *Ecclesiastical Ordinances* of 1541. Calvin divided the church (biblically, he believed) into a fourfold ministry consisting of pastors, teachers, elders, and deacons, plus two committees: the Company of Pastors overseeing doctrinal unity, and the Consistory overseeing disciplinary matters.

Calvin's *Institutes* became one of the most influential texts of the Reformation era, yet as his biographers have pointed out, he was also much occupied with the day-to-day affairs of Geneva, and his primary interest was not in codifying a unified system centering on one doctrine, but in seeing his ideas carried out in practice. The publication history of the *Institutes,* which Calvin first published as a sort of catechism in 1536, shows how he developed his ideas over time and in a somewhat piecemeal fashion. His later editions of the *Institutes* were not just republications of the same original text, but vastly expanded, and sometimes sprawling, improvements on the original. The final 1559 edition, organized into four parts, on (1) knowledge of God as creator, (2) knowledge of Jesus Christ as redeemer, (3) modes of obtaining grace in Christ, and (4) the true versus false church and sacraments, represented a complex theological masterpiece that continues to be read and interpreted by scholars and theologians today.

## Theological Debates, Post-Calvin

Calvin's followers codified his theology into the five doctrines known as the TULIP formulation, argued over the meanings of predestination, and made it a defining mark of the tradition, especially in attempting to differentiate it from other branches of the Protestant Reformation. Explaining and living with such doctrines, however, was not always an easy task for Reformed clergy and laity. Who were the elect?

How did a person know if he or she was predestined to salvation? How was mankind to know anything about a completely other and completely divine God who chose to save some and not others for reasons unknown?

Reformed critics of Calvin's theology, such as Jerome Bolsec (birthdate unknown–1584), questioned the doctrine of predestination, believing that it could lead to apathy, or worse, undue anxiety, and that it detracted from effective preaching, since it suggested that men could do nothing to alter their eternal states. These critics believed that the doctrine was overly harsh in its diminishment of human agency and its ascription of salvation or damnation to God's inscrutable will alone. Theodore Beza (Théodore de Bèze, 1519–1605), the first rector of the academy at Geneva, argued to the contrary. He was particularly adamant that the Bible taught double predestination—in other words, that God predestined men to damnation as well as to salvation. Not all Reformed leaders who accepted Calvin's arguments about predestination as a sign of God's grace agreed with Beza or with Bolsec. The Second Helvetic Confession of 1566, the most important and widely adopted Reformed confession of the late sixteenth century, smoothed over these disagreements, stating that God predestined men to salvation but ignoring whether or not he also predestined them to damnation. The Confession also stated that church polity should be based on the Bible but did not say precisely how, allowing for flexibility as the Reformed tradition spread through different historical contexts.

Controversy over predestination never fully subsided as Calvinism spread beyond the borders of Geneva and Switzerland. A particularly important late-sixteenth- and early-seventeenth-century controversy occurred in the Netherlands, when Jacobus Arminius (1560–1609), a former student of Beza's, challenged the doctrine of double predestination, beginning in 1591. According to Arminius and his followers, God foresaw but did not predetermine who would be saved and who would be damned. Arminians argued that predestination in the form of predetermination (as opposed to foreknowledge) made God tyrannical, arbitrary, and capricious in his choice of whom to save and whom to damn. Humans, according to Arminians, had a part in bringing about their own salvation. The Synod of Dort convened to oppose the Arminian critique and to state the definitive Calvinist position in 1619, and the five doctrines known as TULIP represent its formulations.

Yet Arminianism, as the human agency position came to be known, and debates over theology in the Reformed Tradition, continued to thrive. In England, for instance, controversies between so-called Arminians such as Archbishop William Laud (1573–1645), who placed great importance on the sacraments and ceremonies of the church, and English divines, who emphasized personal devotion and piety, shook the Church of England in the early seventeenth century, leading to the migration of the Pilgrim and Puritan dissenters to the New World. These dissenters, and the English divines who influenced them, were more concerned with the signs of salvation and attaining assurance thereof than their Reformed counterparts elsewhere. They suggested that believers could find assurance by self-examination of their own experiences and behavior, a kind of devotional and practical piety that some scholars term "experimental predestinarianism," and that conflicted with Laud's emphasis on the sacraments. Opponents of both sacramentalism and experimental predestinarianism, however, such as Anne Hutchinson (1591–1643) in the Massachusetts Bay colony, charged that it was essentially Arminianism as well, but their positions often erred toward the other extreme of Antinomianism, the rejection of any authority and signs but the Spirit. "Moderate Calvinists" grappled with balancing the two extremes, while "high Calvinists" vigorously argued for the doctrine of double predestination.

The Westminster Confession of Faith (completed in England in 1647) ignored controversies between double predestinarians and those who argued that God only elected humankind to salvation. It rejected Arminian impositions and reaffirmed the classic Reformed doctrines of divine sovereignty, the imputation of Adam's sin onto mankind, the imputation of Christ's salvation onto the elect, and the perseverance of the saints. It represented the definitive theological position of Reformed English divines, to which Reformed Anglo-Americans also subscribed, and to which some Reformed denominations today continue to adhere. Reformed statements of faith continue to be written and revised, as in the United Church of Christ's "Statement of Faith" (1959), but the heyday of Reformed confession writing ended with the definitive statements of the seventeenth century.

## Reformed Theology in North America

Reformed theology in North America exhibited much of the same dynamism, debates, and variety as it had in Europe. Though some scholars have criticized religious histories of America that begin with the New England divines, the Puritans and their successors exercised a theological influence on future generations that was disproportionate to their relatively small numbers. Such eminent thinkers as Jonathan Edwards (1703–1758) gave the Reformed Tradition in America an international reputation, and the universities, seminaries, and voluntary societies organized by Reformed ministers gave the tradition an intellectual dominance against which many other strains of religious thought in America had to contend and define themselves.

## Puritanism

The Westminster Confession of Faith was completed several decades after the Puritans first began migrating to America, and while it restated accepted and generally noncontroversial positions, the Puritans still grappled with how to balance paradoxes in Calvinist theology: between God's inscrutability and the ability of mankind to know him and to know of him; between absolute sovereignty and divine accommodation; between God's justness and God's mercy; and between election and free will. To address these issues, the Puritans drew on a theology of the covenant derived from close study of the Old Testament and God's dealings with the Israelites. Covenant theology had been first advanced by Reformed theologian Zacharias Ursinus (1534–1583) of Heidelberg, Germany, who distinguished between the legal covenant of works and the salvific covenant of grace. According to covenant theology, God continued to make special agreements with chosen nations. The Puritans who migrated to the New World believed that God had made a covenant with them as his new Israel, whereby he deigned to abide by certain knowable laws governing his conduct, on the condition that his people abide by the rules that he set for them in scripture. Covenant theology suggested that although only the elect were offered the covenant of grace by Christ's atonement, all within a chosen nation were obligated to abide by the covenant of works given by God to Adam. Failure to do so would imperil the nation and would almost surely serve as a sign that the noncomplying individual was not one of the elect.

This was only one sign among many. Puritan theologians devoted much thought to the order of salvation, which included preparing the heart, by humiliation and contrition, for God's saving call to the elect; responding to God's call through faith; justification, in which God imputed Christ's sacrificial righteousness onto the sinner; sanctification, in

which the elect lived a holy life according to God's revealed Word; and finally, glorification in heaven after death. Both the elect and the nonelect could live moral lives according to the covenant of works, but only the elect did so out of gratitude for their regeneration.

Covenant theology and the signs of regeneration laid out by Puritan theologians helped to alleviate some uneasiness with Calvinism's paradoxes; the Puritans' deep piety and awe of an unpredictable God eased, for some, the anxieties that remained. To the Puritans, it was natural and indeed, necessary, that God have the freedom to be unpredictable. Fallen humanity deserved to be condemned; God's choice to redeem even a few was infinitely merciful. In the words of well-known historian of Puritanism Perry Miller: "It was better in Puritan eyes that most men be passed over by this illumination and left to hopeless despair rather than that all men should be born without the hope of beholding it, or that a few should forgo the ecstasy of the vision." As the Puritan settlements grew and spread geographically, the Reformed clergy in New England debated and modified the requirements for church membership and benefits. In the Cambridge Platform of 1648, the New England congregations had affirmed that the only biblical model for the church was the individual congregation, though larger synods could be convened when necessary. As in Reformation-era Zurich and Geneva, the platform gave power to secular magistrates to punish immoral behavior, as well as blasphemy and heresy. The synod also decided that full membership of the church should be restricted to those who were able to offer testimony of saving grace, though all were required to attend church. Although this may have worked for the first generation, full church membership declined over succeeding generations, and a synod convened in 1662 decided, in what came to be known as the Half-way Covenant, that children of the baptized but unconverted ("half-way members" or noncommunicant members who had yet to give saving testimony) could also be baptized, as long as their parents acknowledged the historical faith of the church and agreed to live according to the moral code in God's revealed Word. Solomon Stoddard (1643–1729), pastor of the New England frontier town of Northampton, took the Half-way Covenant even further, by softening the requirements for Communion as well: because only God could know what counted as genuine conversion, the church could not presume to exclude people from the Lord's Supper on the basis of external signs of regeneration. Rather, since the Lord's Supper could itself be a means of grace, it should be open to more than just professed converts. Stoddard's position stirred much controversy.

## Jonathan Edwards

In fact, Stoddard's grandson, Jonathan Edwards, was ambivalent about his grandfather's support of the Half-way Covenant, and much preoccupied by the question of how to discern true conversion, so that one could have confidence in one's salvation. Edwards was at the center of the revivals that swept New England in the mid-eighteenth century, known by most historians as the Great Awakening (although the "greatness" of the revivals and the singularity of the "awakening" have both been disputed). After the deaths of two youths in the 1730s, Edwards urged his Northampton congregants to live morally and to focus on the life to come, establishing prayer meetings and using the tragedies as a means of guiding people to conversion. Edwards's preaching was effective in bringing people to a conviction of their sin and the need for regeneration, and he published an account of the revival that made him and the town of Northampton internationally famous. Yet just as news of the revival spread to England and Scotland, the revival itself ebbed with the suicides of several unstable townspeople who took Edwards's warnings about the very real power of Satan to heart.

Revivals swept America again with the arrival of George Whitefield (1714–1770) in 1740. However, Edwards's experience with the ups and downs of revivalism led him to be more skeptical about the durability of religious enthusiasm than he had been in the 1730s, and to more deeply consider the meaning and signs of true and lasting conversion. Edwards did not support religious experience at the expense of intellectual rigor. Like the seventeenth-century Puritan theologians, he sought to balance piety and intellect, because too excessive a focus on either could lead to the pernicious and recurring challenges to Reformed theology of Antinomianism and Arminianism. Instead, Edwards upheld the paradoxical Calvinist doctrines of both election and free will, modifying and expanding on the ideas of his forefathers for a generation moving toward the Enlightenment. He challenged the optimism of the Enlightenment by reaffirming the doctrine of original sin, yet argued that despite such sin, humans still had free will because nothing external or natural (such as pain or physical constraints) prohibited them from acting according to their moral inclinations. Edwards also reaffirmed the doctrine of election: since God

created and thus determined human moral inclinations, he elected whom he would to be regenerated. Those who were damned were hence paradoxically damned not by external hindrances but by their God-created free wills.

Edwards's definition of regeneration flowed from his understanding of the nature of God and Creation. Unlike some Enlightenment thinkers, who asserted that God's purpose in Creation was human happiness, Edwards argued that God creates the world moment by moment, and that his purpose is to radiate his glory outward as the sun continually radiates its light and warmth. Regeneration consists of God changing the heart of the sinner away from love of self toward love for "being in general," or what Edwards also called the "consent of being to being." Although Satan could imitate religious enthusiasm in those affected by revivals, only God could act directly on the convert's heart through spiritual and not scientifically explicable means, sometimes manifesting in converts' ecstatic sense of being enveloped by God.

## Liberals, New Divinity, and Old Calvinists

Edwards died at the height of his intellectual powers because of a smallpox vaccination gone awry; his successors were left to systematize his theological innovations for future generations. They did so amidst the splintering of the Reformed clergy into rival factions as a result of the mid-eighteenth-century revivals. Those who had opposed the revivals, known as the "Old Lights," believed that the revivals' emphasis on a change of heart was too individualistic and diminished the importance of a life of obedience within the covenanted community. Those who had supported the revivals were known as the "New Lights." By the late eighteenth century, three roughly drawn groups emerged as a result of these divisions in the Anglo-American Reformed Tradition: the Arminian or liberal faction, the moderate or Old Calvinists, and the Edwardseans or New Divinity.

Men such as Jonathan Mayhew (1720–1766), Ebenezer Gay (1696–1787), and Charles Chauncy (1705–1787) led the Arminian or liberal faction. They had opposed the revivals on the grounds that the religious enthusiasm that resulted was not a sign of conversion, and they emphasized the emotions over the intellect. Highly attuned to late-eighteenth-century Enlightenment-driven criticisms of Calvinism by Deists and early Universalists, Liberals softened the Calvinist focus on God's ultimate sovereignty and mankind's inability and focused instead on the importance of virtue and morality. Chauncy even suggested that all might eventually be saved. The Unitarians trace their origins to these early liberalizers of the Reformed Tradition in America.

The Edwardseans or New Divinity consisted of the New Light supporters and students of Jonathan Edwards, and their students in turn, who supported the mid-eighteenth-century revivals, and who played prominent roles as preachers and theologians in the revivals of the late-eighteenth and nineteenth centuries, known as the Second Great Awakening. Samuel Hopkins (1721–1803) was the man primarily responsible for systematizing Edwards's thought into what became known as the "New Divinity." Hopkins grounded Edwards's aesthetic love for "Being in general" into a more specific and prescriptive focus on what he called "disinterested benevolence." According to Hopkins, holiness consisted in the transformation of self-love, which he considered the essence of sin, into love of others. Hopkins's famous idea that believers should be willing to be damned for the glory of God, stemmed from his belief that a too-narrow focus on one's salvation or damnation is selfish, and that one's energies should instead be spent on the amelioration of moral and social ills and the betterment of society. One can see, in Hopkins's theology, Calvin's idea that predestination was a source of comfort meant to take believers' attention away from their own eternal welfare toward the welfare of others and the reformation of the world. The New Divinity men were strong proponents of revivals. They drew on Edwards's distinction between the moral and natural ability of the will, to argue that since everyone had a natural ability to convert, they could blame no one but themselves for failing to do so.

The moderate or Old Calvinists, who grew out of the Old Light opposition to the mid-eighteenth-century revivals, believed that the Edwardseans were metaphysicians whose ideas were too speculative, and they deemphasized the importance of the church and means of grace in helping sinners live moral lives leading to regeneration. Men such as Hopkins believed that the means of grace, such as sermons, prayers, and meditation, damned the unregenerate the more they used them and yet remained unregenerate. In contrast, Old Calvinists believed that the means of grace, offered continually through the church as opposed to in occasional revivals, were effective. They also believed that the unregenerate should be exhorted to behave morally as a means of urging them toward regeneration, as well as ensuring a moral society. The Old Calvinists rejected the New Divinity's belief that self-love was sin and instead believed that

appeals to self-love could encourage the unregenerate toward true piety.

## Princeton, New Haven, and Oberlin Theologies

By the mid-nineteenth century, Princeton became the bastion of conservative Calvinism in America. In 1837 the Presbyterians split into Old School and New School factions, which were roughly the heirs to the Old Calvinist/ Edwardsean split of the late eighteenth and early nineteenth century. The Old School Presbyterians at Princeton saw themselves as the conservators of Calvinism, appealing to the Westminster Confession of Faith and biblical authority. Southern conservatives such as Robert Lewis Dabney (1820–1898) and James Henley Thornwell (1812–1862) also saw themselves as conservators of Calvinist tradition; their literal reading of the Bible's discussions of slavery led them to support the institution as biblically sanctioned, and social hierarchies as a natural result of the depravity of man.

In New Haven, Connecticut, by contrast, Nathaniel William Taylor (1786–1858), who identified as an Edwardsean, nevertheless emphasized the moral agency of mankind more than earlier Edwardseans ever had. Taylor argued that sin was a voluntary though permanent condition of mankind, and that it was humans' continual choice to sin, though they could choose the opposite, that endangered their eternal welfare. Taylor saw himself as balancing free will against original sin, though some Edwardseans and conservative Calvinists accused him of jettisoning that most fundamental of Reformed doctrines in his effort to make Calvinism conform to the ecumenical evangelical goal of urging sinners to voluntarily stop sinning and convert.

Though he was a Presbyterian and later a Congregationalist, Charles Grandison Finney (1792–1875), perhaps the preeminent revivalist of the antebellum era, also faced accusations of jettisoning Calvinism and the doctrine of election. Finney's main interest lay in evangelizing and exhorting sinners to take responsibility for their own conversions. He minced no words in accusing conservative Calvinists of preaching a theology that was not conducive to converting sinners. He felt that the old doctrines encouraged laypeople to simply wait for God to act on their hearts, and to blame God for not doing so if they failed to convert, rather than to blame themselves. Like Taylor, Finney won criticism from those who sought to uphold a more traditional Calvinism subscribing to the Westminster Confession. Yet his theology, which he taught at Oberlin College in Ohio, proved immensely influential, particularly in spurring the antislavery movement's shift from gradual emancipation and colonizationism to immediate abolitionism.

## Protestant Liberalism and Reformed Orthodoxies

The antislavery movement was profoundly influenced by the New Divinity's concept of disinterested benevolence, and by Finney's argument that conversion should be immediate rather than gradual; however, Southern divines' uses of the Bible to justify slavery led some abolitionists to depart from their Reformed upbringings by the time of the Civil War. A few prominent ministers with roots in the Reformed Tradition also departed from their theological heritage in the mid- to late nineteenth century. Horace Bushnell (1802–1876), a graduate of Yale Divinity School and a Congregationalist minister, argued in *Christian Nurture* (1847) against the immediate conversion model of the revivalists, and instead he suggested that children should be educated into the Christian religion, a view that coincided with his understanding of Christian life and society as progressive, rather than static and predicated on before/after conversion experiences. Henry Ward Beecher (1813–1887) also rejected the Calvinism of his forefathers in favor of a Gospel of Love where strict predestination disappeared and sentimentalism prevailed.

In the wake of the publication of Darwin's *Origin of Species* in 1859, and in the aftermath of the Civil War, where theologians on both sides hurtled biblical accusations at each other, and where death on such a grand scale caused some to look for more comfort than orthodox Calvinism seemed to offer, more Reformed denominations and ministers also abandoned basic tenets of Calvinist theology, such as predestination and innate depravity. Yet even as their differences from other mainline denominations blurred and church cooperation spurred the formation of interdenominational councils and unions in the twentieth century, many still identified as part of the Reformed Tradition, highlighting the tradition's adaptability and continuing vitality in the modern world. Bushnell's idea that Christian society should be progressive, and the social ethic that Calvinism spurred among some followers, can be seen in the late-nineteenth-century Social Gospel, and in mainline Protestants' attention to progress and the reform of this world. Today, the Presbyterian Church of the USA (PCUSA) is the largest mainline Reformed denomination, with over two million members, ten thousand congregations, and fourteen thousand ministers. The United Church of Christ, formed in 1957 from the union of the Congregational Christian and Evangelical and Reformed (traditionally German) churches, also falls on the liberal side of the Reformed heritage in America.

On the other hand, the last century has also seen a resurgence of the doctrine of depravity. The two world wars led neoconservative theologians to revise the optimistic progressive visions of the mainline churches and instead promote a more cautious view of human limitations and God's absolute sovereignty. Reformed denominations today that explicitly uphold the tradition's orthodox positions include the Presbyterian Church in America and the Orthodox Presbyterian Church, which have roots in the mid-nineteenth-century Princeton Theology and conservative Southern Presbyterianism, and the Reformed Church of America and the Christian Reformed Church, originally formed by Dutch Calvinists. These denominations hew to the standard confessions of the Reformed Tradition.

Modern-day fundamentalists who identify as Baptists also have been influenced by the Reformed Tradition, and by the Princeton theologians' and Southern Presbyterians' emphasis on biblical inerrancy. Baptists in the colonial and revolutionary era had experienced their own Arminian-Calvinist split; the Calvinist branch of Particular Baptists (believing in particular, as opposed to general, election), was numerically dominant. Calvinist theology continues to influence conservative denominations and denominational subgroups in the highly diverse Baptist tradition today, such as the Primitive Baptists. The Southern Baptist Convention, with more than sixteen million members, does not explicitly hew to the Reformed confessions, preferring to see themselves as biblically based, rather than based in creed, but nevertheless affirms the inerrancy of scripture and the consistency of election with free agency.

A brief comparison of the Web sites of the PCUSA and the Orthodox Presbyterian Church highlights the diversity within American Reformed churches today, and the extent to which they continue to draw on traditional Calvinist beliefs. The PCUSA Web site notes that "Some of the principles articulated by John Calvin remain at the core of Presbyterian beliefs." The Web site's discussion of predestination quotes from the Second Helvetic Confession, typically seen as the most generous of the early Reformed confessions, and suggests that the doctrine of predestination should provide comfort to believers who can never fall from God's grace. The beliefs of the Orthodox Presbyterian Church (OPC) on the other hand, are presented as essentially unchanged from the Synod of Dort and the Westminster Confession, including the depravity of man, the complete sovereignty of

God, and his justness in predestination. Ironically, the PCU-SA's stance is perhaps more akin to Calvin's original intentions for the doctrine of predestination, while the OPC's position aligns with the ways in which Calvin's writings were interpreted by followers such as Theodore Beza and the standard confessions of the Reformed Tradition.

## Ethos of the Reformed Tradition

Whether there is "a" Calvinist or Reformed ethos has been a rich subject of inquiry among scholars. Some have tried to draw connections between Calvinism and various other hallmarks of modernity, such as capitalism, democracy, and social activism. Max Weber most famously described Calvinism, and the doctrine of predestination in particular, as a driving force behind the Protestant work ethic in his 1904–1905 *The Protestant Ethic and the Spirit of Capitalism*. Weber argued that the anxiety people experienced as a result of not knowing whether or not they were of the elect led to a this-worldly asceticism, in which Reformed Protestants interpreted success in this world as a sign of salvation in the next. According to Weber and others who had tried to establish links between Calvinism and capitalism, Calvin's valuation of one's vocation in this world also contributed to the economic energy of countries influenced by the Reformed tradition.

Scholars have argued, too, that Calvin's decentralized, four-part church polity, with its Consistory and Company of Pastors, contributed to republican political theory, where power is spread among several branches of government, led by disinterested magistrates who are also citizens. Some scholars have suggested that Calvin's focus on God as the ultimate sovereign, to whom all humans are beholden, and his insistence on the depravity of all mankind, also contributed to democratic political thought and the concept of checks and balances. Some historians have even depicted the Reformed clergy's support of the American Revolution as evidence of the affinities between Reformed theology and republican government.

Still others have suggested that Calvinism's focus on the sovereignty of God contributed to a social activist, and sometimes millennialist, ethos in which believers have seen themselves as part of God's grand scheme of history, and dedicated their energies to the reform of the world according to his plan. The Reformed Tradition encouraged a deep piety toward the ineffability and "otherness" of God, but unlike the Pietist groups that also developed from the Reformation, it encouraged social action and reformation of the world, and not just of the individual soul. The social and moral reform movements of the antebellum era, many of them supported by Reformed leaders and laypeople, illustrate this kind of social activist orientation. Samuel Hopkins's idea of disinterested benevolence, for instance, embodies the shift from a focus on self to a focus on God's will for the world that is so characteristic of this strain of the Reformed ethos.

On the other hand, more recent scholars such as Philip Benedict, author of a synthesis on the Reformed Tradition, have criticized the connections earlier historians made between Calvinist theology and the hallmarks of modernity. They have argued that extrapolating ethos from theological beliefs, as Weber essentially did, is methodologically faulty because not all laypeople within a tradition necessarily believe every doctrine generated by theologians, or weigh various doctrines' importance in the same way as theologians and ministers. In addition, they have compared countries influenced by the Reformed Tradition with those where Lutheranism and Catholicism prevailed, and shown that capitalism, and republican and democratic political ideas, were not exclusive to the Reformed Tradition.

These scholars have focused instead on the ways in which the Reformed Tradition was a lived religion to lay believers, and on the diversities within the tradition. Self-examination, for instance, which was an essential aspect of experimental predestinarianism, the devotional and practical piety first suggested by English divines in the sixteenth and seventeenth centuries, could lead to profound relief if a believer came to feel that he or she was one of God's elect, but could also lead to profound anxiety and distress if assurances were not so forthcoming. Such anxiety and distress led to the caricature of Calvinist theology by Deist, Universalist, Arminian, and other critics in the late eighteenth and nineteenth centuries as overly harsh and terror-inducing, with a tyrannical and arbitrary God who was easy to fear but hard to worship as just and merciful. Lorenzo Dow, a popular early-nineteenth-century Methodist evangelist in America, for instance, noted that the doctrine of election "tend[ed] to presumption, or despair," and summarized Calvinism with the saying, "You can and you can't—You shall and you shan't—You will and you won't—And you'll be damned if you do—And you'll be damned if you don't." It was partly in response to such accusations that the New Divinity and New Haven divines crafted their theological innovations to the Reformed tradition.

That the Methodists and other populist denominations were much more successful than the Calvinists in gaining adherents in nineteenth-century America has been interpreted by some scholars as a sign of Calvinism's decline after disestablishment. Ann Douglas, for instance, famously argued that Calvinist ministers and women, both essentially disestablished in the nineteenth century, joined arms to influence popular culture with a maudlin sentimentality that drained the rigor from Calvinist theology instead. Others have located the decline of Calvinism later: in his influential synthesis of American religious history, Sydney Ahlstrom, for example, situated the end of the Puritan ethos in the 1960s.

Belief in predestination, with the attendant anxieties the doctrine once produced, has indeed declined among some Reformed denominations and adherents by the twenty-first century. Yet from the disagreements between Bolsec and Beza, to the Arminian controversy of the early seventeenth century, and from the migration of Puritan dissenters to the fracturing of the New England clergy over the mid-eighteenth-century revivals, the Reformed Tradition has never been static or homogenous. Rather, it has always been characterized by rigorous theological debate, variety, and adaptability through the ages.

**See also** *Antinomian Controversy; Bible* entries; *Congregationalists; Dutch Reformed; Education: Colleges and Universities; Great Awakening(s); Lutheran Tradition and Heritage; Methodists: Tradition and Heritage; Pilgrims; Presbyterians* entries; *Puritans; Reformed Denominational Family; Religious Thought: Reformed Protestant.*

Kathryn Gin

**BIBLIOGRAPHY**

Ahlstrom, Sydney E. *A Religious History of the American People.* 2nd ed. New Haven, Conn.: Yale University Press, 2004.

Albanese, Catherine A. *America, Religions and Religion.* 3rd ed. Belmont, Calif.: Wadsworth, 1999.

Applegate, Debby. *The Most Famous Man in America: The Biography of Henry Ward Beecher.* New York: Doubleday, 2006.

Benedict, Philip. *Christ's Churches Purely Reformed: A Social History of Calvinism.* New Haven, Conn.: Yale University Press, 2002.

Conforti, Joseph A. *Jonathan Edwards, Religious Tradition & American Culture.* Chapel Hill: University of North Carolina Press, 1995.

———. *Samuel Hopkins and the New Divinity Movement: Calvinism, the Congregational Ministry, and Reform in New England between the Great Awakenings.* Grand Rapids, Mich.: Christian University Press/Eerdmans, 1981.

Douglas, Ann. *The Feminization of American Culture.* New York: Noonday Press/Farrar, Straus and Giroux, 1998.

Hall, David D. *Worlds of Wonder, Days of Judgment: Popular Religious Belief in Early New England.* New York: Knopf, 1989.

Holifield, E. Brooks. *Theology in America: Christian Thought from the Age of the Puritans to the Civil War.* New Haven, Conn.: Yale University Press, 2003.

Hood, Fred J. *Reformed America: The Middle and Southern States, 1783–1837.* University: University of Alabama Press, 1980.

Kuklick, Bruce. *Churchmen and Philosophers: From Jonathan Edwards to John Dewey.* New Haven, Conn.: Yale University Press, 1985.

Leith, John H. *An Introduction to the Reformed Tradition: A Way of Being the Christian Community.* Rev. ed. Atlanta: John Knox Press, 1981.

Marsden, George M. *Jonathan Edwards: A Life.* New Haven, Conn.: Yale University Press, 2003.

McGrath, Alister E. *A Life of John Calvin: A Study in the Shaping of Western Culture.* Cambridge, Mass.: Basil Blackwell, 1990.

McNeill, John Thomas. *The History and Character of Calvinism.* New York: Oxford University Press, 1967.

Miller, Perry. *The New England Mind: The Seventeenth Century.* Cambridge, Mass.: Harvard University Press, 1983.

Morgan, Edmund Sears. *The Puritan Dilemma: The Story of John Winthrop.* The Library of American Biography. Boston: Little, 1958.

Noll, Mark A. *America's God: From Jonathan Edwards to Abraham Lincoln.* New York: Oxford University Press, 2002.

Stout, Harry S. *The New England Soul: Preaching and Religious Culture in Colonial New England.* New York: Oxford University Press, 1986.

Sweeney, Douglas A., and Allen C. Guelzo. *The New England Theology: From Jonathan Edwards to Edwards Amasa Park.* Grand Rapids, Mich.: Baker Academic, 2006.

Thuesen, Peter J. *Predestination: The American Career of a Contentious Doctrine.* New York: Oxford University Press, 2009.

Weber, Max. *The Protestant Ethic and the Spirit of Capitalism with Other Writings on the Rise of the West.* Translated and introduced by Stephen Kalberg. 4th ed. New York: Oxford University Press, 2009.

Wells, David F., and Roger R. Nicole. *Reformed Theology in America: A History of Its Modern Development.* Grand Rapids, Mich.: Eerdmans, 1985.

# Camp Meetings

Camp meetings are, strictly defined, outdoor religious revival gatherings, lasting for several days, at which attendees camp on-site for the duration of the meeting. Originating in the United States at the beginning of the nineteenth century, camp meetings were aimed toward bringing new converts into the churches and were noted for high levels of emotionalism and strong physical manifestations of religious experience. Although camp meetings had their greatest impact and significance prior to about 1850, they continued to occur in various parts of the United States well beyond that time, and survive, in modified form, to the present day.

## Origins

The camp meeting's origins have been subject to much debate among historians. Outdoor preaching is as old as

Christianity itself, and, in American history, many of the services in the colonial Great Awakening were held out of doors as well. Such services were occasionally called "camp meetings," though they differed in important ways from the nineteenth-century form, and the term itself did not receive widespread use.

Some historians have also identified important European antecedents to the American camp meeting. In particular, scholars have cited the background of seventeenth- and eighteenth-century Scottish "communions," large outdoor gatherings, which displayed many characteristics of the camp meeting, including high levels of emotionalism, and which appear to have inspired some of the earliest camp meeting leaders in the United States.

Still, such specific practices as camping out appear to have been early nineteenth-century American innovations, and, most scholars agree, the camp meeting quickly took on a life of its own in the antebellum United States, developing forms and conventions that clearly distinguished it from colonial and European antecedents.

In general, historians date the first American camp meetings to about 1800, when they emerged as part of the second major religious revival in American history, the Great Revival or the Second Awakening. These meetings took place in Kentucky. The earliest were held in Logan County, in western Kentucky, and from there they quickly spread to other parts of the state. Most notable among these early meetings was a seven-day gathering at Cane Ridge, near Lexington, Kentucky, in August 1801. The meeting drew crowds estimated in the thousands; attendees came from great distances and, bringing their provisions with them, came prepared to spend several days on the site. Nineteenth-century observers and historians alike have often described Cane Ridge as the camp meeting's true birthplace.

Presbyterians took a dominant role in the leadership of these early meetings and, most likely, in the makeup of the congregations, since many of Kentucky's initial settlers—to the extent that they were church members at all—tended to be Presbyterians. Nevertheless, some of the earliest meetings also tended to be interdenominational. Thus, at Cane Ridge, for example, clergy from the Methodist and Baptist denominations joined their Presbyterian counterparts, preaching from various locations around the encampment to a religiously diverse crowd.

The early camp meetings were exciting affairs. Marked by fiery preaching—ministers from different denominations loudly addressing different parts of the crowd simultaneously—lusty singing, and, above all, multitudes of people, in the throes of religious experience, undergoing powerful physical exercises; the scenes were viewed even by friendly observers as approaching chaos. The physical exercises were especially impressive and took several forms, including "falling" helplessly, "barking" or "laughing" uncontrollably, or, most spectacularly, "the jerks." The jerks began with a twitch that would take over the entire body, becoming increasingly violent. According to contemporary observers, at the height of a meeting's excitement, the entire congregation might be affected by the jerks, moving rapidly from one person to the next.

## Evolution

From its Kentucky beginnings, the camp meeting spread widely and rapidly to other parts of the United States. Newly settled frontier regions provided the most fertile ground for camp meetings. Individual churches were difficult to support in thinly populated areas, and the camp meeting, where people could come to a central location for several days of worship, providing their own lodgings, had obvious utility. But camp meetings proved to be popular even in well-established areas and continued to be so throughout the antebellum period.

As the camp meeting evolved, its character changed in major ways. For one thing, despite its early interdenominational history, the practice was to be increasingly identified with the Methodist Church during the first part of the nineteenth century. Baptists and Presbyterians tended to move away from the camp meeting, for a variety of reasons. Many found the more spectacular physical exercises troubling, and the emotionalism incompatible with a true Christian faith. As they accurately pointed out, camp meeting conversions were often attributable more to the excitement of the moment than to any deep-seated religious commitment and were quickly forgotten once the excitement had passed.

Methodism had long prized emotionalism, and Methodists openly embraced that of the camp meeting. They celebrated the exercises as manifestations of the power of God moving among the people. Although by the 1810s, some of the more spectacular exercises had begun to be replaced mainly by shouting, weeping, and, occasionally, jumping, at the height of a meeting's excitement, Methodist camp meetings continued to feature exercises through much of the first half of the nineteenth century.

There were also theological reasons for Presbyterian and Baptist opposition. From the beginning, camp meeting preaching had displayed tendencies toward Arminianism, that is, the view that God has offered salvation to everyone and that each individual has the power to accept or to reject God's call. Holding to Calvinist doctrines of predestination and election, Presbyterian and Baptist leaders became concerned about the potentially subversive impact of the camp meeting itself. Methodism was, however, strongly rooted in Arminian theology, making the camp meeting wholly compatible with the church's doctrinal thrust.

To be sure, Baptist and Presbyterian camp meetings continued to occur here and there throughout the antebellum period. Such other groups as the Adventist followers of William Miller and the Mormons, groups spawned in the religious ferment of the first half of the nineteenth century, also incorporated the camp meeting into their efforts. Nevertheless, the camp meeting was to be most closely identified with the Methodists, who fully embraced it as well.

## Structure

As camp meetings evolved over the first half of the nineteenth century, they developed a body of fairly standardized procedures that was to be maintained throughout the era. These procedures were regular enough that, over the course of the period, several writers produced camp meeting "manuals" prescribing appropriate rules for organizing a meeting—rules that actually codified what had become fairly regular practice.

In general, meetings were scheduled over a long weekend. Although there was some variation, people usually began to arrive at the site on Thursday, with services scheduled to begin that evening, and continuing through Monday or, sometimes, Tuesday morning. In rural, agricultural regions, there was something of a camp meeting season in early autumn, when people had brought in their harvests and could devote several days to religious observance.

The sites themselves tended to take a standard form. The campers' tents surrounded a large central space dominated by a preaching stand and pulpit. A small area in front of the stand, the altar—sometimes called the "mourners' bench" or "anxious seat" (or, by critics, the "glory pen")—was set aside to allow new converts to come forward at appropriate times in the services. There were benches for the congregation, usually divided into sections, men on one side, women on the other—with, in parts of the South, a separate area for slaves, usually behind the stand. The settings could be quite

impressive, and camp meeting locations were often chosen for their potential effect. In wooded areas, canopies of trees overhung the site, creating what some observers described as "a cathedral" in the wilderness; at night, flickering firelight illuminated the services, giving, and intended to give, a kind of sublimity to the proceedings.

The camp meeting day was long. Morning services, usually devoted to prayer, began shortly after sunup and before breakfast. Services continued throughout the day and included sermons, prayers, exhortations, and invitations. Between scheduled services, people gathered in private tents for continuing prayer, singing, and exhortation; or, toward the end of the meeting, "love feasts," in which clergy and laypeople counseled new converts. But the camp meetings were dominated by their evening services, beginning around 7 P.M. and often lasting past midnight. This was when the most spectacular preaching occurred, as ministers graphically laid out the horrors of hell and the joys of heaven, and set forth the ability and duty of every individual to respond to God's offer of salvation. Enthusiastic singing and praying accompanied the preaching. Most important, the evening services were also when most new converts went to the altar, weeping, and then shouting as they found their new faith.

The culmination of the camp meeting came on the final morning when, prior to breaking camp, worshippers gathered for a closing service. Here, members of the congregation proclaimed themselves a community of believers, joining hands and singing as they marched around the campground.

## Camp Meetings, Community, and Society

In many ways, community was the hallmark of the camp meeting. Many participants, reflecting on their experiences, recalled not only the importance of religion to their lives, but also the feeling of happiness resulting from their participation in the camp meeting's religious community. As the practice matured, especially within Methodism, it became an important institution for maintaining a larger sense of denominational ties. Becoming, in many areas, an annual affair, integrated into the institutional calendars of regional denominational bodies, it was intended specifically to provide an occasion for individual congregations and for clergy to come together in a larger fellowship.

In more sparsely settled areas, the camp meeting also had a social dimension not entirely confined to religious purposes. It enabled people to meet with friends who might otherwise live too far away for frequent visiting; many observers noted that the campground was also a courting ground for young men and women. There was definitely a downside to this aspect of the camp meeting. Alcohol was often a problem on the campground, so much so that some states passed laws prohibiting the sale of liquor within a mile or two of religious services. Interloping drunks and "row-dies" occasionally disrupted services, challenging preachers, even threatening violence. Some ministers tried to turn this to their advantage, recounting the conversion of scoffers as a way of showing God's power—or proving their mettle by meeting violence with violence, forcibly restoring order when they felt it had to be restored. Nevertheless, there seem to have been plenty of people attending camp meetings whose purposes were not exactly identical to those of their religious sponsors.

Nonetheless, and despite such problems, the camp meeting remained an important religious tool. The first bishop of the Methodist Episcopal Church in the United States, Francis Asbury (1745–1816), specifically credited the camp meeting for his denomination's spectacular growth and success in the early nineteenth century. Many of his successors did so as well.

## Camp Meeting Religion

From the beginning, the core of camp meeting religion was composed of an Arminian theology, a focus on conversion and religious experience, and an understanding of the church as a community of believers. These ideas both helped shape and were shaped by trends in the larger arena of antebellum American Protestantism. Thus, the Arminianism that dominated camp meeting religion was not only in keeping with Methodism but was also compatible with, and helped to hasten, a more general American rejection, or at least redefinition of older Calvinist ideas of election and predestination, a major development during the first half of the nineteenth century.

In giving a central place to conversion, camp meeting religion carried forward and helped maintain long-standing Protestant traditions stressing individual conversion as a basis for church membership. The "morphology of conversion," as camp meeting participants understood it, cohered with traditional models, in which individuals moved, by stages, from a powerful, often disabling conviction of their sinfulness, through a recognition of God's saving power, and into a new life, based on an assurance of heaven.

Still, some historians have argued that the camp meeting ritualized and dramatized this conversion morphology,

redefining it in communal terms. Thus, as potential converts began to realize their sinful state, usually under preaching, and to make their way out of the general body to the altar, they signaled their separation from the world, and from the life they had known. "Falling" or weeping in front of the stand, they gave concrete form to the helplessness conviction entailed. Finally, with the help of others, they were able to emerge, often shouting or jumping, back into the world of the congregation, giving tangible reality to their new status as members of a community of "saints."

In camp meeting religion, this idea of the church as a community of believers had especially significant interactions with other elements in antebellum American religion. Stressing individual experience and deemphasizing institutional, mediating structures, Protestant tradition has long celebrated such a conception of the church. Camp meeting religion built on this tradition but took it in some remarkably egalitarian directions, and in a variety of ways.

One was the heavy congregational involvement in the services themselves. To be sure, ministers played a crucial role, especially through their function as preachers and teachers. Within the services, however, the role of the laity was critical. Laypeople led many activities, including the love feasts. During the day, private gatherings and other services were usually organized around the personal testimonies of laybelievers and converts, recounting their experiences and describing what religion had meant in their lives. Particularly important was the role of laypeople in the evening services, especially as converts made their way to the altar and underwent the physical torments of conviction. There, they were surrounded by members of the congregation, many of them women, who provided encouragement, praying over them, singing to them, urging them forward, even as the preachers continued to proclaim the horrors of hell and the joys of salvation.

## Gender and Race

Noting the role of women in this process has important implications for understanding the character of the camp meeting as a communal exercise. The American churches of the first half of the nineteenth century were, for the most part, dominated by men, at least insofar as professional, institutional roles were concerned. Nevertheless, in the setting of the meeting, the role of women was both large and critical. They offered testimonies and counseling throughout the services, and, again, they played an essential role in bringing converts into the community. In this, the camp meeting displayed an egalitarianism that belied the male domination of the institutional churches, emphasizing the temporality of worldly categories, at least during the bounded time and space within which the meeting took place.

This transcending of categories was especially visible in the camp meetings' closing ceremonies, in the march around the encampment. Here the lines of gender governing the layout of the campground were broken down, as everyone marched around the site, singing and proclaiming a common assurance of salvation. So, too, could lines of race and color as, often, African American as well as white believers joined in the march.

Race was a complex issue for camp meeting religion. From the beginning, African Americans—and in some places Native Americans—participated regularly in the meetings. African American preachers and exhorters served black congregants, and, early in the form's development, mixed congregations as well. This participation provided an important basis for the growth of Christianity among African Americans. Recognizing its value, leaders of the African Methodist Episcopal Church, after its 1816 departure from white-dominated Methodism, retained the camp meeting as a key tool in their efforts to expand their denomination's reach.

In the South, the camp meeting was also a vehicle for the creation of an autonomous slave religion that came to fruition during the antebellum period. This was a faith that shared much with camp meeting religion generally: its egalitarianism, its Arminianism, and its recognition of physical exercises as manifestations of religious experience. But this faith also developed significant directions of its own. Its egalitarianism, for example, focused on freedom and liberation in a way that related directly to the conditions of enslavement people endured. It stressed an understanding of conversion that involved consolation in this world, as well as assurance of the next. No less critically, as the emphasis on physical experience and conversion dovetailed with an array of African traditions, it helped to encourage syncretistic tendencies in African American religious thought and practices. Thus, African American Christians—and not only slaves in the South—combined African with European elements to create a distinctive theology and ritual practice that powerfully shaped African American religious life.

## The Spiritual Songs

African Americans played a particularly important role in the creation of one of the camp meeting's most significant innovations, the camp meeting spiritual songs. Singing was

critical to the camp meeting, and these songs developed early in the camp meeting's history. They were designed especially for congregational singing in regions where literacy rates were low and were especially useful in the poorly illuminated night services, where hymnbooks would not have been useful anyway.

In form, the songs drew on a fairly small number of well-known English hymns, to which their creators added a brief, highly repetitive refrain, usually following each verse. Sometimes composed on the ground, these refrains also traveled from hymn to hymn, making them quickly to familiar to camp meeting crowds. Leaders would give out the verses; everyone in the congregation could quickly pick up the refrain and join in the singing. The tunes were often borrowed from familiar traditional folksongs, making the songs still easier to learn. Throughout the antebellum period, and beyond, these songs circulated freely in both African American and Anglo-American traditions, even though those traditions would diverge with the continuing development of distinct African American religious forms. Evidence from the meetings indicates that African Americans and Anglo-Americans alike had a role in their creation.

Because they were so easy for everyone to sing, the spirituals enhanced the communal feeling of camp meeting religion and its egalitarian tendencies. Such tendencies were also conveyed in the songs themselves, which often stressed the ties binding church members together, and the saints' sense of distinctiveness from a world of suffering and sin. The songs also reinforced the purposes of the camp meeting by holding out to believers the hope of salvation and the joys that heaven would bring, enhancing their role at the altar. Built on a limited core of ideas and images, especially in their refrains, these songs did much to define the camp meeting's theology and proved to be one of its more enduring legacies.

## Interpretations

The camp meeting has been subject to a variety of scholarly interpretations. Some of the earliest commentators joined camp meetings' critics in condemning what they, too, saw as the meetings' emotionalism and lack of theological sophistication. Many focused on the spectacular physical exercises and even sought to explain those exercises by citing the power of mass hysteria in a social setting. More recent scholars have tended to reject such approaches, looking, instead, to social and cultural factors that might account for the camp meeting's rise and success.

Because of the camp meeting's Kentucky origins and its distinct success in newly settled areas, many scholars have interpreted the practice as a manifestation, or a symptom, of the American frontier environment. Some of these interpretations have leaned heavily on the influential 1896 "frontier thesis" of the historian Frederick Jackson Turner. Prominent in Turner's thesis was the view that the frontier experience strongly shaped American life and culture, encouraging, among other things, individualism, egalitarianism, and anti-intellectualism—all of which, historians have suggested, were embodied in the camp meeting.

Other approaches that emphasize the camp meeting's frontier origins have looked in a slightly different direction. Citing the fragmentation of frontier societies, these interpretations have stressed the communal tendencies of camp meeting ritual and belief and its relationship to desires for community in an otherwise fragile and disordered social environment.

Finally, however, at least a few scholars, while acknowledging the influence of a frontier environment on the camp meeting's origins and development, have suggested that such explanations do not adequately take into account the camp meeting's place in larger traditions of religious practice and, as well, the extent to which the beliefs of camp meeting religion were compatible with larger tendencies in antebellum American religion toward Arminianism and emotionalism, tendencies that went well beyond the camp meeting movement. The camp meeting's meaning and significance ultimately derive from its intimate connections to larger religious trends; and, once established, the practice developed momentum, unrelated to the demands of a frontier environment.

## Survivals

The camp meeting did not disappear after its heyday in the first half of the nineteenth century. Methodists, for example, have continued to sponsor meetings to the present day, though in a very different form from those of the early nineteenth century. Even before the Civil War, camp meetings became increasingly sedate, as many members of the increasingly middle-class denomination came to be dismayed by what they, too, viewed as the emotional excesses of earlier days. In the post–Civil War era, cottages and even hotels began to replace tents for lodging participants, and the term "camp meeting" came to refer more to services offered in ongoing programs of worship and recreation on permanent, church-owned sites.

Even within Methodism, however, a few groups have maintained older camp meeting traditions. African American Methodists in some areas continue to hold camp meetings that display many of the syncretistic forms established in earlier times. The camp meeting proved significant to the growth and spread of the Holiness movement, beginning shortly after the Civil War within Methodism and, later, as it moved out on its own. In addition, since their early twentieth-century origins, Pentecostal groups have also made use of the form. Holiness and Pentecostal meetings, in keeping with the churches' experiential emphases, have retained something of the fervor of earlier versions, including physical exercises, glossolalia, and a distinctive body of religious song. These churches have also tended to develop permanent camp meeting sites, complete with cottages and hotels. Since the late nineteenth century, Holiness and Pentecostal groups have also adopted the term "camp meeting" to refer to protracted urban revivals, doing so deliberately to create a figurative, if not literal, tie to an institution that played such a major role in the development of American religion.

**See also** *Charismatics / Charismatic Movements; Emotion; Evangelicals* entries; *Frontier and Borderlands; Fundamentalism; Glossolalia; Great Awakening(s); Methodists* entries; *Music: African American Spirituals; Pentecostals; Pietism; Revivalism* entries; *Social Gospel.*

Dickson D. Bruce Jr.

## BIBLIOGRAPHY

Boles, John B. *The Great Revival: The Origins of the Southern Evangelical Mind.* Lexington: University Press of Kentucky, 1972.

Bruce, Dickson D., Jr. *And They All Sang Hallelujah: Plain-Folk Camp-Meeting Religion, 1800–1845.* Knoxville: University of Tennessee Press, 1974.

Conkin, Paul K. *Cane Ridge: America's Pentecost.* Madison: University of Wisconsin Press, 1990.

David, Jonathan C. *Together Let Us Sweetly Live: The Singing and Praying Bands.* Urbana: University of Illinois Press, 2007.

Eslinger, Ellen. *Citizens of Zion: The Social Origins of Camp Meeting Revivalism.* Knoxville: University of Tennessee Press, 1999.

Fairchild, Louis. *The Lonesome Plains: Death and Revival on an American Frontier.* College Station: Texas A&M University Press, 2002.

Hatch, Nathan O. *The Democratization of American Christianity.* New Haven, Conn.: Yale University Press, 1989.

Johnson, Charles A. *The Frontier Camp Meeting: Religion's Harvest Time.* Dallas: Southern Methodist University Press, 1955.

Raboteau, Albert J. *Slave Religion: The 'Invisible Institution' in the Antebellum South.* New York: Oxford University Press, 1978.

Schmidt, Leigh Eric. *Holy Fairs: Scottish Communions and American Revivals in the Early Modern Period.* Princeton, N.J.: Princeton University Press, 1989.

Stephens, Randall J. *The Fire Spreads: Holiness and Pentecostalism in the American South.* Cambridge, Mass.: Harvard University Press, 2008.

# Canada: Aboriginal Traditions

Aboriginal religion in Canada (often referred to as "spirituality" by Aboriginal peoples) encompasses a wide range of practices, beliefs, and values among which there are certain commonalities. There are 1.2 million indigenous people in Canada (about 4 percent of the country's population) who are recognized in the Canadian Constitution Act of 1982 as "Aboriginal." These include First Nations, Métis, and Inuit peoples. First Nations are communities traditionally referred to as Indians; the Métis are a distinct ethnic group who are descendants of Cree, Ojibwe, Anishinaabe, or Menominee peoples and eighteenth-century fur traders; and Inuit are indigenous peoples who inhabit the Arctic and subartic regions of Canada. Spirituality operates within these cultures as a vital component of modern life that is quite distinct from that of non-Aboriginals.

## Principles, Symbols, and Practices

First Nations, Métis, and Inuit spiritualities are repositories of distinctive practices and moral principles that help to negotiate people's relationships with the world as it is most broadly conceived. Although there are many variations in religious life among Aboriginal peoples, there are also some distinct shared characteristics. Aboriginal spiritualities, for instance, are not generally reliant upon written texts. Rather, they are oral traditions that make use of memory, story, and public discourse to convey the deepest meanings of human existence. Most traditions maintain a belief in a creator who is responsible for the creation of humanity and the natural world. All hold a profound reverence for the earth (often conceived of as a mother), as well as a belief that all living things possess a spirit that should be respected and protected. From this perspective, people are not simply pragmatically connected with their environment, they are morally bound to it. Thus, all things are related to one another and bear responsibility for one another; and relationships among people are generally governed by the same principles.

Within this matrix of relationships respect for elders is fundamental, as elders are recognized as the preeminent bearers of tribal knowledge and are vital cultural links between the past, present, and future. Certain symbols are also widely shared among Aboriginal peoples. Eagle feathers, for instance, are generally associated with spiritual strength, and with the creator. Circles (as well as medicine wheels, talking circles, and healing circles) signify healing, wholeness, and interdependence; and medicine bundles contain sacred objects that symbolically represent teachings and knowledge that has been received from elders or through ceremonies and fasting. Sweet grass is associated with purification and spiritual strength; tobacco connects the human and spirit worlds; sage is associated with protection from harmful spirits; and cedar is related to healing. Drums signify the center or heartbeat of creation. In some traditions, totem poles, petroglyphs, or masks have sacred significance.

Aside from symbols, there are also religious practices that are found broadly within Aboriginal cultures. Story-telling is a long-standing practice, and while it has suffered in some communities in recent years (due to language loss and the pervasive influence of entertainment technologies in the lives of young people), it continues to varying degrees in all traditions. Among the Métis, for instance, stories of a trickster figure variously named Nanabush (Ojibwe root), Wîsahkêcâhk (Cree root), and Ti-Jean (French Canadian root) are common; and in Tsimshian and Haida stories and art, a multifaceted traditional figure, Raven, continues to appear.

In many traditions, the smoking of a sacred pipe is part of individual and communal ritual and prayer, signifying people's relationships with one another and with the creator. Thanksgiving rituals and sweat lodge ceremonies are enacted for healing or as expressions of gratitude; fasting is believed to deepen spiritual knowledge; and dancing is regarded as a form of prayer. The burning of sacred herbs (for example, sweet grass, tobacco) is also a long-standing practice, often done in the service of physical or spiritual healing. Vision quests (undertaken to achieve spiritual direction at pivotal moments in an individual's life) are carried out to varying degrees among Aboriginal peoples; and pow-wows are a general practice in which people gather to express and celebrate various aspects of culture and spirituality.

Among First Nations peoples of the prairies, the sun dance has remained a vital part of communal life, in spite of government attempts to sabotage it in the late nineteenth and early to mid-twentieth centuries. The sun dance is practiced by Sioux, Dene, and Assiniboine peoples. Among the Cree its counterpart is known as the thirst dance; Anishinaabe refer to it as the rain dance; and Blackfoot refer to it as the medicine dance. The celebration can involve the building of a sacred fire, prayer, dance, drumming, fasting, visions, and sweat ceremonies. On the west coast, the traditional cedar big house or longhouse (used in the past as residences for extended families) is used for various kinds of ceremonies and assemblies; and in central Canada and among Métis, the longhouse has continued to serve as a communal and ceremonial structure. Hereditary chiefs of the Haudenosaunee (the Iroquois League of Peace and Power), for instance, meet in the longhouse.

## Christianity

In addition to these practices and beliefs, the majority of Aboriginal Canadians have some affiliation with Christianity. The timeframe for the adoption of Christianity varied among communities depending on when they came into contact with missionaries, and in most cases conversion could not be isolated from economic factors. The first Aboriginal person to be baptized in Canada was the Mi'kmaq chief, Membertou. In 1610, he and twenty members of his family (none of whom could speak French) were baptized by the Catholic French missionary priest Jessé Fléché (who could speak no Mi'kmaq) in a ceremony that was clearly understood by Membertou as a trading agreement. In the early seventeenth century, the Wendat peoples, who were interested in extending their trading relationships with the French, were introduced to Catholic missionaries who had arrived as part of a package deal under orders from Samuel de Champlain 1567–1635, a French navigator who founded Quebec City. By midcentury, already half of those involved in the fur trade were either converts or catechists, since native Christians were paid the same rate for their furs as the French, an amount that was substantially more than that paid to those who remained unconverted. Likewise, the Inuit of the coast of Labrador were confronted by Moravian missionaries in the late eighteenth century and gradually converted over a span of 150 years. This community was distinct from other Inuit, who tended to convert to the Anglican or Catholic churches. Although there were symmetries between Moravian Christianity and traditional Inuit spirituality that undoubtedly made conversion possible, the Labrador coast Inuit were also induced to conversion by economic incentives. In particular, the Moravians owned seal nets that they loaned to Inuit converts to catch harp seals for a lucrative international trade, the profits of which were shared by the missionaries with the fishermen. The connection between conversion and economics continued into the twentieth century among the Innu of the interior areas of Labrador, for whom the adoption of Catholicism was associated with preferential treatment by missionaries (for example, loans for fishing equipment).

The meeting of Christianity with traditional spiritual frameworks resulted in the emergence of new religious forms, some of which have continued to the present day. The Labrador coast Innu, for instance, have traditionally practiced a ritual called *nalujak* on the Catholic feast of Epiphany, during which masked members of the community visit homes giving presents to children and chastising adults; and a long-standing tradition of meetings involving men only has continued in the context of elected elder's councils associated with the church. Among the Mi'kmaq, the feast of St. Anne (July 26) is a focus for annual gatherings that have been incorporated into a tradition of summer meetings dating to at least as early as the sixteenth century. These meetings, which were convened primarily to conduct business involving a number of bands (for example, wars, treaties, marriages), are now a context for receiving sacraments, celebrating Mi'kmaq culture and spirituality, and conducting intertribal business.

Generally speaking, although conversion occurred broadly among Aboriginal peoples, the influence of Christianity (and especially the Roman Catholic Church) has diminished markedly in recent years due to a number of factors; chief among these is a legacy of cultural assault aimed at all indigenous peoples perpetrated by the Canadian government and a number of churches who united to create an Indian Residential School system that was in place until the 1980s.

## Government Policy and Repression

The world of Aboriginal peoples was dramatically altered by colonial contact, and their religious lives cannot be separated from this context of contact, new relationships, and injustice. In Canada one of the most far-reaching and culturally damaging colonial policies was the Indian Act of 1876, which imposed regulations on Aboriginal peoples that could never have been legally applied to non-Aboriginals. The intention of the act was to "civilize" Aboriginal peoples, to assume control of their lands and their day-to-day lives, and to establish a definition of who was and who was not an "Indian." According to the act, indigenous peoples were not permitted to employ the services of lawyers to advocate for Aboriginal or treaty rights; and they were denied the right to vote until the 1960s. The law, which remains in effect to the present day, requires that Band Councils be elected and defines the limits of band council responsibilities. The imposition of elected councils undermined traditional forms of self-government with lasting implications: because band councils are accountable to the Ministry of Indian Affairs, they have often failed to represent the interests or wishes of their fellow band members. The Iroquois Haudenosaunee (longhouse) tradition, in which chiefs were selected by clan mothers, is a case in point. In communities where the tradition has been sustained, there is often notable conflict between those who support it and those who support elected Band Councils, since the government does not recognize the legitimacy of nonelected councils. The Indian Act also required that all children be registered at birth according to a number of categories of Indian status. According to a 1985 amendment to the law, there are seventeen options. Until the 1985 passing of Bill C-31, An Act to Amend the Indian Act, women could not retain their Indian status if they married a non-Aboriginal man, and children of their unions could not claim Indian status. As a result of Bill C-31, more than 80,000 people regained their status by 1992. At the present time, the Indian Act still reserves government control of education, taxes, land management, and band membership.

The Indian Act was only one of a number of coercive government policies that shaped the lives of native peoples beginning in the late nineteenth century. Others included the institution of Permit and Pass Systems, and the prohibition of religious ceremonies. The Permit System required that financial transactions be subject to government control, including the sale of cattle, grain, hay, firewood, lime, charcoal, and home-grown produce, and the purchase of groceries or clothing. The system was technically in place until 1995 but was virtually inoperative after the 1960s. The Pass System was instituted to oversee and limit the mobility of First Nations people, in order to undermine the possibility of organization among them and to prevent parents from having contact with their children who were attending Residential Schools. The system essentially confined individuals to their Reserves, with the possibility of traveling left to the discretion of Indian agents. "No Trespassing" signs were planted at the edges of Reserves, and those who left their Reserves without a pass were subject to criminal prosecution. Although the Pass System had no basis in the Indian Act (or any other legislation), it remained operative until the 1930s and was not officially dismantled until 1951. Other oppressive measures were given legal sanction. An 1884 amendment to the Indian Act, for example, resulted in prohibitions against a family of practices involving feasting and gift giving known generally as the potlatch, as well as a number of ceremonial dances (for example, the *Tamanawas*) practiced by First Nations in British Columbia. The traditional potlatch ceremony involved a ritual distribution of gifts as a means of extending communal relationships through the celebration of pivotal experiences such as the birth of a child, marriage, or the confirmation of treaties, but the ceremony was regarded by religious and civil authorities as un-Christian and a wanton waste of personal resources. In 1895, ritual acts of physical stamina associated with the thirst (sun) dance were also prohibited, effectively disallowing the dances. These laws were enforced as, for example, in 1904 when a ninety-year-old man who was virtually blind was sentenced to a two-month prison term with hard labor for taking part in traditional ceremonial practices.

Within this context of cultural and religious oppression, religion remained an integral part of people's lives. New religious movements emerged, such as one that occurred in 1904, when a message of imminent salvation circulated throughout southern Saskatchewan, involving a prophecy of the end of the white world. According to the prophesy, the remaining native peoples who lived a traditional lifestyle would have the world to themselves and full access to returned herds of buffalo that had virtually disappeared. Aside from new movements, some traditional practices were also elaborated. Among the Ojibwe, contact precipitated a flourishing of the Midewiwin, healing societies whose members underwent elaborate rituals of initiation in order to prophesy, and to be empowered to communally cure the sick. The Midewiwin is firmly grounded in traditions that predated contact, but these healing societies have become a important vehicle for transmitting tribal knowledge in the postcontact period. Additionally, and in spite of prohibitions, illegal dances and the potlatch were not discontinued in the nineteenth century but were carried on covertly, resurfacing into public view again in the second half of the twentieth century. Sustained government oppression, as well as language loss in the twentieth century, have also taken a toll on traditions of story-telling; many mythic motifs have survived this onslaught, however, and, in many cases, adapted themselves to contemporary contingencies. The hero Kluskap, for instance, became a key player when he was invoked in a 1990 standoff involving the Mi'kmaq and a mining company that intended to destroy a sacred site. Another figure, Wesakechak, appeared as a Cree superhero in a 1996 comic book designed to provide guidance to Aboriginal teenagers among whom suicide rates had become disturbingly high.

## Treaties and Land Claims

Among commonly shared aspects of Aboriginal spirituality in postcolonial Canada is a general recognition of the sacred nature of (1) land and treaty rights, and (2) language, both of which have historically been assaulted by governments and economic interests. There are about 400 treaties involving Aboriginal peoples in Canada. Early treaties involved native pledges of support during times of colonial conflict (such as English-French hostility in the eighteenth century), recognition of harvesting and trade rights, promises of peace, and protections against encroachment on native land. The clearest examples of these kinds of treaties are those collectively referred to as "Peace and Friendship Treaties," negotiated by the British with the Maliseet and Mi'kmaq between 1725 and 1779. Other treaties followed, and in these subsequent cases, the agreements dealt also with issues of land cession and Reserves. Such was the case with the Upper Canada Treaties (1764–1862), the Vancouver Island Treaties (1850–1854), and a series of eleven numbered treaties with Aboriginal peoples in various parts of Ontario, Manitoba, Saskatchewan, Alberta, British Columbia, Yukon, and the Northwest Territories (1871–1921).

Until the early 1980s, the Canadian courts refused to acknowledge the binding nature of these agreements, and harvesting rights, perhaps the most explicit part of the treaties, were consistently undermined by fishing and hunting regulations. Still, in spite of the fact that no Aboriginal person has enjoyed the full benefit of treaty rights, the treaties themselves have continued to be regarded as extremely significant. First Nations, Métis, and Inuit tend to place great value on the knowledge of history as a resource in dealing with issues of identity and for determining present actions. Treaties are a critical part of this knowledge, as they are regarded as structures for regulating native and nonnative relations in the postcolonial period, as well as for potentially creating unity. Many Aboriginal peoples, however, were excluded from the treaty-making process, either because of geographical location (for example, Aboriginals in the northern regions and many First Nations in British Columbia who were situated beyond the parameters of early colonial expansion) or because of lack of status.

Although the Constitution Act affirms the Aboriginal and treaty rights of all three Canadian Aboriginal Peoples, the Métis, for example, do not have a legacy of treaties to which they can turn for recognition of land rights because they were not recognized as a distinct Aboriginal people until the latter part of the twentieth century. Called "Canada's Forgotten People," the Métis have remained outside the pale of treaties, aside from one instance where they were included in the "Half-Breed Adhesion to Treaty No. 3," negotiated in Ontario in 1875. Under pressure from Aboriginal communities who were not included in treaties, the Canadian government has been compelled into land claims negotiations and settlements (also called Comprehensive Claims) that are constitutionally recognized as treaties. In the late 1970s, for instance, Labrador Inuit and Innu began pressing governments to begin treaty discussions. The Inuit were able to secure the Labrador Inuit Land Claims Agreement in 2005. In 1993, the federal government passed the Nunavut Land Claims Agreement Act and the Nunavut Act, as a result of land claims negotiations with Inuit of the Northwest Territories that had begun in the mid-1970s. These acts led to the establishment of Nunavut in 1999, a territory that comprises nearly one-fifth of Canada's land mass; and in 2008, the Canadian parliament passed a second reading of the Tsawwassen First Nation Final Agreement Act, whereby the government would formally recognize Tsawwassen First Nation ownership of its reservation in southern British Columbia.

Treaties and modern agreements were, and are, formal and mutually binding contracts relating to land, natural resources, political power, and economic relations. They are compromises that establish the principle that coercion and/or violence is unacceptable in settling differences, and they have legal weight. For Aboriginal peoples, they are also sacred. In 1991, the Canadian government created the Royal Commission on Aboriginal Peoples (RCAP), a commission whose mandate was to assess a variety of issues relating to the status of Aboriginal peoples in Canada. In the process of its deliberations, RCAP spoke with First Nations, Métis, and Inuit peoples from all over the country. What the commission learned with respect to treaties was that by and large they are regarded as "covenants of trust and obligation," sacred agreements that represent spiritual principles, and that are binding for all time; as one eighteenth-century treaty ratified in New Brunswick put it, "so long as the sun rises and the river flows." Treaties were always enacted within ritualized frameworks replete with religious symbolism (wampum, the smoking of a sacred pipe, and so on) in which government representatives participated. They were consequently placed within a context of mutual respect and responsibility that has religious ramifications. Annual reaffirmations of these sacred agreements occurred on Treaty Day, when band members met with representatives of the British Crown to renew their commitment to peaceful relations and to receive gifts and treaty payments. The practice of celebrating Treaty Days fell into disuse in some communities but has been reinstituted in recent years with events marked by ceremony, processions, church services, drumming, presentations of eagle feathers, and feasting. Contemporary negotiations over Aboriginal and treaty rights maintain this sacred component, as seen during discussions concerning amendments to the Constitution Act that took place in Charlottetown in 1992, where Aboriginal delegates were advised by elders who engaged in prayer throughout the negotiations.

## Land, Spirituality, and Resistance

Treaties and Comprehensive Land Claims relate specifically to land, and issues of Aboriginal rights involving land have historically accounted for a great deal of friction between indigenous Canadians and the wider society. Exasperated by the indifference of government officials in Nova Scotia, for example, Mi'kmaq Grand Chief Louis-Benjamin Peminuit Paul wrote to Queen Victoria in 1841 appealing for assistance for his people who were suffering extreme deprivation: "The Micmacs now receive no presents, but one small Blanket for a whole family. The Governor is a good man but he cannot help us now. We look to you the Queen. The White Wampum [treaties] tell that we hope in you." By the turn of the twentieth century, Canadian authorities had lost patience with First Nations peoples who advocated for recognition of their rights. Thus, the Cree chief Payipwat was imprisoned twice for his advocacy of treaty and religious rights and was unseated as chief by the federal government in 1902 (his band remained faithful to him, in spite of this move, and did not elect another chief until he died in 1908). The relationship between Aboriginal people and the natural environment has continued to be a site of contestation to the present day, as is evident in an ongoing conflict between the Lubicon Lake Cree and the federal government concerning oil and gas development on reserve land in Alberta. The conflict began in the 1970s and has yet to be resolved. Contests over land have been amplified by government initiatives aimed at alienating indigenous peoples from their land. Policies of relocation and centralization throughout the twentieth century were a common practice that were justified in a number of ways, including the desire to assist economically disadvantaged communities and to centralize bands in the interest of efficiently delivering government programs, as well as to secure nonnative access to natural resources. In some cases (for example, the Hebron Inuit), these policies created socially stratified communities where relocated communities found themselves alienated from resident populations. In all instances, relocation decreased the capacity of communities to support themselves economically and caused an increase in illness, government dependence, and other forms of cultural strain. The case of Nova Scotia Mi'kmaq is emblematic. In the 1940s, the Mi'kmaq were resettled on two Reserves at Eskasoni and Shubenacadie with promises of employment, livestock, and better educational and health facilities. It was a disastrous experiment in social engineering. Neither community had the resources to sustain its increased population. Additionally, as RCAP noted, the promised housing did not materialize and many were forced to live in tents (although native laborers were enlisted to build houses for police officers and nonnative government personnel). In one year, an Indian agent's goats ate all the fruit tree saplings that had been planted, and groundwater was poisoned by kerosene that had been poured on seed potatoes to deter residents who were suffering from malnutrition from eating them.

Aboriginal peoples live in abject poverty and suffer from staggering rates of diabetes and other diseases. While 16 percent of Canadians live in poverty, the figure among Aboriginal peoples is 40 percent. In most cases, a long-established delicate economic balance in indigenous communities based on harvesting of various forms has been destroyed within a generation or two through lack of access to natural resources and policies like relocation.

For indigenous people, cultural knowledge is tied to the environment, creating a spiritual link between the person and landscape that has devastating effects when broken. As one Inuk man said in an RCAP interview, nuna (the land) is "my life, nuna is my body." The land provides a connection between people, their history, and their sense of the future, a connection that is often epitomized in ritual spaces, burial grounds, and other symbolic aspects of the natural world.

Such sites have consequently been the focal point of various kinds of religious resistances, ranging from peaceful demonstrations to violent confrontations. In the 1990s, when dredging threatened to destroy a 4,500-year-old system of weirs used for harvesting fish by Wendat and then later, Chippewa peoples near Orillia, Ontario, the response was the creation of the Mnjikaning Fish Fence Circle, a community-based organization that has been able to forge a working relationship with Parks Canada to ensure the protection of the site. Those involved in this diplomatic effort stressed not only the historical significance of the site, but also its spiritual importance and its capacity to bring healing. A similar initiative has occurred in British Columbia, where it is estimated that tens of thousands of sacred sites and others containing First Nations sacred artifacts have been destroyed by urban development. In the 1990s, the First Nations became aware of the critical role these artifacts played in legally establishing Aboriginal rights to the land, and they began pressing the provincial government for control over the way in which developers were destroying these sites. The First Nations have had some success in this respect. The Hul'qumi'num Treaty Group, for instance, was able to pressure the government to prosecute a developer in 2003 for violating the Heritage Conservation Act.

Other disputes have not been so peaceful. In 1990, a demonstration involving a Mi'kmaq warrior society led by Sulian Stone Eagle Herney attempted to disrupt a proposed plan to create a rock quarry on Cape Breton Island, Nova Scotia. The company responsible for the plan, Kelly Rock, was determined to create a "Superquarry" on Kelly's Mountain, a site that is sacred to Mi'kmaq. The warriors had demonstrated against the company in 1989 with little success, and so they mounted another protest in 1990 wearing military fatigues and announcing that they were ready for combat. Kelly Rock decided to abandon the superquarry plan. The same year, a Mohawk demonstration against the development of a golf course on contested land at the Kanestake Reserve near Montreal turned violent. The land in question contained a burial ground and a sacred forest called "the Pines," which the Mohawk occupied in mid-March. Quebec's premier requested police intervention, and an initial attempt to disperse the protesters (involving tear gas and flash-bang grenades) led to an exchange of fire that resulted in the death of a policeman. Paramilitary and military forces were subsequently called into the situation as the resistance extended to the Kanawake Reserve outside of Montreal. For a number of months the situation was charged, with Mohawk warriors and nonnative Quebecers (as well as other First Nations warriors and Canadian troops) in confrontation with one another. When the crisis ended in late September, two elderly men had died in addition to the policeman, and the federal government had purchased the land in question. The warriors' return to the Reserve was accompanied by the burning of tobacco, drumming, and the prayers of elders. Fatalities are not a common result of such conflicts, but they have occurred on a number of occasions. In 1993,

for example, a group of Chippewa set up a protest in an area of Ipperwash Provincial Park, Ontario, that contained a burial ground, and in the resulting clash with authorities, a Chippewa man, Dudley George, was killed.

## Language

Aside from land and treaties, one other facet of sacred value among Aboriginal peoples is language, and as with land and treaties, it has been a contested issue. There are eleven distinctive language families among First Nations peoples, as well as a number of dialects of Inuktitut (Inuit) and Michif (Métis). Within these linguistic families, there are more than fifty languages. A variety of dialects of Inuktitut are spoken throughout the Canadian Arctic. The area between Alberta and Atlantic Canada is home to a number of Algonkian languages, and Iroquoian languages are spoken in Quebec and Ontario. Siouan languages are located in Alberta, Saskatchewan, and Manitoba; and those of the Athapaskan family are spoken in the prairies as well as British Columbia and the Northwest Territories. Tlingit, Haida, and Kutenai are spoken in British Columbia, as are languages of the Salishan, Wakashan, and Tsimshian families; and Michif (the language of the Métis) is spoken in various parts of the country but predominantly in the west and Northwest Territories.

Most of these languages were the objects of a devastating assault perpetrated by the Canadian government, the Roman Catholic Church, and, to varying degrees, the Anglican Church and the United Church of Canada (as well as its founding congregations, the Congregationalist, Presbyterian, and Methodist churches) beginning in the late nineteenth century and lasting almost a century. Nineteenth-century treaties committed the federal government to providing education for First Nations children, and the residential school system was the product of the melding of this obligation with cost-cutting measures. Since schools were already being administered by missionaries associated with Christian churches, the government decided to fulfill its treaty promises by making use of the churches' organizational structures rather than creating its own. Thus, it shouldered the cost of providing facilities, while the churches supplied teachers and general administration. The government's cost of providing education was thus dramatically reduced as it ostensibly fulfilled its treaty obligations. In effect, it was promoting the assimilation of Aboriginal children and undercutting the viability of their cultures: the goal was to "kill the Indian in the child."

During the twentieth century, 150,000 First Nations, Métis, and Inuit children were placed in 132 Indian Residential Schools located in all but three provinces and territories. These children were taken from their homes (often forcibly) and placed in church-administered institutions where they were prohibited from using their own languages and denied contact with family members, while they were trained to assume employment in the lowest economic strata of the society (basic trades and domestic service). They were punished for attempting to leave the schools and for speaking Aboriginal languages; many were sexually abused by teachers and other staff; and some died as a result of poor health conditions in the schools. Although most Residential Schools were shut down in the 1970s, the last school under government control was closed in 1996. It would be another decade (June 2008) before Canadian prime minister Stephen Harper would make a statement of apology in the House of Commons on behalf of all Canadians to the 80,000 surviving students of the Indian Residential School system.

The Residential School System was designed to undermine Aboriginal culture, and more especially, First Nations, Métis, and Inuit language and spirituality. The experiences of the children who were subjected to the system dramatically altered their lives; and the trauma caused by the schools has continued to reverberate within communities, having been directly implicated in a current tide of substance abuse, domestic violence, mental illness, and suicide. Among the most dramatic results of the enterprise has been a general erosion of Aboriginal languages caused by a breakdown in systems of transmission. Essentially, the survival of any language depends on the presence of older speakers who can transmit it to younger generations. The residential school experiment was intended to undermine this relationship, and it was disturbingly successful.

Language is inseparably related to culture, since every language embodies a discreet way of understanding identity, history, and the world in which a community finds itself. One-quarter of Canada's Aboriginal peoples are able to speak their traditional language, with only about 13 percent of these using it daily. At this time, scores of Aboriginal languages are at risk of being lost, including Maliseet, Abenaki, Haida, Kutenai, Tlingit, Tsimshian, Wakashan, most Salishan, and a number of Athapaskan languages. For Aboriginal peoples, language carries spiritual weight. It is the most important aspect of culture, and most regard it as a fundamental gift to human beings from the creator who has placed within it the cultural knowledge necessary to survive and flourish. Further, Aboriginal languages contain the wisdom and knowledge of elders stemming back thousands of years—their visions, teachings, and general understandings of the world. Reverence for elders is inextricably related to language, as are traditions of story-telling, medicine, cosmologies, rituals, and, critically, history. Among the Mi'kmaq, for instance, a spiritually laden and hereditary office of *putus* exists for the sole purpose of interpreting (now missing) wampum records of the eighteenth-century Peace and Friendship Treaties. By means of symbols embedded in language, these "texts" contained specifically Mi'kmaq records of treaty agreements, and traditionally carried authority. This was illustrated when Grand Chief Gabriel Syliboy was tried (and convicted) for possessing pelts in contravention of lands and forests regulations in 1928. The community's principle witness at the trial was the putus.

In the indigenous oral traditions of Canada, spoken languages are irreplaceable because they are structurally distinct from the Indo-European languages of the dominant society, and they are spoken nowhere else. Many, for example, are notably verb-oriented, with verb tenses that do not exist in French or English (Canada's official languages). Many also employ a free ordering of words such that differences in meaning are communicated through changes in intonation. These languages are not translatable. In the wake of the Residential School assault, Aboriginal peoples have recognized that language restoration is the key to intergenerational healing, and hundreds of schools on First Nations across Canada are now administered by band councils, with language instruction ranging from individual classes to full immersion, as at Ohsweken on the Grand River First nation in Ontario (Cree), and Onion Lake First Nation in Saskatchewan (Cayuga). Others have created language institutes to serve their larger communities (for example, Kanien'kehaka Onkwawén:na Raotitiohkwa, a Mohawk cultural and language education center located at Kahnawake, Quebec). The religious lives of First Nations, Métis, and Inuit peoples are, as noted above, extremely rich and diverse, yet language as a sacred structure is a unifying motif that runs through these traditions. For this reason, the Residential School System was a particularly sinister enterprise among colonial and postcolonial assaults on Aboriginal peoples, cutting to the heart of their spirituality. As the Assembly of First Nations succinctly stated in its 1990 document *Principles for Revitalization of First Nations Languages,* "Language is our unique relationship to the Creator, our attitudes, beliefs, values and fundamental notions of what is truth. Our Languages are the cornerstone of who we are as a People. Without our Languages our cultures cannot survive."

**See also** *Canada* entries; *Environment and Ecology: Native American Cultures; Mexico: Indigenous Religions; Missions: Native American; Moravians; Native American Religions* entries.

Jennifer Reid

## BIBLIOGRAPHY

Axtell, James. *Natives and Newcomers: The Cultural Origins of North America.* New York: Oxford University Press, 2001.

Barkwell, Lawrence J., Leah Dorion, and Audreen Hourie, eds. *Metis Legacy: Michif Culture, Heritage, and Folkways.* Saskatoon, Canada: Gabriel Dumont Institute and Pemmican Publications, 2006.

Barman, Jean, Yvonne Hébert, and Don McCaskill, eds. *Indian Education in Canada. Vol. I: The Legacy,* Vancouver: UBC Press, 1986.

Battiste, Marie, ed. *Reclaiming Indigenous Voice and Vision.* Vancouver: University of British Columbia Press, 2000.

Brice-Bennett, ed. *Our Footprints Are Everywhere.* Nain, Canada: Labrador Inuit Association, 1977.

Choquette, Robert. "French Catholicism Comes to the Americas." In *Christianity Comes to the Americas, 1492–1776,* edited by Charles H. Lippy, Robert Choquette, and Stafford Poole. New York: Paragon House, 1992.

Dickason, Olive Patricia. *Canada's First Nations: A History of Founding Peoples from Earliest Times.* Toronto: Oxford University Press, 2002.

Grant, John Webster. *Moon of Wintertime: Missionaries and Indians of Canada in Encounter Since 1534.* Toronto: University of Toronto Press, 1989.

Haig-Brown, Celia. *Resistance and Renewal: Surviving the Indian Residential School.* Vancouver: Tillacum Library/Arsenal Pulp Press, 1988.

Indian and Northern Affairs Canada. *Report of the Royal Commission on Aboriginal Peoples.* 1996. http://www.ainc-inac.gc.ca/ch/rcap/sg/sjm5_e.html.

Inuvialuit Pitqusiit. *The Culture of the Inuvialuit.* Yellowknife, Canada: Northwest Territories Education, 1991.

Mackey, Mary G. Alton. "Remembering the Years of my Life." In *For Seven Generations: An Information Legacy of the Royal Commission on Aboriginal Peoples,* edited by Royal Commission on Aboriginal Peoples. Ottawa, Canada: Libraxus, 1997.

Mercredi, Ovide, and Mary Ellen Turpel. *In the Rapids: Navigating the Future of First Nations.* Toronto: Penguin, 1993.

Miller, J. R. *Sweet Promises: A Reader in Indian-White Relations in Canada.* Toronto: University of Toronto Press, 1991.

———. *Skyscrapers Hide the Heavens: A History of Indian-White Relations in Canada.* Toronto: University of Toronto Press, 2000.

Morrison, Bruce R., and C. Roderick Wilson. *Native Peoples: The Canadian Experience.* Toronto: McClelland and Stewart, 1995.

Paul, Daniel N. *We Were Not the Savages: A Micmac Perspective on the Collision of European and Aboriginal Civilizations.* Halifax, Canada: Nimbus, 1993.

Richling, Barnett. "Images of the 'Heathen' in Northern Labrador." *Études Inuit Studies.* 4, nos. 1–2 (1980): 233–242.

# Canada: Anglicans

The Anglican Church of Canada (ACC) is a self-governing province of the Anglican Communion, a worldwide family of churches that have historical roots in the Church of England. The ACC is characterized by Christian worship according to authorized liturgical texts and a governance structure of bishops and representative synods. It has been known by its present name since 1955. The ACC publishes no confessional statement; its general doctrinal orientation is indicated by its liturgical texts. The theological views of its members are very diverse, but the church is frequently described as liberal and catholic in its center of gravity. The ACC is distinguished from a few much smaller Canadian Anglican bodies, which it regards as schismatic, by being formally recognized by the Archbishop of Canterbury and by being eligible to participate in certain "instruments of unity" of the Anglican Communion. In its institutional operations, the ACC uses much of the vocabulary of the Church of England but adapts it to its different social and legal context. The ACC in 2001 counted 642,000 members.

## *Worship, Ministry, Doctrine*

All public worship is conducted according to authorized liturgical texts by clergy (or sometimes lay ministers) licensed by the local bishop; this is a significant denominational principle. In practice, however, leaders of worship may either expand the liturgical texts with informal comments, liturgical instructions, announcements of events, prayers for local concerns, and other unscripted material, or they may abbreviate the texts in the interest of time or for other reasons. The sermon, music, and ceremony are arranged by congregational worship leaders, taking into account worship space and congregational interests and traditions. As a result, worship in the ACC is far more diverse from congregation to congregation than might be expected from the fact that common texts are used.

The two liturgical texts generally in use and nationally authorized are the *Book of Common Prayer* (BCP), in a Canadian revision of 1959, and the *Book of Alternative Services* (BAS) of 1985. The BCP is a close descendant of the English BCP of 1552, written in mid-Tudor English (including "thou" forms) and reflecting a moderately Reformed Calvinist theology. The BAS is a product of the Liturgical Movement, a school of thought rooted in modern Benedictine monasticism and reflected in the liturgical theology of the Second Vatican Council (1962–1965) of the Roman Catholic Church. The BCP and BAS are thus theologically at variance. Thus, in the Eucharist, the BAS pictures the Church as joining with Christ in a sacrificial offering of bread and wine to God; the BCP avoids all suggestion of material sacrifice. The BAS gives symbolic ritual functions to such objects as oils, candles, and ashes, a practice that the BCP minimizes. The BCP, in its Eucharistic prayer and in speaking of the church as "the blessed company of all faithful people," suggests a Protestant premise of justification by faith alone, which is absent from the BAS.

Liturgical forms for the Eucharist other than the BCP and BAS must be authorized by the local bishop. Common alternatives include three supplementary Eucharistic prayers approved by the General Synod in 1998, rites used in the Iona Community in Scotland, texts developed by and for First Nations Anglicans, and services developed by individual congregations.

By far the most common Sunday service of an ACC congregation is that of Eucharist according to the BAS. Most ACC congregations now welcome all baptized persons (and sometimes unbaptized persons), including children, to take Communion at a Sunday service. In many congregations a rite of prayer and anointing for healing is sometimes made available at the time of Communion. The sacrament of baptism is usually administered as part of a Sunday morning Eucharist; formerly baptism was frequently practiced privately. Many clergy are reluctant to baptize persons not directly connected with their congregation.

Among other worship services, morning prayer (also called matins) and evening prayer (also called evensong), which were popular forms of worship before the 1960s, are now relatively rare outside theological colleges and religious communities. The rite of confirmation, once a prominent part of a bishop's visit to a parish, an important rite of passage for young teens, and a requirement for receiving Communion, is no longer frequent. Praise worship, with tuneful and rhythmic modern Christian songs, unscripted prayer, and physical expressions of an emotive piety, is held in some churches either by itself or within a service of Eucharist.

Almost all ACC churches constructed between 1845 and 1960 are in the architectural style known as gothic revival. Gothic churches evoke a sense of God's transcendence and the authority of the church by using light to draw attention heavenward and by separating laity and clergy into different spaces. But a few prominent churches from this period are in Richardsonian Romanesque or central-plan style.

Surviving church buildings from before 1845 are usually neoclassical in style, though most of these have been gothicized in later renovations. Architectural styles of churches built after 1960 are diverse but are likely to give value to congregational community by stressing horizontal lines in a single room.

There are three orders of ordained ministry: bishop, priest (or presbyter), and deacon. Members of all three orders are considered clergy. A service of ordination is provided for each order sequentially (only deacons can be ordained priests, and only priests can be ordained bishops). By far most clergy are priests. Priests differ from deacons mainly in being authorized to preside at the Eucharist. All priests and deacons in good standing are under the authority of a bishop.

The ACC has no denominationally distinctive doctrinal statement. Its general theological orientation is established principally, if not exclusively, by its authorized liturgical texts. These provide for the recitation of the Apostles' and Nicene Creeds, and for the public reading of scripture, organized by lectionaries that make use of both testaments and sometimes the Apocrypha. In addition, the liturgies contain many statements and prayers implying theological positions, especially concerning the church, ministry, and sacraments. These positions are not necessarily consistent among themselves. Both BCP and BAS frequently adopt a "holy ambiguity" in phrasing so as to comprehend a diversity of belief.

There is no provision for disciplining laypeople for their theological views. In this respect the ACC probably reflects its roots in the established Church of England, which comprehended all citizens by default, and which usually preferred to unify through compromise. Clergy, by contrast, have always been expected to conform to doctrinal standards, although these are now minimal. Clergy during ordination "solemnly promise to conform to the doctrine" of the ACC, but this doctrine is not defined. (Before the 1960s, prospective clergy were required to affirm the Thirty-Nine Articles of Religion of the Church of England, a moderately Reformed statement of 1563.)

The theological center of gravity in the ACC can be called liberal (in that it seeks to accommodate doctrine and the interpretation of scripture to scientific discovery, modern values, and common sense), and catholic (in that it values tradition, and esteems the sacraments and the liturgy as the font of the church's power). This liberal and catholic viewpoint is signaled by the view frequently stated in the

ACC that Anglicanism rests on a three-legged stool of scripture, tradition, and reason, a formula often (though wrongly) ascribed to a sixteenth-century Anglican, Richard Hooker. A spectrum of other theological viewpoints can also be found, including the classical humanistic Reformation Protestantism of the BCP, the experiential piety of the renewal movement, an ecumenical liberal Protestantism, the more conservative strains of both Catholicism and evangelicalism that are represented by an advocacy group called Anglican Essentials Canada, and a doctrinal agnosticism. The theological diversity of the ACC creates tensions and sometimes conflicts. Since 2004, several conservative ACC congregations have broken away because of theological conflict, including St. John's Shaughnessy in Vancouver, which had reputedly been the largest ACC parish.

## Governance

The ACC has four levels of governance: parochial, diocesan, provincial, and national. The diocesan level legally and historically precedes the other three. The dioceses employ most of the clergy, own most of the ACC's property, and exercise the greatest amount of authority. A diocese is a unit of geographical territory under the spiritual authority of a bishop. (Some dioceses also have one or more assistant bishops.) There are twenty-nine dioceses in the ACC, plus an administrative region in the central interior of British Columbia replacing the bankrupt diocese of Cariboo. A diocese has a governing assembly called a synod, composed of the bishop, the clergy, and representatives of the laity. The synod typically meets annually to adopt a budget, receive reports, and approve disciplinary and organizational rules called "canons." The diocesan bishop has the power of veto over the resolutions of the synod. When the episcopal office is vacant, the synod elects a new bishop.

Below the level of the diocese is the parish, which is created, defined, and organized by diocesan authority. It is composed of one or more congregations, which are local communities of Anglicans. The number of parishes in a diocese varies from about a dozen, in the case of the Yukon, to more than 200, in the case of Toronto. A parish typically comes under the pastoral supervision of a priest "incumbent," sometimes called a "rector," who represents the bishop. Parish governing structures and standards vary from diocese to diocese.

Above the level of the diocese is the ecclesiastical province, which is a grouping of dioceses governed by a provincial synod chaired by a metropolitan, with the title of

archbishop, who is elected from among the diocesan bishops. There are currently four provinces; a proposal for a fifth, nongeographical province for First Nations Anglicans is expected to be considered in 2010.

At the national level, the General Synod was created in 1893 and was incorporated in 1921. Its members are clergy and lay delegates from the dioceses, the bishops, and a few others. Under its jurisdiction come doctrine, worship, clergy education and pensions, social issues of national importance, relations with other churches, and missionary work. In practice the General Synod has few means to enforce either its rules or its financial assessments on the dioceses. Its chief officer, who is called the primate, is elected from among the diocesan bishops. A permanent staff is headquartered in Toronto.

Although the ACC is legally independent, it maintains moral, affectionate, and financial bonds with other parts of the Anglican Communion through certain so-called "instruments of unity," notably the Lambeth Conference (a decennial meeting of bishops), the Anglican Consultative Council, and the Primates' Meeting, and through mutual organizations such as Partners in Mission.

## Populations

In the 2001 Canadian census, 2,035,495 persons, or 6.9 percent of the general population, identified themselves with the ACC. This was the fourth largest religious grouping after Roman Catholic (43.2 percent), "no religion" (16.2 percent), and the United Church of Canada (9.6 percent). The figure represented a decline from 1991 (2,188,110, or 7.8 percent). In the 1951 census, 14.7 percent of the general population identified themselves as Anglicans. Many will self-identify as Anglican in census questionnaires who have no institutional connection with the church.

The ACC in 2001 (the most recent year for which numbers are available) counted:

- 642,000 members (a decline from 1.36 million in 1961);
- 227,000 identifiable givers (typically singles and heads of families);
- 2,884 congregations;
- 1,792 parishes;
- 2,048 active clergy (as of July 2000).

About half the members of the church live in Ontario.

With roots in the Church of England and the Church of Ireland, the ACC has had from its beginnings a heavily

Anglo-Saxon and Celtic ethnic identity. Before 1962, when immigration restrictions were eased, Canada's population was overwhelmingly British and western European in ethnic background. Anglican Christianity was appropriately used as an example of an ethnic church in Richard Niebuhr's *Social Sources of Denominationalism* (1929). Occasional efforts to increase French Canadian membership, as in the 1760s and 1840s, were not successful. During the first decades of the twentieth century, the ACC reinforced its ethnic and racial identity ideologically with a rhetoric of British superiority. Multiculturalism has increased substantially in Canada since 1962, but it is not possible to analyze how many Anglicans today have an Anglo-Saxon or Celtic background, since census data includes "Canadian" as a category of ethnic identity. On the basis of casual observation, however, it would appear that persons of British ethnic background remain dominant in the ACC. According to cross-referenced data from the 2001 census, 86 percent of Anglicans were born in Canada.

After British, the largest ethnic group in the ACC is likely indigenous. The Canadian Constitution divides this group into three categories: First Nations, formerly called Indians, representing more than fifty cultural and language groups; Métis or mixed race, and Inuit. There are about one million First Nations people in Canada, of whom an estimated 25 percent are Anglican, and 45,000 Inuit, of whom an estimated 85 percent are Anglican. Among the First Nations groups with strong Anglican connections are the Mi'kmaq, Ojibwe, Cree, Mohawk, Blackfoot, Tsimshian, Kwakiutl, Haida, and Gwich'in. (The last has been called "arguably the most Anglican people in the world.") About 225 congregations have all or nearly all indigenous membership, and there are about 130 indigenous Anglican priests. The Anglican ethnic majority has generally not been comfortable with the cultural diversity represented by indigenous Anglicans. Before 1969 the ACC administered a total of more than thirty First Nations residential schools, whose purpose was to assimilate First Nations children into British culture. Attendance at these schools, or similar schools administered by other Christian denominations, was enforced under the federal Indian Act. A significant change in attitude was marked by a report commissioned by the ACC called *Beyond Traplines* (1969), probably reflecting in part the influence of the Civil Rights Movement in the United States. About the same time, Margaret Craven's *I Heard the Owl Call My Name* (1967), the fictionalized story of what a white Canadian Anglican priest learns from a Kwakiutl congregation, reached the top of the *New York Times* best seller list, and was made into a CBS television movie. Since then indigenous people have gradually been incorporated into ACC structures of decision making, and there are some signs that their inculturated Anglicanism is becoming more widely appreciated and more influential theologically and spiritually. The first bishop of indigenous ethnic identity was elected in 1989. In 2007 Mark MacDonald took office as the first national Aboriginal indigenous bishop.

Ethnic groups other than British and indigenous are most conspicuously represented in the diocese of Toronto, which has Chinese, Filipino, Franco-African, Hispanic, Japanese, Korean, Tamil, and West Indian congregations and a Sudanese fellowship group. Many other congregations in the diocese have a multicultural character. A Hong Kong–born assistant bishop was elected for Toronto in 2006. In Vancouver, however, although the city is ethnically diverse, the ACC has moved in another direction. Since 2003 Japanese and Chinese Anglican parishes have severed their connection with the liberal and predominantly European-descent diocese.

Women were largely though not entirely excluded from church governance until the 1960s. They were conspicuously involved in lay ministries, however. Particularly notable was an independent missionary organization called the Women's Auxiliary (1885–1966), with active branches in most parishes. It sponsored female missionaries for domestic and foreign service, and undertook educational and social ministries. The first women's religious orders were founded in the 1870s; the most active today is the Sisters of St. John the Divine. The first deaconesses were "set aside" in 1895 and were used mainly for missionary, educational, and inner-city social work; their order gradually disappeared when women began to be ordained as deacons after 1969. A proposal to ordain women to the priesthood was raised, discussed, agreed, and implemented between 1968 and 1976. Despite some protest and the loss of a few congregations, the change was absorbed relatively quickly and painlessly, partly because of the diplomatic leadership of the primate, Ted Scott (1991–2004). The first woman bishop, Victoria Matthews was ordained in 1993.

## History to 1867

As the British Empire took control of the regions that now belong to Canada, the Church of England accompanied it. Anglican chaplains served British military personnel, and when colonies were established, congregations were formed with help from London. Religious affairs were controlled by the Colonial Office (working through local governors), the bishop of London, and, beginning in 1701, a Church mission organization called the Society for the Propagation of the Gospel in Foreign Parts (SPG). These authorities did not always work together harmoniously.

Before the American Revolution, the landmark Anglican events can be briefly summarized. In 1578 the first recorded Anglican Eucharist in what is now Canadian territory was celebrated by the chaplain to an adventuring expedition to Frobisher Bay. In 1583 the founder of a short-lived settlement in Newfoundland decreed a religious monopoly for the Church of England. In 1699 the earliest existing Anglican parish was founded in St. John's, Newfoundland. The minister, John Jackson, who was reputedly factious and cantankerous, received SPG sponsorship in 1702. In 1750, St. Paul's, the country's oldest Anglican church building still in use was erected in Halifax, Nova Scotia. In 1763, when England took control of Quebec at the end of the Seven Years War, the governor received royal instructions "that the Church of England may be established both in Principle and Practice." He and his successor ignored the direction: it was not wise for a tiny English occupying force to alienate a province of 70,000 French-speaking Roman Catholics. They did make a minimal provision for Anglican services for the British, and half-heartedly supported some ineffective proselytizing by three francophone Anglican clergy. In 1774, the Quebec Act made no provision for an English church establishment.

Anglican activity increased substantially with the American Revolution. Anglicans comprised a significant minority of the 40,000 persons, generally called loyalists, who left the United States to resettle in the newly reduced British North America (BNA). Their major religious work was forming congregations over a very large territory in a difficult climate, building and furnishing churches, obtaining clergy from the SPG, and developing local lay leadership. In addition, they organized schools, set up groups and guilds, sponsored social activities, developed parish libraries, and set up colleges of higher learning. Anglican leaders were typically "High Church" in the language of the day (the term is now used differently). They extolled the Church of England as the best possible church because of its true evangelical and Protestant doctrine, its episcopate in succession from Christ's apostles, and its historic written liturgy. They highly valued its "establishment," that is, its essential and privileged place in the English constitution. They thought that a strong Church of England would keep BNA loyal to Britain. They curried government privilege, protection, and largesse, and they helped shape the religious policy of the Tory governing elite both in England and in the colonies.

An early political victory for High-Church Anglicans was securing a colonial bishop, whose main role, in addition to teaching, ordaining, disciplining, and confirming, would be administering the government's religious policies and keeping non-Anglican leaders in the shadow. The very idea of an Anglican colonial bishop had been controversial for decades. For one thing, many non-Anglicans had come to the New World precisely to escape persecuting bishops. But even the United States was now accepting bishops consecrated in England, so the risk of giving offense seemed reduced. In 1787 the king signed letters patent creating a single Anglican diocese comprehending virtually all of BNA, including Newfoundland, to be called the diocese of Nova Scotia, and appointing Charles Inglis (1734–1816), former rector of Trinity Church, New York, to be bishop. The diocese has since then been divided many times.

The English government further strengthened the Anglican cause in BNA by providing it with a huge landed endowment—glebes (land set aside as part of a rector's compensation) and, in two provinces, a huge amount (estimated at 3,000,000 acres) of what was called clergy reserve land. In addition to these financial privileges, governments granted the Church of England additional advantages in such areas as marriage legislation, college and university charters and subsidies, and appointments to powerful provincial executive councils and agencies.

Entrenched privileges for the Church of England in BNA were naturally opposed by non-Anglicans, but they were controversial among Anglicans themselves. For their part, High-Church Anglicans predictably defended them. Their greatest champion was John Strachan (1778–1867), who served Upper Canada as a parish priest for thirty-three years, and then twenty-seven years more as bishop. Three Anglican groups opposed official privilege. First were the "Low-Church" Anglicans of the whiggish type then very common south of the border. They denied that the characteristics distinguishing the Church of England from other Protestant churches, such as episcopal governance and a written liturgy, were matters of essential importance. They freely collaborated with other Protestants in politics, education, and civic and charitable activities, a behavior that High-Church Anglicans criticized as religious relativism and disloyalty. Second, the Irish Anglican evangelicals, whose numbers were considerably augmented through immigration between 1830 and 1860, held that true Christians were to be identified by personal characteristics such as respect for scripture, conversion, and opposition to Roman Catholicism, not by the marks of the church institution to which they belonged. Their dislike for High-Church Anglicanism was heightened by a resentment of English ecclesiastical dominance that they carried over from Ireland. A third group were those influenced by the Anglo-Catholic movement that broke out at Oxford University in the 1830s, which stressed the divine authority of the church and its foundation in scripture, early Christian teaching, and tradition, and which strongly criticized the captivity of the English church to the state. Anglo-Catholics were quickly promoted to prominent leadership in the ACC and other colonial churches through the influence of a fundraising group called the Colonial Bishoprics Council, founded in 1841. Anglo-Catholic leaders in BNA such as John Medley (1804–1892), bishop of Fredericton, and George Hills (1816–1895), bishop of British Columbia, publicly opposed a colonial church establishment.

Against such opposition, official privilege for colonial Anglicans could not persist. As power in the provinces of BNA was transferred from Anglican-controlled elites to elected legislatures between the 1820s and the 1850s, the church's special status was gradually dismantled. A final blow was the secularization of the clergy reserve lands in 1854. The arguments among High-Church, Low-Church, evangelical, and Anglo-Catholic Anglicans continued, however, and grew increasingly broad and acrimonious through the nineteenth century. They gave a distinctive character to Anglican conversation, theology, and identity.

Anglican leaders recognized the need for independent financial and decision-making mechanisms. Taking the initiative, and theoretically running the risk of prosecution under English law, John Strachan in Toronto in 1853 created a synod of bishops, clergy, and lay delegates with the power to govern diocesan affairs. Similar bodies, called "diocesan conventions," existed in the Episcopal Church in the U.S.A., but Strachan's Anglican synod was the first in the British Empire. The idea quickly spread to other dioceses, and became the standard form of Anglican self-government in Canada.

In 1863 a decision to liberate colonial Anglicanism from its dependence on the state came from an unexpected corner. The highest court in the British Empire, in a case called *Long v. Gray,* decided that England had no authority in church matters in self-governing colonies. In 1865 it reaffirmed this decision in *Colenso v. Gray,* which protected a bishop from discipline for what was seen by many as theological unorthodoxy. England could no longer create dioceses, appoint bishops, or impose theological, liturgical, or canonical standards on any of its territories that had achieved a local legislature. The Anglican church in BNA was thus demoted to the status of one voluntary religious association among others.

Meanwhile, the Hudson's Bay Company (HBC), under a royal charter of 1670, held the land that is now Manitoba, Saskatchewan, Alberta east of the continental divide, the Yukon, most of the Northwest Territories, northern Ontario, and northern Quebec. This region was known as Rupert's Land, after the first governor of the HBC. In 1820 the first Anglican missionary in this fur-trading empire, John West, began ministering to both European settlers and Cree in the area of what is now Winnipeg. His sponsor was the Church Missionary Society (CMS), which had been formed in 1799 by the group of evangelical Anglicans best known for their campaign against slavery. The CMS contrasted with the High-Church SPG, not least in its being firmly committed to promoting indigenous leadership in its missions. Thus an orphaned Cree child named Sakachuwescam, or Henry Budd, a pupil of West's, would become in 1853 the first native person in North America to be ordained to the Anglican priesthood. Also in 1853 Robert McDonald, who was part Ojibwe was ordained priest; he became perhaps the most effective of all Anglican missionaries among the First Nations. A diocese of Rupert's Land was established in 1849 with gifts from the HBC and the estate of one of its chief factors.

In British Columbia, before gold was discovered on the Fraser River in 1858, Anglican work was confined mainly to two HBC settlements and a CMS mission to the Tsimshian. In that year a diocese was endowed and a bishop was appointed. Church growth was slow during this period.

By 1867, when the dominion of Canada was born, Anglicans were an unprivileged minority, prominent in the east and extremely thin on the ground west of the Great Lakes. They had no national organization. They had almost no formal institutional connections with other Anglicans in the British Empire.

## History since 1867

Shocked at the fragmentation of the British empire-wide Church of England into independent, self-governing churches without common standards, ACC bishops asked the archbishop of Canterbury to invite all Anglican bishops worldwide to discuss the "distress." Despite resistance from many English and American bishops who feared the control of colonials, a conference was held in 1867 at Lambeth Palace, the London residence of the archbishop of Canterbury. This proved to be the first of a series of decennial Lambeth Conferences. These are now considered a major instrument of the unity of the Anglican Communion, although their actual effectiveness has been diversely evaluated.

The ACC's most demanding work for the next half century was in the North West. In 1868 Canada bought the land of the HBC. Learning from the bad example of the Native American battles in the United States, it signed treaties with the First Nations, promising to reserve land for their use and to educate their children. The government contracted out the latter obligation to the ACC and three other Christian denominations. The ACC also had to build churches and train clergy for a flood of European immigrants, totaling about two million over the thirty-five years following the completion of the Canadian Pacific Railway across the continent in 1885. Robert Machray (1834–1901), the second Anglican bishop of Rupert's Land, oversaw this work. Although he generally depended on help from the CMS for native ministry and the SPG and other English agencies for European ministry, Machray moved the churches increasingly toward self-support. He developed lay leadership, created parish vestries, marshaled experienced missionaries to challenging tasks, began parish schools, and organized higher education. He envisioned an indigenous First Nations church (which did not materialize) and supported native missionaries. He upgraded his diocese into an ecclesiastical province and then subdivided the original diocese by persuading the CMS and SPG to endow episcopal salaries.

British Columbia entered Canadian Confederation in 1871. In 1879 two new dioceses were formed, one for the growing European population of the lower mainland and one for native ministries in the north.

From the 1860s to the 1890s hostilities among the church parties dominated the politics of the ACC, as of other parts of the Anglican world. The focal controversy was unauthorized liturgical ceremonial, which could range from modest physical signs of reverence to lavish medievalism. While few Anglicans appreciated the extremes, probably most were inclined to accommodate them as a harmless

deviation. But evangelicals aggressively and vocally sought the suppression of unauthorized ceremonial as un-Anglican, un-Protestant, and un-scriptural. Two opposing camps emerged, called "the Church party" and "the evangelical party." Each party developed its own newspaper, Sunday school curriculum, hymn book, theological school, and mission society. Synods became political battlegrounds. Much of the ceremonial that was controversial then is common in the ACC today.

By the 1880s most Canadian Anglicans wanted an integrated national structure, which most other mainline Protestant denominations had already achieved. The completion of the national railway in 1885 increased the feasibility of what was called "church consolidation." In 1893 Anglican delegates met in Toronto, published a "solemn declaration" of their intent to remain connected with the Church of England, and ratified the plan for consolidation. The General Synod was created, and Machray was elected primate. Western Canadian dioceses, straining to meet the needs of a growing population, hoped for greater sympathy from the wealthier eastern dioceses; others hoped for a stronger denominational contribution to global missions, which were a consuming enthusiasm of the day. Moreover, national church agencies might effect the collaboration of the church parties. Progress was discouraging for many years, however. At first the General Synod had no budget for staff members or office space. Not until 1905 was a Missionary Society of the Church of England in Canada (MSCC) functioning effectively. Later, a Sunday School Commission and a Council for Social Service were established. A Toronto office building was purchased in 1920.

The Church of England in Canada, as it was then called, might serve the young nation, but it saw itself as an expression of the mother church. Union jacks hung from church walls, Sunday worship featured prayers for the royal family and "God save the Queen" (or "King"), and synods wrote respectful addresses to the sovereign. By contrast, the larger United Church of Canada, formed in 1925, had a much keener sense of Canadian national identity and destiny. After World War II, as English Canadians generally developed their sense of independence from England, so did Canadian Anglicans, and in 1955 the name Anglican Church of Canada was adopted.

By the early 1900s, disputes about ritual were giving way to arguments about the theological implications of modern science and scholarship. Theological liberals were reinterpreting scripture and the church's teaching to be compatible with a scientific and modern world view. At first a few liberal clergy and professors were disciplined for their views, but from World War I to the 1950s, the ACC's dominant theology was a liberal evangelicalism that avoided conflicts between science and propositional doctrine by stressing the believer's sense of a personal relationship with an immanent God. A common activistic expression of theological liberalism was the Protestant "social gospel movement." Understanding the "kingdom of God" in Jesus' preaching as a call to build a just and compassionate social order, the ACC supported legislation and interventionist measures for social reform, including temperance laws, Sunday observance, the prohibition of child labor, workers' compensation, film censorship, and, in the 1940s, welfare legislation. A more individualistic expression of theological liberalism was the religion and health movement, which used scientific psychology and personal experience as resources for theological reflection. Clergy were trained for leadership in a therapeutic culture through hospital-based clinical pastoral education.

The liberal agenda gave priority to the modernization of the church not only in theology but also in communication, educational techniques, governance, and administration. In 1931, an Anglican National Commission made dozens of recommendations to make "organized religion" more respectable, responsive, and relevant to "our modern civilization." In the 1960s, the General Synod itself was modernized by management consultants, and the Sunday school curriculum was modernized according to the fashionable educational theories of John Dewey. In 1971 the *Hymn Book,* produced jointly by the ACC and the United Church of Canada, jettisoned traditional hymns such as "Amazing Grace" in favor of more modern hymns such as "God of Concrete, God of Steel."

Anglicans modernized their liturgical texts as well. In the 1960s the ACC was still using a prayer book very similar to the English prayer book of 1552. Influenced by an international and multidenominational school of thought known as the Liturgical Movement, reformers sought a style of worship consonant with the conclusions of modern liturgical scholarship, free of medieval elements, and suitable for a post-Christendom church. Many congregations experimented with trial rites, until in 1985 the General Synod approved the BAS, written in modern English and usually closely resembling the 1979 *Book of Common Prayer of The Episcopal Church in the U.S.A.* The change was controversial since it was hard for many Anglicans to give up a familiar and dear style of worship, and since the BAS was introduced into some parishes with insufficient sensitivity and preparation. The Prayer Book Society of Canada was organized in 1986 to protect and promote the BCP.

In the 1970s and 1980s national staff members and others vigorously advocated for progressive causes, including "corporate social responsibility," the dismantling of apartheid in South Africa, environmental protection, and a fair resolution of First Nations land claims. Their activities provoked a reaction, particularly from business interests and conservative media. After 1990 staff time was generally diverted to other matters, not only because of the resistance or indifference of members but also because of the press of other business, including lawsuits, and the waning clout of the churches in Canadian public life.

In the 1990s, it became known that many children had been abused in Indian residential schools administered in earlier years by the ACC under agreements with the government of Canada. By the end of 2002, claims and lawsuits had been filed by about 1,350 Anglican residential school survivors naming the church and the government as defendants. Though concerned for persons whom it had injured, the church also worried that it could be bankrupted by financial liabilities. In 2003, the ACC reached an agreement with the federal government: Canada would pay 60 percent of the church's liability up to $25 million, and 100 percent of amounts in excess of that. Because the ACC also accepted restrictions on claims and a complex and sometimes humiliating claims process, the Anglican Council of Indigenous People, which had not been consulted, raised energetic protests. Since then some changes have been made in the mechanisms for dispute resolution and in the agreement between the church and the government. The government has also established a Truth and Reconciliation Commission to promote healing.

Discussions as to whether the ACC should bless same-gender unions and ordain gay and lesbian clergy gained traction in the 1970s, and by the 1990s it had become a principal topic at most meetings of the General Synod, the House of Bishops, and the Primate's Theological Commission, and in the denominational press. Definitive action has been stalled by disagreements about the issue itself, a reluctance to alienate more conservative churches in the Anglican Communion, and an uncertainty about whether the blessing of same-gender unions is a matter of "doctrine," for which the General Synod has special procedures. In the meantime, clergy in same-gender relationships and blessings of same-gender unions are informally and quietly countenanced in scattered dioceses. In 2003 the diocese of New Westminster on its own accord publicly began blessing same-gender unions, provoking the separation of some parish churches and widening fissures in the worldwide Anglican Communion. In 2005 Canada legalized same-gender marriages. The matter will return to the General Synod at its next meeting in 2010.

See also *American Revolution; Anglican Tradition and Heritage; Anglicans in Colonial and Revolutionary America; Canada* entries; *Episcopalians* entries; *Mainline Protestants; Polity; Same-Gender Marriage; Worship: Anglican.*

Alan L. Hayes

**BIBLIOGRAPHY**

Boon, Thomas C. B. *The Anglican Church from the Bay to the Rockies.* Toronto: Ryerson Press, 1962.

Carrington, Philip. *The Anglican Church in Canada.* Toronto: Collins, 1963.

*Dictionary of Canadian Biography.* Toronto: University of Toronto Press, 1966–.

Fahey, Curtis. *In His Name: The Anglican Experience in Upper Canada, 1791–1854.* Ottawa, Canada: Carleton University Press, 1991.

Ferguson, Barry, ed. *The Anglican Church and the World of Western Canada, 1820–1970.* Regina, Canada: University of Regina Press, 1991.

Hayes, Alan L. *Anglicans in Canada: Controversies and Identity in Historical Perspective.* Urbana: University of Illinois Press, 2004.

————, ed. *By Grace Co-workers: Building the Anglican Diocese of Toronto, 1780–1989.* Toronto: Anglican Book Centre, 1989.

Katerberg, William. *Modernity and the Dilemma of North American Anglican Identities, 1880–1950.* Montreal: McGill Queen's University Press, 2001.

Knowles, Norman. *Seeds Scattered and Sown: Studies in the History of Canadian Anglicanism.* Toronto: Anglican Book Centre, 2008.

Miller, J. R. *Shingwauk's Vision: A History of Native Residential Schools.* Toronto: University of Toronto Press, 1996.

Millman, Thomas R., and A. R. Kelley. *Atlantic Canada to 1900: A History of the Anglican Church.* Toronto: Anglican Book Centre, 1983.

Peake, Frank A. *The Anglican Church in British Columbia.* Vancouver: Mitchell Press, 1959.

————. *From the Red River to the Arctic: Essays on Anglican Missionary Expansion in the Nineteenth Century.* Toronto: Canadian Church Historical Society, 1989.

Vaudry, Richard. *Anglicans and the Atlantic World: High Churchmen, Evangelicals, and the Quebec Connection.* Montreal: McGill Queen's University Press, 2003.

Westfall, William. *Two Worlds: The Protestant Culture of Nineteenth-century Ontario.* Toronto: McGill-Queen's University Press, 1989.

# Canada: Catholics

Catholics are the largest religious group in Canada, representing 43 percent of the population, or 12,937,000 in number (Canadian Census 2001). Canada is a country of immigrants, and Canadian churches are the churches of immigrants. For more than 400 years, various Catholic groups have immigrated to Canada, beginning with the French, Scots, and Irish, and continuing with the central and eastern Europeans. In the decades immediately following World War II, the southern and eastern Europeans seemed to conclude this influx, yet after changes in the Canadian immigration laws of 1967, Catholic immigrants began arriving from the Caribbean, South America, Middle East, Asia, and Africa. Aboriginal Canadians, like the nation's population as a whole, are estimated to be 43 percent Catholic, and from the beginning have been intimately interlinked with Catholic Christianity. Catholic history in Canada can be divided into three thematic developments: seventeenth- and eighteenth-century Gallicanism; nineteenth-century Romanism; and twentieth-century Canadianism.

## Gallicanism

During the first two centuries, French colonists landed in Canada and promoted Christian evangelization of the Aboriginals. The French Gallican church generated a mystical and heroic spirituality. Gallicanism fostered the canons and customs of the French church limiting papal intervention in French affairs and resisting papal infallibility apart from the consent of the whole church. The first recorded Aboriginal conversions began at Port Royal in Acadia, Nova Scotia, in 1610. The French missionary, L'abbé Jessé Fléché (d. 1611), baptized Chief Memberton and his family and 140 Mi'kmaq and Malecite neophytes. The following year, the Jesuits Pierre Biard (1567–1622) and Énemond Massé (1575–1646) replaced the missionary Fléché, studied the Aboriginal languages, educated neophytes in their native language, and translated the catechism (a systematic presentation of Christian teaching). They began a program of methodical Christian instruction for the Aboriginals.

In Canada, French Catholics settled principally in three locations: at the fortress of Quebec, at the remote sanctuary of Saint Marie among the Hurons, and at Ville Marie (Montreal), where the St. Lawrence, the Ottawa, and the Richelieu Rivers join together. With the fur brigades, enterprising Catholic chaplains penetrated quickly to the heart of the continent at Michilimackinac, sharing the gospel with the

Aboriginals as they went, eventually paddling their canoes down the Mississippi River to the Gulf of Mexico by 1687.

At Quebec in 1608, the layperson Samuel de Champlain (d. 1635) founded Quebec by planting the French flag and evangelizing the Aboriginals nearby. He was followed by missionary volunteers—the Recollets, the Jesuits, the Ursulines, and the Hóspitallers of St. Augustine—who built churches, hospitals, colleges, and schools that dotted the Canadian riverbanks. A multipurpose center for New France, the city of Quebec included government administration, commercial trade, military contingents, and the seat of the new diocese that stretched across North America from the Gulf of the St. Lawrence to the Gulf of Mexico.

As Quebec became the bedrock of French colonials in North America, Jean de Brébeuf (1593–1649), Antoine Daniel (1601–1648), and Ambrose Davost boarded Huron fur canoes and began the tortuous four-week journey up the St. Lawrence, the Ottawa, and the Mattawa Rivers to cross over the height of land on Lake Nipissing and to descend down the French River into the open waters that led to Huronia. When they arrived in 1634, the three Jesuits initiated a mission to 25,000 Hurons, the first Christian mission to this Aboriginal people. Five years later, Jerome Lalemant (1593–1673) and Jesuit companions began construction near Midland, Ontario, of the historic Saint Marie among the Hurons that became the centerplace for inculturation into Aboriginal life.

These famous personages in Catholic history—Jean de Brébeuf, Isaac Jogues (1607–1646), Gabriel Lalemant (1610–1649), Antoine Daniel, Charles Garnier (1606–1649), Noël Chabanel (1613–1649), Jean de Lalonde (d. 1646), and René Goupil (1608–1642)—began the long process of what is now called inculturation. They lived and ate as Hurons, and with great humility learned to speak the Aboriginal languages and respect their culture. The Hurons shared corn, tomatoes, potatoes, squash, and their fishing and hunting methods, and in turn the Euro-Canadians brought from France chickens, pigs, and cattle. Seventy Jesuits and donees lived at Saint Marie among the Hurons at its peak, and the compound became a place for Euro-Huron cultural exchange. Joseph Chihwatenha, Joseph Teondechoren, Paul Atondo, and other Hurons were baptized, evangelized their fellow Hurons, and soon founded Christian villages. Five of the Jesuits died in the service of the gospel in Huronia and three near Auriesville, New York. The eight were canonized by the Catholic Church in 1930 for their heroic sanctity in the face of violence and death.

As Quebec was a multipurpose center, and Huronia a place for European inculturation, so Ville Marie (Montreal) was a location for lay evangelization. Paul de Chomedey Maisonneuve (1612–1676) led the expedition of lay Christian missionaries up the St. Lawrence River to the Aboriginal fur markets at its juncture with the Ottawa River. Maisonneuve and his companions founded Ville Marie; Jeanne Mance (1606–1673) opened the first hospital; and Marguerite Bourgeoys (1620–1700) established the first school and the first uncloistered religious order in North America, the Congrégation-de-Notre Dame (CDN). Unlike Ursuline nuns who lived behind the cloister wall, the CDNs left their convent daily to do apostolic ministry throughout the countryside. The Sulpicians (a Catholic Society of Apostolic Life) in 1657 arrived in Montreal to found the principal church, Notre-Dame-de-Montréal, and the Grand-Séminaire-de-Montréal. In the midst of danger, the Christian faith was lived with a missionary intensity, and Montreal emerged as a center of lay evangelization. Francois de Laval (1623–1708), a descendant of the first Christian Franks in the fifth century, arrived in Quebec in 1659 as its missionary bishop to direct the nascent growth of the Canadian Catholic Church.

French Catholics in Canada enjoyed a century and a half of rustic solitude until the second half of the eighteen century, when the Irish and the Scots immigrated to Newfoundland and Nova Scotia and shattered the devout Gallican tranquility. From Scotland, the impoverished Scottish families sailed to Nova Scotia and Prince Edward Island and appeared to the French as less than proper Catholics. Their priests were not properly attired in Roman clerical dress, and they lacked suitable vestments and appropriate furnishings for religious services.

The Irish during the mid-eighteenth century in Newfoundland were separated by a large expanse of water from the French "Canadiens." The Irish were a minority in Newfoundland and were forced to hide their priests because under British penal laws, if the priests were discovered, homes would be knocked down. By the beginning of the nineteenth century, the Irish became a majority but still faced legal discrimination until a provincial assembly was formed in 1832. In 1850, the jubilant Newfoundland Catholics constructed, on the high ground overlooking the city of St. John's, the classical granite Cathedral of St. John the Baptist as a glistening symbol of the Celtic emergence in Atlantic Canada. In the mid-nineteenth century, the Irish commanded three dioceses, St. John's, Halifax, and Saint

John (New Brunswick), and in turn, the Scots commanded another three dioceses, Charlottetown, Antigonish, and Kingston. Gallican spirituality henceforth was on the wane.

## Romanism

During the first half of the nineteenth century, the Roman Catholic Church filled episcopal sees in Canada with French, Scottish, and Irish bishops for parishioners who demanded their own bishops, and then, Propaganda Fide, the office in charge of missions for the Holy See, drew these different ethnic cultures into one church. During the second half of the nineteenth century, a second wave of immigrants arrived: the Germans, Ukrainians, Polish, and Hungarians. The Roman Church intensified the effort to unify the Canadian Catholic Church.

The period of the romanization of the Canadian church throughout the nineteenth century began with the successive appointments of the first two bishops of Montreal, Jean-Jacques Lartigue (1777–1840) and Ignace Bourget (1799–1885), both ultramontanes (those who affirmed the unilateral authority of the pope). They were the resolute and dynamic leaders of the new ultramontane Canadian spirituality, whose followers believed that a resurgence of the papal spiritual leadership was essential for the survival of Canadian Catholicism. The ultramontanes during the middle of the nineteenth century focused on loyalty to the leadership of Pope Pius IX (1792–1878), or Pio Nono, who reigned supreme for thirty-two years. At the time, Rome was besieged by the Italian republicans who were determined to unite Italy and remove the pope as temporal leader of the Papal States. As Pius IX fought a rearguard action to protect the Papal States against these popular forces, Catholics around the world loved the beleaguered Pio Nono, prayed for him, rose up to his support, and visited Rome to cheer him on. The spontaneous support for the beleaguered pope and the attractiveness of Roman spirituality and Roman devotions was the future of the Catholic Church.

Bishop Bourget hoped to make Montreal a second Rome and to have the Catholic Church direct Quebec schools and social services. He reasoned that as Catholic priests and seminarians appeared in Rome in cassocks and Roman flat hats, this was the way his Montreal clergy should appear. He built the new Saint-Jacques Cathedral (now also named "Notre-Dame, Renne de Monde") as a smaller replica of St. Peter's Basilica in Rome. He recruited

a company of Papal Zoaves to sail to Rome to defend Pio Nono against the Italian republicans. Another Canadian leader of the ultramontane movement was Bishop Michael Fleming (1792–1850) of St. John's, who had built the Cathedral of St. John the Baptist and invited the Irish sisters to Newfoundland to open schools, to educate young women to become the mothers of the Catholic elite, and to fashion a solid parochial culture. Ultramontane J.J. Lynch (1816–1888), the first archbishop of Toronto, formed a coalition with the Ontario premier, Oliver Mowat (1820–1903), and offered Catholic political support to the ruling party in exchange for province-funded Catholic schools.

At St. Boniface on the Red River, the French Oblates arrived in 1845 and took over the western missions under the young bishop Alexandre Taché (1853–1894). The Oblate Fathers were strong ultramontanes and fanned out along the river highways to carry the Christian gospel with untiring zeal to St. Albert, Lac St. Anne, Fort Vermilion, Rocky Mountain House, and Mission, British Columbia. In a short time more than 200 Oblates poured into the mission field to learn native languages, preach the gospel, and open churches and schools. The missionaries suffered from fatigue, rheumatism, asthma, and bladder problems. The famous Parisian editor of *L'univers,* Louis Veuillot (1813–1883), poignantly depicted the well-known, humble missionary bishop of forty-three years, Vital Grandin (1829–1902), as the "lice-covered" bishop, a not uncommon contagion for those doing mission work.

The Irish and Scottish clergy in the eastern Maritime Provinces became a phalanx of English-speaking missionaries mobilizing to evangelize western Canada. By 1900 the Celtic wave gave an Irish green tinge to the blue and white fields of the French Canadian west, and the French Oblates were being replaced by *les Irelandais*. Archbishop Adélard Langevin (1855–1915) of St. Bonifice, Manitoba, became unhappy that the Irish-driven Canadian Catholic Extension Society offered financial help to western Catholics but did not consult him or send the English-speaking seminarians to the Collège St. Boniface. When J. T. McNally (1871–1952) was appointed bishop in Calgary, Archbishop Henry O'Leary (1879–1938) replaced Emile Legal (1849–1920) in Edmonton, and Archbishop James C. McGuigan (1894–1974) replaced Olivier Mathieu (1853–1929) in Regina, the English-speaking clergy and laity replaced the French Canadians as the major players in western Canada. The

French sphere of influence became restricted to Quebec and enclaves of French-speaking peoples at St. Boniface, Gravelbourg, St. Albert, and smaller French-speaking communities in the Canadian West. The Irish and Scottish Canadians had convinced the Holy See that the future of the Canadian church in Ontario and the West lay with the English-speaking parishioners, clergy, and bishops.

## Central and Eastern European Immigrants

The completion of the Canadian Pacific Railroad to the west in 1885 made transportation safe, and the second wave of newcomers, the Germans, Ukrainians, Polish, and Hungarians, were disbursed throughout the West. The settlers could homestead 160 acres for $10. Having staked their claim, settlers bought wagon and team and traveled 60 to 100 miles over the roughest terrain searching through uncharted regions for their land. Arriving at the site, they set up tents to shelter and feed their families until they could erect a sod house and sod barn. In Saskatchewan, German Catholics located themselves at Balgonie, St. Joseph's Colony, and St. Peter's Colony. New life in the wilderness was a challenge for any family newly arrived from Europe.

Many German Catholics came to Canada from the United States. In 1903, eight thousand German Americans trekked from the American Midwest to found St. Peter's Colony, east of Saskatoon. A German-American land company had taken out options on fifty townships—1,800 square miles of rich soil—and then encouraged German-Americans from the United States to claim quarter-sections of 160 acres at $10 each. Within a few years these homesteads were occupied, parish churches and private schools were built, and German Canadian villages were formed. The heart of the colony was St. Peter's Priory, which was founded by Benedictine Fathers from Cluny, Illinois, and St. John's, Minnesota. In 1921, the Holy See declared St. Peter's an abbacy and the abbot served as bishop for the thirty-six German Catholic parishes in the area. The abbey printed a German-language newspaper, *St. Peter's Bote,* with an English edition, the *Prairie Messenger,* still widely read throughout western Canada. Also in 1921, the abbey opened St. Peter's College as a Catholic high school for boys; in 1925, it became affiliated with the University of Saskatchewan and in 1972 offered university education. Métis, French Canadian, Irish, English, and German Protestant families were interspersed among the German Catholics of St. Peter's.

Ukrainian Catholics also played an important role in the Canadian church. In the late nineteenth and early twentieth centuries, 80 percent of the 100,000 Ukrainians who arrived in Canada were Catholic. The Ukrainian Catholics came from Galicia and the Carpatho-Ukraine, while Ukrainian Orthodox came from Bukovina and the eastern Ukraine. The Ukrainian Catholics belonged to the Greek Catholic Church, one of the Eastern churches in union with Rome. At the Union of Brest in 1596, the Ukrainian Catholics recognized the leadership of the Holy See and retained the Byzantine liturgy and their ecclesial traditions, including married priests. Pope Leo XIII (1810–1903) in 1894 forbade married priests from immigrating to North America and deprived Ukrainian Catholics of needed married clergy. Archbishop Langevin of St. Boniface invited the Ukrainians to attend Latin churches, but they refused the invitation. The Ukrainian Catholics preserved their religious traditions in Canada, erecting wayside crosses, constructing Eastern-style churches, and organizing their devotions in accordance with the Byzantine church.

Langevin, after consulting his fellow bishops in Edmonton and Prince Albert, began to understand the need for Ukrainian clergy. The Metropolitan of Lviv, the head of the Catholic Church in the Ukraine, was asked to send celibate clergy, who began to arrive in 1902. This included five Basilian monks and four Sister Servants of Mary Immaculate who came to western Canada. The monks preached devotion to the Eucharist, the Sacred Heart of Jesus, and the Blessed Virgin Mary. The Sister Servants with financial help from the Sulpicians opened the Sacred Heart Academy for girls at Yorkton, Saskatchewan. The priests opened a bilingual school for boys. Ten Redemptorists from Belgium, five French Canadian diocesan priests, and one Oblate joined the Ukrainian priests in becoming Ukrainian clergy in western Canada. Although this was helpful, Ukrainian Catholics preferred Ukrainian married priests who became involved in the politics of parish life and organized reading clubs, drama circles, and co-operatives. For Ukrainian Catholics, Ukrainian nationalism was second only to their Catholic faith.

The First Plenary Council of Quebec in 1909 recommended the Ukrainians be given their own bishop, schools, newspaper, and more Ukrainian priests. The following year Metropolitan Andrei Sheptytsky (1865–1944) of Lviv came to the Eucharistic Congress in Montreal and visited Ukrainian Catholics across Canada. The Ukrainian faithful told

Sheptytsky that they needed a Ukrainian bishop, married priests, and the removal of the bilingual French-speaking priests. Sheptytsky urged them to remain loyal to the Holy See and the universal church. The Canadian Latin churches began supplying funds for their Ukrainian brothers and sisters. Bishop Langevin supported the Ukrainian Catholic newspaper, *Canadian Ruthenian/Canadian Ukrainian,* first published in 1911. The Catholic Church Extension Society contributed money for the construction of churches and bilingual schools.

In 1912, at the request of the Canadian bishops, Pope Pius X (1835–1914) appointed thirty-five-year old Nykyta Budka (1877–1959) from Lviv as the first Canadian eparch (bishop) of 128,000 Ukrainian Catholics. The following year, twenty Ukrainian priests and seminarians arrived in Canada. Budka assured Ukrainian Catholics that their language and way of life would be protected in the Catholic Church and asked parishes to register with the new Ukrainian Catholic eparchy. Initially only twenty-one of ninety-three parishes registered with the bishop. Budka stated that he was not in favor of married priests as he believed that Ukrainian immigrants could not afford married priests, and in any case, married priests from the Ukraine would not move their families to Canada. The Cathedral of St. Nicholas was constructed in Winnipeg, the Taras Shevchenko Reading Club was opened, and the Boyan Drama Circle staged Ukrainian plays.

Setting themselves apart from the Ukrainian Catholics, some of the Ukrainian intelligentsia initiated opposition, but they were badly divided among themselves. Politicians made contact with the Canadian Liberal and the Conservative parties to cultivate their favor. The nonsectarian rural nationalists sought bilingual education and political and economic independence for the Ukrainian community. The urban socialists sought bilingual schools for children and a populist party for the working people. Some of the intelligentsia in 1918 formed the Ukrainian Greek Orthodox Church with the assistance of the Presbyterians at Manitoba College. Bishop Budka imposed a boycott of Ukrainian Catholic parishes that had not registered with the Catholic eparchy.

By 1920 the Ukrainian religious community in Canada had split into the Ukrainian Catholics, Russian Orthodox, Ukrainian Greek Orthodox, who were independent, and the Ukrainian Protestants, who would soon disperse. Non-Catholic Ukrainians criticized the Ukrainian Catholics for excluding married priests, attending Latin services, and having too many or not enough domes on their churches. The complaints continued that Catholic Ukrainian crosses on the dome of their churches were without the second diagonal arm, their sanctuaries were without iconostasis, they used pipe organs, made the sign of the cross only once, observed the Gregorian calendar, and attended Latin schools. These omissions were pointed out to be serious violations of the Ukrainian cultural environment.

In his last years in Canada, Budka guided forty-seven priests and maintained Eastern liturgies in 229 parishes and mission stations. The Ukrainian Catholics through the next half-century created five Byzantine eparchies: in Winnipeg, Edmonton, New Westminster, Saskatoon, and Toronto. The presence of Ukrainian Catholics along with other Europeans helped to soften the language friction between the French- and English-speakers and led the Canadian church toward multiculturalism. By the end of the twentieth century, the Ukrainian Catholic Canadian church numbered 200,000 members, scattered in 350 parishes, in five eparchies, all of which strengthened the presence of the Eastern churches in Canada.

The Polish, driven off their ancestral lands in Prussia, arrived in Canada looking for free land. As farmers they arrived in eastern Ontario and then the Canadian prairies, and as workers they settled in Montreal, Toronto, Hamilton, and Winnipeg. Polish farmers arrived with almost no funds and hired themselves out to learn the dry farming techniques of the prairies and to generate capital for purchases. Meanwhile, their wives and children managed the homestead and produced a subsistence diet of vegetables, fowl, and beef. Polish clergy arrived to rally the newcomers by organizing community festivals where they could share kielbasa and conversation. In 1929 there were 33 Polish parishes and 157 missions ministering to more than 200,000 Canadian Poles. The Polish newcomers erected schools and chose English as the language of instruction (although Polish was also taught).

Count Paul Esterhazy of Hungary (1831–1912) became a Canadian immigration agent and recruited his Hungarian compatriots to come to Saskatchewan. Winnipeg eventually became the center of Hungarian Canadian culture, publishing *Kanadai Magyar Újság.* Sizeable Hungarian communities emerged in the urban centers of Toronto, Montreal, Windsor, Brantford, and Hamilton. The influx of eastern European Catholics paved the way for Canadian Catholics to become multicultural and international, and thus, more Canadian and more Catholic. The Roman ultramontane spirituality that inspired nineteenth-century Catholics became static during the twentieth century, and Canadians, by the end of the century, were forging a new spirituality and new Canadian church.

## Canadianism

During the first half of the twentieth century, the Catholic Church in Canada began to Canadianize itself, and it became apparent that it was now important to integrate into the church the third wave of southern European Catholics, the Italian and Portuguese Canadians. This process of Canadianization was initiated once again during the last half of the twentieth century, with newcomers arriving from Asia, Africa, and South America.

Southern Europe provided Canada with a large number of immigrant Catholics. Italians made up the largest group, with more than 95 percent being Catholic. In the 1890s, several hundred Italian Catholic laborers were working in Montreal, Toronto, and the Okanagan. The diocese of Toronto and the Redemptorists in 1908 renamed the Irish church Our Lady of Mount Carmel for Italian Catholics and, for the Irish, the Redemptorists then constructed another St. Patrick's Church. During the first three decades of the twentieth century, Italian immigrants arriving before World War I numbered almost 150,000. Settling mainly in urban centers, Italian workers accepted employment on the railways, maintaining urban roads and sewers, and laboring in the construction industry. Priests from several orders as well as Carmelite nuns served these immigrants—in Montreal, principally Servites, in Toronto, Franciscans. In 1934, Toronto's Italian community sponsored a Good Friday procession, which continues to this day. This modern-day procession winds its way through the Italian neighborhood south of College Street, starting and ending at the Church of St. Francis of Assisi. Elaborately costumed actors play the roles of Jesus Christ, Judas Iscariot, Mary Magdalene, Jewish Pharisees, Pontius Pilate, and Roman soldiers.

During the 1930s, education became a source of contention between the ecclesial hierarchy and Italian Catholics. The Italian government offered to provide Italian Canadians with classes in Italian language and culture, and the classes were taught in the evening at the Catholic schools and church halls. In 1939, James C. McGuigan (1894–1974), archbishop of Toronto, discovered that the Italian classes had a barely disguised Fascist agenda. Sensing future hostility, the Italian consul early in that year, much to the archbishop's relief, withdrew funding for the classes, and by the time the

Italian Fascists joined Nazi Germany against the western Allies in May 1940, the issue had disappeared. In the three decades following the war, Italy ranked second only to Great Britain as a source for Canadian immigrants, with more than 500,000 settling in Montreal, Toronto, Ottawa, Hamilton, Guelph, Windsor, Thunder Bay, Winnipeg, Edmonton, and Vancouver. In Toronto, forty-five parishes offered religious services in Italian, and ten in Montreal.

The Portuguese arrived in the postwar world to participate in the Canadian economic expansion. The Canadian and Portuguese governments after World War II signed agreements allowing Portuguese railway, construction, and agricultural laborers to work in Canada. In the 1950s, nearly 20,000 Portuguese arrived, almost 90 percent of whom were Catholic. Immigrants came from the island of Sao Miguel in the Azores and settled in Toronto, and others from the continental districts of Portugal came to Montreal. In the following two decades, family sponsorship programs and chain migration boosted the Portuguese community to 140,000, and in Toronto fifteen churches offered religious services in Portuguese, and two in Montreal.

## Canadian Catholic Response during the Depression

The stock market crashed in October 1929 and a world economic Depression descended upon Europe and North America. The economy in the Maritime Provinces of Nova Scotia, New Brunswick, and Prince Edward Island was listless; in Montreal and Toronto, the unemployed took to the streets looking for work; and on the Canadian prairies, the drought intensified the agricultural distress. The Depression intensified the Canadianization of the Catholic Church. In 1933, the Cooperative Commonwealth Federation (CCF) was founded in Regina, Saskatchewan, as a socialist effort to alleviate economic distress. In Montreal, Archbishop George Gauthier condemned the CCF, fearing it was communist-inspired and antireligious.

At Antigonish, Nova Scotia, Fathers Jimmy Tompkins (1870–1953) and Moses Coady (1882–1959) provided a Canadian Catholic response to the Depression by convincing St. Francis Xavier College, in 1930, to open an Extension Department to offer continuing education for working people and teach them how to establish cooperatives. Moses Coady educated farmers, fishermen, and miners to develop the habit of continual learning throughout their adult lives. Jimmy Tompkins (1870–1953) helped set up cooperatives to buy necessities at a reduced rate, and to sell their fish, agricultural products, and manufactured items at a fair price. This Antigonish Movement generated a powerful spirit of sharing, research, cooperation, and hope among the Maritime people. The Maritime Catholics were discovering Canadian Catholic solutions for Canadian problems.

In Toronto, the editor of the *Catholic Register,* Henry Somerville (1889–1953), an English journalist with a diploma in labor studies from Oxford University, introduced Toronto Catholics in the 1920s and 1930s to the papal encyclicals, *Rerum Novarum* and *Quadragesimo Anno.* He taught at St. Augustine's Seminary in Toronto and wrote in the Catholic newspaper that the church was concerned not only about morality but also about social justice. This concern spoke for workers, including living wages, healthy working conditions, and church support for the cause of unions. He also urged that Canadian Catholics must achieve at least a high school education to take up leadership roles in Canadian politics, unions, and society. What Somerville taught, Catherine de Hueck (1896–1985) did by opening a Friendship House in downtown Toronto to provide food for the hungry and shelter for the needy. During the Depression, de Hueck joined the picket line of workers at Laura Secord Company. This action upset Archbishop McGuigan because the company was owned by Sen. Frank O'Connor (1885–1939), a generous benefactor of the archdiocese. After the archbishop castigated her, de Hueck itemized the injustices at the Laura Secord plant and backed them up with passages from *Quadragesimo Anno* advocating a just wage for each worker and affirming the prolabor teaching of *Rerum Novarum.* De Hueck and the archbishop remained friends, and Laura Secord improved their hiring practices.

To alleviate the grinding poverty during the Depression, Basilian Father Eugene Cullinane (1907–1997) was attracted to the CCF because he found it based on the British parliamentary system and on principles similar to Catholic social teachings. During graduate studies at Catholic University of America, he began a dissertation on the social philosophy of the CCF and then taught economics from 1945 to 1948 at St. Thomas More College in Saskatoon. Father Cullinane assessed the CCF to be an expression of Canadian Christian humanism, being neither violent nor against religion. In these controversial years, he was the first Catholic priest to join the CCF. Shortly after, his letter explaining why he joined the CCF, which Bishop Pocock had forbidden him to make public, was mistakenly circulated. Bishop Pocock, without further ceremony, expelled Father Cullinane from the diocese of Saskatoon.

Fathers Isidore Gorski (1930–2005) and Bob Ogle (1928–1998) followed his path and joined the CCF, which by then had broadened its political base to become the New Democratic Party (NDP). The NDP Premier of Saskatchewan Allan Blakeney (1925–) had thirteen Catholic members of the provincial legislature in his government, five of whom were in his cabinet. As historian Teresita Kambeitz has argued, the Catholic Church never stood in unrelenting opposition to the CCF. After the formation of the Canadian Catholic Conference in 1943, the Canadian bishops made it clear that the support of Catholics for the CCF was quite acceptable.

Catholic social teaching in Quebec was fully tested by the asbestos strike of 1949. During the Duplessis regime, Quebec workers were the most poorly paid in the country. The asbestos miners in spring 1949 went on strike to maintain their wages against further cuts. Johns-Manville Company in full-page newspaper ads labeled the strikers as revolutionaries and communists. Facing starvation and expulsion from their homes, the workers asked the church for help. Outside the churches at Sherbrooke and Montreal, $167,000 was collected for the starving families. At the Montreal cathedral, Archbishop Joseph Charbonneau (1892–1959) mounted the pulpit and stated that the working class was a "victim of a conspiracy which seeks to crush it." He declared that "the Church has the duty to intervene."

Archbishop Roy of Quebec City offered his services as a mediator, and the asbestos companies agreed to settle. After the strike, the Jesuit and Dominican editors of their respective journals, who took the side of the workers, were sent into exile. Archbishop Charbonneau was summoned to the apostolic delegate's residence in Ottawa on New Year's Day and told to resign. The archbishop replied that he was a canon lawyer, knew his rights, and would appeal directly to the pope. The delegate countered that this message came directly from the pope: *Roma locuta est, causa finita est.* Charbonneau left Montreal before the end of the month and accepted work in British Columbia as a hospital chaplain.

One pundit alleged the New York firm of Johns-Manville Company had complained to Cardinal Spellman in New York, a very close friend of Pope Pius XII, and thus, Charbonneau was dismissed for interference against the New York firm. Another pundit claimed that the Premier of Quebec, Maurice Duplessis (1890–1959), denounced the archbishop to Rome on behalf of the mine owners. Both opinions were commonly stated without fear or research.

Rather within the month, Charbonneau blamed Quebec's rural bishops. The rural Quebec bishops, fearing the open-minded Franco-Ontarian in their midst, and themselves having strong connections in Rome, denounced Charbonneau as the thin edge of the wedge of modernity and wanted him eliminated before the turmoil of the "Quiet Revolution" ("Revolution Tranquille") swept up river to their rural dioceses.

The rural bishops of Quebec had reason to be concerned. The Quiet Revolution during the 1940s and 1950s percolated slowly through the province of Quebec and only came to a boil in 1960 with the election of the Premier Jean Lesage (1912–1980) of the Liberal Party. The center of the Quiet Revolution was the newly educated professional classes who were eager to gain control of the schools, labor unions, hospitals, and social work. In a society where education, health care, and social work had been controlled by the Catholic Church officials, the laypeople sought their place in public office. The reason the revolution turned out to be "quiet" was that the clergy willingly let go of control in exchange for an advisory role in the future reforms. With breathtaking speed, Premier Jean Lesage, Réne Levesque (1922–1987), and colleagues secularized the medical, social, labor, and pension systems that up until that time were run by the religious orders for the province. Seeing this happen, Cardinal Paul-Émile Léger (1904–1991) of Montreal, maneuvered for influence through chaplains and raised questions to Quebec society on behalf of minorities. These radical changes in Quebec society convinced Catholics that the Second Vatican Council (1962–1965) was a necessary remedy to deal globally with the paradigm shift happening throughout Western society.

At the Second Vatican Council, the three Canadian stars were Cardinal Léger, Metropolitan Maxim Hermaniuk (1911–1996) of Winnipeg, and Archbishop Maurice Baudoux (1902–1974) of St. Boniface. Before the Council, Rome asked the bishops and universities to submit "vota" for the agenda. Cardinal Léger submitted nineteen pages in the vernacular and asked that the church adjust to the modern age and not restore dead structures. Before the first session of the council, he wrote directly to Pope John XXIII (1881–1963) to say that the agenda prepared by the Curia was not adequate and another must be prepared by council members. This was done. Metropolitan Hermaniuk sent submissions asking for equality of the Eastern and Western churches, reunion of the Christian churches, and naming the church by its proper title, "The Catholic Church."

Archbishop Baudoux set up a preparatory commission of outstanding theologians that included four future bishops, Antoine Hacault of St. Boniface, Edouard Gagnon of Saint-Paul, Remi De Roo of Victoria, and Noël Delaquis of Gravelbourg. Archbishop Baudoux was president of the Canadian bishops at the beginning of the council, as Archbishop Flahiff was their president for the last session. The Canadian bishops sat on many council commissions and returned at the end of the council with a heightened awareness of the Christian Church as the sacrament of Christ responding to the needs of the people.

The Second Vatican Council opened up many questions on church life and practice. Two problems surfaced, which the Canadian church has yet to resolve adequately, concerned the participation of women and the status of the Aboriginal Catholics. Since the intervention of Cardinal George Bernard Flahiff (1905–1989) in Rome in 1971, the Canadian church has asked that the role of women be more fully discussed and that women be appointed to administrative positions. Since that time, women have been hired in Canadian parishes and dioceses, in Catholic universities and seminaries, and in liturgies have contributed as lectors, servers, and ministers of bread and cup. In regard to the Aboriginal Catholics, Dean Achiel Peelman (1942–) of St. Paul University in Ottawa revealed his vision that Catholics will never become a Canadian Catholic church until the Aboriginal Catholics take leadership in the church and evangelize the Euro-Canadians.

## Postmodern Canadianism: International Catholicism

While that vision remained a possible future of the Canadian Catholic church as of the early twenty-first century, the day-to-day reality was affected by an arrival of a fourth wave of Catholics to Canada. Canadian laws after 1967 admitted immigrants from around the world by the merit system, opening the way for Asians, Africans, Arabs, and Hispanics. This meant that Catholics from these continents chose to migrate to Canada and carry with them their indigenous cultures. In particular, Chinese Catholics in Toronto have opened four parishes since 1970, and in Vancouver they operate three parishes, and one parish each in Edmonton, Calgary, Ottawa, and Montreal. While the average parish in Toronto baptizes eighty-seven neophytes yearly, Chinese Martyrs' Parish of Toronto since the 1990s has each year consistently baptized 300 to 600 people. Lest one have any doubt about the quality of the catechesis, the pastoral council of Chinese

Martyrs' Parish extended its Rite of Christian Initiation for Adults (RCIA) program from nine to eighteen months.

The Filipinos have a small number of Tagalog-speaking parishes in Canada but, more importantly, have renewed many parishes by their presence in Winnipeg, Toronto, Vancouver, Calgary, and Edmonton. Filipinos attend churches regularly in large numbers and contribute to the reading, serving, and Eucharistic ministry, as well as quickly becoming the backbone of parish social activities. The Vietnamese Catholics have opened eleven parishes from Vancouver to Montreal. These parishes become cultural rallying points for Vietnamese Catholics, as they take over abandoned Canadian churches and renew them or build new ones.

The Tamils have four Catholic communities in Toronto and one in Montreal. Like the Chinese, Vietnamese, Koreans, and Filipinos, the Tamils have charismatic prayer groups that rally the flagging spirits of new Canadians and help them to cope with the daily adjustment demanded. The Korean communities are seven in number and stretch from Vancouver to Montreal. The Koreans have an intensity in their religious practice that makes their faith outstanding.

Furthermore, it is the rising number of Asian, African, and Hispanic students who are making a difference in Canadian seminaries. The missionary work of Canadian men and women around the world during the last one hundred years is bringing to Canada strong believers from around the globe. Since the Second Vatican Council, the Asian bishops have been meeting at regular intervals to formulate Asian theology, which includes the principles of collegiality, subsidiarity, family values, cohesive community spirit, respect for the elderly, and concern for the needy.

## Conclusion

Catholic Canadians arrived in four waves. French Gallicans for two hundred years were in undisputed control of Canadian geography and religion, until Irish and Scottish Catholic rivals settled to the east and to the west of them. In the middle of the nineteenth century, newcomers from central and eastern Europe settled in central and western Canada and helped diffuse the French-Celtic conflict, establishing the foundation of the international church Canadian Catholics profess to be. In the twentieth century, southern Europeans arrived in the well-established cities of Ontario and Quebec and created a more diverse Canadian society. The multicultural picture of Canada and the Canadian Catholic Church was completed after 1970 with the influx

of the Asians, Africans, Arabs, and Hispanics. These ethnic groups from the continents of the world are now integrated into a Catholic history that was established by Aboriginal, Gallican, Roman, and Canadian influences. Canada freely adopted multiculturalism, and the mission of the Catholic Church in Canada fully embraces this multicultural vision.

See also *Anti-Catholicism; Architecture: Roman Catholic; Canada entries; Roman Catholicism: French Influence; Roman Catholicism: Tradition and Heritage; Women Religious; Worship: Roman Catholic.*

Terence J. Fay SJ

## BIBLIOGRAPHY

Akenson, Donald H. *Small Differences: Irish Catholics and Irish Protestants, 1815–1922.* Montreal: McGill-Queens University Press, 1988.

Bumsted, J. M. *The People's Clearance, 1770–1815.* Winnipeg, Canada: University of Manitoba Press, 1982.

Choquette, Robert. *The Oblate Assault on Canada's Northwest.* Ottawa, Canada: University of Ottawa Press, 1995.

Clarke, Brian P. *Piety and Nationalism: Lay Voluntary Associations in Toronto, 1850–1895.* Montreal: McGill-Queens University Press, 1993.

Dixon, Robert T. *Catholic Education and Politics in Ontario.* Vol. 4. Toronto: Catholic Education Foundation of Ontario, 2003.

Fay, Terence J. *A History of Canadian Catholics: Gallicanism, Romanism, and Canadianism.* Montreal: McGill-Queens University Press, 2002.

———. *The New Faces of Canadian Catholics: The Asians.* Ottawa, Canada: Novalis, 2009.

———. "From the Tropics to the Freezer: Filipino Catholics Acclimatize to Canada, 1972–2002." *Historical Studies* 71 (2005): 29–59.

Fox, Thomas C. *Pentecost in Asia.* Maryknoll, N.Y.: Orbis, 2003.

Gauvreau, Michael. *The Catholic Origins of Quebec's Quiet Revolution, 1931–1971.* Montreal: McGill-Queens University Press, 2005.

Greer, Allan. *Mohawk Saint: Catherine Tekakwitha and the Jesuits.* Toronto: Oxford University Press, 2005.

Houston, Cecil J., and William J. Smyth. *Irish Immigration and Canadian Settlement.* Toronto: University of Toronto Press, 1990.

Huel, Raymond J. A. *Proclaiming the Gospel to the Indians and Métis.* Edmonton, Canada: University of Alberta Press and Western Canadian Publishers, 1996.

McCarthy, Martha. *From the Great River: Oblate Missions to the Dene, 1847–1921.* Edmonton, Canada: University of Alberta Press and Western Canadian Publishers, 1995.

McGowan, Mark G. *The Waning of the Green: Catholics, the Irish, and Identity in Toronto, 1887–1922.* Montreal: McGill-Queens University Press, 1999.

McNally, Vincent J. *The Lord's Distant Vineyard: A History of the Oblates in British Columbia.* Edmonton, Canada: University of Alberta Press, 2000

Milloy, John S. *A National Crime: The Canadian Government and the Residential School System, 1879–1896.* Winnipeg, Canada: University of Manitoba Press, 1999.

Murphy, Terrence, and Roberto Perin. *A Concise History of Christianity in Canada*. Toronto: Oxford University Press, 1996.

Murphy, Terrence, and Gerald Storz, eds. *Creed and Culture: English-Speaking Catholics in Canadian Society, 1750–1930*. Montreal: McGill-Queens University Press, 1993.

Perin, Roberto. *Rome in Canada: The Vatican and Canadian Affairs*. Toronto: University of Toronto Press, 1990.

Platt, W. Wallace. *Gentle Eminence: A Life of Cardinal Flahiff*. Montreal: McGill-Queens University Press, 1999.

Power, Michael. *A Promise Fulfilled: The Political History of the Catholic Separate Schools in Ontario*. Toronto: Ontario Catholic School Trustees' Association, 2002.

Simpson, Patricia. *Marguerite Bourgeoys*. 2 vols. Montreal: McGill-Queens University Press, 2005.

Welton, Michael R. *Little Mosie from the Margaree: A Biography of Moses Michael Coady*. Toronto: Thompson Educational Publishing, 2001.

Zucchi, John E. *Italians in Toronto: Development of a National Identity, 1875–1935*. Montreal: McGill-Queens University Press, 1988.

# Canada: Church and State

The changing relationship between church and state in Canada reflects the historical development of a society whose colonial roots are both French Roman Catholic and British Protestant. Although by the mid-nineteenth century the classical pattern of a single established church had been successfully contested, ties between church and state remained strong, with religion functioning as an informal or "shadow" religious establishment composed of a relatively few "mainline" Protestant denominations, with Roman Catholicism dominating in francophone Quebec. Beginning in the 1960s church and state underwent massive restructuring, resulting in a radical differentiation that brought to an end the long-standing overlap between the spiritual and the secular.

As a result, the term *church and state* is now anachronistic to describe the place of religion in contemporary secular and pluralistic Canada and can be more meaningfully reformulated as *religion and public life*. Both terms are fluid and dynamic and at various points will invite comparison with the U.S. experience.

## New France, 1608–1760

As early as 1534, when French adventurer Jacques Cartier erected a cross at Gaspé, Christianity established a symbolic presence in what would become New France, but its actual roots date to 1608, when settlement began in Quebec. Following closely upon the termination of the religious wars in France, the new royal absolutism insisted on a Gallican church that was submissive to the state rather than

to Rome. Although limited toleration of Huguenots granted by the Edict of Nantes remained in effect until 1685, already in 1627 a royal charter to a commercial company stipulated that only French Roman Catholics were to be settled in the colony.

The task of the colonial church, as an arm to the state, was the religious formation and education of settlers and, more dauntingly, the Christianization of the aboriginal population. Motivated by fervid piety and eschatological zeal, male and female religious orders, some newly formed, eagerly undertook this work, and missions to native tribes became part of the network of trading alliances along the north shore of the St. Lawrence. Dependent on the military for protection, priests and missions inevitably found themselves caught up in the military and economic rivalries among European nations and their aboriginal allies. A similar interdependence could be found in the government of New France: senior clergy served as members of the governing council, while church services celebrated major state events such as the birth of a royal heir or a major victory in war.

In return for supporting the government the church received extensive benefits. All state appointments as well as some professions required proof of Roman Catholic baptism, and public morality was regulated by legislation. State financial support was significant, and by 1700 the state treasury provided 40 percent of the church's revenues, as well as offering generous subsidies to the building of ecclesiastical institutions. Church buildings dominated the colonial settlements, and the church functioned as the major patron of music, painting, and the arts.

In theory the partnership between church and state in New France was meant to work to mutual advantage, but as the state extended its power and colonial life became more stable, religious influence weakened. A shortage of priests meant less close contact with the general population, and government authorities found it impossible to enforce such moral regulations as the closing of taverns during church services and holy days. What did not change was the ecclesiastical obedience to state authority so characteristic of the Gallican church. When, after years of war, first Acadia in 1713 and then New France in 1763 fell to Britain, this obedience would be transferred to the new royal authority, a move made easier by Britain's measured pragmatic approach in the treaties and legislative acts that settled the conquest of the French colonies in North America.

## Canada as a British Colony, 1763–1867

### Roman Catholics and the State in Quebec and the Maritimes

The close association between the Roman Catholic Church and the state during the French period laid the foundations for a markedly tolerant attitude toward Roman Catholics in the newly acquired British colony. In England the classical church-state model of one religion had been adjusted by the late seventeenth century to permit some religious, but not civil, rights to minority Protestant religions, and to a lesser extent Roman Catholics. Upon their conquest of Acadia in 1713, the British had not outlawed Roman Catholicism, but in 1751 as war continued with France and concerns mounted about the population's loyalty, it was decided to deport the Acadians to the British colonies to the south.

Eight years later, with the defeat of Quebec and then Montreal, there was no thought of deportation, and despite the opposition of the archbishop of Canterbury and like-minded Protestants, there was no effort to convert the conquered Roman Catholics. What ensued was a relatively lenient practice, which, despite some restrictions on male orders, granted religious freedom to the conquered, thereby encouraging the continuation of cooperation between church and state. When compared with that of New France, ecclesiastical authority was in fact enhanced, for in the vacuum left by the departure of state officials for France, the bishop of Quebec became the population's de facto political and religious leader. Successive bishops recognized the need to maintain cordial relations with the new rulers and willingly sought the support of a government that shared their understanding of the church's conservative social role.

Pragmatic state concerns encouraged this cooperation. As Britain's colonies to the south became increasingly restive, the first two governors, James Murray and Guy Carleton, were anxious to win the hierarchy's respect and goodwill. The Quebec Act (one of the "intolerable" acts that eventually led to war in the American colonies) in 1774 granted unprecedented Roman Catholic rights of freedom of religion, including the right of clergy to collect their accustomed tithes. Although it was subsequently clarified that this did not make Roman Catholicism the established religion, such concessions did ensure the loyalty of the bishop and at least the neutrality of the majority of the *Canadiens* and lower clergy during the American and French revolutionary wars. In Nova Scotia, formerly Acadia, bans prohibiting entry into the priesthood and the ownership of property by

Roman Catholics were repealed in 1783, but there and in the subsequent separate colonies of New Brunswick (1785) and Prince Edward Island (1802) complete civil rights were not extended until 1830, immediately following the British Parliament's passing of the Catholic Emancipation Act.

Although these last two colonies had a substantial Roman Catholic population, it was only in the former New France that the church remained dominant. An influx of 5,000 Protestant loyalists following the formation of the new American republic resulted in the Constitutional Act of 1791, dividing the area into Lower and Upper Canada, each with its own colonial government and religious settlement. Since only a small number of Protestants had settled in Lower Canada, there was little immediate threat to Roman Catholics of any Church of England establishment. Of greater concern, however, was the influence of American and French revolutionary ideas on the colony's political leaders. The new constitutional arrangement had provided an elected assembly where a struggle for democratic rights now challenged the church's traditional conservative role in society, a position strengthened in 1818 by the appointment of the bishop of Quebec to the conservative Legislative Council. In 1837–1838 growing dissatisfaction and increasingly radical rhetoric resulted in several abortive rebellions, an indication that not all the faithful docilely accepted the church's insistence on loyalty to legitimate authority.

In the long term, however, the Roman Catholic Church recovered the place it had enjoyed before the advent of representative institutions in 1791. The failed rebellions and the radical reformers' loss of authority conclusively ended any fears that Lower Canadians might establish a secular state on the model of the American republic. Having won the respect of the British authorities for its conservative leadership during the rebellions, the church also received more freedom to establish new dioceses and bring priests and religious communities from France. Under its strengthened leadership, those distinctly French Canadian elements that had been part of the struggle for sovereignty—language, religion, and law—now became the foundation of a unique socially conservative Roman Catholic identity.

Facilitating this shift was a new constitutional arrangement. In 1841 in response to similar rebellions in Upper Canada but specifically to facilitate economic reform under English Canadian leadership, the Act of Union joined Lower and Upper Canada, now called Canada East and West, under one system of responsible government. To counter the potentially dangerous impact of such a union on Roman

Catholic identity, Bishop Ignace Bourget, recently appointed to the new diocese of Montreal, heartland of Protestant commercial interests in Canada East, instigated a thorough devotional revolution that affected all areas of life. Following the example of France and Italy, where the Church had been battling anticlerical and republican ideas much longer than in French Canada, Catholicism became thoroughly Roman or ultramontane. Unlike countries where Roman Catholicism was a minority faith, in Quebec its dominance allowed it to become a pervasive and public religion. There through means of distinctive architecture and art, rituals, schools, hospitals, and other social institutions, staffed by growing numbers in religious orders, the church was able to create a unique cultural space. Confederation in 1867 would help entrench this, for on the insistence of the Roman Catholic hierarchy, health, education, and social services remained under provincial jurisdiction. Throughout the nineteenth century and well into the twentieth, Quebec's ultramontane public institutions would set it apart not only from Protestant Canada but also from other North American Roman Catholics.

## Protestants and the State, 1750–1867

Whereas Roman Catholicism retained some signs of informal establishment in Quebec, the large numbers of Protestants who came to British North America from Britain and the new American Republic quickly began to either compete for state support or challenge the very idea of establishment. Neither position ended up with a clear victory, and not unlike Roman Catholicism in Quebec, by 1867 although church and state would be formally separate, the churches with the help of the state had achieved a strong public presence and wielded significant cultural authority.

Initially, the same conservative ideals that had inspired the colonial government's support of the Roman Catholic Church in Quebec also favored a Protestant establishment. As articulated most persistently by John Strachan, Anglican bishop of York, Upper Canada, in an age of revolutionary fervor church and state had to work together and create a social order characterized by obedience to authority and sound moral behavior. Thus at a time when in the new American republic churches were being disestablished, in the British colonies to the north a struggling Church of England tried to adapt establishment principles and practices to colonial soil. Legislation to this effect (but also granting freedom of religion to dissenters) had already been

passed in 1758 in Nova Scotia and, upon their formation as separate colonies, would follow in New Brunswick in 1787 and Prince Edward Island in 1802. For Upper Canada, which at its formation had no revenue for church support, the Constitutional Act of 1791 stipulated that one-seventh of the land be set apart for the support "of a Protestant clergy." These "clergy reserves" and a subsequent decision in 1836 to set aside further land for Anglican rectories quickly became a source of much criticism and displeasure among the other Protestant denominations, which greatly outnumbered the Anglican.

Equally contentious in all the colonies were Anglican efforts to educate an elite leadership for church and state. Well before the availability of financial resources, university charters were obtained to erect an exclusively Anglican King's College in Windsor, Nova Scotia, and another, somewhat less exclusive, in York, Upper Canada. Other Anglican entitlements such as the unique right to perform marriages and the exclusion of non-Anglicans from burial in parish cemeteries proved from the beginning to be unenforceable, when three-quarters of the population were members of a different denomination. Moreover, since the majority of Protestants belonged to evangelical denominations, there was strong resistance to any claim that an established church rather than individual conversion and faith provided the proper foundation for a moral social order. In Upper Canada there was the added aggravation of the clergy reserves, as members of the elected assembly decried the impediments these large tracts of undeveloped land posed to a commercializing market economy. By the 1830s the opinion of political reform in Britain had also turned against church establishment, and even the widening missionary movement proved a detriment when the Anglican Society for the Propagation of the Gospel moved its funding priorities from the Maritimes to new fields.

Though only Nova Scotia passed specific legislation, by 1854 church establishment had come to an end in all the colonies, with middle-class reformers now firmly in control and keen to dismantle all privileges of the former social order. In the meantime all religious groups had also acquired complete equality before the law in such areas as the right to conduct marriages, to vote, and to hold military and civil office, and the earlier automatic right of Anglican bishops to sit on the legislative councils had ended. The monopoly of the Anglican King's College in Windsor, Nova Scotia also had been successfully challenged: rival denominational colleges had been founded by Baptists, Methodists, Roman

Catholics, and Presbyterians, and in 1838, Rev. Thomas McCulloch, founder of the Presbyterian Pictou Academy, accepted the presidency of a publicly funded religiously neutral Dalhousie College in Halifax.

In Upper Canada, disestablishment had a more tortuous history, as various denominations contested Anglican privilege by claiming their own right to state financial support. By the 1830s government aid was being received not only by the Church of England but also by the Church of Scotland, the Wesleyan Methodists (for support to aboriginal missions), and the Roman Catholic Church (whose bishop premised his claim on preconquest status). In 1854 the growing strength of voluntarism finally terminated all denominational aid when the conservative administration of John A. Macdonald, Canada's future prime minister, voted the clergy reserves out of existence, with the proceeds to be applied to municipalities. As part of the arrangement and to the indignation of voluntarists, vested rights of the existing clergy were acknowledged in financial allotments to their respective denominations, primarily the Church of England, some to the Church of Scotland, and small amounts to the Roman Catholics and Wesleyan Methodists. Consolidated as a "commutation fund," the Anglican amount was sufficient to support its clergy into the next century.

In higher education similar vestiges of earlier denominational rivalry remained. In response to the Anglican monopoly of King's College, Wesleyan Methodists, the Church of Scotland, Roman Catholics, and the Free Church had all founded their own institutions by the 1840s. In 1849 a reform-minded legislature, sympathetic to resentment at Anglican privilege to public funds in a cash-strapped society, replaced King's College with a secular University of Toronto, but with small annual grants for the denominational colleges.

Unlike the Maritimes, which had no government-funded school system, elementary and secondary education in the Canadas would also retain evidence of an earlier period of cooperation between church and state. Through a series of compromises, what began in a sparsely settled colony as an assortment of individual schools to accommodate the religious beliefs of the local population turned into two distinct publicly funded school systems, Protestant and Roman Catholic. Influenced by reformers such as Horace Mann, Egerton Ryerson, western Canada's superintendent of education and former editor of the Methodist *Christian Guardian,* considered education a state responsibility and in the place of denominational schools advocated a single nonsectarian Christian system. To Toronto's ultramontane bishop Armand de Charbonnel, such a system was only Protestant in disguise, and nothing less than complete Roman Catholic control of their own schools was acceptable. By 1859, with the help of like-minded representatives in the legislature and the support of the Protestant minority in Canada East, both Canadas had publicly funded schools for their respective Roman Catholic and Protestant religious minorities. At Confederation these rights would be entrenched in section 93 of the British North America Act.

This would be the only reference to religion in the new constitutional agreement, and the formal loss of church privilege by then in place was simply assumed. As had been the case with the 1791 amendment to the U.S. Constitution, religion was now a matter of free choice and expression, untrammeled by any established church. In both countries the move to voluntarism ensured a vital Christianity that contrasted favorably with the European tradition of establishment. In each, evangelical Protestants joined forces in a "united front" of interdenominational agencies devoted to such moral goals as temperance, Sabbath observance, and benevolence. Nevertheless in the second half of the nineteenth century it was Canada that struck observers as the more Christian nation. Where in the United States, debates over slavery and the subsequent Civil War fractured the evangelical front, in Canada Confederation in 1867 gave it a new impetus. However, the fact that Canada had not one but two activist forms of Christianity, evangelical Protestantism and ultramontane Roman Catholicism, also ensured that in an age of growing nationalism, religion would be a source of conflict as each group sought to shape the new country's identity.

## Christian Canada, 1867–1967

Roman Catholics, who by 1871 had formed 40.4 percent of the population and feared the corrosive impact of "Americanism" in the newly formed country, emphasized those differences that distinguished them from the Protestant majority. The latter was concentrated in five main denominations: Anglican, Baptist, Congregationalist, Presbyterian, and Methodist (these last two consolidated by internal unions completed, respectively, in 1875 and 1883). Despite their different traditions, all shared a strong sense of evangelical mission, evocatively captured in the country's motto, taken from Psalm 72:8, "And He shall have Dominion from Sea to Sea." As the country expanded, both Catholics and Protestants looked to home missions and institutional growth to extend their presence and in the process encountered new sources of conflict.

For the next century the entry of additional provinces, beginning with Manitoba in 1870 and finalized with Newfoundland in 1949, ensured that religious rights for minorities remained a potential battleground requiring continual political compromise. Faced with religiously mixed constituencies and usually satisfying neither side, federal politicians debated and prevaricated, reluctantly acquiescing in New Brunswick's decision in 1872 to cease providing public funds for Roman Catholic schools but subsequently extending such rights to Manitoba, Saskatchewan, Alberta, and Newfoundland.

At a time when federal and provincial governments were relatively weak and underfunded, the opening of the west to white settlers called for increased cooperation between church and state. By its treaties, the federal government was obliged to provide schooling for Aboriginal children. Convinced that the goal of their education was to be "civilization" and "Christianization," the Department of Indian Affairs in the 1880s undertook to establish and fund a system of church-run residential schools. In contrast to their brief and limited role in the operation of Aboriginal boarding schools in the United States, Protestant and Roman Catholic denominations continued in their role on behalf of the Canadian government until the latter terminated the system in 1969.

Immigration to the west began seriously in the 1890s and in the first decade of the twentieth century brought over a million new settlers representing many different languages and faiths. That same period also saw a rise in urbanization, from 37.5 percent to 45.4 percent of the population. In each case the churches took on the giant's share of providing such basic institutions as schools, hospitals, and settlement houses for the newcomers, in part out of concern to meet their immediate needs but also to implant Christian ideals of citizenship. Anti-Catholicism and nativism combined with loyalty to the British Empire to shape a national vision of a distinctly increasingly Protestant cast. Evangelical concern for social holiness and Victorian values of sobriety and industry, with little distinction between Christ and culture, provided the impetus for large-scale campaigns of moral and social reform, from temperance to Sabbatarianism.

By the 1890s a new impetus to reform emerged in the Social Gospel, originating in American and British thought but flourishing in the less complicated Canadian setting.

Seeking to meet the challenges of large-scale immigration and growing urbanization through reform based on Christian principles of brotherhood and social justice, Social Gospelers looked beyond individual conversion to the moral reform of church and state. Methodists, who previously had favored moral suasion over reform legislation, now joined forces with Presbyterians and other evangelicals in ecumenical organizations such as the Lord's Day Alliance, which in 1906 saw the passing of a federal Lord's Day Act. Despite aggressive campaigns in every province, the achievement of prohibition legislation was more difficult, succeeding only in Prince Edward Island in 1901, until war gave sobriety a moral boost, making every province dry by 1919.

When Canada, with Britain, declared war on August 4, 1914, the churches offered enthusiastic support, often differentiating little between the spheres of Caesar and Christ in their eagerness to promote recruitment. Little tolerance was shown to religious groups of German or Russian background, and in 1917 under the Wartime Elections Act, Mennonites, Hutterites, and Doukhobors lost the franchise, not to be restored until 1920. Resentment also flared up against French Roman Catholics in Quebec, whose ties with Europe were much more distant and who strongly resisted the move to conscription in 1917. The high rate of service overseas by Roman Catholics of Irish origin, on the other hand, spoke of a shared Canadian and British identity with the Protestant majority.

For both Protestants and Roman Catholics the interwar years were a period of readjustment as capitalism evolved toward corporate concentration, forcing the federal government tentatively to take on a more regulatory role. Better equipped to assist those affected by economic downturn, it began to move into areas traditionally under the churches' purview. In the face of such changes, both mainline Protestants and Roman Catholics were able to recast their earlier visions of Christian nationhood and maintain cultural authority. In Canada Protestants were fortunate, for unlike in the United States, except for the relatively small Baptist denomination there were no fundamentalist schisms. Instead a major move to consolidation began in 1902, when, with a view to strengthening their national mission, Methodists, Presbyterians, and Congregationalists entered into union discussions. Postponed until after the war, the union was finalized in 1925, and a new denomination, the United Church of Canada, came into existence by act of Parliament. Presbyterian resistance, however, left some 40 percent continuing as a separate denomination, with both sides turning to the federal and provincial legislatures in protracted battles over property and name rights.

As the country's largest Protestant denomination, the United Church assumed leadership in adapting the earlier evangelical vision of social and moral reform to new realities. Already in 1918, building on the wartime regulation of industry, the General Conference of the Methodist Church had supported a committee report rejecting the capitalist system and calling for complete economic restructuring. In 1933 this radical approach received further impetus with the formation of a new party, the Co-operative Commonwealth Federation (CCF), led by J. S. Woodsworth, a former Methodist minister who since 1921 had served in Parliament as a Labor Independent. With the help of a fellow laborite, Woodsworth had been instrumental in forcing the Liberal government to pass old-age legislation in 1926, and as House Leader of the new CCF, he continued to push for reform, until the declaration of war in 1939 forced him as a pacifist to step down.

The Depression of the 1930s did not raise up radical religious voices only on the left. From 1935 to 1968 Alberta was ruled by the populist Social Credit Party, led successively by two fundamentalist preachers, William Aberhart and Ernest C. Manning, who as premiers freely transmitted their premillennialist Christianity in weekly broadcasts on the province's airwaves. In so doing they ran afoul of the Canadian Broadcasting Act of 1936, whose regulations, in a pattern similar to that in the United States, supported the interests of the mainline denominations. It was they who defined national ideals in civic life and who influenced the country's universities. Since 1907, through the ecumenical Christian Social Service Council and through progressive clergy professors, Protestant denominations played a leading role in developing university research and teaching in the new social sciences. As a result they also had a major input into social policy creation at both the federal and provincial levels and became crucial catalysts in creating a climate of opinion receptive to increased state intervention. Their social understanding of Christianity favored such ideals as universal old-age security and government-funded hospital insurance, and in 1946 the latter became reality under North America's first socialist government, the CCF in Saskatchewan, led by former Baptist minister Tommy Douglas.

In such ways the Protestant denominations were able to recast their earlier partnership with the state. They had historically taken little critical distance from the culture, and thus their cooperation was not without ambiguity. It was only in 1939, for example, that they finally began to plead the cause of Jewish refugees seeking entry into Canada. Even then few questioned their cultural authority. A postwar religious boom resulted in new church development and healthy finances; church attendance among all Protestants continued to outstrip that in the United States; and in Ontario the public education system took new measures to reaffirm the moral teachings of Protestant Christianity. The impact of economic change on communal moral behavior also remained comparatively slow. It was not until 1950, for example, that Ontario legislation made it possible for communities to allow professional sports on Sundays, but even then it took another five years before local plebiscites accepted the change.

In Canada's other informal religious establishment, Roman Catholic Quebec, French Canadians continued to look to the church for leadership in adjusting to accelerated urbanization and corporate capitalism. As a conservative organic society dominated by church-run institutions, their way of life remained distinct from the dominant North American culture. Through the Confederation of Canadian Catholic Laborers, founded in 1921, the church played a pivotal role in the labor movement; its influence became pervasive also through cooperative movements inspired by Catholic social doctrine, especially credit unions, largely managed by priests. In the face of social change Roman Catholic identity remained strong as church-sponsored societies fostered moral behavior, from regular Sunday observance to modest dress and wholesome entertainment.

Although the numbers entering religious life continued to expand, economic and social restructuring also placed inordinate demands on church facilities. Between 1916 and 1931 people receiving care in church-run institutions more than doubled, and in 1921 the church reluctantly agreed to provincial subsidies for social service institutions in return for accountability and government inspection. Following even greater urban expansion after the Second World War, the church increased its dependence on the conservative government of Premier Maurice Duplessis, whose funding favored health, education, and welfare over transportation and natural resource development. Despite outward appearances, the 1940s and 1950s would later be seen as the twilight of Roman Catholic triumphalism, a time when the church's human resources weakened, when unions challenged the low pay of church-run institutions and clergy found themselves on both sides during strikes against several

American-owned companies allied with the Duplessis government.

## The End of "Christian Canada," 1960s to the Present

In both French- and English-speaking Canada, the 1960s proved to be a watershed that saw the dismantling of religious authority in civic life, as traditional church and state ties became untangled. Most dramatic were the changes in Quebec. Faced with the advent of the Keynesian state and increased state intervention to control the social impact of monopoly capitalism, French Canadian Roman Catholics found themselves at a fork in the road. Rather than see the autonomous church-run social institutions that had largely defined their culture come under the control of the federal government and the English-speaking Protestant majority, they opted for a French Canadian provincial state. With the victory of a Liberal government in Quebec in 1960, there followed six years of "Quiet Revolution," in which the state intervened massively in economic life, nationalizing major industries such as hydroelectric power as well as assuming control over formerly church-run social welfare, health, and educational institutions. This happened with little resistance and in many cases with support from a church that, during these same years as a result of Vatican II, was undergoing its own restructuring with a view to clarifying its role within society.

Simultaneously and less self-consciously, the rest of Canada was also experiencing growing differentiation between the spiritual and temporal as a result of the state's increased regulatory role. By 1970, with the implementation of universal medicare, the churches' goal of a more just society, where all had equal access to such essentials as old-age security, medical care, and unemployment insurance, had largely been reached. As was the case in Europe and the United States, the restructuring of the state of which such legislation was a part happened within a context of broad social change. Greater leisure and consumer choices, more women in the labor force, increased reliance on technology, and extensive demographic mobility all worked together to redefine such traditional social structures as marriage, family, and community. In Canada, a milestone in this redefinition was the 1968 Divorce Act, which greatly facilitated divorce and ended a system in place since Confederation whereby divorce had been available only by private acts of Parliament on a case-by-case basis. The decriminalization of homosexuality the following year set in process even more far-reaching changes in social attitudes, leading eventually to full civil rights for gays and lesbians and, in 2005, the passing of controversial legislation that made Canada the third country in the world, after the Netherlands and Belgium, officially to recognize same-sex marriage.

These and other social changes, such as government funding for abortions, became matters of deep division within denominations that had long shared a consensus on moral behavior. Formerly at the center of Canadian culture, they began to readjust their relationship to the state and in the 1960s and 1970s focused increasingly on the "prophetic" rather than the previous civic dimension of their role. Protests by the ecumenical Project North, for example, in 1975 successfully raised awareness of the danger to Aboriginal ways of a government-proposed pipeline in the Mackenzie Valley. Internal tensions intensified the loss of cultural leadership, especially in cases when a concern for social justice meant rejecting the denominations' traditional moral codes. Thus in 1988 the United Church of Canada at a cost to its unity moved to accept the ordination of practicing gays and lesbians and later became the only major denomination formally to support the legalization of same-sex marriage. Those denominations that had never claimed cultural leadership, and whose memberships were smaller and less diverse, largely escaped fragmentation and ambiguity. Becoming more politically active, they joined in like-minded coalitions for a more effective voice to maintain traditional Christian signposts in public life. Foremost in seeking to influence public policy were organizations such as Citizens for Public Justice, the Mennonite Central Committee, and the Evangelical Fellowship of Canada, which in the years since its founding in 1964 became increasingly skilled in moving its constituency from isolation into legal and political engagement.

Compared with the "culture wars" in the United States, the response to social change in Canada has been more muted. Evangelicals, who compose only a tenth of the population, compared with a quarter in the United States, realize that theirs is a society wary of public religious discourse. Unlike the United States, Canada has no civil religion that unites state and society: It has no Puritan forebears who established a "city on a hill," it had no war of independence, and its global role has been modest. Formed in the 1860s for pragmatic reasons, it has been shaped by two religiously dominant groups with conflicting understandings of what it meant to be Christian and Canadian. When in the 1950s and 1960s its culture began dramatically to change and the old ways fell under critique, the authority these two informal religious establishments had long exercised melted away. What emerged was a thoroughly secular society. In 1961 only .05 percent of Canadians reported no religious affiliation; by 2001 this had climbed to 16.2 percent. Polls in the late 1940s registering weekly church or synagogue attendance at 67 percent by 2003 showed a drop to 19 percent, with 43 percent declaring that religion was unimportant as guidance in daily life.

Despite a reference to "the supremacy of God" in its preamble, the Canadian Charter of Rights and Freedoms, which was part of the state's repatriation of its constitution in 1982, accelerated the dismantling of "Christian Canada." In the public school system of Ontario, where a nondenominational Protestant form of religion remained officially normative, a series of challenges in the mid-1980s in the name of religious pluralism and freedom of choice resulted in the eradication of all Christian symbols from the curriculum and holiday celebrations. Provincial legislation setting aside Sunday as a common day of rest, a hallmark of the old informal establishment, was also successfully challenged as being at variance with the practices of believers of other world religions as well as those of no religion.

There remain a few vestiges of the traditional relationship between church and state, notably the British monarch as head of state, the opening of some legislative and municipal sessions with prayer, and tax exemptions for registered religious institutions. Evidence of the churches' historical relationship with public education continues in some provinces. Publicly supported separate schools exist in Saskatchewan, Alberta, the two territories, and Ontario, where controversial legislation in 1985 extended full funding to the final three years of secondary education. Several provinces–British Columbia, Alberta, Saskatchewan, and Manitoba–have chosen to provide partial funding to independent, mostly religious schools. In Newfoundland, on the other hand, voters in 1997 approved the replacement of a publicly funded school system of eight denominations by a single secular system. After forty years of reform and study, Quebec in 1998 also abolished its confessional school boards in favor of integrated secular schools. A lasting, financially costly, and shameful legacy of the old partnership between church and state have been the residential schools. Disclosures in the 1990s of sexual abuse in these church-run institutions have resulted in protracted battles in the courts and large expenditures by the churches for legal costs and compensation to the victims, culminating in the Indian Residential Schools Settlement Agreement in 2007, which finally clarified and settled the obligations of the federal government and the churches.

Accompanying the dismantling of the churches' legacy in public life has been an intentional shift to a multicultural society. In 1832 Jews had been granted political and civic equality in Lower Canada, the first to achieve such status in the British Empire, but it was not until the 1960s that the much-vaunted "Canadian mosaic" emerged. In 1967 a new immigration act welcomed non-Western groups, and in 1971 this was followed by the federal government's adoption of multiculturalism as a national policy. Enshrined a decade later in the Charter as foundational to Canadian social and political imagination, multiculturalism reflects the shift to a secular society, and in public policy has proved to be more receptive to promoting ethnic than religious diversity. This omission of religion from the Canadian diversity model has undermined the country's ability to accommodate the religious practices of people of non-Christian faiths, who have arrived in large numbers since the changed immigration policy. In 2001 these constituted 6.2 percent of the population, and it is estimated that by 2017 this will have almost doubled. In a society that prides itself on ethnic tolerance, controversy continues to erupt over such religious symbols as a Sikh boy taking his *kirpan* to school or Muslim girls wearing the *hijab* at sports events.

Both the secular multiculturalism that subsumes religion under ethnicity and the public's resistance to religious pluralism suggest that Canada's history of religious establishment still casts a long shadow. Alternatively, at a time of global resurgence in public religion, the country's complex past of accommodating Roman Catholics and Protestants also places it in a leading position to promote religious pluralism as a "lively experiment" in a multicultural secular society.

See also *Anglican Tradition and Heritage; Canada entries; Church and State: Early Republic; Education: Colleges and Universities; Establishment, Religious; Freedom, Religious; Roman Catholicism: Tradition and Heritage; Same-Gender Marriage; Social Gospel.*

Marguerite Van Die

## BIBLIOGRAPHY

Bramadat, Paul, and David Seljak, eds. *Religion and Ethnicity in Canada.* Toronto: Pearson Longman, 2005.

Christie, Nancy, and Michael Gauvreau. *A Full-Orbed Christianity: The Protestant Churches and Social Welfare in Canada, 1900–1940.* Montreal /Kingston: McGill-Queen's University Press, 1996.

Farrow, Douglas, ed. *Recognizing Religion in a Secular Society: Essays in Pluralism, Religion, and Public Policy.* Montreal /Kingston: McGill-Queen's University Press, 2004.

Fay, Terence J. *A History of Canadian Catholics: Gallicanism, Romanism, and Canadianism.* Montreal /Kingston: McGill-Queen's University Press, 2002.

Grant, John Webster. *The Church in the Canadian Era.* 2d ed. Burlington, Ontario: Welch Publishing, 1988.

Lyon, David, and Marguerite Van Die, eds., *Rethinking Church, State, and Modernity: Canada Between Europe and America.* Toronto: University of Toronto Press, 2000.

Menendez, Albert J. *Church and State in Canada.* Amherst, N.Y.: Prometheus Books, 1996.

Miedema, Gary R. *For Canada's Sake: Public Religion, Centennial Celebrations, and the Re-making of Canada in the 1960s.* Montreal /Kingston: McGill-Queen's University Press, 2005.

Miller, J. R. *Shingwauk's Vision: A History of Native Residential Schools.* Toronto: University of Toronto Press, 1996.

Moir, John S. *Church and State in Canada 1627–1867.* Toronto: McClelland and Stewart, 1967.

Murphy, Terrence, and Roberto Perin, eds. *A Concise History of Christianity in Canada.* Toronto: Oxford University Press, 1996.

Noll, Mark. "What Happened to Christian Canada?" *Church History* 75:2 (June 2006): 245–273.

Ogilvie, M. H. *Religious Institutions and the Law in Canada.* 2d ed. Toronto: Irwin Law, 2003.

Sissons, C. B. *Church and State in Canadian Education: An Historical Study.* Toronto: Ryerson Press, 1959.

Van Die, Marguerite, ed. *Religion and Public Life in Canada: Historical and Comparative Perspectives.* Toronto: University of Toronto Press, 2001.

Wilson, Alan. *The Clergy Reserves of Upper Canada: A Canadian Mortmain.* Toronto: University of Toronto Press, 1968.

# Canada: Pluralism

Visitors from the United States to the English-speaking segment of Canada often remark that there is little difference between the two countries and point with good reason to the many common religious and cultural institutions as proof. Furthermore, they speak of a common "freedom of religion" in Canadian society and note the similar traditions in organized religion, such as Catholicism. They also see similar problems arising from common religious histories, as recent court cases on both sides of the border testify. Those of a scholarly bent see that similar concepts have been utilized to evaluate socioreligious phenomena, as, for example, Edmund H. Oliver's use of American frontier theory in his authoritative western Canadian Christian history, *Winning of the Frontier* (1930). However, in pressing the point, these American visitors are somewhat baffled by the negative Canadian response to these sociable and linking comments; it is a theme here that part of the reason for such a response

lies in the diversity and pluralism within the Canadian religious domain.

This is not to say that Canadian social concern for religion is more "European," since Canadians join with their American confreres in churches and religious organizations in roughly the same proportion. The Canadian Institute of Public Opinion reported in 1974 that 39 percent of Canadian adults attended church weekly, a figure that compares favorably with 42 percent of American adults. The 1972 Gallup Poll, which provided the American figure, also indicated that this percentage was higher than in Switzerland, Greece, and Germany, and significantly higher than in the Scandinavian countries. Statistics indicate that in 2001, 77.1 percent of Canadians identified themselves as Christian, while 76.5 percent of Americans were similarly self-identified.

However, joining may not indicate much about affiliation, and church attendance, once used by scholars to determine Canadians' religiosity, must now be replaced by more representative instruments: The most recent study of religion arising out of the 2001 census indicates continuing decline of church attendance and rise of nonaffiliation. According to Warren Clark and Grant Schellenberg, in their 2006 survey discussed in *Canadian Social Trends,* adults with no affiliation or who do not attend religious services increased from 31 percent to 43 percent between 1985 and 2004; no affiliation increased from 12 percent to 19 percent. This compares with Barry Kosmin, Egon Mayer, and Ariela Keysar's 2001 survey in the United States, "American Religious Identification Survey (ARIS), which found that 14.1 percent specified "no religion." Furthermore, recently there has been considerable divergence of opinion toward religion by Canadian-born and immigrant communities, with the percentage of those Canadian-born respondents reporting no affiliation rising from 33 percent in 1985 to 48 percent in 2004, while immigrant religious affiliation remained constant. This suggests that with the significant increase in immigration into Canada since 1985, religious values may likewise reflect greater diversity. Jack Jedwab, from the Canadian Studies Association, predicts that Canadian religion will change dramatically over the next five years; the Muslim population alone likely will increase by 160 percent according to his calculations (www.acs-aec.ca/oldsite/Polls/30–03–2005.pdf). To this feature of Canada must now be added the extraordinary rise of private religion. Of those who reported no regular attendance at religious services, 37 percent indicated that they practiced some form of religious activity on a weekly basis.

Still, numerical values may not indicate all dimensions of religiosity in a country; this is certainly the case in Canada. Diversity and pluralism have all along played a key role in the country's makeup, but the numbers tell of a more conservative organizational norm: Although Canadian institutional religion is pluralistic, it has an establishment character. Catholics in Canada make up over 50 percent of those who self-identify as Christian, and three churches—the United, Anglican, and Presbyterian—currently represent about 62 percent of Protestants. Canadian church polity reflects the centralizing tendencies: None of the major institutions is congregational, and the United Church of Canada, while it is the country's largest Protestant denomination and itself formed by corporate union, is far more centralized than, for example, either the Methodist or the Baptist church in the United States.

One way in which pluralism has developed in Canada has been through the key role that the church has always played in the immigration process—by being there as receiver of the homesteaders and by providing whole groups for homesteading. In the former, right from the founding of Canada the church was present to shape cultural developments; in the latter, the radiation from center to periphery has continued to exercise a restraining influence on divisions, with smaller groups following the model of centralized bureaucracy so evident in the larger institutions. Thus pluralistic religion became a feature in the very founding of the nation through the religious groups that were just transported en masse to Canada and encouraged to set up shop there. Both tended to eschew schisms.

In a peculiar way, the conflicts between the French and English have assured an establishment mentality in Canada. When the company of New France was granted the charter in 1627, all colonists were required to be Roman Catholic, even though France had a sizable religious minority in the Huguenots. It was partially this traditional homogeneity in New France that allowed the Roman Catholic hierarchy to support Confederation, as one way of preventing a feared annexation by the United States; and the creation of provinces (including the two most populous, Ontario and Quebec) was a tacit recognition of the counterbalance of Catholic Quebec and Protestant Ontario. The autonomy in cultural and educational matters in Quebec granted to the Roman Catholic hierarchy in exchange for its support for Confederation has guaranteed a self-confident church, which in turn has allowed it to influence public policy and initiate debate across denominational and provincial lines.

While this balance of religious forces might have provided Canada with positive elements for discourse across diversity in the early decades, this did not occur. Rather, a pluralism of viewpoints was reinforced. In fact, from the early days a tone of rancor and competition prevailed and played a role in the mission enterprises and immigration reactions of the churches in the developing West. Protestants looked to it as an arena to extend the Reformation heritage, and Catholics saw it as the logical extension of the church in Quebec. The French hierarchy supported the French language and culture as a means of maintaining the dominance of the Catholic vision in Canada, while Protestant groups labored vigorously so their dreams would not take second place. The one positive result not immediately evident was that settlement on the prairies was intimately tied to the "national" church, in direct contrast with the situation in the United States, where individuals and sects looked to western settlement for religious and personal freedom. Because of these characteristics, it must be recognized that organized religion asserted far more than a voluntary role in the shaping of the Canadian experience.

Another way that pluralism triumphed was through a cluster of ideological concerns with religious dimensions. Some of these concerns were connected with the mission of the church to the masses of immigrants. More than one church official saw the Christianizing of the nation as a necessary ingredient in civilizing it. The church, whether Catholic or Protestant, developed energetic mission programs, at the heart of which was the conviction that moral fiber and strong character were essential in building up the kingdom of God. Such a mission was to blossom mightily during the nineteenth century, when Catholic orders and Protestant mission groups set their sights on continuing the great values of Christian tradition in the new nation of Canada. These two religious orientations differed significantly in the definition of the mission—the ultramontanists of Quebec would look to a strong hierarchy, almost medieval in ideal, from the local parish through the archbishops to the Holy Father in Rome, while the most aggressive Protestants, the Methodists and the Baptists, would brandish millennial visions and actively fight against alcohol and other social vices in their effort to bring about the morally upright Canada of their hopes. Yet both Catholics and Protestants wanted legislation to reflect their concepts, and in many cases government was shaped by their concerns. Ultimately social activism embodied in legislation was to secularize the mission legacy of the churches, giving Canadian governments the appearance of both liberalism and community sensitivity. Especially among Protestants, the moral responsibility built into missions would translate into the material and cultural development of the nation when the original message had withered and died.

This focus on community over the individual has made the Canadian experience far less schismatic and particularist than the American experience; Canada's wild West was very dull indeed when compared with that of its southern neighbor. The Northwest Mounted Police were already there before the settlers arrived, and the sense of extending tradition in a hostile environment applied not only to religion but also to law. Since some of the greatest conflicts were between groups within a religious tradition, the law mediated for them. Because law was held to embody the moral dimensions of society, it transmuted into a kind of supra-value-system for all. Respect for law remains one of the chief traits on which Canadians pride themselves, despite the rapid rise of crime in cities.

Loyalties to community and law have had their impact in turn on the religious life. No authentically Canadian religious group has sprung up. A number of movements and revivals have influenced the whole, but no new group has appeared as a genuinely Canadian religion. Canada's best-known evangelist, Aimee Semple McPherson, did not remain in her homeland but found her greatest success in Los Angeles. Individual initiative in a number of areas always seemed to run counter to the prevailing spirit of the country, with the result that Canada is lauded for its stability and conservatism while being chastised for its reluctance to risk and its resistance to difference. Conversion to a new or radical group is not effectively salable in Canada—only sixty-one groups are noted in the 2001 census of identifiable Christians—in contrast, the United States must have several hundred.

Then, too, religion has not sparked any equivalent of "Manifest Destiny." No religious group has linked its identity with Canada as a nation, and religionists have been far less concerned with the fact of Canada's existence than with its character. Since the inculcated values were the finest from the past, Canada was no "lively experiment." The spiritual patriotism that marks the church in the United States is absent in Canada, and the messianic mythology underlying the Union is exclusive to that domain. The church in Canada has been excited by national achievements, such as construction of the national railway system, but it has scarcely presented the country with a definite

answer as to whether Canada has any destiny, let alone one clear and manifest. The result is that participation in a local religious organization does not provide the average Canadian with an entrée into national identity and seldom links him or her with fellow Canadians in a common national symbol-system. The qualifier *seldom* is deliberate. The Roman Catholic Church may for some Canadians represent that system, while for others it is the United Church. By acknowledging its pluralism legally, however, and by firmly holding to ethnic and racial differences, Canada has effectively moved religion out of national identity. This does not mean that there is no religious dimension to Canadian identity, but that it may be of a diffuse and ambiguous nature. Nevertheless, some aspects of Canadian culture have religious dimensions, and these do foster a kind of civil religion.

## Canadian "Civil Religion"

The most evident example of Canadian civil religion is in the province of Quebec. Quebec society has so embodied a vision of French culture in North America, and has given it form and substance through state festivals, legendary heroes, and popular epics, that elements of a grand destiny appear. This collective direction has continued to play an effective role, even when the province became far more ethnically divided and certainly more secular than in the ultramontane days of New France. It has continued to shape public opinion in the conflict between Quebec and the federal government and the other provinces, ultimately giving birth to the Parti Quebecois and the Bloc Quebeçois, with their separatist agendas.

If, as some have contended, Protestant civic piety is one meaning of civil religion, then the other provinces have had their own form. Even when immigration has brought non-Christian traditions, the mores and customs take on a Protestant civic coloring. Some provinces, such as Alberta, mindful of the serious problems that prejudice and lack of communication between various social groups can have, have instituted major curriculum reforms with a view to incorporating more values in the educational diet. The very will to do this indicates a transorganizational ethic and a certain concept of what Canadians "should be" that harks back to the nation-building images of the missionaries of an earlier time. It also reflects a Canadian identity transcending sectarian consciousness.

If Canadians live in isolated communities strung out along the U.S. border, and if they relate primarily through local group consciousness, one way they are held together is by a collective response to their natural environment (the following poem fragment by F. R. Scott, "Laurentian Shield," from *Events and Signals* [1954]):

> Hidden in wonder and snow, or sudden with
>    summer,
> This land stares at the sun in a huge silence
> Endlessly articulating something we cannot hear.

The image of the land is not always depicted as so alien. Jacques Cartier went to great lengths to describe it as a "new earth," deliberately drawing on Christian allusions. The prolific writings of the Jesuits present a land of natural paradisal dimensions. Even today, with all the scientific knowledge of the northern lights, people are overwhelmed by their dramatic and brilliant display on a cold winter's night, and poets and thinkers have etched the experience in the public's imagination. Thus it is certainly impossible on the basis of artistic and literary traditions to talk of "being Canadian" without noting the connectedness of identity with the land. By extension, the "land" has also been linked to weather: Canada was the land of constant engagement with cold—it tied the country together. A byproduct of the cold is hockey; the sport often overrides the fragmentation of a huge land by uniting disparate sections around the arena. In prairie towns the arena stands out as the largest building in the community, and it dominates the skyline, far beyond any church building. Secularists insist it reflects a much more tangible Canadian religion than Christianity.

If the land is so multivalent and perhaps awe inspiring, the human response posed by experiencing it is fairly simple and straightforward: one is lost. George Grant's *Lament for a Nation: The Defeat of Canadian Nationalism* is famous for the description of what happens to loyalty to Canada in the wake of a liberalism bent on fulfilling its individual entrepreneurial goals regardless of the cost. The result is a book moving for its sense of loss.

Other writers have attributed the loss not so much to the awe-inspiring nature of an unforgiving land or to the inability to relate to its first inhabitants but to slavish attention to U.S. values, culture, and influence. The ambiguity for identity is obvious. Some of Canada's best writers—Margaret Atwood, for example—use losing and victimization as unifying themes in their writing. It is too facile to regard this literature of deprivation as Canada's reaction to living next door to success. The United States throws a long shadow, and existing at a time of doubt and alienation surely helps, but the trait goes back to the way people have looked upon their history. Some see it as a profound expression of the Canadian soul.

## The Religions of the First People, Indian and Inuit

The people whose culture has been most associated with the land and who best have a reason for "being lost" are the people who were there when Europeans arrived. The diversity of religions and religious practices among Canada's Aboriginal population is legendary and quite beyond reduction to a few themes. The main conceptions are treated elsewhere in this collection, but something should be said about the Aboriginal response to the forced assimilation practices of the federal government and their impact on Canadian religion. It was Canada's major churches—Catholic, Anglican, Presbyterian, United—that participated in the discriminatory residential school policy of the federal government; it was they who agreed to set up schools that removed Aboriginal children from their parents, sent them away from their villages, forcefully attempted to undermine Aboriginal languages, and placed many vulnerable children in destructive situations. The result was devastating, leaving a history of alcoholism and abuse in its train. The long-festering sore between Christian traditions and Aboriginal peoples has finally been recognized officially and publicly: in 2005, the federal government set up a fund of $1.7 billion to compensate those who endured the abuses of the policy, and on June 11, 2008, the Canadian government formally apologized to Canadian Aboriginals for the policy.

However, this was not the only religious reality that Europeans brought. They brought traditions that were embraced by Aboriginal peoples. Many Aboriginals married Christians in the early years of migration, forming another largely Catholic people known as Métis. Northwestern and Alaskan Aboriginals came in contact with Orthodox priests from the Russian Orthodox tradition and established firm Orthodox churches. Missionaries founded churches of various kinds funded by European or eastern Canadian churches. Even those who eventually rejected the establishment churches were attracted to aspects of the Christian message, especially the message clothed in evangelical and Pentecostal attire. Or they embraced minority traditions, such as the Bahai. The result is that the Aboriginal community today demonstrates the same pluralism found in the larger Canadian community.

It is important to consider the role of religious reaction among Aboriginal religions themselves. For example, messianic movements have influenced Canadian Indians since the seventeenth century. The Ghost Dance religion and the various nativistic movements are examples. More recently, the Native American Church, with its focus on peyote rituals, has had an impact, especially among the Plains people. This religion has succeeded in overthrowing many of the old ways still practiced by these tribes, notably in Saskatchewan as late as 1982.

Of a different order is the almost universal standing that elders have even when they are in a completely different cultural area. Young educated Indians are attracted to this sophisticated elder, who is able to represent to them the old ways but in a manner that stresses the broad unifying elements. Especially attractive is the herbalist and healer, who combines many of the characteristics sited by believers regardless of which religion they espouse.

Reservations, for all the segregation and loss of status that they imply to their inhabitants, have kept some areas relatively isolated from white prying, allowing some rituals to be carried on. Unfortunately, young Indians leaving the reservations have negative feelings toward them, and the elders are often included in those feelings. The result is that the young have rejected both Christianity and the old ways. Some have turned to atheism or agnosticism. With few skills in an urban society, they have become a disillusioned generation. In some areas of the prairies, the majority of the prison population is native, and alcohol and drug abuse is commonplace.

Canadian willingness to accept some form of collective representation of Aboriginal nations in Parliament might aid Indian identity in a way that would encourage a revival of traditional ways and, since Aboriginal rights are guaranteed in the new Canadian constitution, the Indians' special place in the makeup of the country is basically established. The role their religions will play is a question that has not been faced, but the Indians' fundamental religious connection with the land may have a long-term impact should Canadians define their identity in its terms.

## Immigrant Religion

George Etienne Cartier, one of the fathers of Confederation, in 1865 expressed (as cited in Alistair Sweeny, 1976) the basis of religion for Canadian history as a unity of diversity:

If we unite we will form a political nationality independent of the national origin and religion of individuals. As to the objection that we cannot form a great nation because Lower Canada is chiefly French and Catholic, Upper Canada English and Protestant, and the Maritime provinces mixed it is completely futile.... In our confederation there will be Catholics and Protestants, English and French, Irish and Scotch, and each by its efforts and success will add to the prosperity, the might, and the glory of the new federation.

The fruit of this policy was to accept religion as a formative element in Canadian identity—the Charter of Rights and Freedoms notes that Canada exists under God—yet it ignored the potential conflicts in the prioritizing tendencies of religious commitment. For example, it said nothing about disagreements on what the foundations are of social and ethical norms.

The nature of Canadian immigration has been directly influenced by the national churches: in the early days a majority of the people came to Canada from or through their organizations. The result was that the number of immigrants with little church affiliation was small. Especially when the prairies opened up and the flood to the West began, arrangements for immigration that respected certain "values" allowed churches (for example, the Mennonites) to sanction the movements of whole communities of people onto the land. The result has been churches of national and ethnic consciousness.

The policy was carried out through the active participation of the governments of central Canada for their own reasons. It was, on the one hand, a colonization policy, designed to carry on Canadian national destiny by peopling the prairies. Part of this was motivated by a concern that if Canada did not populate the West, the United States would. Immigrants were part of national establishment policy. In addition, the prospect of a West that required the manufacturing capabilities of eastern Canada was attractive to Toronto and Montreal. But there was also Canadian ideology behind this move; a vast unpopulated land lay open to developing British conceptions of law, justice, and ultimately a distinctive sense of freedom.

Immigrant ethnic and religious diversity was the price the eastern governments were willing to pay, since it not only offset the dreams of the French Catholics but also guaranteed a grateful and submissive foreign contingent. All this took place in a remarkably short period of time, between

1870 and 1920, a factor that made continuity all the more important.

The manner in which traditional forms of religion came to dominate the West can be gauged by a look at the Orthodox Church. Orthodoxy derives from peoples of eastern Europe, Africa, the eastern Mediterranean, and Asia; the distinction from the Roman Catholic Church is usually identified with the schism of 1054, when the Eastern Church broke away from Rome. On occasion, Orthodoxy is known as the Eastern or Byzantine rite, to parallel it with the Western rite of Roman Catholicism.

The use of *rite* is significant, because for these Eastern churches it is the ritual commonality that unites, not the administrative and authoritative jurisdiction. This is demonstrated by the fact that there are believers in Canada who may owe allegiance to the ancient patriarchates of Constantinople, Alexandria, Antioch, or Jerusalem; they may also belong to one of the so-called national churches of Russia, Serbia, Romania, Bulgaria, Cyprus, Greece, Albania, Poland, or the Czech Republic; they could adhere to the autonomous churches of Sinai or Finland or Japan; or they could have recently joined a daughter church formed from one of the aforementioned national churches in Canada and the United States. There is also a small group of believers who do not adhere to this "Byzantine" Orthodoxy but rather follow the non-Chalcedonian doctrine of Christ's nature. (This doctrine places emphasis on the divine in the person of Christ, with the human element reduced to an impersonal humanity.) These Oriental Orthodox—the Armenian, Coptic, Syrian, Ethiopian, and South Indian Orthodox—churches are rejected as noncanonical by the Byzantines.

Probably the largest group practicing the Byzantine rite is the Ukrainian Orthodox Church in Canada, numbering in excess of 140,000 members. Their ancestors came to Canada at the turn of the century in the immigration flood, and most of them were from peasant stock; they have been joined recently by post–World War II immigrants who settled not on the prairies but in the eastern manufacturing centers. They came principally from Galicia in the Ukraine. The first church was established in Gardenton, Manitoba, which is still the scene of an annual pilgrimage. They are not regarded as canonically Orthodox by the other Byzantine rite churches, because Galicia was traditionally under the jurisdiction of the Roman Catholic Church and used the Ruthenian rite. The Galicians have a married clergy, however, and the Church of Rome wished to dispense with that right. They also had used the Ukrainian language in the liturgy. By 1918 an organization called the Ukrainian Greek Brotherhood evolved, and many of its adherents joined the Orthodox Church in Nova Scotia. The church emerged from a growing awareness of solidarity at the turn of the century, and the resulting organization, founded in 1921, follows Orthodox liturgical practice and accepts the seven ecumenical councils. It is also significant that Orthodoxy first came to North America not through immigration but through Russian Orthodox missionary activity among the Aleut in Alaska. The diocese was established in 1799 and by 1905 had an archdiocese in New York. Most of the Orthodox organizations have a North American rather than a Canadian focus.

An entirely different genre of church is associated with the Doukhobors. A pietistic group, the Doukhobors originated in Russia in the eighteenth century. They rejected both the Russian Orthodox Church and the state. It was this conflict that led them to Canada in 1899. Indeed, they were opposed to all the trappings of church, dispensing with priests, liturgies, sections of the Bible, and church edifices, and they resisted any education that would lead them away from the immediacy of the oral tradition and spiritual enlightenment. Their life in the Crimea had centered on communal living and total nonviolence; the latter concept was close to that of the Quakers. When the czar moved to conscript the young men into his army, they resisted. News of the resulting bloodshed reached sympathetic ears in Canada, where Clifford Sifton was looking for strong farmworkers, like the Mennonites who had come earlier. By June 1899 over 7,500 Doukhobors had come to Canada, the largest group migration to the prairies. They immediately moved to communal farms in Saskatchewan, where they faced strong resistance from other immigrants, who envied the huge tracts of land they had been given. Ultimately they had to abandon their communal living and principles of universal peace and brotherhood. Required to give an oath of loyalty before they could get land, some simply "affirmed" and received land; many refused on grounds of religious conviction. This group, the largest, became known as the Orthodox Doukhobors and was led by the mystical Peter V. Verigin. They purchased private land in British Columbia and became quite successful. A third group, seeking a totally untrammeled existence, began a trek across the West to British Columbia and became notorious very quickly. The negative publicity applied to all Doukhobors indiscriminately, and the members in British Columbia were twice banned from voting in federal elections.

Despite the extraordinary nature of their religious convictions and the difficulties in transplanting them to Canada, the Doukhobors have persevered and today represent a Russian group that maintains an almost mystical belief in the homeland and in the principles of communal and nonviolent living.

The Mennonites are another group who arrived on the prairies, but with an entirely different story. Originally an urban people, the Mennonites had been forced to live in rural areas because of their nonviolent and independent church conceptions. They became very productive farmers, achieving their most extensive holdings in Russia, where they enjoyed near self-government. The successors of Alexander I withdrew these privileges, however, and the Mennonites moved to the Canadian prairies, where the government gave them large tracts of land together and made concessions about military service and their own schools. Early in the 1920s thousands of Mennonites immigrated, displaced by the Russian Revolution. The large size of the group meant conflict with other Canadians and splits within the group over policy. Their goal of living an isolated life evaporated under the strain of realities in the Canadian West. Their Christian separation of church from state, the kingdom of God from that of human construction, and distinctive ways of life were all blurred under the pressure of living with others from all over the world.

## Major Religious Diversity

No discussion of Canada's diversity would be complete without some mention of traditions of an entirely different nature—Judaism, Islam, Hinduism, and Buddhism. All have played a role in the development of Canada's religious environment.

Jewish immigrants came to Nova Scotia from New England in the mid-1750s, and Sephardim from England journeyed to Montreal at about the same time. By 1768 they had formed a group called Shearith Israel, similar to one in England. The census of 1901 reported only 16,400 Jews, but a dramatic change came in the next decade when the western Jewish population increased more than fourfold. This shift to the prairies came about through Jewish societies in the East, such as the Colonization Committee of the Young Men's Hebrew Benevolent Society of Montreal, which sponsored the oldest Jewish farm community, in Oxbow, Saskatchewan, in 1892. Farming communities were also established in Alberta and Manitoba. In 1905 many responded to Prime Minister Wilfrid Laurier's speech on the occasion of the condemnation of the Russian pogrom against the Jews of Kishinev, when Laurier promised a "hearty welcome" to Jews who came to Canada. Following World War I, however, Jewish immigration slowed to a trickle, and in the face of the Nazi peril in Europe, Canada virtually shut the door on the problem. Meanwhile, believers moved from farming communities to towns and cities as they sought the social and religious advantages that numbers provided. Today there are synagogues in only two centers outside major cities—Prince Albert, Saskatchewan, and Lethbridge, Alberta.

Most of the first Muslims came to Canada from Lebanon, and they set to work not as farmers but as peddlers. A nucleus made Edmonton, Alberta, their departure point for selling routes to the North. These early families were finally able to construct a mosque, completed in 1938 with the help of a few Christian friends and much sacrifice. After World War II the much less restrictive immigration laws opened the way for additional Muslim immigrants, most of whom were from Pakistan and India. Today the South Asian population constitutes the largest contingent of Muslims in Canada; they are principally centered in urban areas, notably Toronto, Vancouver, and Montreal. A most unusual town in Alberta, Lac La Biche, has a sizable Muslim population, all of whom are Arab, and a mosque that is one of the main sights in town. Edmonton now boasts an Arabic-English bilingual program in its public school system, with classes through high school, and recently a joint Muslim community sponsored the first Chair in Islamic Studies at the University of Alberta.

The earliest Muslim immigrants were Sunnis, and the early preponderance of Muslims in Canada belong to that tradition, but in the twentieth century, largely through the policies of dictator Idi Amin, significant numbers of Ismailis came to Canada from Uganda. They settled in all major urban areas across the country and have had a major impact on Canada's religious diversity. At the same time, when Canada liberalized its immigration policies in the late 1950s, thousands of Muslims from most major Muslim populations came to Canada, bringing that diversity along—including Shias and Ahmadiyas from regions as disparate as Syria, Pakistan, Somalia, and India. The Druze, a sect with roots in Islam, also arrived at this time, contributing to the religious diversity of the country. The arrival of all these groups has not been without controversy, especially after 9/11. Their growing presence jarred some Canadians, and some communities in Quebec passed a policy on just how immigrants were to act and dress. This sparked an inquiry from the provincial government on integrating divergent cultures into its society, with mixed results.

In 2001 in Toronto, a group proposed to establish Sharia law for legal issues, including divorce and custody. The Canadian Council of Muslim Women launched a nationwide debate over this and argued vigorously against such a plan. The Ontario government set up a committee to study the issue but finally rejected the initiative. After 9/11, the Canadian government supported the U.S. "war on terror," including the attack on Afghanistan, to which it contributed forces. However, after 9/11, Muslims were often profiled in airport security and had to deal with widespread antagonism. While not as severe as the curtailing of Muslim freedoms that occurred in the United States, as noted in 2007 by Aisha Pena, Canadians generally supported the curbing of Muslim militants. Wearing the *hijab* was viewed as close to subversive in some areas of the country for a time and became a matter of wider conflict when the *hijab* was banned for girls playing soccer by the national soccer body. Subsequently, public opinion forced the ruling to be rescinded. The agreement to follow the lead of the U.S. president George W. Bush against Muslim jihadists, however, backfired when the Canadian government collaborated with the CIA in September 2002 in sending an innocent citizen, Maher Arar, to Syria to be tortured. The public outcry forced the federal government to admit its collusion in this miscarriage of justice and to negotiate a sizable compensation. As part of the fallout, the Canadian public refused to support the U.S. invasion of Iraq, and Prime Minister Jean Chrétien won widespread praise for his refusal to participate.

Canadians remain divided on how loyal Muslim groups are to Canada, and some have wondered why few moderate voices seem to be heard. No Muslim in Canada has argued publicly, as has Ameer Ali in Australia, about Muslim militancy and the need to embrace a tolerant Islam. In a marked break with this culture of gloom, however, has come the humorous television show entitled *Little Mosque on the Prairie*. A lighthearted take on the foibles and ironies of being Muslim in a small prairie town has captured the imagination of the Canadian public and given Islam a sympathetic audience. (It has since been sold to American television.) Still, the result of most of the recent events has definitely placed Muslims on the defensive, and a sense of unease rests on the Muslim community in Canada today.

The earliest Asian religious believers came to southern Alberta and the coastal regions of British Columbia from Japan at around the turn of the twentieth century. Some worked on the railways; some came to work in the coal mines or to begin farming. A number of the latter settled in Raymond, Alberta. They banded together in 1929 and established the Raymond Buddhist Church, the first in the province. They purchased a former Mormon church and today have one of the finest temples in North America.

When World War II began, the Japanese were rounded up and sent to internment camps in Alberta and in the interior of British Columbia. Their forced evacuation from the coast spurred the building of churches, and new congregations sprang up in Taber, Picture Butte, Coaldale, and Rosemary, with Lethbridge, the largest town, as the center of Japanese activities. After the war, the Alberta churches organized into the Alberta *Kyoku,* or ministerial jurisdiction, as part of four *Kyokus* in Canada: British Columbia, Alberta, Manitoba, and the East. Despite a split and the formation of the Honpa Buddhist Church of Alberta, the Buddhists of the West have maintained an ongoing congregation. Regular and special services of the True Pure Land Buddhist tradition are conducted by resident ministers. Following the federal apology to the Japanese for their incarceration, relations between Buddhist communities and government institutions have been friendlier. Edmonton has had a continuing Dharmadhatu congregation, and that group has also decided to establish a permanent base in Halifax because of a stable community base; meditation rituals were successfully introduced to Canadians, and today followers of Buddhist traditions are found all across the country, with many converts among Caucasians.

The federal government's multicultural policy has encouraged the various ethnic and religious groups to preserve their traditions, and Canada now has congregations of religions as disparate as the Rastafarians, Sikhs, and Hindus, as well as the traditional ancestor worship of the Chinese. The Sikhs suffer from a similar resistance from Canadians as Muslims: Sikhs were implicated in the bombing of a transatlantic flight that killed over three hundred, with the result that the tradition is linked in some minds to militancy and violence. However, some Sikhs continue to wear the turban and the *kirpan,* and the Royal Canadian Mounted Police (RCMP) has loosened rules so that Sikh Mounties may dress in the traditional headdress. This diversity of cultures is most noticeable in western Canada, where summer festivals of ethnic heritage are very popular. While the Canadians support the contributions these various people make to the country, some worry privately that they are challenging the essentially "Christian" character of Canada.

## Material Religion

The coming of so many religious groups to Canada has spawned a dramatic change in the physical landscape of towns and cities. Architecture has shifted dramatically as these influences from abroad attempt to shape a building around the distinctive needs of an immigrant community. Consonant with this new trend, recently the federal government has matched a $30 million initiative of the Aga Khan of the Ismaili tradition to transform the old Canadian War Museum in Ottawa into the Global Centre for Pluralism. Its concern will be research and education specific to the value of pluralist societies.

The concern with documenting this trend has encouraged scholars to move away from conventional evaluations of religion-as-doctrine to the impact of so much pluralism-in-landscape on Canadian identity. Spearheaded by Queen's University scholar William Closson James, and his groundbreaking study of religious pluralism in Kingston, a new way of looking at religion has evolved. Dubbed *material religion*, this trend changes the focus to the artifacts and constructions of religion, and tries to examine the impact of this kind of reality on the larger culture and identity. One has only to visit the many towns and cities and examine their architecture to realize how the landscape of Canada has changed—cities such as Mississauga are rich with temples, mosques, synagogues, and centers that reflect the vitality and variety of religious building. McGill University has developed the Montreal Religious Sites Project as a way to document this growing diversity.

The orientation was given a significant boost by the spectacular success of a turn-of-the-century display at the Provincial Museum of Alberta entitled *Anno Domini: Jesus through the Centuries*. Curated by University of Chicago graduate David Goa, the exhibit brought together a wide variety of material from around the Christian world: images, art, music, and architecture—2,000 years of Christian material engagement with Jesus. Thousands visited the displays that focused not so much on the doctrine of Jesus but on the variety of ways in which the figure of Christ had been portrayed, reflected upon, and embodied in architecture in the Christian West. Certainly another way material religion is expressed is in the spontaneous sanctifying of terrain: one of the most dramatic contemporary examples of how landscape becomes meaningful is ground zero in New York City, but across the Canadian landscape one sees this transformation not only in religious buildings but also in roadside commemorative displays for accident victims.

## Religious Movements

The face of religion in Canada has been decisively changed through a number of movements. A few lasting ones have modified Canadians' social outlook. In the main the impetus for these movements has come from the United States, and only two of significance, the Salvation Army and the Plymouth Brethren, have European origins. Canada has been impressed deeply by the religious ferment of its southern neighbor.

Some of this religious ferment was brought by Americans themselves. Before the War of 1812, eight out of ten residents of Ontario were Americans. Most of the Icelandic, Norwegian, Swedish, and Danish Lutherans who settled on the Canadian prairies came from the Dakotas. Early Congregationalists in Nova Scotia influenced the religious development of that province. The Mormons came directly to southern Alberta to establish a thriving community. Still, much of the religious ferment was a conscious adaptation of American forms to Canada.

Not all are as dramatic as the New Light movement among the Baptists of the Maritimes or the Camp Meeting movement among the Methodists. Anglicans molded their structures according to Episcopal innovations in the United States, and Canadian sectarian congregations used liturgical forms drawn from American evangelism. Strategies for winning converts, such as the huge religious forums of Billy Graham, were first tried in the United States and found an acceptance among Canada's evangelicals. Some groups, such as the Canadian Pentecostals, preferred the boisterous and dramatic evangelists of the United States, and Roman Catholic charismatics found adherents there before trying similar forms in Canada.

Despite this close connection, Canada has not always responded to these movements as has the United States. The revivalism that swept the eastern seaboard of the United States under Jonathan Edwards in the mid-eighteenth century had an impact in Canada, but not as broadly or as deeply. The United States' repeated revivalist history has not found similar expression in Canada.

The church in Canada responded, too, to its own agenda. Most notable was the Church Union movement, the most impressive achievement of which was the union of Presbyterian, Congregational, and Methodist churches in 1925, but which periodically took place between Baptists, Lutherans, and others. Another impact deriving from religion has been the Social Gospel movement. The Anglican, Methodist, and Presbyterian churches were most inspired by the need to make the Gospel relevant to the everyday concerns of humans, although their motivations arose not from conditions that they saw as unique to Canada but as part of a movement that embraced the western world. The ways they responded may well not have come from the United States. In fact, the institutional structures, such as the brotherhoods, the settlements, and the labor churches, were of British derivation rather than American, but many of the themes had American counterparts. Even the antialcohol crusade, well-known in the United States, can be seen as an attempt to apply Gospel interpretations to social problems.

The center of the Canadian Social Gospel movement was not in the Maritimes or in Ontario but in Manitoba, at Wesleyan College in Winnipeg, where staff and students responded to the depression of the 1890s, which saw farmers inundated with unsold grain. Railway rates, tariffs, and a host of related issues became matters on which Christians had to take a stand. When Salem Bland arrived at Wesleyan in 1903, he found fertile ground for his social perspectives, and Methodists in particular dominated the progressive wing of the movement. The best-known Social Gospel clergyman, J. S. Woodsworth, was a Methodist, even though he later resigned from the church. The movement built rapidly. From 1890 to 1914 it dramatically increased its impact on church and labor organizations, but its very success spelled its doom: its impact fostered groups, institutions, and responses that outgrew its religious sources and spread its attitudes through church, labor, and social networks in such a way that by 1928 the movement had given over its formulation to labor and political forces. With the crash of 1929, it was no longer effective. Nevertheless, it has left an important legacy in Canadian society, and its ideas flow with regularity close to the surface of church discussion of issues.

Mention should be made of the Métis movement, led by Louis Riel. (The Métis were communities formed by the marriage of native people and early French trappers.) The Métis movement stood for independence from the federal government and the importance of local cultural difference, and its ideas were little different from those lauded by provincial premiers today. Riel was born in 1844 to a settled Métis family who represented well the combination of Indian and French blood. A devout Roman Catholic, he believed that Providence wanted the western lands to stay under the domination of the people who lived on them, and he fought with messianic vision to resist federal encroachment on Métis land. He often did this in the name of French Canadian and Roman Catholic culture. His sense of destiny for the West ended with his execution for treason in 1885 by the federal government, but his dream of regional power and the rights of French Catholics is as alive as ever in western Canada.

## "New" Religions

Of the welter of new religions that have sprung up in Canada since its inception, several seem to have been more successful than others. The Church of Jesus Christ of Latter-day Saints (Mormons) has made major headway in urban populations, especially in the West. The Bahais have built a national organization and have succeeded in attracting middle-class youth and educated Canadians alike. The Church of Scientology recruited aggressively in the 1970s and established groups across the country, as did the Reverend Moon's Unification Church. Mantra meditation was taught earlier in Canada by transcendental meditation and still has adherents.

Various self-improvement groups operate in Canada, including Silva mind control and the New Light, which are based on certain religious views of the individual. And while Hare Krishna and Divine Light people are not as prevalent as they used to be, those groups attracted a wide range of converts at the end of the last century. Sri Chinmoy adherents are found across Canada, as are Tai Chi Chuan participants. While not new, spiritualist groups and the Unity Church appeal to some Canadians. Sometimes the charismatics are considered a new religion (for example, Toronto's Airport Church), although their message is hardly different from that of the Pentecostals, and it is the closest to traditional Christian inspiration. Canadian animosity toward cults is largely inspired by media reports about non-Canadian groups, such as the Jonestown cult in Guyana, and about kidnapping and deprogramming of adherents. No government in Canada has enacted restraining laws, with the exception of some municipal jurisdictions for the control of street harassment. The groups have free rein in attracting secular or disillusioned persons to their organizations.

The most interesting recent new religious movement group has been that associated with Pastor John de Ruiter. Described now as a "worldwide phenomenon" by Judy Piercey, with converts to his movement in the United States,

Europe, Australia, and now India, Pastor John, as he is known, began as a shoemaker and a part-time Lutheran preacher in the small Alberta town of Stettler. He then moved to Edmonton, where he established a following that is hundreds strong. Seated on a raised dais, and responding to questions from a fixed "asking" seat among his New Age–type followers, he has moved away from Christian references and now concentrates on using silence as an operative religious medium. Believers follow him back to Edmonton from his many tours around the world. From his new building in the west end called the Edmonton College of Integrated Philosophy, he dispenses his tapes and videos to an enlarging circle of devotees—a tour to India garnered him a group from the Osho/Rajneesh ashram.

Some people regard the television evangelists as cultic, in that much of the impact of their message derives from personal appeal. David Mainse's 100 Huntley Street, a Pentecostal TV program, is a good case in point. It has carved out a singular place in the television market and reminds us that technology is continuing to change the environment of religion. Canada has a long and vigorous evangelical tradition, however, and the strong support that evangelists receive from Canadians may only reflect that sympathy. They are a most important fact reflecting the continuous interaction between U.S. and Canadian culture and religion.

**See also** *Anabaptist Denominational Family; Buddhism in North America; Canada* entries; *Eastern Orthodoxy; Islam in North America; Judaism* entries; *Krishna Consciousness; Native American Religions* entries; *New Religious Movements* entries; *Roman Catholicism: French Influence; Sikhs.*

Earle H. Waugh

**BIBLIOGRAPHY**

Ali, Ameer. "The Closing of the Muslim Mind." *Journal of Muslim Minority Affairs* 27, no. 3. (December 2007). 443–453.

Beyer, Peter. "Roman Catholicism in Contemporary Quebec: The Ghosts of Religion Past?" In *The Sociology of Religion: A Canadian Focus,* edited by H. W. Hewitt. Toronto: Butterworths, 1993.

Bibby, R. W. *Restless Gods: The Renaissance of Religion in Canada.* Toronto: Stoddart Publishing, 2002.

Bibby, R. W. *Unitrends.* Toronto: United Church, 1994.

Clark, S. D. *Church and Sect in Canada.* Toronto: University of Toronto Press, 1948.

Clark, Warren, and Grant Schellenberg. "Who's Religious?" *Canadian Social Trends,* no. 81, (Summer 2006).

Coward, Harold, and Leslie Kawamura, eds. *Religion and Ethnicity.* Waterloo, Ont.: Wilfrid Laurier University Press, 1978.

Driedger, Leo. *Mennonite Identity in Conflict.* Lewiston, N.Y.: Edwin Mellen Press, 1988.

Goa, David, Linda Distad, and Matthew Wangler. *Anno Domini: Jesus through the Centuries.* Edmonton: Provincial Museum of Alberta, 2000.

Grant, George M. *Lament for a Nation: The Defeat of Canadian Nationalism.* Ottawa: Carleton University Press, 1982.

Grant, John Webster, ed. *The Churches and the Canadian Experience.* Toronto: Ryerson Press, 1966.

Joosse, Paul. "Silence, Charisma and Power: The Case of John de Ruiter." *Journal of Contemporary Religion* 21, no. 3 (October 2006): 355–371.

Kosmin, Barry A., Egon Mayer, and Ariela Keysar. *American Religious Identification Survey, 2001 Report.* New York: CUNY Graduate Center, 2001.

Olson, Daniel, and C. Kirk Hadaway. "Religious Pluralism and Affiliation among Canadian Counties and Cities." *Journal of the Scientific Study of Religion* 38, no. 4 (1999): 490–508.

O'Toole, Roger. "Religion in Canada: Its Development and Contemporary Situation." *Social Compass* 43, no. 1 (1996): 23–41.

Pena, Aisha. "Protecting Muslim Civil and Human Rights in America: The Role of Islamic, National, and International Organizations." *Journal of Muslim Minority Affairs* 27, no. 3 (December 2007): 387–400.

Piercey, Judy. "The Gospel According to John." CBC National News, Feb. 1, 2002.

Robinson, B.A. "Canadian Data about Christianity." Ontario Consultants on Religious Tolerance. www.religioustolerance.org/can_re11.htm

Sweeny, Alastair. *George Etienne Cartier.* Toronto: McClelland and Stewart, 1976.

Voas, David, Alasdair Crockett, and Daniel V. A. Olsen. "Religious Pluralism and Participation: Why Previous Research Is Wrong." *American Sociological Review* 67, no. 2 (April 2002): 212–230.

Walsh, Henry H. *The Christian Church in Canada.* Toronto: Ryerson Press, 1956.

Waugh, Earle H., Baha Abu-Laban, and Regula Qureshi, eds. *The Muslim Community in North America.* Edmonton: University of Alberta Press, 1983.

# Canada: Protestants and the United Church of Canada

Canadian Protestant identity, like the identity of Canada itself, has been shaped by regionalism, cross-border politics, and the relatively peaceful transition from colonialism to sovereignty. Canadian Protestantism has been largely shaped by a spirit of ecumenism that cumulated in the formation in 1925 of the United Church of Canada (UCC)—a church that positioned itself to be Canada's national church in a way that was distinctly Canadian.

In many respects, the Protestant experience in Canada has resembled that of Protestants in the United States. There are, however, a few notable differences, including the fact that the majority of the population has always been distributed among four or five major denominations. Mark Noll, for example, has suggested that religious allegiances in

Canada differ from those in the United States because of an absence of a significant war on Canadian territory. Noll argues that as a result Canadian religiosity is not as strong as that of its neighbors to the South (both the United States and Mexico underwent bloody civil wars that depended on religious affiliations, metaphors, and differences to foment their national consciousness). In contrast, it should be noted that Canadian historian John Webster Grant points to the War of 1812 as a significant moment in the historical articulation of Canadian national identity, one that is on par with that of the American Revolution. Likewise, the World War II battle of Vimy Ridge is often represented as a moment that had a profound effect on the construction of Canadian national identity. Other scholars have argued that the distinctiveness of Canadian religious identity stems from the historic "unofficial official" status of a few dominant denominations under the shadow of which other Protestant denominations were forced to develop. Some argue that this factor, combined with the scarcity of resources, especially in rural areas, led to a compulsory ecumenism among certain denominational families. Finally, it has been suggested that at the core of Canadian churches lie a laity who have maintained a highly suspicious and resistant attitude toward ecclesiastical control from outside Canada and who are ardently loyal to their chosen denominations.

## Early History

The first sustained Protestant settlement in Canada corresponded with British control of the Maritimes and with primarily economic, rather than spiritual, interests and activities in the new colony. These early settlers included a mix of old-stock British Anglicans and Presbyterians, Lutheran and Reformed settlers from Germany and Switzerland, and some American Congregationalists. While the Church of England dominated the Nova Scotian capital, Halifax, well over half of the rural population were New England Congregationalists. Initially, there was limited missionary work undertaken and few clergy available or willing to serve the scattered Maritime congregations. The expulsion of Francophone Acadians in 1755 created space for the addition of several Free Church advocates who sought to distinguish the colonies from an established Anglican regime. Most notable was Henry Alline (1748–1784), a charismatic, uneducated, sectarian who preached a mystical "new light" revivalism, which reached its peak in around 1775 and emphasized sudden conversion, communion with God, and anti-Calvinism. Historian George Rawlyk has

suggested that Canadian evangelicalism as expressed in Alline's "New Light" movement actually stood as even more radical, anarchistic, democratic, and populist than its American counterpart exemplified during the first Great Awakening. Rawlyk suggested that Alline's radical anarchism stemmed from his movement's freedom from the distinctively American characteristics of civic humanism, republicanism, the covenant ideal, and possessive individualism. After Alline's premature death in 1784, the movement was largely absorbed, albeit without the anti-Calvinism of its founder, by Maritime Baptists and New Light Congregational churches. The legacy of Alline's popular religious expression and revivalism in Atlantic Canada is traceable, though in a modified form, into the twentieth century.

Other early communities in the Maritimes included the American Quakers, who settled in Nova Scotia as early as 1762, and Moravian missionaries, who established missions in Labrador in 1771 working among the Inuit peoples in that region. Neither community was especially large but they did establish a presence and cleared the way for more sustained missionary efforts in the future.

The first Methodists in Atlantic Canada were organized under the leadership of Lawrence Coughlan in Newfoundland (1765) and William Black Jr. in Nova Scotia (1781), who set up the Methodist Church in opposition to the New Light movement. Black initially established his Methodist classes under the direction of the American Methodist Episcopal Church, by which he was ordained. Growing anti-American sentiment in the colonies following the American Revolution led him to redirect the affiliations of the Canadian colony to the Wesleyan Methodists of England.

Former Virginian slave David George organized the first black Baptist churches in Nova Scotia in 1783. George was part of the 1792 emigration of twelve hundred African Canadians who carried a modified version of Alline's New Light theology to Africa. The current Baptist and Methodist churches in Sierra Leone are descended from the churches that were established there by these former residents of Nova Scotia.

In Quebec, following the British conquest of 1759, a plan to anglicize the Francophone population led to an introduction of government-supported, French-speaking Protestant clergy who were largely ignored by Francophones and Anglophones alike for religious and linguistic reasons, respectively. On the eve of the American Revolution, government policy legally recognized the Roman Catholic Church through the Quebec Act (1774), which was implemented with the intent of keeping Quebec British. The legacy of this act resulted in a strong Roman Catholic presence and squashed any hope for anything but a Protestant minority in that province.

Following the establishment of Upper Canada (present-day Ontario) by the Constitutional Act of 1791, the Church of England maintained a semiofficial status as the only recipient of the "clergy reserves," approximately 2,500,000 acres of land set aside for the support of Protestant clergy, despite the fact that it claimed at best only 20 percent of the population in Upper Canada. The clergy reserves system and resulting revenue acknowledged the Anglican Church as the de facto established church in Canada, but this was not without resistance. It should be noted, as historian John S. Moir states, that while many churches were resistant to the Anglican Church's claim to official status, for the most part Protestant denominations (Presbyterians, Methodists, and Congregationalists) stressed British Christian values over and against Enlightenment free-thinking or American-style democracy.

The American Revolution dramatically changed the religious character of Canada, as British Loyalists flooded over the border, offering alternatives to the established Anglican Church in the form of ethnic and evangelical traditions. By 1812 over 80 percent of the population of Upper Canada were loyalists (or late-loyalists), having settled somewhat haphazardly: Quakers in Newmarket and Prince Edward County, Mennonites in the Waterloo and the Niagara peninsula, Scottish Presbyterians in the Glengarry region, and German American Lutherans in Dundas, Addington, and Lennox counties.

The most significant growth following the Revolution was in the Methodist Church. As noted by historian Phyllis Airhart, at the time of establishment in 1791 there were eight hundred Methodists in Canada with four circuits and only six preachers; in a little over half a century Methodism grew to become the second-largest denomination in Canada. Initially, Methodists in Lower and Upper Canada were deeply rooted in the New York network. Unlike their Maritime counterparts, who were closely tied to the English (Wesleyan) Church and were considerably more conventional in their piety and firm in their discouragement of overly emotional outbursts, the Methodists in Upper Canada espoused a revivalist theology that focused on the ecstatic conversion of the individual. The first Methodist Camp meeting in Upper Canada occurred in 1805 and was described by its organizer, itinerant preacher Nathan Bangs,

as quoted in Abel Stevens's 1863 work *Life and Times of Nathan Bangs, D. D.* (p. 152), as if there were "a cloud of divine glory resting upon the congregation." Central to this revivalism was an emphasis on a personal encounter between the individual (radically convicted by sin and isolated from the world) and God.

The conversion experience distinguished evangelicalism from the perceived established churches in Canada, enabling it to gain momentum following the War of 1812. In response to criticism from the Anglican bishop of Toronto, John Strachan (1778–1867), the Methodist Church was among the first of the evangelical churches to Canadianize and separate from their American and European mother churches. An autonomous Canadian Methodist church was established in 1828. Other denominations, such as the Baptists and German Lutherans, were constrained by their dependence on missionary revenue from American supporters.

## Mid-Nineteenth and Early Twentieth Century

Increased religious diversity led to a challenge to the Church of England's claims to the clergy reserves. During the War of 1812, the Presbyterian Church petitioned for a share of the revenue generated by the reserves following the destruction of Niagara on the Lake by the Americans. The Presbyterian claim was based on its status as the national Church of Scotland. Despite Anglican objections, the allocation of the clergy reserves was revised to include both Anglicans and Presbyterians. These two churches understood themselves as the rightful heirs of Canadian religiosity, in contrast to populist evangelicals, who argued from a voluntarist position that the clergy reserves should be secularized. By the 1830s evangelicals had moved from the fringes of society to the center, establishing powerful and successful churches and engaging in political and public debate. As such, their concerns were modified by such individuals as Egerton Ryerson in Upper Canada and Baptist preacher Edward Manning in the Maritimes, who turned their attention to the transformation of social order primarily through the establishment of voluntary societies, newspapers, public education, and denominational colleges.

Several important denominational schools and colleges were formed during this time as a means of providing a balance between evangelicalism and the Enlightenment. According to historian Michael Gauvreau, these two phenomena were not mutually exclusive in Canadian academe. Thomas McCulloch, a Scottish-born Presbyterian minister, founded Pictou Academy in 1816 as a response to what he saw as religious destitution in the colony. Several important Protestant universities were founded during this time, including the Presbyterian Dalhousie University in Halifax (1818) and Queen's University in Kingston (1841), as well as Methodist Mount Allison in Sackville, New Brunswick (1839), and Victoria College in Cobourg, Ontario (1841, today part of the University of Toronto). Despite their smaller demographics, the Baptists established Acadia University in Wolfville, Nova Scotia (1838), and McMaster University in Toronto (1887, moved to its present location in Hamilton, Ontario, in 1930). Many universities in Canada maintained their church affiliations well into the mid-twentieth century, at which point they were forced to at least partly secularize in order to qualify for government funding.

In 1839 the clergy reserves were extended to the four mainline denominations: Anglican, Methodist, Presbyterian, and Roman Catholic. The Baptists refused government funding except in Nova Scotia, where they shocked their Upper Canadian contemporaries by accepting financial support for Acadia University. The question of what constituted Protestantism and who had the right to speak for it became a topic of much debate during this time period. The issue came to the forefront in the public voice of Egerton Ryerson, who ultimately emerged as the official adversary to the Reverend John Strachan. As an advocate for Anglican privilege in regard to the clergy reserves as well as higher education, Strachan was a fervent supporter of the Anglican establishment as the means of maintaining Canada's Christian identity. In contrast, Ryerson sought to redefine Upper Canadian Protestant society as populist. As the founder and editor of the weekly Methodist newspaper *Christian Guardian,* he served as the most prominent defender of "voluntarism," or dependence by the church on voluntary giving. Ryerson also served as the first principal of Victoria College. In 1844 he was named chief superintendent of education in Ontario, where he successfully reformed the provincial education system, making it accessible to all school-aged children while still providing Protestant instruction in public institutions. His influence on Canadian Protestantism specifically and Canadian public life in general can still be felt today. Ryerson is best remembered for having standardized education in Upper Canada; this standardization relied on a central textbook press that used Canadian authors, a library in every school, the formation of an educational journal, and professional development conventions for educators.

Ryerson's energies concerning the secularization of the clergy reserves paid off in 1854, when public debate surrounding their necessity led to the introduction of a bill to secularize them. The bill's intention was to "remove all semblance of connexion between Church and State" and represents the first and only such reference to the separation of church and state in Canadian law.

John S. Moir has suggested that the effects of the secularization of the clergy reserves led to an increased interdenominational cooperation on social and political matters. The Methodists, Baptists, Presbyterians, and evangelical Anglicans petitioned for government legislation of a Lord's Day law. Other ecumenical efforts included the formation of temperance societies, missionary organizations, Bible guilds, and YMCAs and YWCAs. Following Confederation in 1867, a national "vision" promoting a Christian Canada was taken up with increasing vigor by the evangelical movement, which imagined the new Dominion of Canada to be "His Dominion." This reference to Psalm 72:8, which serves as Canada's motto, was suggested by Samuel Tilley, one of the fathers of Confederation: "He shall have dominion from sea to sea, and from the rivers unto the ends of the earth."

## Confederation and Protestant Presence in Western Canada

The decades following Confederation saw the purchase of Rupert's Land (present-day Manitoba) from the Hudson's Bay Company in 1870 and the addition of the province of British Columbia in 1871, which, following the completion of the Canadian Pacific Railroad in 1885, ushered in a new era of expansion and immigration. The Protestant churches undertook the task of evangelizing western Canada as their duty, though it eventually fell to the Presbyterians and the Methodists, with their newly established national offices, to set up missions and churches in the prairies.

The first Protestants in the pre-Confederation West were Scottish Presbyterians on the Red River near Winnipeg. This community was initially served by an Anglican minister until Presbyterian minister John Black arrived in 1851. The Presbyterian presence in the prairies expanded in the 1860s into Prince Albert, Saskatchewan. Likewise the first Methodists were of British stock (Wesleyan missionaries who had been invited by the Hudson's Bay Company to work among the First Nations populations there). The Canadian Methodist Church, however, took responsibility for missions in Edmonton in as early as 1853. As such, both Presbyterians and Methodists were firmly established and ready for evangelism in the West at the time of Confederation (along with Baptists who concentrated their energy on missionary work among non-English-speaking immigrants).

With the completion of the railroad, an increasing number of immigrant churches were built in western Canada. Russian Mennonites arrived in Manitoba in 1874 and would be followed by a second, larger group fleeing the Bolshevik Revolution of the 1920s. Also from Russia, the controversial communal sect the Doukhobors immigrated to Canada in 1899 with the assistance of Canadian Quakers and Tolstoyans. The Doukhobors entered into the public spotlight when a segment of their community defaced public property and organized nude parades in protest against government intrusion into their communal lifestyle and educational practices. The end of the nineteenth century also witnessed the first entry of Mormons into Canada, in 1887 in Cardston, Alberta, where they constructed the first Mormon temple outside the United States.

In British Columbia the Protestant churches lagged behind the activities of the Roman Catholic and Anglican churches, which had established a strong presence in the years following the Fraser River gold rush. The Presbyterians established a church on Vancouver Island in 1861. The Baptist Convention of British Columbia was formed in 1897.

Following Confederation, several Protestant denominations amalgamated. Four groups of Presbyterians merged into the Presbyterian Church in Canada in 1875, followed by further consolidations in 1886. The many disparate Methodist groups came together in two successive waves, in 1874 and 1884, to become the largest single denomination in Canada. At about the same time, two Baptist conventions formed, first Ontario and Quebec, in 1888, and later in the Maritimes the Free Christian Baptists and the Regular Baptists amalgamated into the United Baptist Convention in 1905–1906. It was not until 1944, however, that a national organization, the Baptist Federation of Canada, was formed, representing only a fragment of Canadian Baptists.

Interdenominational ecumenism was also on the mind of Protestant leaders such as Presbyterian minister and principal of Queen's University, George Munro Grant, who in 1874 advocated for a transconfessional "organic union" among Canada's Protestant denominations. This notion of an organic union stemmed from a sense that Canada's national identity was a moral and spiritual concern; an independent Canadian church was deemed necessary in order to maintain social cohesion in the face of increased immigration. Church Union was aggressively pursued by the Congregationalists, Methodists, and Presbyterians beginning in the 1890s. A national church was perceived as a possibility by overlooking theological differences concerning Methodist Arminianism and Presbyterian Calvinism and by limiting the emphasis of creedal statements. This proposal was met with strong opposition, especially from within the rank and file of the Presbyterian Church, who underscored the importance of the Westminster Confession and Scottish identity.

Ecumenism was also expressed in large-scale revivals. Mass evangelism gained popularity following Confederation, and the appearance of American and Canadian evangelists became more prominent after 1884. For example, the Canadian evangelist team of H. T. Crossley and John E. Hunter held revival meetings in major urban centers, converting more than 100,000 people—even Anglican prime minister John A. Macdonald was caught up in the momentum. Evangelists promoted key Protestant causes such as missionary societies, Sunday schools, and temperance, which in many ways became synonymous with Protestantism in nineteenth-century Canada. During the same time period the Woman's Christian Temperance Union established its Canadian branch under the leadership of its first president, Methodist Letitia Youmans. Initially concerned with moderation of alcohol, the temperance movement's objective became one of prohibition, which was temporarily achieved, except in Quebec, during the First World War by government legislation. The temperance movement became a key concern for promoters of the Social Gospel.

## From the Social Gospel to Fundamentalism in Canada

Involvement in social reform movements was seen by many as a natural extension of evangelical commitments to the transformation of Canada into a Christian society. The Social Gospel in Canada was most prominent in the 1910s through to the 1920s. The most active participants in the Social Gospel movement were liberal Methodists and Presbyterians who replaced a theology of atonement and individual salvation with the project of constructing the Kingdom of God on Earth. As a movement, the Social Gospel found its initial home in Canada's theological colleges, especially the Presbyterian Queen's University in Kingston, Methodist Wesley College in Winnipeg, and Baptist McMaster University in Toronto. As in the United States, Christians sought a way to respond to the social problems that accompanied industrialization in urban environments: poor working conditions, unemployment, health problems, and housing shortages.

It can be argued that in Canada, particularly in western Canada, the Social Gospel movement initially maintained a closer tie to evangelical and mainline Protestantism. Ultimately it diffused into the secular political sphere in such a way that it served as the foundation for one of Canada's major political parties, the Cooperative Commonwealth Federation (the socialist-democratic movement out of which Canada's current New Democratic Party evolved). Some of its less radical propositions also found their way into the Liberal Party of Canada through the political leanings of prime ministers William Lloyd Mackenzie King and Lester B. Pearson. Its most lasting effects were manifest in Tommy Douglas, the former Baptist pastor who moved from ministry into politics in the 1930s. Douglas went on to become the first socialist premier of Saskatchewan and leader of the federal New Democratic Party. Douglas is most specifically remembered as having established a universal health care plan in Saskatchewan that was later adopted across Canada.

For the Methodist Church, which continued to rely on its revivalist foundations in the form of teams of professional evangelists, the Social Gospel movement manifested itself in city missions that provided an important space for women, who were barred from ordained ministry, to participate in evangelism. The city revival was also seen both as a way to meet the challenges of the twentieth century—temperance, labor, health and educational reform—and as offering a means of attracting new members to the church.

Among the important proponents of the Social Gospel were Methodist Salem Bland and his student J. S. Woodsworth. Bland, a student of Queen's University's George Munro Grant, taught theology at Wesley College in Winnipeg from 1903 to 1917 until he was dismissed in part for his progressivism. Known as the Social Gospel's "spirit in the West," he was instrumental in moving Social Gospel concerns out of the classroom and the pulpit and into the public domain. Bland's role was crucial in the formation of the Cooperative Commonwealth Federation, whose first leader was former Methodist minister J. S. Woodsworth. Historian Ramsay Cook points out that Woodsworth's career mirrors the path taken by Canadian liberal Protestantism at the beginning of the twentieth century. In 1902 Woodsworth experienced a profound crisis of faith in which he expressed doubt concerning central tenets of church doctrine, including the divinity of Jesus and the authority of the Bible.

Despite his agnosticism, the Manitoba Conference refused Woodsworth's resignation in 1907, stating that there was nothing in his belief system that prevented him from ministering. With this in mind Woodsworth began a process of challenging established doctrines within the Methodist Church and expanding its missionary ministry toward immigrants. By 1914, in his role as leader of the Canadian Welfare League, he questioned whether the church was the ideal venue in which to enact social reform. Eventually, Woodsworth resigned from the Methodist ministry in 1918 as a result of his refusal to support conscription. Along with other Social Gospelers and labor advocates, Woodsworth joined the short-lived Labour Church in Winnipeg, which positioned itself as part church and part educational forum based on Salem Bland's "New Christianity." The Labour Church served as a venue in which the groundwork was laid for the Winnipeg General Strike of 1919. Woodsworth served one year in jail for his involvement in the strike and went on to political involvement with the Cooperative Commonwealth Federation at the federal level.

David Marshall has argued that the Canadian Protestant churches' acceptance of the Social Gospel was a significant contributing factor to its eventual diminution by the end of World War I. Marshall contends that Protestant clergy made a concerted effort to maintain relevancy in light of social, political, and intellectual challenges of modern life, which ultimately undermined the authority of the church in light of contemporary culture. In contrast, Nancy Christie and Michael Gauvreau maintain that while it eventually became subservient to secular interests and leadership, the Protestant churches and the Social Gospel remained influential well into the mid-1930s. The political activities of the Social Gospelers certainly contributed to the secularization of their initially theological mandate. When considered alongside the prevalent theological challenges of Darwinism and biblical higher criticism circulating at denominational colleges at the time, the story of secularizing trends within Canadian Protestantism becomes more prominent.

The denominational colleges were set up with the intention of educating the evangelical elite and training Canadian-born clergy, so as to limit the churches' dependence on European and American theologians. It was from within the theological colleges that the challenges of modern scholarship to the traditional Christian frame of reference were considered. Many of the church colleges offered a theologically liberal curriculum that focused on an attempt to reconcile the church with the concerns of secular society.

Many historians have concluded that this process served as a major contribution to the eventual secularization of Canadian society. Mark A. Noll concludes *A History of Christianity in the United States and Canada,* published by Eerdmans in 1992, his comparative work on Canadian and American Christianity, by suggesting that "the forces of modernity . . . have worked *through* the communal, top-down structures of traditional Canadian religion, while they have worked *alongside* the more fragmented, populist strictures of the American churches" (p. 549).

Nathanael Burwash (1839–1918), a leading Canadian Methodist, stands as the quintessential representative of liberal evangelicalism emerging from within denominational colleges. Burwash, professor of natural theology and chancellor of Victoria College, attempted to align moderate biblical criticism with a conservative understanding of evolution and the belief in the regenerative necessity of conversion. Because of his beliefs, Burwash makes for an interesting object of study, and his life is key to formulating an understanding of pre–World War I Canadian Protestantism. Burwash was also instrumental in the early negotiations on the part of the Methodists for church union.

It was under Burwash's leadership at Victoria that the Methodist Church articulated disapproval regarding higher criticism. In 1890, Hebrew Bible professor George Coulson Workman was asked to resign from his teaching post because of his nontraditional views concerning the messianic prophecy. Following that, in 1909, English Bible professor-elect George Jackson was attacked by a number of prominent laity and ministers, including the general superintendent of the Methodist Church, Albert Carman, for applying higher criticism methods to the Book of Genesis. Burwash successfully defended Jackson at the Methodist General Conference in British Columbia in 1910. With this controversy, Burwash established Victoria College as a cornerstone institution in the teaching of higher criticism in Canada. That same year, the newly elected general superintendent of the Methodist Church, S. D. Chown, ensured that biblical criticism would be taught in all Canadian Methodist colleges. In his position as general superintendent, Chown went on to be active in the final negotiations that brought together the United Church of Canada.

At the opposite end of the spectrum, T. T. Shields, a controversial pastor at Toronto's Jarvis Street Baptist Church, fought to keep higher criticism out of the classrooms at McMaster University, where he held a seat on the board of governors. In 1924 he attacked theology professor L. H.

Marshall for rejecting scriptural inerrancy (the idea that the Bible was literally accurate); atonement theology, which taught that Jesus' sacrificial death was in atonement and satisfaction for the collective sins of humanity; and the innate depravity of humanity, which held that human nature was hopelessly crippled by original sin and irreparably flawed without divine intervention. Shields was censured two years later for his inflammatory accusations against Marshall at the General Council of the Baptist Convention. Jarvis Street Baptist Church was expelled from the Baptist Convention of Ontario and Quebec and formed its own denomination (the Union of Regular Baptists) as well as its own educational institution (Toronto Baptist Seminary), both of which remain active today. At the time of its founding, seventy-seven churches joined Shields's new denomination, an act that attests not only to his popularity and charisma but also to the prevalence of fundamentalism in central Canada in the 1920s. Controversy followed Shields, however, when in 1933 the majority of those churches left to form the Fellowship of Independent Baptist Churches. In 1949 Shields was asked to leave the Union, at which point he established the Conservative Baptist Association of Canada.

Following the spirit of ecumenism, the Canadian Council of Churches was formed in 1944 as a representative body of twelve denominations in Canada (Protestant and Eastern Orthodox). The Council was established as a means of coordinating social service and missionary efforts in Canada and abroad. There are presently twenty-two member churches, which include representation from the major Protestant denominations as well as Anglican, Orthodox, and Roman Catholic traditions. A similar movement can be found among Canadian evangelicals in the Evangelical Fellowship of Canada (EFC), which was founded in 1964 and brought together twenty-four conservative denominations including the Pentecostal Assemblies of Canada and smaller groups such as the Salvation Army, the Mennonite Brethren Church, the Christian Reformed Church, and the Christian and Missionary Alliance Churches. Today, the EFC consists of forty affiliates, five observers (including the Canadian Council of Churches), and individual congregations across Canada.

## United Church of Canada

Formally established on June 10th, 1925, the United Church of Canada was the amalgamation of the Methodist Church, Canada (which at the time was the largest Methodist denomination in Canada), the Congregational

Union of Canada, the Council of Local Union Churches (approximately 3,000 small congregations mostly in the West that had been established in anticipation of church union), and two-thirds of the Presbyterian Church in Canada. Upon founding, it was instantly the largest church in Canada, with over 20 percent of the Canadian population. Later additions were the Methodist Church of Bermuda in 1930 and the Canadian Conference of the Evangelical United Brethren in 1968.

The historian Marguerite Van Die links church union with a decreased emphasis on denominational identity and orthodoxy in light of the emergence of modern evangelism. George Pidgeon, the first moderator of the United Church of Canada and the former moderator of the Presbyterian Church, negotiated two competing narratives arguing that Jesus was not merely a social reformer but also an evangelist interested in individual transformation and union with God. For the most part, the founding members of the United Church were Social Gospelers advocating not just a shift from "salvation of the self" to "salvation of society" but more importantly for a transformation of what "salvation of the self" actually entails. The United Church set itself on an early path toward egalitarianism and began ordaining women in 1936. While it is often criticized by other Protestants as being theologically weak and too quick to accommodate secular society, the United Church continues to be widely recognized as the most tolerant and justice-oriented denomination in Canada.

The optimism of church union was renewed following the Second World War; between 1945 and 1965, the United Church constructed over fifteen hundred churches, saw its enrollment increase by over 25 percent, and had thousands of laypeople join adult Christian education groups. Charles Templeton (1915–2001) was appointed to conduct a national "Crusade for Christ," which rivaled the evangelical campaigns of Billy Graham. Templeton's tumultuous theological journey is representative of a larger dissolution of consensus among Protestants in Canada. Templeton's career had two distinct stages, the first as an old-fashioned revivalist and the second as an advocate for a revised Christianity that drew upon contemporary insights with which to reinterpret doctrines. In a 1958 interview with the Toronto newspaper the *Globe and Mail,* Templeton declared himself an agnostic. This statement resulted in deep backlash from the evangelical community. Templeton went on to become a journalist and ran for leadership of the Liberal Party of Ontario in 1964.

In 1963 the United Church introduced its "New Curriculum," which attempted to provide material for all age groups that engaged with biblical higher criticism and socially relevant material. It can be said that the New Curriculum intensified the polarization between liberal and conservative Christians in Canada and seemingly ends the ecumenist era of Canadian Protestantism. While the curriculum was subsequently taken up and adapted by several liberal denominations (it is comparable to the Anglican Church of Canada's "Parish Education" of 1966), it was widely criticized by conservative churches and ended several decades of Sunday school collaboration between the United Church and Baptists.

The United Church continued to establish itself as an inclusive and liberal-leaning church throughout the second half of the twentieth century. In 1980 Lois Wilson was elected as the first female moderator of the United Church (Wilson went on to have a distinguished career as president of both the Canadian and World Council of Churches as well as serving as a Canadian senator from 1998 to 2002). Other notable moderators have included Robert McClure in 1968 and Anne Squires in 1986 (both nonordained laypeople) and Sang Chul Lee (the first Asian moderator) in 1988.

## Recent Developments

The current configuration of Protestantism in Canada is characterized by a striking decline in membership in the years following the 1960s. From 1960 to 2000 the Canadian census reveals that membership in each of Canada's four major Protestant denominations decreased dramatically: the United Church from 20.1 percent to 9.6 percent, the Anglican Church from 13.2 percent to 6.9 percent, the Presbyterian Church from 4.5 percent to 1.4 percent, and the Lutheran Church from 4 percent to 2 percent. Interestingly, Canadian sociologist Reginald Bibby's statistics reveal that for the most part mainline Protestants continue to identify with their childhood religious affiliations, even in instances where they are not actively engaged with church institutions. In contrast, conservative Protestants are more likely to switch affiliations several times throughout their lifetimes. Conservative Protestants in Canada, as in the United States, are more likely to attend weekly services, to profess categorical beliefs regarding the existence of God, and to pray regularly.

In the mid-1980s and into the 1990s the United Church engaged in lengthy theological debate surrounding its stance on sexuality. After much debate, in 1988 the United Church approved the ordination of openly gay and lesbian candidates for ministry. While this decision led to the departure of some congregations, for the most part the United Church became known as a safe place for people of all sexual orientations. The United Church was actively involved in presenting evidence in favor of same-sex marriage to the Canadian federal government, which went on to legislate same-sex marriage in 2005.

At the other end of the theological spectrum, the 1990s witnessed an influx of visitors to the controversial Toronto Airport Christian Fellowship, originally a member of the Vineyard Church, to receive the "Toronto Blessing" in the form of speaking in tongues, divine healings, "holy laughter," and the experience of being "slain in the spirit."

Current theological concerns among Protestants, especially in the United Church, revolve around the representation of "theological truths" in the public sphere. Popular books and films such as *The Da Vinci Code* have prompted discussion about biblical accuracy and personal morality. As the most vocal institution of liberal Christianity in Canada, the United Church has become the centrifuge of debate. In 1997 Bill Phipps, United Church moderator from 1997 to 2000, entered the media spotlight when, during an interview with the *Ottawa Citizen*, he questioned the divinity of Jesus. More recently, in 2008, Gretta Vosper, United Church minister and founder of the Canadian Centre for Progressive Christianity, published *With or Without God*, in which she posits that language and references to God have outlived their usefulness in the church. Although there have been calls for her resignation, Vosper's congregation understands itself to be a community that is intellectually rigorous, free of absolutist statements, and consistent with a worldview that conforms to accepted scientific and moral norms—a position that they insist the rest of Christianity needs to adopt in order to survive in the twenty-first century.

The core social issues facing Canadian Protestant churches today relate to an attempt to make sense of their pasts while accommodating the future. Partially as a response to decline in membership and also as a reflection of a mandate for multiculturalism in Canada, many of the mainline churches have established themselves as a resource for new immigrants to Canada. For example, in the Presbyterian Church in Canada services are conducted in at least seventeen languages with notable Korean and Ghanaian congregations. Likewise the United Church has continued to represent itself as Canada's national church, not only by engaging in multiculturalism but also by promoting intercultural and multifaith dialogue. In 1996 the United Church established its Ethnic Ministries Council as a means to support ethnic minority congregations and individuals within the church and to provide a venue for new immigrants, as well as for third- and fourth-generation Canadians to participate meaningfully in the denomination.

**See also** *Canada* entries; *Charismatics/Charismatic Movements; Ecumenism; Great Awakening(s); Mainline Protestants; Missions* entries; *Moravians; Native American* entries; *Protestant Liberalism; Revivalism* entries; *Same-Gender Marriage; Sexuality and Sexual Identity.*

Rebekka King

## BIBLIOGRAPHY

Airhart, Phyllis D. *Serving the Present Age: Revivalism, Progressivism, and the Methodist Tradition in Canada*. Montreal-Kingston: McGill-Queen's University Press, 1992.

Bibby, Reginald. *Restless Gods: The Renaissance of Religion in Canada*. Toronto: Stoddart, 2002.

Bramadat, Paul, and David Seljak. *Christianity and Ethnicity in Canada*. Toronto: University of Toronto Press, 2008.

Christie, Nancy, and Michael Gauvreau. *A Full-Orbed Christianity: The Protestant Churches and Social Welfare in Canada, 1900–1940*. Montreal-Kingston: McGill-Queen's University Press, 2001.

Cook, Ramsey. *The Regenerators: Social Criticism in Late Victorian English Canada*. Toronto: University of Toronto Press, 1985.

Gauvreau, Michael. *The Evangelical Century: College and Creed in English Canada from the Great Revival to the Great Depression*. Montreal-Kingston: McGill-Queen's University Press, 1991.

Gauvreau, Michael, and Ollivier Hubert, eds. *The Churches and Social Order in Nineteenth- and Twentieth-Century Canada*. Montreal-Kingston: McGill-Queen's University Press, 2006.

Grant, John Webster. *The Church in the Canadian Era*. Burlington, Ont.: Welch, 1988.

Handy, Robert T. *A History of the Churches in the United States and Canada*. New York: Oxford University Press, 1977.

Marshall, David. *Secularizing the Faith: Canadian Protestant Clergy and the Crisis of Belief, 1850–1940*. Toronto: University of Toronto Press, 1992.

Moir, John S. *Christianity in Canada: Historical Essays*. Edited by Paul Laverdure. Yorkton, Sask.: Redeemer's Voice Press, 2002.

Murphy, Terence, and Roberto Perin. *A Concise History of Christianity in Canada*. New York: Oxford University Press, 1996.

Noll, Mark A. "What Happened to Christian Canada?" *Church History* 75 (June 2006): 245–273.

Rawlyk, George A. *"The Canada Fire": Radical Evangelism in British North America, 1775–1812*. Montreal and Kingston: McGill-Queen's University Press, 1994.

———, ed. *Aspects of the Canadian Evangelical Experience*. Montreal-Kingston: McGill-Queen's University Press, 1997.

———, ed. *The Canadian Protestant Experience, 1760–1990*. Burlington, Ont.: Welch, 1990.

Semple, Neil. *The Lord's Dominion: The History of Canadian Methodism*. Montreal-Kingston, McGill-Queens University Press, 1996.

Stackhouse, John G., Jr. *Canadian Evangelicalism in the Twentieth Century: An Introduction to Its Character.* Toronto: University of Toronto Press, 1993.

Van Die, Marguerite. *An Evangelical Mind: Nathanael Burwash and the Methodist Tradition in Canada, 1839–1918.* Montreal-Kingston: McGill-Queen's University Press, 1989.

———, ed. *Religion and Public Life in Canada: Historical and Comparative Perspectives.* Toronto: University of Toronto Press, 2001.

Westfall, William. *Two Worlds: The Protestant Culture of Nineteenth-Century Ontario.* Montreal-Kingston: McGill-Queen's University Press, 1989.

# Caribbean Religious Culture and Influence

The Caribbean Sea, lying between the North and South American continents, is the setting for the archipelago of islands stretching from Cuba, off the shores of Florida, to Trinidad, which can be seen from the Venezuelan mainland. The geographical location of the Caribbean islands has shaped their historical importance as a crossroads of cultures, races, and religions. Because these many islands sit within the Gulf Stream and the African Equatorial Current, they have been the stage for power and politics stretching from October 12, 1492, down to the early twenty-first century.

The many religious traditions brought to the islands have been impacted by the islands' history and culture, influencing religious beliefs and practices in ways unique to the Caribbean. The impact of these transformations on religion has long been categorized with the term *syncretism.* This term has proven to be problematic, since it includes instances of both embracement and rejection of disparate elements without the intellectual tools to decipher variations in the process. The polemic use of *syncretism* has been especially prevalent in the theological literature of religious elites, for whom one or another set of beliefs is either acceptable or unacceptable. Considered less freighted with the polemics of previous literature, the word *hybridity* has been more recently incorporated. But under any category, transformations and mixing of cultures and religions exercise an undeniable presence in the Caribbean.

Formal religion, it has been claimed, has the capacity to absorb popular expressions in order to reproduce the devotions of the masses within the boundaries of orthodox belief. Jaime Vidal (in *An Enduring Flame,* 1994) not only insists that there is an acceptable form of faith mixture within religions such as Catholicism but also coins an expression, *synthetization,* to describe this acceptable mixture, arguing that this term rather than *syncretization* registers the acceptability of certain kinds of faith mixtures, while differentiating it from the unpalatable jumble of religious beliefs that are not yet reconciled or are incapable of reconciliation with the formal theological system.

What is being ultimately argued is that Christianity's absorption of elements of faith from other religions is indispensable to an analysis of Caribbean religious culture. Consider, for example, the influences from African belief systems that are present in a Catholic devotion like that to the Cuban Our Lady of Charity. Her statues and prayers to her are also found in Santería. Certainly, the term *hybridity* fits both cases. But how does devotion to Our Lady of Charity also result in differing theological conclusions that make such devotions both orthodox to Catholicism and unorthodox at the same time? These differing judgments about the theological dimension in religion are crucial in assessing the influences on Caribbean religious culture and the historical path trod in the process of religious transformations.

A useful analogy to sum up the "breaking point" between an assimilating synthesization and an unacceptable syncretism is the split of the different Romance languages from the common original language, Latin. Following this logic, Gustavo Benavides suggests that when the symbolic languages of religion have become so differentiated that persons accepting the same symbols no longer understand each other, then a new religion has been created (*Enigmatic Powers,* 1995). Crucial to any analysis of Caribbean religions is an empirical test of whether religion is a coherent mixture of different elements or, in fact, a noncommunicating dyad. These are the different currents that run under the cover of Caribbean religious culture and its influences.

## Historical Origins

Even before the arrival of European Christianity with Columbus, the Caribbean had already experienced the encounter of different peoples and religious cultures. Two distinct linguistic groups occupied contiguous regions of the Caribbean. The most numerous were the Arahuacan-speaking Taínos and Taínas, who were also the first people encountered by the Iberians on the major islands of Cuba, Española, and Puerto Rico. In the Lesser Antilles of the Eastern Caribbean, Karina-speaking groups called "Carib" had successfully integrated themselves into the social fabric. One curious aspect of this contact is the linguistic phenomenon found among the peoples of the island of Dominica. A seventeenth-century French missionary assembling a catechism in the native language found that the men used Carib words for certain tools and activities, while the women used the Arahuacan terms for the same things. Anthropologists have concluded this is linguistic evidence that Carib men settled the island by replacing Arahuacan men as husbands in the island population. These intrusions had already taken place in the smaller islands of the Eastern Caribbean and were being resisted in Puerto Rico when the Spaniards arrived. Thus, the cultural differentiations of the Greater and Lesser Antilles began before the European intrusions.

These pre-Columbian differences are not matters of idle trivia. The earliest Spanish documents expanded the cultural divide between these groups to view the Arahuacan Taínos and Taínas as "docile natives" and the Caribs as "hostile cannibals who deserve enslavement." In their famous Valladolid debates of 1550–1551, Bartolomé de Las Casas and Juan Ginés de Sepúlveda discussed whether or not the gravity of "sins against nature" by the American natives legitimized their enslavement. The arguments of Las Casas helped set the cornerstone of contemporary international laws that protect the religious and cultural rights of native peoples.

Speeches in Spain, however, did not erase the contradictions and conflicts among the different peoples and cultures in the colonies of the Caribbean. The distinction between preaching by word and preaching by example was made clear in Las Casas's own commentaries on evangelization. In an encounter with a prospective native convert, Las Casas asked if he had become a Christian. The man answered that he was only a "little bit of a Christian," explaining that he knew only a little bit about drunkenness, adultery, swearing, and lying, but by imitating the Spanish Christians, he would soon be a more complete Christian. The point is well-taken, even if Las Casas exaggerated here the contrast between the preaching of a religion and its actual practice.

## African Presence in the Caribbean

Africans came to the Caribbean first as freemen working on Spanish boats and in the military and later as slaves after Queen Isabella decreed in 1503 that Taínos and Taínas could not be enslaved. The demand for a slave workforce quickly transformed the African presence in the Caribbean into one that was mostly of persons held in chattel slavery. It is also noteworthy that the first black slaves came from Spain and Portugal and not from Africa. Las Casas's early defense of the American natives had led him to suggest that those already slaves could be substituted. Later, he more clearly repudiated the enslavement of Africans on their native soil, condemning such actions with the same

vehemence with which he had defended the American natives. He wrote of the exploitation in Africa in his *History of the Indies,* picturing oppression of peoples of color as a worldwide abuse of human rights everywhere, although these passages were omitted by nineteenth-century editors.

The distinctions between free- and slave-blacks, and between Iberian and African-origin slaves, greatly affected religious influences. For instance, the free-blacks and the Iberian slaves spoke Spanish and understood European culture, law, and religion. The slave-blacks and those taken directly from Africa had little previous exposure to Christianity until arriving in the Caribbean. This divide explains why the rituals of Africa and its linguistic heritage were preserved in the rural slave quarters and not among the domestic servants of colonial cities. The runaway slaves, called *cimarrones,* often lived in the hills and would reproduce a culture and religious expression most familiar to their memories of Africa. Eventually, arguments about fugitive African slaves as savages needing punishment would be extended by Spanish, French, and English authorities to include all black persons, slaves and freemen. Essential to this racist argument was citing rituals of African religion as enduring proof of savagery. On such a religious and cultural basis, the slaveholders conducted hunts to recapture and brutally suppress the *cimarrones.*

Also among these *cimarrones,* another kind of hybridity and racial mixture began in the sixteenth-century Caribbean. The runaway slaves often assimilated into the existing culture of the American natives. Thus, in addition to those who were a mixture of black African race and white European stock, there were peoples of mixed African and Native American ethnicities—the later the were more frequently found in the Caribbean than in Mexico or Peru. It has been suggested that the Taíno-African mixture is present in Haitian Vodun as well as in the cultural and religious practices of the so-called Black Caribs of Honduras and the Garifuna people of Belize. It is the mixed race and attendant religious and cultural heritage of the Garifuna that marks them as a Caribbean nationality. Racial mixtures do not automatically produce cultural transfers with theological results, but racial miscegenation is often the context for religious and cultural miscegenation.

## Religion and Racial Politics

Cultural and religious bias is an ordinary occurrence in human history, and it affects the study of that history.

Accordingly, descriptions of the cultures and religions of the Caribbean need to be filtered through a critique that identifies underlying premises. Thus, some non-Catholic historians perceive the colonial effort of the Spanish in the Caribbean as unrelentingly exploitative. This so-called Black Legend emphasizes the negative aspects and results of Spanish colonization. Carried to the extreme, it interprets everything Spanish and Catholic as wrongful. On the other side, there is a rationalizing approach that emphasizes the positive aspects of Spanish intervention to the point of whitewashing any errors or mistakes. It is labeled as the "White Legend," to contrast it as an opposite type of exaggeration.

Labels derived from sixteenth-century debates have persisted into the twentieth and twenty-first centuries. In 1987 in Hialeah, Florida, where many Cuban exiles live, the city council prohibited killing animals in Santería rituals. Defending the city ordinance, the chaplain of the police department compared the ritual to "the worship of demons" (do Campo 1995: 156). While a Supreme Court decision (*Lukuni v. Hialeah,* 1992) and subsequent federal law (Religious Freedom Restoration Act, 1993) included Santería rituals as the free exercise of religion, this case shows that the categories used by the White and Black Legends' approaches to Caribbean religion persist in the contemporary United States.

The White Legend that supports the role of Christianity as a civilizing force is echoed in the approach of Anglicanism to slave-blacks in the English Caribbean in such places as Jamaica. Beginning in the eighteenth century, organizations such as the Society for the Propagation of the Gospel in Foreign Parts focused on evangelizing the slaves in the Americas. In his 1684 book *Sacred Theory of the Earth,* Thomas Burnet echoed the White Legend notion that supplanting native religion with Christianity was a benign process. The optimism for Anglicans about the potential for African slaves to become Christians stood in contrast with the Calvinist tendency to consider them unredeemable savages.

The failure of these earlier efforts helped spur the abolitionist movement of the early nineteenth century. Member of the British Parliament William Wilberforce (1759–1833) was one of many who cited the cruel mistreatment of African slaves in the Caribbean as a reason for Christians to end the slave trade. As with Las Casas two centuries earlier, Wilberforce found his most bitter opposition came from plantation owners, who considered slavery a necessary component of a profitable economy. Nonetheless, slave trade in the Caribbean was restricted and finally abolished throughout the British Empire in a series of measures adopted by Parliament, beginning in 1807 and concluding in 1833. The religious sentiments that animated the British abolitionist movement spilled over into the U.S. abolitionist movement, which achieved success only after a bloody Civil War (1861–1865).

Without the dramatic examples drawn from the Caribbean, neither the history of the slave trade in Great Britain nor the emancipation of slaves in the United States would have been the same. Even critics who argue for economic rather than religious causes for abolition in the Caribbean recognize that religion exercised a crucial influence in the formation of Caribbean societies. In the case of abolition, as with the Spanish White Legend, the emphasis was on what Christianity did to uplift religion in the Caribbean, neglecting the power of other religious expressions among the slaves. Still, Wilberforce and his allies followed the trail blazed by Las Casas centuries before in urging reform, with a Caribbean scenario as the dramatic example presented on the world stage.

Often divorced from the processes of kings and parliaments, religion among the peoples of color in the Caribbean took on its own character. The most common form of religious hybridity arose from the need of the poor to apply medicines and cures to the sick. Before the invention of the urban pharmacy, ordinary people used plant leaves or seeds with medical properties for teas or for topical use.

Hybridity entered through two doors in the Caribbean. For one, the tropical forests and mountains did not always offer the same set of plants that were familiar to Europeans. Instead, there was an abundance of local and new sources for usage. Often these new Caribbean pharmacological resources had been used by the natives of the Caribbean long before the arrival of Spaniards or Africans. Moreover, at times the Caribbean variation of the plants more closely resembled African equivalents than European variations.

Patterns emerged for certain individuals skilled in recognizing and applying such home remedies to function in the stead of scientifically trained doctors. However, the material application of such herbal remedies was often accompanied by prayers for efficacy that could be traced to the non-Christian experience. As often as not, the practitioners invoked both Christian saints and nature spirits to provide the best path to recovery for the sick. Touching, rubbing, and anointing affected parts frequently accompanied such actions. This type of home medicine became known in the

Spanish-speaking Caribbean as *curanderismo,* and the skilled practitioners were *curanderos/as.* While in the early twenty-first century medical treatments are seldom associated with religion, history suggests that such holistic healing was applied with prayer and blessings. In this way, such home healing with religious overtones became associated with the poor, the rural, and the people of color.

With the twentieth-century efforts to build hospitals and bring scientific methods of care to the Caribbean countryside, the old arguments about savages and civilization, about the ignorant natives and the educated elites, resurfaced. On the one hand, it was argued that *curanderismo* was a vestige of ignorance and superstition. Prayers to spirits unrecognizable to Christian orthodoxy or use of plants with names unfamiliar to hospital doctors became proof that *curanderismo* should be rejected. Instead of proof of commonsense medical insight, the frequent efficacy of such home-style organic treatment was twisted to become evidence of devil worship and the like. This was exacerbated by the tendency among the *curanderos/as* to attribute illness to evil spirits who had taken up abode in the body of the sick.

*Curanderismo* has become part of the fabric of ordinary life in contemporary Caribbean societies. Such skills have become "spiritual capital" and have made such healing into "the business of magic" (Romberg 2003). More clinical approaches to *curanderismo* have emphasized its efficacy over its religious foundation and demonstrated the empowerment of women both as healers and as patients in what has been termed "traditional healing" in Puerto Rico and among the Latino community in the United States. Its persistence argues that *curanderismo* ought to be considered an important element of Caribbean religious culture.

## Political Views of Caribbean religion

The American War of Independence and the French Revolution introduced politics into the Caribbean in ways that affected the perception of religion. While the rivalries between Catholic Spain and France on the one hand and Protestant England and Holland on the other had been present in the sporadic warfare and the piracy of the Caribbean, only in the nineteenth century did the religious cultures indigenous to the islands begin to assume political influence.

The first such manifestation was in the Haitian Revolution. The 1793 beheading of the French king in Paris and the subsequent turmoil that lasted until the final defeat of Napoleon in 1815 allowed a new nation composed mostly of former slaves to emerge on the western part of Española. Ruled by blacks and supported by an army of former slaves, the Haitians repulsed European armies and eventually marched unimpeded into the Spanish eastern section of the island, annexing the colony of Santo Domingo in 1821. Viewing the Vatican, the central apostolic see of Roman Catholicism, with the same suspicion as existed for the European imperial powers, the new Haitian Republic witnessed the emergence of religious practices that were unregulated in the absence of clergy. Although by midcentury an accommodation was reached that allowed for restoration of institutionalized Catholicism, the hiatus had permitted a public role for rituals that exhibited elements of both Catholicism and African religions, known as Vodun, or "Voodoo."

Haiti is not the only site for syncretism of Catholicism and African beliefs. The dichotomy between white free society and black slaves in Cuba permitted a similar syncretism that resulted in the religion of Lukumí, known outside of Cuba as Santería. Both of these forms as well as variations in the Dominican Republic (Gagá) share a common trait of hybridization, although in different measures and in various formulations.

Caribbean religions usually identified as "Afro-Caribbean" often also have been influenced by Spiritualism. Developed from European positivism, Spiritualism emerged in the nineteenth century as a philosophical system with the Enlightenment's view that institutionalized religion was for the masses while rational science was the superior understanding of the elites. Propagated by Masonic organizations, positivism went beyond a passive deism and produced a religion to rival Christianity.

The Spiritualism that arrived in the Caribbean via Spain and France was derived from the writings of Allan Kardec, pseudonym for Hippolyte Leon Denizard Rivail (1804–1869), a French educator. Kardec insisted rational meaning was hidden within all religions. He offered the key to deciphering the progress of human history. Often cast into numerical formulae, the hidden meanings allowed Spiritualists to accept public religions such as Christianity to satisfy social expectations. Often, Spiritualists in the Caribbean were Masons or Free Thinkers who did not attack the church but tolerated it as an inconvenience whose inner esoteric symbolism was a prop for universal rationalism. While Kardec was still fashioning his synthesis of outward material religious symbols and inner spiritualist rational meaning, cases of spirit-tapping stirred public interest in communication with the spirit world. The side result of Kardec's popularity on both sides of the Atlantic was the upper class gathering in a séance to speak with the dead.

In Puerto Rico, as in Cuba and Haiti, contact with spirits was a feature of the religion of the people of color, particularly of black slaves. In search of frequent contact with the dead, Spiritualists of an upper class were brought into symbiotic contact with Afro-Caribbean religions of blacks. Thus, there emerged cross-class religions that incorporated both the "white table," the nonsacrificial séance, with the "red table," or bloody animal sacrifice rituals.

Contact between these traditions was intensified with the migration of black persons to the cities of the Caribbean in the first third of the twentieth century and exploded with the immigration to the United States after World War II. Variations from the Caribbean islands survive among people from a particular culture who have migrated to the United States. There is, for instance, the persistence of Lukumí among Cubans in Miami of all social classes. In addition to these home-and-away linkages, the contact among the major Caribbean groups in cities such as New York has produced religious configurations found only in the United States. Moreover, the Afro-Caribbean variations in the United States attract not only new members from among African Americans with little or no Caribbean background but white people as well.

Jamaica had its own version of syncretism that combined religion with the utopian visions of Marcus Garvey (1887–1940). Garvey, who achieved his greatest successes in New York City, had lived much of his life in Jamaica before becoming an immigrant to the United States. During the Great Depression, he organized the Universal Negro Improvement Association (UNIA), a society in which blacks ran their own businesses and took pride in their African history. Although run from New York, the association popularized the notion of Pan-Africanism and the eventual prosperity of African peoples everywhere to a leading role in world affairs.

While Garvey's organization did not constitute a religion, it was a breeding ground for new religions, some of which appear unconnected to the Caribbean. It may be argued that Garvey's influence could be traced to the Black Muslims, since Elijah Muhammad had been a Garveyite before taking over the Nation of Islam. In Garvey's homeland of Jamaica, his economic and social utopian vision was hitched to a religious framework of salvation and millenarian fulfillment known as the Rastafarian faith. The first publication

promoting the religious dimensions that became the Rasta movement was Leonard P. Howell's *The Promise Key,* published shortly after the November 1930 coronation of the emperor Haile Selassie of Ethiopia in Addis Ababa. Ethiopia has a history dating back to biblical times and protects a Christian faith with unique beliefs and rituals partially explained by isolation from Roman Catholicism. Enlarging on the honorific titles such as "Lion of Judah" invoked in the ceremony, Howell (1898–1981) presented them as fulfillments of prophecies taken eclectically from Judaism and Christianity. His audacity rewarded him with jail time in Jamaica for sedition because he urged recognition of Selassie as a Black Messiah instead of continuing obedience to the English king.

The Rasta grew in numbers in Jamaica. Street preachers promoted a belief in a Black Messiah, using concepts taken from Christianity that were familiar to the new converts, and invoking Garvey's ideas on economic and social power for black people. By 1961, when Haile Selassie visited Jamaica, the Rasta had retreated from troublesome conflict with authorities into communes, where they promoted a return to Africa. Customs such as not cutting hair and letting it grow as dreadlocks and using marijuana, or ganja, in rituals mark members of the Rasta. The Rastafarians have also developed a musical style for songs that mirror their beliefs about the world and the role of blacks. The reggae music with words written and songs performed by Bob Marley are considered representative not only of the Rastafarians but of Jamaican culture.

In the Spanish Caribbean there is a current revival of the Taíno religion. While there was a historical break in continuity between the religion practiced by the natives of the Greater Antilles and groups of Puerto Ricans and Dominicans today, some have organized themselves as part of the Native American peoples. These new Taínos/as attend pow wows and other regional conferences for Native Americans in the contemporary United States. The Neo-Taínos/as intend to restore to contemporary practice the main elements of the religion that had been replaced by the sixteenth-century encounter with Spanish Catholicism. While there are questions as to whether or not these restorations actually reproduce the native religion of the sixteenth century, there is little doubt that such efforts have introduced Taíno/a spirituality into modern society. The revival of native religions is found not only on the Caribbean islands but also among groups of immigrants living in U.S. cities.

Not only traditional domestic customs and grassroots groups can be categorized as Caribbean religious culture. Religious institutions also generated much social influence, especially in politics. In prerevolutionary Cuba (1900–1959) as in the Dominican Republic under the Trujillo's dictatorship (1930–1961), Catholicism was used by tyrants in order to prop up their rule among the people. Their siren song was anticommunism, and at times this effort to frighten church leaders would distract religious attention from issues of social justice and government corruption. In Cuba and the Dominican Republic, however, church members from both Catholic and Protestant denominations eventually opposed the regime, participating in the dramatic overthrow of dictatorships.

In Cuba, the 1959 victory of rebel forces under the leadership of Fidel Castro over Fulgencio Batista's dictatorial regime was quickly followed by religious conflicts between the Catholic Church and the Revolution, when it was backed by the communist government of the Soviet Union. The rush of events produced the Cuban exile community of South Florida and elsewhere. Relations between the Cuban government and the Catholic Church underwent alternating periods of rapprochement and distancing for three decades, affected primarily by the Second Vatican Council, which opened up Catholicism to the theology of liberation. However, the so-called special time produced by the dissolution of the Soviet Union had the greatest impact on Cuban religion. At a party congress in 1993, the Cuban Constitution was changed from describing Cuba as "an atheistic state" to "a secular state." With the implicit censure of religious practice lifted, not only Catholicism and the historic Protestant denominations were invigorated, but also the religions of Lukumí and Spiritualism, which had often functioned secretly at the margins of state and religion. The historic visit of Pope John Paul II to Cuba in 1998 signaled a new epoch in religious influence in Cuba, and the full effects are yet to be experienced, as longtime Cuban leader Fidel Castro remains powerful even after resigning his office for health reasons in 2008.

In Puerto Rico, a U.S. colonial possession since the end of the Spanish-American War of 1898, the 1960 island elections produced a conflict between church and state when the Catholic bishops promoted the formation of a religious party, the Partido de Acción Cristiana (PAC), in opposition to the birth control policies of the established political leader, Luis Muñoz Marín. Although Muñoz Marín won reelection, and the North American bishops were replaced by native Puerto Rican hierarchs, the conflict produced a division among Catholics and fragmented ecumenical participation for decades. Moreover, the political ineptness of the North American bishops in 1960 dimmed the glaring light cast on forced sterilization by a native bishop, Antulio Parrilla Bonilla (1919–1994). In 2000, Puerto Rico had the highest rate (33 percent) of sterilization of women of childbearing age in the world, and endemic poverty made worse by its juxtaposition with the wealth of North American corporations. The ambiguous political status of Puerto Rico—ruled by the U.S. Congress but without voting rights—has stilled the prophetic voice of religious institutions such as the Catholic Church and many Protestant churches with headquarters in the United States.

Catholicism was identified in Puerto Rico from the 1940s through the 1960s with both conservatives and radicals. The revolutionary Nationalist Party leader, Pedro Albizu Campos (1893–1965), promoted a Catholic identity for Puerto Rico. Arguing that the United States was a Protestant country with culture and values inimical to Catholic Puerto Rico, Albizu Campos compared the situation of his homeland to what Ireland had suffered under Protestant British rule for some 400 years, and he urged armed rebellion. The legacy of religious resistance to colonialism acquired an ecumenical character after the Second Vatican Council and the arrival in Puerto Rico of liberation theology from Latin America. Beginning in 1999, successful protests led by religious groups forced the closing of the U.S. Navy base and its target bombing of the inhabited island of Vieques in 2003. Thus, unique among the religions found elsewhere in the Caribbean, many believers in Puerto Rico have come together to confront the moral implications of what they view as a situation of colonialism.

## Diasporic Caribbean Religion

Each of the Caribbean islands has undergone a major out-migration of its people. Too complicated to reduce to any single formula, the twentieth century produced a scattering, or diaspora, of Caribbean peoples. The ties between the sending and receiving groups also allow for continual interchange or religious culture and influence between island homeland and migrant destination.

An example of the phenomenon of import-export of both people and religion is found in Puerto Rican Pentecostalism. Shortly after the U.S. annexation of the island in 1898, growers in faraway Hawaii began to bring displaced Puerto Ricans to the Pacific islands to work the agribusiness fields. Hawaii in 1900 was also a key player in the Holiness movement, which spilled over into the Azusa Street Revival of 1913 in California, thus contributing to the birth of Pentecostalism. Juan L. Lugo, a Puerto Rican Pentecostal convert, returned to Puerto Rico after his acceptance into the Assemblies of God in 1916. The Pentecostal faith grew rapidly in Puerto Rico, and by 1932, Pentecostals outnumbered all other Protestants in Puerto Rico. Eventually, Puerto Rican Pentecostal missionaries would found churches in much of Latin America and most especially in New York City.

Caribbean Pentecostals have not been exempt from the syncretistic elements common in other expressions of the island cultures. Juanita Garcia Peraza (d. 1970) converted to Pentecostalism in the 1940s but became convinced that she was the incarnation of the Holy Spirit. With the name La Diosa Mita, her new religion integrated a strong network of support groups and enterprises to its worship and now has spread outside of Puerto Rico. Also fitting into this category of "Pentecostal heresies" are churches such as Fuentes de Agua Viva (Fountains of Living Water). In New York City, Pentecostals broke with the orthodox preaching that "retarded" children were possessed by the devil and condemned to hell. Instead, such groups as Angels Unaware nurture people of faith and care for children with special needs.

Ana Maria Diaz-Stevens has written convincingly, in "The Saving Grace," of a "matriarchal core" at the heart of diasporic Caribbean religion. Noting that males in migration seldom reach the social status afforded them in their homeland, she states that women have assumed the key role in sustaining faith and family. The same author, in *Oxcart Catholicism on Fifth Avenue,* demonstrated that the presence of large numbers of Caribbean peoples has forced substantial changes on the religious institutions of the diaspora. The changes include the use of typical folk music and the utilization of symbols both secular and religious to identify worship as specifically Caribbean. There is a growing literature that explores the diasporic experience of other groups and other religions.

Thomas Tweed undertakes an analysis of Cuban religious identity in his study of the Shrine of Our Lady of Charity in Miami, Florida. Because it is difficult when not also unlawful for Cubans in the United States to travel to the original shrine, in the Santiago region of Cuba, the Miami complex has developed a set of supports for cultural and religious identity with uniquely diasporic Caribbean characteristics. Likewise, Dominicans in the United States have transferred to American shores the devotion to their national patron, Our Lady of Altagracia. Haitians have incorporated the Polish Our Lady of Czechostowa, the "Black Madonna," into their expression of cultural identity. Without claiming American exceptionalism for Caribbean religion, it appears that many in diaspora have become more religious in the United States than they were in their island homelands.

## Caribbean Religious Forms

Caribbean religious culture has adapted to constantly changing circumstances in multicultural and multiracial societies. Some variations appear as syncretized or hybrid "new" religions that have no match elsewhere. The Rastafarians and the religion of La Diosa Mita fall into this category. Some view Afro-Caribbean religions as imperfect restorations of pristine African religions. The Neo-Taínos made a similar claim to have restored an old religion rather than having created a new one.

Most of Caribbean believers, however, are not members of these specialized religions. Rather, they belong to more familiar Christian churches. They have been affected, however, by the crosswinds and deep currents of religious encounters in multicultural and multiracial Caribbean societies. As suggested in the opening pages, the adaptation or lack thereof to syncretistic elements is the key to understanding Caribbean religious cultures and their influences. Caribbean peoples worship through familiar forms of Christianity but also with unique expressions such as Vodun, Santería, and the Rastafarian faith. Whether on the islands or in diaspora, the lived religion of the Caribbean peoples has proven to be creative and enduring.

**See also** *Abolitionism and Antislavery; African American Religion* entries; *Freedom, Religious; Frontier and Borderlands; Healing; Immigration* entries; *Invisible Institution; Latino American Religion* entries; *Latino/a Religious Practice; Nation(s) of Islam; New Religious Movements: Black Nationalist Movements; Pentecostals* entries; *Santería; Spiritualism; Supreme Court; Voodoo.*

Adán Stevens-Diaz

## BIBLIOGRAPHY

Benavides, Gustavo. "Syncretism and Legitimacy in Latin American Religion." In *Enigmatic Powers,* edited by Anthony M. Stevens-Arroyo and Andrés Pérez y Mena. New York: Bildner Center Books, 1995.

Campo, Orlando do. "The Supreme Court and the Practice of Santeria." In *Enigmatic Powers,* edited by Anthony M. Stevens-Arroyo and Andrés Pérez y Mena. New York: Bildner Center Books, 1995.

Díaz-Stevens, Ana María. *Oxcart Catholicism on Fifth Avenue.* Notre Dame, Ind.: University of Notre Dame Press, 1993.

Díaz-Stevens, Ana María. "The Saving Grace: The Matriarchal Core of Latino Catholicism." *Latino Studies Journal* 4, no. 3 (September 1993): 60–78.

Díaz-Stevens, Ana María, and Anthony M. Stevens-Arroyo. *Recognizing the Latino Resurgence in U.S. Religion: The Emmaus Paradigm.* Boulder, Colo.: Westview Press, 1998.

Hanke, Lewis. *Aristotle and the American Indians: A Study in Race Prejudice in the Modern World.* Bloomington: Indiana University Press, 1959.

Harwood, Alan. *Rx: Spiritist as Needed.* New York: John Wiley and Sons, 1977.

Koss-Chioino, Joan. *Women as Healers, Women as Patients: Mental Health Care and Traditional Healing in Puerto Rico.* Boulder, Colo.: Westview Press, 1992.

McCaffrey, Katherine T. *Military Power and Popular Protest: The U.S. Navy in Vieques, Puerto Rico.* New Brunswick, N.J.: Rutgers University Press, 2002.

Murell, Nathaniel Samuel. "Tuning Hebrew Psalms to Reggae Rhythms: Rastas' Revolutionary Lamentations for Social Change." *Cross Currents* 50 (Winter 2001–02): 4.

Pérez y González, María Elizabeth. "Latinas in the Barrio." In *New York Glory: Religions in the City,* edited by Anna Karpathakis and Tony Carnes. New York: New York University Press, 2000.

Pérez y Mena, Andrés I. "Cuban Santería, Haitian Vodun, Puerto Rican Spiritualism: A Multicultural Inquiry into Syncretism." *Journal for the Scientific Study of Religion* 37, no. 1 (1998): 15–27.

Ramírez de Arellano, Annette B., and Conrad Seipp. *Colonialism, Catholicism, and Contraception: A History of Birth Control in Puerto Rico.* Chapel Hill: University of North Carolina Press, 1983.

Romberg, Raquel. *Witchcraft and Welfare: Spiritual Capital and the Business of Magic in Modern Puerto Rico.* Austin: University of Texas Press, 2003.

Stevens-Arroyo, Anthony M., ed. *Papal Overtures in a Cuban Key: The Pope's Visit and Civic Space for Cuban Religion.* Scranton, Pa.: University of Scranton Press, 2002.

Stevens-Arroyo, Anthony M., and Ana María Díaz-Stevens. *An Enduring Flame: Studies in Latino Popular Religiosity.* New York: Bildner Center Books, 1994.

Stevens-Arroyo, Anthony M., and Andrés I. Pérez y Mena, eds. *Enigmatic Powers: Syncretism with African and Indigenous Peoples' Religions among Latinos.* New York: Bildner Center Books, 1995.

Taylor, Douglas. *The Black Carib of British Honduras.* New York: Wenner Gren Foundation, 1951.

Thompson, Henry Paget. *Into All Lands: The History of the Society for the Propagation of the Gospel in Foreign Lands.* London: SPC, 1951.

Tweed, Thomas A. *Our Lady of the Exile: Diasporic Religion at a Cuban Catholic Shrine in Miami.* New York: Oxford University Press, 1997.

Williams, Eric. *Capitalism and Slavery.* Chapel Hill: University of North Carolina Press, 1994.

# Celebrity Culture

Celebrity culture influenced religious life long before such twentieth-century icons as Billy Graham, Elvis Presley, and the Dalai Lama. Most religions and spiritual movements start around the lives of celebrated individuals. Two thousand years later, the Christian calendar is based on the major events in the life of Jesus of Nazareth. In the Roman Catholic Church, the person performing the central act of worship is referred to as the "celebrant." Long before modern mass media placed entertainers on the national pedestal, Christians looked to the lives of the saints for their celebrity needs. Muslims may not revere the image of their founder, but they certainly seek to emulate the life story of the prophet Muhammad. In the East, the life journey of Siddhartha Gautama, a man born in the sixth century BCE in modern-day Nepal, defines the foundation of the practice of Buddhism. In more recent times, however, the line between religious celebrity and pop stardom has become increasingly blurred. One noteworthy example of this occurred at an event in the San Francisco Bay Area during the 1990s when actress Sharon Stone took the stage to introduce the fourteenth Dalai Lama, His Holiness Tenzin Gyatso, as "the hardest-working man in spirituality."

## History: Religious Figures as Celebrities

In the United States a long tradition of religious individualism and a consumerist approach to personal spirituality has only exaggerated the ancient tendency to personalize the mysterious power of the divine in celebrated individuals. During the colonial period the Boston Congregational Church minister Cotton Mather (1663–1728) was the first American preacher to gain international fame. He went down in history as the best-known American Puritan, in part because of his role in the Salem witchcraft prosecution of 1692, which stimulated widespread public excitement. While Mather was famous, he did little to foster the spirit of individualism and spiritual diversity that would come to characterize American religion and help create its celebrity culture. The colonial preacher best known for the cause of religious liberty was Roger Williams (1603–1683), the founder of the Rhode Island colony.

### The Eighteenth and Nineteenth Centuries

The most renowned preacher of the First Great Awakening, the Calvinist clergyman George Whitefield, established the model for modern mass evangelism. Whitefield (1714–1770) drew thousands of people to hear him preach during his seven pilgrimages to the United States. His call for a "new birth" in Jesus, his ability to ignore denominational differences, and his strategy of taking his message outside church buildings and directly to the people were to become the hallmarks of the American evangelical movement. White-field, an Englishman whose anti-Anglican stance made him popular in the American colonies, advertised his revivals in newspapers and advised his disciples that "the object of our measures is to gain attention." Another celebrated preacher during this period of American religious fervor was Jonathan Edwards (1703–1758), who delivered the "sermon New England would never forget," titled "Sinners in the Hand of an Angry God," and wrote several famous treatises such as *The Nature of True Virtue*.

The next great wave of religious celebrities would come in the first few decades of the nineteenth century, as Protestant revivalists sought to counter the ideas of the Enlightenment and resist the deism of Thomas Jefferson and other leaders of the American Revolution. The best-known preacher of this Second Great Awakening was Charles Grandison Finney (1792–1875), who began his career as a lawyer but wound up testifying to a soul-shaking conversion that convinced him he had "a retainer from the Lord Jesus Christ to plead his cause." He led revivals in the major cities of the East and in the fast-growing towns of the West. Finney developed such a personal popularity that he was forced to defend the whole idea of a religious revival led by man—rather than by God himself. "More than five thousand million have gone down to hell, while the church has been dreaming, and waiting for God to save them without the use of means," Finney wrote.

This period of American religious history also saw the rise of religious reformers, who were reviled as much as celebrated. Chief among them was Joseph Smith, the founder of the Church of Jesus Christ of Latter-day Saints. The story of Smith (1805–1844) is a textbook example of how starting a modern-day religion around the life of a single person can be a mixed blessing. Smith wrote, and many Mormons believe, that God was once a man and that he and his wife, the Heavenly Mother, live near the star Kolob. Smith also preached that Jesus Christ was married. In the 1890s, the church was finally forced to renounce the most well-known of Smith's doctrines—the practice of plural marriage, or polygamy. According to historians, Smith had taken thirty-three wives by the time he was murdered by an angry mob in Carthage, Illinois, in 1844. In recent decades, the Church of Jesus Christ of Latter-day Saints has sought to emphasize what it has in common with mainstream Christian thought, such as its belief that Jesus Christ was born of a virgin and resurrected from the dead, and that humanity can be eternally saved through Christ's sacrificial death.

Mary Baker Eddy provides another example of how the life struggles of a spiritual celebrity can shape the doctrines of a religious movement. Eddy (1821–1910) was often ill as a young woman and found little help in the remedies of her time. She turned to Phineas P. Quimby, who used magnets and hypnotism in his healing treatments, but later developed her own ideas about faith healing, doctrines that were laid down in the Christian Science movement she founded. Another celebrated nineteenth-century woman who would influence the Spiritualist and New Age movements of the twentieth century was Elena Petrovna Gan, better known as Madame Blavatsky (1831–1891), who founded the Theosophical Society in New York City in 1875. During the final years of her life, Blavatsky told some of her students that the real purpose of the Theosophists was to pave the way for the return of the ultimate religious leader, a new world teacher. In 1909, her successors claimed to have found that teacher in India in the form of Jiddu Krishnamurti, a fourteen-year-old boy. Krishnamurti would be raised as the new "World Teacher," only to denounce that messianic role at age thirty-four.

Christian revivalism didn't stop at the end of the Second Great Awakening. The premier celebrity preacher of the second half of the nineteenth century was a shoe salesman from Chicago named Dwight L. Moody. In 1860, Moody (1837–1899) dedicated himself to Christian evangelism, working in army camps during the Civil War and offering words of hope to families displaced and otherwise devastated by the fighting. Moody had no theological training and only a seventh-grade education, but his simple gospel message found an eager audience in the decades following the Civil War. Newspapers devoted significant coverage to his revivals, which filled auditoriums in New York City, Chicago, and other American cities. Encouraged by wealthy contributors and powerful patrons, he founded the Moody Bible Institute and began to train a new generation of Christian revivalists who would continue the message into the twentieth century. Moody is the link between two of America's greatest Protestant religious celebrities, George Whitefield and Billy Graham.

Another Protestant minister of this period, the Reverend Henry Ward Beecher of Brooklyn, New York, exemplified the growing national obsession with religious scandal and celebrity culture. Beecher (1813–1887) was a brother to writer Harriet Beecher Stowe and a preacher of enormous popularity in nineteenth-century America. In the 1840s thousands of people boarded ferries from Manhattan known as "Beecher Boats" to hear his Sunday sermons. Newspaper stories of his alleged sexual affair with the wife of a close friend culminated in 1875 with an adultery trial that received unprecedented saturation coverage in American newspapers. The trial unleashed a media frenzy perhaps not surpassed until the 1995 murder trial of celebrity athlete and actor O.J. Simpson.

## The Late Nineteenth and the Early Twentieth Century

Professional athletes were a major component of celebrity culture in the late nineteenth century and throughout the twentieth century. The first man to make the crossover from the major leagues to the mission field was William Ashley Sunday, better known as Billy Sunday. Sunday (1862–1935) was a popular outfielder in the National League in the 1880s and one of the league leaders in stolen bases. Following his evangelical conversion in the late 1880s, Sunday stopped drinking and partying with his teammates and started speaking before congregations and young people at local chapters of the YMCA. When his audience got too large for church halls, Sunday began erecting huge canvas tents in which to hold his revival meetings. He later erected an eighteen-thousand-seat church hall, known as Billy Sunday's Tabernacle, on the corner of Broadway and 168th Street in New York City. Sunday was the nation's leading Christian celebrity in the first two decades of the twentieth century, but his popularity began to decline after World War I. Movie theaters and movie stars were offering new competition for the revival tent and the celebrity preacher. They were the first in a series of technological revolutions that changed the nature of celebrity culture in America.

Movies, radio, television, and, finally, the Internet each brought about profound changes in twentieth-century America. And those changes began with a woman named Aimee Semple McPherson. Decades before such televangelists as Billy Graham, Pat Robertson, and Jim and Tammy Bakker started mixing show business and conservative Christianity, this pioneering Pentecostal preacher and radio evangelist presided over the lavish opening of her 5,300-seat Angelus Temple in southern California. Just as with other celebrities then and now, her reputation was built up and torn down by a news media hungry for scandal and sensation. Born to a farmer father and mother who worked for the Salvation Army, McPherson (1890–1944) was raised in the desolate countryside of Ontario, Canada. As a young girl, she found her salvation in an Irish immigrant and fiery preacher

named Robert Semple. The couple was swept up in a revival that was just gathering steam in towns and cities across North America. The revival sparked the modern Pentecostal movement, a lively style of Christian worship that stresses faith healing, prophecy, speaking in tongues, and a literalist approach to the Bible. They married in 1908 and two years later took off on a mission to China, but within months of their arrival Robert contracted malaria and died. Looking for security, Aimee married businessman Harold McPherson. She gave birth to a son, but it was not a happy marriage.

During World War I, McPherson crisscrossed America in a "Gospel Car" painted with the slogan, "Where will you spend eternity?" By the 1920s she was a famous faith healer filling auditoriums in Denver, San Diego, and other cities. Her giant Angelus Temple soon rose at Sunset and Glendale boulevards, just down the road from Hollywood. The huge church, described by one visitor as "half like a Roman Coliseum, half like a Parisian Opera House," became one of the city's premier tourist attractions. It was topped with a giant radio tower that sent McPherson's sermons and speeches across southern California. The evangelist's most notorious exploit came in the spring of 1926 when she suddenly vanished while swimming at Venice Beach. Her disappearance and feared death by drowning set off media speculation that only continued to build after she mysteriously reappeared five weeks later in Mexico, amid rumors that she had escaped to have an amorous affair. But by the end of the twentieth century, the religious denomination McPherson founded, the International Church of the Foursquare Gospel, had more than 1,850 U.S. congregations and more than 238,000 members.

McPherson was at her peak in the summer of 1925, when the nation was gripped by one of the watersheds of American cultural history. In Dayton, Tennessee, celebrity attorneys Clarence Darrow (1857–1938) and William Jennings Bryan (1860–1925) faced off in the landmark "monkey trial," in which high school teacher John Scopes was prosecuted for violating a state law that prohibited teaching the theory of evolution. Reporters from across the country descended on Dayton for an event that would define a cultural split between the secular forces of modernism and the waves of religious revivalism that periodically sweep across the United States. This same religious and political divide would persist into the next century, separating the country into a nation of "red states" and "blue states."

Radio and television were also the media that turned two Roman Catholic priests into national celebrities in the

1930s, 1940s, and 1950s. Father Charles Coughlin (1891–1979) was one of the first North American clergymen to use radio to preach a political message, including commentary that was widely viewed as anti-Semitic. Bishop Fulton Sheen (1895–1979) was a television pioneer with his *Life Is Worth Living* show in the early 1950s, which continued in various forms well into the 1960s. Coughlin and Sheen paved the way for an American-born nun Rita Antoinette Rizzo, later known as Mother Angelica (1923–), to viewers of her Eternal Word Television Network (EWTN).

## "Living" Saints: Billy Graham, John Paul II, and Mother Teresa of Calcutta

Perhaps no religious celebrity in twentieth-century America has had as much fame and impact as William Franklin Graham. During that century, Billy Graham probably preached to more people than anyone in the history of the world. Graham's television broadcasts have been viewed by hundreds of millions of people around the world, and millions more have personally witnessed his Christian crusades at massive revival meetings, from Aarhus, Denmark, to Azagorsk, Russia. Graham (1918–) was born on a dairy farm in North Carolina to Scottish Irish parents but was "born again" at a revival meeting sixteen years later. His evangelical career took off in 1944, when Graham, then a young suburban pastor and budding radio evangelist, was invited to speak at the 3,400-seat Orchestra Hall in Chicago before young servicemen from the adjacent USO.

Graham got his first big boost from newspaper czar William Randolph Hearst. Impressed by Graham's anticommunism and strong moral values, Hearst reportedly told his editors to "puff Graham." And they did, running glowing full-page stories about the young preacher in all twenty-two papers of the Hearst chain. During the 1950s Graham was an early supporter of the civil rights movement and Rev. Martin Luther King Jr. That cost him some southern support but improved his reputation among African Americans and the mainstream media. Graham was famous as the pastor to American presidents, and his closest and most controversial political tie was to Richard Nixon. While officially neutral, Graham was a behind-the-scenes force in Nixon's 1960 campaign against John Kennedy, whose Catholicism worried many American evangelicals, and he also dropped clear hints in his support of Nixon's successful 1968 presidential run. Graham stuck by Nixon during much of the Watergate scandal, only to be embarrassed later by the expletive-filled audiotapes secretly recorded in the Oval Office.

In the 1980s Graham remained untouched by the sex-and-money scandals that disgraced a series of major TV evangelists, and he was a strong voice for greater financial accountability in evangelical ministry. His unparalleled popularity landed him on the Gallup Poll's list of "10 Most Admired Men in the World" more than forty times in the last half of the twentieth century. Graham often shared that list with another religious leader who was not born in the United States but whose American pilgrimages drew millions of Roman Catholic spectators and communicants.

Pope John Paul II (1920–2005) presided over a twenty-six-year papacy, in which he played a critical role in the downfall of communism and promoted traditional moral values as an alternative to the materialism of the West. Born as Karol Jozef Wojtyla in Wadowice, Poland, John Paul II had Eastern European roots that would define his pontificate, the second longest after Pope Pius IX, who served from 1846 to 1878. Wojtyla was elected pope in 1978, survived a would-be assassin's bullet in the early years of his pontificate, and pushed onward to become the most-traveled pontiff ever, beginning with his first trip to Mexico in January 1979. Like former president Ronald Reagan, John Paul II was a former actor and charismatic speaker, someone who understood the power of television. His foreign tours, including five highly publicized visits to the United States, featured parades in his bulletproof "pope-mobile" and outdoor masses attended by millions of worshipers. The pope and his tour managers were masters of the photo opportunity, and images of the pope holding a koala bear in Australia, hugging a young AIDS patient in San Francisco, and kissing airport tarmacs around the world were deeply etched in the public mind.

One of the few religious celebrities who could compete with the pope for public renown and respect was another Catholic personality, Mother Teresa of Calcutta. During the last two decades of her life, the diminutive Catholic nun appeared nineteen times on the Gallup Poll of women most admired by the American public. Mother Teresa (1910–1997) was born Agnes Gonxha Bojaxhiu in the summer of 1910 in Skopje, Macedonia. At age eighteen, she joined the Loreto Sisters, a Catholic religious order, and traveled to Ireland and Darjeeling, India. The journey to India began a second conversion in the young nun, who started her own religious order there, the Missionaries of Charity, and devoted herself to compassionate aid for the "poorest of the poor." Unlike many celebrities, religious or otherwise, Mother Teresa did not seek the spotlight. The tireless nun first gained international attention in the 1960s, when she was discovered by the British author and filmmaker Malcolm Muggeridge.

In 1979 she achieved worldwide fame when she was awarded the Nobel Peace Prize for her decades of work with ill and dying people in India and around the world. Even after those accolades, Mother Teresa shunned publicity and downplayed her accomplishments. To avoid the media spotlight, she would often slip unnoticed into San Francisco to visit her main U.S. convent, where between eighty and one hundred sisters quietly prepared for religious life. Yet it was Mother Teresa's renown that made her Missionaries of Charity the most successful Roman Catholic religious order of the late twentieth century. At a time when many Catholic orders were in rapid decline, the Missionaries of Charity grew swiftly around the world, attracting thousands of idealistic young converts. In the process the wrinkled face and soulful eyes of Mother Teresa became synonymous with religious devotion and selfless charity.

Decades before her death, Catholics and non-Catholics alike began calling Mother Teresa "a living saint." The wheels of the official Roman Catholic process towards sainthood began to turn on September 5, 1997, the day of her death. Long before the days of television, *People* magazine, and celebrity Web sites, religious leaders were selected by a painstaking process undertaken in Rome at the offices of the Sacred Congregation for the Causes of Saints. But in the case of Mother Teresa, the process of sainthood had already began. Over his long papacy, Pope John Paul II canonized more than 470 saints and beatified 1,280 candidates as "blessed," more than the combined totals of all his predecessors over the past four hundred years. Saints had almost gone out of style in the 1960s. Pope John XXIII, the pontiff who inaugurated the great liberal reforms of the Second Vatican Council (1962–1965), canonized only 10 of them and beatified 4 candidates during his five years in office. Many church leaders at the time saw Catholic saints—and the miracles performed in their name—as outdated or superstitious remnants from another era. John Paul II and Mother Teresa pushed sainthood back to the center of church life, but not all Catholics saw this as a sign of healthy faith. They complained that the number of canonizations by Rome lacked proper skepticism and represented a resurgent form of personal piety in the Catholic Church. Perhaps the same can be said for the larger rise of celebrity culture in American religion. There is a downside to focusing on individual personalities and choosing religious leaders because

they are photogenic or "great communicators." Both the mystical piety of the Polish pope and the good deeds of the late Calcutta nun were a move towards seeing the church as an agent of social transformation. Celebrity religion can rise at the expense of more complex questions of systematic poverty and social injustice.

## Televangelism and Celebrity: Oral Roberts and the Bakkers

Most of Pope John Paul II's televised images were in the form of news coverage provided at no charge by the mainstream media. Television, in the form of paid programming and dedicated cable networks, was the key force in the rise of the major Protestant media celebrities in the last half of the twentieth century. One pioneer in that field was Oral Roberts (1918–2009), an Oklahoma faith healer who built his *Expect a Miracle* show into the top-rated religious television program of the 1970s. But another religious broadcaster would soon eclipse Roberts. Robert Schuller (1927–) came to southern California with his wife in 1955, right out of his seminary education in Chicago, and began preaching sermons atop the snack bar at the Orange drive-in theater in Garden Grove, as members of the congregation remained in their cars. Schuller was an ordained minister in the Dutch Reform Church, but his message was a hopeful "You can do it" proclamation, heavily influenced by the Positive Thinking ideas of Norman Vincent Peale.

It was a message that thousands of other displaced midwesterners who had broken ties with churches back home were ready to hear. Two decades later, Schuller began building the Crystal Cathedral, a star-shaped, reflective glass church, television studio, and performance hall designed by architect Philip Johnson. Celebrity religion is all about glitz, and the Crystal Cathedral was certainly glitzy. But television, with its enormous power to provide an audience and financial base, creates a kind of church without walls. Schuller's cathedral is not unlike the modern stadium in a sports world dominated by television. Schuller's church provided the set for his *Hour of Power* television show, which began in 1970 and grew to become the most watched one-hour church service in the United States, with some twenty million viewers.

Schuller's show was seen in many parts of the country on the Trinity Broadcasting Network (TBN), which was founded in 1973 by two couples, Paul and Jan Crouch and Jim and Tammy Bakker, and grew to be the largest Christian television network in the world. Crouch and his wife, famous for her towering bouffant hairdo, presided over an eclectic three-ring circus of Christian pop music, soap operas, aerobics classes, and other programming that unapologetically mixed celebrity glitz and gospel message. More traditional evangelicals have condemned the network for its promotion of the "prosperity gospel," the idea that living a Christian life (and contributing financially) will inspire material success. Two of the network's biggest stars, Jim and Tammy Bakker, split off to form their own operation, the Praise the Lord (PTN) network, which would collapse in 1987 in a scandal over embezzlement and sexual harassment. Their downfall—part of a series of televangelism scandals in the 1980s that also brought down the fiery TV preacher Jimmy Swaggart—revealed the shadowy side of celebrity Christianity and the fact that fame and fortune can be a double-edged sword. It also generated a firestorm of media attention in the 1980s, a journalistic free-for-all reminiscent of the newspaper coverage of the Scopes monkey trial back in the steamy summer of 1925.

Jim and Tammy were unapologetic in preaching a prosperity gospel, and they had their own rags-to-riches lives to offer up as testimony. They liked to say, "God wants his people to go first-class," which is exactly what they did with their purchase of luxury cars and lavish homes. On a 2,300-acre pasture in the heart of the Bible Belt, in Fort Mill, South Carolina, the Bakkers built Heritage Village USA, a condo development and Christian theme park. It was also the site for the state-of-the-art television studio from which they broadcast their evangelical variety show, *The PTL Club,* which was seen by millions of viewers. Many of those viewers were "prayer partners" who sent in contributions, and during a two-year period in the 1980s, some $200 million poured in.

It all collapsed after Jim Bakker's March 1987 confession to a 1980 sexual encounter with church secretary Jessica Hahn, who went on to appear topless in the November 1987 edition of *Playboy* magazine. The Bakkers' fall from grace was the perfect storm of consumerism, politics, Christianity, and celebrity culture. Before their downfall, President Ronald Reagan, himself a former show business celebrity, invited the couple to his first inaugural and praised their television network for "carrying out a master plan for people that love."

Jim and Tammy Bakker also partnered with another powerful televangelist, Pat Robertson (1930–), and with his Christian Broadcasting Network (CBN). In fact, the couple began their Christian show business career in 1966 by

staging a children's puppet show on Robertson's fledgling network. Robertson's Christian talk show, *The 700 Club,* was to Christian celebrities what the *Tonight Show* was to secular stars. Robertson was long active in Republican Party politics and made an unsuccessful run for that party's presidential nomination in 1988. But it was another televangelist who first mobilized evangelical voters into a force powerful enough to sway presidential elections, the Reverend Jerry Falwell (1933–2007) and his Moral Majority. Founded in 1979 and credited with helping to bring Ronald Reagan into the White House, the Moral Majority mobilized a new political base with cable television, sophisticated direct-mail techniques, and emotional attacks on his *Old Time Gospel Hour* television show against legalized abortion, gay rights, and other causes. Robertson and Falwell illustrate another side of celebrity Christianity: their fame focused national media attention on them, which inspired the mainstream media to promulgate a series of controversial statements that eventually soured their reputations with many voters.

In the 1990s, Robertson and Falwell were overshadowed by James Dobson, another Christian celebrity and political power broker. Dobson (1936–), a conservative Christian psychologist and radio talk show host, had already been spreading his views on abortion, marriage, and child rearing for more than two decades. His views were broadcast from 2,500 radio stations across North America and 3,000 other outlets around the world. Most of those who contacted his Colorado City–based ministry were not seeking advice on how to vote in the presidential primary. The majority who called in to his *Focus on the Family* show were filing prayer requests or ordering merchandise from Dobson's extensive catalog of books, magazines, videotapes, and audiocassettes on how to save marriages, stay off drugs, avoid fornication, and find Jesus. By the middle of the 1990s his sophisticated telephone marketing system handled nearly four thousand calls and eleven thousand letters a day.

Complementing the radio ministry of Dobson has been the rise of "Christian radio" and its own brand of celebrities: *Christian* music artists. Christian rock dates back to the 1960s, but it became more popular in the 1990s. That was the decade when Billy Graham—who once condemned rock and roll as Satan's music—started asking Christian rock bands to warm up the crowds at his youth crusades. Graham drew tens of thousands of Christian rock fans to his crusades by booking Jars of Clay and DC-Talk, two of the most popular Christian rock bands at that time. These and other evangelical rock bands helped propel "Contemporary

Christian" music to sell more than forty-four million albums in 2000, making it the sixth-best-selling genre in the United States, ahead of jazz, classical, and new age combined.

## Celebrities as Religious Promoters: The Beatles, Richard Gere, and Scientologists

Christians were not the only religionists to tap into the power of celebrity culture in the 1960s. Maharishi Mahesh Yogi (1917–2008) began teaching transcendental meditation in India in 1955 and brought the technique to the United States in 1959. But his big break came in 1967, when the Beatles rock band—at the height of their popularity—attended one of his lectures in Wales in 1967 and visited his ashram in India in 1968, along with Donovan, another rock star. The Beatles soon lost interest. There was a falling out between the Maharishi and the rock band amid rumors that the bearded guru had made inappropriate advances on actress Mia Farrow. John Lennon even wrote a song about the affair, "Sexy Sadie," in which he promised that the Maharishi would "get yours yet." But the image of the meditation teacher dressed in white and surrounded by four smiling young Beatles stuck in the public mind and helped inspire hundreds of thousands of young American spiritual seekers to explore the mysteries of Eastern religion.

Another Beatle, George Harrison, was the real "spiritual" Beatle. Not coincidentally, he was also the first member of the band to take the psychedelic drug LSD in 1964, when he was just twenty-one years old. He later credited that experience with giving him a powerful glimpse into another realm of consciousness, an awareness he would cultivate for the rest of his life through chanting and meditation. Harrison went on to study with another Indian guru, the late Swami Srila Prabhupada, the founder of the International Society for Krishna Consciousness, better known as the Hare Krishna movement. Both the Maharishi and Prabhupada popularized specific types of Hindu religious practice. Maharishi stressed a simple form of silent meditation, while Krishna devotees were known for their shaved heads and chanting. Harrison remained devoted to Krishna, one of the central gods in the Hindu pantheon. Krishna is seen as the incarnation of divine love and beauty, and he is known for his quality of playfulness. "My life belongs to the Lord Krishna," Harrison said in 1974. His 1970 No. 1 hit, "My Sweet Lord," started out chanting the more familiar prayer of "Hallelujah," then subtly switched to "Hare Krishna."

English rock-guitarist, singer-songwriter, and member of the group the Beatles, George Harrison, wearing dark clothing, center, appears with a group of Hare Krishnas on August 29, 1969. References to eastern religion in the Beatles' music played a large role in introducing these religions to Westerners on a wide scale.

The Beatles' endorsement of Maharishi was short-lived, but it had a huge effect on the West's new openness to the religious practices of India and the Far East. Of course, many other factors contributed to this East-meets-West religious syncretism, most notably a loosening of immigration restrictions that allowed a steady stream of Indian gurus, Tibetan monks, and Japanese Zen masters to come to the United States. But the massive popularity of the Beatles among the baby boom generation greatly amplified the impact of the Beatles' journey. The rock band's spiritual search was also reflected in the writings and drug-induced revelations of John Lennon. His reading of a seminal book of the sixties drug culture, *The Psychedelic Experience,* first inspired the band's mystical shift with the song "Tomorrow Never Knows." Like the book, coauthored in 1964 by Timothy Leary, Richard Alpert, and Ralph Metzner, the song was inspired by the *Tibetan Book of the Dead,* a classic Buddhist text. The song appeared on the 1966 album *Revolver,* prefiguring the release of the band's landmark tribute to the psychedelic sixties, *Sgt. Pepper's Lonely Hearts Club Band,* which included the group's tribute to LSD, the song "Lucy in the Sky with Diamonds." Leary, known as the "high priest of LSD," and Alpert, who took his own journey to India and returned as Baba Ram Dass, achieved celebrity status themselves in the 1960s and 1970s. Alpert's religious conversion to a devotional Hindu practice, chronicled in his seminal book *Be Here Now,* furthered the pop culture shift to the exotic mysticism of the East.

Later, in the 1980s and 1990s, celebrities played a large role in helping popularize another ancient Indian religion, Buddhism. The best-known "celebrity Buddhist" to emerge during this period was actor Richard Gere, who was best remembered for his role opposite Julia Roberts in *Pretty Woman,* and his 1999 selection by that bible of celebrity gossip, *People* magazine, as the sexiest man alive. Gere may have been a "celebrity Buddhist," but he is also a serious, longtime practitioner of Tibetan Buddhism. Gere first became interested in Buddhism during an existential crisis in his twenties. He studied under Zen teacher Sasaki Roshi before becoming a student in the 1980s of Tenzin Gyatso (1935–), the 14th Dalai Lama. Since then Gere has devoted much of his energies to the campaign to preserve the Buddhist culture of Tibet and oppose Chinese efforts to weaken the faith of that ancient seat of Buddhist learning. At the same time, the Dalai Lama hardly needed Hollywood stars to promote the Tibetan cause, especially since winning the Nobel Peace Prize in 1989. For the next twenty years, the

Dalai Lama's infectious giggles, self-deprecating humor, and spiritual addresses turned him into one of the world's premier religious celebrities, right beside Mother Teresa of Calcutta and Pope John Paul II. Tickets for the Dalai Lama's appearances were sold on the same Web sites used to promote rock concerts and sporting events.

Better-known new religious movements also have benefited from celebrity endorsement, most notably the Church of Scientology International. Founded in the 1950s by L. Ron Hubbard (1911–1986), a prolific science fiction writer and freelance philosopher, Scientology describes itself as "the only major new religion established in the 20th century" as a bridge to increased awareness and spiritual freedom. Scientology is based on the precepts of Hubbard's 1950 book, *Dianetics: The Modern Science of Mental Health.* Practitioners at Scientology centers around the world hook themselves up to a simple electric device, an "e-meter," for "auditing" sessions that purport to measure thoughts and emotional reactions, known in Scientology parlance as "engrams." Their goal is to attain a psychological and spiritual state called "clear," where they are said to overcome compulsions, repressions, and other self-generated diseases and psychoses. "Clears" are then sold advanced training sessions to become "operating thetans," spiritual beings said to possess such supernatural powers as the ability to leave their bodies. Scientologists purchasing 12.5 hours of advanced auditing, for example, were asked (in February 2001) to make a "donation" of between $12,100 and $15,125. Graduates purportedly achieve "a new viewpoint of sanity and rationality." From the beginning Hubbard encouraged his followers to actively recruit show business celebrities. In a directive issued in early 1955, Hubbard started "Project Celebrity" with a long list of movie stars to be courted, including Groucho Marx, Liberace, and Orson Wells. The church had little initial success in celebrity recruitment but decades later brought into its ranks two of Hollywood's most bankable actors, John Travolta and Tom Cruise. In 2004, Scientology leader David Miscavige expressed his appreciation of Cruise's work to promote the movement by awarding the actor the organization's 20th Anniversary Freedom Medal of Valor.

In the early 1970s the church purchased one of Hollywood's most distinctive buildings, a turreted castle on three acres of formal gardens originally built as the Château Élysée, a long-term residential hotel for movie stars. The church turned the building into its Celebrity Centre. It includes an exclusive hotel and restaurant described as "a safe environment for Celebrities and Scientologists." Travolta has personally endorsed the food and service and has appeared on the cover of a Scientology magazine titled *Celebrity*. In 2000, Travolta released the film *Battlefield Earth*, which was a screen homage, with a $90 million budget, to one of L. Ron Hubbard's science fiction stories. To promote the film, Travolta appeared in bookstores signing copies of Hubbard's book, but the film failed at the box office.

## Celebrities as Religious Figures

While some religious figures became celebrities and others endorsed a religion or spiritual movement, devotion to some celebrities, such as Elvis Presley, took on quasi-religious dimensions. Even in life, Presley (1935–1977) was known as "the King," and he continued to defy death through countless "Elvis sightings" and celebrity impersonations. Numerous shrines have arisen, including the 24 Hour Church of Elvis, which began as an art project in Portland, Oregon, less than a decade after Presley's death. Churches and new religious movements have arisen around the lives of other famous musicians, as well; included among them are the Saint John Coltrane Church in San Francisco and the short-lived Church of Unlimited Devotion, a hippie cult that saw Grateful Dead guitarist Jerry Garcia as an avatar of God.

## Future Prospects

In the twenty-first century American religion and celebrity culture continues an exchange that began in the eighteenth century with George Whitefield taking out newspaper advertisements for his Christian revivals and continued into the new millennium with such Hollywood stars as Sharon Stone and Richard Gere promoting the Dalai Lama. Celebrity culture has no single effect on American religion. In some cases celebrity endorsements allow the promotion of minority faiths and exotic spiritualities—for example, the Beatles' pilgrimage to India or the decision by pop icon Madonna to embrace Jewish mysticism. In others the rise of religious celebrities such as Mother Teresa can inspire a return to more traditional forms of Christian piety. Celebrity fame is, by its very nature, ephemeral, while religious belief appears to be long-lasting. Cable television can raise up religious celebrities—for instance, Jim and Tammy Bakker—and then destroy them with saturation coverage of the latest sex-and-money scandal. Over the past three centuries, technological innovations in mass communication (newspapers, radio, film, and television) have offered new ways to bring celebrity culture into religious life. That trend will no doubt

continue as computers and the Internet reshape the way Americans view themselves, society, and perhaps even their religious beliefs, practices, and communities.

**See also** *Buddhism in North America; Canada: Protestants and the United Church of Canada; Devotionalism; Electronic Church; Film; Great Awakening(s); Internet; Krishna Consciousness; Music: Christian; Popular Religion and Popular Culture* entries; *Radio; Revivalism* entries; *Scientology; Television.*

Don Lattin

**BIBLIOGRAPHY**

Anonymous. "Advancing Scientology on a Fully Epic Scale: Mr. Tom Cruise Awarded Freedom Medal of Valor." *International Scientology News* (December 2002).

Chidester, David. *Authentic Fakes: Religion and American Popular Culture.* Berkeley: University of California Press, 2005.

Cimino, Richard, and Don Lattin. *Shopping for Faith: American Religion in the New Millennium.* San Francisco: Jossey-Bass, 1998.

Falsani, Cathleen. *The God Factor: Inside the Spiritual Lives of Public People.* New York: Farrar, Straus and Giroux, 2007.

Fox, Richard Wightman. *Jesus in America: Personal Savior, Cultural Hero, National Obsession.* San Francisco: HarperSanFrancisco, 2004.

Gaustad, Edwin, and Leigh Schmidt. *The Religious History of America.* Rev. ed. San Francisco: HarperSanFrancisco, 2002.

Kolodiejchuk, Brian, ed. *Mother Teresa: Come Be My Light; The Private Writings of the "Saint of Calcutta."* New York: Doubleday, 2007.

Lattin, Don. "Hark! Hollywood Angels Take Wing." *San Francisco Chronicle,* Dec. 15, 1996.

———. "Mother Teresa Is Dead." *San Francisco Chronicle,* Sept. 6, 1997.

———. "Pope John Paul II: 1920–2005—Beloved, Charismatic and Controversial." *San Francisco Chronicle,* April 3, 2005.

———. "Rock (Music) of Ages: Monterey Crowd Testament to Growth of Christian Sound." *San Francisco Chronicle,* Aug. 2, 1997.

———. "Stuff of Myth and Legend: Age-old Themes in New 'Star Wars' Film. *San Francisco Chronicle,* May 14, 1999.

———. "Sunday Interview with Billy Graham—Superman of the Cloth." *San Francisco Chronicle,* Sept. 21, 1997.

———. "Travolta's Religious Battlefield." *San Francisco Chronicle,* May 15, 2000.

McLeod, Melvin. "Richard Gere: My Journey as a Buddhist." *Shambhala Sun* (May 1999).

Sutton, Matthew Avery. *Aimee Semple McPherson and the Resurrection of Christian America.* Cambridge, Mass.: Harvard University Press. 2007.

# Chabad-Lubavitch

The movement known today as "Chabad," "Chabad-Lubavitch," or "Lubavitch" grew out of the pietistic Hasidic revolution that swept through East European Jewry in the eighteenth century. The charismatic healer, preacher, and popular religious mystic Israel ben Eliezer Ba'al Shem Tov

("Master of the Good Name"), known by his acronym "the Besht" (c. 1700–1760) served as the central figure of this movement, which arose in response to such complex forces as the partition of Poland, anti-Semitic massacres, the stirrings of pseudo-messiahs such as Shabbetai Zevi and Jacob Frank, economic ruin, spiritual despair, and pietistic religious trends throughout the region. Hasidim defied traditional Jewish communal authorities and formed spiritual circles distinguished by their patterns of life and dress, their ecstatic religious practices, the mystical teachings that they communicated, their outreach to the poor and the illiterate, and their self-segregation. At a time when authority and prestige in Jewish life depended heavily upon Talmudic knowledge, early Hasidic masters insisted that God could also be approached through acts of love and devotional prayer.

## Hasidism after "the Besht"

The leading figure in the Hasidic movement following the death of the Besht was his disciple, the charismatic preacher (*maggid*) Dov Baer of Mezhirech (d. 1772). He helped to popularize Hasidism by sending forth emissaries to recruit followers from the Jewish masses throughout Poland, while his personal conduct set the pattern for the institution of the *Zaddik,* the benevolent "spiritual father"–type leader of a Hasidic sect. He also gathered around him a group of significant disciples who studied his teachings and mystical practices. These disciples, following his death, decentralized and diversified Hasidism. They spread through Poland, the Ukraine, and into Russia, establishing Hasidic courts of their own.

Shneur Zalman (1745–1812/1813), one of Dov Baer's disciples, settled in Belarus, establishing a Hasidic court in the town of Lyady. With his broad learning, he developed a new school of Hasidism that placed greater emphasis on scholarship, study, and contemplation. He wrote a path-breaking volume of spiritual guidance, known as the *Tanya,* and sought to impart formerly restricted and esoteric Hasidic teachings throughout all levels of society. Shneur Zalman developed a three-part system of intellectual contemplation, connected to three rungs of the esoteric ten "spheres" (*sfirot*) described by Jewish mystics: "wisdom," "understanding," and (through a union of these two) "knowledge." The Hebrew acronym of these three words is *Chabad,* the name by which the movement came to be known.

Following the death of Shneur Zalman, his son, Dov Ber, settled in the town of Lubavitch, where he became the movement's dynastic leader. As was Hasidic custom, followers of Dov Ber and his descendants became known by the town's name, the home of its central Hasidic court. Chabad also developed centers elsewhere in Russia, generally led by other members of the dynasty.

## Emigration to America and Rabbi Joseph Schneersohn

Chabad Hasidim, like many other fervently Orthodox Jews, feared emigration to America. They considered it a "non-kosher land" where Judaism could not properly be observed. Nevertheless, in the face of persecution, some followers emigrated to America in any case. One of the first to arrive was Rabbi Chaim Yaakov Widerwitz (1835–1911), an ordained follower of the Rebbe ("grand rabbi") of Lubavitch, who was expelled from Moscow in 1891 and became a rabbi in the United States. Subsequently, as conditions for Jews in Russia worsened, others emigrated, some of whom continued to maintain contact with their Rebbe from afar. Synagogues named "Anshe Lubavitch" or named in memory of one of the Chabad Rebbes began to appear on the American scene.

Following World War I and the Bolshevik revolution, the Chabad movement in Russia, along with many other religious groups, was actively persecuted, and more followers emigrated, including Rabbi Israel Jacobson, who arrived in America on December 22, 1925. The fact that many Chabad followers were rabbis made it possible for them to enter the United States outside quota restrictions. Jacobson subsequently helped to bring other Chabad followers to the United States and played a major role in building the movement in North America and raising funds to send back to Chabad headquarters in Europe.

The Sixth Lubavitcher ("of Lubavitch") Rebbe, Rabbi Joseph I. Schneersohn (1880–1950), who became Rebbe upon his father's death in 1920, took a special interest in his growing band of American followers. He corresponded with them, and in 1923 he established an organization of Chabad Hasidim in the United States and Canada (Agudas Chasidim Anshei Chabad) to raise funds, promote Jewish learning, and spread the teachings of the Chabad movement. Following his imprisonment by the Communists, who allegedly sentenced him to death for promoting Judaism underground, and his subsequent expulsion from the Soviet Union in 1927, Rabbi Schneersohn personally visited the United States from September 17, 1929, to July 17, 1930. He toured Jewish communities, raised funds, lectured about Hasidism, spoke out concerning the importance of Jewish education and the laws of family purity, and met with Justice Louis Brandeis and President Herbert Hoover. Unlike many other European rabbis, he expressed optimism concerning American Jewry and its future, believing that young American-born Jews would experience a religious revival. He even considered settling in America. Later, he continued from afar to encourage his American followers, dispatching personal emissaries to promote Chabad and raise funds for the movement.

Rabbi Schneersohn, confined to a wheelchair, was at the Yeshiva (Talmudical academy) that he had established in Otwock, Poland, when the Nazis invaded in 1939, and he soon made his way to Warsaw. There he was caught up in the German bombing and in the suffering experienced by the city's Jews once the Nazis came to power. Thanks to the efforts of his American followers, leading American political figures, and sympathetic Nazi officials (one of whom had a Jewish father), he and his household were saved. They arrived in the United States on March 19, 1940. His daughter, Chaya Mushka, and her husband, Rabbi Menachem Mendel Schneerson (1902–1994), followed a year later from France, which had likewise fallen under Nazi control.

As leader of the Chabad movement, Rabbi Joseph Schneersohn settled in the Crown Heights section of Brooklyn, reestablishing his movement's world headquarters at 770 Eastern Parkway. In the midst of war, and working from the premise that the United States was "no different" from European communities in its potential for Jewish life, he established a *yeshiva,* a network of Jewish all-day and supplementary schools, Jewish summer camps, a publishing house, and other institutions aimed at transforming America into the "new center for Torah and Judaism," replacing Europe. Where other Hasidic leaders who settled in America during and after the war followed an enclave strategy, seeking to secure their followers against dangerous outside influences, Rabbi Joseph Schneersohn advocated an outreach strategy aimed at spreading his movement's mission to all Jews, affiliated and unaffiliated alike, in an effort to strengthen their religious consciousness and commitments in the face of the European catastrophe.

## Movement's Growth under Rabbi Menachem Mendel Schneerson

Rabbi Joseph Schneersohn's death in 1950 set off something of a leadership crisis in the Chabad community. The Rebbe left two learned, eloquent, dynamic, and competing sons-in-law—Rabbi Shmaryahou Gourary and Rabbi Menachem Mendel Schneerson—but no clear heir. Rabbi Gourary was older and had accompanied his father-in-law for some forty years. Rabbi Schneerson had attended university in Berlin and Paris, was more modern in outlook and dress, had assisted his father-in-law in Europe, and had, in the United States, achieved great success as head of the movement's publishing arm (Kehot Publication Society) and educational and social services arms (Merkos L'Inyonei Chinuch and Machne Israel). Rabbi Schneerson's lectures and scholarly writings won him renown among Chabad Hasidim in the United States. Thanks in part to their lobbying, he eventually emerged as victor and was formally installed as the seventh (and, as it turned out, the last) Lubavitcher Rebbe in 1951. Some members of the Gourary branch of the family, especially Barry S. Gourary, the son of Rabbi Shmaryahou, never fully acquiesced. In the 1980s, Barry Gourary fought and lost a widely publicized legal battle against his uncle over ownership of the Chabad library.

Under Rabbi Menachem Mendel Schneerson, the Chabad movement grew in numbers, wealth, and influence, and became a significant force in American Jewish religious life. Chabad emissaries—"the Rebbe's army"—spread through every Jewish community in the United States and also across the world. Chabad became the best-known Hasidic movement in America and among the fastest-growing postwar religious movements of any kind in the United States. While the movement maintains no membership figures, it bills itself as the largest Jewish organization in the world, with institutions in more than seventy countries and forty-eight states. It boasts several hundred thousand active devotees in New York (mostly Brooklyn) and other major Jewish communities, and a much larger number of friends who participate in some of its educational and religious programs and contribute to its work.

## Modernizing Hasidism

Rabbi Menachem Mendel Schneerson made clear, soon after he assumed his position, that he appreciated modernity. Having himself studied mathematics and engineering, he encouraged his followers to utilize new technologies to strengthen their movement and Jewish life in general. Television, satellite communications, and the latest computer gadgetry all, in time, became part of the Chabad arsenal. Today Chabad.org and Lubavitch.com declare that their mission is to "utilize internet technology to unite Jews worldwide, empower them with the knowledge of their 3300 year old tradition, and foster within them a deeper connection to Judaism's rituals and faith." But modernity still has its limits. The Rebbe insisted that the biblical view of creation was correct and opposed both the theory of evolution and scientific claims concerning the antiquity of the world.

Significantly, the Rebbe abandoned the distinctive fur hat and long Hasidic caftan that had been his father-in-law's uniform. He dressed in the somewhat more modern fashion to which he had grown accustomed in Europe, with a black Borsalino felt fedora. This became the uniform for Chabad Hasidic men, distinguishing them both from other Hasidim and from their American neighbors. Chabad women, though always modestly dressed, likewise made more concessions to modern fashion than most of their Hasidic counterparts, without compromising their understanding of what Jewish law demanded.

Rabbi Schneerson possessed deep Jewish learning, and was viewed as brilliant, charismatic, energetic, and a skillful administrator by many of his followers. His literary output fills dozens of volumes, comprising his regular weekly discourses on a range of subjects, occasional lectures, thousands of published letters, scholarly notes, and more. Followers considered his every word and action to be holy and maintained careful records of his activities and conversations.

Rabbi Schneerson devoted the bulk of his energies to strengthening the Chabad movement and Jewish life in general. He initiated a wide range of formal and informal educational and religious endeavors, including well-publicized and sometimes controversial campaigns, to promote the observance of individual commandments, such as the lighting of Sabbath candles by women, the donning of phylacteries (*tefillin*, small boxes containing verses from scripture) by men, and the public celebration of Chanukah by Jews. Chabad frequently borrowed military metaphors to promote these activities, perhaps appropriately given the movement's strict hierarchic organization. Emissaries drove around in "mitzvah tanks," reaching out to the unaffiliated, and children were registered at a young age as "soldiers" in Tzivos Hashem, the Rebbe's "army of the Lord."

### Rabbi Schneerson and the Public Square

While many American Jews believed that the public square should be devoid of religious symbols based on the principle of church-state separation, the Rebbe insisted that public displays of religion were both constitutional and compatible with U.S. tradition. He justified his efforts to promote nonsectarian prayer in the public schools on the basis that Congress opens with a prayer. He promoted Chanukah in the public square according to the same legal basis that justified Christmas trees. Of course, his larger goal was to gain access to secular Jews whose faith he hoped to strengthen. "Where Chanukah lamps were kindled publicly," he exulted in a letter, "the results have been most gratifying in terms of spreading the light of Torah and Mitzvoth [commandments], and reaching out to Jews who could not otherwise have been reached." The United States Supreme Court in *Allegheny County, City of Pittsburgh and Chabad v. ACLU* (1989) strengthened Chabad's hand, ruling that the public display of a menorah did not violate the First Amendment to the Constitution. Thereafter such displays became widespread across the country. By contrast, efforts on the part of Chabad to promote nondenominational prayers and "moments of silence" in the public schools, and to win state aid for parochial schools, failed to win court approval.

Late in his life, Rabbi Schneerson reached out beyond the Jewish community to "influence the nations of the world." While eschewing conversionism, he argued that non-Jews needed to observe a basic moral code set forth in seven laws that, according to Jewish tradition, God commanded Noah to observe following the flood. Chabad's hope for imminent messianic redemption of the world may have sparked this unusual universalistic campaign. An unknown number of non-Jews committed themselves to observing the Noahide laws, some calling themselves "children of Noah."

Rabbi Schneerson became a strong supporter of the state of Israel. His father-in-law, like many fervently Orthodox rabbis of the time, had once opposed Zionism, fearing that secular nationalism would replace religion as the central core of Jewish identity. About a year after the establishment of the state of Israel, however, Kfar Chabad ("Chabad Village") was established in Central Israel as the movement's Israeli headquarters. Over time, Chabad became a force in the country, particularly since the Rebbe's message of tolerance and love for every Jew contrasted with the more insular views of other fervently Orthodox groups. Rabbi Schneerson won thousands of followers in the Jewish state, and without ever traveling there, he exerted substantial influence—so much so that many Israeli leaders visited him in Brooklyn. Throughout the years, he advocated an amendment to Israel's Law of Return so that only Jews by birth and those converted according to strict Jewish law (and not by non-Orthodox rabbis) might claim citizenship. Following the Six Day War, he opposed the Camp David accords and the return of any territory to Israel's Arab neighbors. He encouraged Israel's leaders to imbue the country with Jewish values and to ensure the security of the land. He also encouraged his Israeli followers to serve in the military, which most fervently Orthodox Jews did not. While he often disagreed with the direction of Israel's secular leaders, particularly its Labor governments, he remained a revered figure among his followers and was admired by many Jews from Arab lands who came to appreciate his spirituality, warmth, and leadership.

## Messianism and the Death of Rabbi Schneerson

Rabbi Menachem Mendel Schneerson was a fervent messianist. Not only did he consider the messiah's coming to be imminent, he also believed that Jews, through their own active efforts, could induce the messianic coming. Many Lubavitch faithful had understood the catastrophe of World War II to be the "last labors prior to the arrival of our Messiah" and took solace from the movement's counsel to "be ready for redemption soon!" When that prophecy failed, they experienced grave disappointment. The Rebbe, through his lectures and outreach efforts to Jews around the world, his widely publicized pronouncements, and his interpretation of modern Israel's role in the divine plan, rekindled messianic hopes, spurring his followers to years of selfless commitment as foot soldiers in campaigns to "force" redemption, to bring "Moshiach [messiah] now." Many of these efforts focused on the observance by Jews of a single commandment and returning "lost" Jews to the fold. Personal emissaries (shluchim) dispatched by the Rebbe to set up institutions around the world wherever Jews lived or visited, served, in effect, as lifelong missionaries for his cause. In accordance with Hasidic teachings concerning self-abnegation, they established Chabad centers in communities large and small and modeled a fervently Orthodox lifestyle, often at personal sacrifice, so as to strengthen Jewish religious consciousness and hasten the messiah's coming.

Substantial numbers of Lubavitch followers concluded, as time passed, that the Rebbe himself was the not-yet-revealed messiah, a belief fostered by his childlessness, the rapid worldwide growth of the movement he headed, and, according to some, hints concealed in his public utterances. Rather than dampening these speculations, the Rebbe's death, in 1994, only heightened them, some believers insisting that "our Master, Teacher and Rebbe, King Messiah"

remained alive and would in time be revealed. Some Orthodox critics condemned these beliefs as alien to Judaism, and in time the mainstream leadership of the movement distanced itself from those who refused to declare the Rebbe dead. The messianist minority was also expelled from the movement's Brooklyn headquarters.

With the death of the Rebbe, his gravesite in Queen's, known as his Ohel (a "tent" built over the resting place of a righteous sage), became a site of pilgrimage. Daily, and especially on commemorative days, people come to recite psalms, light candles, and seek the deceased Rebbe's heavenly intercession. A visitor center, meditation area, and study hall have been erected close to the gravesite, and those in need are encouraged to write the Rebbe a letter. The Web site of the Ohel promises that faxes, e-mails, and ordinary letters "are brought to the Ohel shortly after their receipt."

## Chabad after the Rebbe

Some predicted, following the Rebbe's death, that the Chabad movement would split asunder or decline. Few Hasidic groups have historically been able to thrive without a living Rebbe to guide and direct them. Chabad, however, has continued to grow, led by its army of more than four thousand full-time emissary families who oversee Chabad houses in far-flung communities around the world and on more than one hundred college campuses. These emissaries—"dedicated to the welfare of the Jewish people worldwide"—guide, teach, provide hospitality, lead religious services, engage in charitable work, serve addicts, minister to those in jail, and reach out to Jews of every sort.

In recent years, Chabad has created a synagogue movement in the United States that claims the involvement of hundreds of thousands of Jews, most of them not themselves fully observant. In the former Soviet Union, where Chabad's roots lie, it plays a major role in Jewish life on both the local and national levels. In Australia, South Africa, the Far East, and some European countries, its rabbis now lead a significant number of the community's major synagogues. Chabad has also established a popular program of adult Jewish education, known as the Jewish Learning Institute, and claims to be "the largest provider of adult Jewish education in the world."

The economics of Chabad, like those of many centrally driven, highly organized, and fiercely independent proselytizing movements, are somewhat mysterious. Much of the funding is thought to come from Jews outside the movement who have come to respect Chabad's work and achievements. Chabad emissaries are responsible for maintaining their own operations and are encouraged to be entrepreneurial. While campus centers receive some start-up funding, every Chabad House is, in time, expected to fend for itself. What keeps the emissaries going is a strong sense of *esprit de corps* fostered by the movement, coupled with the deep-seated belief that they are carrying forward the Rebbe's work, serving and strengthening the Jewish people, and hastening the coming of the messiah.

See also *Anti-Semitism; Architecture: Jewish; Canada: Pluralism; Hasidism; Holocaust; Judaism entries; Music: Jewish; Religious Thought: Jewish; Torah; Women: Jewish; Worship: Jewish; Zionism.*

Jonathan D. Sarna

**BIBLIOGRAPHY**

Berger, David. *The Rebbe, the Messiah, and the Scandal of Orthodox Indifference.* Oxford, UK: The Littman Library of Jewish Civilization, 2001.

Ehrlich, M. Avrum. *The Messiah of Brooklyn: Understanding Lubavitch Hasidism Past and Present.* Jersey City, N.J.: KTAV Publishing House, 2004.

Feldman, Jan. *Lubavitchers as Citizens: A Paradox of Liberal Democracy.* Ithaca, N.Y.: Cornell University Press, 2003.

Fishkoff, Sue. *The Rebbe's Army: Inside the World of Chabad-Lubavitch.* New York: Schocken Books, 2003.

Harris, Lis. *Holy Days: The World of a Hasidic Family.* New York: Touchstone, 1995.

Hoffman, Edward. *Despite All Odds: The Story of Lubavitch.* New York: Simon and Schuster, 1991.

Mintz, Jerome R. *Hasidic People: A Place in the New World.* Cambridge, Mass.: Harvard University Press, 1992.

Rigg, Bryan Mark. *Rescued from the Reich: How One of Hitler's Soldiers Saved the Lubavitcher Rebbe.* New Haven, Conn.: Yale University Press, 2004.

Shaffir, William. *Life in a Religious Community: The Lubavitcher Chassidim in Montreal.* Toronto, Canada: Holt, Rinehart and Winston, 1974.

*Toldois Chabad B'Artzois Ha'Bris* [History of Chabad in the U.S.A.—1900–1950]. Brooklyn, N.Y.: Kehot Publication Society, 1988 (in Hebrew).

# Charismatics/Charismatic Movements

The word *charismatic* characterizes any Christian in any church tradition who exercises one of the postconversion gifts of the Holy Spirit. These gifts, listed in Romans 12:6–8 and 1 Corinthians 12–14, include, but are not limited to, the ecstatic religious experience of speaking in tongues, the interpretation of tongues, prophecy, healing, and miracles. The term is derived from the Greek word *charisma,* meaning an unmerited gift of grace. The Holy Spirit manifests himself through these gifts for the common good of the body of Christ. Charismatics differ greatly in church background and doctrine but are united in a common experience—the baptism of the Holy Spirit.

The Charismatic movement is a global spiritual renewal over the past one hundred years that has been described by some as the "New Pentecost." Pentecostals believe that the postconversion experience of baptism of the Holy Spirit is available for all believers and is evidenced by *glossolalia* (speaking in tongues). The "New Pentecost" has spread the Pentecostal beliefs and practices to mainline Protestant, Catholic, Orthodox, and nondenominational traditions.

## Three Waves

Charismatic Christianity has no one founder, no one system of theology, no particular type of church government, and no defining liturgy. While scholars differ on which groups should be included in this category, they generally agree that the revival/renewal movement began at the turn of the twentieth century and consists of three phases or waves of the Spirit.

### The First Wave: Classical Pentecostalism (1900–Present)

Numerous revivals marked the turn of the twentieth century around the world: the Welsh Revival of 1904, a revival in India in 1905, and several revivals in the United States between 1901 and 1906. Most scholars identify the 1906 Azusa Street Revival in Los Angeles, California, as the launching pad for the First Wave of the Spirit in the modern era and the catalyst for the extraordinary missionary activity that followed. Few events have influenced modern church history as much as the three and one half years of this revival. It became a magnet that drew people from many racial, ethnic, and denominational backgrounds to Los Angeles to receive the baptism of the Holy Spirit, as evidenced by speaking in tongues. When the participants returned to their home churches to share their experiences, they faced rejection by their denominations. Forced out on their own, the Classic Pentecostals eventually formed the first Pentecostal denominations such the Church of God in Christ, Church of God (Cleveland, Tennessee), the Assemblies of God, the International Church of the Foursquare Gospel, and others. Theologically, most Classic Pentecostals believe that speaking in tongues is the initial physical evidence of Spirit baptism. Historically, they have been very missionary-minded people because they connect their experience with empowerment for evangelism and missionary effort.

### The Second Wave: Charismatic Movement (1960–Present)

The Second Wave, also known as Neo-Pentecostalism, emerged in a dramatic and unexpected fashion in the 1960s when the Pentecostal beliefs and emphasis on the spiritual gifts spread to non-Pentecostal churches. Rather than leaving their own church traditions as the First Wavers did, most Second Wavers chose to stay and bring about a spiritual or charismatic renewal in those churches. The movement spread rapidly. In only ten years, it had penetrated all major Protestant, Roman Catholic, and Orthodox traditions and spawned numerous independent Neo-Pentecostal ministries. Theologically, the Charismatics accept the idea that the spiritual gifts are still valid today. They tend to believe that speaking in tongues usually accompanies Spirit baptism, but they do not give preeminence to this belief in the same way that Classic Pentecostals do.

### The Third Wave: Neo-Charismatic (1981–Present)

The roots of the Neo-Charismatic movement extend back into the 1960s when numerous independent Charismatic churches were formed. The Signs and Wonders Movement, part of the larger Neo-Charismatic movement, developed in the early 1980s from the teachings of John Wimber, the founder of the Vineyard Church and professor at Fuller Theological Seminary in Southern California. C. Peter Wagner, one of Wimber's colleagues at Fuller, coined the phrase "the Third Wave of the Holy Spirit" in 1983. According to Wagner, the Charismatic movement has been replaced by a new stream that seeks the restoration of New Testament Christianity (Acts 3:21). People in this new stream do not like to be labeled as either Pentecostal or Charismatic but prefer terms such as New Apostolic and Restorationist. Theologically, Third Wavers identify Spirit baptism with conversion, emphasizing the continuing nature of the experience rather than one specific event. They stress the gift of prophecy, the miraculous working of the Spirit, power encounters, and the importance of modern day apostles and prophets. Speaking in tongues may be found among Neo-Charismatics, but not in the same way as it was in the first two waves.

### A Global Movement

Each movement began in unique ways, but all share common elements that bind them together. Because of the interconnectiveness of the Pentecostal and Charismatic movements, it is becoming harder and harder to speak of them separately. The terms are often used interchangeably. Some scholars declare that the Charismatic movement is simply Pentecostalism within historic mainline churches and describe Charismatics as Pentecostals dressed in traditional church garb. The Third Wavers, on the other hand, may demonstrate Pentecostal or charismatic characteristics, but they reject Pentecostal terminology.

Because the Charismatic Renewal is so various and widespread, discussing it can be confusing. As the movement spread globally, it filtered through many church traditions and indigenous groups. In some cases, it changed so significantly that the original stream is hard to find. The Pentecostal/Charismatic movement with its multifaceted character constitutes the fastest-growing group of churches within Christianity. It has been estimated that more than six hundred million Pentecostal/Charismatic adherents exist worldwide today. Recognizing that statistics vary according to methods used to collect them, if these figures are in any way correct, they indicate that the Pentecostal, Charismatic, and associated movements have grown to represent one-fourth of all Christians in just over one hundred years.

### Roots of the Charismatic Movement (1950–1960)

The beginning of the Charismatic movement is traced to the spiritual experience of Dennis Bennett (1917–1991), an Episcopal priest from Van Nuys, California, in 1960. However, the roots of the movement go back to the late 1940s and early 1950s, when speaking in tongues and exercising spiritual gifts began appearing periodically in non-Pentecostal churches. From the beginning of the Classical Pentecostal movement, individuals from historic churches sporadically received the baptism of the Holy Spirit. After their experience, they usually resigned or were coerced into leaving their churches. When Harald Bredesen (1918–2006), a Lutheran minister, received the baptism in the Holy Spirit in 1946, leaders in his church requested that he stay. His ministry was a precursor to the Charismatic movement and ignited a revival in 1960 at Yale University, where Episcopal, Lutheran, and Presbyterian students spoke in tongues. Under Bredesen's mentorship, several Charismatic leaders, including Pat Robertson, a Southern Baptist and host of the

Christian television show *The 700 Club;* John Sherrill, founder of the Chosen Books publishing company; and Pat Boone, conservative gospel singer and actor, experienced the baptism of the Holy Spirit.

Bredesen was not alone in this experience. In 1951, Richard Winkler, the rector of the Trinity Episcopal Church in Wheaton, Illinois, became the first Spirit-baptized Episcopal pastor in America. Agnes Sanford, the founder of the Inter Healing Movement; James Brown, a Presbyterian minister; and Tommy Tyson, a Methodist minister, were also part of the early beginnings of the movement. In 1959, *Christian Life* magazine featured several articles about the outpourings of the Spirit in mainline congregations. Although there was noticeable Pentecostal activity in non-Pentecostal arenas, it was sporadic and lacked a sense of cohesion.

## The Immediate Forerunners

The ministries of Kathryn Kuhlman (1907–1976), Oral Roberts (1918–2009), and several other healing evangelists in the late 1940s and 1950s provided a platform for the coming Charismatic movement. In the large healing crusades and charismatic conferences, men and women from many religious, theological, and cultural backgrounds mixed together without difficulty. While most of these evangelists had Classical Pentecostal backgrounds, their ministries were independent of denominational control. Large numbers of mainline Protestants and Catholics were introduced to the Pentecostal experience in their meetings and joined a growing group of believers who fell outside the Classic Pentecostal boundaries.

Oral Roberts, a minister in the Pentecostal Holiness Church (International Pentecostal Holiness Church after 1975), began his healing ministry in 1947 with a citywide meeting in Enid, Oklahoma. From that small beginning, he went on to conduct more than three hundred healing crusades on six continents, ending each meeting by individually praying for the sick. By the mid-1950s, Roberts started filming his healing crusades for his national television program. Americans began to see Pentecostalism in a new light as they heard Roberts's positive messages and witnessed dramatic healings.

To appeal to a broader constituency of Charismatics and Christians, he opened Oral Roberts University, an accredited liberal arts college in Tulsa, Oklahoma, in 1965. Dedicated by Billy Graham two years later, Oral Roberts University was considered the foremost Charismatic university in the United States. To align himself more closely with mainline Charismatics, he changed his religious affiliation to the United Methodist Church in 1968 and began televising prime-time religious variety shows featuring popular celebrities. In 1970, the religion editor of the *New York Times* claimed that Roberts commanded more personal loyalty than any other minister in America. In 1980, Roberts established the City of Faith Medical and Research Center, a huge health facility dedicated to merging prayer and medicine in the healing process. This institution struggled financially for eight years before it closed.

Theologically, Roberts is a classical Pentecostal, but his moderation made him a favorite with many people. Roberts's ability to discern change and adapt to new contexts has extended his influence into the twenty-first century. His trademark message, expect a miracle (from God), has brought hope to millions of people.

Kathryn Kuhlman was probably the most famous woman preacher between 1950 and 1979. She began traveling as an evangelist when she was only sixteen years old. In 1947, her healing ministry started after a woman announced that she had been healed during Kuhlman's sermon on the Holy Spirit. As her healing ministry developed, Kuhlman intentionally avoided some of the techniques used by other healing evangelists. She seldom prayed for people individually; however, she often used the Charismatic gift of the word of knowledge to point out people's medical conditions. She refused to be called a "faith healer" but tried to create an atmosphere of faith and worship where the sick could be healed through the power of the Holy Spirit.

Like Roberts, Kuhlman used the media well and gained nationwide publicity through more than four thousand radio broadcasts, five hundred telecasts, and a variety of printed materials. Dramatic and deliberate, she was a popular guest on talk shows such as the *Tonight Show* and was often featured in major Christian and secular magazines.

The Full Gospel Business Men's Fellowship International helped link the evangelists' message to the mainline churches. In 1951, Demos Shakarian (1913–1993), a Pentecostal layperson, started the first chapter of the nondenominational association of charismatic businessmen in the Los Angeles area, with Oral Roberts as the featured speaker. Using the format of prayer breakfasts and conventions, Shakarian created an atmosphere where Spirit-filled businessmen could evangelize non-Pentecostal professionals. In neutral venues such as hotel ballrooms or convention centers, businessmen from all denominations explored their common faith and enjoyed regular Charismatic fellowship.

In 1967, four women whose husbands were active in the Full Gospel Business Men's Fellowship International organized the Full Gospel Women's Fellowship in Seattle, Washington. The first speaker was Rita Bennett, wife of Dennis Bennett. The organization sponsored local Bible studies and prayer meetings as well as regional, national, and international conferences. Using a name taken from Romans 12:11 in the Amplified Bible, the group reincorporated as Women's Aglow Fellowship International in 1972 (later Aglow International). Organized around the themes of Charismatic spirituality and evangelism, Aglow provided Charismatic women with a place of fellowship and a showcase for their leadership skills.

David du Plessis (1905–1987), a South African Classical Pentecostal minister, was one of the first individuals to grasp what the Spirit could do across ecumenical lines. Dubbed "Mr. Pentecost," he worked to promote unity among Spirit-baptized believers, regardless of their church affiliation. Even when his Pentecostal colleagues frowned on what he was doing, du Plessis served as an unofficial ambassador of Pentecostalism to mainline denominations and the Roman Catholic Church. In 1951, he made a spontaneous visit to the headquarters of the World Council of Churches in New York City. Although he arrived uninvited and unannounced, his efforts to share his Pentecostal faith were warmly received and opened many doors for him to speak and lecture about his Pentecostal experiences.

In his work to promote unity, du Plessis initiated dialogue with the Roman Catholic Church and served as the invited Pentecostal representative at the Second Vatican Council in 1964. Between 1972 and 1982, he cochaired the Roman Catholic and Pentecostal Dialogues with Kilian McDonnell (1921–), an outstanding Charismatic Catholic scholar from St. John's University in Minnesota.

Many people regarded du Plessis as the unofficial father of the Charismatic movement. No other individual did so much to link the movements and bridge the differences as "Mr. Pentecost." Because of his efforts, *Time* magazine listed him as one of the eleven leading shapers and shakers of Christianity in 1974. In recognition of his outstanding service to Christianity, Pope John Paul II awarded him the Good Merit medal in 1983. Du Plessis was the first non-Catholic to receive this honor.

### Birth of the Charismatic Movement (1960)

At 9:00 a.m. on a November day in 1959, Dennis Bennett, an American Episcopal vicar, knelt with some friends and began to pray in an unknown, unlearned language. He had no idea at the time the far-reaching effect this personal experience would have on his life or on church history.

The origin of the Charismatic movement is commonly associated with Bennett's public announcement of his Spirit baptism to the St. Mark's Episcopal Church in Van Nuys, California, on April 3, 1960. Although he received some support, he faced a riot of rejection from a large percentage of his parishioners. They adamantly denounced his Pentecostal activity and called for his resignation from the church. He agreed to resign from St. Mark's but refused to give up the priesthood. Shortly afterward, *Time* and *Newsweek* magazines picked up the story, and Bennett became famous overnight.

After Van Nuys, Bennett accepted a pastoral assignment to the struggling St. Luke's Episcopal Church in Seattle, Washington. With the blessing of his new bishop, he openly shared his experience and an astounding thing happened. The church, which had been closed twice, flourished and grew in attendance under Bennett's leadership. The once nearly bankrupt parish quickly became an important Charismatic center. While the Sunday services remained traditionally Episcopal in worship, the Charismatic prayer meetings were packed with enthusiastic people from all denominations.

The Second Wave spread rapidly throughout the historic churches. By 1963, *Christianity Today* magazine estimated that two thousand Episcopalians in Southern California were speaking in tongues. Charismatic prayer groups popped up all over the United States in Methodist, Baptist, Mennonite, Presbyterian, and other historic churches. In these informal gatherings, participants had the freedom to sing, praise, pray, speak in tongues, and minister to one another with the various gifts of the Holy Spirit. Believing that this move of the Spirit was God's way of renewing existing denominations, the Neo-Pentecostal leaders and David du Plessis encouraged Charismatics to stay in their churches and work for renewal. For this reason, by the 1970s, most mainline churches dropped the term "Neo-Pentecostal" in preference to the more neutral "Charismatic renewal."

### The Catholic Charismatic Renewal

The "Duquesne Weekend" marked the birth of the Charismatic movement in the Roman Catholic Church, but a number of events prepared the way for the leap from Protestant circles into the Catholic world. First, Vatican II, an important Roman Catholic Church Council, adopted an open and receptive position on the work of the Holy Spirit and spiritual gifts in the church. The same council opened the way for interaction between Catholics and Christians of other churches. This was important because non-Catholic Christians would be instrumental in leading many Roman Catholics into the baptism of the Holy Spirit.

A second milestone came at Duquesne University in Pittsburgh, Pennsylvania. A group of teachers experienced an outpouring of the Holy Spirit and spoke in tongues after reading the first chapters of the Book of Acts and two other books, *They Speak with Other Tongues* by John Sherrill and *The Cross and the Switchblade* by David Wilkerson. Soon afterward on February 17, 1967, they sponsored a retreat that has come to be known as the "Duquesne Weekend." During the retreat, a move of the Spirit fell on twenty-five students as they were going to the chapel for prayer. Some of the students praised God in new unlearned languages while others wept for joy. Their Holy Spirit–inspired worship lasted all night. This event not only affected the Roman Catholic Church, but it made the Charismatic movement a pan-Christian experience.

The renewal spread rapidly. Two graduates from Notre Dame University went to investigate the happenings at Duquesne and shared the same Spirit baptism. From there, the Charismatic experience extended to the students and faculties of Michigan State, Iowa State, and several other universities. From the university campuses, the renewal reached into the wider Catholic Church.

Large conferences and renewal gatherings provided unity and integrated the renewal movement into the life of the church. The celebration of a Charismatic Eucharist that blended traditional structure and the spontaneity of the Spirit was a popular feature at Catholic Charismatic Renewal Conferences. The ministry of inner healing gained popularity and produced several new ministries devoted to healing with a number of priests, nuns, and laypeople in charge.

The positive attitude by Catholic leaders toward the renewal promoted growth in the movement. Cardinal Leon-Josef Suenens (1904–1996) of Belgium, a leading voice of the reform movement in Vatican II, described the experience in his book *A New Pentecost* as a "high voltage current of grace which is coursing through the Church" (p. 111). He expressed his belief that the future of the Catholic Church depended on charismatic renewal within its ranks. Another Catholic scholar and prolific writer, Kilian McDonnell

(1921–) of the Order of St. Benedict, felt that the Spirit's charismatic anointing was the key to Christian unity and living a fuller Christian life.

While the Catholic Charismatic Renewal was not without opposition, most Catholic bishops affirmed the movement because of Vatican II. By 1970, a Catholic Charismatic Conference at Notre Dame attracted thirty thousand Catholics who prayed in tongues, prophesied, and rejoiced in what God was doing among them. At a 1975 international conference in Rome, ten thousand pilgrims from more than fifty countries heard Pope Paul VI voice his gratitude for the move of the Holy Spirit in the Catholic Church. By the turn of the twenty-first century, statistics showed more than seventy million Charismatic Catholics in more than 120 nations of the world. To many of those involved, this move of the Holy Spirit was regarded as the answer to Pope John XXIII's prayer at Vatican II for a "New Pentecost."

## The First General Conference on Charismatic Renewal

The first General Conference on Charismatic Renewal convened in Kansas City, Missouri, in the summer of 1977. It was the most inclusive gathering of Spirit-baptized believers to date and the first time that all segments of the modern renewal movement met together. Representatives from the Classic Pentecostal wing, the Protestant Charismatic wing, and the Catholic Charismatic wing attended the historic meeting in a demonstration of grassroots unity never before seen in the United States.

Kevin Ranaghan (a Catholic Charismatic), Larry Christenson (a Protestant Charismatic), and Vinson Synan (a Classic Pentecostal) served as the executive committee for the conference. The morning sessions were divided up according to denominational affiliations, but the afternoon workshops were opened to participants from all church persuasions. At night, the entire body worshipped together in the huge Arrowhead Stadium. The meetings were highlighted by periods of praise and solemn moments of prayer. With fifty thousand participants, the night sessions sometimes resembled an old-fashioned revivalist camp meeting as thousands of Spirit-filled Christians rallied around the theme, "Jesus Is Lord."

The Kansas City conference demonstrated several trends. First, Dr. Pauline E. Parham, daughter-in-law of Charles and Sarah Parham, spoke at one of the main sessions. This hinted at a change in attitudes toward women in the ministry. This change would evidence itself in other charismatic conferences where women like Joyce Meyer, a Word of Faith teacher and author; Marilyn Hickey, inspirational speaker and Bible teacher; and Ruth Carter Stapleton, sister of President Jimmy Carter, were frequent speakers.

The fact that Thomas Zimmerman, general superintendent of the Assemblies of God in America; Leon Joseph Cardinal Suenens, Roman Catholic primate of Belgium; Bishop J. O. Patterson, presiding bishop of the predominantly African American Church of God in Christ; and Anglican archbishop Bill Burrett of South Africa all graced the platform at the same time showed that shared relationships in Jesus Christ created both ecumenical and racial unity. A poignant moment in the conference came when Larry Christenson gave a remarkable prophecy. He declared that the racial struggle in South Africa would end without bloodshed as a white man and black man reached out to each other in Jesus Christ. These words came years before Nelson Mandela and F. W. de Klerk amazed the world with the 1994 bloodless transfer of power in South Africa.

The success of the historic Kansas City conference generated other conferences in the years following. The 1987 Congress on the Holy Spirit and World Evangelization in New Orleans called the Pentecostal and Charismatic movement to a "decade of world evangelization," with the shared goal of winning half of the earth's population to Christ by the year 2000. Other conferences that also fostered evangelism and personal witnessing were held in Indianapolis (1990), Orlando (1995), and St. Louis (2000).

## Media and Literature

Charismatics learned to use the media to their best advantage, and it played an important part in spreading the renewal message. In 1959, Pat Robertson (1930–) founded the first Christian television station, the Christian Broadcasting Network. He contributed much to the development of religious broadcasting. He was the first to use the telethon to raise support for his station and the first to broadcast a Christian talk show on CBN. Both formats remained popular in the early twenty-first century.

In 1973, Paul Crouch (1934–) formed the Trinity Broadcasting network with Jim Bakker (1940–). A few months later, Bakker moved to North Carolina to start his own PTL (Praise the Lord) network. By the late 1970s, numerous Christian centers and evangelistic ministries televised their services and beamed conferences via satellite to cooperating churches across the USA. The increased demand for

teaching materials led to an "audio cassette tape explosion." Audio and video tape libraries distributed millions of Charismatic teaching tapes around the world.

The rapid growth of the Charismatic movement generated the need for popular and scholarly charismatic literature. Dennis Bennett shared his charismatic journey in the book *Nine O'Clock in the Morning.* John Sherrill (1923–) authored and coauthored several Charismatic best sellers. He related his own personal experience in *They Speak with Other Tongues.* He and his wife, Rita, worked with David Wilkerson to write *The Cross and the Switchblade,* the book that influenced the Catholic Charismatic Renewal. The demand for popular Christian fiction in the 1980s was met by works like *This Present Darkness* by Frank Peretti and *The Left Behind* series by Tim LaHaye and Jerry B. Jenkins.

## Problems Develop

The Charismatic experience conditioned believers to expect God to move in unusual ways that were sometimes outside the traditional milieu. The very thing that made the Charismatic movement strong also caused controversies when carried to extremes. New ideas based only on experience caused faulty interpretations of the Bible and led to dangerous excesses. Debates swirled around methods used by well-meaning Charismatic leaders who prayed for the sick or practiced exorcisms.

Although many Charismatics stayed in their original denominations, others eventually left their churches for various reasons and formed new independent Charismatic churches and fellowships. This growing number of independents did not associate with any one particular church or organization and functioned without a safety net of denominational supervision. They met in ad hoc prayer groups, randomly attended teaching conferences, and wandered from group to group in search of the newest teaching. Many leaders in the movement voiced concern over the increasing numbers of "floating" Charismatics.

Don Basham, Bob Mumford, Derek Prince, Charles Simpson, and Ern Baxter, all associated with the Florida-based Christian Growth Ministries, presented what they believed to be the answer to this problem. They began teaching that every Christian, including the leaders, needed to have a "covering" and be under the spiritual guidance of a personal pastor or shepherd. When large numbers of people accepted this teaching and submitted to the authority of the five men, the "Shepherding movement" was born in 1974. It was promoted and popularized in the pages of

Don Basham's *New Wine* magazine and thousands of newsletters, books, and teaching tapes.

Controversy started almost immediately. Charismatic leaders such as Pat Robertson, Demos Shakarian, David du Plessis, and Dennis Bennett all publicly opposed the new movement. Finally, the Shepherding leaders dissolved their association in 1989, thus ending the debate. The hard feelings generated during the ten years of the debate dampened some ecumenical relationships. In 1989, Bob Mumford issued a public apology for his part in the controversial movement, but the damage was done. Some Charismatic leaders never again attended the annual leadership conferences.

In the late 1970s, another controversy arose within the Pentecostal/Charismatic ranks—the "health and wealth" or "prosperity" gospel based on evangelist E. W. Kenyon's writings. Faith teachers Kenneth Hagin, Kenneth Copeland, and others proclaimed that it was God's will for every believer to be financially blessed. All a Christian needed to do was "speak" or "claim" the blessing and God would answer. Opponents felt these teachings overemphasized human faith and caused a lot of condemnation if a person did not receive what he or she had claimed—the tendency being to blame them for their lack of faith. In spite of the debate, the prosperity gospel became very popular. Kenneth Hagin's unaccredited Rhema (spoken word) Bible Training Center in Broken Arrow, Oklahoma, turned out hundreds of graduates who spread the Word of Faith teachings around the world and carried the teaching into the twenty-first century.

By the late 1980s, the Charismatic movement had changed into many different groups and lost much of its cohesion. The very public sex and money scandals associated with televangelists Jim Bakker and Jimmy Swaggart damaged the reputation of Pentecostals and Charismatics. Controversy and media attention swirled around Oral Roberts's dramatic ultimatum to his television audience in 1987 that God would "call him home" if he failed to raise $8 million to support his struggling City of Faith hospital and medical school. Even though Roberts eventually raised more than $9 million, both his fund-raising techniques and the idea that God would kill him created a huge uproar.

## Charismatic Communities

Entire congregations or parishes often became Charismatic; however, in other cases Charismatics sometimes functioned as a subset within a parish. They met in weekly prayer meetings featuring Bible studies, testimonies, and fellowship. Central to these meetings were charismatic expressions of prayer and ministry to each other with the spiritual gifts. In these small groups, Charismatic believers encouraged and strengthened each other in their faith and experience. While church leaders attended these meeting, the laity often took the leadership roles.

The renewal movement also spawned covenant communities, teaching seminars, and discipleship studies that provided special Charismatic ministry to the wider church. A Charismatic Benedictine monastery founded in 1969 in Pecos, New Mexico, and the Word of God Community near the University of Michigan in Ann Arbor are examples of these communities that sprang up across the United States and around the world. Members of these communities separated themselves from the world and lived a life of devotion. Some communities were both evangelistically inclined to attract new membership and socially orientated for the poor and underprivileged. Spirit-filled leaders guided and directed the members in prayer, teaching, and worship. The Word of God community, ecumenical in nature but with a large percentage of Catholic members and under Catholic leadership, was divided into "households" dedicated to university students, married couples, single men, and single women.

Loose-knit fellowships, associations, and networks linked the organizations. The Word of God community sponsored an ecumenical association called the "Sword of the Spirit." The People of Praise Community created the Catholic Renewal Services to coordinate and administer large Charismatic conferences. These Charismatic communities contributed in a positive way to the greater renewal movement. First, they provided discipleship and training for volunteers who manned the large Charismatic conferences. Second, they fostered scholarships and provided an encouraging atmosphere for writing. The Mother of God Community in Gaithersburg, Maryland, was the home base for Peter Hocken and Francis Martin, two leading Catholic scholars.

The communitarian movement was not without controversy. The unity among the groups was shaken by the end of the 1980s when disagreements developed between Word of God and People of Praise communities. The Catholic Church itself found it necessary to examine the activities of some communities because they were too exclusive and interfered with members' private lives.

## Neo-Charismatics or the Third Wave

The Neo-Charismatic movement, or Third Wave, is larger numerically than the first two renewal waves combined. By 2000, an estimated three hundred million members had swelled the ranks of nondenominational or independent charismatic groups not aligned with either the Classic Pentecostal or Charismatic Renewal churches. C. Peter Wagner claimed that the Third Wave was taking place in the straight-line evangelical churches previously untouched by the first two waves.

The Third Wave has been typified by the ministries of John Wimber and C. Peter Wagner. Wimber's teaching led to the Signs and Wonders movement. His teaching declared signs and wonders were normal in the church and were necessary in evangelism and church growth. Wagner is more famous for his New Apostolic Reformation, which stresses the restoration of New Testament offices of apostles and prophets.

There is no one defining form of church government or style for this group. They accept the postconversion gifts of the Holy Spirit including speaking in tongues, prophecy, and healing, but they do not specify any one experience as a requirement for the reception of spiritual gifts. As in other Charismatic churches, worship styles vary, but holy laughter, dancing before the Lord, and Spirit-inspired singing are often found in the services. It can be said that Neo-Charismatics have Pentecostal-like experiences but no Classical Pentecostal or Charismatic affiliations. While they may share slight historical connections to the previous waves, sometimes there are none at all. Neo-Charismatics include organized denominations and fellowships such as the Association of Vineyard Churches, Every Nation, Sovereign Grace Ministries, and others.

## Conclusion

The Charismatic renewal caught the whole church by surprise. At first, Classic Pentecostal denominations were suspect of a revival outside their boundaries; but as time went on, the majority of Pentecostals withdrew their criticisms and embraced the growing renewal movement. By 2000, the Charismatic renewal had encompassed more than 250 distinct ecclesiastical confessions, traditions, and groups of Christianity. The contributions to Christianity of a renewal movement of this size and magnitude are worthy of note.

*Ecumenical Awareness.* The Charismatic renewal produced ecumenical awareness and fellowship across denominational and traditional church lines. Two important events illustrate this impulse: the Kansas City Conference of 1977 and the Roman Catholic-Pentecostal Dialogues.

*Vitality in Worship.* Because of the infusion of charismatic innovations, the church worship has been reinvented. New forms of doctrine, worship, organization, and outreach are reflected in praise and worship music, prayer marches, and innovative uses of mass media and technology.

*New Awareness of Spiritual Gifts.* Those involved in the Charismatic renewal discovered that the spiritual gifts that were available to build and strengthen the early Christian church are still available for the same purpose in churches today.

*Scholarship and Education.* Leaders of the Charismatic renewal such as Larry Christenson and J. Rodman Williams wrote books and educational materials that were influential in the development of Charismatic theology. Kilian McDonnell, the primary historian and adviser to the Catholic Charismatic Renewal, also produced several major works.

*Slower Liberalization of the Church.* The movement significantly reshaped the landscape of the church at large and slowed the liberalization of historic mainline denominations. The emphasis on Jesus as Lord and the work of the Holy Spirit drew churches back to the essentials of Christianity.

*Unity.* Roman Catholics and Protestants found each other in Jesus. Unity based on the shared experience motivated the establishment of closer relationships.

*Concern for Fellow Human Beings.* The charismatic movement muted the divisiveness between churches and church traditions. The work toward reconciliation was fueled by Christian love and desire for unity.

*Evangelization.* The belief that the Holy Spirit was given to empower evangelism inspired the large joint evangelistic efforts during the decade of the 1990s. The goal was to bring millions of people to the Lord before the end of the twentieth century.

*New Vitality.* New energy poured into the churches because of the Charismatic renewal. Charismatic worship services brought life into tired churches and produced significant growth.

*Role of Women.* The Charismatic renewal brought greater freedom for women leaders in the churches and strong ministries with women leaders.

*Prayer.* The renewal waves produced a new interest in prayer and the power of prayer for healing and deliverance.

*Fellowship.* Christian fellowship across church lines has been an important result of the Charismatic renewal. Small groups meeting together for prayer encouraged relationship building and spiritual growth.

*Laity.* The work of the Holy Spirit among all members of the body of Christ was a great equalizer. Spirit-filled laypersons found places of ministry in prayer meetings, small groups, and Charismatic communities.

This movement presents problems for those who wish to study it. First, it is hard to separate the parts from the whole because Charismatics did not form new denominations as did the Classical Pentecostals. Because the movement mixed with other traditions, it is difficult to separate the renewal stream from the larger matrix. Second, the movement, so full of diversity, is still in the process of development. Some churches that started out as Classical Pentecostal or mainline Protestant have blended Charismatic thought and practices with their traditional background to produce something different. In spite of who they are and where they originated, it can be said that this collection of Classic Pentecostals, Charismatics, and Third Wavers makes up a widespread spiritual movement. Together, they have come to constitute a major force in Christendom throughout the world.

**See also** *Ecumenism; Glossolalia; Holiness Denominational Family; Holiness Movement; House Church Movement; Jehovah's Witnesses; Pentecostal Denominational Family; Pentecostals; Pentecostals: African American; Roman Catholicism: The Later Twentieth Century; Serpent Handlers; Television.*

M. Annette Newberry

**BIBLIOGRAPHY**

Anderson, Allan. *An Introduction to Pentecostalism: Global Charismatic Christianity.* Cambridge: Cambridge University Press, 2004.

Bennett, Dennis J. *Nine O'Clock in the Morning: An Episcopal Priest Discovers the Holy Spirit.* South Plainfield, N.J.: Bridge, 1970.

Burgess, Stanley M. "Charismatic Revival and Renewal." In *Encyclopedia of Religious Revivals in America,* edited by Michael McClymond, 99–102. Westport, Conn.: Greenwood, 2007.

———, ed. *Encyclopedia of Pentecostal and Charismatic Christianity.* New York: Routledge, 2006.

Burgess, Stanley M., and Eduard M. Van Der Maas, eds. *The New International Dictionary of Pentecostal Charismatic Movements.* Grand Rapids, Mich: Zondervan, 2001.

du Plessis, David J. *The Spirit Bade Me Go.* Plainfield, N.J.: Logos, 1970.

Harrell, David E. *All Things Are Possible: The Healing and Charismatic Revivals in Modern America.* Bloomington: Indiana University Press, 1975.

Hayford, Jack W. *The Charismatic Century.* New York: Warner Faith, 2006.

Hocken, Peter D. "Charismatic Movement." In *The New International Dictionary of Pentecostal Charismatic Movements,* edited by Stanley

M. Burgess and Eduard M. Van Der Maas, 477–519. Grand Rapids, Mich.: Zondervan, 2001.

Hunter, Harold D., and Cecil M. Robeck. *The Azusa Street Revival and Its Legacy.* Cleveland, Tenn.: Pathway Press, 2006.

Lederle, H. I. *Treasures Old and New.* Peabody, Miss.: Hendrickson, 1988.

McDonnell, Kilian. *Charismatic Renewal and the Churches.* New York: Seabury Press, 1976.

———. *Presence, Power, Praise Documents on the Charismatic Renewal.* 3 vols. Collegeville, Minn.: Liturgical Press, 1980.

Miller, Donald E., and Tetsunao Yamamori. *Global Pentecostalism: The New Face of Christian Social Engagement.* Berkeley: University of California Press, 2007.

Moore, S. David. *The Shepherding Movement: Controversy and Charismatic Ecclesiology.* New York: Continuum, 2003.

Sherrill, John L. *They Speak with Other Tongues.* Grand Rapids, Mich.: Baker, 1964.

Suenens, Leon Joseph. *A New Pentecost.* New York: Seabury Press, 1975.

Synan, Vinson. *The Century of the Holy Spirit: 100 Years of Pentecostal and Charismatic Renewal.* Nashville, Tenn.: Thomas Nelson, 2001.

———. *The Twentieth-Century Pentecostal Explosion.* Altamonte Springs, Fla.: Creation House, 1987.

Thigpen, T. P. "Catholic Charismatic Renewal." In *The New International Dictionary of Pentecostal Charismatic Movements,* edited by Stanley M. Burgess and Eduard M. Van Der Maas, 460–467. Grand Rapids, Mich.: Zondervan, 2001.

Quebedeaux, Richard. *The New Charismatics II.* San Francisco: Harper and Row, 1983.

Wagner, C. Peter. *The Third Wave of the Holy Spirit: Encountering the Power of Signs and Wonders.* Ann Arbor, Mich.: Servant Books, 1988.

# Children and Adolescents

In his 1990 book *The Spiritual Lives of Children,* psychologist Robert Coles writes that children and adolescents use religion to find meaning in their lives, and in doing so they usually achieve greater maturity and growth. He found this was true for many religions: Christian children who deeply feared hell also found personal strength through the ministry of Jesus; Jewish children understood themselves to be Chosen, but also developed compassion for the suffering of others through their understanding of the persecution of Jews; and Muslim children grew in personal autonomy through surrender to Allah. In understanding religion in America, then, one must understand both how religions view children and how children experience religion. Many religious traditions form the religious landscape of the United States, ranging from the Protestantism that has long shaped the public discourse and much of the country's communal imagination to traditions that grew immensely after immigration laws changed to allow greater diversity. Questions arise as to the nature of the experience of children and adolescents in some of those diverse traditions—Protestantism, Catholicism, Judaism, Hinduism, and Islam—before touching on an important moral and spiritual influence on many American children: children's literature.

## Protestant Traditions in Early America

In the early years of America, Protestant assumptions about children were hugely important to the experience of children in the United States. Not only were most children, statistically speaking, raised in Protestant homes of one stripe or another, but also Protestant understandings of children and childhood shaped much about American public education and underlie many of the assumptions of "secular" American society. For instance, the "spare the rod and spoil the child" style of parenting owes its origins to early American understandings of salvation and the best ways to ensure salvation for one's children. Such a strict approach suggests harsh parenting, but seventeenth-century Puritan parents loved their children dearly, as numerous journal entries of parents espousing deep love for their children attest. Thomas Shepard, minister of the First Parish in Newtown (which would become Cambridge), Massachusetts, even feared that his oldest son's life-threatening illness was caused by God because Shepard loved his child too dearly.

Although Puritan parents loved their children, they were simultaneously deeply dubious about their spiritual state. Calvinist theology argued that children were born either among the elect (saved) or not, that no actions on the part of parent or child could affect the child's eternal state. The best that loving parents could hope for were signs indicating that their child was among the saved, and given the lack of self-control that is an inherent part of infancy, those signs were few and far between. Additionally, Puritans believed that children were born tainted with sin, as Anne Bradstreet's description of her own childhood in *The Poems of Mrs. Anne Bradstreet* demonstrates: "Stained from birth with Adam's sinful fact,/ Thence I began to sin as soon as act." Early American Protestants believed that their beloved children were in fact "fallen," deeply tainted by original sin and ruled, not by knowledge of God, but by their baser instincts.

This concern for the spiritual state and fate of Puritan children can be seen in the intense importance that Puritan parents placed on the rite of baptism for their children. For instance, before 1662, only babies whose parents had made a confession of faith and become Communion-receiving members of congregations were eligible to receive baptism. Theoretically, having been baptized in no way affected whether one was saved, but many parents thought baptism encouraged the spiritual potential of their children. In particular, parents who had been baptized themselves but had never experienced saving conversion wished to see their own children receive the sacrament of baptism. In 1662, ministerial delegates from Massachusetts churches decided that while only the converted could take the Lord's Supper, or Communion, anyone who had been baptized might have his or her own child baptized into the church community. This decision, called the Half-Way Covenant, reflected a dramatic shift in the understanding of the role of congregations in the spiritual lives of children. If previously the church had been understood as existing for the already saved, Puritans were moving in the direction of understanding churches as being able to encourage conversion among children by giving them some external markers of grace. In short, parents and communities might be able to help children on the road to grace.

### Evangelical Child Rearing

Within a few generations, Puritan ambivalence about the nature of childhood had largely given way to an evangelical anxiety about childhood. In the increased evangelical fervor of the early eighteenth century, an understanding of childhood took hold that framed it as a time of innate depravity. Parents, then, were responsible for shepherding their children from a position of unrepentant and unknowing evil into Christ. One of the most important ways in which parents, particularly mothers, could do so was through their example of personal piety. If parents allowed themselves to be ruled by their tender feelings for their children, they ran the risk of damaging their children's spiritual growth. A particular fear of evangelical leaders emerged in the paradox that, while parents would not want to frighten their "innocent" children with tales of hellfire and damnation, by failing to warn them about this potential, parents would damn children to just such a fate. Jonathan Edwards, one of the most prominent figures in New England Evangelicalism, responded to criticisms that one should not frighten children with eternal damnation:

> As innocent as children seem to be to us, yet if they are out of Christ, they are not so in God's sight, but are young vipers, and are infinitely more hateful

than vipers, and are in a most miserable condition, as well as grown persons; and they are naturally very selfish and stupid . . . and need much to awaken them. Why should we conceal the truth from them? (In C. C. Goen, *The Great Awakening*)

This trajectory demonstrates an important movement in how American Protestants understood salvation and the spiritual state. If Calvinist Puritans hoped that their children would be saved, but believed both that they could not affect their salvation and that the statistical odds were against salvation, they nonetheless moved quickly into looking for ways to assure themselves that their children would be among the saved. One can see such a trend in the Half-Way Covenant, which suggested strongly that it would benefit children to be within the church community. By the mid-eighteenth century, however, the operating assumption was that children, though they were born inherently depraved, could be and must be brought to Christ by making them very aware that if they did not become godly, they would burn. The message of damnation was harsh, but it was also hopeful, in that it offered parents a way to care spiritually for their children.

How, though, did it feel to be a child in the evangelical world that formed the dominant Protestant culture of the eighteenth and early nineteenth centuries? Certainly, there were children who found the evangelical narrative compelling. Some of the most articulate memories of life under evangelical parenting, however, came from the children of Lyman Beecher, a leading figure in the Second Great Awakening of the early nineteenth century. While his son, Henry Ward Beecher, a famous minister of the second half of the nineteenth century, remembered his profound love for his father and his father's gentle care for him in sickness, he also observed, as quoted by Debby Applegate in *The Most Famous Man in America,* "I don't remember a year of my life, after I was seven or eight Years old, that I did not go about with a feeling of sadness; a feeling that I was in danger of exile from Heaven—all because I was a sinner and I did not want to be." The reaction of people like Henry Ward Beecher to their evangelical upbringing brought about dramatic changes in the American religious landscape. Instead of evangelical fire, Henry Ward Beecher preached a "Gospel of Love" in which "God had a father's heart.... Christ loved me in my sin ... while I was a sinner He did not frown upon me or case me off, but cared for me with unutterable tenderness, and would help me out of sin." Beecher's kinder, gentler Christianity had direct implications for child rearing.

In the words of his older sister, Harriet Beecher Stowe, "Tell a boy that God loves him, and religion has a chance to take hold. Tell a boy that he is under God's wrath and curse ... because somebody ate an apple five thousand years ago, and his religious associations are not so agreeable—especially if he has the answers whipped into him."

## Horace Bushnell and the Gospel of Love

While the evangelical model of parenting certainly continued in some streams of American Protestantism, this new form of Christianity suggested a more nurturing approach to religious training. A leader in this new approach, Horace Bushnell was a Connecticut minister and author who was one of the leaders of a cultural shift away from revival culture. His *Views of Christian Nurture and of Subjects Adjacent Thereof,* first published in 1847, specifically described children as spiritual beings counter to the evangelical model. The industrial revolution contributed to a shift in how Americans understood the family. As important as evangelical mothers were in the spiritual development of their children, their families were patriarchal in structure, with the home and children under the father's control. During the nineteenth century, the domestic sphere began to be cast both as female and as sacred space, while the public world became both male and worldly. For men, the home became a retreat from the cares of the world, but it was the mother who became primarily responsible for child rearing. Simultaneously, a Rousseauian understanding of childhood as a time of innocence began to take hold. This landscape provided fertile ground for Bushnell's ideas to become popular. For Bushnell, as for evangelicals, parents were responsible for their children's spiritual development, but rather than using fear of damnation, he espoused that they model a healthy relationship with God. Parents were to shape their child, understanding that every word uttered and every action performed had the potential to shape their offspring toward or away from Christ. That said, Bushnell also understood children as having an inherent Christian nature from birth—that the child's nature would develop as the child did, slowly, and with proper care, into adult faith. As a result of Bushnell's influence, the Christian home became the primary staging ground of childhood Protestant experience. Bushnell encouraged parents to create religious experiences out of most facets of childhood, including play, birthday celebrations, holidays, and careful attention to religious devotions including Bible study, catechism, and a family altar. These home practices were reinforced with church attendance and community. Children attended worship and Sunday school, were aware of missionaries, and aided, as age appropriate, in the broader missions of the church.

Bushnell's views had a variety of critics and certainly represented a middle-class view of the family. That said, Bushnell's views were broadly culturally pervasive. For instance, Unitarian author Louisa May Alcott valorized the home and parental nurture in her wildly popular series for "young readers," *Little Women, Good Wives,* and *Little Men.* The March family, characterized by deeply loving and highly moral parents, is established from the opening scene as having raised Christian children when the daughters, despite some personal reluctance, sacrifice Christmas presents to the (Civil) war effort; sacrifice personal treats and vanities further to get gifts for their mother, Marmee; and, under her influence, give their Christmas breakfast to the poor. The model of Christian nurture ran counter to the Calvinist understanding of election. While not every person was automatically among the saved, salvation was possible for each person, especially if they were properly nurtured in loving homes and churches. That salvation, however, was not expected to be a life-altering conversion as in the Calvinist model. Instead, it was understood as a slow development of an innocent, childlike faith into a deep and mature one. Many of the liberal Protestants raised in the late nineteenth century felt little of the anxiety or alienation experienced by evangelicals, rather understanding themselves to be secure in both their Christianity and their family settings.

### Protestant Children in the Twentieth Century

If Bushnell's views of childhood characterized the late nineteenth century, the early twentieth century was characterized by a fear that the family and the church were under siege from modern life. Neither, it was argued by ministers and Sunday school societies, could compete against the movies, the radio, jazz, and the marketplace. Christmas, it was feared, was moving from Christ to consumption. Additionally, parents were becoming more secular, so that family devotions and Bible study were on the decline. While many American Protestants became more secular or moved into the realm of "do-it-yourself" spirituality, which left children without formal, communal, religious training, throughout the second half of the twentieth century, evangelicals created a separate youth culture that ran parallel to secular American society. Evangelical youth culture includes literature, Christian heavy metal, and the positing of Christian culture as a form of youth counterculture that proved deeply spiritually satisfying for many who participated.

### Catholicism and the Spiritual Formation of Children

If Protestants debated the inherent nature of children, the Catholic position was more clear. Children were understood to be gifts from God. Though they inherited original sin, they were also of God. Parents, then, were responsible for raising their children in the church, so as to properly spiritually form them. While parents shaped children, children were also understood to have spiritual wisdom to impart to their parents and families, both through the innocence of their questions and through their childlike wonder at the world.

### American Catholicism in the Nineteenth Century

Like their Protestant contemporaries, nineteenth-century Catholic mothers were invested in and responsible for the spiritual health of their children. Mothers were charged with leading the children in family recitations of the rosary, though other forms of home devotions were also encouraged. In addition to home devotions, by the mid-nineteenth century, American Catholics had an additional concern in terms of transmitting their faith to their children. Over the course of the first half of the nineteenth century, support grew for the idea of tax-supported public schools, such that by 1860, every state had some form of a public school system. While these schools guaranteed a basic education, they were also deeply dedicated to shaping moral citizens. Horace Mann, a Boston-based educational reformer, argued that publicly funded schools could offer an education that was nonsectarian, while nevertheless retaining key pieces of Christian moral teachings. The argument was that general precepts of Christianity, such as biblical readings and recitations of the Ten Commandments and the Lord's Prayer, were acceptable and left students to be guided in specifically theological concerns by their parents and ministers. From the Catholic standpoint, however, these practices were unacceptable because the Protestant King James Bible was the biblical text used, and Protestant versions of the Ten Commandments and the Lord's Prayer were the ones recited. To Catholics, even the not explicitly religious material, such as the readers and primers selected, demonstrated a distinct Protestant bias. As a result, Catholics tended not to support the creation of public schools. Starting in the 1840s, bishops began encouraging parents to send children to Catholic schools. Additionally, all states with large Catholic populations had political battles over whether Catholic schools should receive public funds and whether the above-mentioned Protestant elements should be removed from the curriculums.

The conflict over public schools is perhaps best exemplified by a conflict in Boston, in which Catholic public school children publicly demonstrated their loyalty to the church. In March 1859, a ten-year-old Catholic student named Thomas Whall was asked by his teacher, Sophia Shepard, to recite the Ten Commandments. Whall refused, having been instructed by his father not to recite the Protestant version of the commandments. While Massachusetts law required the day to begin with the Protestant form of the commandments, most teachers had the class recite en masse, and Catholic students could simply say the Catholic version, with no one the wiser. Miss Shepard deviated in insisting on individual recitation, and the school board upheld her position. The following weekend, the Whalls' priest urged the Sunday school to avoid Protestant prayers. Additionally, the congregation passed a resolution recommending that the children should use Catholic versions whenever called upon to recite prayers. On Monday, Whall was once again required to recite the King James version of the Ten Commandments. He refused and was beaten until his hands were bloody. After the beating, the principal announced that all students who refused to recite the Ten Commandments would be sent home from school. Hundreds of Catholic students were discharged, and the following week, when they brought Catholic copies of the commandments, they were sent home yet again. The Whall family sued the assistant principal who had administered the beating, but the court ruled in favor of Assistant Principal Cooke.

This incident says quite a bit about Catholic-Protestant relations, but it also demonstrates the devotion of a ten-year-old boy to a sense of Catholic identity. While Catholics had been creating separate educational systems for more than a century, incidents like the Eliot School rebellion encouraged the creation of a separate American Catholic school system. While the purpose of such a system was, in part, to protect schoolchildren from Protestant influence, Catholic schools had internal religious goals as well. In the late nineteenth century, Catholic schools were huge forces in shaping Catholic culture, which was, at that time, deeply devotional. In addition to teaching the secular subjects, Catholic schools offered religious instruction that went well beyond the catechism. Historians have noted that schools were decorated in styles similar to churches, with statues and paintings of saints. Religious devotional objects were used as rewards for academic achievement, and devotions to the saints and to the Virgin Mary became school holidays. As a result, school became sanctified space, designed to encourage the devotional lives of Catholic students and nurture in them a sense of divine figures within their daily lives.

## Catholicism in the Twentieth Century

In the twentieth century, Catholic children continued to be taught that they, like Thomas Whall, might need to defend the faith. In the words of a midcentury teaching sister from Wisconsin, Catholic children were "the smallest of God's soldiers," who were directed by their teachers in "the part they were to play in winning the world for Christ. It will mean a tremendous battle."

The sacrality of the Catholic world did not, in the twentieth century, prevent it from also being fun. Scholar Julie Byrne describes women's basketball as a vital aspect of the Philadelphia Catholic high school and college experience. Catholic girls played basketball, and played it well, beginning in the 1930s and culminating in national women's college basketball championships in the 1970s. Basketball is significant because it models a way in which Catholic girls were encouraged to move out of traditional female roles, to be active athletes in whom their communities took pride. Given popular conceptions of the Catholic Church as repressive to women, this is hardly insignificant. The basketball court was also a place of spirituality, in that before the game, the team and coaches on the court and the parents, classmates, priests, and nuns in the stands would all pray, in the words of the Immaculata College Mighty Macs, "Oh God of Players, hear our prayers to play this game and play it fair." Perhaps most importantly, according to Byrne, the fun that Catholic girls took in basketball complicates the "culture of suffering" that characterizes Catholic women's history by demonstrating a place in which Catholic adolescent girls experienced pleasure in a church-sanctioned setting.

## African American Children and Community Life

The pictures of Christianity traced out above, both Catholic and Protestant, were principally those of white Christianity. While African Americans were certainly affected by the theological trends discussed above, life in the black churches had distinct characteristics, particularly for children. For instance, according to sociologist Cheryl Townsend Gilkes, until the late twentieth century, African American congregations were less likely to have programming explicitly for children and teens. Rather, children participated in adult activities as apprentices to adult positions. As a result, children were able to serve as junior leaders to adult congregations, and their voices were heard in church space. Since one of the primary social goals of black congregations was to provide children with a safe space from the harsh racism of the outside world, communities took special care to nurture and support the talents of youngsters. Children were raised to know that they were the valued future of the church. In fact, the nurturing influence of the church helped to mentor children into leadership roles in the secular world as well. Oprah Winfrey, Aretha Franklin, and Henry Lewis Gates Jr. all had their earliest public roles in their childhood churches. The positive role that the black churches have played in the lives of their children has not been static. There have been times when it has been more or less political and times when churches have failed to reach out to, or meet the needs of, the young people in the community. For many, however, African American churches have offered a deeply affirming recognition of talent.

## The Role of Children in Judaism

Jews have lived in what is now the United States since colonial times; however, for much of that time communities were small, and many families lived as the only Jews in town. Waves of immigration at the beginning and the end of the nineteenth century and in the early decades of the twentieth century have created a sizable American Jewish community, though Jews remain a small percentage of the country's overall population. One of the major concerns of Judaism is *ledor vador,* the transmission of Judaism from generation to generation. Given the importance placed on passing on Judaism, children have been a major focus in American Judaism.

Life-cycle rites are an important aspect of Jewish childhood, particularly the *bris* (Yiddish) or *brit malah* (Hebrew), the ritual circumcision of a Jewish male on his eighth day of life. Through his *bris,* a boy was made part of the covenant between God and the Jewish people. At the age of thirteen, a Jewish boy became a *bar mitzvah* or a son of the commandments. A bar mitzvah took place after years of Jewish education and was marked by the teenager being called to read in Hebrew from the Torah, after which he offered thoughts on what he had read. Families often marked this occasion with some form of celebration, ranging from

offering refreshments to the congregation immediately following the service to a lavish party for the child's friends and the parents' social circles. The bar mitzvah marked the assumption of Jewish adulthood, with all the attendant ritual responsibilities. While thirteen-year-olds were still not considered to be adults in most ways, from that point on, the boy could be counted in a *minyan* (the ten Jews necessary for the recitation of certain prayers), fasted for Yom Kippur (the Day of Atonement), and abstained from certain foods during Passover. The extent to which any given boy observed these restrictions depended on the traditions of his individual Jewish movement and the conventions of his family, and many children observed these rituals before turning thirteen.

Study was a central piece of the Jewish childhood. While the Jewish movements had varied educational goals, traditionally, a boy would be able to read Hebrew, know the contents of the Hebrew Bible and its accompanying Jewish commentary, and be ritually literate. American Jews created a small separate educational system of day schools in areas where their numbers permitted, but communally supported Hebrew schools that provided supplemental religious education were far more common.

Until the twentieth century, the American Jewish community, like those elsewhere, was primarily concerned with the education and ritual lives of boys. Though the Reform movement instituted confirmation ceremonies for both boys and girls in the nineteenth century, generally girls were not formally educated in the Torah or in Hebrew. Instead, they learned how to maintain Jewish homes and became ritually significant mostly in their role as wives and mothers. That tendency began to change in the early years of the twentieth century. Jewish girls gained increasing access to forms of education previously reserved for boys, and in 1922, Rabbi Mordecai Kaplan performed the first *bat mitzvah,* or daughter of the commandment, ceremony for his daughter. While bat mitzvah celebrations were slow to catch on, by the 1970s, most girls in the Reform and Conservative movements received bat mitzvah celebrations and the Jewish education leading up to them. In these ceremonies, girls took a ritual role very similar, if not identical, to those taken by their brothers. Historian Jonathan Sarna suggests that such access to Jewish learning and synagogue ritual gave these girls both a deep connection to Judaism and empowered them, such that many grew up to expand the ritual and leadership roles available to Jewish women. By the late twentieth century, many Orthodox congregations were also offering bat mitzvah celebrations, adapting the ceremony for the restrictions placed on women's ritual leadership.

## Hinduism, Immigration, and Growing Up American

In India, Hinduism is primarily practiced in the home. There is no equivalent to Sunday school; rather, children learn what it is to be Hindu by immersion in a society largely ordered by a Hindu worldview. While changes in Indian society around the turn of the twenty-first century have affected the transmission of Hinduism within India, for Hindus who moved to the United States in the post-1965 waves of immigration, it became a central concern. Scholar Raymond Brady Williams describes the process as one of creating a sacred world that children could enter with their families and communities, apart from the daily world of secular American society. In an attempt to create such a sacred world, American Hindus have brought together many different strands of Hinduism from across the Indian sub-continent, each of which may have different languages, fes-tivals, and traditions. In community settings often borrowed from Christianity and Judaism (Sunday school, summer camp, and community centers similar to the YMCA [origi-nally, the Young Men's Christian Association] and JCC [Jewish Community Center]). Hindu parents inculcated children with Hindu values that they saw as transcending the various differences between forms of Hindu practice. The result was a new American Hinduism, different from what parental generations knew in India but nonetheless the Hinduism most familiar to their children.

In Hindu educational settings and at home, American Hindus taught their children about karma, or the moral consequences of one's actions; dharma, or one's duties and responsibilities according to one's familial status; and values such as moderate appetites, compassion, mediation, and charity. Children were also likely to learn Hindu epics, tales that they might read and discuss in classes, act out in plays, hear as bedtime stories, see in comic book form, or watch as TV miniseries. Classes and summer camps enforced values that were taught at home but that parents worried might not be reinforced by life in the United States.

For the earliest generations of Hindu children growing up in America, educational material was often created for an Indian market and rarely in English. The Hindu worldview, which is tightly interconnected with Indian social systems, often made more sense in an Indian context and was at odds with some American ideology. (The Hindu emphasis on the extended family, for example, contradicts the American value of individualism.) Some American Hindu children found these contradictions inherently confusing, as they experienced both value sets as making inherent cultural sense. In this way, American Hindu children often end up bicultural. Simultaneously, Hindu parents and educators worked to create educational material that was in English and more socially accessible to American-raised children. In the early twenty-first century, however, the question of how to be Hindu in America remained one that each Hindu child found himself or herself working out in relation to families and communities.

## Negotiating America as a Muslim Child

While Muslims have lived in the Americas since the slave trade, the Muslim American community has grown numeri-cally and in visibility since 1965. There are many forms of and approaches to Islam, inflected by factors ranging from country of origin to individual piety. While many American Muslims in the United States became assimilated, the children in more traditional Muslim families often faced similar challenges, regardless of country of origin, principally related to the negotiation of American popular culture and public space.

Observant Muslim families in the United States took care to preserve Islamic customs in their homes, observing life-cycle rituals and dietary rules. They founded schools to ensure that children learned Arabic and studied the Qur'an, included events for children in celebrations for Ramadan and other holidays, and followed Qur'anic instructions to love their children and teach them self-respect. In an American context, however, Muslim parents also had to decide exactly how to allow their children to interact with American popular cul-ture. Individual parents made decisions for their own families, but just as conservative Christians created an alternate popular culture for their youth, Muslims produced Muslim video games, Internet sites, and even a Muslim doll to compete with Barbie. Children in some families were encouraged to partici-pate in prayer five times daily, but that practice as well as holi-day observance and dietary rules proved problematic in the public schools. Children missed school for religious holidays; prayer times sometimes overlapped with class time; and in order to avoid unacceptable meat (that which is not halal meat), children avoided school meals, which limited their access to public aid and made them notably different from their classmates. Similarly, clothing caused problems, as physi-cal education uniforms often did not meet Muslim standards for modesty, particularly for women.

Negotiation of these problems continued into the twenty-first century, as Muslim communities and public schools sought solutions. Aside from policy problems, however, observant Muslim students can feel like outsiders: for instance, observant girls often chose not to wear *hijab* because, even when they were not openly mocked for the practice, looking so different put them on the outside of the social circle, making it difficult to maintain a spiritual practice and be socially accepted. Similarly, Muslim children reported feeling depressed and socially excluded during the anti-Islamic outbursts that followed September 11, 2001.

## Religion, Moral Formation, and Children's Literature

While there are children growing up in many different American religious cultures, there are commonalities of experience among them. A central feature of childhood in twentieth-century America came in the form of literature written specifically for children. Sometimes the literature was explicitly religious, but often the most popular texts used religious themes that were embedded in stories that were not overtly religious. For instance, in 1950, the British Anglican author C. S. Lewis wrote *The Lion, the Witch, and the Wardrobe,* the first of *The Chronicles of Narnia* series. *The Lion, the Witch, and the Wardrobe* is a fantasy novel in which four children enter an enchanted land through the back of an old wardrobe, but it is also a Christological tale in which a magical land is saved by a Christ figure, who is both sacrificed and resurrected. According to *Time* magazine, *The Lion, the Witch, and the Wardrobe* was one of the best English-language children's novels of the twentieth century, and while it is hard to state precisely how it has shaped children's spiritual or moral thinking, it is also part of a genre of widely read books. Madeline L'Engle, an American and liberal Episcopalian author, won the Newberry Medal award in 1963 for her science fiction novel *A Wrinkle in Time.* While L'Engle's Christianity, as portrayed in the novel, is somewhat unconventional, the book tells the story of a battle against darkness, using biblical references, references to God and Jesus, and supernatural figures who are occasionally read as angels. Indeed, the strong Christian home and family of Bushnell's Christian nurture provides an ideal throughout all of L'Engle's work, particularly in her less supernatural and theological work.

Not all literature that presents children with tales featuring morality and the fight of good against evil is inherently Christian. That does not mean, however, that such stories are not important in the shaping of American children. Susan Cooper's *The Dark Is Rising* series, written in the 1960s and 1970s, uses the myths of ancient England as the moral framework. Philip Pullman, the British atheist who authored *The Golden Compass,* was inspired by John Milton's *Paradise Lost.* His novels, which were written beginning in the 1990s for an adolescent market, deal with both the fall of man and with a corrupt church. The resulting books are concerned with both what Pullman refers to as the school of morals and with the dangers of conventional religion. Most famously, and deeply embedded in controversy both in their depiction of witchcraft and about the role of marketing in children's literature, are the Harry Potter books, a series of seven fantasy novels published between 1997 and 2007. While J. K. Rowling makes no explicit religious claims in the books, a pervasive theme throughout the series is the contrast between doing what is right and what is easy, acceptable, or politically expedient. In her 2008 commencement address at Harvard University, she spoke about the role of imagination in moral formation. All of these books have been popular examples of serial fiction, all in a similar literary genre, and they help to shape the moral and/or spiritual experience of children and adolescents. (Indeed, all of the authors deal with themes of adolescent sexuality at some point in their texts.) They are important cultural productions in the spiritual lives of children.

**See also** *Education* entries; *Evangelicals: Nineteenth Century; Literature: Contemporary; Music: Contemporary Christian; Spirituality* entries.

Samira Mehta

## BIBLIOGRAPHY

Applegate, Debby. *The Most Famous Man in America: The Biography of Henry Ward Beecher.* New York: Doubleday, 2006.

Bendroth, Margaret Lamberts. *Growing Up Protestant: Parents, Children, and Mainline Churches.* New Brunswick, N.J.: Rutgers University Press, 2002.

Beste, Jennifer. "The Status of Children within the Roman Catholic Church." In *Children and Childhood in American Religions,* edited by Don S. Browing and Bonnie J. Miller-McLemore. New Brunswick, N.J.: Rutgers University Press, 2009.

Bradstreet, Anne. *The Poems of Mrs. Anne Bradstreet (1612–1672): Together with Her Prose Remains.* Boston: Charles Eliot Norton, Frank Easton Hopkins, The Duodecimos, 1897.

Byrne, Julie. *Oh God of Players: The Story of the Immaculata Mighty Macs.* New York: Columbia University Press, 2003.

Dolan, Jay. *The American Catholic Experience: A History from Colonial Times to the Present.* New York: Doubleday, 1985.

Dorff, Elliot N. "Judaism and Children in the United States." In *Children and Childhood in American Religions,* edited by Don S. Browing and Bonnie J. Miller-McLemore. New Brunswick, N.J.: Rutgers University Press, 2009.

Gilkes, Cheryl Townsend. "The Black Church and Children." In *Children and Childhood in American Religions,* edited by Don S. Browing and Bonnie J. Miller-McLemore. New Brunswick, N.J.: Rutgers University Press, 2009.

Goen, C. C. *The Great Awakening.* Vol. 4 of *The Works of Jonathan Edwards.* New Haven, Conn.: Yale University Press, 1972.

Greven, Philip. *The Protestant Temperament: Patterns of Child Rearing, Religious Experience, and the Self in Early America.* New York: Knopf, 1977.

Hall, David D. *Worlds of Wonder: Days of Judgment: Popular Religious Beliefs in Early New England.* Cambridge, Mass.: Harvard University Press, 1989.

Holifield, E. Brooks. *The Covenant Sealed: The Development of Puritan Sacramental Theology in Old and New England, 1570–1720.* New Haven, Conn.: Yale University Press, 1974.

Luhr, Eileen. *Witnessing Suburbia: Conservatives and Christian Youth Culture.* Berkeley: University of California Press, 2009.

McGreevy, John T. *Catholicism and American Freedom: A History.* New York: Norton, 2003.

Miller, Laura. "Far from Narnia: Philip Pullman's Secular Fantasy for Children." *The New Yorker,* December 26, 2005.

Orsi, Robert A. "Material Children: Making God's Presence Real for Catholic Boys and Girls and for the Adults in Relation to Them." In *Between Heaven and Earth: The Religious Worlds That People Make and the Scholars That Study Them.* Princeton, N.J.: Princeton University Press, 2005.

Sarna, Jonathan. *American Judaism: A History.* New Haven, Conn.: Yale University Press, 2004.

Slater, Peter G. "'From the Cradle to the Coffin': Parental Bereavement and the Shadow of Infant Damnation in Puritan Society." In *Growing Up in America: Children in Historical Perspective,* edited by N. Ray Hinter and Joseph M. Hawes. Urbana: University of Illinois Press, 1985.

Smith, Christian, and Melina Lundquist Denton. *Soul Searching: The Religious and Spiritual Lives of American Teenagers.* New York: Oxford University Press, 2005.

Smith, Jane I. "Children in American Islam." In *Children and Childhood in American Religions,* edited by Don S. Browing and Bonnie J. Miller-McLemore. New Brunswick, N.J.: Rutgers University Press, 2009.

Williams, Raymond Brady. "Hindu Children in the United States." In *Children and Childhood in American Religions,* edited by Don S. Browing and Bonnie J. Miller-McLemore. New Brunswick, N.J.: Rutgers University Press, 2009.

# Christian Science

Christian Science is an indigenous American religious movement founded by Mary Baker Eddy (1821–1910), author of its textbook, *Science and Health with Key to the Scriptures* (1875), and founder, first pastor, and continuing leader of the Church of Christ, Scientist (1879). In the latter half of the nineteenth century, a battle for the hearts and minds of American Protestants between explanations found in secular science and religion motivated new approaches to spiritual explanation, resulting in movements such as Christian Science. Christian Science emerged at a time also marked by a growing interest in spiritual and mental healing, at a juncture between stern Protestantism and religious liberalism. Christian Scientists view Jesus' teachings and his method of healing as scientific demonstrations of divine law, not as supernatural interventions. This law is spiritual, not material, and Christian Scientists believe that it sets aside the claims of material law, obliterating and destroying in human experience all that is unlike God.

## Mary Baker Eddy: Formative Years

Born in 1821 in Bow, New Hampshire, Mary Morse Baker was the youngest of the six children of Mark Baker and Abigail Ambrose. Brought up in a strict religious household,

Mary Baker Eddy founded the indigenous American religious movement Christian Science and is the author of its textbook, *Science and Health with Key to the Scriptures.*

she joined the Congregational Trinitarian Church in 1838, though she rejected the Calvinist dogma of eternal damnation. Eddy later wrote that from her childhood she was impelled by a desire for a knowledge of God as the great relief from human woe, higher and better than matter. Her father was a strict Calvinist who emphasized judgment day and punishment, and her mother was a sympathetic heart who advised her to lean on God's love and seek his guidance through prayer. Her subsequent formulation of Christian Science would reiterate these gendered ideas in her conception of the Father-Mother God. Frail in her early life, she also suffered the loss of her mother and favorite brother in her early adulthood. Married in 1843 to George Glover, she returned home after he died within six months. Widowed with a child at the age of twenty-two, she spent the next two decades battling invalidism. In 1851 her ill health and family troubles caused her only son to move in with another family, who later moved away with him in 1856. She married again in 1853 to itinerant dentist Daniel Patterson but could not travel with him, and she was bedridden for most of the next eight years. In her search for relief, she adopted Graham's pure food cure; visited Dr. Vail's Hydropathic Institute in 1861; studied traditional medicine, homeopathy (using dilutions to heal with substances that would cause symptoms in a healthy person), and mesmerism (healing through the manipulation of magnetic vital forces); and visited Dr. Phineas P. Quimby several times between 1862 and 1865. It was Quimby who had an important effect on her health and well-being. During this time her literary aspirations began to emerge and mature as she contributed poems and incidental narratives to local newspapers and periodicals.

Phineas Quimby, a clockmaker and early student of mesmerism, believed that disease had a mental cause. To him, the impressionable "spiritual matter" of the human mind was the origin of both disease and its cure. He experimented with several methods, including animal magnetism, clairvoyance, and hypnotism, until he developed a suggestive talking cure where he simply sat by his patients, told them what he thought was their disease, and his explanations were the cure. Quimby believed that disease was a deception held in the mind and that the mind could chemically change the body. Through his method of correcting the patient's "errors," he supposed he could change the fluids of the system and establish health. He believed his experiments would be scientifically verified. Eddy was helped by him and continued to explore mental causation, lectured about Quimby's methods, opposing them to deism and spiritualism,

and attempted to recast his techniques into a Christian framework.

Several months after Quimby's death, Mrs. Patterson had a severe fall on the ice in February 1866 on her way to a temperance meeting. It was this event that she later claimed led to her discovery of the decisive curative power of a spiritual understanding of the scriptures. After reading an account of Jesus' healing, she experienced a powerful moment of recognition that life and reality were spiritual and glimpsed the sole reality of the spiritual nature of God: life. She believed this understanding of God's presence healed her. Soon after the experience Patterson deserted her (she was officially divorced in 1873). Socially dislocated, Mrs. Patterson relied on the kindness of friends and family and moved often into boarding houses across New England, all the while studying the scriptures in order to understand and clarify her new conviction that she had discovered the scientific laws of God, revealing Jesus' miracles as demonstrations of the healing power of divine mind.

Her understanding evolved slowly over the next few years. In 1867, students and patients began calling on her to teach them her method and heal them. By 1869 she completed writing her first manuscripts and began teaching organized classes based on them in Lynn, Massachusetts. In 1875 she published a more complete statement of her methodology in her book *Science and Health*.

## Healing Theology

Eddy taught that creation was a dynamic unfolding of God's individual spiritual ideas; revelation was how this process appeared to humanity. Eddy considered the explanation of creation in Genesis chapter 1 to be the spiritual account of God's creation, while the second chapter contained the mortal or material view of creation. The platform of Christian Science rests on discovery of the facts of being as the revelation of absolute truth, making Christian Science closer to evangelical thinking than other mind cure or New Thought theologies. As humans discover their essential spiritual nature of being as the "image and likeness of God," the divine order or kingdom of heaven is revealed with the force of divine law, destroying sin and healing the sick.

Eddy defined God with seven synonyms in *Science and Health*: "infinite Mind, Spirit, Soul, Principle, Life, Truth, Love." Since God is infinite spirit, the only intelligence of the universe, including man, God's true creation cannot be seen by the material senses. In fact, matter itself is ultimately unreal. God is one mind, the only self-existence, and spiritual man is his eternal image or expression. Much like the sunray partakes of the essence of the sun and yet is not the sun, God and man are inexplicably bound together as mind and idea. God, the divine ego, expresses himself in man. As the human yields to this divine mandate, it is saved from the bondage of mortality.

Eddy rejected pantheism—spirit does not enter matter, it supplants its claim to reality: the visible universe and material man are counterfeits of spiritual reality. The material senses, as faculties of "mortal mind," lie to humanity and claim to have power as sin, disease, and death. These are rooted in false beliefs about the nature of creation and exist only in relationship to the lack of human understanding of God's active spiritual law. Christian Science teaches that an understanding of humanity's spiritual relationship to God dispels the claims of the senses and destroys any false claims of "error"—of evil, sin, and sickness. Eddy believed that this was Jesus' method: the savior saw man as God's image and likeness, and this correct view healed the sick and sinning.

Jesus was human, born of a virgin, and "appointed" to appear to humanity in a form they could both understand and perceive. Thus, he was the exemplar, the embodiment of the Christ, God's divine manifestation that actively dispels the illusions of the senses. Moreover, Christian Scientists acknowledge Jesus' atonement, demonstrated in healing the sick and sinning, and overcoming death in resurrection. To be born again means to realize one's true spiritual identity, distinct in the mind that is God, and to constantly bring human thought into an awareness of this spiritual reality.

While the healing of sin remained the goal of Christian Science, healing of the body and the empirical evidence that ensued were powerful advertising. Christian Science practitioners, who practice the Christian Science method full-time, could be called upon to help patients in the healing process through scientific prayer, and paid for their help, making the public practice of Christian Science attractive to students, many of them women. By 1958 there were nearly eleven thousand officially recognized by the church, 90 percent of whom were women. Christian Science teachers, authorized by a board of education that inherited its responsibilities from the earlier Massachusetts Metaphysical College, teach yearly classes of not more than thirty pupils, thus creating and maintaining a cohesive community of student associations that convene annually.

Christian Science conquers "error" by denying its claims to truth. Healing is accomplished through an understanding that disease and any claims of evil are only beliefs or illusions of mortal mind, a limited material view, and practitioners turn from the evidence of the senses in order to accept the consciousness of divine truth and love, so disease will "vanish into its native nothingness." They might argue mentally until they are receptive to accepting the ever-present perfection of the divine mind and its expression: man, in Christian Science, is complete, intact, and flawless in every detail because he is perfectly created, intelligently governed, and tenderly cared for by infinite love. God is omnipotent; therefore there can be no cause and effect other than perfect God and perfect man. Nothing can exist and there is no substance that is contrary to God's nature as divine principle, life, truth, and love. Christian Scientists believe that this type of mental argumentation leads to an understanding of the action of God's law that restores spiritual sense to human consciousness.

## The Church of Christ, Scientist

Though early attempts at proselytizing were problematic and even litigious, Eddy organized the Christian Scientist Association (CSA) of her students in 1876 and continued teaching. In 1877 she married her student and public practitioner of her method, Asa Eddy: he was an important soul mate but died five years later. In 1878 and 1879 Eddy preached in the vestry of the Tabernacle Baptist Church in Boston, but by April 1879 members of her association voted to organize their own church. Its function was to commemorate the word and works of Jesus, including reinstating primitive Christianity with its lost element of healing.

By 1881, the focus of the new movement shifted to Boston, then center of intellectual and religious life in the United States, where Eddy, at the age of sixty, became the church's first official pastor. A year earlier, she had founded and chartered the Massachusetts Metaphysical College, where she and her students held classes into 1889, graduating nearly six hundred students. In Boston Eddy attracted attention among middle-class women, religious seekers from Protestant denominations, and businesspeople. Christian Science has always attracted a large female following—more than 75 percent of the overall membership. Founded by a woman, it offered women relief from suffering and a public profession as healers, readers, and teachers that reinforced the traditional role of women as caregivers, often with significant remuneration. The theology of the Father/Mother God was also undoubtedly attractive to women, and early Christian Science periodicals often focused on women's issues. Eddy chose many of the more dynamic pupils of her college, many of them women, to disseminate her teachings across the United States. In 1884 she taught a class in Chicago, where other mind cure organizations were proliferating, that helped demonstrate the Christian basis of her teachings. Often in her preaching Eddy emphasized the differences between Christian Science and other spiritual healing methods, since many of her students had defected to form their own New Thought groups (which taught the prosperity gospel and positive thinking "mind cure"), even if there were commonalities between their teachings. Emma Curtis Hopkins, who served as editor of the *Christian Science Journal* in 1884–1885, broke away to found the Christian Science Theological Institute in Chicago in the late 1880s and taught many of the subsequent founders of New Thought groups.

The Christian Science church, with its new institutes, academies, and branches spreading across the West, began attracting critical attention in the local and national newspapers and popular periodicals. Its own publishing society was operating by 1883 and issued the bimonthly *Journal of Christian Science.* Soon it was a monthly periodical called the *Christian Science Journal,* with a circulation of ten thousand. By 1886 the National Christian Scientist Association of students was formed. It met yearly through 1890 and established the first reading room in Boston in 1888. By 1890 Eddy dissolved much of the organization, and she removed herself to Concord, New Hampshire, in 1892.

Eddy was a careful organizer. In 1892 the Church of Christ (Scientist) was reorganized with a corporate structure based on a Deed of Trust for the purpose of building a church edifice. The Mother Church polity, once democratically based, was founded on new business models, governed by Eddy, a self-perpetuating board of directors, all male at the time, and twelve first members (whose power was given to the directors exclusively in 1901). New branch churches continued enjoying democratic self-rule. But for the Mother Church, a democratic organizational model would be particularly unwieldy for a growing far-flung international organization. Christian Science was enjoying the limelight at the 1893 World's Parliament of Religions in Chicago, with students of Eddy invited to address a plenary session and hold their own congress. Eddy was in Concord working on her collaborative art project, the painting/poem book *Christ and Christmas,* with illustrative figurative paintings by James Gilman punctuating Eddy's poem, published that year. She was also busy overseeing the planning of the first edifice of the Mother Church in Boston. Completed in late 1894,

the Romanesque revival edifice sparked a building boom across the United States that lasted into the 1920s. The original edifice was soon outgrown, and the members of the Mother Church built a grand extension: a domed classical revival auditorium church rising 224 feet above the street, seating more than four thousand, completed in 1906. Branch churches in their urban settings were often quite distinctive, inspired by the classical revival architecture of Chicago's World's Columbian Exposition of 1893, with imposing Greek classical porches and Roman domes of art glass that gathered the faithful in acoustically superior auditoriums.

The church continued to focus on creating a distinctive identity that became increasingly standardized in the 1890s, particularly with the publication of *The Manual of the Mother Church* in 1895. The *Manual,* which Eddy claimed was divinely inspired, established the rules and standards of the organization and was continually revised by her until her death in 1910. While some of its bylaws were clearly conceived to curb possible rival students, such as Augusta Stetson in New York, the *Manual* nonetheless became an important document in transitioning the church from Eddy's charismatic leadership into an impersonal, legal, institutional form.

In 1895 Eddy ordained the Bible and *Science and Health* the impersonal pastor of the Mother Church and later its branches. This impersonal pastor would safeguard against the heresy that could creep into personal preaching. Thereafter, lay readers, a man and woman, would carry out the worship services in the Mother Church with hymns, scripture reading, suitable music, and a lesson-sermon: selections from the Bible and *Science and Health.* The services ended with a repetition of the scientific statement of being from *Science and Health,* which is still repeated today every Sunday in Christian Science churches:

> There is no life, truth, intelligence, nor substance in matter. All is infinite Mind and its infinite manifestation, for God is All-in-all. Spirit is immortal Truth; matter is mortal error. Spirit is the real and eternal; matter is the unreal and temporal. Spirit is God, and man is His image and likeness. Therefore man is not material; he is spiritual. (P. 468)

Lessons from the Bible and *Science and Health* were established informally by 1888, followed in 1890 with the *Christian Science Quarterly Bible Lessons,* the first subjects adapted from the International Sunday-school Bible lessons, until new topics were introduced in 1898. Also in 1895 a Board of Missionaries was established, replaced by the Board of Lectureship in 1898. The latter provided itinerant lecturers to serve the Christian Science field.

Taking over from the Massachusetts Metaphysical College was a Board of Education, established in 1898 to teach primary (foundational) and normal (teaching) classes. A Committee on Publication responsible for discussing and defending Christian Science in the press was also instituted. Other periodicals also began coming off the presses: the *Christian Science Weekly,* renamed the *Christian Science Sentinel,* in 1898; *Der Herold der Christian Science,* in 1903; and the *Christian Science Monitor,* in 1908. In 1904 Eddy provided for Christian Science organizations on college campuses. The first was at Harvard University.

The standardization of services, publications aimed at the educated middle class, the equal representation of men and women in the pulpits, as well as the new distinctive edifices being built by Christian Science congregations in cities and towns demonstrated to many that Christian Science was well organized and here to stay. Certainly the growing reputation of the *Christian Science Monitor* as a reform-minded international daily paper revealed that the church had a larger mission. Eddy had earlier authorized the opening of Christian Science Dispensaries in 1889, to help anyone without charge. There were thirty such dispensaries when they were closed in 1894. By 1900 Eddy instructed all branch churches to provide public reading rooms, popular with other publishers at the time, so that authorized literature published by the church could be made available in quiet meditative spaces in the bustling business districts of American towns and cities.

## Broader Contexts of Appeal

Christian Science emerged in Gilded Age America at a time of a critical redefinition of religion, as well as a time of growing interest in science. Evangelical Protestantism was increasingly divided over doctrinal distinctions and social functions, unprepared for the rise of industrialism and threats to its cultural hegemony. Catholicism was growing, as was Judaism, and populations were migrating to cities. Christian Science offered an antidote to this fragmentation, decisively positioning itself as the new/old gospel of primitive Christianity and emphasizing Jesus' healing mission as practical in a time when conventional medical therapeutics were often ineffective or even harmful. It was also attractive to women, who were given equality within a church that

valued their self-sufficiency. The vast majority of public practitioners were women, who took their traditional healing role from the home into the public sphere.

Other currents paved the way for Christian Science's rapid growth. Transcendentalism injected an intuitive spirit and a recognition of the spark of the divine in humanity into the purely rational scientism that permeated the Enlightenment. Spiritualism indicated a broader social interest in the materialization of psychic phenomena and the next life. In the larger context of an interest in evolution and vitalism, as opposed to deistic and mechanistic explanations, Christian Science, made up chiefly of members from evangelical churches, espoused a method for humanity to progress and grow spiritward, beyond materialism. And Christian Science's idealism was nonetheless pragmatic: it claimed that to empirically witness a healing of sickness or sin indicated this spiritual growth. Periodicals were filled with testimonials—more than fifty thousand published since the beginning of the movement—and every week Christian Science congregations gathered at their testimony meetings that encouraged them to publicly testify to Christian Science's efficacy. One critique from 1912 suggested that Christian Science's gospel of healing, its religious message, its monistic idealism, its anti-materialistic spirit, its notable originator, as well as the responsive practical mind of the American people, were the reasons for its success.

Christian Science was widely criticized from the pulpit and from the medical establishment. Critics claimed that the new religious and healing movement was a fad, a mask for commerce, a haven for the affluent, an irrational female system, a modern doctrine of subjective idealism (only mind exists), a Gnosticism (spiritual knowledge that frees our divine souls from material bondage), a neo-Hegelianism (God is all substance), and a gloss of Swedenborg (emphasizing spiritual reality and the spiritual interpretation of scripture), among other criticisms. Many criticized the movement for its lack of social activism, which it began to significantly address during wartime.

Christian Science and the implication of its practice to medicine became increasingly an issue. Court cases establishing the difference between prayer and medical treatment were many. While some physicians recognized that Christian Science contributed to healing the nervousness of American women, they balked at its claims to heal organic disease. By 1911, under pressure from an increasingly powerful American Medical Association, Congress was on the verge of prohibiting the practice of Christian Science throughout the

United States, and many feared that Eddy's attitudes about hygiene and contagion were a threat to public sanitation and health. But Christian Scientists began winning court cases, particularly as they not only argued for the efficacy of their method of spiritual healing but defended their constitutional right to religious freedom.

What many clergymen feared was early Christian Science's rapid growth and the conversion of many of their own congregations' prominent members to the new church. The movement continued to develop into a mainstream denomination, through committed memberships whose influence was greater than their numbers might indicate. Due to her students' gratification over sizeable early growth, Eddy forbade the reporting of membership figures, so estimates varied widely. From a Mother Church with 26 members in 1879, by 1906 there were more than 85,000 members. In the late 1920s and into the 1930s, a church or society was being formed every week. The 1926 United States Census counted 1,913 groups, with a membership of more than 200,000, of whom 94 percent were urban and 75.5 percent were women. In 1936 there were more than 2,600 branch churches and societies worldwide, nearly 50 college organizations (which expanded to 200 by 1958), almost 11,000 practitioners, and more than 500 nurses. The 1936 United States census reported nearly 270,000 members in more than 2,100 churches in the United States, and the membership continued to grow. By 1958 there were more than 2,300 congregations in the United States and 700 in other countries, probably peaking with nearly 475,000 members. Since that time there has been a fairly precipitous decline. In 2008, the membership was possibly 200,000 worldwide, with 1,250 congregations in the United States and 500 in other countries, with some new growth in Africa and South America.

## A Religion of the Word

Spiritual healing and new practices of worship created a distinctive religious community and a distinctive Christian Science subjectivity. This was partly a matter of the economic and cultural profile of church members, who were typically literate and middle-class women and men, at least in the great American cities. Indeed, it was largely through extensive publishing activity that the teachings of Christian Science reached the existing membership and new converts. Literature distribution was one of the most popular committees in many branch churches, providing young people social outlets that were church related. All members kept abreast of the publications and bought numerous editions of *Science and Health,* which had more than 225 editions, as Eddy was ever refining and clarifying her writing. This emphasis on the divine and revelatory Word, whether on the printed page or read in the church, was not merely a matter of communication; it was an exercise of a power tantamount to spiritual healing. Even Mark Twain, Christian Science's most acerbic critic in the early twentieth century wrote in *Christian Science* that it was "the first time since the dawn-days of Creation that a Voice has gone crashing through space with such placid and complacent confidence and command" (p. 3).

Christian Science was most radically a religion of the Word, of reading and speaking, with crucial implications for the acoustics of their churches. These edifices were stages upon which the faithful reiterated the Word of God, revealed to reconnect the congregations with the sources of primitive Christianity, with signs following. While early edifices often featured symbolic elements such as the cross and crown motif that embellished the covers of *Science and Health* as well as stained glass windows, most congregations began to eschew overt Christian symbolism by the early 1920s. With the Bible and *Science and Health* the only preachers, quotations from the Bible and Eddy (she limited churches to one out of three specific quotations) became the primary decoration on the walls of branch churches. Eddy's ideas were visionary and dramatic. The reading of the Word became the liturgy, and church services in increasingly impressive edifices allowed the congregations to contemplate the grander verities of spirit, through Christian Science, clearly inscribed in the logic of their church buildings, often under soaring domes of art glass.

Eddy was often criticized for what some critics thought were her prosaic, illogical, and sometimes contradictory statements in *Science and Health.* But her style, expressed through literary, philosophical, and religious tropes and metaphors, was to her an ethical gesture at the service of spiritual truths that she felt could not be adequately expressed in material language. She often addressed the beliefs of mortal mind based in material existence; she addressed the human mind as the relative battleground of suffering and overcoming, where the action of the divine mind through Christ appeared. She also contemplated an absolute realm of spirit, where the divine mind, the true and only reality, knows nothing of sin, disease, and death, thus destroying the beliefs of mortal mind in the human realm. The mortal, the human, and the divine seem to exist, but only the divine truly exists. These ideas led to apparent inconsistencies in her writings, because while mortal mind claims reality, through "animal magnetism," sensuality, sin, and so forth, the human mind is redeemable, and the divine mind has no need of redemption.

These ideas and strongly worded statements became the fundamental basis for disciplined spiritual healing. The Word revealed spiritual ideas and supplanted a material sense of language with the enunciation or utterance of spiritual truth, transforming material appearances through the healing of sin and sickness. Christian Scientists studied the Bible and Eddy's writings daily and in their church services in a sacramental way, for they led the student to understand eternal spiritual truths demonstrated in physical healing and well-being. In Christian Science, the language of the Bible and Eddy's writings were utilized as an autonomous and divine discourse, which aided the student in the realization of the perfect spiritual subject that reflected the perfection of the divine principle, God, even though human language was at best feeble in its ability to describe the infinite beauty and intelligence of the spiritual. The language of Christian Science was found in the "new tongue," which Eddy defined in her 1886 sermon "Christian Healing" as the spiritual language of soul instead of the senses, translating matter into its original language of mind, thus giving a spiritual instead of a material signification.

Eddy's rhetorical strategies in her writings were highly metaphorical and, like Swedenborg, created corresponding spiritual meanings that became the language of Christian Science. Terminology was reinforced through relationships with other members, teachers, and practitioners and through the continuous reiterations from the official texts. Within this discourse, individual freedom and reason were emphasized within fairly strict moral codes, including chastity and temperance, though the renouncing of pleasure through the senses was to ensure pleasure in a different spiritual form. The disciplined argumentative method of Christian Science attempted to prove the scientific lawfulness of Christian spirituality as opposed to its supernaturalness, and claimed the beneficial redemptive healing effect of this spirituality. Living the active spiritual discipline of Christian Science created a process of regeneration through which the reality of God's spiritual creation appeared.

## The Church Matures

Into the twentieth century, the Christian Science church grew steadily in members, influence, and respectability,

even though challenges to its healing method continued. As media attention lessened after Eddy's death, the church began to foster an image of quiet, disciplined spirituality, an emphasis on traditional family values, respect of authority and legal systems, and multigenerational reliance on spiritual healing in families that felt sustained by their religion even in a generally unsupportive social milieu. A new publishing society was built in 1934; subscriptions to and advertising revenues from the *Monitor* increased; and by the early 1960s a vision for a new sixteen-acre complex as headquarters began to take shape, centered on the Mother Church and its extension with a grand new entrance portal and flanked by the publishing house. Completed in 1973, the plan included an office building, a Sunday school building, a twenty-eight-story administration building, and a 670-by-100-foot reflecting pool covering a parking garage.

Also important was the creation of other institutions to care for members' needs. In 1916 the directors established the Christian Science Benevolent Association, one of Eddy's last requests, to maintain places to care for ailing and aged Christian Scientists and create a nurses training program to help minister to Christian Scientists in need. A sanatorium in Chestnut Hill, Massachusetts, was opened in 1919; Pleasant View Home in Concord, New Hampshire, was established in 1927; and the Christian Science Benevolence Association on the Pacific Coast, in San Francisco, was opened in 1930. Several such institutions were also established in the United Kingdom.

Not quite a decade after Eddy's death, leadership challenges to the *Manual* model erupted in the "Great Litigation" or suit in equity. The lawsuits divided the church between the trustees of the Christian Science Publishing Society and the Christian Science Board of Directors between 1919 and 1921, but Eddy's form of church government prevailed. Schisms did occur, such as Augusta Stetson's short-lived "Church Triumphant" and British teacher Annie C. Bill's "Church of the Universal Design," the latter of which advocated a policy of cooperation with medical doctors, and had nearly eighty congregations by the 1930s, though none exist today.

Wartime challenged the church to become increasingly pragmatic. The church established a Relief Fund in Europe between 1914 and 1919, with committees throughout Britain and in France, Switzerland, Holland, and Italy that distributed food, clothing, and more than $2 million to those Christian Scientists and other citizens negatively affected by the war. When the United States entered the war, ten commissioned chaplains served the active armed forces, and Christian Science camp welfare centers were located in Army camps in thirty states.

Christian Scientists officially denounced fascism and defended the democratic system at their annual meeting in 1941, and soon after the gestapo in Germany closed all of the ninety Christian Science churches and reading rooms, arrested members for questioning, and banned public and private meetings. Profession of Christian Science was forbidden. Church services continued in private, and some could hear radio broadcasts of the Mother Church services: radio had been introduced in the early 1920s, with expanded testimonial programming on radio and then television beginning in 1953.

The Mother Church became a registered relief agency during World War II and worked through appointed and local wartime committees between 1939 and 1946. By the end of the war in 1945, more than 378 ministers and chaplains and other workers had served Christian Scientists in the armed forces in the United States and Britain. The camp welfare committees maintained 222 service rest centers on bases in the allied nations, as well as one in Hamburg, Germany, and several in France, Italy, and Belgium that helped reestablish Christian Science activities after the war.

## Christian Science since the Later Twentieth Century

With the rise of improved medical care, and the growth of secularism and religious skepticism, by the 1979 centennial of the founding of the church the relevance of Christian Science's late-nineteenth-century religious language and formulations, approach to scientific terminology, and emphasis on spiritual healing began to be challenged as church membership declined. The 1980s witnessed a new media public relations push by the Boston leadership, who began amassing a media empire that some members felt was at odds with the church's religious mission. Between 1988 and 1993, unable to popularize the daily *Monitor,* they spent hundreds of millions of dollars to diversify into radio, television, cable, and Internet publishing. The church bought an international short-wave radio network, produced excellently reviewed radio and cable television news programs, owned a local Boston television channel, and started *World Monitor,* a glossy monthly news magazine that struggled to find an audience. The church lost more than $325 million on these ventures.

Debates and scandal erupted when the Board of Directors, attracted by a possible $97 million bequest that would expire in 1993 if they did not act, published the book of popular but esoteric teacher and lecturer Bliss Knapp in 1991. Entitled *The Destiny of the Mother Church* (written and privately printed in the 1940s but rejected by church leaders at that time), it proposed that Eddy had been prophesied in the Bible, an idea anathema to most Christian Scientists, who had been warned constantly during their lifetime against any deification of their person. However, these ideas appeared to be supported by a 1943 official pamphlet, and several influential Christian Science teachers had started their own independent groups based on these ideas. Though around five hundred reading rooms refused to carry the book, and members debated and publicly criticized the leadership, the church received $50 million, which offset losses from the media projects.

Other controversies challenged the church. Both federal and state governments and insurance companies have long recognized Christian Science healing. The late 1980s and 1990s saw increased consideration of the issue of the care of children, due to the public outcry over illnesses and deaths of several children receiving Christian Science treatment, brought to the media's attention by one-time church members. With court cases mounting, press attention, and grassroots organizing, early laws protecting spiritual healing began to be questioned and overturned. Controversies concerning religious exemption laws, child neglect and endangerment laws, due process, manslaughter statutes, Medicare, and public policy are again affecting the practice of Christian Science healing.

The move into television prompted the church to use non–Christian Science workers, which also revealed certain underlying social prejudices and caused a debate about the presence of gays and lesbians in the church, who had always been part of the movement but had gone unrecognized and were sometimes openly castigated.

Members of the denomination maintain many institutions in common with other Protestant church bodies, and while not supported directly by the Mother Church, these continue the maintenance of a healing community. Today, Christian Scientists support more than forty-five retirement/nursing facilities worldwide. Members formed historical foundations such as Longyear (1938) and Daystar (1990); Christian Science schools and colleges such as Daycroft (1928–1991) and Principia (1898); and youth organizations such as *Monitor* Youth Forums (1946),

Adventure Unlimited (1962–present), and six summer camps (founded between 1915 and 1955). Emergence International (1985) was created to minister to gay and lesbian Christian Scientists, and several financial support networks and foundations are also available for members.

Some critics propose that the Christian Science approach is anachronistic, particularly in light of the increased success of medicine and the rise of popular secular holistic approaches to healing. Recently, even some church members have suggested that other emphases in Eddy's theological thought should be given a more thorough vetting by the church. Others believe that the church, in attempting to create new audiences for *Science and Health,* was modifying its radicalism and becoming more worldly and new age as the movement entered into the twenty-first century and began to participate in secular mind/body conferences. A renewed emphasis on Eddy's *Science and Health,* translated into seventeen languages, caused the textbook to continue to sell well: more than five hundred thousand copies were sold between 1993 and 1998. Its famous cross and crown emblem is now being offered as an official insignia to identify churches, societies, and reading rooms.

Mary Baker Eddy is one of the most controversial of American religious leaders. Biographers since her time have created idealized and hagiographic accounts of her life, negative psycho-biography, broader contextual narratives, feminist and psychoanalytic readings, and have even used biblical prophecy as a method to explain her relevance, often based on spurious secondary and tertiary sources. Reversing decades of secrecy and guardedness towards independent scholars, in 2000 the church announced the redesign of the publishing society building into the Mary Baker Eddy Library for the Betterment of Humanity, intended to emphasize Eddy's feminist credentials and innovative ideas concerning spirituality and health. The church released all of Eddy's papers to public study. The $50 million research library contains more than 525,000 documents, photographs, and objects concerning Eddy's work and legacy, with state-of-the-art exhibition spaces.

The church today is trying to redefine its distinctive mission of positioning spiritual healing as an effective alternative to medical care, though there is some relaxation of earlier church social mores, including allowing members to use medical treatment. The fact that the church's policies and methods were fixed at the time of Eddy's death has remained somewhat problematic for innovation. Both public lectures and reading rooms were tremendously popular

modes of communication for a variety of groups and publishers at the turn of the last century, but today they are not particularly popular modes of publicity.

In an attempt to focus on its healing ministry, the church has recently put several of its Boston complex's buildings up for lease and has sold two of Eddy's former homes to the independent Longyear Foundation, which supports a museum about Eddy and early workers in the movement and already maintains six of her former homes throughout New England.

Today, with the rise of the Internet, the church has several Web sites, some marketed for youth searching for spiritual answers in today's world (spirituality.com). But many independent groups on the Web now promote Eddy and the study of Christian Science outside officialdom, including the Bookmark, the Aequus Institute, Healing Unlimited, the Mary Baker Eddy Institute, and the Christian Science Endtime Center. All of these groups support historical Christian Science study materials as well as publication and distribution activities of teachers and writers outside and sometimes at odds with current church "authorized" literature.

See also *Architecture: New Religious Movements; Esoteric Movements; Harmonialism and Metaphysical Religion; Healing; Idealist Philosophy; New Age Religion(s); New Religious Movements* entries*; Occult and Metaphysical Religion; Positive Thinking; Science; Scientology; Spiritualism; Transcendentalism; Wicca and Witchcraft.*

Paul Eli Ivey

## BIBLIOGRAPHY

Beasley, Norman. *The Continuing Spirit.* New York: Duell, Sloan, and Pearce, 1956.

———. *The Cross and the Crown: The History of Christian Science.* New York: Duell, Sloan, and Pearce, 1952.

Braden, Charles S. *Christian Science Today: Power, Policy and Practice.* Dallas, Tex.: Southern Methodist University, 1958.

Bridge, Susan. *Monitoring the News, The Brilliant Launch and Sudden Collapse of the Monitor Channel.* Armonk, N.Y.: M. E. Sharpe, 1998.

Canham, Erwin D. *Commitment to Freedom: The Story of the Christian Science Monitor.* Boston: Houghton Mifflin, 1958.

*Christian Science: A Sourcebook of Contemporary Materials.* Boston: Christian Science Publishing Society, 1990.

Eddy, Mary Baker. *Manual of the Mother Church, The First Church of Christ, Scientist, in Boston, Massachusetts.* 89th ed. Boston: Christian Science Publishing Society, 1908.

———. *Prose Works Other than Science and Health with Key to the Scriptures.* Boston: Christian Science Publishing Society, 1925.

———. *Science and Health with Key to the Scriptures.* Boston: Christian Science Publishing Society, 1971. (Orig. pub. 1875; final revision, 1906.)

Fraser, Caroline. *God's Perfect Child, Living and Dying in the Christian Science Church.* New York: Henry Holt, 1999.

Gill, Gillian. *Mary Baker Eddy.* Reading, Mass.: Perseus Books, 1998.

Gottschalk, Stephen. *The Emergence of Christian Science in American Religious Life.* Berkeley: University of California Press, 1973.

———. *Rolling Away the Stone, Mary Baker Eddy's Challenge to Materialism.* Bloomington: Indiana University Press, 2006.

Ivey, Paul Eli. *Prayers in Stone: Christian Science Architecture in the United States, 1894–1930.* Urbana: University of Illinois Press, 1999.

Knee, Stuart E. *Christian Science in the Age of Mary Baker Eddy.* Westport, Conn.: Greenwood, 1994.

Peel, Robert. *Christian Science: Its Encounter with American Culture.* New York: Holt, Rinehart and Winston, 1958.

———. *Health and Medicine in the Christian Science Tradition: Principle, Practice and Challenge.* New York: Crossroads, 1989.

———. *Mary Baker Eddy: The Years of Authority.* New York: Holt, Rinehart and Winston, 1977.

———. *Mary Baker Eddy: The Years of Discovery.* New York: Holt, Rinehart and Winston, 1966.

———. *Mary Baker Eddy: The Years of Trial.* New York: Holt, Rinehart and Winston, 1971.

Schoeplfin, Rennie B. *Christian Science on Trial: Religious Healing in America.* Baltimore: Johns Hopkins University Press, 2003.

Smith, Clifford P. *Historical Sketches from the Life of Mary Baker Eddy and the History of Christian Science.* Boston: Christian Science Publishing Society, 1992.

Steiger, Henry W. *Christian Science and Philosophy.* New York: Philosophical Library, 1948.

Twain, Mark. *Christian Science.* New York: Harper and Brothers, 1907.

# Church and State: Revolutionary Period and Early Republic

Church-state issues have been the subject of heated debates throughout much of U.S. history, often focusing on whether the Constitution requires governmental secularism or whether the federal and state governments can support some religious activities or institutions in a land in which an overwhelming majority of citizens say that they believe in God. These debates often center on the manner in which the framers of the U.S. Constitution and the constitutions of the individual states addressed church-state issues during the American Revolution and in the early republic.

## *Church-State History and the Supreme Court*

In a famous Supreme Court case in the 1940s, Justice Hugo Black recounted a common version of the history of church and state in America. It begins with people fleeing to America to escape religious persecution in Europe. On arrival, they found that traditional European church-state patterns were difficult to cast off, and the colonists often failed to leave religious intolerance completely behind, at least in the early years. They even set up a number of state-supported "established" churches. Eventually, the colonials' "freedom-loving nature" led towards recognizing the importance of the liberty of conscience, which paved the way for intolerance to be replaced by religious freedom.

During the Revolutionary Era, thanks to the efforts of Thomas Jefferson and James Madison (who later became the nation's third and fourth presidents), Virginia set an example for the rest of the colonies, and for the new nation, by casting off its legally established Anglican Church. Moreover, Virginia refused to pass even a broader-based, more ecumenical tax to support religion and instead adopted a now-famous Statute for Religious Freedom drafted by Jefferson. A few years later, Madison, the "father of the Constitution" and the principal architect of the federal Bill of Rights, infused this same spirit into the First Amendment's "establishment clause," which says that *"Congress shall make no law respecting an establishment of religion,"* thus creating, in Jefferson's famous phrase, "a wall of separation between church and state."

In this case, *Everson v. Board of Education* (1947), the Court declared that the constitutional "wall of separation between church and state" meant that the federal and state governments could not provide aid to any one religion, nor could they favor religion over nonreligion. This "no aid" standard has come to be called the "strict separationist" approach to the establishment clause, and it has led the Supreme Court to ban many forms of state support for religious schools and to eliminate official prayers and Bible reading in the public schools on the grounds that these activities constitute a forbidden "establishment of religion."

Because this interpretation of the Constitution has generated a great deal of controversy, and because it appears to have been derived by the Supreme Court justices from their understanding of the intentions of the framers of the establishment clause, the *Everson* case triggered an explosion of church-state historical studies. Opposition to the *Everson* Court's "no aid" interpretation has come from those who believe that a better understanding of the framers' intentions leads to the conclusion that federal and state governments can aid religion as long as that aid does not prefer any one religion over the others. This school of thought has generally been labeled "nonpreferentialism" or "accommodationism" (in the sense that it seeks to allow the government to accommodate the American people's religiosity).

Meanwhile, a third school of thought has argued that both strict separationists and nonpreferentialists have missed the point. For this group, a significant element of the establishment clause's original meaning was to keep the federal government from interfering with the state-supported churches that existed in New England at the time of the Bill of Rights. Looking specifically at the text of the clause, which reads, "Congress shall make no law *respecting* [that is, on the subject of] an establishment of religion," these scholars assert that any law on the general subject of religious establishments—irrespective of whether that law is proestablishment or antiestablishment—would be forbidden. That is, Congress was rendered impotent to interfere with "establishments of religion" in places such as Massachusetts, where many towns collected taxes for the benefit of local (usually Congregational) churches. Accordingly, the clause should be read to insulate the way the states choose to organize their church-state affairs from anything Congress might do.

This "hands-off" approach to the establishment clause has been called "enhanced-federalism" because it bolsters the broader concept of federalism that many scholars have associated with the entire design of the Constitution itself. "Federalism" is a complicated subject, but it generally revolves around the notion that the federal government, having been created by the state governments, possesses only the specific powers that have been expressly delegated to it by the states, thus leaving the states with all governmental power to make laws except to the extent that the Constitution specifically provides otherwise. In this case, the power to decide whether to have an establishment of religion was not delegated to the federal government in the Constitution, and therefore the basic principle of federalism should mean that Congress has no power either to establish a religion or to interfere with religious establishments in the states. The enhanced-federalism approach takes this argument one step further by saying that the addition of the First Amendment's establishment clause was specifically designed to add another layer of protection for church-state practices in the states, in the event that the Congress might become disposed towards interfering with them.

All three of these interpretations—strict separationism, nonpreferentialism, and enhanced federalism—are built on historical foundations. Their proponents believe that a fair reading of the history surrounding the adoption of the First Amendment leads inescapably to their conclusions.

While the arguments among these schools of thought sometimes seem to split historical hairs, the language of scholarly debate has been unrestrained. "False," "frivolous," and "fiction" are just a few of the epithets hurled by prominent scholars at their distinguished adversaries. In light of the fact that these competing theories of the First Amendment have real economic and political consequences (many millions of dollars of funding for religious schools or other "faith-based" institutions, for example), it is important to recognize that many of the books and articles in this field have been written with the goal of presenting historical events in a light that is most favorable to a particular interpretation of the Constitution. While this kind of goal-oriented history writing is not unique to church-state studies, it is especially pronounced in this field, and so all sources (including this article) should be read with particular care.

In thinking about how the Supreme Court and various other commentators have discussed the original meaning of the Constitution's church-state provisions, it may be valuable to note that only some people agree with Justice Black that history is an important element of constitutional interpretation; many others believe that history is either irrelevant or is merely one of many tools to be applied to the understanding of a constantly evolving Constitution. Even those who think that the original meaning of a constitutional provision *is* important do not necessarily agree on how to employ those historical insights.

And so, while many people who debate church-state issues are "originalists" in that they believe that the Constitution should be interpreted in accordance with its original meaning, they differ in where they look for evidence of that meaning. Some scholars have concentrated on the specific intentions of important framers (as can be seen in the *Everson* case's focus on James Madison and Thomas Jefferson); others are more interested in the meaning of words such as *establishment* in legal or theological writings at the time; and yet another group looks for what the constitutional text would have meant to a fully informed member of the general public (and since it is often impossible to get conclusive evidence of what ordinary citizens thought, modern scholars try to create a hypothetical vision of what those people were likely to have been thinking). In evaluating the various arguments about constitutional meaning, readers should think not only about the historical evidence itself but also how that evidence should be applied to the task of constitutional interpretation.

Ever since the *Everson* case, Americans have become accustomed to having the Supreme Court decide church-state issues involving state and local governments as well as those arising at the national level. Even though the establishment clause only refers to laws made by "Congress," and despite a decision by the Supreme Court early in the nineteenth century that the First Amendment did not apply to state or municipal laws, since the *Everson* era, the Supreme Court has consistently held that states, cities, and towns are now bound by the clause as well. Many of the Court's most prominent church-state decisions over the past century have involved state laws, or even the administrative actions of local school boards, rather than acts of Congress.

The legal theory adopted by the Supreme Court to apply the establishment clause (and other elements of the Bill of Rights) to the states is usually called the "incorporation doctrine." It is based on the Court's argument that when the post–Civil War Congress passed the Fourteenth Amendment to the Constitution, that amendment's "due process" clause (which reads, "nor shall any State deprive any person of life, liberty, or property, without due process of law . . .") included the concept that many of the fundamental rights described in the Bill of Rights (that is, the first ten amendments to the Constitution) would henceforth apply to the state governments. Since most church-state issues in the past two hundred years have involved state and local governments rather than Congress, the incorporation doctrine has been extremely influential in shaping modern American views on how the phrase "the separation of church and state" relates to the Constitution. The incorporation doctrine is very well established in American constitutional jurisprudence at this time, although it has been challenged on historical grounds, especially by those who subscribe to the enhanced-federalism approach to the establishment clause. Their argument is that the original goal of the clause was to insulate the states from federal interference with their church-state decisions and, therefore, that the incorporation doctrine effectively reverses that outcome by subjecting state decision making to Supreme Court review.

Finally, it is important to note that the histories of church-state issues in America almost invariably focus on the generally Northern European Protestant immigrants who constituted almost all of the voting population in colonial America. As a result, these histories completely overlook the Native Americans, large numbers of slaves brought forcibly to North America, indentured servants, and any others who did not voluntarily choose to seek their spiritual or financial fortunes in the New World. In fact, colonial and early national laws and constitutions upholding the principle of religious liberty were sometimes drafted by the same people who wrote the "slave codes" that placed severe restrictions on slaves' religious freedom. There are also few, if any, women's voices heard in the early American church-state debates, since those debates generally involved the men who were the leaders of the churches and the states—that is, those who served as members of the clergy and as legislators.

## Church-State Colonial Background

People left Europe for America in the seventeenth and eighteenth centuries for many reasons, from the desire to "get rich quick" to the hope of establishing God's kingdom on earth. The vast majority of these immigrants shared a common cultural background; perhaps 90 percent or more of the colonists at the time of the Revolution were English-speaking Protestants, at least by cultural background. How many of those colonists were actually active churchgoers when the Constitution was adopted has been the subject of lively scholarly debate, with some pointing to a fairly low percentage of colonists' holding formal church memberships and others finding that many people affiliated themselves with churches even if they were not technically members.

The long and complicated relationship of church and state in the various colonies from the time they were founded until the Revolutionary Era is an interesting subject, but one that is well beyond the purview of this article. For present purposes, what may be most valuable to point out is that at the outset of the Revolution, several of the colonies had laws or provisions in their charters or constitutions (that is, their basic governing documents) to raise taxes for specific Protestant denominations; and most, if not all, restricted voting or public office-holding to Christians, limited secular activities on the Sabbath, punished blasphemy, and generally promoted specific forms of Christian beliefs or precepts over others.

Members of churches not receiving tax funding (often called "dissenters") were sometimes but not always permitted to obtain exemptions from paying the official church taxes. The most vocal dissenters were usually the Baptists, but they were joined by some Presbyterians (especially in the South), Quakers, and others. The churches most commonly supported by taxes were the Congregational churches in New England and the Anglican Church in the South, but at various times even the Baptists and Presbyterians were the beneficiaries of religious taxation in parts of New England, where each town voted on which local Protestant church would receive tax support.

During the Revolutionary Era, as the colonies moved towards becoming independent states, they drafted new constitutions, and thus they had the opportunity to consider whether to change their relationship with religion. How these issues were sorted out, especially in large colonies such as Virginia and Massachusetts, has provided considerable raw material for constitutional argumentation, and it is worth a more detailed look.

In Virginia, Anglicanism (that is, the official Church of England) was the "Church by law established," from the colonial period until the Revolutionary Era, as it was in England. Its property was provided by the government, and its priests were essentially civil servants. Originally, all tax-payers were required to pay for the support of the church, but first dissenters were exempted, and then the church taxes were completely abolished in 1779. A remaining question was whether Virginia would adopt a church-funding plan under which there would be a "general assessment" levied on all taxpayers, who could then specify which churches would receive their portions of those religious taxes. Such a plan was discussed off and on for a number of years and was then seriously debated in 1784–1785.

Prominent Virginians were on both sides of the issue, with George Washington and Patrick Henry favoring the church-funding plan and Jefferson and Madison leading the charge against it. One of more than a hundred petitions circulating during this vocal campaign contained an especially powerfully worded and uncompromising argument against any religious taxation; it was written by James Madison but circulated anonymously. Although similar petitions received more signatures, Madison's document, titled, "A Memorial and Remonstrance against Religious Assessments," became very popular with the Baptists, first in Virginia and later in New England, and it has become very influential in modern Supreme Court decisions as well. Calling the general assessment proposal an establishment of religion, Madison wrote at length about the unhappy consequences of having established churches in Europe and America. Ultimately, intense lobbying by the Baptists and Presbyterians, combined with Madison's clever maneuver to elect the formidable Patrick Henry as governor, thus removing his influence from the legislature, meant that the general assessment bill never became law. The legislature then approved the Virginia Statute for Religious Freedom that

had been drafted by Thomas Jefferson, another document to which the Supreme Court has turned for constitutional guidance.

Around the same time, the other southern states— Maryland, Georgia, North Carolina, and South Carolina— generally followed suit, diminishing or eliminating taxes supporting the Church of England. There are a variety of reasons why the Revolutionary state governments would stop supporting the Church of England, not the least of which was that they were at war with England. Additionally, Baptists, Presbyterians, and other dissenters had been protesting the special legal favors that had been granted to the Anglican Church, and there were undoubtedly others, including Jefferson and Madison, who opposed religious taxation as a violation of the basic principle of liberty of conscience. Once formal church taxes were eliminated, the idea of a general assessment was raised in Georgia and Maryland, as it had been in Virginia. While Virginia spurned the concept, the new constitutions in Maryland and Georgia provided for the possibility of general assessments for the support of the churches, although these provisions were never actually implemented.

The political situation was quite different in New England, where the tax-supported Congregational churches were usually stalwart supporters of the patriot cause. When Massachusetts adopted a new constitution in 1780, that document required each town to provide for the support of a Protestant church. Baptists and other dissenters fought against this provision, but proponents of what New Englanders called the Standing Order (which is a complicated term, but generally it refers to the tax-supported churches) ultimately prevailed. This kind of system of local taxation for a Protestant church designated by a majority of the town's voters continued in Massachusetts, New Hampshire, Vermont, and Connecticut until the first part of the nineteenth century. Dissenting Protestants could usually obtain an exemption from the religious taxes, but the tiny Roman Catholic population was usually not given the same benefit.

In sum, then, as the colonies became states during the Revolutionary Era, church-state patterns were altered fairly dramatically in the South, where the politically unpopular Church of England had previously been favored; they were unchanged in Delaware, New Jersey, Pennsylvania, and Rhode Island, where no churches were being publicly supported at the dawn of the Revolutionary Era; and they remained largely unchanged in Massachusetts, Connecticut, Vermont, and New Hampshire, where each town would continue to tax its citizens for the benefit of a Protestant church. In places where the issue was especially controversial, leading citizens stood on both sides of the debate.

It is therefore impossible to say that Revolutionary Americans, as a whole, held any particular view on the question of whether governments should tax citizens to support churches. Many people believed that good government required a religious citizenry because religion—especially the Protestant religion—was essential to morality, and most of the New England states chose to provide tax support for churches as a way of promoting that religiously inspired morality. These taxes were, therefore, understood by their supporters as being no different from taxes for maintaining the roads or the judicial system—all were public services for the benefit of all citizens. At the same time, many other Revolutionary Americans believed that such taxes violated the principle of "liberty of conscience," that they unfairly benefited the demographically dominant churches to the detriment of others, or that they were an improper use of governmental power. Others simply looked for any opportunity to pay smaller amounts of taxes.

Even while the issue of religious taxation was being vigorously debated in various locales, other links between government and religion—such as punishments for Sabbath breaking and blasphemy; restrictions on governmental offices to members of certain religious groups, and legislative and military chaplains; and official days of prayer—continued to be widespread throughout the states and were rarely controversial. To be sure, it is possible to find a few prominent dissenters, such as Roger Williams (the New Englander whose century-old writings on religious liberty were rediscovered during this era) and Baptist leader John Leland, arguing against such practices, but their positions were well outside the mainstream and were often not shared even by other dissenters. That religion (usually Protestantism) was an essential component of society was a widely held view; even Jefferson and Madison helped draft laws in Virginia that would punish Sabbath breakers, and leading Baptists, Presbyterians, and other dissenters strongly favored religious tests for public office. There is, therefore, a complicated backdrop for the church-state issues that would surface at the new nation's constitutional ratifying conventions, in the First Congress, and thereafter.

## The Constitution

Today's church-state debates generally revolve around the establishment clause, but that provision did not appear in the original Constitution. There was, however, a controversial church-state provision approved at the Constitutional Convention: Article VI's prohibition of any religious test for public office (that is, elected and appointed governmental positions, such as legislators or judges). At that time, at least eleven of the thirteen states restricted public office to Protestants or Christians. Some of the antifederalists—that is, those who opposed the adoption of the Constitution or who wanted the Constitution amended in a variety of ways—focused on this lack of a religious test as one of the weaknesses of the original Constitution. They feared the possibility of the government being run by unscrupulous and ungodly men. Since many Americans believed that Protestantism, or at least Christianity, was the essential foundation of morality, they worried that extending public office to nonbelievers was a threat to public safety.

Ultimately, the antifederalists were unsuccessful in removing the "no religious test" clause from the Constitution, but some of them had other church-state concerns in mind. These antifederalists, many of whom belonged to the dissenting churches (and some were even ordained clergy in those churches) saw nothing in the Constitution that would guarantee that they would be free of the kinds of legal disabilities that they had suffered in the colonies. Not only had colonial dissenters been forced on many occasions to pay taxes to support other churches but, in addition, some dissenting ministers were not entitled to perform marriage ceremonies and had even been jailed for preaching without governmentally issued licenses. Rumors also circulated that the Presbyterian Church, which was the legally established Church of Scotland, might seek to become the new nation's official church, or that the Presbyterians and the Congregationalists, who had been holding joint annual meetings, might combine in an effort to create a Calvinist establishment. (These were two of the largest denominations in America at that time, and both churches traced their theological roots to Reformation Era theologian John Calvin.)

Madison and other federalists (that is, those who defended the Constitution and urged its adoption, not necessarily the same "Federalists" who favored John Adams over Thomas Jefferson's "Republicans" ten years later in the presidential election of 1800) generally made two counterarguments: first, that the Constitution did not contain any grant of power by the states to the federal government that would permit it to establish a religion; and second, that there were so many Protestant denominations throughout the states that it would be practically impossible for any one church to obtain enough political power to emerge as the nation's official church.

The federalists' arguments were successful in some states but not in others. By the end of the ratifying conventions, four states had formally proposed amendments relating to the establishment of religion. Three of them—from Virginia, North Carolina, and New York—were almost identical and were modeled on a Virginia proposal that had been adopted at Patrick Henry's urging despite the efforts of Madison and his fellow federalists. The Virginia version read, "No particular religious sect or society ought to be favoured or established by law in preference of others." A few months later, the New Hampshire convention, for which there is no official record of the debate, came up with a very different wording: "Congress shall make no laws touching religion." These proposals joined more than two hundred other amendments suggested by the state conventions. The subject of amendments was expected to be considered by the U.S. Congress soon thereafter at its inaugural session.

Newly elected Congressman James Madison took responsibility for collecting the various proposals and putting together a draft Bill of Rights for Congress to review in 1789. Since Madison had originally opposed amending the Constitution, he did so with some reluctance; and the rest of Congress, which was heavily populated with federalists, was even less enthusiastic about postponing the business of setting up a working federal government to deal with amending the Constitution. The records from the First Congress are sparse and often unreliable, so our knowledge of what transpired is limited, but those records, together with letters written by the members, provide some insight into the amendment process.

For the most part, congressmen from both North and South described Madison's list of amendments with comments such as "froth," "anodyne to the discontented," and "milk and water"—today we might say "Mom and apple pie": noncontroversial principles (free speech, free press, jury trials, due process, and the like) that might calm the antifederalists without actually changing anything. Moreover, the language of the amendments was so broad that the provisions did not even require that there be any agreement among the members of Congress on what it meant, for example, to have a free press or to provide due process of law.

Madison's initial proposal for amendments on the subject of religion included the following: "The civil rights of none shall be abridged on account of religious belief or worship, nor shall any national religion be established, nor shall the full and equal rights of conscience be in any manner, or on any pretext, infringed." (All quotations in this section are from *The Complete Bill of Rights,* edited by Neil H. Cogan.) Somewhat surprisingly, this language did not resemble any of the four proposals for an establishment clause; the nonestablishment language most closely tracked a provision that had been introduced but not approved at the Maryland ratifying convention. All of the amendment proposals were referred to a select committee, which modified Madison's nonestablishment language by dropping the word *national,* which was a term the antifederalists disliked.

Two months after Madison's initial proposals, the Congress finally got around to debating the following language: "no religion shall be established by law, nor shall the equal rights of conscience be infringed." The discussion was desultory at best. In response to the classic federalist argument from Connecticut's Roger Sherman that the Congress had no "authority whatever delegated to them by the constitution to make religious establishments" and that, therefore, the amendment was unnecessary, Madison gave a half-hearted defense of the language: "Whether the words are necessary or not, he did not mean to say, but they had been required by some of the State Conventions, who seemed to entertain an opinion that under the [necessary and proper clause of the Constitution, Congress might be able] to make laws of such a nature as might infringe the rights of conscience, and establish a national religion. . . ."

There followed a very brief debate in which only one other member of Congress appeared to push for the adoption of the clauses; this was Representative Daniel Carroll of Maryland, who said, "As the rights of conscience are, in their nature, of peculiar delicacy, and will little bear the gentlest touch of governmental hand; and as many sects have concurred in opinion that they are not well secured under the present constitution, he said he was much in favor of adopting the words. . . ."

Meanwhile, two congressmen expressed concerns about the nonestablishment clause: Sylvester of New York "feared it might be thought to have a tendency to abolish religion altogether," and Huntington of Connecticut worried that it might be misconstrued. He agreed with Madison, who had said that "the meaning of the words [was] that Congress should not establish a religion, and enforce the legal observation of it by law, and not compel men to worship God in any manner contrary to their conscience." But he was afraid that it "might be taken in such latitude as to be extremely hurtful to the cause of religion," especially in that the federal courts might not be willing to enforce Connecticut's approach to funding churches. In response, Madison urged a return to his original proposal, which would make clear that church-state arrangements in the states would not be affected: "if the word national was inserted before religion, it would satisfy the minds of honorable gentlemen. He believed that the people feared one sect might obtain a pre-eminence, or two combine together, and establish a religion to which they would compel others to conform. He thought if the word national was introduced, it would point the amendment directly to the object it was intended to prevent."

New Hampshire's Livermore then said that his understanding of the amendment was the same as Madison's but, to avoid confusion, it might better be worded, "Congress shall make no laws touching religion, or infringing the rights of conscience," which was virtually identical to his state's proposed amendment. Without further discussion, the members of the House, officially acting as a "committee of the whole" (which meant that the House would later need to vote again when not meeting as a committee), passed Livermore's amendment by a vote of 31–20.

When the House returned to this topic, Representative Ames of Massachusetts proposed an entirely different wording: "Congress shall make no law establishing religion, or to prevent the free exercise thereof, or to infringe the rights of conscience." This version was adopted by the House of Representatives on August 20, 1789. There was no further recorded debate.

The records of the Senate are even less illuminating than those of the House's brief discussions. It appears that the first version adopted by the Senate was "Congress shall make no law establishing one religious sect or society in preference of others," which resembled the proposals from Virginia, North Carolina, and New York. After further unrecorded discussions, the Senate then settled on alternative language, "Congress shall make no law establishing articles of faith or a mode of worship, or prohibiting the free exercise of religion. . . ."

At this point, both House and Senate versions began with the phrase, "Congress shall make no law establishing," and they both ended with a ban on laws "prohibiting the free exercise" of religion. (The "rights of conscience" clause was dropped along the way, perhaps because a similar point was addressed by the "free exercise" clause.) A House-Senate joint conference committee would need to resolve the differences between the prohibition of laws establishing "religion" in the House's language and "articles of faith or a mode of worship" in the Senate's version.

The conference committee, which had to deal with all amendment issues, not just ones relating to religion, included Ellsworth and Sherman of Connecticut, both devoted supporters of that state's Standing Order, as well as Virginia's Madison, who had fought against any tax support for churches in Virginia, and Charles Carroll of Maryland, a Roman Catholic who had grown up under an Anglican establishment that had leveled burdensome taxes on Catholics; so it is difficult to say that the committee members necessarily leaned one way or another on the subject of government support for religion. There is no record of the conference committee's discussions, although it appears that the House agreed to virtually all of the Senate's preferences as long as the Senate would consent to certain House proposals, one of which was a new version of the establishment clause: "Congress shall make no law respecting an establishment of religion." This language then became a part of the "Third Amendment" sent to the states for ratification. It became the First Amendment not because it was first in importance or priority to the framers but because the states failed to ratify the first two proposed amendments.

Before leaving the House and Senate debates on religion, it may be valuable to consider the amendment that Madison called "the most valuable on the whole list." This proposal read, "No state shall infringe the equal rights of conscience, or the freedom of speech or of the press, nor of the right of trial by jury in criminal cases." Unlike the establishment clause, which expressly limited "Congress," Madison's view was that "if there was any reason to restrain the Government of the United States from infringing upon these essential rights, it was equally necessary that they should be secured against the State Governments." One congressman thought it was better to "leave the State Governments to themselves," but, after a minor amendment, the language was adopted by the House. The Senate rejected this proposal without any discussion. It is interesting to speculate about what it would have meant to require the states to respect the rights of conscience or why Madison's proposal omitted a nonestablishment clause in this provision. Unfortunately, there is essentially no record to help address these questions.

This ends the First Congress's brief debate about the establishment clause, which has been identified by many commentators as the foundation of America's national devotion to the principle of the separation of church and state. And since there are very few recorded comments from the discussions about ratification in the state legislatures, these debates represent virtually the entire legislative record for the establishment clause.

## What Did It Mean?

Scholars have vigorously debated what "an establishment of religion" meant to the framers of the Bill of Rights. One of the reasons for the scholarly debate is that the term "establishment of religion" was used in a variety of ways around the time the Bill of Rights was adopted. The documentary record (newspapers, laws, letters, and similar types of writings) shows that some people believed that an establishment of religion only existed when laws specified an officially recognized creed and liturgy. These people denied that the New England Standing Orders constituted "establishments." Others were quite sure that New England's religious taxes did, in fact, create an established religion. Similarly, in the South, some agreed with Madison that general assessments were religious establishments, while others believed that disestablishment had occurred when taxes specifically for the Anglican Church were eliminated.

Justice Black and many strict separationists have generally based their arguments on the positions taken by Madison and Jefferson in Virginia, especially since Madison had said in his "Memorial and Remonstrance" petition that the proposed general assessment would constitute an establishment. To argue that the views of Madison and Jefferson provide an authoritative understanding of the establishment clause, they may point to Madison's role in proposing the Bill of Rights in the First Congress or perhaps to Virginia's church-state actions during the Revolutionary Era as being representative of American thinking at the time. Doing so allows them to see Madison's "Memorial and Remonstrance" as something of an expanded gloss on the establishment clause, including the view that even an ecumenical, nondiscriminatory tax in favor of religion, like the proposed Virginia general assessment, would violate the Constitution. Advocates of strict separation will sometimes also point to Madison and especially to Jefferson to emphasize the role of the establishment clause in creating a secular government inspired by Enlightenment philosophy, a concept that they believe is properly captured in Jefferson's "wall of separation" phrase, which appeared in a letter Jefferson wrote during his presidency to a Baptist group in Connecticut.

Some strict separationists have also examined the use of the word *establishment* and have concluded that Americans at the time of the Bill of Rights conceived of the New England Standing Orders as constituting an establishment of multiple Protestant churches; therefore, they argue, the framers were familiar with the concept of nonpreferential aid to religion and must have wanted to prevent anything of that sort when they adopted the establishment clause. The fact that the Senate explicitly rejected language that sounded nonpreferential (following the proposals from Virginia, North Carolina, and New York, it only banned laws favoring "one religious sect . . . in preference of others") is cited as further support for the strict separationist view.

Those favoring the enhanced-federalism interpretation concur that the town-based religious taxes in New England were establishments of religion because, in their view, one of the central purposes of the establishment clause was to protect those establishments from federal interference. Meanwhile some nonpreferentialists and others have looked at early-nineteenth-century dictionaries and other sources (usually ministers of the Standing Order and other proponents of tax support for religion) and have found that the term *establishment* was most commonly used to describe a single church favored above all others, as in the case of the Church of England. Based on this evidence, they conclude that no "establishment" of religion existed in America at the time of the Constitution. Other nonpreferentialists take a different approach: they admit that the New England states "established" the demographically dominant Congregationalism but that there was no such thing as nonpreferential aid to churches at that time (and, therefore, the establishment clause could not have been meant to ban nonpreferential support for religion). Finally, some nonpreferentialists have latched onto the word *an*, arguing that the First Amendment could have forbidden a broad concept—"the" establishment of religion—but chose instead only to ban "an" establishment, that is, a single established church.

In summary, people at the time of the framing of the Constitution appeared to use the phrase "establishment of religion" in a variety of sometimes inconsistent ways. There seems to be no conclusive way to determine what definition the First Congress had in mind when it adopted the First Amendment, nor is it crystal clear how the American public might have understood the language when it was ratified by the states. This situation has allowed the advocates for various interpretations to pick and choose among various pieces of the documentary record to support their preferred approaches to understanding the establishment clause.

## *Church-State Issues following Adoption of the First Amendment*

### The States

While the religion clauses of the Bill of Rights were largely noncontroversial, church-state issues arising in the various states would hardly be called "milk and water." In the South, where the states had severed financial ties with the Church of England, there were lively disputes over the ownership of state lands previously owned by (or held for the benefit of) the Anglican Church and over the extent to which churches would be entitled to become "incorporated" entities. By becoming incorporated, the churches would receive a charter from the government that would grant them the ability to sue recalcitrant members to collect pledged contributions and to own property separately from the members or a member-elected board of trustees. Incorporation would therefore create an additional amount of institutional stability, as well as provide ministers with some degree of insulation from the members' whims. These ongoing church-state disputes in the South sometimes involved the former dissenters' trying to make sure that the Anglican Church would not work its way back into a favored position. But in other cases, even the dissenters were divided. As their numbers grew and as their members became more influential in their communities, some Baptists and Presbyterians sought to establish colleges, to promote an educated ministry, and to obtain the legal benefits of incorporation. Meanwhile, some of their fellow Baptists and Presbyterians campaigned against both an educated clergy and any governmental involvement in churches at all. Over the course of the nineteenth century, church incorporation became an increasingly well-accepted practice, but it was a heated issue in numerous locales, and it remained a controversial topic in Virginia as late as the 1850s.

In New England, the disputes were especially animated over the continuation of the tax-supported Standing Orders in Massachusetts, Connecticut, New Hampshire, and Vermont. The key elements of the debates between the supporters of the Standing Order and the Baptists and other dissenters who believed that churches should only be supported by voluntary contributions were summarized in an opinion by church-state traditionalist Theophilus Parsons in an 1810 Massachusetts case, *Barnes v. Falmouth*.

The dissenting position had been clearly and frequently articulated by Baptist spokesman Isaac Backus, and Judge Parsons made a point of responding to each of the three major objections to the Massachusetts Standing Order: "that when a man disapproves of any religion . . . to compel him by law to contribute [to it] is an infraction of his liberty of conscience, that to compel a man to pay for public religious instruction [from which he derives no benefit] is unreasonable and intolerant; and that it is antichristian for any state to avail itself of the precepts and maxims of Christianity . . . because the founder of it has declared that his kingdom is not of this world."

Parsons commented on each argument in turn. The first, he said, "mistake[s] a man's conscience for his money. . . . The great error lies in not distinguishing between liberty of conscience in religious opinion and worship, and the right of appropriating money by the state." As to the second objection, he argued that "every man derives the most important benefits" from a religious instruction that is designed to "teach and to enforce . . . a system of correct morals among the people." Finally, since "the Founder . . . did not intend to erect a temporal dominion," Judge Parsons asserted that "it is one great excellence of this religion, that, not pretending to worldly pomp and power, it is calculated . . . to meliorate the conduct and condition of man, under any form of civil government." Parsons's efforts to defend the Massachusetts Standing Order proved to be persuasive; the state's system of religious taxation was perhaps the most solidly entrenched in New England, and it would survive for a generation after Judge Parsons's opinion.

To different degrees in each of the New England states, many factors—from immigration and rapidly changing religious demographics that favored the dissenters to theological disputes within Congregationalism and the beginnings of what would become party politics—made the Standing Order much less politically stable in the nineteenth century than it had been in the Revolutionary Era. Not only were the dissenting denominations growing faster than the Congregational churches, which were usually the tax-supported churches, but the Congregationalists themselves were increasingly divided by politics and, as the nineteenth century advanced, riven by a battle between the more traditional Trinitarians and the increasingly powerful but less orthodox Unitarians. Vermont became the first to abandon compulsory religious taxation (in 1807), followed by Connecticut and New Hampshire about a decade later, with Massachusetts waiting until 1833.

The debates in Vermont and New Hampshire were less heated than in Connecticut and Massachusetts, where the Standing Order was more firmly ensconced. To some extent in Connecticut, and even more so two decades later in Massachusetts, the Trinitarian Congregationalists, who had previously dominated the Standing Order and who had been the most zealous in defending the tax benefits they were receiving, found that they were increasingly losing ground—and the control of their churches—to the Unitarians. As a result, they naturally became less enthusiastic about tax monies going to their former churches. Ultimately, religious taxation ended in New England in 1833, and as was the case every time the religious taxation issue was raised throughout the new nation, prominent and distinguished politicians and clergymen spoke up for each side. As was the case in Virginia during the Revolutionary Era, the rising political power of the Baptists and other dissenting denominations was a significant factor in the movement to abolish religious taxes (and once again the dissenters frequently cited Madison's "Memorial and Remonstrance" as a bold statement in their favor).

The end of compulsory church taxation did not sever all ties between religion and government in any of these states. Many retained religious tests for public office (New Hampshire's provision limiting office holding to Protestants continued until late in the nineteenth century despite numerous challenges in the legislature); laws against blasphemy stayed on the books (although prosecutions died out); legislatures typically had official chaplains; and governors continued to declare days of prayer, fasting, or thanksgiving. The abolition of religious taxes did not necessarily lead to the creation of secular states but was a reflection of increasingly complex political and theological dynamics (almost entirely within Protestantism), such that a majority of voters would no longer support the traditional religious taxation system. Those who may have favored a genuinely secular state (a fairly small number in New England in the first part of the nineteenth century) undoubtedly supported this outcome, but the vastly larger number of Baptists and other dissenters generally saw the end of such taxes instead as a positive step towards creating a Christian commonwealth on what they believed were genuinely biblical principles.

## The Federal Government

In the new nation's first few decades, the federal government periodically addressed church-state issues, and many modern scholars have looked at these events for help in determining what the establishment clause might have meant at that time.

The very first act of the Congress following its approval of the Bill of Rights was to recommend that President Washington declare a day of thanksgiving to thank God for the blessings of the Bill of Rights. Only one congressman is recorded as opposing the concept on establishment clause grounds, and the resolution was adopted. Ever since, almost every president has declared such days (with Jefferson and Jackson being the notable exceptions).

For a significant part of the early national period, church services were routinely held on Sundays in the halls of Congress and other governmental buildings. The First Congress also appointed official chaplains (a Presbyterian minister in the House and an Episcopal priest in the Senate), another practice that has endured throughout essentially all of American history. Nonpreferentialists point to James Madison's service on the House Chaplaincy Committee as evidence that he approved of some links between church and state, while strict separationists cite one of his unpublished writings that appears to have been written much later in his life (called by scholars the "Detached Memoranda"), in which he argued against both chaplains and national days of prayer.

One event that generated little, if any, notice in the early national period has become extremely influential ever since the *Everson* case: Jefferson's "wall of separation" letter to the Baptist association of Danbury, Connecticut, in 1802. The Baptists were fighting against that state's Standing Order, and they wrote to President Jefferson seeking his support. Upon receiving this letter, he told his advisers that his reply would give him the chance he had been seeking to say why he did not declare days of prayer, fasting, or thanksgiving, as Washington and Adams had done. But his advisers talked Jefferson out of doing so because such practices were so popular in New England, even among many of Jefferson's supporters. So he took that argument out of his draft letter, leaving in the more general statement, "I contemplate with sovereign reverence that act of the whole American people" in adopting the religion clauses of the First Amendment, "thus building a wall of separation between Church and State" (quoted in *Church and State in American History,* edited by John F. Wilson and Donald L. Drakeman). This statement has become the rallying cry of the strict separationists, and it has been cited in more than two dozen Supreme Court cases. At the time, however, the Danbury Baptists appear to have disregarded Jefferson's letter, perhaps because the concept of the "separation of church and state" was perceived as a quite radical position at the dawn of the nineteenth century. It appears that Jefferson's letter only came to light decades later when it was included in a published compilation of his papers.

The church incorporation issue arose in the federal government as it did in a variety of states. Churches set up in the federal District of Columbia turned to Congress to approve their charters as incorporated entities. Although Jefferson, as president, signed a law incorporating a Presbyterian church in Georgetown in 1806, five years later Madison vetoed a similar law passed by the Congress on behalf of an Episcopal church on the grounds that it did not respect the appropriate distinction between government and religion. The Episcopal Church had to wait until 1893 for Congress to act again on its incorporation request; in between, however, numerous religious organizations were incorporated in the District of Columbia.

Two more areas of church-state interaction at the federal level bear mentioning, even though they have been cited by modern scholars less frequently than the ones mentioned above: federal funding for Christian missions and the church-state controversy over Sunday mail delivery.

President Washington's administration continued a practice adopted by the Continental Congress and the colonial governments of providing funds to Christian missionaries for their work with Native Americans. Presidents and Congresses throughout the eighteenth and nineteenth centuries appropriated considerable sums that were awarded to a range of religious groups to educate and Christianize Native Americans. These funds paid for the building of religious schools, the salaries of the missionaries, and many other related expenses. Not until late in the nineteenth century were the potential constitutional issues surrounding this practice (such as whether it might constitute an improper "establishment of religion") raised to a significant level, and the practice did not end until the beginning of the twentieth century.

Despite the lack of church-state debate over the direct funding of religious missions, there was a very well-publicized ongoing battle over the issue of whether a proposal to stop mail delivery on Sunday would violate the Constitution. When Congress passed a law in 1810 requiring mail delivery seven days a week, a coalition of Protestant groups protested this failure to observe the Sabbath and lobbied Congress to reverse its decision. The controversy became especially heated in 1829 and 1830, when many thousands

of Americans signed petitions asking Congress to eliminate the Sunday mails. These petitions were part of an organized effort coordinated by some of the nation's leading Protestant churches. Their principal argument was that America, as a Christian nation, was obliged to obey the Ten Commandments' injunction to respect the Sabbath.

The Senate and House committees responsible for the mails were chaired in successive years by the same man, Richard Johnson of Kentucky, who used the opportunity to release very strongly worded reports in support of the Sunday mails and expressing deep concerns about the pernicious influence of religion (and especially clergymen) on the actions of government. These reports became very popular in Jacksonian America (and helped propel Johnson into the vice presidency), but over time, those who sought the elimination of the Sunday mails ultimately prevailed.

In summary, influential interpretations of the establishment clause in the early republic ranged widely from the sharply anticlerical Sunday mails congressional reports to frequent assertions, as in the federal Northwest Ordinance, that "religion, education and morality" are essential components of good government. Even within one presidential administration, two fundamentally different views are evident. For example, Madison put forth a very strict interpretation of the establishment clause when he vetoed the incorporation of a church; meanwhile, one of Madison's appointees to the Supreme Court, Harvard law professor Joseph Story, issued the highly influential *Commentaries on the Constitution* in 1833, proclaiming that "the general, if not universal sentiment in America" at the time of the Constitution was "that Christianity ought to receive encouragement from the State so far as was not incompatible with the private rights of conscience and the freedom of religious worship" (quoted in Wilson and Drakeman, *Church and State in American History*). These differing views have endured ever since, with the strict separationists following in Madison's footsteps and the nonpreferentialists opting instead for Story's outlook.

## Conclusion

Some scholars have located the foundation for modern America's approach to church-state issues in the founding era and the early national period described in this article. To be sure, the establishment clause prohibited Congress from making laws "respecting an establishment of religion," yet the meaning of those words has been the subject of vigorous debate. And some scholars have countered that the now-familiar concept of the separation of church and state actually developed significantly later as waves of Roman Catholic immigrants in the nineteenth century brought an entirely new dynamic to the largely intra-Protestantism church-state debates of the founding era. Those heated and sometimes violent nineteenth-century disputes between Protestants and Catholics centered on the Protestant prayers and Bible reading mandated by many public schools and the related issue of whether there should be state funding for a parallel system of parochial schools established by Catholics. These debates continued through the nineteenth and twentieth centuries, and while the *Everson* case is best known for the Supreme Court's commitment to a strict separationist originalism as the best way to understand the establishment clause, the main issue in that case was whether a state could reimburse parents for bus transportation to the Roman Catholic parochial schools. The *Everson* Court narrowly upheld the reimbursement plan—largely on the grounds that it could be seen as being similar to providing fire and police protection for church buildings—but the opinion's strict separationist legacy has led the Court to strike down public school prayers, many forms of aid to religious schools, and a variety of other state and federal programs supporting religion. This interpretation of the establishment clause, based as it was on the history of the Constitution's framing, has made the study of the relationship of religion and government in the Revolutionary and early national eras highly controversial, frequently politicized, and, as a result, extremely interesting and worthy of further study.

See also *American Revolution; Anglicans in Colonial and Revolutionary America; Atheism, Agnosticism, and Disbelief; Canada: Church and State; Constitution; Deism; Enlightenment; Evangelicals: Colonial America; Establishment, Religious; Freedom, Religious; Politics: Colonial Era; Supreme Court.*

Donald L. Drakeman

**BIBLIOGRAPHY**

Amar, Akhil Reed. *The Bill of Rights.* New Haven, Conn.: Yale University Press, 1998.

Borden, Morton. *Jews, Turks, and Infidels.* Chapel Hill: University of North Carolina Press, 1984.

Bradley, Gerard V. *Church-State Relationships in America.* Westport, Conn.: Greenwood, 1987.

Buckley, Thomas E. *Church and State in Revolutionary Virginia, 1776–1787.* Charlottesville: University of Virginia Press, 1977.

Butler, Jon. *Awash in a Sea of Faith: Christianizing the American People.* Cambridge, Mass.: Harvard University Press, 1990.

Cogan, Neil H., ed. *The Complete Bill of Rights: The Drafts, Debates, Sources, and Origins.* New York: Oxford University Press, 1991.

Cord, Robert L. *Separation of Church and State: Historical Fact and Current Fiction.* New York: Lambeth Press, 1982.

Curry, Thomas J. *The First Freedoms: Church and State in America to the Passage of the First Amendment.* New York: Oxford University Press, 1986.

Drakeman, Donald L. *Church, State and Original Intent.* New York: Cambridge University Press, 2009.

Dreisbach, Daniel. *Thomas Jefferson and the Wall of Separation between Church and State.* New York: New York University Press, 2002.

———, ed. *Religion and Politics in the Early Republic: Jasper Adams and the Church-State Debate.* Lexington: University Press of Kentucky, 1996.

Greenwalt, Kent. *Religion and the Constitution: Establishment and Fairness.* Princeton, N.J.: Princeton University Press, 2008.

Hamburger, Philip A. *Separation of Church and State.* Cambridge, Mass.: Harvard University Press, 2002.

Howe, Mark DeWolfe. *The Garden and the Wilderness: Religion and Government in American Constitutional History.* Chicago: University of Chicago Press, 1965.

Hutchinson, William R. *Religious Pluralism in America.* New Haven, Conn.: Yale University Press, 2003.

Hutson, James H. *Church and State in America: The First Two Centuries.* Cambridge: Cambridge University Press, 2008.

Kramnick, Isaac, and R. Lawrence Moore. *The Godless Constitution: The Case against Religious Correctness.* New York: Norton, 1996.

Levy, Leonard W. *The Establishment Clause: Religion and the First Amendment.* 2nd ed. Chapel Hill: University of North Carolina Press, 1994.

McLoughlin, William G. *New England Dissent, 1630–1833: The Baptists and the Separation of Church and State.* 2 vols. Cambridge, Mass.: Harvard University Press, 1971.

Munoz, Vincent Phillip. *God and the Founders: Madison, Washington, and Jefferson.* Cambridge: Cambridge University Press, 2009.

Noonan, John T., Jr. *The Lustre of Our Country: The American Experience of Religious Freedom.* Berkeley: University of California Press, 1998.

Pfeffer, Leo. *Church, State, and Freedom.* Boston: Beacon, 1953.

Smith, Steven D. *Foreordained Failure: The Quest for a Constitutional Principle of Religious Freedom.* New York: Oxford University Press, 1995.

Stokes, Anson Phelps. *Church and State in the United States.* 3 vols. New York: Harper and Brothers, 1950.

Wilson, John F., ed. *Church and State in America, a Bibliographical Guide: The Colonial and Early National Periods.* New York: Greenwood, 1986.

Wilson, John F., and Donald L. Drakeman, eds. *Church and State in American History.* 3rd ed. Boulder, Colo.: Westview, 2003.

Witte, John. *Religion and the American Constitutional Experiment.* 2nd ed. Boulder, Colo.: Westview, 2005.

# Churches of Christ

Churches of Christ represent a distinct American heritage that originated, along with the Disciples of Christ, in the Stone-Campbell Movement (also known as the "Restoration Movement") in the early nineteenth century. They exist in many parts of the country, but their numbers are strongest in "Bible Belt" states such as Tennessee, Arkansas, and Texas; like many other Christian fellowships, the majority of their members can now be found in Africa, India, and Latin America. This tradition should not be confused with the United Church of Christ or with the Church of Jesus Christ of Latter-day Saints.

## Historical Development

As suggested by its name, the Stone-Campbell Movement was marked by dual leadership. The first leader was Barton W. Stone (1772–1844), who played a pivotal role in the Cane Ridge Revival (near Lexington, Kentucky) in 1801. Stone began his ministerial career as a Presbyterian; disenchanted, however, with creedal and synodical obligations, he withdrew in 1804. His anticreedal, anticlerical followers embraced the generic label of "Christians," and they sought to be governed by scripture and united by holiness. While Stone's movement was still quite new, a similar venture appeared in southwestern Pennsylvania, led by Thomas Campbell (1763–1854) and his son, Alexander (1788–1866). They both departed the Presbyterian fold in 1809, and Alexander ultimately played the leading role in his own anticreedal, anticlerical enterprise. He took a rationalistic approach, treating the Bible (especially the New Testament) as a formula for Christian identity and unity. In an effort to identify with the earliest Christians, his partisans were frequently known as "Disciples."

Alexander Campbell was no revivalist, and Barton Stone was not inclined toward rational formulas. However, despite their differences on these (and other) issues, they joined forces in the winter of 1831–1832, and on the strength of this tenuous unity, their influence spread throughout the Midwest and into the South. Their followers, frequently meeting as "Christians," "Disciples," or "Churches of Christ," labored to strip away the dross of tradition and to "restore" the unity and simplicity of first-century Christianity. Opposed to clerical oversight and creedal definition, this remarkable movement became a diverse and decentralized body during the 1840s and 1850s.

Churches of Christ were ultimately recognized as a separate body in the 1906 Census, but their isolation from the Disciples was realized, de facto, during the final decades of the 1800s. These parties shared common convictions about congregational autonomy, the weekly observance of the Lord's Supper, and the salvific role of adult baptism; nonetheless, they became estranged on predominantly sectional lines, and their earliest tensions were manifested during the

Civil War and Reconstruction eras. Poorer, rural, southern churches were typically opposed to the liturgical use of musical instruments, and this proved to be a leading source of contention. Moreover, in contrast to their wealthier, relatively urban, northern counterparts, the southern churches refused to support the formation of a centrally governed missionary society.

It was not a consistent rule, but the nomenclature of the "Church of Christ" was increasingly applied to the southern churches, and the northern churches were widely known as "Disciples." When the Census was published in 1906, the Churches of Christ had 159,658 members, a figure that was only one-sixth of the Disciples' total. The increasingly liberal Disciples, however, soon suffered another division. Over the course of the next thirty years, a confederation of conservative "Christian Churches" withdrew from their midst and formed a separate fellowship. Aside from their use of musical instruments, these churches strongly resembled the Churches of Christ, and many adopted the "Church of Christ" name; nonetheless, they remained estranged from their noninstrumental counterparts.

Lacking any official corporate structure, the Churches of Christ were loosely organized around the editors of periodical publications. Among them were two primary papers: one was the Texas-based *Firm Foundation,* established by Austin McGary (1846–1928) in 1884; another, from Nashville, was the postwar *Gospel Advocate,* established in 1866 and edited by David Lipscomb (1831–1917). Meanwhile, the Disciples were largely defined by the *Christian Standard,* which was edited by Isaac Errett (1820–1888) from 1866 till 1888. By the turn of the twentieth century, the Churches of Christ were also identified by a growing collection of colleges, and some have survived to the present day. The Nashville Bible School (now known as Lipscomb University) began in 1891, and Abilene (Texas) Christian College was founded in 1906. Two others, Harding College (in Searcy, Arkansas) and Freed-Hardeman College (in Henderson, Tennessee), were founded in 1919.

Until his death, Lipscomb proved to be the most significant representative of the southern movement, and the official dissolution of 1906 was published on the strength of his reluctant testimony. In the region around Nashville (where Lipscomb's influence was strongest), the Churches of Christ tended to be an economically marginalized, countercultural sect, eschewing earthly political systems and eagerly anticipating the premillennial return of Christ. By the end of two world wars, however, the pressures of patriotism had become too great, and the movement was driven toward the mainstream of American Protestant culture. They retained their distinctive opposition to instruments, and they held aloof from the broader Protestant spectrum; nonetheless, in sociological terms, the Churches of Christ had become, by the 1950s, a conservative denomination. Like their fundamentalist and evangelical neighbors, they were deeply concerned about a host of predictable issues, such as Darwinian evolution, the "social gospel," and the menace of communism.

The 1950s and 1960s were particularly heady days for the Churches of Christ. They enjoyed an explosion in numbers, and by 1970 they crested near the two million mark. To answer the call for additional ministers, new preaching schools were established: one of these, the Sunset School of Preaching, began in Lubbock, Texas, in 1961; another, the White's Ferry Road School of Preaching, was founded in West Monroe, Louisiana, in 1964. Graduate programs were added to the religious curriculum at George Pepperdine College (1944, in Los Angeles), Abilene (1953), and Harding (1954, in Memphis). Through the generous donations of numerous churches, the Herald of Truth radio ministries were launched in 1952, and television programs were added the following year. Moreover, missionaries flowed from these new institutions, and a newspaper called *The Christian Chronicle* (founded in 1943) kept the churches informed about the projects that were being completed.

The prosperity of the twentieth century, however, did not guarantee unity among the Churches of Christ. For instance, there was a small coterie who challenged the biblical authorization for Sunday schools: these "nonclass" churches, mostly in Texas, withdrew to form their own fellowship during the 1920s, and they have maintained a separate fellowship ever since. Greater impact, however, was delivered by the "noninstitutional" protest, which reacted against the growing influence of the colleges and the Herald of Truth. Recalling the nineteenth-century arguments against missionary societies, this movement rejected parachurch institutions where religious influence could be centralized. In this dispute, the noninstitutional perspective was forcefully argued by Foy E. Wallace Jr. (1896–1979), who edited various periodicals such as the *Bible Banner* (1938–1949). For their part, the mainstream churches defended their colleges and radio programs; nonetheless, noninstitutional churches still constitute nearly 10 percent of the membership in Churches of Christ.

As the Churches of Christ moved into the second half of the twentieth century, their growth began to stagnate. Many churches sought to distance themselves from a notoriously disputatious heritage, and they began to adopt new points of emphasis. For example, *Mission* magazine appeared from 1967 to 1987, dealing frankly with cultural topics such as racial prejudice, warfare, and feminism. During the 1980s, another movement radiated from the Boston Church of Christ, placing radical emphasis on evangelism and discipleship. Mainstream congregations rejected this impulse, and despite its numerical success it was judged to be manipulative and "cultish." Eventually organized as the International Churches of Christ, this movement became a separate fellowship in 1993.

Predictably, strong, reactionary forces have tried to preserve the "sound doctrines" of the previous generation. In their quest to distinguish themselves from mainstream American Christianity, these churches have been represented by journals such as *The Spiritual Sword,* which began in 1969, and by their own lectureship programs. They rigorously maintain an exclusivist, noninstrumental platform, and they continue to wield considerable influence.

To a significant degree, however, the Churches of Christ have moved away from their prior exclusivism, and many have sought to reverse their historical division with the instrumental Christian Churches/Churches of Christ. This particular quest for unity was stimulated, in large part, by a series of annual "Restoration Forums" that began in Joplin, Missouri, in 1984. Other churches, meanwhile, have reached beyond the borders of the original Stone-Campbell Movement and have embraced a broad range of evangelical associations. Some congregations, inspired by nondenominational "community church" models, have labored to erase entirely the distinctive marks of their tradition. As they entered the twenty-first century, the Churches of Christ had become a rich but fractured heritage, their identity hanging heavily on their colleges and on the continued reportage of *The Christian Chronicle.*

## Distinctive Beliefs and Practices

Despite their debt to Barton Stone, the Churches of Christ have been primarily marked by the early legacy of Alexander Campbell. In his later years, Campbell softened his tone and became relatively ecumenical; Churches of Christ, however, have favored his original mission to overturn denominational creeds and to restore the putative purity of primitive Christianity. In many Churches of Christ, the earliest centuries of Catholic development have been rejected as a time of "apostasy," and the reformations of Martin Luther and John Calvin have been faintly praised as a partial move in a first-century direction. Hence, in this view, the restorative work of Campbell and Stone must be viewed as a decisive moment on the timeline of church history. Mainstream Churches of Christ have historically (but not unanimously) viewed themselves as the complete restoration of the first-century church; according to the cornerstones on many of their buildings, they were "established in A.D. 33." In keeping with these convictions, they have typically refused to classify themselves as a "denomination," believing that they have transcended that sort of category.

In 1816, Campbell delivered a "Sermon on the Law," where he contrasted the Mosaic and Christian "dispensations." He affirmed the abiding value of the Old Testament, but he rejected its normative authority for the restoration he envisioned. It was, he argued, the manifestation of an earlier dispensation, and its jurisdiction had been "fulfilled." This disposition toward the Old Testament, historically, has become a trademark for the Churches of Christ and has mitigated most of the narratives and teachings that transpired before the death of Jesus. Significantly, this attitude has led to a disproportionate focus on the book of Acts and the Pauline epistles, with very little emphasis on the gospels.

Churches of Christ have traditionally used this canon-within-a-canon to identify a coherent biblical "pattern." This pattern can be discerned, first of all, with a tripartite hermeneutic of "direct commands," "approved precedents," and "necessary inferences." In many Churches of Christ, this approach has become the target of ridicule; nonetheless, it has been a distinctive interpretive tool through the years, and it still has vigorous defenders. The "direct commands" are drawn from biblical passages where imperative language is used: Acts 2:38, for instance, is frequently cited as an obligatory commandment from Peter, who said "repent and be baptized, every one of you." Meanwhile, the "approved precedents" are based on reconstructions of first-century practice: Acts 20:7, therefore, sets a normative example for every believer when Paul breaks bread "on the first day of the week." Other precedents, such as head coverings for women (1 Corinthians 11:3–16), can be explained by cultural considerations and are usually overruled. Third, the "necessary inferences" can be devised with simple syllogisms: Acts 2:38, for example, links baptism with repentance, which logically implies mature reflection and logically disqualifies infant baptism.

This hermeneutical strategy undergirds a nexus of distinctive practices in the Churches of Christ, beginning with baptism. In keeping with a literal translation of the Greek word *baptizo* (and the presumed example of the first-century church), it has been important for Churches of Christ to define baptism as a full bodily immersion. More distinctively, however, the purpose of baptism has been carefully defined in sacramental terms, as the means for receiving grace and forgiveness. It is not understood to be a meritorious act; on the contrary, it represents an essential, visible, and salvific moment. Once again, Acts 2:38 has been determinative here, along with Acts 22:16, 1 Peter 3:21, and numerous other passages. Campbell publicly articulated this understanding in 1823, and it became an immediate, decisive, and ongoing point of departure for his movement. Though it is scarcely unique to "Campbellites," this definition of baptism has been central to the historical rivalry between Baptists and Churches of Christ and accounts for its distinctive priority among Campbell's heirs.

From the very beginning, the Churches of Christ have also been marked by fierce assertions of congregational autonomy. Insisting that first-century churches were individually governed by a plurality of elders (1 Timothy 3:1–7; Titus 1:5–9), Campbell and Stone rejected the concept of monarchical bishops and authoritative councils. In this respect, their position was consistent with their Puritan forebears, but, with appeals to first-century practice, their own opinions pressed even further: most famously, Stone rejected the validity of the Springfield Presbytery in 1804, arguing that it should "die, be dissolved, and sink into union with the Body of Christ at large." For his part, Campbell was affiliated with Baptist "associations" during the 1820s, but he also judged them, eventually, to be coercive and unscriptural. As noted above, this persuasion has led the Churches of Christ to be suspicious of any manifestation of centralized authority, including missionary societies, colleges, and radio programs. On the other hand, it has also allowed for remarkable freedom of expression and is largely responsible for the bewildering diversity that presently characterizes the movement.

Most visibly (and perhaps most famously), the Churches of Christ are known for their refusal to use musical instruments during worship assemblies. This issue did not originate with Campbell or Stone and has been explained, above, as a sectional affair. Among Churches of Christ, however, it has been consistently treated as a litmus test for obedience; for many, instruments are unauthorized by the New Testament because they cannot be justified by a direct command, an approved precedent, or a necessary inference. Ephesians 5:19 and Colossians 3:16 are decisive, here, because they command "psalms, hymns, and spiritual songs" without any mention of instruments. As will be noted below, this issue continues to provoke considerable discussion, and many churches have abandoned the traditional position. Nonetheless, it is rare, even in those "progressive" churches, to find instruments used on a regular basis.

## Internal Issues

To some degree, the traditional threefold hermeneutic can be traced to Thomas Campbell's *Declaration and Address* (1809), where he spoke of "express terms," "approved precedent," and "inferences." This approach to the Bible revealed rationalistic assumptions that he and his son, Alexander, had inherited from the Enlightenment. Similarly, in their quest for a coherent, authoritative, first-century pattern, the Churches of Christ have imbibed a modern, rationalistic mindset. They have been optimistic about the clear-cut authority of scriptural data, and they have considered themselves to be exempt from the foibles of human interpretation. Moving far beyond the Campbells, this certitude has led the Churches of Christ to refuse "fellowship" with churches who do not accept the ostensibly "clear" teachings of scripture. They have been reluctant, consequently, to worship or fraternize with Christians from other denominational affiliations.

With the advent of a "postmodern" era, however, these hermeneutical assumptions are being called into question, along with their exclusivist consequences. Some have concluded that the traditional, pattern-seeking strategy has inadvertently neglected crucial biblical themes, leaving Churches of Christ in a theologically shallow position. This concern was expressed as early as 1965 by Thomas H. Olbricht (1929–), who dared to suggest that Campbell had led the movement in a mistaken hermeneutical direction. Moreover, subsequent critics have observed that the genre of biblical literature does not lend itself to systematic, "patternistic" manipulation; Pauline letters, for instance, must be treated according to their epistolary genre with special attention to their occasional character. These suggestions have received a predictably mixed reaction, as traditionalists rightly recognize the threat that a "new hermeneutic" would pose to numerous cherished doctrines. The most celebrated response, *Behold the Pattern,* was published by Goebel Music (1934–) in 1991 and

stoutly defended the traditional hermeneutic. In Music's presentation, he upheld the categories of command, precedent, and inference, and he denounced the critics of the pattern-seeking approach.

Normally, the Churches of Christ have reserved public leadership roles for their male members only. This practice has been predictably called into question, as the broader culture presses in egalitarian directions; nonetheless, there are very few exceptions to this rule, and the traditional hermeneutic, despite its detractors, has proven to be a sturdy constraint. With its customary emphasis on Pauline epistles, it highlights biblical passages such as 1 Corinthians 14:34 and 1 Timothy 2:11–15, where feminine roles would seem to be clearly and sharply curtailed. Egalitarian advocates, with a different hermeneutical approach, have argued that gender equality is an essential feature of the Kingdom of God, and they have cited passages such as Galatians 3:28, where Paul asserts that there is "no male or female" in the fellowship of Christ. Many congregations are revising their views on this subject, but the hermeneutical stakes are significant and the issue has been remarkably contentious.

The Churches of Christ have also been challenged by questions of ecumenicity; as mentioned above, the movement holds diverse opinions about its associations with other fellowships. For those who believe that the Churches of Christ have restored a biblical, first-century pattern, it has been difficult to avoid an exclusivist stance, and this attitude was typical for most of the twentieth century. Once again, however, a traditional position has been modified by hermeneutical considerations, and the Churches of Christ have become increasingly tolerant toward other Christian traditions. This non-denominational impulse was significantly endorsed by Rubel Shelly (1945–), whose book, *I Just Want to Be a Christian,* was published in 1984. More recently, the devotional writings of Max Lucado (1955–) have been featured on the *New York Times* best seller list, and he has provided a public, visible example of nondenominational fraternization. Shelly and Lucado have been strongly rebuked by traditional elements in the Churches of Christ, but those reactionary voices are reaching a shrinking audience.

Though the Churches of Christ are diverse, that diversity has significant limits. These churches remain stridently conservative, and they continue, with near unanimity, to make common assumptions about biblical inerrancy, the substitutionary atonement of Christ, and homosexuality. On these and other issues, there has been no substantial activism toward a liberal point of view.

## Interpretive Theories

One of the earliest chroniclers of the Churches of Christ has been Earl I. West, who began, in 1949, to publish a four-volume series entitled *The Search for the Ancient Order,* which describes the history of the Stone-Campbell Movement from its beginnings until 1950. West interprets the movement as the successful restoration of the first-century church, and he regards the Churches of Christ to be the purest remnant of that original quest. For West, therefore, it is a story about truth and error, and his interpretation is clearly premised on traditional hermeneutical assumptions.

Douglas Foster takes an entirely different approach in his 1994 publication, *Will the Cycle Be Unbroken?* He measures the Churches of Christ against the theories of various sociologists, including the "sect-to-church" typology of Ernst Troeltsch. In Foster's assessment, the Churches of Christ have reached a predictable and respectable stage in the life cycle of a religious movement, and he warns about the likelihood of future fragmentation. Foster insists, however, that the prospect is still theoretical and can yet be resisted: indeed, for him, the central genius of the Stone-Campbell Movement was not its quest for restoration, but its quest for unity. By recovering that priority, Foster says, the Churches of Christ can defy the sociological odds and still retain their identity.

By contrast, David Edwin Harrell Jr. interprets the story of the Churches of Christ as a series of divisions. In his 1973 publication, *The Social Sources of Division in the Disciples of Christ, 1865–1900,* he explains the schism of 1906 in terms of sectional loyalties. He observes that the Churches of Christ took root in poor, rural, southern locations and had little success in the eastern parts of the country. In addition, he has written *The Churches of Christ in the 20th Century* (2000), where he describes the tensions provoked by deeply embedded loyalties and rancorous power struggles. Unlike Foster, Harrell concludes that the mainstream is already splintered in reality, if not in writing, between two evenly matched camps of "progressives" and "conservatives." He does speculate about the eventual "winners" and "losers," but he does not envision a peaceful solution.

The most comprehensive interpretation of the Churches of Christ has come from Richard Hughes, who acknowledges the movement's divisions but proposes a different set of concerns. In his 1996 book, *Reviving the Ancient Faith,* Hughes contrasts the legalistic rationalism of Alexander Campbell with the countercultural, premillennial pietism of Barton Stone. He believes that Campbell overshadowed Stone from the start, and he traces the "unequal fusion" of their influence throughout the 1800s. As mentioned above, the Churches of Christ were driven toward the patriotic mainstream of American Protestantism during the two world wars; in the judgment of Hughes, this constituted a tragic renunciation of the "Stoneite side" of their heritage and was a cultural compromise that neutered their Christian testimony. Hughes revisits this theme in a 2002 publication, *Reclaiming a Heritage,* where he laments the movement's evangelical assimilation and urges the Churches of Christ to reconsider the choice they have made.

## Critical Assessment

The Churches of Christ have inherited a vibrant heritage and a unique historical narrative, but their distinctive doctrinal identity seems to hang on a time-bound hermeneutical scaffold. As the modernist era fades into memory, it will be increasingly difficult for these churches to appeal to the clear-cut authority of biblical patterns. Traditionalists will surely continue to protect the old paths, and they will not be dissuaded by the disapproval of the majority. Their mission, however, will be increasingly difficult, and their ranks seem destined to dwindle.

Progressives will continue to press for hermeneutical changes, but it will be difficult to do this without a change of affiliation. For instance, many congregations have already erased the "Church of Christ" label from their stationery, and some are frankly indifferent about the historic ties they might sever. If they care about the past, they might salvage an ecumenical vision from the earliest days of the movement (as Foster has hoped), or they might recover the countercultural remnants of Barton Stone's legacy (as Hughes has advised). These kinds of options, however, will require a serious commitment to the heritage, and this does not seem likely to happen. The path of least resistance will surely lead the progressive churches into generic evangelicalism.

The most interesting variable, here, could come from other parts of the world. As noted above, the Churches of Christ have a global presence, and most of their churches are now located in Africa, India, and Latin America. In these contexts, many people are deeply impressed with a modern approach to the Bible, and they are happy to search for patterns. Only time can tell what role they will play, as they continue to grow. The picture looks complicated, and it is impossible to make confident assertions about the future of the Churches of Christ.

See also *Bible: Interpretation of; Denominationalism; Disciples of Christ; Missions: Foreign; Stone-Campbell Movement; Women: Ordination of.*

Keith Huey

**BIBLIOGRAPHY**

Casey, Michael W., Jr., and Douglas A. Foster, eds. *The Stone-Campbell Movement: An International Religious Tradition.* Knoxville: University of Tennessee Press, 2002.

Foster, Douglas A. *Will the Cycle Be Unbroken? Churches of Christ Face the 21st Century.* Abilene, Tex.: ACU Press, 1994.

Foster, Douglas A., Mel E. Hailey, and Thomas L. Winter, eds. *Ministers at the Millennium: A Survey of Preachers in Churches of Christ.* Abilene, Tex.: ACU Press, 2000.

Harrell, David Edwin, Jr. *The Churches of Christ in the Twentieth Century: Homer Hailey's Personal Journey of Faith.* Tuscaloosa: University of Alabama Press, 2000.

———. *A Social History of the Disciples of Christ.* 2 vols. Nashville, Tenn.: Disciples of Christ Historical Society, 1966–1973.

Hooper, Robert E. *A Distinct People: A History of Churches of Christ in the Twentieth Century.* West Monroe, La.: Howard Books, 1993.

Hughes, Richard T. *Reviving the Ancient Faith: The Story of Churches of Christ in America.* Grand Rapids, Mich.: Eerdmans, 1996.

# City Missions

A city missions movement developed in the late nineteenth and early twentieth centuries that was an essentially Christian response to the widespread social problems that grew out of the industrial revolution.

## Nineteenth-Century Roots

The industrial revolution of the late nineteenth and early twentieth centuries brought economic opportunity and prosperity to unprecedented numbers of immigrants and Americans, but it was accompanied by widespread social problems such as unemployment, homelessness, crime, substance abuse, and destruction of families. In an era when governments offered little relief, voluntary associations and religious institutions responded to the cries of the urban poor. City missions, or rescue missions as they were often labeled, became the spearhead of a reform movement that offered immediate relief and short-term solutions to complex urban industrial problems.

There was no single city mission that appeared first, proved effective, and then became the prototype mission to be duplicated throughout urban America. On the contrary, small storefront missions appeared almost simultaneously in every industrial city across the nation as soon as space could be secured in areas frequented by the people who lived and struggled to survive on the lowest rungs of the social ladder.

Those outposts designed to attract the least fortunate of the poor offered words of comfort, meals, cups of hot coffee or tea, and a warm and dry place to rest away from inclement weather and people who preyed on the weak. Typically these missions cared for the immediate needs of hurting people. Some missions offered shelter overnight. But for the most part these were short-term care facilities that offered little in the way of long-term solutions to systemic social problems. In brief, these rescue missions were inaugurated and sustained by Christians who ministered in marked contrast to Christians in the Social Gospel movement, who were more keen on changing the social, political, and economic systems that they believed caused the problems.

## Evangelical Beginnings

The inspiration behind the earliest city missions was decidedly evangelical. Indeed, the twin purposes that motivated evangelical Protestants—evangelistic outreach to the unchurched and charity to the poor—worked like two blades of a pair of scissors. The name "mission," which was proudly painted on the front of most of these facilities, had its roots in a biblical mandate to send out evangelists to convert non-Christians, and the impetus to care for the physical needs of shelter, food, and clothing for the poor came from the same Christian Bible.

Consequently, when a city mission opened its doors, it was commonly outfitted with a piano, pulpit, and benches or chairs to seat a few dozen people. There was usually a table to set out food, and where the buildings were large enough there were cots in a separate room so people could sleep overnight in a safe environment.

## Typical City Missions

One of the earliest city missions that became well known because of its New York City location and its longevity (it is still operating) was founded in Manhattan's Bowery

District. Opened in 1872 and originally called the Helping Hand Mission, it was eventually named the McAuley Water Street Mission after its founder, Jerry McAuley. Born in Ireland in 1839, deserted by his parents, and taken to the United States by an older sister, McAuley lived hand-to-mouth on New York's East Side. This abjectly poor immigrant lad turned to petty crime as a means of survival, and he ended up in New York's Sing Sing Prison at age seventeen. While behind bars he converted to Christianity through the preaching and follow-up ministry of a woman prison evangelist. Upon release in 1864, McAuley began evangelistic preaching while he attempted to meet the survival needs of the Lower East Side's poorest people. By 1870 he raised enough money to open a rescue mission with a permanent facility.

In Chicago after the Civil War, a shoe salesman named Dwight L. Moody conducted similar rescue and relief activities among destitute people in the Windy City's rapidly growing slums. In 1876, two women of Free Methodist persuasion, Rachael Bradley and Mary Everhart, began the dual work of evangelism and social welfare in a low-income section of Chicago. Their mission, called The Olive Branch, was rivaled only by the Pacific Garden Mission as the largest and most famous of missions in the upper Midwest. Pacific Garden Mission, founded in 1877, became one of the most famous missions in the United States. Among the men who converted to Christianity at the missions and then went on to distinguish themselves as leading evangelical preachers were Billy Sunday, the major league baseball player, as well as Mel Trotter, Edward Cord, Bill Hadley, and Walter McDonald.

## Meeting Wider Needs

During the 1880s and 1890s these rescue missions spread throughout the United States. By World War I, it is doubtful if there was a city with a population of eighty thousand or more that did not have at least one mission operated and supported by Christians in the local community. As the mission movement spread geographically, it also gradually embraced a wider vision. At first designed to rescue souls through conversion to Jesus Christ and to offer immediate but temporary relief from hunger and homelessness, the missions acquired larger facilities. Toilets, showers, and lockers for clothes were added, and people were allowed to live in the mission for up to a month if they attended the nightly religious services, promised to refrain from consumption of alcohol and tobacco, and were willing to help with chores. The Salvation Army pioneered this type of wider ministry when it made its appearance in the United States in 1880 from England, where it was founded by William and Catherine Booth.

The Salvation Army was a purposively evangelistic and social welfare organization, but it was a Christian organization with a difference. Besides rescuing the spiritually and physically perishing, as the Salvationists labeled destitute people who were not Christians, these urban missionaries invested in longer-term follow-up. People were given food, clothing, and shelter as well as evangelistic preaching, but they were also given wide varieties of rehabilitation opportunities to learn how to earn a living and become self-supporting.

The Roman Catholic Church had always been sensitive to the needs of the poor, and as increasing numbers of Catholic immigrants arrived in America in the late nineteenth century, the Catholic Church rushed to care for their own for two reasons. First, it was a calling of the church to care for the poor. And second, the Catholic Church did not want its own people proselytized to by evangelical Protestants. Consequently, the Catholic Church had missions in every city where Catholic immigrants settled, but these facilities functioned in conjunction with local Catholic churches and always had worship facilities, nuns and priests to serve the people, and quite soon orphanages and schools for the children. In short, although the Catholics reached out to their own poor, their work was more holistic from the outset, and it never looked or functioned like the evangelical city missions. One of the striking examples of this Catholic work was that of Mother Cabrini and her Missionary Sisters, who worked to meet the socio-religious needs of Italian immigrants in the United States beginning in the late nineteenth century.

## Late-Twentieth-Century Changes

The rural depression of the 1920s and the nationwide Great Depression of the 1930s stretched city missions throughout America beyond their limits. Indeed, by the late 1930s, most of these religious organizations suffered from dwindling donations at the time needs were greatest. The New Deal's infant welfare programs helped ease urban poverty. But World War II stimulated the economy and pulled many young men and women into factories and the armed services, thereby easing the strain on the nation's city missions.

As a result, some of the smaller and younger missions permanently closed their doors during the 1940s.

After the war, some of the older city missions continued to serve the homeless and destitute. By the late twentieth century, the city mission movement that had begun as a Protestant evangelical ministry was being complemented by Roman Catholic charities; and by the end of the century, local, state, and federal governments increasingly assumed the task of rescue and rehabilitation at taxpayers' expense and without the Christian religious dimension. To be sure, Christians' efforts to aid the poor did not end in the late 1900s. By the middle of the twentieth century the "mainline" denominations had founded churches in the inner cities with the purpose of offering pastoral care and places of worship for the poor and the newly arrived immigrants. Nevertheless, the rise of the welfare state gradually rivaled but never replaced the charitable efforts of Christians in the inner cities of America.

**See also** *Evangelicals* entries; *Faith-Based Community Organizations; Faith-Based Initiatives; Missions: Domestic; Missions: Foreign; Missions: Native American; Philanthropy; Roman Catholicism: The Age of the Catholic Ghetto; Social Gospel.*

Lyle W. Dorsett

## BIBLIOGRAPHY

Bonner, Arthur. *Jerry McAuley and His Mission.* Neptune, N.J.: Loizeaux Brothers, 1992.

Booth, General. *In Darkest England and the Way Out.* London: Salvation Army, 1890.

Burger, Delores T. *Women Who Changed the Heart of the City: The Untold Story of the Rescue Movement.* Grand Rapids, Mich.: Kregel, 1997.

Conn, Harvie. *The American City and the Evangelical Church: A Historical Overview.* Grand Rapids, Mich.: Baker, 1994.

Dorsett, Lyle. *A Passion for Souls: A Life of D. L. Moody.* Chicago: Moody, 1997.

Ellis, Marc. *A Year at the Catholic Worker.* New York: Paulist Press, 1978.

Henry, Carl F. H. *The Pacific Garden Mission.* Grand Rapids, Mich.: Zondervan, 1942.

Magnuson, Norris. *Salvation in the Slums: Evangelical Social Work 1865–1920.* Metuchen, N.J.: Scarecrow Press and American Theological Library Association, 1977.

McKinley, Edward. *Marching to Glory: The History of the Salvation Army in the United States, 1880–1992.* Grand Rapids, Mich.: Eerdmans, 1992.

Sullivan, Mary Louise. *Mother Cabrini: "Italian Immigrant of the Century."* New York: Center for Migration Studies, 1992.

Woodward, Ralph. *Light in a Dark Place: The Story of Chicago's Oldest Rescue Mission.* Winona Lake, Ill.: Light and Life Press, 1978.

# Civil Religion in the United States

The term *civil religion* comes from the writings of the eighteenth-century French philosopher Jean Jacques Rousseau, although the ideas it denotes are much older and more universal. In writing about the essential ingredients for a successful nation-state, Rousseau suggested that among them would be a shared moral system grounded in some overarching belief in a god whose providence was revealed in the common life of the people. Rousseau recognized that particulars of belief could vary considerably but felt that social cohesion required some sort of religious base to sustain it and to keep a nation viable.

## An American Civil Religion?

In the ancient world, glimmers of what Rousseau had in mind come in the biblical Israel where the people believed that God had entered into a special covenant relationship with them at Sinai, a relationship in which they alone were chosen to receive the way to holiness through the keeping of the commandments. Civil religion is also apparent in the Roman Empire, when the Senate designated emperors as gods. Doing so endowed their rule with a transcendent, extraordinary power. Similar forces were at work in traditional Japan, for example, where the ruling family was also granted status as divine as a way to lift political control to a higher plane. Virtually no nation or people has existed who did not in some way regard themselves as a folk set apart from others, as a people whose collective well-being carried a dimension of divine destiny—although at times perhaps the people could fail to live up to the status God had granted them.

Historians and others had long recognized the close ties between religion and national identity in the United States, but the idea that there was a distinctive American civil religion received classic statement in an essay entitled "Civil Religion in America," published by sociologist Robert Bellah in 1967. Bellah insisted that there was a clearly defined civil religion that existed alongside more traditional religion, complete with its own belief system, rituals, and other apparatus. Drawing on frequent references to God or Providence in presidential inaugural addresses and looking to documents such as the Declaration of Independence and the Constitution as sacred texts, Bellah argued that this civil religion looked to divine intervention in key events of

American history, especially wars. Indeed, many of the ritual celebrations he identified had ties to wars, such as Fourth of July events that recalled Americans to their founding ideals fixed in the War for Independence, or Memorial Day happenings that recalled first those who had lost their lives in the War between the States and later all who sacrificed their lives in the service of the nation. As well, Bellah looked to battlefields as pilgrimage sites where the faithful were revitalized in their commitment to the core ideals of the nation. There was even a hymnody associated with this civil religion, including not simply the national anthem but songs ranging from "America the Beautiful" to "God Bless America." Many of those songs also had originally emerged in times of conflict when national identity was at stake.

Bellah's claims seemed to many the key to understanding how religion and nationalism or at least religion and American identity were linked to one another. But others questioned whether there was actually a discrete civil religion on a par with other religions, or whether what Bellah observed was more varied dimensions of transcendent or religious meaning layered on to political events. In time, those who probed most deeply would come to question whether even those ties adequately explained the nebulous ways religious meaning became attached to political phenomena, and whether at base they worked to link all Americans to a single sense of national purpose and identity. Before exploring the many challenges to the civil religion hypothesis, however, it is helpful to understand exactly what it seeks to delineate—namely, the many ways in which events in the common life of the American people take on a religious or transcendent quality as interpreters attempt to explain their full meaning and significance—and what forces sustain that understanding from one generation to the next.

## Roots of an American Civil Religion

At the time European nations entered an age of conquest and established colonial empires across the globe, ideas of destiny and providence flourished. The Spanish *conquistadores* believed they were executing the will of God in subjugating the indigenous peoples of the New World and forcing them to submit to the Spanish expression of Roman Catholicism. But in the territory within North America that became the United States, English influence was ultimately dominant, and in that age of discovery and colonization England saw itself as a beacon of righteousness, chosen of God and protected by God.

Those ideas penetrated the subconscious of the Puritan settlers who peopled New England in the seventeenth century. In a now well-known sermon preached to the dissenters from the Church of England who were about to establish a foothold in Massachusetts Bay, the early colonial governor and leader John Winthrop spoke of the enterprise as equivalent to building a city on a hill, a biblical image denoting a model civilization that would be a beacon to the world. Others described the Puritan venture as an errand into the wilderness and likened their attempt to create a holy commonwealth to that of ancient Israel. Leaving England in an exodus as the Hebrews had left Egypt, they were journeying through a colonial wilderness as they sought to craft the ideal society in their own promised land. The colonists, like the Hebrews of old, had joined in a covenant with the Almighty and with each other. In this rich mixture of religious language and images with political tasks, elements of a civil religion begin to take shape.

But colonial Puritans moved beyond what Rousseau meant by civil religion's providing a base for social cohesion and common identity. To be sure, cohesion was central, for they were reluctant to allow those whose vision differed to settle in Massachusetts Bay, lest they contaminate the purity of the ideal society. Yet they also tended to see the hand of Providence in historical and natural events, some as signs of blessing and some as signs of chastisement. For example, earthquakes signaled divine displeasure and resulted in calls to repentance; rulers were to exhibit characteristics based on scriptural models; conflicts with the French and Native American peoples appeared as omens of the ultimate confrontation between the forces of good and evil. The English colonial enterprise was, in the familiar phrase, "God's new Israel," and no event was too insignificant to be a medium through which Providence was nudging the people to be faithful to their covenant.

Although popular perception associates the Puritans primarily with New England, much of this thinking permeated the collective subconscious in all areas of English control, particularly because it had roots in an earlier sense of English particularism. Hence, as events moved the colonists towards independence, they carried an overlay of interpretation that fused the political and the religious. From the Stamp Act crisis of 1765 to the Boston Tea Party of 1773, many in the English colonies saw the hand of God at work, steering a righteous people toward independence from a king and parliament given over to iniquity.

The era of the American Revolution or War for Independence became a foundational epoch in crafting a distinctive American civil religion—at least in the eyes of white male colonists who wielded power. The Declaration of Independence and then the Constitution took on the status of a civil scripture, sacred texts that articulated core beliefs in liberty, justice, and equality that would guide all the people, regardless of their European ancestry. It was Providence that crafted this *novus ordo saeculorum* (new order of the ages), making *e pluribus unum* (one out of many)—Latin phrases that still appear on U.S. currency. Few at the time took account of the many who were not part of the one, from white women denied equal rights, to Africans yet held in bondage as property, to indigenous peoples not recognized as citizens. Nonetheless, there was a widespread sense at least among the political and economic elite that the Republic, this experiment in democracy that left behind monarchy and aristocracy, had launched a political order that reflected divine will, with its structures ordered by God to guide the people towards fulfilling their destiny not just in world history but in sacred history. American independence, through the lens of Revolutionary-era civil religion, moved all humanity forward to that day when there would be a new heaven and a new earth.

Hence a lively millennial sensibility and pervasive apocalyptic spirit infused the style of civil religion that took root in the United States. Yale's Ezra Stiles trumpeted how God would bestow great honor and glory on the nation if it remained faithful to the divine will. If not, it would—like the nations of Europe—experience decay. Early on, civic rituals emerged to reinforce this conviction of American uniqueness and righteousness. From liberty poles during the Revolution to celebrations on the Fourth of July, ritual symbols and acts recalled the people to their sacred beginnings. In those celebrations, their commitment to the covenant of liberty became revitalized and the people became empowered anew to live as those chosen by God to be a light to all nations.

Many of these images carried biblical overtones, but none required a theological construction associated with a particular denominational expression of biblical religion, although most Euro-Americans of that age were inclined towards some brand of Protestant Christianity. Even the First Amendment to the Constitution that forbade a national religious establishment and in theory guaranteed to all the free exercise of religion indirectly buttressed the idea that this civil religion was anchored in religious perceptions common to all and shared by all. It mattered not whether one's personal belief bore the marks of a particular denomination—Episcopal, Presbyterian, Congregational, Baptist, Roman Catholic, Methodist, whatever. Specific doctrinal difference need not divide a people nor keep them from fulfilling their destiny, so long as all affirmed belief in an overarching Providence that informed all doctrines and creeds, even as it determined American destiny. Creed was a matter of opinion that amplified on common belief, and opinion could have many expressions.

Also sustaining this melding of the religious and political in the emerging identity of the nation and its people was the assumption widely held in the later eighteenth century that all the particular expressions of religion, despite their differences, inculcated in followers a basic morality that was essential to the common good. George Washington, who was well on his way to quasi-supernatural status in the popular mind even in his own lifetime, captured this well in his famous "farewell address." There he asserted that morality could not exist without religion, nor could government endure without morality. This "religion-in-general" was thus indispensable to the well-being of the new nation. Religions could abound; what mattered was how they worked in tandem to create a moral citizenry who trusted in Providence to guide their collective destiny.

That the new nation was headed in the direction Providence intended and desired received fresh witness when revolutionary impulses spread in Europe. For many, the events leading up to the French Revolution, which erupted in full force less than three months after George Washington took the oath of office as the first American president, heralded another chapter in the unfolding drama of God's plan for humanity. Guided by the American spirit, other peoples would follow, and democratic principles of liberty, justice, and equality would gradually begin to prevail throughout the world. Here, too, are glimpses of that larger millennial hope underpinning these dimensions of a civil religion, for history seemed as if it were everywhere beginning to move towards its final culmination, with the United States standing as the beacon lighting the way. For many, though, as the French experience bordered on anarchy and some of its revolutionary leaders embarked on an assault on all religion, and thus by implication on the foundations of the morality essential to the commonweal, excess seemed likely to trump the righteousness America exemplified and threatened to demolish its place as exemplar to the world. In terms of civil religion, the controversy in the United States over whether to ally with revolutionary France or with a once-misguided Britain brought a significant challenge. After renewed conflict with Britain led to another military outbreak in the War of 1812, the nation began to turn inward. Perhaps the hand of Providence could be discerned moving more in the internal life of the nation than in its efforts to be a model for all peoples.

## The Spirit of Civil Religion in Antebellum America

Other dynamics quickly propelled a more intense intertwining of broadly based religious notions with American nationalism that some later analysts would see as evidence of a stratum of civil religion. With the Louisiana Purchase of 1803, the United States embarked on a policy of expansion that most of the founding generation had not envisioned. After the War of 1812 had reaffirmed the righteousness of the American democratic venture, with Providence guiding the fledgling nation to victory, those with an eye to expansion soon looked to Florida and then to territory farther west as regions where American democracy could establish itself. By the 1840s, Jacksonian Democrats especially talked about Manifest Destiny, the idea that God had ordained the United States would one day span the North American continent from the Atlantic to the Pacific. It was the nation's destiny ordained by God, and nothing human could ultimately stand in its path. Indeed, the idea of national destiny echoed the Calvinist theology that undergirded the Puritans, who had embarked upon an earlier errand to subdue a different wilderness.

Manifest Destiny stirred interest, for example, in annexing Texas (then the Lone Star Republic) in 1845, although Mexico still had a historical claim to the territory. It fueled interest in the Oregon Territory, which at the time included much of what is now the Canadian province of British Columbia. An agreement with Britain added some of that land to the nation in 1846. Already California had declared its independence from Mexico, and expansionists enamored of Manifest Destiny simply presumed that this land would join the American empire. Perhaps the most strident calls to heed the desire of Providence that the nation take in more land came as the United States embarked on war with Mexico in 1848. Indeed, there was little military justification for the conflict. The Mexican Cession of 1850, however, served as confirmation for expansionists that God had destined the nation to grow and take control of more land. Providence had blessed the nation through expansion and

reinforced the conviction that a democracy rooted in ideals of liberty, justice, and equality carried divine endorsement.

Of course, it helped that Manifest Destiny and its ties to democratic ideology flourished as antimonarchical sentiment once again swept through Europe in the wake of Napoleon's defeat and then the democratic "revolutions" of the 1850s. A closer look at the American nation, though, would suggest that Manifest Destiny, as other facets of an American civil religion taking shape in the eras of Revolution and the Early Republic, resonated more with the lived experience of a developing white male economic elite whose personal religious perspectives were shaped primarily by a broadly evangelical Protestantism. By the 1830s, sectional division over both slavery and the evolution of an industrial economy suggested a lack of consensus about the foundational values behind American republican democracy and its destiny. Could a nation that allowed some to hold other humans as property, as slaves, exemplify liberty and equality? Was its destiny less to expand from coast to coast than to founder in the quagmire of hypocrisy? Other religious and ethnic conflict, symbolized in the often violent anti-Catholicism that accompanied a surge in Irish immigration between 1830 and 1860, highlighted additional problems in trying to see the hand of Providence at work in national growth. Was liberty reserved for white Protestant males? It seemed increasingly so, especially to those of the ilk of William Lloyd Garrison, a strong antislavery advocate, and rank-and-file Irish pouring into Boston and other northern port cities seeking employment and hoping to make a new life in a land where justice presumably prevailed.

## Civil War and the Revitalization of a Civil Religion

For those who probe the idea of an American civil religion, the War between the States from 1861 to 1865 looms large. Even at the time, those who sought to find larger meaning in this national inferno sought to understand it in religious terms that would not undercut the American enterprise altogether. President Abraham Lincoln, whose words have received careful study by a host of scholars, recognized the futility of identifying either the Union or the Confederate cause as the only one endorsed by God. In his mind, neither was faultless; both were misguided in trying to claim God for their side. But Lincoln and others also saw in the sectional conflict opportunities to revitalize a national commitment to the founding ideals of liberty, justice, and equality, extending them in theory at least to include those once held as slaves, if the American people were willing to commit themselves anew to those principles. New England pastor and theologian Horace Bushnell, speaking at Yale's commencement ceremonies in 1865, used some traditional Christian language in trying to capture this sentiment. Talking about the obligations both North and South had to the hundreds of thousands who had given their lives in the war as well as about the heritage of democratic ideals, Bushnell saw the Civil War as a kind of baptism, albeit a baptism in blood, that reconsecrated the nation and its people to the core beliefs shared by all. War had renewed the national covenant.

The end of military conflict did not necessarily mean the end of sectional division. In one sense, as historian Charles Reagan Wilson has argued, the Southern states developed a regional civil religion that sought to mythologize the antebellum past, elevate Confederate heroes to the level of demigods, and perpetuate white racial superiority in regional culture as racism and discrimination replaced slavery. The Southern agrarian past evoked something of an Eden for those who glorified the "lost cause" of the Confederacy. As aspects of a regional civil religion emerged, antebellum white culture became idealized, with its evangelical Protestantism seen as a pure expression of truth for both individuals and society.

In the industrializing North, racial discrimination also remained the order of the day. But other issues linked to religion and ethnicity prompted many northerners to question whether there was adequate affirmation of values and beliefs associated with a civil religion. More so than for folk in other regions, massive immigration from central, southern, and eastern Europe that swelled the ranks of the Catholic, Jewish, and Eastern Orthodox population seemed to many northerners a threat to the core values of the nation. Because the rapid industrialization that was transforming the nation's economy centered more in the North and its cities, immigrants flocked to urban areas in the hopes of finding jobs and a secure future.

Josiah Strong, one-time executive secretary of the Evangelical Alliance, captured some of the apprehension of northern Protestants about immigration, urbanization, and industrialization in his *Our Country* that first appeared in 1885. Strong argued that God chose Anglo-Saxon Protestants to fashion American democracy and culture in such a way that the nation itself had special status in the divine plan for all history. The moral values instilled by Anglo-Saxon

Protestants had become endangered with the influx of millions of non-Anglo-Saxon Protestant immigrants. To protect the purity of the nation—to buttress elements of a civil religion—it was necessary to convert new immigrants to evangelical Protestantism in order to Americanize them. Strong did not single out a particular Protestant denomination as best suited for this task; in retrospect, the denomination did not matter. What Strong was promoting was in essence the kind of tie between a broadly held but loosely defined set of religious beliefs and an understanding of the nation as a people set apart by God. In other words, Strong saw as vital to social cohesion a kind of civil religion, albeit in this case one with links to a specific religious heritage, namely, Protestant Christianity. As was the case with New England Puritans in the seventeenth century, for Strong in the later nineteenth century, diversity threatened to contaminate the whole culture because it would render any civil religious sensibility dysfunctional.

By the time Strong wrote, public schools had taken hold in American culture. With roots in Massachusetts in the 1830s, public schools became vehicles for the transmission not only of basic learning thought essential to all Americans, but also of the moral values and political ideals associated with American democracy. The now-renowned McGuffey readers, used for generations to instruct public school children, freely mixed theological notions associated with the broad evangelical Protestantism Strong advocated with patriotic and moral virtues associated with American republican democracy. These two features were so intertwined in the primers that Roman Catholic leaders called for a parish or parochial school system where Catholic children, especially immigrant children, might receive basic education and even learn the moral values and responsibilities of citizenship, but without an overtly Protestant stamp. Parochial schools would demonstrate that Catholics could be good citizens without having to abandon their distinctive religious faith and practice.

Confidence that American political institutions and all the apparatus that accompanied them reflected God's design and will for humanity gained fresh reinforcement at the close of the nineteenth century when the United States engaged in the Spanish-American War. William McKinley, president at the time, made the war a religious crusade as well as a military venture when he recalled that it was while he was praying that God revealed to him the necessity of America's entering the war to bring salvation and civilization to heathen peoples. It mattered not that Cubans and

Filipinos, both of whom were for a time incorporated into the expanding American empire, already were overwhelmingly Roman Catholic Christians. McKinley's Anglo-Saxon Protestant vision of the nation and his effort to impose transcendent meaning on the trumped-up conflict with Spain also lay behind a widely publicized speech given by Albert Beveridge, a Republican senator from Indiana at the turn of the century. Beveridge insisted that divine blessing followed the imposition of American control on other peoples, since a morality sanctioned by God had given birth to American institutions. This later quest for empire was Manifest Destiny with all its ties to aspects of civil religion revamped and repackaged for a new day.

## Global Conflicts Spur Concerns for Cohesion

The new age of American empire crumbled when World War I erupted. But for the United States, the war became another sign that God had chosen American democracy to influence if not dominate the world. Once again connections between religion and national identity suggest the undercurrents of dimensions of a civil religion. American president Woodrow Wilson, who turned the war from a struggle between fading imperial states in Europe into a quest to impress an American-style democracy on yet more peoples, drew readily on religious language in political speeches that were more sermons than public addresses. The son of a Presbyterian seminary professor, Wilson saw the war through a lens that fused his own Calvinist heritage with a conviction that God ordained and guided American democracy to bring true moral values to all humanity. Once again military engagement was vital to linking religion with national identity. Wilson's style and his sermonic tone help support the claim of Bellah and others that a religious substratum in American life constitutes a civil religion.

So, too, the Second World War took on religious dimensions as Hitler and the Nazi-Fascist Axis became identified with virulent evil and the United States and its allies with righteous goodness. Once again apocalyptic currents informed the ties between a civil religion and national identity, for the defeat of Hitler signaled the triumph of liberty, equality, and justice and thus pointed to a new future for all humanity. Yet this time, the religious euphoria quickly became muted. No sooner had the war come to a close than conflict broke out in Korea; more to the point was the emerging Cold War that pitted God-fearing, capitalist, democratic America against the godless communism epitomized by the Soviet Union and its puppet states.

The Cold War provided much fodder for those who insist there is a distinctive American civil religion. In 1954, for example, Congress added the phrase "under God" to the Pledge of Allegiance to the flag. No doctrinal definitions were provided; getting specific would reveal diversity and dissension. But the symbolic import was obvious: the United States was a nation with God on its side while the Soviet empire lacked divine blessing. So, too, when Congress ordered the phrase "in God we trust" to appear on all coins and currency, not just some of it, another symbol of American righteousness appeared. This mid-1950s move cemented the notion of the United States as a moral and upright nation. The most prominent Christian evangelist of the era, Billy Graham, added to the aura of civil religiosity, proclaiming a nondenominational gospel in arenas and stadiums across the nation and even abroad, insisting that simple faith in God, faith that was never carefully explained or articulated, provided a panacea for all social and personal problems and assured those who believed that they carried God's blessing in this life and beyond. The threat of nuclear annihilation at the hands of an expanding Soviet empire required social cohesion in the United States. Centuries earlier, Rousseau had advanced his notion of civil religion as a key ingredient in sustaining that cohesion. The United States did the same in the 1950s by attempting to use religious language in the public square and to cast the American people as righteous and moral, while acknowledging that individuals could hold a range of personal beliefs.

That connection became a central thesis in several sociological studies that appeared in the 1950s. Will Herberg's study entitled *Protestant, Catholic, Jew* (1955) demonstrated that for most Americans, it made no difference whether one was identified with any of the scores of Protestant groups, Roman Catholicism, or one of the branches of Judaism. People regarded all as equally functional and legitimate ways to inculcate the moral values that undergirded good citizens. Differences in fine-tuning beliefs from a theological perspective remained; such was the character of American religious life. But there was a core consensus that crossed all such boundaries. Herberg did not speak about civil religion as such, although he did insist that there was a religion of the American way of life, one based on capitalist free enterprise economics and its concomitant conspicuous consumption. Herberg regretted the prevalence of this culture religion, thinking that it lacked the prophetic dimension and sense of commitment he thought central to the biblical faiths.

Also in the 1950s, W. Lloyd Warner appraised Memorial Day celebrations held across the nation that were replete with parades and patriotic oratory, noting that they represented an "American sacred ceremony" whose function was to integrate the people into a cohesive whole. In his understanding, Abraham Lincoln, whose Gettysburg Address was frequently quoted at Memorial Day assemblies, became a collective representation of the idealized American. Moving from poverty to the presidency, Lincoln illustrated the popular American dream of what anyone could accomplish if committed to the core values of liberty, justice, and equality.

## Forces Undermining an American Civil Religion

Minority voices soon challenged the perception of the United States as a righteous nation knit together and guided by Providence. In the 1950s, the civil rights movement erupted with particular force, reminding Americans of the depth of inequality and injustice that prevailed in a nation where racism was rampant and discrimination legally sanctioned. Civil rights leaders such as Martin Luther King also drew heavily on religious rhetoric to make their case for an end to segregation and racism. In doing so, they demonstrated that whatever dimensions of a civil religion might exist, they did not speak to the lived experience of African Americans. By the 1960s other dissenting voices reminded the nation that women also experienced exclusion, as did gay and lesbian Americans. As concern over U.S. military engagement in Vietnam mounted, those opposed to government policy came to think that political leaders themselves had forgotten the meaning of justice and freedom. To many, the core values of the nation seemed linked only to the lived experience of white males who were part of the nation's political and economic elite. For millions, the extent of dissent appeared to undercut any sense of cohesion and unity.

This social disarray prompted Robert Bellah to create his mythic understanding of the American past in his seminal essay insisting that there was indeed an American civil religion. But Bellah also recognized that the social unrest of the 1960s and 1970s challenged the social cohesion promoted by this civil religion and threatened to render the civil religion dysfunctional. Hence he wrote a more penetrating study, suggesting that the social movements of that age had led to a "broken covenant" in the nation. At the time, even Bellah did not take note of other cultural transformations under way that would make it increasingly difficult to claim that there was a single civil religion at the heart of the national experience.

Those shifts resulted in part from changes in U.S. immigration law in 1965 that allowed millions from Asia, the Middle East, Africa, and Latin America to enter the country. Like those of earlier generations, these immigrants brought with them their native religious expressions. But many of these religions were new to the United States, at least in terms of visibility and increasing numbers of adherents, and they were far removed from the biblical traditions that had once dominated and had informed not only Bellah's understanding of civil religion but also much of the casual connections that gave national experience a religious aura grounded in a broad evangelical Protestant perspective. The numbers of Muslims, Buddhists, Hindus, and Sikhs, for example, began to skyrocket. For them a providential God loosely tied to the biblical tradition, particularly to ancient Israel's understanding of itself as a chosen people, and who worked in the events of history, was altogether alien. Now there were millions more who were part of the American people but for whom the traditional religious construction of the American past or of the American political order had no meaning whatsoever.

Some, such as evangelical leader Jerry Falwell, looked askance at how immigration and other social changes were transforming the texture of American society. Reviving the genre of the jeremiad, a sermon type developed by the Puritans to bemoan presumed declension in the moral fabric of society, Falwell and others identified with the religious right sought to reclaim an understanding of the nation even narrower that Bellah's. Only by curtailing developments such as expanding rights for women and for homosexuals, by evangelizing among newer immigrants, and by restoring overt religious practices in the public schools eliminated by Supreme Court decisions in the 1960s could America once again become a moral nation blessed by God. The religious right associated with groups such as the Moral Majority attempted to infuse civil religious discourse with a decidedly conservative Protestant Christian nuance.

Religious language and symbolism also continued to infuse political rhetoric. In the 1980s, President Ronald Reagan, prior to the collapse of the Soviet bloc, repeatedly referred to the communist nations as an "evil empire" in a way that brought Cold War apocalyptic images to mind. Two decades later, President George W. Bush also drew heavily on apocalyptic imagery in describing Iraq before the American invasion and in reflecting on the terrorist attacks on the World Trade Center in September 2001. Yet efforts to use such language and attempts to revitalize whatever components of a civil religion remained operative in American common life faced increasing challenges by the early twenty-first century, given the expanding religious pluralism and the growing political diversity that had become characteristics of the nation.

## Contemporary Challenges to an American Civil Religion

Of course, some critics had long before raised questions not only about whether an American civil religion existed as the kind of religion that Bellah had posited, but also about whether it was a meaningful construct for looking at links between religion and politics. John Wilson, for example, drew on a wealth of historical and sociological materials and interpretations to suggest decades ago that certain features of American common life had religious dimensions and could from time to time function in religious ways. So presidential addresses could have something of a sermonic dimension, and invocation of God in pledges and on coins could represent an effort to endow the American experience with transcendent meaning. However, Wilson insisted that careful scrutiny did not reveal a full-fledged religion at all, but simply what people in many places across time had done in trying to claim divine sanction for policies and programs.

The many prongs of the civil rights movement suggested as well that the civil religion hypothesis had limitations. If it did not speak to the lived history and experience of Native Americans, African Americans, or even women, for whom did it speak? More and more, it seemed as if efforts to invoke a civil religion echoed the experience only of white men of economic and political privilege. The deep angst about the course of American society unleashed by protests against military engagement in Southeast Asia in the 1960s and 1970s was echoed in concerns about war in Iraq and Afghanistan as well as about how best to combat international terrorism. Then, too, the biblical traditions had always anchored the religious ideas encapsulated in the idea of an American civil religion. With religious groups that denied divine action in history or at least construed history very differently than did the biblical traditions, it was harder to assume that a civil religion resonated in any way with the lived religion of increasingly large numbers of Americans. Certainly Americans identified with one of the many strands of Buddhism, for example, would look at history very differently and tend not to see it as the stage on which Providence was working out a great cosmic scheme for humanity.

Yet the idea of civil religion remains important, even if it is tentative at best. It suggests that Americans, as every people, seek to give larger meaning to their corporate national experience. It signals that Americans struggle to unite diverse peoples within a framework of common values such as liberty, justice, and equality, even while nurturing an extraordinarily wide range of particular religious beliefs and practices. Finally, the notion of civil religion serves to remind Americans that much yet remains to be done if all the diverse peoples who call the United States their homeland are to be united in a cohesive whole.

See also *African American Religion: From the Civil War to Civil Rights; American Revolution; Anti-Catholicism; Civil War; Demographics; Freedom, Religious; Historical Approaches; Immigration entries; Philanthropy; Pledge of Allegiance; Politics entries; Puritans; Religious Right; Sociological Approaches; Sport(s); World War I; World War II.*

Charles H. Lippy

### BIBLIOGRAPHY

Albanese, Catherine L. *Sons of the Fathers: The Civil Religion of the American Revolution.* Philadelphia: Temple University Press, 1976.

Bellah, Robert N. *The Broken Covenant: American Civil Religion in Time of Trial.* New York: Seabury, 1975.

———. "Civil Religion in America." *Daedalus* 96, no. 1 (Winter 1967): 1–21.

Cherry, Conrad, ed. *God's New Israel: Religious Interpretations of American Destiny.* Rev. ed. Chapel Hill: University of North Carolina Press, 1998.

Herberg, Will. *Protestant, Catholic, Jew: An Essay in American Religious Sociology.* Garden City, N.Y.: Doubleday, 1955.

Strong, Josiah. *Our Country.* Edited by Jurgen Herbst. Cambridge, Mass.: Belknap Press of Harvard University Press, 1963.

Warner, W. Lloyd. *American Life: Dream and Reality.* Chicago: University of Chicago Press, 1953.

Wilson, Charles Reagan. *Baptized in Blood: The Religion of the Lost Cause, 1865–1920.* Athens: University of Georgia Press, 1980.

Wilson, John F. *Public Religion in American Culture.* Philadelphia: Temple University Press, 1979.

# Civil War

The Civil War (1861–1865) pitted the Northern United States against the Southern Confederate States of America. The bloodiest war in U.S. history, the military conflict cost approximately 620,000 soldiers and 50,000 civilians their lives. The war's political outcomes included the preservation of the national union and the emancipation of about four million African American slaves, but the Civil War also represented a signal moment in American religious life. Nineteenth-century American public life was infused with a high degree of religious rhetoric, particularly that of evangelical Protestantism. Religion played a prominent role in the rending of the national union, and both the Union and the Confederacy went to war with the sanction of leading ministers in each section, assured that the Christian God had ordained their cause.

## Theological Crisis over Slavery

A devout nation went to war in 1861. A year prior, somewhere between one-third and two-fifths of the American population claimed church membership, with at least double that number regularly participating in church-related activities. While American religion contained a noticeable degree of diversity, the social and political discourse of evangelical Protestantism dominated the landscape. The nation's three most populous denominations, Methodists, Baptists, and Presbyterians, all evangelical in style, accounted for approximately 67 percent of all existing churches, about 63 percent of church seating capacity (which could accommodate roughly 38 percent of the American population at any one time), and nearly 45 percent of the value of all church property. By no means did these three denominations represent all—or the only—evangelicals in antebellum America. Congregationalists, Restorationists, and some Lutherans and Episcopalians exhibited evangelical traits. More than ten million Americans—roughly 40 percent of the 1850 population—identified in some way with evangelicalism.

While antebellum evangelicals enjoyed unprecedented cultural power and authority, their seemingly broad consensus masked deep divisions. No issue was more divisive than slavery. At the core of evangelical belief rested a commitment to the primacy of the Bible as the divinely inspired, authoritative guide for the shaping of Christian life and practice. Moreover, evangelicals shared a common method of biblical interpretation. Emphasizing a literalist hermeneutic—inherited from the Reformed theological tradition, influenced by the common sense moral reasoning of the Scottish Enlightenment, and steeped in the American principle of democratic individualism—American evangelicals believed the Bible to be an eminently readable book that contained easily understandable, God-given teachings that applied to all people at all times. When forced to deal with the morality of American slavery, that literalist method of biblical interpretation led to a theological crisis.

Key passages in both the Old and New Testaments suggested the Holy Writ sanctioned slavery. Southern proslavery divines made much of the biblical warrant for slavery, but many ostensibly antislavery ministers in the North also conceded the biblical imprimatur for slavery. Still, such concessions did not mean that antislavery clergy accepted the pro-slavery biblical argument. While some antislavery activists argued from a radical perspective that a higher human law demanded the Bible be rejected for its endorsement of slavery, more moderate antislavery religious voices held to biblical authority yet attempted to show how the slavery in scripture differed greatly from American slavery. Not only did the American system refuse to recognize such biblical concepts as the Jubilee Year—in Mosaic law, all slaves were set free every seven years—or allow for marriage between slaves but, most significantly, biblical slavery also was not based on racial difference. American slavery clearly was, though few white evangelicals questioned the racist foundations of their society. Thus, antebellum American evangelicals grew deeply divided over the slavery question. Two factions emerged, more or less divided sectionally, both claiming to read the Bible the same way and denouncing the other as sinful.

## Antebellum Church Schisms

The crisis over slavery fractured the nation's three most populous denominations. That religious fracture anticipated and fomented the national fracture that would come in the Civil War. The Presbyterians were the first to divide. In 1837 an "Old School" majority of the Presbyterian General Assembly voted to remove four "New School" synods located in New York and Ohio. The New School was accused of deviating from the denomination's stricter Calvinist roots, embracing more liberal revivalist doctrines, and advocating forms of interdenominational cooperation that modified traditional church polity. While the slavery question was not the primary issue at stake, it was a very closely related secondary matter. Much of the abolitionist agitation in Presbyterian circles came from New School ranks. There was little doubt that the South's presbyteries, overwhelmingly populated with conservatives, supported the Old School on theological grounds. However, following the Old School also gave southerners a chance to rid the denomination of abolitionist influence. The following year, in 1838, a newly formed New School General Assembly claimed roughly 100,000 members, 85 presbyteries, and 1,200 churches, significantly less than the Old School's approximately 127,000 members, 96 presbyteries, and 1,763 churches.

The Presbyterian schism of 1837–1838 could not have happened without southern support for the Old School, but the divisions were not clearly sectional. A few southern presbyteries initially joined the New School, but in the next decade, agitation over slavery proved too much stress for the denomination. In 1857 the New School condemned slaveholding as sinful, prompting twenty-one southern and border state presbyteries—containing approximately fifteen thousand members—to leave the denomination, making the New School a wholly northern denomination. At the same time, an uneasy peace prevailed in the Old School until the start of the Civil War. Then, in 1861, when the General Assembly passed a staunchly Unionist and antislavery platform, southern Presbyterians—most of whom had not attended the General Assembly—responded by creating the Presbyterian Church in the Confederate States of America.

Among Methodists and Baptists, the divisions were more clearly sectional and more obviously about slavery. For Methodists, the issue had loomed large for several years, but it proved ultimately divisive in an 1844 debate about qualifications for bishops. James O. Andrew, bishop of Georgia, had acquired slaves through marriage and inheritance. The national General Conference instructed Andrew to free his slaves, arguing that bishops should not be slaveholders. After much southern protest and debate, the denomination agreed to divide along sectional lines. In 1845, the Methodist Episcopal Church, South, was created.

Baptist schism over slavery occurred almost concurrently. Abolitionism rose throughout the 1830s among northern Baptists, culminating with the 1840 American Baptist Anti-Slavery Convention in New York City. That meeting produced a treatise that denounced slavery as sin and called on southern slave-holding Baptists to repent and free their slaves or risk being cut off from fellowship. For the next few years, the issue came up repeatedly in Baptist meetings. It finally came to a head in the fall of 1844 when a group of Alabama Baptists pressed the General Convention for a ruling on whether slaveholders could serve as missionaries. The denomination's "acting board," located in Boston, answered that they could not appoint such a missionary. Baptists from around the South responded in May 1845 by creating the Southern Baptist Convention.

## Religion, Politics, and Society

Northern and Southern Protestants did not divide solely on how they read slavery in the Bible. They also divided on how they saw God's relationship to American society and the closely linked matter of the relationship between religion and politics. In the 1820s and 1830s the North experienced a wave of revivals. Led by famous evangelists such as Charles Finney (1792–1875), northern evangelicals came to believe that the society around them needed to be perfected through social reform, which would serve to bring about the kingdom of God on earth. At the same time, the North was steeped in the centuries-old Puritan notion of the United States as a covenanted nation like biblical Israel, a people chosen by God for a special purpose in the world. By the late antebellum years, northern Protestants came to believe key social reforms—such as the eradication of slavery—could be best achieved through political activism, particularly through the work of the antislavery Republican Party. As such, the political work of eradicating slavery gained a righteous stamp of approval. From a late antebellum northern religious viewpoint, the pro-slavery South, which stood in the way of the advancing kingdom of God, represented an enemy to be defeated. As armies prepared for war, Protestant ministers throughout the North overwhelmingly supported the Union effort and saw the war as a necessary "American Apocalypse" that would ultimately launch the Christian millennium.

Southern Protestants also came to believe that the Christian God sanctioned their section and, eventually, the Confederate nation. Unlike their counterparts in the North, however, such a view was a departure from historic patterns. For at least a century, dating to the colonial era, Southern evangelicals remained detached from direct political engagement, believing the church a purely spiritual institution that should not meddle with the purely secular affairs of state. This pervasive Southern Protestant doctrine, which achieved its fullest articulation among Southern Presbyterians as the "spirituality of the church," argued that the church's proper role was to aid in the saving of souls and the cultivating of individual piety, not to work for the perfection of society at large.

However, with the rise of more aggressive antislavery activism in the 1830s and the attacks on Southern society that followed, Southern Protestants became increasingly political. Slavery, the bedrock of antebellum white Southern society, was ordained of God. It was not the South that had erred, but the North, which Southerners believed ignored the plain teaching of the Bible about slavery.

The election of Abraham Lincoln (1809–1865) to the U.S. presidency in November 1860 proved decisive in securing Southern religious support for the Confederacy. Southerners convinced of the righteousness of slavery came to believe that an abolitionist conspiracy had taken over the American government. When the Confederacy ratified its constitution in March 1861, in sharp contrast to the U.S. Constitution, the Southern document signaled to all readers that the new nation was "invoking the favor and guidance of Almighty God." Like the North, the people of the South developed the belief that they were a chosen people who participated in a covenant relationship with God. From a Southern religious perspective, the Confederate cause—and war in its name—was a Christian one.

If the Confederate sense of Christian nationhood led Southerners to war convinced of their collective righteousness, God's plan for the South also meant that the nation had to live up to Christian standards. On the eve of the sectional crisis, and then throughout the war, Confederates participated in regular "fast days," ritual observances where ministers—like Old Testament prophets—called upon the nation to repent for its national sins and follow the Christian God. Fast days were also called regularly in the North during the conflict. In that section, they had been something of a regular occurrence dating to Puritan New England. For the South, however, like political preaching more generally, the tradition was much newer. Confederate President Jefferson Davis (1808–1889) called for no less than nine official fast days, and many others were called at the state and local levels. Since slavery was the core institution in the Christian South, fast day sermons often called on white Christian masters to realize the divine trust they had been given. They needed to bring the institution into conformity with biblical standards, making it more charitable, more benevolent, and more humane, or risk divine judgment at the hands of their oppressors—the heretical, abolitionist Union. War was God's way of testing his people.

## Chaplains

Many people in the North and South believed a chaplain system was necessary for good Christian armies and the sustaining of morale in the ranks. Prior to the war, the chaplaincy was relatively small and weak in the American military. In the Civil War, the system expanded greatly, and it has remained a fixture in the U.S. military ever since.

Union and Confederate chaplains both fulfilled one primary duty: they held regular religious services for soldiers. To be sure, chaplains also assisted in hospitals, wrote letters for soldiers, taught classes, delivered mail, carried supplies, and more, but in the main they existed to provide spiritual care. Throughout the war, on both sides, chaplains were in short supply and often complained of unreasonable treatment. In the Union, they earned $145 per month—equivalent to a cavalry captain—but they received private's rations and no forage for their horses. They were not officially accorded officer status until 1864. In mid-1862, Union chaplains began to receive officer's rations and forage but had their salary cut to $100 a month. In the Confederacy, chaplains were paid $80 a month, and they were not allotted uniforms, supplies, a horse, forage, or rations (though they were eventually allowed private's rations).

Hundreds of clergy, both South and North, found their skills best put to use as regular soldiers or officers rather than chaplains. Such was the case for, among others, Leonidas Polk (1806–1864), the Episcopal bishop of Louisiana who became a Confederate lieutenant general; Robert Lewis Dabney (1820–1898), a noted Presbyterian divine who served as chaplain for Confederate general Thomas J. "Stonewall" Jackson (1824–1863)—also a devout Presbyterian—before becoming a staff officer; and John Eaton Jr. (1829–1906), an ordained Presbyterian minister who began the war as a Union chaplain, became a colonel over an African American regiment in 1863, and was then appointed by General Ulysses S. Grant (1822–1885) as superintendent of Negro affairs in Tennessee, foreshadowing the duties undertaken later by the Freedmen's Bureau.

Over the course of the war, approximately 2,300 chaplains served in Union ranks, though no more than 600 ever served at once. Chaplains had long served in the U.S. military, but prior to the war, with a much smaller military, the peacetime number had been capped at 30 men. President Abraham Lincoln believed strongly in the importance and utility of the chaplaincy, seeing religion as cohesive and a morale-building agent. On May 4, 1861, the Union War Department issued orders that provided for the large-scale expansion of the chaplaincy so that each regiment might have spiritual guidance—though that goal was never fully realized.

Initially, federal orders only allowed for ordained Christian ministers to serve as chaplains, the expectation being that chaplains would primarily come from Protestant denominations. Within a year, however, concerns arose about chaplains' lacking proper qualifications for service. In July 1862, Congress responded to the issue by revising the terms of the office to provide for more rigorous standards. These revisions also opened the chaplaincy to clergy from any religious background. Theoretically, it became possible for non-Christian chaplains to serve, but in fact only one Jewish rabbi filled the post (along with one nonordained Jew who had served illegally in 1861). Indeed, representation from non-Protestant traditions proved minimal. Approximately 200,000 soldiers, about 10 percent of the Union army, were Catholic, but only 3 percent of all chaplains were Catholic priests. Overwhelmingly, Methodists provided the largest number of Union chaplains (38 percent), followed by Presbyterians (17 percent), Baptists (12 percent), Episcopalians (10 percent), Congregationalists (9 percent), Unitarian/Universalists (4 percent), and Lutherans (2 percent). African Americans were not permitted to serve as chaplains until 1863. After that date, 14 served, the most prominent of whom was Henry McNeal Turner (1834–1915), a future bishop in the African Methodist Episcopal Church.

The Confederacy (or Confederate States of America, the C.S.A.) did not develop nearly as organized or expansive a chaplaincy as the Union. Over the course of the war, 938 chaplains—14 percent of all Southern clergy—served the Southern cause. Almost half were Methodists (47 percent), but Presbyterians (18 percent), Baptists (16 percent), Episcopalians (10 percent), and Catholics (3 percent) were also represented. In May 1861, the Confederate Congress authorized the creation of a chaplaincy but allowed chaplains few benefits and offered little guidance about formal duties. Confederate President Jefferson Davis and Secretary of War James Seddon (1815–1880), who saw chaplains as inconsequential to military efforts, offered little support for the office. The Confederacy had been created in rebellion against the centralized power of the U.S. government; the C.S.A. simply did not have an efficient bureaucracy for the organizing of chaplains, which Southern leaders saw as tangential to their primary military aims. Moreover, due to a long-standing Southern Protestant commitment to the separation of church and state, many Southerners opposed the creation of military offices for clergy. Because of the widely held "spirituality of the church" view, many Southerners maintained that religious bodies, not the secular government, should provide for soldiers' spiritual care. As a result, the Confederacy's chaplains, while often visible and prominent members of the military, suffered from an ambiguous status.

## Charitable Organizations

In addition to the formal military structure of the chaplaincy, numerous charitable civilian organizations emerged to support the war effort. In most cases, these supporting organizations drew from deep religious roots. An 1864 study estimated that in the Union alone, to that date, approximately $212 million had been raised to support Civil War philanthropy. While charitable societies existed in virtually every town, one of the most visible organizations was the United States Christian Commission. Founded in November 1861 by members of the New York Young Men's Christian Association and led by Philadelphia Presbyterian layman George H. Stuart (1816–1890), the Christian Commission organized roughly five thousand volunteers from a wide variety of evangelical denominations. The Christian Commission offered general support to the armies by visiting sick and wounded soldiers, assisting surgeons, writing letters for soldiers, presiding at revival meetings, sponsoring chaplains, and running soup kitchens to supplement soldiers' diets. It is estimated that the Christian Commission received and distributed more than $6 million along with roughly 1.5 million Bibles, 1 million hymnals, and 39 million tracts among Union ranks.

The United States Sanitary Commission was similarly visible in the Union war effort. Founded in July 1861 following a meeting of the New York City–based Women's Central Association of Relief and led by Unitarian Henry W. Bellows (1814–1882), the Sanitary Commission drew from a liberal Protestant emphasis on humanitarianism. It worked to regulate medical standards, distributed needed supplies to military surgeons, and provided donated food and clothing for soldiers. Over the course of the war, the Sanitary Commission raised an estimated $25 million and helped to drastically lower the rate of disease in Union ranks.

Relief for freedpeople also constituted one of the primary outlets for civilian charity. Devoted primarily to providing educational opportunities for former slaves, by the end of the war, nearly one thousand teachers from variety of organizations were serving freedpeople. The most prominent freedpeople's relief organization was the evangelically minded American Missionary Association (AMA). Founded in 1846 and devoted to abolition of slavery, by 1865 the AMA had 320 workers operating schools for former slaves in every Southern state and almost every major Southern city. Within the next decade their ranks would swell to the thousands, and they assisted in the opening of several hundred schools along with a number of Southern colleges—such as Fisk, Atlanta, Dillard, and Howard—for freedpeople.

In the Confederacy, civilian aid tended to be offered at a more local level, but soldiers and ladies aid societies existed in nearly every Southern town. Leading the way among broader religious relief efforts was the Evangelical Tract Society of the Confederacy, which became a primary dispenser of print among Southern soldiers. Organized in July 1861 in Petersburg, Virginia, it produced an estimated one hundred tracts and fifty million pages of print over the course of the Civil War. One of its primary outlets was the *Army and Navy Messenger,* a newspaper that circulated to soldiers. Several other significant newspapers were sponsored by denominations, including the Baptist *Soldier's Friend* (Atlanta), the Presbyterian *Soldier's Visitor* (Richmond), and the Methodist *Soldier's Paper* (Richmond). These organs collectively encouraged soldiers fighting for what they saw as a Christian cause.

## Revivals

The course and progress of the war surprised both the Union and Confederacy. Neither side expected the war to take more than a few months, nor did they expect much bloodshed. By the end of 1862, it was clear that those expectations were misguided. On April 6 and 7 of that year, the Battle of Shiloh, in western Tennessee, claimed more than twenty-three thousand casualties. To date, it was the bloodiest battle in American history. Just a few months later, on September 17, Union and Confederate armies matched Shiloh's casualties in a single day. In what remains the bloodiest day in American military history, Confederate general Robert E. Lee's (1807–1870) Army of Northern Virginia battled Union general George B. McClellan's (1826–1885) Army of the Potomac at Antietam Creek near Sharpsburg, Maryland, resulting in roughly twenty-three thousand casualties.

Such catastrophic losses—and the knowledge that the war would not be ending in the near future—led many soldiers to look for religious meaning in the conflict. Drawing on a long nineteenth-century tradition of revivalism, including the recent "businessman's revival" of 1857–1858—which primarily spread through the urban centers of the North—Union soldiers stationed in Washington, Chicago, and St. Louis experienced waves of heightened religiosity in 1862. It was not until the next year, 1863, that revivals had their most lasting impact among Union ranks. After significant victories in the siege of Vicksburg (May 18–July 4; nineteen thousand casualties) and the battle at Gettysburg (July 1–3; fifty-one thousand casualties), the Union army was dealt a serious defeat in September at Chickamauga Creek, near Chattanooga, Tennessee. The three-day battle was costly, with thirty-four thousand casualties, and the Union army was forced to retreat to Chattanooga while Confederates held highlands around the city and settled into a siege. As soldiers waited for General Ulysses S. Grant to come and take over command of the army, Union ranks became infused with heightened Christian fervor as soldiers implored God for their deliverance. Then, in late November, when Grant's army won the battle of Chattanooga by unexpectedly running Confederate forces off of their high position—a development that many contemporary observers saw as a miraculous show of divine favor for the Union—soldiers in the ranks became more sure of God's will for the Union. In the winter of 1863–1864, Grant's army camped nearby at Ringgold, Georgia. There, the revival continued among the soldiers, with hundreds baptized in the Chickamauga. The revivals of 1863–1864 strengthened Union resolve, improved morale, and prepared soldiers for the immense amount of bloodshed to come in the next year. For Union troops, revivals seemed linked to military fortunes as well as the promise of nearly certain death. As the army drew closer to victory but the battles grew more fierce—as in the case of 1864's Overland Campaign, which claimed one hundred thousand casualties—revivalism grew more prevalent among soldiers.

Among Confederate ranks, revivals followed a trajectory similar to those in the Union. Periodic revivals spread throughout the Confederate army in 1862 and 1863. Then, following Gettysburg and Vicksburg, revivalism seemed to become a constant fixture for the next several months. The Confederate religious press regularly made mention of revivals in the camp throughout the latter half of 1863 and into 1864. In that time in the Army of Northern Virginia, about seven thousand soldiers (roughly 10 percent of Lee's force) converted to Christianity, and thirty-two of thirty-eight brigades felt some effect of what participants called the "Great Revival." In the Army of Tennessee, a reported eleven of twenty-eight brigades were touched by revival during the Chickamauga-Chattanooga campaign. Then, as they wintered in Dalton, Georgia—near the Union troops who were experiencing their own revival in Ringgold—the revival continued into the spring of 1864. As was the case for Union soldiers, revival sustained Confederates and encouraged them to continue the fight, though for different reasons. Where Northern soldiers experienced victories, Confederates sensed imminent defeat. Yet convinced they served a just God who ordered the universe, Confederate soldiers still believed they had done right in the eyes of the Lord. If God's will required that the Confederacy be defeated, they could face death assured of the righteousness of their cause. In this way, both in North and South, the revivals that began in 1862 and reached their full flourishing in the winter of 1863–1864 contributed considerably to the prolonging of the war.

An estimated one hundred thousand Confederate soldiers converted to Christianity during the war. At least that number, but perhaps as many as two hundred thousand, converted in Union ranks. The experience of revival was relatively similar for soldiers on both sides. Following patterns established decades earlier in American religious history, revivals were a democratic affair. While chaplains and representatives of voluntary organizations aided revivals whenever and wherever possible, neither was ubiquitous enough in camps to provide consistent religious leadership. As such, it was the common soldiers themselves who drove revivals, with much emphasis placed on individual experience and little authority ceded to educated clergy.

Revivals in the camp were also a conspicuously masculine affair, differing greatly from the prior history of American evangelical experience. Throughout the nineteenth century and into the late antebellum period, the common assumption was that church and expressions of piety were particularly feminine in nature. Men were certainly active religious actors, but such expressions of devotion tended to be seen as reserved for women. Revivals in the camp fundamentally changed such views. As large groups of Civil War soldiers responded to gospel messages, their experiences recast evangelicalism and revivalism as masculine in nature. While there were certainly many, many soldiers who remained untouched by revivalist fervor, those who experienced revival often looked at their fellow men as Christian brothers, fit to serve one another in battle.

## Women and the Home Front

As religious gender norms changed for men serving in Civil War armies, so they also changed for women on the home front. Military ranks were closed to women in the Union and Confederacy, but religious activism offered opportunities for service and access to the world of politics. Not only were they the primary movers behind civilian relief efforts but, with an overwhelming number of men away from home, women also became heads of households. Moreover, as numerous churches had to close their doors due to lack of a minister or enough congregants or local military action, women stepped into new leadership roles in their religious communities.

These realities were particularly acute in the Confederacy. The Civil War brought massive destruction to the South, where all the battles other than Gettysburg took place. The toll on Southern religious life was particularly noticeable. Many overarching religious bodies, such as presbyteries, synods, conferences, and conventions had to suspend regularly scheduled meetings due to local military conflict. In other cases, when organizations opted to convene, representation was so thin that quorums could not be gathered. At the local level, many churches had to shut their doors to regular worshippers. In this religious environment, women on the home front worked to provide consistent religious support for those around them, holding prayer and reading groups at private homes. In the process, the site of religious community shifted from the public church to the domestic home.

That change in practice spoke to a larger change that occurred ideologically among religious Confederate women. At the outset of the war they believed that God was on their side and behind their cause. As the war progressed and the tide turned against the Confederacy, its devout women believed their new nation's suffering—like the biblical case of Job—was sent by God as a test designed to strengthen their faith. As the numbers of Confederate dead grew, devout Southern women found themselves suffering on an individual, psychological level. Over time, the loss of loved ones reminded religious women of their own mortality and enabled them to face death without fear. At the same time, however, it also led them to question the religious wisdom they had been taught about the nature of properly Christian social order. It was widely believed in the antebellum white South that God had ordained a system of paternalism and patriarchy that ensured proper relationships in human society. From God almighty, power was extended to white men, who were to exercise benevolent authority over women, children, and black slave dependents. The Civil War, however, caused Southern women to question that entire arrangement. Following God's will and embracing the Confederacy had only brought pain and loss to women at home.

Southern women did not abandon their faith en masse at the end of the war, but their understanding of gender roles, shaped by their experience over the previous four years, had changed to allow for a greater degree of religious autonomy.

## African Americans and Emancipation

Slavery's end came with the Emancipation Proclamation (1863)—which declared slaves in conquered territories free—and the postwar Thirteenth Amendment (1865), which banned involuntary servitude in the United States (the border slave states of Missouri, Kentucky, Maryland, and Delaware, which had never joined the Confederacy, were not bound by the Emancipation Proclamation). These legal changes, which freed approximately four million slaves, launched a revolution in American religious life.

Like whites in the North and South who read Providence into their war effort, African Americans also saw the hand of God at work. However, blacks interpreted the war differently. Like the biblical Hebrews who had been liberated from Egyptian slavery in the Exodus narrative, American blacks had been liberated from the oppression of white masters. When former slaves were given the chance to seize their own religious destiny, apart from white influence, they took it. Autonomous black churches had existed in the North since the late eighteenth century, but in the South most slaves worshipped with whites in biracial churches and were relegated to second-class seating. While those antebellum biracial churches had often provided Southern blacks the only public space where they could speak with authority among whites, their postemancipation actions demonstrated clearly that they no longer wished to practice a religion dictated by their former masters. Almost immediately after the war, a significant percentage of former slaves moved to black denominations, either newly created or linked to those already existing in the North. The Methodist Episcopal Church, South, for example, counted 207,766 African American members in 1860. In 1866, that number dropped to 78,742 members.

## The War's Religious Legacy

On April 9, 1865, Robert E. Lee surrendered to Ulysses S. Grant at Appomattox Courthouse in Virginia, confirming Confederate defeat and bringing an end to the war. Though the military conflict ended, the religious divisions between North and South persisted well beyond the war. In President Abraham Lincoln's Second Inaugural Address, delivered on March 4, just a month prior to Confederate surrender, he perceptively surmised the religious stakes of the conflict, famously stating, "Both read the same Bible and pray to the same God, and each invokes His aid against the other." Lincoln was never baptized, nor did he ever join a church. Yet in his Second Inaugural, Lincoln suggested that neither Union nor Confederate Christians had clearly understood the work of Providence in the Civil War. In so doing, the president sought to repair the deep religious divide that had broken the nation years before.

Most religious Americans, however, stuck to the beliefs they maintained throughout the conflict. Union victory convinced Northerners that they had been right and uniquely blessed by God. The defeated South needed to repent for the division it had brought to the nation and its religious life. The Northern branches of denominations that split before the war refused to consider religious reunion afterward, without Southern confessions for the sins of slave-holding and disunion. That was not something white Southerners were prepared to do in the immediate aftermath of the war. (Methodists did not reunite until 1939, Presbyterians waited until 1983, and Baptists never repaired their schism.) Like Northerners, white Southerners retained their belief in the righteousness of their section and the divine sanction for slave-holding. Although slavery no longer existed legally, the inherent racism of the pro-slavery argument remained quite visible in the creation of a segregationist social order that relegated former slaves to secondary status. Former Confederates did their best to return the South to the antebellum status quo. As such, the theological crisis that had paved the way for the Civil War was never truly resolved.

At the same time, the inability to resolve that theological crisis led to a diminished role for clergy—and organized evangelical religion more broadly—in American society. The language of religion did not disappear from American public life as a result of the Civil War. Rather, it contributed to forging a civic faith, or "civil religion," devoted first to the causes of the nation. In the name of patriotism, American civil religion invented its own sacred days—such as Thanksgiving, celebrated annually in the North from 1863, when Abraham Lincoln called for a national day of Thanksgiving, and finally declared a federal holiday in 1939 by President Franklin D. Roosevelt (1882–1945). Civil religion also sacralized key texts in the national mythology, such as Lincoln's Gettysburg Address (1863) and Second Inaugural (1865). Moreover, civil religion also enshrined memories of its national saints in monuments, as was the case of the Lincoln Memorial, erected in 1922 to mark the legacy of a president martyred in the name of preserving the nation and ending slavery.

The South developed its own form of a civil religion in the "religion of the Lost Cause," which developed from 1865 into the early twentieth century. It had its own rituals, which reminded white Southerners of the righteousness of slavery and the supremacy of their race. In contrast to holidays that celebrated the Union—Thanksgiving and Independence Day, for example, were not regularly observed in the South until long after the Civil War—there were days set aside annually to remember Southern sacrifice, such as Confederate Memorial Day, begun in 1866 and held every June 3. Monuments to Confederate dead sprang up throughout the South, and famous Confederate leaders were enshrined in stained glass windows in Southern churches. Regiments of soldiers gathered annually for sermons on the sectional crisis, and when a Confederate veteran died, strict guidelines regulated the funeral service. Groups like the United Daughters of the Confederacy (founded 1894) and the Sons of Confederate Veterans (founded 1896) organized to preserve Confederate memory. The Ku Klux Klan, perhaps the most notorious racist terrorist organization in American history, was created in 1866 by former Confederate general Nathan Bedford Forrest (1821–1877) and claimed to be preserving a Southern Christian legacy. While none of these forms of memorialization came from a deeply theological foundation, they all drew from religious roots and spoke to the ways religious ideas about the Civil War persisted long after the fighting ceased.

**See also** *Abolitionism and Antislavery; African American Religion entries; American Revolution; Civil Religion in the United States; Cult of Domesticity; Evangelicals: Nineteenth Century; Holidays; Pacifism and Conscientious Objection; Philanthropy; Politics: Nineteenth Century; Revivalism: Nineteenth Century; World War I; World War II; Women entries.*

Luke E. Harlow

**BIBLIOGRAPHY**

Dvorak, Katharine L. *An African-American Exodus: The Segregation of the Southern Churches.* Brooklyn, N.Y.: Carlson, 1991.

Faust, Drew Gilpin. *Mothers of Invention: Women of the Slaveholding South in the American Civil War.* Chapel Hill: University of North Carolina Press, 1996.

Genovese, Eugene D. *A Consuming Fire: The Fall of the Confederacy in the Mind of the White Christian South.* Athens: University of Georgia Press, 1998.

Goen, C. C. *Broken Churches, Broken Nation: Denominational Schisms and the Coming of the Civil War.* Macon, Ga.: Mercer University Press, 1985.

Miller, Randall M., Harry S. Stout, and Charles Reagan Wilson, eds. *Religion in the American Civil War.* New York: Oxford University Press, 1998.

Miller, Robert J. *Both Prayed to the Same God: Religion and Faith in the American Civil War.* Lanham, Md.: Lexington Books, 2007.

Moorhead, James H. *American Apocalypse: Yankee Protestants and the Civil War, 1860–1869.* New Haven, Conn.: Yale University Press, 1978.

Noll, Mark A. *The Civil War as a Theological Crisis.* Chapel Hill: University of North Carolina Press, 2006.

Shattuck, Gardiner H., Jr. *A Shield and a Hiding Place: The Religious Life of the Civil War Armies.* Macon, Ga.: Mercer University Press, 1987.

Snay, Mitchell. *Gospel of Disunion: Religion and Separatism in the Antebellum South.* Cambridge: Cambridge University Press, 1993.

Stout, Harry S. *Upon the Altar of the Nation: A Moral History of the Civil War.* New York: Viking, 2006.

Stowell, Daniel W. *Rebuilding Zion: The Religious Reconstruction of the South, 1863–1877.* New York: Oxford University Press, 1998.

Wilson, Charles Reagan. *Baptized in Blood: The Religion of the Lost Cause, 1865–1920.* Athens: University of Georgia Press, 1980.

Woodworth, Steven E. *While God Is Marching On: The Religious World of Civil War Soldiers.* Lawrence: University Press of Kansas, 2001.

# Common Sense Realism

Common sense realism is a philosophical position that affirms the reality of the objects of our senses and the legitimacy of our knowledge of them. To nonphilosophers this might hardly seem to need affirmation, but in the history of philosophy it has been a controversial assertion, and indeed sometimes even treated with scorn. Nevertheless, common sense realism has been, and still remains, important in the history of American Christian intellectual life.

## Origins: Thomas Reid and the Scottish Enlightenment

Common sense realism arose in reaction against the philosophy known as British empiricism, developed in the late seventeenth and eighteenth centuries by John Locke (1632–1704), George Berkeley (1685–1753), and David Hume (1711–1776). Locke taught that our minds only know "ideas," that is, sensory perceptions, not the external world that provokes them. Berkeley drew the conclusion that nothing really exists except that which perceives or is perceived. What keeps objects in existence when no one is looking? Berkeley, a bishop, had an answer: God perceived them. But Hume took Berkeley's metaphysical idealism to drastically skeptical conclusions. If all we know is a stream of sense impressions, then the outside world is only a fiction. True, in everyday life we cannot help believing that there is an outside world, Hume admitted, but this belief is merely a psychological necessity, not *philosophically* justified. There were no arguments that justified faith in God, Hume claimed; indeed, even belief in causality was merely a custom, and not rigorously justifiable. A person could not be sure that memories represented events that had actually happened, and so did not truly know (in a rigorous sense) that she or he was the same person from one moment to the next. To these disturbing assertions, the metaphysical realism of common sense proposed a rebuttal.

Common sense realism first appeared in Scotland. Hume was a Scot, and his fellow countrymen felt most strongly the urge to find an answer to his skepticism. The original definitive formulation of common sense realism came from Thomas Reid (1710–1796), professor first at the University of Aberdeen and after 1764 at the University of Glasgow. In that year Reid published *An Inquiry into the Human Mind, on the Principles of Common Sense*. In 1785 he completed his *Essays on the Intellectual Powers of Man*.

Reid went back to the first epistemological principle of the British empiricists and challenged it. The objects of knowledge, he insisted, were not ideas in the mind, but sensible things in themselves. He found Locke's notion of representational ideas not only superfluous but a barrier to understanding. The human mind included certain built-in constituents of consciousness that Reid called "common sense." These were fundamental principles of knowledge. They included the axioms of mathematics and logic, belief in causality, trust in our own senses and memory, and belief that other people too exist and that their testimony is entitled to some credence. In sum, they provided the rebuttal to Humean skepticism. A Presbyterian clergyman, Reid accepted the principle that God is no deceiver, so the faculties he has given us are entitled to reliance. The proper task of philosophy, according to Reid, was to accept and deal with the data of experience—not to challenge their validity. Reid and his disciples saw themselves as Baconians, respecting evidence. The validity of inductive reasoning constituted part of their definition of common sense.

Reid termed his basic principles "common" not because they were merely ordinary but because everyone shared them. The word *common* was a powerful one, used for the common law, the common land of a village, the common weal, and the *Book of Common Prayer*. A commoner was a citizen, with a voice in the common affairs, represented in the House of Commons. Reid declared his principles to be "sense" because he considered them rational, as one might speak of "a man of sense." Jane Austen used the word this way when she distinguished between "sense" and "sensibility." Thomas Paine called his great polemic against the British monarchy on behalf of American independence *Common Sense*.

Reid's philosophy of common sense realism figured prominently in the flowering of the Scottish Enlightenment. Reid belonged to the "Moderate" wing of the established Church of Scotland (the Presbyterian Church), a party eager to synthesize Christianity with the Enlightenment. Opposing the Moderates were the Popular, or Evangelical, party, who insisted on a stricter adherence to Calvinism and a more austere lifestyle. These ecclesiastical parties would remain significant in the history of the Presbyterian Church in the United States, recipient of many Scottish influences. Common sense realism demonstrated its strength by appealing to thinkers in both camps.

The impressive roster of famous intellectuals in the Scottish Enlightenment includes Adam Smith, Francis Hutcheson, Hugh Blair, Lord Kames, William Robertson, Adam Ferguson, and the philosopher who transmitted Reid's work to nineteenth-century Britain and America, Dugald Stewart (1753–1828). Out of the work of these thinkers developed much of the social science, history, and cultural studies of later generations. The Scottish Enlightenment had a large and multifaceted influence on the American Enlightenment, partly as a result of the institutional example of the Scottish universities on American higher education. The philosophy of common sense realism permeated these intellectual developments.

## Reasons for Widespread Influence

To appreciate why Reid's ideas exerted such widespread influence, we need to understand the scope of moral philosophy in the eighteenth and nineteenth centuries. Reid succeeded to the chair of moral philosophy at the University of Glasgow upon the departure of Adam Smith. The discipline of moral philosophy as then defined included, along with what we call ethical theory, epistemology and metaphysics on the one hand and, on the other, all of what we consider the social sciences: psychology, sociology, anthropology, and political science. The problem of how we know what is right was thus considered in the context of how we have other kinds of knowledge. The social sciences gained inclusion as illustrations of applied morality. To us it seems an anomaly that Adam Smith wrote both *The Theory of Moral Sentiments* and *The Wealth of Nations*. To his contemporaries, he simply addressed two facets of his assigned subject.

Because moral philosophy addressed not only ethics but also epistemology and the empirical sciences of human behavior, the word *moral* could be applied not only to ethical matters but also to inductive knowledge, as opposed to deductive conclusions. "Moral evidence" meant empirical evidence. From this usage, now obsolete, we retain the expression "moral certainty."

Reid addressed the epistemology of morality in his *Essays on the Active Powers of Man* (1788). Reid believed in a rational moral sense, analogous to the common sense that structured our knowledge of sensory objects. The moral sense intuited principles of morality, such as that promises should be kept, in the same way that common sense intuited that the whole is equal to the sum of its parts and validated the existence of the outside world. Moral principles are objective and rational, declared Reid. Not all his contemporaries agreed with him; in Scotland itself, both Francis Hutcheson and Adam Smith described the moral sense as a feeling, a "sentiment," rather than an intellectual function, although they did not deny the objective reality of moral principles. In the technical language of philosophy, Reid's ethical theory represented a form of deontological intuitionism, one that he presented as compatible with common sense realism in epistemology.

Closely associated with moral philosophy was another academic discipline of former times, natural theology. Natural theology studied the phenomena of natural science in order to demonstrate from them the existence and attributes of the divine creator. The intelligent and benevolent design of the universe seemed obvious to practically everybody then. Even the harshest critics of organized religion, the deists, believed in intelligent design. Indeed, the deists critiqued biblical revelation as unnecessary, given the infinitely more impressive revelation God had provided in the testimony of his creation itself. Pre-Darwinian natural science did not refute natural theology, and although Hume's *Dialogues Concerning Natural Religion* (published posthumously in 1779) presented telling criticisms of natural theology, they did not have much impact on received opinion. Treatises on moral philosophy in the eighteenth and nineteenth centuries often included a section on natural theology. Together, moral philosophy and natural theology served a desire for a science of human nature grounded in a God-given natural morality. The aspiration to value-free social science that

appeared in a later generation had zero appeal for thinkers of the Anglophone Enlightenment.

Scottish common sense realism exerted international influence for several generations—for example, on the French philosophers Victor Cousin and Theodore Jouffroy. But the distinctive synthesis of common sense moral philosophy with natural theology found a particularly receptive audience in the English-speaking countries. It represented a happy synthesis of Protestantism with the Enlightenment, and by no means excluded deists. The American founders shared in the assumptions and vocabulary of this consensus. Thomas Jefferson, Benjamin Franklin, and John Adams, discussing the wording of the American Declaration of Independence, chose to characterize their assertion that all men are created equal as "self-evident"—a favorite term of common sense realism and intuitionist moral philosophy. Later, when Jefferson went to Paris as ambassador to France, he made friends with Reid's leading disciple, Dugald Stewart, and later hoped (vainly) to recruit him for the University of Virginia.

## Common Sense Realism Comes to America

A figure of central importance in the transmission to America of common sense realism and the Scottish Enlightenment in general was John Witherspoon (1723–1794), an evangelical clergyman in the Church of Scotland who in 1768 accepted the presidency of the College of New Jersey, now Princeton University. Besides providing administrative leadership to the college, Witherspoon also taught moral philosophy. His lectures, delivered over a period of many years and eventually published, influenced hundreds of American statesmen, educators, and clergy trained at Princeton between 1768 and 1794. The lectures included a section on "civil polity," or political philosophy, defending natural rights, including the right of resistance to tyranny, and the principle of checks and balances. Witherspoon exerted practical as well as theoretical influence in American politics, for he played a prominent role in the Sons of Liberty during the Revolution, signed the Declaration of Independence (the only clergyman to do so), served in the Continental Congress, and supported the Constitution at the New Jersey state ratification convention.

Witherspoon's *Lectures on Moral Philosophy* (published posthumously in 1801) rejected the metaphysical idealism of Berkeley and Hume in favor of common sense realism. His account of human nature followed Francis Hutcheson's in most respects but tipped it toward ethical intuitionism.

Under his leadership, Princeton moved away from the metaphysical idealism and ethical sentimentalism of its famous earlier president, Jonathan Edwards, and embraced the Scottish philosophical tradition of Thomas Reid.

Witherspoon's Princeton modeled higher education for other American colleges for decades to come. Moral philosophy, defined as Reid and Witherspoon did to include common sense realism in both epistemology and ethics, along with natural theology, constituted the capstone of the nineteenth-century American college curriculum. Because of its effort to synthesize a wide range of human knowledge into an intelligible, natural, moral, and Christian system, the moral philosophy of that time has been called a "Protestant scholasticism." Typically, moral philosophy constituted a required course for seniors, taught by the college president. As it had appealed to both moderates and evangelicals in Scotland, common sense realism bridged denominational and theological differences in the United States. Its prominent advocates included Francis Bowen and James Walker at Unitarian Harvard, Francis Wayland at Baptist Brown, Noah Porter at Congregationalist Yale, Mark Hopkins at Congregationalist Williams, and Archibald Alexander at Presbyterian Princeton Theological Seminary (a new institution, separate from Princeton University). Unless he attended a Catholic institution, practically everyone who went to college in the United States between, say, 1820 and 1870 learned the comprehensive moral philosophy of Scottish common sense.

## Decline of Common Sense Realism

Scottish common sense realism in the United States reached a kind of culmination with James McCosh (1811–1894) of Princeton University. McCosh was a Scottish Presbyterian clergyman, who, like Witherspoon, was invited to take up the presidency of Princeton in 1868, exactly one hundred years after Witherspoon's arrival. McCosh defended what had become the conventional American academic philosophy in *Our Moral Nature* (1893) and *Philosophy of Reality* (1894). McCosh's neighbor at Princeton Theological Seminary, Charles Hodge, invoked common sense realism in his *What is Darwinism?* (1874), an attempt to refute Charles Darwin's theory of evolution. By this time, however, Scottish common sense realism had already fallen under serious criticism and had come to seem old-fashioned.

The dominance enjoyed by Scottish common sense realism declined in both Britain and the United States during the later decades of the nineteenth century. The

James McCosh, a Scottish Presbyterian clergyman, became president of Princeton University in 1868. He defended common sense realism when it came under assault during the late 1800s.

first important attack on it came not from a philosopher but from an historian. Henry Thomas Buckle (1821–1862), in *On Scotland and the Scotch Intellect* (1861), treated Scottish common sense philosophy as socially conservative and an instrument of clerical supremacy. Buckle's argument was based on the premise that deductive reasoning was elitist, while inductive reasoning was democratic. He then identified the Scottish philosophers with deduction, even though the thinkers considered themselves—often rightly—champions of Baconian induction. Buckle's caricature of common sense realism enjoyed a long life in intellectual historiography. Of more immediate effect was the assault that came from within the discipline of philosophy.

The great German philosopher Immanuel Kant (1724–1804) had despised common sense realism, which he dismissed as an appeal to the judgment of the crowd. (Just the opposite of Buckle's criticism, it appears.) Nevertheless William Hamilton (1805–1865), appointed professor of moral philosophy at Edinburgh in 1836, undertook to reconcile Kant with Reid and subsume Kant's views within the framework of Scottish common sense. Hamilton's work provoked one of the most effective rebuttals in the history of philosophy: John Stuart Mill's *An Examination of Sir William Hamilton's Philosophy* (1865). Like Buckle, Mill (1806–1873) considered common sense realism a philosophy of political conservatism; he made its destruction in favor of the phenomenalism of the British empiricists (that is, their belief that we know our perceptions rather than things in themselves) a necessary part of his own liberal political agenda. Not a first-rate thinker, Hamilton proved a sitting duck for Mill. The Edinburgh professor had died, but James McCosh and others went to his defense. Still, the intellectual world of the time soon decided that Mill had demolished not only Hamilton but common sense realism in general. The pedagogical use of Scottish moral philosophy declined to the vanishing point throughout Anglophone higher education. Today, Mill has survived as a great thinker while Hamilton is forgotten. Mill's *Examination of Hamilton* is ignored, too, and not considered one of his major philosophical writings.

Meanwhile in the United States, the isolated genius Charles Sanders Peirce (1839–1914) was pioneering the philosophy of pragmatism along with other original intellectual endeavors. Peirce remained a metaphysical realist of sorts and developed his own argument for the existence of God. But his successors in the pragmatist tradition, William James (1842–1910) and John Dewey (1859–1952), departed further from the concerns of nineteenth-century academic philosophy. They saw the world as fluid and made by human beings, not as fixed and made by God. Like Mill they wanted a metaphysical foundation for democratic participation and did not see it in common sense realism. The rise of separate social sciences, which the pragmatists found hopeful, rendered the old-fashioned comprehensive academic course in moral philosophy obsolete. The version of common sense realism prevailing in American higher education had been Christian, and it is no accident that the secularizing universities of the early twentieth century hastened to leave it behind.

## Twentieth Century: A Philosophical Revival

For most of the twentieth century, common sense realism remained in bad odor in the United States: out of fashion with philosophers, treated with condescension by historians, who followed in Buckle's footsteps. Joseph Blau

(1909–1986), in *Men and Movements in American Philosophy* (1952), expressed the prevailing view of the Scottish-American philosophy of common sense as naive, dogmatic, socially conservative, and the servant of an outmoded religion. Some of the advocates of common sense realism were indeed popularizers and polemicists (the Scotsmen James Beattie and James Oswald, for example) who deserved this treatment, but others were serious philosophers and educators who did not.

Significantly, philosophers and not historians led the revival of respect for Scottish common sense realism. Writing in *A History of American Philosophy* (1977), Elizabeth Flower (1915–1995) emphasized that the Scottish philosophy should be considered part of the Enlightenment, not a reaction against it, and even provided a sympathetic account of James McCosh's restatement of realist metaphysics. Not long afterwards, George Marsden (1939–) started to bring the intellectual historians around, describing the common sense realism of nineteenth-century American education as antielitist, democratic, and supportive toward natural science.

Crucial to the recovery of respect for the common sense realism of past times has been the fact of its being taken seriously in the present. Although common sense realism is now a minority metaphysical viewpoint, some noteworthy twentieth-century philosophers have embraced versions of it. The most famous of these was the Englishman George Edward Moore (1873–1958), usually called G. E. Moore. Moore defended metaphysical realism and, even more impressively, ethical intuitionism. He expounded the latter with extraordinary sophistication and persuasiveness, even in the face of the skepticism of the logical positivists (some of whom were his colleagues at Cambridge University). Moore did not believe in God, the major difference (apart from his greater analytic skill) between him and the earlier philosophers of common sense.

In the United States, common sense realism is still sometimes identified with evangelical Protestantism, including varieties of fundamentalism, but this is by no means invariably the case. Roderick Chisholm (1916–1999) and Amie Thomasson (1973–) have defended forms of common sense realism in recent years without reference to religion. Philosophers who formulate their own versions of common sense realism and synthesize them with Christianity include Alvin Plantinga (1932–) and Nicholas Rescher (1928–). It is a significant commentary on how the cultural climate has changed over the past century that the Protestant Plantinga teaches in a Roman Catholic university and Rescher is a Catholic himself.

**See also** *Atheism, Agnosticism, and Disbelief; Deism; Education: Colleges and Universities; Enlightenment; Ethics; Idealist Philosophy; Philosophical Theology; Philosophy; Pragmatism; Religious Thought* entries.

Daniel Walker Howe

## BIBLIOGRAPHY

Ellingsen, Mark. *A Common Sense Theology: The Bible, Faith, and American Society.* Macon, Ga.: Mercer University Press, 1995.

Flower, Elizabeth, and Murray Murphey. *A History of Philosophy in America.* Vol. I. New York: Putnam, 1977.

Grave, S. A. *The Scottish Philosophy of Common Sense.* Oxford: Oxford University Press, 1960.

Hodge, Charles. *What Is Darwinism?* Edited by Mark A. Noll and David N. Livingstone. Grand Rapids, Mich.: Baker Books, 1994.

Howe, Daniel Walker. "John Witherspoon and the Transatlantic Enlightenment." In *The Atlantic Enlightenment,* edited by Susan Manning and Francis D. Cogliano, 61–80. Aldershot, UK: Ashgate, 2008.

———. *The Unitarian Conscience: Harvard Moral Philosophy, 1805–1861.* With a new introduction. Middletown, Conn. Wesleyan University Press, 1988.

Lemos, Noah. *Common Sense: A Contemporary Defense.* Cambridge: Cambridge University Press, 2004.

Marsden, George. *The Soul of the American University: From Protestant Establishment to Established Nonbelief.* Oxford: Oxford University Press, 1994.

Meyer, D. H. *The Instructed Conscience: The Shaping of the American National Ethic.* Philadelphia: University of Pennsylvania Press, 1972.

Moore, G. E. *Philosophical Papers.* New York: Macmillan, 1959.

Thomasson, Amie. *Ordinary Objects.* Oxford: Oxford University Press, 2007.

Wayland, Francis. *The Elements of Moral Science.* Edited by Joseph L. Blau. Cambridge, Mass.: Harvard University Press, 1963.

Witherspoon, John. *An Annotated Edition of Lectures on Moral Philosophy.* Edited by Jack Scott. Newark, N.J.: University of Delaware Press, 1982.

# Congregationalists

A distinct stream within the sixteenth- and seventeenth-century English Reformation, Congregationalism is an old and influential American religious tradition. More specifically, Congregationalism was part of the Reformed wing of the Protestant Reformation, sharing broadly Calvinist beliefs but also emphasizing the freedom of the local church, formed by the signing of a members' covenant and unhindered by any higher forms of ecclesiastical authority.

At the same time, however, American Congregationalism has always insisted on the necessity of church connection. Since the earliest days of New England settlement, local churches created various forms of mutual oversight, beginning with the Cambridge Platform of 1648 and continuing on through the evolution of a national denominational structure in the late nineteenth century.

But every move toward centralized structure has generated debate and controversy about Congregational identity, especially with the merger that created the United Church of Christ in 1957. Indeed, for a religious tradition with relatively few doctrinal requirements, the nature of "authentic Congregationalism" has remained a constant and often deeply vexing question.

## The English Independents

Congregationalism originated in the dynastic woes of King Henry VIII (1491–1547), who wished an annulment of his first marriage in order to marry the young Anne Boleyn and produce a male heir. He had his way through the Act of Supremacy in 1534, which made him the "supreme head" of the Church of England. But though the act denied the authority of the Roman Catholic pope, it kept old beliefs and institutions intact; the Anglican Church, or Church of England, continued the hierarchical structure and ritual forms it had inherited from sixteenth-century Catholicism.

But Protestant dissenters saw in Henry's marital solution an opportunity to bring about more fundamental change. Those who wished to purify the English church of its Catholic elements—people often referred to in a generally pejorative sense as "Puritans"—began to envision a genuine fellowship of "visible saints," those who had undergone a spiritual change of heart. Under Henry VIII's daughter Elizabeth I (1533–1603), who attempted to chart a middle way between Protestant and Catholic parties within the Church of England, energy for reform swirled out of traditional government structures and into the streets and local churches. Dissenters began to join together in clandestine meetings or "conventicles," providing each other with biblical teaching and spiritual support and increasingly sharp critiques of the established religious order.

What emerged was not a linear debate between Anglicans and Protestants but a many-faceted discussion about the nature of a true church and the role of biblical authority. Most English Protestants accepted the foundational categories of Reformed theology, emphasizing the sovereignty of God, the dependent state of human beings, and the final authority of the Bible in all matters of faith and practice. But they differed on the means of application, especially in regard to worship and ecclesiology. Some, often known as Independents, took a minimalist approach to biblical authority, insisting that only those practices specifically prescribed in scripture were permissible. Echoing in many ways an Anabaptist point of view, they refused to countenance any church order beyond that provided by the New Testament and pressed for simple lay-oriented structures with a minimum of hierarchy. A much larger group of more moderate Presbyterians argued that in matters pertaining to "adiaphora," or "things indifferent," broader Christian principles prevailed. Looking to Calvin's Geneva and the state churches of Scotland as a model, they advocated a limited form of ecclesiastical oversight exercised through a graded system of presbyteries and synods.

By the late 1500s, increasing impatience with Elizabeth's noncommittal policies began to fuel an urge toward entire separation from the Church of England. One of the earliest such was Robert Browne, whose *Treatise of Reformation without tarrying for anie* (1582) argued that godly piety was simply not possible under the Anglican Church and its lax exercise of spiritual discipline. Rejecting any forms of state control, Browne urged his followers not to "tarry for the magistrate" but to create their own churches by signing onto covenants together. Though the intemperate and apparently unstable Browne later recanted his position, his was an important early articulation of basic principles that later would become central to Congregational self-understanding.

During the later years of Elizabeth's reign, pessimism spread. Leading Independents Henry Barrow and John Greenwood were executed in 1593; many others faced prison or banishment. Moreover, when James I took the throne in 1603, he inspired little confidence for positive change; thus, in 1608 a group of self-described Separatists, led by John Robinson and John Smyth, left England for the relative freedom of Holland. Smyth subsequently became a Baptist, but Robinson's group of Pilgrims soldiered on. After a short stay in Leyden, they departed for New England, landing in Plymouth in the winter of 1620.

Non-Separatist Puritans, whose chief spokesmen were William Ames and Henry Jacob, held out for the importance of church connection. They sought to reform the Anglican Church from within, planting seeds of change through small congregational bodies within the existing structure. In their view, as long as the biblical word was preached and the sacraments regularly administered, the Church of England was still a legitimate home for Christian believers. In fact, non-Separatists argued that even the old parish system, which automatically assigned church membership to all those born in a certain geographic area, allowed its members to exercise free consent, and in some

form a covenantal arrangement, by the willing acceptance of their own clergy.

But prospects for reform grew dim under Archbishop William Laud (1573–1645). During the 1630s and 1640s, Laud's High-Church policies and the monarchist agenda of King Charles I sparked a "great migration" of dissenting Protestants to New England. With upwards of twenty thousand new arrivals into Massachusetts Bay, churches grew rapidly—some twenty-nine in Massachusetts alone by 1640. Despite their large-scale departure, the settlers of Massachusetts Bay insisted that they had not abandoned their goal of reforming the English church. Especially as succeeding generations of Puritans settled into their new home across the Atlantic Ocean, they began to envision New England as a "city on a hill," an explicitly godly community, and a righteous example for all the world to follow.

## From Independent to Congregational

New England's Puritans were not the dour, witch-hunting killjoys of American myth and legend. They were in many ways typical Elizabethan English men and women who enjoyed good ale and good company and who also held their religious beliefs with deep personal conviction. Early on they flourished in New England, buoyed by the conviction that they were God's chosen people, with a central role in the unfolding of divine history. This confidence did not always make them easy to accommodate: when smallpox epidemics decimated the local Native American population, Puritan settlers accepted the tragedy as an affirmation of God's providential care.

Very quickly the issues that once divided Independents from Separatists began to blur on New England soil. Without the Church of England as an ecclesiastical foil, questions about what constituted a "true church" needed to be addressed promptly and clearly. The very earliest Puritan settlements in Salem and Charlestown drew on Robert Browne's notion of covenant as the means by which a legitimate church might be gathered, and this soon became a fundamental characteristic of the so-called Congregational Way. As Cotton Mather (1663–1728) described the practice in the late eighteenth century, a group of believers (with the minimum set at seven to follow the procedure laid down in Matthew 18:15–20) met together for a day of prayer and fasting before setting down their intention in a written agreement. These church covenants were sometimes lengthy, sometimes very short, but normally followed a dual pattern, laying out the new congregation's obligations to God and to each other. Then each member signed his or her name at the bottom of the document. Only at this point would the new congregation call a pastor, typically one already marked out as a spiritual leader but named to his new post as one church member among the rest. An ecclesiastical council of representatives from other nearby churches assisted in the ordination and installation of the new pastor, affirming—but not formally approving—the local congregation's choice.

Before long, however, the logic of the pure gathered church required new layers of ecclesiastical oversight. Often referred to as the constitution of American Congregationalism, the 1648 Cambridge Platform directly addressed worries, especially back in England, that New England churches were theologically rudderless. The Cambridge divines affirmed the Westminster Confession of 1643 as the standard of belief and outlined a "mixed polity" that affirmed the autonomy of local churches but within a larger structure of mutual oversight and care. Walking a fine line between Presbyterianism and out-and-out independency, the Platform allowed for the legitimacy of synods and local forms of cooperative supervision, while affirming the spiritual integrity of local congregations.

Churches in Connecticut tended to be less leery of cooperative forms than their coreligionists in Massachusetts. The first settlers in Connecticut, led by Cambridge pastor Thomas Hooker, left the original Puritan colony because they objected to what they saw as authoritarian trends. But the New Haven Colony, established in 1639, rested on a close alliance between church and state. In many ways, in fact, Connecticut leaned toward a more presbyterian polity: the Saybrook Platform of 1708 set up governing bodies with broad powers of ecclesiastical oversight. Under this system, associations composed of pastors and elders and "consociations" of representatives from local churches had the authority to decide disputes between churches and to approve and license new ministers. In Massachusetts, however, the basic form of association was between individual ministers themselves, a practice going back to the formation of the Massachusetts Convention of Congregational Ministers in 1692.

During the nineteenth century, many defenders of Congregational polity began to argue that the denomination's decentralized institutional structure was inherently democratic—and therefore a historical precursor of the United States Constitution. But in fact, the tie between Congregational ecclesiology and American political democracy is far from direct. Though, for example, all church members were

automatically voting members of their congregations and in the larger commonwealth, this privilege did not extend to women or to religious dissenters, who were still required to pay taxes for church support. Ecclesiological outliers, like Baptists and Quakers, or dissonant theological voices like Ann Hutchinson and Roger Williams, faced severe consequences, including banishment and persecution.

Still, contrary to the popular notion that Puritan settlements were theocratic—that is, ruled by the clergy—the government of the Massachusetts Bay colony included separate realms of activity for church and state. That partnership rested on an assumption that godly magistrates and the churches' spiritual leadership would always work cooperatively, maintaining covenant obligations that mirrored those governing local churches.

In the long run, of course, the arrangement was untenable, especially as the ranks of dissenters began to grow; but in the mid-seventeenth century, the obligations of church membership fell equally on all of the colony's inhabitants, whether or not they personally held to Puritan doctrines. Religious dissent was, in effect, illegal.

New England pastors also exercised considerable spiritual and intellectual authority, though within certain limits. In an age still bound by aristocratic assumptions, the minister's status in his community was taken for granted, simply by virtue of his superior training and erudition. Even so, however, evidence from church records shows that laypeople took their own covenant responsibilities very seriously. Though outright opposition to clerical authority was rare, many a disgruntled parishioner found ways to remind a pastor that he ruled only by his congregation's consent.

Spiritual unity was the highest goal, and in the end more important than the right of individual belief that Independents had guarded so carefully in England. Though the English Civil War ultimately brought about the Act of Toleration in 1689, allowing dissenting bodies to exist within a structure dominated by the state Church of England, New England churches resisted its imposition. Put simply, their primary purpose was not to provide a haven of religious liberty for all but to establish and maintain close-knit covenanted communities of visible saints.

## Congregationalists in the Age of Revivals

In its ideal form, Congregational church government required high levels of individual piety and zeal. From early on, new members were required to "give a relation," or publicly testify to a genuine conversion experience, in order to join. Not just the minister and deacons but the entire congregation vetted the spiritual authenticity of each new applicant. Though the practice proved difficult to maintain in its pure form—relatively quickly exceptions were made for women deemed too modest to endure this kind of scrutiny—every effort was made to ensure that the unconverted would not compromise the congregation's spiritual purity.

But zeal did not translate easily across generations. Already in 1662 leaders of Massachusetts Bay had had to make allowances for the children of parents who had not passed the hurdle of church membership. The Half-Way Covenant created in effect a new type of church member, one who had not experienced conversion and who could not participate in the sacrament of Communion but, having publicly owned the church's covenant, could present children for baptism.

This pragmatic solution raised difficult questions of ecclesiology that would roil Congregational churches for the next century or more. Though nearly every New England church eventually accepted the Half-Way standard for membership, disputes divided leading churches and pitted eminent divines against each other in prolonged public debates. One of the most famous voices was that of Northampton pastor Solomon Stoddard (1643–1729), who defended the Half-Way Covenant as a converting ordinance, a way of keeping young families within the spiritual purview of their local church. He was vigorously opposed by Richard and Increase Mather, pastors of Boston's Second Congregational Church, who decried the decline in piety that made the new measure necessary.

The transatlantic religious revival known as the First Great Awakening tilted the scale in the other direction, back toward an insistence on heart piety as a requirement for church membership. During the 1730s and 1740s, under the fiery preaching of itinerating evangelists such as George Whitefield, Gilbert Tennent, and James Davenport, thousands of laypeople experienced dramatic adult conversions and became increasingly critical of the spiritual laxity they saw around them. All across New England Congregational dominance began to splinter, with self-described New Lights insisting on the necessity of a primal experience of grace and the Old Lights wary of the excessive emotionalism that often accompanied such religious "enthusiasm." At one end of the spectrum, Baptists and Separate Congregationalists lobbed insistent criticisms against the spiritually lukewarm clergy and unrevived church members in the established churches; in their view, the common

denominator of any religious fellowship was a personal encounter with Christ. At the other end of the spectrum, churchmen such as Charles Chauncy (1705–1787), who pastored Boston's First Church, argued that spiritual pyrotechnics of the revival were a counterfeit, distracting honest believers from embracing the means of grace already available through the ordinances of a duly gathered local congregation.

The enlarging debate generated a variety of intellectually sophisticated responses, none more influential than those of Northampton pastor Jonathan Edwards (1703–1758). An unapologetic defender of "religious affections" and a thorough scholar with a firm grasp of the Enlightenment critique of revealed religion, Edwards was an unparalleled philosopher and theologian. In his many published treatises and devotional works, Edwards constructed a subtle combination of classic Calvinism with a more modern affirmation of the authenticity of human moral choices.

Though the grandson and for much of his career a disciple of Solomon Stoddard, Edwards decisively parted ways with Stoddard's ecclesiology in the course of the revivals. In Edwards's view, parents who joined the church to have their children baptized were the worst possible influence on the tender faith of young children. He announced to his congregation that he would no longer acknowledge Half-Way members or baptize their offspring; nothing but a genuine change of heart would suffice. In many ways, Edwards's appeal won the day. The Half-Way model fell into disuse by the early nineteenth century, especially with a subsequent groundswell of religious fervor. But questions about what constituted membership in a Congregational church and about the nature of Congregational identity were far from over.

## Nineteenth-Century Setbacks and Successes

The Revolutionary War was an important benchmark in Congregational history. Hundreds of New England clergy sided with the cause of independence, helping to organize militias, providing service as chaplains, and organizing boycotts of British goods. Some clergy, such as John Adams of Durham, New Hampshire, even led raids against British forts; Adams reportedly stored the gunpowder he acquired under his pulpit. But most of all, through fiery sermons and literary skill, the "black regiment" of New England's gowned clergy helped the Revolution to succeed.

In practical terms, however, American independence presented Congregationalists with some serious challenges. By the late 1700s, the New England clergy, sometimes referred to as the Standing Order, were hardly enthusiastic at the prospect of a full Jeffersonian-style democracy, nor were they prepared for the effect of the First Amendment to the United States Constitution, cutting off all religious groups from any forms of government support. When Massachusetts became the last state to encode this principle into its own state constitution in 1833, the heart of the old Congregational order finally faced the unsettling prospect of relying on the voluntary donations of their members for survival.

The Dedham Decision of 1820 was another important defining point in Congregational history. The court case originated in a dispute in Dedham, Massachusetts, between the local parish and the gathered congregation, each claiming the right to name the next minister. By that time many Congregational churches were supported both by a society, defined geographically, and the church, which encompassed the worshipping body of visible saints. In the Dedham case, the church called a conservative pastor who the parish did not support, raising an immediate question about which group would have priority. The Massachusetts Supreme Judicial Court sided with the society, reasoning that the group paying the bills had the prior claim. The worshipping members of the Dedham church, and many others across eastern Massachusetts, were forced to leave their historic properties and build anew.

The Dedham Decision widened a growing divide between Trinitarian and Unitarian groups. By then, deep differences over the role of rationality in religious belief, forged within the fires of the First Great Awakening, had created two separate and increasingly disaffected parties. William Ellery Channing (1780–1842), pastor of Boston's Federal Street Church, laid out the basic differences in a sermon on "Unitarian Christianity" for the ordination of Jared Sparks in 1819. In short order, all of Boston's original Congregational churches—except for Boston's Third or Old South Church—identified with the Unitarian party.

Hampered by disestablishment and division, Congregationalists found it difficult to expand beyond their traditional New England base, though the problem was hardly new in the nineteenth century. When a Puritan congregation from Massachusetts attempted to form a church in Nansemond County, Virginia, in 1649, the colonial authorities forced them to leave—this despite the intercession of Massachusetts governor John Winthrop. Another group from Dorchester, Massachusetts, formed a church in Charlestown, South Carolina, sometime around 1680; in 1752 an

offshoot of this congregation settled in Midway, Georgia. But despite these scattered efforts, by the end of the colonial period, Congregationalism was thoroughly entrenched in New England. Indeed, by the 1830s, nine-tenths of all Congregational churches were located in that region; half a century later, the figure was still around two-thirds, with the vast majority of other Congregationalists in states due west—the so-called "Yankee Exodus" states of New York, Ohio, Illinois, Wisconsin, and Iowa.

Much of that expansion was the ambiguous by-product of an agreement that Congregationalists contracted with Presbyterians in 1801. Under the Plan of Union both groups agreed to pool their resources to allow for more efficient church planting on the frontier. Individual congregations could call a minister from either body and could participate in local presbyteries or ministers' associations regardless of their stated polity. By 1835, some 149 of these "presbygational" churches had been established just in the Western Reserve territory of Ohio; scores of others dotted the Great Lakes and upper Midwest, from New York to Iowa. The Plan of Union also included efforts to evangelize Native Americans and to establish institutions of higher learning. There the partnership was very successful, with an array of colleges stretching from Illinois, Knox, Beloit, Grinnell, and Rockford Colleges in the Midwest to a school that eventually became the University of California in 1868.

But both Presbyterians and Congregationalists found it difficult to compete with Methodists and Baptists. Only lightly invested in money and property, these "upstart" denominations expanded rapidly into the western frontier, soon overtaking Congregationalists in numbers, if not in cultural prestige. Thus, between 1776 and 1850, Methodism emerged as the leading denomination in the United States. Though some 20 percent of all religious adherents in 1776, Congregationalists numbered barely 4 percent by 1850.

Even so, the early nineteenth century was an important time of institution building. In 1810 Congregationalists sponsored the first national foreign missionary society, the American Board of Commissioners for Foreign Missions (ABCFM). Intended as a cooperative venture with Presbyterians, and the Dutch and German Reformed, by 1870 the American Board eventually became a solely Congregational entity, notable for a broad program of educational and humanitarian outreach from the Middle East to Hawaii to Japan. In its early days, the American Board also conducted a far-reaching home missionary program; in 1830 ABCFM missionaries took a public stand opposing the American government's Indian Removal Act, specifically the forcible resettling of Cherokees from their homes in Tennessee and Alabama into the Oklahoma Territory.

In 1826 Congregationalists were lead sponsors of the American Home Missionary Society (AHMS), an organization dedicated to establishing churches in the western frontier. Originally involving Presbyterians and Dutch Reformed supporters, the AHMS also eventually lost its interdenominational character, changing its name to the Congregational Home Missionary Society in 1893. Congregationalists also helped found other organizations that in turn became nondenominational, including the American Tract Society (1825) and the American Education Society (1826).

The American Missionary Association (AMA), formed in 1846, joined the denomination's antislavery zeal with its commitments to education and evangelism. The AMA was an antislavery alternative to the ABCFM, originating in efforts of abolitionists to win the freedom of mutinying slaves on the ship *Amistad* in 1839. In the post–Civil War years, hundreds of AMA missionaries, including scores of young women and ex-slaves, established an educational network of primary and secondary schools across the South. Many of the colleges the AMA helped form became prestigious African American institutions, including Howard, Fisk, Atlanta, and Talladega.

Congregationalists were also pioneers in seminary education. Andover Theological Seminary, founded in 1807, was the first freestanding American theological seminary and in fact the first American graduate school of any kind. Its three-year curriculum also became a standard for ministerial education across all Protestant denominations. Other Congregational seminaries soon followed after Andover, including Bangor (1816), Yale (1822), and Hartford Seminary (1833), carrying forward an intellectual tradition of educated clergy established by the original Puritan settlers, who founded Harvard College in 1636.

Congregationalists also made important contributions to American theological thought. In the late eighteenth and early nineteenth centuries, the New England theology, articulated and taught by the heirs of Jonathan Edwards, defined mainstream Protestant theological discourse. The so-called New Divinity Party—men like Nathaniel Emmons, Samuel Hopkins, and Joseph Bellamy—led a complex debate about Calvinist doctrines of sin and predestination and about the social responsibilities of Christians. In the mid-nineteenth century New Haven pastor Horace Bushnell (1802–1876) laid the groundwork for the development of liberal thought.

In contrast to the more rationalist presuppositions of the New England theology, Bushnell emphasized the poetic, metaphoric nature of religious truth and the immanence of God in human experience. Bushnell's insistence that God lived within the most minute human interactions, described in his ground-breaking book on *Christian Nurture* (1847), laid the groundwork for liberal theories about child rearing and created an important rationale for the expansion of Sunday schools and other forms of religious education.

Other Congregational theologians, led by the faculty at Andover Seminary, developed Bushnell's ideas even further. In the late nineteenth century, the so-called new theology rejected the formal categories of Calvinist thought, emphasizing instead a more optimistic, ethical creed centering on Christ's role as a moral exemplar and affirming human efforts to bring about a just and peaceful social order. By the early twentieth century, these views were no longer those of the radical few, as liberal theology dominated the curriculum of most Congregational seminaries and spread rapidly into church pulpits across the country.

In the late nineteenth and early twentieth centuries, Congregationalists also became identified with a variety of progressive causes. In some cases, the denomination's loose polity allowed for innovative changes at the local level, including the ordination of the first woman to the Protestant ministry, Antoinette Brown Blackwell, in 1853. During the late nineteenth century, many Congregationalists, most notably pastor and writer Washington Gladden, were leading figures in the social gospel movement. This loose coalition of pastors, parish workers, and scholars worked to establish the "kingdom of God on earth" by campaigning for the rights of labor unions and aid to the urban poor.

## Ecumenism

During the late nineteenth and early twentieth centuries, Congregationalists moved toward a more centralized structure. The process officially began at the Albany Convention of 1852, the first national gathering since the Cambridge Synod of 1646. The occasion for this meeting was simmering discontent with the Plan of Union, by then widely perceived as a win for Presbyterians, who had reaped the majority of newly planted churches. ("They have milked our Congregational cows," one critic exclaimed, "and made nothing but Presbyterian butter and cheese.") But in fact, the Plan of Union exposed the weakness of Congregationalism's decentralized polity, especially when isolated and struggling mission churches demanded support. Indeed, one major outcome of the Albany Convention was the formation of the Congregational Church Building Society, an organization that provided funding for new churches in the West.

The Plan of Union also opened Congregationalists to criticism for their relatively open doctrinal stance. Indeed, the more conservative Old School faction of Presbyterians had repudiated the arrangement back in 1834, objecting to a lack of theological rigor among their New England partners. Not surprisingly, when Congregationalists convened again after the Civil War, talk turned to the necessity of some common creedal understanding.

The Boston Council of 1865 extended and further defined the work at Albany, involving some five hundred delegates from the various state organizations. One of the main results was the adoption of the Burial Hill Declaration of Faith at an historic site in Plymouth, the first such common statement since the Cambridge Synod. The Boston Council also adopted a "Statement of Congregational Principles," codifying important points of polity for the first time.

Formal denominational organization came in 1871, with the creation of a permanent body, the National Council of Congregational Churches, in Oberlin, Ohio. The Council, which was composed of equal numbers of lay and clergy representatives chosen by their state organizations, had no formal legislative power over local churches. Its stated purpose was to oversee the work of Congregational missionary organizations, encouraging local churches to support the ABCFM and the AMA and dividing up their overlapping mission fields for maximum efficiency. To offset any lingering perception of sectarianism, the Oberlin meeting also produced a ringing "Declaration on the Unity of the Church," affirming the unity and integrity of "all those who love and serve our common Lord."

Other denominational statements followed. A Commission Creed, adopted in 1883, replaced the Burial Hill Declaration with a more nuanced liberal version. The Kansas City Declaration of Faith, adopted in 1913, put the denomination on record as a socially progressive body, working on behalf of justice, peace, and human "brotherhood."

The push toward greater centralization tracked with a rising denominational consciousness during the early twentieth century. The National Council of 1907, for example, recommended a common legal structure for all of the various local organizations that had evolved to carry on the work of the churches since the seventeenth century, replacing all of the missionary societies, vicinage councils, associations, and consocations with a uniform arrangement of state conferences. A Commission of Nineteen, appointed in 1910, tackled the financial and administrative complexities resulting from the decentralized structure of the denomination's various missionary and educational organizations—in all some ten agencies, including three women's boards and three different home missionary boards. Adoption of their recommendations in 1913 led to a closer relationship between these boards and the local churches represented in the National Council and, by 1929, to mergers that ended the independent existence of the various women's boards.

Congregationalists also courted mergers with other denominations. In 1886, a Permanent Commission on Church Unity voted to unite with the Free Baptist churches, a move that was ultimately unsuccessful. But a few years later, in 1892, the Congregational Methodist Churches, a largely southern body affiliated with the Congregational Churches of Georgia, came under the wing of the National Council. Ensuing years saw a variety of ecumenical proposals—from Episcopalians, Disciples of Christ, Methodist Protestants, United Brethren, and Universalists—but little institutional change. Still, in 1925, the National Council accepted into fellowship the Conference of the Evangelical Protestant Churches of North America, a group of twenty-seven liberal German churches centered around Pittsburgh, Pennsylvania, and Cincinnati, Ohio.

The most important merger occurred in 1931 with the General Convention of the Christian Churches. The Christians, who numbered only around one hundred thousand (compared to slightly less than one million Congregationalists), were a loosely organized group, composed of several different geographic strands. One originated in New England in the early 1800s, under the leadership of Elias Smith and Abner Jones, both fiercely dedicated to liberty of conscience and an absolute minimum of church hierarchy. About that same time in Virginia, James O'Kelly gathered a group in opposition to the hierarchical structure of the Methodist Episcopal Church; Barton W. Stone led a similar protest against the Presbyterian Church in Kentucky. By the late nineteenth century, all three groups had found a common cause and adopted the simple name of "Christians," reflecting their opposition to all forms of sectarian labeling. One large segment of African American churches in the upper South formed an affiliated Afro-Christian Convention in 1892.

Though Christians were on the whole more rural and less affluent than Congregationalists, both groups shared a commitment to organizational simplicity and freedom of thought; the new denomination they formed had a relatively minimal structure. The General Council of

Congregational Christian Churches consolidated all of the missionary boards into two, the American Board of Commissioners for Foreign Missions and the Home Mission Board, and created a Council for Social Action in 1934. Some social conventions, especially around race, remained untouched, however. The Afro-Christian Convention and African American Congregationalists in the South remained segregated, merging to form a single entity, the Convention of the South, in 1950.

The Council for Social Action soon became the focus of controversy. Its primary tasks were to gather and disseminate information about social problems, including labor relations, rural life, international relations, and race. But critics saw an anticapitalist bias in the Council's published materials, a suspicion amplified by an "anti-profit-motive" resolution passed by the General Council in 1934. Spiritual Mobilization, a group founded by Los Angeles pastor James Fifield in 1935, campaigned tirelessly against the denomination's perceived left-leaning agenda throughout the 1940s and 1950s, gathering strength with the rise of anticommunist fervor during the postwar decades.

## UCC, NACC, CCCC

After World War II, the Congregational Christian Churches emerged as a leading voice for ecumenical cooperation. Already in 1891, with the formation of the International Congregational Council (ICC), American Congregationalists had become part of a wide network of sister churches from around the world. The ICC met roughly every decade during the early twentieth century; Americans such as Douglas Horton gave key leadership, but the gatherings themselves incorporated an array of denominational bodies from Great Britain, Canada, India, and the Philippines.

In 1937 leaders of the Congregational Christian churches—Truman Douglass, George M. Gibson, and Douglas Horton—began to discuss the possibility of union with leaders from the Evangelical and Reformed Church, a denomination formed by an earlier merger in 1934 of two German immigrant bodies. After years of negotiation, a Joint Committee on Union issued a Basis of Union in 1947. That July the General Synod of the Evangelical and Reformed Church approved the document, and prospects for merger looked relatively bright.

But on the Congregational Christian side, the Basis of Union proved deeply controversial and led to a series of departures. In 1948, evangelical churches opposed to the denomination's liberal theological stance formed the Conservative Congregational Christian Conference (CCCC).

The CCCC maintained a strong emphasis on liberty of conscience but within a conservative evangelical doctrinal framework. Some fifty years after its founding, the denomination numbered 242 churches and more than forty thousand members.

The National Association of Congregational Churches (NACC) provided a home for congregations and individuals who opposed the 1957 merger for polity reasons. Critics argued that a union with the Evangelical and Reformed Church would impose a Presbyterian structure that was fundamentally at odds with historical Congregationalism. They also argued that the General Council had no legal right to unite with another denomination, as this was the sole prerogative of local churches. The NACC, formed in Evanston, Illinois, in 1955, thus emphasized the authority of the gathered congregation and the right of churches to modify any act by a national body. Fifty years after its founding, the denomination reported more than four hundred churches and sixty-five thousand members.

The final merger leading to the creation of the United Church of Christ (UCC) came after a decade of tumult. In 1949 the General Council put the question of union with the Evangelical and Reformed to local churches, hoping for a 75 percent vote in favor; when the resulting return fell just short (72.8 percent), the Council declared it an acceptable mandate and voted to move ahead. Soon after, the Cadman Memorial Church in Brooklyn, New York, filed suit against Helen Kenyon, the moderator of the General Council, charging the denomination's leaders with a misuse of power. A complex progression of court rulings, appeals, and reversals delayed any other progress toward merger for several years, until the New York Court of Appeals dismissed the Cadman case in 1953. Shortly afterward, in 1956, the General Council of Congregational Churches voted (1,310 to 179) to go ahead with merger plans. After a parallel vote from the General Synod of the Evangelical and Reformed Church, a Uniting General Synod met in Cleveland, Ohio, on June 25, 1957, to form the UCC.

Like many mainline Protestant denominations, the UCC endured substantial membership loss, especially from the 1980s onward. Some of the decline was due to demographic factors—a declining birthrate for one—and some of it was related to a general mainline "malaise" in the face of the resurgent evangelical movement of the mid- to late twentieth century. In 2008 the UCC numbered just over 5,600 churches and 1.2 million members, a precipitous drop from the denomination's high point of 2.2 million members during the early 1960s.

## Conclusion

Congregationalism is an important American tradition, though in some ways a vanishing one. Because of the tradition's historic aversion to creedal or doctrinal requirements, and because of its decentralized structure, Congregationalism was a relatively poor competitor in the American religious marketplace. Over the course of its long existence, the denomination has divided and merged several times, sometimes by choice and sometimes under duress. Consequently, in terms of sheer numbers, Congregationalism no longer enjoys the cultural and intellectual preeminence it once took for granted.

But in many other ways, Congregationalism is so deeply rooted in American religious life that its influence is almost impossible to measure. Its democratic and locally oriented polity is now broadly characteristic of many other denominations, from Baptists to Mennonites; even more hierarchically oriented denominations such as Catholics and Episcopalians have adopted more representative structures than their European counterparts. Congregationalism's historical insistence on toleration for other beliefs—a somewhat ironic legacy of its Puritan founders and their insistence on the freedom of the individual conscience—has also shaped modern acceptance of religious pluralism. The denomination's formidable intellectual contribution has long played a central role in the American historical narrative. Though the Puritans and their descendents are now no longer the first or only story historians tell about the nation's religious past, they are still an important and an intriguing one.

**See also** *American Revolution; Anglican Tradition and Heritage; Architecture: Early America; Congregations; Denominationalism; Ecumenism; Great Awakening(s); Mainline Protestants; Missions: Domestic; New England Region; Pilgrims; Polity; Presbyterians entries; Puritans; Reformed Tradition and Heritage; Unitarians.*

Margaret Lamberts Bendroth

### BIBLIOGRAPHY

Alika, Clifford, and Miya Okawara. "Sho-Chiku-Bai: Japanese American Congregationalists." In *Hidden Histories in the United Church of Christ,* edited by Barbara Brown Zikmund. New York: United Church Press, 1994.

Chrystal, William G. "German Congregationalism." In *Hidden Histories in the United Church of Christ,* edited by Barbara Brown Zikmund. New York: United Church Press, 1994.

Conforti, Joseph. *Samuel Hopkins and the New Divinity Movement: Calvinism, the Congregational Ministry, and Reform in New England between the Great Awakenings.* Grand Rapids, Mich.: Eerdmans, 1981.

Cooper, James F. *Tenacious of Their Liberties: The Congregationalists in Colonial Massachusetts.* New York: Oxford, 1999.

Hambrick-Stowe, Charles. *The Practice of Piety: Puritan Devotional Disciplines in Seventeenth-Century New England.* Chapel Hill: University of North Carolina Press, 1982.

Kuehne, Dale S. *Massachusetts Congregationalist Political Thought, 1760–1790: The Design of Heaven.* Columbia: University of Missouri Press, 1996.

Marsden, George. *Jonathan Edwards: A Life.* New Haven, Conn.: Yale University Press, 2003.

Moore, William F., and Jane Ann Moore. *Owen Lovejoy: His Brother's Blood: Speeches and Writings, 1838–64.* Champaign: University of Illinois Press, 2004.

Morey, Verne Dale. "American Congregationalism: A Critical Bibliography." *Church History* 21 (1952): 323–344.

Mullin, Robert Bruce. *The Puritan as Yankee: A Life of Horace Bushnell.* Grand Rapids, Mich.: Eerdmans, 2002.

Pearson, Samuel C., Jr. "From Church to Denomination: American Congregationalism in the Nineteenth Century." *Church History* 38 (1969): 67–87.

Rohrer, James. *Keepers of the Covenant: Frontier Missions and the Decline of Congregationalism, 1774–1818.* New York: Oxford University Press, 1995.

Sweeney, Douglas. *Nathaniel Taylor: New Haven Theology and the Legacy of Jonathan Edwards.* New York: Oxford, 2003.

Sweet, William Warren. *The Congregationalists: A Collection of Source Materials.* Chicago: University of Chicago Press, 1939.

Stanley, A. Knighton. *The Children Is Crying: Congregationalism among Black People.* New York: Pilgrim Press, 1979.

Stuckey-Kauffman, Priscilla. "Women's Mission Structures and the American Board." In *Hidden Histories in the United Church of Christ,* vol. 2, edited by Barbara Brown Zikmund. New York: United Church Press, 1987.

Von Rohr, John. *The Shaping of American Congregationalism, 1620–1957.* Cleveland, Ohio: Pilgrim Press, 1992.

Walker, Williston. *The Creeds and Platforms of Congregationalism.* New York: Pilgrim Press, 1991. (Orig. pub. 1893.)

Wallace, Dewey D., Jr. "Charles Oliver Brown at Dubuque: A Study in the Ideals of Midwestern Congregationalists in the Late Nineteenth Century." *Church History* 53 (1984): 46–60.

Youngs, J. William T. *The Congregationalists.* Westport, Conn.: Greenwood, 1990.

Zikmund, Barbara. "Chinese Congregationalism." With Dorothy Wong, Rose Lee, and Matthew Fong. In *Hidden Histories in the United Church of Christ,* vol. 2, edited by Barbara Brown Zikmund. New York: United Church Press, 1987.

# Congregations

In the last two decades of the twentieth century, *congregation* became the generic term for local religious institutions in the United States, a term intentionally inclusive of entities known to their own constituents by a great variety of names: church, parish, worship center, ward, synagogue, temple, mosque, Islamic center, *mandir, wat,* meditation center, and *gurdwara,* among other designations. Intending to build on the ordinary sense of the term, scholars define the American congregation as an institution with regular and frequent face-to-face gatherings that are understood by their participants to be religious in nature but are predominantly composed of religious laity (nonprofessionals). The predominance of nonprofessionals, or what this article will call "religious amateurs," is crucial. Congregations may be, but are not necessarily, led by religious professionals, who are disproportionately male. But the majority of those who attend congregations, and do their volunteer work, are women. In this sense, the work of congregations is disproportionately women's work.

Congregations often own the building in which they meet, but many do not, instead renting their meeting spaces from other congregations or from such secular institutions as schools. Thus, there are more "congregations" in America than there are freestanding church buildings. Congregations so defined are widespread and prevalent across the United States, numbering approximately 330,000 in the year 2000.

## The Study of Congregations

Systematic social scientific knowledge of congregations as units of analysis began with the work of H. Paul Douglass in the 1920s, with ironic results. Douglass's studies led to efforts to curtail what was perceived as excessive proliferation of and differentiation among competing congregations, for which interdenominational cooperation was proposed. By the middle third of the twentieth century, congregations were generally regarded as unworthy of the attention of scholars or religious activists. Congregations were seen as especially conducive to bad faith, while seminaries and denominational and interchurch agencies were seen as conducive to religious integrity. Liberal clergy in the 1960s learned that their efforts to promote religiously inspired social change were more likely to be successful the further away they stayed from congregational entanglement.

The focus of scholars' and activists' attention changed in the 1970s as the fortunes of ecumenically inclined denominations and interchurch agencies declined from their 1960s peaks. Some scholars thought "new religious movements" were an exciting research frontier in the face of denominational decline, and conservative religious activists found meaningful engagement in such parachurch agencies as Inter-Varsity Christian Fellowship. But other scholars and church activists insisted that whatever future religion had in the United States, and whatever potential it promised for the betterment of the society, must ultimately rise

on the convictions nurtured and resources generated in congregations. From their point of view, the congregational bedrock of American religion had been rediscovered. Well-endowed foundations, notably the Lilly Endowment, encouraged their aspirations. Meanwhile, by the late 1970s, a small literature on congregations began to emerge, stimulated more by disciplinary agendas within sociology and anthropology (for example, participant observation, symbolic interaction, racial and ethnic studies) and religious studies (especially of non-Christian communities) than by religious agendas. A field of "congregational studies" coalesced by the mid-1980s.

The new field was made up of scholars and religious leaders of different backgrounds looking from different points of view. Historians produced new studies and collected extant ones of local religious communities from colonial times to the present. Some of these were the work of academic researchers, while others were labors of love on the part of dedicated amateurs. Researcher-activists based in divinity schools promoted and encouraged efforts on the part of congregations to understand their own cultures, social processes, and environmental challenges, the better to pursue their mission objectives. Large, well-funded, academically based projects employing the talents of multiple researchers took on the tasks of understanding how Vatican II changed American parishes; how congregations dealt with economic, social, and cultural changes in their communities; why and how most congregations were racially homogeneous (and a very few are heterogeneous); and in what kinds of congregations post-1965 immigrants were involved.

The resulting literature in congregational studies consisted disproportionately of single-case studies. Some projects compared multiple congregations within a single locale or sharing a particular situation (for example, economic downturn in the community). But it was difficult to generalize from these studies because what statisticians call the "sampling frame" from which they were drawn remained unknown. Eventually, Mark Chaves devised a "hypernetwork sampling" technique that in 1998 produced, for the first time, a representative sample of all American congregations in the "National Congregations Study" (NCS). By 2008, the NCS had undergone a second iteration. In the hypernetwork technique, randomly drawn respondents to the General Social Survey were asked if they attended religious services, and those who answered in the affirmative were then asked to name the institution in question. The result was a random sample of congregations, with the chances of a given congregation's inclusion being proportional to its number of constituents. NCS researchers then contacted a key informant in each congregation with a lengthy battery of questions. The 1998 NCS has data on 1,234 congregations, and the 2008 survey has data on 1,506. These data can be used to weight the results of nonrandom but nonetheless large and representative samples of American congregations—for example, the survey conducted by the project on "Organizing Religious Work," directed by Nancy Ammerman in 1997–1999.

Such survey data inform this article. Yet because small groups (either of individuals or institutions) are statistically unlikely to be chosen in random sample surveys such as the General Social Survey, the NCS can tell us little about, for example, congregations of Muslims, Buddhists, and Hindus, to name three important and growing religious communities, each of which accounted for little more than 1 percent of the American population in 2000. So the field of congregational studies will continue to rely on case studies and denominational rosters for much basic information.

## Distributions

About 96 percent of America's 330,000 congregations in 2000 were Christian institutions, and, of them, about 94 percent were Protestant, the remaining Christian congregations being primarily Roman Catholic and Eastern Orthodox. The predominance of Protestant congregations is important, for, as we shall see, they have historically set the tone for other religious communities in the United States. Nonetheless, the number of non-Christian congregations has grown swiftly and significantly since the 1960s to about 12,000 in 2005. At the beginning of the twenty-first century, the largest group of non-Christian congregations comprised Jewish synagogues, temples, and *shuls,* numbering some 3,500. Mosques and Islamic centers numbered between 1,200 and 2,000, Unitarian churches and Buddhist centers each numbered slightly more than 1,000, and there were smaller but rapidly growing numbers of Hindu *mandirs* and Sikh *gurdwaras.*

Congregations vary enormously in the number of participants who compose them, and some of this variation is best explained by norms specific to one or another religious tradition. In general, Catholic parishes serve a thousand or more families, while the majority of Protestant congregations have fewer than a hundred regular attendees. Some Hindu temples serve dispersed populations that span several states, whereas Buddhist centers tend to have smaller constituencies. Synagogues tend to have more member families

than Protestant churches, although with a lower rate of regular attendance. Thus, the congregation gathered for a *shabbat* service in a large synagogue may number no more persons than are found every week in a small to midsize Protestant church. Methodist and Baptist congregations, disproportionately located in rural and small-town locations, tend to be very small, although there are many exceptions to such a generalization.

Most churches are small, but most worshippers attend large churches. In 1998, half of all American congregations had seventy-five or fewer regular attendees, but the average religiously active person attended a church with four hundred or more other worshippers. Thus, there are important differences between characteristics of "the average church" (which is very small) and the church of the "average churchgoer" (which is far larger). ("Average" here refers to the median, not to the arithmetic mean.) Both perspectives matter. Insofar as we are interested in what most churchgoers experience, we must pay attention to larger congregations. Insofar as churches themselves count, as units of representation in denominations or as icons of "religion" in America, we cannot neglect smaller ones.

Starting in the 1970s, such "skewness" became more pronounced. "Megachurches" (defined as congregations with weekly attendance of two thousand or more) attracted a larger proportion of the Protestant churchgoing population, at the expense of smaller congregations. What seemed to be happening was that it became increasingly hard to do what congregations are expected to do on the restricted resources that small congregations can command. In a highly mobile society where even faithful churchgoers find themselves looking for a church in a new hometown, people will be drawn to churches that can provide high-quality Sunday schools, youth programs, and worship music. Small churches will lose members who move away and will find it harder to replace them with people new to the community. But being conservative institutions that enshrine memories of ancestors, small churches do not easily die. They plod along with ever fewer members and programs. The end result is an increasingly skewed distribution with a few large churches attracting a rising percentage of the churchgoing population and a large and only slowly diminishing number of small churches serving a declining percentage.

## Structural Types: Congregation, Parish, and Temple

The size distribution of American congregations not only tracks the increasing differentiation between megachurches and the ordinary run of Protestant congregations. It also coincides with religiously defined differences in local religious institutions that may be obscured by the use of the generic term *congregation*. Strictly speaking, from an ecclesiastical point of view, a congregation is an assembly or gathering of voluntarily participating believers. In the congregational traditions, especially among Baptists and Jews, the congregation is, as the etymology of the word suggests, defined socially, by those who assemble to comprise it. (In the Roman Catholic tradition, a "congregation" is a religious order whose members take "simple" rather than "solemn" vows. Not only is that a different usage than the generic term that is the topic of this article, it is an opposed term, insofar as a Catholic "congregation" consists entirely of religious specialists whereas the congregation as we are discussing it consists primarily of religious amateurs.) The Baptist or Jewish congregation is autonomous, governed by its laity through a board of elders, deacons, or trustees. It hires (and fires) religious professionals. "Congregation" is a bottom-up concept for the local branch of the people of God.

Because the congregation is a voluntary association, most of its work is carried out by religious amateurs in groups dedicated to activities (rehearsing choral anthems, teaching Sunday school, counting the offering, assembling the monthly newsletter, maintaining the building, and cooking soup and sewing clothes for the needy) that draw on their talents and provide them with a meaningful connection to their faith. Congregations tend to be busy places where the religious content of many activities may not be immediately obvious to the outside observer.

Because they are defined socially, as voluntary gatherings, rather than administratively, by ecclesiastical mandate, and depend on the unpaid labor of their members, congregations are especially subject to what sociologists call the principle of "homophily," the pattern by which like chooses like. Because friendship choices in American society are heavily determined by race, congregations tend to be racially and ethnically homogeneous or, to use a less benign word, segregated. According to sociologist Michael Emerson, only 5 percent of American Protestant congregations in 1998 could fairly claim to be multiracial.

The local unit of the Roman Catholic Church that is parallel to "congregation" in the sense of this article is the "parish." In the Catholic tradition, parishes are defined spatially, in terms of the place, especially the neighborhood, in which they are located, rather than socially, in terms of the people who compose them. When the neighborhood is

segregated, so is the parish. Yet because of their somewhat less voluntary constitution, Catholic parishes are more likely to be multiracial than Protestant congregations. In the past, the rectory was home to a corps of priests who served the parish. Today, the priest-parishioner ratio has greatly declined with the reduction in priestly vocations and the growth of the Catholic population (especially due to immigration). Many parishes now have only one resident priest; some have none. The constituent population of Catholic parishes is much higher than that of most Protestant congregations, and the disparity is growing.

An important exception to the spatial definition of the Catholic parish occurred as a result of the great migration of a century ago (roughly 1880–1920), when American bishops authorized "national parishes," defined by the immigrant group whom they served (and who often funded their construction). Thus, many American cities have a heritage of "German," "Italian," and "Polish" Catholic parishes that at one time enjoyed ecclesiastic sanction. But pressures toward Americanization, especially during and after World War I, brought about a renewed stress on the territorial definition of the parish. During the 1920s, the church became less willing to designate national parishes for Catholic immigrants. The typical pattern at the end of the twentieth century was for a territorially defined parish to offer masses in more than one language, Spanish being the most widespread.

The Protestant congregation and the Catholic parish are venues for ritual observances (a "service of worship" or a "mass") on the part of an assembly of the religiously defined community in a space large enough to accommodate their numbers. A third type of local religious institution may be called the "temple," using this term more in the manner of Mormons and Hindus than Reform Jews (for whom "temple" is a synonym for "synagogue"). Many rituals in Hindu and Buddhist temples consist of esoteric interactions between individuals or families and religious specialists; some important rituals are conducted by priests in the absence of any lay devotees. Some of the most sacred of Mormon rituals are conducted in the temple with only a small number of people present. Because of the relatively small numbers of Hindus in the United States and their dispersed pattern of residence, some of the largest and most prominent Hindu temples in the United States are devoted to the service of multiple deities. Thus, *pujas* in service to several gods, each involving a handful of participants, occur simultaneously on the temple grounds. If the main worship event in a Protestant church can give it the air of a movie theater, the profusion of parallel worship activities in a Hindu temple can make it feel a bit like a trade fair.

## De Facto Congregationalism

Notwithstanding these hallowed differences across religious traditions, Stephen Warner proposed in 1994 that a process of "de facto congregationalism" was at work in American religion at large. American Protestants' beliefs (for example, about the Bible) and practices (for example, hymn singing) were decreasingly aligned with their denominational affiliation and increasingly with the congregation they attended. For their part, many Protestant congregations made decreasing public reference to their denominational affiliation, identification of which began to appear in ever smaller type on their signboards. Individual Catholics felt increasingly free to attend a parish other than the one territorially defined for them. Canon law was relaxed to make territoriality only a "determining" principle instead of being "constitutive" of the parish. "Magnet" or "niche" parishes were developed by entrepreneurial priests to serve diverse Catholic constituencies: Irish, African American, gay and lesbian, progressive and conservative, those who fought to extend Vatican II reforms and those who harked back to the Tridentine (or Latin) Mass. Naming one's parish was no longer a shortcut way of referring to where one lived; it became a signal of one's values.

Warner's de facto congregationalism extended to new, often non-Christian, communities in the United States as well. Members of immigrant groups who initially came together to create suitable worship spaces in their new homeland often found that the space served them as well as a place to speak their home country language and eat their home country food in the company of their fellows. As often the immigrant group's most prominent public space in their new American home, the religious institution recommended itself for the observance of ceremonies that are not, in their religion, strictly speaking religious, for example, weddings in some Buddhist traditions. As their children grew up speaking English and adopting ways of American youth, the parents' religious space provided a critical mass of people of somewhat similar backgrounds or ethnicities to undergird the norms they wanted their children to respect. Finding themselves unable to explain what to their children seemed exotic religious beliefs and practices, immigrant parents recognized that new programs of religious education were called for. Pursuing these ends, they found that they needed to raise money, and for that purpose they learned how to take advantage of tax deductions for religious contributions. Some found it necessary to honor donors and to specify the names of those who would be eligible for the services their emerging institutions intended to provide. The congregational pattern of the Protestant majority (and of Jews, the largest and most well-established non-Christian minority) recommended itself to them.

De facto congregationalism is an instance of a process sociologists call "institutional isomorphism." (The paradigmatic case is the widespread adoption of the organizational form known as "bureaucracy.") Pressures toward isomorphism can come from law (for instance, qualifying for Internal Revenue Service recognition as a 501(c)3 nonprofit organization) and from expectations on the part of interested parties. An imam of an Islamic center may learn from members of the interfaith clergy association ways to address the Muslim community's needs. A doctor who invites a coworker's family to her son's wedding may be asked if the wedding is going to take place in her Buddhist temple. But not all processes toward congregationalism come from American pressure or models. Innovations in religious organization take place all over the modern world, wherever religion is decreasingly taken for granted. Several Hindu movements (for example, Chinmaya Mission, Swadhyay Parivar, and the Swaminarayan sect) organized themselves in India in ways that, intentionally or not, turned out to be well suited to American conditions, especially because of their focus on explicit instruction in rites that Hindu temples ordinarily take as culturally given.

The adoption of congregational organization in the United States can appear as an unwelcome devolution, compromising religious ideals. The practice of maintaining local membership rolls offends many Muslims' concept of the *ummah,* the worldwide community of faith. The local Islamic center is supposed to be open to all Muslims, not just dues-paying "members." The power of lay trustees over temple expenditures and personnel decisions comports badly with the deference owed to the *bhikku-sangha,* the community of monks, in the Theravada Buddhist tradition. The expectation that the family is supposed to show up at the mission every Sunday is not what many immigrant Hindus learned from their religiously observant parents. Congregationalism is the wrong way to organize religious life not only for some new immigrant communities but also for some old-stock American denominations. United Methodists pride themselves on their system of assigning clergy to congregations for brief terms and under conditions that guarantee that poorer congregations are not left to rely on their own limited resources; congregational autonomy would undermine these commitments. In the face of the controversy over the ordination of non-celibate homosexual clergy, the Episcopal Church contested the claims of dissident congregations that they own the property they occupy. Although it is not simply a matter of Americanization, the concept of de facto congregationalism engendered controversy.

## Functions: What Congregations Do

It should be obvious that the chief function of congregations is religious worship (although Buddhists may not use that term for their devotional ceremonies). Not only Chaves's and Ammerman's data showed as much, but also the case study literature that preceded these large-scale surveys. Yet it is also a well-established generalization about American congregations of whatever religious affiliation that they tend to be multifunctional. Their activities typically include not only worship but also religious education for children and adults, mutual care, social activities (or "fellowship"), cultural preservation or articulation, outreach and community service, and encouragement of members' civic and political participation. The activities in the middle of this list, especially mutual care and fellowship, have been underresearched. We know that those toward the top (worship and education) are nearly universal among American congregations, whereas those toward the bottom (community service and civic participation) are especially associated with the historical mainline Protestant tradition. Yet the prestige of that tradition and the early precedent it established for "religion" in America gives those activities normative weight as part of what Ammerman called the "template" for American congregations. Chaves gave special attention to the aesthetic component of worship as third in prominence (after worship and education) of congregational functions. Ammerman categorized congregational functions somewhat differently, but she agreed that congregations are places where the culture of the group (including its music, cuisine, and storytelling) is reproduced.

What occasioned more controversy is how political, civic, and service activities figured in the picture. In the post-1960s "restructuring" of American religion depicted by Robert Wuthnow, the "declining significance of denominationalism" was accompanied by the "growth of special purpose groups," and one implication was that Americans'

religious interests were increasingly expressed in terms of specific, especially political, agendas. The rise of the religious right in the 1980s suggested to many onlookers that these purposes were increasingly partisan. Chaves's 1998 data confirmed the findings of numerous case studies that congregations do not devote much of their effort to political and civic activism. Among Protestants, individuals who attend mainline churches were somewhat more likely to be encouraged to get involved in civic affairs, whereas those attending conservative churches were more likely to receive voter guides. Jews and black Protestants were more likely to hear speeches by political candidates in their congregations and to be encouraged to register to vote. Catholics were more likely to be recruited for a demonstration or protest march. But in all cases, such activities were the exception rather than the rule.

Another controversy arose from the "charitable choice" and "faith-based initiatives" policies of, respectively, the Clinton and George W. Bush administrations. Some advocates of these policies suggested that the governmentally provided "safety net" for economically distressed families could be supplanted by congregations' social service provisions—for example, soup kitchens, clothing banks, and warming shelters. The data are clear and consistent. Monetary and human resources devoted to social service activity are a small fraction of those expended by congregations. A small minority of the members of the typical congregation are involved in such efforts, and they are more likely to be found among mainline Protestant than conservative Protestant congregations and in larger ones rather than smaller ones. The programs that do exist are important for many congregations' sense of their mission, but they are most typically and effectively carried out in collaboration with organizational partners—religious, secular, and governmental.

Is the religiously provided social service glass half empty or half full? Chaves stressed that those who expect congregations to take up the slack of a shrunken welfare state suffer from a fundamental misunderstanding of the magnitude of the task. But Ammerman stressed how much social service work is in fact done through congregations, especially channeling volunteer efforts through organizational partners. Given the agreed-on finding that congregations spend their time on a welter of diverse activities—parenting classes, youth groups, Bible studies, new members classes, support groups, 12-step groups, prayer groups, missionary societies, building maintenance crews, choir rehearsals, hospital visits, meal preparation, and a host of others, in addition to their primary activity of planning and conducting worship events—it was remarkable that three-fourths of religiously active Americans in 1998 attended congregations that featured some social service programs.

**See also** *Civil Religion in the United States; Demographics; Denominationalism; Ecumenism; Emerging Church Movement; Ethnographic and Anthropological Approaches; Faith-Based Community Organizations; Historical Approaches; House Church Movement; Independent Bible and Community Churches; Megachurches; Ministry, Professional; Philanthropy; Polity; Seeker Churches; Sociological Approaches; Unaffiliated; Worship* entries.

R. Stephen Warner

## BIBLIOGRAPHY

Ammerman, Nancy Tatom. *Bible Believers: Fundamentalists in the Modern World.* New Brunswick, N.J.: Rutgers University Press, 1987.

———. *Pillars of Faith: American Congregations and Their Partners.* Berkeley: University of California Press, 2005.

Becker, Penny Edgell. *Congregations in Conflict: Cultural Models of Local Religious Life.* Cambridge: Cambridge University Press, 1999.

Cadge, Wendy. "De Facto Congregationalism and the Religious Organizations of Post-1965 Immigrants to the United States: A Revised Approach." *Journal of the American Academy of Religion* 76, no. 2 (2008): 344–374.

Carroll, Jackson W., Carl S. Dudley, and William McKinney, eds. *Handbook for Congregational Studies.* Nashville, Tenn.: Abingdon Press, 1986.

Chaves, Mark. *Congregations in America.* Cambridge, Mass.: Harvard University Press, 2004.

Ebaugh, Helen Rose, and Janet Saltzman Chafetz. *Religion and the New Immigrants: Continuities and Adaptations in Immigrant Congregations.* Walnut Creek, Calif.: Altamira, 2000.

Emerson, Michael O., and Rodney M. Woo. *People of the Dream: Multiracial Congregations in the United States.* Princeton, N.J.: Princeton University Press, 2006.

Gremillion, Joseph, and Jim Castelli. *The Emerging Parish: The Notre Dame Study of Catholic Life since Vatican II.* San Francisco: Harper and Row, 1987.

McGreevy, John T. *Parish Boundaries: The Catholic Encounter with Race in the Twentieth-Century Urban North.* Chicago: University of Chicago Press, 1996.

Warner, R. Stephen. *New Wine in Old Wineskins: Evangelicals and Liberals in a Small-Town Church.* Berkeley: University of California Press, 1988.

———. "The Place of the Congregation in the American Religious Configuration." In *American Congregations,* vol. 2, *New Perspectives in the Study of Congregations,* edited by James P. Wind and James W. Lewis, 54–99. Chicago: University of Chicago Press, 1994.

Wind, James P., and James W. Lewis, eds. *American Congregations.* 2 vols. Chicago: University of Chicago Press, 1994.

Wuthnow, Robert. *The Restructuring of American Religion: Society and Faith since World War II.* Princeton, N.J.: Princeton University Press, 1988.

# Constitution

The United States was the first modern nation to adopt a written constitution limiting governmental power and the first to enshrine religious liberty among its constitutional values. The U.S. Constitution contains no reference to a deity or any invocation of any divine power; the only reference to religion in the original Constitution is the provision that there be no religious test for holding public office. When the Bill of Rights was added, its first words expanded religious protection and symbolized the new nation's commitment to religious liberty: "Congress shall make no law respecting an establishment of religion or prohibiting the free exercise thereof." Of course, as James Madison recognized, words on parchment do not themselves make a constitution. Yet over the years the United States has managed, imperfectly but with reasonable success, to maintain both an extraordinary level of religious intensity and diversity by making the guarantees part of the way American society is constituted.

## Adoption of the Constitution and the Bill of Rights

By the time of Independence, the American states had become quite religiously heterogeneous. Many of the new states retained some kinds of religious establishments, although by the late eighteenth century they tended to be far more relaxed than many of their more comprehensive European counterparts. The Church of England had been established in the five southern colonies, as was the Congregational Church in three New England ones. In the Middle Atlantic states there was no establishment, but there were religious qualifications for office. Pennsylvania, with no establishment, did not grant religious freedom to "papists." Most states still required licensing of ministers and punished blasphemy, sacrilege, or criticizing the doctrine of the Trinity. Many required attending church and keeping the Sabbath. But by 1776, the trend was toward multiple Protestant establishments that provided public support for several churches, and establishment had come to mean support of religion generally through taxation, rather than support for a particular religion or penalties on nonbelievers or members of other faiths. But support was growing in many states, most notably Virginia, for the abolition of religious assessments. James Madison's famous *Memorial and Remonstrance against Religious Assessments* both articulated and reflected this sentiment.

Under the Articles of Confederation, Congress ratified several treaties making reference to religious liberties. The Northwest Ordinance of 1787 guaranteed that "No person, demeaning himself in a peaceable and orderly manner, shall ever be molested on account of his mode of worship or religious sentiments." The same ordinance funded religiously based education in the Northwest Territories. The Continental Congress made references to God and Christian practices.

The U.S. Constitution was adopted by the Convention on September 12, 1787, and ratified by the states on June 21, 1789. However, antifederalists had conditioned their support upon a promise that the first Congress would adopt a Bill of Rights, including a religious liberty guarantee. Among the advocates of such a guarantee, the growing Baptist minority played a particularly important role. Baptists, who had suffered both discrimination and oppression during the colonial era, took the leadership in advocating for a formal guarantee of religious freedom. Virginia's Bill for Religious Liberty, first proposed by Thomas Jefferson in 1779 and finally adopted in 1786, became a model for the national conversation over a religious liberty guarantee in the new federal Constitution. Virginia's bill provided

> That no man shall be compelled to frequent or support any religious worship, place, or ministry whatsoever, nor shall be enforced, restrained, molested, or burdened in his body or goods, nor shall otherwise suffer on account of his religious opinions or belief; but that all men shall be free to profess, and by argument to maintain, their opinions in matters of religion, and that the same shall in nowise diminish, enlarge, or affect their civil capacities.

The creation of the Bill of Rights is embedded in conflict between federalists, who advocated a strong central government, and the antifederalists, who favored greater state autonomy. The debate over a Bill of Rights was dominated by concerns over its implications for the power of the new government. Many federalists considered a Bill of Rights not only superfluous but also seriously misleading because it might imply that the newly created national government had excessive power that needed to be restrained. In their view, the Constitution had already created a government of delegated powers, which lacked authority to take any actions that were not specifically authorized. Nevertheless, the commitment had been made

to win antifederalist support, and the new Congress set out to draft a Bill of Rights.

Originally twelve rights were proposed, including the religious freedom draft offered by James Madison on June 8, 1789: "the civil rights of none shall be abridged on account of religious belief or worship, nor shall any national religion be established, nor shall the full and equal rights of conscience be in any manner, or on any pretext infringed." Ultimately two of the proposed amendments were rejected, and after several revisions, the religious rights guarantee was moved to the First Amendment and rephrased to read, "Congress shall make no law respecting an establishment of religion or prohibiting the free exercise thereof." Members of Congress generally supported an amendment prohibiting a national religious establishment and guaranteeing religious liberty, but they devoted very little time or energy to analyzing its implications. The Bill of Rights was adopted on September 25, 1789, and ratified on December 15, 1791.

## No Religious Tests

The problem of governing a religiously diverse nation had clearly been on the minds of the framers of the original Constitution. Article VI, section 3, provided that

> The Senators and Representatives before mentioned, and the Members of the several State Legislatures, and all executive and judicial Officers, both of the United States and of the several States, shall be bound by Oath or Affirmation, to support this Constitution; but no religious Test shall ever be required as a Qualification to any Office or public Trust under the United States.

The provision for either an oath or affirmation reflects the recognition that some citizens have religious scruples against taking oaths, and others would object to invoking the name of a deity they did not recognize. Even more significantly, the prohibition against a religious test for public office was a departure from the common practice of requiring officeholders to swear to holding particular beliefs (usually the existence of God and/or faith in Jesus Christ, the Trinity, or divine reward and punishment). At the time this provision was adopted, eleven of the thirteen new States had religious requirements for public office.

There has been no significant litigation under this provision of the U.S. Constitution. However, religious tests and oaths continued to be common requirements for public office in several states until ruled unconstitutional as a violation of the First Amendment's establishment clause in 1961. In *Torcaso v. Watkins* (367 U.S. 488), the Supreme Court struck down a Maryland law requiring a public officeholder to swear to a belief in the existence of God, because it privileged one kind of religious expression.

## The First Amendment Religion Clauses

The opening sentence of the Bill of Rights provided that "Congress shall make no law respecting an establishment of religion or prohibiting the free exercise thereof." These words are typically divided into the establishment clause and the free exercise clause. (Grammarians note that they are not clauses at all.) The establishment clause offers protection against government-imposed religious obligations, and the free exercise clause offers protection against government-imposed burdens to religious practice. Constitutional scholars debate whether the two clauses should be considered as a single guarantee or treated separately and, if so, whether they might logically conflict with each other.

For almost a century, there was no significant litigation under these clauses. The one important nineteenth-century case to reach the Supreme Court was the case of *Reynolds v. United States,* 98 U.S. 145 (1887), in which the justices upheld a Utah law against polygamy and articulated a very constricted understanding of religious free exercise. Beginning in the 1930s, the religion clauses have been a major source of constitutional jurisprudence. Religious advocacy groups, beginning with the Jehovah's Witnesses Watchtower Bible and Tract Society and the American Jewish Congress, played a large role both in supporting litigation and in shaping constitutional doctrine, usually in support of separationist principles. Since the 1980s, conservative advocacy groups such as the Rutherford Institute and the American Center for Law and Justice have advocated successfully for a constitutional understanding that permits government to accommodate religious interests.

## Contemporary Constitutional Disputes

Like all constitutional disputes, the religion clause conflicts reflect different interpretations of the Constitution's language. The following sections survey contemporary religion clause jurisprudence as it relates to the guarantee's specific words and phrases.

## Congress

The First Amendment begins with the phrase, "Congress shall make no law...." As the word *Congress* indicates, these guarantees originally bound only the lawmaking power of the federal government, leaving the states free to regulate religion as they saw fit. Some scholars have argued that the religion clauses had less to do with protecting religious freedom than with guaranteeing the autonomy of individual states to create whatever establishments they wished or regulate religious practice as they chose. However, the adoption of the Fourteenth Amendment after the Civil War extended the protections of life, liberty, and property against state infringement as well as national. And by the middle of the twentieth century, most of the guarantees of the Bill of Rights were "incorporated" into the Fourteenth Amendment. The Supreme Court incorporated the free exercise clause in the case of *Catewell v. Connecticut,* 310 U.S. 396 (1940), striking down a state law requiring a license for religious solicitation and the subsequent conviction of Jehovah's Witnesses proselytizers for breach of the peace. In the case of *Everson v. Board of Education,* 330 U.S. 1 (1947), a five to four majority of the Supreme Court incorporated the establishment clause while upholding New Jersey's policy of offering public transportation of schoolchildren to parochial as well as public schools. Since that time, it has been settled constitutional understanding that the religion clauses of the First Amendment apply equally to the states and to the federal government—or so it had seemed until 2002, when Justice Clarence Thomas suggested reversing that understanding. In a concurring opinion in *Zelman v. Simmons-Harris,* 538 U.S. 639 (2002), upholding an Ohio school voucher plan that provided students public funds for attending private (including religious) schools, Justice Thomas seemed to be making a variation of that argument, suggesting that while states could establish religions, they could not interfere with religious liberty. And when the Court voted five to four to uphold a display of the Ten Commandments among many monuments on display on the grounds of the Texas State capitol in *Van Orden v. Perry,* 545 U.S. 677 (2005), Justice Thomas wrote a concurring opinion reemphasizing his belief that the establishment clause should apply only to the national government. This suggestion would reverse more than seventy-five years of settled constitutional understanding and dramatically change the conditions of religious liberty within the United States.

## "Respecting an Establishment"

Beyond the question of states rights, there remain major disagreements over the interpretation of the words "respecting an establishment of religion." Since colonial practice left no single understanding of a religious establishment, we are left with no definitive understanding of what kinds of public policies constitute an illegal establishment, much less about the broader sweep of the language "respecting an establishment." Traditionally, approaches to the establishment clause fall into two categories: accommodation of religion and separation of church and state. Those favoring separation of church and state take their imagery from Thomas Jefferson's famous call for a "wall of separation" between church and state and envision religious and governmental functions as operating in separate spheres. Those favoring accommodation argue for a benevolent governmental stance toward religion, as symbolized by Justice William O. Douglas's words, "we are a religious people whose institutions presume a Supreme Being" (*Zorach v. Clauson,* 343 U.S. 306 [1952]). In this view, both state and federal governments may voluntarily act to enhance opportunities for religious expression and may publicly recognize the religious culture of the American people, as long as they do not favor one religion over another.

In the process of deciding concrete establishment clause disputes, various justices have attempted to articulate what is at the heart of an illegal establishment. The following paragraphs describe some of these attempts, none of which are mutually exclusive.

Expenditure of public funds for religious purposes is the starting place, if only because Madison was so adamant about it in his *Memorial and Remonstrance against Religious Assessments.* Yet religious institutions have received public funds from the beginning of American history down to the present time, so this point has never been taken literally. As early as *Everson v. Board of Education,* 330 U.S. 1 (1947), the Supreme Court majority expressed concern about the expenditure of tax funds for transporting students to private religious schools but nevertheless upheld a New Jersey law providing bus fare for both public and parochial schoolchildren. The often contradictory series of Supreme Court cases about parochial school funding is inconclusive: *Zelman v. Simmons-Harris,* 536 U.S. 639 (2002), most recently, upheld state allocation of vouchers for children attending private religious schools. Since some expenditures of money are permissible and others are not, money alone does not seem to be the definitive factor indicating a religious establishment.

The longest-running "test" for establishment is the *Lemon* test, used, ignored, and criticized since it was announced in the case of *Lemon v. Kurtzman,* 403 U.S. 602 (1977). According to this "test," a challenged activity is acceptable under the establishment clause as long as it has a secular purpose and an effect that neither advances nor burdens religion and does not excessively entangle government and religion. The *Lemon* test reflects the separationist view that the establishment clause requires religious neutrality (secular purpose and religiously neutral effects), while accommodationists argue that the test is too stringent and that state and federal governments should be able to advance religion in nondiscriminatory ways. The *Lemon* test is the most comprehensive approach to establishment clause jurisprudence, but it seemed to have fallen out of use until it reappeared in the 2005 Ten Commandments cases. In *McCreary County v. American Civil Liberties Association,* 545 U.S. 844 (2005), the majority explicitly referred to the *Lemon* test in striking down Kentucky's Ten Commandments display because it had an obviously religious purpose. In contrast, in the Texas Ten Commandments case *Van Orden v. Perry,* 545 U.S. 677 (2005), decided at the same time, the absence of an obviously religious purpose was one of the reasons the justices upheld the constitutionality of the monument.

As an alternative to the *Lemon* test, some judges suggest that religious coercion is the real danger to which the establishment clause is aimed; its goal is to protect freedom of conscience or freedom of religious choice. For example, in *McCollum v. Board of Education,* 333 U.S. 203 (1948), the justices struck down state programs offering religious education during the public school day because the programs relied on the coercive power of state compulsory education laws to foster religious education. In 1992, Justice Anthony Kennedy relied on this approach in his majority opinion in *Lee v. Weisman,* 505 U.S. 577 (1992). Kennedy argued that graduation invocations *coerced* students to participate in a religious event—and the coercion is all the more serious for young people, who are especially susceptible to group pressure and the pressure of school authorities.

Another explanation of the establishment clause is that it is an attempt to prevent religious conflict by avoiding institutional entanglement between church and state. Advocates of this view recall the dangers to civil peace when religious conflicts spill over into political ones, as they have often done throughout history. Particularly when tax money is involved, there is a danger of politicizing sectarian conflicts. Moreover, the institutional entanglement between church and state can easily compromise the integrity and autonomy of religious institutions. The concern is a practical one, as Justice Souter argued in his 2002 *Zelman* dissent. In his view, accepting government money puts a church in a double bind: government requires some accountability to be sure the church is not using the money for illegal purposes. But that accountability involves the government in regulating and overseeing the activities of religious institutions. Thus, he explained, to accept vouchers, religious schools had to agree not to prefer their own church members, not to teach certain doctrines, and not to discriminate. All of those requirements potentially interfere with religious autonomy, so the entanglement endangers religious freedom.

One of the most thoughtful approaches to establishment is Justice Sandra Day O'Connor's "endorsement test," which she first introduced in her concurring opinion in *Lynch v. Donnelly,* 465 U.S. 668 (1984). Her opinion contends that the heart of an establishment clause violation is government endorsement of religion in a way that would make others feel excluded or give the impression that they were less than equal citizens. This test might inquire whether a Jew or a Muslim could feel less than equal seeing a Christmas nativity scene on public property, or whether a nonreligious person might feel excluded by the inclusion of invocations at public school graduation ceremonies, or whether a Hindu seeing an official posting of the Ten Commandments might experience a sense of "otherness" and exclusion.

Both separationists and accommodationists insist that the establishment clause requires religious neutrality, but they differ immensely on what that neutrality entails. Separationists insist that the establishment clause requires that government be not only absolutely neutral among religions but also between religion and nonreligion—hence, "religion blind." Seen in this light, one of the reasons the majority upheld private school vouchers in the *Zelman* case is because the voucher program provided money for public, community, and private religious and nonreligious schools on an absolutely neutral basis. Similarly, the majority opinion in *Rosenberger v. Rector of the University of Virginia,* 515 U.S. 819 (1995) emphasizes that the university's student activity money had to be distributed with absolute neutrality to student publications, irrespective of their religious content. Accommodationists understand neutrality only as demanding neutrality among various religious sects, while government is permitted to recognize, accommodate, and benefit religions in general, as long as it does so in a nonsectarian way. Thus, the heart of the clause is no religious discrimination. Laws granting military exemptions for religious conscientious objectors rest on this view, as does the funding of

military chaplains, as do laws protecting workers from religious discrimination.

Finally, Justice Antonin Scalia has advocated a historical approach to establishment clause jurisprudence, arguing that courts should be guided by the general understandings prevailing at the time the Bill of Rights was adopted. Moreover, contemporary understanding should give great weight to American traditions, including the enormous role that religion plays in the lives of the American people. Scalia makes this point in both *Lee v. Weisman* and *McCreary,* and Justice Rehnquist argued forcefully for a historical approach in his dissent in *Wallace v. Jaffre,* 472 U.S. 38 (1985) and again in *Van Orden v. Perry,* 545 U.S. 677 (2005). Dissenting in that case, Justice John Paul Stevens offers a powerful refutation of this view, noting how the framers' experiences of religious diversity were so much more restrictive than contemporary experience and how deeply their approaches would offend contemporary sensibilities.

While the establishment clause has been the source of a far greater number of constitutional conflicts than the free exercise clause, many observers claim that it is really the "dependent clause," intended to enhance the general theme of religious freedom as articulated in the free exercise clause.

### "Of Religion"

Because the First Amendment singles out religion for special protection, the word *religion* serves as the threshold or gatekeeper to both constitutional guarantees, but the constitutional language gives no clue about what constitutes a religion. Most of the time, this threshold is passed without controversy, but occasionally courts are asked to decide whether the claim is a genuinely *religious* one. That question puts judges in the awkward role of deciding what counts as a religion for First Amendment purposes and what criteria to use for making the judgment.

Defining religion for purposes of the First Amendment constitutes a paradox, because no definitions are neutral. Every effort to define a religion privileges some particular kind of belief or practice and discounts others. History is singularly unhelpful. The authors of the Bill of Rights probably had a very limited understanding of what was a legitimate religion—often excluding the beliefs and practices of Native Americans—and they had little experience thinking (in Madison's phrase) of "Jews, Turks, and infidels. . . ."

The earliest judicial attempts to define religion emphasized belief—particularly belief in a supreme being. But by the mid-twentieth century, this definition already seemed woefully outmoded. In *Torcao v. Watkins,* 367 U.S. 488 (1961), the Supreme Court rejected such a definition and focused instead on the function of a religion and, especially, on the claims of conscience to which religions give rise. James Madison's earliest drafts of the First Amendment religion clauses had proposed the phrase "freedom of conscience." Furthermore, Madison's *Memorial and Remonstrance against Religious Assessments* defined religion as "the duty we owe to our Creator." The Court relied on this kind of reasoning in refusing to limit conscientious objector status to those whose objections to war were based on a belief in a supreme being during the Vietnam War era. In *United States v. Seeger,* 380 U.S. 163 (1964) and *Welch v. United States,* 398 U.S. 333 (1970), the Court relied on broader understanding that nontheistic beliefs function as religions and give rise to commands of conscience.

Important as this insight is, it does not encompass the full range of religious experience. Moreover, it provides little observable evidence of the kind the legal system prefers. Not surprisingly, then, judges have attempted to identify religion by observable behaviors, including the collective practices of religious communities—worship services and other rituals, institutionalized ways of propagating the faith to future generations, clergy or some other form of teaching or leadership, festivals and holidays or life-cycle events, for example. By the early twenty-first century, the trend seems to be to seek a family of characteristics, rather than a single essential element in identifying a religion. These may include some or all of the following: ultimate ideas; metaphysical beliefs; moral or ethical systems; comprehensiveness of beliefs; and accoutrements of religion, including such things as founders or teachers, writings, gathering places, ceremonies and rituals, organizational structure, festivals, and efforts at propagation. Of course, not every religion or individual religious person partakes of every one of these characteristics. Some conventionally religious persons are almost totally ignorant of the doctrine of their faith or unburdened by its moral commandments; others may partake in the spiritual life of their faith and ignore its communal manifestations. Still, taken in various combinations, these indicators help identify a wide range of religious phenomena.

### "Exercise of Religion"

The very first free exercise case to reach the Supreme Court was *Reynolds v. United States,* 98 U.S. 145 (1878), upholding a federal law against religiously inspired polygamy. Chief Justice Waite, writing for the Court, made a distinction between beliefs and actions, the former beyond government purview, the latter subject to regulation. Yet constitutional observers remind us that the First Amendment does not protect "religion" in the abstract, or even abstract beliefs, but the *exercise* of religion. However, identifying a religious exercise proves to be even more difficult than attempting to define religion. The scope of religiously motivated behaviors is virtually incalculable. Religious codes dictate a variety of means by which people worship: kneeling, standing, eating, fasting, ingesting alcoholic beverages or hallucinogenic drugs, making symbolic sacrifices or sacrificing live animals, covering or uncovering their heads or feet in houses of worship, singing, meditating, chanting, preaching, and speaking in tongues, to name only a few. Religions frequently mandate certain kinds of personal care, including bathing, hygiene, dressing, health care, diet, and hairstyle. Religious mandates cover comportment in the world at large in such areas as social responsibility, education, child rearing, relations between the sexes, medical practices, appropriate employment, financial decisions, and countless other aspects of life. Religious practices include ceremonial activities performed in religious institutions and secular practices motivated by religious faith—both obligatory and optional practices, practices sanctioned by recognized churches and those based upon individual conscience, as well as the folk practices of religious communities. And to add further complications, free exercise protection also covers the actions of religions institutions—including financial management, employment practices, social services, zoning, and architecture.

### "Prohibiting"

The First Amendment provides that "Congress shall make no law . . . prohibiting the free exercise [of religion]." To "prohibit" a religious exercise—making it a crime or subject to a civil penalty—is indeed a very serious infringement on religious liberty, but it is only one of the ways in which liberty may be trammeled. At least since *Sherbert v. Verner,* 374 U.S. 398 (1963), the Court has understood that clause to prevent unjustified burdens to religion. In effect, the word *prohibiting* has come to mean "burdening," and thus the showing of a burden to religion is the threshold to free exercise protection. But what constitutes a burden, and how serious must it be to present a constitutionally cognizable problem? How can courts distinguish a major impediment to religion from a minor annoyance?

Harms to religious freedom are experienced in a variety of ways. Some laws literally prohibit a religious exercise. For example, in the case of *Church of the Lukumi Babalu Aye v. Hialeah,* 308 U.S. 520 (1993), the Supreme Court struck down a local ordinance that prohibited religious animal sacrifice while permitting most other nonreligious reasons for killing animals. Some condition government benefits on behavior inconsistent with religion, such as South Carolina's refusal to grant unemployment benefits to a Seventh-day Adventist who would not work on her Sabbath (*Sherbert v. Verner,* 374 U.S. 398 [1963]). Others make a religious practice impossible, such as the National Forest Service decision to build a logging road through land held sacred by local Native Americans (upheld in *Lyng v. Northwest Indian Cemetery Protective Association,* 5485 U.S. 439 [1988]). Some penalties or burdens on religious exercise or intentionally targeted at religious practices, but most are unintended burdens created when otherwise valid secular laws have the effect of burdening a religious practice. The difference may have great constitutional significance.

## "No Law"

The wording of the First Amendment is stark: "Congress shall make *no* law...." Not even constitutional literalists have taken "no law" to mean "no law." This statement has never been taken literally; both state and federal government do prohibit various religious exercises deemed a threat to life or safety. To use a common example, nobody doubts that the state could prohibit human sacrifice, no matter how religiously sincere its motivation or how important it might be to its adherents. The real question is, under what conditions may government prohibit or otherwise burden a religious exercise? How are legislatures and courts to balance the protection of religious liberties against other important public interests?

Ordinarily, when a law is challenged, the state must only show that the law is reasonably related to legitimate interests, not necessarily that it is the best way to achieve them. In this kind of balancing, dominant interests generally prevail over minority interests. Furthermore, the person challenging the constitutionality of a law bears the burden of proof. Failing to overcome this burden leaves the law intact.

To put extra weight on the side of religious freedom, the courts developed the compelling state interest test. When a religious right is burdened, the burden of proof reverts to the state to show that the public interest in burdening the religion is not only important, but *genuinely compelling,* and that no less burdensome strategies are available for achieving that interest. This method reflects the view that the whole point of having a Bill of Rights is to remove certain liberties from the ordinary balancing of the political process. Furthermore, in these cases the ordinary burden of proof is reversed, so that laws burdening religious freedom are to be unconstitutional, and its defenders bear the burden of establishing its constitutionality. Such laws are subjected to "strict scrutiny," requiring their defenders to show (1) that the challenged law served not just an important public purpose, but a genuinely compelling one; (2) that the law was well tailored to achieve that purpose; and (3) that the purpose could not be achieved by some less burdensome legislative method.

Beginning in the 1963 case of *Sherbert v. Verner,* the Supreme Court ruled that only a compelling state interest was sufficient to justify burdening religious freedom, thus requiring the state to provide unemployment benefits for a Seventh-day Adventist who lost her job because she was not available to work on her Sabbath. In *Wisconsin v. Yoder,* 406 U.S. 205 (1972), upholding the free exercise right of Amish families to be exempt from state compulsory education laws, Chief Justice Warren Burger phrased the point by saying, "only those interests of the highest order and those not otherwise served can overbalance legitimate claims to the free exercise of religion."

That approach remained constitutional doctrine until the ruling in *Employment Division, Department of Human Resources of Oregon v. Smith,* 494 U.S. 872 (1990), in which the Court majority ruled that the free exercise clause did not require exemptions from state drug laws for sacramental use of peyote in religious services. In this case, the majority held that the compelling state interest test was no longer necessary to justify unintentional burdens to religion stemming from valid secular neutral laws. Justice Scalia's majority opinion ruled that the free exercise clause is directly breached only by laws that specifically target religious practice for unfavorable treatment, not by generally applicable, religiously neutral laws. Consequently, laws inadvertently burdening religious exercise need not be justified by a compelling state interest.

The argument over balancing religious rights against other important interests is bound up with the distinction between intentional (or targeted) burdens on religion and those that are the incidental results of other laws. Even apparently neutral laws can inadvertently burden someone's religious interests. For example, compulsory education laws were not adopted to impose burdens on the Amish (*Yoder*); narcotics laws were not intended to forbid the rituals of the Native American Church (*Smith*) or of Brazilian immigrant religious communities (*O Centro Spiritu Beneficiente Uniao Do Vegetal v. Ashcroft,* 546 U.S. 418 (2006). Military uniform regulations were not intended to burden Jewish men who are required to keep their heads covered (*Goldman v. Weinberger,* 475 U.S. 503 [1986]); nor were drivers' license photograph requirements imposed to burden Muslim women religiously required to cover their faces in public. Yet all of these laws imposed incidental burdens on religious practices.

Persons who claim to be burdened by secular laws usually do not ask that the law be withdrawn or overturned; they most often request exemptions. Religious exemptions to ordinary laws and policies are so common we often do not notice them at all. Legislation is full of religious exemptions, including laws that exempt churches from some provisions of the Civil Rights Act and from zoning ordinances, that exempt persons with religious objections from vaccination requirements, and even those that exempt Communion rituals from laws regarding serving alcohol to minors. These policies are sometimes criticized as violating the establishment clause by giving preferences to religion (Estate *of Thornton v. Caldor,* 472 U.S. 703 [1985]). Free exercise disputes center not on whether legislators and administrators *may* grant exemptions but on whether the constitution *requires* exemptions from otherwise valid, secular neutral laws in order to accommodate religious needs.

The question is thus whether the First Amendment requires that persons acting on sincere religious motives be granted exemptions from such laws. What kinds of justifications are sufficient to override religious burdens and refuse exemptions? The controversial *Smith* decision reversed the long-standing understanding that such exemptions were required unless there were a compelling state interest to the contrary. While Justice Antonin Scalia's majority opinion denied any free exercise *right* to religious exemptions, he insisted that legislatures are free to grant them as part of the normal political process. He recognized that this approach moves religious protection from the courts back to the political process. "Values that are protected against government interferences through enshrinement in the Bill of Rights are not thereby banished from the political process." He readily admits that

> leaving accommodation to the political process will place at a relative disadvantage those religious practices that are not widely engaged in; but that unavoidable consequences of democratic government must be preferred to a system in which each conscience is a law unto itself. . . . (*Unemployment Division, Department of Human Resources of Oregon v Smith,* 494 U.S. 872 [1990])

Hence, much of his argument turns on his preference for political solutions within the democratic process, rather than on judicial solutions. Critics of the *Smith* decision are appalled that this ruling removes this kind of religious protection from the status of a constitutional right and makes it simply a matter for negotiation within the political process.

## Legislative Efforts to Restore Compelling State Interest

Almost immediately after the announcement of the *Smith* decision, a broad coalition of religious advocates, concerned about its potentially devastating implications for the rights of religious minorities, petitioned Congress to reverse the effects of the decision legislatively. In November 1993 Congress adopted and the president signed the Religious Freedom Restoration Act (RFRA), which legislatively restored the compelling state interest standard in cases where state or federally supported programs were involved. The key section of the bill states that government may restrict a person's free exercise of religion only if government can show that such a restriction "(1) is essential to further a compelling governmental interest; and (2) is the least restrictive means of furthering that compelling governmental interest" standard.

Congress relied on its authority under its Fourteenth Amendment power to "enforce by appropriate legislation" constitutional guarantees. The law was challenged in the case of *City of Boerne v. Flores,* 521 U.S. 507 (1997), a conflict between a church renovation plan and city's decision to preserve it unchanged as a historical landmark. Flores, the Catholic bishop overseeing the church, argued that the act required deference to the church's religious exercise unless the city could show a compelling state interest to the contrary. However, when the case reached the Supreme Court, a majority struck down the act as violating the separation of powers by infringing on the judicial power. The majority ruled that while the Fourteenth Amendment grants Congress the power to enforce a constitutional right, the RFRA went beyond enforcement and, in fact, altered the meaning of the right, thus usurping both judicial power and the prerogatives of states. As Justice Kennedy wrote, "Legislation which alters the Free Exercise Clause's meaning cannot be said to be enforcing the clause. Congress does not enforce a constitutional right by changing what the right is."

After the demise of the RFRA, many states adopted their own versions of the statute, enhancing religious rights protection under state laws or constitutions. In 2000 Congress adopted the much more limited Religious Land Use and Institutionalized Persons Act of 2000 (RLUIPA), which forbids the federal government from implementing land use regulations that impose a substantial burden on the religious exercise of a person or on the religious exercise of a person confined to an institution, "unless that action is in furtherance of a compelling governmental interest and is the least restrictive means of furthering that compelling governmental interest." Rather than resting on Fourteenth Amendment grounds as the RFRA had, this law was based on the commerce and spending clauses, since it extends to all programs that receive federal money. In *Cutter V. Wilkinson,* 544 U.S. 709 (2005), the Supreme Court upheld this law against an establishment clause challenge.

## Proposed Constitutional Amendments Regarding Religion

From time to time various religious advocates have proposed constitutional amendments regarding religion, but none has come even near passage. The closest were reactions to the Supreme Court's decisions in 1961 and 1963 that prohibited religious exercises in the public schools. In *Engle v. Vitale,* 370 U.S. 421 (1962), the Court struck down New York's Board of Regent's prayer, composed by state officials and promulgated for recital in the public schools. Two years later the Court struck down the common practice of public school Bible readings. (*Abington School District v. Schempp,* 374 U.S. 203 [1963]).

Almost immediately after those rulings, and continuing into the twenty-first century, there have been persistent efforts to reverse the impact of these decisions by constitutional amendments. Nearly every congressional session has seen the introduction of constitutional amendments to authorize prayers in public schools, religious symbols on government property, and tax dollars for private religious schools. A typical version is the amendment President Reagan sent to Congress in 1982, which read, "Nothing in this Constitution shall be construed to prohibit individual or group prayer in public schools or other public institutions. No person shall be required by the United States or by any State to participate in prayer." Similar proposals have occasionally received favorable hearings in congressional committees, but none has made it through the first stage of the amendment process.

Proposed constitutional amendments banning abortions and limiting marriage to one man and one woman reflect religious sentiments but are not overtly religious. Thus far none has succeeded. More extreme amendments have also been proposed—including one declaring the United States to be a Christian nation and one in 2008 declaring Islam not to be a religion. Such proposals are usually understood to be political statements and have not been taken seriously as genuine candidates for consideration.

**See also** *Church and State: Revolutionary Period and Early Republic; Education: Court Cases; Establishment, Religious; Pacifism and Conscientious Objection; Pluralism; Politics: Colonial Era; Politics: Nineteenth Century; Politics: Twentieth Century; Supreme Court.*

Bette Evans

## BIBLIOGRAPHY

Alley, Robert S. *The Constitution and Religion: Leading Supreme Court Cases on Church and State.* Amherst, N.Y.: Prometheus Books, 1999.

Conkle, Daniel O. *Constitutional Law: Religion Clause.* New York: Foundation Press, 2003.

Eisgruber, Christopher, and Lawrence Sager. *Religious Freedom and the Constitution.* Cambridge, Mass.: Harvard University Press, 2007.

Evans, Bette Novit. *Interpreting the Free Exercise Clause.* Chapel Hill: University of North Carolina Press, 1998.

Feldman, Noah. *Divided by God: America's Church-State Problem and What We Should Do about It.* New York: Farrar, Straus and Giroux, 2005.

Feldman, Steven. *Law and Religion: A Critical Anthology.* New York: New York University Press, 2000.

Greenawalt, Kent. *Religion and the Constitution.* Vol. I, *Free Exercise and Fairness.* Princeton, N.J.: Princeton University Press, 2006.

Kamnick, Isaac, and Lawrence Moore. *The Godless Constitution: A Moral Defense of the Secular State.* New York: Norton, 2005.

McConnell, Michael W., John Garvey, and Thomas Berg. *Religion and the Constitution.* New York: Aspen, 2006.

Smith, Steven. *Foreordained Failure.* New York: Oxford University Press, 1995.

Sullivan, Winnifred Fallers. *The Impossibility of Religious Freedom.* Princeton, N.J.: Princeton University Press, 2005.

Witte, John. *Religion and the American Constitutional Experiment.* Boulder, Colo.: Westview, 2005.

# Cult of Domesticity

In the early-nineteenth-century United States, a set of ideals regarding womanhood and the home emerged that was commonly called the cult of domesticity. Americans who subscribed to this widespread ideology, found in sermons, novels, and magazines, believed the ideal woman possessed the qualities of piety, purity, submissiveness, and domesticity. This "true woman," as she was called, was suited to life in the home, a private domain removed from the public world of politics and economics. The true woman was an embodiment of virtue, whose moral goodness originated in her innately pious nature. Such perceptions of women's spirituality led to an increasing association between women and Christianity in the nineteenth century that ultimately granted women a degree of religious authority in American culture. From the 1830s through 1880s, the cult of domesticity profoundly constrained women's lives, governing how women evaluated themselves and were evaluated by others. At the same time, the cult of domesticity credited American women with a moral influence that enabled them to shape and at times challenge U.S. culture.

## Separate Spheres

The cult of domesticity emerged in the context of changing political and economic structures. The nineteenth century saw the United States transform from a fledgling agricultural democracy into an industrialized global power. The new republic contended with ever-expanding national borders, large-scale immigration, and growing tensions between federal power and state sovereignty. In the same period, a process of industrialization was taking hold in the urban Northeast, beginning along the Erie Canal in upstate New York. In the midst of political uncertainty and economic upheaval, a new middle class arose. The members of this class—doctors, lawyers, managers, teachers, office workers, and their families—performed newly important functions in the changing society. The urban factory began to replace the rural subsistence farm as the center of economic production in the United States, dramatically altering women's relationship to the economy. In the agricultural economy, women were vital producers who grew food, spun and sewed clothes, and made other goods that their families required for survival. In the emerging industrial economy, women of the upper and middle classes, who no longer needed to produce their own food or clothes, became consumers, purchasing necessities and accumulating material commodities such as furniture, books, decorations, and clothes that showcased their taste and class status.

As these transformations took place, Americans began to conceive of men's and women's familial and national roles in new ways. Many Americans came to believe that society was divided into two separate spheres: the public sphere, associated with the political and professional worlds, and the private sphere, equated with the home and family. Men toiled at financial and political endeavors in the rough and ruthless public sphere. Women assumed responsibility for the family's moral education, health, comfort, and happiness in the safe and serene private sphere. Ministers, doctors, and others claimed that women had physically and morally delicate natures that would be corrupted or damaged by voting, working, or otherwise participating in the fields of government and finance. Many Americans rationalized that women's exclusion from the public sphere not only protected the "weaker" sex but also preserved the home as a moral refuge from the arduous and depraved world. In effect, the ideology of separate spheres allowed Americans to maintain certain cultural values, particularly the Christian values of modesty, obedience, and meekness, which conflicted with the self-interest necessary for attaining success in a developing capitalist society. In the private sphere, women ostensibly upheld the traditional religious ideals of American society, while men pursued wealth and political power in the public sphere.

## True Womanhood

The ideal of the true woman emerged with this transformation in women's roles. In the cult of true womanhood, femininity came to be equated with familial and religious devotion. Women's identities as daughters, sisters, wives, mothers, and Christians formed the basis of their cultural value. True womanhood demanded that the completed woman be pious, pure, submissive, and domestic. Magazines, advice manuals, novels, and religious literature helped create and popularize the cult of domesticity and instructed women in the best ways to embody the essential qualities of true womanhood.

Religion, specifically Protestant Christianity, formed the basis of the true woman's virtue. It was the source of her femininity as well as her power in society. In magazines such as *Godey's Lady's Book,* edited by Sarah Josepha Hale (1788–1879), perhaps the century's most influential domestic arbiter, women read that religious reverence enhanced a woman's personal attractiveness. Women were informed that they would find fulfillment only when their lives were absorbed in Christianity. That process of fulfillment would begin sometime in adolescence, when girls were expected to undergo a personal Christian conversion. A lack of religious interest or conviction in women was considered an anomaly and an affront to femininity. Irreligion made a woman revolting, because her faith was the foundation of her chastity, obedience, and domesticity.

Purity was equally essential for the true woman. Women were expected to remain chaste until marriage, when they would bestow on their husbands the gift of their virginity. Without purity, a woman was deemed a "fallen woman" or "fallen angel." Unworthy of respect, the fallen woman was no longer considered a woman at all. In popular books and magazines, women's sexual activity brought about insanity, illness, and death. Death, in fact, was often considered preferable to seduction. The threat of impurity was serious enough that advice manuals suggested that young women should avoid sitting beside or reading from the same book as men.

The ideal of women's submission, a distinctly feminine virtue, was frequently justified through Christian teachings, both Protestant and Catholic. Piety and purity were desired characteristics in men, but society expected and forgave their failings in these categories. Obedience, however, was demanded only of women. As men made decisions and took action, women were expected to passively conform. Many Americans claimed that this sexual hierarchy was established in the Bible. Others, such as George Burnap in *The Sphere and Duties of Woman* (1854), asserted that women needed and wanted protectors. Submission asked that the true woman serve her husband's, father's, and brother's desires in a state of continual dependence.

Finally, the true woman exemplified domesticity. The home was the true woman's domain; it belonged to her and she belonged in it. The cult of domesticity insisted that women make the home a warm, tasteful refuge from business and politics, a place to nurture children and ease a husband's burdens. From housekeeping manuals such as *The American Woman's Home* (1869), written by the popular authors and sisters Catharine Beecher (1800–1878) and Harriet Beecher Stowe (1811–1896), women received advice on everything from caring for the sick to polishing furniture. Home decoration, food preparation, cleaning, and children's education became moral duties that reflected a woman's virtue and her family's Christian devotion.

## Image and Reality

The image of the true woman was demanding and demeaning—it required women to live up to an exacting model of womanhood in which they remained explicitly subordinate to men. Moreover, the ideal was unrealistic. As much praise as they might receive for their feminine virtue, women were often plagued by feelings that they had failed to fulfill society's expectations. Even Beecher, a popular writer and the daughter of the celebrated and influential minister Lyman Beecher (1775–1863), could not fully adhere to the ideals of domesticity. Catharine submitted neither to conversion nor to marriage as her father and society expected.

Furthermore, the prevailing image of the true woman was white, middle-class, and Protestant, reflecting the context of the industrializing U.S. Northeast in which the ideology of domesticity emerged. Women who differed from the true woman by religion, race, class, or region acutely felt their exclusion from this pervasive feminine norm. Catholic and Jewish women, for instance, were largely barred from acceptance as true women by widespread anti-Catholicism and anti-Semitism. Within the largely immigrant Catholic and Jewish communities, true womanhood represented not only an impossible ideal, given the need for many women to support their families by working outside the home, but also a departure from traditional religious values and practices. In Catholicism, the church, not the home, was the center of moral and religious education, and celibacy, rather than marriage, was celebrated as the paradigm of purity. Assimilation to Protestant ideals signified a rejection of the church's authority and teachings, and as such Catholic Americans cultivated their own distinctly Catholic model of domesticity. In Orthodox Judaism, men were responsible for the spiritual needs of the family, while women, prohibited from studying the Talmud and excluded from full membership in the congregation, supported the family physically and economically. In contrast to American Catholicism, the American Jewish Reform movement largely adopted the tenets of true womanhood, revising women's roles at home and in the temple.

Similarly, and perhaps more starkly, racial difference obstructed admission to true womanhood. Free and enslaved African American women were frequently sexualized in U.S. culture, perceived alternately as seductresses and victims of male lust. This supposed impurity barred black women from the category of true womanhood. In her narrative *Incidents in the Life of a Slave Girl* (1861), escaped slave Harriet Jacobs shows how the standards of true womanhood are impossible to maintain within the system of slavery. Assailed by her owner's sexual advances, Jacobs's only method of preserving her purity is to choose another white man as her lover and hopeful protector.

Catholic, Jewish, and African American women were not alone in their anxieties. Women who lived in the U.S. South and West, women who sewed or laundered clothes for wages, women who toiled on farms, immigrant women, and Asian American and Latina women all felt their unquestionable deviation from the feminine standard. Still, the true woman remained a pervasive ideal and a symbol of national belonging with which U.S. women struggled throughout the century.

## The Feminization of American Religion

Womanhood became nearly synonymous with Christian virtue in the nineteenth century. The true woman's piety was the source of her purity and her selfless obedience. Even the virtue of domesticity, women were reminded, was religious in origin; St. Paul himself had allocated the home and its cultivation to women. As femininity was increasingly viewed as an effect of women's natural religiosity, religion came to be seen as the province of women. Churches and religious organizations began to be viewed not only as appropriate outlets for female activity but also, along with the family, as part of the feminine sphere. The association of women with the church reflected a revolution occurring within Protestant Christianity, sometimes called the feminization of American religion. Scholars have used the term "feminization" to describe both a sentimentalizing trend in Christian theology and the transformation of women's roles within religious organizations that occurred during the nineteenth century. It should be noted that this feminization was largely rejected by Catholics through the 1860s, who endorsed the patriarchal parish and household over and against what they viewed as a nationalized culture of domesticity. In Protestant communities, however, women's power and presence increased during the nineteenth century, instilling in women a new consciousness about their moral responsibility. As religion became feminized, Protestant women were ascribed and assumed the role of spiritual guardians, taking upon themselves the task of developing and defending the Christian home and the Christian nation.

## Theological Transformations

In the first decades of the nineteenth century, the United States experienced the Second Great Awakening, a period of religious fervor and activity distinguished by the popularity of evangelical revivals and the proliferation of new Christian sects and denominations, including Mormonism and Shakerism. In the wake of this spiritual enthusiasm, the major Protestant Christian denominations began to adopt increasingly emotional models of religious practice. In 1800, Protestants were likely to explain their faith in terms of dogma, a system of beliefs the members of a particular church were required to accept. By the 1870s, Protestants were likely to describe their faith through the family values and civic responsibilities they advocated and practiced. This new emphasis on social values indicated a transformation from the repressive and patriarchal Calvinistic models that had dominated the American religious scene to a more sentimental and accommodating Protestantism. This change was reflected in Methodist, Baptist, Presbyterian, Congregationalist, Episcopal, and Unitarian churches with new policies and programs, such as infant baptism and children's Sunday school instruction. Interpretations of the figure of Jesus Christ similarly began to shift. In sermons and religious literature, ministers conceived of a new Christ defined by love, selfless sacrifice, and forgiveness. This modest and meek Christ was viewed as an affectionate companion, as the popular nineteenth-century hymn "Nearer My God, to Thee" illustrates. Nineteenth-century Americans likewise celebrated God's compassion. A mother's mercy as well as a father's authority comprised God's essence, according to Theodore Parker (1810–1860), a prominent reformer and Unitarian minister. As the church and its theology began to exemplify domestic virtues, Americans became increasingly conscious of a vital, distinctly feminine, religious responsibility.

## Women and the Church

Although the ministers and theologians who constituted the church hierarchy remained overwhelmingly male, women's prominence within religious communities expanded throughout the nineteenth century. Church congregations frequently included more women than men, and their female members exerted powerful influence over the direction of the church. Realizing women were the chief consumers of religion in society, Protestant ministers routinely addressed women's particular concerns, praising women's innocence, maternal inclinations, and quiet endurance of the various burdens that accompanied marriage and child rearing. Within the church community, women's presence was felt everywhere. Women taught and frequently supervised Sunday school and wrote popular hymns; and in the West, where congregations had fewer members, women occasionally participated in church services.

Beyond their individual churches, women became important members of religious organizations and reform movements. In temperance, antislavery, and religious tract societies, women raised funds, licked envelopes, and solicited support from their husbands and other family members. Women also channeled their sense of piety into missionary work, laboring most often within the United States to provide Christian instruction to indigenous communities. Some particularly daring women (who were able to find husbands who shared their religious enthusiasm and ambition) became missionaries in foreign lands such as China and the Holy Land. Cultural assumptions about female piety and virtue enabled women to assume an energetic role within the church and its endeavors. As she gained a sense of religious responsibility, the nineteenth-century woman began to see herself as a "new Eve," charged with improving and perhaps even perfecting American society.

## The Christian Home

This new Eve sought to reform America starting at home. Her home was a space for reflecting Christian values and influencing others' moral actions. In *The American Woman's Home,* Beecher and Stowe included drawings for a home church, a house that may be converted at a moment's notice into a small chapel complete with steeple. Stowe and Beecher's image illustrates how many nineteenth-century Americans viewed the home and the true woman as extensions of the church's moral authority. In the Christian home, bed-making, cooking, and needlework were viewed as morally uplifting activities. Such tasks absorbed women in productive pursuits that left little time for sinful activities, and they created a pleasant environment that induced brothers, husbands, and sons to stay home and forgo the dangerous temptations (alcohol, gambling, sex) of the outside world. With her family comfortable and content at home, the true woman could bring her family closer to God. The tasks women performed at home—child care, nursing, gardening, mending clothes, financial management—aimed to make

the Christian family the foundation of society. Ideally, as women wielded their influence in the home, their families would embrace Christian values. Collectively, these families would constitute a Christian neighborhood and eventually a Christian nation. The new Eve could improve her society simply by setting the proper example for her family.

## Sentiment and Social Reform

Women expanded their moral influence beyond the home through popular literature and social reform efforts. Although many ministers, teachers, and mothers expressed concerns about the dangers of women writing and reading, women's literary endeavors were accepted for the most part as an appropriate extension of women's moral facility. Women became enthusiastic writers and readers of domestic or sentimental fiction, which sought to instruct women and children in Christian virtue, general usefulness, and social responsibility. Sentimental novels, such as Susan Warner's (1819–1885) best seller *The Wide, Wide World* (1850), scripted the community and the nation as one large home in which sympathy and Christian duty formed the basis for social action. Conceived as an extended Sunday sermon or biblical parable, *The Wide, Wide World* asked readers to extend compassion toward the friendless child heroine Ellen Montgomery and to interpret her eventual happy marriage as a reward for her faith and humility. Although men were not considered a suitable audience for women writers, they evidently consumed women's fiction and helped solidify its incredible popularity. In fact, nineteenth-century women writers were more widely read than theologians, causing some scholars to suggest that domestic fiction had replaced theology as Americans' primary spiritual guide.

In conjunction with their literary endeavors, U.S. women increasingly channeled their piety and moral influence into social reform. This intrusion into the public sphere was justified, women argued, because society had violated Christian commandments and teachings through adultery, slavery, and excessive alcohol consumption. Feminine intervention was necessary to defend the family against the immoralities of male-dominated society. Seeking to eradicate prostitution and limit opportunities for adultery, the New York Female Moral Reform Society was founded in 1834. In addition to preaching to prostitutes and praying in brothels, the society published a popular national weekly, *The Advocate of Moral Reform,* which was staffed with women writers and editors.

Women also joined the antislavery movement, participating in the work of the American Anti-Slavery Society. Among the more famous female abolitionists were Lydia Maria Child (1802–1880), a notable author of fiction, housekeeping advice, and children's literature, and Sarah Grimké (1792–1893) and Angelina Grimké Weld (1805–1879), sisters and public lecturers on the antislavery circuit. The temperance movement, which sought to curb or prohibit the consumption of alcohol in the United States, likewise attracted large numbers of women. Temperance appealed to women as a family issue, because drinking reputedly took money and men away from the home. By participating in these reform societies, women expanded their collective power while remaining within the bounds of conventional femininity.

## The Little Lady and the Big War

Women's writing and religious reform efforts often complemented each other and at times even merged. Stowe's novel *Uncle Tom's Cabin* (1852), the most popular book of the nineteenth century and the most famous example of literary activism in U.S. history, has often been credited with hastening the U.S. Civil War. Upon meeting Stowe, President Abraham Lincoln famously called her the "little lady who made this big war." Stowe herself claimed the novel was written by God, excusing her interference in the intense public debate over slavery as an act of Christian piety. *Uncle Tom's Cabin,* in fact, employs the values of domesticity and true womanhood to persuade its readers to join the antislavery cause. Written explicitly in response to the Fugitive Slave Law of 1850, which required northerners to return escaped slaves to the South, *Uncle Tom's Cabin* depicts slavery above all as a destroyer of families and an affront to domestic life. As such, Stowe implies, slavery demands women's attention and intervention. The novel calls upon true women to recognize slavery's incompatibility with Christianity and exert their moral influence over husbands, fathers, and sons.

## Moral Crusaders

As women endeavored to improve society through literature and social reforms, they changed the meaning of domesticity. Submissiveness, one of the central tenets of true womanhood from the 1830s to the 1860s, gradually diminished in importance as women embraced "moral authority" as a feminine prerogative. As a consequence, women's attempts to transform the nation through moral suasion gave way to increasing social and political activism, particularly following the U.S. Civil War.

Most notably, women converted their sense of moral righteousness into public action through the temperance crusades of the 1870s. Women temperance crusaders organized marches on the street and prayer meetings inside bars to protest the consumption of alcohol. In 1874, the crusaders formed the Woman's Christian Temperance Union (WCTU), which eventually boasted more than 176,000 members, making it the largest association of women in the nation. The WCTU expanded its reform efforts under the direction of President Frances Willard (1839–1898) to include child care for working women and immigrant aid. Willard developed a protofeminist platform for the WCTU, even campaigning for limited woman's suffrage. Under the banner of "Home Protection," Willard argued that women needed the vote to make alcohol consumption illegal.

Despite its basis in women's presumed moral superiority, women's activism existed in tension with the ideals of domesticity. In uniting the temperance cause with the woman's suffrage movement, Willard illuminated the inherent limitations of domesticity. Proponents of domesticity declared that women were supposed to influence men quietly in the home, not on the podium. Women's rights activists might argue that suffrage would enable women to protect the family, but the political equality woman's suffrage would establish between men and women conflicted with conventional morality. As early as 1837, Beecher had expressed her disapproval of the Grimké sisters' lecturing before "promiscuous"—mixed male and female—audiences. The Grimkés, however, felt that women had an obligation to speak out not only against slavery's wrongs but also against the subordination of women. The fundamental tension between these points of view persisted throughout the nineteenth century, causing many women's rights activists to abandon the tenets of domesticity. This impasse would prove to be the cult of domesticity's undoing. By the 1880s, the ideal of the true woman was becoming outmoded, the symbol of an old-fashioned moral framework that could no longer forward women's interests.

## Domesticity's Interpreters

In the twentieth and twenty-first centuries, the cult of domesticity has served as a subject of heated debate. Critics have struggled to understand how deeply the ideology of domesticity affected the lives of Americans and whether such ideas of womanhood ultimately served conservative or radical ends. Many of domesticity's original interpreters, including Barbara Welter, conceived of domesticity as a lived reality for nineteenth-century women, whose experiences deserved to be studied alongside political and economic histories. Subsequent critics, among them Nancy Cott, Ann Douglas, and Jane Tompkins, argued that domesticity and "separate spheres" were not realities but, rather, ideologies that deeply affected American political and religious culture. In Cott's view, domesticity and its consequent sex segregation created a sisterhood, at least among white, middle-class, northeastern women. Douglas, by contrast, perceived the cult of domesticity as a symptom of general cultural degeneration, in which feminized religion and sentimental fiction affirmed an unjust economic system and encouraged women to embrace confining roles. Countering Douglas's analysis, Tompkins suggested that domesticity, in its very conventionality, provided women with the means to mold, challenge, and transform mainstream cultural values. More recently, Amy Kaplan has proposed that the cult of domesticity was intertwined with the histories of national expansion, or Manifest Destiny, making domesticity a vital part of U.S. political history and foreign policy. Gradually, the cult of domesticity has come to be seen as an important element of nineteenth-century culture in the United States, neither separate from political, economic, and religious histories nor the cause of cultural deterioration. The cult of domesticity was a complicated and integral component of nineteenth-century U.S. culture, a powerful and popular ideology that had the potential to serve both conservative and radical ends.

**See also** *Abolitionism and Antislavery; Benevolent Empire; Children and Adolescents; Evangelicals: Nineteenth Century; Feminism; Gender; Marriage and Family; Literature: Early Republic and "the American Renaissance"; Masculinity; Religious Thought: Feminist; Sexuality and Sexual Identity; Women* entries.

Molly Robey

## BIBLIOGRAPHY

Carby, Hazel V. *Reconstructing Womanhood: The Emergence of the Afro-American Woman Novelist.* New York: Oxford University Press, 1987.
Cott, Nancy. *The Bonds of Womanhood: "Woman's Sphere" in New England, 1780–1835.* New Haven, Conn.: Yale University Press, 1977.
Douglas, Ann. *The Feminization of American Culture.* New York: Knopf, 1977.
Epstein, Barbara Leslie. *The Politics of Domesticity: Women, Evangelism, and Temperance in Nineteenth-Century America.* Middletown, Conn.: Wesleyan University Press, 1981.
Kaplan, Amy. "Manifest Domesticity." *American Literature* 70, no. 3 (September 1998): 581–606.
McDannell, Colleen. *The Christian Home in Victorian America, 1840–1900.* Bloomington: Indiana University Press, 1986.
Sklar, Kathryn Kish. *Catharine Beecher: A Study in American Domesticity.* New Haven, Conn.: Yale University Press, 1973.
Tompkins, Jane. *Sensational Designs: The Cultural Work of American Fiction, 1790–1860.* New York: Oxford University Press, 1985.
Welter, Barbara. *Dimity Convictions: The American Woman in the Nineteenth Century.* Athens: Ohio University Press, 1976.

# Death and Burial Practices

Death and burial practices in America have been as varied as the people who have populated the land. From the beginning of European settlement, attitudes toward death, beliefs about the afterlife, and practices surrounding death and burial were important markers of identity separating native from colonist, Protestant from Catholic, Calvinist from Anglican, and African from European.

Among European Americans, there has never been a single "American way of death." Although American death practices and beliefs are far from homogeneous, it is possible to identify widespread patterns that reflect broadly shared religious and cultural values. As these values have changed, so have the practices and beliefs related to death and burial. In the early years of European settlement, the growing wealth in the colonies led to greater materialism and optimism, which were reflected in opulent funerals and an anticipation of salvation. In the nineteenth century the idealization of the domestic sphere found expression in images of death as a natural homecoming. The acceptance of embalming during the Civil War ushered in the professional role of undertaker and the removal of the body from family control. By the mid-twentieth century, death itself had been largely removed from the home and took place in the company of medical specialists and life-prolonging technologies. Critics of these "death-denying" practices gained enough popular support in the 1960s to demand substantial reform in the care of the dying and the disposal of the dead. As a result, Americans today can choose not only between burial and cremation, but also

from an array of traditional and novel religious and secular rituals and symbols to create a personally meaningful farewell.

## Death in Early America

European settlers in the New World brought with them Catholic and Protestant religious traditions, which they aggressively introduced to the Native Americans. For the many Spanish and French Catholic colonists, a good death depended on the availability of a priest to administer the sacrament of last rites to the dying and perform the funeral mass. The last rites offered sinners a final chance to repent and receive forgiveness before their postmortem journey. Though necessary for the forgiveness of sins, the sacrament did not guarantee a direct entry into heaven. Apart from the saintly, most were destined to spend time in the state of purgatory expiating their sins, and the prayers of the faithful at funeral mass were believed to shorten this duration. Whereas these Catholic practices were eventually accepted by many Native Americans as they suffered devastating death tolls from epidemics under Spanish and French rule, Protestant missionaries had much less success. Protestant colonists rejected the existence of purgatory and the ability of the living to affect the destiny of the dead through prayers and other meritorious acts. Consequently, those of the Anglican and Reformed traditions simplified the sacramental and liturgical systems of the Roman Catholic Church to varying degrees. The most radical reforms were made by the Puritans in New England, who expressly forbade the superstitious ceremonialism.

## Puritans' Approaches to Death

Seventeenth-century Puritans approached death with anxious fear of damnation, because the doctrines of depravity and predestination made any certainty of salvation impossible. John Calvin's insistence on the utter depravity of man derived from the assertion that because all had inherited Adam's guilt, none could merit salvation. Damnation was simply the logical outcome of divine justice. Through God's pure gift of grace some had been selected for salvation, but this knowledge was utterly beyond human capacity. Puritan ministers used death as a didactic tool, describing it in ghastly images of decomposition and hellfire to motivate their congregants toward conversion. Educated in the terrors of hell and unable to discern their predetermined fate, they were understandably terrified of the destiny awaiting them. In the context of belief in depravity, predestination, and the inscrutability of God, the sinner best approached death through stringent introspection and repentance. Appalled by their wretchedness, sinners had no choice but to rely entirely on God's mercy. As depicted in deathbed narratives, despair was the appropriate attitude of the dying. Ironically, doubt of salvation was the best assurance of salvation, because any suggestion that one deserved otherwise was a sure sign of self-delusion.

The first Puritans encountered death frequently and dealt with it efficiently. Families washed and dressed their own dead and laid them out at home or at the church for a few days prior to burial. The dead were buried at a central graveyard with no prayers or ceremony. Excessive displays of emotion, such as wearing black, were forbidden, and there is little evidence of grave markers. Mourners gathered at the family home afterward for a meal.

The stark simplicity of the Puritan funeral did not last long, however. By the 1650s signs of elaboration were apparent, and growing class distinctions were expressed through expensive funeral garments. Those who could afford to do so would send mourning gloves as an invitation to the funeral and give attendees mourning rings. Coffins were upgraded from simple to expensive woods and lined with cloth. The burial was accompanied by a funeral sermon often including a eulogy, and graves were marked with tombstones displaying winged skulls, bones, and hourglasses. The growing expense and formality of the Puritan funeral drew criticism, but it did not abate. The doctrines of depravity and predestination had not disappeared as the famous 1741 sermon by Jonathan Edwards, "Sinners in the Hands of an Angry God," makes clear. But because the

enthusiastic revivals of the eighteenth century (the Great Awakening) offered all sinners an opportunity to accept Jesus, salvation likewise could be attained through human agency.

## Domestication of Death

In the nineteenth century fear of divine justice and damnation was eclipsed by peaceful images of death and a loving, merciful God. Letters, diaries, and sermons of this period indicate that death was a constant preoccupation, valued as a forewarning to the wayward sinner. Even though the unconverted were still destined for damnation, the faithful expressed confidence that a heavenly home awaited them. Heaven, pictured as an idealized earthly home where family and friends are reunited, seemed familiar and close by. Enslaved Africans had long thought of death as a return to their homeland in Africa, and their descendents who converted to Christianity routinely spoke of death as a homecoming and reunion in heaven. For example, the well-known slave spiritual "Swing Low, Sweet Chariot" declares,

Swing low, sweet chariot, Coming for to carry me home.
I looked over Jordan and what did I see, Coming for to carry me home?
A band of angels coming after me, Coming for to carry me home.
If you get there before I do, Coming for to carry me home.
Tell all my friends I'm coming too, Coming for to carry me home.

African Americans' belief that heaven was familiar can also be seen in the everyday objects they buried with their loved ones, who would need them on the other side.

In the nineteenth century European Americans also pictured death as a homecoming. The similarity and closeness between the spirit and earthly worlds became the basis for the spiritualist movement of the nineteenth century. Mediums traveled the country offering Americans a channel of communication with their beloved dead. Influenced by Romanticism, nineteenth-century Americans embraced death as a natural process that delivered the dying from earthly suffering rather than a punishment to be dreaded. Family and friends gathered around the bedside to witness the release of the soul as an edifying experience. Care of the dead continued to be the purview of the family: the family washed, dressed, wrapped, and laid out the body, keeping close vigil until the church service and burial. Keeping vigil showed great respect for the dead, but it also served the practical function of ensuring that no one was buried prematurely, a common fear at this time. The emphasis on familial bonds was expressed in elaborate displays of sentimentality at the funeral and an extended public mourning period. As in the previous century, class distinctions were apparent in the degree of ornamentation surrounding the funeral, especially in the expense of the coffin and tombstone.

The disappearance of fearful images of decay and damnation can be clearly seen in the cemeteries of the nineteenth century. The tombstone engravings of New England had changed almost universally from skulls and hourglasses to cherubs and willow branches by the 1760s. The end of the eighteenth century also witnessed the first urban cemetery. Known first as "The New Burying Ground" and later as Grove Street Cemetery, it was built in 1796 in New Haven, Connecticut, but urban crowding and fear of disease pushed the dead farther from the living. A rural cemetery movement sought to integrate death with a cultivated natural setting that was both sanitary and peaceful. Mt. Auburn Cemetery, opened in 1831 outside of Boston, was a popular destination for locals and tourists. Designed as a beautiful garden where the living could commune with the dead in a natural setting, the rural cemetery expressed romanticized views of both nature and family. Families could purchase family plots to ensure they would remain together eternally. Following the model of Mt. Auburn, several dozen rural cemeteries, such as Laurel Hill Cemetery in Philadelphia and Spring Grove Cemetery in Cincinnati, were created across the country. By the latter decades of the nineteenth century, however, the rural cemetery was supplanted by the open expanse of the lawn-park cemetery with flush grave markers, which continues to dominate today. Unlike the often neglected graveyards of the early colonists, modern cemeteries required constant maintenance well beyond the care of family members. From the cemetery movement emerged the role of cemetery superintendent, one of many death professions to develop in the late nineteenth century.

## The Modern Funeral

The Civil War was a turning point for burial practices in the United States. With so many soldiers dying far from home, Americans began to accept embalming in order to bring their dead home for burial. Embalming allowed families to view their dead one last time and be assured that they were buried in a fitting manner. Far from a modern practice, embalming had long been rejected by Christians on the grounds that it desecrated the body. When weighed against the practical problems created by the war, the religious opposition faded. The 1865 public

procession and viewing of President Abraham Lincoln's embalmed body helped to popularize the practice. The scientific and technological allure of embalming also appealed to the modernizing impulse of the time. Although embalmers originally did their work at the family home, they soon insisted that the dead be brought to specialized facilities with the necessary equipment. Funeral parlors were designed to resemble the family home and minimize the disruption created by the physical removal of the dead from the control of the family. Undertakers organized themselves as legitimate professionals—funeral directors—in the 1880s and claimed authority over the care and handling of the dead. Many Americans resisted the transformation of funeral rituals, but wealthy Americans living in urban areas were the first to accept their expertise and pay for a refined funeral, as they sought to distinguish themselves from the commoner. It would be several decades before the majority of Americans would accept the modern funeral form.

By the early twentieth century, reliance on funeral professionals and acceptance of embalming had become the norm among urban Americans. Increasing urbanization and mobility, which disrupted local communities and their traditions, was one of many major social changes aiding this development. As families became more dispersed, embalming was essential for delaying the funeral long enough for everyone to gather. Because of rising life expectancy, Americans had less experience with death, and they turned to professionals for guidance. A similar shift was occurring in the care of the dying. Whereas doctors previously had made house calls, the modern hospital provided more efficacious treatment of disease. The dying were now in the hands of professionals with specialized knowledge and technology for staving off death. With their traditional caregiver role supplanted by doctors and nurses, Americans became unfamiliar with death and increasingly reliant on funeral directors to guide them.

Once the funeral industry began to disseminate ideas about proper preparation, display, and disposal of the body, as well as patterns of mourning, many Americans came to believe that they needed the expertise of a professional funeral director to guide them. The funeral director assured clients of a dignified farewell. In the United States, funeral directors successfully established not only the practice of embalming, but also the use of cosmetics and facial reconstruction to create a serene image of the restful dead. The elaborate preparation of the body and its placement in a costly, sturdy, but beautifully crafted casket were undertaken for the benefit of the mourners, who took comfort in having a final picture of their loved one in repose. Cemeteries further added the practice of covering the casket with a grave liner or vault to ensure even greater protection of the peaceful dead. Together, the removal of the body from the home and the family's control, the practice of embalming and the use of makeup, and the body-preserving caskets served to mask the reality of death or at least push it to a more manageable distance. The funeral director arranged all the details of the funeral for the family, who could grieve free of disturbing images of decay. Public mourning practices greatly declined in the early decades of the twentieth century when extended or excessive grieving became viewed as a sign of psychological distress.

These modern practices of embalming and display combined with Christian beliefs in the afterlife with little difficulty. Efforts to sanitize death had no effect on the postmortem journey of the soul or the future resurrection of the body. The emergence of the American funeral industry did affect the clergy, however. The explicitly religious aspects of the funeral were retained: a church service with a theologically focused sermon and eulogy, followed by the burial in a local cemetery accompanied by prayers. But these rituals were increasingly overshadowed by the larger drama orchestrated by the funeral director. This loss of authority became even more obvious when Americans began holding the funeral service at the funeral home chapel to save themselves the expense and trouble of transporting the body elsewhere.

Although the funeral industry was able to wield considerable power in defining the ideal form of the modern funeral, its influence was by no means absolute. In rural parts of the country, families continued to care for the dead in the context of the local community and traditional Christianity. Even in urban areas, some religious and ethnic groups maintained control of their dead much longer than Anglo Protestants. For example, Orthodox and Conservative Jews refused to accept embalming and relied on their own burial societies, known as the *Chevra Kadisha,* to care for the dead. The *Chevra Kadisha* ritualistically washes and dresses the body and maintains a vigil until the burial, which takes place within three days. Jews have also resisted the elaborate casket in favor of a simple pine coffin. More recently, American Muslim communities have organized networks to care for their own dead in a similar manner. Today, many funeral homes will accommodate these traditional practices by inviting these groups to care for their dead within the rented space of the funeral home, thus giving limited control back to the family.

## Critique and Reform

Even though the funeral industry's practices had been criticized since its inception, by the 1950s piercing critiques were drawing much public attention. In her 1963 bestseller *The American Way of Death,* Jessica Mitford criticized the opulent materialism of the modern funeral, which sought to mask death through makeup and euphemisms. She condemned the industry's exploitation of grieving families and argued for a more authentic funeral experience. Mitford singled out embalming as an especially bizarre American anomaly. In response to public outrage, legislation was enacted in the 1980s to better regulate the funeral industry. Death professionals were required to provide detailed information about prices and forced to inform families that embalming was not legally necessary. These changes were insufficient for some consumers, who sought to bypass the industry entirely by creating local cremation and burial societies that offered inexpensive, no-frills options for disposal of the dead.

Concurrent with consumer demand for greater transparency in the funeral industry, the number of Americans requesting cremation rose dramatically. The practice was first introduced to the American public in 1876 as a more scientific and modern means of disposal, but it was widely rejected until the 1960s, when disgust with the funeral industry and the weakening of religious ties allowed cremation to become a viable alternative. Cremation took hold first on the West Coast, where religious affiliation is lowest, and has only slowly caught on in the southern Bible Belt. In 1950 the cremation rate was just 4 percent, but the number had risen to over 32 percent by 2005 and is projected to surpass 57 percent by 2025. The current cremation rate in the United States is substantially lower than in other Western countries: 72 percent in the United Kingdom and 56 percent in Canada. By comparison, Americans remain strongly tied to the practice of embalming, display, and burial, but the recent surge in the cremation rate indicates that American funeral practices are undergoing major changes.

The popularity of cremation has created significant challenges for both religious communities and the funeral industry. As noted earlier, the Abrahamic traditions have long required burial of the dead on theological grounds. Orthodox Jews, Muslims, and Orthodox Christians continue to reject cremation, as does the Church of Jesus Christ of Latter-day Saints. Protestant Christians, especially African Americans, strongly prefer burial to cremation as do a slight majority of Catholics, but enough religiously affiliated Americans prefer cremation to push their religious communities to end restrictions on the practice. The Roman Catholic Church relaxed its absolute ban on cremation in 1963, but insisted that the body be present for the funeral mass. Because the presence of the body for the service required embalming and purchase or rental of a casket, cost-conscious Catholics often ignored the rule and proceeded directly with cremation. Rather than deny the funeral mass in these cases, in 1997 the church allowed cremated remains to be present at the funeral mass, but it has continued to insist that burial is the expected form of Christian disposal. Increasingly, Protestant and Catholic churches are adapting to the cremation trend by constructing scattering gardens and columbaria on their grounds, not unlike the ancient Christian practice of burying the faithful inside or close to the sanctuary.

From a financial perspective, immediate or direct cremation cuts sharply into industry profits. It requires no embalming, no facial reconstruction, no refrigeration, no casket (other than a cardboard box), no formal attire, no burial plot, and no memorial tombstone. To counter their losses, funeral professionals have creatively marketed new products and services to cremation customers as memorializing activities needed for grief facilitation. These activities include holding a viewing prior to cremation, which necessitates embalming and a casket; holding a memorial service, preferably at the nondenominational chapel of the funeral parlor; and purchasing a beautiful urn. In addition to holding a memorial service, families are encouraged to do some kind of memorializing activity around the disposition or scattering of the cremated remains. Here the options are large and expanding rapidly: burial in a cemetery plot is quite common, but many families will want to scatter the cremated remains at a site that was personally meaningful to the deceased. Whatever they choose, funeral directors encourage families to purchase some kind of stationary memorial marker where they can return as needed to spend time with the dead. Now that the industry has had to branch out beyond embalming and casket sales to survive, technologically savvy funeral directors are even offering video memorials and webcasting of services in real time. Just as embalming opened the door to the professionalized care of the dead, the practice of cremation is creating an opening for the development of new death rituals. The dizzying array of choices now available appeals to the consumer seeking an alternative to the traditional funerary rites.

## Personalizing Funerals

Today, American funeral practices are quickly diversifying as growing numbers of Americans seek a meaningful farewell to loved ones. The formal, professionally orchestrated, theologically focused funeral of the 1950s no longer achieves this goal for many Americans. Far from following a prescribed religious or professional script, contemporary death rituals are created out of the interactions among family, funeral professionals, and clergy. The demand for new death rituals is part of a much larger shift in American religiosity, which began in the counterculture of the 1960s. Spiritual seeking and denominational switching have loosened the commitment to the traditional religious forms in favor of a more flexible eclectic religiosity. Regardless of religious affiliation, the most recent trend in funeral practices has been toward greater personalization. Contemporary death rituals are designed to express the personality, values, and lifestyle of the deceased and to celebrate his or her life.

Thanks to the creativity and innovation of families and funeral entrepreneurs, the options for personalizing death rituals are expanding rapidly. For example, there are "theme" funerals complete with theatrical backdrops and props and "artistic" funerals in which everyone takes a turn at decorating the casket or urn. More common, families decorate the ritual space with photographs or create a slideshow that is featured during the service. The choice of readings and music is an obvious place to reflect the personality of the deceased. Although traditional scripture passages such as Psalm 23, "The Lord is my shepherd," are very common, scripture is often juxtaposed with a contemporary song. A more subtle change in the funeral or memorial service is the central place now given to eulogizing. With the exception of the early Puritans, eulogies have long been part of the American funeral, but until now their significance has been secondary to the religious message delivered by the clergy. For the religiously unaffiliated, the entire service may consist of eulogies prepared by invited loved ones or a "shared eulogy" in which anyone is invited to speak at the service. Expression of feelings is further encouraged through a cyber memorial placed on the Internet where photos, videos, and shared reflections can be posted well after the actual funeral. Finally, the burial or scattering of the cremated remains is an obvious arena for a personalized farewell. Possibilities range from incorporating ashes into jewelry, artwork, and fireworks to scattering cremated remains over a favorite beach or golf course.

Personal values, such as environmental concerns, are also expressed in the new death practices. Cremation has long been advocated as eco-friendlier than burial because it avoids the use of embalming fluids, the waste of precious materials in caskets and grave liners, and the use of land. For the environmentally conscious, cremated remains may be mixed with concrete and added to an artificial reef. However, concerns about pollution and energy conservation have caused some Americans to reject cremation in favor of "green burials," or "woodland burials," which are already common in Great Britain. In 2008 some thirteen green burial sites were operating in the United States, although the exact criteria for this designation have not yet been determined. At a minimum, these sites promote plant and animal life and prohibit embalming toxins, metals, concrete, and precious woods. Some do not even allow grave markers, but they do map the burial sites using global positioning devices. Loved ones are intimately involved in the green burial process by carrying the body to the actual burial. They are free to ritualize the burial in any manner they choose, including a traditional religious service held at the gravesite. Green burials bring together two contemporary American values: environmental conservation and nature-based spirituality.

As traditional religious forms are being renegotiated, there are seemingly endless possibilities for how Americans dispose of and memorialize their dead. Some new practices, such as space burial, cryogenics, or do-it-yourself burials, are too expensive or burdensome to gain many adherents. Others, such as the spontaneous shrines created in the wake of tragic deaths, have been quickly embraced by Americans and will become even more common. What most distinguishes American funeral practices in the twenty-first century is their celebration of the life of the deceased as the central narrative that brings meaning to death and life.

**See also** *Food and Diet; Latino/a Religious Practice; Lived Religion; Popular Religion and Popular Culture* entries.

Kathleen Garces-Foley

## BIBLIOGRAPHY

Cremation Association of North America (CANA). "Final 2005 Statistics and Projections to the Year 2025." CANA, Chicago, 2007.

Farrell, James. *Inventing the American Way of Death, 1830–1920.* Philadelphia: Temple University Press, 1980.

Garces-Foley, Kathleen, ed. *Death and Religion in a Changing World.* Armonk, N.Y.: M. E. Sharpe, 2006.

Grimes, Ronald. *Deeply into the Bone.* Berkeley: University of California Press, 2000.

Harris, Mark. *Grave Matters: A Journey through the Modern Funeral Industry to the Natural Way of Burial.* New York: Scribner, 2007.

Jackson, Charles O. *Passing: The Vision of Death in America.* Westport, Conn.: Greenwood Press, 1977.

Laderman, Gary. *Rest in Peace: A Cultural History of Death and the Funeral Home in Twentieth-Century America.* New York: Oxford University Press, 1991.

———. *The Sacred Remains.* New Haven, Conn.: Yale University Press, 1996.

Mitford, Jessica. *The American Way of Death.* New York: Simon and Schuster, 1963.

Prothero, Stephen R. *Purified by Fire: A History of Cremation in America.* Berkeley: University of California Press, 2001.

Stannard, David E. *The Puritan Way of Death: A Study in Religion, Culture, and Social Change.* New York: Oxford University Press, 1977.

# Death of God Theology

Death of God theology as a cultural and philosophical movement reached its pinnacle in the United States in the 1960s, but it has its roots in European intellectual history after the Enlightenment.

The theology emerged from the conviction that God had become culturally irrelevant in modern discourse and paradigms of selfhood. This movement stems from an increasingly secular worldview in discussions of morality, self-identity, and cultural issues. In spite of this theology's provocative name, the notion of the death of God is not necessarily related to an atheist perspective, although it can be. More specifically, Death of God theology maintains that the view of God as a superior metaphysical being is no longer widely accepted, because the vision of God as a transcendent or providential being controlling the events of the world has essentially died. In a general sense, this view involves a move from transcendence to immanence: instead of religious paradigms, people now turn to scientific, pragmatic, or social explanations of the world. In the contemporary era the idea of God has meaning only in relation to what is known through human existence.

Death of God theology overlaps with some separate but closely related intellectual movements. The rejection of otherworldly sources of meaning places a strong emphasis on human experience and culture as the true sources of reality and is therefore very much compatible with existentialism. Furthermore, Death of God theology correlates with the death of a certain type of Western metaphysical thinking. Rather than suggesting that philosophy can determine a category of absolutes, philosophical thinking is instead engaged in inquiry that relates to individual perspective and experience. The rejection of a traditional understanding of God—and thus a supreme grounding principle—suggests that things have value only to the extent to which they relate to other things in existence, an idea known as perspectivism. These ideas were considered in the views of existentialist thinkers such as Martin Heidegger and Paul Tillich in their expositions of how issues of ultimate Being must be considered in the context of the individual subject's being and experiences contained therein.

## Nietzsche and the Death of God

At the forefront of the Death of God theological movement was the nineteenth-century German philosopher Friedrich Nietzsche (1844–1900). Nietzsche continued certain themes in his writings that also are prevalent in German Romanticism—human creativity, self-expression, and nature. In *The Gay Science* (1882) and *Thus Spoke Zarathustra* (1883–1885), Nietzsche describes characters who proclaim that "God is dead." In both of these works, the characters in question are social outcasts who realize that the general community is not ready to recognize that God is dead. As sobering as this declaration may be initially, Nietzsche argues that human beings should ultimately view it as a moment of possibility. He views the Christian moral system as an outdated source of "slave-morality" that breeds resentment, pessimism, and self-doubt. Even though God has no real influence in modern-day culture, Nietzsche argues, people still cling to an antiquated view of the world that teaches them to doubt themselves and turn to an otherworldly God for solace—even though for all intents and purposes this God is dead. This realization is an important step in beginning the process of self-overcoming and the establishment of the *Übermensch* (the overman/superman), who for Nietzsche was the most enlightened and empowered version of the human being.

Nietzsche's influence on continental Europe and eventually the English-speaking world was significant. For one thing, many of the thinkers who followed Nietzsche interpreted his perspectivism and rejection of otherworldly sources of meaning as a basis for social critique and change. Without the perceived existence of a God who commands moral directives and metaphysical truth, the socially and politically constructed value of the world is given much more emphasis.

## Death of God Theology in the Twentieth Century

The Death of God movement took shape in the United States in the context of the social and political climate of the 1960s. It was represented by various voices.

### Gabriel Vahanian

Operating from a Christian theological perspective, Gabriel Vahanian (1927–) in his *The Death of God* (1961) suggested that Americans were entering a "post-Christian" era. In his view, the death of God was only figurative, a cultural phenomenon marked by recent trends in secularism and pluralism that arose in the context of the twentieth century. For example, theologian Walter Rauschenbusch's idea of the "social gospel" at the beginning of the century provided an eschatological vision that pertained more to earthly matters of social justice, not otherworldly salvation. For authors like Rauschenbusch, Vahanian argued, the idea of God as a supreme or transcendent being was no longer essential. This idea led to an indeterminate era of "religiosity" in which doctrinal or theocentric religions were superseded by superficial forms. Some of Vahanian's examples included "do-it-yourself" religions that were most concerned about psychological and emotional well-being, or a watered-down view of God as the "Cosmic Pal," a being who was little more than a calming influence amid the tumult of daily life. Vahanian suggested that in the contemporary age human beings would describe God in a manner that was most beneficial to their needs, and that ultimately these conceptualizations of religion would reflect anthropological need rather than religious awareness. He asserted that these movements shifted religion's influence away from the "transcendentalist" ideals of traditional Christianity and the Bible and toward "immanentist" ones, as defined by earthly goods and cultural institutions. Trends in Christian existentialism and humanism have only furthered the immanentist mindset, because their descriptions of the religious event downplay crucial theological moments, such as Jesus' death on the cross, in favor of anthropological observations.

Vahanian viewed this modern take on religion as superficial, if not idolatrous, and in need of an overhaul. In spite of his objections to the current culture, he observed that, ironically, the tradition of Christianity itself caused its inception to a certain extent. In serving as the foundation of a civilization that eventually developed to the current secular state, it ultimately demonstrated its own majesty through the folly of the human condition. Echoing the nineteenth-century Danish philosopher Søren Kierkegaard, Vahanian suggested that the death of God demonstrated the true futility of the human condition, and ultimately human beings were even more dependent on God as the supreme living being than ever before.

## Thomas J. J. Altizer

At the other end of the spectrum of Death of God theology was Thomas J. J. Altizer (1927–). Along with theologian William Hamilton, Altizer represented the more radical voice of the movement in the 1960s. Read widely in academic and popular culture circles alike, he was featured in two *Time* magazine articles in 1965 and 1966. The later article, "Is God Dead?" was published during the Easter season and fomented a national backlash. Many of Altizer's public appearances throughout the country were met with protests, including an appearance on the *Merv Griffin Show* that abruptly ended when the studio audience began calling for Altizer's death. Unlike Vahanian, Altizer viewed the death of God as a literal event. In spite of its seemingly sacrilegious nature, Altizer's *Gospel of Christian Atheism* (1966) suggested that the death of God was actually a "Christian confession of faith" made possible by the very death of Jesus on the cross.

Following Nietzsche, Altizer viewed the death of God as the absolute moment of possibility for human beings. Altizer explained the death of God as a specific historical event that occurred when Jesus was crucified. He suggested that the radical Christian understands that God died along with Christ, and this death was in fact a final event. The true implications of this historical event have been overshadowed in traditional Christianity through the portrayal of the living transcendent God and the subsequent moral implications. To its detriment, the Christian tradition had understood itself as a tradition of sin and redemption, interlaced with supernatural elements. As an alternative Altizer offered a Hegelian interpretation of history, suggesting that the radical Christian vision involved a dialectical mode of understanding in which the profane event of God's death was actually a mode of entrance to divinity. The world would be redeemed not as a supernatural act of God's grace, but as part of the dialectical process of history itself. The Incarnation and Crucifixion were dual but necessary

moments in the singular process of God's "self-annihilation" that negated the existence of God as only transcendent or wholly other. Only after God died on the cross, as a true human being, could absolute Spirit reach the world in a specific and determinate way.

When traditional Christianity viewed the sacrifice of God as a moral event that took place because of the shortcomings of humanity, it failed to appreciate that God's own death was a deliberate act of self-annihilation and was the only event that makes true reconciliation possible. In Altizer's view God's death on the cross was part of a divine process, a gradual metamorphosis of Spirit into flesh. The death of God was also the moment of epiphany in which the world knew Christ and was thereby the possibility of transformation. Only an event as radical as God's death could allow for true atonement: if God were a mere author of history, controlling its every event, the possibility for true reconciliation would not be possible. Insofar as God himself died and was also annihilated by this alien Spirit, then all forms of alien otherness would also be subject to this dialectical reversal. In this line of thought Altizer maintained that Satan himself was the "eschatological epiphany of Christ" and ultimately would be himself annihilated, and this would be made possible only by the death or annihilation of God.

## Dietrich Bonhoeffer and Karl Barth

Like Nietzsche, Altizer and Hamilton saw the death of God as a ground for possibility, also describing the concept as a type of "radical theology" made necessary because of a perceived nihilism or complacency within contemporary culture. This emptiness was most dangerous because it created a false sense of security, even in times of great urgency. They cited the example of Dietrich Bonhoeffer (1906–1945), who wrote in his 1944 letters from prison that people must learn to live as if God were not there. The presence of Nazi Germany showed that "God is weak and powerless in the world," and only once people make that realization and act on the basis of it could God continue to help them. Bonhoeffer described this realization of the death of God as a kind of "coming of age" process.

The Protestant theologian Karl Barth (1886–1968) represents an interesting foil to the Death of God theologians of the 1960s. On the one hand, as members of the Confessing Church in Germany, both Bonhoeffer and Barth criticized "liberal theology" because it placed too much emphasis on personal experience in the interpretation of religion. The contemporary events of Nazi Germany should cause one to be highly critical of the human being's ability to do good. Barth emphasized the "humanity of God" as a central tenet of the Christian tradition, but believed that nineteenth-century thinkers such as Friedrich Schleiermacher and Ludwig von Feuerbach overemphasized the anthropocentric nature of this concept to the detriment of the tradition. Barth viewed the humanity of Jesus Christ as paramount, but it was solely because of his existence as the Redeemer of humankind. For Barth, subjectivism and cultural relativism as presences in religious thought needed to be corrected by a more precise interpretation of Reform theology. Although Bonhoeffer also believed in the value of Reform theology as the basis of the criticism of contemporary complacency, it was precisely the "coming of age" realization of the powerlessness—or "death"—of God in human culture that was central in his willingness to participate in the plot to assassinate Adolf Hitler.

## Continuing Relevance of Death of God Theology

The problem of evil in the world introduces another important voice in Death of God theology, that of Rabbi Richard Rubenstein (1924–), who believed the death of God occurred within a specific historical event, the Holocaust. Rubenstein's *After Auschwitz* (1966; 2nd ed., 1992) was a revolutionary work that considered the problems of a post-Holocaust Jewish theology. Up to that point, Jewish thought was primarily conceived as following a covenantal model of election: God promises to act in history on behalf of the people of Israel as long as they keep the Commandments. Following from Deuteronomy 28, the people shall be "blessed" or "cursed" based on how well they maintain God's laws. God is viewed as a transcendent God who is an invisible author of history and the events that take place are an act of God's will. This logic poses a significant problem in the wake of the Holocaust, because it suggests that God willed the Holocaust to happen and that somehow Jews themselves are to blame for it.

Rubenstein argues that this notion of Jewish election or "chosenness" is no longer tenable after the Holocaust, and that the idea of God as a transcendent God who works through history is now dead. As a result, Jewish identity and the meaning of the covenant made at Mount Sinai must be radically reconceived. God should now be perceived as a God of nature who participates in its ebb and flow but does not control it. Although God's divinity exists everywhere, like the changing of the seasons, it is still subject to a basic state of flux. This explains how God exists immanently, not transcendently, and its paradigmatic example is found in Zionism, which Rubenstein explains as the Jewish people's yearning to return to their ancient homeland and union with the earth. Rubenstein is also heavily influenced by German philosopher Georg Hegel, but he ultimately suggests that Hegel's quest for continuity is inadequate. Drawing from the Kabbalah and other mystical traditions, Rubenstein suggests that God should be conceived as a Holy Nothingness without limit or end (En-Sof). God is not a tangible being or thing controlling the events of world; instead God is a "no-thing" that exists as the primordial ground of nature.

Death of God theology continues into the twenty-first century, although not with the same fervor of the 1960s. In addition to its contemporary applications by the thinkers noted here, it has been a significant influence within the circles of postmodernism, secular humanism, and existentialism. Over time, the idea of God as being real but dead—as illustrated by notions of "Christian atheism" or "Death of God theology"—was simply replaced by a more explicitly secular vernacular. In the latter part of the twentieth century, religious thought and religious ethics took more of a pragmatic turn. Because of both the moral and epistemological difficulties of proving the metaphysics of God's existence or death, such propositions are viewed as less important than the social and political impacts of such beliefs.

**See also** *Holocaust; Neo-Orthodoxy; Philosophical Theology; Philosophy; Postmodernism; Religious Thought* entries.

Christy Flanagan

## BIBLIOGRAPHY

Altizer, Thomas J. J. *The Gospel of Christian Atheism.* Philadelphia: Westminster, 1966.

Altizer, Thomas J. J., and William Hamilton. *Radical Theology and the Death of God.* Indianapolis: Bobbs-Merrill, 1966.

Barth, Karl. *The Humanity of God,* translated by Thomas Wieser and John Newton Thomas. Louisville: John Knox Press, 1960.

Bonhoeffer, Dietrich. *Letters and Papers from Prison.* New York: Touchstone, 1997.

Caputo, John D., and Gianni Vattimo. *After the Death of God,* edited by Jeffrey W. Robbins. New York: Columbia University Press, 2007.

Heidegger, Martin. "The Word of Nietzsche: 'God Is Dead.'" In *The Question Concerning Technology, and Other Essays,* translated by William Lovitt. New York: Harper and Row, 1977.

Nietzsche, Friedrich. *The Portable Nietzsche,* edited and translated by Walter Kaufmann. New York: Viking Penguin, 1954.

Rubenstein, Richard. *After Auschwitz: History, Theology, and Contemporary Judaism.* 2nd ed. Baltimore: Johns Hopkins University Press, 1992.

Tillich, Paul. *The Essential Tillich: An Anthology of the Writings of Paul Tillich*, edited by F. Forrester Church. Chicago: University of Chicago Press, 1987.

Vahanian, Gabriel. *The Death of God: The Culture of Our Post-Christian Era*. New York: George Braziller, 1961.

# Deism

Deism, sometimes referred to as "rational religion" or the "religion of nature," is the belief in a God disclosed in nature and by reason rather than in sacred scripture and by supernatural revelation. Deists typically reject scriptural inerrancy, miracles, providence, and ecclesial institutions, but accept the existence of a First Cause, the importance of virtuous behavior, and, less unanimously, an afterlife.

Originating in England, deism emerged from the context of the late seventeenth- and eighteenth-century Enlightenment. Deistic texts were appearing in the American colonies by the mid-eighteenth century, scandalizing orthodox Christians but attracting a lively following among young people and intellectuals. Although enthusiasm for deism waned in the first two decades of the nineteenth century, it gained surprising momentum, thanks especially to the tireless agitation of America's most influential deist, Elihu Palmer (1764–1806), in the opening years of the Republic. Deism in the late colonial and early Republic periods became a rallying cry for freethinkers, religious-minded people disgruntled with Christianity, and radical republicans. In addition to Palmer, the leading American deists or deist sympathizers were Benjamin Franklin, Thomas Jefferson, Ethan Allen, Thomas Paine, and Philip Freneau. The young nation's first five presidents seem more deistic than orthodox in their religious sensibilities.

## Basic Principles

There was no universal agreement among the individual proponents of deism, any more than there is universal agreement among adherents of the major faith traditions. Moreover, the borders between eighteenth-century deism and liberal Christianity, on the one hand, and outright free thought, on the other, were sometimes difficult to establish. Some liberal Christians endorsed positions that sounded more deist than Christian, and charges of "infidelity" and "atheism" were frequently hurled at deists by their detractors. But there was a handful of core beliefs that nearly all deists of the period embraced. These principles can be grouped into two categories: critical and constructive.

## Critical Deism

British and American deists consistently condemned revealed religion in general and Christianity in particular on two counts. (Early on, it was fashionable for deist authors to level their supernaturalist criticisms at Islam as a safe but transparent stand-in for Christianity.) First, deists argued that doctrines such as miracles, the divinity of Jesus, the Resurrection, and the Trinity were irrational. They ran counter to human experience—how can an enfleshed human being walk on water without sinking? How can a man dead three days be revived? And they violated the canons of reason—how can an entity be fully human and fully divine at one and the same time? Moreover, they argued, sacred scripture was full of unbelievable tales, self-contradictions, and sheer nonsense. As Elihu Palmer sarcastically asked in his deist masterpiece *Principles of Nature* (1801), if God condemned the serpent to crawl on his belly as punishment for tempting Eve, what was the serpent's mode of locomotion prior to the divine curse? In short, the deists argued that no rational person could be expected to take the claims of revealed religion seriously. Indeed, any proposition based on a supposed revelation rather than experience or reason was immediately suspect.

But the irrationality of Christian doctrine was not the only point of deistic attack. Many but not all deists also criticized what they saw as the immorality of Christianity. All of them insisted that the church was an oppressive social institution that retained its power by intimidating, encouraging superstition, and collaborating with the state. Likewise, all of them rejected the doctrine of original sin as offensive to both reason and moral sensibilities. And nearly all of them also condemned the Old Testament as a morally dubious document that legitimizes wholesale slaughter and slavery and depicts God as fickle and vengeful. But some of them went even further by condemning the moral precepts taught by Jesus through word and example in the New Testament. Benjamin Franklin and Thomas Jefferson thought that the ethical precepts taught by Jesus were sublime. But Elihu Palmer believed that the scripture portrayed Jesus as petty (blighting the fig tree), unconcerned with private property (destroying a herd of swine into which demons were driven), and advocating unworthy behavior such as meekness or humility in the face of evil. Although Palmer's fierce denunciation of Jesus as moral teacher was extreme, most other deists agreed with his claim that the New Testament neither offered a systematic ethic nor taught anything particularly new. As they saw it, the maxims attributed to Jesus by the New Testament authors had been expressed earlier and more cogently by Greek and Roman philosophers.

## Constructive Deism

Deists were first and foremost influenced by three fundamental Enlightenment principles: John Locke's empiricism, which held that all knowledge originates with experience; Isaac Newton's mechanism, which held that the universe is analogous to a cosmic machine and operates according to fixed natural law; and Francis Bacon's insistence that the true purpose of knowledge is to promote individual happiness, social progress, and development of the useful arts and industry. But the deists pushed these principles even further than their originators. Locke and Bacon, for example, were at least nominal Christians. Newton left open the possibility that God periodically intervened in miraculous ways in the operations of the cosmic machine, and he pored over sacred scripture scrutinizing prophetic texts.

Reason, experience, orderliness, a high regard for the concrete and practical over the abstract and speculative, and the reduction of religion to virtue were the primary ingredients of the deistic worldview. Experience disclosed patterns in nature that served as the basis for the natural sciences. The ability of the human mind to discern natural order attested to the fact that humans were rational creatures. Thus the orderliness of the human mind was a reflection of the larger orderliness throughout the universe. Just as the physical realm obeyed predictable laws of nature (as Newton demonstrated), so too did the psychological realm (as Locke demonstrated).

Deists were in unanimous agreement that the orderliness of both nature and mind pointed to the existence of an equally orderly and rational divine Architect. Few of them felt it necessary to offer rigorous arguments for their belief in God. At best they occasionally appealed to conventional arguments from design or causation. They concluded for the most part that the existence of a God as First Cause was evident from a consideration of nature and mind as opposed to sacred scripture or religious traditions. The Book of Nature was where God and God's ways were to be found. Moreover, they considered the study of nature to be one of the highest expressions of religious veneration.

Like many Enlightenment figures, the deists had little use for metaphysical speculation. Reason for them, as for Bacon, was primarily instrumental, a tool by which to expand human ability to manipulate matter and promote good works. An understanding of natural law was a necessary condition for harnessing nature in the service of humankind. It was also essential to the liberation of humans from the religious superstition and political oppression that stood in the way of progress and felicity. So they were content to posit the existence of God as First Cause without speculating more closely about God's nature or whether there was an ultimate purpose or plan to God's creation of the world. This apparent indifference to God as anything but a convenient *deus ex machina* was just one of the signature characteristics that prompted the charges of atheism and infidelity so often leveled against the deists. (The primary cause of such charges, of course, was deism's repudiation of Christianity.) Although the accusation of atheism was unwarranted, it is true that the deist God was so minimalistic that the eloquent hymns to the Supreme Architect occasionally written by deists have a rather hollow ring to them.

Virtue was just as important to deists as reason and nature. All deists agreed that the best way to show reverence for the God of nature was by virtuous living, although they insisted that any assumption of a divine command foundation for virtue was incorrect. Practicing virtue may have been the most appropriate way to worship God, but virtue had no necessary connection to God except insofar as it reflected the rational order of nature.

For the most part what the deists meant by virtue was prudence and moderation—two practices they felt best accorded with reason. Benjamin Franklin, for example, famously worked out a moral calculus by which to habituate himself (and others who cared to try it) to moderate and prudent behavior. Ethan Allen and Thomas Paine, who in their private lives were anything but exemplars of either prudence or moderation, adamantly advocated both in their writings. Elihu Palmer, the closest thing to a systematic ethicist among the deists, defended the moral principle of "reciprocal justice," a prudential promise of mutual respect, as the foundation of morality.

After the 1789 French Revolution deists in both Great Britain and the United States, inspired by the ideals of radical republicanism, tended to espouse freedom of conscience, separation of church and state, elimination of slavery, emancipation of women, and universal suffrage. Their admiration for radical political principles earned them at least as much public censure as did their religious heterodoxy. In the United States opposition to what was seen as the social threat of deism was so great that Thomas Jefferson found it politically expedient to publicly distance himself from it. Thomas Paine, one of the French Revolution's most ardent supporters and one of deism's most fiery champions, came to symbolize in the popular imagination the intertwining of political radicalism and religious free thought. Two generations after Paine's death, Theodore Roosevelt still referred to him as a "filthy little atheist."

## British Origins

Edward Herbert, Lord Cherbury (1583–1648), is generally credited with the birth of deism. Herbert, a British diplomat, was horrified by the ferocious sectarian fighting in the Thirty Years' War (1618–1648). In his *De religione gentilium* (Of Pagan Religion), published posthumously, he seeks to distill sectarian differences into a system of belief about which Protestant and Roman Catholic adversaries in the war, despite their sectarian differences, could agree. He argues that the most widespread and therefore agreeable religious beliefs are the following: (1) God exists; (2) God deserves worship; (3) virtue is the chief part of religion; (4) it is appropriate for humans to repent of their sins; and (5) virtue and vice will be rewarded and punished in an afterlife. These five principles, while failing to satisfy the sectarians to whom they were directed, became the foundations of deism.

Herbert's *De religione gentilium* was influential primarily because it inspired more polemical and widely read successors. In 1696 John Toland (1670–1722) published *Christianity Not Mysterious* in which he explicitly denies Christian articles of faith such as miracles and revelation. For Toland, all human knowledge, including religious beliefs, has to be based on experience and display logical coherency. The creator of the universe is as orderly and rational as the creation itself, and religious inquirers have no need for appeals to the supernatural to understand either the world or God.

Anthony Collins (1676–1729) raised the polemical defense of deism to a new level when he attacked ecclesiastical authority in his 1724 *Discourse on the Grounds and Reasons of the Christian Religion*. Collins argues that sacred scripture is incomprehensible and irrational, and that it retains its privileged position only through the conniving of superstitious priestcraft. In *Discourses on the Miracles of Our Lord* (1729), Thomas Woolston (1668–1733) argues that the New Testament's account of Jesus' miracles is "broken, elliptical and absurd."

On both the British and American sides of the Atlantic, the most influential British deist was Matthew Tindal (1657–1733), whose *Christianity as Old as the Creation* (1730) soon became recognized as the "Deist Bible." Tindal repeats the denunciations of revealed religion indulged in by his predecessors. He denies the divinity of Jesus, questions the ethical value of the Bible (he argues, for example, that sacred scripture paints a morally unworthy portrait of the Deity), and thunders against the influence of the church. He also provides a methodological rule of thumb that was embraced by subsequent deists: the only way in which supposedly "revealed" truths can be taken seriously is if they do not violate experience or reason. There is no other standard of truth other than empirical knowledge and the canons of logic. If any religionist claims as true a proposition that is "above" reason, much less "contrary" to reason, his claim is to be rejected immediately as confusion, superstition, or deliberate deception. This rule of thumb is most famously defended in David Hume's chapter "Of Miracles" in his 1748 *An Essay Concerning Human Understanding*.

British deism, while generating a relatively steady stream of polemical texts and broadsides from the late seventeenth century through the end of the eighteenth century, never fueled as acrimonious a public debate as its American counterpart. This relative calm stemmed in part from the prevalence of "liberal Christianity" in Great Britain during the period, defended by thinkers such as John Locke, Samuel Clarke, John Tillotson, and William Wollaston, who saw no necessary tension between reason and revelation, as well as the influence of Enlightenment empiricism on British churchmen and intellectuals. But what struck most British Christians as a minor annoyance (or, for some, an entertainment) tended to outrage the faithful, especially those in the Calvinist tradition, in America.

## Deism in America

The writings of British deists trickled into the American colonies slowly. But by mid-eighteenth century their influence was being felt at Yale, Harvard, Princeton, and William and Mary. New England Congregationalist minister and future president of Yale Ezra Stiles wrote in 1759 that "Deism has got such Head in this Age of Licentious Liberty" that there was no choice for Christians but to "conquer and demolish it." Stiles, like most other American clergy, undoubtedly exaggerated the hold that deism had on the colonies. But it is true that by the end of the century worried college administrators throughout the young Republic considered their campuses to be hotbeds of impiety. Nor was deism an exclusively academic fad. Thanks to the polemical works of several apologists, deism was embraced by a sizable minority from Georgia to Massachusetts. Philadelphia and New York City appear to have been the two areas where deists were most active. Moreover, frequent denunciations in newspapers, pamphlets, and sermons, as well as well-attended debates between deists and orthodox spokespersons, kept the religion of nature in the public eye. Most people in the colonies and early Republic were not deists. But most had heard of deism, and some, such as Benjamin Franklin, were undoubtedly converted to it after reading antideistic polemics.

## Benjamin Franklin and Thomas Jefferson

Benjamin Franklin (1706–1790) and Thomas Jefferson (1743–1826) each endorsed private religious views that bore some resemblance to deism. Franklin confesses in his posthumous *Autobiography* that he abandoned his parents' Calvinism for deism while still a youth. Although occasionally attending Presbyterian or Anglican services as an adult, his religious convictions appear to have been more deistic than Christian. In his early "A Dissertation on Liberty and Necessity" (1725), he defends a mechanistic universe worldview that implicitly denounces Christian doctrines of free will and divine providence. Three years later, his "Articles of Belief and Acts of Religion" outlines a straightforwardly deist catechism that Franklin seems to have more or less adhered to for the rest of his life. But though he was widely rumored to be an "infidel," Franklin issued few public statements of personal belief during his lifetime and played no major role in the popularization of natural religion in America.

Thomas Jefferson was another deist sympathizer who was reticent about public expressions of his religious belief. Unlike Franklin, however, Jefferson was excoriated both during his lifetime and afterward as an infidel. As late as 1830 the Philadelphia Public Library refused to catalog his collected works on the grounds that he had died a freethinker. Much of the rancor against Jefferson was politically motivated, associated as he was in the Federalist press after 1789 with French-style radical republicanism. But posthumously published correspondence by Jefferson, as well as his private redaction of the New Testament that expunged all supernatural references and retained Jesus' moral teachings, show that he endorsed natural religion.

## Revolutionary Deists: Ethan Allen, Thomas Paine, Elihu Palmer, and Philip Freneau

America's first open defense of deism was written by the Revolutionary War hero Ethan Allen (1737–1789). His *Reason, the Only Oracle of Man* appeared in 1784. Although written in a tediously cumbersome style, the book was widely read and quickly earned Allen the anger and contempt of orthodox Christians. (Yale College president Timothy Dwight thundered that Allen was enlisted "in Satan's cause.") Little is original in the book's criticism of Christianity and defense of deism. But especially noteworthy is the number of pages Allen devotes to denying the divinity of Jesus and arguing for the moral unworthiness of the God of the Old Testament. It is contrary to reason, he argues, to presume that "God should become a man and that man should become a God." Moreover, God should be held to the same moral standards as humans, "for the rules of justice are essentially the same whether applied to the one or to the other, having their uniformity in the eternal truth and reason of things."

*The Age of Reason* (1795) by Thomas Paine (1737–1809) is the best-known defense of deism penned by an American. As derivative as Allen's book but less difficult to read, *The Age of Reason* is important more for its public notoriety than its arguments. Predictably, Paine defends the "true theology" of natural philosophy: the "word of God is the creation we behold." He offers an argument for the existence of a divine First Cause, argues that miracles are "tricks to amuse and make the people stare and wonder," and condemns the church for its immorality. This condemnation does not extend, however, to Jesus, whom Paine believes to have advocated a morality of a "most benevolent kind." It is St. Paul, "that manufacturer of quibbles," who perverted Jesus' originally sublime message. Paine's book was greeted with outrage by the faithful, even though, ironically, Paine intended it as much as a response to the dogmatic atheism of the French revolutionaries as to orthodox Christianity. It is one of the few eighteenth-century defenses of rational religion still in print.

Undoubtedly the most original American deist was Elihu Palmer. A Presbyterian minister who renounced the pulpit for the law, Palmer devoted the last thirteen years of his life to spreading deism up and down the eastern seaboard. He lectured tirelessly; founded deistical societies in New York, Maryland, New Jersey and Pennsylvania; edited two widely read deistical newspapers; advocated founding "Temples of Reason," alternatives to Christian churches that would provide for the spiritual needs of deists; and agitated for republican political principles aimed against the "double despotism" of church and state. In 1801 he published *Principles of Nature,* a distillation and refinement of his thought. The book went through three editions before Palmer's death in 1806 and became known as the "American Bible of Deism." It is the most sophisticated defense of natural religion written on the American side of the Atlantic.

Much of Palmer's *Principles* is a recital of familiar themes: a denunciation of revealed religion and a defense of the God of nature. What makes the book distinctive is Palmer's defense of an ethic based exclusively on naturalistic grounds. Earlier (and later) deists all insisted on the importance of virtue and the irrelevance for morality of a supernaturalistic God. But none of them offered a sustained argument on how to ground an ethic that claimed independence from religion. Palmer filled that gap by arguing that a naturalistic ethic rested on the twin principles of "reciprocal justice" and "universal benevolence." According to Palmer, humans are sentient creatures who naturally pursue pleasure and avoid pain. Pleasure promotes and pain destroys well-being. Reason dictates that the sensible person will act to maximize the chance for pleasure and minimize the possibility of pain, recognize that his actions toward others are reciprocated in kind, and conclude that his own best chance for well-being therefore lies in encouraging others to treat him well by treating them well. Elements of Christianity's "golden rule" are evident in all this. But the crucial point is that Palmer intended to defend morality on the basis of human nature and self-interest rather than scriptural injunction or religious tradition.

The final American deist worthy of mention is Philip Freneau (1752–1832), sometimes called the "poet of the American Revolution." Freneau, an anti-Federalist politician, journalist, and occasional civil servant, was an acquaintance of Palmer and corresponded with Paine. His defense of deism was expressed in verse and pithy parables that appeared first in newspapers and magazines and then in book-length collections. In "On Superstition," for example, he advises readers to "turn from her [superstition's] detested ways," and encourages cultivation of "the reasoning power, celestial guest/The stamp upon the soul impress'd." Like his fellow deists, he also insists that virtue is the highest form of veneration and that its practice maximizes happiness. Finally, Freneau predicts the coming of a "new age" in which reason will demolish political despotism and "dread superstition," the "worst plague of human race." Then he concludes that "the sun of happiness, and peace" will "shine on earth and never cease."

## Decline of Deism

By the time Freneau died in 1832 deism in the United States had pretty much run its course. To a certain extent it died out as a clearly defined movement because it had succeeded in getting at least some of its message absorbed by the wider culture. Unitarianism, milder in rhetoric and more agreeable to popular sensibilities, gradually adopted much of the antisupernaturalism endorsed by deism. Christian apologists, learning from deists the importance of reconciling notions of the divinity with the physical world, began to pay more attention to natural theology. And deism's criticisms of oppressive religious institutions and social practices began to seem a bit less radical when progressive movements such as abolitionism were endorsed by at least some Christian leaders.

But deism's decline in the second quarter of the nineteenth century was also attributable to the fact that the Enlightenment ethos from which it sprang gave ground in the United States to a new wave of Christian revivalism—the so-called Second Great Awakening—which tended toward anti-intellectualism and emphasized personal and emotionally turbulent piety. In addition, American transcendentalism, though not Christian, likewise called into question the Enlightenment conviction that reason was the best tool for understanding reality. The generation of infidels that immediately succeeded the deists—for example, Abner Kneeland, Robert Owen, and Frances Wright—were more influenced by the utopianism of Henri Saint-Simon and Charles Fourier than by Enlightenment ideals.

Finally, the rational religion advocated by deists was simply too impersonal to satisfy the popular religious imagination. Critical deism's savaging of supernaturalism in general and Christianity in particular appealed primarily to a generation of rebellious youth, many of whom returned to conventional religion with the passing of years, and to a small number of lifelong skeptics such as Thomas Paine. Constructive deism's God as a distant First Cause and virtue as the highest form of worship appealed only to a relatively small group of intellectuals. Such principles were too abstract for the general populace to find fulfilling. Deism always remained more a philosophical school than a religion, despite the efforts of deist popularizers such as Elihu Palmer.

**See also** *American Revolution; Atheism, Agnosticism, and Disbelief; Church and State: Revolutionary Period and Early Republic; Enlightenment; Evangelicals: Colonial America; Politics: Colonial Era; Transcendentalism.*

Kerry Walters

## BIBLIOGRAPHY

Gay, Peter, ed. *Deism: An Anthology.* New York: Van Nostrand, 1968.
Holmes, David. *The Faiths of the Founding Fathers.* New York: Oxford University Press, 2006.
Koch, G. Adolf. *Republican Religion: The American Revolution and the Cult of Reason.* New York: Henry Holt, 1933.

May, Henry. *The Enlightenment in America.* New York: Oxford University Press, 1976.

Morais, Herbert A. *Deism in Eighteenth-Century America.* New York: Russell and Russell, 1960.

Turner, James. *Without God, Without Creed: The Origins of Unbelief in America.* Baltimore: Johns Hopkins University Press, 1985.

Walters, Kerry, ed. *The American Deists: Voices of Reason and Dissent in the Early Republic.* Lawrence: University Press of Kansas, 1992.

———. *Benjamin Franklin and His Gods.* Carbondale: University of Illinois Press, 1998.

———. *Elihu Palmer's Principles of Nature: Text and Commentary.* Wolfeboro, N.H.: Longwood Academic, 1990.

———. *Rational Infidels: The American Deists.* Durango, Colo.: Longwood Academic, 1992.

Waring, E. Graham, ed. *Deism and Natural Religion: A Sourcebook.* New York: Frederick Ungar, 1967.

# Demographics

Demography is the statistical study and description of human populations. In its formal or narrow sense, it generates statistics that illustrate the conditions and processes of life in communities: births, deaths, migrations, education, income, race, family structure, spatial distribution, change, and the like. Like mathematics, however, demography is not ultimately about *numbers;* it is about *relations.* Thus economists, anthropologists, historians, and others borrow its tools. Religious demography analyzes the relationship between religion and the biological, economic, social, and cultural processes influencing a population across space and time.

Religion in America has long presented observers from abroad with a canvas of such kaleidoscopic dazzle as to provoke frustration and wonder in anyone who makes an effort to comprehend the whole. Little wonder that they wonder, for the United States is perhaps the most religiously complex nation in history. Most of the religions of the world are present, interacting internally with their own constituents and externally with one another, at least indirectly. These religions navigate the currents of a wider and partly secular culture. They deal with the inheritance of often obscure historical developments. And they respond to a dynamic, evolving present. Prudent analysts even within the United States cannot hope to comprehend all of this. But demography can help.

## Challenges in Assembling and Interpreting Data

The work of demography is not without problems. All statistics harbor their own ambiguities, non sequiturs, and capacity to mislead. To convey even highly selective aspects of America's religious history through statistics means at times indulging in risky calculations and generalizations.

For example, membership statistics for the seventeenth and eighteenth centuries are elusive, erratic, and difficult to compare. In most instances, therefore, one must gain a sense of a religion's size and proportion in this era by counting churches. What is referred to as a "church," however, may be an impressive building and its constituents, or instead a modest chapel-of-ease, an even more humble preaching station, or merely a loose collection of the like-minded. The term *church* thus varies in meaning in different periods and among different denominations.

Religious statistics after 1800 begin to inspire more confidence, but difficulties persist. *Membership* rather than *church* may seem at first glance a more accurate gauge for determining denominational strength. But *member,* like *church,* contains a span of meanings.

Religious bodies differ in their inclusiveness when they construe membership. Some churches tally everyone. Others count only those who remain in good standing, or who donate, or who are heads of families, or who are free persons, or who have been "born again." Some groups offer only estimates of their membership; others have no interest or few resources to keep records. Some bodies oppose the idea of enumeration on philosophical grounds. Maddeningly for the historical demographer, various churches periodically recalibrate their methods of tabulation.

One must, then, keep in mind qualitative variances in historical religious statistics, whether thinking of members or of churches (or synagogues, temples, centers, and mosques). The count of one hundred Pentecostal churches is not equivalent to that of one hundred Roman Catholic churches, but rather less, for a single Catholic church typically serves many more communicants than a Pentecostal one. Conversely, one hundred Baptist members will not be the equivalent of one hundred Roman Catholics, but a good deal more, because a Baptist group may count only adult baptized believers, whereas Catholics, who baptize their infants, claim the entire baptized family. By comparing denominations by both number of churches and size of membership and by complementing the demography with an informed historical awareness of the groups under discussion, one can achieve informed and balanced impressions.

A contrasting method of estimating religious affiliation offers an additional perspective. Here the measure is not how religious organizations enumerate their churches or membership, but how people identify themselves religiously in response to surveys. This approach has the virtue of offering a direct glimpse into how contemporary Americans think of their religious attachments, beliefs, and practices. But like any method it has its limitations.

In light of the problems and necessity of religious demography what resources are available for guidance? And what demographic portrait of the nation emerges?

## Sources

Selections from among the more important resources for helping to craft an understanding of the country's always-in-motion religious demography are listed in the bibliography. Three among them are examples of a strong starting point, especially if used jointly, because they employ demography in treating different but essential and complementary dimensions of religious life in America. The first work adopts the tools of geography, cartography, and narrative history; the second analyzes religion and contemporary public life; and the third reports private contemporary religious self-understanding.

Oxford University Press's *New Historical Atlas of Religion in America,* coauthored by Edwin Scott Gaustad and Philip L. Barlow, includes hundreds of color maps and graphs on dozens of religious groups. It is the most extensive effort to date to interpret the nation's institutional religious past to the end of the twentieth century through the combined means of statistical data, narrative history, and an array of maps. These maps place various "filters" over assembled data in order to depict a range of insights. Constructed maps, like assembled statistics and written history, are acts (or failures) of the imagination, using and arranging the building blocks of symbolized "facts." Maps thus bear their own dangers and distortions, all the while offering irreplaceable possibilities for visualizing enormous quantities of information and otherwise obscure spatial relationships. Maps are "white lies that tell the truth of the landscape."

The second recommended beginning point is AltaMira Press's "Religion by Region" series, under the general editorship of Mark Silk. The series is not a work of history, but a historically conscious exploration of religion and public life in the contemporary United States. More than fifty authors working with eight editors contributed to the series, which devotes an independently edited book to each of eight regions, supplemented by a summary volume reintegrating the sectional dynamics into a national story. Each volume begins with a chapter on its region's secular and religious demography, and then integrates this demography with qualitative analysis of religion's encounters with politics, education, and other elements of the public sphere. The series demonstrates real regional differences and local religious-cultural accents that persist despite the homogenizing effects of modern mobility and mass communication.

The U.S. Religious Landscape Survey, conducted in 2007 under the auspices of the Pew Forum on Religion and Public Life, is a third resource for those beginning an exploration of America's religions. It is through this lens that this essay looks at the contemporary self-understanding of adult Americans in their relation to region. The study is based on interviews with a sample of more than 35,000 adults, eighteen years and older. The Pew Forum intends this survey to serve as a baseline for additional periodic surveys on a similarly large scale. Responses from participants provide researchers with estimates of the size of religious groups in the country, as well as a picture of additional demographic traits and basic social, political, and religious beliefs, attitudes, and practices. The Pew survey differs from previous polls by managing to ask a large sampling of people a large number of questions on religion, as opposed to asking a large sampling of people a small number of questions, or a small sampling of people a large number of questions. The survey's results provide an opportunity to examine the relationship among religious affiliation, religious and secular beliefs and practices, and factors such as age, ethnicity, place of birth, family size, regional distribution, and income and educational levels.

## History

Analysts of the "present," including the religious and demographic present, must be historically informed: the present was formed by the past and is itself always becoming the past. Alertly or unaware, persons and institutions in the present are ever encountering and in dialogue with the consequences of the past. Each day and moment one engages not merely what "is," but what "has become" and what "is becoming."

This is not the space for a developed and balanced demographic-religious account of the nation's past—an exceedingly large task. What follows, instead, is an abbreviated sketch of several demographically inflected dynamics, focusing on immigration, nationality, ethnicity, and denomination or other institutional grouping. This approach intentionally ignores important elements such as gender, age, family structure, and wealth, leaving these to be exemplified in the subsequent treatment of early twentieth-century America. This narrowed demographic sample of the earlier period will, however, illustrate the churning denominational and ethnic change that has always characterized American religious history.

## Colonial Demography

As citizens and observers of the new United States worked to grasp the meaning and fallout of the successful revolt from the British monarchy, the young Republic both enabled and witnessed an era of bewildering social ferment. Federal and state disestablishment of religion, religious experimentation, missionary outreach at home and abroad, denominational cooperation and competition in the face of stupendous territorial expansion, and much else preoccupied the nervous and exuberant citizens. Grasping certain religious implications of democracy, ordinary people by the thousands embraced the camp meeting methods, the simplified theologies, and the proximity of unschooled "farmer-preachers" and circuit riders. These developments transformed the religious landscape in a single generation: upstart Baptists and Methodists, despite the efforts of urbane and rooted Episcopalians, Presbyterians, and Congregationalists, became by 1830 the largest denominations in three-quarters of the counties in the country, which had thrust westward to Missouri, Arkansas, and Louisiana. Immigration had even more impact than conversion in the long term, coming in great waves throughout the nineteenth century.

Indeed, immigration defined the continent from its first peopling, when Siberian tribes made their way across a land bridge into North America and south across the Plains and to wider dispersion, before ceding the continent in the modern era to the onslaught of European germs, guns, and numbers. During the seventeenth and eighteenth centuries these Europeans laid down an immigrant foundation along the eastern shores of North America, dominated by a comparatively rich mixture of Protestants from northern Europe. These Protestants attempted at times a valiant missionary outreach, but as a whole additional immigration controlled their increase.

Despite decades of scholars' efforts to dismantle the dominance of New England in the telling of America's early religious past, the migration of the Puritans into Plymouth and Massachusetts Bays in the early seventeenth century left an imprint slow to fade in the American psyche. The compact geography of Massachusetts and Connecticut, coupled with the size of the immigration and cultural homogeneity of the immigrants, etched an enduring way of thinking, acting, and worshipping on the colonies, affecting family, school, church, and government. Historian Sydney Ahlstrom has estimated that Puritanism formed the moral and religious background for perhaps 75 percent of the population declaring independence from England in 1776. The colonists' later migrations into the Midwest and their literary legacy disproportionately colored the country's collective memory.

Even in New England, however, outcroppings of Separate Congregationalists began to grow strong, eventually developing into Separate Baptist churches. After 1710 Baptists were the largest group within the religious grab bag of Rhode Island.

The colonial reality outside New England was religiously diverse indeed. Beyond even the legal support they enjoyed, Anglicans predominated numerically along most of the coast south from Maryland and Virginia through South Carolina, though giving ground to religious invaders in the Piedmont and mountain areas as the century wore on. Roman Catholics had arrived shortly after the Puritans, founding and sustaining a presence in Maryland, which, though never exclusively Catholic, remained the central place of residence for Catholics through the end of the colonial period. Already by 1690, however, their original strength had contracted so much that they remained predominant only in the colony's southernmost counties. Outside the British colonies on the Atlantic seaboard, nineteenth-century Protestant missionaries, carrying their Bibles to the Southwest, would discover that Spanish Catholics had preceded them by more than two hundred years, beginning with the founding of Santa Fe in 1610. Authorities recalled French Jesuits from their long-standing mission stations in 1764 in the face of war and eventual defeat at the hands of Great Britain. The vast Louisiana Territory was sold to the young United States in 1803, but French language, culture, and place names continued to suffuse the Mississippi River Valley from its upper reaches in Minnesota southward to St. Louis and New Orleans.

## Demography of the New Republic

By 1790 Quakers still predominated in counties in West Jersey, in adjacent southeastern Pennsylvania, and in North and South Carolina. Lutherans, German Reformed, and Presbyterians eclipsed them after the mid-eighteenth century by occupying the hinterlands. Great diversity thrived among the Germans of Pennsylvania, where most Lutherans shared church buildings with the German Reformed, and where Amish, Mennonites, and various German sects thrived. The Dutch Reformed, settlers of New Netherland before the English wrested control from them in the 1660s, retained at the end of the eighteenth century strength in the New York counties west of Massachusetts and Vermont. Methodists were beginning to bare their comparative numerical strength on the Delmarva Peninsula in the southern portions of Delaware and Maryland.

The colonies' major involuntary immigration, from Africa, deserves its own extended treatment (as does the major involuntary internal migration of Native Americans). During the two centuries preceding 1808, when the slave trade was outlawed, nearly half a million blacks were brought to what was to become the United States. The African population in the eighteenth century was concentrated in Maryland, Virginia, South Carolina, and Georgia. Slaves shaped their traditional religious practices—quickly forced underground–to respond to the new environment. Eventually these traditions gave way to a hybrid orientation formed of both African (in some cases Islamic) and Christian elements. Some traditions, such as Santería imported via Cuba and the voodoo traditions imported via Haiti, especially to New Orleans, have had a long life. As the nineteenth century approached, the population of the young nation had grown to approximately five million. One in five was black—90 percent of them still slaves.

Despite some indifference or hostility to the religion of their masters, the era between the Revolutionary and Civil Wars would bring a mass conversion to Christianity, which in turn was affected by new styles and forms emerging from an African heritage. Some free and slave groups began a transition from worshipping on the plantation or in white churches to starting their own congregations and forming their own denominations.

The early nineteenth century brought immigrants from new places of origin, permanently changing the religious mix. Irish Roman Catholics came in streams from the 1820s onward. Stimulated after 1845 by famine and disease in Ireland, they came in torrents. In the ten years following 1845 nearly two million people—a fourth of Ireland's population—arrived in the United States, by which time they accounted for 43 percent of all foreign-born citizens. To the alarm of the Protestant immigrants and children of immigrants who preceded them, this very suddenly made Catholicism the country's largest denomination, which it would remain. This is no small statement in view of the explosion of Methodist and Baptist converts during the preceding decades. In the northeastern United States the Irish newcomers overwhelmed even the Congregationalist heirs of the once-dominant Puritans. Contests over politics and the nature of education were tense if unsurprising; violence sometimes flared.

## The Later Nineteenth Century

As potent as the Irish wave was, others came, too—in such numbers that by century's end the Irish portion of the nation's foreign-born had plummeted from 43 percent to 16 percent. Hailing this time from eastern Europe, many of these Austrians, Hungarians, Italians, Russians, and Poles were Catholics as well. They were also poor, taxing the capacities of the ecclesiastical hierarchy and bringing rivalries both among ethnic Catholic groups and between Catholics and Protestants. Ponder the implications: the Catholic population exploded from about fifty thousand at the beginning of the century, half of them in Maryland, to twelve million people, dispersed across the nation, by the century's end.

The human floodtide from eastern and southern Europe in the second half of the nineteenth century brought more than Catholics. Jews, fewer than four thousand around 1800, had by 1900 become more than a million. Not all the arrivals were religious, to be sure, just as with other groups. But enough were religious to establish more than a thousand synagogues, principally in New York and other eastern seaports. Even before the Civil War, however, German Jews had pushed westward, founding under the vision and perseverance of Isaac Mayer Wise an influential center of learning in Cincinnati and a new religious expression. Reform Judaism, as it was known, strove for a religious vitality relevant to the modern world and the American setting.

Yet another gush of nineteenth-century newcomers—this time Lutherans—came from Scandinavia. Perhaps a quarter-million strong in 1800, Lutherans had long prospered along the Hudson River Valley and in eastern Pennsylvania, especially from the time of their great national organizer, Henry Melchior Mühlenberg, in the 1740s. By 1900 their numbers had swelled to two million, and the majority of the new arrivals were settling not in Pennsylvania or in urban centers like the Catholics and Jews, but in the upper Midwest—in Wisconsin, Minnesota, and the Dakotas. There they established a cultural fiefdom sufficiently enduring that, a century later, humorist Garrison Keillor could draw smiles rather than outrage by quipping, when asked whether someone in his home state of

Minnesota was a Lutheran: "Of course she's a Lutheran. Everyone here is. Even the Catholics."

By the end of the nineteenth century the largest non-Catholic body remained the Methodists, 5.5 million strong, who around 1812 had surpassed the Baptists, but who before the Great Depression would surrender to them their lead by ever greater margins. In 1900 Baptists could claim 4.5 million adherents, Lutherans and Presbyterians 1.7 million each, Christians/Disciples 800,000, Episcopalians 700,000, and Congregationalists 600,000. Along with the Catholics, these denominations, for all the breathless commotion and change, were by 1900 the largest and arguably the most influential religious organizations in the United States. If these figures suggest anything, however, it is a dynamic religious picture. The fleet pace of change would not lessen in the coming century.

## The Twentieth Century

Immigration into the United States continued apace during the first decade and a half of the twentieth century. Arriving Greeks and Russians, for example, elevated the numbers of the Eastern Orthodox above the few who had settled in Alaska when it was still Russian territory, later trickling south as far as San Francisco. World War I, however, crimped Europeans' ability to leave the continent even as it heightened Americans' concerns about the prospect of them doing so. By 1924 these concerns had enabled passage of the National Origins Act, a quota system favoring immigrants from northern and western Europe. This legislation constricted not only immigrants from elsewhere, but immigration as such, because northern and western European countries at the time harbored fewer "huddled masses yearning to be free." Although the rate of immigration began to rise again in the 1930s, not until the end of the century would the flow reach the torrent it had at the century's beginning.

For the next forty years the National Origins Act checked the arrival of Catholics and Jews from eastern and southern Europe, and Hindus, Muslims, and Buddhists from India and Asia. Immigrants from Mexico and South and Central America, however, continued to stream in, rendering American Catholicism ever more Hispanic.

The first half of the twentieth century witnessed steady progress for most of the established faiths. Membership in churches increased impressively from 40 percent of the population in 1900 to 60 percent by midcentury. Catholics had more than doubled their population, to 30 million, by

that time. Baptists had quadrupled theirs, to 16 million. Methodists had grown from 5 million to 9 million; Lutherans from less than 2 million to more than 4 million; Presbyterians from 1.5 million to almost 3 million. Mainline religion seemed on a decades-long incline.

The 1960s and 1970s presented a very different picture, brought on by several conditions. Among the most important was an emergent cultural malaise. So long had the historic Protestant mainline seemed to dominate the culture and to champion cooperation with it that it seemed almost to become the culture. The newer generation, fully at home in American society, had an increasingly difficult time discerning what it had to gain by church membership. With seeming suddenness it was the conservative churches—demanding in discipline and sacrifice and unambiguous in theology, identity, and moral claims—that were growing in numbers and in public awareness. Scholars debated the causes, but the trend of mainline decline held through the end of the century. Congregationalist and Presbyterian growth peaked around 1960, Lutheran and Episcopalian growth around 1970, and Methodist growth around 1980.

While these liberal-leaning denominations were bleeding members, groups such as the Southern Baptists, Mormons, and Pentecostals were experiencing a surge. By the end of the century, the Southern Baptist Convention alone was claiming nearly 20 million adherents; the Latter-day Saints, 4.2 million; and the Pentecostal Assemblies of God, 2.6 million. The charismatic yearning for and experience of spiritual gifts, such as healing and speaking in tongues, spread widely beyond formally Pentecostal denominations, gaining influence even within Catholicism and the mainline churches.

Evangelical, fundamentalist, and Pentecostal bodies, especially, later discovered religious outlets of contested magnitude and effectiveness in the "Electronic Church." This movement was a product of the television age, succeeding the religious radio broadcasting of the previous half-century and entwined with a still-active revivalism. Another distinctively (not uniquely) Evangelical and Pentecostal phenomenon emerged in and after the 1950s: "megachurches," each of which boasted two thousand or more reliable weekly attendees. By the beginning of the twenty-first century, more than thirteen hundred such churches were thriving, fifty of them with congregants ranging from ten thousand to almost fifty thousand. More than half of such churches were nondenominational; perhaps 20 percent had attachments to the Southern Baptists, and another 10 percent each associated with the Assemblies of God and with historically African American denominations. During the latter decades of the twentieth century the movement spread abroad; half of the ten largest Protestant megachurches were by 2008 in South Korea.

Another new aspect of the 1960s and 1970s was the reaction against the establishment culture and, amid social tumult, the rise of new and zealous sects and movements, often experimental in nature. Prominent among them were hard-to-measure New Age inclinations and a strong interest in selective parts of Native American spirituality.

Intersecting with these developments was a new tide and new pattern of immigration, enabled by the Immigration and Nationality Act of 1965. By equalizing immigration policies skewed since 1924, the act enabled a flood of new immigration from non-European nations that changed the ethnic and religious demography—and the consciousness and self-identity—of the country. Immigration doubled between 1965 and 1970 and doubled again between 1970 and 1990. The United States was now host to a significant number of Muslims. Citizens encountered chanting, shaven, and brightly clad devotees of the International Society for Krishna Consciousness at every airport. Asian-born Buddhists, once thought confined to Hawaii, California, and graduate centers where the world's religions were quietly explored, were now discovered in cities throughout the land. One's new doctor in many urban centers seemed as likely as not to be from India, and thus perhaps of Hindu background. This influx of immigrants tightened selectively after the terrorist attacks on the country on September 11, 2001, a national trauma that sparked debate about immigration, legal and otherwise, and about the security of the nation's borders. Nevertheless, a year after the attacks the United States was still accepting immigrants at the fastest rate since the 1850s. One in nine U.S. residents was foreign-born. Of these, 52 percent were from Latin America, 26 percent from Asia, and only 16 percent and 3 percent, respectively, from Europe and Africa.

## A Contemporary Portrait

The contours and dynamics of immigration and of ethnic and denominational movements provide an essential perspective on the development of American religion. A better grasp of the realities of people's lives and religion, however, requires many demographic lenses. One such lens is the U.S. Religious Landscape Survey, noted earlier, in which a large sampling of American adults responded in 2007 to extensive queries on their religious self-identity and their attitudes

### U.S. Religions by Major Groups

| Religious Group | Percentage of Total Population |
|---|---|
| **Christian** | **78.4** |
| Protestant | 51.3 |
| *Evangelical* | *26.3* |
| Baptists (evangelical) | 10.8 |
| Pentacostal | 3.4 |
| Nondenominational (evangelical) | 3.4 |
| *Mainline* | *18.1* |
| Methodist | 5.4 |
| Lutheran | 2.8 |
| Baptist (mainline) | 1.9 |
| Presbyterian (mainline) | 1.9 |
| Anglican/Episcopal (mainline) | 1.4 |
| *Historically Black Churches* | *6.9* |
| Catholic | 23.9 |
| Mormon | 1.7 |
| Jehovah's Witnesses | 0.7 |
| Orthodox | 0.6 |
| **Jewish** | **1.7** |
| Reform | 0.7 |
| Conservative | 0.5 |
| Orthodox | less than .3 |
| Other Jewish groups | less than .3 |
| Jewish, not further specified | less than .3 |
| **Buddhist** | **0.7** |
| Theravada | less than .3 |
| Mahayana (Zen) | less than .3 |
| Vajrayana (Tibetan) | less than .3 |
| Other Buddhist groups | less than .3 |
| **Muslim** | **0.6** |
| Sunni | 0.3 |
| Shia | less than .3 |
| Other Muslim groups | less than .3 |
| **Hindu** | **0.4** |
| **Other world religions** | **less than .3** |
| **Unitarian and other liberal faiths** | **0.7** |
| **Native American** | **less than .3** |
| **Unaffiliated** | **16.1** |
| Atheist | 1.6 |
| Agnostic | 2.4 |
| "Nothing in particular" | 12.1 |
| *Secular* | *6.3* |
| *Religious* | *5.8* |
| **Don't know/refused to answer** | **0.8** |

*Source:* U.S. Religious Landscape Survey, 2007

toward religion. The ensuing report summarized key findings. Among them:

• America's religious complexion is diverse—not startling news. Its breakdown in major groupings is displayed in the table above.

• Religious attachment in the United States is increasingly fluid. By 2007 more than a quarter (28 percent) of adult Americans had abandoned the religion of their youth, exchanging it for another or simply discarding organized religion altogether. If switches from one denomination to another within Protestant ranks are included, the percentage skyrockets: almost half (44 percent) of adults had either changed, dropped, or newly claimed affiliation to a particular religious group. Jehovah's Witnesses had the lowest retention rate: only 37 percent of those who were raised as such still identified themselves as Witnesses.

• African Americans were the most likely of the major racial and ethnic groups to report a formal religious affiliation.

• In view of their declining proportion, Protestants seemed destined to become the nation's largest religious minority rather than its longtime religious majority (51 percent and falling as of 2007).

• One-third of respondents who indicated they were raised as Catholics no longer claimed the label, meaning that one in ten adult Americans were former Catholics. However, 2.6 percent of the adult population had converted to Catholicism, and the losses were further offset by immigrants, a disproportionate number of whom were Catholic. The composition of American Catholicism thus was rapidly transforming, becoming more Hispanic.

• The demographics of age distribution may offer a glimpse into the future. Among Americans ages eighteen to twenty-nine, for example, one in four said they were not affiliated, whereas only 8 percent of those over age seventy were unattached. This trend portends a deep societal change if it continues among the young and as those currently in this age bracket proceed through their thirties, forties, and fifties. Similarly, 62 percent of those over age seventy were Protestant, but only 43 percent among those ages eighteen to twenty-nine. Finally, half of Jews and "mainline" Protestants were age fifty and above, as compared with 40 percent in the population as a whole.

Scrutiny of the survey suggests the importance of gender. Although the general population was only 48 percent male, 70 percent of atheists and 64 percent of agnostics were male. Only 13 percent of women claimed no affiliation with a particular religion, whereas this was true of nearly one in five men. Hindus (61 percent) and Jews and Unitarians (54 percent) were disproportionately male. By contrast, 60 percent of historically black Protestants and Jehovah's Witnesses, 59 percent of Adventists, and 58 percent of Greek Orthodox were female.

Family is also important to the character of affiliation. Hindus (79 percent) and Mormons (71 percent) were by far the most married. Next closest were the Greek Orthodox

and Reform Jews (61 percent each). Members of the historically black Protestant churches (33 percent) were the least married, followed by New Age adherents (38 percent), atheists (39 percent), and agnostics (41 percent). Nearly four in ten married people had spouses who belonged to a different denomination or religion. Hindus and Mormons, again, were the most likely to be married to someone of their faith (90 percent and 83 percent, respectively). Hindus were the least divorced or separated (5 percent); New Age and uncategorized Christians were the most (19 percent).

Mormons were dramatically more likely than any other group to have large families; 10 percent of Mormon adults in 2007 reported having four or more children living at home. The next highest was Muslims (6 percent), with Catholics, black Protestants, and the religiously unaffiliated following (4 percent). Conservative Jews led in having no children at home (82 percent), followed by atheists, agnostics, and Greek Orthodox (all at 75 percent).

The relation of religion to education and wealth warrants careful thought. Seventy-four percent of Hindus graduated from college, compared with 59 percent of Jews (66 percent of Reform Jews), 48 percent of Buddhists, 42 percent of atheists, 34 percent of mainline Protestants (53 percent of Episcopalians), 28 percent of Mormons, 26 percent of Catholics, 24 percent of Muslims, and 20 percent of evangelicals (31 percent of evangelical Presbyterians). An astounding proportion of Hindus, nearly half, attained some postgraduate education, many in the field of medicine. Jews, both Reform and Conservative, followed (35 percent), and then Unitarians and other liberal faiths (29 percent) and Episcopalians (25 percent).

At 55 percent, Reform Jews had by far the greatest percentage of practitioners earning more than $100,000 a year. They were followed by Conservative Jews and Hindus (both at 43 percent). These religious categories markedly exceeded the remaining ones. Among Christians, 35 percent of Episcopalians and 30 percent of the Greek Orthodox earned $100,000 a year or more. Holiness and Pentecostals, at 7 percent, had the fewest in this category.

Race matters. Muslims were the most racially diverse faith in the nation: 37 percent reported themselves to be white, followed by black (24 percent), Asian (20 percent), "other/mixed" (15 percent), and Hispanic (4 percent). Among Protestants, Adventists exceeded even Pentecostals as the most racially diverse group: 45 percent white, 26 percent Latino, 21 percent black, 4 percent Asian, and 4 percent other/mixed. More than half of all American Buddhists (53 percent) were white; almost a third

(32 percent) were Asian. Lutherans were the denomination with the highest percentage of white members (96 percent); Unitarians were next (88 percent). Those in the historically black traditions (principally several Baptist and Methodist denominations) had, of course, the greatest percentage of black members (97 percent and 96 percent, respectively). Twenty-nine percent of Catholics were Hispanic, as were 24 percent of Jehovah Witnesses. Indeed, the proportion of blacks and Hispanics who were Jehovah's Witnesses were twice their proportion in the general population.

Americans may separate church and state, but not religion and society. The historically black churches were more decidedly Democratic in their politics than any other grouping, with 78 percent either firmly or "leaning" Democratic. They were followed by the Buddhists (67 percent), Jews (65 percent), and Muslims and Hindus (63 percent each). Sixty-five percent of Mormons were firmly in or inclining toward the Republican Party, as were 50 percent of evangelicals. Mainline Protestants were nearly evenly split: 31 percent Republican, 10 percent leaning Republican, 29 percent Democratic, and 14 percent leaning Democratic. Jews, who made up only 1.7 percent of the general populace, were more than any other group disproportionately represented in Congress: 7.4 percent of the House and 13.1 percent of the Senate.

## Engaging Demographic Data Critically

The full survey, along with those of comparable breadth (such as the periodic American Religious Identification Surveys) or others of more specialized focus, should be used critically and imaginatively. Doing so will induce further inquiry into the lives and cultures that lie behind the data, using tools such as history, theology, anthropology, biography, and religious studies. Readers should think about what such surveys mask as well as what they reveal. Beyond providing answers, they should generate new questions. Examples follow.

### Limitations to Survey Data

The social scientists who engineered the 2007 U.S. Religious Landscape Survey are sophisticated in recognizing some of its limitations. They note that it is a study of adults, who represent only three-fourths of the American public, and that many respondents bring a lack of clarity in terms of what religious group they belong, thereby somewhat blurring the picture. They further note that some 8 percent of adults in the country are not proficient in English, which

means that even though addressed by the survey in certain ways, the survey may modestly undercount, for example and especially, the proportion of Catholics among Hispanics.

Some limitations are intrinsic to surveys of religion based on self-reporting by individuals. For example, the approach is restricted to the modern era, making historical comparisons problematic. A second difficulty is that how people portray themselves when asked, while important, may not represent their behavior. The number who report going to church, temple, or mosque on a weekly or monthly basis is consistent over time. That number, however, is also notoriously inflated when researchers compare it with the number of people who actually attend the services. Similarly, a person, when asked, may respond that she is a Muslim or Methodist, and even that her religion is very important to her, and yet she may live showing little evidence of those claims. According to Muslim and Jewish demographers, most national telephone surveys undercount their respective adherents. Thus valuable telephone surveys do not resolve all issues. Reports from the religious institutions themselves about the strength and size of their memberships remain a significant source of information.

Another characteristic of the Religious Landscape Survey is that questions of belief are deliberately broad or simple: "Do you believe in God or a universal spirit? How certain are you of this belief?" "Which statement comes closer to your own views?: 'My religion is the one, true faith leading to eternal life' OR 'Many religions can lead to eternal life'?" The use of simplicity was surely wise in engaging 35,000 people at length by telephone, and the results are useful for their gross characterizations of tendencies among various demographic groups, such as Quakers or Buddhists or people in their twenties or fifties. Responses to such questions, however, can scarcely convey any conceptual or theological depth or sophistication on the part of the faithful.

Moreover, the simplicity of the questions on belief may lure analysts into thinking they understand something they do not. Instead, the questions should provoke further thought. One of the more interesting questions asked was whether one subscribed to the statement "My religion is the one, true faith leading to eternal life." Jehovah's Witnesses had far and away the greatest portion of adherents (80 percent) who concurred. Mormons, at 57 percent, were second, and evangelicals, at 36 percent, were third. The significance of this question is implied when the answers are juxtaposed with those from the religions that tend not to think in such terms. Eighty-nine percent of Hindus, 86 percent of Buddhists, 83 percent of mainline Protestants, and 79 percent of Catholics affirmed a counterproposal: "Many religions can lead to eternal life." But are respondents hearing the question in the same sense? If not, do their responses carry similar meaning? Mormons, for example, distinguish among concepts such as immortality, salvation, and exaltation or eternal life.

The same item on the survey raises other issues: what, for example, is the meaning of "religion" in the statement "many religions can lead to eternal life"? When 70 percent of Americans affirmed the statement, did they have in mind that other *denominations* within, say, Christianity have access to eternal life, or also that other *religions,* such as Hinduism or Islam, did as well? The question occurred to the survey's administrators. A follow-up study conducted in 2008 pursued the issue, learning that 80 percent of those Christians who believed many religions could lead to eternal life named at least one non-Christian religion that was able to do so.

A closer look at these intriguing findings suggests how demographic truths may induce yet further inquiry. For example, the survey reports that more than half (57 percent) of those in evangelical churches believed that other religions can lead to eternal life. Although this proportion is lower than those for many groups, it is an impressive figure. Nearly two-thirds of this group of evangelicals who so believed also believed that Judaism could bring eternal life, and one-third of them held that Islam or Hinduism could do so as well, with fewer still (26 percent) indicating that atheists could achieve the goal. These findings are intriguing for their own sake, but they raise a separate and basic question: what is an evangelical?

This question has been asked and addressed many times. A common understanding is that evangelicals are people who exhibit at least several of a cluster of traits. The most important of these traits are a high regard for the inspiration and authority of the Bible, a belief in the necessity of accepting Jesus as one's personal savior and of being "born again," and a commitment to evangelizing, to sharing the "good news" of the Gospel. But if a quarter of those in evangelical churches believe that even atheists may be saved and two-thirds of them believe that Jews can, then what, again, is an evangelical? Why proselytize to those who can otherwise be saved? Is, or is not, a born-again experience necessary for salvation? A related question is what does it mean to categorize entire denominations as "mainline

Protestant" or "evangelical" (as the survey does for purposes of national analysis) when views toward salvation are so inclusive (as documented by the survey) among significant segments of "evangelicals"? Conversely, labeling United Methodists as "mainline Protestant" is an understandable but problematic choice, when Methodists in the South think and behave much more like evangelicals than Methodists in Michigan or Colorado.

## Religious Affiliation and Unaffiliation

The survey's respondents who indicated no religious affiliation (the "Nones," as the American Religious Identification Survey labeled them) are particularly intriguing and ripe for further analysis because of both their size and their momentum. They seem to be a social weathervane. The Nones are the fastest-growing of any category of respondents in the survey. At 16.1 percent of the total population, their proportion is more than double the number who said they were not affiliated with any particular religion as children. So widespread and long-rooted have they been in the Pacific Northwest that observers have designated the region the "None Zone." They are emerging even more rapidly in the Northeast.

Indeed, the group is growing everywhere. Despite this growth, half of those who were unaffiliated as children reported being attached to a specific religion today. Taking into account the numbers thereby injected into the ranks of the religiously affiliated, while also accounting for the dramatic growth among the unaffiliated, one can conclude that a great many people who were attached as children are surrendering their affiliation. Awareness of their increase has been widening among scholars, and, increasingly, the public, since the beginning of the twenty-first century. This publicity of itself may have contributed to a higher rate of reporting in more recent surveys, making Nones feel more confident and free to announce themselves.

The unaffiliated are as diverse as any of the religious groupings such as Jews or evangelicals. Only a quarter of the Nones construe themselves as atheists or agnostics. Two-thirds of them (12.1 percent of the adult population) describe their religion as "nothing in particular," though half of these suggest that religion is somewhat or very important to them. "Spiritual but not religious" is often their mantra, especially among people in their teens, twenties, and thirties.

The lack of institutional commitment of those in this group who are not atheists may be explained variously. The explanations are based in part on survey responses, in part on other research, and in part on speculation in need of testing. Some Nones are in transition, moving by stages into or away from a denomination. Some are active seekers. Some are faintly attached to a vestige of their parents' or grandparents' loyalties. Some claim the benefits of religious feeling shorn of the burden of organized religious action or what they experience as the confinement of specific creeds. Many have constructed an eclectic, do-it-yourself religion; recall the radically individualistic "Sheilaism" made famous by sociologist Robert N. Bellah and his colleagues in *Habits of the Heart* (1985). Perhaps some of this impulse is a by-product of contemporary global connectedness, the presence in the United States of a radical diversity and pluralism (the celebration of diversity), and a waning cultural regard for institutions generally.

## What of the Future?

The startling willingness of adult Americans to exchange religious allegiances or to surrender them altogether has prompted questions among the religious, the irreligious, and observers of all stripes. Is religion growing less relevant to the lives of Americans? Is the religious commitment that remains increasingly shallow, a sort of hobby or fashion statement rather than a fundamental commitment? Is the country inclining toward the way of Europe, where Christianity has grown pale and its great cathedrals have become museums? Is secularism the future? Is "denomination" still a meaningful category?

The importance of denominations and particular religions may indeed dwindle further, and yet they continue to claim the loyalty of scores of millions of citizens. Many Catholics and Baptists, Eastern Orthodox and Jehovah's Witness, Jews, Muslims, Mormons, Episcopalians, Lutherans, and others intend to continue to enact their belief and practice through their denominational traditions. It is not implausible that this allegiance will erode in the acids of modernity and American pluralism, but neither is it implausible that a reaction will set in to the radical individualism of the culture. The country has a long history of groups that refused to call themselves a church but that have assumed over time explicit or implicit denominational traits. The rapidly growing Pentecostal movement is a case in point, as are the fiercely independent Churches of Christ.

One thing does seem certain: American religion in the future will more than ever enact its dynamics in international contexts. This is so because critical masses of imported religions already thrive within the country's borders. It is so because Christianity's demographic center of gravity and zeal has shifted from Europe, and is shifting from the United States, toward the southern hemisphere. It is so because internal division sometimes forges new international ties, as the Episcopalian experience demonstrates. Although theological conservatives are a minority in the Episcopal Church, they constitute a large majority among Anglicans worldwide. Seven hundred conservative parishes in the United States and Canada defected in 2008 over issues surrounding homosexuality. They formed a new church affiliated with overseas Anglicans.

The importance of international contexts for the future is further revealed by attention to Europe, which has so many ties to the United States. In Europe, Islam is, through immigration and high birthrates, beginning to fill the religious hole once filled by Christianity. In addition, international politics and economics dictate that the United States will need to grow accustomed to a more equitable role in world affairs than it has known since the beginning of the twentieth century. And yet despite all this, the United States is, as of the early twenty-first century, virtually unique among wealthy, technologically developed nations: it remains a religiously still-vibrant civilization. It is both three-quarters Christian *and* the most religiously diverse of all countries.

As for other demographic trends, they bear watching. The next pandemic, the next economic collapse or expansion, a war brought closer to home, another technological revolution—who knows when these or other imponderables will unleash a flow of emigration or launch or cut off a tide of immigration (and to and from what parts of the world?). Who knows how such events might alter the American birthrate, or its psyche, or its interest in the sacred?

The future has a way of mocking predictions. If there is a heaven for deists, Thomas Jefferson has had cause to recalibrate one of his. After all, he once predicted that, within a generation, most young Americans of his day would have become Unitarians.

**See also** *Economics; Emotion; Ethnographic and Anthropological Approaches; Feminist Studies; Geographical Approaches; Historical Approaches; History of Religion Approaches; Lived Religion; Marriage and Family; Material Culture Approaches; Politics* entries; *Religious Studies; Sociological Approaches; Unaffiliated.*

Philip L. Barlow

## BIBLIOGRAPHY

Balmer, Randall, and Mark Silk, eds. *Religion and Public Life in the Middle Atlantic Region: Fount of Diversity.* Walnut Creek, Calif.: AltaMira Press, 2006.

Barlow, Philip, and Mark Silk, eds. *Religion and Public Life in the Midwest: America's Common Denominator?* Walnut Creek, Calif.: AltaMira Press, 2006.

Bonomi, Patricia U., and Peter R. Eisenstadt. "Church Adherence in the Eighteenth-Century British Colonies." *William and Mary Quarterly* 39 (1982): 245–286.

Gaustad, Edwin Scott, and Philip L. Barlow. *New Historical Atlas of Religion in America.* New York: Oxford University Press, 2001.

Jones, Dale E., et al. *Religious Congregations and Membership in the United States 2000.* Cincinnati: Glenmary Research Center, 2002.

Killen, Patricia O'Connell, and Mark Silk, eds. *Religion and Public Life in the Pacific Northwest: The None Zone.* Walnut Creek, Calif.: AltaMira Press, 2004.

Kosmin, Barry A., and Ariela Keysar. "American Religious Identification Survey 2008." www.americanreligionsurvey-aris.org.

Lindsey, William, and Mark Silk, eds. *Religion and Public Life in the Southern Crossroads: Shutdown States.* Walnut Creek, Calif.: AltaMira Press, 2005.

Pew Forum on Religion and Public Life. *U.S. Religious Landscape Survey.* Washington, D.C.: Pew Research Center, 2008. http://religions.pewforum.org.

Roof, Wade Clark, and Mark Silk, eds. *Religion and Public Life in the Pacific Region: Fluid Identities.* Walnut Creek, Calif.: AltaMira Press, 2005.

Shipps, Jan, and Mark Silk. *Religion and Public Life in the Mountain West: Sacred Landscapes in Transition.* Walnut Creek, Calif.: AltaMira Press, 2004.

Silk, Mark, and Andrew Walsh. *One Nation, Divisible.* Lanham, Md.: Rowman and Littlefield, 2008.

Walsh, Andrew, and Mark Silk. *Religion and Public Life in New England: Steady Habits Changing Slowly.* Walnut Creek, Calif.: AltaMira Press, 2004.

Weis, Rev. Frederick Lewis. *The Colonial Churches and the Colonial Clergy of the Middle and Southern Colonies, 1607–1776.* Lancaster, Mass.: Society of the Descendants of the Colonial Clergy, 1938.

———. *The Colonial Clergy and the Colonial Churches of New England.* Lancaster, Mass.: Society of the Descendants of the Colonial Clergy, 1936.

———. *The Colonial Clergy of Maryland, Delaware, and Georgia.* Lancaster, Mass.: Society of the Descendants of the Colonial Clergy, 1950.

———. *The Colonial Clergy of Virginia, North Carolina, and South Carolina.* Lancaster, Mass.: Society of the Descendants of the Colonial Clergy, 1955.

# Denominationalism

In a 1972 mapping of religion, sociologist Andrew M. Greeley discerned denominationalism to be such a central, stable facet of American life that he titled his volume *The Denominational Society.* The United States, he believed, was one of four denominationally defined societies (along with Canada, Holland, and Switzerland). Although subsequent developments and more recent scholarship contest this characterization as overstated, his use of the rubrics *denominational* and *denominationalism* points both to the historic importance of this dimension of American religion and to the multivalent character of the terms themselves.

Employed in academic and popular discourse alike, the terms can be shorthand for religious identity or affiliation (as, for example, of military chaplains). The rubrics describe the diversity in American organizational religious life—the named or "denominated" faith communities. They point to the major Protestant divisions and traditions: mainline, evangelical, and historically black denominations. The terms also sometimes refer to religions that coalesce around or organize themselves through regional or national assemblies, leadership, or bureaucracy—that is, for Protestant-normed patterns of religious organization, uniting congregations within regional judicatories into national or global polities. The collective term *denominationalism* can stand for the salience or societal clout of the collectivity of mainline Protestant bodies. Sociologists employ the single term *denomination* typologically, and so compare it with other "ideal types"—cults, sects, and churches.

In several ways, then, the term *denominationalism* identifies a distinctive way of being religious. It indicates, for example, that a faith, ethic, tradition, single-purpose cause, or parachurch entity has developed into a multipurpose, multifunctional entity with some measure of centralization and corporate structure. It also has an identifiable membership and affiliated congregations, leadership, and regional and national judicatories. Similarly, denominationalism can function as a theory or theology of the church that discerns individual denominations as branches of the one vine (Christ). Alternatively, as an Internet search will reveal, denominationalism renders theological judgment, a denunciatory rubric for religious division, elitism, diversity, sectarianism, and schism. Denominationalism, denominational, and denomination can mean many things.

## An Invention of Modernity

The denomination is an invention of modernity. It emerged in Western societies as they searched for stratagems and policies other than coercion and repression for coping with the religious diversity and discord that emerged from the sixteenth-century reformations and seventeenth-century religious wars. English contributions—explorations of tolerance or comprehension after the Restoration and particularly after the Glorious Revolution, the Acts of Toleration, the writings of John Locke and colleagues, and the path-breaking efforts of newly tolerated English Presbyterians, Congregationalists, Baptists, and Quakers—played a vital role in the North American denomination. "Denomination" *named* voluntary religious organizations (initially Christian) operating under conditions of religious pluralism, codes of civility, and some measure of toleration. The collective term *denominationalism* references the existence and coexistence of tolerated voluntary religious bodies, their uneasy competition with one another establishing a larger pattern, the production thereby of an organizational field, and the emergence of a set of beliefs or practices that govern participation in the denominational order.

In their American context, both the denominational organizational field and individual denominations have evolved significantly over time, acting and reacting to other creatures of modernity, especially political parties, the press, and free enterprise, along with volunteer organizations and all levels of civil government. The relation and similarity of denomination to political parties and free enterprise have been especially marked and important. Sometimes the recipient of practice and precept from business and politics, denominationalism also has contributed to these sectors. The malleability, porosity, and dynamic character of denominationalism stem in no small way from denominations' highly successful missional efforts in American society, from pressures to stay current with communication idioms and systems, from the freedom they have enjoyed to experiment, and from their capture of intellectual, cultural, and political elites.

Denominations' culturally adaptive and sensitive character—embracing slavery in the South but abolition in the North—has earned both plaudits and denunciation. Here it is important to underscore the culturally adaptive and elastic character of the larger organizational ecology and its similarity to other sectors of modernity. Just as individual newspapers and magazines make up the free press, individual businesses make up capitalist free enterprise, and individual parties make up representative democracy, individual denominations make up the organizational ecology of denominationalism. These four creatures of modernity have tended to evolve together and to influence one another. That the denomination looks bureaucratic and has resembled the corporation for the last century is not surprising. It resembles the current business form of the day,

and also the current form of the political party and of the press. And no less than these other systems, denominationalism functions with sets of practices, understandings, and norms. Just as free enterprise evidenced its operative policy in corporate practice and democratic politics in partisan behavior, so denominationalism defined itself through the activities of the several denominations, in how they interacted, in the boundaries they set, and in their efforts to shape American society.

## Denominational Styles and Stages of Denominationalism

Five denominational styles emerged from the eighteenth to the twenty-first century. The first style, ethnic voluntarism, or provincial voluntarism, took root in the revivalism or awakening of the eighteenth century, shaping the religious pluralism of the middle colonies. The second style arose from the religious free-for-all of the early national period. Popular evangelistic movements were patterned after the purposive missionary association, seeking converts across the whole society. The third style, a churchly or confessional style, appeared in the Civil War era, invigorated by both immigrant religiosity and nativism. It assumed both high church and primitivist expressions and sought deeper foundations for belief and polity (in Romanticism and other popular theory). The fourth style emerged in the late nineteenth and early twentieth centuries. Protestantism reinvented itself for world evangelism by adopting corporate and managerial processes and forms. A fifth style, still defining itself, emerged in the late twentieth century, as conservative-evangelical movements and historically black denominations enlarged the mainstream and newer and non-Christian movements began negotiating their place in American society as well.

This typology serves a variety of purposes. First, it indicates that denominationalism and the denomination reinvent themselves over time. This dynamism should caution against equating denominationalism with its mainstream, bureaucratized image. Second, each stage models a normative style, thereby drawing boundaries, sometimes explicitly, sometimes implicitly, determining which movements belonged and which did not. Over time, the denominational system enlarged itself, again prompting the question of whether that is happening now. Third, at least in several stages the transformative impulses operated from the margins, importing a new dynamic into the religious picture and effectively enlarging the system by carving out new space for denominational formation and identity. Fourth, implicit in such renewal, the typology draws attention to renewal impulses that underlay and guided each new stage. Fifth, the schema suggests that also shaping denominations were interactions with business, politics, communication systems, and culture generally, and that denominational patterns of leadership, organization, decision making, and "business" looked very much like their counterparts in the American social, economic, and political orders. A sixth possible value, but one that cannot be probed here, is that to some extent movements new to the American scene may recapitulate some if not all of the stages. That said, the schema does not accurately describe individual denominations for any period. Instead, it "idealizes"; it identifies a predominant denominational style, and it accents the denominational profiles, purposes, and dynamic principles most powerfully operative for a specific era. Specific denominations adjusted these goals and principles in view of their own context, relative maturity, and confessional self-understanding.

## Ethnic Voluntarism

The ethnic ferment of the middle colonies, under conditions of toleration, set the stage for the first stage or style of denominationalism in what has been called the First Great Awakening. Various factors preconditioned colonial society's capacity to yield this new form of the church. The first factor was religious pluralism. Living side by side in the middle colonies were the Dutch Reformed, Quaker, Scottish, Scotch-Irish and Irish Presbyterian, English Baptist, Anglican, transplanted New England Congregationalist, and various German-speaking persuasions (Dunker, Lutheran, Reformed, Moravian, Schwenckfelder, Mennonite). African Americans, then seldom Christianized, and Jews also had their places. The second factor, as already noted, was policies or practices of toleration or of land grants to groups seeking asylum that implicitly permitted religious practice. William Penn's policies were of immense importance, as were English precepts.

The impetus for and form of *ethnic* voluntarism lay in immigration and whatever measure of religious heritage the immigrants brought with them. The dynamism for ethnic *voluntarism* lay in the waves of revival that *imported* pietism unleashed and in the religious reactions to pietism. Congregations and associations, quasi-independent because of the sheer distance to "proper" authority, accomplished through their problem-solving two related but distinguishable social

transactions: establishing new ethnic communities and legitimating them religiously as German-American Moravians, Scottish-American Presbyterians, and Dutch Reformed.

Most imported religion has come to American shores with little in the way of trained and credentialed leadership or the capacity to create such (the Puritans being the notable exception). Middle colony immigrants, modeling a pattern, found themselves largely fending for themselves religiously. They drew on their (often lay) memories of church practice and structure. They pressed someone into leadership, gathered in one another's homes, wrote religious authorities in the homeland pleading for proper preachers, and put in place processes by which to recognize authority. When preachers came or a community selected one of their own to serve, they founded congregations. The newly installed preachers, perhaps with laity, reached out to the leadership from congregations of the same apparent "persuasion" to initiate presbyteries, consistories, or their tradition's counterpart. And around these modest structures converged the immigrant community, ordering itself religiously while adhering to colonial authority and further pleading to some home country judicatory for additional ministers, print resources, and adjudication of disputes that threatened the community.

The formation of religious communities began in the early stages of immigration and settlement, but took off with the itinerant, revivalistic, conversionist, pietist practices that surfaced in Dutch settlements under Theodore J. Frelinghuysen in the 1720s. It then continued among Presbyterians under William and Gilbert Tennent in the 1730s and appeared in quite diverse confessional forms thereafter, spreading across the colonies tracking the several decades of itinerations by George Whitefield. Pietism's tactics proved highly effective in stimulating both new religious identity and community as well as angry reactive responses, themselves community-strengthening, from existing and more confessionally oriented leaders. Formative but controversial were pietism's emotional invitational preaching; expectations of conversion and a morally regenerate life thereafter; allowance for lay testimony; encouragement of prayer, Bible reading, and disciplining small groups (conventicles); itinerant preaching (beyond the community to which the minister might be called); focus in sermon and witness on sin and salvation; blunt criticisms of worldliness in other laity and of unfruitful and unconverted ministers; and willingness to experiment with new ways of training and credentialing leadership.

This repertoire, known thereafter as revivalism, proved to be of enduring value in forming a (religious) community, in part because it authorized local or indigenous processes and leadership generation, in effect allowing a community to declare its religious independence from its European home base or its alignment with more evangelical resource centers (Halle, in the case of pietism). Meanwhile, an elective, voluntary, ethnic denominational identity emerged, because most of this pietist community formation occurred within lines of kinship, language, national origin, religious tradition, and race. These communities, however, understood their new identity not in sociological terms but in pneumatological and eschatological terms.

Others, particularly in congregations based on the then-normative Protestant-confessional model, took great exception to what they saw as pietism's censorious criticism, emotionalism (enthusiasm), lax theology, irregular lay activity, and untrained/unauthorized ministries. These confessional communities filed disciplinary charges at their headquarters in Edinburgh and Amsterdam and read the enthusiast pietists out of their synods or assemblies. Religious energy and division yielded ethnic identity and cohesion. Thus among Presbyterians both the Awakening New Side and the more confessional Old Side offered versions of Celtic-American ethnicity, each organizing along received polity lines.

Denominations at this stage consisted of a few congregations loosely tied together by small, periodic leadership gatherings. These pastor-led associations concerned themselves with care of congregations, problem solving, leadership supply and credentials, hymnals and service books, catechism, and the like. Denominations did not elaborate a public theology. Nor did they see themselves caring for the whole of colonial society or seek to transform the social order. They remained largely dependent on European resources (either pietist or confessional) for preachers and materials. Insofar as perceptions of belonging within a denominational field (denominationalism) existed, they did so quite vaguely in a sense of alignment with or against the Awakening or within a confessional or pietist realm.

## Purposive Missionary Associations

A second denominationalism derived its primary impulse from pietistic revivalism as well, in what has been termed the Second Great Awakening. But it was conceived in relation to the new nation, and it invented mechanisms to missionize the entire society. This civic theology harnessed revivalistic energies to build a Christian America. The then-mainline denominations (Congregationalists, Presbyterians, Episcopalians), each regionally dominant, supplied the vision of a Christian America and the main institutions needed for enculturation (voluntary societies, colleges). More marginal and newer bodies (Baptists, Methodists, Christians) supplied the expansive, energetic evangelism that transgressed lines of language, ethnicity, *and* race and aspired to Christianize (convert) the whole society. The camp meeting epitomized its missionary dynamic.

Presbyterians and Congregationalists provided the leadership and the intellectual framework that guided denominations. The new nation needed, they thought, a common moral framework for the good order that a republic required. To elaborate such, they drew heavily on Reformed theological traditions, Puritan covenantal notions, Scottish moral philosophy, and the rubrics of republicanism. When integrated, this new paradigm assigned to the several denominations, and themselves especially, the responsibility for creating and overseeing a Christian America.

Notwithstanding Congregational and Presbyterian presumptions—and they graciously included Episcopalians as well—other movements supplied both the human resources and the effective model for implementing such high policy and grand aims. The popular, even though despised, evangelistic movements—Baptists, Methodists, and Christians (Restorationists)—suffused denominationalism with their missionary energy.

The popular denominations adapted pietism's revivalistic repertoire to open, inclusive missionary purpose. In doing so, they raced settlers into western lands. Missionary impulse shaped these denominations. To be sure, the new denominationalism and even its signature camp meeting could only breach but not eradicate or transcend the social barriers (class, ethnicity, region, language, race, and slavery). Meanwhile, language- and race-specific denominations emerged—African Methodist and Baptist, as well as German- and Scandinavian-speaking. They, too, took on the new aggressive, competitive style. And increasingly so did the Presbyterians and Congregationalists.

The Reformed denominations' more highly developed institutions, as well as their theological notion of covenant, combined with the revivalistic energies of popular movements such as Methodism to provide a highly effective ecumenical drive toward building a Christian America that transcended denominational allegiances. The missionary self-understanding demanded new mobile entrepreneurial leadership skills, a new vernacular, new communication media, and a new, more elastic organization. Mission and covenant were combined in an incredible institution-building effort, much of which went into transforming the denominations from modest associational structures into engines for national ministerial deployment and governance. They became powerful democratizing and creative forces. The three mainline denominations invested significantly in establishing voluntary societies that focused nationally on urgent causes (distributing Bibles, forming Sunday schools, furthering various reforms). Other denominations also mounted their own voluntary society endeavors. Denominational publishing houses provided congregations and Sunday schools with lessons, newspapers, and magazines. Colleges, sometimes founded more on promise than on prospect, trained denominational ministers and lay elites. And from the local level women and men joined the denominational and interdenominational reform and mission societies to deal with the urban poor, seamen, prostitutes, slaves, and slavery. In doing so, denominations would Christianize the continent. A purposive missionary association generated structure and procedure faster than formal theologies and ecclesiastical polities could adjust. The adjustment would yield other styles of denominationalism.

## Confessional Denominationalism

The third style of denominationalism, confessional, culminated in transatlantic fellowships: the Lambeth Conference (1867), World Presbyterian Alliance (1877), Methodist Ecumenical Conference (1881), International Congregational Council (1891), and Baptist World Alliance (1905). Various impulses, some international and some American, stimulated more pronounced awareness of doctrinal, liturgical, or polity identity and generated a style of denominationalism that competed with purposive denominationalism. In the first impulse, the dynamism, cultural power, and seductive appeal of American revivalistic evangelicalism induced emulation and adaptation within some communions that traditionally defined their identities in other ways—notably the Reformed, Lutheran, and Anglican churches (as well as Catholicism and Judaism). Within some of these confessional Protestant churches, the leaders who emerged drew on their respective traditions to critique camp meeting style revivalism, the "new measures" advanced by Charles Grandison Finney, expansive voluntarism generally, and associated denominational practices. Especially articulate and important were the Mercersburg theologians,

Philip Schaff and John W. Nevin. In various works they parodied revivalism as a "methodistical" scheme. They deemed signature elements of purposive missionary denominationalism alien to their German Reformed tradition and its converting ordinances—catechism and the sacraments. Similarly, Charles Philip Krauth spoke for confessional Lutheranism and John Henry Hobart and Calvin Colton for proper Anglicanism, in each instance moving their denominations or a newly formed one (Missouri Synod) onto proper confessional foundations. These spokespersons appealed to their respective doctrinal heritages, but drew variously on currents of romanticism, which valued tradition, confessions, sacraments, mystery, catechism, and other hallmarks of ecclesial identity.

A second impulse of confessionalism derived from the differences over slavery within evangelical denominations. Presbyterians divided in 1837, and Methodists and Baptists in the early 1840s. In each instance various factors drove the schisms, but slavery or antislavery was at least in the background for Presbyterians, or in the foreground for Methodists and Baptists. Once divided, the rival churches rationalized their causes and explained their purposes theologically, confessionally, and biblically. In fights over turf—Methodists and Presbyterians reunited only in the mid-twentieth century and Baptists never have—each defended its polity by proclaiming first principles, appealing to the teachings of its founder, and reverting to tradition.

A third and related impulse toward a churchly or confessional orientation was centered on the voluntary associations that were a hallmark of purposive missionary organizations and, in part, their dedication to the antislavery cause. Among Presbyterians, old-school theologians such as Charles Hodge saw such institutions as ecclesially anomalous. Organized interdenominationally, overseen by interlocking boards of donors, and accountable only to themselves, they were involved in a range of churchly matters (Bibles, Sunday schools, tracts, missions) and within churchly contexts that should have been the denomination's domain. On what basis and by what authority did they do the church's business? Motivating the old school and driving the 1837 division were associated concerns—a missional concordat struck with the Congregationalists earlier in the century, Finney's "new measures," discipline cases, and antislavery. After the division the old school restructured itself denominationally, in order to bring under ecclesial authority the functions and tasks launched by the interdenominational voluntary societies. Mission, Sunday school, tract, temperance, and various other societies became *intra*denominational operations. Other movements echoed the Presbyterian brief against voluntary or missionary societies and sought to bring such ventures under church control, a pattern to be widely emulated. Similarly, antimission Baptists and Restorationists denounced voluntary societies as unbiblical, articulating a kind of nonconfessional confessionalism. Of long-term significance were the kindred efforts and primitivist ideas of Landmark Baptists, who leapt back to the New Testament and repudiated intervening centuries of Christian tradition to warrant ecclesiologies of localism and close communion.

**Corporate Organization**

The fourth style of denominationalism drew on both prior styles to achieve accountability over, while affirming and increasing, the effectiveness of the powerful voluntary, purposive missionary societies created by evangelical Protestantism. During the Civil War, mobilization of the religious community by women and men to supply, support, nurse, and minister had demonstrated the extraordinary delivery capacities of a focused, popularly based, vertically integrated, nationally managed organization. Like northern businesses, denominations had experienced firsthand in the war effort the payoff of top-down control and corporate organization. In part emulating the business community, in part capitalizing on its own experience, mainstream Protestantism undertook significant structural reforms in the late nineteenth and early twentieth centuries. Denominations sought to bring under judicatory control the complex of voluntary societies—men's and women's—by which they had done their business. In doing so, denominations established a *corporate board and agency system*—in effect, they carried out a "managerial revolution."

This revolution was aimed at checking the parallel, self-guided, trustee-accountable societies that ran denominational programs. More positively, the revolution sought to increase the effectiveness of the array of enterprises being undertaken on the denomination's behalf and in doing so to coordinate their efforts under denominational authority. The problem? With their self-perpetuating boards, own staffs, distinct collections or appeals for funds across the denomination, and prerogatives over programs, denominational societies functioned beyond denominational control.

By legislative action or by more gradual initiatives, denominations reorganized themselves internally, provided denominational oversight for the former voluntary societies, and created a corporate board structure. Elaborate

procedures coordinated finance, communications, and publication programs. The churches experimented with new modes of collaboration between agencies and local churches, especially in areas of program and finance. Every level of the church, from congregational to state to regional to national, structured itself with the same bodies, with the same names, with the same duties. The changes created national power centers, essentially bureaucratic in nature. Gradually the churches began staffing agencies with professionals, requiring higher degrees of specialization and expertise, and exploring new schemes of systematic finance.

Thus the mainstream denominations came into being, and as a collective system they effectively dominated American society and culture until the mid-twentieth century. Their various authority systems, bureaucratic program structure, and professionalized leadership aligned them with American society generally, and especially with business and government. By midcentury, their professional elites were collaborating with African Americans in leading society and the denominations themselves toward overcoming segregation and racism. And they began to accommodate women and minorities in the ministry. Thus mainstream Protestantism seemed to be poised for continued societal leadership. Instead, as noted, it found itself upstaged by conservative and evangelical movements. Badly divided itself and facing a much more pluralistic society, it effectively disestablished itself.

**Post-Christian Denominationalism?**

The fifth style of denominationalism might be variously dated. It may have emerged with the 1965 Immigration Act, which opened the door to Asian and Middle Eastern immigrants, or with Vatican II and the 1960 election of John F. Kennedy to the presidency, or with the civil rights movement and Rev. Martin Luther King's "I have a dream" speech in 1963, or with the urban and Vietnam War crises in the late sixties, or with the election of Ronald Reagan to the White House in 1980 and the ascendancy of conservative evangelicalism.

Characterizing this new style is difficult because, standing within it, scholars do not yet see its contours or its understandings and practices. This style formed within mainstream Protestantism; however, interactions among denominations of all kinds have resulted in a cross-fertilization in societal roles, operational styles, program features, communication systems, outreach mechanisms, and organizational purposes. Unclear at this juncture is whether these interactions are producing a new form of denominationalism or its demise. Even less clear is whether the increased pluralism in American society and the importance of non-Protestant and non-Christian religions augur an even more dramatic reconstitution of denominationalism.

Not yet apparent, then, is the operative theory for the fifth style and whether it is Protestant, Judeo-Christian, or pluralistic. More evident are efforts across religious traditions to experiment with contemporary cultural forms, delivery systems, and communication networks. However, experiments with technique and technology stress existing associations and traditional expectations of leadership. Culture wars, immigration, war and terrorism, and the global economy further pressure denominational systems. In places, religious life charts a nondenominational course; elsewhere a hyperdenominationalism results. Will institutional ferment produce a religiously plural American denominationalism, a denominationalism stratified globally, or a Protestant denominationalism adjusted to minority status in North American society?

## The Modern Denomination

The modern denomination, at least as typified by mainstream Protestantism, exhibits internal features that lend themselves to sometimes differing overall impressions. In fact, denominations function with complex or multiple authority systems, each part of which proves capable of pulling in its own distinct direction, pressing for interests intrinsic to its domain. A religious authority system—theologically warranted, biblically based, confessionally labeled, or constitutionally protected—shapes a denomination. Denominations sometime proclaim this system in their names—the African Methodist *Episcopal* Church, the Associate Reformed *Presbyterian* Church, the Evangelical *Congregational* Christian Conference. The names locate a significant, perhaps primary, source of authority—in the congregation, in presbyteries, in bishops (the episcopacy). And the religious authority systems have yielded distinctive political structures or polities—episcopal, presbyterial, congregational, Actually, denominations within each of these distinctive polity types usually borrow aspects of the other two.

Sometimes the leading or teaching function is effectively undertaken by a second system—an administrative, agency, or board apparatus. Often mimicked at every level in the denomination with offices, commissions, or committees, this system implements much of the program, publishing, mission, social action, employee care (pensions, insurance), and

financing (stewardship and expenditure) for the denomination. Theoretically accountable to the religious authority system, boards and agencies often function like corporations. Their general secretaries operate as CEOs, their staffs effectively chart denominational policy, and their initiatives are redirected by bishops, conferences, or conventions only with great effort.

Such campaigns disclose yet a third internal system, congregations and regional or middle judicatories. The latter, variously termed association, presbytery, conference, diocese, region, or synod, functions administratively between congregations and the national or international structures and authority. At this level, church officials decide to ordain, hire, and dismiss clergy; conduct problem solving; mount educational, training, and outreach programs; and negotiate denominational style, ethos, and identity. Bishops, presidents, clerks, district superintendents, and their staffs interact with pastors and congregations in quite complex ways, behaving in effect like congregations' regional service centers. This level deals with charges of clerical misconduct either through denominational judicial procedures or through civil or criminal proceedings, or through both. Findings can sometimes be appealed to other levels, but much denominational judicial, disciplinary, and personnel activity focuses on the regional judicatory

Congregations and regional judicatories generate a fourth internal system, a national, continental, or even global assembly. These assemblies, which are usually unicameral, function as congresses. Some permit messengers from every congregation, while others are confined to representative delegates. The assemblies initiate constitutional change, vote on offices, authorize new hymnals or doctrinal statements, set missional policy, speak on public issues, and the like. Even in nonconnectional or congregational denominations, the national assembly becomes the most visible public, media-covered event. This system provides for some lay and congregational roles in denominational decision making, property holding, and financial administration.

Closely related and perhaps emerging as yet another internal system are caucuses, struggle groups, and organized campaigns—the ecclesial counterparts to political action groups, think tanks, and legislative caucuses.

Caucuses, regional judicatories, and national assemblies draw leadership from yet another denominational system, the church's professionals and, in particular, the clergy. Ministers, priests, and rabbis have no state authorizing or professionally controlled associations through which clergy can be credentialed or advance their professional interests. However, at least in some instances the regional or national assembly has functioned as a denomination-specific professional society, despite the presence of laity. Laity serve in these bodies in a representative capacity, sometimes for a single session, while the clergy enjoy an ongoing membership. Regional judicatories function like professional organizations or the state bar.

Other professionals and specialists within denominations—religious educators, missionaries, deacons and deaconesses, musicians, urban ministers, college and military chaplains, evangelists, information officers, fiscal officers, large-church pastors, agency administrators, and even judicatory staff—have to create their own professional organizations. Typically, they have done so in more loosely structured and less regularly attended annual gatherings, and they may seek their professional recognition through some other denominational connection, perhaps in relation to a national board or agency. Denominations are, then, complex systems.

## Perspectives

In recent years sociology, particularly the sociology of religion, has probed denominations extensively. The ideal typology locates a denomination on a spectrum—church, denomination, sect (perhaps in several categories), cult (sometimes), and mysticism (in some versions). Sociology also examines denominations in studies of societal composition and evolution, secularization, pluralism, and religious preference (rational choice).

However, history, not sociology, offers the oldest perspective on denominations. Chronicling and publishing its own story is one signal that a religious movement understands itself as a denomination. And early efforts to depict American religion did so by narrating the histories of the several denominations, an encyclopedic practice that continues. The most important of such efforts, guided by German-born theologian and historian Philip Schaff, founder of the American Society of Church History (1888), undertook to survey American religion by studying individual denominations (or denominational families) for inclusion in the thirteen-volume American Church History Series (1893–1897). Histories of individual denominations, for much of the twentieth century left almost exclusively to insiders and amateurs, have resurfaced as sophisticated period or region-specific case studies.

Among newer perspectives, the field of organizational studies and some examinations of voluntarism, voluntary associations, not-for-profits, and nongovernmental organizations include denominations in their purview. Bringing these several perspectives together and adding anthropology is the emerging field of congregational studies. Once more neglected than the denomination, the congregation is now studied as the shaper, instrument, and expression of American religiosity. Congregational studies often offer fresh views from the bottom-up of the denomination and its leadership. When they look across the panorama of American religion, congregational studies can measure the overall health of the denominational system and assess the degree to which newer and non-Christian religious impulses take on congregational form (de facto congregationalism), a probable indicator of their assuming denominational shape as well.

Christian theology and ethics, whose intellectual domains include ecclesiology and institutional social policy, have rather neglected the denomination and denominationalism. The notable exception is James M. Gustafson's *Treasure in Earthen Vessels: The Church as a Human Community*. And when theology has taken up the topic, it has tended to render judgment and offer criticism. In the early and mid-twentieth century, such assessments derived from ecumenical and neo-orthodox perspectives. Denominationalism was an emblem of Christian division and disunity and the ethical failure of the church to be the church made one in Christ. And as porous, culturally sensitive institutions that accommodated, and occasionally championed, some of the worst of human practices (slavery, war, segregation, class prejudice, exploitation of workers, sexism, and homophobia), denominations compromised the gospel with the world, a theological scandal.

The person who most forcefully synthesized these ecumenical and neo-orthodox judgments, H. Richard Niebuhr, was among the first to analyze the collective phenomenon of American denominationalism. He found that each denomination established and shaped itself around social impulses of class, caste, nationality, region, ethnicity, and language. These socially partial origins and denominations' difficulty in surmounting them earned Niebuhr's scathing reproach in *The Social Sources of Denominationalism* (1957), and his work and views still typify perceptions of denominationalism. He pointed out that the "evil of denominationalism" lay in the conditions that made the emergence of sects necessary. Churches had failed to transcend the social conditions that made them into "caste-organizations," to "sublimate their loyalties" to standards and institutions that had little relevance, if any, to the Christian ideal, and to fight the temptation to give first priority to their own self-preservation and expansion.

Niebuhr's usage of church, denomination, and sect made popular the typological categories advanced by social scientists such as Ernst Troeltsch. Niebuhr proposed the categories of denomination and denominationalism as most apt for understanding American society. He wrote at the highpoint of mainline Protestant ascendancy in national affairs, perhaps in world affairs. Consequently, Niebuhr emphasized denominational conformity to society and culture and compromise of an egalitarian, inclusive, world-denying Christian ethic. He later revisited the denomination's relation to society in various works. In *Christ and Culture* (1951) he set forth a fivefold typology aimed at characterizing the longer saga of Christianity's relation to the state, the social order, and culture.

## Status

The complexity of denominationalism makes its status in American society in part a definitional issue. However, a variety of developments suggest, if not its decline, then certainly the destabilization of the central societal role to which Andrew Greeley pointed; this can be discerned from the U.S. Religious Landscape Survey by the Pew Forum on Religion and Public Life and from several works by commentators on the American religious institution scene, such as Robert Wuthnow and Nancy Ammerman. The following are some considerations that call the centrality of denominationalism in the American religious spectrum into question.

• The growing North American religious pluralism may require other categories than "denominationalism" to recognize the importance and the unique patterns of the local and translocal institutionalization of non-Protestant Christian, Jewish, Buddhist, Muslim, Hindu, Native American, and New Age faiths, and various types of the unaffiliated.

• Protestantism breaks into three traditions—mainline, evangelical, and historically black—each denominationally divided, but together slipping to only 51 percent of total reported membership, a trajectory possibly indicating Protestant minority status in the future.

• Membership in mainline Protestant denominations has eroded (and aged) over the last half-century, and the importance, prestige, and power of mainline denominational leadership is now contested, and often bested—for example, in the access of religious leaders to the White House.

• Conservative, evangelical, and fundamentalist bodies and their leadership have experienced corresponding growth, vigor, visibility, and political prowess, with their collective membership exceeding that of the mainline churches and constituting over a quarter of the overall American population.

• Membership growth in Latin America, the Caribbean, Africa, and Asia, and stagnation or decline in North America threaten long-standing patterns of assembly, governance, ethos, worship, and morality (on homosexuality especially).

• Denominational ethos, values, commitment, and cohesion now contend with denomination switching—a quarter of adults are no longer a part of the religion in which they were raised, and that figure climbs to 44 percent if switching among Protestant bodies is tracked.

• Evidence of the weakening of denominational identity and allegiance are the marriages across religious, confessional, and denominational lines (37 percent); persons retaining a sense of being Methodist or Presbyterian but no actual membership; disaffiliation in younger age cohorts; and adherents experimenting with various spiritualities and meditative practices.

• Protestant denominations contend with similar patterns of congregational independence or diffidence, reflected in the selection of nonstandard educational materials or hymnals, the diversion of collections to local or nondenominational projects, the resistance to denominational programs, and the removal of denominational signage.

• Competing for congregational business and competing with denominational agencies are an array of independent and parachurch publishing houses, curriculum suppliers, music licensers, bookstore chains, program franchisers, consultants, and training outfits.

• Megachurches, some independent or nondenominational and some remaining denominationally affiliated (often loosely), now boast resources comparable to small denominations, with sophisticated broadcast, Internet, and digital presences and the capacity to meet needs once supplied by denominations.

• Coalitions of megacongregations or their church plantings coalesce into denomination-like entities or function more loosely as quasi-denominations, offering training events and inspirational gatherings for prospective clergy.

- Single-purpose lobbying, humanitarian, and mission organizations are claiming the resources once channeled through congregational structures and through denominations and denominational programs. Examples are Focus on the Family, World Vision, Promise Keepers, Institute on Religion and Democracy, and Habitat for Humanity.

- Similar single-purpose struggle, ideological, or caucus groups within denominations, especially within mainline ones, turn assemblies and conferences into contentious culture war gatherings. They tend to align into broad progressive or conservative camps and establish connections to similar camps in other denominations or through religious political action or coalition-forming entities, such as the Institute of Religion and Democracy.

- Older interdenominational organizations—such as the National and the World Council of Churches—that once harmonized the leadership of the mainline, function within the ambit of culture wars, tending to retain the allegiance of the more progressive and to function as a foil for the more conservative denominational leaders.

- Marginal membership attachment, congregational independence, culture war sentiments, and societal prejudices engender indifference, suspicion, and sometimes hostility toward the centers and symbols of denominational identity, at times resulting in tax resistance or other forms of revolt.

- Media ministries, the newer virtual alliances, and political action efforts that trade on religious sensibilities enlarge the marketplace within which religious expression and affiliation occur and induce consumption or invite appropriation of multiple beliefs, value systems, and ethical practices.

- Such public or digital visualizations of North America and of the world heighten awareness of American religious diversity, test tolerance levels, stimulate post–September 11 fears, and erode faith in or adherence to putative societal norms within which Protestant denominationalism has functioned.

- Because denominational loyalty is tested on so many fronts, denominational leaders, ordination committees, and seminaries find themselves forced to accent confessional particularities, resulting in the strange phenomenon of hyperdenominationalism contending with postdenominationalism.

## An End to Denominationalism?

Corrosive forces are eroding the dominance, indeed the salience, of Protestant denominations, particularly those that might be termed mainline or traditional. Should one then conclude that America is no longer a denominational society? Or even that the end of denominationalism looms, as a chorus of doomsayers prophesizes? Such judgments may seem appropriate to Protestant leaders anguishing over numerical declines or to those outside mainstream denominations who have found megachurches, parachurch organizations, media ministries, or virtual spirituality to be the most effective religious modality for the twenty-first century.

The historian, however, can ask whether the crisis interpretive mood obscures the longer saga of denomination and denominationalism and overlooks the earlier declarations of its doom. Denominationalism has itself differed over time, as noted. Adequate definitions of denomination and denominationalism can no longer be equated with mainline Protestantism or with bureaucratic-corporate forms. Such definitions need to recognize the changing modalities of denominational structure and governance over the course of the American denominational experience and leave open the possibility that some of the newer and non-Christian movements will participate in the reshaping of denominationalism.

Indeed, the catalogue of social strains prompts the question of whether denominationalism is, in fact, undergoing reconstitution, whether the denominational system is broadening beyond evangelical and historically black churches and Judaism, and whether immigrant, non-Christian, and newer religious impulses are organizing themselves in what might be termed a denominational pattern (the once Protestant-normed pattern of American religious organization functioning as a denominational organizational field). Will newer movements embrace a denominational identity or label (what sociologists term "institutional isomorphism") to claim space in the religious marketplace? Will they coalesce as voluntary communities in patterns of de facto congregationalism? Will they seek nonprofit status, advertise in newspapers or in the *Yellow Pages,* and establish trustees and lay leadership cadres, committees, or boards? Will one or more of the leaders function in such congregational communities in minister-like capacities? Will the congregations gradually emulate their neighboring churches with Sunday schools and an array of other community-building or outreach functions? To support such multipurpose activities will leaders and congregations collaborate with counterparts to build some translocal form of denominational organization? And will such denominationalizing impulses be welcomed, recognized, or even accommodated to by existing denominations and by American society? Will the many studies, institutes, conferences, and institutes now exploring religious diversity function as signals and means of accommodation, as did Vatican II, JFK's presidency, the "discovery" of a Judeo-Christian tradition, and Will Herberg's landmark declaration in his classic book *Protestant, Catholic, Jew* of a wider denominationalism? The questions are many; the answers are few.

**See also** *Civil Religion in the United States; Congregations; Demographics; Ecumenism; Emerging Church Movement; Historical Approaches; House Church Movement; Independent Bible and Community Churches; Megachurches; Ministry, Professional; Philanthropy; Polity; Seeker Churches; Sociological Approaches; Unaffiliated.*

Russell E. Richey

**BIBLIOGRAPHY**

Ammerman, Nancy Tatom. *Pillars of Faith: American Congregations and Their Partners.* Berkeley: University of California Press, 2005.

Demerath, N. J., III, et al., eds. *Sacred Companies: Organizational Aspects of Religion and Religious Aspects of Organizations.* New York: Oxford University Press, 1998.

Gustafson, James M. *Treasure in Earthen Vessels: The Church as a Human Community.* New York: Harper and Row, 1961.

Harrison, Paul M. *Authority and Power in the Free Church Tradition: A Social Case Study of the American Baptist Convention.* Princeton, N.J.: Princeton University Press, 1959.

Mullin, Robert, Bruce Mullin, and Russell E. Richey, eds. *Reimagining Denominationalism.* New York: Oxford University Press, 1994.

Newman, William M., and Peter L. Halvorson. *Atlas of American Religion: The Denominational Era, 1776–1990.* Walnut Creek, Calif.: AltaMira Press, 2000.

Niebuhr, H. Richard. *Christ and Culture.* New York: Harper and Brothers, 1951.

———. *The Social Sources of Denominationalism.* New York: Living Age Books/Meridian Books, Inc., 1957 [orig. pub. 1929].

Pew Forum on Religion and Public Life. *U.S. Religious Landscape Survey.* Washington, D.C.: Pew Research Center, 2008.

Richey, Russell E. "Institutional Forms of Religion." *Encyclopedia of Religion in America,* 3 vols., ed. Charles H. Lippy and Peter W. Williams, 1:31–50. New York: Scribner, 1988.

———, ed. *Denominationalism.* Nashville: Abingdon Press, 1977.

Roozen, David A., and James R. Nieman. *Church, Identity and Change: Theology and Denominational Structures in Unsettled Times.* Grand Rapids, Mich.: Eerdmans, 2005.

Tipton, Steven M. *Public Pulpits: Methodists and Mainline Churches in the Moral Argument of American Life.* Chicago: University of Chicago Press, 2007.

Wind, James P., and James W. Lewis, eds. *American Congregations.* 2 vols. Chicago: University of Chicago Press, 1994.

Wuthnow, Robert. *America and the Challenges of Religious Diversity.* Princeton, N.J.: Princeton University Press, 2005.

# Devotionalism

Devotionalism refers to the many ways in which religious worshippers relate to sacred figures, such as deities, persons, spirits, or objects. Sometimes known as popular piety, devotions are found in many religions and are practiced by a wide variety of believers.

Individuals and communities employ various media when practicing devotion to a sacred figure such as God, saints, goddesses, or gurus. Among these media are candles, incense, oils, flowers, songs, prayers, beads, and icons. Some devotions can be considered private because they are practiced in a domestic setting. In examples of public devotions, Roman Catholics attend Benediction (a ceremony during which the consecrated host used in Communion is displayed and adored), Jews gather as family and friends for Sabbath, and Buddhists go to public temples to pay personal homage to the Buddha. In the United States, devotionalism has long been practiced by a wide range of individuals and communities, from Native Americans to Catholics. Protestants, because of their resistance to material images (with the exception of the cross) have been less inclined to devotionalism, but they are not without the practice, particularly Hispanic Protestants. Adherents of other religions more recently present in North America (for example, Hindus, Buddhists, Jains, and Sikhs) have their own forms of devotionalism that are practiced in places of public worship as well as in private settings.

Devotionalism balances the theological and intellectual aspects of religion with concrete images, prayers, and practices that support the faith of believers. Employing material aids such as statues, altars, oils, and flowers, worshippers bring to mind the divine. Many popular devotions originate with and are practiced by ordinary believers. Sometimes institutional representatives or clergy view such devotions as secondary forms of worship. In 2001 Pope John Paul II (1978–2005) defined popular piety as an expression of faith that avails itself of certain cultural elements proper to a specific environment—elements that are capable of interpreting and questioning the sensibilities of those who live in that same environment.

Devotionalism and popular religion often go hand-in-hand, although they may be separated by their originating sources. Devotions are frequently led by, or approved by, religious officials such as priests, ministers, rabbis, or bishops. Popular religion usually comprises practices created by ordinary believers and is not led by religious authorities. Often these practices are created on the margins of organized religion, and yet once established they are regularly tolerated or embraced by institutions. These practices may be described as extraliturgical for those traditions that have institutionalized and structured liturgy or worship. Over time, some practices of popular piety make their way into official liturgical ritual.

Pilgrimages are another form of devotionalism found in many religions practiced in the United States. American devotees may make a sacred journey to a place reputed to be holy because the transcendent or divine is believed to have touched that place in a special way. Thus, for example, Muslims visit Mecca in a pilgrimage to Saudi Arabia known as the *hajj*, Jews visit the remains of the second temple in Jerusalem at the Western Wall, and Catholics visit the healing waters of Lourdes in France.

Some of the risks of popular piety, according to religious officials, are demeaning sacred objects, misunderstanding the meaning of images or practices, attributing magical powers to objects or rituals, elevating these objects and rituals above sanctioned practices, substituting these objects and rituals for approved practices, or investing them with authority that supersedes the authority of approved texts or rituals.

## Christian Devotionalism

The Protestant Reformation discouraged the use of icons, statues, and religious images. At the same time, it encouraged Bible reading and personal prayer. Many Protestants read, pray, and study the Bible. For many, private devotionalism extends to reading religiously inspired books and, in the contemporary era, listening to Christian radio and watching Christian television shows.

The religious revivals of the eighteenth and nineteenth centuries included devotionalism as well as preaching and prayer. For example, the American preacher Jonathan Edwards (1703–1758) and the British evangelist George Whitfield (1714–1770) led a revival called the Great Awakening, during which crowds gathered not only to pray but also to dance, scream, and contort their bodies, all as signs of their devotion to the Lord. In the Second Great Awakening, preachers such as Charles Grandison Finney (1792–1875) and James McGready (1758–1817), often in outdoor campground revivals, stirred people's emotions with their fiery preaching. These same practices are followed today in many evangelical churches.

In the 1800s public schools in America initiated readings from the King James Version of the Bible. At the beginning of the nineteenth century, *The Christian Century,* a popular American publication representing mainline Protestantism, published a devotional guide entitled *The Daily Altar* that encouraged Americans to take just a few minutes daily to pray and reflect on spiritual matters. The guide included Bible readings, poetry, and inspirational texts. The use of these publications differentiated liberal Protestants from fundamentalists, who preferred only the Bible for their mediation and prayer. Henry Emerson Fosdick (1878–1969), a liberal Protestant author of four tracts on devotion, found that there were as many different ways of praying as there were individuals. Liberal Protestants accommodated contemporary culture in their devotional life, whereas fundamentalists resisted it in their spirituality while still embracing its advantages in their everyday lives. In either case, private devotions were required to keep the spirit of God alive and active in one's life. Spiritual writer Rueben Torrey (1856–1928) once observed that "no two things are more essential to a spirit-filled life than Bible reading and secret prayer." In 1962 the Supreme Court ruled that the subjection of students to official prayer is not allowed in public school classrooms. Prayer at civic public assemblies has been challenged but still finds its way into presidential inaugurations.

As for the visual arts, in his popular paintings inspired by Bible stories Warner Sallman (1892–1968) portrayed Jesus in everyday life. These pious paintings captured the imagination of millions of Christians, who displayed prints of them in their homes. Sallman's painting "Head of Christ" (1940) has been reproduced over one billion times and would be recognized by most Americans, Christian or not. Although critics dismiss art of this genre as commercial and sentimental, such art inspired devotionalism among Protestants, who traditionally had eschewed religious images, as well as among Catholics, who enjoyed a long tradition of religious art. Led by David Morgan, contemporary scholars are reexamining this art to assess its social and religious influence.

Catholics have regularly practiced a variety of devotions. Many of these center on Mary, the mother of Jesus, who is the focus of intense devotion. Catholics revere Mary and often ask her intercession with her son Jesus. Statues of Mary abound in churches and are often found in the homes of Catholics. The church devotes the month of May to Mary, and in many Catholic schools and parishes, in a May ceremony her statue is crowned with flowers by a schoolchild. Theologically, Mary is not divine but human, like all other humans. Nevertheless, some Catholics accord her privilege and homage that rivals that given to Jesus. The church has bestowed on her more titles than on Jesus. Commemorated on December 8, the Feast of the Immaculate Conception is based on the belief that Mary was from her conception without the stain of original sin, the only human besides Jesus to be so conceived. In 1854 Pope Pius IX declared the dogma of the Immaculate Conception, and in 1951 Pope Pius XII solemnly declared Mary's "Assumption"—that is, that Mary was assumed bodily into heaven at her death. This belief has fostered the notion that Mary was more than human or, at the least, a specially favored one.

One of the most popular and enduring prayers recited by Catholics is the rosary, sometimes called "Our Lady's Prayer." The rosary is prayed while holding a string of fifty-five beads connected in a circle. Five additional beads lead from the circle to a crucifix. Catholics touch each bead as they pray the "decades" (ten beads). The main prayer recited, "Hail Mary," is a tribute and petition to Mary:

Hail Mary, full of grace,

The Lord is with thee.

Blessed art thou among women

and blessed is the fruit of thy womb, Jesus.

Holy Mary, Mother of God,

Pray for us sinners now,

and at the hour of our death. Amen.

Every Catholic recognizes this prayer, and most have it committed to memory. It was a mainstay of the pre–Vatican II church (before 1962). Even though rosaries continue to sell well in religious goods stores, today many younger Catholics do not own rosary beads, could not name the various mysteries that accompany the rosary, and may only encounter "Hail Mary" during the wake of a deceased Catholic, when the priest, deacon, or perhaps a layperson leads the mourners in this prayer.

"Novenas," devotional prayers recited over a nine-day period that are devoted exclusively to Mary, have also been a form of popular piety among Catholics. These prayers might be conducted by a group or said privately by an individual. Novenas said over the course of the first Friday in the month of nine months in a row were very popular in the pre–Vatican II church and continue to be a prayer form today for some Catholics.

Devotion to Jesus takes many forms among Catholics, from prayer cards with artistic depictions of Jesus to statues of the Sacred Heart of Jesus, which is graphically depicted in the plaster form. The devotion to the Sacred Heart began in France in the late seventeenth century in response to the visions reported by Margaret Mary Alacoque, a Visitandine nun. Pope Pius IX (1846–1878) popularized the devotions throughout the church, beatified (the step before canonization as a saint) the French nun, and created the Feast of the Sacred Heart, which is celebrated throughout the church. American Catholics took up the practice of reverence to the Sacred Heart, creating Societies of the Sacred Heart, which promoted devotions and encouraged Catholics to have statues of the Sacred Heart in their homes.

Eucharistic adoration is another form of Catholic devotion to Jesus. American Catholics appropriated European practices for the "Blessed Sacrament"—that is, the "host" (the small wafer Catholics receive at Communion). The host is displayed in an elaborate holder or chalice, called a "monstrance." It is worshipped in a ritual known as the Benediction during visits to the Blessed Sacrament, which is kept in a receptacle called a "tabernacle" outside of liturgical celebrations. In perpetual adoration the host is displayed in the church for Catholics to worship at all hours of the day. These are just some of the devotional practices surrounding what Catholics believe to be the body of Christ.

The veneration of saints is another form of Catholic devotionalism. Catholics revere saints as model Christians. Many religious orders (groups of nuns, brothers, or priests) were founded to imitate a particular saint (for example, the Franciscans follow the twelfth-century Saint Francis of Assisi and the Jesuits follow the sixteenth-century Saint Ignatius of Loyola). Catholics believe that the saints not only provide a model for spiritual life but also can intercede for them with God. Specific saints have been identified as particularly helpful in specific domains. Thus Saint Lucy, a martyr whose eyes were gouged out, helps believers' eyesight; Saint Anthony, a medieval Franciscan monk, helps to find lost items; and Saint Jude the Apostle, often depicted with a flame around his head, is the patron of hopeless causes to whom many critically ill people turn for help.

Catholic devotionalism was addressed by the bishops and the pope at the Second Vatican Council (1962–1965). In *Sacrosanctum Concilium* the Council stated, "Such devotions should be so drawn up that they harmonize with the liturgical seasons, accord with the sacred liturgy, and are in some ways derived from it, lead the people to it, since in fact the liturgy by its very nature is far superior to any of them."

Some observers interpreted the council documents as a signal that Catholics should limit their expressions of devotion to Mary. Concerned that Marian piety might suffer a serious decline, Pope Paul VI issued *Marialis Cultus* (Devotion to Mary) in 1974 in an attempt to renew devotion to the mother of Jesus. To further encourage continued esteem for Mary among Catholics, in 1987 Pope John Paul II issued *Redemptoris Mater* (Mother of the Redeemer), in which he declared 1988 a "Marian Year." This year of remembrance of Mary was not designed to undermine the council's guidance in understanding Mary. Instead, it was "meant to promote a new and more careful reading of what the Council said about the Blessed Virgin Mary, Mother of God, in the mystery of Christ and of the Church. . . . Here we speak not only of the doctrine of faith but also of the life of faith, and thus of authentic 'Marian spirituality,' seen in the light of Tradition, and especially the spirituality to which the Council exhorts us."

Mary continues to play a significant role in Catholic piety, as testified by the millions who practice personal devotion to her. The church dedicates several feast days in the liturgical calendar to Mary. That devotion even carries over into the public world of the Internet. The Web site "Catholic Online" (www.catholic.org) carries a dedication to Our Lady of Guadalupe, and numerous other Web sites are also dedicated to those who are devoted to Mary. The Virgin Mary thus remains a key figure in Catholic art, theology, devotion, and piety. Interpretations of her today are not as uniform as they were in the 1950s, but her importance to Catholic culture cannot be underestimated.

Although Protestants and Catholics have been the most prominent religious communities in the history of the United States, recently they have been joined by members of other religions, most of them immigrants. The Pluralism Project, headed by Diana Eck of Harvard University, has identified the locations of these groups and mapped a multireligious America. The following sections describe some of these religious communities and some aspects of their devotionalism.

## Hindu Devotionalism

Much of the Hindu community practices a ritual devotion known as *bhakti,* a word derived from ancient Sanskrit that means devotion focused on a deity. The two major gods, Shiva and Vishnu, are the primary subjects of intense devotion, but other gods and goddesses (Ganesh and Devi are two prominent examples) receive significant devotional attention as well. *Puja,* a devotional ceremony for a god or goddess, can be conducted in the temple or at home, either with a group

Hinduism is filled with devotions to gods and goddesses. Here, a young Hindu prays in front of a Lingam, symbol of the god Shiva. These symbols, often made of stone, are found throughout India, usually in temples, and are the objects of devotion. Hindus anoint them with oil, place garlands of flowers on them, and pray before them. Shiva is the creator god whose symbol resembles male and female organs of creation. In Hinduism, the two major gods, Shiva and Vishnu, are the primary subjects of intense devotion, but other gods and goddesses receive significant devotional attention as well.

or alone, led by a priest or a layperson. *Puja* often includes flowers to adorn a god or goddess image, oil to anoint the image, and food as an offering. For the convenience of worshippers, Hindu temples in the United States sometimes combine the most popular gods, Shiva and Vishnu, which are normally worshipped in separate temples in India.

American Hindus continue to practice traditions that originated in India but adjust them to suit the U.S. context. The community's Hawaii-based publication, *Hinduism Today,* reaches out to Hindus outside of India, many of whom are second- or third-generation Hindus living in cultures dominated by other religions.

Hindus revere their gurus (wise teachers) and practice devotion to them by bringing gifts of flowers, money, and other goods. One popular guru is Sri Sathya Sai Baba (1926–) who lives in India but has many American Hindu and non-Hindu devotees. His followers believe that he is an *avatar,* an incarnation of the divine being. Seeing him in person is considered *darshan,* the equivalent of seeing a god. Numerous Web sites are devoted to Sai Baba, and devotees from around the world travel to his home in Puttatarthi, Andhra Pradesh, India. Many attribute miraculous healings and other extraordinary happenings to his power. Skeptics abound as well. The Sai Organization sponsors civic activities designed to improve conditions for individuals and communities. For example, in 2008 it sponsored a free medical camp to provide medical screenings. The event was acknowledged by a proclamation from the mayor of Saint Louis declaring June 7, 2008, "St. Louis Medical Camp Day."

Krishna, an incarnation of God, is a major figure from the Indian literature, especially the *Mahabharata.* Devotees to Krishna say prayers to the god, decorate his statue, and invoke his blessing. A worldwide movement called Hare Krishna attracted American followers and has proved controversial in its methods of obtaining and retaining members.

## Buddhist Devotionalism

Even though the Buddha discouraged devotion to him, some forms of Buddhism exhibit elements of devotionalism. The Buddha taught that the *dharma* (the way to enlightenment) is far more important than any form of devotion. Nevertheless, Buddhists practice a deep devotion to the Buddha as well as to his teachings. The Buddha himself said that "respect and homage paid to those who are worthy of it, is a great blessing." Buddhist temples house statues of the Buddha. Thus devotional expressions of reverence and gratitude play a role in Buddhist spirituality. In some parts of the world, *stupas,* containing relics of the Buddha, are revered pilgrimage sites.

In many Buddhist communities another aspect of devotionalism is ancestors, whose pictures and memories are cherished through offerings such as flowers and food.

In Buddhist centers and temples in the United States, as elsewhere in the world, there are often prayer wheels containing sacred scriptures. Devotees can spin the wheels to gain merit. Some centers and temples also have prominent bells that are used in ceremonies. Especially over the last fifty years or so, Buddhists have constructed gathering places in many states to serve a diverse immigrant and indigenous population of followers. These vary from Zen centers and simple converted residences to elaborate temples, some of which are associated with monasteries. Some structures have exquisitely designed gardens that house statues of the Buddha. Rituals vary from quiet mediation to chanting, mirroring the types of Buddhism practiced in countries such as Sri Lanka, Vietnam, South Korea, China, and Japan.

Many Americans, both Buddhist and non-Buddhist, practice *Vipassana* meditation, which originated in South Asian *Theravadan* Buddhism. This exercise is intended to calm the spirit and focus the mind. Directed toward the connection between mind and body, the meditation offers techniques to help one see reality or one's permanent nature. It is intended to purify the mind, allowing one to live in peace.

The Nichiren Buddhist Church of America, which has its origins in a form of Japanese Buddhism, practices a chant called *daimoku* that emphasizes the importance of the Buddhist text, the *Lotus Sutra.* Buddhists conduct these chants in groups or individually at home in front of a scroll (a *gohonzon*) representing the *Lotus Sutra.* Many also use strings of beads similar to a rosary to aid their concentration. These rituals are conducted by laity without the leadership of a monk or priest. They also have devotional regard for *lamas* (Tibetan or Mongolian Buddhist monks), some of whom they consider incarnations of *bodhisattvas* (enlightened beings).

## Jain Devotionalism

The Jain community in North America is small but fervent, with temples dotting the American landscape. When Jains pray, they use a set of 108 beads, each of which represents a quality of the supreme beings. Jains visit temples but also offer rituals and prayers in their homes. They bow and recite *mantras* (prayers) several times a day, the most common of which is the *Nasvkar Mantra,* which reminds Jains that one is not to cling to worldly life. Among the rituals practiced by Jains is the *pratikraman,* in which the devotee acknowledges and repents of his or her mistakes and asks forgiveness. They also read their scriptures and meditate regularly. Jains revere monks and nuns, bowing down before them in an act called *vandana.* This act humbles the person and inspires him or her to emulate nuns and monks. If no monk or nun is available, they bow in the direction of the northeast to *arihantas* (those whose souls are about to liberated and who live far away). Jains also assume a steady posture to control the body during meditation and to indicate the superiority of the soul over the body.

## African Diaspora Devotionalism

African rituals and devotions are practiced in America by descendants of Africans. The practice of Santería, brought to the United States via Cuba, which, in turn, received it from West Africa, includes forms of devotionalism. Santería, a form of African religion that incorporates aspects of Catholicism, is practiced in Cuba and parts of the United States in Caribbean-American communities. Practitioners interact with *orishas* (the elemental powers of life) in rituals and devotions. Yoruba rituals are often carried out in the homes of senior priests or priestesses. In Hispanic neighborhoods in New York or Miami, small stores sell candles, beads, oils, and statues of saints that are used in the devotion practiced in Santería.

Devotionalism also plays a role in African American churches in the United States. Wednesday night prayer meetings are common, as well as the use of devotional literature meant to inform and inspire. African slaves were introduced to Christianity as far back as the American revivals. Many became Christians, affiliating in particular with the Methodists and Baptists. They also conducted their own spirited devotions in secret in slave dwellings.

## Mormon Devotionalism

The Church of Jesus Christ of Latter-day Saints has rituals that are closed to nonmembers. Many of the church's temples are striking examples of architecture that stand out for their beauty and size. These temples have multiple rooms, bereft of liturgical symbols, and most are reserved exclusively for Mormons and devoted to various forms of worship. The first of these temples was built in 1836 in Kirtland, Ohio, and the best known is located in Salt Lake City, Utah, where the Mormon Tabernacle Choir regularly performs. In addition to the formal ceremonies in the temple, Mormons hold a "Family Home Evening" each Monday, during which they recite devotionals found in church manuals, learn elements of the faith, and participate in family activities.

## Jewish Devotionalism

Jewish worship usually takes place communally in a temple or synagogue; however, Jews do practice particular devotions individually or in groups. Before prayer, Jews customarily center their thoughts. The practice is called *kavvanah,* a term that generally translates as the intention to direct one's prayers to God, close or cover one's eyes, and concentrate on the prayer and its meaning in order to avoid making the prayer simply routine. Jewish prayer books are called *siddurim.* Traditionally, ten adults (a *minyan*) are required if prayers are recited outloud. Orthodox Jews permit only men in this count, whereas Conservative and Reform Judaism permit both men and women to participate. Prayers may also be read silently by an individual. The prayers should be read or recited in Hebrew, the "sacred tongue." Thus most American Jews seek to learn at least enough Hebrew to recite the prayers. A young Jew coming of age demonstrates his or her proficiency in the language at his or her *bar mitzvah* (for boys) or *bat mitzvah* (for girls). Orthodox and Hassidic Jews permit only the boy's ceremony.

Many Jews in America mark their homes by attaching a *mezuzah* to their doorpost. Derived from the Hebrew word for doorpost, a *mezuzah* contains a small scroll with biblical passages, *shema,* taken from the books of Deuteronomy and Exodus. Occupants and guests touch the *mezuzah* as they enter or exit the home, reminding them of their dependence upon God.

*Shabbat* (or Sabbath, from the Hebrew word for rest) is observed from sunset on Friday night through Saturday at sunset. Those observing *Shabbat* light the Sabbath candles, bless members of the family, recite the *kiddush,* a blessing recited over the wine and special bread (hallah), and refrain from certain kinds of work in order to devote time to prayer and contemplation. Families often celebrate this religious observance with guests. Orthodox and Conservative Jews often adhere more strictly to these practices than Reform Jews, who may or may not perform the rituals of *Shabbat* and may or may not refrain from work.

*Zekhut Abot* is a devotion to ancestors whom Jews believe will pray on their behalf. This devotion can be practiced at any time, but it is especially popular during the high holy days of Rosh Hashanah (New Year's Day) and Yom Kippur (Day of Atonement).

Jews recognize 613 religious commandments, *mitsvot,* inscribed in the Torah. They include everything from hanging the *mezuzah* to circumcision practices to keeping kosher. Although many American Jews may not abide by the majority of these *mitsvot,* these laws are the basis of traditional Judaism and the foundation of many present-day devotional practices that are still observed.

Part of Jewish law revolves around the proper preparation of food. Some observant Jews follow these laws, keeping kosher homes in which meat and dairy dishes cannot be mixed for consumption and must be served on separate dishware. The preparation of kosher foods is approved by rabbis before the foods are sold. Kosher foods are often packaged in America with a notation authenticating that they have been prepared according to these rules.

## Muslim Devotionalism

Islam forbids images of God because the religion holds that God (Allah) is completely transcendent and thus is not part of creation; creation is completely separate from God and is designed to give praise to God. For Muslims, devotion means living in God's presence and striving for a blameless life. Islam does not include icons, because Muslims are careful not to present images of God or to equate any material thing with God. The only images permitted are quotations from the Qu'ran and nonrepresentational art that is usually in a geometric form that depicts infinite patterns, indicating the expansiveness of God. However, some Muslims, particularly in the Sufi tradition, practice elaborate dance rituals accompanied by music.

One of the "five pillars of Islam" (the requirements of the religion) is that adherents pray five times a day. *Islam* means "submit," and Muslims are asked to submit to God. Before prayer, Muslims participate in a purification ritual, using water to cleanse the body externally, which also symbolizes internal purification. Bowing in the direction of Mecca, worshippers perform a specified number of movements while reciting verses of the Qu'ran. Often they perform this ritual on a prayer rug. These prayers can be performed at a mosque but usually are conducted in private settings.

In North America the number of Muslims has grown in recent decades, In recent years American presidents have noted Eid, the Muslim celebrations marking the breaking of the fast at the end of Ramadan (*Eid al-Fitr*) and commemorating Abraham's complete faithfulness when God asked him to sacrifice his son Isaac (*Eid al-Adha*). In 2001

the U.S. Postal Service issued a stamp commemorating the feasts. Some observant Muslims follow dietary laws (halal), similar in nature to Jewish dietary laws, including avoidance of pork and shellfish, and requiring certain procedures for the slaughtering of animals. Halal foods have a notation indicating that the food has been properly prepared, as determined by a religious authority.

## Native American Devotionalism

Native Americans practiced their religions long before America was settled by Europeans, and they continue to maintain these practices today. Because this community is so diverse, any attempt to describe all of their devotional practices is not practical, but some commonalities are found among the many tribes that make up this population. Unlike many religious communities—in particular, Christian ones—Native Americans do not make a clear demarcation between the natural and the supernatural. Thus the material and the spiritual coexist so that sacrality is identified within the natural environment. Many tribes have also selectively adapted Christian practices to accommodate their own worldview. This religious syncretism includes practices derived from at least two (and sometimes more) traditions.

Native Americans often find their deities in nature, so they have a particular reverence for elements of nature such as streams, mountains, and valleys. In the past and sometimes today, this reverence may be displayed by paying special homage to nature. For example, in the ritual surrounding death the Catawba Nation would blow ashes on the dead to appease the spirit. The Muskogee Indians maintained a sacred fire that connected them to the Maker of Breath and their ancestors and therefore had to be kept unpolluted. The Natchez observed a cult of the sun as a deity who had a son who came to earth and brought them special customs and eventually resided in a stone that was preserved in a temple and revered. Other tribes used (and continue to use) special structures called "sweat lodges" in their rituals. Even though many Native Americans have embraced mainstream forms of Christianity, they continue to practice their own ancient devotions as well. Many tribes also perform holy dances that put them in touch with and pay homage to the spirits.

## Conclusion

The diverse American religious landscape has given rise to multiple forms of devotionalism. With the exception of Native American traditions and, to a degree, Mormonism, all of these expressions of religiosity have been developed elsewhere and then adopted and adapted for the American context. Generally, devotions that are particular to a world religion and developed over time in both the place of origin of the religion and in locales around the world where the religion is widely practiced make their way to the United States via immigrants. These religious adherents adopt and alter devotions as is appropriate to the American context, usually without losing the qualities and particularities that define them. Thus a Jew from Israel would recognize devotions practiced by American Jews, and Catholics from other countries would recognize the devotions of American Catholics. The same applies to Buddhists, Hindus, Jains, Muslims, and others. These practices are not unique to American communities but are specific expressions of often universal practices. These are, after all, transnational communities.

Nor are devotional practices usually unalloyed. Many religious traditions combine a variety of beliefs that may include some semblance of magic, fate, and the occult. Sometimes even a trained observer cannot separate the superstition from the genuine devotion. But believers hold that their devotionalism bears fruit in this life and likely in the next. Thus those who practice devotion in its many forms believe that saints grant favors, gurus help on the path to enlightenment and liberation from the bonds of earthly life, and prayers uttered in secret are heard by God. One does not need to be an official of the religion to participate in and benefit from devotion. It complements the texts, rituals, and teachings of the religion and connects believers to the sacred in a myriad of ways that suit a variety of spiritual interests. In no country on earth is this religious expression more varied than in the United States, home of the most diverse religious population the world has ever witnessed.

The link between devotionalism and "lived religion" is a close one. Studying the doctrines of religion differs from observing the practices, including devotions, in which ordinary believers engage ("lived religion") whether sanctioned or unsanctioned by religious officials. Devotionalism is sometimes embraced by institutional religion and sometimes resisted. When embraced, it can become integral to the religion. In any case, it represents a vibrant, living, and changing dimension of religious expression. Some forms of devotion have significant roots in the tradition and long histories, but some forms come and go, following cultural patterns and serving a spiritual need for a limited time and often for a particular audience.

**See also** *Celebrity Culture; Latino/a Religious Practice; Lived Religion; Spirituality; Spirituality: Contemporary Trends; Worship* entries.

Chester Gillis

## BIBLIOGRAPHY

Ball, Ann. *Encyclopedia of Catholic Devotions and Practices.* Huntington, Ind.: Our Sunday Visitor, 2003.

Cort, John E. "Singing the Glory of Ascetisim: Devotion of Asceticism in Jainism." *Journal of the American Academy of Religion* 70 (December 2002): 719–742.

Eck, Diana. *A New Religious America: How a "Christian Country" Has Become the World's Most Diverse Nation.* San Francisco: Harper, 2001.

Haddad, Yvonne, Jane Smith, and John Esposito, eds. *Religion and Immigration: Christian, Jewish, and Muslim Experiences in the United States.* Lanham, Md.: AltaMira Press, 2003.

Hammer, Reuven. *Entering Jewish Prayer: A Guide to Personal Devotion and the Worship Service.* New York: Schocken, 1995.

McDannell, Colleen. *Material Christianity: Religion and Popular Culture in America.* 2nd ed. New Haven, Conn.: Yale University Press, 1998.

———, ed. *Religions of the United States in Practice.* 2 vols. Princeton, N.J.: Princeton University Press, 2001.

McGreevy, John T. "Bronx Miracle." *American Quarterly* 52 (September 2000): 405–443.

Morgan, David, ed. *Icons of American Protestantism: The Art of Warner Sallman.* New Haven, Conn.: Yale University Press, 1996.

———. *Key Words in Religion, Media and Culture.* New York: Routledge, 2008.

Murphy, Joseph M. *Working the Spirit: Ceremonies of the African Diaspora.* Boston: Beacon Press, 1995.

Neusner, Jacob, ed. *World Religions in America.* 3rd ed. Louisville, Ky.: Westminster John Knox, 2003.

Orsi, Robert. *The Madonna of 115th Street: Faith and Community in Italian Harlem, 1880–1950.* 2nd ed. New Haven, Conn.: Yale University Press, 2002.

Ostrander, Richard. "The Battery and the Windmill: Two Models of Protestant Devotionalism in Early-Twentieth-Century America." *Church History* 65 (March 1996): 42–61.

O'Toole, James M., ed. *Habits of Devotion: Catholic Religious Practice in Twentieth-Century America.* Ithaca, N.Y.: Cornell University Press, 2005.

Phan, Peter C., ed. *Directory on Popular Piety and the Liturgy: Principles and Guidelines, A Commentary.* Collegeville, Minn.: Liturgical Press, 2005.

Taves, Ann. *The Household of Faith: Roman Catholic Devotions in Mid-Nineteenth-Century America.* Notre Dame, Ind.: University of Notre Dame Press, 1986.

# Disciples of Christ

Disciples of Christ is a Protestant denomination in the Reformed tradition. It has its roots within the Stone-Campbell movement on the American frontier in the early nineteenth century. Officially known as the Christian Church (Disciples of Christ), the denomination is composed of about 3,850 congregations and 700,000 members in the United States and Canada. Disciples congregations are also found in Australia and New Zealand, but in Britain Disciples congregations have joined the United Church.

The denomination describes itself as "a movement for wholeness in a fragmented world." As such a movement, it provides the means for its individual congregations to cooperate in a variety of educational, mission, service, and advocacy programs. Representatives of congregations gather for deliberation and worship in a biennial general assembly. The denomination is a member of the National Council of Churches USA and the World Council of Churches. It also participates in Churches Uniting in Christ and maintains fraternal relationships with many church bodies.

## Origins

The Disciples' early leadership was motivated by the profound conviction that the multiplicity of denominations was contrary to biblical teaching and an impediment to Christian evangelism. This conviction drove a commitment to the restoration of the unity of the church, which Disciples believed could be achieved on the basis of a simple affirmation that Jesus is the Christ and a return to the practices of earliest Christianity. Early Disciples shared the widespread belief among Anglo-American Protestants that divisions among denominations were caused by distinctive beliefs and practices that were largely irrelevant to the Christian message. Christian evangelism required an appeal to the Bible alone, leaving to individual interpretation issues that were not clearly mandated or prohibited in scripture.

These views were shared by several restorationist movements of the period. Disciples were most closely associated with two of these movements: that of Thomas Campbell (1763–1854) and his son, Alexander (1788–1866), in Pennsylvania and Virginia, and that of Barton Stone (1772–1844) in Kentucky. After 1832 the leaders of these groups agreed to unite their efforts. Initially linked by the writing and preaching of a few influential leaders, most notably Alexander Campbell, the Disciples of Christ congregations were in fact independent; they recognized no authority beyond the local congregation. Campbell's journal, *The Millennial Harbinger,* reflected his postmillennial views, which were shared by many Americans of this period.

This movement for unity grew rapidly in the nineteenth century, with individual congregations adopting a variety of names: Christian Church, Disciples of Christ, and Churches of Christ. However, the nascent denomination eventually faced division within its own ranks, caused not only by social and cultural factors as American society changed, but also by inherent tensions between its appeal for church unity and its effort to mandate or prohibit specific church organization

and practices based on biblical interpretation. The Churches of Christ, which rejected instrumental music on biblical grounds, were separately enumerated from 1906. Another group of Christian Churches became disillusioned with the growing theological liberalism and denominational development among Disciples and so separated in 1971.

## Distinctive Beliefs and Practices

Because most early leaders among the Disciples had Presbyterian backgrounds, many of their theological positions are rooted in that tradition. Their worship pattern also follows that tradition and includes scripture readings, hymns, prayers, a sermon, and communion. But to this tradition Disciples have brought their own distinctive understandings, reflecting both their reading of the Bible and the social conditions of their time and place. Many of those views continue to shape Disciple thought and practice today. Insisting on the sole authority of the scripture in matters of faith and practice, for example, Disciples reject all creeds, including the Apostles' and Nicene creeds, as determinative in church life and as tests of fellowship. Instead, they insist on the primitive affirmation that "Jesus is the Christ" as the only doctrinal requirement for church membership. Similarly, although early Disciples shared with Presbyterians and other Protestants of the time an understanding of faith as belief in the testimony of scripture that should lead the believer to repentance and baptism, they derive from this idea the conviction that Christian commitment is the product of reason rather than emotion and tend to be suspicious of sudden, supernatural conversion experiences.

Disciples have developed distinctive views of baptism, communion, and clerical status based on their understanding of the earliest Christian practices, as reflected in Acts of the Apostles. Alexander Campbell became convinced that a believer's baptism by immersion was scripturally mandated. He allowed himself to be immersed, and thereafter he and other Disciples insisted that immersion was the only proper mode of entry into the church. That position prevailed well into the twentieth century, although early in that century several congregations began to adopt a position of "open membership"—that is, persons who had been baptized as infants were admitted into full Communion without immersion. Controversial at the time, that position is today the practice of the vast majority of Disciples of Christ congregations, and Disciples recognize the validity of baptism regardless of when or how it is administered.

For Disciples, celebration of the Lord's Supper was a central element in the life of the earliest church. Thus they insist that the service of Communion be celebrated no less often than weekly. Their theological understanding of the service differs little from that of other Reformed tradition Protestants, but it occupies a more central place in their common life. The Disciples' separation from Presbyterians was caused in part by the Disciples' conviction that the invitation to the table should be extended to all Christians—a view not generally held at the time. From the outset, Disciples therefore have insisted that the invitation to communion is an invitation from the Lord and that all Christians are welcome regardless of denominational affiliation.

The democratization of American society in the early nineteenth century reinforced for Disciples the Protestant principle of the priesthood of believers. In addition to ordained pastoral leadership, their congregations are served by lay persons commonly designated as elders and deacons. Earlier it was common to ordain elders as well as pastors, but this practice is not in place today. Deacons have always been regarded as lay persons. Although early Disciples restricted clerical offices to men, today women serve in all positions of church leadership, both lay and clerical. Disciples reject hierarchical conceptions of clergy, but early Disciples sometimes used the term *bishop* to designate the pastoral leader of a congregation. Such usage is now rare.

## Denominational Development

The Disciples of Christ evolved from those groups within the broader Stone–Campbell tradition who were more sympathetic to the tradition's appeal for ecumenism and more open to social and cultural changes that marked America's transition from a rural and agricultural society to an urban and industrial one. As the movement grew, the need for organizational structure beyond the congregational level became apparent to many, including Alexander Campbell himself, and a general convention of Disciples was convened in 1849 with delegates from congregations in eleven states. This gathering granted voting rights in this and subsequent conventions to all who chose to participate. It approved the work of the American Christian Bible Society and created the American Christian Missionary Society to encourage evangelism. Similar organizations followed at the state level, and a Christian Woman's Board of Missions and a Foreign Christian Missionary Society were founded after the Civil War. The convention and the societies, although dependent on individual support, became the foundation of a developing denominational structure.

The Disciples' claim that all questions on the life of the church could be resolved by an appeal to the teachings of scripture was soon shown to be problematic; too often they found the scripture to be silent or ambiguous on issues on which there was disagreement. Even though their very modest and weak cooperative structure enabled Disciples to avoid formal division over slavery during the Civil War era, the profound tensions engendered by that crisis were evident in controversies during the postwar era that led to division by the end of the century. One source of conflict was the work of the societies created for activities beyond the congregational level. Although those who took the name Churches of Christ insisted that the societies lacked biblical warrant and therefore were unacceptable, Disciples regarded them as an appropriate means of cooperation in Christian work beyond the scope of a single congregation. They argued that the societies were organized as private corporations, made no claims to be churches, and therefore posed no problems for a biblical ecclesiology, which, for them, focused on the congregational community. Another major conflict arose when prosperity permitted larger churches to introduce organs. Conservatives within the movement rejected them as unscriptural, whereas Disciples of Christ welcomed this enhancement of worship as useful and not prohibited in scripture. In these and several less significant controversies, Disciples have come to accept new ways of conducting church life, which they regard as sensible when they are not clearly contrary to scripture. Their position represents an appeal both to scripture and to reason and experience, reflecting the pragmatic temperament of the society in which their position was shaped.

Disciples, like most American Protestants, were caught up in the modernist–fundamentalist controversy of the 1920s and 1930s. For Disciples, the controversy arose from disagreements over the conduct of foreign missions, as well as over the presentation of the denominational position at home. However, because Disciples had no creed by which to test the orthodoxy of individuals, this struggle centered largely on biblical interpretation and attitudes toward newer forms of biblical criticism.

Beginning in the latter years of the nineteenth century, traditional assumptions about interpretation of scripture were assaulted by a group of scholars whose approach was later called "higher criticism." That approach opened the books of scripture to examination of their historical background and reliability, authorship, date, and literary characteristics, among other things. In doing so, it threatened the rather legalistic use of scripture by earlier Disciples, as well as their conviction that all matters in dispute among Christians might be resolved by a simple appeal to a consistently clear and unambiguous text. Consequently, the Disciples' initial reaction was quite negative. J. W. McGarvey (1829–1911) became professor of sacred scripture at the College of the Bible in 1865, and from that influential post he defended a view of scripture as presenting a fixed pattern of truth that Christians were simply to accept and implement. By means of his academic post and as a columnist for the *Christian Standard,* McGarvey had a profound impact on Disciples during the latter years of the century. For many, his *Standard* filled the place occupied earlier by Alexander Campbell's *Millennial Harbinger.* However, as Disciples students moved from denominational schools into major universities, they began to be shaped by the newer biblical studies. Just as McGarvey was an example of the older biblical scholarship, Herbert Lockwood Willett (1864–1944) was representative of the new. Like McGarvey, Willett studied at Bethany College as an undergraduate. However, Willett went on to pursue his studies at Yale University, where he embraced the newer biblical scholarship. From there, he followed William Rainey Harper, one of the most distinguished biblical scholars of the time, to the University of Chicago. There, Willett completed a doctoral degree in biblical studies and became the first dean of the Disciples Divinity House. He and his successors in that post provided a critical center for the education of Disciples leaders in the newer approach to Bible study over the next half-century. They created the Campbell Institute, a national organization of Disciples sympathetic to the newer scholarship, and popularized these views in *The Scroll.*

In the early years of the twentieth century, the two methods of biblical study reflecting conservative and liberal theological temperaments struggled for dominance among Disciples, but increasingly the newer views were favored by Disciples. The newer biblical studies liberated them from much of their earlier biblical legalism and rendered possible an effective dialogue between Bible and culture, as well as effective cooperation with other denominational groups in ecumenical affairs. By mid-century the newer approach was clearly dominant in the churches and seminaries of the denomination. Disciples moved decisively toward what was becoming the liberal mainstream of American Protestantism.

In 1957 the denomination appointed a Panel of Scholars. Composed of some of the denomination's ablest scholars and reflecting the theological ferment and transformation of the time, this group met for three years to restudy the doctrines and practices of Disciples and to analyze practical issues and problems confronting the church from a theological perspective. The panel completed its work and published its findings and recommendations in 1963. The panel's work was valued, and its published reports were widely studied throughout the denomination. The concerns that underlay appointment of the panel also led to the creation of a continuing theological study group, the Association of Disciples for Theological Discussion (ADTD). The ADTD, an association of Disciples scholars from private and state universities as well as denominational colleges and seminaries, began to meet annually in 1957. It identifies and analyzes common problems and encourages theological dialogue both among its members and within the denomination as a whole.

In parallel with their twentieth-century theological transformation and related to it, Disciples undertook a succession of institutional adjustments designed to provide a more effective and coherent denominational organization and ministry. The earlier general convention had simply provided a venue in which their various societies conducted annual meetings. Seeking greater coherence for denominational programs, Disciples replaced the general convention in 1917 with an International Convention to which the societies submitted reports and from which they received recommendations. A cooperative program of fund-raising was then created to support all denominational programs. In 1950 Disciples further strengthened their management of cooperative programs by forming a Council of Agencies, in which all of the organizations reporting to the International Convention worked to achieve agreement on programs and funding. The council proposed further structural reorganization, and in 1960 the International Convention appointed a Commission on Restructure. In 1967 the commission presented a Design for the Christian Church (Disciples of Christ), which was ratified the following year. This document provided for the creation of a General Assembly to replace the convention and for regional assemblies, and it designated the old agencies as general units of the church. The chief executive officer of the church is called the general minister and president. Although congregations retain independence, corporate unity is reinforced through decisions made by elected representatives from congregations and regions.

## Attitude Toward Learning

Insisting that the Bible alone was sufficient for understanding faith and church and that theology represented an imposition of human opinion upon the simple message of the Bible, Disciples initially emphasized study of the Bible within the context of a liberal arts education. Theological seminaries were founded rather late in the development of the denomination. The Disciples' first college-level institution was Bacon College in Kentucky. Named for Francis Bacon, this college of arts and sciences also included courses in biblical studies, as did Campbell's Bethany College in western Virginia, the Disciples' second college. Bacon College later merged into what is today Transylvania University, and these two schools established a pattern that generally has been followed by other colleges of this denomination—combining the study of arts and sciences with the study of scripture.

In post–Civil War America, as state universities experienced more rapid growth than church-related colleges, Disciples sought to expand the inclusion of biblical studies in liberal arts curricula by establishing denomination-funded "Bible chairs" in state universities. These chairs, funded by the denomination, entered into agreements with the universities, enabling them to offer courses in Bible and related religious studies that were considered part of the institution's curriculum. The first such chair was established at the University of Michigan, and subsequently in Missouri, Kansas, Texas, Virginia, Georgia, and elsewhere. Some of these programs continue, although many have been replaced by religious studies programs of the universities themselves.

Theological education among Disciples evolved from the biblical studies departments in their liberal arts colleges, as it became apparent that the preparation of parish clergy in an urbanizing and modernizing America required a more demanding curriculum. Transylvania's Department of Bible became the College of the Bible in 1865, and today is known as Lexington Theological Seminary. Similar developments occurred in other Disciple colleges and universities, and more recently the seminaries have become independently governed institutions. Today Disciples maintain four seminaries: Brite Divinity School in Fort Worth, Texas; Christian Theological Seminary in Indianapolis, Indiana;

Lexington Theological Seminary in Lexington, Kentucky; and Phillips Theological Seminary in Tulsa, Oklahoma. All of these seminaries draw faculty from many denominations and serve students from many other denominations, as well as those from the Disciples.

The Bible chair pattern of establishing close relationships with non-Disciple educational institutions has been replicated at the graduate level. In 1894 Disciples established a Divinity House in association with the Divinity School of the University of Chicago, and similar institutions have been established in association with Yale Divinity School, Vanderbilt Divinity School, and Claremont Theological Cluster and Graduate Theological Union in California. As a result of these relationships, a large portion of the faculty of Disciples seminaries and college-level religious studies programs is drawn from these schools, especially Chicago and Yale, and significant numbers of parish clergy are similarly educated in these and other ecumenical institutions. This distinctive pattern of ministerial education undoubtedly reinforces the ecumenical commitment of contemporary Disciples.

## Ecumenical Relationships

Advocacy of Christian unity has been central to the proclamation of Disciples since their beginning. The denomination has been shaped by Thomas Campbell's assertion in 1809 "that the Church of Christ upon earth is essentially, intentionally and constitutionally one; consisting of all those in every place that profess their faith in Christ and obedience to him in all things according to the Scriptures, and that manifest the same by their tempers and conduct." The centrality of the Disciples' advocacy of Christian unity thrust the denomination into the forefront of the ecumenical movement, beginning in mission fields where Disciples were early advocates of comity agreements and interdenominational schools and programs. In 1910 Disciples created an ecumenical office, now the Council on Christian Unity, and they also enthusiastically endorsed the church federation movement. Indeed, they were founding members of the Federal Council of Churches, the National Council of Churches USA, and the World Council of Churches. More recently Disciples participated in the Consultation on Church Union, and since its formation in 2002 they have participated in Churches Uniting in Christ. They maintain close relationships with many denominations and share with the United Church of Christ a common program of mission. Disciples also cultivate relationships with other groups tracing their history to the Stone-Campbell movement. For example, the denomination participates in the World Convention of Churches of Christ, which was formed in 1930 and conducts mass meetings every four years. And it supports the Disciples of Christ Historical Society, the major repository for materials related to the Stone-Campbell movement.

## Roles of Women and Minorities

The early role of women in the Disciples reflected the common patriarchal patterns of the early nineteenth century. However, women were occasionally ordained in the latter years of that century. Meanwhile, women founded the first Disciple missionary society and have been active in all areas of church life over the history of the denomination. Today, Disciple seminaries reflect the gender balance of American society, and women exercise pastoral and congregational leadership throughout the denomination where they serve as pastors, elders, and deacons. Disciples selected Sharon E. Watkins as their first female general minister and president in 2005.

Similarly, the role of minorities in the church initially followed and more recently anticipated the trajectory of American society generally. African Americans were attracted to the new denomination and to pastoral responsibilities early in its history. However, during the Jim Crow era a separate National Convention was created by this increasingly segregated community. Agreement was reached in 1960 to merge the National and International Conventions, and the merger was formalized in 1969. Disciples congregations are now including more and more members with diverse racial and ethnic backgrounds, but support groups within the denomination continue to address the special interests of those congregations identifying themselves as African American, Asian American, or Hispanic. Yet all participate in the General Assembly and the work of the denomination at local and regional levels. Those congregations serving immigrant communities are among the most rapidly growing within the denomination.

## Impact on American Religious Life

The Disciples of Christ both reflected and contributed to shaping the democratic ethos of the early nineteenth century. Their insistence upon the right and duty of the individual Christian to study, to think, and to respond with integrity to the Gospel located them among a variety of religious, political, and economic forces contributing to the democratization of American society. Although the denomination developed in an age of revivalism and participated in that movement, their conviction that faith is born of reason rather than of intense experience and their concern with Christian nurture offers Americans an alternative understanding of the process whereby one enters into Christian life.

The Disciples' insistence on the centrality of Communion in worship, a view they adopted through the classic Protestant appeal to scripture, links them to the Anglican and Catholic traditions, even as other aspects of their worship life link them to the Reformed tradition. And yet Disciples combine their understanding of worship as involving the eucharistic celebration with the affirmation that every Christian of every tradition should be welcomed to the table in the name of the Lord. They bring these somewhat disparate views to ecumenical discussions whether with other Protestant churches or with the Catholic Church.

The Disciples' conviction that divisions within the church are unscriptural has encouraged them to assume a leadership role in the ecumenical movement where their participation and enthusiastic support have been consistent. And yet Disciples, like many other Americans, have generally shown more interest in cooperative action than in reaching unity grounded in common theological commitments, and their suspicion of unity based on creedal formulations has presented problems for them when engaging in ecumenical dialogue. They have supported church federations and councils at every level, their mission churches have generally entered into united churches whenever possible, and they comfortably cooperate with other Protestant denominations in union congregations in North America. They conduct their mission program cooperatively with the United Church of Christ and have held national meetings together with that body. Only since mid-twentieth century, however, have Disciples been prepared and willing to engage in the serious theological discussions required for effective participation in Christian ecumenism today.

See also *Churches of Christ; Stone-Campbell Movement.*

Samuel C. Pearson

## BIBLIOGRAPHY

Blakemore, William Barnett, general ed. *The Renewal of Church: The Panel of Scholars Reports.* Vol. 1, *The Reformation of Tradition,* ed. Ronald E. Osborn; Vol. 2, *The Reconstruction of Theology,* ed. Ralph G. Wilburn; Vol. III, *The Revival of the Churches,* ed. William Barnett Blakemore. St. Louis: Bethany Press, 1963.

Boring, M. Eugene. *Disciples and the Bible: A History of Disciples Biblical Interpretation in North America.* St. Louis: Chalice Press, 1997.

Campbell, A. *The Christian System, in Reference to the Union of Christians, and a Restoration of Primitive Christianity, as Plead in the Current Reformation.* Bethany, Va., 1839.

Foster, Douglas A., Paul M. Blowers, Anthony L. Dunnavant, and D. Newell Williams, eds., *The Encyclopedia of the Stone–Campbell Movement,* Grand Rapids, Mich.: Eerdmans, 2004.

Harrell, David Edwin, Jr. *A Social History of the Disciples of Christ.* Vol. I, *Quest for a Christian America: The Disciples of Christ and American Society to 1866.* Nashville: Disciples of Christ Historical Society, 1966; Vol. II, *The Social Sources of Division in the Disciples of Christ, 1865–1900.* Atlanta: Publishing Systems, 1973.

Hatch, Nathan O. *The Democratization of American Christianity.* New Haven, Conn.: Yale University Press, 1989.

Lawrence, Kenneth, ed. *Classic Themes of Disciples Theology: Rethinking the Traditional Affirmations of the Christian Church (Disciples of Christ).* Fort Worth: Texas Christian University Press, 1986.

Toulouse, Mark G. *Joined in Discipleship: The Shaping of Contemporary Disciples Identity.* St. Louis: Chalice Press, 1997.

Tucker, William E., and Lester G. McAllister. *Journey in Faith: A History of the Christian Church (Disciples of Christ).* St. Louis: Bethany Press, 1975.

Williams, D. Newell, ed. *A Case Study of Mainstream Protestantism: The Disciples' Relation to American Culture, 1880–1989.* Grand Rapids, Mich.: Eerdmans, 1991.

Young, Charles Alexander. *Historical Documents Advocating Christian Union.* Chicago: Christian Century Co., 1904.

# Dispensationalism

Originating in nineteenth-century England, dispensationalism is a system of Bible prophecy interpretation adopted by many evangelical and fundamentalist American Protestants. Popularized by televangelists, megachurch pastors, and the mass media beginning in the 1970s, dispensationalism gained a wide following. As millions of Americans embraced this scheme of prophetic interpretation, it, in turn, influenced their view of world affairs and public policy issues.

Dispensationalism is one variant of a broader scheme of prophetic interpretation known as premillennialism. According to this view, Christ's thousand-year millennial reign (Revelations 20:1–6) will come about entirely by supernatural means, and only after humanity has sunk to unprecedented levels of wickedness, culminating in a final apocalyptic battle in which the forces of evil are forever vanquished.

## Historical Background

Throughout history, Christians have struggled to interpret the Bible's prophetic and eschatological passages. St. Augustine, formulating what would become the orthodox Catholic view, saw the prophecies as a revelation of all sacred and secular history, culminating in the triumph of righteousness. With the Reformation, Protestant leaders generally adopted this view as well. In all eras, however, some interpreters held that the prophecies referred to events still in the future. The early Christians anticipated Christ's return in their own lifetime. Sixteenth-century Anabaptists preached that the millennium was at hand. Late sixteenth- and seventeenth-century religious radicals in England believed that the millennium would come as papal pomp and ritual—and their remnants in the Church of England—were overthrown and a purified believers' church established. Cotton Mather and other New England Puritans shared such millennialist expectations.

This futurist reading of the prophetic scriptures survived on the fringes of British religious life into the nineteenth century. The Scotsman Edward Irving, a popular London preacher in the 1820s and 1830s, formulated elements of what came to be called dispensationalism in the early 1830s in *The Morning Watch,* a prophecy magazine. John Nelson Darby (1800–1882), a leader of a British dissenting sect known as the Plymouth Brethren, made significant contributions as well. Organizing the Bible's prophetic and apocalyptic texts in sequential form, Darby and other early shapers of dispensationalism believed they had found the key to God's plan for the Jews and for Gentile Christians, and to events that would unfold in the end times. According to this scheme, God has dealt with his chosen people, the Jews, and with the rest of humanity in a series of seven epochs, or dispensations, each with its distinctive plan of salvation, beginning with the Age of Innocence in the Garden of Eden and continuing through the present dispensation, the Church Age.

Introducing dispensationalism's most distinctive feature, the founders of this interpretive system taught that the Church Age would end with the Rapture, when all true believers would disappear to join Christ in the air. (The word *rapture* is etymologically related to *raptor,* the bird of prey that swoops down to snatch mice and other small creatures.) The texts undergirding this doctrine include I Thessalonians 4:16–17: "For the Lord himself shall descend from heaven with a shout, . . . and the dead in Christ shall rise first: Then we which are alive and remain shall be caught up together with them in the clouds to meet the Lord in the air: and so shall we ever be with the Lord."

The Second Coming of Christ is a core Christian dogma, reflected in the Nicene Creed (CE 325), which is translated in the Anglican Book of Common Prayer as:

"And he shall come again with glory to judge both the quick and the dead." However, the Rapture as an eschatological event prior to the Second Coming represents one of dispensationalism's distinctive contributions to prophetic interpretation.

Heeding Jesus' warnings in Matthew 24:36 against date setting ("of that day and hour knoweth no man"), dispensationalists avoided a pitfall that has discredited many prophecy interpreters. In the 1830s, for example, William Miller of New York, after studying time sequences mentioned in the book of Daniel and translating the "days" into years, began to preach that Christ would return "around 1843 or 1844." An even more precise date soon emerged: October 22, 1843 (later revised to 1844). Miller won many followers, but when the predicted dates passed uneventfully, the movement collapsed. (From its ashes, however, arose the Seventh-day Adventist Church, whose followers still study the prophecies, though carefully avoiding date setting.)

Although dispensationalists generally eschew date setting, they also teach that Jesus' Mount of Olives discourse recorded in Matthew 24, along with other biblical passages, reveal telltale signs by which believers can know that the end is near. These signs include wars, wickedness, natural disasters, and the return of the Jews to Palestine, the land promised by God to Abraham (Genesis 15:18), and the rebuilding there of the Jewish Temple destroyed by the Romans in CE 70. For Pentecostals, renewal of the spiritual gifts granted to believers at Pentecost, including divine healing and speaking in tongues (glossolalia), is further evidence of the approaching end.

This avoidance of date setting, combined with the insistence that the Rapture is imminent, helps explain dispensationalism's enduring appeal and its powerful spur to the evangelistic effort. Believers exist in a state of intense anticipation, carrying on their daily lives and yet convinced that the Rapture may occur at any moment. Anxiously looking to their own readiness, they urgently implore others to accept Christ before it is too late and scan the headlines for signs that the long-awaited event is, indeed, drawing ever closer.

After the Rapture, according to the dispensationalist system, will come the Great Tribulation foretold by Jesus (Matthew 24:21–22), when a demonic figure, the Antichrist, will arise. First presenting himself as a peacemaker, the Antichrist (called the "Beast" in Revelation) will soon reveal his true intentions and establish a global dictatorship in which all who resist his power, represented by the number 666 (Revelation 13:18), will be persecuted and slaughtered.

The Antichrist's reign, though brutal, will be brief. After seven years, as the Antichrist's armies gather at Har-Megiddo (Armageddon), an ancient battle site in Israel, Christ and the raptured saints will return to earth in full battle mode. Once he defeats the Antichrist and slaughters his armies (Revelation 19:11–21), Christ will inaugurate his millennial reign of justice and peace in the rebuilt Jewish Temple in Jerusalem. After a short-lived final rebellion, the Antichrist will be defeated forever. After a solemn Last Judgment, when all who have ever lived confront their eternal destiny, the great human drama that began in the Garden of Eden will come to a close. The damned will suffer endless torment in hell; the redeemed will rejoice forever in God's presence in heaven.

## Dispensationalism Comes to America

Dispensationalism won adherents among evangelical Protestants in late nineteenth-century Britain and North America, where Darby made several evangelistic tours. Early U.S. dispensationalists included the evangelist Dwight L. Moody; the Chicago businessman William E. Blackstone, whose *Jesus Is Coming* (1898) sold more than a million copies; and James Brookes, a Presbyterian minister in St. Louis. Through Brookes's prison ministry, Cyrus Scofield (1843–1921) became not only an evangelical Christian but also a committed dispensationalist. After fleeing an embezzlement accusation and abandoning a wife and children in Kansas, Scofield was in a St. Louis prison on forgery charges at the time of his conversion. After prison, he settled in Dallas as a Congregationalist pastor. There, Scofield edited a prophecy magazine, preached at prophecy conferences, and conducted a Bible correspondence course. In 1909 Oxford University Press published his annotated version of the King James Bible, with a running commentary reflecting the dispensationalist interpretation. Eventually selling millions of copies, the "Scofield Bible" played a seminal role in spreading dispensationalism.

Dispensationalism, with its confident assumption of the Bible's divine inspiration and inerrancy, appealed to evangelicals dismayed by theological modernism and critical biblical scholarship. The fundamentalist movement, coalescing around a series of treatises published as *The Fundamentals: A Testimony of Truth* (1910–1915), proved particularly receptive to dispensationalism.

## Other Systems of Prophetic Interpretation

Although highly influential, dispensationalism and premillennialism more generally are not the only ways in which

Christians past and present have interpreted biblical prophecy. Indeed, these often cryptic texts have stirred much controversy over the centuries. The Catholic, Reformed, and Lutheran traditions are generally amillennial, viewing the prophecies as unfolding over a long span of time or as allegories of the perennial conflict between good and evil. Although they anticipate Christ's return, amillennialists reject the idea of a literal thousand-year earthly reign as well as other details of dispensationalism's end-time scenario. Righteousness will finally triumph, they affirm, but the details remain unknowable.

Another interpretive mode, postmillennialism, views the prophesied era of justice and peace as gradually attainable in the present age through Christian effort, rather than emerging only after a final apocalyptic confrontation between righteousness and evil. The eighteenth-century New England theologian Jonathan Edwards espoused postmillennialism, believing that the triumph of righteousness could be achieved through prayer, evangelism, and other pious endeavors. Much nineteenth-century reform activity, including the temperance and antislavery movements, was inspired by this vision of a purified society achieved by means of earnest Christian striving.

Postmillennialism appealed to liberal Protestants and reformers of the late nineteenth and early twentieth centuries. Leaders of the Social Gospel movement such as W. D. P. Bliss, Washington Gladden, and Walter Rauschenbusch argued that Christ's kingdom could be advanced by remedying the social evils and injustices so rampant in urban-industrial America. The mainstream Protestant denominations and their ecumenical organization, the Federal (later National) Council of Churches, embraced postmillennialism as a theological rationale for their social activism.

Meanwhile, other groups—notably the Church of Jesus Christ of Latter-day Saints (Mormons), Seventh-day Adventists, and Jehovah's Witnesses—taught particular versions of end-time belief. Many Pentecostalists, while emphasizing glossolalia and other "gifts of the spirit" as evidence of Christ's near return, also believe in ongoing prophetic revelations, whereas most dispensationalists hold that information about the end-times is confined to the Bible.

## Dispensationalism from World War I through the Cold War

From the 1920s through the 1960s dispensationalism retained a loyal following among fundamentalists and evangelicals. Bible schools and seminaries such as the Philadelphia School of the Bible (founded by Cyrus Scofield and William L. Pettingill in 1911), Bible Institute of Los Angeles, Dallas Theological Seminary, and Chicago's Moody Bible Institute became dispensationalist bastions. Among the prominent ministers, evangelists, and writers who espoused dispensationalism were Isaac Haldeman, pastor of Manhattan's First Baptist Church; Arno Gaebelein, editor of the prophecy magazine *Our Hope;* the British revivalist G. Campbell Morgan, who frequently toured America; Harry A. Ironside, pastor of Chicago's Moody Memorial Church; Reuben A. Torrey of Los Angeles's Church of the Open Door; James M. Gray, the longtime president of the Moody Bible Institute; and Philadelphia's Donald Grey Barnhouse, whose *Bible Study Hour* radio program and *Eternity* magazine exerted broad influence.

Historical developments seemed to confirm the dispensationalist scenario. Progressive-era optimism and President Woodrow Wilson's vision of a peaceful, democratic world faded in the disillusioned 1920s. The 1917 Bolshevik Revolution in Russia stirred interest in prophecies of a mysterious northern kingdom, Gog, that would be destroyed by God after it invaded the land of Israel (Ezekiel 38). Some prophecy writers had long identified Russia as Gog, and with the atheistic communists in power such speculation intensified. Britain's 1917 Balfour Declaration supporting the establishment of a Jewish homeland in Palestine also captured the attention of dispensationalists; they had long viewed the Jews' return to Palestine as a crucial end-time sign. As early as 1891, businessman William Blackstone had persuaded prominent U.S. political and corporate leaders to sign a manifesto calling for a Jewish homeland in Palestine "to further the purposes of God concerning His ancient people." The Balfour Declaration seemed to be a momentous step toward this long-anticipated prophetic fulfillment.

World War II, with its global scale and massive casualties, appeared to fulfill Jesus' prophecy of "wars and rumours of wars" (Matthew 24:6) in the last days. And Adolf Hitler and Benito Mussolini for a time seemed possible candidates for the Antichrist. After 1945 Wilbur M. Smith of the Moody Bible Institute and other dispensationalists looked upon the atomic bomb as the instrument that would lead to the earth's fiery destruction, as foretold in II Peter 3:10. The postwar founding of the United Nations and moves toward European unification were interpreted as preludes to the Antichrist's global dictatorship. Meanwhile, the Cold War struggle with the Soviet Union heightened the attention given to Russia's end-time role. As telecommunications satellites soared into orbit, dispensationalists identified the technology by which the Antichrist would attract a worldwide following. Wherever dispensationalists looked, it seemed, end-time signs were proliferating.

## Dispensationalism in the Contemporary United States

Despite its wide acceptance by conservative Protestants, dispensationalism remained marginal throughout the 1960s, with only limited penetration of the larger culture. This situation changed dramatically after 1970, as world events combined with political and cultural developments at home to expand the influence of dispensationalism. In a backlash against the antiwar activism, campus turmoil, and counterculture provocations of the 1960s, conservative churches burgeoned in the 1970s and beyond. While liberal, mainstream denominations lost members, evangelical churches grew dramatically. The nation's largest Protestant denomination, the evangelical Southern Baptist Convention, grew by 23 percent between 1970 and 1985. Membership in the Assemblies of God church, a product of the Pentecostal revival of the early twentieth century, increased by 300 percent over the same period. The nondenominational Calvary Chapel movement, launched by Chuck Smith in Costa Mesa, California, in 1965, spread like wildfire; eight hundred Calvary Chapels could be found worldwide by 2000. Nondenominational suburban megachurches (churches with two thousand or more members), most of them fervently evangelical, proliferated as well.

As conservative Protestantism grew, premillennial dispensationalism, with its emphasis on human sinfulness, the futility of reform effort, and God's absolute sovereignty over the course of history, also gained ground. Chuck Smith, for example, promoted dispensationalism not only through the hundreds of Calvary Chapels worldwide but also through paperbacks, films, audio- and videotapes, and eventually the Internet.

Changes in mass communications further facilitated the diffusion of dispensationalism. Religious programming on television, once confined to local preachers and soporific Sunday public service programs on network television, now exploded as evangelical, fundamentalist, and Pentecostal preachers, supported by viewer contributions, seized the initiative. Exploiting cable and communications satellites, Jerry Falwell's *Old Time Gospel Hour,* Pat Robertson's Christian Broadcasting Network (1961), and Paul Crouch's Trinity Broadcasting Network (1973) provided potent new venues for promulgating evangelical Christianity and dispensationalism specifically.

The paperback revolution, the emergence of book marketing outlets (such as Borders, Barnes and Noble, Wal-Mart, and Amazon.com), and the explosive growth of Christian (mostly evangelical) bookstores were all factors in the mass marketing of dispensationalism. Hal Lindsey's *The Late Great Planet Earth* signaled what lay ahead. Lindsey, a Mississippi River tugboat operator who found God, studied dispensationalism at Dallas Theological Seminary, and joined Campus Crusade for Christ (an evangelical ministry founded by Bill Bright in 1951), sensed his opportunity when his sermons on Bible prophecy at the University of California, Los Angeles, drew standing-room-only crowds. *The Late Great Planet Earth,* a slangy version of dispensationalism full of allusions to current events, was issued as an inexpensive paperback by Zondervan, a religious publisher in Grand Rapids, Michigan. It went on to become the nonfiction bestseller of the 1970s.

As dispensationalism entered the cultural mainstream, other popularizers produced their own paperbacks, and many became bestsellers. John Walvoord of Dallas Theological Seminary published *Armageddon, Oil, and the Middle East Crisis* in 1974. In the years that followed, the veteran televangelist Jack Van Impe produced a stream of prophecy paperbacks, including *Signs of the Times* (1979) and *11:59 and Counting* (1984). Arthur Bloomfield's *How to Recognize the Antichrist* (1975), John Wesley White's *The Coming World Dictator* (1981), and Doug Clark's *Shockwaves of Armageddon* (1982) typified the scores of dispensationalist paperbacks that flooded the market in these years. In a 1996 poll 42 percent of Americans either "strongly agreed" (28 percent) or "moderately agreed" (14 percent) with the statement "the world will end in a battle in Armageddon between Jesus and the Antichrist."

The entertainment industry seized this lucrative new marketing opportunity. *The Omen* (1976), a film starring Gregory Peck, treated the boyhood of the Antichrist, who in later sequels became a powerful industrialist and ultimately world dictator. Bob Dylan's brief interlude as a born-again Christian resulted in two songs about the Second Coming: "When He Returns" (1979) and "Are You Ready?" (1980). The 1991 movie *The Rapture* featured Mimi Rodgers as a sexually promiscuous hedonist who experienced the cosmic event that is dispensationalism's centerpiece. *The Omega Code,* another Antichrist movie, received a full-scale Hollywood release in 1999.

Dispensationalism's mass market penetration culminated in the *Left Behind* novels by Tim LaHaye and Jerry B. Jenkins. In *Left Behind* (1995), the central characters, having missed the Rapture, convert to Christ. Successive volumes cover the Antichrist's rise, the Tribulation, and Christ's return at Armageddon—the key elements of the dispensationalist scenario. Enjoying sales of some seventy million copies and many translations, the twelve-volume series became a marketing juggernaut. The tie-in products included a movie, a "prequel," DVDs, audio- and videotapes, a videogame, a children's version, a Bible study series, greeting cards, and T-shirts. In 2002 the Bantam Dell Publishing Group signed LaHaye to a multimillion-dollar, four-book contract. The new (ghost-written) series was entitled *Babylon Rising*.

## Dispensationalism's Political Significance

From the beginning, dispensationalism had political implications, because believers monitored current events for end-time signs. In the Balfour Declaration, Bolshevik Revolution, rise of fascism, World War II, atomic bomb, and beginnings of a global political and corporate order, dispensationalists saw the unfolding of a divine plan. They supported Zionism as a step toward the prophesied reestablishment of a Jewish nation and restoration of the Jewish Temple on Temple Mount (also sacred to Muslims). They opposed Russia not only as a Cold War adversary, but also as a nation whose end-time destruction is foretold in scripture. They dismissed nuclear disarmament efforts, because the Bible predicts the earth's destruction.

Lindsey's *The Late Great Planet Earth* was intensely political. He foresaw a nuclear World War III and urged preparation for war with Russia and Communist China, which he linked to the 200 million-man army that dispensationalists believe will advance across the Euphrates River in the end-time (Revelation 9:14–16). He interpreted Israel's occupation of the West Bank in the 1967 war as a fulfillment of God's promise to Abraham, and dismissed any Mideast peace initiative that involved a Palestinian state, shared governance of Jerusalem, or Israeli withdrawal from the occupied territories. Many other dispensationalist popularizers echoed the same themes.

Along with the larger evangelical movement, post-1970 dispensationalists were increasingly politicized under the influence of Jerry Falwell's Moral Majority, Pat Robertson's Christian Coalition, James Dobson's Family Research Council, Tim LaHaye's Council on National Policy, Beverly LaHaye's Concerned Women for America, Donald Wildmon's American Family Association, Gary Bauer's American Values organization, the Southern Baptists' Ethics and Religious Liberty Commission led by the powerful Washington lobbyist Richard Land, and a host of other political pressure groups. Indeed, the dispensationalist insistence that unfolding events have profound prophetic significance added a note of eschatological urgency to the newly politicized evangelical wing of American Protestantism.

With the end of the Cold War, the dispensationalists increasingly turned their attention to the movement toward European unity, the continued expansion of the UN and other international bodies, the rise of a global corporate order, and the spread of computer-based information technologies. All were seen as forerunners of the Antichrist's rule. Spreading fears of global warming and other environmental hazards were linked to prophecies in the book of Revelation of nightmarish disruptions in the natural order. The *Roe* v. *Wade* abortion decision, the ban on prayer in public schools, the barring of creationist dogma from public school science classes, judicial protection of pornography on First Amendment grounds, and the greater cultural visibility of gays and lesbians were all cited as evidence of the growing end-time wickedness foretold by Christ.

Above all, post–Cold War dispensationalist popularizers focused on the Middle East. Dispensationalists such as Falwell, Robertson, Lindsey, Michael Evans, and John Hagee redoubled their calls for unqualified support of Israel's territorial claims and dismissed the claims of Palestinians and the Muslim world generally as contradictory to God's prophetic plan. After the terrorist attacks on the United States on September 11, 2001, the anti-Muslim theme intensified. In *Beyond Iraq: The Next Move* (2003), Michael Evans, founder of the Jerusalem Prayer Team and other pro-Israel groups, dismissed Islam as "a religion conceived in the pit of Hell." John Hagee, a San Antonio televangelist, megachurch pastor, and founder of a lobby called Christians United for Israel, struck the same note. Tom DeLay, a dispensationalist who served as Republican majority leader of the U.S. House of Representatives until scandal forced his resignation in 2006, tirelessly fought to align U.S. foreign policy with what he saw as God's end-time plan, denouncing any peace effort that required concessions by Israel.

The growth and political influence of dispensationalism were not, however, unopposed. The mainstream liberal denominations, though weakened, remained influential, rejecting the apocalyptic militancy of dispensationalism and continuing to promote peace, social justice, and environmental protection—causes dispensationalists viewed as naïve at best and demonic at worst. Resistance to dispensationalism arose even within the evangelical camp, as some called for a recovery of the lost nineteenth-century tradition of engagement with social reform causes. In his book *The Scandal of the Evangelical Mind* (1994), the evangelical historian Mark Noll criticized dispensationalism as theologically unsound and a travesty of evangelicalism's tradition of rigorous biblical exegesis. Two movements from the 1970s, Ronald Sider's Evangelicals for Social Action and Jim Wallis's evangelical Sojourners, rejected both dispensationalism's theology and its political agenda. They urged social action on issues such as poverty, peace, and environmental protection. As the George W. Bush administration came to a close in 2008, amid widespread disillusionment with the Iraq War and uneasiness over the direction of public policy, some evidence suggested that the political mobilization of religious conservatives, energized by dispensationalist beliefs, might be waning. Few observers, however, were prepared to predict that the influence of dispensationalism in the public sphere would soon end.

## Conclusion

Crossing the Atlantic from Britain, dispensationalism took root among American evangelicals in the late nineteenth and early twentieth centuries. It was energized by the post-1970 growth and political mobilization of religious conservatives. Exploiting changes in U.S. church life, mass marketing, and communications technologies, popularized versions of this system of prophetic interpretation spread rapidly in the late twentieth and early twenty-first centuries. From obscure beginnings, dispensationalism had become a major force not only in American religious life but also in the nation's popular culture, politics, and foreign policy.

**See also** *Adventism and Millennialism; Adventist and Millennialist Denominational Families; Apocalypticism; Bible* entries; *Evangelicals* entries; *Fundamentalism; Jehovah's Witnesses; Religious Right; Seventh-day Adventists.*

Paul S. Boyer

**BIBLIOGRAPHY**

Anderson, Robert Mapes. *Vision of the Disinherited: The Making of American Pentecostalism.* New York: Oxford University Press, 1979.
Armerding, Carl Edwin, and W. Ward Gasque. *Dreams, Visions, and Oracles: The Layman's Guide to Biblical Prophecy.* Grand Rapids, Mich.: Baker Book House, 1977.

Boyer, Paul. *When Time Shall Be No More: Prophecy Belief in Modern American Culture.* Cambridge, Mass.: Harvard University Press, 1992.
Findlay, James F., Jr. *Dwight L. Moody: American Evangelist, 1837–1899.* Chicago: University of Chicago Press, 1969.
Frykholm, Amy Johnson. *Rapture Culture: Left Behind in Evangelical America.* New York: Oxford University Press, 2004.
Patterson, Mark, and Andrew Walker. "Irving, Albury, and the Origins of the Pre-Tribulation Rapture," in *Christian Millennarianism: From the Early Church to Waco,* edited by Stephen Hunt. Bloomington: Indiana University Press, 2001.
Rossing, Barbara R. *The Rapture Exposed: The Message of Hope in the Book of Revelation.* Boulder, Colo.: Westview Press, 2004.
Sandeen, Ernest. *The Roots of Fundamentalism: British and American Millenarianism, 1800–1930.* Chicago: University of Chicago Press, 1970.
Tatford, Frederick A. *God's Program of the Ages.* Grand Rapids, Mich.: Kregel, 1967.
Weber, Timothy P. *Living in the Shadow of the Second Coming: American Premillennialism, 1875–1975.* New York: Oxford University Press, 1979.
———. *On the Road to Armageddon: How Evangelicals Became Israel's Best Friend.* Grand Rapids, Mich.: Baker Academic Books, 2004.
Wilson, Dwight. *Armageddon Now! The Premillenarian Response to Russia and Israel Since 1917.* Grand Rapids, Mich.: Baker Book House, 1977.

# Dutch Reformed

The term *Reformed* refers to those Protestant churches that emerged from the Swiss Reformation, especially from the influence of John Calvin of Geneva and to a lesser extent Ulrich Zwingli of Zurich. The Calvinist churches on the European continent usually assumed the name "Reformed." Those in the British Isles became known as "Presbyterian." The Dutch Reformed churches in America originated in Holland and belong to this broader movement.

## European Background

The Reformed wing of the Reformation was the most international of the Protestant churches of the sixteenth century. The movement began in Switzerland and spread not only to Holland but also to England, Scotland, Ireland, Wales, France, Germany, Poland, Hungary, and other areas of Europe, and to North America.

Like other Protestants of the Reformation, the Dutch Reformed believed in the three basic doctrines of the Protestant movement: the authority of the Bible for the church and the life of the believer, salvation by God's grace and not by human works, and the priesthood of all believers. Each of these ideas had distinctive implications for the Reformed churches. For example, the emphasis on the Bible led to intense study of it, higher levels of literacy and education so people could read and understand the Bible, and disputes about the Bible's authority and meaning. The focus on salvation by God's grace alone led Reformed leaders, including the Dutch, to advocate God's predestination and election of those who were saved (perhaps no doctrine proved to be more contentious than that of predestination). Finally, by stressing the priesthood of all believers, Reformed Christians launched not only an attack on hierarchical forms of authority but also an affirmation of more democratic and egalitarian forms of authority in both church and civil affairs.

In worship, these Reformed Protestants sought to "reform" or restore the church and its worship to the New Testament's description of early Christian practices. The sermon (the Word of God proclaimed) replaced the sacrament of the Lord's Supper (the Word of God sacramentally presented) as the heart of Reformed worship services. These services were long in duration and simplified to include preaching, the singing of psalms, and extended prayers. Like other Protestants, the Reformed reduced the number of sacraments from the seven in the Roman Catholic tradition to only two—the Lord's Supper and baptism of both infants and adults. For the Lord's Supper, the Reformed held that the bread and wine *symbolized* the presence of Jesus Christ.

In their organization of the church, Reformed Protestants differed from both the Roman Catholic Church and their Protestant cousins. Like all Protestants, they rejected the Roman Catholic emphasis on the authoritative teaching role of the church and its tradition and emphasized the definitive superiority of the Bible (*Sola Scriptura* or the Bible alone). The Reformed leaders also rejected the role of bishops (which Lutherans and Anglicans retained) but still ordained ministers (which many of the Anabaptist groups did not). What distinguished Reformed church government from those of the Roman Catholic and other Protestant traditions was its understanding of power as delegated and balanced. Reformed churches were not radically democratic, vesting final authority in congregations. Instead, the churches were representative democracies—much like the republican governments spawned in their wake. The ministry of the entire church was divided between ministers and teachers (sometimes called teaching elders), elders (sometimes called ruling elders), and deacons (supervisors of ministries of compassion to the poor, the

sick, and the needy). This division of power was evident in the organization of the congregation; authority rested with the minister, the consistory or session, and the congregation itself. Groups of congregations were governed by a balanced relationship between congregations, classes or presbyteries, synods, and a general assembly or general synod (usually defined by national boundaries). Unifying their understanding of the church (and, by implication, their understanding of society), Reformed Protestants believed in the separation and balance of powers—all clearly defined in a constitution.

Reformed Protestants also differed sharply from the Roman Catholic tradition in the frequent Protestant emphasis on stipulated and codified confessions. These human-constructed statements of faith were viewed as subordinate to the authority of scripture, but their authority and interpretation were always subject to challenge and debate. Lutherans and Anglicans had their own confessions or doctrinal standards. For the Dutch Reformed the confessional standards became the Belgic Confession (1561), the Heidelberg Catechism (1563), and the canons of the Synod of Dort (1618–1619).

The Reformed tradition has often been described as a "confessional" tradition, and the Dutch Reformed are particularly vivid examples of this impulse in Protestantism. Indeed, the Dutch Reformed churches in America are known for the importance they give to confessions and Christian doctrine. For the Dutch Reformed, ideas about God truly matter. Their history and even present-day practice are molded by the desire to think clearly and correctly about divine truths; more generally, they prize intellectual rigor in all areas of life.

## Dutch Reformed in Colonial America

When Dutch Protestants began to migrate to North America, they brought with them the marks of their tradition in Holland, as well as urgent practical concerns. The first Dutch Reformed churches were founded in New York, New Jersey, and Delaware during the seventeenth century. They were some of the earliest Reformed congregations in North America.

The sponsor of Dutch migration was the Dutch West India Company, whose interests were primarily economic and commercial. Initially it shied away from sponsoring any church, but the director of New Netherland (later New York), Peter Minuit, took the lead in appointing the first pastor, Jonas Michaelius (1577–1638). Michaelius founded "the church in the fort" (now known as Collegiate Church) in 1628, marking the beginning of the Dutch Reformed Church in America.

The most pressing economic challenge for every colony was the need for immigrants to support its life and welfare. The population of Dutch immigrants did grow in New York and New Jersey, but that growth created the most pressing ecclesiastical need—more ministers. The Classis of Amsterdam controlled the Dutch Reformed congregations in America. This control included the power to ordain ministers, which made the supply of ministers even more problematic. Dutch Reformed churches also faced the dilemma of serving a diverse population. New York—and the middle colonies more generally—had the most diverse population of all the American colonies. Some Dutch Reformed churches attempted to reach out beyond the Dutch population, but because services were conducted in Dutch, their efforts were largely futile.

In 1664 the Dutch Reformed lost their privileged status in New York when the English conquered the colony. They protested—successfully—the English desire to establish or strengthen the Church of England in the colony. Their victory was ironic, however, for in protecting their own liberty they had to accept legal protection for all other churches as well. This is an early example of how the experience of diversity produced the reality of toleration in American history.

Migration from Holland waned during the late seventeenth century and so did the Dutch Reformed churches in numbers and vitality. By 1700 New York had fifty churches, and twenty-nine were Dutch Reformed. What the Dutch Reformed may have lacked in numerical and spiritual strength, they made up for in economic influence and social prestige. Dutch families occupied a central role in the development of New York and New Jersey's political, social, and economic life well into the twentieth century.

In 1720 Theodore J. Frelinghuysen (1787–1862), a young German pastor, came to New Jersey. Frelinghuysen was a pietist who advocated individual conversion and personal appropriation of faith. His evangelistic preaching revived Dutch churches just before the First Great Awakening of the 1730s and 1740s spread through the colonies.

The ticklish problem of ecclesiastical independence became a source of contention. Some Dutch Reformed pastors wanted freedom from the Classis of Amsterdam and petitioned for autonomy in 1738. Other Dutch Reformed pastors opposed the initiative and wanted Amsterdam to maintain its power to ordain ministers for the colonies and regulate colonial church life. They also wanted Dutch Reformed ministers to be trained at New York's King College (now Columbia University).

The Classis of Amsterdam proposed a compromise. It granted the Dutch Reformed in the colonies the right to establish a coetus—an association of churches without ecclesiastical autonomy. The Coetus Party eventually broke with Amsterdam and formed its own classis in 1754, which angered its opponents, the Conferentie Party. John Henry Livingston (1746–1825), who became known as "the father of the Reformed church," brought the two parties together in 1771, but complete freedom from the Classis of Amsterdam was won only through the colonies' American War of Independence. This victory was symbolized by the founding of the New Brunswick Theological Seminary in New Jersey in 1784, one year after the end of the American Revolution.

## Dutch Reformed in the New Nation

The year 1784 also brought the formation of a synod and classis, and in 1792 the Dutch Reformed organized themselves as the Reformed Protestant Dutch Church. In 1867 the name was changed to the Reformed Church in America (RCA)—the name it uses to this day.

Although the Dutch Reformed largely supported the American Revolution, they found themselves at the fringes of the increasingly English-speaking population. They argued about whether to continue to use Dutch in worship services and attempted to work with Presbyterians and the German Reformed to reach more people, but evangelistic efforts foundered and the new denomination remained almost exclusively Dutch.

That situation did not, however, stifle the theological discussion and division. In 1822 the True Dutch Reformed broke away and protested the influence of revivalism and evangelical Arminianism in softening the strict Calvinism of the Dutch Reformed churches. The schismatic group nearly disappeared, but then its forces grew with the migration of conservative Dutch Reformed Protestants from Holland. In 1834 conservative Calvinists in Holland broke with the state church. They sought a more vital piety, strict application of moral laws to regulate Christian life, and a rigorous interpretation of Christian orthodoxy. But they were met by religious and political oppression, and life worsened in Holland because of the onset of an agricultural depression in the 1840s.

In 1846–1847 these conservatives began what is known as the second Dutch migration to North America. One group, led by Albertus Van Raalte (1811–1876), founded Holland, Michigan, and other communities in the region. Hendrik Scholte (1805–1868) led another group that settled in central Iowa. Both contingents tried to remain independent of the Dutch Reformed Church, but only Scholte's group succeeded. Van Raalte and his supporters united with the Dutch Reformed in 1850.

The debate over the boundaries of Calvinist doctrine persisted, and 1857 saw the most significant and enduring split in the Dutch Reformed churches. At first, the breakaway group, led by Gijsbert Haan (1801–1874), was known as the True Holland Reformed Church. Eventually, however, it became the Christian Reformed Church (CRC). The CRC began with few members, but during the late nineteenth century it grew because of more Dutch immigration and a dispute in the Reformed Church in America over Freemasonry.

## Dutch Reformed in the Twentieth Century

As these two branches of the Dutch Reformed tradition entered into the twentieth century, they were virtually identical in their geographical distribution. They shared an eastern bloc (New York and New Jersey), a midwestern contingent (Michigan, Illinois, Wisconsin, and Iowa), and a western constituency (California). After World War II, another wave of Dutch immigration to Canada and especially Ontario gave the Christian Reformed Church numerical strength across the border and validated its formal name as the Christian Reformed Church in North America. In the early twenty-first century Canadian members of the Christian Reformed Church constituted about one-quarter of its membership.

Throughout the nineteenth century the eastern churches of both denominations exerted considerable influence, but by the end of the twentieth century the two churches found the majority of their members, financial support, and spiritual vitality in the Midwest and West. This significant shift stemmed largely from demographic factors, especially the dramatic growth of California, and economic factors, particularly the significant financial prosperity of the middle and western parts of twentieth-century America.

Three important results flowed from this alteration of the Dutch Reformed landscape. First, both denominations found themselves struggling with and adjusting to the various forms of twentieth-century evangelicalism. Because of their roots in scholastic and rigorous forms of Calvinism, the Dutch Reformed have had an uneasy relationship with evangelicalism—the dominant influence in American Protestantism. Because evangelicalism was especially powerful in their growing strongholds in the Midwest and West, it was inevitable that the Dutch Reformed would encounter and adjust to it, in manifold ways. For example, during the last quarter of the twentieth and into the twenty-first century, a large proportion of their ministers—especially in the West—were trained at Fuller Theological Seminary, an evangelical institution in California. But the influence worked both ways. In the late twentieth century Fuller's president, Richard Mouw, was recruited from Calvin College and the Christian Reformed Church.

Second, both denominations sought to adjust to modern streams of thought and practice—often slowly and gradually, but inexorably. They were not completely spared the debates over theological liberalism and fundamentalism that swept through many mainline Protestant denominations. The Christian Reformed Church underwent three divisions: the formation of the Protestant Reformed Church (1924–1926), the Orthodox Christian Reformed Church (1988), and the United Reformed Churches of North America (1996). Nevertheless, the Calvinist theological affirmation of culture enabled the Dutch Reformed to address modern science and contemporary thought from a critical, constructive, and explicitly Christian stance. For example, Hope College of the Reformed Church in America and Calvin College of the Christian Reformed Church distinguished themselves in the fields of science and the humanities—two hotly contested areas of debate in other Protestant denominations.

Third, both denominations struggled over ethnicity—the issue that gave the churches their popular name, Dutch Reformed. Throughout the twentieth century, congregations, seminaries, and colleges remained strongly tied to the Dutch ethnic base, except in the East and eventually in California. Leaders recognized the diminishing numerical and economic strength of the Dutch population, but the powerful influence of ethnicity prevailed throughout the century. In one crucial area, the Dutch Reformed churches relinquished their Dutch heritage; gradually, worship services were conducted in English. At the same time, ethnicity probably played the most important role in limiting more serious ecclesiastical divisions or mitigating them when they did occur. These Dutch Calvinists often fought fiercely among themselves, in part because they had so much in common—blood as well as belief.

## Twentieth-Century Theological Developments

Theologically, the Reformed Church in America and the Christian Reformed Church agree on common doctrinal standards—the Belgic Confession, the Heidelberg Catechism, and the Canons of the Synod of Dort. Although united on this Calvinist theological platform, the Reformed Church in America has been more moderate in its Calvinism, more ecumenically minded, and more willing to adjust its positions to address issues in American society.

Perhaps the most significant theological difference between the Reformed Church in America and the Christian Reformed Church during the twentieth century was their stance toward culture. The Calvinist tradition has always advocated a positive attitude toward the world as the product of God's creative design. In confronting its defects and deficiencies, the Reformed Church in America has tended to support the church's role as a transformer of culture. In doing so, it has aligned itself more often with other mainline Protestant theological movements of the last century, including neo-orthodoxy, the theology of Karl Barth, liberation theology, and other theological currents.

By contrast, the Christian Reformed Church has been decisively shaped by the theology of Abraham Kuyper (1837–1920). Kuyper, who served as prime minister of the Netherlands from 1901 to 1905, was known for his theological insistence on applying Christian principles to the social order. In doing so, Kuyper emphasized the role of the church as a creative agency for Christian alternatives to secular culture rather than the transformer of existing institutions. An even more rigorous form of Kuyperian thought was advocated by Herman Dooyweerd (1894–1977) of the Free University of Amsterdam. The Kuyperian impact on the Christian Reformed Church has been pervasive and profound, making its voice and mission in American culture both distinctive and critically distant.

## Missionary Activities

Dutch Reformed churches, with their strong emphasis on the sovereignty of God, would seem to be unlikely candidates for participation in the powerful missionary movement of American Protestantism, which has been shaped largely by Arminian theological ideas. And yet the Dutch Reformed churches' involvement in missionary work far outstrips their comparatively small size and contrasts sharply with their inability to move beyond their Dutch ethnic base.

In the past, Reformed Church in America missionaries have undertaken pioneering work in India, China, Japan, and Saudi Arabia, and their work continues in Japan, India, Saudi Arabia, Africa, and Mexico. In the twentieth century, the denomination also joined forces with other Reformed churches and other Christian bodies to pursue a variety of goals: evangelism, medical care, relief work, and social and economic reform.

Likewise, the Christian Reformed Church launched its own missionary effort in the twentieth century. It remains involved in work with Native Americans and in Japan, South America, Nigeria, Mexico, and Taiwan.

## Ecumenism

The distinctive theological accents of the Dutch Reformed churches have shaped their relationships with one another and other churches. Relations between the RCA and the CRC have been more competitive than cordial.

The Reformed Church in America has had close connections with American Presbyterians. In fact, it considered a proposed merger with the southern wing of American Presbyterians, but finally rejected the proposal in 1969. The RCA has been an active participant in ecumenical discussions and a member of the National Council of Churches, the World Council of Churches, and the World Alliance of Reformed Churches.

By contrast, the Christian Reformed Church has focused its ecumenical attention more narrowly and more confessionally. The CRC was a member of the North American Presbyterian and Reformed Council until 2001, and it has been a member of the Reformed Ecumenical Council and the World Alliance of Reformed Churches. Both churches are affiliated with the National Association of Evangelicals.

## Social Issues

Three social issues have dominated the agenda of American Protestantism in the twentieth century—war, race, and gender/sex. Like most Protestant churches, the RCA and CRC supported World Wars I and II, were divided over the Vietnam War, and maintained a critical distance on the war in the Middle East during the early twenty-first century. Because neither denomination had a significant African American membership, the issues of civil rights and race were recognized as important but as somewhat distant. By contrast, the role of women in the church and homosexuality have been far more heated and divisive issues. The Reformed Church in America has ordained women for the ministry since 1978. The Christian Reformed Church voted to ordain women in 1995, a decision marked by years of dissension and ultimately the defection of several congregations to other denominations. Homosexuality has been a difficult theological and ethical issue for both churches, and in the early twenty-first century it is unclear whether or how the churches' traditional teaching against homosexuality will change.

## Education

The influence of the Dutch Reformed on education in American life has been extraordinary. Measured against their immigrant beginnings, bounded by Dutch customs and language, the Dutch Reformed have nevertheless shaped American education through their institutions and a significant group of influential thinkers. During the colonial era, the Dutch Reformed (the Coetus Party) helped found Queens College (Rutgers), which became the State University of New Jersey in 1945, and they took the initiative in theological education by founding the New Brunswick Theological Seminary in 1784, the first theological seminary in the United States.

The second wave of Dutch immigration quickly led the Reformed Church in America to establish Hope College in Holland, Michigan, in 1866, and a second school for educating ministers, Western Theological Seminary, in 1884. The Reformed Church took over the sponsorship of Central College in Pella, Iowa, in 1916, a Baptist school established in 1853, and founded Northwestern College in 1882 in Orange City, Iowa.

The Christian Reformed Church was barely surviving after the Civil War, but in 1874 it founded Calvin College and Calvin Theological Seminary in Grand Rapids, Michigan. In 1955 the Christian Reformed established Dordt College in Sioux Center, Iowa, as well as several smaller colleges in the United States and Canada.

Perhaps the most noteworthy and characteristically Christian Reformed activity in education has been its extensive network of primary and secondary Christian schools. The Reformed Church supported public schools, but the Christian Reformed created their own. These schools are not sponsored by the denomination itself but mainly by Christian Reformed parents—a product of the Christian Reformed conviction that education is part of the responsibility parents assume in baptizing a child. The schools constitute the largest Protestant private school system in the nation.

The geographic center of Dutch Reformed vitality in higher education is western Michigan—Hope College and Western Theological Seminary in Holland (RCA) and, a mere thirty miles away in Grand Rapids, Calvin College and Calvin Theological Seminary (CRC).

These institutions have produced an extraordinary number of leaders in various areas of American intellectual, economic, and social life. For example, the Christian Reformed Church spawned Louis Berkhof (theologian), Richard DeVos (Amway co-founder), Peter De Vries (novelist), Vern Ehrlers (member of Congress), William Frankena (philosopher), Paul Henry (member of Congress), Bill Hybels (minister, Willow Creek Association), George Marsden (historian), Richard Mouw (theologian), Alvin Plantinga (philosopher), Patricia Rozema (filmmaker), Leonard Schrader (filmmaker), Paul Schrader (filmmaker), Lewis Smedes (theologian), the Staal brothers (professional hockey players), and Nicholas Wolterstorff (philosopher).

The Reformed Church in America and its educational institutions have produced a similar list of individuals who have left their mark on American life, including Meredith Arwady (opera star), M. R. DeHaan (founder of the *Radio Bible Class*), Vern Den Herder (professional football player), Max De Pree (writer and business leader), Everett Dirksen (U.S. senator), Peter Hoekstra (member of Congress), Jim Kaat (baseball player), James Muilenburg (biblical scholar), A. J. Muste (pacifist leader), Norman Vincent Peale (minister), Ruth Peale (*Guideposts* magazine), Theodore Roosevelt (president), Philip Schuler (leader in the American Revolution), Robert Schuller (TV evangelist), Richard Smalley (Nobel laureate in chemistry), Martin Van Buren (president), and Guy Vander Jagt (member of Congress).

Grand Rapids itself has become an enormously successful religious publishing center, which has an international influence. Four Christian Reformed families, all highly competitive, founded four book publishing firms—Baker, Eerdmans, Kregel, and Zondervan. Zondervan was bought by HarperCollins, but the other three remain under family control. Nearby Muskegon is home to Bible Gateway, one of the most widely used Internet resources for studying the Bible.

In the early twenty-first century the two major denominations of the Dutch Reformed tradition in America were each composed of some 300,000 members. Rarely have so many emerged from so few to accomplish so much.

**See also** *Antinomian Controversy; Calvinist/Reformed Tradition and Heritage; Congregationalists; Pilgrims; Presbyterians* entries; *Puritans; Reformed Denominational Family; Religious Thought: Reformed Protestant.*

John M. Mulder

## BIBLIOGRAPHY

Balmer, Randall H. *A Perfect Babel of Confusion: Dutch Religion and English Culture in the Middle Colonies.* New York: Oxford University Press, 1989.

Bratt, James D. *Dutch Calvinism in Modern America.* Grand Rapids, Mich.: Eerdmans, 1984.

De Jong, Gerald. *The Dutch Reformed Church in the American Colonies.* Grand Rapids, Mich.: Eerdmans, 1978.

De Klerk, Peter, and Richard R. De Ridder, eds. *Perspectives on the Christian Reformed Church.* Grand Rapids, Mich.: Baker Book House, 1983.

Finney, Paul Corby, ed. *Seeing beyond the Word: Visual Arts and the Calvinist Tradition.* Grand Rapids, Mich.: Eerdmans, 1999.

Smidt, Corwin, et al. *Divided by a Common Heritage: The Christian Reformed Church and the Reformed Church in America.* Grand Rapids, Mich.: Eerdmans, 2006.

Swierenga, Robert P., and Elton Bruins. *Family Quarrels in the Dutch Reformed Churches in the Nineteenth Century.* Grand Rapids, Mich.: Eerdmans, 1999.

VandenBerge, Peter, ed. *Historical Directory of the Reformed Church in America, 1628–1965.* New Brunswick, N.J.: Reformed Church in America, 1966.

van Hinte, Jacob. *Netherlands in America.* Grand Rapids, Mich.: Baker Book House, 1985.

Willis, David, and Michael Welker, eds. *Toward the Future of Reformed Theology.* Grand Rapids, Mich.: Eerdmans, 1999.

# Index

*Bold page numbers indicate primary treatment of a subject. Italic page numbers indicate illustrations. Alphabetization is letter-by-letter (e.g., "Churches Uniting in Christ" precedes "Church of England").*

divisions with national Baptist groups, 227–228

early black congregations and regional organizations, 27–28, 29, 30, 34, 224–225, 1883

National Baptist Convention, 34, 41, 45, 224, 226–228

non-national Baptist denominations, 228–229, 1830

political activism, 39, 41

Southern, 254

women, 43, 226–227

women's ordination, 2341

African Canadians, 396

Appalachian mountain religion, 138, 139, 140, 141

Black Primitive Baptist music, 1455

British roots of, 2119

camp meetings, 349

in Canada, 399, 401

church and state, 451–452, 453, 457

church architecture, 143–144, 162, 187, 188, 190, 199

civil rights and, 41

colonial period and American Revolution, 70, 96, 216, 217, 256–258, 1553, 1555–1556

congregations, 498, 499

denominations, **230–238**

American Baptist Churches in USA, 231–238

colonial period, 230–231, 1828

diversity of, 238

general Baptists, 231

theological differences, 230

evangelicalism, 799

faith-based initiatives, 248

fundamentalism, 883

in Great Plains Region, 933

Latino American religion, 1190, 1192, 1193

as Mainline Protestants. See Mainline Protestants

millennialism, 14

in Mountain West and Prairie Region, 1434, 1435

Old Baptist hymnody, 1454–1455

Reformed tradition, 345

Regulators vs. Anglicans, 2248–2249

schools, 665

sectarian, **238–246**

associationalism and Great Awakening, 239–240

contributions, 245–246

early Baptist history, 239

Free Will Baptists, 240–241

interpretive constructs, 244–245

Landmark Baptists, 243–244

nineteenth century and modern mission movement, 241–242

other sectarian Baptists, 244

Primitive Baptists, 242

Two-Seed-in-the-Spirit Baptists, 242, 245

slavery and, 477

in South, 2118, 2120

Southern (SBC), **246–254**

beginnings of Convention, 248–249, 260, 2122

beliefs, 7, 246–248

confession of faith, 251

conservatism, 2123

continuing issues, 253–254, 266, 267

controversies, 251–253, 264–265, 280, 477

cooperative program, 250

development of Convention agencies, 249

educational programs, 250

fundamentalism-liberalism divide, 252–253, 265, 891

Landmarkism, 252–253

Latino American religion, 1190, 1192

racial issues, 252, 1855

same-gender marriage, 2074

women's ordination, 2341, 2348

women's role, 2310

tradition and heritage, 14, 16, **254–268**

nineteenth century, 258–263, 1559

origins of Baptist tradition, 255–256

twentieth century, 263–266

twenty-first-century trends, 266–267

women's ordination, 2341

Baptist University of the Américas, 1192

Baraka, Amiri, 1243, 1259

Barclay, Henry, 108

Barker, Benjamin, 1862

Barlow, Joel, 1465

Barnes, Albert, 1763

Barnett, Ruth, 6

Barrett, Ellen, 1920

Barrow, Henry, 489

Barry, E. J., 229

Barth, John, 1255

Barth, Karl, 296, 524–525, 1533, 1534–1535, 1536, 1929, 2184

Bartram, John, 712

Bartram, William, 712

Baseball, 2157

Basham, Don, 429, 430

Basílica de Nuestra Señora de Guadalupe (Mexico), 201–202, 2202

Bass, Sarah. See Allen, Sarah (Bass)

Bastian, Jean-Pierre, 1399

Bates, Daisy, 1345

Bates, Joseph, 24, 2065

Bateson, Gregory, 1546

Batista, Fulgencio, 409

Battle, Kathleen, 1451

Battle Creek Sanitarium, 2067

Baudet, Henri, 63

Baudoux, Maurice, 375

Bauer, Gary, 1873

*Bauhaus,* 168

Baulieu, Etienne-Emile, 9

Baur, Ferdinand Christian, 1302

Bavarian Illuminati, 271

Bavinck, Herman, 299

Bawa Muhaiyadeen Fellowship, 2335

Baxter, Ern, 429

Bayley, Daniel, 1477

Bayne, Stephen, 102

BCP. See Book of Common Prayer

Beachy, Moses, 80

Bean, Joel & Hannah, 1815–1816

Beanite and Conservative Friends, 1816, 1819

Bearden, Romare, 2288, *2289*

Bear's Lodge, 709–710, 934

Beatles, 411, 417–418

Beat movement, 317, 1258–1259, 2401

Beauchamp, Tom, 303

Beaux-Arts architecture, 190, *191*

Beccaria, Cesare, 696

Bednarowski, Mary Farrell, 2311

Beecher, Catharine, 512, 514, 1262–1263, 1318, 1415, 1685, 2144

Beecher, Edward, 2193

Beecher, Henry Ward

celebrity culture, 412–413

children and adolescents, 434

covenant, concept of, 2355

missions, 1411

popular religion and popular culture, 1714, 1717–1718

Presbyterians, 1762

Protestant liberalism, 1785, 1789

religious press, 1862

science, 2040

sentimental romantics and, 2021

Social Gospel, 2094

sports, 2154–2155

theology of, 345

Beecher, Lyman

abolitionism, 2, 3, 1761

anti-Catholicism, 113–114, 1266, 1558, 1689, 1970

apocalypticism, 131

Benevolent Empire, 274, 277, 278

Calvinism, 2224

children and adolescents, 434

ecumenism, 600

evangelicals, 802

family history, 1762

food and diet, 854

in Great Lakes region, 922

missions, 1413

in New England, 1557, 1559

Old Northwest evangelicals, 922

"Plea for the Churches," 905, 1434

"Plea for the West," 922, 1639–1640, 1687

politics, 1685

Presbyterians, 1760, 1761, 1762

revivalism, 1, 2, 3, 1761, 1941

social reform, 1413

Beijing Platform (1995), 2337

Beissel, Conrad, 81, 1476–1477, 2235–2236

Belgic Confession (1561), 339, 570, 573, 1927

Beliefnet, 1867

politics, 1687, 1688
Presbyterians, 1763
religious press, 1014, 1862
social reform, 2099
Garvey, Marcus, 37, 408, 1239, 1566, 1571–1573, *1572*, 1574, 1830
Gates, Henry Louis, 1239, 1451
Gates, J. M., 1463
*Gates of Prayer* (Jewish reform), 2375
Gaustad, Edwin, 989, 1432
Gautama, Siddhartha (Buddha). *See* Buddhism
Gauthier, George, 373
Gauvreau, Michael, 397, 400
Gay. *See* Sexuality and sexual identity
Gay, Ebenezer, 343
Gay marriage. *See* Same-gender marriage
Gay theology, **1908–1910**. *See also* Sexuality and sexual identity
Gearhart, Sally Miller, 1919
Geertz, Clifford, 779, 1527, 1741, 1876
Gelineau, Joseph, 1488
Gender, **895–903**. *See also* Women
Anglicans, issues of, 102–103
demographics, 537
diversity, 899–900
emotion, 692
feminism. *See* Feminism
food and religion, 859–860
gay marriage. *See* Same-gender marriage
hegemonic masculinity, 900
history, 896–898
Islam, 1089–1090
Judaism, 1162
"men" vs. mankind, 900–901
muscular Christianity, 900
Oneness Pentecostalism, 1621
Progressivism, 1777–1778
secularization and, 2115
sexual identity, varieties of, 901–902. *See also* Sexuality and sexual identity
womanist. *See* Womanist theology
women, 898–899. *See also* Women
General Association of Regular Baptist Churches (GARBC), 236
General Baptists, 230, 231, 239, 241
General Convention of 1789, 111
General Theological Seminary, 737–738
General War-Time Commission, 2355
Generation X, 683
Genesis. *See* Bible; Scriptures
Genesis flood, 813–814
*The Genesis Flood* (Whitcomb & Morris), 813–814
Genetically modified organisms, 2045
Geneva Bible, 283
Gennarelli, Thomas, 304–305
*Gentlemen's Agreement* (film), 125
Geoghan, John, 1994
Geographical approaches, **903–910**
Anglicanism, 904–905
cartography, 908–909
Catholicism, 906

denominational geography at end of nineteenth century, 906–907
denominational geography in early republic, 905–906
ghettoization and Native Americans, 908
influence on religion, 903–904
Methodists, 906, 933–934
Mormons, 906
physical geography and region, 907–908
religious settlement, 904–905
relocation, effects of, 904–905
sacred space, 909–910
space vs. time, 910
George I (king, England), 159
George III (king, England), 131
George, David, 27–28, 30, 225, 261, 396
George, Dudley, 358
Georgetown University, 199
Gerbi, Antonelli, 63
Gere, Richard, 318, 418
Gérente, Alfred, 1275
Gerhard, Johann, 1301
Gerhardt, Paul, 1301
German Baptists, 234–235, 262
German Nazarene painting style, 1278
German Reformed churches, 1839–1843, 2384. *See also* Reformed denominational family
Germ theory, 2044
Gerovich, Eliezer, 1483
Gerrish, Brian A., 1929
Gettysburg College, 1306
Gezari, Temima, 174
Ghandi, Mahatma, 41
Ghost Dances
anthropological approaches and, 777–778
in Canada, 389
economics, 592–593
environment and ecology, 701
freedom, religious, 865
Great Awakening and, 914
in Mountain West and Prairie Region, 1433
Native American religion, 1512–1513, *1513*, 1522, 1523
new religious movements, 1578–1579
pluralism, 1671, 1689
politics, 1683
religious thought, 1881
violence and terror, 2252
Gibbon, Edward, 696
Gibbons, James, 1932, 1973
Gibbs, James, 144, 158, 160–161, 162, 166–167, 187
Gibson, George M., 495
Gibson, Mel, 127, 1724
Gilded Age, 739–745, 1863–1864, 2090, 2172
Gilkes, Cheryl Townsend, 436–437, 1897
Gillow, Eugenio, 1384, 1399
Gilman, Charlotte Perkins, 1271–1272
Gilson, Etienne, 1542, 1934
Ginsberg, Allen, 1258–1259
Ginsburg, Ruth Bader, 2331
Girard, Chuck, 1467

Girard, René, 1451
Glacken, Clarence, 1529
Gladden, Washington, 493, 925, 1479, 1866, 2086, 2091–2092, 2101, 2155
Glazer, Nathan, 1156
Gleason, Philip, 1541–1542
Glide Memorial United Methodist Church (San Francisco), 334
Global Gag Rule, 10, 11
Globalization
immigration, 1063
philanthropy, 1642–1643
Glorious Revolution of 1688, 71, 95, 1679, 1803
Glossolalia, **910–913**
Charismatics/Charismatic movements, 912–913
in Christian tradition, 911
definition of, 910–911
Delphic oracle, 910
in early Pentecostalism, 288, 425, 912–913
forms of, 910–911
heteroglossa, 910
in literature, 1239
miracles and, 911
in modern times, 427, 428, 911–912, 2393
New Testament phenomenon, 911
Pentecostals, 1627, 1628
revivalism and, 1951
zenoglossa, 911
Gloucester, John, 29
Glover, Joseph, 1860
Glover, Rebecca, 1344
Gnosis, 751
Goa, David, 393
Goble, D. H., 1454
Goddard, Dwight, 317
Goddess worship, 1539
Godefroy, Maximilian, 199
GodMen, 1323, 1324, 1325, 1326, 1327, 1328
Gogarten, Friedrich, 1535
Goizueta, Roberto S., 1223–1224, 1915, 1916
Goldfarb, Abraham, 1485
*Goldman v. Weinberger* (1986), 1845
Goldstein, Elyse, 1904–1905
Goldstein, Joseph, 318
Goldwater, Barry, 1870
Gómez Farías, Valentín, 1381
González, Ambrosio, 1191
González, Justo, 1194, 1195, 1917
Gonzalez, Michelle A., 1223, 1916
Goodhue, Bertram, 190, 1279
Goodhue, Harry Wright, 1280
Goodman, Andrew, 42
*Goodridge v. Department of Public Health* (Mass. 2003), 2028, 2030
"Good Wife," 2344
Good works, 1112
Gordon, A. J., 20
Gordon, Thomas, 1861
Gore, Al, 254, 267
Gore, Charles, 101
Gorham, Jabez, 1275

Greeley, Andrew, 541, 549, 1195, 2110, 2113, 2114, 2133

Greeley, Dana McLean, 2228, 2230

Green, Arthur, 1912

Green Acre community, 222

Greenacre retreat center, 1565

Greenberg, Blu, 1912, 2310

Green Corn ceremony, 1505–1506, 1517

Greene, Graham, 1934

Greene, Nathaniel, 69

Greenough, Horatio, 90

Gregorian calendar, 2369

Gregorian chant, 2361

Gregory (Moravian), 1427

Gregory VII (pope), 2018

Grentzel, Charles, 1548

Grenz, Stanley, 1891

Griffin, David Ray, 301

Griffith, D. W., 1277

Griffith, R. Marie, 2113

Griggs, Sutton, 1270

Grimké, Angelina & Sarah, 2, 279, 515, 831, 1415, 2304, 2324, 2346

*Griswold v. Connecticut* (1965), 6

Gropius, Walter, 168, 174

Gross, Rita, 897, 2311

Groton School, 621, 744, 2155

Grow, Henry, 185

Gruber, Eberhard Ludwig, 58

Grundtvig, N. F. S., 1296, 1303

Guadalupe. *See* Virgin of Guadalupe

Guadalupe Hidalgo, Treaty of, 1179, 1266, 1975, 2007

Guan Gong temple (New York City), *150,* 151

Guilday, Peter, 1979

Guilford College, 1820

Gulick, Luther, 2156

Gulley, Philip, 1234

Gulsrud, Mark, 1281

Gunananda, Mohottivatte, 326

Gurdjieff, G. I., 758

*Gurdwara* (Sikh place of worship), 155

Gurney, Joseph John, 1812–1813

Gurney, Marion, 1977

Gurneyite Friends, 1812–1814, 1815–1816

Guru Dev, 2211–2212

Guru Gobind Singh, 2082

Guru Nanak, 2081

Gusfield, Joseph, 2109

Gustafson, James M., 548

Gutiérrez, Cerefino, 200

Gutterson, Henry Higby, 152, 185

Gutzlaff, Karl, 1303

Guyart, Marie (Marie of the Incarnation), 2315

Guzmán, Nuño de, 1378

Haan, Gijsbert, 572

Habitat for Humanity, 1643

Hacault, Antoine, 375

Hadassah, 2330, 2404

Haddad, Yvonne, 2335

Hadith of Gabriel, 1093

Hadley, Norval, 1818

Hae-Jong Kim, 1357

Hagee, John, 568

Hagin, Kenneth, 430

Haidu, Katsugoro, 150

Haile Selassie I (king, Ethiopia), 408, 1574, 1575

Hairston, Jester, 1452

Haitian Revolution, 407

Hakluyt, Richard, 64

Hale, Apollos, 16, 19

Hale, Sarah Josepha, 511

Haley, Alex, 1243

Half-Way Covenant, 342, 343, 433, 434, 435, 491, 784, 1371

Hall, David, 183, 1331, 2115, 2139, 2151

Hall, G. Stanley, 2172, 2356

Hall, Prince, 29

Hall church, 163, 164

Halloween, 1012

Ham, Mordecai, 1950

Hamer, Dean, 2046

Hamer, Fannie Lou, 290

Hamilton, Alexander, 1962

Hamilton, William, 212, 486–487, 524

Hammans, William, 1248

Hampton University Ministers' Conference, 43

Hand, Wayland, 847

Handsome Lake. *See* Ganioda'yo (Handsome Lake)

Handy, Robert, 989, 1311, 2090

Hansen, Marcus Lee, 1321

Hansen, Walter, 1191

Hanukkah, 1160

Harding, Rachael, 1898

Harding, Vincent, 1895

Hare, R. M., 303

Hare, Robert, 2136

Hare, William Hobart, 745

Hare Krishna. *See* Krishna Consciousness

Hargis, Billy James, 1836, 1848, 1869, 1870

Harkness, Georgia, 1357, 2348

Harlem Negro Apostolate, 1958

Harlem Renaissance, 38, 1230, 1243, 2288

Harmandir (Golden Temple), 2082

Harmonia (New York), 2136

Harmonialism and metaphysical religion, **937–943**

antebellum popular culture, 1716

architecture, *182,* 182–183, 185–186

Christian Science, 939–940

Divine Science, 941

Eddy, Mary Baker, 939–940

Hopkins, Emma Curtis, 939–941

megachurches, 942

New Thought, early contexts of, 938

new visions of divine, 1580

nineteenth century, 207

pietism, 1659–1660

as popular religion, 1708–1709

Quimby, Phineas P., 938–939

Religious Science, 942

religious thought, 1885–1886

Science of Mind (SOM), 942

Unity, 941–942

Harmonic convergence, 1545

Harmony Society, 1577, 2237–2238

Harnack, Adolf von, 295, 296, 1534

Harper, Stephen, 359

Harper, William Rainey, 285, 561

Harper's Ferry raid, 3, 2021. *See also* Brown, John

Harrell, David Edwin, Jr., 465, 2165

Harris, Barbara, 43, 102, 2349

Harris, Benjamin, 1860

Harris, Elizabeth, 1808

Harris, Howell, 1366

Harris, Neil, 2262

Harris, Sam, 213, 1532

Harris, Samuel, 1418

Harris, Thomas Lake, 2136

Harris, William Torrey, 613, 1038

Harrison, George, 417, *417*

Harrison, Peter, 160, 169

Harrison, William Henry, 1512

Harry Frank Guggenheim Foundation, 1857

Harry Potter series, 439

Hart-Cellar Immigration Act of 1965. *See* Immigration and Nationality Act of 1965

Harte, Bret, 2259

Hartshorne, Charles, 1531, 1891

Harvard University

anti-Semitism at, 123

Catholics at, 1984

Congregationalists at, 493

education, 628, 662, 664

establishment of, 216

music, 1459

in New England, 1553

Unitarians at, 2224

Harvey, Graham, 1530

Harwood, Thomas & Emily, 1191

Hasidism, **943–948**. *See also* Judaism, *subheading:* Orthodox

Chabad-Lubavitch. *See* Chabad-Lubavitch

divorce, 946

family, education, and work, 946–947

Jewish culture, 1122–1123

Nazis and, 944

opponents of, 944

origins, European, 943–944

persecution and violence, 944–945

physical appearance, 946

rebbes, 946

relationships with other groups, 947–948

in United States, 945–946

women, 2331

World War I, 944

World War II, 944

Zionism, 947

Haskalah, 2403

Haskell, Thomas, 2107

Hastings, Thomas, 14

Hatch, Nathan, 2165

Hate speech. *See* Anti-Catholicism; Anti-Semitism

Hauerwas, Stanley, 1358, 1890

NOT FOR CIRCULATION

NOT FOR CIRCULATION